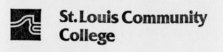

THE NORTON
INTRODUCTION
TO
LITERATURE

Combined Shorter Edition

Carl E. Bain · Jerome Beaty
J. Paul Hunter

EMORY UNIVERSITY

THE NORTON
INTRODUCTION
TO
LITERATURE

Combined Shorter Edition

W · W · NORTON & COMPANY · INC.
NEW YORK

First Edition

Library of Congress Cataloging in Publication Data

Bain, Carl E   comp.
The Norton introduction to literature.

1. Literature—Collections. I. Beaty, Jerome,
1924–   joint comp. II. Hunter, J. Paul,
1934–   joint comp. III. Title.
PN6014.B27 1973   808.8   73–5878
ISBN 0–393–09347–6
ISBN 0–393–09334–4 (pbk.)

PRINTED IN THE UNITED STATES OF AMERICA
1 2 3 4 5 6 7 8 9 0

iv

Contents

Fiction

I. The Story in Focus: Subjects and Forms

II. A Middle Distance: A Kind and Its Varieties

xi

III. The Larger Frame: Stories in Contexts

Poetry

I. The Poem in Focus: Subject and Tone

II. The Middle Distance: Craft, Form, and Kind

III. The Larger Frame: Poems in Contexts

Drama

I. The Play in Focus: Audience and Action

II. The Middle Distance: The Page and the Stage

III. The Larger Frame: Contexts of the Play

The Limits of Literature

Foreword

Using This Book

This book is an anthology: a generous collection of what the editors
think are, for the most part, enjoyable, stimulating, and significant literary works. With all literature to choose from, the editors had to use
additional criteria to limit the selection. Among these criteria are the
type of audience, considerations of similarity and variety, and illustra-
tive utility.

We assume an audience of English-speaking, reasonably literate,
late-20th-century readers with some experience of literature but not
necessarily with specific literary or other background in common.
Judging in purely qualitative terms, we have perhaps "over-repre-
sented" 20th-century, especially recent-20th-century works, but we
feel these are the most readily enjoyable and comprehensible works,
requiring intelligence and awareness but not necessarily as much specific information and experience. We have tried to include some works
that are familiar to at least some students and to many instructors. We
have also tried to include the excellent but unfamiliar, the forgotten,
undiscovered, or new, the seldom if ever anthologized, for surely one
of the pleasures of reading is the joy of discovery.

We have also tried to include a wide variety of works—in subject
matter, in form, in tone, in attitude, in effect. Yet, where offered a
choice among equally excellent possibilities, we have chosen works
that interact with each other by comparability of subject matter, form,
tone, or effect; for reading, like other experiences, is in large measure
comparative. Some even say that one can have a pure experience—
feeling fur, for example—only once, and that all subsequent fur-feel-
ings are comparisons with the first one. Any alert reader will find
multiple instances of comparable works, not only those deliberately
juxtaposed by the editors but works from widely separated sections
and even from different genres.

Where other considerations—excellence, appropriateness to audience, variety, and comparability—have been satisfied, we have chosen
from among works that best illustrate an appropriate and appropriately
timed critical or pedagogical point. This is not only an anthology but a
textbook; the works are not only selected but arranged or ordered to
introduce the reader to the serious study of literature. Any selection of
excellent literary works may be read in many meaningful orders, and
this anthology is, we trust, no exception, but in a bound book some one
order is fixed. We divide literature into genres—fiction, drama, poetry
—and within each genre proceed in a pattern as parallel as the nature
and exigencies of the genres permit. Each begins with works to be
read, or "closely read" discretely and analytically as suggested below,
but all or many of them are also grouped by subject matter or theme—

xxv

elements readily accessible to all regardless of past reading experience. The early subject matter groupings of stories and plays also introduce and incorporate matters of structure; since the formal elements in poems are more complex, fixed, and defined, these are introduced in groups separate from and subsequent to the subject-matter groups. The second major section of each collection specifically addresses itself to some secondary ways of understanding a literary work in the genre: the relation of a short story to rites and patterns of initiation, the specific elements of language, meter, and forms in a poem, and the relation between a play as a literary work and its actualization upon the stage. The final major section within each genre presents works in biographical or historical contexts: works by a single author, works from a historical period or contiguous periods, and so on.

The arrangement is not meant to classify the works. What it does suggest is a method for introducing students to the serious study of literature. It begins with considerations that assume no specific literary method or experience but assume expectations aroused by certain human situations—subject matter or theme; it builds toward making conscious certain literary expectations, those of form and kind; and finally it introduces contextual expectations—those created by the author's other works, by the norms of a period or a tradition, the historical realities. All these elements and expectations operate simultaneously and interact, of course, and it would be not only possible but desirable to return to works placed early in the selections with the accumulated experience of having read through the entire anthology to discover just what has been gained by heightened awareness of form, kind, and context.

The pattern of arrangement and implied method here described is followed in general within each genre. More specific and detailed description of the order within each genre, with variations and varied emphases necessitated by the inherent differences between genres, appears in sections called "Note on Arrangement" at the end of each separate preface. Since one of our principles—indeed, perhaps, our first principle—is that the study of literature is the reading of literature, we have preferred to fill the pages available to us with literary works, and to let understanding, awareness, and engagement grow out of that reading. At the same time, we recognize the necessity of some assistance. The works are annotated—as is customary in Norton anthologies—in order to free the instructor from spending valuable class time in glossing the texts. Each genre is preceded by a preface, which is designed to raise some general questions about what to expect. Each genre is followed by a section entitled "The Elements of Fiction," "The Elements of Poetry," or "The Elements of Drama," which contain brief essays on such topics as, for example, "Audience," "Tone," or "Character": these essays may be read as introductory chapters to sections of the anthology, as a glossary of literary terms and the necessary technical vocabulary, or ignored. Finally, the teachers manuals may be drawn on for classroom questions or writing topics.

Literature in the Classroom

Questions of definition and theory are apt to become, over the years, central for a teacher, but for a student the central questions are, at the beginning, practical: how to read literature with enjoyment, interest,

and understanding and how to relate it to life beyond the classroom. Of course, no universal how-to formula exists, not only because all individual readers differ from one another but also because different works of literature demand different approaches. Still, there are common grounds among readers and common grounds among works, for although every work is *in a sense* unique, many things about it are not unique at all, and in approaching any work of literature a reader may save himself many difficulties by using some common tools. Ultimately, one's experience with a work is very personal—and at its furthest reaches private—but the experience begins communally. No private insight occurs if the reader does not first participate in a sharing with the writer, and that sharing depends upon uses of language which are agreed on and discoverable. The classroom and the textbook represent places and ways of delineating and articulating what is public and shareable.

But where does one begin? "Read, read, read, read, my unlearned reader" is the advice *Tristram Shandy* offers, and the literal and intense following of that advice is assumed by nearly every college teacher. For almost half a century the *close reading* approach to literature has dominated the college classroom, asking that each student read completely, carefully, analytically each individual literary work, making sure to know exactly the significance of each word, each phrase, each part, each transition. Over the years this approach has undergone many variations and shifts of emphasis and has been known by many names ("the new criticism" and "formalism" are two of the most popular and lasting), but its premises remain fairly constant: that any literary work is a self-existent whole which will reveal its own laws, meanings, and implications if it is approached intensely and sensitively. "Close reading" emphasizes the knowledge of basic tools and the asking of basic questions: What, literally, does each line, or sentence, or unit of dialogue say? What kind of vocabulary (or "diction") does the work use, and how specialized is it? What images does it use, and what are their emotional connotations? How does the setting contribute to the total effect? Who is telling the story, or speaking the dialogue, or addressing us in the poem, and how does knowledge of that speaker color our responses to what he or she says? All such questions mean to get at the work's final effect, helping to explain not only what the work "says" but what responses it evokes, intellectual and emotional, and they articulate both what a reader first feels impressionistically and point toward new areas of feeling and response, extending the range of the work's effect.

A second popular approach to literature is *generic*, and in classroom practice the generic and close-reading approaches often quietly merge. The generic approach assumes that each genre (in the sense that we are using the term to distinguish fiction, poetry, and drama) has some identifying characteristics which may be usefully isolated—that, for example, all plays have some elements in common which differentiate them from stories and poems—and that a reader who knows these characteristics may test an individual work against them to evaluate the work, to clarify it, and to learn at the same time more about the genre as a genre. The generic approach assumes that the writer and reader both approach a work in a certain genre with specific—if not always fully conscious—expectations and that part of the effect depends on whether, and how, those expectations are satisfied. Knowing

what to expect, even when one's expectation is not fulfilled—in fact, especially when one's expectation is not fulfilled—puts the reader on a common ground with the author. The writer may, and often does, re-contour that ground quickly, but for a moment at least the common-ness of ground allows communication to begin. Writers who choose to write drama rather than fiction commit themselves to the materials and possibilities of the dramatic genre, and this commitment enables the reader to concentrate on terms, problems, and questions that relate especially to drama. The generic approach is primarily an admission that *groups* of works have something in common and that recognizing the *nature* of the grouping provides the basis for further study and consideration.

Some generic critics believe that there are "essential" characteristics of each genre and that the differences between genres are deeply rooted in the ultimate order of the world or of human nature. Others simply find genres a convenient way of describing tendencies. Either group may use the generic approach as a tool for reading individual works, and either may extend the genre distinction to smaller units. Distinctive groups within genres, sometimes called subgenres or types or kinds, often have specific characteristics. Drama is, for example, traditionally divided into comedy and tragedy, each with character-istics which can be described, and many smaller groups are also recog-nized as having clear group identity: romantic comedy, black comedy, tragicomedy, melodrama, revenge plays, heroic plays, absurd plays are a few of the kinds of drama which provide expectations more specific than those of drama itself. Similarly there are many kinds of fiction (mystery stories, for example, or initiation stories, as well as novels, romances, and novellas) and of poetry (epic, pastoral, satiric, confes-sional, etc.); writers often choose their kind with great care and pre-cision, to impose specific tasks upon themselves and to guarantee com-munication with the reader through a well defined common area of expectation. Even when the writer's choice of kind is arbitrary, capri-cious, or unconscious, the reader can profit from sensible comparisons and contrasts between an individual work and the norm of the group, and when a writer sets out deliberately to make his own unique kind the reader who knows the conventions of the other kinds will see more clearly what is going on.

Other classroom approaches to literature have gone in and out of fashion: the *biographical* approach (which emphasizes the relation of a work to the events and psychological patterns of an author's life), the *historical* approach (which emphasizes the development of forms and strategies and the passing on of techniques from one writer to an-other), and the *thematic* approach (which groups works by the sub-jects that they deal with or ideas that they present, rather than by genre, form, or style) have been among the more popular ones. The close-reading and generic approaches—often modified to fit the special interests or needs of a particular moment or a particular instructor—have, however, dominated the literature classroom for many years, and whatever concessions to fashion are made usually occur within the general framework of the close-reading and generic approaches. The selections in Sections I and II of the Norton Introduction to each genre are arranged so as to be especially convenient for these approaches.

In the last few years there has been a growing restlessness about these traditional approaches, and many attempts at experimentation

reflect uncertainty about classroom method. The uncertainty is not so much disillusionment with what the close-reading and generic approaches can do, but a worry about what they cannot do; it is not so much a matter of replacing traditional methods as of supplementing them so that literature may seem more integrally related to other things. Students and teachers alike often weary of tool-sharpening, especially if they are not sure what larger tasks the tools are good for; most actors, athletes, and lovers can put up with strenuous discipline if they have a performance in view, but few are enchanted by practice for its own sake.

Seeing the relation of literature to other art and to the larger culture of which it is part is chiefly a matter of thinking about literature in context, related to a specific time and place—besides having "universal" and "timeless" aspects. Students who insist on knowing how a work relates to political or social or moral questions are, in an important sense, addressing the same issues as scholars trying to "place" a work in its whole cultural setting. (All of the more important critical and scholarly movements of the last few years—phenomenology, structuralism, psychological criticism, contextualism, neo-historicism—share the concern with literature as existing in time and having a specific relationship to the immediate cultural context which it reflects and addresses.) Seeing how one work of an author relates to other works, how specific events shape and control both the theme and the form of a work, how persuasive devices work upon a reader or audience in a specific emotional context, how the ideas of one time may be translated into a world with different assumptions and pressures—all these possibilities represent attempts to expand beyond the self-existent world of an individual work and the galaxy of a particular genre or kind. And such larger concerns often correct and clarify as well as expand, for reading many works by one writer (or knowing more about events to which the author refers) often corrects mistakes or reveals resonances which are not discoverable when one reads the work in isolation. Section III of the Norton Introduction to each genre is arranged to facilitate the investigation of such temporal and cultural matters. As editors, we have tried to arrange this book so that students and teachers can take advantage of classroom procedures already in use and adventure a little beyond what is already familiar or what they already do well.

C. E. B.
J. B.
J. P. H.

Acknowledgments

If you are old enough to edit a textbook, you are indebted to literally hundreds of people—family, colleagues, teachers, and students. We are. If you cannot thank them wittily, it is more important anyway to thank them sincerely. We do.

In the preparation of this book we have acquired many new indebtednesses which should be acknowledged. Our colleagues at Emory University, especially in the Department of English and the University Library, continue to be lodes of information, encouragement, and wisdom. Special thanks are due to Debbie Hunter and Shawn Beaty for many hours of capable assistance. Particular information was solicited from and provided by Mr. John Shaw of the Florida State University Library. A place of honor was earned by Mrs. Carolyn Breecher, formerly of the Emory University English Department, for many services and for the engaging wit with which they were performed.

On several occasions during the preparation of this work a retreat from everyday was needed. The Ossabaw Island Project provided it, and we wish to thank the Ossabaw Island Foundation and particularly Mr. and Mrs. Clifford B. West and Mr. and Mrs. Charles B. Wood for the provision and for the grace with which it was offered.

At W. W. Norton & Company, Ann Holler, Carol Paradis, Mill Jonakait, Calvin Towle, and John Benedict have provided assistance and encouragement in many ways and on many occasions.

Arrangements have been made for suitable expressions of gratitude for the assistance and encouragement of our wives at a more appropriate time and place.

Fiction

EDITED BY

JEROME BEATY

A Preface to Fiction

> We are all like Scheherazade's husband, in that we want to know
> what happens next. . . . And now the story can be defined. It is a narra-
> tive of events arranged in their time sequence. . . . Qua story, it can have
> only one merit: that of making the audience want to know what happens
> next. And conversely it can only have one fault: that of making the
> audience not want to know what happens next. . . . It is the lowest and
> simplest of literary organisms. Yet it is the highest factor common to all
> the very complicated organisms known as [fiction].
>
> —E. M. Forster, *Aspects of the Novel*

Reading fiction, as Forster describes it, is a spectator sport, like
watching a football game, a chess match, or any other human process
that moves from event to event in time. It touches on something that
happens to all of us: we want to know what's going to happen next
and how it will all come out.

But watching a game need not be a passive, mindless experience. It
is anticipatory and, if only vicariously, participatory, and the more you
know and understand, the more you think, the more you are engaged.
When "your" team has the ball on its own twenty-six, third down and
three to go, you want to know whether it will make it or not, how it
will come out. Even the casual observer will ask himself more than
this: will it be a running play or a pass? A real fan will try to guess
what kind of pass, what kind of running play, and he'll try to take into
account the score, the time left, the strengths and weaknesses of both
teams, the patterns that have been run on the last two or three plays
and in similar situations. Why? In part the satisfaction of guessing right
or the excitement of being surprised, but also to participate more, to
become engaged, not only intellectually but emotionally.

And that is the purpose of studying fiction: to make reading something other than a passive, mindless experience; not only to learn the
rules of the game but the possibilities and varieties, to see more,
anticipate more, participate more—to become engaged intellectually
and emotionally.

Because the question of what happens next is both elementary and
universal, we might begin the study of fiction by watching how stories
arouse, direct, and satisfy this expectation. Some stories have quite
obvious, immediate, and direct designs on our expectations:

"Off there to the right—somewhere—is a large island," said Whitney.
"It's rather a mystery—"

"What island is it?" Rainsford asked.

"The old charts call it 'Ship-Trap Island,' " Whitney replied. "A suggestive name, isn't it? Sailors have a curious dread of the place. I don't
know why. Some superstition—"

1

Others have designs as immediate and only a little less obvious:

> People were telling one another that a newcomer had been seen on the promenade—a lady with a dog. Dmitri Dmitrich Gurov had been a fortnight in Yalta, and was accustomed to its ways, and he, too, had begun to take an interest in fresh arrivals. . . .
> "If she's here without her husband, and without any friends," thought Gurov, "it wouldn't be a bad idea to make her acquaintance."

As we read beyond the opening sentences or paragraphs of a story, anticipation of what is to happen next or to be revealed next continues to be part of our reading process, as does attention to details that might serve as "clues," and a third mental activity becomes involved—retention or memory. In trying to anticipate or guess with the author, we must not only know what's going on now, we must know what has happened earlier. This is true not only in order to help us to guess right but to help us to participate, to enjoy even wrong guesses. In *The Most Dangerous Game,* for example, just after Rainsford hears from Whitney about the mysterious Ship-Trap Island, the conversation turns to hunting, and we learn of Rainsford's rather insensitive attitude toward the animals he hunts. Soon thereafter Rainsford falls into the sea and is washed up on the dreaded island. He hears shots and the sound of what seems to be an animal thrashing about. He comes to a strange, castle-like structure. At this point, we remember both parts of the earlier conversation: the mystery and superstition about the island, so we can anticipate something like a ghost story, and the conversation about hunting, so we can appreciate what turns out to be the actual course of events. Our mind keeps working on both possibilities, and, through this mental activity and participation, intensifies our response through complexity of anticipation. Most stories supply "clues" to what is to happen, so that the events and endings will seem, in retrospect, "inevitable" or convincing; most will also supply or embody "false" clues, alternative possibilities, so that the events and ending will in some ways be "surprising." In most stories the "right" guess does more than convince or surprise: it often informs and illuminates the story's perception of reality. The second part of the Whitney-Rainsford conversation, for example, not only heightens our suspense and helps us to guess right but also leads us to understand and to feel the perception of the sanctity of all life which is embodied in this short story.

Attention, anticipation, retention—so essential in reading for what Forster calls "story"—are the same activities, exercised in the same way and largely on the same material, that inform our understanding of and response to all elements of fiction. Story, then, "the lowest and simplest of literary organisms," which makes "the audience want to know what happens next," is not only the highest factor common to all fiction but also engages a wide range of the mental and emotional activities involved in reading fiction. By studying what is involved in reading for story, expectation, or wanting to know what happens next, we are led to consider virtually all the aspects of reading literature.

Forster defines story as "a narrative of events *arranged in their time sequence*." The time of the events within the story we may call "fictional time." When the fictional events are in fact arranged sequentially, they parallel the act of reading, which is itself temporal, sequential: we are a few seconds older when we read the second sentence of a story than we were when we began reading (and we are more "experienced"; the "experience" we have gained is at least the experience of having read the first sentence). The form of the work is similarly sequential—the second sentence is fixed in space on the page and therefore in time, always following the first and preceding the third. We may call this "formal time." The simplest and most common time-structure is that in which fictional time and formal time move forward sequentially, parallel to each other, so that the fictional events in the second sentence follow those in the first sentence just as our reading of the second sentence follows our reading of the first. All the stories in Section I of this collection except the last, *Sonny's Blues*, move sequentially forward in fictional time.

Our reading between the first sentence of a story and the last, though sequential, is actually multidimensional: as we read on, we remember all or some of what went before, so that by the middle of the story we are not reading quite the same way we were at the beginning, and at the end we are reading in still another manner. We remember Whitney describing Ship-Trap Island as mysterious and we remember the discussion of hunting. When we come to the castle-like structure we remember both, but when we discover General Zaroff and his "game," we "forget" about the hints of mystery and get involved in anticipating what is to happen next in the game (or to the game). When we find that out and finish the story, the "mystery" of the island is long forgotten, but the conversation about hunting, the hunter, and the hunted takes on a new dimension in our mind.

Even in these sequential stories the time-structure is not quite so one-directional as we have suggested. The hunting conversation, for example, deals with Rainsford's past experiences, expeditions that occurred before the first moment in the story—the first fictional moment. So, too, Gurov's past affairs in "real" time and in the formal time-structure of the story follow the first paragraphs, but in fictional time, in the supposed life of Dmitri Dmitrich Gurov, they precede the time of the opening of the story. When we get to *Criers and Kibitzers, Kibitzers and Criers* and *The Dead*, however, this fictional past emerges as a much more important consideration—it is what happened in that fictional past that we find out about at the end of the story. We have discovered in our reading not "what happened next" but "what had happened earlier," in the fictional past; we read not toward an *outcome* but toward a *revelation*.

A mystery story is a story of revelation, but one reads a mystery story more like an outcome story, anticipating what is to happen next. What happens next, however, in formal time is actually a revelation about the fictional past: we discover who done it. There is thus in a mystery story suspense about the revelation comparable to the sus-

pense in other stories about the outcome. This does not seem to be the case in reading *Criers and Kibitzers* or *The Dead*. In these stories, and especially in *The Dead*, there is almost no way to anticipate nor invitation to anticipate the revelation at the end. There is therefore little if any thrusting forward of the reader's attention. The pace seems slower; the reader, diverting less attention to anticipating what is to come, concentrates his attention more fully on the passage before his eyes. For some readers, indeed, it seems as if nothing happens in such stories.

Something is happening, however. The very absence of "story," of exciting events, and the dwelling on everyday details and events in the lives or ordinary people in a rather ordinary society (that of Chicago Jewish shopkeepers or shabby-genteel, "cultured" Dubliners) builds up convincing *verisimilitude*, "life-likeness," or realism. Both the imitation and the perception of reality convince. This in itself creates a kind of interest, projecting not so much forward through the story as outward to our own lives and to our own perceptions of reality. Our lives and perceptions create a kind of expectation, not of what happens next but of confirmation or authentication—yes, this is the way it is, and this, and this. We get interested in what *comes* next even if not in what *happens* next. And, just as in an outcome story we look forward to both inevitability and surprise, so in these stories we look forward to confirmation of our expectations and some reinterpretation, a deepening of a perception or an enrichment or even a new perception. The revelation becomes as important as an outcome: it completes the structure of the story, patterns and proportions the detail, and clinches our responses with affirmation or surprise. Just as, when we finish *The Most Dangerous Game*, the early discussion of hunting gains significance, so when we finish *The Dead* the discussion of the opera stars of yesteryear gains significance. When Mr. Greenspahn and Gabriel Conroy learn something about the fictional past, they must reinterpret their experiences, including those that took place in the story in the fictional present, and so must we. Stories of revelation virtually force us to reread them in our mind.

It is important at this point to insist that calling attention to differences in the use of the time element in stories is not an attempt to classify or pigeonhole. Just as there is a kind of anticipation in the stories of revelation, a review of details in stories of outcome, and elements of the fictional past (events that occurred before the story opened) in essentially sequential, outcome stories like *The Lady with the Dog*, so too there is verisimilitude in the Chekhov story and a rather fully embodied world-view, a perception of reality that relates to and perhaps modifies our own perceptions. The elements of fiction appear in a variety of compounds.

Stories like *The Lottery* and *Bartleby the Scrivener*, for example, represent a somewhat different compound of elements than do the stories of outcome and of revelation. In reading these stories we may have questions about what is to happen next or even of what has happened in the fictional past, but the primary question seems to be what is happening in the fictional present, what in the devil is

going on in the story. Though there is in the stories a good deal of verisimilitude of detail, there are also actions which are so weird, grotesque, or unusual that we do not read these stories as we do revelation stories, to confirm or illuminate reality in any literal sense. The mixture of the everyday setting and detail with the extraordinary, scarcely credible behavior suggests something like the mixture of dreams, not so much the unreal as the surreal, and projects some of our attention outside the story, making us search for some explanation, some relation to reality. We seek an *interpretation* rather than an *outcome* or *revelation*.

Fictional time in all the stories we have mentioned so far is essentially sequential—even revelations about what happened before the story began (Gretta's early love) taking place in the fictional present (Gretta in the Dublin hotel telling Gabriel about her early love). In other stories, however, a scene from the fictional past, a time before the opening of the story, may be presented not as a revelation but as a flashback: we are moved bodily, as it were, into the past. Several scenes in *Sonny's Blues,* for example, take place in a fictional time prior to that of the opening paragraphs of the story. This treatment of time can be used to delay outcome and heighten suspense about what is to happen next, but it is also mimetic: for, if "real" time, historical time, is linear and one-directional, our mental time, the thoughts and images that flow through our minds at any given moment are not only responses to present stimuli but are also projections about the future and flashes of memory out of the past. In the flashback, as in the workings of the mind, there is also an implied causality—something in the present triggers a memory out of the past, something from the past influences behavior in the present.

What may be called "psychological time"—images of the past and future mingling with those of the fictional present—operates as a determining factor in another time-dimension of fiction, duration. Joyce's long novel *Ulysses,* largely detailing the relatively insignificant movements and significant mental processes of three characters, takes place in a single day. One of the shortest stories in this collection, *The Sin of Jesus,* spans many months of fictional time; a longer, though still very short story, *The Egg,* spans years; one of the longest, *The Dead,* takes place in only a few hours, as does one of the shortest, *Debut.* Within stories, too, a scene that requires only a few minutes of fictional time may be dwelt on for pages while months if not years may be passed over in a sentence. If one were to read *Ulysses* through with attention from cover to cover in one sitting, the elapsed time might be almost exactly equal to the elapsed fictional time, but even in that novel there are moments of fictional time which would take more than a real moment to read and hours of fictional time could be disposed of in a few moments of reading time. Once we are inside the story we accept these conventions; we no longer worry about the discrepancy between real and fictional time.

Another reason for our acceptance of "unrealistic" duration in fictional time is that it is a function of the focus of narration or point of view—how the story is told to us. At one extreme of "how a story is

told to us" is the unmediated, the *dramatic*. When we watch a play we see the actor-character move about the stage and hear directly what he is saying. Each movement and line of dialogue is not only sequential, parallel to real time directionally, but it is also equal to real time in duration.

When fiction approaches the unmediated, scenic, durational equivalency of a play it too is called dramatic. The opening of *The Most Dangerous Game*, for example, except for the stage directions telling us who speaks which lines, is dramatic:

> "Off there to the right—somewhere—is a large island," said Whitney.
> "It's rather a mystery—"
> "What island is it?" Rainsford asked.
> "The old charts call it 'Ship-Trap Island,'" Whitney replied. . . .

It is possible to write an entire story in the form of dialogue with stage directions; it would then approach the condition of drama. It is also possible to approach the durational and unmediated nature of drama through means other than dialogue and for the most part not available to a playwright. For example, one or more characters could write letters. However, as soon as the letter-writer began describing an action that took place before the time of the writing he would be writing narrative. The letter-writer would become a narrator, an intermediary filtering, focusing, and describing the action for us.

When Gretta or a letter-writer narrates, when and if they refer to themselves, they of course speak in the first person. Some entire stories are presented that way. All such stories, all first-person narration, are therefore dramatic: though the actions within the story are narrated (and are treated with all kinds of durational and even sequential varieties of fictional time) the actual action of the story is the telling (or writing) of the story, not the narrated events within the telling.

Such unmediated, dramatically written or uttered fictions resemble drama in another way: the narrator is a character, no more reliable, necessarily, than a character in a play. Thus when Polonius says "To thine own self be true . . . ," Shakespeare may or may not stand behind the statement; it is wholly that of the character. Similarly, the painter who narrates *The Beldonald Holbein* disclaims responsibility for what happens to Mrs. Brash, but we need not believe him any more— or any less— than we do Polonius. There are some differences, however. The play *Hamlet* is not mediated by Polonius: there are speeches and actions outside his sight and knowledge, words and actions of other characters which come to us not through him but directly. But in *The Beldonald Holbein* everything we see or hear, the very words of the story, we get only from the first-person narrator; even the other characters' words and actions are told to us by him.

It is possible to use a third-person point of view in a way that closely approaches that of the first-person narrator, making him "a camera" (but often a camera that thinks). This means that whenever that character who is being used as the "camera," the point of view, leaves a room the story must go with him, that if anyone's thoughts are to be

directly revealed they are only those of that one character. In *Criers and Kibitzers*, for example, we are always with Mr. Greenspahn; we can only see and hear what he sees and hears, and the only mind we enter is his. This centered consciousness, as we may call it, also gives the appearance of dramatic presentation: there seems to be no one mediating between the action—sights, events, thoughts—and us. Whether there is mediation in fact, however, is difficult to establish. Are the words and images of the story those of Mr. Greenspahn? Would he be capable of "writing" this story? Or do we assume a mediator, a narrator, some other writer (who may or may not be the author)?

We know a story has an author. We know in first-person narration whose "words" we are supposed to be reading (the painter in *The Beldonald Holbein*, the lawyer in *Bartleby the Scrivener*). In third-person narration lines are often harder to draw. Philip, in *The Basement Room*, for example, is almost as much a centered consciousness as Mr. Greenspahn: the action follows him; almost all the sights or thoughts we get are his; even the language, if not the boy's, seems appropriate to a grown-up Philip. The narrator is clearly not Philip, however. He survives Philip; he sometimes sees him from the outside ("you could almost see the small unformed face hardening"). Yet he never identifies himself, never tells us how "he" knows what he knows that Philip does not (that the police sergeant "wished his wife were with him," for example). Such a narrator, especially when he assumes the prerogative of knowing anything at any time without bothering to explain how he came by such information, is sometimes called the omniscient narrator. Some stories in this collection—*O Yes* and *The Artificial Nigger*, for example—make use of the prerogative of fictional omniscience to enter the consciousnesses of more than one character; most, however, are either first-person narratives or use a centered consciousness.

Is the narrator "reliable" or "unreliable"? Does the story mean what it appears to mean? The use of some kind of non-omniscient mediator or filter, a point of view that makes the fiction approach the condition of dramatic utterance with all the ambivalence of dramatic utterance, has been the dominant mode of fiction for the past hundred years. Though such dramatic narrative is associated with the theory and practice of Henry James, it is not a matter of mere influence—nor of fashion or accident. It clearly has something to do with the assumption in Western culture during this period that perception is subjective, that not only does each man perceive his own reality and not reality or truth itself, but that mankind taken as a whole cannot objectively see "what's really out there;" he can only perceive within the limits determined by his senses and his brain. Even science becomes, seen thus, a fiction or myth about the external, nonhuman world put in communal, human terms, an ordered imitation of a perceived reality.

Awareness of the manipulation of formal and fictional time and of point of view (and of other "Elements of Fiction" such as "Genre," "Form," "Focus," "Style," and "Theme" discussed at the end of the

anthology of fiction) serves to inform and intensify our expectations, our intellectual and emotional response to reading stories, our attention, anticipation, and retention as we read. We need not divorce Scheherazade—or cut her head off: we still want to know what happens next. Reading fiction may be as exciting as watching a game; may, like watching, become even more exciting as we learn more and more about the "rules" and variations; may involve us in vicarious participation. But reading fiction well engages more of our being than do spectator sports, and we are left with more than knowledge of the outcome once it's over. For a game is a game because it is unreal; its rules, though they may have evolved over a long period of time, are wholly artificial, and, despite what amateur coaches and sportswriters and their lesser followers say, life is not a football game. Games are, after all is said and done, "irrelevant," deliberately simplified and controlled escapes from the complexities of life.

When we were discussing stories of revelation earlier, we mentioned that anticipation had been transformed from the question of what happened next to whether the next detail would be convincingly "true" or whether our view of reality was to be confirmed or challenged. We suggested that though this was often the dominant question or expectation in such stories, it was ultimately a question raised by all the stories in this collection, even those where anticipation of what happens next is most intensely present. This is the dimension that literature has and football and other games do not. Stories offer a perception of reality. Sometimes it approaches a "message"—all living things are sacred; sometimes it is an exploration of a theme—the essential otherness and/or incomprehensibility of others; sometimes it is a definition of reality or an aspect of reality, of life or maturity, which we may or may not accept. It is not the "truth" of the perception in the sense of our agreement or conversion that is at the heart of the experience of literature, but the human or subjective truth: if we had those eyes rather than our own and were there rather than where we are, are we convinced that this is what we might see or how we might see? Whenever we say yes we have expanded our consciousness, we have been able to escape or transcend our own eyes, our own past and conditions, and we are able to see, to a greater or lesser extent, a new world or the world in a new way. The "relevance," then, is in the difference. There is value in a story that confirms our view of reality if it deepens it or sharpens it or highlights that which we might have missed. But there is as much relevance in those stories that are strange but moving, convincingly unacceptable—never will our vision be quite so narrow again, our understanding so parochial. Apprehension of otherness is the only means of defining the self.

Note on Arrangement

Though this collection of stories is designed to be as flexible as possible, so that the stories may be read profitably in any order, there is a rationale that controls the fixed order here.

The stories in Section I are arranged fundamentally according to the way in which the reader's attention—and therefore expectation—is controlled by the element of time or sequence. The first six stories proceed more or less chronologically from the first moment of fictional time to the last, revealing what happens (and what does not happen) next. The time sequence itself in the next four stories is also linear or sequential, but in the first two—*Criers and Kibitzers* and *The Dead* —the revelation toward which the story moves is not something that is to happen next but something that has happened in the past, before the story began. In *The Lottery* and *Bartleby* there are mystifying or perplexing elements about what is going on in the fictional present or about what it all means. The final story in the section, *Sonny's Blues*, cuts back and forth in time.

A second principle of arrangement within this section is focus of narration or point of view. The first three stories center on a single character through whose eyes or mind or over whose shoulder all or almost all the action is seen but who is spoken of in the third person. *The Sin of Jesus* seems to focus on a single consciousness too, but there is clearly a narrator other than the character focused on, someone who refers to himself as distinct from the character. *The Beldonald Holbein,* like *Bartleby* and *Sonny's Blues,* is narrated in the first person, though the "I" is not the central character in the action.

The Lady with the Dog and *Souls Belated* deal with similar subject matter—love, marriage, fidelity. The arrangement in Section I invites consideration of the stories in terms of time, focus, and subject.

The stories in Section II are of a particular type or kind—initiation stories—which define the kind inductively, indicate a range of possibilities within that kind, and educate the reader's expectations in identifying and reading stories of that kind. The first three stories deal specifically with a child's discovering that an adult or adults he admires is not so admirable as he thought. The next three deal with children or young people facing what might be called "otherness." In *The Egg* the narrator recounts his and his family's experiences when he was growing up, experiences from which he infers what "life" is all about. The boy, Ike McCaslin, in *The Old People* is doubly initiated: not only into manhood or into the adult "tribe" but also into his role as the "chief" or proper heir to the tribal lands.

The first two stories in this section are English; all but one of the remainder directly or indirectly involve racial confrontation. Albert Murray's *Train Whistle Guitar* and Kristin Hunter's *Debut,* with the final story of Section I, James Baldwin's *Sonny's Blues,* deal directly with black experience described by black writers.

Though the stories in Section III may be read as independent works, they are placed in a larger context or "frame" that to some extent modifies or enriches them. The Lawrence stories, from the three decades of his writing career, raise issues about how or what reading several works by an author contributes to our understanding of the individual works and initial questions about changes or development in an author's canon. There is a pair of stories in which the second

echoes or responds to the first substantively or formally, thereby raising issues of tradition and literary history. The final pair of stories implies a framework larger than that of the author's canon or literary tradition, namely, the entire social or historical background against which the story is set or within which it is written and the interaction between that background and the story.

This is an anthology meant to stimulate interest in the reading of fiction, and a textbook meant to inform and stimulate thought and discussion about formal and contextual aspects of fiction. Methods are suggested, not determined; issues raised, not resolved. This is an invitation to years of further serious study and delight, an introduction to fiction.

The dates following the stories usually refer to first volume publication; a *p* preceding the date indicates date of periodical publication. Translators are indicated in initial footnotes, except in the case of the Soviet translation of *The Lady with the Dog*.

J. B.

I

RICHARD CONNELL

The Most Dangerous Game

"Off there to the right—somewhere—is a large island," said Whitney. "It's rather a mystery—"

"What island is it?" Rainsford asked.

"The old charts call it 'Ship-Trap Island,'" Whitney replied. "A suggestive name, isn't it? Sailors have a curious dread of the place. I don't know why. Some superstition—"

"Can't see it," remarked Rainsford, trying to peer through the dank tropical night that was palpable as it pressed its thick warm blackness in upon the yacht.

"You've good eyes," said Whitney, with a laugh, "and I've seen you pick off a moose moving in the brown fall bush at four hundred yards, but even you can't see four miles or so through a moonless Caribbean night."

"Nor four yards," admitted Rainsford. "Ugh! It's like moist black velvet."

"It will be light in Rio," promised Whitney. "We should make it in a few days. I hope the jaguar guns have come from Purdey's. We should have some good hunting up the Amazon. Great sport, hunting."

"The best sport in the world," agreed Rainsford.

"For the hunter," amended Whitney. "Not for the jaguar."

"Don't talk rot, Whitney," said Rainsford. "You're a big-game hunter, not a philosopher. Who cares how a jaguar feels?"

"Perhaps the jaguar does," observed Whitney.

"Bah! They've no understanding."

"Even so, I rather think they understand one thing—fear. The fear of pain and the fear of death."

"Nonsense," laughed Rainsford. "This hot weather is making you soft, Whitney. Be a realist. The world is made up of two classes—the hunters and the huntees. Luckily, you and I are hunters. Do you think we've passed that island yet?"

"I can't tell in the dark. I hope so."

"Why?" asked Rainsford.

"The place has a reputation—a bad one."

"Cannibals?" suggested Rainsford.

"Hardly. Even cannibals wouldn't live in such a God-forsaken place. But it's gotten into sailor lore, somehow. Didn't you notice that the crew's nerves seemed a bit jumpy today?"

"They were a bit strange, now you mention it. Even Captain Nielsen—"

"Yes, even that tough-minded old Swede, who'd go up to the devil himself and ask him for a light. Those fishy blue eyes held a look I never saw there before. All I could get out of him was: 'This place has

an evil name among sea-faring men, sir.' Then he said to me, very gravely: 'Don't you feel anything?'—as if the air about us was actually poisonous. Now, you mustn't laugh when I tell you this—I did feel something like a sudden chill.

"There was no breeze. The sea was as flat as a plate-glass window. We were drawing near the island then. What I felt was a—a mental chill; a sort of sudden dread."

"Pure imagination," said Rainsford. "One superstitious sailor can taint the whole ship's company with his fear."

"Maybe. But sometimes I think sailors have an extra sense that tells them when they are in danger. Sometimes I think evil is a tangible thing—with wave lengths, just as sound and light have. An evil place can, so to speak, broadcast vibrations of evil. Anyhow, I'm glad we're getting out of this zone. Well, I think I'll turn in now, Rainsford."

"I'm not sleepy," said Rainsford. "I'm going to smoke another pipe up on the after deck."

"Good night, then, Rainsford. See you at breakfast."

"Right. Good night, Whitney."

There was no sound in the night as Rainsford sat there, but the muffled throb of the engine that drove the yacht swiftly through the darkness, and the swish and ripple of the wash of the propeller.

Rainsford, reclining in a steamer chair, indolently puffed on his favorite brier. The sensuous drowsiness of the night was on him. "It's so dark," he thought, "that I could sleep without closing my eyes; the night would be my eyelids—"

An abrupt sound startled him. Off to the right he heard it, and his ears, expert in such matters, could not be mistaken. Again he heard the sound, and again. Somewhere, off in the blackness, some one had fired a gun three times.

Rainsford sprang up and moved quickly to the rail, mystified. He strained his eyes in the direction from which the reports had come, but it was like trying to see through a blanket. He leaped upon the rail and balanced himself there, to get greater elevation; his pipe, striking a rope, was knocked from his mouth. He lunged for it; a short, hoarse cry came from his lips as he realized he had reached too far and had lost his balance. The cry was pinched off short as the blood-warm waters of the Caribbean Sea closed over his head.

He struggled up to the surface and tried to cry out, but the wash from the speeding yacht slapped him in the face and the salt water in his open mouth made him gag and strangle. Desperately he struck out with strong strokes after the receding lights of the yacht, but he stopped before he had swum fifty feet. A certain cool-headedness had come to him; it was not the first time he had been in a tight place. There was a chance that his cries could be heard by some one aboard the yacht, but that chance was slender, and grew more slender as the yacht raced on. He wrestled himself out of his clothes, and shouted with all his power. The lights of the yacht became faint and ever-vanishing fireflies; then they were blotted out entirely by the night.

Rainsford remembered the shots. They had come from the right, and doggedly he swam in that direction, swimming with slow, deliberate strokes, conserving his strength. For a seemingly endless time he fought the sea. He began to count his strokes; he could do possibly a hundred more and then—

Rainsford heard a sound. It came out of the darkness, a high scream-ing sound, the sound of an animal in an extremity of anguish and terror.

He did not recognize the animal that made the sound; he did not try to; with fresh vitality he swam toward the sound. He heard it again; then it was cut short by another noise, crisp, staccato.

"Pistol shot," muttered Rainsford, swimming on.

Ten minutes of determined effort brought another sound to his ears —the most welcome he had ever heard—the muttering and growling of the sea breaking on a rocky shore. He was almost on the rocks before he saw them; on a night less calm he would have been shattered against them. With his remaining strength he dragged himself from the swirling waters. Jagged crags appeared to jut into the opaqueness; he forced himself upward, hand over hand. Gasping, his hands raw, he reached a flat place at the top. Dense jungle came down to the very edge of the cliffs. What perils that tangle of trees and under-brush might hold for him did not concern Rainsford just then. All he knew was that he was safe from his enemy, the sea, and that utter weariness was on him. He flung himself down at the jungle edge and tumbled headlong into the deepest sleep of his life.

When he opened his eyes he knew from the position of the sun that it was late in the afternoon. Sleep had given him new vigor; a sharp hunger was picking at him. He looked about him, almost cheerfully.

"Where there are pistol shots, there are men. Where there are men, there is food," he thought. But what kind of men, he wondered, in so forbidding a place? An unbroken front of snarled and ragged jungle fringed the shore.

He saw no sign of a trail through the closely knit web of weeds and trees; it was easier to go along the shore, and Rainsford floundered along by the water. Not far from where he had landed, he stopped.

Some wounded thing, by the evidence a large animal, had thrashed about in the underbrush; the jungle weeds were crushed down and the moss was lacerated; one patch of weeds was stained crimson. A small, glittering object not far away caught Rainsford's eye and he picked it up. It was an empty cartridge.

"A twenty-two," he remarked. "That's odd. It must have been a fairly large animal too. The hunter had his nerve with him to tackle it with a light gun. It's clear that the brute put up a fight. I suppose the first three shots I heard was when the hunter flushed his quarry and wounded it. The last shot was when he trailed it here and finished it."

He examined the ground closely and found what he had hoped to find—the print of hunting boots. They pointed along the cliff in the direction he had been going. Eagerly he hurried along, now slipping on a rotten log or a loose stone, but making headway; night was be-ginning to settle down on the island.

Bleak darkness was blacking out the sea and jungle when Rains-ford sighted the lights. He came upon them as he turned a crook in the coast line, and his first thought was that he had come upon a village, for there were many lights. But as he forged along he saw to his great astonishment that all the lights were in one enormous build-ing—a lofty structure with pointed towers plunging upward into the gloom. His eyes made out the shadowy outlines of a palatial château; it was set on a high bluff, and on three sides of it cliffs dived down to where the sea licked greedy lips in the shadows.

"Mirage," thought Rainsford. But it was no mirage, he found, when he opened the tall spiked iron gate. The stone steps were real enough; the massive door with a leering gargoyle for a knocker was real enough; yet about it all hung an air of unreality.

He lifted the knocker, and it creaked up stiffly, as if it had never before been used. He let it fall, and it startled him with its booming loudness. He thought he heard steps within; the door remained closed. Again Rainsford lifted the heavy knocker, and let it fall. The door opened then, opened as suddenly as if it were on a spring, and Rainsford stood blinking in the river of glaring gold light that poured out. The first thing Rainsford's eyes discerned was the largest man Rainsford had ever seen—a gigantic creature, solidly made and black-bearded to the waist. In his hand the man held a long-barreled revolver, and he was pointing it straight at Rainsford's heart.

Out of the snarl of beard two small eyes regarded Rainsford.

"Don't be alarmed," said Rainsford, with a smile which he hoped was disarming. "I'm no robber. I fell off a yacht. My name is Sanger Rainsford of New York City."

The menacing look in the eyes did not change. The revolver pointed as rigidly as if the giant were a statue. He gave no sign that he understood Rainsford's words, or that he had even heard them. He was dressed in uniform, a black uniform trimmed with gray astrakhan.

"I'm Sanger Rainsford of New York," Rainsford began again. "I fell off a yacht. I am hungry."

The man's only answer was to raise with his thumb the hammer of his revolver. Then Rainsford saw the man's free hand go to his forehead in a military salute, and he saw him click his heels together and stand at attention. Another man was coming down the broad marble steps, an erect, slender man in evening clothes. He advanced to Rainsford and held out his hand.

In a cultivated voice marked by a slight accent that gave it added precision and deliberateness, he said: "It is a very great pleasure and honor to welcome Mr. Sanger Rainsford, the celebrated hunter, to my home."

Automatically Rainsford shook the man's hand.

"I've read your book about hunting snow leopards[1] in Tibet, you see," explained the man. "I am General Zaroff."

Rainsford's first impression was that the man was singularly handsome; his second was that there was an original, almost bizarre quality about the general's face. He was a tall man past middle age, for his hair was a vivid white; but his thick eyebrows and pointed military mustache were as black as the night from which Rainsford had come. His eyes, too, were black and very bright. He had high cheek bones, a sharp-cut nose, a spare, dark face, the face of a man used to giving orders, the face of an aristocrat. Turning to the giant in uniform, the general made a sign. The giant put away his pistol, saluted, withdrew.

"Ivan is an incredibly strong fellow," remarked the general, "but he has the misfortune to be deaf and dumb. A simple fellow, but, I'm afraid, like all his race, a bit of a savage."

"Is he Russian?"

"He is a Cossack,"[2] said the general, and his smile showed red lips and pointed teeth. "So am I."

1. The ounce, native to the Himalayas, and quite rare.
2. From the southern part of European Russia, the Cossacks were known as exceptionally fine horsemen and light cavalrymen and, under the Czars, were feared for their ruthless raids.

"Come," he said, "we shouldn't be chatting here. We can talk later. Now you want clothes, food, rest. You shall have them. This is a most restful spot."

Ivan had reappeared, and the general spoke to him with lips that moved but gave forth no sound.

"Follow Ivan, if you please, Mr. Rainsford," said the general. "I was about to have my dinner when you came. I'll wait for you. You'll find that my clothes will fit you, I think."

It was to a huge, beam-ceilinged bedroom with a canopied bed big enough for six men that Rainsford followed the silent giant. Ivan laid out an evening suit, and Rainsford, as he put it on, noticed that it came from a London tailor who ordinarily cut and sewed for none below the rank of duke.

The dining room to which Ivan conducted him was in many ways remarkable. There was a medieval magnificence about it; it suggested a baronial hall of feudal times with its oaken panels, its high ceiling, its vast refectory table where twoscore men could sit down to eat. About the hall were the mounted heads of many animals—lions, tigers, elephants, moose, bears; larger or more perfect specimens Rainsford had never seen. At the great table the general was sitting, alone.

"You'll have a cocktail, Mr. Rainsford," he suggested. The cocktail was surpassingly good; and, Rainsford noted, the table appointments were of the finest—the linen, the crystal, the silver, the china.

They were eating *borsch*, the rich, red soup with whipped cream so dear to Russian palates. Half apologetically General Zaroff said: "We do our best to preserve the amenities of civilization here. Please forgive any lapses. We are well off the beaten track, you know. Do you think the champagne has suffered from its long ocean trip?"

"Not in the least," declared Rainsford. He was finding the general a most thoughtful and affable host, a true cosmopolite. But there was one small trait of the general's that made Rainsford uncomfortable. Whenever he looked up from his plate he found the general studying him, appraising him narrowly.

"Perhaps," said General Zaroff, "you were surprised that I recognized your name. You see, I read all books on hunting published in English, French, and Russian. I have but one passion in my life, Mr. Rainsford, and it is the hunt."

"You have some wonderful heads here," said Rainsford as he ate a particularly well cooked filet mignon. "That Cape buffalo[3] is the largest I ever saw."

"Oh, that fellow. Yes, he was a monster."

"Did he charge you?"

"Hurled me against a tree," said the general. "Fractured my skull. But I got the brute."

"I've always thought," said Rainsford, "that the Cape buffalo is the most dangerous of all big game."

For a moment the general did not reply; he was smiling his curious red-lipped smile. Then he said slowly: "No. You are wrong, sir. The Cape buffalo is not the most dangerous big game." He sipped his wine. "Here in my preserve on this island," he said in the same slow tone, "I hunt more dangerous game."

Rainsford expressed his surprise. "Is there big game on this island?"

The general nodded. "The biggest."

3. Big, quick, intelligent, when separated from the herd ("rogue"), one of the most dangerous of African game animals.

"Really?"

"Oh, it isn't here naturally, of course. I have to stock the island."

"What have you imported, general?" Rainsford asked. "Tigers?"

The general smiled. "No," he said. "Hunting tigers ceased to interest me some years ago. I exhausted their possibilities, you see. No thrill left in tigers, no real danger. I live for danger, Mr. Rainsford."

The general took from his pocket a gold cigarette case and offered his guest a long black cigarette with a silver tip; it was perfumed and gave off a smell like incense.

"We will have some capital hunting, you and I," said the general. "I shall be most glad to have your society."

"But what game—" began Rainsford.

"I'll tell you," said the general. "You will be amused, I know. I think I may say, in all modesty, that I have done a rare thing. I have invented a new sensation. May I pour you another glass of port, Mr. Rainsford?"

"Thank you, general."

The general filled both glasses, and said: "God makes some men poets. Some He makes kings, some beggars. Me He made a hunter. My hand was made for the trigger, my father said. He was a very rich man with a quarter of a million acres in the Crimea, and he was an ardent sportsman. When I was only five years old he gave me a little gun, specially made in Moscow for me, to shoot sparrows with. When I shot some of his prize turkeys with it, he did not punish me; he complimented me on my marksmanship. I killed my first bear in the Caucasus when I was ten. My whole life has been one prolonged hunt. I went into the army—it was expected of noblemen's sons—and for a time commanded a division of Cossack cavalry, but my real interest was always the hunt. I have hunted every kind of game in every land. It would be impossible for me to tell you how many animals I have killed."

The general puffed at his cigarette.

"After the debacle in Russia[4] I left the country, for it was imprudent for an officer of the Czar to stay there. Many noble Russians lost everything. I, luckily, had invested heavily in American securities, so I shall never have to open a tea room in Monte Carlo or drive a taxi in Paris. Naturally, I continued to hunt—grizzlies in your Rockies, crocodiles in the Ganges, rhinoceroses in East Africa. It was in Africa that the Cape buffalo hit me and laid me up for six months. As soon as I recovered I started for the Amazon to hunt jaguars, for I had heard they were unusually cunning. They weren't." The Cossack sighed. "They were no match at all for a hunter with his wits about him, and a high-powered rifle. I was bitterly disappointed. I was lying in my tent with a splitting headache one night when a terrible thought pushed its way into my mind. Hunting was beginning to bore me! And hunting, remember, had been my life. I have heard that in America business men often go to pieces when they give up the business that has been their life."

"Yes, that's so," said Rainsford.

The general smiled. "I had no wish to go to pieces," he said. "I must do something. Now, mine is an analytical mind, Mr. Rainsford. Doubtless that is why I enjoy the problems of the chase."

4. The Revolution of 1917 which overthrew the Czar and prepared the way for Communist rule.

"No doubt, General Zaroff."

"So," continued the general, "I asked myself why the hunt no longer fascinated me. You are much younger than I am, Mr. Rainsford, and have not hunted as much, but you perhaps can guess the answer."

"What was it?"

"Simply this: hunting had ceased to be what you call 'a sporting proposition.' It had become too easy. I always got my quarry. Always. There is no greater bore than perfection."

The general lit a fresh cigarette.

"No animal had a chance with me any more. That is no boast; it is a mathematical certainty. The animal had nothing but his legs and his instinct. Instinct is no match for reason. When I thought of this it was a tragic moment for me, I can tell you."

Rainsford leaned across the table, absorbed in what his host was saying.

"It came to me as an inspiration what I must do," the general went on.

"And that was?"

The general smiled the quiet smile of one who had faced an obstacle and surmounted it with success. "I had to invent a new animal to hunt," he said.

"A new animal? You're joking."

"Not at all," said the general. "I never joke about hunting. I needed a new animal. I found one. So I bought this island, built this house, and here I do my hunting. The island is perfect for my purposes—there are jungles with a maze of trails in them, hills, swamps—"

"But the animal, General Zaroff?"

"Oh," said the general, "it supplies me with the most exciting hunting in the world. No other hunting compares with it for an instant. Every day I hunt, and I never grow bored now, for I have a quarry with which I can match my wits."

Rainsford's bewilderment showed in his face.

"I wanted the ideal animal to hunt," explained the general. "So I said: 'What are the attributes of an ideal quarry?' And the answer was, of course: 'It must have courage, cunning, and, above all, it must be able to reason.'"

"But no animal can reason," objected Rainsford.

"My dear fellow," said the general, "there is one that can."

"But you can't mean—" gasped Rainsford.

"And why not?"

"I can't believe you are serious, General Zaroff. This is a grisly joke."

"Why should I not be serious? I am speaking of hunting."

"Hunting? Good God, General Zaroff, what you speak of is murder."

The general laughed with entire good nature. He regarded Rainsford quizzically. "I refuse to believe that so modern and civilized a young man as you seem to be harbors romantic ideas about the value of human life. Surely your experiences in the war—"

"Did not make me condone cold-blooded murder," finished Rainsford stiffly.

Laughter shook the general. "How extraordinarily droll you are!" he said. "One does not expect nowadays to find a young man of the educated class, even in America, with such a naïve, and, if I may say so, mid-Victorian point of view. It's like finding a snuff-box in a limousine. Ah, well, doubtless you had Puritan ancestors. So many Americans ap-

pear to have had. I'll wager you'll forget your notions when you go hunting with me. You've a genuine new thrill in store for you, Mr. Rainsford."

"Thank you, I'm a hunter, not a murderer."

"Dear me," said the general, quite unruffled, "again that unpleasant word. But I think I can show you that your scruples are quite ill founded."

"Yes?"

"Life is for the strong, to be lived by the strong, and, if need be, taken by the strong. The weak of the world were put here to give the strong pleasure. I am strong. Why should I not use my gift? If I wish to hunt, why should I not? I hunt the scum of the earth—sailors from tramp ships—lascars, blacks, Chinese, whites, mongrels—a thorough-bred horse or hound is worth more than a score of them."

"But they are men," said Rainsford hotly.

"Precisely," said the general. "That is why I use them. It gives me pleasure. They can reason, after a fashion. So they are dangerous."

"But where do you get them?"

The general's left eyelid fluttered down in a wink. "This island is called Ship-Trap," he answered. "Sometimes an angry god of the high seas sends them to me. Sometimes, when Providence is not so kind, I help Providence a bit. Come to the window with me."

Rainsford went to the window and looked out toward the sea.

"Watch! Out there!" exclaimed the general, pointing into the night. Rainsford's eyes saw only blackness, and then, as the general pressed a button, far out to sea Rainsford saw the flash of lights.

The general chuckled. "They indicate a channel," he said, "where there's none: giant rocks with razor edges crouch like a sea monster with wide-open jaws. They can crush a ship as easily as I crush this nut." He dropped a walnut on the hardwood floor and brought his heel grinding down on it. "Oh, yes," he said, casually, as if in answer to a question, "I have electricity. We try to be civilized here."

"Civilized? And you shoot down men?"

A trace of anger was in the general's black eyes, but it was there for but a second, and he said, in his most pleasant manner: "Dear me, what a righteous young man you are! I assure you I do not do the thing you suggest. That would be barbarous. I treat these visitors with every consideration. They get plenty of good food and exercise. They get into splendid physical condition. You shall see for yourself tomorrow."

"What do you mean?"

"We'll visit my training school," smiled the general. "It's in the cellar. I have about a dozen pupils down there now. They're from the Spanish bark San Lucar that had the bad luck to go on the rocks out there. A very inferior lot, I regret to say. Poor specimens and more accustomed to the deck than to the jungle."

He raised his hand, and Ivan, who served as waiter, brought thick Turkish coffee. Rainsford, with an effort, held his tongue in check.

"It's a game, you see, pursued the general blandly. "I suggest to one of them that we go hunting. I give him a supply of food and an excellent hunting knife. I give him three hours' start. I am to follow, armed only with a pistol of the smallest caliber and range. If my quarry eludes me for three whole days, he wins the game. If I find him"—the general smiled—"he loses."

"Suppose he refuses to be hunted?"

"Oh," said the general, "I give him his option, of course. He need not play that game if he doesn't wish to. If he does not wish to hunt, I turn him over to Ivan. Ivan once had the honor of serving as official knouter[5] to the Great White Czar,[6] and he has his own ideas of sport. Invariably, Mr. Rainsford, invariably they choose the hunt."

"And if they win?"

The smile on the general's face widened. "To date I have not lost," he said.

Then he added, hastily: "I don't wish you to think me a braggart, Mr. Rainsford. Many of them afford only the most elementary sort of problem. Occasionally I strike a tartar. One almost did win. I eventually had to use the dogs."

"The dogs?"

"This way, please. I'll show you."

The general steered Rainsford to a window. The lights from the windows sent a flickering illumination that made grotesque patterns on the courtyard below, and Rainsford could see moving about there a dozen or so huge black shapes; as they turned toward him, their eyes glittered greenly.

"A rather good lot, I think," observed the general. "They are let out at seven every night. If anyone should try to get into my house—or out of it—something extremely regrettable would occur to him." He hummed a snatch of song from the Folies Bergère.[7]

"And now," said the general, "I want to show you my new collection of heads. Will you come with me to the library?"

"I hope," said Rainsford, "that you will excuse me tonight, General Zaroff. I'm really not feeling at all well."

"Ah, indeed?" the general inquired solicitously. "Well, I suppose that's only natural, after your long swim. You need a good, restful night's sleep. Tomorrow you'll feel like a new man, I'll wager. Then we'll hunt, eh? I've one rather promising prospect—"

Rainsford was hurrying from the room.

"Sorry you can't go with me tonight," called the general. "I expect rather fair sport—a big, strong black. He looks resourceful—Well, good night, Mr. Rainsford; I hope you have a good night's rest."

The bed was good, and the pajamas of the softest silk, and he was tired in every fiber of his being, but nevertheless Rainsford could not quiet his brain with the opiate of sleep. He lay, eyes wide open. Once he thought he heard stealthy steps in the corridor outside his room. He sought to throw open the door; it would not open. He went to the window and looked out. His room was high up in one of the towers. The lights of the château were out now; and it was dark and silent, but there was a fragment of sallow moon, and by its wan light he could see, dimly, the courtyard; there, weaving in and out in the pattern of shadow, were black, noiseless forms; the hounds heard him at the window and looked up, expectantly, with their green eyes. Rainsford went back to bed and lay down. By many methods he tried to put himself to sleep. He had achieved a doze when, just as morning began to come, he heard, far off in the jungle, the faint report of a pistol.

---

5. In Czarist Russia the official flogger of criminals.

6. Probably Nicholas II (1868–1918) who was overthrown by the Revolution and executed; "White" designates those op-posed to the Communists, or "Reds."

7. Paris theater and music hall which in 1918 reestablished itself as the scene for revues, spectaculars, etc.

General Zaroff did not appear until luncheon. He was dressed fault-lessly in the tweeds of a country squire. He was solicitous about the state of Rainsford's health.

"As for me," sighed the general, "I do not feel so well. I am worried, Mr. Rainsford. Last night I detected traces of my old complaint."

To Rainsford's questioning glance the general said: "Ennui. Bore-dom."

Then, taking a second helping of *crêpes suzette,* the general ex-plained: "The hunting was not good last night. The fellow lost his head. He made a straight trail that offered no problems at all. That's the trouble with these sailors; they have dull brains to begin with, and they do not know how to get about in the woods. They do excessively stupid and obvious things. It's most annoying. Will you have another glass of Chablis, Mr. Rainsford?"

"General," said Rainsford firmly, "I wish to leave this island at once."

The general raised his thickets of eyebrows; he seemed hurt. "But, my dear fellow," the general protested, "you've only just come. You've had no hunting—"

"I wish to go today," said Rainsford. He saw the dead black eyes of the general on him, studying him. General Zaroff's face suddenly brightened.

He filled Rainsford's glass with venerable Chablis from a dusty bottle.

"Tonight," said the general, "we will hunt—you and I."

Rainsford shook his head. "No, general," he said, "I will not hunt."

The general shrugged his shoulders and delicately ate a hothouse grape. "As you wish, my friend," he said. "The choice rests entirely with you. But may I not venture to suggest that you will find my idea of sport more diverting than Ivan's?"

He nodded toward the corner to where the giant stood, scowling, his thick arms crossed on his hogshead of a chest.

"You don't mean—" cried Rainsford.

"My dear fellow," said the general, "have I not told you I always mean what I say about hunting? This is really an inspiration. I drink to a foeman worthy of my steel—at last."

The general raised his glass, but Rainsford sat staring at him.

"You'll find this game worth playing," the general said enthusiasti-cally. "Your brain against mine. Your woodcraft against mine. Your strength and stamina against mine. Outdoor chess! And the stake is not without value, eh?"

"And if I win—" began Rainsford huskily.

"I'll cheerfully acknowledge myself defeated if I do not find you by midnight of the third day," said General Zaroff. "My sloop will place you on the mainland near a town."

The general read what Rainsford was thinking.

"Oh, you can trust me," said the Cossack. "I will give you my word as a gentleman and a sportsman. Of course you, in turn, must agree to say nothing of your visit here."

"I'll agree to nothing of the kind," said Rainsford.

"Oh," said the general, "in that case—But why discuss that now? Three days hence we can discuss it over a bottle of Veuve Cliquot,[8] unless—"

The general sipped his wine.

8. A fine champagne; Chablis, above, is a very dry white Burgundy table wine; Chambertin, later, is a highly esteemed red Burgundy wine.

Then a businesslike air animated him. "Ivan," he said to Rainsford, "will supply you with hunting clothes, food, a knife. I suggest you wear moccasins; they leave a poorer trail. I suggest too that you avoid the big swamp in the southeast corner of the island. We call it Death Swamp. There's quicksand there. One foolish fellow tried it. The deplorable part of it was that Lazarus followed him. You can imagine my feelings, Mr. Rainsford. I loved Lazarus; he was the finest hound in my pack. Well, I must beg you to excuse me now. I always take a siesta after lunch. You'll hardly have time for a nap, I fear. You'll want to start, no doubt. I shall not follow till dusk. Hunting at night is so much more exciting than by day, don't you think? Au revoir, Mr. Rainsford, au revoir."

General Zaroff, with a deep, courtly bow, strolled from the room.

From another door came Ivan. Under one arm he carried khaki hunting clothes, a haversack of food, a leather sheath containing a long-bladed hunting knife; his right hand rested on a cocked revolver thrust in the crimson sash about his waist. . . .

Rainsford had fought his way through the bush for two hours. "I must keep my nerve. I must keep my nerve," he said through tight teeth.

He had not been entirely clear-headed when the château gates snapped shut behind him. His whole idea at first was to put distance between himself and General Zaroff, and, to this end, he had plunged along, spurred on by the sharp rowels of something very like panic. Now he had got a grip on himself, had stopped, and was taking stock of himself and the situation.

He saw that straight flight was futile; inevitably it would bring him face to face with the sea. He was in a picture with a frame of water, and his operations, clearly, must take place within that frame.

"I'll give him a trail to follow," muttered Rainsford, and he struck off from the rude paths he had been following into the trackless wilderness. He executed a series of intricate loops; he doubled on his trail again and again, recalling all the lore of the fox hunt, and all the dodges of the fox. Night found him leg-weary, with hands and face lashed by the branches, on a thickly wooded ridge. He knew it would be insane to blunder on through the dark, even if he had the strength. His need for rest was imperative and he thought: "I have played the fox, now I must play the cat of the fable."[9] A big tree with a thick trunk and outspread branches was nearby, and, taking care to leave not the slightest mark, he climbed up into the crotch, and stretching out on one of the broad limbs, after a fashion, rested. Rest brought him new confidence and almost a feeling of security. Even so zealous a hunter as General Zaroff could not trace him there, he told himself; only the devil himself could follow that complicated trail through the jungle after dark. But, perhaps, the general was a devil—

An apprehensive night crawled slowly by like a wounded snake, and sleep did not visit Rainsford, although the silence of a dead world was on the jungle. Toward morning when a dingy gray was varnishing the sky, the cry of some startled bird focused Rainsford's attention in that direction. Something was coming through the bush, coming slowly, carefully, coming by the same winding way Rainsford had

9. The fox boasts of his many tricks to elude the hounds; the cat responds he knows only one—to climb the nearest tree—but that this is worth more than all the fox's tricks.

come. He flattened himself down on the limb, and through a screen of leaves almost as thick as tapestry, he watched. The thing that was approaching was a man.

It was General Zaroff. He made his way along with his eyes fixed in utmost concentration on the ground before him. He paused, almost beneath the tree, dropped to his knees and studied the ground. Rainsford's impulse was to hurl himself down like a panther, but he saw that the general's right hand held something metallic—a small automatic pistol.

The hunter shook his head several times, as if he were puzzled. Then he straightened up and took from his case one of his black cigarettes; its pungent incense-like smoke floated up to Rainsford's nostrils.

Rainsford held his breath. The general's eyes had left the ground and were traveling inch by inch up the tree. Rainsford froze there, every muscle tensed for a spring. But the sharp eyes of the hunter stopped before they reached the limb where Rainsford lay; a smile spread over his brown face. Very deliberately he blew a smoke ring into the air; then he turned his back on the tree and walked carelessly away, back along the trail he had come. The swish of the underbrush against his hunting boots grew fainter and fainter.

The pent-up air burst hotly from Rainsford's lungs. His first thought made him feel sick and numb. The general could follow a trail through the woods at night; he could follow an extremely difficult trail; he must have uncanny powers; only by the merest chance had the Cossack failed to see his quarry.

Rainsford's second thought was even more terrible. It sent a shudder of cold horror through his whole being. Why had the general smiled? Why had he turned back?

Rainsford did not want to believe what his reason told him was true, but the truth was as evident as the sun that had by now pushed through the morning mists. The general was playing with him! The general was saving him for another day's sport! The Cossack was the cat; he was the mouse.[1] Then it was that Rainsford knew the full meaning of terror.

"I will not lose my nerve. I will not."

He slid down from the tree, and struck off again into the woods. His face was set and he forced the machinery of his mind to function. Three hundred yards from his hiding place he stopped where a huge dead tree leaned precariously on a smaller, living one. Throwing off his sack of food, Rainsford took his knife from its sheath and began to work with all his energy.

The job was finished at last, and he threw himself down behind a fallen log a hundred feet away. He did not have to wait long. The cat was coming again to play with the mouse.

Following the trail with the sureness of a bloodhound, came General Zaroff. Nothing escaped those searching black eyes, no crushed blade of grass, no bent twig, no mark, no matter how faint, in the moss. So intent was the Cossack on his stalking that he was upon the thing Rainsford had made before he saw it. His foot touched the protruding bough that was the trigger. Even as he touched it, the general sensed his danger and leaped back with the agility of an ape. But he was not quite quick enough; the dead tree, delicately adjusted to rest on the

1. A cat, sure of his prey, plays with a mouse before killing him.

cut living one, crashed down and struck the general a glacing blow on the shoulder as it fell; but for his alertness, he must have been smashed beneath it. He staggered, but he did not fall; nor did he drop his revolver. He stood there, rubbing his injured shoulder, and Rainsford, with fear again gripping his heart, heard the general's mocking laugh ring through the jungle.

"Rainsford," called the general, "if you are within sound of my voice, as I suppose you are, let me congratulate you. Not many men know how to make a Malay man-catcher. Luckily, for me, I too have hunted in Malacca. You are proving interesting, Mr. Rainsford. I am going now to have my wound dressed; it's only a slight one. But I shall be back. I shall be back."

When the general, nursing his bruised shoulder, had gone, Rainsford took up his flight again. It was flight now, a desperate, hopeless flight, that carried him on for some hours. Dusk came, then darkness, and still he pressed on. The ground grew softer under his moccasins; the vegetation grew ranker, denser; insects bit him savagely. Then, as he stepped forward, his foot sank into the ooze. He tried to wrench it back, but the muck sucked viciously at his foot as if it were a giant leech. With a violent effort, he tore his foot loose. He knew where he was now. Death Swamp and its quicksand.

His hands were tight closed as if his nerve were something tangible that someone in the darkness was trying to tear from his grip. The softness of the earth had given him an idea. He stepped back from the quicksand a dozen feet or so and, like some huge prehistoric beaver, he began to dig.

Rainsford had dug himself in in France[2] when a second's delay meant death. That had been a placid pastime compared to his digging now. The pit grew deeper; when it was above his shoulders, he climbed out and from some hard saplings cut stakes and sharpened them to a fine point. These stakes he planted in the bottom of the pit with the points sticking up. With flying fingers he wove a rough carpet of weeds and branches and with it he covered the mouth of the pit. Then, wet with sweat and aching with tiredness, he crouched behind the stump of a lightning-charred tree.

He knew his pursuer was coming; he heard the padding sound of feet on the soft earth, and the night breeze brought him the perfume of the general's cigarette. It seemed to Rainsford that the general was coming with unusual swiftness; he was not feeling his way along, foot by foot. Rainsford, crouching there, could not see the general, nor could he see the pit. He lived a year in a minute. Then he felt an impulse to cry aloud with joy, for he heard the sharp crackle of the breaking branches as the cover of the pit gave way; he heard the sharp scream of pain as the pointed stakes found their mark. He leaped up from his place of concealment. Then he cowered back. Three feet from the pit a man was standing, with an electric torch in his hand.

"You've done well, Rainsford," the voice of the general called. "Your Burmese tiger pit has claimed one of my best dogs. Again you score. I think, Mr. Rainsford, I'll see what you can do against my whole pack. I'm going home for a rest now. Thank you for a most amusing evening."

2. During World War I he had quickly dug a hole or trench to shelter himself from exploding shells, bullets, etc.

At daybreak Rainsford, lying near the swamp, was awakened by a sound that made him know that he had new things to learn about fear. It was a distant sound, faint and wavering, but he knew it. It was the baying of a pack of hounds.

Rainsford knew he could do one of two things. He could stay where he was and wait. That was suicide. He could flee. That was postponing the inevitable. For a moment he stood there, thinking. An idea that held a wild chance came to him, and, tightening his belt, he headed away from the swamp.

The baying of the hounds drew nearer, then still nearer, nearer, ever nearer. On a ridge Rainsford climbed a tree. Down a watercourse, not a quarter of a mile away, he could see the bush moving. Straining his eyes, he saw the lean figure of General Zaroff; just ahead of him Rainsford made out another figure whose wide shoulders surged through the tall jungle weeds; it was the giant Ivan, and he seemed pulled forward by some unseen force; Rainsford knew that Ivan must be holding the pack in leash.

They would be on him any minute now. His mind worked frantically. He thought of a native trick he had learned in Uganda. He slid down the tree. He caught hold of a springy young sapling and to it he fastened his hunting knife, with the blade pointing down the trail; with a bit of wild grapevine he tied back the sapling. Then he ran for his life. The hounds raised their voices as they hit the fresh scent. Rainsford knew now how an animal at bay feels.

He had to stop to get his breath. The baying of the hounds stopped abruptly, and Rainsford's heart stopped too. They must have reached the knife.

He shinned excitedly up a tree and looked back. His pursuers had stopped. But the hope that was in Rainsford's brain when he climbed died, for he saw in the shallow valley that General Zaroff was still on his feet. But Ivan was not. The knife, driven by the recoil of the springing tree, had not wholly failed.

Rainsford had hardly tumbled to the ground when the pack took up the cry again.

"Nerve, nerve, nerve!" he panted, as he dashed along. A blue gap showed between the trees dead ahead. Ever nearer drew the hounds. Rainsford forced himself on toward that gap. He reached it. It was the shore of the sea. Across a cove he could see the gloomy gray stone of the château. Twenty feet below him the sea rumbled and hissed. Rainsford hesitated. He heard the hounds. Then he leaped far out into the sea. . . .

When the general and his pack reached the place by the sea, the Cossack stopped. For some minutes he stood regarding the blue-green expanse of water. He shrugged his shoulders. Then he sat down, took a drink of brandy from a silver flask, lit a perfumed cigarette, and hummed a bit from "Madame Butterfly."

General Zaroff had an exceedingly good dinner in his great paneled dining hall that evening. With it he had a bottle of Pol Roger and half a bottle of Chambertin. Two slight annoyances kept him from perfect enjoyment. One was the thought that it would be difficult to replace Ivan; the other was that his quarry had escaped him; of course the American hadn't played the game—so thought the general as he tasted his after-dinner liqueur. In his library he read, to soothe himself, from

the works of Marcus Aurelius.[3] At ten he went up to his bedroom. He was deliciously tired, he said to himself, as he locked himself in. There was a little moonlight, so, before turning on his light, he went to the window and looked down at the courtyard. He could see the great hounds, and he called: "Better luck another time," to them. Then he switched on the light.

A man, who had been hiding in the curtains of the bed, was standing there.

"Rainsford!" screamed the general. "How in God's name did you get here?"

"Swam," said Rainsford. "I found it quicker than walking through the jungle."

The general sucked in his breath and smiled. "I congratulate you," he said. "You have won the game."

Rainsford did not smile. "I am still a beast at bay," he said, in a low, hoarse voice. "Get ready, General Zaroff."

The general made one of his deepest bows. "I see," he said. "Splendid! One of us is to furnish a repast for the hounds. The other will sleep in this very excellent bed. On guard, Rainsford. . . ."

He had never slept in a better bed, Rainsford decided.

1924

ANTON CHEKHOV

The Lady with the Dog

1

People were telling one another that a newcomer had been seen on the promenade—a lady with a dog. Dmitri Dmitrich Gurov had been a fortnight in Yalta, and was accustomed to its ways, and he, too, had begun to take an interest in fresh arrivals. From his seat in Vernet's outdoor café, he caught sight of a young woman in a toque, passing along the promenade; she was fair and not very tall; after her trotted a white pomeranian.

Later he encountered her in the municipal park, and in the square, several times a day. She was always alone, wearing the same toque, and the pomeranian always trotted at her side. Nobody knew who she was, and people referred to her simply as "the lady with the dog."

"If she's here without her husband, and without any friends," thought Gurov, "it wouldn't be a bad idea to make her acquaintance."

He was not yet forty, but had a twelve-year-old daughter and two schoolboy sons. He had been talked into marrying in his second year at college, and his wife now looked nearly twice as old as he was. She was a tall, black-browed woman, erect, dignified, imposing, and, as she said of herself, a "thinker." She was a great reader, omitted the "hard sign"[1] at the end of words in her letters, and called her husband "Dimitri" instead of Dmitri; and though he secretly considered her shallow, narrow-minded, and dowdy, he stood in awe of her, and dis-

3. Roman Emperor (161–180 A.D.), Stoic philosopher, writer, and humanitarian, who, though good to the poor and opposed to the cruelty of gladiatorial shows, persecuted early Christians.

1. Conventional sign that was used following consonants; to omit it was then "progressive," and it has in fact been eliminated in the reformed alphabet adopted by the Soviet government.

liked being at home. It was long since he had first begun deceiving her and he was now constantly unfaithful to her, and this was no doubt why he spoke slightingly of women, to whom he referred as *the lower race*.

He considered that the ample lessons he had received from bitter experience entitled him to call them whatever he liked, but without this "lower race" he could not have existed a single day. He was bored and ill-at-ease in the company of men, with whom he was always cold and reserved, but felt quite at home among women, and knew exactly what to say to them, and how to behave; he could even be silent in their company without feeling the slightest awkwardness. There was an elusive charm in his appearance and disposition which attracted women and caught their sympathies. He knew this and was himself attracted to them by some invisible force.

Repeated and bitter experience had taught him that every fresh intimacy, while at first introducing such pleasant variety into everyday life, and offering itself as a charming, light adventure, inevitably developed, among decent people (especially in Moscow, where they are so irresolute and slow to move), into a problem of excessive complication leading to an intolerably irksome situation. But every time he encountered an attractive woman he forgot all about this experience, the desire for life surged up in him, and everything suddenly seemed simple and amusing.

One evening, then, while he was dining at the restaurant in the park, the lady in the toque came strolling up and took a seat at a neighboring table. Her expression, gait, dress, coiffure, all told him that she was from the upper classes, that she was married, that she was in Yalta for the first time, alone and bored. . . . The accounts of the laxity of morals among visitors to Yalta are greatly exaggerated, and he paid no heed to them, knowing that for the most part they were invented by people who would gladly have transgressed themselves, had they known how to set about it. But when the lady sat down at a neighboring table a few yards away from him, the stories of easy conquests, of excursions to the mountains, came back to him, and the seductive idea of a brisk transitory liaison, an affair with a woman whose very name he did not know, suddenly took possession of his mind.

He snapped his fingers at the pomeranian, and when it trotted up to him, shook his forefinger at it. The pomeranian growled. Gurov shook his finger again.

The lady glanced at him and instantly lowered her eyes.

"He doesn't bite," she said, and blushed.

"May I give him a bone?" he asked, and on her nod of consent added in friendly tones: "Have you been in Yalta long?"

"About five days."

"And I am dragging out my second week here."

Neither spoke for a few minutes.

"The days pass quickly, and yet one is so bored here," she said, not looking at him.

"It's the thing to say it's boring here. People never complain of boredom in God-forsaken holes like Belyev or Zhizdra, but when they get here it's: 'Oh, the dullness! Oh, the dust!' You'd think they'd come from Granada,[2] to say the least."

2. City in southern Spain, site of the Alhambra and once capital of the Moorish kingdom.

She laughed. Then they both went on eating in silence, like complete strangers. But after dinner they left the restaurant together, and embarked upon the light, jesting talk of people free and contented, for whom it is all the same where they go, or what they talk about. They strolled along, remarking on the strange light over the sea. The water was a warm, tender purple, the moonlight lay on its surface in a golden strip. They said how close it was, after the hot day. Gurov told her he was from Moscow, that he was really a philologist,[3] but worked in a bank; that he had at one time trained himself to sing in a private opera company, but had given up the idea; that he owned two houses in Moscow. . . . And from her he learned that she had grown up in Petersburg, but had got married in the town of S., where she had been living two years, that she would stay another month in Yalta, and that perhaps her husband, who also needed a rest, would join her. She was quite unable to explain whether her husband was a member of the gubernia[4] council, or on the board of the Zemstvo,[5] and was greatly amused at herself for this. Further, Gurov learned that her name was Anna Sergeyevna.

Back in his own room he thought about her, and felt sure he would meet her the next day. It was inevitable. As he went to bed he reminded himself that only a very short time ago she had been a schoolgirl, like his own daughter, learning her lessons; he remembered how much there was of shyness and constraint in her laughter, in her way of conversing with a stranger—it was probably the first time in her life that she found herself alone, and in a situation in which men could follow her and watch her, and speak to her, all the time with a secret aim she could not fail to divine. He recalled her slender, delicate neck, her fine gray eyes.

"And yet there's something pathetic about her," he thought to himself as he fell asleep.

2

A week had passed since the beginning of their acquaintance. It was a holiday. Indoors it was stuffy, but the dust rose in clouds out of doors, and people's hats blew off. It was a thirsty day and Gurov kept going to the outdoor café for fruit-drinks and ices to offer Anna Sergeyevna. The heat was overpowering.

In the evening, when the wind had dropped, they walked to the pier to see the steamer come in. There were a great many people strolling about the landing-place; some, bunches of flowers in their hands, were meeting friends. Two peculiarities of the smart Yalta crowd stood out distinctly—the elderly ladies all tried to dress very young, and there seemed to be an inordinate number of generals about.

Owing to the roughness of the sea the steamer arrived late, after the sun had gone down, and it had to maneuver for some time before it could get alongside the pier. Anna Sergeyevna scanned the steamer and passengers through her lorgnette, as if looking for someone she knew, and when she turned to Gurov her eyes were glistening. She talked a great deal, firing off abrupt questions and forgetting immediately what it was she had wanted to know. Then she lost her lorgnette in the crush.

The smart crowd began dispersing, features could no longer be

3. In the older sense, classical scholar.
4. Czarist province.
5. In Czarist Russia an elective provincial council responsible for local government.

made out, the wind had quite dropped, and Gurov and Anna Serge-yevna stood there as if waiting for someone else to come off the steamer. Anna Sergeyevna had fallen silent, every now and then smelling her flowers, but not looking at Gurov.

"It's turned out a fine evening," he said. "What shall we do? We might go for a drive."

She made no reply.

He looked steadily at her and suddenly took her in his arms and kissed her lips, and the fragrance and dampness of the flowers closed round him, but the next moment he looked behind him in alarm—had anyone seen them?

"Let's go to your room," he murmured.

And they walked off together, very quickly.

Her room was stuffy and smelled of some scent she had bought in the Japanese shop. Gurov looked at her, thinking to himself: "How full of strange encounters life is!" He could remember carefree, good-natured women who were exhilarated by love-making and grateful to him for the happiness he gave them, however short-lived; and there had been others—his wife among them—whose caresses were insincere, affected, hysterical, mixed up with a great deal of quite unnecessary talk, and whose expression seemed to say that all this was not just love-making or passion, but something much more significant; then there had been two or three beautiful, cold women, over whose features flitted a predatory expression, betraying a determination to wring from life more than it could give, women no longer in their first youth, capricious, irrational, despotic, brainless, and when Gurov had cooled to these, their beauty aroused in him nothing but repulsion, and the lace trimming on their underclothes reminded him of fish-scales.

But here the timidity and awkwardness of youth and inexperience were still apparent; and there was a feeling of embarrassment in the atmosphere, as if someone had just knocked at the door. Anna Ser-geyevna, "the lady with the dog," seemed to regard the affair as something very special, very serious, as if she had become a fallen woman, an attitude he found odd and disconcerting. Her features lengthened and drooped, and her long hair hung mournfully on either side of her face. She assumed a pose of dismal meditation, like a repentant sinner in some classical painting.

"It isn't right," she said. "You will never respect me anymore."

On the table was a watermelon. Gurov cut himself a slice from it and began slowly eating it. At least half an hour passed in silence.

Anna Sergeyevna was very touching, revealing the purity of a decent, naïve woman who had seen very little of life. The solitary candle burning on the table scarcely lit up her face, but it was obvious that her heart was heavy.

"Why should I stop respecting you?" asked Gurov. "You don't know what you're saying."

"May God forgive me!" she exclaimed, and her eyes filled with tears. "It's terrible."

"No need to seek to justify yourself."

"How can I justify myself? I'm a wicked, fallen woman, I despise myself and have not the least thought of self-justification. It isn't my husband I have deceived, it's myself. And not only now, I have been deceiving myself for ever so long. My husband is no doubt an honest, worthy man, but he's a flunkey. I don't know what it is he does at his

office, but I know he's a flunkey. I was only twenty when I married him, and I was devoured by curiosity, I wanted something higher. I told myself that there must be a different kind of life. I wanted to live, to live. . . . I was burning with curiosity . . . you'll never understand that, but I swear to God I could no longer control myself, nothing could hold me back, I told my husband I was ill, and I came here. . . . And I started going about like one possessed, like a madwoman . . . and now I have become an ordinary, worthless woman, and everyone has the right to despise me."

Gurov listened to her, bored to death. The naïve accents, the remorse, all was so unexpected, so out of place. But for the tears in her eyes, she might have been jesting or play-acting.

"I don't understand," he said gently. "What is it you want?"

She hid her face against his breast and pressed closer to him.

"Do believe me, I implore you to believe me," she said. "I love all that is honest and pure in life, vice is revolting to me, I don't know what I'm doing. The common people say they are snared by the devil. And now I can say that I have been snared by the devil, too."

"Come, come," he murmured.

He gazed into her fixed, terrified eyes, kissed her, and soothed her with gentle affectionate words, and gradually she calmed down and regained her cheerfulness. Soon they were laughing together again.

When, a little later, they went out, there was not a soul on the promenade, the town and its cypresses looked dead, but the sea was still roaring as it dashed against the beach. A solitary fishing-boat tossed on the waves, its lamp blinking sleepily.

They found a droshky[6] and drove to Oreanda.

"I discovered your name in the hall, just now," said Gurov, "written up on the board. Von Diederitz. Is your husband a German?"

"No. His grandfather was, I think, but he belongs to the Orthodox church himself."

When they got out of the droshky at Oreanda they sat down on a bench not far from the church, and looked down at the sea, without talking. Yalta could be dimly discerned through the morning mist, and white clouds rested motionless on the summits of the mountains. Not a leaf stirred, the grasshoppers chirruped, and the monotonous hollow roar of the sea came up to them, speaking of peace, of the eternal sleep lying in wait for us all. The sea had roared like this long before there was any Yalta or Oreanda, it was roaring now, and it would go on roaring, just as indifferently and hollowly, when we have passed away. And it may be that in this continuity, this utter indifference to life and death, lies the secret of our ultimate salvation, of the stream of life on our planet, and of its never-ceasing movement toward perfection.

Side by side with a young woman, who looked so exquisite in the early light, soothed and enchanted by the sight of all this magical beauty—sea, mountains, clouds and the vast expanse of the sky—Gurov told himself that, when you came to think of it, everything in the world is beautiful really, everything but our own thoughts and actions, when we lose sight of the higher aims of life, and of our dignity as human beings.

Someone approached them—a watchman, probably—looked at them and went away. And there was something mysterious and beautiful

6. Horse-drawn, four-wheeled open carriage.

even in this. The steamer from Feodosia could be seen coming toward the pier, lit up by the dawn, its lamps out.

"There's dew on the grass," said Anna Sergeyevna, breaking the silence.

"Yes. Time to go home."

They went back to the town.

After this they met every day at noon on the promenade, lunching and dining together, going for walks, and admiring the sea. She complained of sleeplessness, of palpitations, asked the same questions over and over again, alternately surrendering to jealousy and the fear that he did not really respect her. And often, when there was nobody in sight in the square or the park, he would draw her to him and kiss her passionately. The utter idleness, these kisses in broad daylight, accompanied by furtive glances and the fear of discovery, the heat, the smell of the sea, and the idle, smart, well-fed people continually crossing their field of vision, seemed to have given him a new lease on life. He told Anna Sergeyevna she was beautiful and seductive, made love to her with impetuous passion, and never left her side, while she was always pensive, always trying to force from him the admission that he did not respect her, that he did not love her a bit, and considered her just an ordinary woman. Almost every night they drove out of town, to Oreanda, the waterfall, or some other beauty spot. And these excursions were invariably a success, each contributing fresh impressions of majestic beauty.

All this time they kept expecting her husband to arrive. But a letter came in which he told his wife that he was having trouble with his eyes, and implored her to come home as soon as possible. Anna Sergeyevna made hasty preparations for leaving.

"It's a good thing I'm going," she said to Gurov. "It's the intervention of fate."

She left Yalta in a carriage, and he went with her as far as the railway station. The drive took nearly a whole day. When she got into the express train, after the second bell had been rung, she said:

"Let me have one more look at you. . . . One last look. That's right."

She did not weep, but was mournful, and seemed ill, the muscles of her cheeks twitching.

"I shall think of you . . . I shall think of you all the time," she said. "God bless you! Think kindly of me. We are parting for ever, it must be so, because we ought never to have met. Good-bye—God bless you."

The train steamed rapidly out of the station, its lights soon disappearing, and a minute later even the sound it made was silenced, as if everything were conspiring to bring this sweet oblivion, this madness, to an end as quickly as possible. And Gurov, standing alone on the platform and gazing into the dark distance, listened to the shrilling of the grasshoppers and the humming of the telegraph wires, with a feeling that he had only just waked up. And he told himself that this had been just one more of the many adventures in his life, and that it, too, was over, leaving nothing but a memory. . . . He was moved and sad, and felt a slight remorse. After all, this young woman whom he would never again see had not been really happy with him. He had been friendly and affectionate with her, but in his whole behavior, in the tones of his voice, in his very caresses, there had been a shade of irony, the insulting indulgence of the fortunate male, who was, moreover, almost twice her age. She had insisted in calling him good, remarkable,

high-minded. Evidently he had appeared to her different from his real self, in a word he had involuntarily deceived her. . . .

There was an autumnal feeling in the air, and the evening was chilly.

"It's time for me to be going north, too," thought Gurov, as he walked away from the platform. "High time!"

3

When he got back to Moscow it was beginning to look like winter, the stoves were heated every day, and it was still dark when the children got up to go to school and drank their tea, so that the nurse had to light the lamp for a short time. Frost had set in. When the first snow falls, and one goes for one's first sleigh-ride, it is pleasant to see the white ground, the white roofs; one breathes freely and lightly, and remembers the days of one's youth. The ancient lime-trees and birches, white with rime, have a good-natured look, they are closer to the heart than cypresses and palms, and beneath their branches one is no longer haunted by the memory of mountains and the sea.

Gurov had always lived in Moscow, and he returned to Moscow on a fine frosty day, and when he put on his fur-lined overcoat and thick gloves, and sauntered down Petrovka Street, and when, on Saturday evening, he heard the church bells ringing, his recent journey and the places he had visited lost their charm for him. He became gradually immersed in Moscow life, reading with avidity three newspapers a day, while declaring he never read Moscow newspapers on principle. Once more he was caught up in a whirl of restaurants, clubs, banquets, and celebrations, once more glowed with the flattering consciousness that well-known lawyers and actors came to his house, that he played cards in the Medical Club opposite a professor.

He had believed that in a month's time Anna Sergeyevna would be nothing but a vague memory, and that hereafter, with her wistful smile, she would only occasionally appear to him in dreams, like others before her. But the month was now well over and winter was in full swing, and all was as clear in his memory as if he had only parted with Anna Sergeyevna the day before. And his recollections grew ever more insistent. When the voices of his children at their lessons reached him in his study through the evening stillness, when he heard a song, or the sounds of a musical-box in a restaurant, when the wind howled in the chimney, it all came back to him: early morning on the pier, the misty mountains, the steamer from Feodosia, the kisses. He would pace up and down his room for a long time, smiling at his memories, and then memory turned into dreaming, and what had happened mingled in his imagination with what was going to happen. Anna Sergeyevna did not come to him in his dreams, she accompanied him everywhere, like his shadow, following him everywhere he went. When he closed his eyes, she seemed to stand before him in the flesh, still lovelier, younger, tenderer than she had really been, and looking back, he saw himself, too, as better than he had been in Yalta. In the evenings she looked out at him from the bookshelves, the fireplace, the corner; he could hear her breathing, the sweet rustle of her skirts. In the streets he followed women with his eyes, to see if there were any like her. . . .

He began to feel an overwhelming desire to share his memories with someone. But he could not speak of his love at home, and outside his home who was there for him to confide in? Not the tenants living in his house, and certainly not his colleagues at the bank. And what

was there to tell? Was it love that he had felt? Had there been anything exquisite, poetic, anything instructive or even amusing about his relations with Anna Sergeyevna? He had to content himself with uttering vague generalizations about love and women, and nobody guessed what he meant, though his wife's dark eyebrows twitched as she said:

"The role of a coxcomb doesn't suit you a bit, Dimitri."

One evening, leaving the Medical Club with one of his card-partners, a government official, he could not refrain from remarking:

"If you only knew what a charming woman I met in Yalta!"

The official got into his sleigh, and just before driving off turned and called out:

"Dmitri Dmitrich!"

"Yes?"

"You were quite right, you know—the sturgeon was just a *leetle* off."

These words, in themselves so commonplace, for some reason infuriated Gurov, seemed to him humiliating, gross. What savage manners, what people! What wasted evenings, what tedious, empty days! Frantic card-playing, gluttony, drunkenness, perpetual talk always about the same thing. The greater part of one's time and energy went on business that was no use to anyone, and on discussing the same thing over and over again, and there was nothing to show for it all but a stunted, earth-bound existence and a round of trivialities, and there was nowhere to escape to, you might as well be in a madhouse or a convict settlement.

Gurov lay awake all night, raging, and went about the whole of the next day with a headache. He slept badly on the succeeding nights, too, sitting up in bed, thinking, or pacing the floor of his room. He was sick of his children, sick of the bank, felt not the slightest desire to go anywhere or talk about anything.

When the Christmas holidays came, he packed his things, telling his wife he had to go to Petersburg in the interests of a certain young man, and set off for the town of S. To what end? He hardly knew himself. He only knew that he must see Anna Sergeyevna, must speak to her, arrange a meeting, if possible.

He arrived at S. in the morning and engaged the best room in the hotel, which had a carpet of gray military frieze, and a dusty ink-pot on the table, surmounted by a headless rider, holding his hat in his raised hand. The hall porter told him what he wanted to know: von Diederitz had a house of his own in Staro-Goncharnaya Street. It wasn't far from the hotel, he lived on a grand scale, luxuriously, kept carriage-horses, the whole town knew him. The hall porter pronounced the name "Drideritz."

Gurov strolled over to Staro-Goncharnaya Street and discovered the house. In front of it was a long gray fence with inverted nails hammered into the tops of the palings.

"A fence like that is enough to make anyone want to run away," thought Gurov, looking at the windows of the house and the fence.

He reasoned that since it was a holiday, her husband would probably be at home. In any case it would be tactless to embarrass her by calling at the house. And a note might fall into the hands of the husband, and bring about catastrophe. The best thing would be to wait about on the chance of seeing her. And he walked up and down the street, hovering in the vicinity of the fence, watching for his chance. A beggar entered the gate, only to be attacked by dogs; then, an hour

later, the faint, vague sounds of a piano reached his ears. That would be Anna Sergeyevna playing. Suddenly the front door opened and an old woman came out, followed by a familiar white pomeranian. Gurov tried to call to it, but his heart beat violently, and in his agitation he could not remember its name.

He walked on, hating the gray fence more and more, and now ready to tell himself irately that Anna Sergeyevna had forgotten him, had already, perhaps, found distraction in another—what could be more natural in a young woman who had to look at this accursed fence from morning to night? He went back to his hotel and sat on the sofa in his room for some time, not knowing what to do, then he ordered dinner, and after dinner, had a long sleep.

"What a foolish, restless business," he thought, waking up and looking toward the dark windowpanes. It was evening by now. "Well, I've had my sleep out. And what am I to do in the night?"

He sat up in bed, covered by the cheap gray quilt, which reminded him of a hospital blanket, and in his vexation he fell to taunting himself.

"You and your lady with a dog . . . there's adventure for you! See what you get for your pains."

On his arrival at the station that morning he had noticed a poster announcing in enormous letters the first performance at the local theater of *The Geisha*.[7] Remembering this, he got up and made for the theater.

"It's highly probable that she goes to first-nights," he told himself.

The theater was full. It was a typical provincial theater, with a mist collecting over the chandeliers, and the crowd in the gallery fidgeting noisily. In the first row of the stalls[8] the local dandies stood waiting for the curtain to go up, their hands clasped behind them. There, in the front seat of the Governor's box, sat the Governor's daughter, wearing a boa, the Governor himself hiding modestly behind the drapes, so that only his hands were visible. The curtain stirred, the orchestra took a long time tuning up their instruments. Gurov's eyes roamed eagerly over the audience as they filed in and occupied their seats.

Anna Sergeyevna came in, too. She seated herself in the third row of the stalls and when Gurov's glance fell on her, his heart seemed to stop, and he knew in a flash that the whole world contained no one nearer or dearer to him, no one more important to his happiness. This little woman, lost in the provincial crowd, in no way remarkable, holding a silly lorgnette in her hand, now filled his whole life, was his grief, his joy, all that he desired. Lulled by the sounds coming from the wretched orchestra, with its feeble, amateurish violinists, he thought how beautiful she was . . . thought and dreamed. . . .

Anna Sergeyevna was accompanied by a tall, round-shouldered young man with small whiskers, who nodded at every step before taking the seat beside her and seemed to be continually bowing to someone. This must be her husband, whom, in a fit of bitterness, at Yalta, she had called a "flunkey." And there really was something of the lackey's servility in his lanky figure, his side-whiskers, and the little bald spot on the top of his head. And he smiled sweetly, and the badge of some scientific society gleaming in his buttonhole was like the number on a footman's livery.

7. Operetta by Sidney Jones (1861–1946) which toured Eastern Europe in 1898–99.   8. Seats at the front of a theater, near the stage and separated from nearby seats by a railing.

The husband went out to smoke in the first interval, and she was left alone in her seat. Gurov, who had taken a seat in the stalls, went up to her and said in a trembling voice, with a forced smile: "How d'you do?"

She glanced up at him and turned pale, then looked at him again in alarm, unable to believe her eyes, squeezing her fan and lorgnette in one hand, evidently struggling to overcome a feeling of faintness. Neither of them said a word. She sat there, and he stood beside her, disconcerted by her embarrassment, and not daring to sit down. The violins and flutes sang out as they were tuned, and there was a tense sensation in the atmosphere, as if they were being watched from all the boxes. At last she got up and moved rapidly toward one of the exits. He followed her and they wandered aimlessly along corridors, up and down stairs; figures flashed by in the uniforms of legal officials, high-school teachers, and civil servants, all wearing badges; ladies' coats hanging on pegs, flashed by; there was a sharp draft, bringing with it an odor of cigarette stubs. And Gurov, whose heart was beating violently, thought:

"What on earth are all these people, this orchestra for? . . ."

The next minute he suddenly remembered how, after seeing Anna Sergeyevna off that evening at the station, he had told himself that all was over, and they would never meet again. And how far away the end seemed to be now!

She stopped on a dark narrow staircase over which was a notice bearing the inscription "To the upper circle."

"How you frightened me!" she said, breathing heavily, still pale and half-stunned. "Oh, how you frightened me! I'm almost dead! Why did you come? Oh, why?"

"But, Anna," he said, in low, hasty tones. "But, Anna. . . . Try to understand . . . do try. . . ."

She cast him a glance of fear, entreaty, love, and then gazed at him steadily, as if to fix his features firmly in her memory.

"I've been so unhappy," she continued, taking no notice of his words. "I could think of nothing but you the whole time, I lived on the thoughts of you. I tried to forget—why, oh, why did you come?"

On the landing above them were two schoolboys, smoking and looking down, but Gurov did not care, and, drawing Anna Sergeyevna toward him, began kissing her face, her lips, her hands.

"What are you doing, oh, what are you doing?" she said in horror, drawing back. "We have both gone mad. Go away this very night, this moment. . . . By all that is sacred, I implore you. . . . Somebody is coming."

Someone was ascending the stairs.

"You must go away," went on Anna Sergeyevna in a whisper. "D'you hear me, Dmitri Dmitrich? I'll come to you in Moscow. I have never been happy, I am unhappy now, and I shall never be happy—never! Do not make me suffer still more! I will come to you in Moscow, I swear it! And now we must part! My dear one, my kind one, my darling, we must part."

She pressed his hand and hurried down the stairs, looking back at him continually, and her eyes showed that she was in truth unhappy. Gurov stood where he was for a short time, listening, and when all was quiet went to look for his coat, and left the theater.

4

And Anna Sergeyevna began going to Moscow to see him. Every two or three months she left the town of S., telling her husband that she was going to consult a specialist on female diseases, and her husband believed her and did not believe her. In Moscow she always stayed at the "Slavyanski Bazaar," sending a man in a red cap to Gurov the moment she arrived. Gurov went to her, and no one in Moscow knew anything about it.

One winter morning he went to see her as usual (the messenger had been to him the evening before, but had not found him at home). His daughter was with him for her school was on the way, and he thought he might as well see her to it.

"It is three degrees above zero,"[9] said Gurov to his daughter, "and yet it is snowing. You see it is only above zero close to the ground, the temperature in the upper layers of the atmosphere is quite different."

"Why doesn't it ever thunder in winter, Papa?"

He explained this, too. As he was speaking, he kept reminding himself that he was going to a rendezvous and that not a living soul knew about it, or, probably, ever would. He led a double life—one in public, in the sight of all whom it concerned, full of conventional truth and conventional deception, exactly like the lives of his friends and acquaintances, and another which flowed in secret. And, owing to some strange, possibly quite accidental chain of circumstances, everything that was important, interesting, essential, everything about which he was sincere and never deceived himself, everything that composed the kernel of his life, went on in secret, while everything that was false in him, everything that composed the husk in which he hid himself and the truth which was in him—his work at the bank, discussions at the club, his "lower race," his attendance at anniversary celebrations with his wife—was on the surface. He began to judge others by himself, no longer believing what he saw, and always assuming that the real, the only interesting life of every individual goes on as under cover of night, secretly. Every individual existence revolves around mystery, and perhaps that is the chief reason that all cultivated individuals insisted so strongly on the respect due to personal secrets.

After leaving his daughter at the door of her school Gurov set off for the "Slavyanski Bazaar." Taking off his overcoat in the lobby, he went upstairs and knocked softly on the door. Anna Sergeyevna, wearing the gray dress he liked most, exhausted by her journey and by suspense, had been expecting him since the evening before. She was pale and looked at him without smiling, but was in his arms almost before he was fairly in the room. Their kiss was lingering, prolonged, as if they had not met for years.

"Well, how are you?" he asked. "Anything new?"

"Wait. I'll tell you in a minute. . . . I can't. . . ."

She could not speak, because she was crying. Turning away, she held her handkerchief to her eyes.

"I'll wait till she's had her cry out," he thought, and sank into a chair.

He rang for tea, and a little later, while he was drinking it, she was

9. Probably Réaumur thermometer; about 39 degrees Fahrenheit.

still standing there, her face to the window. She wept from emotion, from her bitter consciousness of the sadness of their life; they could only see one another in secret, hiding from people, as if they were thieves. Was not their life a broken one?

"Don't cry," he said.

It was quite obvious to him that this love of theirs would not soon come to an end, and that no one could say when this end would be. Anna Sergeyevna loved him ever more fondly, worshipped him, and there would have been no point in telling her that one day it must end. Indeed, she would not have believed him.

He moved over and took her by the shoulders, intending to fondle her with light words, but suddenly he caught sight of himself in the looking-glass.

His hair was already beginning to turn gray. It struck him as strange that he should have aged so much in the last few years. The shoulders on which his hands lay were warm and quivering. He felt a pity for this life, still so warm and exquisite, but probably soon to fade and droop like his own. Why did she love him so? Women had always believed him different from what he really was, had loved in him not himself but the man their imagination pictured him, a man they had sought for eagerly all their lives. And afterwards when they discovered their mistake, they went on loving him just the same. And not one of them had ever been happy with him. Time had passed, he had met one woman after another, become intimate with each, parted with each, but had never loved. There had been all sorts of things between them, but never love.

And only now, when he was gray-haired, had he fallen in love properly, thoroughly, for the first time in his life.

He and Anna Sergeyevna loved one another as people who are very close and intimate, as husband and wife, as dear friends love one another. It seemed to them that fate had intended them for one another, and they could not understand why she should have a husband, and he a wife. They were like two migrating birds, the male and the female, who had been caught and put into separate cages. They forgave one another all that they were ashamed of in the past, in their present, and felt that this love of theirs had changed them both.

Formerly, in moments of melancholy, he had consoled himself by the first argument that came into his head, but now arguments were nothing to him, he felt profound pity, desired to be sincere, tender.

"Stop crying, my dearest," he said. "You've had your cry, now stop. . . . Now let us have a talk, let us try and think what we are to do."

Then they discussed their situation for a long time, trying to think how they could get rid of the necessity for hiding, deception, living in different towns, being so long without meeting. How were they to shake off these intolerable fetters?

"How? How?" he repeated, clutching his head. "How?"

And it seemed to them that they were within an inch of arriving at a decision, and that then a new, beautiful life would begin. And they both realized that the end was still far, far away, and that the hardest, the most complicated part was only just beginning.

1899

EDITH WHARTON

Souls Belated

Their railway carriage had been full when the train left Bologna;
but at the first station beyond Milan their only remaining companion
—a courtly person who ate garlic out of a carpetbag—had left his
crumb-strewn seat with a bow.

Lydia's eye regretfully followed the shiny broadcloth of his retreating back till it lost itself in the cloud of touts and cab drivers hanging
about the station; then she glanced across at Gannett and caught the
same regret in his look. They were both sorry to be alone.

"*Par-ten-za!*"[1] shouted the guard. The train vibrated to a sudden
slamming of doors; a waiter ran along the platform with a tray of fos-
silized sandwiches; a belated porter flung a bundle of shawls and
bandboxes into a third-class carriage; the guard snapped out a brief
Partenza! which indicated the purely ornamental nature of his first
shout; and the train swung out of the station.

The direction of the road had changed, and a shaft of sunlight struck
across the dusty red-velvet seats into Lydia's corner. Gannett did not
notice it. He had returned to his *Revue de Paris*,[2] and she had to rise
and lower the shade of the farther window. Against the vast horizon of
their leisure such incidents stood out sharply.

Having lowered the shade, Lydia sat down, leaving the length of
the carriage between herself and Gannett. At length he missed her
and looked up.

"I moved out of the sun," she hastily explained.

He looked at her curiously: the sun was beating on her through the
shade.

"Very well," he said pleasantly; adding, "You don't mind?" as he
drew a cigarette case from his pocket.

It was a refreshing touch, relieving the tension of her spirit with the
suggestion that, after all, if he could *smoke*—! The relief was only
momentary. Her experience of smokers was limited (her husband had
disapproved of the use of tobacco) but she knew from hearsay that men
sometimes smoked to get away from things; that a cigar might be the
masculine equivalent of darkened windows and a headache. Gannett,
after a puff or two, returned to his review.

It was just as she had foreseen; he feared to speak as much as she
did. It was one of the misfortunes of their situation that they were never
busy enough to necessitate, or even to justify, the postponement of unpleasant discussions. If they avoided a question it was obviously, uncon-
cealably because the question was disagreeable. They had unlimited
leisure and an accumulation of mental energy to devote to any subject
that presented itself; new topics were in fact at a premium. Lydia sometimes had premonitions of a famine-stricken period when there would be
nothing left to talk about, and she had already caught herself doling
out piecemeal what, in the first prodigality of their confidences, she
would have flung to him in a breath. Their silence therefore might
simply mean that they had nothing to say; but it was another disad-
vantage of their position that it allowed infinite opportunity for the

1. "Departing," equivalent of "All aboard."   2. Intellectual, literary review revived in 1894.

classification of minute differences. Lydia had learned to distinguish between real and factitious silences; and under Gannett's she now detected a hum of speech to which her own thoughts made breathless answer.

How could it be otherwise, with that thing between them? She glanced up at the rack overhead. The *thing* was there, in her dressing bag, symbolically suspended over her head and his. He was thinking of it now, just as she was; they had been thinking of it in unison ever since they had entered the train. While the carriage had held other travelers they had screened her from his thoughts; but now that he and she were alone she knew exactly what was passing through his mind; she could almost hear him asking himself what he should say to her.

The thing had come that morning, brought up to her in an innocent-looking envelope with the rest of their letters, as they were leaving the hotel at Bologna. As she tore it open, she and Gannett were laughing over some ineptitude of the local guidebook—they had been driven, of late, to make the most of such incidental humors of travel. Even when she had unfolded the document she took it for some unimportant business paper sent abroad for her signature, and her eye traveled inattentively over the curly *Whereases* of the preamble until a word arrested her: Divorce. There it stood, an impassable barrier, between her husband's name and hers.

She had been prepared for it, of course, as healthy people are said to be prepared for death, in the sense of knowing it must come without in the least expecting that it will. She had known from the first that Tillotson meant to divorce her—but what did it matter? Nothing mattered, in those first days of supreme deliverance, but the fact that she was free; and not so much (she had begun to be aware) that freedom had released her from Tillotson as that it had given her to Gannett. This discovery had not been agreeable to her self-esteem. She had preferred to think that Tillotson had himself embodied all her reasons for leaving him; and those he represented had seemed cogent enough to stand in no need of reinforcement. Yet she had not left him till she met Gannett. It was her love for Gannett that had made life with Tillotson so poor and incomplete a business. If she had never, from the first, regarded her marriage as a full canceling of her claims upon life, she had at least, for a number of years, accepted it as a provisional compensation,—she had made it "do." Existence in the commodious Tillotson mansion in Fifth Avenue—with Mrs. Tillotson senior commanding the approaches from the second-story front windows—had been reduced to a series of purely automatic acts. The moral atmosphere of the Tillotson interior was as carefully screened and curtained as the house itself: Mrs. Tillotson senior dreaded ideas as much as a draft in her back. Prudent people liked an even temperature; and to do anything unexpected was as foolish as going out in the rain. One of the chief advantages of being rich was that one need not be exposed to unforeseen contingencies: by the use of ordinary firmness and common sense one could make sure of doing exactly the same thing every day at the same hour. These doctrines, reverentially imbibed with his mother's milk, Tillotson (a model son who had never given his parents an hour's anxiety) complacently expounded to his wife, testifying to his sense of their importance by the regularity with which he wore galoshes on damp days, his punctuality at meals, and his elaborate

precautions against burglars and contagious diseases. Lydia, coming from a smaller town, and entering New York life through the portals of the Tillotson mansion, had mechanically accepted this point of view as inseparable from having a front pew in church and a parterre[3] box at the opera. All the people who came to the house revolved in the same small circle of prejudices. It was the kind of society in which, after dinner, the ladies compared the exorbitant charges of their children's teachers, and agreed that, even with the new duties on French clothes, it was cheaper in the end to get everything from Worth,[4] while the husbands, over their cigars, lamented municipal corruption, and decided that the men to start a reform were those who had no private interests at stake.

To Lydia this view of life had become a matter of course, just as lumbering about in her mother-in-law's landau had come to seem the only possible means of locomotion, and listening every Sunday to a fashionable Presbyterian divine the inevitable atonement for having thought oneself bored on the other six days of the week. Before she met Gannett her life had seemed merely dull; his coming made it appear like one of those dismal Cruikshank prints[5] in which the people are all ugly and all engaged in occupations that are either vulgar or stupid.

It was natural that Tillotson should be the chief sufferer from this readjustment of focus. Gannett's nearness had made her husband ridiculous, and a part of the ridicule had been reflected on herself. Her tolerance laid her open to a suspicion of obtuseness from which she must, at all costs, clear herself in Gannett's eyes.

She did not understand this until afterwards. At the time she fancied that she had merely reached the limits of endurance. In so large a charter of liberties as the mere act of leaving Tillotson seemed to confer, the small question of divorce or no divorce did not count. It was when she saw that she had left her husband only to be with Gannett that she perceived the significance of anything affecting their relations. Her husband, in casting her off, had virtually flung her at Gannett: it was thus that the world viewed it. The measure of alacrity with which Gannett would receive her would be the subject of curious speculation over afternoon tea tables and in club corners. She knew what would be said—she had heard it so often of others! The recollection bathed her in misery. The men would probably back Gannett to "do the decent thing"; but the ladies' eyebrows would emphasize the worthlessness of such enforced fidelity; and after all, they would be right. She had put herself in a position where Gannett "owed" her something; where, as a gentleman, he was bound to "stand the damage." The idea of accepting such compensation had never crossed her mind; the so-called rehabilitation of such a marriage had always seemed to her the only real disgrace. What she dreaded was the necessity of having to explain herself; of having to combat his arguments; of calculating, in spite of herself, the exact measure of insistence with which he pressed them. She knew not whether she most shrank from his insisting too much or too little. In such a case the nicest sense of proportion might be at fault; and how easily to fall into the error of taking her resistance for a test of his sincerity! Whichever way she turned, an ironical implica-

3. Part of theater beneath balcony at back of main floor; "orchestra circle."
4. Charles F. Worth (1825–1895), Anglo-French dress designer, for years the leading arbiter of women's styles.

5. George Cruikshank (1792–1878), caricaturist, satirist, and book illustrator (including *Oliver Twist* and *Uncle Tom's Cabin*).

tion confronted her: she had the exasperated sense of having walked into the trap of some stupid practical joke.

Beneath all these preoccupations lurked the dread of what he was thinking. Sooner or later, of course, he would have to speak; but that, in the meantime, he should think, even for a moment, that there was any use in speaking, seemed to her simply unendurable. Her sensitiveness on this point was aggravated by another fear, as yet barely on the level of consciousness; the fear of unwillingly involving Gannett in the trammels[6] of her dependence. To look upon him as the instrument of her liberation; to resist in herself the least tendency to a wifely taking possession of his future, had seemed to Lydia the one way of maintaining the dignity of their relation. Her view had not changed, but she was aware of a growing inability to keep her thoughts fixed on the essential point—the point of parting with Gannett. It was easy to face as long as she kept it sufficiently far off: but what was this act of mental postponement but a gradual encroachment on his future? What was needful was the courage to recognize the moment when, by some word or look, their voluntary fellowship should be transformed into a bondage the more wearing that it was based on none of those common obligations which make the most imperfect marriage in some sort a center of gravity.

When the porter, at the next station, threw the door open, Lydia drew back, making way for the hoped-for intruder; but none came, and the train took up its leisurely progress through the spring wheat fields and budding copses. She now began to hope that Gannett would speak before the next station. She watched him furtively, half-disposed to return to the seat opposite his, but there was an artificiality about his absorption that restrained her. She had never before seen him read with so conspicuous an air of warding off interruption. What could he be thinking of? Why should he be afraid to speak? Or was it her answer that he dreaded?

The train paused for the passing of an express, and he put down his book and leaned out of the window. Presently he turned to her with a smile.

"There's a jolly old villa out here," he said.

His easy tone relieved her, and she smiled back at him as she crossed over to his corner.

Beyond the embankment, through the opening in a mossy wall, she caught sight of the villa, with its broken balustrades, its stagnant fountains, and the stone satyr closing the perspective of a dusky grass walk.

"How should you like to live there?" he asked as the train moved on.

"There?"

"In some such place, I mean. One might do worse, don't you think so? There must be at least two centuries of solitude under those yew trees. Shouldn't you like it?"

"I—I don't know," she faltered. She knew now that he meant to speak.

He lit another cigarette. "We shall have to live somewhere, you know," he said as he bent above the match.

Lydia tried to speak carelessly. "*Je n'en vois pas la nécessité!*[7] Why not live everywhere, as we have been doing?"

"But we can't travel forever, can we?"

---

6. Shackles; confining or restricting circumstances.

7. I don't see why (lit.: I don't see the necessity for it).

"Oh, forever's a long word," she objected, picking up the review he had thrown aside.

"For the rest of our lives then," he said, moving nearer.

She made a slight gesture which caused his hand to slip from hers. "Why should we make plans? I thought you agreed with me that it's pleasanter to drift."

He looked at her hesitatingly. "It's been pleasant, certainly; but I suppose I shall have to get at my work again some day. You know I haven't written a line since—all this time," he hastily amended.

She flamed with sympathy and self-reproach. "Oh, if you mean *that* —if you want to write—of course we must settle down. How stupid of me not to have thought of it sooner! Where shall we go? Where do you think you could work best? We oughtn't to lose any more time."

He hesitated again. "I had thought of a villa in these parts. It's quiet; we shouldn't be bothered. Should you like it?"

"Of course I should like it." She paused and looked away. "But I thought—I remember your telling me once that your best work had been done in a crowd—in big cities. Why should you shut yourself up in a desert?"

Gannett, for a moment, made no reply. At length he said, avoiding her eye as carefully as she avoided his: "It might be different now; I can't tell, of course, till I try. A writer ought not to be dependent on his *milieu;* it's a mistake to humor oneself in that way; and I thought that just at first you might prefer to be—"

She faced him. "To be what?"

"Well—quiet. I mean—"

"What do you mean by 'at first'?" she interrupted.

He paused again. "I mean after we are married."

She thrust up her chin and turned toward the window. "Thank you!" she tossed back at him.

"Lydia!" he exclaimed blankly; and she felt in every fiber of her averted person that he had made the inconceivable, the unpardonable mistake of anticipating her acquiescence.

The train rattled on and he groped for a third cigarette. Lydia remained silent.

"I haven't offended you?" he ventured at length, in the tone of a man who feels his way.

She shook her head with a sigh. "I thought you understood," she moaned. Their eyes met and she moved back to his side.

"Do you want to know how not to offend me? By taking it for granted, once for all, that you've said your say on the odious question and that I've said mine, and that we stand just where we did this morning before that—that hateful paper came to spoil everything between us!"

"To spoil everything between us? What on earth do you mean? Aren't you glad to be free?"

"I was free before."

"Not to marry me," he suggested.

"But I don't *want* to marry you!" she cried.

She saw that he turned pale. "I'm obtuse, I suppose," he said slowly. "I confess I don't see what you're driving at. Are you tired of the whole business? Or was I simply a—an excuse for getting away? Perhaps you didn't care to travel alone? Was that it? And now you want to chuck me?" His voice had grown harsh. "You owe me a straight answer, you know; don't be tenderhearted!"

Her eyes swam as she leaned to him. "Don't you see it's because I care—because I care so much? Oh, Ralph! Can't you see how it would humiliate me? Try to feel it as a woman would! Don't you see the misery of being made your wife in this way? If I'd known you as a girl—that would have been a real marriage! But now—this vulgar fraud upon society—and upon a society we despised and laughed at—this sneaking back into a position that we've voluntarily forfeited: don't you see what a cheap compromise it is? We neither of us believe in the abstract 'sacredness' of marriage; we both know that no ceremony is needed to consecrate our love for each other; what object can we have in marrying, except the secret fear of each that the other may escape, or the secret longing to work our way back gradually—oh, very gradually—into the esteem of the people whose conventional morality we have always ridiculed and hated? And the very fact that, after a decent interval, these same people would come and dine with us—the women who talk about the indissolubility of marriage, and who would let me die in a gutter today because I am 'leading a life of sin'—doesn't that disgust you more than their turning their backs on us now? I can stand being cut by them, but I couldn't stand their coming to call and asking what I meant to do about visiting that unfortunate Mrs. So-and-so!"

She paused, and Gannett maintained a perplexed silence.

"You judge things too theoretically," he said at length, slowly. "Life is made up of compromises."

"The life we ran away from—yes! If we had been willing to accept them"—she flushed—"we might have gone on meeting each other at Mrs. Tillotson's dinners."

He smiled slightly. "I didn't know that we ran away to found a new system of ethics. I supposed it was because we loved each other."

"Life is complex, of course; isn't it the very recognition of that fact that separates us from the people who see it *tout d'une pièce?*[8] If *they* are right—if marriage is sacred in itself and the individual must always be sacrificed to the family—then there can be no real marriage between us, since our—our being together is a protest against the sacrifice of the individual to the family." She interrupted herself with a laugh. "You'll say now that I'm giving you a lecture on sociology! Of course one acts as one can—as one must, perhaps—pulled by all sorts of invisible threads; but at least one needn't pretend, for social advantages, to subscribe to a creed that ignores the complexity of human motives—that classifies people by arbitrary signs, and puts it in everybody's reach to be on Mrs. Tillotson's visiting list. It may be necessary that the world should be ruled by conventions—but if we believed in them, why did we break through them? And if we don't believe in them, is it honest to take advantage of the protection they afford?"

Gannett hesitated. "One may believe in them or not; but as long as they do rule the world it is only by taking advantage of their protection that one can find a *modus vivendi*."[9]

"Do outlaws need a *modus vivendi?*"

He looked at her hopelessly. Nothing is more perplexing to man than the mental process of a woman who reasons her emotions.

She thought she had scored a point and followed it up passionately. "You do understand, don't you? You see how the very thought of the thing humiliates me! We are together today because we choose to be

8. All of a piece.   9. Way of living.

—don't let us look any farther than that!" She caught his hands. *"Promise* me you'll never speak of it again; promise me you'll never *think* of it even," she implored, with a tearful prodigality of italics.

Through what followed—his protests, his arguments, his final unconvinced submission to her wishes—she had a sense of his but half-discerning all that, for her, had made the moment so tumultuous. They had reached that memorable point in every heart history when, for the first time, the man seems obtuse and the woman irrational. It was the abundance of his intentions that consoled her, on reflection, for what they lacked in quality. After all, it would have been worse, incalculably worse, to have detected any overreadiness to understand her.

2

When the train at nightfall brought them to their journey's end at the edge of one of the lakes, Lydia was glad that they were not, as usual, to pass from one solitude to another. Their wanderings during the year had indeed been like the flight of outlaws: through Sicily, Dalmatia, Transylvania[1] and Southern Italy they had persisted in their tacit avoidance of their kind. Isolation, at first, had deepened the flavor of their happiness, as night intensifies the scent of certain flowers; but in the new phase on which they were entering, Lydia's chief wish was that they should be less abnormally exposed to the action of each other's thoughts.

She shrank, nevertheless, as the brightly-looming bulk of the fashionable Anglo-American hotel on the water's brink began to radiate toward their advancing boat its vivid suggestion of social order, visitors' lists, Church services, and the bland inquisition of the *table d'hôte*.[2] The mere fact that in a moment or two she must take her place on the hotel register as Mrs. Gannett seemed to weaken the springs of her resistance.

They had meant to stay for a night only, on their way to a lofty village among the glaciers of Monte Rosa; but after the first plunge into publicity, when they entered the dining room, Lydia felt the relief of being lost in a crowd, of ceasing for a moment to be the center of Gannett's scrutiny; and in his face she caught the reflection of her feeling. After dinner, when she went upstairs, he strolled into the smoking room, and an hour or two later, sitting in the darkness of her window, she heard his voice below and saw him walking up and down the terrace with a companion cigar at his side. When he came up he told her he had been talking to the hotel chaplain—a very good sort of fellow.

"Queer little microcosms, these hotels! Most of these people live here all summer and then migrate to Italy or the Riviera. The English are the only people who can lead that kind of life with dignity—those soft-voiced old ladies in Shetland shawls somehow carry the British Empire under their caps. *Civis Romanus sum.*[3] It's a curious study—there might be some good things to work up here."

He stood before her with the vivid preoccupied stare of the novelist on the trail of a "subject." With a relief that was half painful she no-

---

1. Dalmatia, then part of Austria (now Yugoslavia) along Adriatic coast; Transylvania, then part of Hungary (now of Rumania).

2. Table at hotel where all the guests eat together.
3. "I am a citizen of Rome," i.e., a member of the dominant nation.

ticed that, for the first time since they had been together, he was hardly aware of her presence.

"Do you think you could write here?"

"Here? I don't know." His stare dropped. "After being out of things so long one's first impressions are bound to be tremendously vivid, you know. I see a dozen threads already that one might follow——"

He broke off with a touch of embarrassment.

"Then follow them. We'll stay," she said with sudden decision.

"Stay here?" he glanced at her in surprise, and then, walking to the window, looked out upon the dusky slumber of the garden.

"Why not?" she said at length, in a tone of veiled irritation.

"The place is full of old cats in caps who gossip with the chaplain. Shall you like—I mean, it would be different if——"

She flamed up.

"Do you suppose I care? It's none of their business."

"Of course not; but you won't get them to think so."

"They may think what they please."

He looked at her doubtfully.

"It's for you to decide."

"We'll stay," she repeated.

Gannett, before they met, had made himself known as a successful writer of short stories and of a novel which had achieved the distinction of being widely discussed. The reviewers called him "promising," and Lydia now accused herself of having too long interfered with the fulfillment of his promise. There was a special irony in the fact, since his passionate assurances that only the stimulus of her companionship could bring out his latent faculty had almost given the dignity of a "vocation" to her course: there had been moments when she had felt unable to assume, before posterity, the responsibility of thwarting his career. And, after all, he had not written a line since they had been together: his first desire to write had come from renewed contact with the world! Was it all a mistake then? Must the most intelligent choice work more disastrously than the blundering combinations of chance? Or was there a still more humiliating answer to her perplexities? His sudden impulse of activity so exactly coincided with her own wish to withdraw, for a time, from the range of his observation, that she wondered if he too were not seeking sanctuary from intolerable problems.

"You must begin tomorrow!" she cried, hiding a tremor under the laugh with which she added, "I wonder if there's any ink in the inkstand?"

Whatever else they had at the Hotel Bellosguardo, they had, as Miss Pinsent said, "a certain tone." It was to Lady Susan Condit that they owed this inestimable benefit; an advantage ranking in Miss Pinsent's opinion above even the lawn tennis courts and the resident chaplain. It was the fact of Lady Susan's annual visit that made the hotel what it was. Miss Pinsent was certainly the last to underrate such a privilege: "It's so important, my dear, forming as we do a little family, that there should be someone to give *the tone;* and no one could do it better than Lady Susan—an earl's daughter and a person of such determination. Dear Mrs. Ainger now—who really *ought,* you know, when Lady Susan's away—absolutely refuses to assert herself." Miss Pinsent sniffed derisively. "A bishop's niece!—my dear, I saw her once actually give in to some South Americans—and before us all. She gave up her seat at

table to oblige them—such a lack of dignity! Lady Susan spoke to her very plainly about it afterwards."

Miss Pinsent glanced across the lake and adjusted her auburn front.[4]

"But of course I don't deny that the stand Lady Susan takes is not always easy to live up to—for the rest of us, I mean. Monsieur Grossart, our good proprietor, finds it trying at times, I know—he has said as much, privately, to Mrs. Ainger and me. After all, the poor man is not to blame for wanting to fill his hotel, is he? And Lady Susan is so difficult—so very difficult—about new people. One might almost say that she disapproves of them beforehand, on principle. And yet she's had warnings—she very nearly made a dreadful mistake once with the Duchess of Levens, who dyed her hair and—well, swore and smoked. One would have thought that might have been a lesson to Lady Susan." Miss Pinsent resumed her knitting with a sigh. "There are exceptions, of course. She took at once to you and Mr. Gannett—it was quite remarkable, really. Oh, I don't mean that either—of course not! It was perfectly natural—we *all* thought you so charming and interesting from the first day—we knew at once that Mr. Gannett was intellectual, by the magazines you took in; but you know what I mean. Lady Susan is so very—well, I won't say prejudiced, as Mrs. Ainger does—but so prepared *not* to like new people, that her taking to you in that way was a surprise to us all, I confess."

Miss Pinsent sent a significant glance down the long laurustinus[5] alley from the other end of which two people—a lady and gentleman— were strolling toward them through the smiling neglect of the garden.

"In this case, of course, it's very different; that I'm willing to admit. Their looks are against them; but, as Mrs. Ainger says, one can't exactly tell them so."

"She's very handsome," Lydia ventured, with her eyes on the lady, who showed, under the dome of a vivid sunshade, the hourglass figure and superlative coloring of a Christmas chromo.[6]

"That's the worst of it. She's too handsome."

"Well, after all, she can't help that."

"Other people manage to," said Miss Pinsent skeptically.

"But isn't it rather unfair of Lady Susan—considering that nothing is known about them?"

"But, my dear, that's the very thing that's against them. It's infinitely worse than any actual knowledge."

Lydia mentally agreed that, in the case of Mrs. Linton, it possibly might be.

"I wonder why they came here?" she mused.

"That's against them too. It's always a bad sign when loud people come to a quiet place. And they've brought van loads of boxes—her maid told Mrs. Ainger's that they meant to stop indefinitely."

"And Lady Susan actually turned her back on her in the salon?"

"My dear, she said it was for our sakes: that makes it so unanswerable! But poor Grossart *is* in a way! The Lintons have taken his most expensive suite, you know—the yellow damask drawing room above the portico—and they have champagne with every meal!"

They were silent as Mr. and Mrs. Linton sauntered by; the lady with

---

4. Band(s) of false hair or set of false curls worn over forehead.

5. Tall evergreens that grow in the

Mediterranean section of Europe.

6. Colored lithograph.

tempestuous brows and challenging chin; the gentleman, a blond strip-
ling, trailing after her, head downward, like a reluctant child dragged
by his nurse.

"What does your husband think of them, my dear?" Miss Pinsent
whispered as they passed out of earshot.

Lydia stooped to pick a violet in the border.

"He hasn't told me."

"Of your speaking to them, I mean. Would he approve of that? I
know how very particular nice Americans are. I think your action might
make a difference; it would certainly carry weight with Lady Susan."

"Dear Miss Pinsent, you flatter me!"

Lydia rose and gathered up her book and sunshade.

"Well, if you're asked for an opinion—if Lady Susan asks you for
one—I think you ought to be prepared," Miss Pinsent admonished her
as she moved away.

3

Lady Susan held her own. She ignored the Lintons, and her little
family, as Miss Pinsent phrased it, followed suit. Even Mrs. Ainger
agreed that it was obligatory. If Lady Susan owed it to the others not
to speak to the Lintons, the others clearly owed it to Lady Susan to
back her up. It was generally found expedient, at the Hotel Bellosguardo, to adopt this form of reasoning.

Whatever effect this combined action may have had upon the
Lintons, it did not at least have that of driving them away. Monsieur
Grossart, after a few days of suspense, had the satisfaction of seeing
them settle down in his yellow damask *premier*[7] with what looked like
a permanent installation of palm trees and silk cushions, and a gratifying continuance in the consumption of champagne. Mrs. Linton trailed
her Doucet[8] draperies up and down the garden with the same challenging air, while her husband, smoking innumerable cigarettes, dragged
himself dejectedly in her wake; but neither of them, after the first encounter with Lady Susan, made any attempt to extend their acquaintance. They simply ignored their ignorers. As Miss Pinsent resentfully
observed, they behaved exactly as though the hotel were empty.

It was therefore a matter of surprise, as well as of displeasure, to
Lydia, to find, on glancing up one day from her seat in the garden, that
the shadow which had fallen across her book was that of the enigmatic
Mrs. Linton.

"I want to speak to you," that lady said, in a rich hard voice that
seemed the audible expression of her gown and her complexion.

Lydia started. She certainly did not want to speak to Mrs. Linton.

"Shall I sit down here?" the latter continued, fixing her intensely-
shaded eyes on Lydia's face, "or are you afraid of being seen with me?"

"Afraid?" Lydia colored. "Sit down, please. What is it that you wish
to say?"

Mrs. Linton, with a smile, drew up a garden chair and crossed one
openwork[9] ankle above the other.

"I want you to tell me what my husband said to your husband last
night."

7. The first floor above the ground
floor.
8. Jacques Doucet (1853–1929), French
dress designer and manufacturer.
9. Stockings—knit, lace, etc.—in which
the pattern left openings in the material;
at one time shocking. The London *Daily
News* said in September 1890, "Openwork
stockings will be the only wear when the
weather gets a bit warmer."

Lydia turned pale.

"My husband—to yours?" she faltered, staring at the other.

"Didn't you know they were closeted together for hours in the smoking room after you went upstairs? My man didn't get to bed until nearly two o'clock and when he did I couldn't get a word out of him. When he wants to be aggravating I'll back him against anybody living!" Her teeth and eyes flashed persuasively upon Lydia. "But you'll tell me what they were talking about, won't you? I know I can trust you—you look so awfully kind. And it's for his own good. He's such a precious donkey and I'm so afraid he's got into some beastly scrape or other. If he'd only trust his own old woman! But they're always writing to him and setting him against me. And I've got nobody to turn to." She laid her hand on Lydia's with a rattle of bracelets. "You'll help me, won't you?"

Lydia drew back from the smiling fierceness of her brows.

"I'm sorry—but I don't think I understand. My husband has said nothing to me of—of yours."

The great black crescents above Mrs. Linton's eyes met angrily.

"I say—is that true?" she demanded.

Lydia rose from her seat.

"Oh, look here, I didn't mean that, you know—you mustn't take one up so! Can't you see how rattled I am?"

Lydia saw that, in fact, her beautiful mouth was quivering beneath softened eyes.

"I'm beside myself!" the splendid creature wailed, dropping into her seat.

"I'm so sorry," Lydia repeated, forcing herself to speak kindly; "but how can I help you?"

Mrs. Linton raised her head sharply.

"By finding out—there's a darling!"

"Finding what out?"

"What Trevenna told him."

"Trevenna—?" Lydia echoed in bewilderment.

Mrs. Linton clapped her hand to her mouth.

"Oh, Lord—there, it's out! What a fool I am! But I supposed of course you knew; I supposed everybody knew." She dried her eyes and bridled. "Didn't you know that he's Lord Trevenna? I'm Mrs. Cope."

Lydia recognized the names. They had figured in a flamboyant elopement which had thrilled fashionable London some six months earlier.

"Now you see how it is—you understand, don't you?" Mrs. Cope continued on a note of appeal. "I knew you would—that's the reason I came to you. I suppose *he* felt the same thing about your husband; he's not spoken to another soul in the place." Her face grew anxious again. "He's awfully sensitive, generally—he feels our position, he says—as if it wasn't *my* place to feel that! But when he does get talking there's no knowing what he'll say. I know he's been brooding over something lately, and I *must* find out what it is—it's to his interest that I should. I always tell him that I think only of his interest; if he'd only trust me! But he's been so odd lately—I can't think what he's plotting. You will help me, dear?"

Lydia, who had remained standing, looked away uncomfortably.

"If you mean by finding out what Lord Trevenna has told my husband, I'm afraid it's impossible."

"Why impossible?"

"Because I infer that it was told in confidence."

Mrs. Cope stared incredulously.

"Well, what of that? Your husband looks such a dear—anyone can see he's awfully gone on you. What's to prevent your getting it out of him?"

Lydia flushed.

"I'm not a spy!" she exclaimed.

"A spy—a spy? How dare you?" Mrs. Cope flamed out. "Oh, I don't mean that either! Don't be angry with me—I'm so miserable." She essayed a softer note. "Do you call that spying—for one woman to help out another? I do need help so dreadfully! I'm at my wits' end with Trevenna, I am indeed. He's such a boy—a mere baby, you know; he's only two-and-twenty." She dropped her orbed lids. "He's younger than me—only fancy, a few months younger. I tell him he ought to listen to me as if I was his mother; oughtn't he now? But he won't, he won't! All his people are at him, you see—oh, I know *their* little game! Trying to get him away from me before I can get my divorce—that's what they're up to. At first he wouldn't listen to them; he used to toss their letters over to me to read; but now he reads them himself, and answers 'em too, I fancy; he's always shut up in his room, writing. If I only knew what his plan is I could stop him fast enough—he's such a simpleton. But he's dreadfully deep too—at times I can't make him out. But I know he's told your husband everything—I knew that last night the minute I laid eyes on him. And I *must* find out—you must help me—I've got no one else to turn to!"

She caught Lydia's fingers in a stormy pressure.

"Say you'll help me—you and your husband."

Lydia tried to free herself.

"What you ask is impossible; you must see that it is. No one could interfere in—in the way you ask."

Mrs. Cope's clutch tightened.

"You won't, then? You won't?"

"Certainly not. Let me go, please."

Mrs. Cope released her with a laugh.

"Oh, go by all means—pray don't let me detain you! Shall you go and tell Lady Susan Condit that there's a pair of us—or shall I save you the trouble of enlightening her?"

Lydia stood still in the middle of the path, seeing her antagonist through a mist of terror. Mrs. Cope was still laughing.

"Oh, I'm not spiteful by nature, my dear; but you're a little more than flesh and blood can stand! It's impossible, is it? Let you go, indeed! You're too good to be mixed up in my affairs, are you? Why, you little fool, the first day I laid eyes on you I saw that you and I were both in the same box—that's the reason I spoke to you."

She stepped nearer, her smile dilating on Lydia like a lamp through a fog.

"You can take your choice, you know; I always play fair. If you'll tell I'll promise not to. Now then, which is it to be?"

Lydia, involuntarily, had begun to move away from the pelting storm of words; but at this she turned and sat down again.

"You may go," she said simply. "I shall stay here."

4

She stayed there for a long time, in the hypnotized contemplation, not of Mrs. Cope's present, but of her own past. Gannett, early that morning, had gone off on a long walk—he had fallen into the habit of taking these mountain tramps with various fellow lodgers; but even had he been within reach she could not have gone to him just then. She had to deal with herself first. She was surprised to find how, in the last months, she had lost the habit of introspection. Since their coming to the Hotel Bellosguardo she and Gannett had tacitly avoided themselves and each other.

She was aroused by the whistle of the three o'clock steamboat as it neared the landing just beyond the hotel gates. Three o'clock! Then Gannett would soon be back—he had told her to expect him before four. She rose hurriedly, her face averted from the inquisitorial façade of the hotel. She could not see him just yet; she could not go indoors. She slipped through one of the overgrown garden alleys and climbed a steep path to the hills.

It was dark when she opened their sitting-room door. Gannett was sitting on the window ledge smoking a cigarette. Cigarettes were now his chief resource: he had not written a line during the two months they had spent at the Hotel Bellosguardo. In that respect, it had turned out not to be the right *milieu* after all.

He started up at Lydia's entrance.

"Where have you been? I was getting anxious."

She sat down in a chair near the door.

"Up the mountain," she said wearily.

"Alone?"

"Yes."

Gannett threw away his cigarette: the sound of her voice made him want to see her face.

"Shall we have a little light?" he suggested.

She made no answer and he lifted the globe from the lamp and put a match to the wick. Then he looked at her.

"Anything wrong? You look done up."

She sat glancing vaguely about the little room, dimly lit by the pallid-globed lamp, which left in twilight the outlines of the furniture, of his writing table heaped with books and papers, of the tea roses and jasmine drooping on the mantelpiece. How like home it had all grown—how like home!

"Lydia, what is wrong?" he repeated.

She moved away from him, feeling for her hatpins and turning to lay her hat and sunshade on the table.

Suddenly she said: "That woman has been talking to me."

Gannett stared.

"That woman? What woman?"

"Mrs. Linton—Mrs. Cope."

He gave a start of annoyance, still as she perceived, not grasping the full import of her words.

"The deuce! She told you—?"

"She told me everything."

Gannett looked at her anxiously.

"What impudence! I'm so sorry that you should have been exposed to this, dear."

"Exposed!" Lydia laughed.

Gannett's brow clouded and they looked away from each other.

"Do you know *why* she told me? She had the best of reasons. The first time she laid eyes on me she saw that we were both in the same box."

"Lydia!"

"So it was natural, of course, that she should turn to me in a difficulty."

"What difficulty?"

"It seems she has reason to think that Lord Trevenna's people are trying to get him away from her before she gets her divorce—"

"Well?"

"And she fancied he had been consulting with you last night as to— as to the best way of escaping from her."

Gannett stood up with an angry forehead.

"Well—what concern of yours was all this dirty business? Why should she go to you?"

"Don't you see? It's so simple. I was to wheedle his secret out of you."

"To oblige that woman?"

"Yes; or, if I was unwilling to oblige her, then to protect myself."

"To protect yourself? Against whom?"

"Against her telling everyone in the hotel that she and I are in the same box."

"She threatened that?"

"She left me the choice of telling it myself or of doing it for me."

"The beast!"

There was a long silence. Lydia had seated herself on the sofa, beyond the radius of the lamp, and he leaned against the window. His next question surprised her.

"When did this happen? At what time, I mean?"

She looked at him vaguely.

"I don't know—after luncheon, I think. Yes, I remember; it must have been at about three o'clock."

He stepped into the middle of the room and as he approached the light she saw that his brow had cleared.

"Why do you ask?" she said.

"Because when I came in, at about half-past three, the mail was just being distributed, and Mrs. Cope was waiting as usual to pounce on her letters; you know she was always watching for the postman. She was standing so close to me that I couldn't help seeing a big official-looking envelope that was handed to her. She tore it open, gave one look at the inside, and rushed off upstairs like a whirlwind, with the director shouting after her that she had left all her other letters behind. I don't believe she ever thought of you again after that paper was put into her hand."

"Why?"

"Because she was too busy. I was sitting in the window, watching for you, when the five o'clock boat left, and who should go on board, bag and baggage, valet and maid, dressing bags and poodle, but Mrs. Cope and Trevenna. Just an hour and a half to pack up in! And you should have seen her when they started. She was radiant—shaking hands with everybody—waving her handkerchief from the deck—distributing bows and smiles like an empress. If ever a woman got what she wanted just in the nick of time that woman did. She'll be Lady Trevenna within a week, I'll wager."

"You think she has her divorce?"

"I'm sure of it. And she must have got it just after her talk with you."

Lydia was silent.

At length she said, with a kind of reluctance, "She was horribly angry when she left me. It wouldn't have taken long to tell Lady Susan Condit."

"Lady Susan Condit has not been told."

"How do you know?"

"Because when I went downstairs half an hour ago I met Lady Susan on the way—"

He stopped, half smiling.

"Well?"

"And she stopped to ask if I thought you would act as patroness to a charity concert she is getting up."

In spite of themselves they both broke into a laugh. Lydia's ended in sobs and she sank down with her face hidden. Gannett bent over her, seeking her hands.

"That vile woman— I ought to have warned you to keep away from her; I can't forgive myself! But he spoke to me in confidence; and I never dreamed—well, it's all over now."

Lydia lifted her head.

"Not for me. It's only just beginning."

"What do you mean?

She put him gently aside and moved in her turn to the window Then she went on, with her face turned toward the shimmering blackness of the lake, "You see of course that it might happen again at any moment."

"What?"

"This—this risk of being found out. And we could hardly count again on such a lucky combination of chances, could we?"

He sat down with a groan.

Still keeping her face toward the darkness, she said, "I want you to go and tell Lady Susan—and the others."

Gannett, who had moved toward her, paused a few feet off.

"Why do you wish me to do this?" he said at length, with less surprise in his voice than she had been prepared for.

"Because I've behaved basely, abominably, since we came here: letting these people believe we were married—lying with every breath I drew—"

"Yes, I've felt that too," Gannett exclaimed with sudden energy.

The words shook her like a tempest: all her thoughts seemed to fall about her in ruins.

"You—you've felt so?"

"Of course I have." He spoke with low-voiced vehemence. "Do you suppose I like playing the sneak any better than you do? It's damnable."

He had dropped on the arm of a chair, and they stared at each other like blind people who suddenly see.

"But you have liked it here," she faltered.

"Oh, I've liked it—I've like it." He moved impatiently. "Haven't you?"

"Yes," she burst out; "that's the worst of it—that's what I can't bear. I fancied it was for your sake that I insisted on staying—because you thought you could write here; and perhaps just at first that really was the reason. But afterwards I wanted to stay myself—I loved it." She broke into a laugh. "Oh, do you see the full derision of it? These peo-

ple—the very prototypes of the bores you took me away from, with the same fenced-in view of life, the same keep-off-the-grass morality, the same little cautious virtues and the same little frightened vices—well, I've clung to them, I've delighted in them, I've done my best to please them. I've toadied Lady Susan, I've gossiped with Miss Pinsent, I've pretended to be shocked with Mrs. Ainger. Respectability! It was the one thing in life that I was sure I didn't care about, and it's grown so precious to me that I've stolen it because I couldn't get it in any other way."

She moved across the room and returned to his side with another laugh.

"I who used to fancy myself unconventional! I must have been born with a cardcase in my hand.[1] You should have seen me with that poor woman in the garden. She came to me for help, poor creature, because she fancied that, having 'sinned,' as they call it, I might feel some pity for others who had been tempted in the same way. Not I! She didn't know me. Lady Susan would have been kinder, because Lady Susan wouldn't have been afraid. I hated the woman—my one thought was not to be seen with her—I could have killed her for guessing my secret. The one thing that mattered to me at that moment was my standing with Lady Susan!"

Gannett did not speak.

"And you—you've felt it too!" she broke out accusingly. "You've enjoyed being with these people as much as I have; you've let the chaplain talk to you by the hour about The Reign of Law and Professor Drummond.[2] When they asked you to hand the plate in church I was watching you—*you wanted to accept.*"

She stepped close, laying her hand on his arm.

"Do you know, I begin to see what marriage is for. It's to keep people away from each other. Sometimes I think that two people who love each other can be saved from madness only by the things that come between them—children, duties, visits, bores, relations—the things that protect married people from each other. We've been too close together—that has been our sin. We've seen the nakedness of each other's souls."

She sank again on the sofa, hiding her face in her hands.

Gannett stood above her perplexedly: he felt as though she were being swept away by some implacable current while he stood helpless on its bank.

At length he said, "Lydia, don't think me a brute—but don't you see yourself that it won't do?"

"Yes, I see it won't do," she said without raising her head.

His face cleared.

"Then we'll go tomorrow."

"Go—where?"

"To Paris; to be married."

For a long time she made no answer; then she asked slowly, "Would they have us here if we were married?"

"Have us here?"

"I mean Lady Susan—and the others."

"Have us here? Of course they would."

---

1. I.e., a member of that part of society (the upper class) that makes formal social calls and leaves calling cards.
2. Henry Drummond (1851–1897), Scottish clergyman who attempted to reconcile science and religion and published *Natural Law in the Spiritual World* (1893).

"Not if they knew—at least, not unless they could pretend not to know."

He made an impatient gesture.

"We shouldn't come back here, of course; and other people needn't know—no one need know."

She sighed. "Then it's only another form of deception and a meaner one. Don't you see that?"

"I see we're not accountable to any Lady Susans on earth!"

"Then why are you ashamed of what we are doing here?"

"Because I'm sick of pretending that you're my wife when you're not—when you won't be."

She looked at him sadly.

"If I were your wife you'd have to go on pretending. You'd have to pretend that I'd never been—anything else. And our friends would have to pretend that they believed what you pretended."

Gannett pulled off the sofa tassel and flung it away.

"You're impossible," he groaned.

"It's not I—it's our being together that's impossible. I only want you to see that marriage won't help it."

"What will help it then?"

She raised her head.

"My leaving you."

"Your leaving me?" He sat motionless, staring at the tassel which lay at the other end of the room. At length some impulse of retaliation for the pain she was inflicting made him say deliberately:

"And where would you go if you left me?"

"Oh!" she cried.

He was at her side in an instant.

"Lydia—Lydia—you know I didn't mean it; I couldn't mean it! But you've driven me out of my senses; I don't know what I'm saying. Can't you get out of this labyrinth of self-torture? It's destroying us both."

"That's why I must leave you."

"How easily you say it!" He drew her hands down and made her face him. "You're very scrupulous about yourself—and others. But have you thought of me? You have no right to leave me unless you've ceased to care—"

"It's because I care—"

"Then I have a right to be heard. If you love me you can't leave me."

Her eyes defied him.

"Why not?"

He dropped her hands and rose from her side.

"Can you?" he said sadly.

The hour was late and the lamp flickered and sank. She stood up with a shiver and turned toward the door of her room.

5

At daylight a sound in Lydia's room woke Gannett from a troubled sleep. He sat up and listened. She was moving about softly, as though fearful of disturbing him. He heard her push back one of the creaking shutters; then there was a moment's silence, which seemed to indicate that she was waiting to see if the noise had roused him.

Presently she began to move again. She had spent a sleepless night, probably, and was dressing to go down to the garden for a breath of air.

Gannett rose also; but some undefinable instinct made his movements as cautious as hers. He stole to his window and looked out through the slats of the shutter.

It had rained in the night and the dawn was gray and lifeless. The cloud-muffled hills across the lake were reflected in its surface as in a tarnished mirror. In the garden, the birds were beginning to shake the drops from the motionless laurustinus boughs.

An immense pity for Lydia filled Gannett's soul. Her seeming intellectual independence had blinded him for a time to the feminine cast of her mind. He had never thought of her as a woman who wept and clung: there was a lucidity in her intuitions that made them appear to be the result of reasoning. Now he saw the cruelty he had committed in detaching her from the normal conditions of life; he felt, too, the insight with which she had hit upon the real cause of their suffering. Their life was "impossible," as she had said—and its worst penalty was that it had made any other life impossible for them. Even had his love lessened, he was bound to her now by a hundred ties of pity and self-reproach; and she, poor child, must turn back to him as Latude returned to his cell.[3]

A new sound startled him: it was the stealthy closing of Lydia's door. He crept to his own and heard her footsteps passing down the corridor. Then he went back to the window and looked out.

A minute or two later he saw her go down the steps of the porch and enter the garden. From his post of observation her face was invisible, but something about her appearance struck him. She wore a long traveling cloak and under its folds he detected the outline of a bag or bundle. He drew a deep breath and stood watching her.

She walked quickly down the laurustinus alley toward the gate; there she paused a moment, glancing about the little shady square. The stone benches under the trees were empty, and she seemed to gather resolution from the solitude about her, for she crossed the square to the steamboat landing, and he saw her pause before the ticket office at the head of the wharf. Now she was buying her ticket. Gannet turned his head a moment to look at the clock: the boat was due in five minutes. He had time to jump into his clothes and overtake her—

He made no attempt to move; an obscure reluctance restrained him. If any thought emerged from the tumult of his sensations, it was that he must let her go if she wished it. He had spoken last night of his rights: what were they? At the last issue, he and she were two separate beings, not made one by the miracle of common forbearances, duties, abnegations, but bound together in a *noyade*[4] of passion that left them resisting yet clinging as they went down.

After buying her ticket, Lydia had stood for a moment looking out across the lake; then he saw her seat herself on one of the benches near the landing. He and she, at that moment, were both listening for the same sound: the whistle of the boat as it rounded the nearest promontory. Gannett turned again to glance at the clock: the boat was due now.

Where would she go? What would her life be when she had left him? She had no near relations and few friends. There was money enough . . . but she asked so much of life, in ways so complex and immaterial. He thought of her as walking barefooted through a stony waste. No one

---

3. Jean Henry de Latude (1725–1805),   a period of 35 years.
an adventurer who kept escaping and get-   4. Flood, drowning.
ting put back in various French jails over

would understand her—no one would pity her—and he, who did both, was powerless to come to her aid.

He saw that she had risen from the bench and walked toward the edge of the lake. She stood looking in the direction from which the steamboat was to come; then she turned to the ticket office, doubtless to ask the cause of the delay. After that she went back to the bench and sat down with bent head. What was she thinking of?

The whistle sounded; she started up, and Gannett involuntarily made a movement toward the door. But he turned back and continued to watch her. She stood motionless, her eyes on the trail of smoke that preceded the appearance of the boat. Then the little craft rounded the point, a dead white object on the leaden water: a minute later it was puffing and backing at the wharf.

The few passengers who were waiting—two or three peasants and a snuffy priest—were clustered near the ticket office. Lydia stood apart under the trees.

The boat lay alongside now; the gangplank was run out and the peasants went on board with their baskets of vegetables, followed by the priest. Still Lydia did not move. A bell began to ring querulously; there was a shriek of steam, and someone must have called to her that she would be late, for she started forward, as though in answer to a summons. She moved waveringly, and at the edge of the wharf she paused. Gannett saw a sailor beckon to her; the bell rang again and she stepped upon the gangplank.

Halfway down the short incline to the deck she stopped again; then she turned and ran back to the land. The gangplank was drawn in, the bell ceased to ring, and the boat backed out into the lake. Lydia, with slow steps, was walking toward the garden.

As she approached the hotel she looked up furtively and Gannett drew back into the room. He sat down beside a table; a Bradshaw[5] lay at his elbow, and mechanically, without knowing what he did, he began looking out the trains to Paris.

1899

ISAAC BABEL

The Sin of Jesus

Arina was a servant at the hotel. She lived next to the main staircase, while Seryoga, the janitor's helper, lived over the back stairs. Between them there was shame. On Palm Sunday[1] Arina gave Seryoga a present—twins. Water flows, stars shine, a man lusts, and soon Arina was big again, her sixth month was rolling by—they're slippery, a woman's months. And now, Seryoga must go into the army. There's a mess for you!

So Arina goes and says: "No sense, Seryoga. There's no sense in my waiting for you. For four years we'll be parted, and in four years, whichever way you look at it, I'll be sure to bring two or three more into this world. It's like walking around with your skirt turned up, working at the hotel. Whoever stops here, he's your master, let him be a Jew, let him be anybody at all. By the time you come home, my

5. *Continental Railway Guide.* George Bradshaw (1801–1853) compiled numerous railroad guide timetables.

1. Sunday before Easter, commemorating Jesus' entry into Jerusalem.

insides will be no good any more. I'll be a used-up woman, no match for you."

"That's so," Seryoga nodded.

"There's many that want me. Trofimych the contractor—but he's no gentleman. And Isai Abramych, the warden of Nikolo-Svyatsky Church, a feeble old man, but anyway I'm sick to the stomach of your murderous strength. I tell you this now, and I say it like I would at confession, I've got the wind plain knocked out of me. I'll spill my load in three months, then I'll take the baby to the orphanage and marry the old man."

When Seryoga heard this, he took off his belt and beat her like a hero, right on the belly.

"Look out there," Arina says to him, "go soft on the belly. It's your stuffing, no one else's."

There was no end to the beating, no end to the man's tears and the woman's blood, but that is neither here nor there.

Then the woman came to Jesus Christ.

"So on and so forth," she says, "Lord Jesus, I am the woman from the Hotel Madrid and Louvre, the one on Tverskaya Street. Working at the hotel, it's just like going around with your skirt up. Just let a man stop there, and he's your lord and master, let him be a Jew, let him be anyone at all. There is another slave of yours walking the earth, the janitor's helper, Seryoga. Last year on Palm Sunday I bore him twins."

And so she described it all to the Lord.

"And what if Seryoga were not to go into the army after all?" the Saviour suggested.

"Try and get away with it—not with the policeman around. He'll drag him off as sure as daylight."

"Oh yes, the policeman," the Lord bowed His head, "I never thought of him. Then perhaps you ought to live in purity for a while?"

"For four years?" the woman cried. "To hear you talk, all people should deny their animal nature. That's just your old ways all over again. And where will the increase come from?[2] No, you'd better give me some sensible advice."

The Lord's cheeks turned scarlet, the woman's words had touched a tender spot. But He said nothing. You cannot kiss your own ear—even God knows that.

"I'll tell you what, God's servant, glorious sinner, maiden Arina," the Lord proclaimed in all His glory, "I have a little angel here in heaven, hanging around uselessly. His name is Alfred. Lately he's gotten out of hand altogether, keeps crying and nagging all the time: 'What have you done to me, Lord? Why do you turn me into an angel in my twentieth year, and me a hale young fellow?' So I'll give you Alfred the angel as a husband for four years. He'll be your prayer, he'll be your protection, and he'll be your solace. And as for offspring, you've nothing to worry about—you can't bear a duckling from him, let alone a baby, for there's a lot of fun in him, but no seriousness."

"That's just what I need," the maid Arina wept gratefully. "Their seriousness takes me to the doorstep of the grave three times every two years."

2. In *I Corinthians* 3:6–7, Paul says of himself and his fellow minister Apollos: "I have planted, Apollos watered; but God gave the increase. So then neither is he that planteth any thing, neither he that watereth; but God that giveth the increase."

"You'll have a sweet respite, God's child Arina. May your prayer be light as a song. Amen."

And so it was decided. Alfred was brought in—a frail young fellow, delicate, two wings fluttering behind his pale-blue shoulders, rippling with rosy light like two doves playing in heaven. Arina threw her hefty arms about him, weeping out of tenderness, out of her woman's soft heart.

"Alfred, my soul, my consolation, my bridegroom . . ."

In parting, the Lord gave her strict instructions to take off the angel's wings every night before he went to bed. His wings were attached to hinges, like a door, and every night she was to take them off and wrap them in a clean sheet, because they were brittle, his wings, and could snap as he tossed in bed—for what were they made of but the sighs of babes, no more than that.

For the last time the Lord blessed the union, while the choir of bishops, called in for the occasion, rendered thunderous praises. No food was served, not a crumb—that wasn't the style in heaven—and then Arina and Alfred, their arms about each other, ran down a silken ladder, straight back to earth. They came to Petrovka, the street where nothing but the best is sold. The woman would do right by her Alfred for he, if one might say so, not only lacked socks, but was altogether as natural as when his mother bore him. And she bought him patent-leather half-boots, checked jersey trousers, a fine hunting jacket, and an electric-blue vest.

"The rest," she says, "we'll find at home."

That day Arina begged off from work. Seryoga came and raised a fuss, but she did not even come out to him, only said from behind her locked door:

"Sergey Nifantyich, I am at present a-washing my feet and beg you to retire without further noise."

He went away without a word—the angel's power was already beginning to manifest itself!

In the evening Arina set out a supper fit for a merchant—the woman had devilish vanity! A half-pint of vodka, wine on the side, a Danube herring with potatoes, a samovar of tea. When Alfred had partaken of all these earthly blessings, he keeled over in a dead sleep. Quick as a wink, Arina lifted off his wings from the hinges, packed them away, and carried him to bed in her arms.

There it lies, the snowy wonder on the eiderdown pillows of her tattered, sinful bed, sending forth a heavenly radiance: moon-silver shafts of light pass and repass, alternate with red ones, float across the floor, sway over his shining feet. Arina weeps and rejoices, sings and prays. Arina, thou hast been granted a happiness unheard of on this battered earth. Blessed art thou among women!

They had drunk the vodka to the last drop, and now it took effect. As soon as they fell asleep, she went and rolled over on top of Alfred with her hot, six-months-big belly. Not enough for her to sleep with an angel, not enough that nobody beside her spat at the wall, snored and snorted—that wasn't enough for the clumsy, ravening slut. No, she had to warm her belly too, her burning belly big with Seryoga's lust. And so she smothered him in her fuddled sleep, smothered him like a week-old babe in the midst of her rejoicing, crushed him under her bloated weight, and he gave up the ghost, and his wings, wrapped in her sheet, wept pale tears.

Dawn came—and all the trees bowed low to the ground. In distant northern forests each fir tree turned into a priest, each fir tree bent its knees in silent worship.

Once more the woman stands before the Lord's throne. She is broad in the shoulders, mighty, the young corpse drooping in her huge red arms.

"Behold, Lord . . ."

But here the gentle heart of Jesus could endure no more, and He cursed the woman in His anger:

"As it is on earth, so shall it be with you, Arina, from this day on."

"How is it then, Lord?" the woman replied in a scarcely audible voice. "Was it I who made my body heavy, was it I that brewed vodka on earth, was it I that created a woman's soul, stupid and lonely?"

"I don't wish to be bothered with you," exclaimed the Lord Jesus. "You've smothered my angel, you filthy scum."

And Arina was thrown back to earth on a putrid wind, straight down to Tverskaya Street, to the Hotel Madrid and Louvre, where she was doomed to spend her days. And once there, the sky was the limit. Seryoga was carousing, drinking away his last days, seeing as he was a recruit. The contractor Trofimych, just come from Kolomna, took one look at Arina, hefty and red-cheeked: "Oh, you cute little belly," he said, and so on and so forth.

Isai Abramych, the old codger, heard about this cute little belly, and he was right there too, wheezing toothlessly:

"I cannot wed you lawfully," he said, "after all that happened. However, I can lie with you the same as anyone."

The old man ought to be lying in cold mother earth instead of thinking of such things, but no, he too must take his turn at spitting into her soul. It was as though they had all slipped the chain—kitchen-boys, merchants, foreigners. A fellow in trade—he likes to have his fun.

And that is the end of my tale.

Before she was laid up, for three months had rolled by in the meantime, Arina went out into the the back yard, behind the janitor's rooms, raised her monstrous belly to the silken sky, and said stupidly:

"See, Lord, what a belly! They hammer at it like peas falling in a colander. And what sense there's in it I just can't see. But I've had enough."

With His tears Jesus laved Arina when He heard these words. The Saviour fell on His knees before her.

"Forgive me, little Arina. Forgive your sinful God for all He has done to you . . ."

But Arina shook her head and would not listen.

"There's no forgiveness for you, Jesus Christ," she said. "No forgiveness, and never will be."

1922

HENRY JAMES

The Beldonald Holbein[1]

1

Mrs. Munden had not yet been to my studio on so good a pretext as when she first put it to me that it would be quite open to me—should I only care, as she called it, to throw the handkerchief[2]—to paint her beautiful sister-in-law. I needn't go here, more than is essential, into the question of Mrs. Munden, who would really, by the way, be a story in herself. She has a manner of her own of putting things, and some of those she has put to me—! Her implication was that Lady Beldonald had not only seen and admired certain examples of my work, but had literally been prepossessed in favor of the painter's "personality." Had I been struck with this sketch I might easily have imagined that Lady Beldonald was throwing *me* the handkerchief. "She hasn't done," my visitor said, "what she ought."

"Do you mean she has done what she oughtn't?"

"Nothing horrid—oh dear, no." And something in Mrs. Munden's tone, with the way she appeared to muse a moment, even suggested to me that what she "oughtn't" was perhaps what Lady Beldonald had too much neglected. "She hasn't got on."

"What's the matter with her?"

"Well, to begin with, she's American."

"But I thought that was the way of ways to get on."

"It's one of them. But it's one of the ways of being awfully out of it too. There are so many!"

"So many Americans?" I asked.

"Yes, plenty of *them*," Mrs. Munden sighed. "So many ways, I mean, of being one."

"But if your sister-in-law's way is to be beautiful—?"

"Oh, there are different ways of that too."

"And she hasn't taken the right way?"

"Well," my friend returned, as if it were rather difficult to express, "she hasn't done with it—"

"I see," I laughed; "what she oughtn't!"

Mrs. Munden in a manner corrected me, but it *was* difficult to express. "My brother, at all events, was certainly selfish. Till he died she was almost never in London; they wintered, year after year, for what he supposed to be his health—which it didn't help, since he was so much too soon to meet his end—in the south of France and in the dullest holes he could pick out, and when they came back to England he always kept her in the country. I must say for her that she always behaved beautifully. Since his death she has been more in London, but on a stupidly unsuccessful footing. I don't think she quite understands. She hasn't what *I* should call a life. It may be, of course, that she doesn't want one. That's just what I can't exactly find out. I can't make out how much she knows."

"I can easily make out," I returned with hilarity, "how much *you* do!"

"Well, you're very horrid. Perhaps she's too old."

1. Hans Holbein the Younger (1497?–1543), most famous of the family of German painters, noted for portraits considered "severely," even "passionately," objective.
2. To indicate willingness.

"Too old for what?' I persisted.

"For anything. Of course she's no longer even a little young; only preserved—oh, but preserved, like bottled fruit, in syrup! I want to help her, if only because she gets on my nerves, and I really think the way of it would be just the right thing of yours at the Academy and on the line."[3]

"But suppose," I threw out, "she should get on *my* nerves?"

"Oh, she will. But isn't that all in the day's work, and don't great beauties always—?"

"*You* don't," I interrupted; but I at any rate saw Lady Beldonald later on—the day came when her kinswoman brought her, and then I understood that her life had its center in her own idea of her appearance. Nothing else about her mattered—one knew her all when one knew that. She is indeed in one particular, I think, sole of her kind—a person whom vanity has had the odd effect of keeping positively safe and sound. This passion is supposed surely, for the most part, to be a principle of perversion and injury, leading astray those who listen to it and landing them, sooner or later, in this or that complication; but it has landed her ladyship nowhere whatever—it has kept her from the first moment of full consciousness, one feels, exactly in the same place. It has protected her from every danger, has made her absolutely proper and prim. If she is "preserved," as Mrs. Munden originally described her to me, it is her vanity that has beautifully done it—putting her years ago in a plate-glass case and closing up the receptacle against every breath of air. How shouldn't she be preserved, when you might smash your knuckles on this transparency before you could crack it? And she *is*—oh, amazingly! Preservation is scarce the word for the rare condition of her surface. She looks *naturally* new, as if she took out every night her large, lovely, varnished eyes and put them in water. The thing was to paint her, I perceived, *in* the glass case—a most tempting, attaching feat; render to the full the shining, interposing plate and the general show-window effect.

It was agreed, though it was not quite arranged, that she should sit to me. If it was not quite arranged, this was because, as I was made to understand from an early stage, the conditions for our start must be such as should exclude all elements of disturbance, such, in a word, as she herself should judge absolutely favorable. And it seemed that these conditions were easily imperiled. Suddenly, for instance, at a moment when I was expecting her to meet an appointment—the first—that I had proposed, I received a hurried visit from Mrs. Munden, who came on her behalf to let me know that the season happened just not to be propitious and that our friend couldn't be quite sure, to the hour, when it would again become so. Nothing, she felt, would make it so but a total absence of worry.

"Oh, a 'total absence,' " I said, "is a large order! We live in a worrying world."

"Yes; and she feels exactly that—more than you'd think. It's in fact just why she mustn't have, as she has now, a particular distress on at the very moment. She wants to look, of course, her best, and such things tell on her appearance."

3. The Royal Academy of Arts, the artistic "establishment" of Britain, holds an annual exhibition at Burlington House, Piccadilly, London; competition is fierce and to "hang on the line" there is to have arrived.

I shook my head. "Nothing tells on her appearance. Nothing reaches it in any way; nothing gets *at* it. However, I can understand her anxiety. But what's her particular distress?"

"Why, the illness of Miss Dadd."

"And who in the world's Miss Dadd?"

"Her most intimate friend and constant companion—the lady who was with us here that first day."

"Oh, the little round, black woman who gurgled with admiration?"

"None other. But she was taken ill last week, and it may very well be that she'll gurgle no more. She was very bad yesterday and is no better today, and Nina is much upset. If anything happens to Miss Dadd she'll have to get another, and, though she has had two or three before, that won't be so easy."

"Two or three Miss Dadds? Is it possible? And still wanting another!" I recalled the poor lady completely now. "No; I shouldn't indeed think it would be easy to get another. But why is a succession of them necessary to Lady Beldonald's existence?"

"Can't you guess?" Mrs. Munden looked deep, yet impatient. "They help."

"Help what? Help whom?"

"Why, every one. You and me for instance. To do what? Why, to think Nina beautiful. She has them for that purpose; they serve as foils, as accents serve on syllables, as terms of comparison. They make her 'stand out.' It's an effect of contrast that must be familiar to you artists; it's what a woman does when she puts a band of black velvet under a pearl ornament that may require, as she thinks, a little showing off."

I wondered. "Do you mean she always has them black?"

"Dear no; I've seen them blue, green, yellow. They may be what they like, so long as they're always one other thing."

"Hideous?"

Mrs. Munden hesitated. "Hideous is too much to say; she doesn't really require them as bad as that. But consistently, cheerfully, loyally plain. It's really a most happy relation. She loves them for it."

"And for what do they love *her?*"

"Why, just for the amiability that they produce in her. Then, also, for their 'home.' It's a career for them."

"I see. But if that's the case," I asked, "why are they so difficult to find?"

"Oh, they must be safe; it's all in that: her being able to depend on them to keep to the terms of the bargain and never have moments of rising—as even the ugliest woman will now and then (say when she's in love)—superior to themselves."

I turned it over. "Then if they can't inspire passions the poor things mayn't even at least feel them?"

"She distinctly deprecates it. That's why such a man as you may be, after all, a complication."

I continued to muse. "You're very sure Miss Dadd's ailment isn't an affection that, being smothered, has struck in?" My joke, however, was not well timed, for I afterwards learned that the unfortunate lady's state had been, even while I spoke, such as to forbid all hope. The worst symptoms had appeared; she was not destined to recover; and a week later I heard from Mrs. Munden that she would in fact "gurgle" no more.

2

All this, for Lady Beldonald, had been an agitation so great that access to her apartment was denied for a time even to her sister-in-law. It was much more out of the question, of course, that she should unveil her face to a person of my special business with it; so that the question of the portrait was, by common consent, postponed to that of the installation of a successor to her late companion. Such a successor, I gathered from Mrs. Munden, widowed, childless, and lonely, as well as inapt for the minor offices, she had absolutely to have; a more or less humble *alter ego*[4] to deal with the servants, keep the accounts, make the tea and arrange the light. Nothing seemed more natural than that she should marry again, and obviously that might come; yet the predecessors of Miss Dadd had been contemporaneous with a first husband, and others formed in her image might be contemporaneous with a second. I was much occupied in those months, at any rate, so that these questions and their ramifications lost themselves for a while to my view, and I was only brought back to them by Mrs. Munden's coming to me one day with the news that we were all right again—her sister-in-law was once more "suited." A certain Mrs. Brash, an American relative whom she had not seen for years, but with whom she had continued to communicate, was to come out to her immediately; and this person, it appeared, could be quite trusted to meet the conditions. She was ugly—ugly enough, without abuse of it, and she was unlimitedly good. The position offered her by Lady Beldonald was, moreover, exactly what she needed; widowed also, after many troubles and reverses, with her fortune of the smallest and her various children either buried or placed about, she had never had time or means to come to England, and would really be grateful in her declining years for the new experience and the pleasant light work involved in her cousin's hospitality. They had been much together early in life, and Lady Beldonald was immensely fond of her—would have in fact tried to get hold of her before had not Mrs. Brash been always in bondage to family duties, to the variety of her tribulations. I dare say I laughed at my friend's use of the term "position"—the position, one might call it, of a candlestick or a sign-post, and I dare say I must have asked if the special service the poor lady was to render had been made clear to her. Mrs. Munden left me, at all events, with the rather droll image of her faring forth, across the sea, quite consciously and resignedly to perform it.

The point of the communication had, however, been that my sitter was again looking up and would doubtless, on the arrival and due initiation of Mrs. Brash, be in form really to wait on me. The situation must, further, to my knowledge, have developed happily, for I arranged with Mrs. Munden that our friend, now all ready to begin, but wanting first just to see the things I had most recently done, should come once more, as a final preliminary, to my studio. A good foreign friend of mine, a French painter, Paul Outreau, was at the moment in London, and I had proposed, as he was much interested in types, to get together for his amusement a small afternoon party. Everyone came, my big room was full, there was music and a modest spread; and I have not forgotten the light of admiration in Outreau's expressive

4. "Other self"; companion.

face as, at the end of half an hour, he came up to me in his enthusiasm.

"*Bonté divine, mon cher—que cette vieille est donc belle!*"[5]

I had tried to collect all the beauty I could, and also all the youth, so that for a moment I was at a loss. I had talked to many people and provided for the music, and there were figures in the crowd that were still lost to me. "What old woman do you mean?"

"I don't know her name—she was over by the door a moment ago. I asked somebody and was told, I think, that she's American."

I looked about and saw one of my guests attach a pair of fine eyes to Outreau very much as if she knew he must be talking of her. "Oh, Lady Beldonald! Yes, she's handsome; but the great point about her is that she has been 'put up,' to keep, and that she wouldn't be flattered if she knew you spoke of her as old. A box of sardines is only 'old' after it has been opened. Lady Beldonald never has yet been—but I'm going to do it." I joked, but I was somehow disappointed. It was a type that, with his unerring sense for the *banal,* I shouldn't have expected Outreau to pick out.

"You're going to paint her? But, my dear man, she *is* painted—and as neither you nor I can do it. *Où est-elle donc?*"[6] He had lost her, and I saw I had made a mistake. "She's the greatest of all the great Holbeins."

I was relieved. "Ah, then, not Lady Beldonald! But do I possess a Holbein, of *any* price, unawares?"

"There she is—there she is! Dear, dear, dear, what a head!" And I saw whom he meant—and what: a small old lady in a black dress and a black bonnet, both relieved with a little white, who had evidently just changed her place to reach a corner from which more of the room and of the scene was presented to her. She appeared unnoticed and unknown, and I immediately recognized that some other guest must have brought her and, for want of opportunity, had as yet to call my attention to her. But two things, simultaneously with this and with each other, struck me with force; one of them the truth of Outreau's description of her, the other the fact that the person bringing her could only have been Lady Beldonald. She *was* a Holbein—of the first water;[7] yet she was also Mrs. Brash, the imported "foil," the indispensable "accent," the successor to the dreary Miss Dadd! By the time I had put these things together—Outreau's "American" having helped me—I was in just such full possession of her face as I had found myself, on the other first occasion, of that of her patroness. Only with so different a consequence. I couldn't look at her enough, and I stared and stared till I became aware she might have fancied me challenging her as a person unpresented. "All the same," Outreau went on, equally held, "*c'est une tête à faire.*[8] If I were only staying long enough for a crack at her! But I tell you what"—and he seized my arm—"bring her over!"

"Over?"

"To Paris. She'd have a *succès fou.*"[9]

"Ah, thanks, my dear fellow," I was now quite in a position to say; "she's the handsomest thing in London, and"—for what I might do with her was already before me with intensity—"I propose to keep her to myself." It was before me with intensity, in the light of Mrs. Brash's distant perfection of a little white old face, in which every wrinkle was

5. "Good gracious, dear friend, how beautiful that old woman is!"
6. "Where is she, then?"
7. Best quality.
8. "That's a (fine) head to paint."
9. Wild success.

the touch of a master; but something else, I suddenly felt, was not less so, for Lady Beldonald, in the other quarter, and though she couldn't have made out the subject of our notice, continued to fix us, and her eyes had the challenge of those of the woman of consequence who has missed something. A moment later I was close to her, apologizing first for not having been more on the spot at her arrival, but saying in the next breath uncontrollably, "Why, my dear lady, it's a Holbein!"

"A Holbein? What?"

"Why, the wonderful sharp old face—so extraordinarily, consummately drawn—in the frame of black velvet. That of Mrs. Brash, I mean—isn't it her name?—your companion."

This was the beginning of a most odd matter—the essence of my anecdote; and I think the very first note of the oddity must have sounded for me in the tone in which her ladyship spoke after giving me a silent look. It seemed to come to me out of a distance immeasurably removed from Holbein. "Mrs. Brash is not my 'companion' in the sense you appear to mean. She's my rather near relation and a very dear old friend. I *love* her—and you must know her."

"Know her? Rather! Why, to see her is to want, on the spot, to 'go' for her. She also must sit for me."

"*She?* Louisa Brash?" If Lady Beldonald had the theory that her beauty directly showed it when things were not well with her, this impression, which the fixed sweetness of her serenity had hitherto struck me by no means as justifying, gave me now my first glimpse of its grounds. It was as if I had never before seen her face invaded by anything I should have called an expression. This expression, moreover, was of the faintest—was like the effect produced on a surface by an agitation both deep within and as yet much confused. "Have you told her so?" she then quickly asked, as if to soften the sound of her surprise.

"Dear no, I've but just noticed her—Outreau a moment ago put me onto her. But we're both so taken, and he also wants—"

"To *paint* her?" Lady Beldonald uncontrollably murmured.

"Don't be afraid we shall fight for her," I returned with a laugh for this tone. Mrs. Brash was still where I could see her without appearing to stare, and she mightn't have seen I was looking at her, though her protectress, I am afraid, could scarce have failed of this perception. "We must each take our turn, and at any rate she's a wonderful thing, so that, if you'll take her to Paris, Outreau promises her there—"

"*There?*" my companion gasped.

"A career bigger still than among *us*, as he considers that we haven't half their eye. He guarantees her a *succès fou*."

She couldn't get over it. "Louisa Brash? In Paris?"

"They do see," I exclaimed, "more than we; and they live extraordinarily, don't you know, *in* that. But she'll do something here too."

"And what will she do?"

If, frankly, now, I couldn't help giving Mrs. Brash a longer look, so after it I could as little resist sounding my interlocutress. "You'll see. Only give her time."

She said nothing during the moment in which she met my eyes; but then: "Time, it seems to me, is exactly what you and your friend want. If you haven't talked with her—"

"We haven't seen her? Oh, we see bang off—with a click like a steel spring. It's our trade; it's our life; and we should be donkeys if we

made mistakes. That's the way I saw you yourself, my lady, if I may say so; that's the way, with a long pin straight through your body, I've got you. And just so I've got *her*."

All this, for reasons, had brought my guest to her feet; but her eyes, while we talked, had never once followed the direction of mine. "You call her a Holbein?"

"Outreau did, and I of course immediately recognized it. Don't *you?* She brings the old boy to life! It's just as I should call you a Titian.[1] You bring *him* to life."

She couldn't be said to relax, because she couldn't be said to have hardened; but something at any rate on this took place in her—something indeed quite disconnected from what I would have called her. "Don't you understand that she has always been supposed—?" It had the ring of impatience; nevertheless, on a scruple, it stopped short.

I knew what it was, however, well enough to say it for her if she preferred. "To be nothing whatever to look at? To be unfortunately plain—or even if you like repulsively ugly? Oh yes, I understand it perfectly, just as I understand—I have to as a part of my trade—many other forms of stupidity. It's nothing new to one that ninety-nine people out of a hundred have no eyes, no sense, no taste. There are whole communities impenetrably sealed. I don't say your friend is a person to make the men turn round in Regent Street.[2] But it adds to the joy of the few who do see that they have it so much to themselves. Where in the world can she have lived? You must tell me all about that —or rather, if she'll be so good, *she* must."

"You mean then to speak to her—?"

I wondered as she pulled up again. "Of her beauty?"

"Her beauty!" cried Lady Beldonald so loud that two or three persons looked round.

"Ah, with every precaution of respect!" I declared in a much lower tone. But her back was by this time turned to me, and in the movement, as it were, one of the strangest little dramas I have ever known was well launched.

3

It was a drama of small, smothered, intensely private things, and I knew of but one other person in the secret; yet that person and I found it exquisitely susceptible of notation, followed it with an interest the mutual communication of which did much for our enjoyment, and were present with emotion at its touching catastrophe. The small case —for so small a case—had made a great stride even before my little party separated, and in fact within the next ten minutes.

In that space of time two things had happened; one of which was that I made the acquaintance of Mrs. Brash, and the other that Mrs. Munden reached me, cleaving the crowd, with one of her usual pieces of news. What she had to impart was that, on her having just before asked Nina if the conditions of our sitting had been arranged with me, Nina had replied, with something like perversity, that she didn't propose to arrange them, that the whole affair was "off" again, and that

1. Tinziano Vecelli or Vecellio (*c.* 1490–1576), generally considered the greatest painter of the Venetian High Renaissance, his painting full of drama, vitality, heroic dignity; a series of paintings of a woman-turned-goddess, "Danaë," is often considered to stress decorative rather than spiritual values.

2. A handsome, broad street in London, part of which is in the most fashionable shopping district of the city.

she preferred not to be, for the present, further pressed. The question for Mrs. Munden was naturally what had happened and whether I understood. Oh, I understood perfectly, and what I at first most understood was that even when I had brought in the name of Mrs. Brash intelligence was not yet in Mrs. Munden. She was quite as surprised as Lady Beldonald had been on hearing of the esteem in which I held Mrs. Brash's appearance. She was stupefied at learning that I had just in my ardor proposed to the possessor of it to sit to me. Only she came round promptly—which Lady Beldonald really never did. Mrs. Munden was in fact wonderful; for when I had given her quickly "Why, she's a Holbein, you know," she took it up, after a first fine vacancy, with an immediate abysmal "Oh, *is* she?" that, as a piece of social gymnastics, did her the greatest honor; and she was in fact the first in London to spread the tidings. For a face-about it was magnificent. But she was also the first, I must add, to see what would really happen —though this she put before me only a week or two later.

"It will kill her, my dear—that's what it will do!"

She meant neither more nor less than that it would kill Lady Beldonald if I were to paint Mrs. Brash; for at this lurid light had we arrived in so short a space of time. It was for me to decide whether my aesthetic need of giving life to my idea was such as to justify me in destroying it in a woman after all, in most eyes, so beautiful. The situation was, after all, sufficiently queer; for it remained to be seen what I should positively gain by giving up Mrs. Brash. I appeared to have in any case lost Lady Beldonald, now too "upset"—it was always Mrs. Munden's word about her and, as I inferred, her own about herself— to meet me again on our previous footing. The only thing, I of course soon saw, was to temporize—to drop the whole question for the present and yet so far as possible keep each of the pair in view. I may as well say at once that this plan and this process gave their principal interest to the next several months. Mrs. Brash had turned up, if I remember, early in the new year, and her little wonderful career was in our particular circle one of the features of the following season. It was at all events for myself the most attaching; it is not my fault if I am so put together as often to find more life in situations obscure and subject to interpretation than in the gross rattle of the foreground. And there were all sorts of things, things touching, amusing, mystifying—and above all such an instance as I had never yet met—in this funny little fortune of the useful American cousin. Mrs. Munden was promptly at one with me as to the rarity and, to a near and human view, the beauty and interest of the position. We had neither of us ever before seen that degree and that special sort of personal success come to a woman for the first time so late in life. I found it an example of poetic, of absolutely retributive, justice; so that my desire grew great to work it, as we say, on those lines. I had seen it all from the original moment at my studio; the poor lady had never known an hour's appreciation—which, moreover, in perfect good faith, she had never missed. The very first thing I did after producing so unintentionally the resentful retreat of her protectress had been to go straight over to her and say almost without preliminaries that I should hold myself immeasurably obliged if she would give me a few sittings. What I thus came face to face with was, on the instant, her whole unenlightened past, and the full, if foreshortened, revelation of what among us all was now unfailingly in store for her. To turn the handle and start that

tune[3] came to me on the spot as a temptation. Here was a poor lady who had waited for the approach of old age to find out what she was worth. Here was a benighted being to whom it was to be disclosed in her fifty-seventh year (I was to make that out) that she had something that might pass for a face. She looked much more than her age, and was fairly frightened—as if I had been trying on her some possibly heartless London trick—when she had taken in my appeal. That showed me in what an air she had lived and—as I should have been tempted to put it had I spoken out—among what children of darkness. Later on I did them more justice; saw more that her wonderful points must have been points largely the fruit of time, and even that possibly she might never in all her life have looked so well as at this particular moment. It might have been that if her hour had struck I just happened to be present at the striking. What had occurred, all the same, was at the worst a sufficient comedy.

The famous "irony of fate" takes many forms, but I had never yet seen it take quite this one. She had been "had over" on an understanding, and she was not playing fair. She had broken the law of her ugliness and had turned beautiful on the hands of her employer. More interesting even perhaps than a view of the conscious triumph that this might prepare for her, and of which, had I doubted of my own judgment, I could still take Outreau's fine start as the full guarantee—more interesting was the question of the process by which such a history could get itself enacted. The curious thing was that, all the while, the reasons of her having passed for plain—the reasons for Lady Beldonald's fond calculation, which they quite justified—were written large in her face, so large that it was easy to understand them as the only ones she herself had ever read. What was it, then, that actually made the old stale sentence mean something so different?—into what new combinations, what extraordinary language, unknown but understood at a glance, had time and life translated it? The only thing to be said was that time and life were artists who beat us all, working with recipes and secrets that we could never find out. I really ought to have, like a lecturer or a showman, a chart or a blackboard to present properly the relation, in the wonderful old tender, battered, blanched face, between the original elements and the exquisite final "style." I could do it with chalks, but I can scarcely do it thus. However, the thing was, for any artist who respected himself, to *feel* it—which I abundantly did; and then not to conceal from *her* that I felt it—which I neglected as little. But she was really, to do her complete justice, the last to understand; and I am not sure that, to the end—for there was an end—she quite made it all out or knew where she was. When you have been brought up for fifty years on black, it must be hard to adjust your organism, at a day's notice, to gold-color. Her whole nature had been pitched in the key of her supposed plainness. She had known how to be ugly—it was the only thing she had learnt save, if possible, how not to mind it. Being beautiful, at any rate, took a new set of muscles. It was on the prior theory, literally, that she had developed her admirable dress, instinctively felicitous, always either black or white, and a matter of rather severe squareness and studied line. She was magnificently neat; everything she showed had a way of looking both old and fresh; and there was on every occasion the same picture in her

3. As an organ-grinder does.

draped head—draped in low-falling black—and the fine white plaits (of a painter's white, somehow) disposed on her chest. What had happened was that these arrangements, determined by certain considerations, lent themselves in effect much better to certain others. Adopted as a kind of refuge, they had really only deepened her accent. It was singular, moreover, that, so constituted, there was nothing in her aspect of the ascetic or the nun. She was a good, hard, sixteenth-century figure, not withered with innocence, bleached rather by life in the open. She was, in short, just what we had made of her, a Holbein for a great museum; and our position, Mrs. Munden's and mine, rapidly became that of persons having such a treasure to dispose of. The world—I speak of course mainly of the art-world—flocked to see it.

4

"But has she any idea herself, poor thing?" was the way I had put it to Mrs. Munden on our next meeting after the incident at my studio; with the effect, however, only of leaving my friend at first to take me as alluding to Mrs. Brash's possible prevision of the chatter she might create. I had my own sense of that—this prevision had been *nil;* the question was of her consciousness of the office for which Lady Beldonald had counted on her and for which we were so promptly proceeding to spoil her altogether.

"Oh, I think she arrived with a goodish notion," Mrs. Munden had replied when I had explained; "for she's clever too, you know, as well as good-looking, and I don't see how, if she ever really *knew* Nina, she could have supposed for a moment that she was not wanted for whatever she might have left to give up. Hasn't she moreover always been made to feel that she's ugly enough for anything?" It was even at this point already wonderful how my friend had mastered the case, and what lights, alike for its past and its future, she was prepared to throw on it. "If she has seen herself as ugly enough for anything, she has seen herself—and that was the only way—as ugly enough for Nina; and she has had her own manner of showing that she understands without making Nina commit herself to anything vulgar. Women are never without ways for doing such things—both for communicating and receiving knowledge—that I can't explain to you, and that you wouldn't understand if I could, as you must *be* a woman even to do that. I dare say they've expressed it all to each other simply in the language of kisses. But doesn't it, at any rate, make something rather beautiful of the relation between them as affected by our discovery?"

I had a laugh for her plural possessive. "The point is, of course, that if there was a conscious bargain, and our action on Mrs. Brash is to deprive her of the sense of keeping her side of it, various things may happen that won't be good either for her or for ourselves. She may conscientiously throw up the position."

"Yes," my companion mused—"for she *is* conscientious. Or Nina, without waiting for that, may cast her forth."

I faced it all. "Then *we* should have to keep her."

"As a regular model?" Mrs. Munden was ready for anything. "Oh, that would be lovely!"

But I further worked it out. "The difficulty is that she's *not* a model,

hang it—that she's too good for one, that she's the very thing herself. When Outreau and I have each had our go, that will be all; there'll be nothing left for anyone else. Therefore it behoves us quite to understand that our attitude's a responsibility. If we can't do for her positively more than Nina does—"

"We must let her alone?" My companion continued to muse. "I see!"

"Yet don't," I returned, "see too much. We *can* do more."

"Than Nina?" She was again on the spot. "It wouldn't, after all, be difficult. We only want the directly opposite thing—and which is the only one the poor dear can give. Unless, indeed," she suggested, "we simply retract—we back out."

I turned it over. "It's too late for that. Whether Mrs. Brash's peace is gone, I can't say. But Nina's is."

"Yes, and there's no way to bring it back that won't sacrifice her friend. We can't turn round and say Mrs. Brash *is* ugly can we? But fancy Nina's not having *seen!*" Mrs. Munden exclaimed.

"She doesn't see now," I answered. "She can't, I'm certain, make out what we mean. The woman, for *her* still, is just what she always was. But she has, nevertheless, had her stroke, and her blindness, while she wavers and gropes in the dark, only adds to her discomfort. Her blow was to see the attention of the world deviate."

"All the same, I don't think, you know," my interlocutress said, "that Nina will have made her a scene, or that, whatever we do, she'll ever make her one. That isn't the way it will happen, for she's exactly as conscientious as Mrs. Brash."

"Then what *is* the way?" I asked.

"It will just happen in silence"

"And what will 'it,' as you call it, be?"

"Isn't that what we want really to see?"

"Well," I replied after a turn or two about, "whether we want it or not, it's exactly what we *shall* see; which is a reason the more for fancying, between the pair there—in the quiet, exquisite house, and full of superiorities and suppressions as they both are—the extraordinary situation. If I said just now that it's too late to do anything but accept, it's because I've take the full measure of what happened at my studio. It took but a few moments—but she tasted of the tree."[4]

My companion wondered. "Nina?"

"Mrs. Brash." And to have to put it so ministered, while I took yet another turn, to a sort of agitation. Our attitude *was* a responsibility.

But I had suggested something else to my friend, who appeared for a moment detached. "Should you say she'll hate her worse if she *doesn't* see?"

"Lady Beldonald? Doesn't see what *we* see, you mean, than if she does? Ah, I give *that* up!" I laughed. "But what I can tell you is why I hold that, as I said just now, we can do most. We can do this: we can give to a harmless and sensitive creature hitherto practically disinherited—and give with an unexpectedness that will immensely add to its price—the pure joy of a deep draught of the very pride of life, of an acclaimed personal triumph in our superior, sophisticated world."

Mrs. Munden had a glow of response for my sudden eloquence. "Oh, it will be beautiful!"

4. Tree of knowledge of good and evil, *Genesis* 3:5–6.

5

Well, that is what, on the whole, and in spite of everything, it really was. It has dropped into my memory a rich little gallery of pictures, a regular panorama of those occasions that were the proof of the privilege that had made me for a moment—in the words I have just recorded— lyrical. I see Mrs. Brash on each of these occasions practically en- throned and surrounded and more or less mobbed; see the hurrying and the nudging and the pressing and the staring; see the people "making up" and introduced, and catch the word when they have had their turn; hear it above all, the great one—"Ah yes, the famous Holbein!"— passed about with that perfection of promptitude that makes the mo- tions of the London mind so happy a mixture of those of the parrot and the sheep. Nothing would be easier, of course, than to tell the whole little tale with an eye only for that silly side of it. Great was the silliness, but great also as to this case of poor Mrs. Brash, I will say for it, the good nature. Of course, furthermore, it took in particular "our set," with its positive child-terror of the *banal*, to be either so foolish or so wise; though indeed I've never quite known where our set begins and ends, and have had to content myself on this score with the indi- cation once given me by a lady next whom I was placed at dinner: "Oh, it's bounded on the north by Ibsen and on the south by Sargent!"[5] Mrs. Brash never sat to me; she absolutely declined; and when she declared that it was quite enough for her that I had with that fine precipitation invited her, I quite took this as she meant it, for before we had gone very far our understanding, hers and mine, was complete. Her attitude was as happy as her success was prodigious. The sacrifice of the portrait was a sacrifice to the true inwardness of Lady Beldonald, and did much, for the time, I divined, toward muffling their domestic tension. All that was thus in her power to say—and I heard of a few cases of her having said it—was that she was sure I would have painted her beautifully if she hadn't prevented me. She couldn't even tell the truth, which was that I certainly would have done so if Lady Beldonald hadn't; and she never could mention the subject at all before that per- sonage. I can only describe the affair, naturally, from the outside, and heaven forbid indeed that I should try too closely to reconstruct the possible strange intercourse of these good friends at home.

My anecdote, however, would lose half such point as it may possess were I to omit all mention of the charming turn that her ladyship ap- peared gradually to have found herself able to give to her deportment. She had made it impossible I should myself bring up our old, our original question, but there was real distinction in her manner of now accepting certain other possibilities. Let me do her that justice; her effort at magnanimity must have been immense. There couldn't fail, of course, to be ways in which poor Mrs. Brash paid for it. How much she had to pay we were, in fact, soon enough to see; and it is my intimate conviction that, as a climax, her life at last was the price. But while she lived, at least—and it was with an intensity, for those wondrous weeks, of which she had never dreamed—Lady Beldonald herself faced the music. This is what I mean by the possibilities, by the sharp actuali- ties indeed, that she accepted. She took our friend out, she showed her at home, never attempted to hide or to betray her, played her no trick whatever so long as the ordeal lasted. She drank deep, on *her*

5. Henrik Ibsen (1828–1906), Norwegian dramatist, and John Singer Sargent (1856– 1906), American painter, both realists, the playwright harsher and darker.

side too, of the cup[6]—the cup that for her own lips could only be bitterness. There was, I think, scarce a special success of her companion's at
which she was not personally present. Mrs. Munden's theory of the
silence in which all this would be muffled for them was, none the less,
and in abundance, confirmed by our observations. The whole thing was
to be the death of one or the other of them, but they never spoke of it
at tea. I remember even that Nina went so far as to say to me once, looking me full in the eyes, quite sublimely, "I've made out what you mean
—she *is* a picture." The beauty of this, moreover, was that, as I am
persuaded, she hadn't really made it out at all—the words were the
mere hypocrisy of her reflective endeavor for virtue. She couldn't possibly have made it out; her friend was as much as ever "dreadfully
plain" to her; she must have wondered to the last what on earth possessed us. Wouldn't it in fact have been, after all, just this failure of
vision, this supreme stupidity in short, that kept the catastrophe so long
at bay? There was a certain sense of greatness for her in seeing so many
of us so absurdly mistaken; and I recall that on various occasions, and
in particular when she uttered the words just quoted, this high serenity,
as a sign of the relief of her soreness, if not of the effort of her conscience, did something quite visible to my eyes, and also quite unprecedented, for the beauty of her face. She got a real lift from it—such a
momentary discernible sublimity that I recollect coming out on the
spot with a queer, crude, amused "Do you know I believe I could paint
you *now?*"

  She was a fool not to have closed with me then and there; for what
has happened since has altered everything—what was to happen a little
later was so much more than I could swallow. This was the disappearance of the famous Holbein from one day to the other—producing a
consternation among us all as great as if the Venus of Milo[7] had suddenly vanished from the Louvre. "She has simply shipped her straight
back"—the explanation was given in that form by Mrs. Munden, who
added that any cord pulled tight enough would end at last by snapping. At the snap, in any case, we mightily jumped, for the master-
piece we had for three or four months been living with had made us feel
its presence as a luminous lesson and a daily need. We recognized
more than ever that it had been, for high finish, the gem of our collection—we found what a blank it left on the wall. Lady Beldonald might
fill up the blank, but *we* couldn't. That she did soon fill it up—and,
heaven help us, *how?*—was put before me after an interval of no great
length, but during which I had not seen her. I dined on the Christmas
of last year at Mrs. Munden's, and Nina, with a "scratch lot,"[8] as our
hostess said, was there, and, the preliminary wait being longish, approached me very sweetly. "I'll come to you tomorrow if you like," she
said; and the effect of it, after a first stare at her, was to make me look
all round. I took in, in these two motions, two things; one of which was
that, though now again so satisfied herself of her high state, she could
give me nothing comparable to what I should have got had she taken
me up at the moment of my meeting her on her distinguished concession; the other that she was "suited" afresh, and that Mrs. Brash's successor was fully installed. Mrs. Brash's successor was at the other side of

6. Jesus, at Gethsemane after his betrayal, three times prays that his trial and
sufferings pass if it is God's will: "O my
Father, if it be possible, let this cup pass
from me." (*Matthew* 26:39)
  7. Famous damaged Greek statue of the
goddess of love, now in the Louvre (Paris).
  8. Group assembled at the last minute.

the room, and I became conscious that Mrs. Munden was waiting to see my eyes seek her. I guessed the meaning of the wait; what was *one*, this time, to say? Oh, first and foremost, assuredly, that it was immensely droll, for this time, at least, there was no mistake. The lady I looked upon, and as to whom my friend, again quite at sea, appealed to me for a formula, was as little a Holbein, or a specimen of any other school, as she was, like Lady Beldonald herself, a Titian. The formula was easy to give, for the amusement was that her prettiness—yes, literally, prodigiously, her prettiness—was distinct. Lady Beldonald had been magnificent—had been almost intelligent. Miss What's-her-name continues pretty, continues even young, and doesn't matter a straw! She matters so ideally little that Lady Beldonald is practically safer, I judge, than she has ever been. There has not been a symptom of chatter about this person, and I believe her protectress is much surprised that we are not more struck.

It was, at any rate, strictly impossible to me to make an appointment for the day as to which I have just recorded Nina's proposal; and the turn of events since then has not quickened my eagerness. Mrs. Munden remained in correspondence with Mrs. Brash—to the extent, that is, of three letters, each of which she showed me. They so told, to our imagination, her terrible little story that we were quite prepared—or thought we were—for her going out like a snuffed candle. She resisted, on her return to her original conditions, less than a year; the taste of the tree, as I had called it, had been fatal to her; what she had contentedly enough lived without before for half a century she couldn't now live without for a day. I know nothing of her original conditions—some minor American city—save that for her to have gone back to them was clearly to have stepped out of her frame. We performed, Mrs. Munden and I, a small funeral service for her by talking it all over and making it all out. It wasn't—the minor American city—a market for Holbeins, and what had occurred was that the poor old picture, banished from its museum and refreshed by the rise of no new movement to hang it, was capable of the miracle of a silent revolution, of itself turning, in its dire dishonor, its face to the wall. So it stood, without the intervention of the ghost of a critic, till they happened to pull it round again and find it mere dead paint.[9] Well, it had had, if that is anything, its season of fame, its name on a thousand tongues and printed in capitals in the catalogue. *We* had not been at fault. I haven't, all the same, the least note of her—not a scratch. And I did her so in intention! Mrs. Munden continues to remind me, however, that this is not the sort of rendering with which, on the other side, after all, Lady Beldonald proposes to content herself. She has come back to the question of her own portrait. Let me settle it then at last. Since she *will* have the real thing—well, hang it, she shall!

1903

9. In painting, dead-color is the first, preparatory layer of paint; here a pun.

STANLEY ELKIN

Criers and Kibitzers, Kibitzers and Criers

Greenspahn cursed the steering wheel shoved like the hard edge of someone's hand against his stomach. Goddamn lousy cars, he thought. Forty-five hundred dollars and there's not room to breathe. He thought sourly of the smiling salesman who had sold it to him, calling him Jake all the time he had been in the showroom: Lousy *podler*.[1] He slid across the seat, moving carefully as though he carried something fragile, and eased his big body out of the car. Seeing the parking meter, he experienced a dark rage. They don't let you live, he thought. *I'll put your nickels in the meter for you, Mr. Greenspahn*, he mimicked the Irish cop. Two dollars a week for the lousy grubber. Plus the nickels that were supposed to go into the meter. And they talked about the Jews. He saw the cop across the street writing out a ticket. He went around his car, carefully pulling at the handle of each door, and he started toward his store.

"Hey there, Mr. Greenspahn," the cop called.

He turned to look at him. "Yeah?"

"Good morning."

"Yeah. Yeah. Good morning."

The grubber came toward him from across the street. Uniforms, Greenspahn thought, only a fool wears a uniform.

"Fine day, Mr. Greenspahn," the cop said.

Greenspahn nodded grudgingly.

"I was sorry to hear about your trouble, Mr. Greenspahn. Did you get my card?"

"Yeah, I got it. Thanks." He remembered something with flowers on it and rays going up to a pink Heaven. A picture of a cross yet.

"I wanted to come out to the chapel but the brother-in-law was up from Cleveland. I couldn't make it."

"Yeah," Greenspahn said. "Maybe next time."

The cop looked stupidly at him, and Greenspahn reached into his pocket.

"No. No. Don't worry about that, Mr. Greenspahn. I'll take care of it for now. Please, Mr. Greenspahn, forget it this time. It's okay."

Greenspahn felt like giving him the money anyway. Don't mourn for me, *podler*, he thought. Keep your two dollars' worth of grief.

The cop turned to go. "Well, Mr. Greenspahn, there's nothing anybody can say at times like this, but you know how I feel. You got to go on living, don't you know."

"Sure," Greenspahn said. "That's right, Officer." The cop crossed the street and finished writing the ticket. Greenspahn looked after him angrily, watching the gun swinging in the holster at his hip, the sun flashing brightly on the shiny handcuffs. *Podler*, he thought, afraid for his lousy nickels. There'll be an extra parking space sooner than he thinks.

He walked toward his store. He could have parked by his own place but out of habit he left his car in front of a rival grocer's. It was an old and senseless spite. Tomorrow he would change. What difference did it make, one less parking space? Why should he walk?

He felt bloated, heavy. The bowels, he thought. I got to move them

1. Vaguely pejorative term; peddler (with implications of chiseler).

soon or I'll bust. He looked at the street vacantly, feeling none of the old excitement. What did he come back for, he wondered suddenly, sadly. He missed Harold. Oh my God. Poor Harold, he thought. I'll never see him again. I'll never see my son again. He was choking, a big pale man beating his fist against his chest in grief. He pulled a handkerchief from his pocket and blew his nose. That was the way it was, he thought. He would go along flat and empty and dull, and all of a sudden he would dissolve in a heavy, choking grief. The street was no place for him. His wife was crazy, he thought, swiftly angry. "Be busy. Be busy," she said. What was he, a kid, that because he was making up some-body's lousy order everything would fly out of his mind? The bottom dropped out of his life and he was supposed to go along as though nothing had happened. His wife and the cop, they had the same psychology. Like in the movies after the horse kicks your head in you're supposed to get up and ride him so he can throw you off and finish the job. If he could get a buyer he would sell, and that was the truth.

Mechanically he looked into the windows he passed. The displays seemed foolish to him now, petty. He resented the wooden wedding cakes, the hollow watches. The manikins were grotesque, giant dolls. Toys, he thought bitterly. Toys. That he used to enjoy the displays him-self, had even taken a peculiar pleasure in the complicated tiers of cans, in the amazing pyramids of apples and oranges in his own window, seemed incredible to him. He remembered he had liked to look at the little living rooms in the window of the furniture store, the wax models sitting on the couches offering each other tea. He used to look at the expensive furniture and think, *Merchandise.* The word had sounded rich to him, and mysterious. He used to think of camels on a desert, their bellies slung with heavy ropes. On their backs they carried *merchandise.* What did it mean, any of it? Nothing. It meant nothing.

He was conscious of someone watching him.

"Hello, Jake."

It was Margolis from the television shop.

"Hello, Margolis. How are you?"

"Business is terrible. You picked a hell of a time to come back."

A man's son dies and Margolis says business is terrible. Margolis, he thought, jerk, son of a bitch.

"You can't close up a minute. You don't know when somebody might come in. I didn't take coffee since you left," Margolis said.

"You had it rough, Margolis. You should have said something, I would have sent some over."

Margolis smiled helplessly, remembering the death of Greenspahn's son.

"It's okay, Margolis." He felt his anger tug at him again. It was something he would have to watch, a new thing with him but already familiar, easily released, like something on springs.

"Jake," Margolis whined.

"Not now, Margolis," he said angrily. He had to get away from him. He was like a little kid, Greenspahn thought. His face was puffy, swollen, like a kid about to cry. He looked so meek. He should be holding a hat in his hand. He couldn't stand to look at him. He was afraid Margolis was going to make a speech. He didn't want to hear it. What did he need a speech? His son was in the ground. Under all that earth. Under all that dirt. In a metal box. Airtight, the funeral director

told him. Oh my God, *airtight. Vacuum-sealed.* Like a can of coffee. His son was in the ground and on the street the models in the windows had on next season's dresses. He would hit Margolis in his face if he said one word.

Margolis looked at him and nodded sadly, turning his palms out as if to say, "I know. I know." Margolis continued to look at him and Greenspahn thought, He's taking into account, that's what he's doing. He's taking into account the fact that my son has died. He's figuring it in and making apologies for me, making an allowance, like he was doing an estimate in his head what to charge a customer.

"I got to go, Margolis."

"Sure, me too," Margolis said, relieved. "I'll see you, Jake.   The man from R.C.A. is around back with a shipment. What do I need it?"

Greenspahn walked to the end of the block and crossed the street. He looked down the side street and saw the *shul* where that evening he would say prayers for his son.

He came to his store, seeing it with distaste. He looked at the signs, like the balloons in comic strips where they put the words, stuck inside against the glass, the letters big and red like it was the end of the world, the big whitewash numbers on the glass thickly. A billboard, he thought.

He stepped up to the glass door and looked in. Frank, his produce man, stood by the fruit and vegetable bins taking the tissue paper off the oranges. His butcher, Arnold, was at the register talking to Shirley, the cashier. Arnold saw him through the glass and waved extravagantly. Shirley came to the door and opened it. "Good morning there, Mr. Greenspahn," she said.

"Hey, Jake, how are you?" Frank said.

"How's it going, Jake?" Arnold said.

"Was Siggie in yet? Did you tell him about the cheese?"

"He ain't yet been in this morning, Jake," Frank said.

"How about the meat? Did you place the order?"

"Sure, Jake," Arnold said. "I called the guy Thursday."

"Where are the receipts?" he asked Shirley.

"I'll get them for you, Mr. Greenspahn. You already seen them for the first two weeks you were gone. I'll get last week's."

She handled him a slip of paper. It was four hundred and seventy dollars off the last week's low figure. They must have had a picnic, Greenspahn thought. No more though. He looked at them, and they watched him with interest. "So," he said. "So."

"Nice to have you back, Mr. Greenspahn," Shirley told him, smiling.

"Yeah," he said, "yeah."

"We got a shipment yesterday, Jake, but the *schvartze*[2] showed up drunk. We couldn't get it all put up," Frank said.

Greenspahn nodded. "The figures are low," he said.

"It's business. Business has been terrible. I figure it's the strike," Frank said.

"In West Virginia the miners are out and you figure that's why my business is bad in this neighborhood?"

"There are repercussions," Frank said. "All industries are affected."

"Yeah," Greenspahn said, "yeah. The pretzel industry. The canned chicken noodle soup industry."

2. Black man.

"Well, business has been lousy, Jake," Arnold said testily.

"I guess maybe it's so bad, now might be a good time to sell. What do you think?" Greenspahn said.

"Are you really thinking of selling, Jake?" Frank asked.

"You want to buy my place, Frank?"

"You know I don't have that kind of money, Jake," Frank said uneasily.

"Yeah," Greenspahn said, "yeah."

Frank looked at him, and Greenspahn waited for him to say something else, but in a moment he turned and went back to the oranges. Some thief, Greenspahn thought. Big shot. I insulted him.

"I got to change," he said to Shirley. "Call me if Siggie comes in."

He went into the toilet off the small room at the rear of the store. He reached for the clothes he kept there on a hook on the back of the door and saw, hanging over his own clothes, a woman's undergarments. A brassiere hung by one cup over his trousers. What is it here, a locker room? Does she take baths in the sink? he thought. Fastidiously he tried to remove his own clothes without touching the other garments, but he was clumsy, and the underwear, together with his trousers, tumbled in a heap to the floor. They looked, lying there, strangely obscene to him, as though two people, desperately in a hurry, had dropped them quickly and were somewhere near him even now, perhaps behind the very door, making love. He picked up his trousers and changed his clothes. Taking a hanger from a pipe under the sink, he hung the clothes he had worn to work and put the hanger on the hook. He stooped to pick up Shirley's underwear. Placing it on the hook, his hand rested for a moment on the brassiere. He was immediately ashamed. He was terribly tired. He put his head through the loop of his apron and tied the apron behind the back of the old blue sweater he wore even in summer. He turned the sink's single tap and rubbed his eyes with water. Bums, he thought. Bums. You put up mirrors to watch the customers so they shouldn't get away with a stick of gum, and in the meanwhile Frank and Arnold walk off with the whole store. He sat down to try to move his bowels and the apron hung down from his chest like a barber's sheet. He spread it across his knees. I must look like I'm getting a haircut, he thought irrelevantly. He looked suspiciously at Shirley's underwear. My movie star. He wondered if it was true what Arnold told him, that she used to be a 26-girl.[3] Something was going on between her and that Arnold. Two bums, he thought. He knew they drank together after work. That was one thing, bad enough, but were they screwing around in the back of the store? Arnold had a family. You couldn't trust a young butcher. It was too much for him. Why didn't he just sell and get the hell out? Did he have to look for grief? Was he making a fortune that he had to put up with it? It was crazy. All right, he thought, a man in business, there were things a man in business put up with. But this? It was crazy. Everywhere he was beset by thieves and cheats. They kept pushing him, pushing him. What did it mean? Why did they do it? All right, he thought, when Harold was alive was it any different? No, of course not, he knew plenty then too. But it didn't make as much difference. Death is an education, he thought. Now there wasn't any reason to put up

---

3. Girl who operates a barroom dice game.

with it. What did he need it? On the street, in the store, he saw every-thing. Everything. It was as if everybody else were made out of glass. Why all of a sudden was he like that?

Why? he thought. Jerk, because they're hurting *you*, that's why.

He stood up and looked absently into the toilet. "Maybe I need a laxative," he said aloud. Troubled, he left the toilet.

In the back room, his "office," he stood by the door to the toilet and looked around. Stacked against one wall he saw four or five cases of soups and canned vegetables. Against the meat locker he had pushed a small table, his desk. He went to it to pick up a pencil. Underneath the telephone was a pad of note paper. Something about it caught his eye and he picked up the pad. On the top sheet was writing, his son's. He used to come down on Saturdays sometimes when they were busy; evidently this was an order he had taken down over the phone. He looked at the familiar writing and thought his heart would break. Harold, Harold, he thought. My God, Harold, you're dead. He touched the sprawling, hastily written letters, the carelessly spelled words, and thought absently, He must have been busy. I can hardly read it. He looked at it more closely. "He was in a hurry," he said, starting to sob. "My God, *he* was in a hurry." He tore the sheet from the pad, and folding it, put it into his pocket. In a minute he was able to walk back out into the store.

In the front Shirley was talking to Siggie, the cheese man. Seeing him up there leaning casually on the counter, Greenspahn felt a quick anger. He walked up the aisle toward him.

Siggie saw him coming. "*Shalom* Jake," he called.

"I want to talk to you."

"Is it important, Jake, because I'm in some terrific hurry. I still got deliveries."

"What did you leave me?"

"The same, Jake. The same. A couple pounds blue. Some Swiss. Delicious," he said, smacking his lips.

"I been getting complaints, Siggie."

"From the Americans, right? Your average American don't know from cheese. It don't mean nothing." He turned to go.

"Siggie, where you running?"

"Jake, I'll be back tomorrow. You can talk to me about it."

"Now."

He turned reluctantly. "What's the matter?"

"You're leaving old stuff. Who's your wholesaler?"

"Jake, Jake," he said. "We already been over this. I pick up the re-turns, don't I?"

"That's not the point."

"Have you ever lost a penny on account of me?"

"Siggie, who's your wholesaler? Where do you get the stuff?"

"I'm cheaper than the dairy, right? Ain't I cheaper than the dairy? Come on, Jake. What do you want?"

"Siggie, don't be a jerk. Who are you talking to? Don't be a jerk. You leave me cheap, crummy cheese, the dairies are ready to throw it away. I get everybody else's returns. It's old when I get it. Do you think a customer wants a cheese it goes off like a bomb two days after she gets it home? And what about the customers who don't return it? They think I'm gypping them and they don't come back. I don't want

the *schlak*[4] stuff. Give me fresh or I'll take from somebody else."

"I couldn't give you fresh for the same price, Jake. You know that."

"The same price."

"Jake," he said, amazed.

"The same price. Come on, Siggie, don't screw around with me."

"Talk to me tomorrow. We'll work something out." He turned to go.

"Siggie," Greenspahn called after him. "Siggie." He was already out of the store. Greenspahn clenched his fists. "The bum," he said.

"He's always in a hurry, that guy," Shirley said.

"Yeah, yeah," Greenspahn said. He started to cross to the cheese locker to see what Siggie had left him.

"Say, Mr. Greenspahn," Shirley said, "I don't think I have enough change."

"Where's the *schvartze?* Send him to the bank."

"He ain't come in yet. Shall I run over?"

Greenspahn poked his fingers in the cash drawer. "You got till he comes," he said.

"Well," she said, "if you think so."

"What do we do, a big business in change? I don't see customers stumbling over each other in the aisles."

"I told you, Jake," Arnold said, coming up behind him. "It's business. Business is lousy. People ain't eating."

"Here," Greenspahn said, "give me ten dollars. I'll go myself." He turned to Arnold. "I seen some stock in the back. Put it up, Arnold."

"I should put up the stock?" Arnold said.

"You told me yourself, business is lousy. Are you here to keep off the streets or something? What is it?"

"What do you pay the *schvartze* for?"

"He ain't here," Greenspahn said. "When he comes in I'll have him cut up some meat, you'll be even."

He took the money and went out into the street. It was lousy, he thought. You had to be able to trust them or you could go crazy. Every retailer had the same problem; he winked his eye and figured, All right, so I'll allow a certain percentage for shrinkage. You made it up on the register. But in his place it was ridiculous. They were professionals. Like the Mafia or something. What did it pay to aggravate himself, his wife would say. Now he was back he could watch them. *Watch* them. He couldn't stand even to be in the place. They thought they were getting away with something, the *podlers*.

He went into the bank. He saw the ferns. The marble tables where the depositors made out their slips. The calendars, carefully changed each day. The guard, a gun on his hip and a white carnation in his uniform. The big safe, thicker than a wall, shiny and open, in the back behind the sturdy iron gate. The tellers behind their cages, small and quiet, as though they went about barefooted. The bank officers, gray-haired and well dressed, comfortable at their big desks, solidly official behind their engraved name-plates. That was something, he thought. A bank. A bank was something. And no shrinkage.

He gave his ten-dollar bill to a teller to be changed.

"Hello there, Mr. Greenspahn. How are you this morning? We haven't seen you lately," the teller said.

"I haven't been in my place for three weeks," Greenspahn said.

---

4. Cheap, low quality.

"Say," the teller said, "that's quite a vacation."

"My son passed away."

"I didn't know," the teller said. "I'm very sorry, sir."

He took the rolls the teller handed him and stuffed them into his pocket. "Thank you," he said.

The street was quiet. It looks like a Sunday, he thought. There would be no one in the store. He saw his reflection in a window he passed and realized he had forgotten to take his apron off. It occurred to him that the apron somehow gave him the appearance of being very busy. An apron did that, he thought. Not a business suit so much. Unless there was a briefcase. A briefcase and an apron, they made you look busy. A uniform wouldn't. Soldiers didn't look busy, policemen didn't. A fireman did, but he had to have that big hat on. *Schmo*, he thought, a man your age walking in the street in an apron. He wondered if the vice-presidents at the bank had noticed his apron. He felt the heaviness again.

He was restless, nervous, disappointed in things.

He passed the big plate window of "The Cookery," the restaurant where he ate his lunch, and the cashier waved at him, gesturing that he should come in. He shook his head. For a moment when he saw her hand go up he thought he might go in. The men would be there, the other business people, drinking cups of coffee, cigarettes smearing the saucers, their sweet rolls cut into small, precise sections. Even without going inside he knew what it would be like. The criers and the kibitzers. The criers, earnest, complaining with a peculiar vigor about their businesses, their gas mileage, their health; their despair articulate, dependably lamenting their lives, vaguely mourning conditions, their sorrow something they could expect no one to understand. The kibitzers, deaf to grief, winking confidentially at the others, their voices high-pitched in kidding or lowered in conspiracy to tell of triumphs, of men they knew downtown, of tickets fixed, or languishing goods moved suddenly and unexpectedly, of the windfall that was life; their fingers sticky, smeared with the sugar from their rolls.

What did he need them, he thought. Big shots. What did they know about anything? Did they lose sons?

He went back to his place and gave Shirley the silver.

"Is the *schvartze* in yet?" he asked.

"No, Mr. Greenspahn."

I'll dock him, he thought. I'll dock him.

He looked around and saw that there were several people in the store. It wasn't busy, but there was more activity than he had expected. Young housewives from the university. Good shoppers, he thought. Good customers. They knew what they could spend and that was it. There was no monkey business about prices. He wished his older customers would take lessons from them. The ones who came in wearing their fur coats and who thought because they knew him from his old place that entitled them to special privileges. In a supermarket. Privileges. Did A&P give discounts? The National? What did they want from him?

He walked around straightening the shelves. Well, he thought, at least it wasn't totally dead. If they came in like this all day he might make a few pennies. A few pennies, he thought. A few dollars. What difference does it make?

A salesman was talking to him when he saw her. The man was trying

to tell him something about a new product, some detergent, ten cents off on the box, something, but Greenspahn couldn't take his eyes off her.

"Can I put you down for a few trial cases, Mr. Greenspahn? In Detroit when the stores put it on the shelves . . ."

"No," Greenspahn interrupted him. "Not now. It don't sell. I don't want it."

"But, Mr. Greenspahn, I'm trying to tell you. This is something new. It hasn't been on the market more than three weeks."

"Later, later," Greenspahn said. "Talk to Frank, don't bother me."

He left the salesman and followed the woman up the aisle, stopping when she stopped, turning to the shelves, pretending to adjust them. One egg, he thought. She touches one egg, I'll throw her out.

It was Mrs. Frimkin, the doctor's wife. An old customer and a chiseler. An expert. For a long time she hadn't been in because of a fight they'd had over a thirty-five-cent delivery charge. He had to watch her. She had a million tricks. Sometimes she would sneak over to the eggs and push her finger through two or three of them. Then she would smear a little egg on the front of her dress and come over to him complaining that he'd ruined her dress, that she'd picked up the eggs "in good faith," thinking they were whole. "In good faith," she'd say. He'd have to give her the whole box and charge her for a half dozen just to shut her up. An expert.

He went up to her. He was somewhat relieved to see that she wore a good dress. She risked the egg trick only in a housecoat.

"Jake," she said, smiling at him.

He nodded.

"I heard about Harold," she said sadly. "The doctor told me. I almost had a heart attack when I heard." She touched his arm. "Listen," she said. "We don't know. We just don't know. Mrs. Baron, my neighbor from when we lived on Drexel, didn't she fall down dead in the street? Her daughter was getting married in a month. How's your wife?"

Greenspahn shrugged. "Something I can do for you, Mrs. Frimkin?"

"What am I, a stranger? I don't need help. Fix, fix your shelves. I can take what I need."

"Yeah," he said, "yeah. Take." She had another trick. She came into a place, his place, the A&P, it didn't make any difference, and she priced everything. She even took notes. He knew she didn't buy a thing until she was absolutely convinced she couldn't get it a penny cheaper some place else.

"I only want a few items. Don't worry about me," she said.

"Yeah," Greenspahn said. He could wring her neck, the lousy *podler*.

"How's the fruit?" she asked.

"You mean confidentially?"

"What else?"

"I'll tell you the truth," Greenspahn said. "It's so good I don't like to see it get out of the store."

"Maybe I'll buy a banana."

"You couldn't go wrong," Greenspahn said.

"You got a nice place, Jake. I always said it."

"So buy something," he said.

"We'll see," she said mysteriously. "We'll see."

They were standing by the canned vegetables and she reached out her hand to lift a can of peas from the shelf. With her palm she made a big thing of wiping the dust from the top of the can and then stared

at the price stamped there. "Twenty-seven?" she asked, surprised.

"Yeah," Greenspahn said. "It's too much?"

"Well," she said.

"I'll be damned," he said. "I been in the business twenty-two years and I never did know what to charge for a tin of peas."

She looked at him suspiciously, and with a tight smile gently replaced the peas. Greenspahn glared at her, and then, seeing Frank walk by, caught at his sleeve, pretending he had business with him. He walked up the aisle holding Frank's elbow, conscious that Mrs. Frimkin was looking after them.

"The lousy *podler*," he whispered.

"Take it easy, Jake," Frank said. "She could be a good customer again. So what if she chisels a little? I was happy to see her come in."

"Yeah," Greenspahn said, "happy." He left Frank and went toward the meat counter. "Any phone orders?" he asked Arnold.

"A few, Jake. I can put them up."

"Never mind," Greenspahn said. "Give me." He took the slips Arnold handed him. "While it's quiet I'll do them."

He read over the orders quickly and in the back of the store selected four cardboard boxes with great care. He picked the stock from the shelves and fit it neatly into boxes, taking a kind of pleasure in the diminution of the stacks. Each time he put something into a box he had the feeling that there was that much less to sell. At the thick butcher's block behind the meat counter, bloodstains so deep in the wood they seemed almost a part of its grain, he trimmed fat from a thick roast. Arnold, beside him, leaned heavily against the paper roll. Greenspahn was conscious that Arnold watched him.

"Bernstein's order?" Arnold asked.

"Yeah," Greenspahn said.

"She's giving a party. She told me. Her husband's birthday."

"Happy birthday."

"Yeah," Arnold said. "Say, Jake, maybe I'll go eat."

Greenspahn trimmed the last piece of fat from the roast before he looked up at him. "So go eat," he said.

"I think so," Arnold said. "It's slow today. You know?"

Greenspahn nodded.

"Well, I'll grab some lunch. Maybe it'll pick up in the afternoon."

He took a box and began filling another order. He went to the canned goods in high, narrow, canted towers. That much less to sell, he thought bitterly. It was endless. You could never liquidate. There were no big deals in the grocery business. He thought hopelessly of the hundreds of items in his store, of all the different brands, the different sizes. He was terribly aware of each shopper, conscious of what each put into the shopping cart. It was awful, he thought. He wasn't selling diamonds. He wasn't selling pianos. He sold bread, milk, eggs. You had to have volume or you were dead. He was losing money. On his electric, his refrigeration, the signs in his window, his payroll, his specials, his stock. It was the chain stores. They had the parking. They advertised. They gave stamps. Two percent right out of the profits—it made no difference to them. They had the tie-ins. Fantastic. Their own farms, their own dairies, their own bakeries, their own canneries. Everything. The bastards. He was committing suicide to fight them.

In a little while Shirley came up to him. "Is it all right if I get my lunch now, Mr. Greenspahn?"

Why did they ask him? Was he a tyrant? "Yeah, yeah. Go eat. I'll watch the register."

She went out, and Greenspahn, looking after her, thought, Something's going on. First one, then the other. They meet each other. What do they do, hold hands? He fit a carton of eggs carefully into a box. What difference does it make? A slut and a bum.

He stood at the checkout counter, and pressing the orange key, watched the *No Sale* flag shoot up into the window of the register. He counted the money sadly.

Frank was at the bins trimming lettuce. "Jake, you want to go eat I'll watch things," he said.

"Not yet," Greenspahn said.

An old woman came into the store and Greenspahn recognized her. She had been in twice before that morning and both times had bought two tins of the coffee Greenspahn was running on a special. She hadn't bought anything else. Already he had lost twelve cents on her. He watched her carefully and saw with a quick rage that she went again to the coffee. She picked up another two tins and came toward the checkout counter. She wore a bright red wig which next to her very white, ancient skin gave her the appearance of a clown. She put the coffee down on the counter and looked up at Greenspahn timidly. He made no effort to ring up the sale. She stood for a moment and then pushed the coffee toward him.

"Sixty-nine cents a pound," she said. "Two pounds is a dollar thirty-eight. Six cents tax is a dollar forty-four."

"Lady," Greenspahn said, "don't you ever eat? Is that all you do is drink coffee?" He stared at her.

Her lips began to tremble and her body shook. "A dollar forty-four," she said. "I have it right here."

"This is your sixth can, lady. I lose money on it. Do you know that?"

The woman continued to tremble. It was as though she were very cold.

"What do you do, lady? Sell this stuff door-to-door? Am I your wholesaler?"

Her body continued to shake, and she looked out at him from behind faded eyes as though she were unaware of the terrible movements of her body, as though they had, ultimately, nothing to do with her, that really she existed, hiding, crouched, somewhere behind the eyes. He had the impression that, frictionless, her old bald head bobbed beneath the wig. "All right," he said finally, "a dollar forty-four. I hope you have more luck with the item than I had." He took the money from her and watched her as she accepted her package wordlessly and walked out of the store. He shook his head. It was all a pile of crap, he thought. He had a vision of the woman on back porches, standing silently at back doors open on their chains, sadly extending the coffee.

He wanted to get out. Frank could watch the store. If he stole, he stole.

"Frank," he said, "it ain't busy. Watch things. I'll eat."

"Go on, Jake. Go ahead. I'm not hungry, I got a cramp. Go ahead."

"Yeah."

He walked toward the restaurant. On his way he had to pass a National; seeing the crowded parking lot, he felt his stomach tighten. He paused at the window and pressed his face against the glass and looked in at the full aisles. Through the thick glass he saw women

moving silently through the store. He stepped back and read the advertisements on the window. My fruit is cheaper, he thought. My meat's
the same, practically the same.

He moved on. Passing the familiar shops, he crossed the street and
went into "The Cookery." Pushing open the heavy glass door, he heard
the babble of the lunchers, the sound rushing to his ears like the noise
of a suddenly unmuted trumpet. Criers and kibitzers, he thought. Kibitzers and criers.

The cashier smiled at him. "We haven't seen you, Mr. G. Somebody
told me you were on a diet," she said.

Her too, he thought. A kibitzer that makes change.

He went toward the back. "Hey, Jake, how are you?" a man in a booth
called. "Sit by us."

He nodded at the men who greeted him, and pulling a chair from
another table, placed it in the aisle facing the booth. He sat down and
leaned forward, pulling the chair's rear legs into the air so that the
waitress could get by. Sitting there in the aisle, he felt peculiarly like
a visitor, like one there only temporarily, as though he had rushed up
to the table merely to say hello or to tell a joke. He knew what it was.
It was the way kibitzers sat. The others, cramped in the booth but
despite this giving the appearance of lounging there, their lunches begun or already half eaten, somehow gave him the impression that they
had been there all day.

"You missed it, Jake," one of the men said. "We almost got Traub
here to reach for a check last Friday. Am I lying, Margolis?"

"He almost did, Jake. He really almost did."

"At the last minute he jumped up and down on his own arm and
broke it."

The men at the table laughed, and Greenspahn looked at Traub sitting little and helpless between two big men. Traub looked down
shame-faced into his Coca-Cola.

"It's okay, Traub," the first man said. "We know. You got all those
daughters getting married and having big weddings at the same time.
It's terrible. Traub's only got one son. And do you think he'd have the
decency to get married so Traub could one time go to a wedding and
just enjoy himself? No, *he's* not *old* enough. But he's old enough to
turn around and get himself bar mitzvah'd, right, Traub? The lousy
kid."

Greenspahn looked at the men in the booth and at many-daughtered
Traub, who seemed as if he were about to cry. Kibitzers and criers, he
thought. Everywhere it was the same. At every table. The two kinds of
people like two different sexes that had sought each other out. Sure,
Greenspahn thought, would a crier listen to another man's complaints?
Could a kibitzer kid a kidder? But it didn't mean anything, he thought.
Not the jokes, not the grief. It didn't mean anything. They were like
birds making noises in a tree. But try to catch them in a deal. They'd
murder you. Every day they came to eat their lunch and make their
noises. Like cowboys on television hanging up their gun belts to go to
a dance.

But even so, he thought, they were the way they pretended to be.
Nothing made any difference to them. Did they lose sons? Not even the
money they earned made any difference to them finally.

"So I was telling you," Margolis said, "the guy from the Chamber of
Commerce came around again today."

"He came to me too," Paul Gold said.

"Did you give?" Margolis asked.

"No, of course not."

"Did he hit you yet, Jake? Throw him out. He wants contributions for decorations. Listen, those guys are on the take from the paper-flower people. It's fantastic what they get for organizing the big stores downtown. My cousin on State Street told me about it. I told him, I said, 'Who needs the Chamber of Commerce? Who needs Easter baskets and colored eggs hanging from the lamppost?' "

"Not when the ring trick still works, right, Margolis?" Joe Fisher said.

Margolis looked at his lapel and shrugged slightly. It was the most modest gesture Greenspahn had ever seen him make. The men laughed. The ring trick was Margolis' invention. "A business promotion," he had told Greenspahn. "Better than Green Stamps." He had seen him work it. Margolis would stand at the front of his store and signal to some guy who stopped for a minute to look at the TV sets in his window. He would rap on the glass with his ring to catch his attention. He would smile and say something to him, anything. It didn't make any difference; the guy in the street couldn't hear him. As Greenspahn watched, Margolis had turned to him and winked slyly as if to say, "Watch this. Watch how I get this guy." Then he had looked back at the customer outside, and still smiling broadly had said, "Hello, schmuck. Come on in, I'll sell you something. That's right, jerk, press your greasy nose against the glass to see who's talking to you. Shade your eyes. That-a-jerk. Come on in, I'll sell you something." Always the guy outside would come into the store to find out what Margolis had been saying to him. "Hello there, sir." Margolis would say, grinning. "I was trying to tell you that the model you were looking at out there is worthless. Way overpriced. If the boss knew I was talking to you like this I'd be canned, but what the hell? We're all working people. Come on back here and look at a real set."

Margolis was right. Who needed the Chamber of Commerce? Not the kibitzers and criers. Not even the Gold boys. Criers. Greenspahn saw the other one at another table. Twins, but they didn't even look like brothers. Not even they needed the paper flowers hanging from the lamppost. Paul Gold shouting to his brother in the back, "Mr. Gold, please show this gentleman something stylish." And they'd go into the act, putting on a thick Yiddish accent for some white-haired old man with a lodge button in his lapel, giving him the business. Greenspahn could almost hear the old man telling the others at the Knights of Columbus Hall, "I picked this suit up from a couple of Yids on Fifty-third, real greenhorns. But you've got to hand it to them. Those people really know material."

Business was a kind of game with them, Greenspahn thought. Not even the money made any difference.

"Did I tell you about these two kids who came in to look at rings?" Joe Fisher said. "Sure," he went on, "two kids. Dressed up. The boy's a regular *mensch*.[5] I figure they've been downtown at Peacock's and Field's. I think I recognized the girl from the neighborhood. I say to her boy friend—a nice kid, a college kid, you know, he looks like he ain't been bar mitzvah'd yet—'I got a ring here I won't show you the

---

5. Man; grown-up.

price. Will you give me your check for three hundred dollars right now? No appraisal? No bringing it to Papa on approval? No nothing?'

" 'I'd have to see the ring,' he tells me.

"Get this. I put my finger over the tag on a ring I paid eleven hundred for. *A big ring.* You got to wear smoked glasses just to look at it. Paul, I mean it, this is some ring. I'll give you a price for your wife's anniversary. No kidding, this is some ring. Think seriously about it. We could make it up into a beautiful cocktail ring. Anyway, this kid stares like a big dummy, I think he's turned to stone. He's scared. He figures something's wrong a big ring like that for only three hundred bucks. His girl friend is getting edgy, she thinks the kid's going to make a mistake, and she starts shaking her head. Finally he says to me, listen to this, he says, 'I wasn't looking for anything that large. Anyway, it's not a blue stone.' Can you imagine? Don't tell me about shoppers. I get prizes."

"What would you have done if he said he wanted the ring?" Traub asked.

"What are you, crazy? He was strictly from wholesale. It was like he had a sign on his suit. Don't you think I can tell a guy who's trying to get a price idea from a real customer?"

"Say, Jake," Margolis said, "ain't that your cashier over there with your butcher?"

Greenspahn looked around. It was Shirley and Arnold. He hadn't seen them when he came in. They were sitting across the table from each other—evidently they had not seen him either—and Shirley was leaning forward, her chin on her palms. Sitting there, she looked like a young girl. It annoyed him. It was ridiculous. He knew they met each other. What did he care? It wasn't his business. But to let themselves be seen. He thought of Shirley's brassiere hanging in his toilet. It was reckless. They were reckless people. All of them, Arnold and Shirley and the men in the restaurant. Reckless people.

"They're pretty thick with each other, ain't they?" Margolis said.

"How should I know?" Greenspahn said.

"What do you run over there at that place of yours, a lonely hearts club?"

"It's not my business. They do their work."

"Some work," Paul Gold said.

"I'd like a job like that," Joe Fisher said.

"Ain't he married?" Paul Gold said.

"I'm not a policeman," Greenspahn said.

"Jake's jealous because he's not getting any," Joe Fisher said.

"Loudmouth," Greenspahn said, "I'm a man in mourning."

The others at the table were silent. "Joe was kidding," Traub, the crier, said.

"Sure, Jake," Joe Fisher said.

"Okay," Greenspahn said. "Okay."

For the rest of the lunch he was conscious of Shirley and Arnold. He hoped they would not see him, or if they did that they would make no sign to him. He stopped listening to the stories the men told. He chewed on his hamburger wordlessly. He heard someone mention George Stein, and he looked up for a moment. Stein had a grocery in a neighborhood that was changing. He had said that he wanted to get out. He was looking for a setup like Greenspahn's. He could speak to him. Sure, he thought. Why not? What did he need the aggravation?

What did he need it? He owned the building the store was in. He could live on the rents. Even Joe Fisher was a tenant of his. He could speak to Stein, he thought, feeling he had made up his mind about something. He waited until Arnold and Shirley had finished their lunch and then went back to his store.

In the afternoon Greenspahn thought he might be able to move his bowels. He went into the toilet off the small room at the back of the store. He sat, looking up at the high ceiling. In the smoky darkness above his head he could just make out the small, square tin ceiling-plates. They seemed pitted, soiled, like patches of war-ruined armor. Agh, he thought, the place is a pigpen. The sink bowl was stained dark, the enamel chipped, long fissures radiating like lines on the map of some wasted country. The single faucet dripped steadily. Greenspahn thought sadly of his water bill. On the knob of the faucet he saw again a faded blue S. S, he thought, what the hell does S stand for? H hot, C cold. What the hell kind of faucet is S? Old clothes hung on a hook on the back of the door. A man's blue wash pants hung inside out, the zipper split like a peeled banana, the crowded concourse of seams at the crotch like carelessly sewn patches.

He heard Arnold in the store, his voice raised exaggeratedly. He strained to listen.

"*Forty-five,*" he heard Arnold say.

"*Forty-five, Pop.*" He was talking to the old man. Deaf, he came in each afternoon for a piece of liver for his supper. "*I can't give you two ounces. I told you. I can't break the set.*" He heard a woman laugh. Shirley? Was Shirley back there with him? What the hell, he thought. It was one thing for them to screw around with each other at lunch, but they didn't have to bring it into the store. "*Take eight ounces. Invite someone over for dinner. Take eight ounces. You'll have for four days. You won't have to come back.*" He was a wise guy, that Arnold. What did he want to do, drive the old man crazy? What could you do? The old man liked a small slice of liver. He thought it kept him alive.

He heard footsteps coming toward the back room and voices raised in argument.

"I'm sorry," a woman said, "I don't know how it got there. Honest. Look, I'll pay. I'll pay you for it."

"You bet, lady," Frank's voice said.

"What do you want me to do?" the woman pleaded.

"I'm calling the cops," Frank said.

"For a lousy can of salmon?"

"It's the principle. You're a crook. You're a lousy thief, you know that? I'm calling the cops. We'll see what jail does for you."

"Please," the woman said. "Mister, please. This whole thing is crazy. I never did anything like this before. I haven't got any excuse, but please, can't you give me a chance?" The woman was crying.

"No chances," Frank said. "I'm calling the cops. You ought to be ashamed, lady. A woman dressed nice like you are. What are you, sick or something? I'm calling the cops." He heard Frank lift the receiver.

"Please," the woman sobbed. "My husband will kill me. I have a little kid, for Christ's sake."

Frank replaced the phone.

"Ten bucks," he said quietly.

"What's that?"

"Ten bucks and you don't come in here no more."

"I haven't got it," she said.

"All right, lady. The hell with you. I'm calling the cops."

"You bastard," she said.

"Watch your mouth," he said. "Ten bucks."

"I'll write you a check."

"Cash," Frank said.

"Okay, okay," she said. "Here."

"Now get out of here, lady." Greenspahn heard the woman's foot-steps going away. Frank would be fumbling now with his apron, trying to get the big wallet out of his front pocket. Greenspahn flushed the toilet and waited.

"Jake?" Frank asked, frightened.

"Who was she?"

"Jake, I never saw her before, honest. Just a tramp. She gave me ten bucks. She was just a tramp, Jake."

"I told you before. I don't want trouble," Greenspahn said angrily. He came out of the toilet. "What is this, a game with you?"

"Look, I caught her with the salmon. Would you want me to call the cops for a can of salmon? She's got a kid."

"Yeah, you got a big heart, Frank."

"I would have let you handle it if I'd seen you. I looked for you, Jake."

"You shook her down. I told you before about that."

"Jake, it's ten bucks for the store. I get so damned mad when some-body like that tries to get away with something."

"*Podler*," Greenspahn shouted. "You're through here."

"Jake," Frank said. "She was a tramp." He held the can of salmon in his hand and offered it to Greenspahn as though it were evidence.

Greenspahn pushed his hand aside. "Get out of my store. I don't need you. Get out. I don't want a crook in here."

"Who are you calling names, Jake?"

Greenspahn felt his rage, immense, final. It was on him at once, like an animal that had leaped upon him in the dark. His body shook with it. Frightened, he warned himself uselessly that he must be calm. A *podler* like that, he thought. He wanted to hit him in the face.

"Please, Frank. Get out of here," Greenspahn said.

"Sure," Frank screamed. "Sure, sure," he shouted. Greenspahn, startled, look at him. He seemed angrier than even himself. Green-spahn thought of the customers. They would hear him. What kind of a place, he thought. What kind of a place? "Sure," Frank yelled, "fire me, go ahead. A regular holy man. A saint! What are you, God? He smells everybody's rottenness but his own. Only when your own son—may he rest—when your own son slips five bucks out of the cash drawer, that you don't see."

Greenspahn could have killed him. "Who says that?"

Frank caught his breath.

"Who says that?" Greenspahn repeated.

"Nothing, Jake. It was nothing. He was going on a date probably. That's all. It didn't mean nothing."

"Who calls him a thief?"

"Nobody. I'm sorry."

"My dead son? You call my dead son a thief?"

"Nobody called anybody a thief. I didn't know what I was saying."

"In the ground. Twenty-three years old and in the ground. Not even a wife, not even a business. Nothing. He had nothing. He wouldn't take. Harold wouldn't take. Don't call him what you are. He should be alive today. You should be dead. You should be in the ground where he is. *Podler. Mumser*,"[6] he shouted. "*I saw the lousy receipts, liar*," he screamed.

In a minute Arnold was there and was putting his arm around him. "Calm down, Jake. Come on now, take it easy. What happened back here?" he asked Frank.

Frank shrugged.

"Get him away," Greenspahn pleaded. Arnold signaled Frank to get out and led Greenspahn to the chair near the table he used as a desk.

"You all right now, Jake? You okay now?"

Greenspahn was sobbing heavily. In a few moments he looked up. "All right," he said. "The customers. Arnold, please. The customers."

"Okay, Jake. Just stay back here and wait till you feel better."

Greenspahn nodded. When Arnold left him he sat for a few minutes and then went back into the toilet to wash his face. He turned the tap and watched the dirty basin fill with water. It's not even cold, he thought sadly. He plunged his hands into the sink and scooped up warm water, which he rubbed into his eyes. He took a handkerchief from his back pocket and unfolded it and patted his face carefully. He was conscious of laughter outside the door. It seemed old, brittle. For a moment he thought of the woman with the coffee. Then he remembered. The porter, he thought. He called his name. He heard footsteps coming up to the door.

"That's right, Mr. Greenspahn," the voice said, still laughing.

Greenspahn opened the door. His porter stood before him in torn clothes. His eyes, red, wet, looked as though they were bleeding. "You sure told that Frank," he said.

"You're late," Greenspahn said. "What do you mean coming in so late?"

"I been to Harold's grave," he said.

"What's that?"

"I been to Mr. Harold's grave," he repeated. "I didn't get to the funeral. I been to his grave cause of my dream."

"Put the stock away," Greenspahn said. "Some more came in this afternoon."

"I will," he said. "I surely will." He was an old man. He had no teeth and his gums lay smooth and very pink in his mouth. He was thin. His clothes hung on him, the sleeves of the jacket rounded, puffed from absent flesh. Through the rents in shirt and trousers Greenspahn could see the grayish skin, hairless, creased, the texture like the pit of a peach. Yet he had a strength Greenspahn could only wonder at, and could still lift more stock than Arnold or Frank or even Greenspahn himself.

"You'd better start now," Greenspahn said uncomfortably.

"I tell you about my dream, Mr. Greenspahn?"

"No dreams. Don't tell me your dreams."

"It was about Mr. Harold. Yes, sir, about him. Your boy that's dead, Mr. Greenspahn."

6. Bastard.

"I don't want to hear. See if Arnold needs anything up front."

"I dreamed it twice. That means it's true. You don't count a dream less you dream it twice."

"Get away with your crazy stories. I don't pay you to dream."

"That time on Halsted I dreamed the fire. I dreamed that twice."

"Yeah," Greenspahn said, "the fire. Yeah."

"I dreamed that dream twice. Them police wanted to question me. Same names, Mr. Greenspahn, me and your boy we got the same names."

"Yeah. I named him after you."

"I tell you that dream, Mr. Greenspahn? It was a mistake. Frank was supposed to die. Just like you said. Just like I heard you say it just now. And he will. Mr. Harold told me in the dream. Frank he's going to sicken and die his own self." The porter looked at Greenspahn, the red eyes filling with blood. "If you want it," he said. "That's what I dreamed, and I dreamed about the fire on Halsted the same way. Twice."

"You're crazy. Get away from me."

"That's a true dream. It happened just that very way."

"Get away. Get away," Greenspahn shouted.

"My name's Harold, too."

"You're crazy. Crazy."

The porter went off. He was laughing. What kind of a madhouse? Were they all doing it on purpose? Everything to aggravate him? For a moment he had the impression that this was what it was. A big joke, and everybody was in on it but himself. He was being *kibitzed* to death. Everything. The cop. The receipts. His cheese man. Arnold and Shirley. The men in the restaurant. Frank and the woman. The *schvartze.* Everything. He wouldn't let it happen. What was he, crazy or something? He reached into his pocket for his handkerchief, but pulled out a piece of paper. It was the order Harold had taken down over the phone and left on the pad. Absently he unfolded it and read it again. Something occurred to him. As soon as he had the idea he knew it was true. The order had never been delivered. His son had forgotten about it. It couldn't be anything else. Otherwise would it still have been on the message pad? Sure, he thought, what else could it be? Even his son. What did he care? What the hell did he care about the business? Greenspahn was ashamed. It was a terrible thought to have about a dead boy. Oh God, he thought. Let him rest. He was a boy, he thought. Twenty-three years old and he was only a boy. No wife. No business. Nothing. Was the five dollars so important? In helpless disgust he could see Harold's sly wink to Frank as he slipped the money out of the register. Five dollars, Harold, *five dollars,* he thought, as though he were admonishing him. "Why didn't you come to me, Harold?" he sobbed. "Why didn't you come to your father?"

He blew his nose. It's crazy, he thought. Nothing pleases me. Frank called him God. Some God, he thought. I sit weeping in the back of my store. The hell with it. The hell with everything. Clear the shelves, that's what he had to do. Sell the groceries. Get rid of the meats. Watch the money pile up. Sell, sell, he thought. That would be something. Sell everything. He thought of the items listed on the order his son had taken down. Were they delivered? He felt restless. He hoped they were delivered. If they weren't they would have to be sold again. He was very weary. He went to the front of the store.

It was almost closing time. Another half hour. He couldn't stay to close up. He had to be in *shul* before sundown. He had to get to the *minion*[7] They would have to close up for him. For a year. If he couldn't sell the store, for a year he wouldn't be in his own store at sundown. He would have to trust them to close up for him. Trust who? he thought. My Romeo, Arnold? Shirley? The crazy *schvartze?* Only Frank could do it. How could he have fired him? He looked for him in the store. He was talking to Shirley at the register. He would go up and talk to him. What difference did it make? He would have had to fire all of them. Eventually he would have to fire everybody who ever came to work for him. He would have to throw out his tenants, even the old ones, and finally whoever rented the store from him. He would have to keep on firing and throwing out as long as anybody was left. What difference would one more make?

"Frank," he said. "I want you to forget what we talked about before."

Frank looked at him suspiciously. "It's all right," Greenspahn reassured him. He led him by the elbow away from Shirley. "Listen," he said, "we were both excited before. I didn't mean it what I said."

Frank continued to look at him. "Sure, Jake," he said finally. "No hard feelings." He extended his hand.

Greenspahn took it reluctantly. "Yeah," he said.

"Frank," he said, "do me a favor and close up the place for me. I got to get to the *shul* for the *minion*."

"I got you, Jake."

Greenspahn went to the back to change his clothes. He washed his face and hands and combed his hair. Carefully he removed his working clothes and put on the suit jacket, shirt and tie he had worn in the morning. He walked back into the store.

He was about to leave when he saw that Mrs. Frimkin had come into the store again. That's all right, he told himself, she can be a good customer. He needed some of the old customers now. They could drive you crazy, but when they bought, they bought. He watched as she took a cart from the front and pushed it through the aisles. She put things in the cart as though she were in a hurry. She barely glanced at the prices. That was the way to shop, he thought. It was a pleasure to watch her. She reached into the frozen-food locker and took out about a half-dozen packages. From the towers of canned goods on his shelves she seemed to take down only the largest cans. In minutes her shopping cart was overflowing. That's some order, Greenspahn thought. Then he watched as she went to the stacks of bread at the bread counter. She picked up a packaged white bread, and first looking around to see if anyone was watching her, bent down quickly over the loaf, cradling it to her chest as though it were a football. As she stood, Greenspahn saw her brush crumbs from her dress, then put the torn package into her cart with the rest of her purchases.

She came up to the counter where Greenspahn stood and unloaded the cart, pushing the groceries toward Shirley to be checked out. The last item she put on the counter was the wounded bread. Shirley punched keys quickly. As she reached for the bread, Mrs. Frimkin put out her hand to stop her. "Look," she said, "what are you going to charge me for the bread? It's damaged. Can I have it for ten cents?"

7. Group of at least ten male Jews necessary for religious, in this case mourning, ceremonies.

Shirley turned to look at Greenspahn.

"Out," he said. "Get out, you *podler*. I don't want you coming in here any more. You're a thief," he shouted. "A thief."

Frank came rushing up. "Jake, what is it? What is it?"

"Her. That one. A crook. She tore the bread. I seen her."

The woman looked at him defiantly. "I don't have to take that," she said. "I can make plenty of trouble for you. You're crazy. I'm not going to be insulted by somebody like you."

"Get out of here," Greenspahn shouted, "before I have you locked up."

The woman backed away from him, and when he stepped forward she turned and fled.

"Jake," Frank said, putting his hand on Greenspahn's shoulder. "That was a big order. So she tried to get away with a few pennies. What does it mean? You want me to find her and apologize?"

"Look," Greenspahn said, "she comes in again I want to know about it. I don't care what I'm doing. I want to know about it. She's going to pay me for that bread."

"Jake," Frank said.

"No," he said. "I mean it."

"Jake, it's ten cents."

"*My* ten cents. No more," he said. "I'm going to *shul*."

He waved Frank away and went into the street. Already the sun was going down. He felt urgency. He had to get there before the sun went down.

That night Greenspahn had the dream for the first time.

He was in the synagogue waiting to say prayers for his son. Around him were the old men, the *minion*, their faces brittle and pale. He recognized them from his youth. They had been old even then. One man stood by the window and watched the sun. At a signal from him the others would begin. There was always some place in the world where the prayers were being said, he thought, some place where the sun had just come up or just gone down, and he supposed there was always a *minion* to watch it and to mark its progress, the prayers following God's bright bird, going up in sunlight or in darkness, always, everywhere. He knew the men never left the *shul*. It was the way they kept from dying. They didn't even eat, but there was about the room the foul lemony smell of urine. Sure, Greenspahn thought in the dream, stay in the *shul*. That's right. Give the *podlers* a wide berth. All they have to worry about is God. Some worry, Greenspahn thought. The man at the window gave the signal and they all started to mourn for Greenspahn's son, their ancient voices betraying the queer melody of the prayers. The rabbi looked at Greenspahn and Greenspahn, imitating the old men, began to rock back and forth on his heels. He tried to sway faster than they did. I'm younger, he thought. When he was swaying so quickly that he thought he would be sick were he to go any faster, the rabbi smiled at him approvingly. The man at the window shouted that the sun was approaching the danger point in the sky and that Greenspahn had better begin as soon as he was ready.

He looked at the strange thick letters in the prayer book. "Go ahead," the rabbi said, "think of Harold and tell God."

He tried then to think of his son, but he could recall him only as he was when he was a baby standing in his crib. It was unreal, like a photo-

graph. The others knew what he was thinking and frowned. "Go ahead," the rabbi said.

Then he saw him as a boy on a bicycle, as once he had seen him at dusk as he looked out from his apartment, riding the gray sidewalks, slapping his buttocks as though he were on a horse. The others were not satisfied.

He tried to imagine him older but nothing came of it. The rabbi said, "Please, Greenspahn, the sun is almost down. You're wasting time. Faster. Faster."

All right, Greenspahn thought. All right. Only let me think. The others stopped their chanting.

Desperately he thought of the store. He thought of the woman with the coffee, incredibly old, older than the old men who prayed with him, her wig fatuously red, the head beneath it shaking crazily as though even the weight and painted fire of the thick, bright hair were not enough to warm it.

The rabbi grinned.

He thought of the *schvartze,* imagining him on an old cot, on a damp and sheetless mattress, twisting in a fearful dream. He saw him bent under the huge side of red, raw meat he carried to Arnold.

The others were still grinning, but the rabbi was beginning to look a little bored. He thought of Arnold, seeming to watch him through the *schvartze's* own red, mad eyes, as Arnold chopped at the fresh flesh with his butcher's axe.

He saw the men in the restaurant. The criers, ignorant of hope, the *kibitzers,* ignorant of despair. Each with his pitiful piece broken from the whole of life, confidently extending only half of what there was to give.

He saw the cheats with their ten dollars and their stolen nickels and their luncheon lusts and their torn breads.

All right, Greenspahn thought. He saw Shirley naked but for her brassiere. It was evening and the store was closed. She lay with Arnold on the butcher's block.

"The boy," the rabbi said impatiently, "*the boy.*"

He concentrated for a long moment while all of them stood by silently. Gradually, with difficulty, he began to make something out. It was Harold's face in the coffin, his expression at the very moment of death itself, before the undertakers had had time to tamper with it. He saw it clearly. It was soft, puffy with grief; a sneer curled the lips. It was Harold, twenty-three years old, wifeless, jobless, sacrificing nothing even in the act of death, leaving the world with his life not started.

The rabbi smiled at Greenspahn and turned away as though he now had other business.

"No," Greenspahn called, "wait. Wait."

The rabbi turned and with the others looked at him.

He saw it now. They all saw it. The helpless face, the sly wink, the embarrassed, slow smug smile of guilt that must, volitionless as the palpitation of a nerve, have crossed Harold's face when he had turned, his hand in the register, to see Frank watching him.

1965

JAMES JOYCE

The Dead

Lily, the caretaker's daughter, was literally run off her feet. Hardly had she brought one gentleman into the little pantry behind the office on the ground floor and helped him off with his overcoat than the wheezy hall-door bell clanged again and she had to scamper along the bare hallway to let in another guest. It was well for her she had not to attend to the ladies also. But Miss Kate and Miss Julia had thought of that and had converted the bathroom upstairs into a ladies' dressing-room. Miss Kate and Miss Julia were there, gossiping and laughing and fussing, walking after each other to the head of the stairs, peering down over the banisters and calling down to Lily to ask who had come.

It was always a great affair, the Misses Morkan's annual dance. Everybody who knew them came to it, members of the family, old friends of the family, the members of Julia's choir, any of Kate's pupils that were grown up enough, and even some of Mary Jane's pupils too. Never once had it fallen flat. For years and years it had gone off in splendid style, as long as anyone could remember; ever since Kate and Julia, after the death of their brother Pat, had left the house in Stoney Batter and taken Mary Jane, their only niece, to live with them in the dark, gaunt house on Usher's Island, the upper part of which they had rented from Mr. Fulham, the corn-factor[1] on the ground floor. That was a good thirty years ago if it was a day. Mary Jane, who was then a little girl in short clothes, was now the main prop of the household, for she had the organ in Haddington Road. She had been through the Academy[2] and gave a pupils' concert every year in the upper room of the Antient Concert Rooms.[3] Many of her pupils belonged to the better-class families on the Kingstown and Dalkey line. Old as they were, her aunts also did their share. Julia, though she was quite gray, was still the leading soprano in Adam and Eve's,[4] and Kate, being too feeble to go about much, gave music lessons to beginners on the old square piano in the back room. Lily, the caretaker's daughter, did housemaid's work for them. Though their life was modest, they believed in eating well; the best of everything: diamond-bone sirloins, three-shilling[5] tea and the best bottled stout. But Lily seldom made a mistake in the orders, so that she got on well with her three mistresses. They were fussy, that was all. But the only thing they would not stand was back answers.

Of course, they had good reason to be fussy on such a night. And then it was long after ten o'clock and yet there was no sign of Gabriel and his wife. Besides they were dreadfully afraid that Freddy Malins might turn up screwed.[6] They would not wish for worlds that any of Mary Jane's pupils should see him under the influence; when he was like that it was something very hard to manage him. Freddy Malins always came late, but they wondered what could be keeping Gabriel: and that was what brought them every two minutes to the banisters to ask Lily had Gabriel or Freddy come.

1. Dealer in grain.
2. Royal Academy of Music.
3. Hall in Dublin for musical or dramatic performances.

4. Church in Dublin.
5. A shilling, now 12 cents, was worth about a quarter.
6. Drunk.

"O, Mr. Conroy," said Lily to Gabriel when she opened the door for him, "Miss Kate and Miss Julia thought you were never coming. Goodnight, Mrs. Conroy."

"I'll engage they did," said Gabriel, "but they forget that my wife here takes three mortal hours to dress herself."

He stood on the mat, scraping the snow from his goloshes, while Lily led his wife to the foot of the stairs and called out:

"Miss Kate, here's Mrs. Conroy."

Kate and Julia came toddling down the dark stairs at once. Both of them kissed Gabriel's wife, said she must be perished alive, and asked was Gabriel with her.

"Here I am as right as the mail, Aunt Kate! Go on up. I'll follow," called out Gabriel from the dark.

He continued scraping his feet vigorously while the three women went upstairs, laughing, to the ladies' dressing-room. A light fringe of snow lay like a cape on the shoulders of his overcoat and like toecaps on the toes of his goloshes; and, as the buttons of his overcoat slipped with a squeaking noise through the snow-stiffened frieze, a cold, fragrant air from out-of-doors escaped from crevices and folds.

"Is it snowing again, Mr. Conroy?" asked Lily.

She had preceded him into the pantry to help him off with his overcoat. Gabriel smiled at the three syllables she had given his surname and glanced at her. She was a slim, growing girl, pale in complexion and with hay-colored hair. The gas in the pantry made her look still paler. Gabriel had known her when she was a child and used to sit on the lowest step nursing[7] a rag doll.

"Yes, Lily," he answered, "and I think we're in for a night of it."

He looked up at the pantry ceiling, which was shaking with the stamping and shuffling of feet on the floor above, listened for a moment to the piano and then glanced at the girl, who was folding his overcoat carefully at the end of a shelf.

"Tell me, Lily," he said in a friendly tone, "do you still go to school?"

"O no, sir," she answered. "I'm done schooling this year and more."

"O, then," said Gabriel gaily, "I suppose we'll be going to your wedding one of these fine days with your young man, eh?"

The girl glanced back at him over her shoulder and said with great bitterness:

"The men that is now is only all palaver and what they can get out of you."

Gabriel colored, as if he felt he had made a mistake and, without looking at her, kicked off his goloshes and flicked actively with his muffler at his patent-leather shoes.

He was a stout, tallish young man. The high color of his cheeks pushed upwards even to his forehead, where it scattered itself in a few formless patches of pale red; and on his hairless face there scintillated restlessly the polished lenses and the bright gilt rims of the glasses which screened his delicate and restless eyes. His glossy black hair was parted in the middle and brushed in a long curve behind his ears where it curled slightly beneath the groove left by his hat.

When he had flicked luster into his shoes he stood up and pulled his waistcoat down more tightly on his plump body. Then he took a coin rapidly from his pocket.

---

7. Fondling.

"O Lily," he said, thrusting it into her hands, "it's Christmas-time, isn't it? Just . . . here's a little. . . ."

He walked rapidly towards the door.

"O no, sir!" cried the girl, following him. "Really, sir, I wouldn't take it."

"Christmas-time! Christmas-time!" said Gabriel, almost trotting to the stairs and waving his hand to her in deprecation.

The girl, seeing that he had gained the stairs, called out after him: "Well, thank you, sir."

He waited outside the drawing-room door until the waltz should finish, listening to the skirts that swept against it and to the shuffling of feet. He was still discomposed by the girl's bitter and sudden retort. It had cast a gloom over him which he tried to dispel by arranging his cuffs and the bows of his tie. He then took from his waistcoat pocket a little paper and glanced at the headings he had made for his speech. He was undecided about the lines from Robert Browning, for he feared they would be above the heads of his hearers. Some quotation that they would recognize from Shakespeare or from the Melodies[8] would be better. The indelicate clacking of the men's heels and the shuffling of their soles reminded him that their grade of culture differed from his. He would only make himself ridiculous by quoting poetry to them which they could not understand. They would think that he was airing his superior education. He would fail with them just as he had failed with the girl in the pantry. He had taken up a wrong tone. His whole speech was a mistake from first to last, an utter failure.

Just then his aunts and his wife came out of the ladies' dressing-room. His aunts were two small, plainly dressed old women. Aunt Julia was an inch or so the taller. Her hair, drawn low over the tops of her ears, was gray; and gray also, with darker shadows, was her large flaccid face. Though she was stout in build and stood erect, her slow eyes and parted lips gave her the appearance of a woman who did not know where she was or where she was going. Aunt Kate was more vivacious. Her face, healthier than her sister's, was all puckers and creases, like a shriveled red apple, and her hair, braided in the same old-fashioned way, had not lost its ripe nut color.

They both kissed Gabriel frankly. He was their favorite nephew, the son of their dead elder sister, Ellen, who had married T. J. Conroy of the Port and Docks.

"Gretta tells me you're not going to take a cab back to Monkstown tonight, Gabriel," said Aunt Kate.

"No," said Gabriel, turning to his wife, "we had quite enough of that last year, hadn't we? Don't you remember, Aunt Kate, what a cold Gretta got out of it? Cab windows rattling all the way, and the east wind blowing in after we passed Merrion. Very jolly it was. Gretta caught a dreadful cold."

Aunt Kate frowned severely and nodded her head at every word.

"Quite right, Gabriel, quite right," she said. "You can't be too careful."

"But as for Gretta there," said Gabriel, "she'd walk home in the snow if she were let."

Mrs. Conroy laughed.

"Don't mind him, Aunt Kate," she said. "He's really an awful bother, what with green shades for Tom's eyes at night and making him do the

---

8. *Irish Melodies* by Thomas Moore (1779–1852).

dumbbells, and forcing Eva to eat the stir-about.[9] The poor child! And she simply hates the sight of it! . . . O, but you'll never guess what he makes me wear now!"

She broke out into a peal of laughter and glanced at her husband, whose admiring and happy eyes had been wandering from her dress to her face and hair. The two aunts laughed heartily, too, for Gabriel's solicitude was a standing joke with them.

"Goloshes!" said Mrs. Conroy. "That's the latest. Whenever it's wet underfoot I must put on my goloshes. Tonight even, he wanted me to put them on, but I wouldn't. The next thing he'll buy me will be a diving suit."

Gabriel laughed nervously and patted his tie reassuringly, while Aunt Kate nearly doubled herself, so heartily did she enjoy the joke. The smile soon faded from Aunt Julia's face and her mirthless eyes were directed towards her nephew's face. After a pause she asked:

"And what are goloshes, Gabriel?"

"Goloshes, Julia!" exclaimed her sister. "Goodness me, don't you know what goloshes are? You wear them over your . . . over your boots, Gretta, isn't it?"

"Yes," said Mrs. Conroy. "Guttapercha[1] things. We both have a pair now. Gabriel says everyone wears them on the Continent."

"O, on the Continent," murmured Aunt Julia, nodding her head slowly.

Gabriel knitted his brows and said, as if he were slightly angered:

"It's nothing very wonderful, but Gretta thinks it very funny because she says the word reminds her of Christy Minstrels."[2]

"But tell me, Gabriel," said Aunt Kate, with brisk tact. "Of course, you've seen about the room. Gretta was saying . . ."

"O, the room is all right," replied Gabriel. "I've taken one in the Gresham."[3]

"To be sure," said Aunt Kate, "by far the best thing to do. And the children, Gretta, you're not anxious about them?"

"O, for one night," said Mrs. Conroy. "Besides, Bessie will look after them."

"To be sure," said Aunt Kate again. "What a comfort it is to have a girl like that, one you can depend on! There's that Lily, I'm sure I don't know what has come over her lately. She's not the girl she was at all."

Gabriel was about to ask his aunt some questions on this point, but she broke off suddenly to gaze after her sister, who had wandered down the stairs and was craning her neck over the banisters.

"Now, I ask you," she said almost testily, "where is Julia going? Julia! Julia! Where are you going?"

Julia, who had gone half way down one flight, came back and announced blandly:

"Here's Freddy."

At the same moment a clapping of hands and a final flourish of the pianist told that the waltz had ended. The drawing-room door was opened from within and some couples came out. Aunt Kate drew Gabriel aside hurriedly and whispered into his ear:

"Slip down, Gabriel, like a good fellow and see if he's all right, and

9. Porridge or similar hot cereal.
1. Rubber-like substance.
2. Negro minstrel group, founded by Edwin T. Christy, which performed from the 1860s.
3. Fashionable Dublin hotel.

don't let him up if he's screwed. I'm sure he's screwed. I'm sure he is."

Gabriel went to the stairs and listened over the banisters. He could hear two persons talking in the pantry. Then he recognized Freddy Malins' laugh. He went down the stairs noisily.

"It's such a relief," said Aunt Kate to Mrs. Conroy, "that Gabriel is here. I always feel easier in my mind when he's here. . . . Julia, there's Miss Daly and Miss Power will take some refreshment. Thanks for your beautiful waltz, Miss Daly. It made lovely time."

A tall wizen-faced man, with a stiff grizzled moustache and swarthy skin, who was passing out with his partner, said:

"And may we have some refreshment, too, Miss Morkan?"

"Julia," said Aunt Kate summarily, "and here's Mr. Browne and Miss Furlong. Take them in, Julia, with Miss Daly and Miss Power."

"I'm the man for the ladies," said Mr. Browne, pursing his lips until his moustache bristled and smiling in all his wrinkles. "You know, Miss Morkan, the reason they are so fond of me is—"

He did not finish his sentence, but, seeing that Aunt Kate was out of earshot, at once led the three young ladies into the back room. The middle of the room was occupied by two square tables placed end to end, and on these Aunt Julia and the caretaker were straightening and smoothing a large cloth. On the sideboard were arrayed dishes and plates, and glasses and bundles of knives and forks and spoons. The top of the closed square piano served also as a sideboard for viands and sweets. At a smaller sideboard in one corner two young men were standing, drinking hop-bitters.[4]

Mr. Browne led his charges thither and invited them all, in jest, to some ladies' punch, hot, strong and sweet. As they said they never took anything strong, he opened three bottles of lemonade[5] for them. Then he asked one of the young men to move aside, and, taking hold of the decanter, filled out for himself a goodly measure of whisky. The young men eyed him respectfully while he took a trial sip.

"God help me," he said, smiling, "it's the doctor's orders."

His wizened face broke into a broader smile, and the three young ladies laughed in musical echo to his pleasantry, swaying their bodies to and fro, with nervous jerks of their shoulders. The boldest said:

"O, now, Mr. Browne, I'm sure the doctor never ordered anything of the kind."

Mr. Browne took another sip of his whisky and said, with sidling mimicry:

"Well, you see, I'm like the famous Mrs. Cassidy, who is reported to have said: 'Now, Mary Grimes, if I don't take it, make me take it, for I feel I want it.'"

His hot face had leaned forward a little too confidentially and he had assumed a very low Dublin accent so that the young ladies, with one instinct, received his speech in silence. Miss Furlong, who was one of Mary Jane's pupils, asked Miss Daly what was the name of the pretty waltz she had played; and Mr. Browne, seeing that he was ignored, turned promptly to the two young men who were more appreciative.

A red-faced young woman, dressed in pansy,[6] came into the room, excitedly clapping her hands and crying:

4. An unfermented liquor flavored with hops.
5. A carbonated citrus drink.
6. Probably the colors of the pansy—purple, yellow, and white.

"Quadrilles! Quadrilles!"[7]

Close on her heels came Aunt Kate, crying:

"Two gentlemen and three ladies, Mary Jane!"

"O, here's Mr. Bergin and Mr. Kerrigan," said Mary Jane. "Mr. Kerrigan, will you take Miss Power? Miss Furlong, may I get you a partner, Mr. Bergin. O, that'll just do now."

"Three ladies, Mary Jane," said Aunt Kate.

The two young gentlemen asked the ladies if they might have the pleasure, and Mary Jane turned to Miss Daly.

"O, Miss Daly, you're really awfully good, after playing for the last two dances, but really we're so short of ladies tonight."

"I don't mind in the least, Miss Morkan."

"But I've a nice partner for you, Mr. Bartell D'Arcy, the tenor. I'll get him to sing later on. All Dublin is raving about him."

"Lovely voice, lovely voice!" said Aunt Kate.

As the piano had twice begun the prelude to the first figure Mary Jane led her recruits quickly from the room. They had hardly gone when Aunt Julia wandered slowly into the room, looking behind her at something.

"What is the matter, Julia?" asked Aunt Kate anxiously. "Who is it?"

Julia, who was carrying in a column of table napkins, turned to her sister and said, simply, as if the question had surprised her:

"It's only Freddy, Kate, and Gabriel with him."

In fact right behind her Gabriel could be seen piloting Freddy Malins across the landing. The latter, a young man of about forty, was of Gabriel's size and build, with very round shoulders. His face was fleshy and pallid, touched with color only at the thick hanging lobes of his ears and at the wide wings of his nose. He had coarse features, a blunt nose, a convex and receding brow, tumid and protruded lips. His heavy-lidded eyes and the disorder of his scanty hair made him look sleepy. He was laughing heartily in a high key at a story which he had been telling Gabriel on the stairs and at the same time rubbing the knuckles of his left fist backwards and forwards into his left eye.

"Good evening, Freddy," said Aunt Julia.

Freddy Malins bade the Misses Morkan good evening in what seemed an offhand fashion by reason of the habitual catch in his voice and then, seeing that Mr. Browne was grinning at him from the sideboard, crossed the room on rather shaky legs and began to repeat in an undertone the story he had just told to Gabriel.

"He's not so bad, is he?" said Aunt Kate to Gabriel.

Gabriel's brows were dark but he raised them quickly and answered:

"O, no, hardly noticeable."

"Now, isn't he a terrible fellow!" she said. "And his poor mother made him take the pledge[8] on New Year's Eve. But come on, Gabriel, into the drawing-room."

Before leaving the room with Gabriel she signaled to Mr. Browne by frowning and shaking her forefinger in warning to and fro. Mr. Browne nodded in answer and, when she had gone, said to Freddy Malins:

"Now, then, Teddy, I'm going to fill you out a good glass of lemonade just to buck you up."

Freddy Malins, who was nearing the climax of his story, waved the

---

7. A French-originated square dance, usually with four couples and five figures.   8. Swear off drink.

offer aside impatiently but Mr. Browne, having first called Freddy Malins' attention to a disarray in his dress, filled out and handed him a full glass of lemonade. Freddy Malins' left hand accepted the glass mechanically, his right hand being engaged in the mechanical read-justment of his dress. Mr. Browne, whose face was once more wrinkling with mirth, poured out for himself a glass of whisky while Freddy Malins exploded, before he had well reached the climax of his story, in a kink of high-pitched bronchitic laughter and, setting down his un-tasted and overflowing glass, began to rub the knuckles of his left fist backwards and forwards into his left eye, repeating words of his last phrase as well as his fit of laughter would allow him.

Gabriel could not listen while Mary Jane was playing her Academy piece, full of runs and difficult passages, to the hushed drawing-room. He liked music but the piece she was playing had no melody for him and he doubted whether it had any melody for the other listeners, though they had begged Mary Jane to play something. Four young men, who had come from the refreshment-room to stand in the doorway at the sound of the piano, had gone away quietly in couples after a few minutes. The only persons who seemed to follow the music were Mary Jane herself, her hands racing along the keyboard or lifted from it at the pauses like those of a priestess in momentary imprecation, and Aunt Kate standing at her elbow to turn the page.

Gabriel's eyes, irritated by the floor, which glittered with beeswax under the heavy chandelier, wandered to the wall above the piano. A picture of the balcony scene in *Romeo and Juliet* hung there and be-side it was a picture of the two murdered princes in the Tower[9] which Aunt Julia had worked in red, blue and brown wools when she was a girl. Probably in the school they had gone to as girls that kind of work had been taught for one year. His mother had worked for him as a birthday present a waistcoat of purple tabinet,[1] with little foxes' heads upon it, lined with brown satin and having round mulberry buttons. It was strange that his mother had had no musical talent though Aunt Kate used to call her the brains carrier of the Morkan family. Both she and Julia had always seemed a little proud of their serious and ma-tronly sister. Her photograph stood before the pierglass.[2] She held an open book on her knees and was pointing out something in it to Con-stantine who, dressed in a man-o'-war suit, lay at her feet. It was she who had chosen the names of her sons for she was very sensible of the dignity of family life. Thanks to her, Constantine was now senior curate in Balbriggan and, thanks to her, Gabriel himself had taken his degree in the Royal University.[3] A shadow passed over his face as he remem-bered her sullen opposition to his marriage. Some slighting phrases she had used still rankled in his memory; she had once spoken of Gretta as being country cute and that was not true of Gretta at all. It was Gretta who had nursed her during all her last long illness in their house at Monkstown.

He knew that Mary Jane must be near the end of her piece for she was playing again the opening melody with runs of scales after every bar and while he waited for the end the resentment died down in his heart. The piece ended with a trill of octaves in the treble and a final

9. *Romeo and Juliet*, Act II, sc. ii; the Prince of Wales (Edward V) and the Duke of York were slain in the Tower of London by order of Richard III. See Shakespeare's play.

1. Poplin-like fabric of silk and wool.
2. Tall mirror set between windows.
3. Established in 1882, an examining body without residence or attendance re-quired.

deep octave in the bass. Great applause greeted Mary Jane as, blushing and rolling up her music nervously, she escaped from the room. The most vigorous clapping came from the four young men in the doorway who had gone away to the refreshment-room at the beginning of the piece but had come back when the piano had stopped.

Lancers[4] were arranged. Gabriel found himself partnered with Miss Ivors. She was a frank-mannered talkative young lady, with a freckled face and prominent brown eyes. She did not wear a low-cut bodice and the large brooch which was fixed in the front of her collar bore on it an Irish device and motto.

When they had taken their places she said abruptly:

"I have a crow to pluck[5] with you."

"With me?" said Gabriel.

She nodded her head gravely.

"What is it?" asked Gabriel, smiling at her solemn manner.

"Who is G. C.?" answered Miss Ivors, turning her eyes upon him.

Gabriel colored and was about to knit his brows, as if he did not understand, when she said bluntly:

"O, innocent Amy! I have found out that you write for *The Daily Express*.[6] Now, aren't you ashamed of yourself?"

"Why should I be ashamed of myself?" asked Gabriel, blinking his eyes and trying to smile.

"Well, I'm ashamed of you," said Miss Ivors frankly. "To say you'd write for a paper like that. I didn't think you were a West Briton."

A look of perplexity appeared on Gabriel's face. It was true that he wrote a literary column every Wednesday in *The Daily Express*, for which he was paid fifteen shillings. But that did not make him a West Briton surely. The books he received for review were almost more welcome than the paltry check. He loved to feel the covers and turn over the pages of newly printed books. Nearly every day when his teaching in the college was ended he used to wander down the quays to the second-hand booksellers, to Hickey's on Bachelor's Walk, to Web's or Massey's on Aston's Quay, or to O'Clohissey's in the by-street. He did not know how to meet her charge. He wanted to say that literature was above politics. But they were friends of many years' standing and their careers had been parallel, first at the University and then as teachers: he could not risk a grandiose phrase with her. He continued blinking his eyes and trying to smile and murmured lamely that he saw nothing political in writing reviews of books.

When their turn to cross had come he was still perplexed and inattentive. Miss Ivors promptly took his hand in a warm grasp and said in a soft friendly tone:

"Of course, I was only joking. Come, we cross now."

When they were together again she spoke of the University question[7] and Gabriel felt more at ease. A friend of hers had shown her his review of Browning's poems. That was how she had found out the secret: but she liked the review immensely. Then she said suddenly:

"O, Mr. Conroy, will you come for an excursion to the Aran Isles[8]

---

4. Form of quadrille.
5. "Bone to pick."
6. Conservative, rather pro-English newspaper; a "West Briton," below, was a pro-English Irishman.
7. The problem of how to offer Roman Catholics equal opportunities for higher education.

8. Islands west of Ireland where old Irish traditions and language remained. Connacht (below) is a section of the west coast of Ireland; Galway is a city and county in the west; Oughterard a village near Galway, and the Shannon, a river mentioned at the end of the story, empties in the west just south of Galway Bay.

this summer? We're going to stay there a whole month. It will be splendid out in the Atlantic. You ought to come. Mr. Clancy is coming, and Mr. Kilkelly and Kathleen Kearney. It would be splendid for Gretta too if she'd come. She's from Connacht, isn't she?"

"Her people are," said Gabriel shortly.

"But you will come, won't you?" said Miss Ivors, laying her warm hand eagerly on his arm.

"The fact is," said Gabriel, "I have just arranged to go—"

"Go where?" asked Miss Ivors.

"Well, you know, every year I go for a cycling tour with some fellows and so—"

"But where?" asked Miss Ivors.

"Well, we usually go to France or Belgium or perhaps Germany," said Gabriel awkwardly.

"And why do you go to France and Belgium," said Miss Ivors, "instead of visiting your own land?"

"Well," said Gabriel, "it's partly to keep in touch with the languages and partly for a change."

"And haven't you your own language to keep in touch with—Irish?" asked Miss Ivors.

"Well," said Gabriel, "if it comes to that, you know, Irish is not my language."

Their neighbors had turned to listen to the cross-examination. Gabriel glanced right and left nervously and tried to keep his good humor under the ordeal which was making a blush invade his forehead.

"And haven't you your own land to visit," continued Miss Ivors, "that you know nothing of, your own people, and your own country?"

"O, to tell you the truth," retorted Gabriel suddenly, "I'm sick of my own country, sick of it!"

"Why?" asked Miss Ivors.

Gabriel did not answer for his retort had heated him.

"Why?" repeated Miss Ivors.

They had to go visiting together and, as he had not answered her, Miss Ivors said warmly:

"Of course, you've no answer."

Gabriel tried to cover his agitation by taking part in the dance with great energy. He avoided her eyes for he had seen a sour expression on her face. But when they met in the long chain he was surprised to feel his hand firmly pressed. She looked at him from under her brows for a moment quizzically until he smiled. Then, just as the chain was about to start again, she stood on tiptoe and whispered into his ear:

"West Briton!"

When the lancers were over Gabriel went away to a remote corner of the room where Freddy Malins' mother was sitting. She was a stout feeble old woman with white hair. Her voice had a catch in it like her son's and she stuttered slightly. She had been told that Freddy had come and that he was nearly all right. Gabriel asked her whether she had had a good crossing. She lived with her married daughter in Glasgow and came to Dublin on a visit once a year. She answered placidly that she had had a beautiful crossing and that the captain had been most attentive to her. She spoke also of the beautiful house her daughter kept in Glasgow, and of all the friends they had there. While her tongue rambled on Gabriel tried to banish from his mind all memory of the unpleasant incident with Miss Ivors. Of course the girl or woman,

or whatever she was, was an enthusiast but there was a time for all things. Perhaps he ought not to have answered her like that. But she had no right to call him a West Briton before people, even in joke. She had tried to make him ridiculous before people, heckling him and staring at him with her rabbit's eyes.

He saw his wife making her way towards him through the waltzing couples. When she reached him she said into his ear:

"Gabriel, Aunt Kate wants to know won't you carve the goose as usual. Miss Daly will carve the ham and I'll do the pudding."

"All right," said Gabriel.

"She's sending in the younger ones just as soon as this waltz is over so that we'll have the table to ourselves."

"Were you dancing?" asked Gabriel.

"Of course I was. Didn't you see me? What row had you with Molly Ivors?"

"No row. Why? Did she say so?"

"Something like that. I'm trying to get that Mr. D'Arcy to sing. He's full of conceit, I think."

"There was no row," said Gabriel moodily, "only she wanted me to go for a trip to the west of Ireland and I said I wouldn't."

His wife clasped her hands excitedly and gave a little jump.

"O, do go, Gabriel," she cried. "I'd love to see Galway again."

"You can go if you like," said Gabriel coldly.

She looked at him for a moment, then turned to Mrs. Malins and said:

"There's a nice husband for you, Mrs. Malins."

While she was threading her way back across the room Mrs. Malins, without adverting to the interruption, went on to tell Gabriel what beautiful places there were in Scotland and beautiful scenery. Her son-in-law brought them every year to the lakes and they used to go fishing. Her son-in-law was a splendid fisher. One day he caught a beautiful big fish and the man in the hotel cooked it for their dinner.

Gabriel hardly heard what she said. Now that supper was coming near he began to think again about his speech and about the quotation. When he saw Freddy Malins coming across the room to visit his mother Gabriel left the chair free for him and retired into the embrasure of the window. The room had already cleared and from the back room came the clatter of plates and knives. Those who still remained in the drawing-room seemed tired of dancing and were conversing quietly in little groups. Gabriel's warm trembling fingers tapped the cold pane of the window. How cool it must be outside! How pleasant it would be to walk out alone, first along by the river and then through the park! The snow would be lying on the branches of the trees and forming a bright cap on the top of the Wellington Monument.[9] How much more pleasant it would be there than at the supper table!

He ran over the headings of his speech: Irish hospitality, sad memories, the Three Graces,[1] Paris, the quotation from Browning. He repeated to himself a phrase he had written in his review: "One feels that one is listening to a thought-tormented music." Miss Ivors had praised the review. Was she sincere? Had she really any life of her own behind all her propagandism? There had never been any ill-feeling be-

9. Statue of the Irish-born Duke of Wellington (Arthur Wellesley, 1769–1852), victor over Napoleon.

1. Sister goddesses in Greek mythology: Aglaia (Brilliance), Euphrosyne (Joy), Thalia (Bloom).

tween them until that night. It unnerved him to think that she would be at the supper table, looking up at him while he spoke with her critical quizzing eyes. Perhaps she would not be sorry to see him fail in his speech. An idea came into his mind and gave him courage. He would say, alluding to Aunt Kate and Aunt Julia: "Ladies and Gentlemen, the generation which is now on the wane among us may have had its faults but for my part I think it had certain qualities of hospitality, of humor, of humanity, which the new and very serious and hypereducated generation that is growing up around us seems to me to lack." Very good: that was one for Miss Ivors. What did he care that his aunts were only two ignorant old women?

A murmur in the room attracted his attention. Mr. Browne was advancing from the door, gallantly escorting Aunt Julia, who leaned upon his arm, smiling and hanging her head. An irregular musketry of applause escorted her also as far as the piano and then, as Mary Jane seated herself on the stool, and Aunt Julia, no longer smiling, half turned so as to pitch her voice fairly into the room, gradually ceased. Gabriel recognized the prelude. It was that of an old song of Aunt Julia's—*Arrayed for the Bridal*.[2] Her voice, strong and clear in tone, attacked with great spirit the runs which embellish the air and though she sang very rapidly she did not miss even the smallest of the grace notes.[3] To follow the voice, without looking at the singer's face, was to feel and share the excitement of swift and secure flight. Gabriel applauded loudly with all the others at the close of the song and loud applause was borne in from the invisible supper table. It sounded so genuine that a little color struggled into Aunt Julia's face as she bent to replace in the music stand the old leather-bound songbook that had her initials on the cover. Freddy Malins, who had listened with his head perched sideways to hear her better, was still applauding when everyone else had ceased and talking animatedly to his mother who nodded her head gravely and slowly in acquiescence. At last, when he could clap no more, he stood up suddenly and hurried across the room to Aunt Julia whose hand he seized and held in both his hands, shaking it when words failed him or the catch in his voice proved too much for him.

"I was just telling my mother," he said, "I never heard you sing so well, never. No, I never heard your voice so good as it is tonight. Now! Would you believe that now? That's the truth. Upon my word and honor that's the truth. I never heard your voice sound so fresh and so . . . so clear and fresh, never."

Aunt Julia smiled broadly and murmured something about compliments as she released her hand from his grasp. Mr. Browne extended his open hand towards her and said to those who were near him in the manner of a showman introducing a prodigy to an audience:

"Miss Julia Morkan, my latest discovery!"

2. Song by George Linley to music from Bellini's opera *I Puritani*. Marvin Magalaner in *Time of Apprenticeship* gives the words thus:
Array'd for the bridal, in beauty behold her,
A white wreath entwineth a forehead most fair;
I envy the zephyrs that softly enfold her, enfold her,
And play with the locks of her beautiful hair.

May life to her prove full of sunshine and love, full of love, yes! yes! yes!
Who would not love her
Sweet star of the morning! shining so bright,
Earth's circle adorning, fair creature of light,
Fair creature of light.
   3. Notes added for ornament, not necessary for the melody.

He was laughing very heartily at this himself when Freddy Malins turned to him and said:

"Well, Browne, if you're serious you might make a worse discovery. All I can say is I never heard her sing half so well as long as I am coming here. And that's the honest truth."

"Neither did I," said Mr. Browne. "I think her voice has greatly improved."

Aunt Julia shrugged her shoulders and said with meek pride:

"Thirty years ago I hadn't a bad voice as voices go."

"I often told Julia," said Aunt Kate emphatically, "that she was simply thrown away in that choir. But she never would be said by me."

She turned as if to appeal to the good sense of the others against a refractory child while Aunt Julia gazed in front of her, a vague smile of reminiscence playing on her face.

"No," continued Aunt Kate, "she wouldn't be said or led by anyone, slaving there in that choir night and day, night and day. Six o'clock on Christmas morning! And all for what?"

"Well, isn't it for the honor of God, Aunt Kate?" asked Mary Jane, twisting round on the piano stool and smiling.

Aunt Kate turned fiercely on her niece and said:

"I know all about the honor of God, Mary Jane, but I think it's not at all honorable for the pope to turn the women out of the choirs that have slaved there all their lives and put little whipper-snappers of boys over their heads. I suppose it is for the good of the Church if the pope does it. But it's not just, Mary Jane, and it's not right."

She had worked herself into a passion and would have continued in defense of her sister for it was a sore subject with her but Mary Jane, seeing that all the dancers had come back, intervened pacifically:

"Now, Aunt Kate, you're giving scandal to Mr. Browne who is of the other persuasion."

Aunt Kate turned to Mr. Browne, who was grinning at this allusion to his religion, and said hastily:

"O, I don't question the pope's being right. I'm only a stupid old woman and I wouldn't presume to do such a thing. But there's such a thing as common everyday politeness and gratitude. And if I were in Julia's place I'd tell that Father Healey straight up to his face . . ."

"And besides, Aunt Kate," said Mary Jane, "we really are all hungry and when we are hungry we are all very quarrelsome."

"And when we are thirsty we are also quarrelsome," added Mr. Browne.

"So that we had better go to supper," said Mary Jane, "and finish the discussion afterwards."

On the landing outside the drawing-room Gabriel found his wife and Mary Jane trying to persuade Miss Ivors to stay for supper. But Miss Ivors, who had put on her hat and was buttoning her cloak, would not stay. She did not feel in the least hungry and she had already overstayed her time.

"But only for ten minutes, Molly," said Mrs. Conroy. "That won't delay you."

"To take a pick itself," said Mary Jane, "after all your dancing."

"I really couldn't," said Miss Ivors.

"I am afraid you didn't enjoy yourself at all," said Mary Jane hopelessly.

"Ever so much, I assure you," said Miss Ivors, "but you really must let me run off now."

"But how can you get home?" asked Mrs. Conroy.

"O, it's only two steps up the quay."

Gabriel hesitated a moment and said:

"If you will allow me, Miss Ivors, I'll see you home if you are really obliged to go."

But Miss Ivors broke away from them.

"I won't hear of it," she cried. "For goodness' sake go in to your suppers and don't mind me. I'm quite well able to take care of myself."

"Well, you're the comical girl, Molly," said Mrs. Conroy frankly.

"*Beannacht libh*,"[4] cried Miss Ivors, with a laugh, as she ran down the staircase.

Mary Jane gazed after her, a moody puzzled expression on her face, while Mrs. Conroy leaned over the banisters to listen for the hall door. Gabriel asked himself was he the cause of her abrupt departure. But she did not seem to be in ill humor: she had gone away laughing. He stared blankly down the staircase.

At the moment Aunt Kate came toddling out of the supper room, almost wringing her hands in despair.

"Where is Gabriel?" she cried. "Where on earth is Gabriel? There's everyone waiting in there, stage to let, and nobody to carve the goose!"

"Here I am, Aunt Kate!" cried Gabriel, with sudden animation, "ready to carve a flock of geese, if necessary."

A fat brown goose lay at one end of the table and at the other end, on a bed of creased paper strewn with sprigs of parsley, lay a great ham, stripped of its outer skin and peppered over with crust crumbs, a neat paper frill round its shin and beside this was a round of spiced beef. Between these rival ends ran parallel lines of side dishes: two little minsters[5] of jelly, red and yellow; a shallow dish full of blocks of blancmange[6] and red jam, a large green leaf-shaped dish with a stalk-shaped handle, on which lay bunches of purple raisins and peeled almonds, a companion dish on which lay a solid rectangle of Smyrna figs, a dish of custard topped with grated nutmeg, a small bowl full of chocolates and sweets wrapped in gold and silver papers and a glass vase in which stood some tall celery stalks. In the center of the table there stood, as sentries to a fruit stand which upheld a pyramid of oranges and American apples, two squat old-fashioned decanters of cut glass, one containing port and the other dark sherry. On the closed square piano a pudding in a huge yellow dish lay in waiting and behind it were three squads of bottles of stout and ale and minerals, drawn up according to the colors of their uniforms, the first two black, with brown and red labels, the third and smallest squad white, with transverse green sashes.

Gabriel took his seat boldly at the head of the table and, having looked to the edge of the carver, plunged his fork firmly into the goose. He felt quite at ease now for he was an expert carver and liked nothing better than to find himself at the head of a well-laden table.

"Miss Furlong, what shall I send you?" he asked. "A wing or a slice of the breast?"

"Just a small slice of the breast."

4. Blessings be with you—Good-bye.
5. Probably shaped somewhat like a

cathedral or large church.
6. Sweet jelly-like molded dessert.

"Miss Higgins, what for you?"

"O, anything at all, Mr. Conroy."

While Gabriel and Miss Daly exchanged plates of goose and plates of ham and spiced beef Lily went from guest to guest with a dish of hot floury potatoes wrapped in a white napkin. This was Mary Jane's idea and she had also suggested applesauce for the goose but Aunt Kate had said that plain roast goose without any applesauce had always been good enough for her and she hoped she might never eat worse. Mary Jane waited on her pupils and saw that they got the best slices and Aunt Kate and Aunt Julia opened and carried across from the piano bottles of stout and ale for the gentlemen and bottles of minerals for the ladies. There was a great deal of confusion and laughter and noise, the noise of orders and counter-orders, of knives and forks, of corks and glass stoppers. Gabriel began to carve second helpings as soon as he had finished the first round without serving himself. Everyone protested loudly so that he compromised by taking a long draft of stout for he had found the carving hot work. Mary Jane settled down quietly to her supper but Aunt Kate and Aunt Julia were still toddling round the table, walking on each other's heels, getting in each other's way and giving each other unheeded orders. Mr. Browne begged of them to sit down and eat their suppers and so did Gabriel but they said there was time enough, so that, at last, Freddy Malins stood up and, capturing Aunt Kate, plumped her down on her chair amid general laughter.

When everyone had been well served Gabriel said, smiling:

"Now, if anyone wants a little more of what vulgar people call stuffing let him or her speak."

A chorus of voices invited him to begin his own supper and Lily came forward with three potatoes which she had reserved for him.

"Very well," said Gabriel amiably, as he took another preparatory draught, "kindly forget my existence, ladies and gentlemen, for a few minutes."

He set to his supper and took no part in the conversation with which the table covered Lily's removal of the plates. The subject of talk was the opera company which was then at the Theatre Royal. Mr. Bartell D'Arcy, the tenor, a dark-complexioned young man with a smart moustache, praised very highly the leading contralto of the company but Miss Furlong thought she had a rather vulgar style of production. Freddy Malins said there was a Negro chieftain singing in the second part of the Gaiety[7] pantomime who had one of the finest tenor voices he had ever heard.

"Have you heard him?" he asked Mr. Bartell D'Arcy across the table.

"No," answered Mr. Bartell D'Arcy carelessly.

"Because," Freddy Malins explained, "now I'd be curious to hear your opinion of him. I think he has a grand voice."

"It takes Teddy to find out the really good things," said Mr. Browne familiarly to the table.

"And why couldn't he have a voice too?" asked Freddy Malins sharply. "Is it because he's only a black?"

Nobody answered this question and Mary Jane led the table back to the legitimate opera. One of her pupils had given her a pass for

7. Dublin theater.

Mignon.[8] Of course it was very fine, she said, but it made her think of poor Georgina Burns. Mr. Browne could go back farther still, to the old Italian companies that used to come to Dublin—Tietjens, Ilma de Murzka, Campanini, the great Trebelli, Giuglini, Ravelli, Aramburo.[9] Those were the days, he said, when there was something like singing to be heard in Dublin. He told too of how the top gallery of the old Royal used to be packed night after night, of how one night an Italian tenor had sung five encores to *Let me like a Soldier fall*,[1] introducing a high C every time, and of how the gallery boys would sometimes in their enthusiasm unyoke the horses from the carriage of some great *prima donna,* and pull her themselves though the streets to her hotel. Why did they never play the grand old operas now, he asked, *Dinorah, Lucrezia Borgia?*[2] Because they could not get the voices to sing them: that was why.

"O, well," said Mr. Bartell D'Arcy, "I presume there are as good singers today as there were then."

"Where are they?" asked Mr. Browne defiantly.

"In London, Paris, Milan," said Mr. Bartell D'Arcy warmly. "I suppose Caruso,[3] for example, is quite as good, if not better than any of the men you have mentioned."

"Maybe so," said Mr. Browne. "But I may tell you I doubt it strongly."

"O, I'd give anything to hear Caruso sing," said Mary Jane.

"For me," said Aunt Kate, who had been picking a bone, "there was only one tenor. To please me, I mean. But I suppose none of you ever heard of him."

"Who was he, Miss Morkan?" asked Mr. Bartell D'Arcy politely.

"His name," said Aunt Kate, "was Parkinson. I heard him when he was in his prime and I think he had then the purest tenor voice that was ever put into a man's throat."

"Strange," said Mr. Bartell D'Arcy. "I never even heard of him."

"Yes, yes, Miss Morkan is right," said Mr. Browne. "I remember hearing of old Parkinson but he's too far back for me."

"A beautiful, pure, sweet, mellow English tenor," said Aunt Kate with enthusiasm.

Gabriel having finished, the huge pudding was transferred to the table. The clatter of forks and spoons began again. Gabriel's wife served out spoonfuls of the pudding and passed the plates down the table. Midway down they were held up by Mary Jane, who replenished them with raspberry or orange jelly or with blancmange and jam. The pudding was of Aunt Julia's making and she received praises for it from all quarters. She herself said that it was not quite brown enough.

"Well, I hope, Miss Morkan," said Mr. Browne, "that I'm brown enough for you because, you know, I'm all brown."

All the gentlemen, except Gabriel, ate some of the pudding out of compliment to Aunt Julia. As Gabriel never ate sweets the celery had

8. Opera (1866) by Ambroise Thomas based on Goethe's *Wilhelm Meister.*

9. A list of sopranos and tenors, several of them identified with roles in *Lucrezia Borgia.* Theresa Johanna Alexandra Tietjens (1831–1877); Ilma de Murzka (1836–1889); Italo Campanini (1845–1896), as well known in his day as Caruso later; Zelia Trebelli (1838–1892); Antonio Giuglini and Antonio Aramburo (dates uncertain); Ravelli not identified.

1. From the opera *Maritana* by William Vincent Wallace and Edward Fitzball.

2. *Dinorah,* original title of Giacomo Meyerbeer's *Le Pardon de Poermel;* *Lucrezia Borgia,* Gaetano Donizetti's opera based on Hugo.

3. Enrico Caruso (1873–1921), most admired Italian tenor of his time.

been left for him. Freddy Malins also took a stalk of celery and ate it with his pudding. He had been told that celery was a capital thing for the blood and he was just then under doctor's care. Mrs. Malins, who had been silent all through the supper, said that her son was going down to Mount Melleray[4] in a week or so. The table then spoke of Mount Melleray, how bracing the air was down there, how hospitable the monks were and how they never asked for a penny-piece from their guests.

"And do you mean to say," asked Mr. Browne incredulously, "that a chap can go down there and put up there as if it were a hotel and live on the fat of the land and then come away without paying anything?"

"O, most people give some donation to the monastery when they leave," said Mary Jane.

"I wish we had an institution like that in our Church," said Mr. Browne candidly.

He was astonished to hear that the monks never spoke, got up at two in the morning and slept in their coffins. He asked what they did it for.

"That's the rule of the order," said Aunt Kate firmly.

"Yes, but why?" asked Mr. Browne.

Aunt Kate repeated that it was the rule, that was all. Mr. Browne still seemed not to understand. Freddy Malins explained to him, as best he could, that the monks were trying to make up for the sins committed by all the sinners in the outside world. The explanation was not very clear for Mr. Browne grinned and said:

"I like that idea very much but wouldn't a comfortable spring bed do them as well as a coffin?"

"The coffin," said Mary Jane, "is to remind them of their last end."

As the subject had grown lugubrious it was buried in a silence of the table during which Mrs. Malins could be heard saying to her neighbor in an indistinct undertone:

"They are very good men, the monks, very pious men."

The raisins and almonds and figs and apples and oranges and chocolates and sweets were now passed about the table and Aunt Julia invited all the guests to have either port or sherry. At first Mr. Bartell D'Arcy refused to take either but one of his neighbors nudged him and whispered something to him upon which he allowed his glass to be filled. Gradually as the last glasses were being filled the conversation ceased. A pause followed, broken only by the noise of the wine and by unsettlings of chairs. The Misses Morkan, all three, looked down at the tablecloth. Someone coughed once or twice and then a few gentlemen patted the table gently as a signal for silence. The silence came and Gabriel pushed back his chair and stood up.

The patting at once grew louder in encouragement and then ceased altogether. Gabriel leaned his ten trembling fingers on the tablecloth and smiled nervously at the company. Meeting a row of upturned faces he raised his eyes to the chandelier. The piano was playing a waltz tune and he could hear the skirts sweeping against the drawing-room door. People, perhaps, were standing in the snow on the quay outside, gazing up at the lighted windows and listening to the waltz music. The air was pure there. In the distance lay the park where the trees

---

4. Location of Trappist monastery; though the Trappists are a very strict order, they do not sleep in their coffins, as the even stricter Carthusians are said to do—see Matthew Arnold, "Stanzas from the Grande Chartreuse": "And where they sleep, that wooden bed,/Which shall their coffin be, when dead!"

were weighted with snow. The Wellington Monument wore a gleaming cap of snow that flashed westward over the white field of Fifteen Acres.[5]

He began:

"Ladies and Gentlemen,

"It has fallen to my lot this evening, as in years past, to perform a very pleasing task but a task for which I am afraid my poor powers as a speaker are all too inadequate."

"No, no!" said Mr. Browne.

"But, however that may be, I can only ask you tonight to take the will for the deed and to lend me your attention for a few moments while I endeavor to express to you in words what my feelings are on this occasion.

"Ladies and Gentlemen, it is not the first time that we have gathered together under this hospitable roof, around this hospitable board. It is not the first time that we have been the recipients—or perhaps, I had better say, the victims—of the hospitality of certain good ladies."

He made a circle in the air with his arm and paused. Everyone laughed or smiled at Aunt Kate and Aunt Julia and Mary Jane who all turned crimson with pleasure. Gabriel went on more boldly:

"I feel more strongly with every recurring year that our country has no tradition which does it so much honor and which it should guard so jealously as that of its hospitality. It is a tradition that is unique as far as my experience goes (and I have visited not a few places abroad) among the modern nations. Some would say, perhaps, that with us it is rather a failing than anything to be boasted of. But granted even that, it is, to my mind, a princely failing, and one that I trust will long be cultivated among us. Of one thing, at least, I am sure. As long as this one roof shelters the good ladies aforesaid—and I wish from my heart it may do so for many and many a long year to come—the tradition of genuine warm-hearted courteous Irish hospitality, which our forefathers have handed down to us and which we in turn must hand down to our descendants, is still alive among us."

A hearty murmur of assent ran round the table. It shot through Gabriel's mind that Miss Ivors was not there and that she had gone away discourteously: and he said with confidence in himself:

"Ladies and Gentlemen,

"A new generation is growing up in our midst, a generation actuated by new ideas and new principles. It is serious and enthusiastic for these new ideas and its enthusiasm, even when it is misdirected, is, I believe, in the main sincere. But we are living in a skeptical and, if I may use the phrase, a thought-tormented age: and sometimes I fear that this new generation, educated or hypereducated as it is, will lack those qualities of humanity, of hospitality, of kindly humor which belonged to an older day. Listening tonight to the names of all those great singers of the past it seemed to me, I must confess, that we were living in a less spacious age. Those days might, without exaggeration, be called spacious days: and if they are gone beyond recall let us hope, at least, that in gatherings such as this we shall still speak of them with pride and affection, still cherish in our hearts the memory of those dead and gone great ones whose fame the world will not willingly let die."

"Hear, hear!" said Mr. Browne loudly.

---

5. Part of Phoenix Park, Dublin.

"But yet," continued Gabriel, his voice falling into a softer inflection, "there are always in gatherings such as this sadder thoughts that will recur to our minds: thoughts of the past, of youth, of changes, of absent faces that we miss here tonight. Our path through life is strewn with many such sad memories: and were we to brood upon them always we could not find the heart to go on bravely with our work among the living. We have all of us living duties and living affections which claim, and rightly claim, our strenuous endeavors.

"Therefore, I will not linger on the past. I will not let any gloomy moralizing intrude upon us here tonight. Here we are gathered together for a brief moment from the bustle and rush of our everyday routine. We are met here as friends, in the spirit of good-fellowship, as colleagues, also to a certain extent, in the true spirit of *camaraderie*, and as the guests of—what shall I call them?—the Three Graces of the Dublin musical world."

The table burst into applause and laughter at this allusion. Aunt Julia vainly asked each of her neighbors in turn to tell her what Gabriel had said.

"He says we are the Three Graces, Aunt Julia," said Mary Jane.

Aunt Julia did not understand but she looked up, smiling, at Gabriel, who continued in the same vein:

"Ladies and Gentlemen,

"I will not attempt to play tonight the part that Paris played on another occasion. I will not attempt to choose between them.[6] The task would be an invidious one and one beyond my poor powers. For when I view them in turn, whether it be our chief hostess herself, whose good heart, whose too good heart, has become a byword with all who know her, or her sister, who seems to be gifted with perennial youth and whose singing must have been a surprise and a revelation to us all tonight, or, last but not least, when I consider our youngest hostess, talented, cheerful, hard-working and the best of nieces, I confess, Ladies and Gentlemen, that I do not know to which of them I should award the prize."

Gabriel glanced down at his aunts and, seeing the large smile on Aunt Julia's face and the tears which had risen to Aunt Kate's eyes, hastened to his close. He raised his glass of port gallantly, while every member of the company fingered a glass expectantly, and said loudly:

"Let us toast them all three together. Let us drink to their health, wealth, long life, happiness and prosperity and may they long continue to hold the proud and self-won position which they hold in their profession and the position of honor and affection which they hold in our hearts."

All the guests stood up, glass in hand, and turning towards the three seated ladies, sang in unison, with Mr. Browne as leader:

> *For they are jolly gay fellows,*
> *For they are jolly gay fellows,*
> *For they are jolly gay fellows,*
> *Which nobody can deny.*

Aunt Kate was making frank use of her handkerchief and even Aunt Julia seemed moved. Freddy Malins beat time with his pudding-fork

---

6. The son of Priam, who abducted Helen and caused the Trojan War, Paris had to choose the fairest from among three goddesses, Hera, Aphrodite, and Athena.

and the singers turned towards one another, as if in melodious conference, while they sang with emphasis:

> *Unless he tells a lie,*
> *Unless he tells a lie,*

Then, turning once more towards their hostesses, they sang:

> *For they are jolly gay fellows,*
> *For they are jolly gay fellows,*
> *For they are jolly gay fellows,*
> *Which nobody can deny.*

The acclamation which followed was taken up beyond the door of
the supper room by many of the other guests and renewed time after
time, Freddy Malins acting as officer with his fork on high.

The piercing morning air came into the hall where they were standing so that Aunt Kate said:

"Close the door, somebody. Mrs. Malins will get her death of cold."

"Browne is out there, Aunt Kate," said Mary Jane.

"Browne is everywhere," said Aunt Kate, lowering her voice.

Mary Jane laughed at her tone.

"Really," she said archly, "he is very attentive."

"He has been laid on[7] here like the gas," said Aunt Kate in the same
tone, "all during the Christmas."

She laughed herself this time good-humoredly and then added
quickly:

"But tell him to come in, Mary Jane, and close the door. I hope to
goodness he didn't hear me."

At that moment the hall door was opened and Mr. Browne came in
from the doorstep, laughing as if his heart would break. He was dressed
in a long green overcoat with mock astrakhan cuffs and collar and wore
on his head an oval fur cap. He pointed down the snow-covered quay
from where the sound of shrill prolonged whistling was borne in.

"Teddy will have all the cabs in Dublin out," he said.

Gabriel advanced from the little pantry behind the office, struggling
into his overcoat and, looking round the hall, said:

"Gretta not down yet?"

"She's getting on her things, Gabriel," said Aunt Kate.

"Who's playing up there?" asked Gabriel.

"Nobody. They're all gone."

"O no, Aunt Kate," said Mary Jane. "Bartell D'Arcy and Miss
O'Callaghan aren't gone yet."

"Someone is fooling at the piano anyhow," said Gabriel.

Mary Jane glanced at Gabriel and Mr. Browne and said with a
shiver:

"It makes me feel cold to look at you two gentlemen muffled up like
that. I wouldn't like to face your journey home at this hour."

"I'd like nothing better this minute," said Mr. Browne stoutly, "than
a rattling fine walk in the country or a fast drive with a good spanking
goer between the shafts."

"We used to have a very good horse and trap[8] at home," said Aunt
Julia sadly.

---

7. "On tap."   8. Two-wheeled light carriage with springs.

"The never-to-be-forgotten Johnny," said Mary Jane, laughing.

Aunt Kate and Gabriel laughed too.

"Why, what was wonderful about Johnny?" asked Mr. Browne.

"The late lamented Patrick Morkan, our grandfather, that is," explained Gabriel, "commonly known in his later years as the old gentleman, was a glue-boiler."

"O, now, Gabriel," said Aunt Kate, laughing, "he had a starch mill."

"Well, glue or starch," said Gabriel, "the old gentleman had a horse by the name of Johnny. And Johnny used to work in the old gentleman's mill, walking round and round in order to drive the mill. That was all very well; but now comes the tragic part about Johnny. One fine day the old gentleman thought he'd like to drive out with the quality[9] to a military review in the park."

"The Lord have mercy on his soul," said Aunt Kate compassionately.

"Amen," said Gabriel. "So the old gentleman, as I said, harnessed Johnny and put on his very best tall hat and his very best stock collar and drove out in grand style from his ancestral mansion somewhere near Back Lane, I think."

Everyone laughed, even Mrs. Malins, at Gabriel's manner and Aunt Kate said:

"O, now, Gabriel, he didn't live in Back Lane, really. Only the mill was there."

"Out from the mansion of his forefathers," continued Gabriel, "he drove with Johnny. And everything went on beautifully until Johnny came in sight of King Billy's[1] statue: and whether he fell in love with the horse King Billy sits on or whether he thought he was back again in the mill, anyhow he began to walk round the statue."

Gabriel paced in a circle round the hall in his goloshes amid the laughter of the others.

"Round and round he went," said Gabriel, "and the old gentleman, who was a very pompous old gentleman, was highly indignant. 'Go on, sir! What do you mean, sir? Johnny! Johnny! Most extraordinary conduct! Can't understand the horse!'"

The peal of laughter which followed Gabriel's imitation of the incident was interrupted by a resounding knock at the hall door. Mary Jane ran to open it and let in Freddy Malins. Freddy Malins, with his hat well back on his head and his shoulders humped with cold, was puffing and steaming after his exertions.

"I could only get one cab," he said.

"O, we'll find another along the quay," said Gabriel.

"Yes," said Aunt Kate. "Better not keep Mrs. Malins standing in the draft."

Mrs. Malins was helped down the front steps by her son and Mr. Browne and, after many maneuvers, hoisted into the cab. Freddy Malins clambered in after her and spent a long time settling her on the seat, Mr. Browne helping him with advice. At last she was settled comfortably and Freddy Malins invited Mr. Browne into the cab. There was a good deal of confused talk, and then Mr. Browne got into the cab. The cabman settled his rug over his knees, and bent down for the address. The confusion grew greater and the cabman was directed differently by Freddy Malins and Mr. Browne, each of whom had his head out through a window of the cab. The difficulty was to know where to drop Mr. Browne along the route, and Aunt Kate, Aunt Julia and

---

9. Members of the upper class.
1. William of Orange, who, in 1690, defeated the Irish Catholics at the Battle of Boyne.

Mary Jane helped the discussion from the doorstep with cross-directions and contradictions and abundance of laughter. As for Freddy Malins he was speechless with laughter. He popped his head in and out of the window every moment to the great danger of his hat, and told his mother how the discussion was progressing, till at last Mr. Browne shouted to the bewildered cabman above the din of everybody's laughter:

"Do you know Trinity College?"

"Yes, sir," said the cabman.

"Well, drive bang up against Trinity College gates," said Mr. Browne, "and then we'll tell you where to go. You understand now?"

"Yes, sir," said the cabman.

"Make like a bird for Trinity College."

"Right, sir," said the cabman.

The horse was whipped up and the cab rattled off along the quay amid a chorus of laughter and adieus.

Gabriel had not gone to the door with the others. He was in a dark part of the hall gazing up the staircase. A woman was standing near the top of the first flight, in the shadow also. He could not see her face but he could see the terra-cotta and salmon-pink panels of her skirt which the shadow made appear black and white. It was his wife. She was leaning on the banisters, listening to something. Gabriel was surprised at her stillness and strained his ear to listen also. But he could hear little save the noise of laughter and dispute on the front steps, a few chords struck on the piano and a few notes of a man's voice singing.

He stood still in the gloom of the hall, trying to catch the air that the voice was singing and gazing up at his wife. There was grace and mystery in her attitude as if she were a symbol of something. He asked himself what is a woman standing on the stairs in the shadow, listening to distant music, a symbol of. If he were a painter he would paint her in that attitude. Her blue felt hat would show off the bronze of her hair against the darkness and the dark panels of her skirt would show off the light ones. *Distant Music* he would call the picture if he were a painter.

The hall door was closed; and Aunt Kate, Aunt Julia and Mary Jane came down the hall, still laughing.

"Well, isn't Freddy terrible?" said Mary Jane. "He's really terrible."

Gabriel said nothing but pointed up the stairs towards where his wife was standing. Now that the hall door was closed the voice and the piano could be heard more clearly. Gabriel held up his hand for them to be silent. The song seemed to be in the old Irish tonality and the singer seemed uncertain both of his words and of his voice. The voice, made plaintive by distance and by the singer's hoarseness, faintly illuminated the cadence of the air with words expressing grief:

> O, the rain falls on my heavy locks
> And the dew wets my skin,
> My babe lies cold . . .[2]

2. The Irish and Scottish ballad, *The Lass of Aughrim*, about a girl abandoned by her lover and father of her child who refuses to see her and keeps her standing with the baby in her arms, in the rain, appears in many versions. The stanza closest to the portion quoted here reads:

Oh Gregory, don't you remember
One night on the hill,
When we swapped rings off each other's hands,
Sorely against my will?
Mine was of the beaten gold,
Yours was but black tin.
The dew wets my yellow locks,
The rain wets my skin,
The babe's cold in my arms,
Oh Gregory, let me in!

"O," exclaimed Mary Jane. "It's Bartell D'Arcy singing and he wouldn't sing all the night. O, I'll get him to sing a song before he goes."

"O, do, Mary Jane," said Aunt Kate.

Mary Jane brushed past the others and ran to the staircase, but before she reached it the singing stopped and the piano was closed abruptly.

"O, what a pity!" she cried. "Is he coming down, Gretta?"

Gabriel heard his wife answer yes and saw her come down towards them. A few steps behind her were Mr. Bartell D'Arcy and Miss O'Callaghan.

"O, Mr. D'Arcy," cried Mary Jane, "it's downright mean of you to break off like that when we were all in raptures listening to you."

"I have been at him all the evening," said Miss O'Callaghan, "and Mrs. Conroy, too, and he told us he had a dreadful cold and couldn't sing."

"O, Mr. D'Arcy," said Aunt Kate, "now that was a great fib to tell."

"Can't you see that I'm as hoarse as a crow?" said Mr. D'Arcy roughly.

He went into the pantry hastily and put on his overcoat. The others, taken aback by his rude speech, could find nothing to say. Aunt Kate wrinkled her brows and made signs to the others to drop the subject. Mr. D'Arcy stood swathing his neck carefully and frowning.

"It's the weather," said Aunt Julia, after a pause.

"Yes, everybody has colds," said Aunt Kate readily, "everybody."

"They say," said Mary Jane, "we haven't had snow like it for thirty years; and I read this morning in the newspapers that the snow is general all over Ireland."

"I love the look of snow," said Aunt Julia sadly.

"So do I," said Miss O'Callaghan. "I think Christmas is never really Christmas unless we have the snow on the ground."

"But poor Mr. D'Arcy doesn't like the snow," said Aunt Kate, smiling.

Mr. D'Arcy came from the pantry, fully swathed and buttoned, and in a repentant tone told them the history of his cold. Everyone gave him advice and said it was a great pity and urged him to be very careful of his throat in the night air. Gabriel watched his wife, who did not join in the conversation. She was standing right under the dusty fanlight[3] and the flame of the gas lit up the rich bronze of her hair, which he had seen her drying at the fire a few days before. She was in the same attitude and seemed unaware of the talk about her. At last she turned towards them and Gabriel saw that there was color on her cheeks and that her eyes were shining. A sudden tide of joy went leaping out of his heart.

"Mr. D'Arcy," she said, "what is the name of that song you were singing?"

"It's called *The Lass of Aughrim*," said Mr. D'Arcy, "but I couldn't remember it properly. Why? Do you know it?"

"*The Lass of Aughrim*," she repeated. "I couldn't think of the name."

"It's a very nice air," said Mary Jane. "I'm sorry you were not in voice tonight."

---

3. Semicircular window over door or large window in which the wooden part holding the panes are arranged in the shape of a fan.

"Now, Mary Jane," said Aunt Kate, "don't annoy Mr. D'Arcy. I won't have him annoyed."

Seeing that all were ready to start she shepherded them to the door, where goodnight was said:

"Well, goodnight, Aunt Kate, and thanks for the pleasant evening."

"Goodnight, Gabriel. Goodnight, Gretta!"

"Goodnight, Aunt Kate, and thanks ever so much. Goodnight, Aunt Julia."

"O, goodnight, Gretta, I didn't see you."

"Goodnight, Mr. D'Arcy. Goodnight, Miss O'Callaghan."

"Goodnight, Miss Morkan."

"Goodnight, again."

"Goodnight, again."

"Goodnight, all. Safe home."

"Goodnight. Good night."

The morning was still dark. A dull, yellow light brooded over the houses and the river; and the sky seemed to be descending. It was slushy underfoot; and only streaks and patches of snow lay on the roofs, on the parapets of the quay and on the area railings. The lamps were still burning redly in the murky air and, across the river, the palace of the Four Courts[4] stood out menacingly against the heavy sky.

She was walking on before him with Mr. Bartell D'Arcy, her shoes in a brown parcel tucked under one arm and her hands holding her skirt up from the slush. She had no longer any grace of attitude, but Gabriel's eyes were still bright with happiness. The blood went bounding along his veins; and the thoughts went rioting through his brain, proud, joyful, tender, valorous.

She was walking on before him so lightly and so erect that he longed to run after her noiselessly, catch her by the shoulders and say something foolish and affectionate into her ear. She seemed to him so frail that he longed to defend her against something and then to be alone with her. Moments of their secret life together burst like stars upon his memory. A heliotrope envelope was lying beside his breakfast cup and he was caressing it with his hand. Birds were twittering in the ivy and the sunny web of the curtain was shimmering along the floor: he could not eat for happiness. They were standing on the crowded platform and he was placing a ticket inside the warm palm of her glove. He was standing with her in the cold, looking in through a grated window at a man making bottles in a roaring furnace. It was very cold. Her face, fragrant in the cold air, was quite close to his; and suddenly he called out to the man at the furnace:

"Is the fire hot, sir?"

But the man could not hear with the noise of the furnace. It was just as well. He might have answered rudely.

A wave of yet more tender joy escaped from his heart and went coursing in warm flood along his arteries. Like the tender fire of stars moments of their life together, that no one knew of or would ever know of, broke upon and illumined his memory. He longed to recall to her those moments, to make her forget the years of their dull existence together and remember only their moments of ecstasy. For the years, he felt, had not quenched his soul or hers. Their children, his writing, her household cares had not quenched all their souls' tender

4. Irish law courts.

fire. In one letter that he had written to her then he had said: "Why is it that words like these seem to me so dull and cold? Is it because there is no word tender enough to be your name?"

Like distant music these words that he had written years before were borne towards him from the past. He longed to be alone with her. When the others had gone away, when he and she were in the room in the hotel, then they would be alone together. He would call her softly:

"Gretta!"

Perhaps she would not hear at once: she would be undressing. Then something in his voice would strike her. She would turn and look at him. . . .

At the corner of Winetavern Street they met a cab. He was glad of its rattling noise as it saved him from conversation. She was looking out of the window and seemed tired. The others spoke only a few words, pointing out some building or street. The horse galloped along wearily under the murky morning sky, dragging his old rattling box after his heels, and Gabriel was again in a cab with her, galloping to catch the boat, galloping to their honeymoon.

As the cab drove across O'Connell Bridge Miss O'Callaghan said:

"They say you never cross O'Connell Bridge without seeing a white horse."

"I see a white man this time," said Gabriel.

"Where?" asked Mr. Bartell D'Arcy.

Gabriel pointed to the statue, on which lay patches of snow. Then he nodded familiarly to it and waved his hand.

"Goodnight, Dan,"[5] he said gaily.

When the cab drew up before the hotel, Gabriel jumped out and, in spite of Mr. Bartell D'Arcy's protest, paid the driver. He gave the man a shilling over his fare. The man saluted and said:

"A prosperous New Year to you, sir."

"The same to you," said Gabriel cordially.

She leaned for a moment on his arm in getting out of the cab and while standing at the curbstone, bidding the others goodnight. She leaned lightly on his arm, as lightly as when she had danced with him a few hours before. He had felt proud and happy then, happy that she was his, proud of her grace and wifely carriage. But now, after the kindling again of so many memories, the first touch of her body, musical and strange and perfumed, sent through him a keen pang of lust. Under cover of her silence he pressed her arm closely to his side; and, as they stood at the hotel door, he felt that they had escaped from their lives and duties, escaped from home and friends and run away together with wild and radiant hearts to a new adventure.

An old man was dozing in a great hooded chair in the hall. He lit a candle in the office and went before them to the stairs. They followed him in silence, their feet falling in soft thuds on the thickly carpeted stairs. She mounted the stairs behind the porter, her head bowed in the ascent, her frail shoulders curved as with a burden, her skirt girt tightly about her. He could have flung his arms about her hips and held her still, for his arms were trembling with desire to seize her and only the stress of his nails against the palms of his hands held the wild impulse of his body in check. The porter halted on the stairs to settle his gutter-

5. The bridge is named after the Irish patriot Daniel O'Connell (1775–1847).

ing candle. They halted, too, on the steps below him. In the silence Gabriel could hear the falling of the molten wax into the tray and the thumping of his own heart against his ribs.

The porter led them along a corridor and opened a door. Then he set his unstable candle down on a toilet table and asked at what hour they were to be called in the morning.

"Eight," said Gabriel.

The porter pointed to the tap of the electric light and began a muttered apology, but Gabriel cut him short.

"We don't want any light. We have light enough from the street. And I say," he added, pointing to the candle, "you might remove that handsome article, like a good man."

The porter took up his candle again, but slowly, for he was surprised by such a novel idea. Then he mumbled goodnight and went out. Gabriel shot the lock to.

A ghastly light from the street lamp lay in a long shaft from one window to the door. Gabriel threw his overcoat and hat on a couch and crossed the room towards the window. He looked down into the street in order that his emotion might calm a little. Then he turned and leaned against a chest of drawers with his back to the light. She had taken off her hat and cloak and was standing before a large swinging mirror, unhooking her waist.[6] Gabriel paused for a few moments, watching her, and then said:

"Gretta!"

She turned away from the mirror slowly and walked along the shaft of light towards him. Her face looked so serious and weary that the words would not pass Gabriel's lips. No, it was not the moment yet.

"You looked tired," he said.

"I am a little," she answered.

"You don't feel ill or weak?"

"No, tired: that's all."

She went on to the window and stood there, looking out. Gabriel waited again and then, fearing that diffidence was about to conquer him, he said abruptly:

"By the way, Gretta!"

"What is it?"

"You know that poor fellow Malins?" he said quickly.

"Yes. What about him?"

"Well, poor fellow, he's a decent sort of chap, after all," continued Gabriel in a false voice. "He gave me back that sovereign[7] I lent him, and I didn't expect it, really. It's a pity he wouldn't keep away from that Browne, because he's not a bad fellow, really."

He was trembling now with annoyance. Why did she seem so abstracted? He did not know how he could begin. Was she annoyed, too, about something? If she would only turn to him or come to him of her own accord! To take her as she was would be brutal. No, he must see some ardor in her eyes first. He longed to be master of her strange mood.

"When did you lend him the pound?" she asked, after a pause.

Gabriel strove to restrain himself from breaking out into brutal language about the sottish Malins and his pound. He longed to cry to her

---

6. Blouse.

7. Once a coin worth one pound (now $2.40, earlier in the century almost $5) and still used as synonym for pound.

from his soul, to crush her body against his, to overmaster her. But he said:

"O, at Christmas, when he opened that little Christmas-card shop in Henry Street."

He was in such a fever of rage and desire that he did not hear her come from the window. She stood before him for an instant, looking at him strangely. Then, suddenly raising herself on tiptoe and resting her hands lightly on his shoulders, she kissed him.

"You are a very generous person, Gabriel," she said.

Gabriel, trembling with delight at her sudden kiss and at the quaintness of her phrase, put his hands on her hair and began smoothing it back, scarcely touching it with his fingers. The washing had made it fine and brilliant. His heart was brimming over with happiness. Just when he was wishing for it she had come to him of her own accord. Perhaps her thoughts had been running with his. Perhaps she had felt the impetuous desire that was in him, and then the yielding mood had come upon her. Now that she had fallen to him so easily, he wondered why he had been so diffident.

He stood, holding her head between his hands. Then, slipping one arm swiftly about her body and drawing her towards him, he said softly:

"Gretta, dear, what are you thinking about?"

She did not answer nor yield wholly to his arm. He said again softly:

"Tell me what it is, Gretta. I think I know what is the matter. Do I know?"

She did not answer at once. Then she said in an outburst of tears:

"O, I am thinking about that song, *The Lass of Aughrim*."

She broke loose from him and ran to the bed and, throwing her arms across the bed rail, hid her face. Gabriel stood stock-still for a moment in astonishment and then followed her. As he passed in the way of the cheval-glass[8] he caught sight of himself in full length, his broad, well-filled shirt-front, the face whose expression always puzzled him when he saw it in a mirror, and his glimmering gilt-rimmed eyeglasses. He halted a few paces from her and said:

"What about the song? Why does that make you cry?"

She raised her head from her arms and dried her eyes with the back of her hand like a child. A kinder note than he had intended went into his voice.

"Why, Gretta?" he asked.

"I am thinking about a person long ago who used to sing that song."

"And who was the person long ago?" asked Gabriel, smiling.

"It was a person I used to know in Galway when I was living with my grandmother," she said.

The smile passed away from Gabriel's face. A dull anger began to gather again at the back of his mind and the dull fires of his lust began to glow angrily in his veins.

"Someone you were in love with?" he asked ironically.

"It was a young boy I used to know," she answered, "named Michael Furey. He used to sing that song, *The Lass of Aughrim*. He was very delicate."

___

8. Full-length mirror that turns or pivots in its frame.

Gabriel was silent. He did not wish her to think that he was interested in this delicate boy.

"I can see him so plainly," she said, after a moment. "Such eyes as he had: big, dark eyes! And such an expression in them—an expression!"

"O, then, you are in love with him?" said Gabriel.

"I used to go out walking with him," she said, "when I was in Galway."

A thought flew across Gabriel's mind.

"Perhaps that was why you wanted to go to Galway with that Ivors girl?" he said coldly.

She looked at him and asked in surprise:

"What for?"

Her eyes made Gabriel feel awkward. He shrugged his shoulders and said:

"How do I know? To see him, perhaps."

She looked away from him along the shaft of light towards the window in silence.

"He is dead," she said at length. "He died when he was only seventeen. Isn't it a terrible thing to die so young as that?"

"What was he?" asked Gabriel, still ironically.

"He was in the gasworks," she said.

Gabriel felt humiliated by the failure of his irony and by the evocation of this figure from the dead, a boy in the gasworks. While he had been full of memories of their secret life together, full of tenderness and joy and desire, she had been comparing him in her mind with another. A shameful consciousness of his own person assailed him. He saw himself as a ludicrous figure, acting as a pennyboy[9] for his aunts, a nervous, well-meaning sentimentalist, orating to vulgarians and idealizing his own clownish lusts, the pitiable fatuous fellow he had caught a glimpse of in the mirror. Instinctively he turned his back more to the light lest she might see the shame that burned upon his forehead.

He tried to keep up his tone of cold interrogation, but his voice when he spoke was humble and indifferent.

"I suppose you were in love with this Michael Furey, Gretta," he said.

"I was great with him at that time," she said.

Her voice was veiled and sad. Gabriel, feeling now how vain it would be to try to lead her whither he had purposed, caressed one of her hands and said, also sadly:

"And what did he die of so young, Gretta? Consumption, was it?"

"I think he died for me," she answered.

A vague terror seized Gabriel at this answer, as if, at that hour when he had hoped to triumph, some impalpable and vindictive being was coming against him, gathering forces against him in its vague world. But he shook himself free of it with an effort of reason and continued to caress her hand. He did not question her again, for he felt that she would tell him of herself. Her hand was warm and moist: it did not respond to his touch, but he continued to caress it just as he had caressed her first letter to him that spring morning.

"It was in the winter," she said, "about the beginning of the winter

9. Errand boy; one who does odd jobs for a penny.

when I was going to leave my grandmother's and come up here to the convent. And he was ill at the time in his lodgings in Galway and wouldn't be let out, and his people in Oughterard were written to. He was in decline, they said, or something like that. I never knew rightly."

She paused for a moment and sighed.

"Poor fellow," she said. "He was very fond of me and he was such a gentle boy. We used to go out together, walking, you know, Gabriel, like the way they do in the country. He was going to study singing only for his health. He had a very good voice, poor Michael Furey."

"Well; and then?" asked Gabriel.

"And then when it came to the time for me to leave Galway and come up to the convent he was much worse and I wouldn't be let see him so I wrote him a letter saying I was going up to Dublin and would be back in the summer, and hoping he would be better then."

She paused for a moment to get her voice under control, and then went on:

"Then the night before I left, I was in my grandmother's house in Nuns' Island, packing up, and I heard gravel thrown up against the window. The window was so wet I couldn't see, so I ran downstairs as I was and slipped out the back into the garden and there was the poor fellow at the end of the garden, shivering."

"And did you not tell him to go back?" asked Gabriel.

"I implored of him to go home at once and told him he would get his death in the rain. But he said he did not want to live. I can see his eyes as well as well! He was standing at the end of the wall where there was a tree."

"And did he go home?" asked Gabriel.

"Yes, he went home. And when I was only a week in the convent he died and he was buried in Oughterard, where his people came from. O, the day I heard that, that he was dead!"

She stopped, choking with sobs, and, overcome by emotion, flung herself face downward on the bed, sobbing in the quilt. Gabriel held her hand for a moment longer, irresolutely, and then, shy of intruding on her grief, let it fall gently and walked quietly to the window.

She was fast asleep.

Gabriel, leaning on his elbow, looked for a few moments unresentfully on her tangled hair and half-open mouth, listening to her deep-drawn breath. So she had had that romance in her life: a man had died for her sake. It hardly pained him now to think how poor a part he, her husband, had played in her life. He watched her while she slept, as though he and she had never lived together as man and wife. His curious eyes rested long upon her face and on her hair: and, as he thought of what she must have been then, in that time of her first girlish beauty, a strange, friendly pity for her entered his soul. He did not like to say even to himself that her face was no longer beautiful, but he knew that it was no longer the face for which Michael Furey had braved death.

Perhaps she had not told him all the story. His eyes moved to the chair over which she had thrown some of her clothes. A petticoat string dangled to the floor. One boot stood upright, its limp upper fallen down: the fellow of it lay upon its side. He wondered at his riot of emotions of an hour before. From what had it proceeded? From his aunt's supper, from his own foolish speech, from the wine and dancing,

the merry-making when saying goodnight in the hall, the pleasure of the walk along the river in the snow. Poor Aunt Julia! She, too, would soon be a shade with the shade of Patrick Morkan and his horse. He had caught that haggard look upon her face for a moment when she was singing *Arrayed for the Bridal*. Soon, perhaps, he would be sitting in that same drawing-room, dressed in black, his silk hat on his knees. The blinds would be drawn down and Aunt Kate would be sitting beside him, crying and blowing her nose and telling him how Julia had died. He would cast about in his mind for some words that might console her, and would find only lame and useless ones. Yes, yes: that would happen very soon.

The air of the room chilled his shoulders. He stretched himself cautiously along under the sheets and lay down beside his wife. One by one, they were all becoming shades. Better pass boldly into that other world, in the full glory of some passion, than fade and wither dismally with age. He thought of how she who lay beside him had locked in her heart for so many years that image of her lover's eyes when he had told her that he did not wish to live.

Generous tears filled Gabriel's eyes. He had never felt like that himself towards any woman, but he knew that such a feeling must be love. The tears gathered more thickly in his eyes and in the partial darkness he imagined he saw the form of a young man standing under a dripping tree. Other forms were near. His soul had approached that region where dwell the vast hosts of the dead. He was conscious of, but could not apprehend, their wayward and flickering existence. His own identity was fading out into a gray impalpable world: the solid world itself, which these dead had one time reared and lived in, was dissolving and dwindling.

A few light taps upon the pane made him turn to the window. It had begun to snow again. He watched sleepily the flakes, silver and dark, falling obliquely against the lamplight. The time had come for him to set out on his journey westward. Yes, the newspapers were right: snow was general all over Ireland. It was falling on every part of the dark central plain, on the treeless hills, falling softly upon the Bog of Allen[1] and, farther westward, softly falling into the dark mutinous Shannon waves. It was falling, too, upon every part of the lonely churchyard on the hill where Michael Furey lay buried. It lay thickly drifted on the crooked crosses and headstones, on the spears of the little gate, on the barren thorns. His soul swooned slowly as he heard the snow falling faintly through the universe and faintly falling, like the descent of their last end, upon all the living and the dead.

1914

SHIRLEY JACKSON

The Lottery

The morning of June 27th was clear and sunny, with the fresh warmth of a full-summer day; the flowers were blossoming profusely and the grass was richly green. The people of the village began to gather in the square, between the post office and the bank, around ten o'clock; in some towns there were so many people that the lottery took two days and

1. A few miles southwest of Dublin.

had to be started on June 26th, but in this village, where there were only about three hundred people, the whole lottery took less than two hours, so it could begin at ten o'clock in the morning and still be through in time to allow the villagers to get home for noon dinner.

The children assembled first, of course. School was recently over for the summer, and the feeling of liberty sat uneasily on most of them; they tended to gather together quietly for a while before they broke into boisterous play, and their talk was still of the classroom and the teacher, of books and reprimands. Bobby Martin had already stuffed his pockets full of stones, and the other boys soon followed his example, selecting the smoothest and roundest stones; Bobby and Harry Jones and Dickie Delacroix—the villagers pronounced this name "Dellacroy" —eventually made a great pile of stones in one corner of the square and guarded it against the raids of the other boys. The girls stood aside, talking among themselves, looking over their shoulders at the boys, and the very small children rolled in the dust or clung to the hands of their older brothers or sisters.

Soon the men began to gather, surveying their own children, speaking of planting and rain, tractors and taxes. They stood together, away from the pile of stones in the corner, and their jokes were quiet and they smiled rather than laughed. The women, wearing faded house dresses and sweaters, came shortly after their menfolk. They greeted one another and exchanged bits of gossip as they went to join their husbands. Soon the women, standing by their husbands, began to call to their children, and the chidren came reluctantly, having to be called four or five times. Bobby Martin ducked under his mother's grasping hand and ran, laughing, back to the pile of stones. His father spoke up sharply, and Bobby came quickly and took his place between his father and his oldest brother.

The lottery was conducted—as were the square dances, the teenage club, the Halloween program—by Mr. Summers, who had time and energy to devote to civic activities. He was a round-faced, jovial man and he ran the coal business, and people were sorry for him, because he had no children and his wife was a scold. When he arrived in the square, carrying the black wooden box, there was a murmur of conversation among the villagers, and he waved and called, "Little late today, folks." The postmaster, Mr. Graves, followed him, carrying a three-legged stool, and the stool was put in the center of the square and Mr. Summers set the black box down on it. The villagers kept their distance, leaving a space between themselves and the stool, and when Mr. Summers said, "Some of you fellows want to give me a hand?" there was a hesitation before two men, Mr. Martin and his oldest son, Baxter, came forward to hold the box steady on the stool while Mr. Summers stirred up the papers inside it.

The original paraphernalia for the lottery had been lost long ago, and the black box now resting on the stool had been put into use even before Old Man Warner, the oldest man in town, was born. Mr. Summers spoke frequently to the villagers about making a new box, but no one liked to upset even as much tradition as was represented by the black box. There was a story that the present box had been made with some pieces of the box that had preceded it, the one that had been constructed when the first people settled down to make a village here. Every year, after the lottery, Mr. Summers began talking again about a new box, but every year the subject was allowed to fade off without

anything's being done. The black box grew shabbier each year; by now it was no longer completely black but splintered badly along one side to show the original wood color, and in some places faded or stained.

Mr. Martin and his oldest son, Baxter, held the black box securely on the stool until Mr. Summers had stirred the papers thoroughly with his hand. Because so much of the ritual had been forgotten or discarded, Mr. Summers had been successful in having slips of paper substituted for the chips of wood that had been used for generations. Chips of wood, Mr. Summers had argued, had been all very well when the village was tiny, but now that the population was more than three hundred and likely to keep on growing, it was necessary to use something that would fit more easily into the black box. The night before the lottery, Mr. Summers and Mr. Graves made up the slips of paper and put them in the box, and it was then taken to the safe of Mr. Summers' coal company and locked up until Mr. Summers was ready to take it to the square next morning. The rest of the year, the box was put away, sometimes one place, sometimes another; it had spent one year in Mr. Graves's barn and another year underfoot in the post office, and sometimes it was set on a shelf in the Martin grocery and left there.

There was a great deal of fussing to be done before Mr. Summers declared the lottery open. There were the lists to make up—of heads of families, heads of households in each family, members of each household in each family. There was the proper swearing-in of Mr. Summers by the postmaster, as the official of the lottery; at one time, some people remembered, there had been a recital of some sort, performed by the official of the lottery, a perfunctory, tuneless chant that had been rattled off duly each year; some people believed that the official of the lottery used to stand just so when he said or sang it, others believed that he was supposed to walk among the people, but years and years ago this part of the ritual had been allowed to lapse. There had been, also, a ritual salute, which the official of the lottery had had to use in addressing each person who came up to draw from the box, but this also had changed with time, until now it was felt necessary only for the official to speak to each person approaching. Mr. Summers was very good at all this; in his clean white shirt and blue jeans, with one hand resting carelessly on the black box, he seemed very proper and important as he talked interminably to Mr. Graves and the Martins.

Just as Mr. Summers finally left off talking and turned to the assembled villagers, Mrs. Hutchinson came hurriedly along the path to the square, her sweater thrown over her shoulders, and slid into place in the back of the crowd. "Clean forgot what day it was," she said to Mrs. Delacroix, who stood next to her, and they both laughed softly. "Thought my old man was out back stacking wood," Mrs. Hutchinson went on, "and then I looked out the window and the kids was gone, and then I remembered it was the twenty-seventh and came a-running." She dried her hands on her apron, and Mrs. Delacroix said, "You're in time, though. They're still talking away up there."

Mrs. Hutchinson craned her neck to see through the crowd and found her husband and children standing near the front. She tapped Mrs. Delacroix on the arm as a farewell and began to make her way through the crowd. The people separated good-humoredly to let her through; two or three people said, in voices just loud enough to be heard across the crowd, "Here comes your Missus, Hutchinson," and "Bill, she made it after all." Mrs. Hutchinson reached her husband,

and Mr. Summers, who had been waiting, said cheerfully, "Thought we were going to have to get on without you, Tessie." Mrs. Hutchinson said, grinning, "Wouldn't have me leave m'dishes in the sink, now, would you, Joe?," and soft laughter ran through the crowd as the people stirred back into position after Mrs. Hutchinson's arrival.

"Well, now," Mr. Summers said soberly, "guess we better get started, get this over with, so's we can go back to work. Anybody ain't here?"

"Dunbar," several people said. "Dunbar, Dunbar."

Mr. Summers consulted his list. "Clyde Dunbar," he said. "That's right. He's broke his leg, hasn't he? Who's drawing for him?"

"Me, I guess," a woman said, and Mr. Summers turned to look at her. "Wife draws for her husband," Mr. Summers said. "Don't you have a grown boy to do it for you, Janey?" Although Mr. Summers and everyone else in the village knew the answer perfectly well, it was the business of the official of the lottery to ask such questions formally. Mr. Summers waited with an expression of polite interest while Mrs. Dunbar answered.

"Horace's not but sixteen yet," Mrs. Dunbar said regretfully. "Guess I gotta fill in for the old man this year."

"Right," Mr. Summers said. He made a note on the list he was holding. Then he asked, "Watson boy drawing this year?"

A tall boy in the crowd raised his hand. "Here," he said. "I'm drawing for m'mother and me." He blinked his eyes nervously and ducked his head as several voices in the crowd said things like "Good fellow, Jack," and "Glad to see your mother's got a man to do it."

"Well," Mr. Summers said, "guess that's everyone. Old Man Warner make it?"

"Here," a voice said, and Mr. Summers nodded.

A sudden hush fell on the crowd as Mr. Summers cleared his throat and looked at the list. "All ready?" he called. "Now, I'll read the names —heads of families first—and the men come up and take a paper out of the box. Keep the paper folded in your hand without looking at it until everyone has had a turn. Everything clear?"

The people had done it so many times that they only half listened to the directions; most of them were quiet, wetting their lips, not looking around. Then Mr. Summers raised one hand high and said, "Adams." A man disengaged himself from the crowd and came forward. "Hi, Steve," Mr. Summers said, and Mr. Adams said, "Hi, Joe." They grinned at one another humorlessly and nervously. Then Mr. Adams reached into the black box and took out a folded paper. He held it firmly by one corner as he turned and went hastily back to his place in the crowd, where he stood a little apart from his family, not looking down at his hand.

"Allen," Mr. Summers said. "Anderson. . . . Bentham."

"Seems like there's no time at all between lotteries any more," Mrs. Delacroix said to Mrs. Graves in the back row. "Seems like we got through with the last one only last week."

"Time sure goes fast," Mrs. Graves said.

"Clark. . . . Delacroix."

"There goes my old man," Mrs. Delacroix said. She held her breath while her husband went forward.

"Dunbar," Mr. Summers said, and Mrs. Dunbar went steadily to the box while one of the women said, "Go on, Janey," and another said, "There she goes."

"We're next," Mrs. Graves said. She watched while Mr. Graves came around from the side of the box, greeted Mr. Summers gravely, and selected a slip of paper from the box. By now, all through the crowd there were men holding the small folded papers in their large hands, turning them over and over nervously. Mrs. Dunbar and her two sons stood together, Mrs. Dunbar holding the slip of paper.

"Harburt. . . . Hutchinson."

"Get up there, Bill," Mrs. Hutchinson said, and the people near her laughed.

"Jones."

"They do say," Mr. Adams said to Old Man Warner, who stood next to him, "that over in the north village they're talking of giving up the lottery."

Old Man Warner snorted. "Pack of crazy fools," he said. "Listening to the young folks, nothing's good enough for *them*. Next thing you know, they'll be wanting to go back to living in caves, nobody work any more, live *that* way for a while. Used to be a saying about 'Lottery in June, corn be heavy soon.' First thing you know, we'd all be eating stewed chickweed and acorns. There's *always* been a lottery," he added petulantly. "Bad enough to see young Joe Summers up there joking with everybody."

"Some places have already quit lotteries," Mrs. Adams said.

"Nothing but trouble in *that*," Old Man Warner said stoutly. "Pack of young fools."

"Martin." And Bobby Martin watched his father go forward. "Overdyke. . . . Percy."

"I wish they'd hurry," Mrs. Dunbar said to her older son. "I wish they'd hurry."

"They're almost through," her son said.

"You get ready to run tell Dad," Mrs. Dunbar said.

Mr. Summers called his own name and then stepped forward precisely and selected a slip from the box. Then he called, "Warner."

"Seventy-seventh year I been in the lottery," Old Man Warner said as he went through the crowd. "Seventy-seventh time."

"Watson." The tall boy came awkwardly through the crowd. Someone said, "Don't be nervous, Jack," and Mr. Summers said, "Take your time, son."

"Zanini."

After that, there was a long pause, a breathless pause, until Mr. Summers, holding his slip of paper in the air, said, "All right, fellows." For a minute, no one moved, and then all the slips of paper were opened. Suddenly, all the women began to speak at once, saying, "Who is it?," "Who's got it?," "Is it the Dunbars?," "Is it the Watsons?" Then the voices began to say, "It's Hutchinson. It's Bill," "Bill Hutchinson's got it."

"Go tell your father," Mrs. Dunbar said to her older son.

People began to look around to see the Hutchinsons. Bill Hutchinson was standing quiet staring down at the paper in his hand. Suddenly, Tessie Hutchinson shouted to Mr. Summers, "You didn't give him time enough to take any paper he wanted. I saw you. It wasn't fair."

"Be a good sport, Tessie," Mrs. Delacroix called, and Mrs. Graves said, "All of us took the same chance."

"Shut up, Tessie," Bill Hutchinson said.

"Well, everyone," Mr. Summers said, "that was done pretty fast, and now we've got to be hurrying a little more to get done in time." He consulted his next list. "Bill," he said, "you draw for the Hutchinson family. You got any other households in the Hutchinsons?"

"There's Don and Eva," Mrs. Hutchinson yelled. "Make *them* take their chance!"

"Daughters draw with their husbands' families, Tessie," Mr. Summers said gently. "You know that as well as anyone else."

"It wasn't *fair*," Tessie said.

"I guess not, Joe," Bill Hutchinson said regretfully. "My daughter draws with her husband's family, that's only fair. And I've got no other family except the kids."

"Then, as far as drawing for families is concerned, it's you," Mr. Summers said in explanation, "and as far as drawing for households is concerned, that's you, too. Right?"

"Right," Bill Hutchinson said.

"How many kids, Bill?" Mr. Summers asked formally.

"Three," Bill Hutchinson said. "There's Bill, Jr., and Nancy, and little Dave. And Tessie and me."

"All right, then," Mr. Summers said. "Harry, you got their tickets back?"

Mr. Graves nodded and held up the slips of paper. "Put them in the box, then," Mr. Summers directed. "Take Bill's and put it in."

"I think we ought to start over," Mrs. Hutchinson said, as quietly as she could. "I tell you it wasn't *fair*. You didn't give him time enough to choose. *Every*body saw that."

Mr. Graves had selected the five slips and put them in the box, and he dropped all the papers but those onto the ground, where the breeze caught them and lifted them off.

"Listen, everybody," Mrs. Hutchinson was saying to the people around her.

"Ready, Bill?" Mr. Summers asked, and Bill Hutchinson, with one quick glance around at his wife and children, nodded.

"Remember," Mr. Summers said, "take the slips and keep them folded until each person has taken one. Harry, you help little Dave." Mr. Graves took the hand of the little boy, who came willingly with him up to the box. "Take a paper out of the box, Davy," Mr. Summers said. Davy put his hand into the box and laughed. "Take just *one* paper." Mr. Summers said. "Harry, you hold it for him." Mr. Graves took the child's hand and removed the folded paper from the tight fist and held it while little Dave stood next to him and looked up at him wonderingly.

"Nancy next," Mr. Summers said. Nancy was twelve, and her school friends breathed heavily as she went forward, switching her skirt, and took a slip daintily from the box. "Bill, Jr.," Mr. Summers said, and Billy, his face red and his feet over-large, nearly knocked the box over as he got a paper out. "Tessie," Mr. Summers said. She hesitated for a minute, looking around defiantly, and then set her lips and went up to the box. She snatched a paper out and held it behind her.

"Bill," Mr. Summers said, and Bill Hutchinson reached into the box and felt around, bringing his hand out at last with the slip of paper in it.

The crowd was quiet. A girl whispered, "I hope it's not Nancy," and the sound of the whisper reached the edges of the crowd.

"It's not the way it used to be," Old Man Warner said clearly. "People ain't the way they used to be."

"All right," Mr. Summers said. "Open the papers. Harry, you open little Dave's."

Mr. Graves opened the slip of paper and there was a general sigh through the crowd as he held it up and everyone could see that it was blank. Nancy and Bill, Jr., opened theirs at the same time, and both beamed and laughed, turning around to the crowd and holding their slips of paper above their heads.

"Tessie," Mr. Summers said. There was a pause, and then Mr. Summers looked at Bill Hutchinson, and Bill unfolded his paper and showed it. It was blank.

"It's Tessie," Mr. Summers said, and his voice was hushed. "Show us her paper, Bill."

Bill Hutchinson went over to his wife and forced the slip of paper out of her hand. It had a black spot on it, the black spot Mr. Summers had made the night before with the heavy pencil in the coal-company office. Bill Hutchinson held it up, and there was a stir in the crowd.

"All right, folks," Mr. Summers said. "Let's finish quickly."

Although the villagers had forgotten the ritual and lost the original black box, they still remembered to use stones. The pile of stones the boys had made earlier was ready; there were stones on the ground with the blowing scraps of paper that had come out of the box. Mrs. Delacroix selected a stone so large she had to pick it up with both hands and turned to Mrs. Dunbar. "Come on," she said. "Hurry up."

Mrs. Dunbar had small stones in both hands, and she said, gasping for breath, "I can't run at all. You'll have to go ahead and I'll catch up with you."

The children had stones already, and someone gave little Davy Hutchinson a few pebbles.

Tessie Hutchinson was in the center of a cleared space by now, and she held her hands out desperately as the villagers moved in on her. "It isn't fair," she said. A stone hit her on the side of the head.

Old Man Warner was saying, "Come on, come on, everyone." Steve Adams was in the front of the crowd of villagers, with Mrs. Graves beside him.

"It isn't fair, it isn't right," Mrs. Hutchinson screamed, and then they were upon her.

1948

HERMAN MELVILLE

Bartleby, the Scrivener

A STORY OF WALL STREET

I am a rather elderly man. The nature of my avocations for the last thirty years has brought me into more than ordinary contact with what would seem an interesting and somewhat singular set of men, of whom as yet nothing that I know of has ever been written:—I mean the law-copyists or scriveners. I have known very many of them, professionally and privately, and if I pleased, could relate divers histories, at which good-natured gentlemen might smile, and sentimental souls might

weep. But I waive the biographies of all other scriveners for a few passages in the life of Bartleby, who was a scrivener the strangest I ever saw or heard of. While of other law-copyists I might write the complete life, of Bartleby nothing of that sort can be done. I believe that no materials exist for a full and satisfactory biography of this man. It is an irreparable loss to literature. Bartleby was one of those beings of whom nothing is ascertainable, except from the original sources, and in his case those are very small. What my own astonished eyes saw of Bartleby, *that* is all I know of him, except, indeed, one vague report which will appear in the sequel.

Ere introducing the scrivener, as he first appeared to me, it is fit I make some mention of myself, my *employées,* my business, my chambers, and general surroundings; because some such description is indispensable to an adequate understanding of the chief character about to be presented.

Imprimis:[1] I am a man who, from his youth upwards, has been filled with a profound conviction that the easiest way of life is the best. Hence, though I belong to a profession proverbially energetic and nervous, even to turbulence, at times, yet nothing of that sort have I ever suffered to invade my peace. I am one of those unambitious lawyers who never addresses a jury, or in any way draws down public applause; but in the cool tranquillity of a snug retreat, do a snug business among rich men's bonds and mortgages and title-deeds. All who know me, consider me an eminently *safe* man. The late John Jacob Astor,[2] a personage little given to poetic enthusiasm, had no hesitation in pronouncing my first grand point to be prudence; my next, method. I do not speak it in vanity, but simply record the fact, that I was not unemployed in my profession by the late John Jacob Astor; a name which, I admit, I love to repeat, for it hath a rounded and orbicular sound to it, and rings like unto bullion. I will freely add that I was not insensible to the late John Jacob Astor's good opinion.

Some time prior to the period at which this little history begins, my avocations had been largely increased. The good old office, now extinct in the State of New York, of a Master in Chancery,[3] had been conferred upon me. It was not a very arduous office, but very pleasantly remunerative. I seldom lose my temper; much more seldom indulge in dangerous indignation at wrongs and outrages; but I must be permitted to be rash here and declare, that I consider the sudden and violent abrogation of the office of Master in Chancery, by the new Constitution, as a—premature act; inasmuch as I had counted upon a life-lease of the profits, whereas I only received those of a few short years. But this is by the way.

My chambers were up stairs at No. —— Wall Street. At one end they looked upon the white wall of the interior of a spacious skylight shaft, penetrating the building from top to bottom. This view might have been considered rather tame than otherwise, deficient in what landscape painters call "life." But if so, the view from the other end of my chambers offered, at least, a contrast, if nothing more. In that direction my windows commanded an unobstructed view of a lofty brick wall, black by age and everlasting shade; which wall required no spyglass to

---

1 In the first place.
2. New York fur merchant and land owner (1763–1848) who died the richest man in the United States.

3. A court of chancery can temper the law, applying "dictates of conscience" or "the principles of natural justice"; the office of Master was abolished in 1847.

bring out its lurking beauties, but for the benefit of all near-sighted spectators, was pushed up to within ten feet of my window panes. Owing to the great height of the surrounding buildings, and my chambers being on the second floor, the interval between this wall and mine not a little resembled a huge square cistern.

At the period just preceding the advent of Bartleby, I had two persons as copyists in my employment, and a promising lad as an office-boy. First, Turkey; second, Nippers; third, Ginger Nut. These may seem names the like of which are not usually found in the Directory.[4] In truth they were nicknames, mutually conferred upon each other by my three clerks, and were deemed expressive of their respective persons or characters. Turkey was a short, pursy[5] Englishman of about my own age, that is, somewhere not far from sixty. In the morning, one might say, his face was of a fine florid hue, but after twelve o'clock, meridian —his dinner hour—it blazed like a grate full of Christmas coals; and continued blazing—but, as it were, with a gradual wane—till 6 o'clock, P.M. or thereabouts, after which I saw no more of the proprietor of the face, which gaining its meridian with the sun, seemed to set with it, to rise, culminate, and decline the following day, with the like regularity and undiminished glory. There are many singular coincidences I have known in the course of my life, not the least among which was the fact, that exactly when Turkey displayed his fullest beams from his red and radiant countenance, just then, too, at that critical moment, began the daily period when I considered his business capacities as seriously disturbed for the remainder of the twenty-four hours. Not that he was absolutely idle, or averse to business then; far from it. The difficulty was, he was apt to be altogether too energetic. There was a strange, inflamed, flurried, flighty recklessness of activity about him. He would be incautious in dipping his pen into his inkstand. All his blots upon my documents were dropped there after twelve o'clock, meridian. Indeed, not only would he be reckless and sadly given to making blots in the afternoon, but some days he went further, and was rather noisy. At such times, too, his face flamed with augmented blazonry, as if cannel coal had been heaped on anthracite.[6] He made an unpleasant racket with his chair; spilled his sand-box; in mending his pens, impatiently split them all to pieces, and threw them on the floor in a sudden passion; stood up and leaned over his table, boxing his papers about in a most indecorous manner, very sad to behold in an elderly man like him. Nevertheless, as he was in many ways a most valuable person to me, and all the time before twelve o'clock, meridian, was the quickest, steadiest creature too, accomplishing a great deal of work in a style not easy to be matched—for these reasons, I was willing to overlook his eccentricities, though indeed, occasionally, I remonstrated with him. I did this very gently, however, because, though the civilest, nay, the blandest and most reverential of men in the morning, yet in the afternoon he was disposed, upon provocation, to be slightly rash with his tongue, in fact, insolent. Now, valuing his morning services as I did, and resolved not to lose them; yet, at the same time made uncomfortable by his inflamed ways after twelve o'clock; and being a man of peace, unwilling by my admonitions to call forth unseemly retorts from him; I took upon me, one Saturday noon (he was always worse

---

4. Post Office Directory.
5. Fat, shortwinded.

6. A fast, bright-burning coal heaped on slow-burning, barely glowing coal.

on Saturdays), to hint to him, very kindly, that perhaps now that he was growing old, it might be well to abridge his labors; in short, he need not come to my chambers after twelve o'clock, but, dinner over, had best go home to his lodgings and rest himself till tea-time. But no; he insisted upon his afternoon devotions. His countenance became intolerably fervid, as he oratorically assured me—gesticulating with a long ruler at the other end of the room—that if his services in the morning were useful, how indispensable, then, in the afternoon?

"With submission, sir," said Turkey on this occasion, "I consider myself your right-hand man. In the morning I but marshal and deploy my columns; but in the afternoon I put myself at their head, and gallantly charge the foe, thus!"—and he made a violent thrust with the ruler.

"But the blots, Turkey," intimated I.

"True,—but, with submission, sir, behold these hairs! I am getting old. Surely, sir, a blot or two of a warm afternoon is not to be severely urged against gray hairs. Old age—even if it blot the page—is honorable. With submission, sir, we *both* are getting old."

This appeal to my fellow-feeling was hardly to be resisted. At all events, I saw that go he would not. So I made up my mind to let him stay, resolving, nevertheless, to see to it, that during the afternoon he had to do with my less important papers.

Nippers, the second on my list, was a whiskered, sallow, and, upon the whole, rather piratical-looking young man of about five and twenty. I always deemed him the victim of two evil powers—ambition and indigestion. The ambition was evinced by a certain impatience of the duties of a mere copyist, an unwarrantable usurpation of strictly professional affairs, such as the original drawing up of legal documents. The indigestion seemed betokened in an occasional nervous testiness and grinning irritability, causing the teeth to audibly grind together over mistakes committed in copying; unnecessary maledictions, hissed, rather than spoken, in the heat of business; and especially by a continual discontent with the height of the table where he worked. Though of a very ingenious mechanical turn, Nippers could never get this table to suit him. He put chips under it, blocks of various sorts, bits of pasteboard, and at last went so far as to attempt an exquisite adjustment by final pieces of folded blotting-paper. But no invention would answer. If, for the sake of easing his back, he brought the table lid at a sharp angle well up towards his chin, and wrote there like a man using the steep roof of a Dutch house for his desk:—then he declared that it stopped the circulation in his arms. If now he lowered the table to his waistbands, and stooped over it in writing, then there was a sore aching in his back. In short, the truth of the matter was, Nippers knew not what he wanted. Or, if he wanted any thing, it was to be rid of a scrivener's table altogether. Among the manifestations of his diseased ambition was a fondness he had for receiving visits from certain ambiguous-looking fellows in seedy coats, whom he called his clients. Indeed I was aware that not only was he, at times, considerable of a ward-politician, but he occasionally did a little business at the Justices' courts, and was not unknown on the steps of the Tombs.[7] I have good reason to believe, however, that one individual who called upon him at my chambers, and who, with a grand air, he insisted was his client, was no other than a dun,[8] and the alleged title-deed, a bill.

7. Prison in New York City.   8. Bill collector.

But with all his failings, and the annoyances he caused me, Nippers, like his compatriot Turkey, was a very useful man to me; wrote a neat, swift hand; and, when he chose, was not deficient in a gentlemanly sort of deportment. Added to this, he always dressed in a gentlemanly sort of way: and so, incidentally, reflected credit upon my chambers. Whereas with respect to Turkey, I had much ado to keep him from being a reproach to me. His clothes were apt to look oily and smell of eating-houses. He wore his pantaloons very loose and baggy in summer. His coats were execrable; his hat not to be handled. But while the hat was a thing of indifference to me, inasmuch as his natural civility and deference, as a dependent Englishman, always led him to doff it the moment he entered the room, yet his coat was another matter. Concerning his coats, I reasoned with him; but with no effect. The truth was, I suppose, that a man with so small an income, could not afford to sport such a lustrous face and a lustrous coat at one and the same time. As Nippers once observed, Turkey's money went chiefly for red ink. One winter day I presented Turkey with a highly-respectable looking coat of my own, a padded gray coat, of a most comfortable warmth, and which buttoned straight up from the knee to the neck. I thought Turkey would appreciate the favor, and abate his rashness and obstreperousness of afternoons. But no. I verily believe that buttoning himself up in so downy and blanket-like a coat had a pernicious effect upon him; upon the same principle that too much oats are bad for horses. In fact, precisely as a rash, restive horse is said to feel his oats, so Turkey felt his coat. It made him insolent. He was a man whom prosperity harmed.

Though concerning the self-indulgent habits of Turkey I had my own private surmises, yet touching Nippers I was well persuaded that whatever might be his faults in other respects, he was, at least, a temperate young man. But indeed, nature herself seemed to have been his vintner,[9] and at his birth charged him so thoroughly with an irritable, brandy-like disposition, that all subsequent potations were needless. When I consider how, amid the stillness of my chambers, Nippers would sometimes impatiently rise from his seat, and stooping over his table, spread his arms wide apart, seize the whole desk, and move it, and jerk it, with a grim, grinding motion on the floor, as if the table were a perverse voluntary agent, intent on thwarting and vexing him; I plainly perceive that for Nippers, brandy and water were altogether superfluous.

It was fortunate for me that, owing to its peculiar cause—indigestion—the irritability and consequent nervousness of Nippers, were mainly observable in the morning, while in the afternoon he was comparatively mild. So that Turkey's paroxysms only coming on about twelve o'clock, I never had to do with their eccentricities at one time. Their fits relieved each other like guards. When Nippers' was on, Turkey's was off; and *vice versa*. This was a good natural arrangement under the circumstances.

Ginger Nut, the third on my list, was a lad some twelve years old. His father was a carman,[1] ambitious of seeing his son on the bench instead of a cart, before he died. So he sent him to my office as student at law, errand boy, and cleaner and sweeper, at the rate of one dollar a

---

9. Wine-seller.

1. Driver of wagon or cart that hauls goods.

week. He had a little desk to himself, but he did not use it much. Upon inspection, the drawer exhibited a great array of the shells of various sorts of nuts. Indeed, to this quick-witted youth the whole noble science of the law was contained in a nutshell. Not the least among the employments of Ginger Nut, as well as one which he discharged with the most alacrity, was his duty as cake and apple purveyor for Turkey and Nippers. Copying law papers being proverbially a dry, husky sort of business, my two scriveners were fain to moisten their mouths very often with Spitzenbergs[2] to be had at the numerous stalls nigh the Custom House and Post Office. Also, they sent Ginger Nut very frequently for that peculiar cake—small, flat, round, and very spicy—after which he had been named by them. Of a cold morning when business was but dull, Turkey would gobble up scores of these cakes, as if they were mere wafers—indeed they sell them at the rate of six or eight for a penny—the scrape of his pen blending with the crunching of the crisp particles in his mouth. Of all the fiery afternoon blunders and flurried rashnesses of Turkey, was his once moistening a ginger-cake between his lips, and clapping it on to a mortgage for a seal. I came within an ace of dismissing him then. But he mollified me by making an oriental bow, and saying—"With submission, sir, it was generous of me to find you in[3] stationery on my own account."

Now my original business—that of a conveyancer and title hunter,[4] and drawer-up of recondite documents of all sorts—was considerably increased by receiving the master's office. There was now great work for scriveners. Not only must I push the clerks already with me, but I must have additional help. In answer to my advertisement, a motionless young man one morning stood upon my office threshold, the door being open, for it was summer. I can see that figure now—pallidly neat, pitiably respectable, incurably forlorn! It was Bartleby.

After a few words touching his qualifications, I engaged him, glad to have among my corps of copyists a man of so singularly sedate an aspect, which I thought might operate beneficially upon the flighty temper of Turkey, and the fiery one of Nippers.

I should have stated before that ground glass folding-doors divided my premises into two parts, one of which was occupied by my scriveners, the other by myself. According to my humor I threw open these doors, or closed them. I resolved to assign Bartleby a corner by the folding-doors, but on my side of them, so as to have this quiet man within easy call, in case any trifling thing was to be done. I placed his desk close up to a small side-window in that part of the room, a window which originally had afforded a lateral view of certain grimy backyards and bricks, but which, owing to subsequent erections, commanded at present no view at all, though it gave some light. Within three feet of the panes was a wall, and the light came down from far above, between two lofty buildings, as from a very small opening in a dome. Still further to a satisfactory arrangement, I procured a high green folding screen, which might entirely isolate Bartleby from my sight, though not remove him from my voice. And thus, in a manner, privacy and society were conjoined.

At first Bartleby did an extraordinary quantity of writing. As if long famishing for something to copy, he seemed to gorge himself on my

2. Red-and-yellow American apple.
3. Supply you with.
4. Lawyer who draws up deeds for transferring property, and one who searches out legal control of title deeds.

documents. There was no pause for digestion. He ran a day and night line, copying by sunlight and by candlelight. I should have been quite delighted with his application, had he been cheerfully industrious. But he wrote on silently, palely, mechanically.

It is, of course, an indispensable part of a scrivener's business to verify the accuracy of his copy, word by word. Where there are two or more scriveners in an office, they assist each other in this examination, one reading from the copy, the other holding the original. It is a very dull, wearisome, and lethargic affair. I can readily imagine that to some sanguine temperaments it would be altogether intolerable. For example, I cannot credit that the mettlesome poet Byron would have contentedly sat down with Bartleby to examine a law document of, say, five hundred pages, closely written in a crimpy hand.

Now and then, in the haste of business, it had been my habit to assist in comparing some brief document myself, calling Turkey or Nippers for this purpose. One object I had in placing Bartleby so handy to me behind the screen, was to avail myself of his services on such trivial occasions. It was on the third day, I think, of his being with me, and before any necessity had arisen for having his own writing examined, that, being much hurried to complete a small affair I had in hand, I abruptly called to Bartleby. In my haste and natural expectancy of instant compliance, I sat with my head bent over the original on my desk, and my right hand sideways, and somewhat nervously extended with the copy, so that immediately upon emerging from his retreat, Bartleby might snatch it and proceed to business without the least delay.

In this very attitude did I sit when I called to him, rapidly stating what it was I wanted him to do—namely, to examine a small paper with me. Imagine my surprise, nay, my consternation, when without moving from his privacy, Bartleby, in a singularly mild, firm voice, replied, "I would prefer not to."

I sat awhile in perfect silence, rallying my stunned faculties. Immediately it occurred to me that my ears had deceived me, or Bartleby had entirely misunderstood my meaning. I repeated my request in the clearest tone I could assume. But in quite as clear a one came the previous reply, "I would prefer not to."

"Prefer not to," echoed I, rising in high excitement, and crossing the room with a stride. "What do you mean? Are you moon-struck?[5] I want you to help me compare this sheet here—take it," and I thrust it towards him.

"I would prefer not to," said he.

I looked at him steadfastly. His face was leanly composed; his gray eye dimly calm. Not a wrinkle of agitation rippled him. Had there been the least uneasiness, anger, impatience or impertinence in his manner; in other words, had there been anything ordinarily human about him, doubtless I should have violently dismissed him from the premises. But as it was, I should have as soon thought of turning my pale plaster-of-paris bust of Cicero[6] out-of-doors. I stood gazing at him awhile, as he went on with his own writing, and then reseated myself at my desk. This is very strange, thought I. What had one best do? But my business hurried me. I concluded to forget the matter for the present, reserving

---

5. Crazy.
6. Marcus Tullius Cicero (106–43 B.C.), pro-republican Roman statesman, barrister, writer, who ranks with Demosthenes and Burke as orator.

it for my future leisure. So calling Nippers from the other room, the paper was speedily examined.

A few days after this, Bartleby concluded four lengthy documents, being quadruplicates of a week's testimony taken before me in my High Court of Chancery. It became necessary to examine them. It was an important suit, and great accuracy was imperative. Having all things arranged I called Turkey, Nippers and Ginger Nut from the next room, meaning to place the four copies in the hands of my four clerks, while I should read from the original. Accordingly Turkey, Nippers and Ginger Nut had taken their seats in a row, each with his document in hand, when I called to Bartleby to join this interesting group.

"Bartleby! quick, I am waiting."

I heard a slow scrape of his chair legs on the uncarpeted floor, and soon he appeared standing at the entrance of his hermitage.

"What is wanted?" said he mildly.

"The copies, the copies," said I hurriedly. "We are going to examine them. There"—and I held towards him the fourth quadruplicate.

"I would prefer not to," he said, and gently disappeared behind the screen.

For a few moments I was turned into a pillar of salt,[7] standing at the head of my seated column of clerks. Recovering myself, I advanced towards the screen, and demanded the reason for such extraordinary conduct.

"*Why* do you refuse?"

"I would prefer not to."

With any other man I should have flown outright into a dreadful passion, scorned all further words, and thrust him ignominiously from my presence. But there was something about Bartleby that not only strangely disarmed me, but in a wonderful manner touched and disconcerted me. I began to reason with him.

"These are your own copies we are about to examine. It is labor saving to you, because one examination will answer for your four papers. It is common usage. Every copyist is bound to help examine his copy. Is it not so? Will you not speak? Answer!"

"I prefer not to," he replied in a flute-like tone. It seemed to me that while I had been addressing him, he carefully revolved every statement that I made; fully comprehended the meaning; could not gainsay the irresistible conclusion; but, at the same time, some paramount consideration prevailed with him to reply as he did.

"You are decided, then, not to comply with my request—a request made according to common usage and common sense?"

He briefly gave me to understand that on that point my judgment was sound. Yes: his decision was irreversible.

It is not seldom the case that when a man is browbeaten in some unprecedented and violently unreasonable way, he begins to stagger in his own plainest faith. He begins, as it were, vaguely to surmise that, wonderful as it may be, all the justice and all the reason is on the other side. Accordingly, if any disinterested persons are present, he turns to them for some reinforcement for his own faltering mind.

"Turkey," said I, "what do you think of this? Am I not right?"

"With submission, sir," said Turkey, with his blandest tone, "I think that you are."

---

7. Struck dumb; in *Genesis* 19:26, Lot's wife defies God's command and "looked back from behind him, and she became a pillar of salt."

"Nippers," said I, "what do *you* think of it?"

"I think I should kick him out of the office."

(The reader of nice perceptions will here perceive that, it being morning, Turkey's answer is couched in polite and tranquil terms, but Nippers replies in ill-tempered ones. Or, to repeat a previous sentence, Nippers's ugly mood was on duty, and Turkey's off.)

"Ginger Nut," said I, willing to enlist the smallest suffrage[8] in my behalf, "what do *you* think of it?"

"I think, sir, he's a little *luny*," replied Ginger Nut, with a grin.

"You hear what they say," said I, turning towards the screen, "come forth and do your duty."

But he vouchsafed no reply. I pondered a moment in sore perplexity. But once more business hurried me. I determined again to postpone the consideration of this dilemma to my future leisure. With a little trouble we made out to examine the papers without Bartleby, though at every page or two, Turkey deferentially dropped his opinion that this proceeding was quite out of the common; while Nippers, twitching in his chair with a dyspeptic nervousness, ground out between his set teeth occasional hissing maledictions against the stubborn oaf behind the screen. And for his (Nippers's) part, this was the first and the last time he would do another man's business without pay.

Meanwhile Bartleby sat in his hermitage, oblivious to everything but his own peculiar business there.

Some days passed, the scrivener being employed upon another lengthy work. His late remarkable conduct led me to regard his ways narrowly. I observed that he never went to dinner; indeed that he never went anywhere. As yet I had never of my personal knowledge known him to be outside of my office. He was a perpetual sentry in the corner. At about eleven o'clock though, in the morning, I noticed that Ginger Nut would advance toward the opening in Bartleby's screen, as if silently beckoned thither by a gesture invisible to me where I sat. The boy would then leave the office jingling a few pence, and reappear with a handful of ginger-nuts which he delivered in the hermitage, receiving two of the cakes for his trouble.

He lives, then, on ginger-nuts, thought I; never eats a dinner, properly speaking; he must be a vegetarian then; but no; he never eats even vegetables, he eats nothing but ginger-nuts. My mind then ran on in reveries concerning the probable effects upon the human constitution of living entirely on ginger-nuts. Ginger-nuts are so called because they contain ginger as one of their peculiar constituents, and the final flavoring one. Now what was ginger? A hot, spicy thing. Was Bartleby hot and spicy? Not at all. Ginger, then, had no effect upon Bartleby. Probably he preferred it should have none.

Nothing so aggravates an earnest person as a passive resistance. If the individual so resisted be of a not inhumane temper, and the resisting one perfectly harmless in his passivity; then, in the better moods of the former, he will endeavor charitably to construe to his imagination what proves impossible to be solved by his judgment. Even so, for the most part, I regarded Bartleby and his ways. Poor fellow! thought I, he means no mischief; it is plain he intends no insolence; his aspect sufficiently evinces that his eccentricities are involuntary. He is useful to me. I can get along with him. If I turn him away, the chances are he

---

8. Favorable vote.

will fall in with some less indulgent employer, and then he will be
rudely treated, and perhaps driven forth miserably to starve. Yes. Here
I can cheaply purchase a delicious self-approval. To befriend Bartleby;
to humor him in his strange wilfulness, will cost me little or nothing,
while I lay up in my soul what will eventually prove a sweet morsel
for my conscience. But this mood was not invariable with me. The
passiveness of Bartley sometimes irritated me. I felt strangely goaded
on to encounter him in new opposition, to elicit some angry spark from
him answerable to my own. But indeed I might as well have essayed
to strike fire with my knuckles against a bit of Windsor soap.[9] But one
afternoon the evil impulse in me mastered me, and the following little
scene ensued:

"Bartleby," said I, "when those papers are all copied, I will compare
them with you."

"I would prefer not to."

"How? Surely you do not mean to persist in that mulish vagary?"

No answer.

I threw open the folding-doors near by, and turning upon Turkey
and Nippers, exclaimed in an excited manner—

"He says, a second time, he won't examine his papers. What do you
think of it, Turkey?"

It was afternoon, be it remembered. Turkey sat glowing like a brass
boiler, his bald head steaming, his hands reeling among his blotted
papers.

"Think of it?" roared Turkey; "I think I'll just step behind his
screen, and black his eyes for him!"

So saying, Turkey rose to his feet and threw his arms into a puglistic
position. He was hurrying away to make good his promise, when I
detained him, alarmed at the effect of incautiously rousing Turkey's
combativeness after dinner.

"Sit down, Turkey," said I, "and hear what Nippers has to say.
What do you think of it, Nippers? Would I not be justified in immediately dismissing Bartleby?"

"Excuse me, that is for you to decide, sir. I think his conduct quite
unusual, and indeed unjust, as regards Turkey and myself. But it may
only be a passing whim."

"Ah," exclaimed I, "you have strangely changed your mind then—you
speak very gently of him now."

"All beer," cried Turkey; "gentleness is effects of beer—Nippers and
I dined together today. You see how gentle *I* am, sir. Shall I go and
black his eyes?"

"You refer to Bartleby, I suppose. No, not today, Turkey," I replied;
"pray, put up your fists."

I closed the doors, and again advanced towards Bartleby. I felt additional incentives tempting me to my fate. I burned to be rebelled
against again. I remembered that Bartleby never left the office.

"Bartleby," said I, "Ginger Nut is away; just step round to the Post
Office, won't you? (it was but a three minutes' walk,) and see if there
is anything for me."

"I would prefer not to."

"You *will* not?"

"I *prefer* not."

9. Scented soap, usually brown.

I staggered to my desk, and sat there in a deep study. My blind inveteracy returned. Was there any other thing in which I could procure myself to be ignominiously repulsed by this lean, penniless wight?—my hired clerk? What added thing is there, perfectly reasonable, that he will be sure to refuse to do?

"Bartleby!"

No answer.

"Bartleby," in a louder tone.

No answer.

"Bartleby," I roared.

Like a very ghost, agreeably to the laws of magical invocation, at the third summons, he appeared at the entrance of his hermitage.

"Go to the next room, and tell Nippers to come to me."

"I prefer not to," he respectfully and slowly said, and mildly disappeared.

"Very good, Bartleby," said I, in a quiet sort of serenely severe self-possessed tone, intimating the unalterable purpose of some terrible retribution very close at hand. At the moment I half intended something of the kind. But upon the whole, as it was drawing towards my dinner-hour, I thought it best to put on my hat and walk home for the day, suffering much from perplexity and distress of mind.

Shall I acknowledge it? The conclusion of this whole business was, that it soon became a fixed fact of my chambers, that a pale young scrivener, by the name of Bartleby, had a desk there; that he copied for me at the usual rate of four cents a folio (one hundred words); but he was permanently exempt from examining the work done by him, that duty being transferred to Turkey and Nippers, one of compliment doubtless to their superior acuteness; moreover, said Bartleby was never on any account to be dispatched on the most trivial errand of any sort; and that even if entreated to take upon him such a matter, it was generally understood that he would prefer not to—in other words, that he would refuse point-blank.

As days passed on, I became considerably reconciled to Bartleby. His steadiness, his freedom from all dissipation, his incessant industry (except when he chose to throw himself into a standing revery behind his screen), his great stillness, his unalterableness of demeanor under all circumstances, made him a valuable acquisition. One prime thing was this,—*he was always there;*—first in the morning, continually through the day, and the last at night. I had a singular confidence in his honesty. I felt my most precious papers perfectly safe in his hands. Sometimes to be sure I could not, for the very soul of me, avoid falling into sudden spasmodic passions with him. For it was exceeding difficult to bear in mind all the time those strange peculiarities, privileges, and unheard of exemptions, forming the tacit stipulations on Bartleby's part under which he remained in my office. Now and then, in the eagerness of dispatching pressing business, I would inadvertently summon Bartleby, in a short, rapid tone, to put his finger, say, on the incipient tie of a bit of red tape with which I was about compressing some papers. Of course, from behind the screen the usual answer, "I prefer not to," was sure to come; and then, how could a human creature with the common infirmities of our nature, refrain from bitterly exclaiming upon such perverseness—such unreasonableness? However, every added repulse of this sort which I received only tended to lessen the probability of my repeating the inadvertence.

Here it must be said, that according to the custom of most legal gentlemen occupying chambers in densely-populated law buildings, there were several keys to my door. One was kept by a woman residing in the attic, which person weekly scrubbed and daily swept and dusted my apartments. Another was kept by Turkey for convenience sake. The third I sometimes carried in my own pocket. The fourth I knew not who had.

Now, one Sunday morning I happened to go to Trinity Church, to hear a celebrated preacher, and finding myself rather early on the ground, I thought I would walk round to my chambers for a while. Luckily I had my key with me; but upon applying it to the lock, I found it resisted by something inserted from the inside. Quite surprised, I called out; when to my consternation a key was turned from within; and thrusting his lean visage at me, and holding the door ajar, the apparition of Bartleby appeared, in his shirt sleeves, and otherwise in a strangely tattered dishabille, saying quietly that he was sorry, but he was deeply engaged just then, and—preferred not admitting me at present. In a brief word or two, he moreover added, that perhaps I had better walk round the block two or three times, and by that time he would probably have concluded his affairs.

Now, the utterly unsurmised appearance of Bartleby, tenanting my law-chambers of a Sunday morning, with his cadaverously gentlemanly *nonchalance*, yet withal firm and self-possessed, had such a strange effect upon me, that incontinently I slunk away from my own door, and did as desired. But not without sundry twinges of impotent rebellion against the mild effrontery of this unaccountable scrivener. Indeed, it was his wonderful mildness, chiefly, which not only disarmed me, but unmanned me, as it were. For I consider that one, for the time, is sort of unmanned when he tranquilly permits his hired clerk to dictate to him, and order him away from his own premises. Furthermore, I was full of uneasiness as to what Bartleby could possibly be doing in my office in his shirt sleeves, and in an otherwise dismantled condition of a Sunday morning. Was anything amiss going on? Nay, that was out of the question. It was not to be thought of for a moment that Bartleby was an immoral person. But what could he be doing there?— copying? Nay again, whatever might be his eccentricities, Bartleby was an eminently decorous person. He would be the last man to sit down to his desk in any state approaching to nudity. Besides, it was Sunday; and there was something about Bartleby that forbade the supposition that he would by any secular occupation violate the proprieties of the day.

Nevertheless, my mind was not pacified; and full of a restless curiosity, at last I returned to the door. Without hindrance I inserted my key, opened it, and entered. Bartleby was not to be seen. I looked round anxiously, peeped behind his screen; but it was very plain that he was gone. Upon more closely examining the place, I surmised that for an indefinite period Bartleby must have ate, dressed, and slept in my office, and that too without plate, mirror, or bed. The cushioned seat of a ricketty old sofa in one corner bore the faint impress of a lean, reclining form. Rolled away under his desk, I found a blanket under the empty grate, a blacking box[1] and brush; on a chair, a tin basin, with soap and a ragged towel; in a newspaper a few crumbs of

---

1. Box of black shoe polish.

ginger-nuts and a morsel of cheese. Yes, thought I, it is evident enough that Bartleby has been making his home here, keeping bachelor's hall all by himself. Immediately then the thought came sweeping across me, What miserable friendlessness and loneliness are here revealed! His poverty is great; but his solitude, how horrible! Think of it. Of a Sunday, Wall Street is deserted as Petra;[2] and every night of every day it is an emptiness. This building too, which of weekdays hums with industry and life, at nightfall echoes with sheer vacancy, and all through Sunday is forlorn. And here Bartleby makes his home; sole spectator of a solitude which he has seen all populous—a sort of innocent and transformed Marius brooding among the ruins of Carthage![3]

For the first time in my life a feeling of overpowering stinging melancholy seized me. Before, I had never experienced aught but a not-unpleasing sadness. The bond of a common humanity now drew me irresistibly to gloom. A fraternal melancholy! For both I and Bartleby were sons of Adam. I remembered the bright silks and sparkling faces I had seen that day, in gala trim, swan-like sailing down the Mississippi of Broadway; and I contrasted them with the pallid copyist, and thought to myself, Ah, happiness courts the light, so we deem the world is gay; but misery hides aloof, so we deem that misery there is none. These sad fancyings—chimeras, doubtless, of a sick and silly brain—led on to other and more special thoughts, concerning the eccentricities of Bartleby. Presentiments of strange discoveries hovered round me. The scrivener's pale form appeared to me laid out, among uncaring strangers, in its shivering winding sheet.

Suddenly I was attracted by Bartleby's closed desk, the key in open sight left in the lock.

I mean no mischief, seek the gratification of no heartless curiosity, thought I; besides, the desk is mine, and its contents too, so I will make bold to look within. Everything was methodically arranged, the papers smoothly placed. The pigeonholes were deep, and removing the files of documents, I groped into their recesses. Presently I felt something there, and dragged it out. It was an old bandanna handkerchief, heavy and knotted. I opened it, and saw it was a savings' bank.

I now recalled all the quiet mysteries which I had noted in the man. I remembered that he never spoke but to answer; that though at intervals he had considerable time to himself, yet I had never seen him reading—no, not even a newspaper; that for long periods he would stand looking out, at his pale window behind the screen, upon the dead brick wall; I was quite sure he never visited any refectory or eating house; while his pale face clearly indicated that he never drank beer like Turkey, or tea and coffee even, like other men; that he never went anywhere in particular that I could learn; never went out for a walk, unless indeed that was the case at present; that he had declined telling who he was, or whence he came, or whether he had any relatives in the world; that though so thin and pale, he never complained of ill health. And more than all, I remembered a certain unconscious air of

2. Once a flourishing Middle Eastern trade center, long in ruins.

3. Gaius (or Caius) Marius (157–86 B.C.), Roman consul and general, expelled from Rome in 88 B.C. by Sulla; when an officer of Sextilius, the governor, forbade him to land in Africa, Marius replied, "Go tell him that you have seen Caius Marius sitting in exile among the ruins of Carthage," applying the example of the fortune of that city to the change of his own condition. The image was so common that a few years after "Bartleby," Dickens apologizes for using it: ". . . like that lumbering Marius among the ruins of Carthage, who has sat heavy on a thousand millions of similes . . ." ("The Calais Night-Mail," in *The Uncommercial Traveller*).

pallid—how shall I call it?—of pallid haughtiness, say, or rather an austere reserve about him, which had positively awed me into my tame compliance with his eccentricities, when I had feared to ask him to do the slightest incidental thing for me, even though I might know, from his long-continued motionlessness, that behind his screen he must be standing in one of those dead-wall reveries of his.

Revolving all these things, and coupling them with the recently discovered fact that he made my office his constant abiding place and home, and not forgetful of his morbid moodiness; revolving all these things, a prudential feeling began to steal over me. My first emotions had been those of pure melancholy and sincerest pity; but just in proportion as the forlornness of Bartleby grew and grew to my imagination, did that same melancholy merge into fear, that pity into repulsion. So true it is, and so terrible too, that up to a certain point the thought or sight of misery enlists our best affections; but, in certain special cases, beyond that point it does not. They err who would assert that invariably this is owing to the inherent selfishness of the human heart. It rather proceeds from a certain hopelessness of remedying excessive and organic ill. To a sensitive being, pity is not seldom pain. And when at last it is perceived that such pity cannot lead to effectual succor, common sense bids the soul be rid of it. What I saw that morning persuaded me that the scrivener was the victim of innate and incurable disorder. I might give alms to his body; but his body did not pain him; it was his soul that suffered, and his soul I could not reach.

I did not accomplish the purpose of going to Trinity Church that morning. Somehow, the things I had seen disqualified me for the time from churchgoing. I walked homeward, thinking what I would do with Bartleby. Finally, I resolved upon this;—I would put certain calm questions to him the next morning, touching his history, &c., and if he declined to answer them openly and unreservedly (and I supposed he would prefer not), then to give him a twenty-dollar bill over and above whatever I might owe him, and tell him his services were no longer required; but that if in any other way I could assist him, I would be happy to do so, especially if he desired to return to his native place, wherever that might be, I would willingly help to defray the expenses. Moreover, if, after reaching home, he found himself at any time in want of aid, a letter from him would be sure of a reply.

The next morning came.

"Bartleby," said I, gently calling to him behind his screen.

No reply.

"Bartleby," said I, in a still gentler tone, "come here; I am not going to ask you to do anything you would prefer not to do—I simply wish to speak to you."

Upon this he noiselessly slid into view.

"Will you tell me, Bartleby, where you were born?"

"I would prefer not to."

"Will you tell me *anything* about yourself?"

"I would prefer not to."

"But what reasonable objection can you have to speak to me? I feel friendly towards you."

He did not look at me while I spoke, but kept his glance fixed upon my bust of Cicero, which as I then sat, was directly behind me, some six inches above my head.

"What is your answer, Bartleby?" said I, after waiting a consider-

able time for a reply, during which his countenance remained immovable, only there was the faintest conceivable tremor of the white attenuated mouth.

"At present I prefer to give no answer," he said, and retired into his hermitage.

It was rather weak in me I confess, but his manner on this occasion nettled me. Not only did there seem to lurk in it a certain calm disdain, but his perverseness seemed ungrateful, considering the undeniable good usage and indulgence he had received from me.

Again I sat ruminating what I should do. Mortified as I was at his behavior, and resolved as I had been to dismiss him when I entered my office, nevertheless I strangely felt something superstitious knocking at my heart, and forbidding me to carry out my purpose, and denouncing me for a villain if I dared to breathe one bitter word against this forlornest of mankind. At last, familiarly drawing my chair behind his screen, I sat down and said: "Bartleby, never mind then about revealing your history; but let me entreat you, as a friend, to comply as far as may be with the usages of this office. Say now you will help to examine papers tomorrow or next day: in short, say now that in a day or two you will begin to be a little reasonable:—say so, Bartleby."

"At present I would prefer not to be a little reasonable," was his mildly cadaverous reply.

Just then the folding-doors opened, and Nippers approached. He seemed suffering from an unusually bad night's rest, induced by severer indigestion than common. He overheard those final words of Bartleby.

"*Prefer not*, eh?" gritted Nippers—"I'd *prefer* him, if I were you, sir," addressing me—"I'd *prefer* him; I'd give him preferences, the stubborn mule! What is it, sir, pray, that he *prefers* not to do now?"

Bartleby moved not a limb.

"Mr. Nippers," said I, "I'd prefer that you would withdraw for the present."

Somehow, of late I had got into the way of involuntarily using this word "prefer" upon all sorts of not exactly suitable occasions. And I trembled to think that my contact with the scrivener had already and seriously affected me in a mental way. And what further and deeper aberration might it not yet produce? This apprehension had not been without efficacy in determining me to summary means.

As Nippers, looking very sour and sulky, was departing, Turkey blandly and deferentially approached.

"With submission, sir," said he, "yesterday I was thinking about Bartleby here, and I think that if he would but prefer to take a quart of good ale every day, it would do much towards mending him and enabling him to assist in examining his papers."

"So you have got the word too," said I, slightly excited.

"With submission, what word, sir?" asked Turkey, respectfully crowding himself into the contracted space behind the screen, and by so doing making me jostle the scrivener. "What word, sir?"

"I would prefer to be left alone here," said Bartleby, as if offended at being mobbed in his privacy.

"*That's* the word, Turkey," said I—"*that's* it."

"Oh, *prefer*? oh yes—queer word. I never use it myself. But, sir, as I was saying, if he would but prefer—"

"Turkey," interrupted I, "you will please withdraw."

"Oh certainly, sir, if you prefer that I should."

As he opened the folding-door to retire, Nippers at his desk caught a glimpse of me, and asked whether I would prefer to have a certain paper copied on blue paper or white. He did not in the least roguishly accent the word *prefer*. It was plain that it involuntarily rolled from his tongue. I thought to myself, surely I must get rid of a demented man, who already has in some degree turned the tongues, if not the heads of myself and clerks. But I thought it prudent not to break the dismission at once.

The next day I noticed that Bartleby did nothing but stand at his window in his dead-wall revery. Upon asking him why he did not write, he said that he had decided upon doing no more writing.

"Why, how now? what next?" exclaimed I, "do no more writing?"

"No more."

"And what is the reason?"

"Do you not see the reason for yourself," he indifferently replied.

I looked steadfastly at him, and perceived that his eyes looked dull and glazed. Instantly it occurred to me, that his unexampled diligence in copying by his dim window for the first few weeks of his stay with me might have temporarily impaired his vision.

I was touched. I said something in condolence with him. I hinted that of course he did wisely in abstaining from writing for a while; and urged him to embrace that opportunity of taking wholesome exercise in the open air. This, however, he did not do. A few days after this, my other clerks being absent, and being in a great hurry to dispatch certain letters by the mail, I thought that, having nothing else earthly to do, Bartleby would surely be less inflexible than usual, and carry these letters to the post office. But he blankly declined. So, much to my inconvenience, I went myself.

Still added days went by. Whether Bartleby's eyes improved or not, I could not say. To all appearance, I thought they did. But when I asked him if they did, he vouchsafed no answer. At all events, he would do no copying. At last, in reply to my urgings, he informed me that he had permanently given up copying.

"What!" exclaimed I; "suppose your eyes should get entirely well—better than ever before—would you not copy then?"

"I have given up copying," he answered, and slid aside.

He remained, as ever, a fixture in my chamber. Nay—if that were possible—he became still more of a fixture than before. What was to be done? He would do nothing in the office: why should he stay there? In plain fact, he had now become a millstone[4] to me, not only useless as a necklace, but afflictive to bear. Yet I was sorry for him. I speak less than truth when I say that, on his own account, he occasioned me uneasiness. If he would but have named a single relative or friend, I would instantly have written, and urged their taking the poor fellow away to some convenient retreat. But he seemed alone, absolutely alone in the universe. A bit of wreck in the mid-Atlantic. At length, necessities connected with my business tyrannized over all other considerations. Decently as I could, I told Bartleby that in six days' time he must unconditionally leave the office. I warned him to take measures, in the interval, for procuring some other abode. I offered to assist him in this endeavor, if he himself would but take the first step towards a removal. "And when you finally quit me, Bartleby," added I, "I shall

---

4. Heavy stone for grinding grain. See *Matthew* 18:6: "But whoso shall offend one of these little ones which believe in me, it were better for him that a millstone were hanged about his neck, and that he were drowned in the depth of the sea."

see that you go not away entirely unprovided. Six days from this hour, remember."

At the expiration of that period, I peeped behind the screen, and lo! Bartleby was there.

I buttoned up my coat, balanced myself; advanced slowly towards him, touched his shoulder, and said, "The time has come; you must quit this place; I am sorry for you; here is money; but you must go."

"I would prefer not," he replied, with his back still towards me.

"You *must*."

He remained silent.

Now I had an unbounded confidence in this man's common honesty. He had frequently restored to me sixpences and shillings[5] carelessly dropped upon the floor, for I am apt to be very reckless in such shirt-button affairs. The proceeding then which followed will not be deemed extraordinary.

"Bartleby," said I, "I owe you twelve dollars on account; here are thirty-two; the odd twenty are yours.—Will you take it?" and I handed the bills towards him.

But he made no motion.

"I will leave them here then," putting them under a weight on the table. Then taking my hat and cane and going to the door I tranquilly turned and added—"After you have removed your things from these offices, Bartleby, you will of course lock the door—since everyone is now gone for the day but you—and if you please, slip your key underneath the mat, so that I may have it in the morning. I shall not see you again; so good-bye to you. If hereafter in your new place of abode I can be of any service to you, do not fail to advise me by letter. Good-bye, Bartleby, and fare you well."

But he answered not a word; like the last column of some ruined temple, he remained standing mute and solitary in the middle of the otherwise deserted room.

As I walked home in a pensive mood, my vanity got the better of my pity. I could not but highly plume myself on my masterly management in getting rid of Bartleby. Masterly I call it, and such it must appear to any dispassionate thinker. The beauty of my procedure seemed to consist in its perfect quietness. There was no vulgar bullying, no bravado of any sort, no choleric hectoring, and striding to and fro across the apartment, jerking out vehement commands for Bartleby to bundle himself off with his beggarly traps.[6] Nothing of the kind. Without loudly bidding Bartleby depart—as an inferior genius might have done —I *assumed* the ground that depart he must; and upon that assumption built all I had to say. The more I thought over my procedure, the more I was charmed with it. Nevertheless, next morning, upon awakening, I had my doubts,—I had somehow slept off the fumes of vanity. One of the coolest and wisest hours a man has is just after he awakes in the morning. My procedure seemed as sagacious as ever,—but only in theory. How it would prove in practice—there was the rub. It was truly a beautiful thought to have assumed Bartleby's departure; but, after all, that assumption was simply my own, and none of Bartleby's. The great point was, not whether I had assumed that he would quit me, but whether he would prefer so to do. He was more a man of preferences than assumptions.

After breakfast, I walked downtown, arguing the probabilities *pro*

---

5. Coins now worth six cents and 12 cents but once worth twice that.

6. Personal belongings, luggage.

and *con.* One moment I thought it would prove a miserable failure, and Bartleby would be found all alive at my office as usual; the next moment it seemed certain that I should see his chair empty. And so I kept veering about. At the corner of Broadway and Canal Street, I saw quite an excited group of people standing in earnest conversation.

"I'll take odds he doesn't," said a voice as I passed.

"Doesn't go?—done!" said I, "put up your money."

I was instinctively putting my hand in my pocket to produce my own, when I remembered that this was an election day. The words I had overheard bore no reference to Bartleby, but to the success or non-success of some candidate for the mayoralty. In my intent frame of mind, I had, as it were, imagined that all Broadway shared in my excitement, and were debating the same question with me. I passed on, very thankful that the uproar of the street screened my momentary absent-mindedness.

As I had intended, I was earlier than usual at my office door. I stood listening for a moment. All was still. He must be gone. I tried the knob. The door was locked. Yes, my procedure had worked to a charm; he indeed must be vanished. Yet a certain melancholy mixed with this: I was almost sorry for my brilliant success. I was fumbling under the door mat for the key, which Bartleby was to have left there for me, when accidentally my knee knocked against a panel, producing a summoning sound, and in response a voice came to me from within—"Not yet; I am occupied."

It was Bartleby.

I was thunderstruck. For an instant I stood like the man who, pipe in mouth, was killed one cloudless afternoon long ago in Virginia, by summer lightning; at his own warm open window he was killed, and remained leaning out there upon the dreamy afternoon, till some one touched him, when he fell.

"Not gone!" I murmured at last. But again obeying that wondrous ascendancy which the inscrutable scrivener had over me, and from which ascendency, for all my chafing, I could not completely escape, I slowly went downstairs and out into the street, and while walking round the block, considered what I should next do in this unheard-of perplexity. Turn the man out by an actual thrusting I could not; to drive him away by calling him hard names would not do; calling in the police was an unpleasant idea; and yet, permit him to enjoy his cadaverous triumph over me,—this too I could not think of. What was to be done? or, if nothing could be done, was there anything further that I could *assume* in the matter? Yes, as before I had prospectively assumed that Bartleby would depart, so now I might retrospectively assume that departed he was. In the legitimate carrying out of this assumption, I might enter my office in a great hurry, and pretending not to see Bartleby at all, walk straight against him as if he were air. Such a proceeding would in a singular degree have the appearance of a home-thrust.[7] It was hardly possible that Bartleby could withstand such an application of the doctrine of assumptions. But upon second thoughts the success of the plan seemed rather dubious. I resolved to argue the matter over with him again.

"Bartleby," said I, entering the office, with a quietly severe expression, "I am seriously displeased. I am pained, Bartleby. I had thought better of you. I had imagined you of such a gentlemanly organization,

7. Thrust that reaches its mark.

that in any delicate dilemma a slight hint would suffice—in short, an assumption. But it appears I am deceived. Why," I added, unaffectedly starting, "you have not even touched that money yet," pointing to it, just where I had left it the evening previous.

He answered nothing.

"Will you, or will you not, quit me?" I now demanded in a sudden passion, advancing close to him.

"I would prefer *not* to quit you," he replied, gently emphasizing the *not*.

"What earthly right have you to stay here? Do you pay any rent? Do you pay my taxes? Or is this property yours?"

He answered nothing.

"Are you ready to go on and write now? Are your eyes recovered? Could you copy a small paper for me this morning? or help examine a few lines? or step round to the post office? In a word, will you do anything at all, to give a coloring to your refusal to depart the premises?"

He silently retired into his hermitage.

I was now in such a state of nervous resentment that I thought it but prudent to check myself at present from further demonstrations. Bartleby and I were alone. I remembered the tragedy of the unfortunate Adams and the still more unfortunate Colt in the solitary office of the latter; and how poor Colt, being dreadfully incensed by Adams, and imprudently permitting himself to get wildly excited, was at unawares hurried into his fatal act—an act which certainly no man could possibly deplore more than the actor himself. Often it had occurred to me in my ponderings upon the subject, that had that altercation taken place in the public street, or at a private residence, it would not have terminated as it did. It was the circumstance of being alone in a solitary office, up stairs, of a building entirely unhallowed by humanizing domestic associations—an uncarpeted office, doubtless, of a dusty, haggard sort of appearance;—this it must have been, which greatly helped to enhance the irritable desperation of the hapless Colt.[8]

But when this old Adam[9] of resentment rose in me and tempted me concerning Bartleby, I grappled him and threw him. How? Why, simply by recalling the divine injunction: "A new commandment[1] give I unto you, that ye love one another." Yes, this it was that saved me. Aside from higher considerations, charity often operates as a vastly wise and prudent principle—a great safeguard to its possessor. Men have committed murder for jealousy's sake, and anger's sake, and hatred's sake, and selfishness' sake, and spiritual pride's sake; but no man that ever I heard of, ever committed a diabolical murder for sweet charity's sake. Mere self-interest, then, if no better motive can be enlisted, should, especially with high-tempered men, prompt all beings to charity and philanthropy. At any rate, upon the occasion in question, I strove to drown my exasperated feelings towards the scrivener by benevolently construing his conduct. Poor fellow, poor fellow! thought I, he don't mean anything; and besides, he has seen hard times, and ought to be indulged.

I endeavored also immediately to occupy myself, and at the same time to comfort my despondency. I tried to fancy that in the course of

8. In 1841, John C. Colt, brother of the famous gunmaker, unintentionally killed Samuel Adams, a printer, when he hit him on the head during a fight.
9. Sinful element in human nature; see, e.g., "Invocation of Blessing on the Child," in the *Book of Common Prayer*: "Grant that the old Adam in this child may be so buried, that the new man may be raised up in him." Christ is sometimes called the "new Adam."
1. In *John* 13:34, where, however, the phrasing is "I give unto . . ."

the morning, at such time as might prove agreeable to him, Bartleby, of his own free accord, would emerge from his hermitage, and take up some decided line of march in the direction of the door. But no. Half-past twelve o'clock came; Turkey began to glow in the face, overturn his inkstand, and become generally obstreperous; Nippers abated down into quietude and courtesy; Ginger Nut munched his noon apple; and Bartleby remained standing at his window in one of his profoundest dead-wall reveries. Will it be credited? Ought I to acknowledge it? That afternoon I left the office without saying one further word to him.

Some days now passed, during which, at leisure intervals I looked a little into "Edwards on the Will," and "Priestley on Necessity."[2] Under the circumstances, those books induced a salutary feeling. Gradually I slid into the persuasion that these troubles of mine touching the scrivener, had been all predestinated from eternity, and Bartleby was billeted upon me for some mysterious purpose of an all-wise Providence, which it was not for a mere mortal like me to fathom. Yes, Bartleby, stay there behind your screen, thought I; I shall persecute you no more; you are harmless and noiseless as any of these old chairs; in short, I never feel so private as when I know you are here. At least I see it, I feel it; I penetrate to the predestinated purpose of my life. I am content. Others may have loftier parts to enact; but my mission in this world, Bartleby, is to furnish you with office-room for such period as you may see fit to remain.

I believe that this wise and blessed frame of mind would have con-tinued with me, had it not been for the unsolicited and uncharitable remarks obtruded upon me by my professional friends who visited the rooms. But thus it often is, that the constant friction of illiberal minds wears out at last the best resolves of the more generous. Though to be sure, when I reflected upon it, it was not strange that people entering my office should be struck by the peculiar aspect of the unaccountable Bartleby, and so be tempted to throw out some sinister observations concerning him. Sometimes an attorney having business with me, and calling at my office, and finding no one but the scrivener there, would undertake to obtain some sort of precise information from him touching my whereabouts; but without heeding his idle talk, Bartleby would remain standing immovable in the middle of the room. So after con-templating him in that position for a time, the attorney would depart, no wiser than he came.

Also, when a Reference[3] was going on, and the room full of lawyers and witnesses and business was driving fast; some deeply occupied legal gentleman present, seeing Bartleby wholly unemployed, would request him to run round to his (the legal gentleman's) office and fetch some papers for him. Thereupon, Bartleby would tranquilly decline, and yet remain idle as before. Then the lawyer would give a great stare, and turn to me. And what could I say? At last I was made aware that all through the circle of my professional acquaintance, a whisper of wonder was running round, having reference to the strange creature I kept at my office. This worried me very much. And as the idea came

2. Jonathan Edwards (1703–1758), New England Calvinist theologian and re-vivalist, in *The Freedom of the Will* (1754), argued that man is not in fact free, for though he chooses according to the way he sees things, that way is pre-determined (by biography, environment, and character), and he acts out of per-sonality rather than by will. Joseph Priest-ley (1733–1804), Dissenting preacher, scientist, grammarian, and philosopher, in *The Doctrine of Philosophical Necessity* (1777), argued that free will is theo'ogi-cally objectionable, metaphysically incom-prehensible, and morally undesirable.

3. Consultation or committee meeting.

upon me of his possibly turning out a long-lived man, and keep occupying my chambers, and denying my authority; and perplexing my visitors; and scandalizing my professional reputation; and casting a general gloom over the premises; keeping soul and body together to the last upon his savings (for doubtless he spent but half a dime a day), and in the end perhaps outlive me, and claim possession of my office by right of his perpetual occupancy: as all these dark anticipations crowded upon me more and more, and my friends continually intruded their relentless remarks upon the apparition in my room; a great change was wrought in me. I resolved to gather all my faculties together, and forever rid me of this intolerable incubus.

Ere revolving any complicated project, however, adapted to this end, I first simply suggested to Bartleby the propriety of his permanent departure. In a calm and serious tone, I commended the idea to his careful and mature consideration. But having taken three days to meditate upon it, he apprised me that his original determination remained the same; in short, that he still preferred to abide with me.

What shall I do? I now said to myself, buttoning up my coat to the last button. What shall I do? what ought I to do? what does conscience say I *should* do with this man, or rather ghost. Rid myself of him, I must; go, he shall. But how? You will not thrust him, the poor, pale, passive mortal,—you will not thrust such a helpless creature out of your door? you will not dishonor yourself by such cruelty? No, I will not, I cannot do that. Rather would I let him live and die here, and then mason up his remains in the wall. What then will you do? For all your coaxing, he will not budge. Bribes he leaves under your own paperweight on your table; in short, it is quite plain that he prefers to cling to you.

Then something severe, something unusual must be done. What! surely you will not have him collared by a constable, and commit his innocent pallor to the common jail? And upon what ground could you procure such a thing to be done?—a vagrant, is he? What! he a vagrant, a wanderer, who refuses to budge? It is because he will *not* be a vagrant, then, that you seek to count him *as* a vagrant. That is too absurd. No visible means of support: there I have him. Wrong again: for indubitably he *does* support himself, and that is the only unanswerable proof that any man can show of his possessing the means so to do. No more then. Since he will not quit me, I must quit him. I will change my offices; I will move elsewhere; and will give him fair notice, that if I find him on my new premises I will then proceed against him as a common trespasser.

Acting accordingly, next day I thus addressed him: "I find these chambers too far from the City Hall; the air is unwholesome. In a word, I propose to remove my offices next week, and shall no longer require your services. I tell you this now, in order that you may seek another place."

He made no reply, and nothing more was said.

On the appointed day I engaged carts and men, proceeded to my chambers, and having but little furniture, everything was removed in a few hours. Throughout, the scrivener remained standing behind the screen, which I directed to be removed the last thing. It was withdrawn; and being folded up like a huge folio, left him the motionless occupant of a naked room. I stood in the entry watching him a moment, while something from within me upbraided me.

I re-entered, with my hand in my pocket—and—and my heart in my mouth.

"Good-bye, Bartleby; I am going—good-bye, and God some way bless you; and take that," slipping something in his hand. But it dropped upon the floor, and then,—strange to say—I tore myself from him whom I had so longed to be rid of.

Established in my new quarters, for a day or two I kept the door locked, and started at every footfall in the passages. When I returned to my rooms after any little absence, I would pause at the threshold for an instant, and attentively listen, ere applying my key. But these fears were needless. Bartleby never came nigh me.

I thought all was going well, when a perturbed-looking stranger visited me, inquiring whether I was the person who had recently occupied rooms at No. — Wall Street.

Full of forebodings, I replied that I was.

"Then sir," said the stranger, who proved a lawyer, "you are responsible for the man you left there. He refuses to do any copying; he refuses to do anything; he says he prefers not to; and he refuses to quit the premises."

"I am very sorry, sir," said I, with assumed tranquillity, but an inward tremor, "but, really, the man you allude to is nothing to me—he is no relation or apprentice of mine, that you should hold me responsible for him."

"In mercy's name, who is he?"

"I certainly cannot inform you. I know nothing about him. Formerly I employed him as a copyist; but he has done nothing for me now for some time past."

"I shall settle him then,—good morning, sir."

Several days passed, and I heard nothing more; and though I often felt a charitable prompting to call at the place and see poor Bartleby, yet a certain squeamishness of I know not what withheld me.

All is over with him, by this time, thought I at last, when through another week no further intelligence reached me. But coming to my room the day after, I found several persons waiting at my door in a high state of nervous excitement.

"That's the man—here he comes," cried the foremost one, whom I recognized as the lawyer who had previously called upon me alone.

"You must take him away, sir, at once," cried a portly person among them, advancing upon me, and whom I knew to be the landlord of No. — Wall Street. "These gentlemen, my tenants, cannot stand it any longer; Mr. B——" pointing to the lawyer, "has turned him out of his room, and he now persists in haunting the building generally, sitting upon the banisters of the stairs by day, and sleeping in the entry by night. Everybody is concerned; clients are leaving the offices; some fears are entertained of a mob; something you must do, and that without delay."

Aghast at this torrent, I fell back before it, and would fain have locked myself in my new quarters. In vain I persisted that Bartleby was nothing to me—no more than to anyone else. In vain:—I was the last person known to have anything to do with him, and they held me to the terrible account. Fearful then of being exposed in the papers (as one person present obscurely threatened) I considered the matter, and at length said, that if the lawyer would give me a confidential interview with the scrivener, in his (the lawyer's) own room, I would that afternoon strive my best to rid them of the nuisance they complained of.

Going upstairs to my old haunt, there was Bartleby silently sitting upon the banister at the landing.

"What are you doing here, Bartleby?" said I.

"Sitting upon the banister," he mildly replied.

I motioned him into the lawyer's room, who then left us.

"Bartleby," said I, "are you aware that you are the cause of great tribulation to me, by persisting in occupying the entry after being dismissed from the office?"

No answer.

"Now one of two things must take place. Either you must do something, or something must be done to you. Now what sort of business would you like to engage in? Would you like to re-engage in copying for someone?"

"No; I would prefer not to make any change."

"Would you like a clerkship in a drygoods store?"

"There is too much confinement about that. No, I would not like a clerkship; but I am not particular."

"Too much confinement," I cried, "why you keep yourself confined all the time!"

"I would prefer not to take a clerkship," he rejoined, as if to settle that little item at once.

"How would a bartender's business suit you? There is no trying of the eyesight in that."

"I would not like it at all; though, as I said before, I am not particular."

His unwonted wordiness inspirited me. I returned to the charge.

"Well then, would you like to travel through the country collecting bills for the merchants? That would improve your health."

"No, I would prefer to be doing something else."

"How then would going as a companion to Europe, to entertain some young gentleman with your conversation,—how would that suit you?"

"Not at all. It does not strike me that there is anything definite about that. I like to be stationary. But I am not particular."

"Stationary you shall be then," I cried, now losing all patience, and for the first time in all my exasperating connection with him fairly flying into a passion. "If you do not go away from these premises before night, I shall feel bound—indeed I *am* bound—to—to—to quit the premises myself!" I rather absurdly concluded, knowing not with what possible threat to try to frighten his immobility into compliance. Despairing of all further efforts, I was precipitately leaving him, when a final thought occurred to me—one which had not been wholly unindulged before.

"Bartleby," said I, in the kindest tone I could assume under such exciting circumstances, "will you go home with me now—not to my office, but my dwelling—and remain there till we can conclude upon some convenient arrangement for you at our leisure? Come, let us start now, right away."

"No: at present I would prefer not to make any change at all."

I answered nothing; but effectually dodging everyone by the suddenness and rapidity of my flight, rushed from the building, ran up Wall Street toward Broadway, and jumping into the first omnibus was soon removed from pursuit. As soon as tranquillity returned I distinctly perceived that I had now done all that I possibly could, both in respect to the demands of the landlord and his tenants, and with regard to my own desire and sense of duty, to benefit Bartleby, and shield him

from rude persecution. I now strove to be entirely carefree and quiescent; and my conscience justified me in the attempt; though indeed it was not so successful as I could have wished. So fearful was I of being again hunted out by the incensed landlord and his exasperated tenants, that, surrendering my business to Nippers, for a few days I drove about the upper part of the town and through the suburbs, in my rockaway; crossed over to Jersey City and Hoboken, and paid fugitive visits to Manhattanville and Astoria. In fact I almost lived in my rockaway for the time.

When again I entered my office, lo, a note from the landlord lay upon the desk. I opened it with trembling hands. It informed me that the writer had sent to the police, and had Bartleby removed to the Tombs as a vagrant. Moreover, since I knew more about him than anyone else, he wished me to appear at that place, and make a suitable statement of the facts. These tidings had a conflicting effect upon me. At first I was indignant; but at last almost approved. The landlord's energetic, summary disposition had led him to adopt a procedure which I do not think I would have decided upon myself; and yet as a last resort, under such peculiar circumstances, it seemed the only plan.

As I afterwards learned, the poor scrivener, when told that he must be conducted to the Tombs, offered not the slightest obstacle, but in his pale unmoving way, silently acquiesced.

Some of the compassionate and curious bystanders joined the party; and headed by one of the constables arm in arm with Bartleby, the silent procession filed its way through all the noise, and heat, and joy of the roaring thoroughfares at noon.

The same day I received the note I went to the Tombs, or to speak more properly, the Halls of Justice. Seeking the right officer, I stated the purpose of my call, and was informed that the individual I described was indeed within. I then assured the functionary that Bartleby was a perfectly honest man, and greatly to be compassionated, however unaccountably eccentric. I narrated all I knew, and closed by suggesting the idea of letting him remain in as indulgent confinement as possible till something less harsh might be done—though indeed I hardly knew what. At all events, if nothing else could be decided upon, the alms-house must receive him. I then begged to have an interview.

Being under no disgraceful charge, and quite serene and harmless in all his ways, they had permitted him freely to wander about the prison, and especially in the inclosed grass-platted yards thereof. And so I found him there, standing all alone in the quietest of the yards, his face towards a high wall, while all around, from the narrow slits of the jail windows, I thought I saw peering out upon him the eyes of murderers and thieves.

"Bartleby!"

"I know you," he said, without looking round,—"and I want nothing to say to you."

"It was not I that brought you here, Bartleby," said I, keenly pained at his implied suspicion. "And to you, this should not be so vile a place. Nothing reproachful attaches to you by being here. And see, it is not so sad a place as one might think. Look, there is the sky, and here is the grass."

"I know where I am," he replied, but would say nothing more, and so I left him.

As I entered the corridor again, a broad meat-like man, in an apron,

accosted me, and jerking his thumb over his shoulder said—"Is that your friend?"

"Yes."

"Does he want to starve? If he does, let him live on the prison fare, that's all."

"Who are you?" asked I, not knowing what to make of such an un-officially-speaking person in such a place.

"I am the grub-man. Such gentlemen as have friends here, hire me to provide them with something good to eat."

"Is this so?" said I, turning to the turnkey.

He said it was.

"Well then," said I, slipping some silver into the grub-man's hands (for so they called him). "I want you to give particular attention to my friend there; let him have the best dinner you can get. And you must be as polite to him as possible."

"Introduce me, will you?" said the grub-man, looking at me with an expression which seemed to say he was all impatience for an oppor-tunity to give a specimen of his breeding.

Thinking it would prove of benefit to the scrivener, I acquiesced; and asking the grub-man his name, went up with him to Bartleby.

"Bartleby, this is Mr. Cutlets; you will find him very useful to you."

"Your sarvant, sir, your sarvant," said the grub-man, making a low salutation behind his apron. "Hope you find it pleasant here, sir;—spacious grounds—cool apartments, sir—hope you'll stay with us some time—try to make it agreeable. May Mrs. Cutlets and I have the pleas-ure of your company to dinner, sir, in Mrs. Cutlets' private room?"

"I prefer not to dine today," said Bartleby, turning away. "It would disagree with me; I am unused to dinners." So saying he slowly moved to the other side of the inclosure, and took up a position fronting the dead-wall.

"How's this?" said the grub-man, addressing me with a stare of astonishment. "He's odd, ain't he?"

"I think he is a little deranged," said I, sadly.

"Deranged? deranged is it? Well now, upon my word, I thought that friend of yourn was a gentleman forger; they are always pale and genteel-like, them forgers. I can't help pity 'em—can't help it, sir. Did you know Monroe Edwards?" he added touchingly, and paused. Then, laying his hand pityingly on my shoulder, sighed, "he died of con-sumption at Sing Sing. So you weren't acquainted with Monroe?"

"No, I was never socially aquainted with any forgers. But I cannot stop longer. Look to my friend yonder. You will not lose by it. I will see you again."

Some few days after this, I again obtained admission to the Tombs, and went through the corridors in quest of Bartleby; but without finding him.

"I saw him coming from his cell not long ago," said a turnkey, "may be he's gone to loiter in the yards."

So I went in that direction.

"Are you looking for the silent man?" said another turnkey passing me. "Yonder he lies—sleeping in the yard there. 'Tis not twenty minutes since I saw him lie down."

The yard was entirely quiet. It was not accessible to the common prisoners. The surrounding walls, of amazing thickness, kept off all sounds behind them. The Egyptian character of the masonry weighed

upon me with its gloom. But a soft imprisoned turf grew under foot. The heart of the eternal pyramids, it seemed, wherein, by some strange magic, through the clefts, grass seed, dropped by birds, had sprung.

Strangely huddled at the base of the wall, his knees drawn up, and lying on his side, his head touching the cold stones, I saw the wasted Bartleby. But nothing stirred. I paused; then went close up to him; stooped over, and saw that his dim eyes were open; otherwise he seemed profoundly sleeping. Something prompted me to touch him. I felt his hand, when a tingling shiver ran up my arm and down my spine to my feet.

The round face of the grub-man peered upon me now. "His dinner is ready. Won't he dine today, either? Or does he live without dining?"

"Lives without dining," said I, and closed the eyes.

"Eh!—He's asleep, ain't he?"

"With kings and counsellors,"[4] murmured I.

There would seem little need for proceeding further in this history. Imagination will readily supply the meager recital of poor Bartleby's interment. But ere parting with the reader, let me say, that if this little narrative has sufficiently interested him, to awaken curiosity as to who Bartleby was, and what manner of life he led prior to the present narrator's making his acquaintance, I can only reply, that in such curiosity I fully share, but am wholly unable to gratify it. Yet here I hardly know whether I should divulge one little item of rumor, which came to my ear a few months after the scrivener's decease. Upon what basis it rested, I could never ascertain; and hence, how true it is I cannot now tell. But inasmuch as this vague report has not been without a certain strange suggestive interest to me, however sad, it may prove the same with some others; and so I will briefly mention it. The report was this: that Bartleby had been a subordinate clerk in the Dead Letter Office at Washington, from which he had been suddenly removed by a change in the administration. When I think over this rumor, I cannot adequately express the emotions which seize me. Dead letters! does it not sound like dead men? Conceive a man by nature and misfortune prone to a pallid hopelessness, can any business seem more fitted to heighten it than that of continually handling these dead letters, and assorting them for the flames? For by the cartload they are annually burned. Sometimes from out the folded paper the pale clerk takes a ring:—the finger it was meant for, perhaps, molders in the grave; a banknote sent in swiftest charity:—he whom it would relieve, nor eats nor hungers any more; pardon for those who died despairing; hope for those who died unhoping; good tidings for those who died stifled by unrelieved calamities. On errands of life, these letters speed to death.

Ah Bartleby! Ah humanity!

p. 1853

---

4. I.e., dead. See *Job* 3:13–14: ". . . then had I been at rest, With kings and counsellors of the earth, which built desolate places for themselves."

JAMES BALDWIN

Sonny's Blues

I read about it in the paper, in the subway, on my way to work. I read it, and I couldn't believe it, and I read it again. Then perhaps I just stared at it, at the newsprint spelling out his name, spelling out the story. I stared at it in the swinging lights of the subway car, and in the faces and bodies of the people, and in my own face, trapped in the darkness which roared outside.

It was not to be believed and I kept telling myself that, as I walked from the subway station to the high school. And at the same time I couldn't doubt it. I was scared, scared for Sonny. He became real to me again. A great block of ice got settled in my belly and kept melting there slowly all day long, while I taught my classes algebra. It was a special kind of ice. It kept melting, sending trickles of ice water all up and down my veins, but it never got less. Sometimes it hardened and seemed to expand until I felt my guts were going to come spilling out or that I was going to choke or scream. This would always be at a moment when I was remembering some specific thing Sonny had once said or done.

When he was about as old as the boys in my classes his face had been bright and open, there was a lot of copper in it; and he'd had wonderfully direct brown eyes, and great gentleness and privacy. I wondered what he looked like now. He had been picked up, the evening before, in a raid on an apartment downtown, for peddling and using heroin.

I couldn't believe it: but what I mean by that is that I couldn't find any room for it anywhere inside me. I had kept it outside me for a long time. I hadn't wanted to know. I had had suspicions, but I didn't name them, I kept putting them away. I told myself that Sonny was wild, but he wasn't crazy. And he'd always been a good boy, he hadn't ever turned hard or evil or disrespectful, the way kids can, so quick, so quick, especially in Harlem. I didn't want to believe that I'd ever see my brother going down, coming to nothing, all that light in his face gone out, in the condition I'd already seen so many others. Yet it had happened and here I was, talking about algebra to a lot of boys who might, every one of them for all I knew, be popping off needles every time they went to the head.[1] Maybe it did more for them than algebra could.

I was sure that the first time Sonny had ever had horse,[2] he couldn't have been much older than these boys were now. These boys, now, were living as we'd been living then, they were growing up with a rush and their heads bumped abruptly against the low ceiling of their actual possibilities. They were filled with rage. All they really knew were two darknesses, the darkness of their lives, which was now closing in on them, and the darkness of the movies, which had blinded them to that other darkness, and in which they now, vindictively, dreamed, at once more together than they were at any other time, and more alone.

When the last bell rang, the last class ended, I let out my breath. It seemed I'd been holding it for all that time. My clothes were wet—I may have looked as though I'd been sitting in a steam bath, all dressed

---

1. Lavatory.   2. Heroin.

up, all afternoon. I sat alone in the classroom a long time. I listened to the boys outside, downstairs, shouting and cursing and laughing. Their laughter struck me for perhaps the first time. It was not the joyous laughter which—God knows why—one associates with children. It was mocking and insular, its intent was to denigrate. It was disenchanted, and in this, also, lay the authority of their curses. Perhaps I was listening to them because I was thinking about my brother and in them I heard my brother. And myself.

One boy was whistling a tune, at once very complicated and very simple, it seemed to be pouring out of him as though he were a bird, and it sounded very cool and moving through all that harsh, bright air, only just holding its own through all those other sounds.

I stood up and walked over to the window and looked down into the courtyard. It was the beginning of the spring and the sap was rising in the boys. A teacher passed through them every now and again, quickly, as though he or she couldn't wait to get out of that courtyard, to get those boys out of their sight and off their minds. I started collecting my stuff. I thought I'd better get home and talk to Isabel.

The courtyard was almost deserted by the time I got downstairs. I saw this boy standing in the shadow of a doorway, looking just like Sonny. I almost called his name. Then I saw that it wasn't Sonny, but somebody we used to know, a boy from around our block. He'd been Sonny's friend. He'd never been mine, having been too young for me, and, anyway, I'd never liked him. And now, even though he was a grown-up man, he still hung around that block, still spent hours on the street corners, was always high and raggy. I used to run into him from time to time and he'd often work around to asking me for a quarter or fifty cents. He always had some real good excuse, too, and I always gave it to him, I don't know why.

But now, abruptly, I hated him. I couldn't stand the way he looked at me, partly like a dog, partly like a cunning child. I wanted to ask him what the hell he was doing in the school courtyard.

He sort of shuffled over to me, and he said, "I see you got the papers. So you already know about it."

"You mean about Sonny? Yes, I already know about it. How come they didn't get you?"

He grinned. It made him repulsive and it also brought to mind what he'd looked like as a kid. "I wasn't there. I stay away from them people."

"Good for you." I offered him a cigarette and I watched him through the smoke. "You come all the way down here just to tell me about Sonny?"

"That's right." He was sort of shaking his head and his eyes looked strange, as though they were about to cross. The bright sun deadened his damp dark brown skin and it made his eyes look yellow and showed up the dirt in his kinked hair. He smelled funky.[3] I moved a little away from him and I said, "Well, thanks. But I already know about it and I got to get home."

"I'll walk you a little ways," he said. We started walking. There were a couple of kids still loitering in the courtyard and one of them said goodnight to me and looked strangely at the boy beside me.

"What're you going to do?" he asked me. "I mean, about Sonny?"

"Look. I haven't seen Sonny for over a year. I'm not sure I'm going to do anything. Anyway, what the hell *can* I do?"

3. Obnoxious.

"That's right," he said quickly, "ain't nothing you can do. Can't much help old Sonny no more, I guess."

It was what I was thinking and so it seemed to me he had no right to say it.

"I'm surprised at Sonny, though," he went on—he had a funny way of talking, he looked straight ahead as though he were talking to himself—"I thought Sonny was a smart boy, I thought he was too smart to get hung."

"I guess he thought so too," I said sharply, "and that's how he got hung. And how about you? You're pretty goddamn smart, I bet."

Then he looked directly at me, just for a minute. "I ain't smart," he said. "If I was smart, I'd have reached for a pistol a long time ago."

"Look. Don't tell *me* your sad story, if it was up to me, I'd give you one." Then I felt guilty—guilty, probably, for never having supposed that the poor bastard *had* a story of his own, much less a sad one, and I asked, quickly, "What's going to happen to him now?"

He didn't answer this. He was off by himself some place.

"Funny thing," he said, and from his tone we might have been discussing the quickest way to get to Brooklyn, "when I saw the papers this morning, the first thing I asked myself was if I had anything to do with it. I felt sort of responsible."

I began to listen more carefully. The subway station was on the corner, just before us, and I stopped. He stopped, too. We were in front of a bar and he ducked slightly, peering in, but whoever he was looking for didn't seem to be there. The juke box was blasting away with something black and bouncy and I half watched the barmaid as she danced her way from the juke box to her place behind the bar. And I watched her face as she laughingly responded to something someone said to her, still keeping time to the music. When she smiled one saw the little girl, one sensed the doomed, still-struggling woman beneath the battered face of the semi-whore.

"I never *give* Sonny nothing," the boy said finally, "but a long time ago I come to school high and Sonny asked me how it felt." He paused, I couldn't bear to watch him, I watched the barmaid, and I listened to the music which seemed to be causing the pavement to shake. "I told him it felt great." The music stopped, the barmaid paused and watched the juke box until the music began again. "It did."

All this was carrying me some place I didn't want to go. I certainly didn't want to know how it felt. It filled everything, the people, the houses, the music, the dark, quicksilver barmaid, with menace; and this menace was their reality.

"What's going to happen to him now?" I asked again.

"They'll send him away some place and they'll try to cure him." He shook his head. "Maybe he'll even think he's kicked the habit. Then they'll let him loose"—he gestured, throwing his cigarette into the gutter. "That's all."

"What do you mean, that's *all*?"

But I knew what he meant.

"I *mean*, that's *all*." He turned his head and looked at me, pulling down the corners of his mouth. "Don't you know what I mean?" he asked, softly.

"How the hell *would* I know what you mean?" I almost whispered it, I don't know why.

"That's right," he said to the air, "how would *he* know what I mean?"

He turned toward me again, patient and calm, and yet I somehow felt him shaking, shaking as though he were going to fall apart. I felt that ice in my guts again, the dread I'd felt all afternoon; and again I watched the barmaid, moving about the bar, washing glasses, and singing. "Listen. They'll let him out and then it'll just start all over again. That's what I mean."

"You mean—they'll let him out. And then he'll just start working his way back in again. You mean he'll never kick the habit. Is that what you mean?"

"That's right," he said, cheerfully. "*You* see what I mean."

"Tell me," I said at last, "why does he want to die? He must want to die, he's killing himself, why does he want to die?"

He looked at me in surprise. He licked his lips. "He don't want to die. He wants to live. Don't nobody want to die, ever."

Then I wanted to ask him—too many things. He could not have answered, or if he had, I could not have borne the answers. I started walking. "Well, I guess it's none of my business."

"It's going to be rough on old Sonny," he said. We reached the subway station. "This is your station?" he asked. I nodded. I took one step down. "Damn!" he said, suddenly. I looked up at him. He grinned again. "Damn it if I didn't leave all my money home. You ain't got a dollar on you, have you? Just for a couple of days, is all."

All at once something inside gave and threatened to come pouring out of me. I didn't hate him any more. I felt that in another moment I'd start crying like a child.

"Sure," I said. "Don't sweat." I looked in my wallet and didn't have a dollar, I only had a five. "Here," I said. "That hold you?"

He didn't look at it—he didn't want to look at it. A terrible, closed look came over his face, as though he were keeping the number on the bill a secret from him and me. "Thanks," he said, and now he was dying to see me go. "Don't worry about Sonny. Maybe I'll write him or something."

"Sure," I said. "You do that. So long."

"Be seeing you," he said. I went on down the steps.

And I didn't write Sonny or send him anything for a long time. When I finally did, it was just after my little girl died, he wrote me back a letter which made me feel like a bastard.

Here's what he said:

Dear brother,

You don't know how much I needed to hear from you. I wanted to write you many a time but I dug how much I must have hurt you and so I didn't write. But now I feel like a man who's been trying to climb up out of some deep, real deep and funky hole and just saw the sun up there, outside. I got to get outside.

I can't tell you much about how I got here. I mean I don't know how to tell you. I guess I was afraid of something or I was trying to escape from something and you know I have never been very strong in the head (smile). I'm glad Mama and Daddy are dead and can't see what's happened to their son and I swear if I'd known what I was doing I would never have hurt you so, you and a lot of other fine people who were nice to me and who believed in me.

I don't want you to think it had anything to do with me being a

musician. It's more than that. Or maybe less than that. I can't get anything straight in my head down here and I try not to think about what's going to happen to me when I get outside again. Sometime I think I'm going to flip and *never* get outside and sometime I think I'll come straight back. I tell you one thing, though, I'd rather blow my brains out than go through this again. But that's what they all say, so they tell me. If I tell you when I'm coming to New York and if you could meet me, I sure would appreciate it. Give my love to Isabel and the kids and I was sure sorry to hear about little Gracie. I wish I could be like Mama and say the Lord's will be done, but I don't know it seems to me that trouble is the one thing that never does get stopped and I don't know what good it does to blame it on the Lord. But maybe it does some good if you believe it.

Your brother,
Sonny

Then I kept in constant touch with him and I sent him whatever I could and I went to meet him when he came back to New York. When I saw him many things I thought I had forgotten came flooding back to me. This was because I had begun, finally, to wonder about Sonny, about the life that Sonny lived inside. This life, whatever it was, had made him older and thinner and it had deepened the distant stillness in which he had always moved. He looked very unlike my baby brother. Yet, when he smiled, when we shook hands, the baby brother I'd never known looked out from the depths of his private life, like an animal waiting to be coaxed into the light.

"How you been keeping?" he asked me.

"All right. And you?"

"Just fine." He was smiling all over his face. "It's good to see you again."

"It's good to see you."

The seven years' difference in our ages lay between us like a chasm: I wondered if these years would ever operate between us as a bridge. I was remembering, and it made it hard to catch my breath, that I had been there when he was born; and I had heard the first words he had ever spoken. When he started to walk, he walked from our mother straight to me. I caught him just before he fell when he took the first steps he ever took in this world.

"How's Isabel?"

"Just fine. She's dying to see you."

"And the boys?"

"They're fine, too. They're anxious to see their uncle."

"Oh, come on. You know they don't remember me."

"Are you kidding? Of course they remember you."

He grinned again. We got into a taxi. We had a lot to say to each other, far too much to know how to begin.

As the taxi began to move, I asked, "You still want to go to India?"

He laughed. "You still remember that. Hell, no. This place is Indian enough for me."

"It used to belong to them," I said.

And he laughed again. "They damn sure knew what they were doing when they got rid of it."

Years ago, when he was around fourteen, he'd been all hipped on the idea of going to India. He read books about people sitting on rocks,

naked, in all kinds of weather, but mostly bad, naturally, and walking barefoot through hot coals and arriving at wisdom. I used to say that it sounded to me as though they were getting away from wisdom as fast as they could. I think he sort of looked down on me for that.

"Do you mind," he asked, "if we have the driver drive alongside the park? On the west side—I haven't seen the city in so long."

"Of course not," I said. I was afraid that I might sound as though I were humoring him, but I hoped he wouldn't take it that way.

So we drove along, between the green of the park and the stony, lifeless elegance of hotels and apartment buildings, toward the vivid, killing streets of our childhood. These streets hadn't changed, though housing projects jutted up out of them now like rocks in the middle of a boiling sea. Most of the houses in which we had grown up had vanished, as had the stores from which we had stolen, the basements in which we had first tried sex, the rooftops from which we had hurled tin cans and bricks. But houses exactly like the houses of our past yet dominated the landscape, boys exactly like the boys we once had been found themselves smothering in these houses, came down into the streets for light and air and found themselves encircled by disaster. Some escaped the trap, most didn't. Those who got out always left something of themselves behind, as some animals amputate a leg and leave it in the trap. It might be said, perhaps, that I had escaped, after all, I was a school teacher; or that Sonny had, he hadn't lived in Harlem for years. Yet, as the cab moved uptown through streets which seemed, with a rush, to darken with dark people, and as I covertly studied Sonny's face, it came to me that what we both were seeking through our separate cab windows was that part of ourselves which had been left behind. It's always at the hour of trouble and confrontation that the missing member aches.

We hit 110th Street and started rolling up Lenox Avenue. And I'd known this avenue all my life, but it seemed to me again, as it had seemed on the day I'd first heard about Sonny's trouble, filled with a hidden menace which was its very breath of life.

"We almost there," said Sonny.

"Almost." We were both too nervous to say anything more.

We live in a housing project. It hasn't been up long. A few days after it was up it seemed uninhabitably new, now, of course, it's already rundown. It looks like a parody of the good, clean, faceless life—God knows the people who live in it do their best to make it a parody. The beat-looking grass lying around isn't enough to make their lives green, the hedges will never hold out the streets, and they know it. The big windows fool no one, they aren't big enough to make space out of no space. They don't bother with the windows, they watch the TV screen instead. The playground is most popular with the children who don't play at jacks, or skip rope, or roller skate, or swing, and they can be found in it after dark. We moved in partly because it's not too far from where I teach, and partly for the kids; but it's really just like the houses in which Sonny and I grew up. The same things happen, they'll have the same things to remember. The moment Sonny and I started into the house I had the feeling that I was simply bringing him back into the danger he had almost died trying to escape.

Sonny has never been talkative. So I don't know why I was sure he'd be dying to talk to me when supper was over the first night. Everything went fine, the oldest boy remembered him, and the young-

est boy liked him, and Sonny had remembered to bring something for each of them; and Isabel, who is really much nicer than I am, more open and giving, had gone to a lot of trouble about dinner and was genuinely glad to see him. And she's always been able to tease Sonny in a way that I haven't. It was nice to see her face so vivid again and to hear her laugh and watch her make Sonny laugh. She wasn't, or, anyway, she didn't seem to be, at all uneasy or embarrassed. She chatted as though there were no subject which had to be avoided and she got Sonny past his first, faint stiffness. And thank God she was there, for I was filled with that icy dread again. Everything I did seemed awkward to me, and everything I said sounded freighted with hidden meaning. I was trying to remember everything I'd heard about dope addiction and I couldn't help watching Sonny for signs. I wasn't doing it out of malice. I was trying to find out something about my brother. I was dying to hear him tell me he was safe.

"Safe!" my father grunted, whenever Mama suggested trying to move to a neighborhood which might be safer for children. "Safe, hell! Ain't no place safe for kids, nor nobody."

He always went on like this, but he wasn't, ever, really as bad as he sounded, not even on weekends, when he got drunk. As a matter of fact, he was always on the lookout for "something a little better," but he died before he found it. He died suddenly, during a drunken weekend in the middle of the war, when Sonny was fifteen. He and Sonny hadn't ever got on too well. And this was partly because Sonny was the apple of his father's eye. It was because he loved Sonny so much and was frightened for him, that he was always fighting with him. It doesn't do any good to fight with Sonny. Sonny just moves back, inside himself, where he can't be reached. But the principal reason that they never hit it off is that they were so much alike. Daddy was big and rough and loud-talking, just the opposite of Sonny, but they both had—that same privacy.

Mama tried to tell me something about this, just after Daddy died. I was home on leave from the army.

This was the last time I ever saw my mother alive. Just the same, this picture gets all mixed up in my mind with pictures I had of her when she was younger. The way I always see her is the way she used to be on a Sunday afternoon, say, when the old folks were talking after the big Sunday dinner. I always see her wearing pale blue. She'd be sitting on the sofa. And my father would be sitting in the easy chair, not far from her. And the living room would be full of church folks and relatives. There they sit, in chairs all around the living room, and the night is creeping up outside, but nobody knows it yet. You can see the darkness growing against the windowpanes and you hear the street noises every now and again, or maybe the jangling beat of a tambourine from one of the churches close by, but it's real quiet in the room. For a moment nobody's talking, but every face looks darkening, like the sky outside. And my mother rocks a little from the waist, and my father's eyes are closed. Everyone is looking at something a child can't see. For a minute they've forgotten the children. Maybe a kid is lying on the rug, half asleep. Maybe somebody's got a kid in his lap and is absent-mindedly stroking the kid's head. Maybe there's a kid, quiet and big-eyed, curled up in a big chair in the corner. The silence, the darkness coming, and the darkness in the faces frighten the child

obscurely. He hopes that the hand which strokes his forehead will never stop—will never die. He hopes that there will never come a time when the old folks won't be sitting around the living room, talking about where they've come from, and what they've seen, and what's happened to them and their kinfolk.

But something deep and watchful in the child knows that this is bound to end, is already ending. In a moment someone will get up and turn on the light. Then the old folks will remember the children and they won't talk any more that day. And when light fills the room, the child is filled with darkness. He knows that every time this happens he's moved just a little closer to that darkness outside. The darkness outside is what the old folks have been talking about. It's what they've come from. It's what they endure. The child knows that they won't talk any more because if he knows too much about what's happened to *them,* he'll know too much too soon, about what's going to happen to *him.*

The last time I talked to my mother, I remember I was restless. I wanted to get out and see Isabel. We weren't married then and we had a lot to straighten out between us.

There Mama sat, in black, by the window. She was humming an old church song, *Lord, you brought me from a long ways off.* Sonny was out somewhere. Mama kept watching the streets.

"I don't know," she said, "if I'll ever see you again, after you go off from here. But I hope you'll remember the things I tried to teach you."

"Don't talk like that," I said, and smiled. "You'll be here a long time yet."

She smiled, too, but she said nothing. She was quiet for a long time. And I said, "Mama, don't you worry about nothing. I'll be writing all the time, and you be getting the checks. . . ."

"I want to talk to you about your brother," she said, suddenly. "If anything happens to me he ain't going to have nobody to look out for him."

"Mama," I said, "ain't nothing going to happen to you *or* Sonny. Sonny's all right. He's a good boy and he's got good sense."

"It ain't a question of his being a good boy," Mama said, "nor of his having good sense. It ain't only the bad ones, nor yet the dumb ones that gets sucked under." She stopped, looking at me. "Your Daddy once had a brother," she said, and she smiled in a way that made me feel she was in pain. "You didn't never know that, did you?"

"No," I said, "I never knew that," and I watched her face.

"Oh, yes," she said, "your Daddy had a brother." She looked out of the window again. "I know you never saw your Daddy cry. But *I* did —many a time, through all these years."

I asked her, "What happened to his brother? How come nobody's ever talked about him?"

This was the first time I ever saw my mother look old.

"His brother got killed," she said, "when he was just a little younger than you are now. I knew him. He was a fine boy. He was maybe a little full of the devil, but he didn't mean nobody no harm."

Then she stopped and the room was silent, exactly as it had sometimes been on those Sunday afternoons. Mama kept looking out into the streets.

"He used to have a job in the mill," she said, "and, like all young folks, he just liked to perform on Saturday nights. Saturday nights, him and your father would drift around to different place, go to dances and

things like that, or just sit around with people they knew, and your father's brother would sing, he had a fine voice, and play along with himself on his guitar. Well, this particular Saturday night, him and your father was coming home from some place, and they were both a little drunk and there was a moon that night, it was bright like day. Your father's brother was feeling kind of good, and he was whistling to himself, and he had his guitar slung over his shoulder. They was coming down a hill and beneath them was a road that turned off from the highway. Well, your father's brother, being always kind of frisky, decided to run down this hill, and he did, with that guitar banging and clanging behind him, and he ran across the road, and he was making water behind a tree. And your father was sort of amused at him and he was still coming down the hill, kind of slow. Then he heard a car motor and that same minute his brother stepped from behind the tree, into the road, in the moonlight. And he started to cross the road. And your father started to run down the hill, he says he don't know why. This car was full of white men. They was all drunk, and when they seen your father's brother they let out a great whoop and holler and they aimed the car straight at him. They was having fun, they just wanted to scare him, the way they do sometimes, you know. But they was drunk. And I guess the boy, being drunk, too, and scared, kind of lost his head. By the time he jumped it was too late. Your father says he heard his brother scream when the car rolled over him, and he heard the wood of that guitar when it give, and he heard them strings go flying, and he heard them white men shouting, and the car kept on a-going and it ain't stopped till this day. And, time your father got down the hill, his brother weren't nothing but blood and pulp."

Tears were gleaming on my mother's face. There wasn't anything I could say.

"He never mentioned it," she said, "because I never let him mention it before you children. Your Daddy was like a crazy man that night and for many a night thereafter. He says he never in his life seen anything as dark as that road after the lights of that car had gone away. Weren't nothing, weren't nobody on that road, just your Daddy and his brother and that busted guitar. Oh, yes. Your Daddy never did really get right again. Till the day he died he weren't sure but that every white man he saw was the man that killed his brother."

She stopped and took out her handkerchief and dried her eyes and looked at me.

"I ain't telling you all this," she said, "to make you scared or bitter or to make you hate nobody. I'm telling you this because you got a brother. And the world ain't changed."

I guess I didn't want to believe this. I guess she saw this in my face. She turned away from me, toward the window again, searching those streets.

"But I praise my Redeemer," she said at last, "that He called your Daddy home before me. I ain't saying it to throw no flowers at myself, but, I declare, it keeps me from feeling too cast down to know I helped your father get safely through this world. Your father always acted like he was the roughest, strongest man on earth. And everybody took him to be like that. But if he hadn't had *me* there—to see his tears!"

She was crying again. Still, I couldn't move. I said, "Lord, Lord, Mama, I didn't know it was like that."

"Oh, honey," she said, "there's a lot that you don't know. But you

are going to find out." She stood up from the window and came over to me. "You got to hold on to your brother," she said, "and don't let him fall, no matter what it looks like is happening to him and no matter how evil you gets with him. You going to be evil with him many a time. But don't you forget what I told you, you hear?"

"I won't forget," I said. "Don't you worry, I won't forget. I won't let nothing happen to Sonny."

My mother smiled as though she were amused at something she saw in my face. Then, "You may not be able to stop nothing from happening. But you got to let him know you's *there*."

Two days later I was married, and then I was gone. And I had a lot of things on my mind and I pretty well forgot my promise to Mama until I got shipped home on a special furlough for her funeral.

And, after the funeral, with just Sonny and me alone in the empty kitchen, I tried to find out something about him.

"What do you want to do?" I asked him.

"I'm going to be a musician," he said.

For he had graduated, in the time I had been away, from dancing to the juke box to finding out who was playing what, and what they were doing with it, and he had bought himself a set of drums.

"You mean, you want to be a drummer?" I somehow had the feeling that being a drummer might be all right for other people but not for my brother Sonny.

"I don't think," he said, looking at me very gravely, "that I'll ever be a good drummer. But I think I can play a piano."

I frowned. I'd never played the role of the older brother quite so seriously before, had scarcely ever, in fact, *asked* Sonny a damn thing. I sensed myself in the presence of something I didn't really know how to handle, didn't understand. So I made my frown a little deeper as I asked: "What kind of musician do you want to be?"

He grinned. "How many kinds do you think there are?"

"Be *serious*," I said.

He laughed, throwing his head back, and then looked at me. "I *am* serious."

"Well, then, for Christ's sake, stop kidding around and answer a serious question. I mean, do you want to be a concert pianist, you want to play classical music and all that, or—or what?" Long before I finished he was laughing again. "For Christ's *sake*, Sonny!"

He sobered, but with difficulty. "I'm sorry. But you sound so— *scared!*" and he was off again.

"Well, you may think it's funny now, baby, but it's not going to be so funny when you have to make your living at it, let me tell you *that*." I was furious because I knew he was laughing at me and I didn't know why.

"No," he said, very sober now, and afraid, perhaps, that he'd hurt me, "I don't want to be a classical pianist. That isn't what interests me. I mean"—he paused, looking hard at me, as though his eyes would help me to understand, and then gestured helplessly, as though perhaps his hand would help—"I mean, I'll have a lot of studying to do, and I'll have to study *everything*, but, I mean, I want to play *with*—jazz musicians." He stopped. "I want to play jazz," he said.

Well, the word had never before sounded as heavy, as real, as it sounded that afternoon in Sonny's mouth. I just looked at him and I

was probably frowning a real frown by this time. I simply couldn't see why on earth he'd want to spend his time hanging around nightclubs, clowning around on bandstands, while people pushed each other around a dance floor. It seemed—beneath him, somehow. I had never thought about it before, had never been forced to, but I suppose I had always put jazz musicians in a class with what Daddy called "good-time people."

"Are you *serious?*"

"Hell, *yes*, I'm serious."

He looked more helpless than ever, and annoyed, and deeply hurt.

I suggested, helpfully: "You mean—like Louis Armstrong?"

His face closed as though I'd struck him. "No. I'm not talking about none of that old-time, down home crap."

"Well, look, Sonny, I'm sorry, don't get mad. I just don't altogether get it, that's all. Name somebody—you know, a jazz musician you admire."

"Bird."

"Who?"

"Bird! Charlie Parker![4] Don't they teach you nothing in the god-damn army?"

I lit a cigarette. I was surprised and then a little amused to discover that I was trembling. "I've been out of touch," I said. "You'll have to be patient with me. Now. Who's this Parker character?"

"He's just one of the greatest jazz musicians alive," said Sonny, sullenly, his hands in his pockets, his back to me. "Maybe *the* greatest," he added, bitterly, "that's probably why *you* never heard of him."

"All right," I said, "I'm ignorant. I'm sorry. I'll go out and buy all the cat's records right away, all right?"

"It don't," said Sonny, with dignity, "make any difference to me. I don't care what you listen to. Don't do me no favors."

I was beginning to realize that I'd never seen him so upset before. With another part of my mind I was thinking that this would probably turn out to be one of those things kids go through and that I shouldn't make it seem important by pushing it too hard. Still, I didn't think it would do any harm to ask: "Doesn't all this take a lot of time? Can you make a living at it?"

He turned back to me and half leaned, half sat, on the kitchen table. "Everything takes time," he said, "and—well, yes, sure, I can make a living at it. But what I don't seem to be able to make you understand is that it's the only thing I want to do."

"Well, Sonny," I said, gently, "you know people can't always do exactly what they *want* to do—"

"*No*, I don't know that," said Sonny, surprising me. "I think people *ought* to do what they want to do, what else are they alive for?"

"You getting to be a big boy," I said desperately, "it's time you started thinking about your future."

"I'm thinking about my future," said Sonny, grimly. "I think about it all the time."

I gave up. I decided, if he didn't change his mind, that we could always talk about it later. "In the meantime," I said, "you got to finish school." We had already decided that he'd have to move in with

4. Charlie ("Bird") Parker (1920–1955); for whom Birdland in New York was named, perhaps the greatest saxophonist and innovator of jazz; cofounder, with Dizzy Gillespie, of the new jazz, once called "bebop"; narcotics addict.

Isabel and her folks. I knew this wasn't the ideal arrangement because Isabel's folks are inclined to be dicty[5] and they hadn't especially wanted Isabel to marry me. But I didn't know what else to do. "And we have to get you fixed up at Isabel's."

There was a long silence. He moved from the kitchen table to the window. "That's a terrible idea. You know it yourself."

"Do you have a *better* idea?"

He just walked up and down the kitchen for a minute. He was as tall as I was. He had started to shave. I suddenly had the feeling that I didn't know him at all.

He stopped at the kitchen table and picked up my cigarettes. Looking at me with a kind of mocking, amused defiance, he put one between his lips. "You mind?"

"You smoking already?"

He lit the cigarette and nodded, watching me through the smoke. "I just wanted to see if I'd have the courage to smoke in front of you." He grinned and blew a great cloud of smoke to the ceiling. "It was easy." He looked at my face. "Come on, now. I bet you was smoking at my age, tell the truth."

I didn't say anything but the truth was on my face, and he laughed. But now there was something very strained in his laugh. "Sure. And I bet that ain't all you was doing."

He was frightening me a little. "Cut the crap," I said. "We already decided that you was going to go and live at Isabel's. Now what's got into you all of a sudden?"

"*You* decided it," he pointed out. "*I* didn't decide nothing." He stopped in front of me, leaning against the stove, arms loosely folded. "Look, brother. I don't want to stay in Harlem no more, I really don't." He was very earnest. He looked at me, then over toward the kitchen window. There was something in his eyes I'd never seen before, some thoughtfulness, some worry all his own. He rubbed the muscle of one arm. "It's time I was getting out of here."

"Where do you want to *go*, Sonny?"

"I want to join the army. Or the navy, I don't care. If I say I'm old enough, they'll believe me."

Then I got mad. It was because I was so scared. "You must be crazy. You goddamn fool, what the hell do you want to go and join the *army* for?"

"I just told you. To get out of Harlem."

"Sonny, you haven't even finished *school*. And if you really want to be a musician, how do you expect to study if you're in the *army*?"

He looked at me, trapped, and in anguish. "There's ways. I might be able to work out some kind of deal. Anyway, I'll have the G.I. Bill when I come out."

"*If* you come out." We stared at each other. "Sonny, please. Be reasonable. I know the setup is far from perfect. But we got to do the best we can."

"I ain't learning nothing in school," he said. "Even when I go." He turned away from me and opened the window and threw his cigarette out into the narrow alley. I watched his back. "At least, I ain't learning nothing you'd want me to learn." He slammed the window so hard I thought the glass would fly out, and turned back to me. "And I'm sick of the stink of these garbage cans!"

5. Snobbish, bossy.

"Sonny," I said, "I know how you feel. But if you don't finish school now, you're going to be sorry later that you didn't." I grabbed him by the shoulders. "And you only got another year. It ain't so bad. And I'll come back and I swear I'll help you do *whatever* you want to do. Just try to put up with it till I come back. Will you please do that? For me?"

He didn't answer and he wouldn't look at me.

"Sonny. You hear me?"

He pulled away. "I hear you. But you never hear anything *I* say."

I didn't know what to say to that. He looked out of the window and then back at me. "OK," he said, and sighed. "I'll try."

Then I said, trying to cheer him up a little, "They got a piano at Isabel's. You can practice on it."

And as a matter of fact, it did cheer him up for a minute. "That's right," he said to himself. "I forgot that." His face relaxed a little. But the worry, the thoughtfulness, played on it still, the way shadows play on a face which is staring into the fire.

But I thought I'd never hear the end of that piano. At first, Isabel would write me, saying how nice it was that Sonny was so serious about his music and how, as soon as he came in from school, or wherever he had been when he was supposed to be at school, he went straight to that piano and stayed there until suppertime. And, after supper, he went back to that piano and stayed there until everybody went to bed. He was at the piano all day Saturday and all day Sunday. Then he bought a record player and started playing records. He'd play one record over and over again, all day long sometimes, and he'd improvise along with it on the piano. Or he'd play one section of the record, one chord, one change, one progression, then he'd do it on the piano. Then back to the record. Then back to the piano.

Well, I really don't know how they stood it. Isabel finally confessed that it wasn't like living with a person at all, it was like living with sound. And the sound didn't make any sense to her, didn't make any sense to any of them—naturally. They began, in a way, to be afflicted by this presence that was living in their home. It was as though Sonny were some sort of god, or monster. He moved in an atmosphere which wasn't like theirs at all. They fed him and he ate, he washed himself, he walked in and out of their door; he certainly wasn't nasty or unpleasant or rude, Sonny isn't any of those things; but it was as though he were all wrapped up in some cloud, some fire, some vision all his own; and there wasn't any way to reach him.

At the same time, he wasn't really a man yet, he was still a child, and they had to watch out for him in all kinds of ways. They certainly couldn't throw him out. Neither did they dare to make a great scene about that piano because even they dimly sensed, as I sensed, from so many thousands of miles away, that Sonny was at that piano playing for his life.

But he hadn't been going to school. One day a letter came from the school board and Isabel's mother got it—there had, apparently, been other letters but Sonny had torn them up. This day, when Sonny came in, Isabel's mother showed him the letter and asked where he'd been spending his time. And she finally got it out of him that he'd been down in Greenwich Village, with musicians and other characters, in a white girl's apartment. And this scared her and she started to scream at him and what came up, once she began—though she denies it to this

day—was what sacrifices they were making to give Sonny a decent home and how little he appreciated it.

Sonny didn't play the piano that day. By evening, Isabel's mother had calmed down but then there was the old man to deal with, and Isabel herself. Isabel says she did her best to be calm but she broke down and started crying. She says she just watched Sonny's face. She could tell, by watching him, what was happening with him. And what was happening was that they penetrated his cloud, they had reached him. Even if their fingers had been a thousand times more gentle than human fingers ever are, he could hardly help feeling that they had stripped him naked and were spitting on that nakedness. For he also had to see that his presence, that music, which was life or death to him, had been torture for them and that they had endured it, not at all for his sake, but only for mine. And Sonny couldn't take that. He can take it a little better today than he could then but he's still not very good at it and, frankly, I don't know anybody who is.

The silence of the next few days must have been louder than the sound of all the music ever played since time began. One morning, before she went to work, Isabel was in his room for something and she suddenly realized that all of his records were gone. And she knew for certain that he was gone. And he was. He went as far as the navy would carry him. He finally sent me a postcard from some place in Greece and that was the first I knew that Sonny was still alive. I didn't see him any more until we were both back in New York and the war had long been over.

He was a man by then, of course, but I wasn't willing to see it. He came by the house from time to time, but we fought almost every time we met. I didn't like the way he carried himself, loose and dreamlike all the time, and I didn't like his friends, and his music seemed to be merely an excuse for the life he led. It sounded just that weird and disordered.

Then we had a fight, a pretty awful fight, and I didn't see him for months. By and by I looked him up, where he was living, in a furnished room in the Village, and I tried to make it up. But there were lots of other people in the room and Sonny just lay on his bed, and he wouldn't come downstairs with me, and he treated these other people as though they were his family and I weren't. So I got mad and then he got mad, and then I told him that he might just as well be dead as live the way he was living. Then he stood up and he told me not to worry about him any more in life, that he *was* dead as far as I was concerned. Then he pushed me to the door and the other people looked on as though nothing were happening, and he slammed the door behind me. I stood in the hallway, staring at the door. I heard somebody laugh in the room and then the tears came to my eyes. I started down the steps, whistling to keep from crying, I kept whistling to myself, *You going to need me, baby, one of these cold, rainy days.*

I read about Sonny's trouble in the spring. Little Grace died in the fall. She was a beautiful little girl. But she only lived a little over two years. She died of polio and she suffered. She had a slight fever for a couple of days, but it didn't seem like anything and we just kept her in bed. And we would certainly have called the doctor, but the fever dropped, she seemed to be all right. So we thought it had just been a cold. Then, one day, she was up, playing, Isabel was in the kitchen fixing lunch for the two boys when they'd come in from school, and she

heard Grace fall down in the living room. When you have a lot of children you don't always start running when one of them falls, unless they start screaming or something. And, this time, Gracie was quiet. Yet, Isabel says that when she heard that *thump* and then that silence, something happened in her to make her afraid. And she ran to the living room and there was little Grace on the floor, all twisted up, and the reason she hadn't screamed was that she couldn't get her breath. And when she did scream, it was the worst sound, Isabel says, that she'd ever heard in all her life, and she still hears it sometimes in her dreams. Isabel will sometimes wake me up with a low, moaning, strangled sound and I have to be quick to awaken her and hold her to me and where Isabel is weeping against me seems a mortal wound.

I think I may have written Sonny the very day that little Grace was buried. I was sitting in the living room in the dark, by myself, and I suddenly thought of Sonny. My trouble made his real.

One Saturday afternoon, when Sonny had been living with us, or anyway, been in our house, for nearly two weeks, I found myself wandering aimlessly about the living room, drinking from a can of beer, and trying to work up courage to search Sonny's room. He was out, he was usually out whenever I was home, and Isabel had taken the children to see their grandparents. Suddenly I was standing still in front of the living room window, watching Seventh Avenue. The idea of searching Sonny's room made me still. I scarcely dared to admit to myself what I'd be searching for. I didn't know what I'd do if I found it. Or if I didn't.

On the sidewalk across from me, near the entrance to a barbecue joint, some people were holding an old-fashioned revival meeting. The barbecue cook, wearing a dirty white apron, his conked[6] hair reddish and metallic in the pale sun, and a cigarette between his lips, stood in the doorway, watching them. Kids and older people paused in their errands and stood there, along with some older men and a couple of very tough-looking women who watched everything that happened on the avenue, as though they owned it, or were maybe owned by it. Well, they were watching this, too. The revival was being carried on by three sisters in black, and a brother. All they had were their voices and their Bibles and a tambourine. The brother was testifying[7] and while he testified two of the sisters stood together, seeming to say, amen, and the third sister walked around with the tambourine outstretched and a couple of people dropped coins into it. Then the brother's testimony ended and the sister who had been taking up the collection dumped the coins into her palm and transferred them to the pocket of her long black robe. Then she raised both hands, striking the tambourine against the air, and then against one hand, and she started to sing. And the two other sisters and the brother joined in.

It was strange, suddenly, to watch, though I had been seeing these meetings all my life. So, of course, had everybody else down there. Yet, they paused and watched and listened and I stood still at the window. " *'Tis the old ship of Zion,*" they sang, and the sister with the tambourine kept a steady, jangling beat, "*it has rescued many a thousand!*" Not a soul under the sound of their voices was hearing this song for the first time, not one of them had been rescued. Nor had they seen much in the way of rescue work being done around them. Neither

6. Processed: straightened and greased. 7. Publicly professing belief.

did they especially believe in the holiness of the three sisters and the brother, they knew too much about them, knew where they lived, and how. The woman with the tambourine, whose voice dominated the air, whose face was bright with joy, was divided by very little from the woman who stood watching her, a cigarette between her heavy, chapped lips, her hair a cuckoo's nest, her face scarred and swollen from many beatings, and her black eyes glittering like coal. Perhaps they both knew this, which was why, when, as rarely, they addressed each other, they addressed each other as Sister. As the singing filled the air the watching, listening faces underwent a change, the eyes focusing on something within; the music seemed to soothe a poison out of them; and time seemed, nearly, to fall away from the sullen, belligerent, battered faces, as though they were fleeing back to their first condition, while dreaming of their last. The barbecue cook half shook his head and smiled, and dropped his cigarette and disappeared into his joint. A man fumbled in his pockets for change and stood holding it in his hand impatiently, as though he had just remembered a pressing appointment further up the avenue. He looked furious. Then I saw Sonny, standing on the edge of the crowd. He was carrying a wide, flat notebook with a green cover, and it made him look, from where I was standing, almost like a schoolboy. The coppery sun brought out the copper in his skin, he was very faintly smiling, standing very still. Then the singing stopped, the tambourine turned into a collection plate again. The furious man dropped in his coins and vanished, so did a couple of the women, and Sonny dropped some change in the plate, looking directly at the woman with a little smile. He started across the avenue, toward the house. He has a slow, loping walk, something like the way Harlem hipsters walk, only he's imposed on this his own half-beat. I had never really noticed it before.

I stayed at the window, both relieved and apprehensive. As Sonny disappeared from my sight, they began singing again. And they were still singing when his key turned in the lock.

"Hey," he said.

"Hey, yourself. You want some beer?"

"No. Well, maybe." But he came up to the window and stood beside me, looking out. "What a warm voice," he said.

They were singing *If I could only hear my mother pray again!*

"Yes," I said, "and she can sure beat that tambourine."

"But what a terrible song," he said, and laughed. He dropped his notebook on the sofa and disappeared into the kitchen. "Where's Isabel and the kids?"

"I think they went to see their grandparents. You hungry?"

"No." He came back into the living room with his can of beer. "You want to come some place with me tonight?"

I sensed, I don't know how, that I couldn't possibly say no. "Sure. Where?"

He sat down on the sofa and picked up his notebook and started leafing through it. "I'm going to sit in with some fellows in a joint in the Village."

"You mean, you're going to play, tonight?"

"That's right." He took a swallow of his beer and moved back to the window. He gave me a sidelong look. "If you can stand it."

"I'll try," I said.

He smiled to himself and we both watched as the meeting across

the way broke up. The three sisters and the brother, heads bowed, were singing *God be with you till we meet again*. The faces around them were very quiet. Then the song ended. The small crowd dispersed. We watched the three women and the lone man walk slowly up the avenue.

"When she was singing before," said Sonny, abruptly, "her voice reminded me for a minute of what heroin feels like sometimes—when it's in your veins. It makes you feel sort of warm and cool at the same time. And distant. And—and sure." He sipped his beer, very deliberately not looking at me. I watched his face. "It makes you feel—in control. Sometimes you've got to have that feeling."

"Do you?" I sat down slowly in the easy chair.

"Sometimes." He went to the sofa and picked up his notebook again. "Some people do."

"In order," I asked, "to play?" And my voice was very ugly, full of contempt and anger.

"Well"—he looked at me with great, troubled eyes, as though, in fact, he hoped his eyes would tell me things he could never otherwise say—"they *think* so. And *if* they think so—!"

"And what do *you* think?" I asked.

He sat on the sofa and put his can of beer on the floor. "I don't know," he said, and I couldn't be sure if he were answering my question or pursuing his thoughts. His face didn't tell me. "It's not so much to *play*. It's to *stand* it, to be able to make it at all. On any level." He frowned and smiled: "In order to keep from shaking to pieces."

"But these friends of yours," I said, "they seem to shake themselves to pieces pretty goddamn fast."

"Maybe." He played with the notebook. And something told me that I should curb my tongue, that Sonny was doing his best to talk, that I should listen. "But of course you only know the ones that've gone to pieces. Some don't—or at least they haven't *yet* and that's just about all *any* of us can say." He paused. "And then there are some who just live, really, in hell, and they know it and they see what's happening and they go right on. I don't know." He sighed, dropped the notebook, folded his arms. "Some guys, you can tell from the way they play, they on something *all* the time. And you can see that, well, it makes something real for them. But of course," he picked up his beer from the floor and sipped it and put the can down again, "they *want* to, too, you've got to see that. Even some of them that say they don't—*some, not all*."

"And what about you?" I asked—I couldn't help it. "What about you? Do *you* want to?"

He stood up and walked to the window and I remained silent for a long time. Then he sighed. "Me," he said. Then: "While I was downstairs before, on my way here, listening to that woman sing, it struck me all of a sudden how much suffering she must have had to go through—to sing like that. It's *repulsive* to think you have to suffer that much."

I said: "But there's no way not to suffer—is there, Sonny?"

"I believe not," he said and smiled, "but that's never stopped anyone from trying." He looked at me. "Has it?" I realized, with this mocking look, that there stood between us, forever, beyond the power of time or forgiveness, the fact that I had held silence—so long!—when he had needed human speech to help him. He turned back to the

window. "No, there's no way not to suffer. But you try all kinds of ways to keep from drowning in it, to keep on top of it, and to make it seem—well, like *you*. Like you did something, all right, and now you're suffering for it. You know?" I said nothing. "Well you know," he said, impatiently, "why *do* people suffer? Maybe it's better to do something to give it a reason, *any* reason."

"But we just agreed," I said, "that there's no way not to suffer. Isn't it better, then, just to—take it?"

"But nobody just takes it," Sonny cried, "that's what I'm telling you! *Everybody* tries not to. You're just hung up on the *way* some people try—it's not *your* way!"

The hair on my face began to itch, my face felt wet. "That's not true," I said, "that's not true. I don't give a damn what other people do, I don't even care how they suffer. I just care how *you* suffer." And he looked at me. "Please believe me," I said, "I don't want to see you— die—trying not to suffer."

"I won't," he said flatly, "die trying not to suffer. At least, not any faster than anybody else."

"But there's no need," I said, trying to laugh, "is there? in killing yourself."

I wanted to say more, but I couldn't. I wanted to talk about will power and how life could be—well, beautiful. I wanted to say that it was all within; but was it? or, rather, wasn't that exactly the trouble? And I wanted to promise that I would never fail him again. But it would all have sounded—empty words and lies.

So I made the promise to myself and prayed that I would keep it.

"It's terrible sometimes, inside," he said, "that's what's the trouble. You walk these streets, black and funky and cold, and there's not really a living ass to talk to, and there's nothing shaking, and there's no way of getting it out—that storm inside. You can't talk it and you can't make love with it, and when you finally try to get with it and play it, you realize *nobody's* listening. So *you've* got to listen. You got to find a way to listen."

And then he walked away from the window and sat on the sofa again, as though all the wind had suddenly been knocked out of him. "Sometimes you'll do *anything* to play, even cut your mother's throat." He laughed and looked at me. "Or your brother's." Then he sobered. "Or your own." Then: "Don't worry. I'm all right now and I think I'll *be* all right. But I can't forget—where I've been. I don't mean just the physical place I've been, I mean where I've *been*. And *what* I've been."

"What have you been, Sonny?" I asked.

He smiled—but sat sideways on the sofa, his elbow resting on the back, his fingers playing with his mouth and chin, not looking at me. "I've been something I didn't recognize, didn't know I could be. Didn't know anybody could be." He stopped, looking inward, looking helplessly young, looking old. "I'm not talking about it now because I feel *guilty* or anything like that—maybe it would be better if I did, I don't know. Anyway, I can't really talk about it. Not to you, not to anybody," and now he turned and faced me. "Sometimes, you know, and it was actually when I was most *out* of the world, I felt that I was in it, that I was *with* it, really, and I could play or I didn't really have to *play*, it just came out of me, it was there. And I don't know how I played, thinking about it now, but I know I did awful things, those times, sometimes, to people. Or it wasn't that I *did* anything to them—it was that they

weren't real." He picked up the beer can; it was empty; he rolled it between his palms: "And other times—well, I needed a fix, I needed to find a place to lean, I needed to clear a space to *listen*—and I couldn't find it, and I—went crazy, I did terrible things to *me,* I was terrible *for* me." He began pressing the beer can between his hands, I watched the metal begin to give. It glittered, as he played with it like a knife, and I was afraid he would cut himself, but I said nothing. "Oh well. I can never tell you. I was all by myself at the bottom of something, stinking and sweating and crying and shaking, and I smelled it, you know? *my* stink, and I thought I'd die if I couldn't get away from it and yet, all the same, I knew that everything I was doing was just locking me in with it. And I didn't know," he paused, still flattening the beer can, "I didn't know, I still *don't* know, something kept telling me that maybe it was good to smell your own stink, but I didn't think that *that* was what I'd been trying to do—and—who can stand it?" and he abruptly dropped the ruined beer can, looking at me with a small, still smile, and then rose, walking to the window as though it were the lodestone rock. I watched his face, he watched the avenue. "I couldn't tell you when Mama died—but the reason I wanted to leave Harlem so bad was to get away from drugs. And then, when I ran away, that's what I was running from—really. When I came back, nothing had changed, *I* hadn't changed, I was just—older." And he stopped, drumming with his fingers on the windowpane. The sun had vanished, soon darkness would fall. I watched his face. "It can come again," he said, almost as though speaking to himself. Then he turned to me. "It can come again," he repeated. "I just want you to know that."

"All right," I said, at last. "So it can come again. All right."

He smiled, but the smile was sorrowful. "I had to try to tell you," he said.

"Yes," I said. "I understand that."

"You're my brother," he said, looking straight at me, and not smiling at all.

"Yes," I repeated, "yes. I understand that."

He turned back to the window, looking out. "All that hatred down there," he said, "all that hatred and misery and love. It's a wonder it doesn't blow the avenue apart."

We went to the only nightclub on a short, dark street, downtown. We squeezed through the narrow, chattering, jampacked bar to the entrance of the big room, where the bandstand was. And we stood there for a moment, for the lights were very dim in this room and we couldn't see. Then, "Hello, boy," said a voice and an enormous black man, much older than Sonny or myself, erupted out of all that atmospheric lighting and put an arm around Sonny's shoulder. "I been sitting right here," he said, "waiting for you."

He had a big voice, too, and heads in the darkness turned toward us.

Sonny grinned and pulled a little away, and said, "Creole, this is my brother. I told you about him."

Creole shook my hand. "I'm glad to meet you, son," he said, and it was clear that he was glad to meet me *there,* for Sonny's sake. And he smiled, "You got a real musician in *your* family," and he took his arm from Sonny's shoulder and slapped him, lightly, affectionately, with the back of his hand.

"Well. Now I've heard it all," said a voice behind us. This was an-

other musician, and a friend of Sonny's, a coal-black, cheerful-looking man, built close to the ground. He immediately began confiding to me, at the top of his lungs, the most terrible things about Sonny, his teeth gleaming like a lighthouse and his laugh coming up out of him like the beginning of an earthquake. And it turned out that everyone at the bar knew Sonny, or almost everyone; some were musicians, working there, or nearby, or not working, some were simply hangers-on, and some were there to hear Sonny play. I was introduced to all of them and they were all very polite to me. Yet, it was clear that, for them, I was only Sonny's brother. Here, I was in Sonny's world. Or, rather: his kingdom. Here, it was not even a question that his veins bore royal blood.

They were going to play soon and Creole installed me, by myself, at a table in a dark corner. Then I watched them, Creole, and the little black man, and Sonny, and the others, while they horsed around, standing just below the bandstand. The light from the bandstand spilled just a little short of them and, watching them laughing and gesturing and moving about, I had the feeling that they, nevertheless, were being most careful not to step into that circle of light too suddenly: that if they moved into the light too suddenly, without thinking, they would perish in flame. Then, while I watched, one of them, the small black man, moved into the light and crossed the bandstand and started fooling around with his drums. Then—being funny and being, also, extremely ceremonious—Creole took Sonny by the arm and led him to the piano. A woman's voice called Sonny's name and a few hands started clapping. And Sonny, also being funny and being ceremonious, and so touched, I think, that he could have cried, but neither hiding it nor showing it, riding it like a man, grinned, and put both hands to his heart and bowed from the waist.

Creole then went to the bass fiddle and a lean, very bright-skinned brown man jumped up on the bandstand and picked up his horn. So there they were, and the atmosphere on the bandstand and in the room began to change and tighten. Someone stepped up to the microphone and announced them. Then there were all kinds of murmurs. Some people at the bar shushed others. The waitress ran around, frantically getting in the last orders, guys and chicks got closer to each other, and the lights on the bandstand, on the quartet, turned to a kind of indigo. Then they all looked different there. Creole looked about him for the last time, as though he were making certain that all his chickens were in the coop, and then he—jumped and struck the fiddle. And there they were.

All I know about music is that not many people ever really hear it. And even then, on the rare occasions when something opens within, and the music enters, what we mainly hear, or hear corroborated, are personal, private, vanishing evocations. But the man who creates the music is hearing something else, is dealing with the roar rising from the void and imposing order on it as it hits the air. What is evoked in him, then, is of another order, more terrible because it has no words, and triumphant, too, for that same reason. And his triumph, when he triumphs, is ours. I just watched Sonny's face. His face was troubled, he was working hard, but he wasn't with it. And I had the feeling that, in a way, everyone on the bandstand was waiting for him, both waiting for him and pushing him along. But as I began to watch Creole, I realized that it was Creole who held them all back. He had them on a short rein. Up there, keeping the beat with his whole body, wailing on

the fiddle, with his eyes half closed, he was listening to everything, but he was listening to Sonny. He was having a dialogue with Sonny. He wanted Sonny to leave the shoreline and strike out for the deep water. He was Sonny's witness that deep water and drowning were not the same thing—he had been there, and he knew. And he wanted Sonny to know. He was waiting for Sonny to do the things on the keys which would let Creole know that Sonny was in the water.

And, while Creole listened, Sonny moved, deep within, exactly like someone in torment. I had never before thought of how awful the relationship must be between the musician and his instrument. He has to fill it, this instrument, with the breath of life, his own. He has to make it do what he wants it to do. And a piano is just a piano. It's made out of so much wood and wires and little hammers and big ones, and ivory. While there's only so much you can do with it, the only way to find this out is to try; to try and make it do everything.

And Sonny hadn't been near a piano for over a year. And he wasn't on much better terms with his life, not the life that stretched before him now. He and the piano stammered, started one way, got scared, stopped; started another way, panicked, marked time, started again; then seemed to have found a direction, panicked again, got stuck. And the face I saw on Sonny I'd never seen before. Everything had been burned out of it, and, at the same time, things usually hidden were being burned in, by the fire and fury of the battle which was occurring in him up there.

Yet, watching Creole's face as they neared the end of the first set, I had the feeling that something had happened, something I hadn't heard. Then they finished, there was scattered applause, and then, without an instant's warning, Creole started into something else, it was almost sardonic, it was *Am I Blue*.[8] And, as though he commanded, Sonny began to play. Something began to happen. And Creole let out the reins. The dry, low, black man said something awful on the drums, Creole answered, and the drums talked back. Then the horn insisted, sweet and high, slightly detached perhaps, and Creole listened, commenting now and then, dry, and driving, beautiful and calm and old. Then they all came together again, and Sonny was part of the family again. I could tell this from his face. He seemed to have found, right there beneath his fingers, a damn brand-new piano. It seemed that he couldn't get over it. Then, for a while, just being happy with Sonny, they seemed to be agreeing with him that brand-new pianos certainly were a gas.

Then Creole stepped forward to remind them that what they were playing was the blues. He hit something in all of them, he hit something in me, myself, and the music tightened and deepened, apprehension began to beat the air. Creole began to tell us what the blues were all about. They were not about anything very new. He and his boys up there were keeping it new, at the risk of ruin, destruction, madness, and death, in order to find new ways to make us listen. For, while the tale of how we suffer, and how we are delighted, and how we may triumph is never new, it always must be heard. There isn't any other tale to tell, it's the only light we've got in all this darkness.

And this tale, according to that face, that body, those strong hands on those strings, has another aspect in every country, and a new depth

8. By Grant Clark and Harry Akst, sung by Ethel Waters in 1929 film, "On with the Show," brilliantly recorded by Billie Holiday, and a favorite blues piece.

in every generation. Listen, Creole seemed to be saying, listen. Now these are Sonny's blues. He made the little black man on the drums know it, and the bright, brown man on the horn. Creole wasn't trying any longer to get Sonny in the water. He was wishing him Godspeed. Then he stepped back, very slowly, filling the air with the immense suggestion that Sonny speak for himself.

Then they all gathered around Sonny and Sonny played. Every now and again one of them seemed to say, amen. Sonny's fingers filled the air with life, his life. But that life contained so many others. And Sonny went all the way back, he really began with the spare, flat statement of the opening phrase of the song. Then he began to make it his. It was very beautiful because it wasn't hurried and it was no longer a lament. I seemed to hear with what burning he had made it his, with what burning we had yet to make it ours, how we could cease lamenting. Freedom lurked around us and I understood, at last, that he could help us to be free if we would listen, that he would never be free until we did. Yet, there was no battle in his face now, I heard what he had gone through, and would continue to go through until he came to rest in earth. He had made it his: that long line, of which we knew only Mama and Daddy. And he was giving it back, as everything must be given back, so that, passing through death, it can live forever. I saw my mother's face again, and felt, for the first time, how the stones of the road she had walked on must have bruised her feet. I saw the moonlit road where my father's brother died. And it brought something else back to me, and carried me past it, I saw my little girl again and felt Isabel's tears again, and I felt my own tears begin to rise. And I was yet aware that this was only a moment, that the world waited outside, as hungry as a tiger, and that trouble stretched above us, longer than the sky.

Then it was over. Creole and Sonny let out their breath, both soaking wet, and grinning. There was a lot of applause and some of it was real. In the dark, the girl came by and I asked her to take drinks to the bandstand. There was a long pause, while they talked up there in the indigo light and after awhile I saw the girl put a Scotch and milk on top of the piano for Sonny. He didn't seem to notice it, but just before they started playing again, he sipped from it and looked toward me, and nodded. Then he put it back on top of the piano. For me, then, as they began to play again, it glowed and shook above my brother's head like the very cup of trembling.[9]

1965

---

9. See *Isaiah* 51:17, 22–23: "Awake, awake, stand up, O Jerusalem, which hast drunk at the hand of the Lord the cup of his fury; thou hast drunken the dregs of the cup of trembling, and wrung them out. . . . Behold, I have taken out of thine hand the cup of trembling, even the dregs of the cup of my fury; thou shalt no more drink it again: But I will put it into the hand of them that afflict thee; . . . ."

II

ANGUS WILSON

Raspberry Jam

"How are your funny friends at Potter's Farm, Johnnie?" asked his
aunt from London.

"Very well, thank you, Aunt Eva," said the little boy in the window
in a high prim voice. He had been drawing faces on his bare knee and
now put down the indelible pencil. The moment that he had been
dreading all day had arrived. Now they would probe and probe with
their silly questions and the whole story of that dreadful tea party with
his old friends would come tumbling out. There would be scenes and
abuse and the old ladies would be made to suffer further. This he could
not bear, for although he never wanted to see them again and had
come, in brooding over the afternoon's events, almost to hate them, to
bring them further misery, to be the means of their disgrace would
be worse than any of the horrible things that had already happened.
Apart from his fear of what might follow he did not intend to pursue
the conversation himself, for he disliked his aunt's bright patronizing
tone. He knew that she felt ill at ease with children and would soon
lapse into that embarrassing "leg pulling" manner which some grown
ups used. For himself, he did not mind this but if she made silly jokes
about the old ladies at Potter's Farm he would get angry and then
Mummy would say all that about his having to learn to take a joke and
about his being highly strung and where could he have got it from,
not from her.

But he need not have feared. For though the grown ups continued
to speak of the old ladies as "Johnnie's friends," the topic soon became
a general one. Many of the things the others said made the little boy
bite his lip, but he was able to go on drawing on his knee with the
feigned abstraction of a child among adults.

"My dear," said Johnnie's mother to her sister, "you really must
meet them. They're the *most* wonderful pair of freaks. They live in a
great barn of a farmhouse. The inside's like a museum, full of old junk
mixed up with some really lovely things all mouldering to pieces. The
family's been there for hundreds of years and they're madly proud of it.
They won't let anyone do a single thing for them, although they're
both well over sixty, and of course the result is that the place is in the
most *frightful* mess. It's really rather ghastly and one oughtn't to laugh,
but if you could *see* them, my dear. The elder one, Marian, wears a
long tweed skirt almost to the ankles, she had a terrible hunting accident or something, and a school blazer. The younger one's said to have
been a beauty, but she's really rather sinister now, inches thick in
enamel[1] and rouge and dressed in all colors of the rainbow, with dyed
red hair which is constantly falling down. Of course, Johnnie's made

1. Cosmetic facial preparation to make the skin appear smooth.

175

tremendous friends with them and I must say they've been immensely kind to him, but what Harry will say when he comes back from Germany, I can't think. As it *is*, he's always complaining that the child is too much with women and has no friends of his own age.

"I don't honestly think you need worry about that, Grace," said her brother Jim, assuming the attitude of the sole male in the company, for of the masculinity of old Mr. Codrington their guest he instinctively made little. "Harry ought to be very pleased with the way old Miss Marian's encouraged Johnnie's cricket and riding; it's pretty uphill work, too. Johnnie's not exactly a Don Bradman or a Gordon Richards,[2] are you, old man? I like the old girl, personally. She's got a bee in her bonnet about the Bolsheviks, but she's stood up to those damned council people[3] about the drainage like a good 'un; she does no end for the village people as well and says very little about it."

"I don't like the sound of 'doing good to the village' very much," said Eva; "it usually means patronage and disappointed old maids meddling in other people's affairs. It's only in villages like this that people can go on serving out sermons with gifts of soup."

"Curiously enough, Eva old dear," Jim said, for he believed in being rude to his progressive sister, "in this particular case you happen to be wrong. Miss Swindale is extremely broadminded. You remember, Grace," he said, addressing his other sister, "what she said about giving money to old Cooper, when the rector protested it would only go on drink—'You have a perfect right to consign us all to hell, rector, but you must allow us the choice of how we get there.' Serve him damn well right for interfering too."

"Well, Jim darling," said Grace, "I must say she could hardly have the nerve to object to drink—the poor old thing has the most dreadful bouts herself. Sometimes when I can't get gin from the grocer's it makes me absolutely livid to think of all that secret drinking and they say it only makes her more and more gloomy. All the same I suppose *I* should drink if I had a sister like Dolly. It must be horrifying when one's family-proud like she is to have such a skeleton in the cupboard. I'm sure there's going to be the most awful trouble in the village about Dolly before she's finished. You've heard the squalid story about young Tony Calkett, haven't you? My dear, he went round there to fix the lights and apparently Dolly invited him up to her bedroom to have a cherry brandy of all things and made the *most* unfortunate proposals. Of course I know she's been very lonely and it's all a ghastly tragedy really, but Mrs. Calkett's a terrible silly little woman and a very jealous mother and she won't see it that way at all. The awful thing is that both the Miss Swindales give me the creeps rather. I have a dreadful feeling when I'm with them that I don't know who's the keeper and who's the lunatic. In fact, Eva my dear, they're both really rather horrors and I suppose I ought never to let Johnnie go near them."

"I think you have no cause for alarm, Mrs. Allingham," put in old Mr. Codrington in a purring voice. He had been waiting for some time to take the floor, and now that he had got it he did not intend to relinquish it. Had it not been for the small range of village society he would not have been a visitor at Mrs. Allingham's, for, as he frequently remarked, if there was one thing he deplored more than her vulgarity it was her loquacity. "No one delights in scandal more than I do, but it is

2. Now Sir Donald Bradman (b. 1908) an Australian, the Ted Williams–Babe Ruth of cricket; and Sir Gordon Richards, jockey, holder of single season British and career world records for wins.

3. Borough, county, or district administrators.

always a little distorted, a trifle *exagéré*,[4] indeed where would be its charm, if it were not so! No doubt Miss Marian has her solaces, but she remains a noble-hearted woman. No doubt Miss Dolly is often a trifle naughty," he dwelt on this word caressingly, "but she really only uses the privilege of one, who has been that rare thing, a beautiful woman. As for Tony Calkett it is really time that that young man ceased to be so unnecessarily virginal. If my calculations are correct, and I have every reason to think they are, he must be twenty-two, an age at which modesty should have been put behind one long since. No, dear Mrs. Allingham, you should rejoice that Johnnie has been given the friendship of two women who can still, in this vulgar age, be honored with a name that, for all that it has been cheapened and degraded, one is still proud to bestow—the name of a lady." Mr. Codrington threw his head back and stared round the room as though defying anyone to deny him his own right to this name. "Miss Marian will encourage him in the manlier virtues, Miss Dolly in the arts. Her own water colors, though perhaps lacking in strength, are not to be despised. She has a fine sense of color, though I could wish that she was a little less bold with it in her costume. Nevertheless with that red-gold hair there is something splendid about her appearance, something especially wistful to an old man like myself. Those peacock-blue linen gowns take me back through Conder's fans and Whistler's rooms to Rossetti's Monna Vanna.[5] Unfortunately as she gets older the linen is not overclean. We are given a Monna Vanna with the collected dust of age, but surely," he added with a little cackle, "it is dirt that lends patina to a picture. It is interesting that you should say you are uncertain which of the two sisters is a trifle peculiar, because, in point of fact, both have been away, as they used to phrase it in the servants' hall of my youth. Strange," he mused, "that one's knowledge of the servants' hall should always belong to the period of one's infancy, be, as it were, eternally outmoded. I have no conception of how they may speak of an asylum in the servants' hall of today. No doubt Johnnie could tell us. But, of course, I forget that social progress has removed the servants' hall from the ken of all but the most privileged children. I wonder now whether that is a loss or a blessing in disguise."

"A blessing without any doubt at all," said Aunt Eva, irrepressible in the cause of Advance. "Think of all the appalling inhibitions we acquired from servants' chatter. I had an old nurse who was always talking about ghosts and dead bodies and curses on the family in a way that must have set up terrible phobias in me. I still have those ugly, morbid nightmares about spiders," she said, turning to Grace.

"I refuse," said Mr. Codrington in a voice of great contempt, for he was greatly displeased at the interruption, "to believe that any dream of yours could be ugly; morbid, perhaps, but with a sense of drama and artistry that would befit the dreamer. I confess that if I have inhibitions, and I trust I have many, I cling to them. I should not wish to give way unreservedly to what is so unattractively called the libido, it suggests a state of affairs in which beach pajamas are worn and jitterbugging is compulsory. No, let us retain the fantasies, the imaginative

---

4. Exaggerated
5. Charles Conder (1868–1909), English artist with decorative style, who, about 1895, was the rage in arty circles for his pastoral, artificial fan designs; James Abbott McNeill Whistler (1834–1903), American painter who in the 1860s introduced the fad of Japanese prints and bric-à-brac:

Gabriel Charles Dante (usually called Dante Gabriel) Rossetti (1828–1882), famous English painter and poet, painted "Monna Vanna" in 1866, which, along with "The Beloved" and "Sibylla Palmifera" of the same year, is his best work in oils. All are associated with the esthetic and decadent movements of the late nineteenth century.

games of childhood, even at the expense of a little fear, for they are the true magnificence of the springtime of life."

"Darling Mr. Codrington," cried Grace, "I do pray and hope you're right. It's exactly what I keep on telling myself about Johnnie, but I really don't know. Johnnie, darling, run upstairs and fetch Mummy's bag." But his mother need not have been so solicitous about Johnnie's overhearing what she had to say, for the child had already left the room. "There you are, Eva," she said, "he's the strangest child. He slips away without so much as a word. I must say he's very good at amusing himself, but I very much wonder if all the funny games he plays aren't very bad for him. He's certainly been very peculiar lately, strange silences and sudden tears, and, my dear, the awful nightmares he has! About a fortnight ago, after he'd been at tea with the Miss Swindales, I don't know whether it was something he'd eaten there, but he made the most awful sobbing noise in the night. Sometimes I think it's just temper, like Harry. The other day at tea I only offered him some jam, my best home-made raspberry too, and he just screamed at me."

"You should take him to a child psychologist," said her sister.

"Well, darling, I expect you're right. It's so difficult to know whether they're frauds, everyone recommends somebody different. I'm sure Harry would disapprove too, and then think of the expense. . . . You know how desperately poor we are, although I think I manage as well as anyone could" . . . At this point Mr. Codrington took a deep breath and sat back, for on the merits of her household management Grace Allingham was at her most boring and could by no possible stratagem be restrained.

Upstairs, in the room which had been known as the nursery until his eleventh birthday, but was now called his bedroom, Johnnie was playing with his farm animals. The ritual involved in the game was very complicated and had a long history. It was on his ninth birthday that he had been given the farm set by his father. "Something a bit less babyish than those woolly animals of yours," he had said, and Johnnie had accepted them, since they made in fact no difference whatever to the games he played; games at which could Major Allingham have guessed he would have been distinctly puzzled. The little ducks, pigs, and cows of lead no more remained themselves in Johnnie's games than had the pink woolen sheep and green cloth horses of his early childhood. Johnnie's world was a strange compound of the adult world in which he had always lived and a book world composed from Grimm, the Arabian Nights, Alice's adventures, natural history books, and more recently the novels of Dickens and Jane Austen. His imagination was taken by anything odd—strange faces, strange names, strange animals, strange voices and catchphrases—all these appeared in his games. The black pig and the white duck were keeping a hotel; the black pig was called that funny name of Granny's friend—Mrs. Gudgeon-Rogers. She was always holding her skirt tight round the knees and warming her bottom over the fire—like Mrs. Coates, and whenever anyone in the hotel asked for anything she would reply, "Darling, I can't stop now. I've simply got to fly," like Aunt Sophie, and then she would fly out of the window. The duck was an Echidna, or Spiny Anteater, who wore a picture hat and a fish train[6] like in the picture of Aunt

---

6. Wide-brimmed woman's hat with feathers or flowers, etc.; train of a formal gown shaped like a fish tail.

Eleanor; she used to weep a lot, because, like Granny, when she described her games of bridge, she was "vulnerable"[7] and she would yawn at the hotel guests and say "Lord I am tired," like Lydia Bennet.[8] The two collie dogs had "been asked to leave," like in the story of Mummy's friend Gertie who "got tight" at the Hunt Ball, they were going to be divorced and were consequently wearing "co-respondent[9] shoes." The lady collie who was called Minnie Mongelheim kept on saying, "That chap's got a proud stomach. Let him eat chaff," like Mr. F's Aunt in *Little Dorrit*.[1] The sheep, who always played the part of a bore, kept on and on talking like Daddy about "leg cuts and fine shots to cover"[2]; sometimes when the rest of the animal guests got too bored the sheep would change into Grandfather Graham and tell a funny story about a Scotsman so that they were bored in a different way. Finally the cat who was a grand vizier and worked by magic would say, "All the ways round here belong to me" like the Red Queen,[3] and he would have all the guests torn in pieces and flayed alive until Johnnie felt so sorry for them that the game would come to an end. Mummy was already saying that he was getting too old for the farm animals: one always seemed to be getting too old for something. In fact the animals were no longer necessary to Johnnie's games, for most of the time now he liked to read and when he wanted to play games he could do so in his head without the aid of any toys, but he hated the idea of throwing things away because they were no longer needed. Mummy and Daddy were always throwing things away and never thinking of their feelings. When he had been much younger Mummy had given him an old petticoat to put in the dustbin, but Johnnie had taken it to his room and hugged it and cried over it, because it was no longer wanted. Daddy had been very upset. Daddy was always being upset at what Johnnie did. Only the last time that he was home there had been an awful row, because Johnnie had tried to make up like old Mrs. Langdon and could not wash the blue paint off his eyes. Daddy had beaten him and looked very hurt all day and said to Mummy that he'd "rather see him dead than grow up a cissie." No, it was better not to do imitations oneself, but to leave it to the animals.

This afternoon, however, Johnnie was not attending seriously to his game, he was sitting and thinking of what the grown ups had been saying and of how he would never see his friends, the old ladies, again, and of how he never, never wanted to. This irrevocable separation lay like a black cloud over his mind, a constant darkness which was lit up momentarily by forks of hysterical horror, as he remembered the nature of their last meeting.

The loss of his friendship was a very serious one to the little boy. It had met so completely the needs and loneliness which are always great

---

7. Having won one game of a two-game "rubber" in bridge, where failing to make a bid carries an increased penalty and making some difficult bids carries an increased bonus.

8. Youngest and flightiest of the sisters in Jane Austen's *Pride and Prejudice*.

9. In law, the party who is charged with committing adultery with the partner being sued for divorce.

1. In Charles Dickens' novel *Little Dorrit* (1855–1857), the senile old lady who "had no name but Mr. F's Aunt" periodically interrupts conversations "totally uncalled for by anything said by anybody"; at one point, Book II, Chap. 9, she offers the hero, Arthur Clennam, a piece of toast and is angered by his holding it without eating it; her angry shout is slightly misquoted—"He has a proud stomach, this chap. . . . Give him a meal of chaff"—but she does repeat it several times.

2. Cricket strokes.

3. In Chap. 2 of Lewis Carroll's *Through the Looking-Glass*, Alice claims to have lost her way, but the Red Queen replies, "I don't know what you mean by your way. . . . : all the ways about here belong to me . . . ," and the Red Queen is fond of sentencing people to having their heads cut off.

in a child isolated from other children and surrounded by unimaginative adults. In a totally unself-conscious way, half crazy as they were and half crazy even though the child sensed them to be, the Misses Swindale possessed just those qualities of which Johnnie felt most in need. To begin with they were odd and fantastic and highly colored, and more important still they believed that such peculiarities were nothing to be ashamed of, indeed were often a matter for pride. "How delightfully odd," Miss Dolly would say in her drawling voice, when Johnnie told her how the duck-billed platypus had chosen spangled tights when Queen Alexandra had ordered her to be shot from a cannon at Brighton Pavilion.[4] "What a delightfully extravagant creature that duck-billed platypus is, *caro*[5] Gabriele, for Miss Dolly had brought back a touch of Italian here and there from her years in Florence, whilst in Johnnie she fancied a likeness to the angel Gabriel. In describing her own dresses, too, which she would do for hours on end, extravagance was her chief commendation. "As for that gold and silver brocade ball dress," she would say and her voice would sink to an awed whisper, "it was richly fantastic." To Miss Marian, with her more brusque, masculine nature, Johnnie's imaginative powers were a matter of far greater wonder than to her sister and she treated them with even greater respect. In her bluff, simple way like some old-fashioned religious army officer or overgrown but solemn schoolboy, she too admired the eccentric and unusual. "What a lark!" she would say, when Johnnie told her how the Crown Prince had slipped in some polar bears dressed in pink ballet skirts to sing "Ta Ra Ra boomdeay"[6] in the middle of a boring school concert which his royal duties had forced him to attend. "What a nice chap he must be to know." In talking of her late father, the general, whose memory she worshipped and of whom she had a never-ending flow of anecdotes, she would give an instance of his warmhearted but distinctly eccentric behavior and say in her gruff voice, "Wasn't it rum? That's the bit I like best." But in neither of the sisters was there the least trace of that self-conscious whimsicality which Johnnie had met and hated in so many grown ups. They were the first people he had met who liked what he liked and as he liked it.

Their love of lost causes and their defense of the broken, the worn out, and the forgotten met a deep demand in his nature, which had grown almost sickly sentimental in the dead practical world of his home. He loved the disorder of the old eighteenth-century farm house, the collection of miscellaneous objects of all kinds that littered the rooms, and thoroughly sympathized with the sisters' magpie propensity to collect dress ends, feathers, string, old whistles, and broken cups. He grew excited with them in their fights to prevent drunken old men being taken to workhouses and cancerous old women to hospitals, though he sensed something crazy in their constant fear of intruders, Bolsheviks, and prying doctors. He would often try to change the conversation when Miss Marian became excited about spies in the village, or told him of how torches had been flashing all night in the garden and of how the vicar was slandering her father's memory in a whispering campaign. He felt deeply embarrassed when Miss Dolly insisted on

---

4. Alexandra (1844–1925), queen consort of Edward VII, was from a boisterous and carefree Danish family. Beautiful and graceful in her early years, she became lame and deaf in 1867. The Royal Pavillion at Brighton, about 50 miles south of London, once the palace of George IV, holds 2,000 people for concerts, etc.

5. Dear.

6. Highly successful nonsense song of the 1890s, adapted by Henry J. Sayers from a risqué nightclub song which was sung in 1891 in London to a shrieking, kicking chorus line.

looking into all the cupboards and behind the curtains to see, as she said, "if there were any eyes or ears where they were not wanted. For, *caro* Gabriele, those who hate beauty are many and strong, those who love it are few."

It was, above all, their kindness and their deep affection which held the love-starved child. His friendship with Miss Dolly had been almost instantaneous. She soon entered into his fantasies with complete intimacy, and he was spellbound by her stories of the gaiety and beauty of Mediterranean life. They would play dressing-up games together and enacted all his favorite historical scenes. She helped him with his French too, and taught him Italian words with lovely sounds; she praised his painting and helped him to make costume designs for some of his "characters." With Miss Marian, at first, there had been much greater difficulty. She was an intensely shy woman and took refuge behind a rather forbidding bluntness of manner. Her old-fashioned military airs and general "manly" tone, copied from her father, with which she approached small boys, reminded Johnnie too closely of his own father. "Head up, me lad," she would say, "shoulders straight." Once he had come very near to hating her, when after an exhibition of his absentmindedness she had said, "Take care, Johnnie, head in the air. You'll be lost in the clouds, me lad, if you're not careful." But the moment after she had won his heart for ever, when with a little chuckle she continued, "Jolly good thing if you are, you'll learn things up there that we shall never know." On her side, as soon as she saw that she had won his affection, she lost her shyness and proceeded impulsively to load him with kindness. She loved to cook his favorite dishes for him and give him his favorite fruit from their kitchen garden. Her admiration for his precocity and imagination was open-eyed and childlike. Finally they had found a common love of Dickens and Jane Austen, which she had read with her father, and now they would sit for hours talking over the characters in their favorite books.

Johnnie's affection for them was intensely protective, and increased daily as he heard and saw the contempt and dislike with which they were regarded by many persons in the village. The knowledge that "they had been away" was nothing new to him when Mr. Codrington had revealed it that afternoon. Once Miss Dolly had told him how a foolish doctor had advised her to go into a home, "for you know, *caro*, ever since I returned to these gray skies my health has not been very good. People here think me strange, I cannot attune myself to the cold northern soul. But it was useless to keep me there, I need beauty and warmth of color, and there it was so drab. The people, too, were unhappy crazy creatures and I missed my music so dreadfully." Miss Marian had spoken more violently of it on one of her "funny" days, when from the depredations caused by the village boys to the orchard she had passed on to the strange man she had found spying in her father's library and the need for a high wall round the house to prevent people peering through the telescopes from Mr. Hatton's house opposite. "They're frightened of us, though, Johnnie," she had said. "I'm too honest for them and Dolly's too clever. They're always trying to separate us. Once they took me away against my will. They couldn't keep me, I wrote to all sorts of big pots,[7] friends of Father's, you know, and they had to release me." Johnnie realized, too, that when his mother had said that she never knew which was the keeper, she had spoken

7. Persons of importance, big shots.

more truly than she understood. Each sister was constantly alarmed for the other and anxious to hide the other's defects from an un-under-standing world. Once when Miss Dolly had been telling him a long story about a young waiter who had slipped a note into her hand the last time she had been in London, Miss Marian called Johnnie into the kitchen to look at some pies she had made. Later she had told him not to listen if Dolly said "soppy[8] things" because being so beautiful she did not realize that she was no longer young. Another day when Miss Marian had brought in the silver-framed photo of her father in full dress uniform and had asked Johnnie to swear an oath to clear the general's memory in the village, Miss Dolly had begun to play a mazurka on the piano. Later, she too, had warned Johnnie not to take too much notice when her sister got excited. "She lives a little too much in the past, Gabriele. She suffered very much when our father died. Poor Marian, it is a pity perhaps that she is so good, she has had too little of the pleasures of life. But we must love her very much, *caro*, very much."

Johnnie had sworn to himself to stand by them and to fight the wicked people who said they were old and useless and in the way. But now, since that dreadful tea-party, he could not fight for them any longer, for he knew why they had been shut up and felt that it was justified. In a sense, too, he understood that it was to protect others that they had to be restrained, for the most awful memory of all that terrify-ing afternoon was the thought that he had shared with pleasure for a moment in their wicked game.

It was certainly most unfortunate that Johnnie should have been in-vited to tea on that Thursday, for the Misses Swindale had been drink-ing heavily on and off for the preceding week, and were by that time in a state of mental and nervous excitement that rendered them far from normal. A number of events had combined to produce the greatest sense of isolation in these old women whose sanity in any event hung by a precarious thread. Miss Marian had been involved in an unpleasant scene with the vicar over the new hall for the Young People's Club. She was, as usual, providing the cash for the building and felt extremely happy and excited at being consulted about the decorations. Though she did not care for the vicar, she set out to see him, determined that she would accommodate herself to changing times. In any case, since she was the benefactress, it was, she felt, particularly necessary that she should take a back seat, to have imposed her wishes in any way would have been most ill-bred. It was an unhappy chance that caused the vicar to harp upon the need for new fabrics for the chairs and even to digress upon the ugliness of the old upholstery, for these chairs had come from the late General Swindale's library. Miss Marian was imme-diately reminded of her belief that the vicar was attempting secretly to blacken her father's memory, nor was the impression corrected when he tactlessly suggested that the question of her father's taste was unim-portant and irrelevant. She was more deeply wounded still to find in the next few days that the village shared the vicar's view that she was at-tempting to dictate to the boys' club by means of her money. "After all," as Mrs. Grove at the Post Office said, "it's not only the large sums that count, Miss Swindale, it's all the boys' sixpences[9] that they've saved up." "You've too much of your father's ways in you, that's the

---

8. Foolishly sentimental.   9. Once worth more than a dime, now about six cents.

trouble, Miss Swindale," said Mr. Norton, who was famous for his bluntness, "and they won't do nowadays."

She had returned from this unfortunate morning's shopping to find Mrs. Calkett on the doorsteps. Now the visit of Mrs. Calkett was not altogether unexpected, for Miss Marian had guessed from chance remarks of her sister's that something "unfortunate" had happened with young Tony. When, however, the sharp-faced unpleasant little woman began to complain about Miss Dolly with innuendos and veiledly coarse suggestions, Miss Marian could stand it no longer and drove her away harshly. "How dare you speak about my sister in that disgusting way, you evil-minded little woman," she said. "You'd better be careful or you'll find yourself charged with libel." When the scene was over, she felt very tired. It was dreadful of course that anyone so mean and cheap should speak thus of anyone so fine and beautiful as Dolly, but it was also dreadful that Dolly should have made such a scene possible.

Things were not improved, therefore, when Dolly returned from Brighton at once elevated by a new conquest and depressed by its subsequent results. It seemed that the new conductor on the Southdown, "that charming dark Italian-looking boy I was telling you about, my dear," had returned her a most intimate smile and pressed her hand when giving her change. Her own smiles must have been embarrassingly intimate, for a woman in the next seat had remarked loudly to her friend, "These painted old things. Really, I wonder the men don't smack their faces." "I couldn't help smiling," remarked Miss Dolly, "she was so evidently *jalouse*,[1] my dear. I'm glad to say the conductor did not hear, for no doubt he would have felt it necessary to come to my defense, he was so completely *épris*."[2] But, for once, Miss Marian was too vexed to play ball, she turned on her sister and roundly condemned her conduct, ending up by accusing her of bringing misery to them both and shame to their father's memory. Poor Miss Dolly just stared in bewilderment, her baby blue eyes round with fright, tears washing the mascara from her eyelashes in black streams down the wrinkled vermilion of her cheeks. Finally she ran crying up to her room.

That night both the sisters began to drink heavily. Miss Dolly lay like some monstrous broken doll, her red hair streaming over her shoulders, her corsets unloosed and her fat body poking out of an old pink velvet ball dress—pink with red hair was always so audacious— through the most unexpected places in bulges of thick blue-white flesh. She sipped at glass after glass of gin, sometimes staring into the distance with bewilderment that she should find herself in such a condition, sometimes leering pruriently at some pictures of Johnny Weissmuller[3] in swimsuits that she had cut out of *Film Weekly*. At last she began to weep to think that she had sunk to this. Miss Marian sat at her desk and drank more deliberately from a cut glass decanter of brandy. She read solemnly through her father's letters, their old-fashioned, earnest Victorian sentiments swimming ever more wildly before her eyes. But, at last, she, too, began to weep as she thought of how his memory would be quite gone when she passed away, and of how she had broken the promise that she had made to him on his deathbed to stick to her sister through thick and thin.

So they continued for two or three days with wild spasms of drink-

---

1. Jealous.
2. Smitten, taken.
3. Olympic champion swimmer, 1924 and 1928, sometime holder of 75 speed records in swimming, who broke into films in 1932 and became the most famous film Tarzan (and male sex symbol).

ing and horrible, sober periods of remorse. They cooked themselves odd scraps in the kitchen, littering the house with unwashed dishes and cups, but never speaking, always avoiding each other. They didn't change their clothes or wash, and indeed made little alteration in their appearance. Miss Dolly put fresh rouge on her cheeks periodically and some pink roses in her hair which hung there wilting; she was twice sick over the pink velvet dress. Miss Marian put on an old scarlet hunting waistcoat of her father's, partly out of maudlin sentiment and partly because she was cold. Once she fell on the stairs and cut her forehead against the banisters; the red and white handkerchief which she tied round her head gave her the appearance of a tipsy pirate. On the fourth day, the sisters were reconciled and sat in Miss Dolly's room. That night they slept, lying heavily against each other on Miss Dolly's bed, open-mouthed and snoring, Miss Marian's deep guttural rattle contrasting with Miss Dolly's high-pitched whistle. They awoke on Thursday morning, much sobered, to the realization that Johnnie was coming to tea that afternoon.

It was characteristic that neither spoke a word of the late debauch. Together they went out into the hot July sunshine to gather raspberries for Johnnie's tea. But the nets in the kitchen garden had been disarranged and the birds had got the fruit. The awful malignity of this chance event took some time to pierce through the fuddled brains of the two ladies, as they stood there grotesque and obscene in their staring pink and clashing red, with their heavy pouchy faces and bloodshot eyes showing up in the hard, clear light of the sun. But when the realization did get home it seemed to come as a confirmation of all the beliefs of persecution which had been growing throughout the drunken orgy. There is little doubt that they were both a good deal mad when they returned to the house.

Johnnie arrived punctually at four o'clock, for he was a small boy of exceptional politeness. Miss Marian opened the door to him, and he was surprised at her appearance in her red bandana and her scarlet waistcoat, and especially by her voice which, though friendly and gruff as usual, sounded thick and flat. Miss Dolly, too, looked more than usually odd with one eye closed in a kind of perpetual wink, and with her pink dress falling off her shoulders. She kept on laughing in a silly, high giggle. The shock of discovering that the raspberries were gone had driven them back to the bottle and they were both fairly drunk. They pressed upon the little boy, who was thirsty after his walk, two small glasses in succession, one of brandy, the other of gin, though in their sober mood the ladies would have died rather than have seen their little friend take strong liquor. The drink soon combined with the heat of the day and the smell of vomit that hung around the room to make Johnnie feel most strange. The walls of the room seemed to be closing in and the floor to be moving up and down like sea waves. The ladies' faces came up at him suddenly and then receded, now Miss Dolly's with great blobs of blue and scarlet and her eyes winking and leering, now Miss Marian's a huge white mass with her moustache grown large and black. He was only conscious by fits and starts of what they were doing or saying. Sometimes he would hear Miss Marian speaking in a flat, slow monotone. She seemed to be reading out her father's letters, snatches of which came to him clearly and then faded away. "There is so much to be done in our short sojourn on this earth, so much that may be done for good, so much for evil. Let us earnestly

endeavor to keep the good steadfastly before us," then suddenly, "Major Campbell has told me of his decision to leave the regiment. I pray God hourly that he may have acted in full consideration of the Higher Will to which . . . ," and once grotesquely, "Your Aunt Maud was here yesterday, she is a maddening woman and I consider it a just judgment upon the Liberal party that she should espouse its cause." None of these phrases meant anything to the little boy, but he was dimly conscious that Miss Marian was growing excited, for he heard her say, "That was our father. As Shakespeare says, 'He was a man take him all in all,'[4] Johnnie. We loved him, but there were those who sought to destroy him, for he was too big for them. But their day is nearly ended. Always remember that, Johnnie." It was difficult to hear all that the elder sister said, for Miss Dolly kept on drawling and giggling in his ear about a black *charmeuse*[5] evening gown she had worn, and a young donkeyboy she had danced with in the fiesta at Asti. "*E come era bello, caro Gabriele, come era bello.*[6] And afterwards . . . but I must spare the ears of one so young the details of the *arte dell' amore*,"[7] she added with a giggle and then with drunken dignity, "it would not be immodest I think to mention that his skin was like velvet. Only a few lire,[8] too, just imagine." All this, too, was largely meaningless to the boy, though he remembered it in later years.

For a while he must have slept, since he remembered that later he could see and hear more clearly though his head ached terribly. Miss Dolly was seated at the piano playing a little jig and bobbing up and down like a mountainous pink blancmange, whilst Miss Marian more than ever like a pirate was dancing some sort of a hornpipe. Suddenly Miss Dolly stopped playing. "Shall we show him the prisoner?" she said solemnly. "Head up, shoulders straight," said Miss Marian in a parody of her old manner, "you're going to be very honored, me lad. Promise you'll never betray that honor. You shall see one of the enemy punished. Our father gave us close instructions, 'Do good to all,' he said, 'but if you catch one of the enemy, remember you are a soldier's daughters.' We shall obey that command." Meanwhile Miss Dolly had returned from the kitchen, carrying a little bird which was pecking and clawing at the net in which it had been caught and shrilling incessantly—it was a little bullfinch. "You're a very beautiful little bird," Miss Dolly whispered, "with lovely soft pink feathers and pretty gray wings. But you're a very naughty little bird too, *tanto cattivo*.[9] You came and took the fruit from us which we'd kept for our darling Gabriele." She began feverishly to pull the rose breast feathers from the bird, which piped more loudly and squirmed. Soon little trickles of red blood ran down among the feathers. "Scarlet and pink a very daring combination," Miss Dolly cried. Johnnie watched from his chair, his heart beating fast. Suddenly Miss Marian stepped forward and holding the bird's head she thrust a pin into its eyes. "We don't like spies around here looking at what we are doing," she said in her flat, gruff voice. "When we find them we teach them a lesson so that they don't spy on us again." Then she took out a little pocket knife and cut into the bird's breast; its wings were beating more feebly now and its claws only moved spasmodically, whilst its chirping was very faint. Little

4. *Hamlet*, Act I, sc. ii, 187 (" . . . take him *for* all in all").
5. Soft, light silk cloth with satin finish.
6. And how handsome he was, dear Gabriel, how handsome he was.
7. The art of love.
8. Unit of Italian currency, once worth almost 20 cents but since 1950 worth only one sixth of a cent.
9. Very naughty.

yellow and white strings of entrails began to peep out from where she had cut. "Oh!" cried Miss Dolly, "I like the lovely colors, I don't like these worms." But Johnnie could bear it no longer, white and shaking he jumped from his chair and seizing the bird he threw it on the floor and then he stamped on it violently until it was nothing but a sodden crimson mass. "Oh, Gabriele, what have you done? You've spoiled all the soft, pretty colors. Why it's nothing now, it just looks like a lump of raspberry jam. Why have you done it, Gabriele?" cried Miss Dolly. But little Johnnie gave no answer, he had run from the room.

1950

GRAHAM GREENE

The Basement Room

1

When the front door had shut them out and the butler Baines had turned back into the dark heavy hall, Philip began to live. He stood in front of the nursery door, listening until he heard the engine of the taxi die out along the street. His parents were gone for a fortnight's holiday; he was "between nurses," one dismissed and the other not arrived; he was alone in the great Belgravia[1] house with Baines and Mrs. Baines.

He could go anywhere, even through the green baize door to the pantry or down the stairs to the basement living room. He felt a stranger in his home because he could go into any room and all the rooms were empty.

You could only guess who had once occupied them: the rack of pipes in the smoking-room beside the elephant tusks, the carved wood tobacco jar; in the bedroom the pink hangings and pale perfumes and the three-quarter finished jars of cream which Mrs. Baines had not yet cleared away; the high glaze on the never-opened piano in the drawing room, the china clock, the silly little tables and the silver: but here Mrs. Baines was already busy, pulling down the curtains, covering the chairs in dust-sheets.

"Be off out of here, Master Philip," and she looked at him with her hateful peevish eyes, while she moved round, getting everything in order, meticulous and loveless and doing her duty.

Philip Lane went downstairs and pushed at the baize door; he looked into the pantry, but Baines was not there, then he set foot for the first time on the stairs to the basement. Again he had the sense: this is life. All his seven nursery years vibrated with the strange, the new experience. His crowded busy brain was like a city which feels the earth tremble at a distant earthquake shock. He was apprehensive, but he was happier than he had ever been. Everything was more important than before.

Baines was reading a newspaper in his shirtsleeves. He said: "Come in, Phil, and make yourself at home. Wait a moment and I'll do the honors," and going to a white cleaned cupboard he brought out a bottle of ginger-beer[2] and half a Dundee cake.[3] "Half-past eleven in the morning," Baines said. "It's opening time,[4] my boy," and he cut

---

1. Fashionable district in the West End of London, next to Pimlico, mentioned later.

2. Ginger-flavored carbonated drink.
3. Spicy cake decorated with almonds.
4. Hour when pubs open to serve drink.

the cake and poured out the ginger-beer. He was more genial than Philip had ever known him, more at his ease, a man in his own home.

"Shall I call Mrs. Baines?" Philip asked, and he was glad when Baines said no. She was busy. She liked to be busy, so why interfere with her pleasure?

"A spot of drink at half-past eleven," Baines said, pouring himself out a glass of ginger-beer, "gives an appetite for chop and does no man any harm."

"A chop?" Philip asked.

"Old Coasters,"[5] Baines said, "call all food chop."

"But it's not a chop?"

"Well, it might be, you know, cooked with palm oil. And then some paw-paw[6] to follow."

Philip looked out of the basement window at the dry stone yard, the ashcan and the legs going up and down beyond the railings.

"Was it hot there?"

"Ah, you never felt such heat. Not a nice heat, mind, like you get in the park on a day like this. Wet," Baines said, "corruption." He cut himself a slice of cake. "Smelling of rot," Baines said, rolling his eyes round the small basement room, from clean cupboard to clean cupboard, the sense of bareness, of nowhere to hide a man's secrets. With an air of regret for something lost he took a long draught of ginger-beer.

"Why did father live out there?"

"It was his job," Baines said, "same as this is mine now. And it was mine then too. It was a man's job. You wouldn't believe it now, but I've had forty niggers under me, doing what I told them to."

"Why did you leave?"

"I married Mrs. Baines."

Philip took the slice of Dundee cake in his hand and munched it round the room. He felt very old, independent and judicial; he was aware that Baines was talking to him as man to man. He never called him Master Philip as Mrs. Baines did, who was servile when she was not authoritative.

Baines had seen the world; he had seen beyond the railings, beyond the tired legs of typists, the Pimlico parade to and from Victoria.[7] He sat there over his ginger pop with the resigned dignity of an exile; Baines didn't complain; he had chosen his fate; and if his fate was Mrs. Baines he had only himself to blame.

But today, because the house was almost empty and Mrs. Baines was upstairs and there was nothing to do, he allowed himself a little acidity.

"I'd go back tomorrow if I had the chance."

"Did you ever shoot a nigger?"

"I never had any call to shoot," Baines said. "Of course I carried a gun. But you didn't need to treat them bad. That just made them stupid. Why," Baines said, bowing his thin gray hair with embarrassment over the ginger pop, "I loved some of those damned niggers. I couldn't help loving them. There they'd be, laughing, holding hands; they liked to touch each other; it made them feel fine to know the other fellow was around.

"It didn't mean anything we could understand; two of them would go about all day without loosing hold, grown men; but it wasn't love; it didn't mean anything we could understand."

---

5. White men living on Africa's Gold Coast in the late nineteenth and early twentieth century.

6. Papaya.

7. Railway and subway (underground) stations.

"Eating between meals," Mrs. Baines said. "What would your mother say, Master Philip?"

She came down the steep stairs to the basement, her hands full of pots of cream and salve, tubes of grease and paste. "You oughtn't to encourage him, Baines," she said, sitting down in a wicker armchair and screwing up her small ill-humored eyes at the Coty lipstick, Pond's cream, the Leichner rouge and Cyclax powder and Elizabeth Arden astringent.

She threw them one by one into the wastepaper basket. She saved only the cold cream. "Telling the boy stories," she said. "Go along to the nursery, Master Philip, while I get lunch."

Philip climbed the stairs to the baize door. He heard Mrs. Baines's voice like the voice in a nightmare when the small Price light[8] has guttered in the saucer and the curtains move; it was sharp and shrill and full of malice, louder than people ought to speak, exposed.

"Sick to death of your ways, Baines, spoiling the boy. Time you did some work about the house," but he couldn't hear what Baines said in reply. He pushed open the baize door, came up like a small earth animal in his gray flannel shorts into a wash of sunlight on a parquet floor, the gleam of mirrors dusted and polished and beautified by Mrs. Baines.

Something broke downstairs, and Philip sadly mounted the stairs to the nursery. He pitied Baines; it occurred to him how happily they could live together in the empty house if Mrs. Baines were called away. He didn't want to play with his Meccano[9] sets; he wouldn't take out his train or his soldiers; he sat at the table with his chin on his hands: this is life; and suddenly he felt responsible for Baines, as if he were the master of the house and Baines an aging servant who deserved to be cared for. There was not much one could do; he decided at least to be good.

He was not surprised when Mrs. Baines was agreeable at lunch; he was used to her changes. Now it was "another helping of meat, Master Philip," or "Master Philip, a little more of this nice pudding." It was a pudding he liked, Queen's pudding[1] with a perfect meringue, but he wouldn't eat a second helping lest she might count that a victory. She was the kind of woman who thought that any injustice could be counterbalanced by something good to eat.

She was sour, but she liked making sweet things; one never had to complain of a lack of jam or plums; she ate well herself and added soft sugar to the meringue and the strawberry jam. The half light through the basement window set the motes moving above her pale hair like dust as she sifted the sugar, and Baines crouched over his plate saying nothing.

Again Philip felt responsibility. Baines had looked forward to this, and Baines was disappointed: everything was being spoilt. The sensation of disappointment was one which Philip could share; knowing nothing of love or jealousy or passion, he could understand better than anyone this grief, something hoped for not happening, something promised not fulfilled, something exciting turning dull. "Baines," he said, "will you take me for a walk this afternoon?"

"No," Mrs. Baines said, "no. That he won't. Not with all the silver to clean."

---

8. Not identified.
9. Building toys similar to Erector sets.

1. Custard made of breadcrumbs, eggs, milk, and raspberry jam, usually topped with browned meringue.

"There's a fortnight to do it in," Baines said.

"Work first, pleasure afterwards." Mrs. Baines helped herself to some more meringue.

Baines suddenly put down his spoon and fork and pushed his plate away. "Blast," he said.

"Temper," Mrs. Baines said softly, "temper. Don't you go breaking any more things, Baines, and I won't have you swearing in front of the boy. Master Philip, if you've finished you can get down." She skinned the rest of the meringue off the pudding.

"I want to go for a walk," Philip said.

"You'll go and have a rest."

"I will go for a walk."

"Master Philip," Mrs. Baines said. She got up from the table, leaving her meringue unfinished, and came toward him, thin, menacing, dusty in the basement room. "Master Philip, you do as you're told." She took him by the arm and squeezed it gently; she watched him with a joyless passionate glitter and above her head the feet of the typists trudged back to the Victoria offices after the lunch interval.

"Why shouldn't I go for a walk?" But he weakened; he was scared and ashamed of being scared. This was life; a strange passion he couldn't understand moving in the basement room. He saw a small pile of broken glass swept into a corner by the wastepaper basket. He looked to Baines for help and only intercepted hate; the sad hopeless hate of something behind bars.

"Why shouldn't I?" he repeated.

"Master Philip," Mrs. Baines said, "you've got to do as you're told. You mustn't think just because your father's away there's nobody here to—"

"You wouldn't dare," Philip cried, and was startled by Baines's low interjection, "There's nothing she wouldn't dare."

"I hate you," Philip said to Mrs. Baines. He pulled away from her and ran to the door, but she was there before him; she was old, but she was quick.

"Master Philip," she said, "you'll say you're sorry." She stood in front of the door quivering with excitement. "What would your father do if he heard you say that?"

She put a hand out to seize him, dry and white with constant soda, the nails cut to the quick, but he backed away and put the table between them, and suddenly to his surprise she smiled; she became again as servile as she had been arrogant. "Get along with you, Master Philip," she said with glee. "I see I'm going to have my hands full till your father and mother come back."

She left the door unguarded and when he passed her she slapped him playfully. "I've got too much to do today to trouble about you. I haven't covered half the chairs," and suddenly even the upper part of the house became unbearable to him as he thought of Mrs. Baines moving round shrouding the sofas, laying out the dust-sheets.

So he wouldn't go upstairs to get his cap but walked straight out across the shining hall into the street, and again, as he looked this way and looked that way, it was life he was in the middle of.

2

It was the pink sugar cakes in the window on a paper doily, the ham, the slab of mauve sausage, the wasps driving like small torpedoes across the pane that caught Philip's attention. His feet were tired by

pavements; he had been afraid to cross the road, had simply walked first in one direction, then in the other. He was nearly home now; the square was at the end of the street; this was a shabby outpost of Pimlico, and he smudged the pane with his nose, looking for sweets, and saw between the cakes and ham a different Baines. He hardly recognized the bulbous eyes, the bald forehead. It was a happy, bold and buccaneering Baines, even though it was, when you looked closer, a desperate Baines.

Philip had never seen the girl. He remembered Baines had a niece and he thought that this might be her. She was thin and drawn, and she wore a white mackintosh; she meant nothing to Philip; she belonged to a world about which he knew nothing at all. He couldn't make up stories about her, as he could make them up about withered Sir Hubert Reed, the Permanent Secretary, about Mrs. Wince-Dudley, who came up once a year from Penstanley in Suffolk with a green umbrella and an enormous black handbag, as he could make them up about the upper servants in all the houses where he went to tea and games. She just didn't belong; he thought of mermaids and Undine; but she didn't belong there either, nor to the adventures of Emil,[2] nor to the Bastables.[3] She sat there looking at an iced pink cake in the detachment and mystery of the completely disinherited, looking at the half-used pots of powder which Baines had set out on the marble-topped table between them.

Baines was urging, hoping, entreating, commanding, and the girl looked at the tea and the china pots and cried. Baines passed his handkerchief across the table, but she wouldn't wipe her eyes; she screwed it in her palm and let the tears run down, wouldn't do anything, wouldn't speak, would only put up a silent despairing resistance to what she dreaded and wanted and refused to listen to at any price. The two brains battled over the teacups loving each other, and there came to Philip outside, beyond the ham and wasps and dusty Pimlico pane, a confused indication of the struggle.

He was inquisitive and he didn't understand and he wanted to know. He went and stood in the doorway to see better, he was less sheltered than he had ever been; other people's lives for the first time touched and pressed and molded. He would never escape that scene. In a week he had forgotten it, but it conditioned his career, the long austerity of his life; when he was dying he said, "Who is she?"

Baines had won; he was cocky and the girl was happy. She wiped her face, she opened a pot of powder, and their fingers touched across the table. It occurred to Philip that it would be amusing to imitate Mrs. Baines's voice and call "Baines" to him from the door.

It shriveled them; you couldn't describe it in any other way; it made them smaller, they weren't happy any more and they weren't bold. Baines was the first to recover and trace the voice, but that didn't make things as they were. The sawdust was spilled out of the afternoon; nothing you did could mend it, and Philip was scared. "I didn't mean . . ." He wanted to say that he loved Baines, that he had only wanted to laugh at Mrs. Baines. But he had discovered that you couldn't laugh at Mrs. Baines. She wasn't Sir Hubert Reed, who used steel nibs and carried a pen-wiper in his pocket; she wasn't Mrs. Wince-Dudley; she was darkness when the night-light went out in a draught; she was

2. In *Emil and the Detectives*, a children's book by Erich Kastner.

3. Children in some of Edith Nesbit's (1858–1924) stories of magic for children.

the frozen blocks of earth he had seen one winter in a graveyard when someone said, "They need an electric drill"; she was the flowers gone bad and smelling in the little closet room at Penstanley. There was nothing to laugh about. You had to endure her when she was there and forget about her quickly when she was away, suppress the thought of her, ram it down deep.

Baines said, "It's only Phil," beckoned him in and gave him the pink iced cake the girl hadn't eaten, but the afternoon was broken, the cake was like dry bread in the throat. The girl left them at once; she even forgot to take the powder; like a small blunt icicle in her white mackintosh she stood in the doorway with her back to them, then melted into the afternoon.

"Who is she?" Philip asked. "Is she your niece?"

"Oh, yes," Baines said, "that's who she is; she's my niece," and poured the last drops of water on to the coarse black leaves in the teapot.

"May as well have another cup," Baines said.

"The cup that cheers," he said hopelessly, watching the bitter black fluid drain out of the spout.

"Have a glass of ginger pop, Phil?"

"I'm sorry. I'm sorry, Baines."

"It's not your fault, Phil. Why, I could believe it wasn't you at all, but her. She creeps in everywhere." He fished two leaves out of his cup and laid them on the back of his hand, a thin soft flake and a hard stalk. He beat them with his hand: "Today," and the stalk detached itself, "tomorrow, Wednesday, Thursday, Friday, Saturday, Sunday," but the flake wouldn't come, stayed where it was, drying under his blows, with a resistance you wouldn't believe it to possess. "The tough one wins," Baines said.

He got up and paid the bill and out they went into the street. Baines said, "I don't ask you to say what isn't true. But you needn't mention to Mrs. Baines you met us here."

"Of course not," Philip said, and catching something of Sir Hubert Reed's manner, "I understand, Baines." But he didn't understand a thing; he was caught up in other people's darkness.

"It was stupid," Baines said. "So near home, but I hadn't time to think, you see. I'd got to see her."

"Of course, Baines."

"I haven't time to spare," Baines said. "I'm not young. I've got to see that she's all right."

"Of course you have, Baines."

"Mrs. Baines will get it out of you if she can."

"You can trust me, Baines," Philip said in a dry important Reed voice; and then, "Look out. She's at the window watching." And there indeed she was, looking up at them, between the lace curtains, from the basement room, speculating. "Need we go in, Baines?" Philip asked, cold lying heavy on his stomach like too much pudding; he clutched Baines's arm.

"Careful," Baines said softly, "careful."

"But need we go in, Baines? It's early. Take me for a walk in the park."

"Better not."

"But I'm frightened, Baines."

"You haven't any cause," Baines said. "Nothing's going to hurt you. You just run along upstairs to the nursery. I'll go down by the area and talk to Mrs. Baines." But even he stood hesitating at the top of the stone steps, pretending not to see her where she watched between the curtains. "In at the front door, Phil, and up the stairs."

Philip didn't linger in the hall; he ran, slithering on the parquet Mrs. Baines had polished, to the stairs. Through the drawing-room doorway on the first floor he saw the draped chairs; even the china clock on the mantel was covered like a canary's cage; as he passed it, it chimed the hour, muffled and secret under the duster.[4] On the nursery table he found his supper laid out: a glass of milk and a piece of bread and butter, a sweet biscuit and a little cold Queen's pudding without the meringue. He had no appetite; he strained his ears for Mrs. Baines's coming, for the sound of voices, but the basement held its secrets; the green baize door shut off that world. He drank the milk and ate the biscuit, but he didn't touch the rest, and presently he could hear the soft precise footfalls of Mrs. Baines on the stairs: she was a good servant, she walked softly; she was a determined woman, she walked precisely.

But she wasn't angry when she came in; she was ingratiating as she opened the night nursery door—"Did you have a good walk, Master Philip?"—pulled down the blinds, laid out his pajamas, came back to clear his supper. "I'm glad Baines found you. Your mother wouldn't have liked your being out alone." She examined the tray. "Not much appetite, have you, Master Philip? Why don't you try a little of this nice pudding? I'll bring you up some more jam for it."

"No, no, thank you, Mrs. Baines," Philip said.

"You ought to eat more," Mrs. Baines said. She sniffed round the room like a dog. "You didn't take any pots out of the wastepaper basket in the kitchen, did you, Master Philip?"

"No," Philip said.

"Of course you wouldn't. I just wanted to make sure." She patted his shoulder and her fingers flashed to his lapel; she picked off a tiny crumb of pink sugar. "Oh, Master Philip," she said, "that's why you haven't any appetite. You've been buying sweet cakes. That's not what your pocket money's for."

"But I didn't," Philip said. "I didn't."

She tasted the sugar with the tip of her tongue.

"Don't tell lies to me, Master Philip. I won't stand for it any more than your father would."

"I didn't, I didn't," Philip said. "They gave it me. I mean Baines," but she had pounced on the word "they." She had got what she wanted; there was no doubt about that, even when you didn't know what it was she wanted. Philip was angry and miserable and disappointed because he hadn't kept Baines's secret. Baines oughtn't to have trusted him; grown-up people should keep their own secrets, and yet here was Mrs. Baines immediately entrusting him with another.

"Let me tickle your palm and see if you can keep a secret." But he put his hand behind him; he wouldn't be touched. "It's a secret between us, Master Philip, that I know all about them. I suppose she was having tea with him," she speculated.

"Why shouldn't she?" he said, the responsibility for Baines weighing on his spirit, the idea that he had got to keep her secret when he

4. Light cloth cover to keep off dust.

hadn't kept Baines's making him miserable with the unfairness of life. "She was nice."

"She was nice, was she?" Mrs. Baines said in a bitter voice he wasn't used to.

"And she's his niece."

"So that's what he said," Mrs. Baines struck softly back at him like the clock under the duster. She tried to be jocular. "The old scoundrel. Don't you tell him I know, Master Philip." She stood very still between the table and the door, thinking very hard, planning something. "Promise you won't tell. I'll give you that Meccano set, Master Philip. . . . "

He turned his back on her; he wouldn't promise, but he wouldn't tell. He would have nothing to do with their secrets, the responsibilities they were determined to lay on him. He was only anxious to forget. He had received already a larger dose of life than he had bargained for, and he was scared. "A 2A Meccano set, Master Philip." He never opened his Meccano set again, never built anything, never created anything, died, the old dilettante, sixty years later, with nothing to show rather than preserve the memory of Mrs. Baines's malicious voice saying goodnight, her soft determined footfalls on the stairs to the basement, going down, going down.

3

The sun poured in between the curtains and Baines was beating a tattoo on the water-can. "Glory, glory," Baines said. He sat down on the end of the bed and said, "I beg to announce that Mrs. Baines has been called away. Her mother's dying. She won't be back till tomorrow."

"Why did you wake me up so early?" Philip said. He watched Baines with uneasiness; he wasn't going to be drawn in; he'd learned his lesson. It wasn't right for a man of Baines's age to be so merry. It made a grown person human in the same way that you were human. For if a grown-up could behave so childishly, you were liable too to find yourself in their world. It was enough that it came at you in dreams: the witch at the corner, the man with a knife. So "It's very early," he complained, even though he loved Baines, even though he couldn't help being glad that Baines was happy. He was divided by the fear and the attraction of life.

"I want to make this a long day," Baines said. "This is the best time." He pulled the curtains back. "It's a bit misty. The cat's been out all night. There she is, sniffing round the area. They haven't taken in any milk at 59. Emma's shaking out the mats at 63." He said, "This was what I used to think about on the Coast: somebody shaking mats and the cat coming home. I can see it today," Baines said, "just as if I was still in Africa. Most days you don't notice what you've got. It's a good life if you don't weaken." He put a penny on the washstand. "When you've dressed, Phil, run and get a *Mail* from the barrow[5] at the corner. I'll be cooking the sausages."

"Sausages?"

"Sausages," Baines said. "We're going to celebrate today. A fair bust." He celebrated at breakfast, reckless, cracking jokes, unaccountably merry and nervous. It was going to be a long, long day, he kept

5. (News)stand.

on coming back to that: for years he had waited for a long day, he had sweated in the damp Coast heat, changed shirts, gone down with fever, lain between the blankets and sweated, all in the hope of this long day, that cat sniffing round the area, a bit of mist, the mats beaten at 63. He propped the *Mail* in front of the coffeepot and read pieces aloud. He said, "Cora Down's been married for the fourth time." He was amused, but it wasn't his idea of a long day. His long day was the Park, watching the riders in the Row, seeing Sir Arthur Stillwater pass beyond the rails ("He dined with us once in Bo; up from Freetown,[6] he was governor there"), lunch at the Corner House for Philip's sake (he'd have preferred himself a glass of stout and some oysters at the York bar), the Zoo, the long bus ride home in the last summer light: the leaves in the Green Park were beginning to turn and the motors nuzzled out of Berkeley Street with the low sun gently glowing on their wind-screens. Baines envied no one, not Cora Down, or Sir Arthur Stillwater, or Lord Sandale, who came out on to the steps of the Army and Navy and then went back again because he hadn't got anything to do and might as well look at another paper. "I said don't let me see you touch that black again." Baines had led a man's life; everyone on top of the bus pricked their ears when he told Philip all about it.

"Would you have shot him?" Philip asked, and Baines put his head back and tilted his dark respectable man-servant's hat to a better angle as the bus swerved round the artillery memorial.

"I wouldn't have thought twice about it. I'd have shot to kill," he boasted, and the bowed figure went by, the steel helmet, the heavy cloak, the down-turned rifle and the folded hands.

"Have you got the revolver?"

"Of course I've got it," Baines said. "Don't I need it with all the burglaries there've been?" This was the Baines whom Philip loved: not Baines singing and carefree, but Baines responsible, Baines behind barriers, living his man's life.

All the buses streamed out from Victoria like a convoy of airplanes to bring Baines home with honor. "Forty blacks under me," and there waiting near the area steps was the proper conventional reward, love at lighting-up time.

"It's your niece," Philip said, recognizing the white mackintosh, but not the happy sleepy face. She frightened him like an unlucky number; he nearly told Baines what Mrs. Baines had said; but he didn't want to bother, he wanted to leave things alone.

"Why, so it is," Baines said. "I shouldn't wonder if she was going to have a bite of supper with us." But he said they'd play a game, pretend they didn't know her, slip down the area steps, "and here," Baines said, "we are," lay the table, put out the cold sausages, a bottle of beer, a bottle of ginger pop, a flagon of harvest burgundy. "Everyone his own drink," Baines said. "Run upstairs, Phil, and see if there's been a post."

Philip didn't like the empty house at dusk before the lights went on. He hurried. He wanted to be back with Baines. The hall lay there in quiet and shadow prepared to show him something he didn't want to see. Some letters rustled down, and someone knocked. "Open in the name of the Republic." The tumbrils rolled, the head bobbed in the

6. Inland city and coastal capital, respectively, of Sierra Leone, West Africa, then a British colony. The Row, above, is Rotten Row, area for horseback riding in Hyde Park; the Zoo, below, is in Regent's Park. These and Green Park, also mentioned, are all London public parks.

bloody basket. Knock, knock, and the postman's footsteps going away. Philip gathered the letters. The slit in the door was like the grating in a jeweler's window. He remembered the policeman he had seen peer through. He had said to his nurse, "What's he doing?" and when she said, "He's seeing if everything's all right," his brain immediately filled with images of all that might be wrong. He ran to the baize door and the stairs. The girl was already there and Baines was kissing her. She leaned breathless against the dresser.[7]

"This is Emmy, Phil."

"There's a letter for you, Baines."

"Emmy," Baines said, "it's from her." But he wouldn't open it. "You bet she's coming back."

"We'll have supper, anyway," Emmy said. "She can't harm that."

"You don't know her," Baines said. "Nothing's safe. Damn it," he said, "I was a man once," and he opened the letter.

"Can I start?" Philip asked, but Baines didn't hear; he presented in his stillness and attention an example of the importance grown-up people attached to the written word: you had to write your thanks, not wait and speak them, as if letters couldn't lie. But Philip knew better than that, sprawling his thanks across a page to Aunt Alice who had given him a doll he was too old for. Letters could lie all right, but they made the lie permanent: they lay as evidence against you; they made you meaner than the spoken word.

"She's not coming back till tomorrow night," Baines said. He opened the bottles, he pulled up the chairs, he kissed Emmy again against the dresser.

"You oughtn't to," Emmy said, "with the boy here."

"He's got to learn," Baines said, "like the rest of us," and he helped Philip to three sausages. He only took one himself; he said he wasn't hungry; but when Emmy said she wasn't hungry either he stood over her and made her eat. He was timid and rough with her; he made her drink the harvest burgundy because he said she needed building up; he wouldn't take no for an answer, but when he touched her his hands were light and clumsy too, as if he were afraid to damage something delicate and didn't know how to handle anything so light.

"This is better than milk and biscuits, eh?"

"Yes," Philip said, but he was scared, scared for Baines as much as for himself. He couldn't help wondering at every bite, at every draught of the ginger pop, what Mrs. Baines would say if she ever learned of this meal; he couldn't imagine it, there was a depth of bitterness and rage in Mrs. Baines you couldn't sound. He said, "She won't be coming back tonight?" but you could tell by the way they immediately understood him that she wasn't really away at all; she was there in the basement with them, driving them to longer drinks and louder talk, biding her time for the right cutting word. Baines wasn't really happy; he was only watching happiness from close to instead of from far away.

"No," he said, "she'll not be back till late tomorrow." He couldn't keep his eyes off happiness; he'd not played around as much as other men, he kept on reverting to the Coast as if to excuse himself for his innocence; he wouldn't have been so innocent if he had lived his life in London, so innocent when it came to tenderness. "If it was you,

7. Sideboard or table used in kitchen for food preparation and storing dishes and utensils.

Emmy," he said, looking at the white dresser, the scrubbed chairs, "this'd be like a home." Already the room was not quite so harsh; there was a little dust in corners, the silver needed a final polish, the morning's paper lay untidily on a chair. "You'd better go to bed, Phil; it's been a long day."

They didn't leave him to find his own way up through the dark shrouded house; they went with him, turning on lights, touching each other's fingers on the switches; floor after floor they drove the night back; they spoke softly among the covered chairs; they watched him undress, they didn't make him wash or clean his teeth, they saw him into bed and lit his night-light and left his door ajar. He could hear their voices on the stairs, friendly, like the guests he heard at dinner parties when they moved down to the hall, saying good night. They belonged; wherever they were they made a home. He heard a door open and a clock strike, he heard their voices for a long while, so that he felt they were not far away and he was safe. The voices didn't dwindle, they simply went out, and he could be sure that they were still somewhere not far from him, silent together in one of the many empty rooms, growing sleepy together as he grew sleepy after the long day.

He had just time to sigh faintly with satisfaction, because this too perhaps had been life, before he slept and the inevitable terrors of sleep came round him: a man with a tricolor hat[8] beat at the door on His Majesty's service, a bleeding head lay on the kitchen table in a basket, and the Siberian wolves crept closer. He was bound hand and foot and couldn't move; they leaped around him breathing heavily; he opened his eyes and Mrs. Baines was there, her gray untidy hair in threads over his face, her black hat askew. A loose hairpin fell on the pillow and one musty thread brushed his mouth. "Where are they?" she whispered. "Where are they?"

4

Philip watched her in terror. Mrs. Baines was out of breath as if she had been searching all the empty rooms, looking under loose covers.

With her untidy gray hair and her black dress buttoned to her throat, her gloves of black cotton, she was so like the witches of his dreams that he didn't dare to speak. There was a stale smell in her breath.

"She's here," Mrs. Baines said; "you can't deny she's here." Her face was simultaneously marked with cruelty and misery; she wanted to "do things" to people, but she suffered all the time. It would have done her good to scream, but she daren't do that: it would warn them. She came ingratiatingly back to the bed where Philip lay rigid on his back and whispered, "I haven't forgotten the Meccano set. You shall have it tomorrow, Master Philip. We've got secrets together, haven't we? Just tell me where they are."

He couldn't speak. Fear held him as firmly as any nightmare. She said, "Tell Mrs. Baines, Master Philip. You love your Mrs. Baines, don't you?" That was too much; he couldn't speak, but he could move his mouth in terrified denial, wince away from her dusty image.

She whispered, coming closer to him, "Such deceit. I'll tell your father. I'll settle with you myself when I've found them. You'll smart; I'll see you smart." Then immediately she was still, listening. A board

8. Red, white, and blue, colors of French revolutionaries.

had creaked on the floor below, and a moment later, while she stooped listening above his bed, there came the whispers of two people who were happy and sleepy together after a long day. The night-light stood beside the mirror and Mrs. Baines could see bitterly there her own reflection, misery and cruelty wavering in the glass, age and dust and nothing to hope for. She sobbed without tears, a dry, breathless sound; but her cruelty was a kind of pride which kept her going; it was her best quality, she would have been merely pitiable without it. She went out of the door on tiptoe, feeling her way across the landing, going so softly down the stairs that no one behind a shut door could hear her. Then there was complete silence again; Philip could move; he raised his knees; he sat up in bed; he wanted to die. It wasn't fair, the walls were down again between his world and theirs; but this time it was something worse than merriment that the grown people made him share; a passion moved in the house he recognized but could not understand.

It wasn't fair, but he owed Baines everything: the Zoo, the ginger pop, the bus ride home. Even the supper called on his loyalty. But he was frightened; he was touching something he touched in dreams: the bleeding head, the wolves, the knock, knock, knock. Life fell on him with savagery: you couldn't blame him if he never faced it again in sixty years. He got out of bed, carefully from habit put on his bedroom slippers, and tiptoed to the door: it wasn't quite dark on the landing below because the curtains had been taken down for the cleaners and the light from the street came in through the tall windows. Mrs. Baines had her hand on the glass doorknob; she was very carefully turning it; he screamed, "Baines, Baines."

Mrs. Baines turned and saw him cowering in his pajamas by the banisters; he was helpless, more helpless even than Baines, and cruelty grew at the sight of him and drove her up the stairs. The nightmare was on him again and he couldn't move; he hadn't any more courage left for ever; he'd spent it all, had been allowed no time to let it grow, no years of gradual hardening; he couldn't even scream.

But the first cry had brought Baines out of the best spare bedroom and he moved quicker than Mrs. Baines. She hadn't reached the top of the stairs before he'd caught her round the waist. She drove her black cotton gloves at his face and he bit her hand. He hadn't time to think, he fought her savagely like a stranger, but she fought back with knowledgeable hate. She was going to teach them all and it didn't really matter whom she began with; they had all deceived her; but the old image in the glass was by her side, telling her she must be dignified, she wasn't young enough to yield her dignity; she could beat his face, but she mustn't bite; she could push, but she mustn't kick.

Age and dust and nothing to hope for were her handicaps. She went over the banisters in a flurry of black clothes and fell into the hall; she lay before the front door like a sack of coals which should have gone down the area into the basement. Philip saw; Emmy saw; she sat down suddenly in the doorway of the best spare bedroom with her eyes open as if she were too tired to stand any longer. Baines went slowly down into the hall.

It wasn't hard for Philip to escape; they'd forgotten him completely; he went down the back, the servants' stairs because Mrs. Baines was in the hall; he didn't understand what she was doing lying there; like the startling pictures in a book no one had read to him, the things he didn't understand terrified him. The whole house had been turned

over to the grown-up world; he wasn't safe in the night nursery; their passions had flooded it. The only thing he could do was to get away, by the back stair, and up through the area, and never come back. You didn't think of the cold, of the need of food and sleep; for an hour it would seem quite possible to escape from people forever.

He was wearing pajamas and bedroom slippers when he came up into the square, but there was no one to see him. It was that hour of the evening in a residential district when everyone is at the theater or at home. He climbed over the iron railings into the little garden: the plane-trees spread their large pale palms between him and the sky. It might have been an illimitable forest into which he had escaped. He crouched behind a trunk and the wolves retreated; it seemed to him between the little iron seat and the tree trunk that no one would ever find him again. A kind of embittered happiness and self-pity made him cry; he was lost; there wouldn't be any more secrets to keep; he surrendered responsibility once and for all. Let grown-up people keep to their world and he would keep to his, safe in the small garden between the plane-trees. "In the lost childhood of Judas Christ was betrayed"; you could almost see the small unformed face hardening into the deep dilettante selfishness of age.

Presently the door of 48 opened and Baines looked this way and that; then he signaled with his hand and Emmy came; it was as if they were only just in time for a train, they hadn't a chance at saying good-bye; she went quickly by, like a face at a window swept past the platform, pale and unhappy and not wanting to go. Baines went in again and shut the door; the light was lit in the basement, and a policeman walked round the square, looking into the areas. You could tell how many families were at home by the lights behind the first-floor[9] curtains.

Philip explored the garden: it didn't take long: a twenty-yard square of bushes and plane-trees, two iron seats and a gravel path, a padlocked gate at either end, a scuffle of old leaves. But he couldn't stay: something stirred in the bushes and two illuminated eyes peered out at him like a Siberian wolf, and he thought how terrible it would be if Mrs. Baines found him there. He'd have no time to climb the railings; she'd seize him from behind.

He left the square at the unfashionable end and was immediately among the fish-and-chip shops, the little stationers selling Bagatelle,[1] among the accommodation addresses[2] and the dingy hotels with open doors. There were few people about because the pubs were open, but a blowzy woman carrying a parcel called out to him across the street and the commissionaire[3] outside a cinema would have stopped him if he hadn't crossed the road. He went deeper: you could go farther and lose yourself more completely here than among the plane-trees. On the fringe of the square he was in danger of being stopped and taken back: it was obvious where he belonged: but as he went deeper he lost the marks of his origin. It was a warm night: any child in those free-living parts might be expected to play truant from bed. He found a kind of camaraderie even among grown-up people; he might have been a neighbor's child as he went quickly by, but they weren't going to tell on him, they'd been young once themselves. He picked up a protective

9. I.e., second floor, the first floor above the ground floor.
1. Game resembling billiards, sometimes called "semi-billiards."
2. Houses where rooms can be hired for short periods; brothels.
3. Doorman.

coating of dust from the pavements, of smuts from the trains which passed along the backs in a spray of fire. Once he was caught in a knot of children running away from something or somebody, laughing as they ran; he was whirled with them round a turning and abandoned, with a sticky fruit-drop in his hand.

He couldn't have been more lost; but he hadn't the stamina to keep on. At first he feared that someone would stop him; after an hour he hoped that someone would. He couldn't find his way back, and in any case he was afraid of arriving home alone; he was afraid of Mrs. Baines, more afraid than he had ever been. Baines was his friend, but something had happened which gave Mrs. Baines all the power. He began to loiter on purpose to be noticed, but no one noticed him. Families were having a last breather on the doorsteps, the refuse bins had been put out and bits of cabbage stalks soiled his slippers. The air was full of voices, but he was cut off; these people were strangers and would always now be strangers; they were marked by Mrs. Baines and he shied away from them into a deep class-consciousness. He had been afraid of policemen, but now he wanted one to take him home; even Mrs. Baines could no nothing against a policeman. He sidled past a constable who was directing traffic, but he was too busy to pay him any attention. Philip sat down against a wall and cried.

It hadn't occurred to him that that was the easiest way, that all you had to do was to surrender, to show you were beaten and accept kindness. . . . It was lavished on him at once by two women and a pawnbroker. Another policeman appeared, a young man with a sharp incredulous face. He looked as if he noted everything he saw in pocketbooks and drew conclusions. A woman offered to see Philip home, but he didn't trust her: she wasn't a match for Mrs. Baines immobile in the hall. He wouldn't give his address; he said he was afraid to go home. He had his way; he got his protection. "I'll take him to the station," the policeman said, and holding him awkwardly by the hand (he wasn't married; he had his career to make) he led him round the corner, up the stone stairs into the little bare overheated room where Justice waited.

5

Justice waited behind a wooden counter on a high stool; it wore a heavy moustache; it was kindly and had six children ("three of them nippers like yourself"); it wasn't really interested in Philip, but it pretended to be, it wrote the address down and sent a constable to fetch a glass of milk. But the young constable was interested; he had a nose for things.

"Your home's on the telephone, I suppose," Justice said. "We'll ring them up and say you are safe. They'll fetch you very soon. What's your name, sonny?"

"Philip."

"Your other name."

"I haven't got another name." He didn't want to be fetched; he wanted to be taken home by someone who would impress even Mrs. Baines. The constable watched him, watched the way he drank the milk, watched him when he winced away from questions.

"What made you run away? Playing truant, eh?"

"I don't know."

"You oughtn't to do it, young fellow. Think how anxious your father and mother will be."

"They are away."

"Well, your nurse."

"I haven't got one."

"Who looks after you, then?" That question went home. Philip saw Mrs. Baines coming up the stairs at him, the heap of black cotton in the hall. He began to cry.

"Now, now, now," the sergeant said. He didn't know what to do; he wished his wife were with him; even a policewoman might have been useful.

"Don't you think it's funny," the constable said, "that there hasn't been an inquiry?"

"They think he's tucked up in bed."

"You are scared, aren't you?" the constable said. "What scared you?"

"I don't know."

"Somebody hurt you?"

"No."

"He's had bad dreams," the sergeant said. "Thought the house was on fire, I expect. I've brought up six of them. Rose is due back. She'll take him home."

"I want to go home with you," Philip said; he tried to smile at the constable, but the deceit was immature and unsuccessful.

"I'd better go," the constable said. "There may be something wrong."

"Nonsense," the sergeanat said. "It's a woman's job. Tact is what you need. Here's Rose. Pull up your stockings, Rose. You're a disgrace to the Force. I've got a job of work for you." Rose shambled in: black cotton stockings drooping over her boots, a gawky Girl Guide[4] manner, a hoarse hostile voice. "More tarts, I suppose."

"No, you've got to see this young man home." She looked at him owlishly.

"I won't go with her," Philip said. He began to cry again. "I don't like her."

"More of that womanly charm, Rose," the sergeant said. The telephone rang on his desk. He lifted the receiver. "What? What's that?" he said. "Number 48? You've got a doctor?" He put his hand over the telephone mouth. "No wonder this nipper wasn't reported," he said. "They've been too busy. An accident. Woman slipped on the stairs."

"Serious?" the constable asked. The sergeant mouthed at him; you didn't mention the word death before a child (didn't he know? he had six of them), you made noises in the throat, you grimaced, a complicated shorthand for a word of only five letters anyway.

"You'd better go, after all," he said, "and make a report. The doctor's there."

Rose shambled from the stove; pink apply-dapply cheeks, loose stockings. She stuck her hands behind her. Her large morgue-like mouth was full of blackened teeth. "You told me to take him and now just because something interesting . . . I don't expect justice from a man . . ."

"Who's at the house?" the constable asked.

"The butler."

"You don't think," the constable said, "he saw . . ."

"Trust me," the sergeant said. "I've brought up six. I know 'em through and through. You can't teach me anything about children."

"He seemed scared about something."

4. Member of the British organization similar to Girl Scouts.

"Dreams," the sergeant said.

"What name?"

"Baines."

"This Mr. Baines," the constable said to Philip, "you like him, eh? He's good to you?" They were trying to get something out of him; he was suspicious of the whole roomful of them; he said "yes" without conviction because he was afraid at any moment of more responsibilities, more secrets.

"And Mrs. Baines?"

"Yes."

They consulted together by the desk: Rose was hoarsely aggrieved; she was like a female impersonator, she bore her womanhood with an unnatural emphasis even while she scorned it in her creased stockings and her weather-exposed face. The charcoal shifted in the stove; the room was overheated in the mild late summer evening. A notice on the wall described a body found in the Thames, or rather the body's clothes: wool vest,[5] wool pants, wool shirt with blue stripes, size ten boots, blue serge suit worn at the elbows, fifteen-and-a-half celluloid collar. They couldn't find anything to say about the body, except its measurements, it was just an ordinary body.

"Come along," the constable said. He was interested, he was glad to be going, but he couldn't help being embarrassed by his company, a small boy in pajamas. His nose smelled something, he didn't know what, but he smarted at the sight of the amusement they caused: the pubs had closed and the streets were full again of men making as long a day of it as they could. He hurried through the less-frequented streets, chose the darker pavements, wouldn't loiter, and Philip wanted more and more to loiter, pulling at his hand, dragging with his feet. He dreaded the sight of Mrs. Baines waiting in the hall: he knew now that she was dead. The sergeant's mouthings had conveyed that; but she wasn't buried, she wasn't out of sight; he was going to see a dead person in the hall when the door opened.

The light was on in the basement, and to his relief the constable made for the area steps. Perhaps he wouldn't have to see Mrs. Baines at all. The constable knocked on the door because it was too dark to see the bell, and Baines answered. He stood there in the doorway of the neat bright basement room and you could see the sad complacent plausible sentence he had prepared wither at the sight of Philip; he hadn't expected Philip to return like that in the policeman's company. He had to begin thinking all over again; he wasn't a deceptive man; if it hadn't been for Emmy he would have been quite ready to let the truth lead him where it would.

"Mr. Baines?" the constable asked.

He nodded; he hadn't found the right words; he was daunted by the shrewd knowing face, the sudden appearance of Philip there.

"This little boy from here?"

"Yes," Baines said. Philip could tell that there was a message he was trying to convey, but he shut his mind to it. He loved Baines, but Baines had involved him in secrets, in fears he didn't understand. The glowing morning thought, "This is life," had become under Baines's tuition the repugnant memory, "That was life": the musty hair across the mouth, the breathless cruel tortured inquiry, "Where are they," the heap of black cotton tipped into the hall. That was what happened

5. Undershirt.

when you loved: you got involved; and Philip extricated himself from
life, from love, from Baines, with a merciless egotism.

There had been things between them, but he laid them low, as a
retreating army cuts the wires, destroys the bridges. In the abandoned
country you may leave much that is dear—a morning in the Park, an
ice at a corner house, sausages for supper—but more is concerned in
the retreat than temporary losses. There are old people who, as the
tractors wheel away, implore to be taken, but you can't risk the rear-
guard for their sake: a whole prolonged retreat from life, from care,
from human relationships is involved.

"The doctor's here," Baines said. He nodded at the door, moistened
his mouth, kept his eyes on Philip, begging for something like a dog
you can't understand. "There's nothing to be done. She slipped on
these stone basement stairs. I was in here. I heard her fall." He
wouldn't look at the notebook, at the constable's tiny spidery writing
which got a terrible lot on one page.

"Did the boy see anything?"

"He can't have done. I thought he was in bed. Hadn't he better go
up? It's a shocking thing. Oh," Baines said, losing control, "it's a
shocking thing for a child."

"She's through there?" the constable asked.

"I haven't moved her an inch," Baines said.

"He'd better then——"

"Go up the area and through the hall," Baines said and again he
begged dumbly like a dog: one more secret, keep this secret, do this
for old Baines, he won't ask another.

"Come along," the constable said. "I'll see you up to bed. You're a
gentleman; you must come in the proper way through the front door
like the master should. Or will you go along with him, Mr. Baines,
while I see the doctor?"

"Yes," Baines said, "I'll go." He came across the room to Philip,
begging, begging, all the way with his soft old stupid expression: this
is Baines, the old Coaster; what about a palm-oil chop, eh?; a man's
life; forty niggers; never used a gun; I tell you I couldn't help loving
them: it wasn't what we call love, nothing we could understand. The
messages flickered out from the last posts at the border, imploring,
beseeching, reminding: this is your old friend Baines; what about an
eleven's,[6] a glass of ginger pop won't do you any harm; sausages; a
long day. But the wires were cut, the messages just faded out into the
enormous vacancy of the neat scrubbed room in which there had
never been a place where a man could hide his secrets.

"Come along, Phil, it's bedtime. We'll just go up the steps . . ." Tap,
tap, tap, at the telegraph; you may get through, you can't tell, somebody may mend the right wire. "And in at the front door."

"No," Philip said, "no. I won't go. You can't make me go. I'll fight.
I won't see her."

The constable turned on them quickly. "What's that? Why won't
you go?"

"She's in the hall," Philip said. "I know she's in the hall. And she's
dead. I won't see her."

"You moved her then?" the constable said to Baines. "All the way
down here? You've been lying, eh? That means you had to tidy up. . . .
Were you alone?"

6. Eleven o'clock tea and snack.

"Emmy," Philip said, "Emmy." He wasn't going to keep any more secrets: he was going to finish once and for all with everything, with Baines and Mrs. Baines and the grown-up life beyond him; it wasn't his business and never, never again, he decided, would he share their confidences and companionship. "It was all Emmy's fault," he protested with a quaver which reminded Baines that after all he was only a child; it had been hopeless to expect help there; he was a child; he didn't understand what it all meant; he couldn't read this shorthand of terror; he'd had a long day and he was tired out. You could see him dropping asleep where he stood against the dresser, dropping back into the comfortable nursery peace. You couldn't blame him. When he woke in the morning, he'd hardly remember a thing.

"Out with it," the constable said, addressing Baines with professional ferocity, "who is she?" just as the old man sixty years later startled his secretary, his only watcher, asking, "Who is she? Who is she?" dropping lower and lower into death, passing on the way perhaps the image of Baines: Baines hopeless, Baines letting his head drop, Baines "coming clean."

1936

ALBERT MURRAY

Train Whistle Guitar

Lil' Buddy's color was that sky blue in which hens cackled; it was that smoke blue in which dogs barked and mosquito hawks lit on barbed-wire fences. It was the color above meadows. It was my color too because it was a boy's color. It was whistling blue and hunting blue, and it went with baseball, and that was old Lil' Buddy again, and that blue beyond outfields was exactly what we were singing about when we used to sing that old one about it ain't gonna rain no more no more.[1]

Steel blue was a man's color. That was the clean, oil-smelling color of rifle barrels and railroad iron. That was the color that went with Luzana Cholly, and he had a steel-blue 32–20 on a 44 frame.[2] His complexion was not steel blue but leather brown like dark rawhide, but steel blue was the color that went with what he was. His hands were just like rawhide, and when he was not dressed up he smelled like green oak steam. He had on slick starched blue denim overalls then, and when he was dressed up he wore a black broadcloth box-back coat with hickory-striped peg-top pants, and he smelled like the barber shop and new money.

Luzana Cholly was there in that time and place as far back as I can remember, even before Lil' Buddy was. Because I can remember when I didn't know Lil' Buddy at all. I can remember when that house they moved to was built (Lil' Buddy's papa and mama were still living together when they came to Gasoline Point from Choctaw County, which was near the Mississippi line), and I can also remember when that street (which was called Chattanooga Lookout Street) was

---

1. Dance song with both mountaineer and Negro versions that moved west from Kentucky and other Southern states and dates at least from the 1870s: "It ain't gonna rain, it ain't gonna snow,/It ain't gonna rain no mo';/Come on ev'rybody now,/Ain't gonna rain no mo'."

2. A smaller caliber barrel (32–20) on a larger mounting, more common in 1920s.

pushed all the way through to the AT&N[3] cut. That was before I had ever even heard of Lil' Buddy, and my buddy then was old Willie Marlowe. Lil' Buddy didn't come until after Willie Marlowe had gone to Detroit, Michigan, and that was not until after Mister One-Arm Will had been dead and buried for about nine months.

I can remember him there in that wee time when I couldn't even follow the stories I knew later they were telling about him, when it was only just grown folks talking, and all I could make of it was *Luzana, they are talking something about old Luzana again, and I didn't know what,* to say nothing of where Louisiana was. But old Luze was there even then and I could see him very clearly when they said his name because I had already seen him coming up that road that came by that house with the chinaberry yard, coming from around the bend and down in the railroad bottom; and I had already heard whatever that was he was picking on his guitar and heard that holler too. That was always far away and long coming. It started low like it was going to be a song, and then it jumped all the way to the very top of his voice and broke off, and then it started again, and this time was already at the top, and then it gave some quick jerking squalls and died away in the woods, the water, and the darkness (you always heard it at night), and Mama always said he was whooping and hollering like somebody back in the rosin-woods country, and Papa said it was one of them old Luzana swamp hollers. I myself always thought it was like a train, like a bad train saying look out this is me, and here I come, and I'm coming through.

That was even before I was big enough to climb the chinaberry tree. That was when they used to talk about the war and the Kaiser,[4] and I can remember that there was a war book with Germans in it, and I used to see sure-enough soldiers marching in the Mardi Gras parades. Soldier Boy Crawford was still wearing his Army coat then, and he was the one who used to tell about how Luze used to play his guitar in France, telling about how they would be going through some French town like the ones called Nancy and Saint Die and old Luze would drop out of the company and go and play around in the underground wine shops until he got as much cognac and as many French Frogs[5] as he wanted and then he would turn up in the company again and Capt'n would put him out by himself on the worst outpost he could find in No Man's Land and old Luze would stay out there sometimes for three or four days and nights knocking off patrol after patrol, and one time in another place, which was the Hindenburg Line,[6] old Luze was out there again and there were a few shots late in the afternoon and then it was all quiet until about three o'clock the next morning and then all hell broke loose, and the Capt'n thought that a whole German battalion was about to move in, and he sent five patrols out to find out what was happening, but when they got there all they found was old Luze all dug in and bristling with enough ammunition to blow up kingdom come; he had crawled around all during the afternoon collecting hand grenades and a mortar and two machine guns and even a light two-wheel cannon, and when they asked him what was going on he told them that he had fallen off to sleep and when he woke up he didn't know whether or not any Germans had snuck up so he thought

---

3. Alabama, Tennessee, and Northern Railroad.
4. Wilhelm II (1859–1941), ruler of Germany during World War I, 1914–1918.

5. Derogatory term for French.
6. Strong defense line established by the Germans in 1916 and the scene of heavy fighting, especially in 1917.

he'd better lay himself down a little light barrage. The next morning they found out that old Luze had wiped out a whole German platoon but when the Capt'n sent for him to tell him he was going to give him a medal, old Luze had cut out and was off somewhere picking the guitar and drinking cognac and chasing the mademoiselles again. He went through the whole war like that and he came out of the Army without a single scratch, didn't even get flat feet.

I heard a lot of stories about the war and I used to draw pictures of them fighting with bayonets in the Argonne Forest,[7] and Soldier Boy Crawford used to look at them and shake his head and give me a nickel and say that some day I was going to be a soldier too.

I used to draw automobiles too, especially the Hudson Super-Six, like old Long George Nisby had; he said it would do sixty on a straightaway, and he had a heavy blasting cut-out on it that jarred the ground. Old Man Perc Stranahan had a Studebaker but he was a white man and he didn't have a cut-out, and he drove as slow as a hearse. Old Gander said Old Man Perc always drove like he was trying to sneak up on something but he never was going to catch it like that. The cars I didn't like then were the flat-engine Buick and the old humpbacked Hupmobile. I liked the Maxwell and the Willys Knight and the Pierce Arrow.

I was playing train then too, and the trains were there before the automobiles were (there were many more horses and buggies in that part of town than there were automobiles then). I couldn't sit up in my nest in the chinaberry tree and see the trains yet, because I could not climb it yet, but I saw them when Papa used to take me to the L&N[8] bottom to see them come by and I knew them all, and the Pan American was the fastest and Number Four was the fastest that ran in the daytime. Old Luzana could tell you all about the Southern Pacific and the Santa Fe, but that was later. But I already knew something about the Southern Pacific because Cousin Roberta had already gone all the way to Los Angeles, California, on the Sunset Limited.

I used to be in bed and hear the night trains coming by. The Crescent came by at nine-thirty and if you woke up way in the middle of the night you could hear Number Two. I was in my warm bed in that house, and I could hear the whistle coming even before it got to Chickasabogue Bridge and it had a bayou sound then, and then I could hear the engine batting it hell-for-leather on down the line bound for Mobile and New Orleans, and the next time the whistle came it was for Three Mile Creek. It was getting on into the beel[9] then. I played train by myself in the daytime then, looking out the window along the side of the house like an engineer looking down along the drivers.

I used to hear old Stagolee playing the piano over in Hot Water Shorty's jook[1] at night too, even then, especially on Saturday night. They rocked all night long, and I was lying in my warm quilted bed by the window. Uncle Jimmy's bed was by the window on the other side of the fireplace. When it was cold, you could wake up way in the night and still see the red embers in the ashes, and hear the wind whining outside, and sometimes you could hear the boat whistles too, and I could lie listening from where I was and tell you when it was a

7. **Forest in northeast France near Belgian border where Allies, including Americans, launched an offensive, September–November 1918.**

8. **Louisville and Nashville Railroad.**
9. *Beal*, mouth of creek or valley.
1. Roadhouse, juke-joint.

launch pulling a log raft or a tugboat pulling a barge or a riverboat like the *Nettie Queen,* and sometimes it was a big ship like the *Luchenback* called the Looking Back, which was all the way down at the city wharf at the foot of Government Street.

I knew a lot about the big ships because Uncle Jimmy worked on the wharf. That was before the state docks were built and the big Gulfgoing and ocean-going ships didn't come on past Mobile then unless they were going up to Chickasaw to be overhauled, but I had already seen them and had been on ships from England and France and Holland and naturally there were always ships from the Caribbean and South America because that was where the fruit boats came from.

All I could do was see old Luzana Cholly and hear him coming. I didn't really know him then, but I knew that he was blue steel and that he was always going and coming and that he had the best walk in the world, because I had learned how to do that walk and was already doing the stew out of it[2] long before Lil' Buddy ever saw it. They were calling me Mister Man, and that was when somebody started calling me The Little Blister, because they said I was calling myself blister trying to say Mister. Aun Tee called me My Mister and Mama called me My Little Man, but she had to drop the little part off when Lil' Buddy came, and that was how everybody started calling me The Man, although I was still nothing but a boy, and I said to myself old Luzana is the man, old Luzana is the one I want to be like.

Then I was getting to be big enough to go everywhere by myself and I was going to school. That was when I knew about Dunkin's Hill and going up through Egerton Lane. That was the short way to school, because that was the way the bell sound came. Buddy Babe and Sister Babe and old double-jointed, ox-jawed Jack Johnson all went that way too, but when it rained you couldn't get across the bottom, and that was when everybody went the Shelton way, going through behind Stranahan's store and Good Hope Baptist to the old car line and then along that red clay road by the Hillside store.

Then Lil' Buddy was there and it was sky blue and we were blue hunters and every day was for whistling and going somewhere to do something you had to be rawhide to do, and some day we were going to live in times and places that were blue steel too. We found out a lot about old Luzana then, and then we not only knew him we knew how to talk to him.

The best time (except when he was just sitting somewhere strumming on his guitar) was when he was on his way to the Gambling Woods. (So far as anybody knew, gambling and guitar picking and grabbing freight trains were the only steady jobs he ever had or ever would have, except during the time he was in the Army and the times he was in jail—and he not only had been in jail, he had been in the penitentiary!) We were his good luck when he was headed for a skin game, and we always used to catch him late Saturday afternoon right out there where Gins Alley came into the oil-tank road, because he would be coming from Miss Pauline's cookshop then. The Gambling Woods trail started right out across from Sargin' Jeff's. Sometimes old Luze would have the guitar slung across his back even then, and naturally he had his famous 32-20 in the holster under his right arm.

"Say now hey Mister Luzana," I would holler at him.

---

2. Doing it expertly.

"Mister Luzana Cholly one-time," Lil' Buddy always said, and he said that was what old Luze's swamp holler said too.

"Mister Luzana Cholly all night long," I would say then.

"Nobody else!" he would holler back at us then, "nobody else but."

"The one and only Mister Luzana Cholly from Booze Ana Bolly come Solly go Molly hit 'em with the fun folly."

"Talk to me, little ziggy,[3] talk to me."

"Got the world in a jug," I might say then.

"And the stopper in your hand,"[4] old Lil' Buddy would say.

"You tell 'em, little crust busters, 'cause I ain't got the heart."

"He's a man among men."

"And Lord God among women!"

"Well tell the dy ya,"[5] old Luze would say then, standing wide-legged, laughing, holding a wad of Brown's Mule chewing tobacco in with his tongue at the same time. Then he would skeet[6] a stream of amber juice to one side like a batter does when he steps up to the plate and then he would wipe the back of his leathery hand across his mouth and squint his eyes.

"Tell the dy-damn-ya!"

"Cain't tell no more," Lil' Buddy would say then, and old Luze would frown and wink at me.

"How come, little sooner,[7] how goddam come?"

" 'Cause money talks."

"Well shut my mouth and call me suitcase."

"Ain't nobody can do that."

"I knowed you could tell 'em little ziggabo, I knowed good and damn well you could tell 'em."

"But we ain't gonna tell 'em no more."

"We sure ain't."

"Talk ain't no good if you ain't got nothing to back it up with."

Old Luze would laugh again and we would stand waiting and then he would run his hands deep down into his pockets and come out with two quarters between his fingers. He would throw them into the air and catch them again, one in each hand, and then he would cross his hands and flip one to me and one to Lil' Buddy.

"Now talk," he would say then. "Now talk, but don't say too much and don't talk too loud, and handle your money like the white folks does."

We were going to be like him even before we were going to be like cowboys. And we knew that blue steel was also root hog or die poor,[8] which was what we were going to have to do whether we liked it or not. Lil' Buddy said it was not just how rough-and-ready old hard-cutting Luze was and how nobody, black or white, was going to do him any dirt and get away with it, and all that. It was that too, but it was also something else. It was also the way he could do whatever he was doing and make it look so easy that he didn't even seem to have to think about it, and once he did it, that seemed to be just about the only real way to do it.

Old Luze did everything his own way just like old Satch[9] played

3. Prison slang variant of "jig," "jiga-boo," derogatory name for a black.

4. The two lines of dialogue are a common blues line.

5. Possibly Gullah phrase with variants used in songs, e.g., "Kushie Dye-yo."

6. Squirt.

7. Mongrel or bastard.

8. Work hard or die poor.

9. Satchell Paige, famed, almost legendary Negro league baseball player who was already in his forties when the major leagues admitted Negroes.

baseball his way. But we knew that we wanted to be like him for more reasons than that too. Somehow or other just as he always seemed to be thirty-five years old and blue steel because he had already been so many places and done so many things you'd never heard of before, he also always seemed to be absolutely alone and not needing anybody else, self-sufficient, independent, dead sure, and at the same time so unconcerned.

Mama said he was don't-carified, and that was it too (if you know the full meaning of the Negro meaning of that expression). He was living in blue steel and his way was don't-carified, because he was blue steel too. Lil' Buddy said hellfied, and he didn't mean hell-defying either, you couldn't say he was hell-defying all the time, and you couldn't say he went for bad either, not even when he was doing that holler he was so notorious for. That *was* hell-defying in a way, but it was really I don't give a damn if I *am* hell-defying, and he was not going for bad because he didn't need to, since everybody, black and white, who knew anything about him at all already knew that when he made a promise it meant if it's the last thing I do, if it's the last thing I do on this earth—and they knew that could mean I'll kill you and pay for you as much as it meant anything else. Because the idea of going to jail didn't scare him at all, and the idea of getting shot at didn't seem to scare him either. *Because all he ever said about that was if they shoot at me they sure better not miss me, they sure better get me the first time.*

He was a Negro who was an out and out Nigger in the very best meaning of the word as Negroes use it among themselves (who are the only ones who can), and nobody in that time and that place seemed to know what to make of him. White folks said he was crazy, but what they really meant or should have meant was that he was confusing to them, because if they knew him well enough to say he was crazy they also had to know enough about him to know that he wasn't even foolhardy, not even careless, not even what they wanted to mean by biggity. The funny thing, as I remember it now, was how their confusion made them respect him in spite of themselves. Somehow or other it was as if they respected him precisely because he didn't care anything about them one way or the other. They certainly respected the fact that he wasn't going to take any foolishness off of them.

Negroes said he was crazy too, but they meant their own meaning. They did not know what to make of him, but when they said he was crazy they almost did, because when they said it they really meant something else. They were not talking so much about what he did, but how he was doing it. They were talking about something like poetic madness, and that was the way they had of saying that he was doing something unheard of, doing the hell out of it, and getting away with whatever it was. You could tell that was what they meant by the very way they said it, by the sound of it, and by the way they were shaking their heads and laughing when they said it.

The way he always operated as a lone wolf and the unconcerned-, not the Negro-ness as such, were the main things then. (Naturally Lil' Buddy and I knew about Negroes and white folks, and we knew that there was something generally wrong with white folks, but it didn't seem so very important then. We knew that if you hit a white boy he would turn red and call you nigger that did not sound like the Nigger the Negroes said and he would run and get as many other white boys

as he could and come back at you, and we knew that a full-grown white had to get somebody to back him up too, but we didn't really think about it much, because there were so many other things we were doing then.)

Nobody ever said anything about old Luzana's papa and mama, and when you suddenly wondered about them you realized that he didn't seem to have or need any family at all, it really was as if he had come full-grown out of the swamp somewhere. And he didn't seem to need a wife either. But that was because he was not going to settle down yet. Because he had lived with more women from time to time and place to place than the average man could even shake a stick at.

We knew somehow or other that the Negro-ness had something to do with the way we felt about him too, but except for cowboys and the New York Yankees and one or two other things, almost everything was Negro then; that is, everything that mattered was. So the Negro part was only natural, although I can see something special about it too now.

When you boil it all down, I guess the main thing was how when you no more than just said his name, *Louisiana Charlie, old Luzana Cholly, old Luze,* that was enough to make you know not only him and how he looked and talked and walked that sporty limp walk, but his whole way of being, and how you knew right off the bat that he all alone and unconcerned in his sharp-edged and rough-backed steel had made it what it was himself.

That was what old Lil' Buddy and I were going to do too, make a name for ourselves. Because we knew even then (and I already knew it before he came) that doing that was exactly what made you the kind of man we wanted to be. Mama said I was her little man, and Aun Tee always called me her little mister, but I wasn't anybody's man and mister yet and I knew it, and when I heard the sound of the name that Mama taught me how to write I always felt funny, and I always jumped even when I didn't move. That was in school, and I wanted to hide, and I always said *they are looking for me, they are trying to see who I am,* and I had to answer because it would be the teacher calling the roll, and I said Present, and it sounded like somebody else.

And when I found out what I found out about me and Aun Tee and knew that she was my flesh and blood mama, I also found out that I didn't know my real name at all, because I didn't know who my true father was. So I said *My name is Reynard the Fox,* and Lil' Buddy said *My name is Jack the Rabbit and my home is in the briar patch.*[1] That was old Luzana too, and when you heard that holler coming suddenly out of nowhere just as old Luze himself always seemed to come, it was just like it was coming from the briar patch.

So when Mama said what she said about me and Aun Tee at that wake that time and I heard it and had to believe it, I wished that old Luzana had been my real papa, but I didn't tell anybody that, not even Lil' Buddy although Lil' Buddy was almost in the same fix because he didn't have a mama any more and he didn't really love his papa because it was his papa that ran his mama away.

But we were buddies and we both did old Luzana's famous walk and we were going to be like him, and the big thing that you had to

1. Reynard and Jack are traditional names for the fox and rabbit: the briar patch episode appears in the Uncle Remus story, by Joel Chandler Harris (1848–1908) in which the shrewd Br'er Rabbit, caught by Br'er Fox, pleads not to be thrown into the briar patch; so of course the fox throws him in and the rabbit escapes crying, "Bred en bawn in a brier-patch, Br'er Fox, bred en bawn in a brier-patch."

do to really get like him was to grab yourself a fast armful of fast freight train and get long gone from here. That was the real way to learn about the world, and we wanted to learn everything about it that we could. That was when we started practicing on the switch engine. That was down in the oilyards. You had to be slick to do even that because naturally your folks didn't want you doing stuff like that, because there was old Peg Leg Nat. Old Peg Leg butt-headed Nat could hop a freight almost as good as old Luzana could. He called himself mister-some-big-shit-on-a-stick. He spent most of his time fishing and sometimes he would come around pushing a wheelbarrow selling fresh fish, shrimps, and crabs, but every now and then he would strike out for somewhere on a freight just like old Luze did. Mama used to try to scare us with old Nat, telling us that a peg leg was just what messing around with freight trains would get you, and for a while she did scare us, but not for long, because then we found out that it never would have happened to old Nat if he hadn't been drunk and showing off. And anybody could see that getting his leg cut off hadn't stopped old Nat himself anyway since he could still beat any two-legged man we knew doing it except old Luze himself. Naturally we had to think about it, and naturally it did slow us up for a while, but it didn't really stop us. Because there was still old Luze, and that was who we were anyway, not old Peg Leg Nat.

Then that time when I found out all about me and Aun Tee, I was going to run away, and Lil' Buddy was ready too. Then old Lil' Buddy found out that old Luze was getting ready to get moving again and we were all set and just waiting and then it was the day itself.

I will always remember that one.

I had on my brogan shoes and I had on my corduroy pants under my overalls with my jumper tucked in. I had on my blue baseball cap too and my rawhide wristband and I had my pitching glove folded in my hip pocket. Lil' Buddy had on just about the same thing except that he was carrying his first-base pad instead of his catcher's mitt. We had our other things and something to eat rolled up in our blanket rolls so that we could sling them over our shoulders and have our arms free.

Lil' Buddy had gotten his papa's pearl-handled .38 Smith & Wesson, and we both had good jackknives. We had some hooks and twine to fish with too, just in case, and of course we had our trusty old slingshots for birds.

It was May and school was not out yet, and so not only were we running away, we were playing hooky too. It was hot, and with that many clothes on we were sweating, but you had to have them, and that was the best way to carry them.

There was a thin breeze that came across the railroad from the river, the marsh, and Pole Cat Bay, but the sun was hot and bright, and you could see the rails downright shimmering under the high and wide open sky. We had always said that we were going to wait until school was out, but this was our chance now, and we didn't care about school much any more anyhow. This was going to be school now anyway, except it was going to be much better.

We were waiting in the thicket under the hill. That was between where the Dodge mill road came down and where the oil spur started, and from where we were, we could see up and down the clearing as far as we needed to, to the south all the way across Three Mile Creek bridge to the roundhouse, and where Mobile was, and to the north all

the way up past that mill to the Chickasabogue Bridge. We knew just about from where old Luzana was going to come running, because we had been watching him do it for a long time now. We had that part down pat.

I don't know how long we had been waiting because we didn't have a watch but it had been a long time, and there was nothing to do but wait then.

"I wish it would hurry up and come on," Lil' Buddy said.

"Me too," I said.

"Got to get to splitting."

We were squatting on the blanket rolls, and Lil' Buddy was smoking another Lucky Strike, smoking the way we both used to smoke them in those old days, letting it hang dangling in the corner of your mouth, and tilting your head to one side with one eye squinted up like a gambler.

"Goddam it, watch me nail that sapsucker," he said.

"Man, you watch me."

You could smell the May woods there then, the dogwood, the honeysuckle, and the warm smell of the undergrowth; and you could hear the birds too, the jays, the thrushes, and even a woodpecker somewhere on a dead tree. I felt how moist and cool the soft dark ground was there in the shade, and you could smell that smell too, and smell the river and the marsh too.

Lil' Buddy finished the cigarette and flipped it out into the sunshine, and then sat with his back against a sapling and sucked his teeth. I looked out across the railroad to where the gulls were circling over the marsh and the river.

"Goddam it, when I come back here to this burg, I'm goddam man and a half," Lil' Buddy said all of a sudden.

"And don't care who knows it," I said.

"Boy, Chicago."

"Man, Detroit."

"Man, Philadelphia."

"Man, New York."

"Boy, I kinda wish old Gander was going too."

"I kinda wish so too."

"Old cat-eyed Gander."

"Old big-toed Gander."

"Old Gander is all right."

"Man, who you telling."

"That son of a bitch know his natural stuff."

"That bastard can steal lightning if he have to."

"Boy, how about that time."

"Man, hell yeah."

"Boy, but old Luze though."

"That Luze takes the cake for everything."

"Hot damn, boy we going!"

"It won't be long now."

"Boy, Los Angeles."

"Boy, St. Louis."

"Man, you know we going."

"Boy, you just watch me swing the sapsucker."

"Boy, snag it."

"Goddam."

"I'm going to natural-born kick that son of a bitch."

"Kick the living guts out of it."

"Boy and when we get back!" I said that and I could see it, coming back on the Pan American I would be carrying two suitcases and have a money belt and an underarm holster, and I would be dressed fit to kill.

"How long you think it will take us to get fixed to come back?" I said.

"Man, I don't know and don't care."

"You coming back when old Luze come back?"

"I don't know."

I didn't say anything else then. Because I was trying to think about how it was really going to be then. Because what I had been thinking about before was how I wanted it to be. I didn't say anything because I was thinking about myself then, thinking: *I always said I was going but I don't really know whether I want to go or not now. I want to go and I don't want to go.* I tried to see what was really going to happen and I couldn't, and I tried to forget it and think about something else, but I couldn't do that either.

I looked over at Lil' Buddy again. Who was lying back against the tree with his hands behind his head and his eyes closed. Whose legs were crossed, and who was resting easy like a ballplayer rests before time for the game to start. I wondered what he was really thinking. Did he really mean it when he said he did not know and didn't care? You couldn't tell what he was thinking, but you could tell that he wasn't going to back out now, no matter how he was feeling about it.

So I said to myself goddam it if Lil' Buddy can make it I can too, and I had more reason to be going away than he did anyway. *I had forgotten about that. I had forgotten all about it. And then I knew that I still loved Papa and they had always loved me and they had always known about me and Aun Tee.*

But I couldn't back out then, because what I had found out wasn't the real reason for going anyway. Old Luze was really the reason, old Luze and blue steel, old Luze and rawhide, old Luze and ever-stretching India Rubber.

"Hey Lebud."

"Hey."

"Going to the big league."

"You said it."

"Skipping city."

"You tell 'em."

"Getting further."

"Ain't no lie."

"Long gone."

"No crap."

That was when Lil' Buddy said my home is in the briar patch. My name is Jack the Rabbit and my natural home is in the briar patch. And I said it too, and I said that was where I was bred and born.

"Goddam it to hell," Lil' Buddy said then, "why don't it come on?"

"Son of a bitch," I said.

Then I was leaning back against my tree looking out across the sandy clearing at the sky and there were clean white pieces of clouds that looked like balled-up sheets in a washtub, and the sky was blue like rinse water with bluing in it, and I was thinking about Mama again, and hoping that it was all a dream.

But then the train was really coming and it wasn't a dream at all, and Lil' Buddy jumped up.

"Come on."

"I'm here."

The engine went by, and we were running across the clearing. My ears were ringing and I was sweating, and my collar was hot and my pants felt as if the seat had been ripped away. There was nothing but the noise and we were running into it, and then we were climbing up the hill and running along the slag and cinders. We were trotting along in reach of it then. We remembered to let an empty boxcar go by, and when the next gondola came, Lil' Buddy grabbed the front end and I got the back. I hit the hotbox with my right foot and stepped onto the step and pulled up. The wind was in my ears then, but I knew about that from practicing. I climbed on up the ladder and got down on the inside, and there was Lil' Buddy coming back toward me.

"Man, what did I tell you!"

"Did you see me lam into that sucker?"

"Boy, we low more nailed it."

"I bet old Luze will be kicking it any minute now."

"Cool hanging it."

"Boy, yair," I said, but I was thinking I hope old Luze didn't change his mind. I hope we don't miss him. I hope we don't have to start out all by ourselves.

"Going boy."

"Yeah."

"*Going,*
don't know where I'm going
but I'm going
Say now I'm going
don't know when I'm going
but I'm going."

We crawled up into the left front corner out of the wind, and there was nothing to do but wait then. We knew that she was going to have to pull into the hole for Number Four when she got twelve miles out, and that was when we were going to get to the open boxcar.

We got the cigarettes out and lit up, and there was nothing but the rumbling noise that the wide-open car made then, and the faraway sound of the engine and the low-rolling smoke coming back. That was just sitting there, and after we got a little more used to the vibration, nothing at all was happening except being there. You couldn't even see the scenery going by.

It was just being there and being in that time, and you never really remember anything about things like that except the sameness and the way you felt, and all I can remember now about that part is this nothingness of doing nothing and the feeling not of going but of being taken.

All I could see after we went through the bridge was the sky and the bare floor and the sides of the gondola, and all I can remember about myself is how I wished that something would happen, because I definitely did not want to be going then, and I was lost even though I knew good and well that I was not even twelve miles from home yet. Because although we certainly had been many times farther away and stayed longer, this already seemed to be farther and longer than all the other times put together.

Then we could tell that it was beginning to slow down, and we stood up and started getting ready. And then it was stopping and we were ready, and we climbed over and got down and started running

for it. That was still in the bayou country and beyond the train smell there was the sour-sweet smell of the swamp. We were running on hard pounded slag then, and with the train quiet and waiting for Number Four, you could hear the double running of our feet echoing through the cypresses and the marshland.

The wide roadbed was almost half as high as the telegraph wires, and along the low right-of-way where the black creosote poles went along, you could see the blue and white lilies floating on the slimy green water. We came hustling hot to get to where we knew the empty car was, and then there we were.

And there old Luzana himself was.

He stood looking down at us from the door with an unlighted cigarette in his hand. We stopped dead in our tracks. I knew exactly what was going to happen then. It was suddenly so quiet that you could hear your heart pounding inside your head, and I was so embarrassed I didn't know what to do and I thought *now he's going to call us a name. Now he's never going to have anything to do with us anymore.*

We were just standing there waiting and he just let us stand there and feel like two puppies with their tails tucked between their legs, and then he started talking.

"It ain't like that. It ain't like that. It just ain't like that, it just ain't."

And he was shaking his head not only as if we couldn't understand him but also as if we couldn't even hear him.

"It ain't. Oh, but it ain't."

We didn't move. Lil' Buddy didn't even dig his toe into the ground.

"So this is what y'all up to. Don't say a word, not a word. Don't open your mouth."

I could have sunk right on down into the ground.

"What the hell y'all think y'all doing? Tell me that. Tell me. Don't say a word. Don't say a goddam mumbling word to me."

We weren't even about to say anything.

"I got a good mind to whale the sawdust out of you both. That's just what I oughta do."

But he didn't move. He just stood looking down.

"Well, I'll be a son of a bitch."

That was all he had said then, and then he jumped down, walked us back to where the switch frog was, and then there was nothing but just shamefaced waiting. Then Number Four came by and then finally we heard the next freight coming south and when it got there and slowed down for the switch he was standing waiting for a gondola and when it came he picked me up and put me on and then he picked Lil' Buddy up and put him on and then he caught the next car and came to where we were.

So we came slowpoking it right on back and got back in Gasoline Point before the whistles even started blowing for one o'clock. Imagine that. All of that had happened and it wasn't really afternoon yet. I could hardly believe it.

We came on until the train all but stopped for Three Mile Creek bridge and then he hopped down and took us off. He led us down the hill and went to a place the hobos used under the bridge. He sat down and lit another cigarette and flipped the match into the water and watched it float away and then he was looking at us and then he motioned for us to sit down too.

That was when he really told us what hitting the road was, and what blue steel was. He was talking evenly then, not scolding, just

telling us man to boys, saying he was talking for our own good because doing what we were trying to do was more than a notion. He was talking quietly and evenly but you still couldn't face him, I know I couldn't and Lil' Buddy naturally couldn't because he never looked anybody straight in the eye anyway.

We were back and sitting under Three Mile Creek bridge and he was not really angry and then we were all eating our something-to-eat and then we could talk too, but we didn't have much to say that day. He was doing the talking and all we wanted to do was ask questions and listen.

That was when he told us all about the chain gang and the penitentiary and the white folks, and you could see everything he said and you were there too, but you were not really in it this time because it was happening to him, not you, and it was him and you were not him, you were you. You could be rawhide and you could be blue steel but you couldn't really be Luzana Cholly, because he himself was not going to let you.

Then he was talking about going to school and learning to use your head like the smart white folks. You had to be a rawhide but you had to be patent leather too, then you would really be nimble, then you would really be not only a man but a big man. He said we had a lot of spunk and that was good but it wasn't good enough, it wasn't nearly enough.

And then he was talking about Negroes and white folks again, and he said the young generation of Negroes were supposed to be like Negroes and be like white folks too and still be Negroes. He sat looking out across the water then, and then we heard another freight coming and he got up and got ready and he said we could watch him but we'd better not try to follow him.

Then we were back up on the hill again and the train was coming and he stood looking at us with the guitar slung over his shoulder and then he put his hands on our shoulders and looked straight at us, and we had to look at him then, and we knew that we were not to be ashamed in front of him any more.

"*Make old Luze proud of you,*" *he said then, and he was almost pleading.* "*Make old Luze glad to take his hat off to you some of these days. You going further than old Luze ever even dreamed of. Old Luze ain't been nowhere. Old Luze don't know from nothing.*"

And then the train was there and we watched him snag it and then he was waving good-bye.

p. 1953

TILLIE OLSEN

O Yes

For Margaret Heaton, who always taught.

1

They are the only white people there, sitting in the dimness of the Negro church that had once been a corner store, and all through the bubbling, swelling, seething of before the services, twelve-year-old Carol clenches tight her mother's hand, the other resting lightly on her friend, Parialee Phillips, for whose baptism she has come.

The white-gloved ushers hurry up and down the aisle, beckoning people to their seats. A jostle of people. To the chairs angled to the left for the youth choir, to the chairs angled to the right for the ladies' choir, even up to the platform, where behind the place for the dignitaries and the mixed choir, the new baptismal tank gleams—and as if pouring into it from the ceiling, the blue-painted River of Jordan, God standing in the waters, embracing a brown man in a leopard skin and pointing to the letters of gold:

REJOICE

GOD   IS   LOVE

I AM THE WAY   THE TRUTH   THE LIFE

At the clear window, the crucified Christ embroidered on the starched white curtain leaps in the wind of the sudden singing. And the choirs march in. Robes of wine, of blue, of red.

"We stands and sings too," says Parialee's mother, Alva, to Helen; though already Parialee has pulled Carol up. Singing, little Lucinda Phillips fluffs out her many petticoats; singing, little Bubbie bounces up and down on his heels.

Any day now I'll reach that land of freedom,
                                    Yes, o yes
Any day now, know that promised land

The youth choir claps and taps to accent the swing of it. Beginning to tap, Carol stiffens. "Parry, look. Somebody from school."

"Once more once," says Parialee, in the new way she likes to talk now.

"Eddie Garlin's up there. He's in my math."

"Couple cats from Franklin Jr. chirps in the choir. No harm or alarm."

Anxiously Carol scans the faces to see who else she might know, who else might know her, but looks quickly down to Lucinda's wide skirts, for it seems Eddie looks back at her, sullen or troubled, though it is hard to tell, faced as she is into the window of curtained sunblaze.

I know my robe will fit me well
I tried it on at the gates of hell

If it were a record she would play it over and over, Carol thought, to untwine the intertwined voices, to search how the many rhythms rock apart and yet are one glad rhythm.

When I get to heaven gonna sing and shout
Nobody be able to turn me out

"That's Mr. Chairback Evans going to invocate," Lucinda leans across Parry to explain. "He don't invoke good like Momma."

"Shhhh."

"Momma's the only lady in the church that invocates. She made the prayer last week. (Last month, Lucy.) I made the children's 'nouncement last time. (That was way back Thanksgiving.) And Bubbie's 'nounced too. Lots of times."

"Lucy-inda. SIT!"

Bible study announcements and mixed-choir practice announcements and Teen Age Hearts meeting announcements.

If Eddie said something to her about being there, worried Carol, if he talked to her right in front of somebody at school.

Messengers of Faith announcements and Mamboettes announcement and Committee for the Musical Tea.

Parry's arm so warm. Not realizing, starting up the old game from grade school, drumming a rhythm on the other's arm to see if the song could be guessed. "Parry, guess."

But Parry is pondering the platform.

The baptismal tank? "Parry, are you scared . . . the baptizing?"

"This cat? No." Shaking her head so slow and scornful, the barrette in her hair, sun fired, strikes a long rail of light. And still ponders the platform.

New Strangers Baptist Church invites you and Canaan Fair Singers announcements and Battle of Song and Cosmopolites meet. "O Lord, I couldn't find no ease," a solo. The ladies' choir:

> *O what you say seekers, o what you say seekers,*
> *Will you never turn back no more?*

The mixed choir sings:

> *Ezekiel saw that wheel of time*
> *Every spoke was of humankind . . .*

And the slim worn man in the pin-stripe suit starts his sermon On the Nature of God. How God is long-suffering. Oh, how long he has suffered. Calling the roll of the mighty nations, that rose and fell and now are dust for grinding the face of man.

O voice of drowsiness and dream to which Carol does not need to listen. As long ago. Parry warm beside her too, as it used to be, there in the classroom at Mann Elementary, and the feel of drenched in sun and dimness and dream. Smell and sound of the chalk wearing itself away to nothing, rustle of books, drumming tattoo of fingers on her arm: *Guess.*

And as the preacher's voice spins happy and free, it is the used-to-be play-yard. Tag. Thump of the volley ball. Ecstasy of the jump rope. Parry, do pepper. Carol, do pepper. Parry's bettern Carol, Carol's bettern Parry. . . .

Did someone scream?

It seemed someone screamed—but all were sitting as before, though the sun no longer blared through the windows. She tried to see up where Eddie was, but the ushers were standing at the head of the aisle now, the ladies in white dresses like nurses or waitresses wear, the men holding their white-gloved hands up so one could see their palms.

"And God is Powerful," the preacher was chanting. "Nothing for him to scoop out the oceans and pat up the mountains. Nothing for him to scoop up the miry clay and create man. Man, I said, create Man."

The lady in front of her moaned "O yes" and others were moaning "O yes."

"And when the earth mourned the Lord said, Weep not, for all will be returned to you, every dust, every atom. And the tired dust settles back, goes back. Until that Judgment Day. That great day."

"O yes."

The ushers were giving out fans. Carol reached for one and Parry said: "What *you* need one for?" but she took it anyway.

"You think Satchmo can blow; you think Muggsy can blow; you

think Dizzy can blow?"[1] He was straining to an imaginary trumpet now, his head far back and his voice coming out like a trumpet.

"Oh Parry, he's so good."

"Well. Jelly jelly."

"Nothing to Gabriel on that great getting-up morning. And the horn wakes up Adam, and Adam runs to wake up Eve, and Eve moans; Just one more minute, let me sleep, and Adam yells, Great Day, woman, don't you know it's the Great Day?"

"*Great Day, Great Day,*" the mixed choir behind the preacher rejoices:

> *When our cares are past*
> *when we're home at last . . .*

"And Eve runs to wake up Cain." Running round the platform, stooping and shaking imaginary sleepers, "and Cain runs to wake up Abel." Looping, scalloping his voice—"Grea-aaa-aat Daaaay." All the choirs thundering:

> *Great Day*
> *When the battle's fought*
> *And the victory's won*

Exultant spirals of sound. And Carol caught into it (Eddie forgotten, the game forgotten) chanting with Lucy and Bubbie: "*Great Day.*"

"Ohhhhhhhhhh," his voice like a trumpet again, "the re-unioning. Ohhhhhhhhh, the rejoicing. After the ages immemorial of longing."

Someone *was* screaming. And an awful thrumming sound with it, like feet and hands thrashing around, like a giant jumping of a rope.

"*Great Day.*" And no one stirred or stared as the ushers brought a little woman out into the aisle, screaming and shaking, just a little shrunk-up woman, not much taller than Carol, the biggest thing about her her swollen hands and the cascades of tears wearing her face.

The shaking inside Carol too. Turning and trembling to ask: "What? . . . that lady?" But Parry still ponders the platform; little Lucy loops the chain of her bracelet round and round; and Bubbie sits placidly, dreamily. Alva Phillips is up fanning a lady in front of her; two lady ushers are fanning other people Carol cannot see. And her mother, her mother looks in a sleep.

Yes. He raised up the dead from the grave. He made old death behave.

Yes. Yes. From all over, hushed.   *O Yes*

He was your mother's rock. Your father's mighty tower. And he gave us a little baby. A little baby to love.

                                                        I am so glad

Yes, your friend, when you're friendless. Your father when you're fatherless. Way maker. Door opener.

                                                                Yes

When it seems you can't go on any longer, he's there. You can, he says, you can.

                                                                Yes

And that burden you been carrying—ohhhhh that burden—not for always will it be. No, not for always.

                                                        Stay with me, Lord

1. Louis Armstrong (1900–1971); Francis ("Muggsy") Spanier (1906–1967); John ("Dizzy") Gillespie (b. 1917), all famous black jazz trumpeters.

I will put my Word in you and it is power. I will put my Truth in you and it is power.

O Yes

Out of your suffering I will make you to stand as a stone. A tried stone. Hewn out of the mountains of ages eternal.

Yes

Ohhhhhhhhhhh. Out of the mire I will lift your feet. Your tired feet from so much wandering. From so much work and wear and hard times.

Yes

From so much journeying—and never the promised land. And I'll wash them in the well your tears made. And I'll shod them in the gospel of peace, and of feeling good. Ohhhhhhhhh.

O Yes.

Behind Carol, a trembling wavering scream. Then the thrashing. Up above, the singing:

> *They taken my blessed Jesus and flogged him to the woods*
> *And they made him hew out his cross and they dragged him to*
> *   Calvary*
> *Shout brother, Shout shout shout. He never cried a word.*

Powerful throbbing voices. Calling and answering to each other.

> *They taken my blessed Jesus and whipped him up the hill*
> *With a knotty whip and a raggedy thorn he never cried a word*
> *Shout, sister. Shout shout shout. He never cried a word.*

> *Go tell the people the Saviour has risen*
> *Has risen from the dead and will live forevermore*
> *   And won't have to die no more.*

Halleloo.

> *   Shout, brother, shout*
> *   We won't have to die no more!*

A single exultant lunge of shriek. Then the thrashing. All around a clapping. Shouts with it. The piano whipping, whipping air to a froth. Singing now.

> *   I once was lost who now am found*
> *   Was blind who now can see*

On Carol's fan, a little Jesus walked on wondrously blue waters to where bearded disciples spread nets out of a fishing boat. If she studied the fan—became it—it might make a wall around her. If she could make what was happening (*what* was happening?) into a record small and round to listen to far and far as if into a seashell—the stamp and rills and spirals all tiny (but never any screaming).

> *   wade wade in the water*

> *   Jordan's water is chilly and wild*
> *   I've got to get home to the other side*
> *   God's going to trouble the waters*

Ladders of screamings. The music leaps and prowls. Drumming feet of ushers running. And still little Lucy fluffs her skirts, loops the chain on her bracelet; still Bubbie sits and rocks dreamily; and only eyes turn for an instant to the aisle—as if nothing were happening. "Mother,

let's go home," Carol begs, but her mother holds her so tight. Alva
Phillips, strong Alva, rocking too and chanting, *O Yes.* No, do not
look.

> *Wade,*
> *Sea of trouble all mingled with fire*
> *Come on my brethren it's time to go higher*
> *Wade wade*

The voices in great humming waves, slow, slow (when did it become
the humming?), everyone swaying with it too, moving like in slow
waves and singing, and up where Eddie is, a new cry, wild and open,
"O help me, Jesus," and when Carol opens her eyes she closes them
again, quick, but still can see the new known face from school (not
Eddie), the thrashing, writhing body, struggling against the ushers
with the look of grave and loving support on their faces, and hear the
torn, tearing cry: "Don't take me away, life everlasting, don't take me
away."

And now the rhinestones in Parry's hair glitter wicked, the white
hands of the ushers, fanning, foam in the air; the blue-painted waters
of Jordan swell and thunder; Christ spirals on his cross in the window,
and she is drowned under the sluice of the slow singing and the sway.

So high up and forgotten the waves and the world, so stirless the
deep cool green and the wrecks of what had been. Here now Hostess
Foods, where Alva Phillips works her nights—but different from that
time Alva had taken them through before work, for it is all sunken
under water, the creaking loading platform where they had left the
night behind; the closet room where Alva's swaddles of sweaters,
boots, and cap hung, the long hall lined with pickle barrels, the sharp
freezer door swinging open.

Bubbles of breath that swell. A gulp of numbing air. She swims into
the chill room where the huge wheels of cheese stand, and Alva swims
too, deftly oiling each machine: slicers and wedgers and the convey,
that at her touch start to roll and grind. The light of day blazes up and
Alva is holding a cup, saying: Drink this, baby.

"DRINK IT." Her mother's voice and the numbing air demanding
her to pay attention. Up through the waters and into the car.

"That's right, lambie, now lie back." Her mother's lap.

"Mother."

"Shhhhh. You almost fainted, lambie."

Alva's voice. "You gonna be all right, Carol . . . Lucy, I'm telling you
for the last time, you and Buford get back into that church. Carol is
fine."

"Lucyinda, if I had all your petticoats I could float." Crying. "Why
didn't you let me wear my full skirt with the petticoats, Mother."

"Shhhhh, lamb." Smoothing her cheek. "Just breathe, take long deep
breaths."

". . . How you doing now, you little ol' consolation prize?" It is
Parry, but she does not come in the car or reach to Carol through the
open window: "No need to cuss and fuss. You going to be sharp as a
tack, Jack."

Answering automatically: "And cool as a fool."

Quick, they look at each other.

"Parry, we have to go home now, don't we, Mother? I almost fainted,

didn't I, Mother? . . . Parry, I'm sorry I got sick and have to miss your baptism."

"Don't feel sorry. I'll feel better you not there to watch. It was our mommas wanted you to be there, not me."

"Parry!" Three voices.

"Maybe I'll come over to play kickball after. If you feeling better. Maybe. Or bring the pogo." Old shared joys in her voice: "Or any little thing."

In just a whisper: "Or any little thing. Parry. Good-bye, Parry."

And why does Alva have to talk now?

"You all right? You breathin' deep like your momma said? Was it too close 'n hot in there? Did something scare you, Carrie?"

Shaking her head to lie, "No."

"I blame myself for not paying attention. You not used to people letting go that way. Lucy and Bubbie, Parialee, they used to it. They been coming since they lap babies."

"Alva, that's all right. Alva, Mrs. Phillips."

"You *was* scared. Carol, it's something to study about. You'll feel better if you understand."

Trying not to listen.

"You not used to hearing what people keeps inside, Carol. You know how music can make you feel things? Glad or sad or like you can't sit still? That was religion music, Carol."

"I have to breathe deep, Mother said."

"Not everybody feels religion the same way. Some it's in their mouth, but some it's like a hope in their blood, their bones. And they singing songs every word that's real to them, Carol, every word out of they own life. And the preaching finding lodgment in their hearts."

The screaming was tuning up in her ears again, high above Alva's patient voice and the waves lapping and fretting.

"Maybe somebody's had a hard week, Carol, and they locked up with it. Maybe a lot of hard weeks bearing down."

"Mother, my head hurts."

"And they're home, Carol, church is home. Maybe the only place they can feel how they feel and maybe let it come out. So they can go on. And it's all right."

"Please, Alva. Mother, tell Alva my head hurts."

"Get Happy, we call it, and most it's good feeling, Carol, when you got all that locked up inside you."

"Tell her we have to go home. It's all right, Alva. Please, Mother. Say good-bye. Good-bye."

When I was carrying Parry and her father left me, and I fifteen years old, one thousand miles away from home, sin-sick and never really believing, as still I don't believe all, scorning, for what have it done to help, waiting there in the clinic and maybe sleeping, a voice called: Alva, Alva. So mournful and so sweet: Alva. Fear not, I have loved you from the foundation of the universe. And a little small child tugged on my dress. He was carrying a parade stick, on the end of it a star that outshined the sun. Follow me, he said. And the real sun went down and he hidden his stick. How dark it was, how dark. I could feel the darkness with my hands. And when I could see, I screamed. Dump trucks run, dumping bodies in hell, and a convey line run, never

ceasing with souls, weary ones having to stamp and shove them along, and the air like fire. Oh I never want to hear such screaming. Then the little child jumped on a motorbike making a path no bigger than my little finger. But first he greased my feet with the hands of my momma when I was a knee baby. They shined like the sun was on them. Eyes he placed all around my head, and as I journeyed upward after him, it seemed I heard a mourning: "Mama Mama you must help carry the world." The rise and fall of nations I saw. And the voice called again Alva Alva, and I flew into a world of light, multitudes singing, Free, free, I am so glad.

2

Helen began to cry, telling her husband about it.

"You and Alva ought to have your heads examined, taking her there cold like that," Len said. "All right, wreck my best handkerchief. Anyway, now that she's had a bath, her Sunday dinner. . . ."

"And been fussed over," seventeen-year-old Jeannie put in.

"She seems good as new. Now *you* forget it, Helen."

"I can't. Something . . . deep happened. If only I or Alva had told her what it would be like. . . . But I didn't realize."

You don't realize a lot of things, Mother, Jeannie said, but not aloud.

"So Alva talked about it after instead of before. Maybe it meant more that way."

"Oh Len, she didn't listen."

"You don't know if she did or not. Or what there was in the experience for her. . . ."

Enough to pull that kid apart two ways even more, Jeannie said, but still not aloud.

"I was so glad she and Parry were going someplace together again. Now that'll be between them too. Len, they really need, miss each other. What happened in a few months? When I think of how close they were, the hours of makebelieve and dressup and playing ball and collecting. . . ."

"Grow up, Mother." Jeannie's voice was harsh. "Parialee's collecting something else now. Like her own crowd. Like jivetalk and rhythmand-blues. Like teachers who treat her like a dummy and white kids who treat her like dirt; boys who think she's really something and chicks who. . . ."

"Jeannie, I know. It hurts."

"Well, maybe it hurts Parry too. Maybe. At least she's got a crowd. Just don't let it hurt Carol though, 'cause there's nothing she can do about it. That's all through, her and Parialee Phillips, put away with their paper dolls."

"No, Jeannie, no."

"It's like Ginger and me. Remember Ginger, my best friend in Horace Mann. But you hardly noticed when it happened to us, did you . . . because she was white? Yes, Ginger, who's got two kids now, who quit school year before last. Parry's never going to finish either. What's she got to do with Carrie any more? They're going different places. Different places, different crowds. And they're sorting. . . ."

"Now wait, Jeannie. Parry's just as bright, just as capable."

"They're in junior high, Mother. Don't you know about junior high? How they sort? And it's all where you're going. Yes and Parry's colored

and Carrie's white. And you have to watch everything, what you wear and how you wear it and who you eat lunch with and how much homework you do and how you act to the teacher and what you laugh at. . . . And run with your crowd."

"It's that final?" asked Len. "Don't you think kids like Carol and Parry can show it doesn't *have* to be that way."

"They can't. They can't. They don't let you."

"No need to shout," he said mildly. "And who do you mean by 'they' and what do you mean by 'sorting'?"

How they sort. A foreboding of comprehension whirled within Helen. What was it Carol had told her of the Welcome Assembly the first day in junior high? The models showing How to Dress and How Not to Dress and half the girls in their loved new clothes watching their counterparts up on the stage—*their* straight skirt, their sweater, their earrings, lipstick, hairdo—"How Not to Dress," "a bad reputation for your school." It was nowhere in Carol's description, yet picturing it now, it seemed to Helen that a mute cry of violated dignity hung in the air. Later there had been a story of going to another Low 7 homeroom on an errand and seeing a teacher trying to wipe the forbidden lipstick off a girl who was fighting back and cursing. Helen could hear Carol's frightened, self-righteous tones: ". . . and I hope they expel her; she's the kind that gives Franklin Jr. a bad rep; she doesn't care about anything and always gets into fights." Yet there was nothing in these incidents to touch the heavy comprehension that waited. . . . Homework, the wonderings those times Jeannie and Carol needed help: "What if there's no one at home to give the help, and the teachers with their two hundred and forty kids a day can't or don't or the kids don't ask and they fall hopelessly behind, what then?"—but this too was unrelated. And what had it been that time about Parry? "Mother, Melanie and Sharon won't go if they know Parry's coming." Then of course you'll go with Parry, she's been your friend longer, she had answered, but where was it they were going and what had finally happened? Len, my head hurts, she felt like saying, in Carol's voice in the car, but Len's eyes were grave on Jeannie who was saying passionately:

"If you think it's so goddam important why do we have to live here where it's for real; why don't we move to Ivy like Betsy (yes, I know, money), where it's the deal to be buddies, in school anyway, three colored kids and their father's a doctor or judge or something big wheel and one always gets elected President or head song girl or something to prove oh how we're democratic. . . . What do you want of that poor kid anyway? Make up your mind. Stay friends with Parry —but be one of the kids. Sure. Be a brain—but not a square. Rise on up, college prep, but don't get separated. Yes, stay one of the kids, but. . . ."

"Jeannie. You're not talking about Carol at all, are you, Jeannie? Say it again. I wasn't listening. I was trying to think."

"She will not say it again," Len said firmly, "you look about ready to pull a Carol. One a day's our quota. And you, Jeannie, we'd better cool it. Too much to talk about for one session. . . . Here, come to the window and watch the Carol and Parry you're both so all worked up about."

In the wind and the shimmering sunset light, half the children of the block are playing down the street. Leaping, bouncing, hallooing, tug-

ging the kites of spring. In the old synchronized understanding, Carol
and Parry kick, catch, kick, catch. And now Parry jumps on her pogo
stick (the last time), Carol shadowing her, and Bubbie, arching his
body in a semicircle of joy, bounds after them, high, higher, higher.

And the months go by and supposedly it is forgotten, except for the
now and then when, self-important, Carol will say: I really truly did
nearly faint, didn't I, Mother, that time I went to church with Parry?

And now seldom Parry and Carol walk the hill together. Melanie's
mother drives by to pick up Carol, and the several times Helen has
suggested Parry, too, Carol is quick to explain: "She's already left" or
"She isn't ready; she'll make us late."

And after school? Carol is off to club or skating or library or someone's house, and Parry can stay for kickball only on the rare afternoons
when she does not have to hurry home where Lucy, Bubbie, and the
cousins wait to be cared for, now Alva works the four to twelve-thirty
shift.

No more the bending together over the homework. All semester the
teachers have been different, and rarely Parry brings her books home,
for where is there space or time and what is the sense? And the phone
never rings with: what you going to wear tomorrow, are you bringing
your lunch, or come on over, let's design some clothes for the Katy
Keane comic-book contest. And Parry never drops by with Alva for
Saturday snack to or from grocery shopping.

And the months go by and the sorting goes on and seemingly it is
over until that morning when Helen must stay home from work, so
swollen and feverish is Carol with mumps.

The afternoon before, Parry had come by, skimming up the stairs,
spilling books and binders on the bed: Hey frail, lookahere and wail,
your momma askin for homework, what she got against YOU? . . .
looking quickly once then not looking again and talking fast. . . .
Hey, you bloomed. You gonna be your own pumpkin, hallowe'en?
Your momma know yet it's mu-umps? And lumps. Momma says: no
distress, she'll be by tomorrow morning see do you need anything
while your momma's to work. . . . (Singing: *whole lotta shakin goin
on.*) All your 'signments is inside; Miss Rockface says the teachers
to write 'em cause I mightn't get it right all right.

But did not tell: Does your mother work for Carol's mother? Oh,
you're neighbors! Very well, I'll send along a monitor to open
Carol's locker but you're only to take these things I'm writing
down, nothing else. Now say after me: Miss Campbell is   trusting
me to be   a good responsible girl. And go   right to Carol's house.
After school. Not stop anywhere   on the way. Not lose anything.
And only take. What's written on the list.

You really gonna mess with that book stuff? Sign on *mine* says
do-not-open-until-eX-mas. . . . That Mrs. Fernandez doll she didn't
send nothin, she was the only, says feel better and read a book to
report if you feel like and I'm the most for takin care for you; she's
my most, wish I could get her but she only teaches 'celerated. . . .
Flicking the old read books on the shelf but not opening to mock-
declaim as once she used to . . . Vicky, Eddie's g.f.[2] in Rockface
office, she's on suspended for sure, yellin to Rockface: you bitchkitty
don't you give me no more bad shit. That Vicky she can sure sling-

2. Girl friend.

ating-ring it. Staring out the window as if the tree not there in which they had hid out and rocked so often. . . . For sure. (*Keep mo-o-vin.*[3]) Got me a new pink top and lilac skirt. Look sharp with this purple? Cinching in the wide belt as if delighted with what newly swelled above and swelled below. Wear it Saturday night to Sweet's, Sounds of Joy, Leroy and Ginny and me goin if Momma'll stay home. IF. (*Shake my baby shake.*) How come old folks still likes to party? Huh? Asking of Rembrandt's weary old face looking from the wall.[4] How come (softly) you long-gone you. Touching her face to his quickly, lightly. NEXT mumps is your buddybud Melanie's turn to tote your stuff. I'm gettin the hoovus groovus. Hey you so unneat, don't care what you bed with. Removing the books and binders, ranging them on the dresser one by one, marking lipstick faces— bemused or mocking or amazed—on each paper jacket. Better. Fluffing out smoothing the quilt with exaggerated energy. Any little thing I can get, cause I gotta blow. Tossing up and catching their year-ago, arm-in-arm graduation picture, replacing it deftly, upside down, into its mirror crevice. Joe. Bring you joy juice or fizz water or kickapoo? Adding a frown line to one bookface. Twanging the paper fishkite, the Japanese windbell overhead, setting the mobile they had once made of painted eggshells and decorated straws to twirling and rocking. And is gone.

She talked to the lipstick faces after, in her fever, tried to stand on her head to match the picture, twirled and twanged with the violent overhead.

Sleeping at last after the disordered night. Having surrounded herself with the furnishings of that world of childhood she no sooner learned to live in comfortably, then had to leave.

The dollhouse stands there to arrange and rearrange; the shell and picture card collections to re-sort and remember; the population of dolls given away to little sister, borrowed back, propped all round to dress and undress and caress.

She has thrown off her nightgown because of the fever, and her just budding breast is exposed where she reaches to hold the floppy plush dog that had been her childhood pillow.

Not for anything would her mother have disturbed her. Except that in the unaccustomedness of a morning at home, in the bruised restlessness after the sleepless night, Helen clicks on the radio—and the storm of singing whirls into the room:

> . . . *of trouble all mingled with fire*
> *Come on my brethren we've got to go higher*
> *Wade, wade. . . .*

And Carol runs down the stairs, shrieking and shrieking. "Turn it off, Mother, turn it off." Hurling herself at the dial and wrenching it so it comes off in her hand.

"Ohhhhh," choked and convulsive, while Helen tries to hold her, to quiet.

"Mother, why did they sing and scream like that?"

"At Parry's church?"

---

3. Words from "Whole Lotta Shakin' Goin' On" mentioned earlier in the passage and continued later; a famous Elvis Presley record.

4. Rembrandt van Rijn (1600–1669), the great Dutch painter, produced perhaps 100 self-portraits.

"Yes." Rocking and strangling the cries. "I hear it all the time." Clinging and beseeching. ". . . What was it, Mother? Why?"

Emotion, Helen thought of explaining, *a characteristic of the religion of all oppressed peoples, yes your very own great-grandparents*—thought of saying. And discarded.

Aren't you now, haven't you had feelings in yourself so strong they had to come out some way? ("what howls restrained by decorum")—thought of saying. And discarded.

Repeat Alva: *hope . . . every word out of their own life. A place to let go. And church is home.* And discarded.

The special history of the Negro people—history?—just you try living what must be lived every day—thought of saying. And discarded.

And said nothing.

And said nothing.

And soothed and held.

"Mother, a lot of the teachers and kids don't like Parry when they don't even know what she's like. Just because. . ." Rocking again, convulsive and shamed. "And I'm not really her friend any more."

No news. Betrayal and shame. Who betrayed? Whose shame? Brought herself to say aloud: "But may be friends again. As Alva and I are."

The sobbing a whisper. "That girl Vicky who got that way when I fainted, she's in school. She's the one keeps wearing the lipstick and they wipe it off and she's always in trouble and now maybe she's expelled. Mother."

"Yes, lambie."

"She acts so awful outside but I remember how she was in church and whenever I see her now I have to wonder. And hear . . . like I'm her, Mother, like I'm her." Clinging and trembling. "Oh why do I have to feel it happens to me too?

"Mother, I want to forget about it all, and not care,—like Melanie. Why can't I forget? *Oh why is it like it is and why do I have to care?*"

Caressing, quieting.

Thinking: *caring asks doing. It is a long baptism into the seas of humankind, my daughter. Better immersion than to live untouched. . . . Yet how will you sustain?*

Why is it like it is?

Sheltering her daughter close, mourning the illusion of the embrace. *And why do I have to care?*

While in her, her own need leapt and plunged for the place of strength that was not—where one could scream or sorrow while all knew and accepted, and gloved and loving hands waited to support and understand.

1956

KRISTIN HUNTER

Debut

"Hold *still*, Judy," Mrs. Simmons said around the spray of pins that protruded dangerously from her mouth. She gave the thirtieth tug to the tight sash at the waist of the dress. "Now walk over there and turn around slowly."

The dress, Judy's first long one, was white organdy over taffeta, with

spaghetti straps that bared her round brown shoulders and a floating skirt and a wide sash that cascaded in a butterfly effect behind. It was a dream, but Judy was sick and tired of the endless fittings she had endured so that she might wear it at the Debutantes' Ball. Her thoughts leaped ahead to the Ball itself . . .

"*Slowly,* I said!" Mrs. Simmons' dark, angular face was always grim, but now it was screwed into an expression resembling a prune. Judy, starting nervously, began to revolve by moving her feet an inch at a time.

Her mother watched her critically. "No, it's still not right. I'll just have to rip out that waistline seam again."

"Oh, Mother!" Judy's impatience slipped out at last. "Nobody's going to notice all those little details."

"They will too. They'll be watching you every minute, hoping to see something wrong. You've got to be the *best.* Can't you get that through your head?" Mrs. Simmons gave a sigh of despair. "You better start noticin' 'all those little details' yourself. I can't do it for you all your life. Now turn around and stand up straight."

"Oh, Mother," Judy said, close to tears from being made to turn and pose while her feet itched to be dancing, "I can't stand it any more!"

"You can't stand it, huh? How do you think *I* feel?" Mrs. Simmons said in her harshest tone.

Judy was immediately ashamed, remembering the weeks her mother had spent at the sewing machine, pricking her already tattered fingers with needles and pins, and the great weight of sacrifice that had been borne on Mrs. Simmons' shoulders for the past two years so that Judy might bare hers at the Ball.

"All right, take it off," her mother said. "I'm going to take it up the street to Mrs. Luby and let her help me. It's got to be right or I won't let you leave the house."

"Can't we just leave it the way it is, Mother?" Judy pleaded without hope of success. "I think it's perfect."

"You would," Mrs. Simmons said tartly as she folded the dress and prepared to bear it out of the room. "Sometimes I think I'll never get it through your head. You got to look just right and act just right. That Rose Griffin and those other girls can afford to be careless, maybe, but you can't. You're gonna be the darkest, poorest one there."

Judy shivered in her new lace strapless bra and her old, childish knit snuggies. "You make it sound like a battle I'm going to instead of just a dance."

"It is a battle," her mother said firmly. "It starts tonight and it goes on for the rest of your life. The battle to hold your head up and get someplace and be somebody. We've done all we can for you, your father and I. Now you've got to start fighting some on your own." She gave Judy a slight smile; her voice softened a little. "You'll do all right, don't worry. Try and get some rest this afternoon. Just don't mess up your hair."

"All right, Mother," Judy said listlessly.

She did not really think her father had much to do with anything that happened to her. It was her mother who had ingratiated her way into the Gay Charmers two years ago, taking all sorts of humiliation from the better-dressed, better-off, lighter-skinned women, humbly making and mending their dresses, fixing food for their meetings, addressing more mail and selling more tickets than anyone else. The club had put it off as long as they could, but finally they had to admit Mrs. Simmons

to membership because she worked so hard. And that meant, of course, that Judy would be on the list for this year's Ball.

Her father, a quiet carpenter who had given up any other ambitions years ago, did not think much of Negro society or his wife's fierce determination to launch Judy into it. "Just keep clean and be decent," he would say. "That's all anybody has to do."

Her mother always answered, "If that's all *I* did we'd still be on relief," and he would shut up with shame over the years when he had been laid off repeatedly and her days' work and sewing had kept them going. Now he had steady work but she refused to quit, as if she expected it to end at any moment. The intense energy that burned in Mrs. Simmons' large dark eyes had scorched her features into permanent irony. She worked day and night and spent her spare time scheming and planning. Whatever her personal ambitions had been, Judy knew she blamed Mr. Simmons for their failure; now all her schemes revolved around their only child.

Judy went to her mother's window and watched her stride down the street with the dress until she was hidden by the high brick wall that went around two sides of their house. Then she returned to her own room. She did not get dressed because she was afraid of pulling a sweater over her hair—her mother would notice the difference even if it looked all right to Judy—and because she was afraid that doing anything, even getting dressed, might precipitate her into the battle. She drew a stool up to her window and looked out. She had no real view, but she liked her room. The wall hid the crowded tenement houses beyond the alley, and from its cracks and bumps and depressions she could construct any imaginary landscape she chose. It was how she had spent most of the free hours of her dreamy adolescence.

"Hey, can I go?"

It was the voice of an invisible boy in the alley. As another boy chuckled, Judy recognized the familiar ritual; if you said yes, they said, "Can I go with you?" It had been tried on her dozens of times. She always walked past, head in the air, as if she had not heard. Her mother said that was the only thing to do; if they knew she was a lady, they wouldn't dare bother her. But this time a girl's voice, cool and assured, answered.

"If you think you're big enough," it said.

It was Lucy Mae Watkins; Judy could picture her standing there in a tight dress with bright, brazen eyes.

"I'm big enough to give you a baby," the boy answered.

Judy would die if a boy ever spoke to her like that, but she knew Lucy Mae could handle it. Lucy Mae could handle all the boys, even if they ganged up on her, because she had been born knowing something other girls had to learn.

"Aw, you ain't big enough to give me a shoe-shine," she told him.

"Come here and I'll show you how big I am," the boy said.

"Yeah, Lucy Mae, what's happenin'?" another boy said. "Come here and tell us."

Lucy Mae laughed. "What I'm puttin' down is too strong for little boys like you."

"Come here a minute, baby," the first boy said. "I got a cigarette for you."

"Aw, I ain't studyin' your cigarettes," Lucy Mae answered. But her voice was closer, directly below Judy. There were the sounds of a

scuffle and Lucy Mae's muffled laughter. When she spoke her voice sounded raw and cross. "Come on now, boy. Cut it out and give me the damn cigarette." There was more scuffling, and the sharp crack of a slap, and then Lucy Mae said, "Cut it out, I said. Just for that I'm gonna take 'em all." The clack of high heels rang down the sidewalk with a boy's clumsy shoes in pursuit.

Judy realized that there were three of them down there. "Let her go, Buster," one said. "You can't catch her now."

"Aw, hell, man, she took the whole damn pack," the one called Buster complained.

"That'll learn you!" Lucy Mae's voice mocked from down the street. "Don't mess with nothin' you can't handle."

"Hey, Lucy Mae. Hey, I heard Rudy Grant already gave you a baby," a second boy called out.

"Yeah. Is that true, Lucy Mae?" the youngest one yelled.

There was no answer. She must be a block away by now.

For a moment the hidden boys were silent; then one of them guffawed directly below Judy, and the other two joined in the secret male laughter that was oddly high-pitched and feminine.

"Aw man, I don't know what you all laughin' about," Buster finally grumbled. "That girl took all my cigarettes. You got some, Leroy?"

"Naw," the second boy said.

"Me neither," the third one said.

"What we gonna do? I ain't got but fifteen cent. Hell, man, I want more than a feel for a pack of cigarettes." There was an unpleasant whine in Buster's voice. "Hell, for a pack of cigarettes I want a bitch to come across."

"She will next time, man," the boy called Leroy said.

"She better," Buster said. "You know she better. If she pass by here again, we gonna jump her, you hear?"

"Sure, man," Leroy said. "The three of us can grab her easy."

"Then we can all three of us have some fun. Oh, *yeah*, man," the youngest boy said. He sounded as if he might be about fourteen.

Leroy said, "We oughta get Roland and J.T. too. For a whole pack of cigarettes she oughta treat all five of us."

"Aw, man, why tell Roland and J.T.?" the youngest voice whined. "They ain't in it. Them was *our* cigarettes."

"They was *my* cigarettes, you mean," Buster said with authority. "You guys better quit it before I decide to cut you out."

"Oh, man, don't do that. We with you, you know that."

"Sure, Buster, we your aces, man."

"All right, that's better." There was a minute of silence.

Then, "What we gonna do with the girl, Buster?" the youngest one wanted to know.

"When she come back we gonna jump the bitch, man. We gonna jump her and grab her. Then we gonna turn her every way but loose." He went on, spinning a crude fantasy that got wilder each time he retold it, until it became so secretive that their voices dropped to a low indistinct murmur punctuated by guffaws. Now and then Judy could distinguish the word "girl" or the other word they used for it; these words always produced the loudest guffaws of all. She shook off her fear with the thought that Lucy Mae was too smart to pass there again today. She had heard them at their dirty talk in the alley before and had always been successful in ignoring it; it had nothing to do with

her, the wall protected her from their kind. All the ugliness was on their side of it, and this side was hers to fill with beauty.

She turned on her radio to shut them out completely and began to weave her tapestry to its music. More for practice than anything else, she started by picturing the maps of the places to which she intended to travel, then went on to the faces of her friends. Rose Griffin's sharp, Indian profile appeared on the wall. Her coloring was like an Indian's too and her hair was straight and black and glossy. Judy's hair, naturally none of these things, had been "done" four days ago so that tonight it would be "old" enough to have a gloss as natural-looking as Rose's. But Rose, despite her handsome looks, was silly; her voice broke constantly into high-pitched giggles and she became even sillier and more nervous around boys.

Judy was not sure that she knew how to act around boys either. The sisters kept boys and girls apart at the Catholic high school where her parents sent her to keep her away from low-class kids. But she felt that she knew a secret: tonight, in that dress, with her hair in a sophisticated upsweep, she would be transformed into a poised princess. Tonight all the college boys her mother described so eagerly would rush to dance with her, and then from somewhere *the boy* would appear. She did not know his name; she neither knew nor cared whether he went to college, but she imagined that he would be as dark as she was, and that there would be awe and diffidence in his manner as he bent to kiss her hand . . .

A waltz swelled from the radio; the wall, turning blue in deepening twilight, came alive with whirling figures. Judy rose and began to go through the steps she had rehearsed for so many weeks. She swirled with a practiced smile on her face, holding an imaginary skirt at her side; turned, dipped, and flicked on her bedside lamp without missing a fraction of the beat. Faster and faster she danced with her imaginary partner, to an inner music that was better than the sounds on the radio. She was "coming out," and tonight the world would discover what it had been waiting for all these years.

"Aw, git it, baby." She ignored it as she would ignore the crowds that lined the streets to watch her pass on her way to the Ball.

"Aw, do your number." She waltzed on, safe and secure on her side of the wall.

"Can I come up there and do it with you?"

At this she stopped, paralyzed. Somehow they had come over the wall or around it and into her room.

"Man, I sure like the view from here," the youngest boy said. "How come we never tried this view before?"

She came to life, ran quickly to the lamp and turned it off, but not before Buster said, "Yeah, and the back view is fine, too."

"Aw, she turned off the light," a voice complained.

"Put it on again, baby, we don't mean no harm."

"Let us see you dance some more. I bet you can really do it."

"Yeah, I bet she can shimmy on down."

"You know it, man."

"Come on down here, baby," Buster's voice urged softly, dangerously. "I got a cigarette for you."

"Yeah, and he got something else for you, too."

Judy, flattened against her closet door, gradually lost her urge to

scream. She realized that she was shivering in her underwear. Taking a deep breath, she opened the closet door and found her robe. She thought of going to the window and yelling down, "You don't have a thing I want. Do you understand?" But she had more important things to do.

Wrapping her hair in protective plastic, she ran a full steaming tub and dumped in half a bottle of her mother's favorite cologne. At first she scrubbed herself furiously, irritating her skin. But finally she stopped, knowing she would never be able to get cleaner than this again. She could not wash away the thing they considered dirty, the thing that made them pronounce "girl" in the same way as the other four-letter words they wrote on the wall in the alley; it was part of her, just as it was part of her mother and Rose Griffin and Lucy Mae. She relaxed then because it was true that the boys in the alley did not have a thing she wanted. She had what they wanted, and the knowledge replaced her shame with a strange, calm feeling of power.

After her bath she splashed on more cologne and spent forty minutes on her makeup, erasing and retracing her eyebrows six times until she was satisfied. She went to her mother's room then and found the dress, finished and freshly pressed, on its hanger.

When Mrs. Simmons came upstairs to help her daughter she found her sitting on the bench before the vanity mirror as if it were a throne. She looked young and arrogant and beautiful and perfect and cold.

"Why, you're dressed already," Mrs. Simmons said in surprise. While she stared, Judy rose with perfect, icy grace and glided to the center of the room. She stood there motionless as a mannequin.

"I want you to fix the hem, Mother," she directed. "It's still uneven in back."

Her mother went down obediently on her knees, muttering, "It looks all right to me." She put in a couple of pins. "That better?"

"Yes," Judy said with a brief glance at the mirror. "You'll have to sew it on me, Mother. I can't take it off now. I'd ruin my hair."

Mrs. Simmons went to fetch her sewing things, returned and surveyed her daughter. "You sure did a good job on yourself, I must say," she admitted grudgingly. "Can't find a thing to complain about. You'll look as good as anybody there."

"Of course, Mother," Judy said as Mrs. Simmons knelt and sewed. "I don't know what you were so worried about." Her secret feeling of confidence had returned, stronger than ever, but the evening ahead was no longer the vague girlish fantasy she had pictured on the wall; it had hard, clear outlines leading up to a definite goal. She would be the belle of the Ball because she knew more than Rose Griffin and her silly friends; more than her mother, more, even, then Lucy Mae, because she knew better than to settle for a mere pack of cigarettes.

"There," her mother said, breaking the thread. She got up. "I never expected to get you ready this early. Ernest Lee won't be here for another hour."

"That silly Ernest Lee," Judy said, with a new contempt in her young voice. Until tonight she had been pleased by the thought of going to the dance with Ernest Lee; he was nice, she felt comfortable with him, and he might even be the awe-struck boy of her dream. He was a dark, serious neighborhood boy who could not afford to go to college;

Mrs. Simmons had reluctantly selected him to take Judy to the dance because all the Gay Charmers' sons were spoken for. Now, with an undertone of excitement, Judy said, "I'm going to ditch him after the first dance, Mother. You'll see. I'm going to come home with one of the college boys."

"It's very nice, Ernest Lee," she told him an hour later when he handed her the white orchid, "but it's rather small. I'm going to wear it on my wrist, if you don't mind." And then, dazzling him with a smile of sweetest cruelty, she stepped back and waited while he fumbled with the door.

"You know, Edward, I'm not worried about her any more," Mrs. Simmons said to her husband after the children were gone. Her voice became harsh and grating. "Put down that paper and listen to me! Aren't you interested in your child?—That's better," she said as he complied meekly. "I was saying, I do believe she's learned what I've been trying to teach her, after all."

p. 1968

FLANNERY O'CONNOR

The Artificial Nigger

Mr. Head awakened to discover that the room was full of moonlight. He sat up and stared at the floor boards—the color of silver—and then at the ticking on his pillow, which might have been brocade, and after a second, he saw half of the moon five feet away in his shaving mirror, paused as if it were waiting for his permission to enter. It rolled forward and cast a dignifying light on everything. The straight chair against the wall looked stiff and attentive as if it were awaiting an order and Mr. Head's trousers, hanging to the back of it, had an almost noble air, like the garment some great man had just flung to his servant; but the face on the moon was a grave one. It gazed across the room and out the window where it floated over the horse stall and appeared to contemplate itself with the look of a young man who sees his old age before him.

Mr. Head could have said to it that age was a choice blessing and that only with years does a man enter into that calm understanding of life that makes him a suitable guide for the young. This, at least, had been his own experience.

He sat up and grasped the iron posts at the foot of his bed and raised himself until he could see the face on the alarm clock which sat on an overturned bucket beside the chair. The hour was two in the morning. The alarm on the clock did not work but he was not dependent on any mechanical means to awaken him. Sixty years had not dulled his responses; his physical reactions, like his moral ones, were guided by his will and strong character, and these could be seen plainly in his features. He had a long tube-like face with a long rounded open jaw and a long depressed nose. His eyes were alert but quiet, and in the miraculous moonlight they had a look of composure and of ancient wisdom as if they belonged to one of the great guides of men. He might have been Vergil summoned in the middle of the night to go to Dante, or better, Raphael, awakened by a blast of God's light to fly

to the side of Tobias.[1] The only dark spot in the room was Nelson's pallet, underneath the shadow of the window.

Nelson was hunched over on his side, his knees under his chin and his heels under his bottom. His new suit and hat were in the boxes that they had been sent in and these were on the floor at the foot of the pallet where he could get his hands on them as soon as he woke up. The slop jar, out of the shadow and made snow-white in the moonlight, appeared to stand guard over him like a small personal angel. Mr. Head lay back down, feeling entirely confident that he could carry out the moral mission of the coming day. He meant to be up before Nelson and to have the breakfast cooking by the time he awakened. The boy was always irked when Mr. Head was the first up. They would have to leave the house at four to get to the railroad junction by five-thirty. The train was to stop for them at five forty-five and they had to be there on time for this train was stopping merely to accommodate them.

This would be the boy's first trip to the city though he claimed it would be his second because he had been born there. Mr. Head had tried to point out to him that when he was born he didn't have the intelligence to determine his whereabouts but this had made no impression on the child at all and he continued to insist that this was to be his second trip. It would be Mr. Head's third trip. Nelson had said, "I will've already been there twict and I ain't but ten."

Mr. Head had contradicted him.

"If you ain't been there in fifteen years, how you know you'll be able to find your way about?" Nelson had asked. "How you know it hasn't changed some?"

"Have you ever," Mr. Head had asked, "seen me lost?"

Nelson certainly had not but he was a child who was never satisfied until he had given an impudent answer and he replied, "It's nowhere around here to get lost at."

"The day is going to come," Mr. Head prophesied, "when you'll find you ain't as smart as you think you are." He had been thinking about this trip for several months but it was for the most part in moral terms that he conceived it. It was to be a lesson that the boy would never forget. He was to find out from it that he had no cause for pride merely because he had been born in a city. He was to find out that the city is not a great place. Mr. Head meant him to see everything there is to see in a city so that he would be content to stay at home for the rest of his life. He fell asleep thinking how the boy would at last find out that he was not as smart as he thought he was.

He was awakened at three-thirty by the smell of fatback frying and he leaped off his cot. The pallet was empty and the clothes boxes had been thrown open. He put on his trousers and ran into the other room. The boy had a corn pone on cooking and had fried the meat. He was sitting in the half-dark at the table, drinking cold coffee out of a can. He had on his new suit and his new gray hat pulled low over his eyes. It was too big for him but they had ordered it a size large because they expected his head to grow. He didn't say anything but his entire figure suggested satisfaction at having arisen before Mr. Head.

1. Vergil, Publius Vergilius Maro (70–19 B.C.), author of the *Aeneid*, in *The Divine Comedy* of Dante Alighieri (1265–1321), is summoned by Beatrice (*Inferno*, II, 49–70) to assist Dante and serves as his guide through Hell and Purgatory; the angel Raphael in the Book of Tobit in the *Apocrypha* serves as Tobias's instructor and companion in the overcoming of the demon Asmodeus.

Mr. Head went to the stove and brought the meat to the table in the skillet. "It's no hurry," he said. "You'll get there soon enough and it's no guarantee you'll like it when you do neither," and he sat down across from the boy whose hat teetered back slowly to reveal a fiercely expressionless face, very much the same shape as the old man's. They were grandfather and grandson but they looked enough alike to be brothers and brothers not too far apart in age, for Mr. Head had a youthful expression by daylight, while the boy's look was ancient, as if he knew everything already and would be pleased to forget it.

Mr. Head had once had a wife and daughter and when the wife died, the daughter ran away and returned after an interval with Nelson. Then one morning, without getting out of bed, she died and left Mr. Head with sole care of the year-old child. He had made the mistake of telling Nelson that he had been born in Atlanta. If he hadn't told him that, Nelson couldn't have insisted that this was going to be his second trip.

"You may not like it a bit," Mr. Head continued. "It'll be full of niggers."

The boy made a face as if he could handle a nigger.

"All right," Mr. Head said. "You ain't ever seen a nigger."

"You wasn't up very early," Nelson said.

"You ain't ever seen a nigger," Mr. Head repeated. "There hasn't been a nigger in this county since we run that one out twelve years ago and that was before you were born." He looked at the boy as if he were daring him to say he had ever seen a Negro.

"How you know I never saw a nigger when I lived there before?" Nelson asked. "I probably saw a lot of niggers."

"If you seen one you didn't know what he was," Mr. Head said, completely exasperated. "A six-month-old child don't know a nigger from anybody else."

"I reckon I'll know a nigger if I see one," the boy said and got up and straightened his slick sharply creased gray hat and went outside to the privy.

They reached the junction some time before the train was due to arrive and stood about two feet from the first set of tracks. Mr. Head carried a paper sack with some biscuits and a can of sardines in it for their lunch. A coarse-looking orange-colored sun coming up behind the east range of mountains was making the sky a dull red behind them, but in front of them it was still gray and they faced a gray transparent moon, hardly stronger than a thumbprint and completely without light. A small tin switch box and a black fuel tank were all there was to mark the place as a junction; the tracks were double and did not converge again until they were hidden behind the bends at either end of the clearing. Trains passing appeared to emerge from a tunnel of trees and, hit for a second by the cold sky, vanish terrified into the woods again. Mr. Head had had to make special arrangements with the ticket agent to have this train stop and he was secretly afraid it would not, in which case, he knew Nelson would say, "I never thought no train was going to stop for you." Under the useless morning moon the tracks looked white and fragile. Both the old man and the child stared ahead as if they were awaiting an apparition.

Then suddenly, before Mr. Head could make up his mind to turn back, there was a deep warning bleat and the train appeared, gliding very slowly, almost silently around the bend of trees about two hundred yards down the track, with one yellow front light shining. Mr.

Head was still not certain it would stop and he felt it would make an even bigger idiot of him if it went by slowly. But he and Nelson, however, were prepared to ignore the train if it passed them.

The engine charged by, filling their noses with the smell of hot metal and then the second coach came to a stop exactly where they were standing. A conductor with the face of an ancient bloated bulldog was on the step as if he expected them, though he did not look as if it mattered one way or the other to him if they got on or not. "To the right," he said.

Their entry took only a fraction of a second and the train was already speeding on as they entered the quiet car. Most of the travelers were still sleeping, some with their heads hanging off the chair arms, some stretched across two seats, and some sprawled out with their feet in the aisle. Mr. Head saw two unoccupied seats and pushed Nelson toward them. "Get in there by the winder," he said in his normal voice which was very loud at this hour of the morning. "Nobody cares if you set there because it's nobody in it. Sit right there."

"I heard you," the boy muttered. "It's no use in you yelling," and he sat down and turned his head to the glass. There he saw a pale ghost-like face scowling at him beneath the brim of a pale ghost-like hat. His grandfather, looking quickly too, saw a different ghost, pale but grinning, under a black hat.

Mr. Head sat down and settled himself and took out his ticket and started reading aloud everything that was printed on it. People began to stir. Several woke up and stared at him. "Take off your hat," he said to Nelson and took off his own and put it on his knee. He had a small amount of white hair that had turned tobacco-colored over the years and this lay flat across the back of his head. The front of his head was bald and creased. Nelson took off his hat and put it on his knee and they waited for the conductor to come ask for their tickets.

The man across the aisle from them was spread out over two seats, his feet propped on the window and his head jutting into the aisle. He had on a light blue suit and a yellow shirt unbuttoned at the neck. His eyes had just opened and Mr. Head was ready to introduce himself when the conductor came up from behind and growled, "Tickets."

When the conductor had gone, Mr. Head gave Nelson the return half of his ticket and said, "Now put that in your pocket and don't lose it or you'll have to stay in the city."

"Maybe I will," Nelson said as if this were a reasonable suggestion.

Mr. Head ignored him. "First time this boy has ever been on a train," he explained to the man across the aisle, who was sitting up now on the edge of his seat with both feet on the floor.

Nelson jerked his hat on again and turned angrily to the window.

"He's never seen anything before," Mr. Head continued. "Ignorant as the day he was born, but I mean for him to get his fill once and for all."

The boy leaned forward, across his grandfather and toward the stranger. "I was born in the city," he said. "I was born there. This is my second trip." He said it in a high positive voice but the man across the aisle didn't look as if he understood. There were heavy purple circles under his eyes.

Mr. Head reached across the aisle and tapped him on the arm. "The thing to do with a boy," he said sagely, "is to show him all it is to show. Don't hold nothing back."

"Yeah," the man said. He gazed down at his swollen feet and lifted

the left one about ten inches from the floor. After a minute he put it down and lifted the other. All through the car people began to get up and move about and yawn and stretch. Separate voices could be heard here and there and then a general hum. Suddenly Mr. Head's serene expression changed. His mouth almost closed and a light, fierce and cautious both, came into his eyes. He was looking down the length of the car. Without turning, he caught Nelson by the arm and pulled him forward. "Look," he said.

A huge coffee-colored man was coming slowly forward. He had on a light suit and a yellow satin tie with a ruby pin in it. One of his hands rested on his stomach which rode majestically under his buttoned coat, and in the other he held the head of a black walking stick that he picked up and set down with a deliberate outward motion each time he took a step. He was proceeding very slowly, his large brown eyes gazing over the heads of the passengers. He had a small white mustache and white crinkly hair. Behind him there were two young women, both coffee-colored, one in a yellow dress and one in a green. Their progress was kept at the rate of his and they chatted in low throaty voices as they followed him.

Mr. Head's grip was tightening insistently on Nelson's arm. As the procession passed them, the light from a sapphire ring on the brown hand that picked up the cane reflected in Mr. Head's eye, but he did not look up nor did the tremendous man look at him. The group proceeded up the rest of the aisle and out of the car. Mr. Head's grip on Nelson's arm loosened. "What was that?" he asked.

"A man," the boy said and gave him an indignant look as if he were tired of having his intelligence insulted.

"What kind of a man?" Mr. Head persisted, his voice expressionless.

"A fat man," Nelson said. He was beginning to feel that he had better be cautious.

"You don't know what kind?" Mr. Head said in a final tone.

"An old man," the boy said and had a sudden foreboding that he was not going to enjoy the day.

"That was a nigger," Mr. Head said and sat back.

Nelson jumped up on the seat and stood looking backward to the end of the car but the Negro had gone.

"I'd of thought you'd know a nigger since you seen so many when you was in the city on your first visit," Mr. Head continued. "That's his first nigger," he said to the man across the aisle.

The boy slid down into the seat. "You said they were black," he said in an angry voice. "You never said they were tan. How do you expect me to know anything when you don't tell me right?"

"You're just ignorant is all," Mr. Head said and he got up and moved over in the vacant seat by the man across the aisle.

Nelson turned backward again and looked where the Negro had disappeared. He felt that the Negro had deliberately walked down the aisle in order to make a fool of him and he hated him with a fierce raw fresh hate; and also, he understood now why his grandfather disliked them. He looked toward the window and the face there seemed to suggest that he might be inadequate to the day's exactions. He wondered if he would even recognize the city when they came to it.

After he had told several stories, Mr. Head realized that the man he was talking to was asleep and he got up and suggested to Nelson that they walk over the train and see the parts of it. He particularly

wanted the boy to see the toilet so they went first to the men's room and examined the plumbing. Mr. Head demonstrated the ice-water cooler as if he had invented it and showed Nelson the bowl with the single spigot where the travelers brushed their teeth. They went through several cars and came to the diner.

This was the most elegant car in the train. It was painted a rich egg-yellow and had a wine-colored carpet on the floor. There were wide windows over the tables and great spaces of the rolling view were caught in miniature in the sides of the coffee pots and in the glasses. Three very black Negroes in white suits and aprons were running up and down the aisle, swinging trays and bowing and bending over the travelers eating breakfast. One of them rushed up to Mr. Head and Nelson and said, holding up two fingers, "Space for two!" but Head replied in a loud voice, "We eaten before we left!"

The waiter wore large brown spectacles that increased the size of his eye whites. "Stan' aside then please," he said with an airy wave of the arm as if he were brushing aside flies.

Neither Nelson nor Mr. Head moved a fraction of an inch. "Look," Mr. Head said.

The near corner of the diner, containing two tables, was set off from the rest by a saffron-colored curtain. One table was set but empty but at the other, facing them, his back to the drape, sat the tremendous Negro. He was speaking in a soft voice to the two women while he buttered a muffin. He had a heavy sad face and his neck bulged over his white collar on either side. "They rope them off," Mr. Head explained. Then he said, "Let's go see the kitchen," and they walked the length of the diner but the black waiter was coming fast behind them.

"Passengers are not allowed in the kitchen!" he said in a haughty voice. "Passengers are NOT allowed in the kitchen!"

Mr. Head stopped where he was and turned. "And there's good reason for that," he shouted into the Negro's chest, "because the cockroaches would run the passengers out!"

All the travelers laughed and Mr. Head and Nelson walked out, grinning. Mr. Head was known at home for his quick wit and Nelson felt a sudden keen pride in him. He realized the old man would be his only support in the strange place they were approaching. He would be entirely alone in the world if he were ever lost from his grandfather. A terrible excitement shook him and he wanted to take hold of Mr. Head's coat and hold on like a child.

As they went back to their seats they could see through the passing windows that the countryside was becoming speckled with small houses and shacks and that a highway ran alongside the train. Cars sped by on it, very small and fast. Nelson felt that there was less breath in the air than there had been thirty minutes ago. The man across the aisle had left and there was no one near for Mr. Head to hold a conversation with so he looked out the window, through his own reflection, and read aloud the names of the buildings they were passing. "The Dixie Chemical Corp!" he announced. "Southern Maid Flour! Dixie Doors! Southern Belle Cotton Products! Patty's Peanut Butter! Southern Mammy Cane Syrup!"

"Hush up!" Nelson hissed.

All over the car people were beginning to get up and take their luggage off the overhead racks. Women were putting on their coats and hats. The conductor stuck his head in the car and snarled, "Firstop-

ppppmry,"[2] and Nelson lunged out of his sitting position, trembling. Mr. Head pushed him down by the shoulder.

"Keep your seat," he said in dignified tones. "The first stop is on the edge of town. The second stop is at the main railroad station." He had come by this knowledge on his first trip when he had got off at the first stop and had had to pay a man fifteen cents to take him into the heart of town. Nelson sat back down, very pale. For the first time in his life, he understood that his grandfather was indispensable to him.

The train stopped and let off a few passengers and glided on as if it had never ceased moving. Outside, behind rows of brown rickety houses, a line of blue buildings stood up, and beyond them a pale rose-gray sky faded away to nothing. The train moved into the railroad yard. Looking down, Nelson saw lines and lines of silver tracks multiplying and criss-crossing. Then before he could start counting them, the face in the window stared out at him, gray but distinct, and he looked the other way. The train was in the station. Both he and Mr. Head jumped up and ran to the door. Neither noticed that they had left the paper sack with the lunch in it on the seat.

They walked stiffly through the small station and came out of a heavy door into the squall of traffic. Crowds were hurrying to work. Nelson didn't know where to look. Mr. Head leaned against the side of the building and glared in front of him.

Finally Nelson said, "Well, how do you see what all it is to see?"

Mr. Head didn't answer. Then as if the sight of people passing had given him the clue, he said, "You walk," and started off down the street. Nelson followed, steadying his hat. So many sights and sounds were flooding in on him that for the first block he hardly knew what he was seeing. At the second corner, Mr. Head turned and looked behind him at the station they had left, a putty-colored terminal with a concrete dome on top. He thought that if he could keep the dome always in sight, he would be able to get back in the afternoon to catch the train again.

As they walked along, Nelson began to distinguish details and take note of the store windows, jammed with every kind of equipment— hardware, drygoods, chicken feed, liquor. They passed one that Mr. Head called his particular attention to where you walked in and sat on a chair with your feet upon two rests and let a Negro polish your shoes. They walked slowly and stopped and stood at the entrances so he could see what went on in each place but they did not go into any of them. Mr. Head was determined not to go into any city store because on his first trip here, he had got lost in a large one and had found his way out only after many people had insulted him.

They came in the middle of the next block to a store that had a weighing machine in front of it and they both in turn stepped up on it and put in a penny and received a ticket. Mr. Head's ticket said, "You weigh 120 pounds. You are upright and brave and all your friends admire you." He put the ticket in his pocket, surprised that the machine should have got his character correct but his weight wrong, for he had weighed on a grain scale not long before and knew he weighed 110. Nelson's ticket said, "You weigh 98 pounds. You have a great destiny ahead of you but beware of dark women." Nelson did not know any women and he weighed only 68 pounds but Mr. Head pointed out that

2. "First stop, Emory," station in suburban Atlanta.

the machine had probably printed the number upsidedown, meaning the 9 for a 6.

They walked on and at the end of five blocks the dome of the terminal sank out of sight and Mr. Head turned to the left. Nelson could have stood in front of every store window for an hour if there had not been another more interesting one next to it. Suddenly he said, "I was born here!" Mr. Head turned and looked at him with horror. There was a sweaty brightness about his face. "This is where I come from!" he said.

Mr. Head was appalled. He saw the moment had come for drastic action. "Lemme show you one thing you ain't seen yet," he said and took him to the corner where there was a sewer entrance. "Squat down," he said, "and stick you head in there," and he held the back of the boy's coat while he got down and put his head in the sewer. He drew it back quickly, hearing a gurgling in the depths under the sidewalk. Then Mr. Head explained the sewer system, how the entire city was underlined with it, how it contained all the drainage and was full of rats and how a man could slide into it and be sucked along down endless pitchblack tunnels. At any minute any man in the city might be sucked into the sewer and never heard from again. He described it so well that Nelson was for some seconds shaken. He connected the sewer passages with the entrance to hell and understood for the first time how the world was put together in its lower parts. He drew away from the curb.

Then he said, "Yes, but you can stay away from the holes," and his face took on that stubborn look that was so exasperating to his grandfather. "This is where I come from!" he said.

Mr. Head was dismayed but he only muttered, "You'll get your fill," and they walked on. At the end of two more blocks he turned to the left, feeling that he was circling the dome; and he was correct for in a half-hour they passed in front of the railroad station again. At first Nelson did not notice that he was seeing the same stores twice but when they passed the one where you put your feet on the rests while the Negro polished your shoes, he perceived that they were walking in a circle.

"We done been here!" he shouted. "I don't believe you know where you're at!"

"The direction just slipped my mind for a minute," Mr. Head said and they turned down a different street. He still did not intend to let the dome get too far away and after two blocks in their new direction, he turned to the left. This street contained two- and three-story wooden dwellings. Anyone passing on the sidewalk could see into the rooms and Mr. Head, glancing through one window, saw a woman lying on an iron bed, looking out, with a sheet pulled over her. Her knowing expression shook him. A fierce-looking boy on a bicycle came driving down out of nowhere and he had to jump to the side to keep from being hit. "It's nothing to them if they knock you down," he said. "You better keep closer to me."

They walked on for some time on streets like this before he remembered to turn again. The houses they were passing now were all unpainted and the wood in them looked rotten; the street between was narrower. Nelson saw a colored man. Then another. Then another. "Niggers live in these houses," he observed.

"Well come on and we'll go somewhere else," Mr. Head said. "We

didn't come to look at niggers," and they turned down another street but they continued to see Negroes everywhere. Nelson's skin began to prickle and they stepped along at a faster pace in order to leave the neighborhood as soon as possible. There were colored men in their undershirts standing in the doors and colored women rocking on the sagging porches. Colored children played in the gutters and stopped what they were doing to look at them. Before long they began to pass rows of stores with colored customers in them but they didn't pause at the entrances of these. Black eyes in black faces were watching them from every direction. "Yes," Mr. Head said, "this is where you were born—right here with all these niggers."

Nelson scowled. "I think you done got us lost," he said.

Mr. Head swung around sharply and looked for the dome. It was nowhere in sight. "I ain't got us lost either," he said. "You're just tired of walking."

"I ain't tired, I'm hungry," Nelson said. "Give me a biscuit."

They discovered then that they had lost the lunch.

"You were the one holding the sack," Nelson said. "I would have kepaholt of it."

"If you want to direct this trip, I'll go on by myself and leave you right here," Mr. Head said and was pleased to see the boy turn white. However, he realized they were lost and drifting farther every minute from the station. He was hungry himself and beginning to be thirsty and since they had been in the colored neighborhood, they had both begun to sweat. Nelson had on his shoes and he was unaccustomed to them. The concrete sidewalks were very hard. They both wanted to find a place to sit down but this was impossible and they kept on walking, the boy muttering under his breath, "First you lost the sack and then you lost the way," and Mr. Head growling from time to time, "Anybody wants to be from this nigger heaven can be from it!"

By now the sun was well forward in the sky. The odor of dinners cooking drifted out to them. The Negroes were all at their doors to see them pass. "Whyn't you ast one of these niggers the way?" Nelson said. "You got us lost."

"This is where you were born," Mr. Head said. "You can ast one yourself if you want to."

Nelson was afraid of the colored men and he didn't want to be laughed at by the colored children. Up ahead he saw a large colored woman leaning in a doorway that opened onto the sidewalk. Her hair stood straight out from her head for about four inches all around and she was resting on bare brown feet that turned pink at the sides. She had on a pink dress that showed her exact shape. As they came abreast of her, she lazily lifted one hand to her head and her fingers disappeared into her hair.

Nelson stopped. He felt his breath drawn up by the woman's dark eyes. "How do you get back to town?" he said in a voice that did not sound like his own.

After a minute she said, "You in town now," in a rich low tone that made Nelson feel as if a cool spray had been turned on him.

"How do you get back to the train?" he said in the same reed-like voice.

"You can catch you a car," she said.

He understood she was making fun of him but he was too paralyzed even to scowl. He stood drinking in every detail of her. His eyes

traveled up from her great knees to her forehead and then made a triangular path from the glistening sweat on her neck down and across her tremendous bosom and over her bare arm back to where her fingers lay hidden in her hair. He suddenly wanted her to reach down and pick him up and draw him against her and then he wanted to feel her breath on his face. He wanted to look down and down into her eyes while she held him tighter and tighter. He had never had such a feeling before. He felt as if he were reeling down through a pitchblack tunnel.

"You can go a block down yonder and catch you a car take you to the railroad station, Sugarpie," she said.

Nelson would have collapsed at her feet if Mr. Head had not pulled him roughly away. "You act like you don't have any sense!" the old man growled.

They hurried down the street and Nelson did not look back at the woman. He pushed his hat sharply forward over his face which was already burning with shame. The sneering ghost he had seen in the train window and all the foreboding feelings he had on the way returned to him and he remembered that his ticket from the scale had said to beware of dark women and that his grandfather's had said he was upright and brave. He took hold of the old man's hand, a sign of dependence that he seldom showed.

They headed down the street toward the car tracks where a long yellow rattling trolley was coming. Mr. Head had never boarded a streetcar and he let that one pass. Nelson was silent. From time to time his mouth trembled slightly but his grandfather, occupied with his own problems, paid him no attention. They stood on the corner and neither looked at the Negroes who were passing, going about their business just as if they had been white, except that most of them stopped and eyed Mr. Head and Nelson. It occurred to Mr. Head that since the streetcar ran on tracks, they could simply follow the tracks. He gave Nelson a slight push and explained that they would follow the tracks on into the railroad station, walking, and they set off.

Presently to their great relief they began to see white people again and Nelson sat down on the sidewalk against the wall of a building. "I got to rest myself some," he said. "You lost the sack and the direction. You can just wait on me to rest myself."

"There's the tracks in front of us," Mr. Head said. "All we got to do is keep them in sight and you could have remembered the sack as good as me. This is where you were born. This is your old home town. This is your second trip. You ought to know how to do," and he squatted down and continued in this vein but the boy, easing his burning feet out of his shoes, did not answer.

"And standing there grinning like a chim-pan-zee while a nigger woman gives you directions. Great Gawd!" Mr. Head said.

"I never said I was nothing but born here," the boy said in a shaky voice. "I never said I would or wouldn't like it. I never said I wanted to come. I only said I was born here and I never had nothing to do with that. I want to go home. I never wanted to come in the first place. It was all your big idea. How you know you ain't following the tracks in the wrong direction?"

This last had occurred to Mr. Head too. "All these people are white," he said.

"We ain't passed here before," Nelson said. This was a neighbor-

hood of brick buildings that might have been lived in or might not. A few empty automobiles were parked along the curb and there was an occasional passer-by. The heat of the pavement came up through Nelson's thin suit. His eyelids began to droop, and after a few minutes his head tilted forward. His shoulders twitched once or twice and then he fell over on his side and lay sprawled in an exhausted fit of sleep.

Mr. Head watched him silently. He was very tired himself but they could not both sleep at the same time and he could not have slept anyway because he did not know where he was. In a few minutes Nelson would wake up, refreshed by his sleep and very cocky, and would begin complaining that he had lost the sack and the way. You'd have a mighty sorry time if I wasn't here, Mr. Head thought; and then another idea occurred to him. He looked at the sprawled figure for several minutes; presently he stood up. He justified what he was going to do on the grounds that it is sometimes necessary to teach a child a lesson he won't forget, particularly when the child is always reasserting his position with some new impudence. He walked without a sound to the corner about twenty feet away and sat down on a covered garbage can in the alley where he could look out and watch Nelson wake up alone.

The boy was dozing fitfully, half conscious of vague noises and black forms moving up from some dark part of him into the light. His face worked in his sleep and he had pulled his knees up under his chin. The sun shed a dull dry light on the narrow street; everything looked like exactly what it was. After a while Mr. Head, hunched like an old monkey on the garbage can lid, decided that if Nelson didn't wake up soon, he would make a loud noise by bamming his foot against the can. He looked at his watch and discovered that it was two o'clock. Their train left at six and the possibility of missing it was too awful for him to think of. He kicked his foot backwards on the can and a hollow boom reverberated in the alley.

Nelson shot up onto his feet with a shout. He looked where his grandfather should have been and stared. He seemed to whirl several times and then, picking up his feet and throwing his head back, he dashed down the street like a wild maddened pony. Mr. Head jumped off the can and galloped after but the child was almost out of sight. He saw a streak of gray disappearing diagonally a block ahead. He ran as fast as he could, looking both ways down every intersection, but without sight of him again. Then as he passed the third intersection completely winded, he saw about half a block down the street a scene that stopped him altogether. He crouched behind a trash box to watch and get his bearings.

Nelson was sitting with both legs spread out and by his side lay an elderly woman, screaming. Groceries were scattered about the sidewalk. A crowd of women had already gathered to see justice done and Mr. Head distinctly heard the old woman on the pavement shout, "You've broken my ankle and your daddy'll pay for it! Every nickel! Police! Police!" Several of the women were plucking at Nelson's shoulder but the boy seemed too dazed to get up.

Something forced Mr. Head from behind the trash box and forward, but only at a creeping pace. He had never in his life been accosted by a policeman. The women were milling around Nelson as if they might suddenly all dive on him at once and tear him to pieces, and the old woman continued to scream that her ankle was broken and to call for

an officer. Mr. Head came on so slowly that he could have been taking a backward step after each forward one, but when he was about ten feet away, Nelson saw him and sprang. The child caught him around the hips and clung panting against him.

The women all turned on Mr. Head. The injured one sat up and shouted, "You sir! You'll pay every penny of my doctor's bill that your boy has caused. He's a juve-nile delinquent! Where is an officer? Somebody take this man's name and address!"

Mr. Head was trying to detach Nelson's fingers from the flesh in the back of his legs. The old man's head had lowered itself into his collar like a turtle; his eyes were glazed with fear and caution.

"Your boy has broken my ankle!" the old woman shouted. "Police!"

Mr. Head sensed the approach of the policeman from behind. He stared straight ahead at the women who were massed in their fury like a solid wall to block his escape. "This is not my boy," he said. "I never seen him before."

He felt Nelson's fingers fall out of his flesh.

The women dropped back, staring at him with horror, as if they were so repulsed by a man who could deny his own image and likeness that they could not bear to lay hands on him. Mr. Head walked on, through a space they silently cleared, and left Nelson behind. Ahead of him he saw nothing but a hollow tunnel that had once been the street.

The boy remained standing where he was, his neck craned forward and his hands hanging by his sides. His hat was jammed on his head so that there were no longer any creases in it. The injured woman got up and shook her fist at him and the others gave him pitying looks, but he didn't notice any of them. There was no policeman in sight.

In a minute he began to move mechanically, making no effort to catch up with his grandfather but merely following at about twenty paces. They walked on for five blocks in this way. Mr. Head's shoulders were sagging and his neck hung forward at such an angle that it was not visible from behind. He was afraid to turn his head. Finally he cut a short hopeful glance over his shoulder. Twenty feet behind him, he saw two small eyes piercing into his back like pitchfork prongs.

The boy was not of a forgiving nature but this was the first time he had ever had anything to forgive. Mr. Head had never disgraced himself before. After two more blocks, he turned and called over his shoulder in a high desperately gay voice, "Let's us go get a Co' Cola somewheres!"

Nelson, with a dignity he had never shown before, turned and stood with his back to his grandfather.

Mr. Head began to feel the depth of his denial. His face as they walked on became all hollows and bare ridges. He saw nothing they were passing but he perceived that they had lost the car tracks. There was no dome to be seen anywhere and the afternoon was advancing. He knew that if dark overtook them in the city, they would be beaten and robbed. The speed of God's justice was only what he expected for himself, but he could not stand to think that his sins would be visited upon Nelson and that even now, he was leading the boy to his doom.

They continued to walk on block after block through an endless section of small brick houses until Mr. Head almost fell over a water spigot sticking up about six inches off the edge of a grass plot. He had not had a drink of water since early morning but he felt he did not

deserve it now. Then he thought that Nelson would be thirsty and they would both drink and be brought together. He squatted down and put his mouth to the nozzle and turned a cold stream of water into his throat. Then he called out in the high desperate voice, "Come on and getcher some water!"

This time the child stared through him for nearly sixty seconds. Mr. Head got up and walked on as if he had drunk poison. Nelson, though he had not had water since some he had drunk out of a paper cup on the train, passed by the spigot, disdaining to drink where his grandfather had. When Mr. Head realized this, he lost all hope. His face in the waning afternoon light looked ravaged and abandoned. He could feel the boy's steady hate, traveling at an even pace behind him and he knew that (if by some miracle they escaped being murdered in the city) it would continue just that way for the rest of his life. He knew that now he was wandering into a black strange place where nothing was like it had even been before, a long old age without respect and an end that would be welcome because it would be the end.

As for Nelson, his mind had frozen around his grandfather's treachery as if he were trying to preserve it intact to present at the final judgment. He walked without looking to one side or the other, but every now and then his mouth would twitch and this was when he felt, from some remote place inside himself, a black mysterious form reach up as if it would melt his frozen vision in one hot grasp.

The sun dropped down behind a row of houses and hardly noticing, they passed into an elegant suburban section where mansions were set back from the road by lawns with birdbaths on them. Here everything was entirely deserted. For blocks they didn't pass even a dog. The big white houses were like partially submerged icebergs in the distance. There were no sidewalks, only drives and these wound around and around in endless ridiculous circles. Nelson made no move to come nearer to Mr. Head. The old man felt that if he saw a sewer entrance he would drop down into it and let himself be carried away; and he could imagine the boy standing by, watching with only a slight interest, while he disappeared.

A loud bark jarred him to attention and he looked up to see a fat man approaching with two bulldogs. He waved both arms like someone shipwrecked on a desert island. "I'm lost!" he called. "I'm lost and can't find my way and me and this boy have got to catch this train and I can't find the station. Oh Gawd I'm lost! Oh hep me Gawd I'm lost!"

The man, who was bald-headed and had on golf knickers, asked him what train he was trying to catch and Mr. Head began to get out his tickets, trembling so violently he could hardly hold them. Nelson had come up to within fifteen feet and stood watching.

"Well," the fat man said, giving him back the tickets, "you won't have time to get back to town to make this but you can catch it at the suburb stop. That's three blocks from here," and he began explaining how to get there.

Mr. Head stared as if he were slowly returning from the dead and when the man had finished and gone off with the dogs jumping at his heels, he turned to Nelson and said breathlessly, "We're going to get home!"

The child was standing about ten feet away, his face bloodless under the gray hat. His eyes were triumphantly cold. There was no **light**

in them, no feeling, no interest. He was merely there, a small figure, waiting. Home was nothing to him.

Mr. Head turned slowly. He felt he knew now what time would be like without seasons and what heat would be like without light and what man would be like without salvation. He didn't care if he never made the train and if it had not been for what suddenly caught his attention, like a cry out of the gathering dusk, he might have forgotten there was a station to go to.

He had not walked five hundred yards down the road when he saw, within reach of him, the plaster figure of a Negro sitting bent over on a low yellow brick fence that curved around a wide lawn. The Negro was about Nelson's size and he was pitched forward at an unsteady angle because the putty that held him to the wall had cracked. One of his eyes was entirely white and he held a piece of brown watermelon.

Mr. Head stood looking at him silently until Nelson stopped at a little distance. Then as the two of them stood there, Mr. Head breathed, "An artificial nigger!"

It was not possible to tell if the artificial Negro were meant to be young or old; he looked too miserable to be either. He was meant to look happy because his mouth was stretched up at the corners but the chipped eye and the angle he was cocked at gave him a wild look of misery instead.

"An artificial nigger!" Nelson repeated in Mr. Head's exact tone.

The two of them stood there with their necks forward at almost the same angle and their shoulders curved in almost exactly the same way and their hands trembling identically in their pockets. Mr. Head looked like an ancient child and Nelson like a miniature old man. They stood gazing at the artificial Negro as if they were faced with some great mystery, some monument to another's victory that brought them together in their common defeat. They could both feel it dissolving their differences like an action of mercy. Mr. Head had never known before what mercy felt like because he had been too good to deserve any, but he felt he knew now. He looked at Nelson and understood that he must say something to the child to show that he was still wise and in the look the boy returned he saw a hungry need for that assurance. Nelson's eyes seemed to implore him to explain once and for all the mystery of existence.

Mr. Head opened his lips to make a lofty statement and heard himself say, "They ain't got enough real ones here. They got to have an artificial one."

After a second, the boy nodded with a strange shivering about his mouth, and said, "Let's go home before we get ourselves lost again."

Their train glided into the suburb stop just as they reached the station and they boarded it together, and ten minutes before it was due to arrive at the junction, they went to the door and stood ready to jump off if it did not stop; but it did, just as the moon, restored to its full splendor, sprang from a cloud and flooded the clearing with light. As they stepped off, the sage grass was shivering gently in shades of silver and the clinkers under their feet glittered with a fresh black light. The treetops, fencing the junction like the protecting walls of a garden, were darker than the sky which was hung with gigantic white clouds illuminated like lanterns.

Mr. Head stood very still and felt the action of mercy touch him

again but this time he knew that there were no words in the world that could name it. He understood that it grew out of agony, which is not denied to any man and which is given in strange ways to children. He understood it was all a man could carry into death to give his Maker and he suddenly burned with shame that he had so little of it to take with him. He stood appalled, judging himself with the thoroughness of God, while the action of mercy covered his pride like a flame and consumed it. He had never thought himself a great sinner before but he saw now that his true depravity had been hidden from him lest it cause him despair. He realized that he was forgiven for sins from the beginning of time, when he had conceived in his own heart the sin of Adam, until the present, when he had denied poor Nelson. He saw that no sin was too monstrous for him to claim as his own, and since God loved in proportion as He forgave, he felt ready at that instant to enter Paradise.

Nelson, composing his expression under the shadow of his hat brim, watched him with a mixture of fatigue and suspicion, but as the train glided past them and disappeared like a frightened serpent into the woods, even his face lightened and he muttered, "I'm glad I've went once, but I'll never go back again!"

1955

SHERWOOD ANDERSON

The Egg

My father was, I am sure, intended by nature to be a cheerful, kindly man. Until he was thirty-four years old he worked as a farm-hand for a man named Thomas Butterworth whose place lay near the town of Bidwell, Ohio. He had then a horse of his own, and on Saturday evenings drove into town to spend a few hours in social intercourse with other farmhands. In town he drank several glasses of beer and stood about in Ben Head's saloon—crowded on Saturday evenings with visiting farmhands. Songs were sung and glasses thumped on the bar. At ten o'clock father drove home along a lonely country road, made his horse comfortable for the night, and himself went to bed, quite happy in his position in life. He had at that time no notion of trying to rise in the world.

It was in the spring of his thirty-fifth year that father married my mother, then a country schoolteacher, and in the following spring I came wriggling and crying into the world. Something happened to the two people. They became ambitious. The American passion for getting up in the world took possession of them.

It may have been that mother was responsible. Being a schoolteacher she had no doubt read books and magazines. She had, I presume, read of how Garfield,[1] Lincoln, and other Americans rose from poverty to fame and greatness, and as I lay beside her—in the days of her lying-in —she may have dreamed that I would some day rule men and cities. At any rate she induced father to give up his place as a farmhand, sell his horse, and embark on an independent enterprise of his own. She

---

1. James Abram Garfield (1831–1881), twentieth President of the United States, was born on a frontier farm in Ohio, spent his early years in poverty, worked as farmer, canal boatman, carpenter, sent himself through Williams College, to become teacher, principal, Congressman, President; like Lincoln, he was assassinated.

was a tall silent woman with a long nose and troubled gray eyes. For herself she wanted nothing. For father and myself she was incurably ambitious.

The first venture into which the two people went turned out badly. They rented ten acres of poor stony land on Grigg's Road, eight miles from Bidwell, and launched into chicken-raising. I grew into boyhood on the place and got my first impression of life there. From the beginning they were impressions of disaster, and if, in my turn, I am a gloomy man inclined to see the darker side of life, I attribute it to the fact that what should have been for me the happy joyous days of childhood were spent on a chicken farm.

One unversed in such matters can have no notion of the many and tragic things that can happen to a chicken. It is born out of an egg, lives for a few weeks as a tiny fluffy thing such as you will see pictured on Easter cards, then becomes hideously naked, eats quantities of corn and meal bought by the sweat of your father's brow, gets diseases called pip, cholera, and other names, stands looking with stupid eyes at the sun, becomes sick and dies. A few hens and now and then a rooster, intended to serve God's mysterious ends, struggle through to maturity. The hens lay eggs out of which come other chickens and the dreadful cycle is thus made complete. It is all unbelievably complex. Most philosophers must have been raised on chicken farms. One hopes for so much from a chicken and is so dreadfully disillusioned. Small chickens, just setting out on the journey of life, look so bright and alert and they are in fact so dreadfully stupid. They are so much like people they mix one up in one's judgments of life. If disease does not kill them, they wait until your expectations are thoroughly aroused and then walk under the wheels of a wagon—to go squashed and dead back to their maker. Vermin infest their youth, and fortunes must be spent for curative powders. In later life I have seen how a literature has been built up on the subject of fortunes to be made out of the raising of chickens. It is intended to be read by the gods who have just eaten of the tree of the knowledge of good and evil.[2] It is a hopeful literature and declares that much may be done by simple ambitious people who own a few hens. Do not be led astray by it. It was not written for you. Go hunt for gold on the frozen hills of Alaska, put your faith in the honesty of a politician, believe if you will that the world is daily growing better and that good will triumph over evil, but do not read and believe the literature that is written concerning the hen. It was not written for you.

I, however, digress. My tale does not primarily concern itself with the hen. If correctly told it will center on the egg. For ten years my father and mother struggled to make our chicken farm pay and then they gave up that struggle and began another. They moved into the town of Bidwell, Ohio, and embarked in the restaurant business. After ten years of worry with incubators that did not hatch, and with tiny— and in their own way lovely—balls of fluff that passed on into semi-naked pullethood and from that into dead henhood, we threw all aside and, packing our belongings on a wagon, drove down Grigg's Road toward Bidwell, a tiny caravan of hope looking for a new place from which to start on our upward journey through life.

2. See *Genesis* 2:9 and 3, esp. 3:22–23: "And the Lord God said, Behold, the man is become as one of us, to know good and evil; and now, lest he put forth his hand, and take also of the tree of life, and eat, and live for ever:/ Therefore the Lord God sent him forth from the Garden of Eden, to till the ground from whence he was taken."

We must have been a sad-looking lot, not, I fancy, unlike refugees fleeing from a battlefield. Mother and I walked in the road. The wagon that contained our goods had been borrowed for the day from Mr. Albert Griggs, a neighbor. Out of its sides stuck the legs of cheap chairs, and at the back of the pile of beds, tables, and boxes filled with kitchen utensils was a crate of live chickens, and on top of that the baby carriage in which I had been wheeled about in my infancy. Why we stuck to the baby carriage I don't know. It was unlikely other children would be born and the wheels were broken. People who have few possessions cling tightly to those they have. That is one of the facts that make life so discouraging.

Father rode on top of the wagon. He was then a bald-headed man of forty-five, a little fat, and from long association with mother and the chickens he had become habitually silent and discouraged. All during our ten years on the chicken farm he had worked as a laborer on neighboring farms and most of the money he had earned had been spent for remedies to cure chicken diseases, on Wilmer's White Wonder Cholera Cure or Professor Bidlow's Egg Producer or some other preparations that mother found advertised in the poultry papers. There were two little patches of hair on father's head just above his ear. I remember that as a child I used to sit looking at him when he had gone to sleep in a chair before the stove on Sunday afternoons in the winter. I had at that time already begun to read books and have notions of my own, and the bald path that led over the top of his head was, I fancied, something like a broad road, such a road as Caesar might have made on which to lead his legions out of Rome and into the wonders of an unknown world. The tufts of hair that grew above father's ears were, I thought, like forests. I fell into a half-sleeping, half-waking state and dreamed I was a tiny thing going along the road into a far beautiful place where there were no chicken farms and where life was a happy eggless affair.

One might write a book concerning our flight from the chicken farm into town. Mother and I walked the entire eight miles—she to be sure that nothing fell from the wagon and I to see the wonders of the world. On the seat of the wagon beside father was his greatest treasure. I will tell you of that.

On a chicken farm, where hundreds and even thousands of chickens come out of eggs, surprising things sometimes happen. Grotesques are born out of eggs as out of people. The accident does not often occur—perhaps once in a thousand births. A chicken is, you see, born that has four legs, two pairs of wings, two heads, or what not. The things do not live. They go quickly back to the hand of their maker that has for a moment trembled. The fact that the poor little things could not live was one of the tragedies of life to father. He had some sort of notion that if he could but bring into henhood or roosterhood a five-legged hen or a two-headed rooster his fortune would be made. He dreamed of taking the wonder about the county fairs and of growing rich by exhibiting it to other farmhands.

At any rate, he saved all the little monstrous things that had been born on our chicken farm. They were preserved in alcohol and put each in its own glass bottle. These he had carefully put into a box, and on our journey into town it was carried on the wagon seat beside him. He drove the horses with one hand and with the other clung to the box. When we got to our destination, the box was taken down at once and

the bottles removed. All during our days as keepers of a restaurant in the town of Bidwell, Ohio, the grotesques in their little glass bottles sat on a shelf back of the counter. Mother sometimes protested, but father was a rock on the subject of his treasure. The grotesques were, he declared, valuable. People, he said, liked to look at strange and wonderful things.

Did I say that we embarked in the restaurant business in the town of Bidwell, Ohio? I exaggerated a little. The town itself lay at the foot of a low hill and on the shore of a small river. The railroad did not run through the town and the station was a mile away to the north at a place called Pickleville. There had been a cider mill and pickle factory at the station, but before the time of our coming they had both gone out of business. In the morning and in the evening busses came down to the station along a road called Turner's Pike from the hotel on the main street of Bidwell. Our going to the out-of-the-way place to embark in the restaurant business was mother's idea. She talked of it for a year and then one day went off and rented an empty store building opposite the railroad station. It was her idea that the restaurant would be profitable. Traveling men, she said, would be always waiting around to take trains out of town and town people would come to the station to await incoming trains. They would come to the restaurant to buy pieces of pie and drink coffee. Now that I am older I know that she had another motive in going. She was ambitious for me. She wanted me to rise in the world, to get into a town school and become a man of the towns.

At Pickleville father and mother worked hard, as they always had done. At first there was the necessity of putting our place into shape to be a restaurant. That took a month. Father built a shelf on which he put tins of vegetables. He painted a sign on which he put his name in large red letters. Below his name was the sharp command—"EAT HERE"—that was so seldom obeyed. A showcase was bought and filled with cigars and tobacco. Mother scrubbed the floor and the walls of the room. I went to school in the town and was glad to be away from the farm, from the presence of the discouraged, sad-looking chickens. Still I was not very joyous. In the evening I walked home from school along Turner's Pike and remembered the children I had seen playing in the town schoolyard. A troop of little girls had gone hopping about and singing. I tried that. Down along the frozen road I went hopping solemnly on one leg. "Hippity Hop To The Barber Shop,"[3] I sang shrilly. Then I stopped and looked doubtfully about. I was afraid of being seen in my gay mood. It must have seemed to me that I was doing a thing that should not be done by one who, like myself, had been raised on a chicken farm where death was a daily visitor.

Mother decided that our restaurant should remain open at night. At ten in the evening a passenger train went north past our door followed by a local freight. The freight crew had switching to do in Pickleville, and when the work was done they came to our restaurant for hot coffee and food. Sometimes one of them ordered a fried egg. In the morning at four they returned north-bound and again visited us. A little trade began to grow up. Mother slept at night and during the day tended the restaurant and fed our boarders while father slept. He slept in the same bed mother had occupied during the night and I went off to the town of Bidwell and to school. During the long nights,

3. Children's song and dance: "Hippety hop to the barber shop to buy a stick of candy./ One for you, and one for me, and one for Sister Annie."

while mother and I slept, father cooked meats that were to go into sandwiches for the lunch baskets of our boarders. Then an idea in regard to getting up in the world came into his head. The American spirit took hold of him. He also became ambitious.

In the long nights when there was little to do, father had time to think. That was his undoing. He decided that he had in the past been an unsuccessful man because he had not been cheerful enough and that in the future he would adopt a cheerful outlook on life. In the early morning he came upstairs and got into bed with mother. She woke and the two talked. From my bed in the corner I listened.

It was father's idea that both he and mother should try to entertain the people who came to eat at our restaurant. I cannot now remember his words, but he gave the impression of one about to become in some obscure way a kind of public entertainer. When people, particularly young people from the town of Bidwell, came into our place, as on very rare occasions they did, bright entertaining conversation was to be made. From father's words I gathered that something of the jolly inn-keeper effect was to be sought. Mother must have been doubtful from the first, but she said nothing discouraging. It was father's notion that a passion for the company of himself and mother would spring up in the breasts of the younger people of the town of Bidwell. In the evening bright happy groups would come singing down Turner's Pike. They would troop shouting with joy and laughter into our place. There would be song and festivity. I do not mean to give the impression that father spoke so elaborately of the matter. He was, as I have said, an uncommunicative man. "They want some place to go. I tell you they want some place to go," he said over and over. That was as far as he got. My own imagination has filled in the blanks.

For two or three weeks this notion of father's invaded our house. We did not talk much, but in our daily lives tried earnestly to make smiles take the place of glum looks. Mother smiled at the boarders and I, catching the infection, smiled at our cat. Father became a little fever-ish in his anxiety to please. There was, no doubt, lurking somewhere in him, a touch of the spirit of the showman. He did not waste much of his ammunition on the railroad men he served at night, but seemed to be waiting for a young man or woman from Bidwell to come in to show what he could do. On the counter in the restaurant there was a wire basket kept always filled with eggs, and it must have been before his eyes when the idea of being entertaining was born in his brain. There was something pre-natal about the way eggs kept themselves connected with the development of his idea. At any rate, an egg ruined his new impulse in life. Late one night I was awakened by a roar of anger coming from father's throat. Both mother and I sat upright in our beds. With trembling hands she lighted a lamp that stood on a table by her head. Downstairs the front door of our restaurant went shut with a bang and in a few minutes father tramped up the stairs. He held an egg in his hand and his hand trembled as though he were having a chill. There was a half-insane light in his eyes. As he stood glaring at us I was sure he intended throwing the egg at either mother or me. Then he laid it gently on the table beside the lamp and dropped on his knees beside mother's bed. He began to cry like a boy, and I, carried away by his grief, cried with him. The two of us filled the little upstairs room with our wailing voices. It is ridiculous, but of the pic-ture we made I can remember only the fact that mother's hand con-

tinually stroked the bald path that ran across the top of his head. I have forgotten what mother said to him and how she induced him to tell her of what had happened downstairs. His explanation also has gone out of my mind. I remember only my own grief and fright and the shiny path over father's head glowing in the lamplight as he knelt by the bed.

As to what happened downstairs. For some unexplainable reason I know the story as well as though I had been a witness to my father's discomfiture. One in time gets to know many unexplainable things. On that evening young Joe Kane, son of a merchant of Bidwell, came to Pickleville to meet his father, who was expected on the ten-o-clock evening train from the South. The train was three hours late and Joe came into our place to loaf about and to wait for its arrival. The local freight train came in and the freight crew were fed. Joe was left alone in the restaurant with father.

From the moment he came into our place the Bidwell young man must have been puzzled by my father's actions. It was his notion that father was angry at him for hanging around. He noticed that the restaurant-keeper was apparently disturbed by his presence and he thought of going out. However, it began to rain and he did not fancy the long walk to town and back. He bought a five-cent cigar and ordered a cup of coffee. He had a newspaper in his pocket and took it out and began to read. "I'm waiting for the evening train. It's late," he said apologetically.

For a long time father, whom Joe Kane had never seen before, remained silently gazing at his visitor. He was no doubt suffering from at attack of stage fright. As so often happens in life he had thought so much and so often of the situation that now confronted him that he was somewhat nervous in its presence.

For one thing, he did not know what to do with his hands. He thrust one of them nervously over the counter and shook hands with Joe Kane. "How-de-do," he said. Joe Kane put his newspaper down and stared at him. Father's eyes lighted on the basket of eggs that sat on the counter and he began to talk. "Well," he began hesitatingly, "well, you have heard of Christopher Columbus, eh?" He seemed to be angry. "That Christopher Columbus was a cheat," he declared emphatically. "He talked of making an egg stand on its end. He talked, he did, and then he went and broke the end of the egg."[4]

My father seemed to his visitor to be beside himself at the duplicity of Christopher Columbus. He muttered and swore. He declared it was wrong to teach children that Christopher Columbus was a great man when, after all, he cheated at the critical moment. He had declared he would make an egg stand on end and then, when his bluff had been called, he had done a trick. Still grumbling at Columbus, father took an egg from the basket on the counter and began to walk up and down. He rolled the egg between the palms of his hands. He smiled

---

4. Washington Irving, attributing it to the 16th-century Italian historian Benzoni, recounts, in *The Life and Voyages of Christopher Columbus,*

the well-known anecdote of the egg. A shallow courtier . . . impatient of the honors paid to Columbus . . . abruptly asked him whether he thought that, in case he had not discovered the Indies, there were not other men in Spain who would have been capable of the enterprise? To this Columbus made no immediate reply, but, taking an egg, invited the company to make it stand on one end. Everyone attempted it, but in vain; whereupon he struck it upon the table so as to break the end, and left it standing on the broken part: illustrating in this simple manner that when he had once shown the way to the New World nothing was easier than to follow it.

genially. He began to mumble words regarding the effect to be produced on an egg by the electricity that comes out of the human body. He declared that, without breaking its shell and by virtue of rolling it back and forth in his hands, he could stand the egg on its end. He explained that the warmth of his hands and the gentle rolling movement he gave the egg created a new center of gravity, and Joe Kane was mildly interested. "I have handled thousands of eggs," father said. "No one knows more about eggs than I do."

He stood the egg on the counter and it fell on its side. He tried the trick again and again, each time rolling the egg between the palms of his hands and saying the words regarding the wonders of electricity and the laws of gravity. When after a half-hour's effort he did succeed in making the egg stand for a moment, he looked up to find that his visitor was no longer watching. By the time he had succeeded in calling Joe Kane's attention to the success of his effort, the egg had rolled over and lay on its side.

Afire with the showman's passion and at the same time a good deal disconcerted by the failure of his first effort, father now took the bottles containing the poultry monstrosities down from their place on the shelf and began to show them to his visitor. "How would you like to have seven legs and two heads like this fellow?" he asked, exhibiting the most remarkable of his treasures. A cheerful smile played over his face. He reached over the counter and tried to slap Joe Kane on the shoulder as he had seen men do in Ben Head's saloon when he was a young farmhand and drove to town on Saturday evenings. His visitor was made a little ill by the sight of the body of the terribly deformed bird floating in the alcohol in the bottle and got up to go. Coming from behind the counter, father took hold of the young man's arm and led him back to his seat. He grew a little angry and for a moment had to turn his face away and force himself to smile. Then he put the bottles back on the shelf. In an outburst of generosity he fairly compelled Joe Kane to have a fresh cup of coffee and another cigar at his expense. Then he took a pan and filling it with vinegar, taken from a jug that sat beneath the counter, he declared himself about to do a new trick. "I will heat this egg in this pan of vinegar," he said. "Then I will put it through the neck of a bottle without breaking the shell. When the egg is inside the bottle it will resume its normal shape and the shell will become hard again. Then I will give the bottle with the egg in it to you. You can take it about with you wherever you go. People will want to know how you got the egg in the bottle. Don't tell them. Keep them guessing. That is the way to have fun with this trick."

Father grinned and winked at his visitor. Joe Kane decided that the man who confronted him was mildly insane but harmless. He drank the cup of coffee that had been given him and began to read his paper again. When the egg had been heated in vinegar, father carried it on a spoon to the counter and going into a back room got an empty bottle. He was angry because his visitor did not watch him as he began to do his trick, but nevertheless went cheerfully to work. For a long time he struggled, trying to get the egg to go through the neck of the bottle. He put the pan of vinegar back on the stove, intending to reheat the egg, then picked it up and burned his fingers. After a second bath in the hot vinegar, the shell of the egg had been softened a little, but not enough for his purpose. He worked and worked and a spirit of des-

perate determination took possession of him. When he thought that at last the trick was about to be consummated, the delayed train came in at the station and Joe Kane started to go nonchalantly out at the door. Father made a last desperate effort to conquer the egg and make it do the thing that would establish his reputation as one who knew how to entertain guests who came into his restaurant. He worried the egg. He attempted to be somewhat rough with it. He swore and the sweat stood out on his forehead. The egg broke under his hand. When the contents spurted over his clothes, Joe Kane, who had stopped at the door, turned and laughed.

A roar of anger rose from my father's throat. He danced and shouted a string of inarticulate words. Grabbing another egg from the basket on the counter, he threw it, just missing the head of the young man as he dodged through the door and escaped.

Father came upstairs to mother and me with an egg in his hand. I do not know what he intended to do. I imagine he had some idea of destroying it, of destroying all eggs, and that he intended to let mother and me see him begin. When, however, he got into the presence of mother, something happened to him. He laid the egg gently on the table and dropped on his knees by the bed as I have already explained. He later decided to close the restaurant for the night and to come upstairs and get into bed. When he did so, he blew out the light and after much muttered conversation both he and mother went to sleep. I suppose I went to sleep also, but my sleep was troubled. I awoke at dawn and for a long time looked at the egg that lay on the table. I wondered why eggs had to be and why from the egg came the hen who again laid the egg. The question got into my blood. It has stayed there, I imagine, because I am the son of my father. At any rate, the problem remains unsolved in my mind. And that, I conclude, is but another evidence of the complete and final triumph of the egg—at least as far as my family is concerned.

1920

WILLIAM FAULKNER

The Old People

At first there was nothing. There was the faint, cold, steady rain, the gray and constant light of the late November dawn, with the voices of the hounds converging somewhere in it and toward them. Then Sam Fathers, standing just behind the boy as he had been standing when the boy shot his first running rabbit with his first gun and almost with the first load it ever carried, touched his shoulder and he began to shake, not with any cold. Then the buck was there. He did not come into sight; he was just there, looking not like a ghost but as if all of light were condensed in him and he were the source of it, not only moving in it but disseminating it, already running, seen first as you always see the deer, in that split second after he has already seen you, already slanting away in that first soaring bound, the antlers even in that dim light looking like a small rocking-chair balanced on his head.

"Now," Sam Fathers said, "shoot quick, and slow."

The boy did not remember that shot at all. He would live to be

eighty, as his father and his father's twin brother and their father in his turn had lived to be, but he would never hear that shot nor remember even the shock of the gun-butt. He didn't even remember what he did with the gun afterward. He was running. Then he was standing over the buck where it lay on the wet earth still in the attitude of speed and not looking at all dead, standing over it shaking and jerking, with Sam Fathers beside him again, extending the knife. "Don't walk up to him in front," Sam said. "If he ain't dead, he will cut you all to pieces with his feet. Walk up to him from behind and take him by the horn first, so you can hold his head down until you can jump away. Then slip your other hand down and hook your fingers in his nostrils."

The boy did that—drew the head back and the throat taut and drew Sam Fathers' knife across the throat and Sam stooped and dipped his hands in the hot smoking blood and wiped them back and forth across the boy's face. Then Sam's horn rang in the wet gray woods and again and again; there was a boiling wave of dogs about them, with Tennie's Jim and Boon Hogganbeck whipping them back after each had had a taste of the blood, then the men, the true hunters—Walter Ewell whose rifle never missed, and Major de Spain and old General Compson and the boy's cousin, McCaslin Edmonds, grandson of his father's sister, sixteen years his senior and, since both he and McCaslin were only children and the boy's father had been nearing seventy when he was born, more his brother than his cousin and more his father than either —sitting their horses and looking down at them: at the old man of seventy who had been a Negro for two generations now but whose face and bearings were still those of the Chickasaw chief who had been his father; and the white boy of twelve with the prints of the bloody hands on his face, who had nothing to do now but stand straight and not let the trembling show.

"Did he do all right, Sam?" his cousin McCaslin said.

"He done all right," Sam Fathers said.

They were the white boy, marked forever, and the old dark man sired on both sides by savage kings, who had marked him, whose bloody hands had merely formally consecrated him to that which, under the man's tutelage, he had already accepted, humbly and joyfully, with abnegation and with pride too; the hands, the touch, the first worthy blood which he had been found at last worthy to draw, joining him and the man forever, so that the man would continue to live past the boy's seventy years and then eighty years, long after the man himself had entered the earth as chiefs and kings entered it;—the child, not yet a man, whose grandfather had lived in the same country and in almost the same manner as the boy himself would grow up to live, leaving his descendants in the land in his turn as his grandfather had done, and the old man past seventy whose grandfathers had owned the land long before the white men ever saw it and who had vanished from it now with all their kind, what of blood they left behind them running now in another race and for a while even in bondage and now drawing toward the end of its alien and irrevocable course, barren, since Sam Fathers had no children.

His father was Ikkemotubbe himself, who had named himself Doom. Sam told the boy about that—how Ikkemotubbe, old Issetibbeha's sister's son, had run away to New Orleans in his youth and returned seven years later with a French companion calling himself the Chevalier Soeur-Blonde de Vitry, who must have been the Ikkemotubbe of his

family too and who was already addressing Ikkemotubbe as *Du Homme;*[1]—returned, came home again, with his foreign Aramis[2] and the quadroon slave woman who was to be Sam's mother, and a gold-laced hat and coat and a wicker wine-hamper containing a litter of month-old puppies and a gold snuff-box filled with a white powder resembling fine sugar. And how he was met at the River landing by three or four companions of his bachelor youth, and while the light of a smoking torch gleamed on the glittering braid of the hat and coat Doom squatted in the mud of the land and took one of the puppies from the hamper and put a pinch of the white powder on its tongue and the puppy died before the one who was holding it could cast it away. And how they returned to the Plantation where Issetibbeha, dead now, had been succeeded by his son, Doom's fat cousin Moke-tubbe, and the next day Moketubbe's eight-year-old son died suddenly and that afternoon, in the presence of Moketubbe and most of the others (the People, Sam Fathers called them) Doom produced another puppy from the wine-hamper and put a pinch of the white powder on its tongue and Moketubbe abdicated and Doom became in fact The Man which his French friend already called him. And how on the day after that, during the ceremony of accession, Doom pronounced a marriage between the pregnant quadroon and one of the slave men which he had just inherited (that was how Sam Fathers got his name, which in Chickasaw had been Had-Two-Fathers) and two years later sold the man and woman and the child who was his own son to his white neighbor, Carothers McCaslin.

That was seventy years ago. The Sam Fathers whom the boy knew was already sixty—a man not tall, squat rather, almost sedentary, flabby-looking though he actually was not, with hair like a horse's mane which even at seventy showed no trace of white and a face which showed no age until he smiled, whose only visible trace of Negro blood was a slight dullness of the hair and the fingernails, and something else which you did notice about the eyes, which you noticed because it was not always there, only in repose and not always then—something not in their shape nor pigment but in their expression, and the boy's cousin McCaslin told him what that was: not the heritage of Ham, not the mark of servitude but of bondage; the knowledge that for a while that part of his blood had been the blood of slaves. "Like an old lion or a bear in a cage," McCaslin said. "He was born in the cage and has been in it all his life; he knows nothing else. Then he smells something. It might be anything, any breeze blowing past anything and then into his nostrils. But there for a second was the hot sand or the cane-brake that he never even saw himself, might not even know if he did see it and probably does know he couldn't hold his own with it if he got back to it. But that's not what he smells then. It was the cage he smelled. He hadn't smelled the cage until that minute. Then the hot sand or the brake blew into his nostrils and blew away, and all he could smell was the cage. That's what makes his eyes look like that."

"Then let him go!" the boy cried. "Let him go!"

His cousin laughed shortly. Then he stopped laughing, making the sound that is. It had never been laughing. "His cage ain't McCaslins',"

---

1. Apparently inaccurate French form for "The Man," with overtones of nobility. French nobility usually have, following their title, *de* or *d'* followed by a place name indicating their residence or seat—e.g., Duc d'Orléans. Even if "The Man," *l'homme*, were preceded by *de*, the proper form would be *de l'homme.*

2. One of Alexandre Dumas' three musketeers.

he said. "He was a wild man. When he was born, all his blood on both sides, except the little white part, knew things that had been tamed out of our blood so long ago that we have not only forgotten them, we have to live together in herds to protect ourselves from our own sources. He was the direct son not only of a warrior but of a chief. Then he grew up and began to learn things, and all of a sudden one day he found out that he had been betrayed, the blood of the warriors and chiefs had been betrayed. Not by his father," he added quickly. "He probably never held it against old Doom for selling him and his mother into slavery, because he probably believed the damage was already done before then and it was the same warriors' and chiefs' blood in him and Doom both that was betrayed through the black blood which his mother gave him. Not betrayed by the black blood and not wilfully betrayed by his mother, but betrayed by her all the same, who had bequeathed him not only the blood of slaves but even a little of the very blood which had enslaved it; himself his own battleground, the scene of his own vanquishment and the mausoleum of his defeat. His cage aint us," McCaslin said. "Did you ever know anybody yet, even your father and Uncle Buddy, that ever told him to do or not do anything that he ever paid any attention to?"

That was true. The boy first remembered him as sitting in the door of the plantation blacksmith-shop, where he sharpened plow-points and mended tools and even did rough carpenter-work when he was not in the woods. And sometimes, even when the woods had not drawn him, even with the shop cluttered with work which the farm waited on, Sam would sit there, doing nothing at all for half a day or a whole one, and no man, neither the boy's father and twin uncle in their day nor his cousin McCaslin after he became practical though not yet titular master, ever to say to him, "I want this finished by sundown" or "why wasn't this done yesterday?" And once each year, in the late fall, in November, the boy would watch the wagon, the hooped canvas top erected now, being loaded—the food, hams and sausage from the smokehouse, coffee and flour and molasses from the commissary, a whole beef killed just last night for the dogs until there would be meat in camp, the crate containing the dogs themselves, then the bedding, the guns, the horns and lanterns and axes, and his cousin McCaslin and Sam Fathers in their hunting clothes would mount to the seat and with Tennie's Jim sitting on the dog-crate they would drive away to Jefferson, to join Major de Spain and General Compson and Boon Hogganbeck and Walter Ewell and go on into the big bottom of the Tallahatchie where the deer and bear were, to be gone two weeks. But before the wagon was even loaded the boy would find that he could watch no longer. He would go away, running almost, to stand behind the corner where he could not see the wagon and nobody could see him, not crying, holding himself rigid except for trembling, whispering to himself: "Soon now. Soon now. Just three more years" (or two more or one more) "and I will be ten. Then Cass said I can go."

White man's work, when Sam did work. Because he did nothing else: farmed no allotted acres of his own, as the other ex-slaves of old Carothers McCaslin did, performed no field-work for daily wages as the younger and newer Negroes did—and the boy never knew just how that had been settled between Sam and old Carothers, or perhaps with old Carothers' twin sons after him. For, although Sam lived among the Negroes, in a cabin among the other cabins in the quarters, and con-

sorted with Negroes (what of consorting with anyone Sam did after the boy got big enough to walk alone from the house to the blacksmith-shop and then to carry a gun) and dressed like them and talked like them and even went with them to the Negro church now and then, he was still the son of that Chickasaw chief and the Negroes knew it. And, it seemed to the boy, not only Negroes. Boon Hogganbeck's grand-mother had been a Chickasaw woman too, and although the blood had run white since and Boon was a white man, it was not chief's blood. To the boy at least, the difference was apparent immediately you saw Boon and Sam together, and even Boon seemed to know it was there—even Boon, to whom in his tradition it had never occurred that anyone might be better born than himself. A man might be smarter, he admitted that, or richer (luckier, he called it) but not better born. Boon was a mastiff, absolutely faithful, dividing his fidelity equally between Major de Spain and the boy's cousin McCaslin, absolutely dependent for his very bread and dividing that impartially too between Major de Spain and McCaslin, hardy, generous, courageous enough, a slave to all the appetites and almost unratiocinative. In the boy's eyes at least it was Sam Fathers, the Negro, who bore himself not only toward his cousin McCaslin and Major de Spain but toward all white men, with gravity and dignity and without servility or recourse to that impenetrable wall of ready and easy mirth which Negroes sustain between themselves and white men, bearing himself toward his cousin McCaslin not only as one man to another but as an older man to a younger.

He taught the boy the woods, to hunt, when to shoot and when not to shoot, when to kill and when not to kill, and better, what to do with it afterward. Then he would talk to the boy, the two of them sitting beneath the close fierce stars on a summer hilltop while they waited for the hounds to bring the fox back within hearing, or beside a fire in the November or December woods while the dogs worked out a coon's trail along the creek, or fireless in the pitch dark and heavy dew of April mornings while they squatted beneath a turkey-roost. The boy would never question him; Sam did not react to questions. The boy would just wait and then listen and Sam would begin, talking about the old days and the People whom he had not had time ever to know and so could not remember (he did not remember ever having seen his father's face), and in place of whom the other race into which his blood had run supplied him with no substitute.

And as he talked about those old times and those dead and vanished men of another race from either that the boy knew, gradually to the boy those old times would cease to be old times and would become a part of the boy's present, not only as if they had happened yesterday but as if they were still happening, the men who walked through them actually walking in breath and air and casting an actual shadow on the earth they had not quitted. And more: as if some of them had not hap-pened yet but would occur tomorrow, until at last it would seem to the boy that he himself had not come into existence yet, that none of his race nor the other subject race which his people had brought with them into the land had come here yet; that although it had been his grandfather's and then his father's and uncle's and was now his cousin's and someday would be his own land which he and Sam hunted over, their hold upon it actually was as trivial and without reality as the now faded and archaic script in the chancery book[3] in Jefferson which

3. Public records or archives.

allocated it to them and that it was he, the boy, who was the guest here and Sam Fathers' voice the mouthpiece of the host.

Until three years ago there had been two of them, the other a full-blood Chickasaw, in a sense even more incredibly lost than Sam Fathers. He called himself Jobaker, as if it were one word. Nobody knew his history at all. He was a hermit, living in a foul little shack at the forks of the creek five miles from the plantation and about that far from any other habitation. He was a market hunter and fisherman and he consorted with nobody, black or white; no Negro would even cross his path and no man dared approach his hut except Sam. And perhaps once a month the boy would find them in Sam's shop—two old men squatting on their heels on the dirt floor, talking in a mixture of Negroid English and flat hill dialect and now and then a phrase of that old tongue which as time went on and the boy squatted there too listening, he began to learn. Then Jobaker died. That is, nobody had seen him in some time. Then one morning Sam was missing, nobody, not even the boy, knew when nor where, until that night when some Negroes hunting in the creek bottom saw the sudden burst of flame and approached. It was Jobaker's hut, but before they got anywhere near it, someone shot at them from the shadows beyond it. It was Sam who fired, but nobody ever found Jobaker's grave.

The next morning, sitting at breakfast with his cousin, the boy saw Sam pass the dining-room window and he remembered then that never in his life before had he seen Sam nearer the house than the blacksmith-shop. He stopped eating even; he sat there and he and his cousin both heard the voices from beyond the pantry door, then the door opened and Sam entered, carrying his hat in his hand but without knocking as anyone else on the place except a house servant would have done, entered just far enough for the door to close behind him and stood looking at neither of them—the Indian face above the nigger clothes, looking at something over their heads or at something not even in the room.

"I want to go," he said. "I want to go to the Big Bottom to live."

"To live?" the boy's cousin said.

"At Major de Spain's and your camp, where you go to hunt," Sam said. "I could take care of it for your all while you aint there. I will build me a little house in the woods, if you rather I didn't stay in the big one."

"What about Isaac here?" his cousin said. "How will you get away from him? Are you going to take him with you?" But still Sam looked at neither of them, standing just inside the room with that face which showed nothing, which showed that he was an old man only when it smiled.

"I want to go," he said. "Let me go."

"Yes," the cousin said quietly. "Of course. I'll fix it with Major de Spain. You want to go soon?"

"I'm going now," Sam said. He went out. And that was all. The boy was nine then; it seemed perfectly natural that nobody, not even his cousin McCaslin, should argue with Sam. Also, since he was nine now, he could understand that Sam could leave him and their days and nights in the woods together without any wrench. He believed that he and Sam both knew that this was not only temporary but that the exigencies of his maturing, of that for which Sam had been training him all his life some day to dedicate himself, required it. They had settled that

one night last summer while they listened to the hounds bringing a fox back up the creek valley; now the boy discerned in that very talk under the high, fierce August stars a presage, a warning, of this moment to-day. "I done taught you all there is of this settled country," Sam said. "You can hunt it good as I can now. You are ready for the Big Bottom now, for bear and deer. Hunter's meat," he said. "Next year you will be ten. You will write your age in two numbers and you will be ready to become a man. Your pa" (Sam always referred to the boy's cousin as his father, establishing even before the boy's orphanhood did that relation between them not of the ward to his guardian and kinsman and chief and head of his blood, but of the child to the man who sired his flesh and his thinking too.) "promised you can go with us then." So the boy could understand Sam's going. But he couldn't understand why now, in March, six months before the moon for hunting.

"If Jobaker's dead like they say," he said, "and Sam hasn't got any-body but us at all kin to him, why does he want to go to the Big Bottom now, when it will be six months before we get there?"

"Maybe that's what he wants," McCaslin said. "Maybe he wants to get away from you a little while."

But that was all right. McCaslin and other grown people often said things like that and he paid no attention to them, just as he paid no attention to Sam saying he wanted to go to the Big Bottom to live. After all, he would have to live there for six months, because there would be no use in going at all if he was going to turn right around and come back. And, as Sam himself had told him, he already knew all about hunting in this settled country that Sam or anybody else could teach him. So it would be all right. Summer, then the bright days after the first frost, then the cold and himself on the wagon with McCaslin this time and the moment would come and he would draw the blood, the big blood which would make him a man, a hunter, and Sam would come back home with them and he too would have outgrown the child's pursuit of rabbits and 'possums. Then he too would make one before the winter fire, talking of the old hunts and the hunts to come as hunters talked.

So Sam departed. He owned so little that he could carry it. He walked. He would neither let McCaslin send him in the wagon, nor take a mule to ride. No one saw him go even. He was just gone one morning, the cabin which had never had very much in it, vacant and empty, the shop in which there never had been very much done, standing idle. Then November came at last, and now the boy made one—himself and his cousin McCaslin and Tennie's Jim, and Major de Spain and General Compson and Walter Ewell and Boon and old Uncle Ash to do the cooking, waiting for them in Jefferson with the other wagon, and the surrey in which he and McCaslin and General Compson and Major de Spain would ride.

Sam was waiting at the camp to meet them. If he was glad to see them, he did not show it. And if, when they broke camp two weeks later to return home, he was sorry to see them go, he did not show that either. Because he did not come back with them. It was only the boy who returned, returning solitary and alone to the settled familiar land, to follow for eleven months the childish business of rabbits and such while he waited to go back, having brought with him, even from his brief first sojourn, an unforgettable sense of the big woods—not a quality dangerous or particularly inimical, but profound, sentient, gi-

gantic and brooding, amid which he had been permitted to go to and fro at will, unscathed, why he knew not, but dwarfed and, until he had drawn honorably blood worthy of being drawn, alien.

Then November, and they would come back. Each morning Sam would take the boy out to the stand allotted him. It would be one of the poorer stands of course, since he was only ten and eleven and twelve and he had never even seen a deer running yet. But they would stand there, Sam a little behind him and without a gun himself, as he had been standing when the boy shot the running rabbit when he was eight years old. They would stand there in the November dawns, and after a while they would hear the dogs. Sometimes the chase would sweep up and past quite close, belling and invisible; once they heard the two heavy reports of Boon Hogganbeck's old gun with which he had never killed anything larger than a squirrel and that sitting, and twice they heard the flat unreverberant clap of Walter Ewell's rifle, following which you did not even wait to hear his horn.

"I'll never get a shot," the boy said. "I'll never kill one."

"Yes, you will," Sam said. "You wait. You'll be a hunter. You'll be a man."

But Sam wouldn't come out. They would leave him there. He would come as far as the road where the surrey waited, to take the riding horses back, and that was all. The men would ride the horses and Uncle Ash and Tennie's Jim and the boy would follow in the wagon with Sam, with the camp equipment and the trophies, the meat, the heads, the antlers, the good ones, the wagon winding on among the tremendous gums and cypresses and oaks where no axe save that of the hunter had ever sounded between the impenetrable walls of cane and brier—the two changing yet constant walls just beyond which the wilderness whose mark he had brought away forever on his spirit even from that first two weeks seemed to lean, stooping a little, watching them and listening, not quite inimical because they were too small, even those such as Walter and Major de Spain and old General Compson who had killed many deer and bear, their sojourn too brief and too harmless to excite to that, but just brooding, secret, tremendous, almost inattentive.

Then they would emerge, they would be out of it, the line as sharp as the demarcation of a doored wall. Suddenly skeleton cotton- and corn-fields would flow away on either hand, gaunt and motionless beneath the gray rain; there would be a house, barns, fences, where the hand of man had clawed for an instant, holding, the wall of the wilderness behind them now, tremendous and still and seemingly impenetrable in the gray and fading light, the very tiny orifice through which they had emerged apparently swallowed up. The surrey would be waiting, his cousin McCaslin and Major de Spain and General Compson and Walter and Boon dismounted beside it. Then Sam would get down from the wagon and mount one of the horses and, with the others on a rope behind him, he would turn back. The boy would watch him for a while against that tall and secret wall, growing smaller and smaller against it, never looking back. Then he would enter it, returning to what the boy believed, and thought that his cousin McCaslin believed, was his loneliness and solitude.

2

So the instant came. He pulled trigger and Sam Fathers marked his face with the hot blood which he had spilled and he ceased to be a

child and became a hunter and a man. It was the last day. They broke camp that afternoon and went out, his cousin and Major de Spain and General Compson and Boon on the horses. Walter Ewell and the Negroes in the wagon with him and Sam and his hide and antlers. There could have been (and were) other trophies in the wagon. But for him they did not exist, just as for all practical purposes he and Sam Fathers were still alone together as they had been that morning. The wagon wound and jolted between the slow and shifting yet constant walls from beyond and above which the wilderness watched them pass, less than inimical now and never to be inimical again since the buck still and forever leaped, the shaking gun-barrels coming constantly and forever steady at last, crashing, and still out of his instant of immortality the buck sprang, forever immortal;—the wagon jolting and bouncing on, the moment of the buck, the shot, Sam Fathers and himself and the blood with which Sam had marked him forever one with the wilderness which had accepted him since Sam said that he had done all right, when suddenly Sam reined back and stopped the wagon and they all heard the unmistakable and unforgettable sound of a deer breaking cover.

Then Boon shouted from beyond the bend of the trail and while they sat motionless in the halted wagon, Walter and the boy already reaching for their guns, Boon came galloping back, flogging his mule with his hat, his face wild and amazed as he shouted down at them. Then the other riders came around the bend, also spurring.

"Get the dogs!" Boon cried. "Get the dogs! If he had a nub on his head, he had fourteen points! Laying right there by the road in that pawpaw[4] thicket! If I'd a knowed he was there, I could have cut his throat with my pocket knife!"

"Maybe that's why he run," Walter said. "He saw you never had your gun." He was already out of the wagon with his rifle. Then the boy was out too with his gun, and the other riders came up and Boon got off his mule somehow and was scrabbling and clawing among the duffel[5] in the wagon, still shouting, "Get the dogs! Get the dogs!" And it seemed to the boy too that it would take them forever to decide what to do—the old men in whom the blood ran cold and slow, in whom during the intervening years between them and himself the blood had become a different and colder substance from that which ran in him and even in Boon and Walter.

"What about it, Sam?" Major de Spain said. "Could the dogs bring him back?"

"We wont need the dogs," Same said. "If he dont hear the dogs behind him, he will circle back in here about sundown to bed."

"All right," Major de Spain said. "You boys take the horses. We'll go on out to the road in the wagon and wait there." He and General Compson and McCaslin got into the wagon and Boon and Walter and Sam and the boy mounted the horses and turned back and out of the trail. Sam led them for an hour through the gray and unmarked afternoon whose light was little different from what it had been at dawn and which would become darkness without any graduation between. Then Sam stopped them.

"This is far enough," he said. "He'll be coming upwind, and he dont want to smell the mules." They tied the mounts in a thicket. Sam led

4. Papaw, tree of custard apple family.   5. Campers' personal gear.

them on foot now, unpathed through the markless afternoon, the boy pressing close behind him, the two others, or so it seemed to the boy, on his heels. But they were not. Twice Sam turned his head slightly and spoke back to him across his shoulder, still walking: "You got time. We'll get there fore he does."

So he tried to go slower. He tried deliberately to decelerate the dizzy rushing of time in which the buck which he had not even seen was moving, which it seemed to him must be carrying the buck farther and farther and more and more irretrievably away from them even though there were no dogs behind him now to make him run, even though, according to Sam, he must have completed his circle now and was heading back toward them. They went on; it could have been another hour or twice that or less than half, the boy could not have said. Then they were on a ridge. He had never been in here before and he could not see that it was a ridge. He just knew that the earth had risen slightly because the underbrush had thinned a little, the ground sloping invisibly away toward a dense wall of cane. Sam stopped. "This is it," he said. He spoke to Walter and Boon: "Follow this ridge and you will come to two crossings. You will see the tracks. If he crosses, it will be at one of these three."

Walter looked about for a moment. "I know it," he said. "I've even seen your deer. I was in here last Monday. He aint nothing but a yearling."

"A yearling?" Boon said. He was panting from the walking. His face still looked a little wild. "If the one I saw was any yearling, I'm still in kindergarden."

"Then I must have seen a rabbit," Walter said. "I always heard you quit school altogether two years before the first grade."

Boon glared at Walter. "If you dont want to shoot him, get out of the way," he said. "Set down somewhere. By God, I—"

"Aint nobody going to shoot him standing here," Sam said quietly.

"Sam's right," Walter said. He moved, slanting the worn, silver-colored barrel of his rifle downward to walk with it again. "A little more moving and a little more quiet too. Five miles is still Hoggan-beck range, even if he wasn't downwind." They went on. The boy could still hear Boon talking, though presently that ceased too. Then once more he and Sam stood motionless together against a tremendous pin oak in a little thicket, and again there was nothing. There was only the soaring and somber solitude in the dim light, there was the thin murmur of the faint cold rain which had not ceased all day. Then, as if it had waited for them to find their positions and become still, the wilderness breathed again. It seemed to lean inward above them, above himself and Sam and Walter and Boon in their separate lurking-places, tremendous, attentive, impartial and omniscient, the buck moving in it somewhere, not running yet since he had not been pursued, not frightened yet and never fearsome but just alert also as they were alert, perhaps already circling back, perhaps quite near, perhaps conscious also of the eye of the ancient immortal Umpire. Because he was just twelve then, and that morning something had happened to him: in less than a second he had ceased forever to be the child he was yesterday. Or perhaps that made no difference, perhaps even a city-bred man, let alone a child, could not have understood it; perhaps only a country-bred one could comprehend loving the life he spills. He began to shake again.

"I'm glad it's started now," he whispered. He did not move to speak; only his lips shaped the expiring words: "Then it will be gone when I raise the gun—"

Nor did Sam. "Hush," he said.

"Is he that near?" the boy whispered. "Do you think—"

"Hush," Sam said. So he hushed. But he could not stop the shaking. He did not try, because he knew it would go away when he needed the steadiness—had not Sam Fathers already consecrated and absolved him from weakness and regret too?—not from love and pity for all which lived and ran and then ceased to live in a second in the very midst of splendor and speed, but from weakness and regret. So they stood motionless, breathing deep and quiet and steady. If there had been any sun, it would be near to setting now; there was a condensing, a densifying, of what he had thought was the gray and unchanging light until he realized suddenly that it was his own breathing, his heart, his blood—something, all things, and that Sam Fathers had marked him indeed, not as a mere hunter, but with something Sam had had in his turn of his vanished and forgotten people. He stopped breathing then; there was only his heart, his blood, and in the following silence the wilderness ceased to breathe also, leaning, stooping overhead with its breath held, tremendous and impartial and waiting. Then the shaking stopped too, as he had known it would, and he drew back the two heavy hammers of the gun.

Then it had passed. It was over. The solitude did not breathe again yet; it had merely stopped watching him and was looking somewhere else, even turning its back on him, looking on away up the ridge at another point, and the boy knew as well as if he had seen him that the buck had come to the edge of the cane and had either seen or scented them and faded back into it. But the solitude did not breathe again. It should have suspired again then but it did not. It was still facing, watching, what it had been watching and it was not here, not where he and Sam stood; rigid, not breathing himself, he thought, cried *No! No!*, knowing already that it was too late, thinking with the old despair of two and three years ago: *I'll never get a shot.* Then he heard it—the flat single clap of Walter Ewell's rifle which never missed. Then the mellow sound of the horn came down the ridge and something went out of him and he knew then he had never expected to get the shot at all.

"I reckon that's it," he said. "Walter got him." He had raised the gun slightly without knowing it. He lowered it again and had lowered one of the hammers and was already moving out of the thicket when Sam spoke.

"Wait."

"Wait?" the boy cried. And he would remember that—how he turned upon Sam in the truculence of a boy's grief over the missed opportunity, the missed luck. "What for? Dont you hear that horn?"

And he would remember how Sam was standing. Sam had not moved. He was not tall, squat rather and broad, and the boy had been growing fast for the past year or so and there was not much difference between them in height, yet Sam was looking over the boy's head and up the ridge toward the sound of the horn and the boy knew that Sam did not even see him; that Sam knew he was still there beside him but he did not see the boy. Then the boy saw the buck. It was coming down the ridge, as if it were walking out of the very sound of the horn

which related its death. It was not running, it was walking, tremendous, unhurried, slanting and tilting its head to pass the antlers through the undergrowth, and the boy standing with Sam beside him now instead of behind him as Sam always stood, and the gun still partly aimed and one of the hammers still cocked.

Then it saw them. And still it did not begin to run. It just stopped for an instant, taller than any man, looking at them; then its muscles suppled, gathered. It did not even alter its course, not fleeing, not even running, just moving with that winged and effortless ease with which deer move, passing within twenty feet of them, its head high and the eye not proud and not haughty but just full and wild and unafraid, and Sam standing beside the boy now, his right arm raised at full length, palm-outward, speaking in that tongue which the boy had learned from listening to him and Jobaker in the blacksmith shop, while up the ridge Walter Ewell's horn was still blowing them in to a dead buck.

"Oleh, Chief," Sam said. "Grandfather."

When they reached Walter, he was standing with his back toward them, quite still, bemused almost, looking down at his feet. He didn't look up at all.

"Come here, Sam," he said quietly. When they reached him he still did not look up, standing above a little spike buck which had still been a fawn last spring. "He was so little I pretty near let him go," Walter said. "But just look at the track he was making. It's pretty near big as a cow's. If there were any more tracks here beside the ones he is laying in, I would swear there was another buck here that I never even saw."

3

It was dark when they reached the road where the surrey waited. It was turning cold, the rain had stopped, and the sky was beginning to blow clear. His cousin and Major de Spain and General Compson had a fire going. "Did you get him?" Major de Spain said.

"Got a good-sized swamp-rabbit with spike horns," Walter said. He slid the little buck down from his mule. The boy's cousin McCaslin looked at it.

"Nobody saw the big one?" he said.

"I dont even believe Boon saw it," Walter said. "He probably jumped somebody's stray cow in that thicket." Boon started cursing, swearing at Walter and at Sam for not getting the dogs in the first place and at the buck and all.

"Never mind," Major de Spain said. "He'll be here for us next fall. Let's get started home."

It was after midnight when they let Walter out at his gate two miles from Jefferson and later still when they took General Compson to his house and then returned to Major de Spain's, where he and McCaslin would spend the rest of the night, since it was still seventeen miles home. It was cold, the sky was clear now; there would be a heavy frost by sunup and the ground was already frozen beneath the horses' feet and the wheels and beneath their own feet as they crossed Major de Spain's yard and entered the house, the warm dark house, feeling their way up the dark stairs until Major de Spain found a candle and lit it, and into the strange room and the big deep bed, the still cold sheets until they began to warm to their bodies and at last the shaking stopped

and suddenly he was telling McCaslin about it while McCaslin listened, quietly until he had finished. "You dont believe it," the boy said. "I know you dont—"

"Why not?" McCaslin said. "Think of all that has happened here, on this earth. All the blood hot and strong for living, pleasuring, that has soaked back into it. For grieving and suffering too, of course, but still getting something out of it for all that, getting a lot out of it, because after all you dont have to continue to bear what you believe is suffering; you can always choose to stop that, put an end to that. And even suffering and grieving is better than nothing; there is only one thing worse than not being alive, and that's shame. But you cant be alive forever, and you always wear out life long before you have exhausted the possibilities of living. And all that must be somewhere; all that could not have been invented and created just to be thrown away. And the earth is shallow; there is not a great deal of it before you come to the rock. And the earth dont want to just keep things, hoard them; it wants to use them again. Look at the seed, the acorns, at what happens even to carrion when you try to bury it: it refuses too, seethes and struggles too until it reaches light and air again, hunting the sun still. And they—" the boy saw his hand in silhouette for a moment against the window beyond which, accustomed to the darkness now, he could see sky where the scoured and icy stars glittered "—they dont want it, need it. Besides, what would it want, itself, knocking around out there, when it never had enough time about the earth as it was, when there is plenty of room about the earth, plenty of places still unchanged from what they were when the blood used and pleasured in them while it was still blood?"

"But we want them," the boy said. "We want them too. There is plenty of room for us and them too."

"That's right," McCaslin said. "Suppose they dont have substance, cant cast a shadow—"

"But I saw it!" the boy cried. "I saw him!"

"Steady," McCaslin said. For an instant his hand touched the boy's flank beneath the covers. "Steady. I know you did. So did I. Sam took me in there once after I killed my first deer."

1942

III

D. H. LAWRENCE

Odour of Chrysanthemums

1

The small locomotive engine, Number 4, came clanking, stumbling down from Selston with seven full wagons. It appeared round the corner with loud threats of speed, but the colt that it startled from among the gorse, which still flickered indistinctly in the raw afternoon, out-distanced it at a canter. A woman, walking up the railway line to Underwood, drew back into the hedge, held her basket aside, and watched the footplate of the engine advancing. The trucks thumped heavily past, one by one, with slow inevitable movement, as she stood insignificantly trapped between the jolting black wagons and the hedge; then they curved away towards the coppice where the withered oak leaves dropped noiselessly, while the birds, pulling at the scarlet hips beside the track, made off into the dusk that had already crept into the spinney. In the open, the smoke from the engine sank and cleaved to the rough grass. The fields were dreary and forsaken, and in the marshy strip that led to the whimsey, a reedy pit-pond, the fowls had already abandoned their run among the alders, to roost in the tarred fowl-house. The pit-bank loomed up beyond the pond, flames like red sores licking its ashy sides, in the afternoon's stagnant light. Just beyond rose the tapering chimneys and the clumsy black headstocks of Brinsley Colliery. The two wheels were spinning fast up against the sky, and the winding engine rapped out its little spasms. The miners were being turned up.

The engine whistled as it came into the wide bay of railway lines[1] beside the colliery, where rows of trucks stood in harbor.

Miners, single, trailing and in groups, passed like shadows diverging home. At the edge of the ribbed level of sidings squat a low cottage, three steps down from the cinder track. A large bony vine clutched at the house, as if to claw down the tiled roof. Round the bricked yard grew a few wintry primroses. Beyond, the long garden sloped down to a bush-covered brook course. There were some twiggy apple trees, winter-crack trees, and ragged cabbages. Beside the path hung dishevelled pink chrysanthemums, like pink cloths hung on bushes. A woman came stooping out of the felt-covered fowl-house, half-way down the garden. She closed and padlocked the door, then drew herself erect, having brushed some bits from her white apron.

She was a tall woman of imperious mien, handsome, with definite black eyebrows. Her smooth black hair was parted exactly. For a few moments she stood steadily watching the miners as they passed along the railway: then she turned towards the brook course. Her face was

---

1. Flat, level area of railroad tracks, probably bending away.

calm and set, her mouth was closed with disillusionment. After a moment she called:

"John!" There was no answer. She waited, and then said distinctly: "Where are you?"

"Here!" replied a child's sulky voice from among the bushes. The woman looked piercingly through the dusk.

"Are you at that brook?" she asked sternly.

For answer the child showed himself before the raspberry-canes that rose like whips. He was a small, sturdy boy of five. He stood quite still, defiantly.

"Oh!" said the mother, conciliated. "I thought you were down at that wet brook—and you remember what I told you——"

The boy did not move or answer.

"Come, come on in," she said more gently, "it's getting dark. There's your grandfather's engine coming down the line!"

The lad advanced slowly, with resentful, taciturn movement. He was dressed in trousers and waistcoat of cloth that was too thick and hard for the size of the garments. They were evidently cut down from a man's clothes.

As they went slowly towards the house he tore at the ragged wisps of chrysanthemums and dropped the petals in handfuls along the path.

"Don't do that—it does look nasty," said his mother. He refrained, and she, suddenly pitiful, broke off a twig with three or four wan flowers and held them against her face. When mother and son reached the yard her hand hesitated, and instead of laying the flower aside, she pushed it in her apron-band. The mother and son stood at the foot of the three steps looking across the bay of lines at the passing home of the miners. The trundle of the small train was imminent. Suddenly the engine loomed past the house and came to a stop opposite the gate.

The engine-driver, a short man with round gray beard, leaned out of the cab high above the woman.

"Have you got a cup of tea?" he said in a cheery, hearty fashion.

It was her father. She went in, saying she would mash.[2] Directly, she returned.

"I didn't come to see you on Sunday," began the little gray-bearded man.

"I didn't expect you," said his daughter.

The engine-driver winced; then, reassuming his cheery, airy manner, he said:

"Oh, have you heard then? Well, and what do you think——?"

"I think it is soon enough," she replied.

At her brief censure the little man made an impatient gesture, and said coaxingly, yet with dangerous coldness:

"Well, what's a man to do? It's no sort of life for a man of my years, to sit at my own hearth like a stranger. And if I'm going to marry again it may as well be soon as late—what does it matter to anybody?"

The woman did not reply, but turned and went into the house. The man in the engine-cab stood assertive, till she returned with a cup of tea and a piece of bread and butter on a plate. She went up the steps and stood near the footplace of the hissing engine.

"You needn't 'a' brought me bread an' butter," said her father. "But a cup of tea"—he sipped appreciatively—"it's very nice." He sipped

2. Prepare (tea).

for a moment or two, then: "I hear as Walter's got another bout on," he said.

"When hasn't he?" said the woman bitterly.

"I heerd tell of him in the 'Lord Nelson'[3] braggin' as he was going to spend that b—— afore he went: half a sovereign[4] that was."

"When?" asked the woman.

"A' Sat'day night—I know that's true."

"Very likely," she laughed bitterly. "He gives me twenty-three shillings."

"Aye, it's a nice thing, when a man can do nothing with his money but make a beast of himself!" said the gray-whiskered man. The woman turned her head away. Her father swallowed the last of his tea and handed her the cup.

"Aye," he sighed, wiping his mouth. "It's a settler, it is——"

He put his hand on the lever. The little engine strained and groaned, and the train rumbled towards the crossing. The woman again looked across the metals. Darkness was settling over the spaces of the railway and trucks; the miners, in gray somber group, were still passing home. The winding engine pulsed hurriedly, with brief pauses. Elizabeth Bates looked at the dreary flow of men, then she went indoors. Her husband did not come.

The kitchen was small and full of firelight; red coals piled glowing up the chimney mouth. All the life of the room seemed in the white, warm hearth and the steel fender reflecting the red fire. The cloth was laid for tea; cups glinted in the shadows. At the back, where the lowest stairs protruded into the room, the boy sat struggling with a knife and a piece of white wood. He was almost hidden in the shadow. It was half-past four. They had but to await the father's coming to begin tea. As the mother watched her son's sullen little struggle with the wood, she saw herself in his silence and pertinacity; she saw the father in her child's indifference to all but himself. She seemed to be occupied by her husband. He had probably gone past his home, slunk past his own door, to drink before he came in, while his dinner spoiled and wasted in waiting. She glanced at the clock, then took the potatoes to strain them in the yard. The garden and fields beyond the brook were closed in uncertain darkness. When she rose with the saucepan, leaving the drain steaming into the night behind her, she saw the yellow lamps were lit along the high road that went up the hill away beyond the space of the railway lines and the field.

Then again she watched the men trooping home, fewer now and fewer.

Indoors the fire was sinking and the room was dark red. The woman put her saucepan on the hob, and set a batter-pudding near the mouth of the oven. Then she stood unmoving. Directly, gratefully, came quick young steps to the door. Someone hung on the latch a moment, then a little girl entered and began pulling off her outdoor things, dragging a mass of curls, just ripening from gold to brown, over her eyes with her hat.

Her mother chid her for coming late from school, and said she would have to keep her at home the dark winter days.

3. A public house, pub.
4. A sovereign is an English pound, then worth $4.86+; there are 20 shillings (see below) to the pound.

"Why, mother, it's hardly a bit dark yet. The lamp's not lighted, and my father's not home."

"No, he isn't. But it's a quarter to five! Did you see anything of him?"

The child became serious. She looked at her mother with large wistful blue eyes.

"No, mother, I've never seen him. Why? Has he come up an' gone past, to Old Brinsley? He hasn't, mother, 'cos I never saw him."

"He'd watch that," said the mother bitterly, "he'd take care as you didn't see him. But you may depend upon it, he's seated in the 'Prince o' Wales.' He wouldn't be this late."

The girl looked at her mother piteously.

"Let's have our teas, mother, should we?" said she.

The mother called John to table. She opened the door once more and looked out across the darkness of the lines. All was deserted: she could not hear the winding engines.

"Perhaps," she said to herself, "he's stopped to get some ripping[5] done."

They sat down to tea. John, at the end of the table near the door, was almost lost in the darkness. Their faces were hidden from each other. The girl crouched against the fender slowly moving a thick piece of bread before the fire. The lad, his face a dusky mark on the shadow, sat watching her who was transfigured in the red glow.

"I do think it's beautiful to look in the fire," said the child.

"Do you?" said her mother. "Why?"

"It's so red, and full of little caves—and it feels so nice, and you can fair smell it."

"It'll want mending directly," replied her mother, "and then if your father comes he'll carry on and say there never is a fire when a man comes home sweating from the pit. A public house is always warm enough."

There was silence till the boy said complainingly: "Make haste, our Annie."

"Well, I am doing! I can't make the fire do it no faster, can I?"

"She keeps wafflin'[6] it about so's to make 'er slow," grumbled the boy.

"Don't have such an evil imagination, child," replied the mother.

Soon the room was busy in the darkness with the crisp sound of crunching. The mother ate very little. She drank her tea determinedly, and sat thinking. When she rose her anger was evident in the stern unbending of her head. She looked at the pudding in the fender, and broke out:

"It is a scandalous thing as a man can't even come home to his dinner! If it's crozzled[7] up to a cinder I don't see why I should care. Past his very door he goes to get to a public house, and here I sit with his dinner waiting for him——"

She went out. As she dropped piece after piece of coal on the red fire, the shadows fell on the walls, till the room was almost in total darkness.

"I canna see," grumbled the invisible John. In spite of herself, the mother laughed.

---

5. Coal-mining term for taking down the roof of an underground road in order to make it higher.

6. Waving.
7. Shriveled.

"You know the way to your mouth," she said. She set the dustpan outside the door. When she came again like a shadow on the hearth, the lad repeated, complaining sulkily:

"I canna see."

"Good gracious!" cried the mother irritably, "you're as bad as your father if it's a bit dusk!"

Nevertheless, she took a paper spill from a sheaf on the mantelpiece and proceeded to light the lamp that hung from the ceiling in the middle of the room. As she reached up, her figure displayed itself just rounding with maternity.

"Oh, mother——!" exclaimed the girl.

"What?" said the woman, suspended in the act of putting the lamp-glass over the flame. The copper reflector shone handsomely on her, as she stood with uplifted arm, turning to face her daughter.

"You've got a flower in your apron!" said the child, in a little rapture at this unusual event.

"Goodness me!" exclaimed the woman, relieved. "One would think the house was afire." She replaced the glass and waited a moment before turning up the wick. A pale shadow was seen floating vaguely on the floor.

"Let me smell!" said the child, still rapturously, coming forward and putting her face to her mother's waist.

"Go along, silly!" said the mother, turning up the lamp. The light revealed their suspense so that the woman felt it almost unbearable. Annie was still bending at her waist. Irritably, the mother took the flowers out from her apron-band.

"Oh, mother—don't take them out!" Annie cried, catching her hand and trying to replace the sprig.

"Such nonsense!" said the mother, turning away. The child put the pale chrysanthemums to her lips, murmuring:

"Don't they smell beautiful!"

Her mother gave a short laugh.

"No," she said, "not to me. It was chrysanthemums when I married him, and chrysanthemums when you were born, and the first time they ever brought him home drunk, he'd got brown chrysanthemums in his buttonhole."

She looked at the children. Their eyes and their parted lips were wondering. The mother sat rocking in silence for some time. Then she looked at the clock.

"Twenty minutes to six!" In a tone of fine bitter carelessness she continued: "Eh, he'll not come now till they bring him. There he'll stick! But he needn't come rolling in here in his pit-dirt, for *I* won't wash him. He can lie on the floor—Eh, what a fool I've been, what a fool! And this is what I came here for, to this dirty hole, rats and all, for him to slink past his very door. Twice last week—he's begun now——"

She silenced herself, and rose to clear the table.

While for an hour or more the children played, subduedly intent, fertile of imagination, united in fear of the mother's wrath, and in dread of their father's homecoming, Mrs. Bates sat in her rocking-chair making a "singlet" of thick cream-colored flannel, which gave a dull wounded sound as she tore off the gray edge. She worked at her sewing with energy, listening to the children, and her anger wearied itself, lay down to rest, opening its eyes from time to time and steadily watching,

its ears raised to listen. Sometimes even her anger quailed and shrank, and the mother suspended her sewing, tracing the footsteps that thudded along the sleepers outside; she would lift her head sharply to bid the children "hush," but she recovered herself in time, and the footsteps went past the gate, and the children were not flung out of their play-world.

But at last Annie sighed, and gave in. She glanced at her wagon of slippers, and loathed the game. She turned plaintively to her mother.

"Mother!"—but she was inarticulate.

John crept out like a frog from under the sofa. His mother glanced up.

"Yes," she said, "just look at those shirtsleeves!"

The boy held them out to survey them, saying nothing. Then somebody called in a hoarse voice away down the line, and suspense bristled in the room, till two people had gone by outside, talking.

"It is time for bed," said the mother.

"My father hasn't come," wailed Annie plaintively. But her mother was primed with courage.

"Never mind. They'll bring him when he does come—like a log." She meant there would be no scene. "And he may sleep on the floor till he wakes himself. I know he'll not go to work tomorrow after this!"

The children had their hands and faces wiped with a flannel.[8] They were very quiet. When they had put on their nightdresses, they said their prayers, the boy mumbling. The mother looked down at them, at the brown silken bush of intertwining curls in the nape of the girl's neck, at the little black head of the lad, and her heart burst with anger at their father, who caused all three such distress. The children hid their faces in her skirts for comfort.

When Mrs. Bates came down, the room was strangely empty, with a tension of expectancy. She took up her sewing and stitched for some time without raising her head. Meantime her anger was tinged with fear.

2

The clock struck eight and she rose suddenly, dropping her sewing on her chair. She went to the stair-foot door, opened it, listening. Then she went out, locking the door behind her.

Something scuffled in the yard, and she started, though she knew it was only the rats with which the place was overrun. The night was very dark. In the great bay of railway lines, bulked with trucks, there was no trace of light, only away back she could see a few yellow lamps at the pit-top, and the red smear of the burning pit-bank on the night. She hurried along the edge of the track, then, crossing the converging lines, came to the stile by the white gates, whence she emerged on the road. Then the fear which had led her shrank. People were walking up to New Brinsley; she saw the lights in the houses; twenty yards farther on were the broad windows of the 'Prince of Wales,' very warm and bright, and the loud voices of men could be heard distinctly. What a fool she had been to imagine that anything had happened to him! He was merely drinking over there at the 'Prince of Wales.' She faltered. She had never yet been to fetch him, and she never would go. So she continued her walk toward the long straggling line of houses, standing back on the highway. She entered a passage between the dwellings.

8. Washrag.

"Mr. Rigley?—Yes! Did you want him? No, he's not in at this minute."

The raw-boned woman leaned forward from her dark scullery and peered at the other, upon whom fell a dim light through the blind of the kitchen window.

"Is it Mrs. Bates?" she asked in a tone tinged with respect.

"Yes. I wondered if your Master was at home. Mine hasn't come yet."

" 'Asn't 'e! Oh, Jack's been 'ome an' 'ad 'is dinner an' gone out. 'E's just gone for 'alf an hour afore bed-time. Did you call at the 'Prince of Wales'?"

"No——"

"No, you didn't like——! It's not very nice." The other woman was indulgent. There was an awkward pause. "Jack never said nothink about—about your Master," she said.

"No!—I expect he's stuck in there!"

Elizabeth Bates said this bitterly, and with recklessness. She knew that the woman across the yard was standing at her door listening, but she did not care. As she turned:

"Stop a minute! I'll just go an' ask Jack if 'e knows anythink," said Mrs. Rigley.

"Oh no—I wouldn't like to put——!"

"Yes, I will, if you'll just step inside an' see as th' childer doesn't come downstairs and set theirselves afire."

Elizabeth Bates, murmuring a remonstrance, stepped inside. The other woman apologized for the state of the room.

The kitchen needed apology. There were little frocks and trousers and childish undergarments on the squab[9] and on the floor, and a litter of playthings everywhere. On the black American cloth[1] of the table were pieces of bread and cake, crusts, slops, and a teapot with cold tea.

"Eh, ours is just as bad," said Elizabeth Bates, looking at the woman, not at the house. Mrs. Rigley put a shawl over her head and hurried out, saying:

"I shanna be a minute."

The other sat, noting with faint disapproval the general untidiness of the room. Then she fell to counting the shoes of various sizes scattered over the floor. There were twelve. She sighed and said to herself: "No wonder!"—glancing at the litter. There came the scratching of two pairs of feet on the yard, and the Rigleys entered. Elizabeth Bates rose. Rigley was a big man, with very large bones. His head looked particularly bony. Across his temple was a blue scar, caused by a wound got in the pit, a wound in which the coal-dust remained blue like tattooing.

" 'Asna 'e come whoam yit?" asked the man, without any form of greeting, but with deference and sympathy. "I couldna say wheer he is—'e's non ower theer!"—he jerked his head to signify the 'Prince of Wales.'

" 'E's 'appen[2] gone up to th' 'Yew,' " said Mrs. Rigley.

There was another pause. Rigley had evidently something to get off his mind:

"Ah left 'im finishin' a stint," he began. "Loose-all[3] 'ad bin gone about ten minutes when we com'n away, an' I shouted: 'Are ter comin', Walt?' an' 'e said: 'Go on, Ah shanna be but a'ef a minnit,' so we com'n

---

9. Sofa.
1. Enameled oilcloth.
2. Perhaps.

3. Signal to quit work and come to the surface.

ter th' bottom, me an' Bowers, thinkin' as 'e wor just behint, an' 'ud come up i' th' next bantle[4]——"

He stood perplexed, as if answering a charge of deserting his mate. Elizabeth Bates, now again certain of disaster, hastened to reassure him:

"I expect 'e's gone up to th' 'Yew Tree,' as you say. It's not the first time. I've fretted myself into a fever before now. He'll come home when they carry him."

"Ay, isn't it too bad!" deplored the other woman.

"I'll just step up to Dick's an' see if 'e *is* theer," offered the man, afraid of appearing alarmed, afraid of taking liberties.

"Oh, I wouldn't think of bothering you that far," said Elizabeth Bates, with emphasis, but he knew she was glad of his offer.

As they stumbled up the entry, Elizabeth Bates heard Rigley's wife run across the yard and open her neighbor's door. At this, suddenly all the blood in her body seemed to switch away from her heart.

"Mind!"[5] warned Rigley. "Ah've said many a time as Ah'd fill up them ruts in this entry, sumb'dy 'll be breakin' their legs yit."

She recovered herself and walked quickly along with the miner.

"I don't like leaving the children in bed, and nobody in the house," she said.

"No, you dunna!" he replied courteously. They were soon at the gate of the cottage.

"Well, I shanna be many minnits. Dunna you be frettin' now, 'e'll be all right," said the butty.[6]

"Thank you very much, Mr. Rigley," she replied.

"You're welcome!" he stammered, moving away. "I shanna be many minnits."

The house was quiet. Elizabeth Bates took off her hat and shawl, and rolled back the rug. When she had finished, she sat down. It was a few minutes past nine. She was startled by the rapid chuff of the winding engine at the pit, and the sharp whirr of the brakes on the rope as it descended. Again she felt the painful sweep of her blood, and she put her hand to her side, saying aloud: "Good gracious!—it's only the nine o'clock deputy going down," rebuking herself.

She sat still, listening. Half an hour of this, and she was wearied out.

"What am I working myself up like this for?" she said pitiably to herself, "I s'll only be doing myself some damage."

She took out her sewing again.

At a quarter to ten there were footsteps. One person! She watched for the door to open. It was an elderly woman, in a black bonnet and a black woollen shawl—his mother. She was about sixty years old, pale, with blue eyes, and her face all wrinkled and lamentable. She shut the door and turned to her daughter-in-law peevishly.

"Eh, Lizzie, whatever shall we do, whatever shall we do!" she cried.

Elizabeth drew back a little, sharply.

"What is it, mother?" she said.

The elder woman seated herself on the sofa.

"I don't know, child, I can't tell you!"—she shook her head slowly. Elizabeth sat watching her, anxious and vexed.

"I don't know," replied the grandmother, sighing very deeply.

4. An open seat or car of the lift or elevator that takes the miners to the surface.

5. Watch out.
6. Buddy, fellow worker.

"There's no end to my troubles, there isn't. The things I've gone through, I'm sure it's enough———!" She wept without wiping her eyes, the tears running.

"But, mother," interrupted Elizabeth, "what do you mean? What is it?"

The grandmother slowly wiped her eyes. The fountains of her tears were stopped by Elizabeth's directness. She wiped her eyes slowly.

"Poor child! Eh, you poor thing!" she moaned. "I don't know what we're going to do, I don't—and you as you are—it's a thing, it is indeed!"

Elizabeth waited.

"Is he dead?" she asked, and at the words her heart swung violently, though she felt a slight flush of shame at the ultimate extravagance of the question. Her words sufficiently frightened the old lady, almost brought her to herself.

"Don't say so, Elizabeth! We'll hope it's not as bad as that; no, may the Lord spare us that, Elizabeth. Jack Rigley came just as I was sittin' down to a glass afore going to bed, an' 'e said: ' 'Appen you'll go down th' line, Mrs. Bates. Walt's had an accident. 'Appen you'll go an' sit wi' 'er till we can get him home.' I hadn't time to ask him a word afore he was gone. An' I put my bonnet on an' come straight down, Lizzie. I thought to myself: 'Eh, that poor blessed child, if anybody should come an' tell her of a sudden, there's no knowin' what'll 'appen to 'er.' You mustn't let it upset you, Lizzie—or you know what to expect. How long is it, six months—or is it five, Lizzie? Ay!"—the old woman shook her head—"time slips on, it slips on! Ay!"

Elizabeth's thoughts were busy elsewhere. If he was killed—would she be able to manage on the little pension and what she could earn? —she counted up rapidly. If he was hurt—they wouldn't take him to the hospital—how tiresome he would be to nurse!—but perhaps she'd be able to get him away from the drink and his hateful ways. She would—while he was ill. The tears offered to come to her eyes at the picture. But what sentimental luxury was this she was beginning? She turned to consider the children. At any rate she was absolutely necessary for them. They were her business.

"Ay!" repeated the old woman, "it seems but a week or two since he brought me his first wages. Ay—he was a good lad, Elizabeth, he was, in his way. I don't know why he got to be such a trouble, I don't. He was a happy lad at home, only full of spirits. But there's no mistake he's been a handful of trouble, he has! I hope the Lord'll spare him to mend his ways. I hope so, I hope so. You've had a sight o' trouble with him, Elizabeth, you have indeed. But he was a jolly enough lad wi' me, he was, I can assure you. I don't know how it is. . . ."

The old woman continued to muse aloud, a monotonous irritating sound, while Elizabeth thought concentratedly, startled once, when she heard the winding-engine chuff quickly, and the brakes skirr with a shriek. Then she heard the engine more slowly, and the brakes made no sound. The old woman did not notice. Elizabeth waited in suspense. The mother-in-law talked, with lapses into silence.

"But he wasn't your son, Lizzie, an' it makes a difference. Whatever he was, I remember him when he was little, an' I learned to understand him and to make allowances. You've got to make allowances for them———"

It was half-past ten, and the old woman was saying: "But it's trouble from beginning to end; you're never too old for trouble, never too old for that——" when the gate banged back, and there were heavy feet on the steps.

"I'll go, Lizzie, let me go," cried the old woman, rising. But Elizabeth was at the door. It was a man in pit-clothes.

"They're bringin' 'im, Missis," he said. Elizabeth's heart halted a moment. Then it surged on again, almost suffocating her.

"Is he—is it bad?" she asked.

The man turned away, looking at the darkness:

"The doctor says 'e'd been dead hours. 'E saw 'im i' th' lamp-cabin."

The old woman, who stood just behind Elizabeth, dropped into a chair, and folded her hands, crying: "Oh, my boy, my boy!"

"Hush!" said Elizabeth, with a sharp twitch of a frown. "Be still, mother, don't waken th' children: I wouldn't have them down for anything!"

The old woman moaned softly, rocking herself. The man was drawing away. Elizabeth took a step forward.

"How was it?" she asked.

"Well, I couldn't say for sure," the man replied, very ill at ease. " 'E wor finishin' a stint an' th' butties 'ad gone, an' a lot o' stuff come down atop 'n 'im.'

"And crushed him?" cried the widow, with a shudder.

"No," said the man, "it fell at th' back of 'im. 'E wor under th' face, an' it niver touched 'im. It shut 'im in. It seems 'e wor smothered."

Elizabeth shrank back. She heard the old woman behind her cry:

"What?—what did 'e say it was?"

The man replied, more loudly: " 'E wor smothered!"

Then the old woman wailed aloud, and this relieved Elizabeth.

"Oh, mother," she said, putting her hand on the old woman, "don't waken th' children, don't waken th' children."

She wept a little, unknowing, while the old mother rocked herself and moaned. Elizabeth remembered that they were bringing him home, and she must be ready. "They'll lay him in the parlor," she said to herself, standing a moment pale and perplexed.

Then she lighted a candle and went into the tiny room. The air was cold and damp, but she could not make a fire, there was no fireplace. She set down the candle and looked round. The candlelight glittered on the luster-glasses[7] on the two vases that held some of the pink chrysanthemums, and on the dark mahogany. There was a cold, deathly smell of chrysanthemums in the room. Elizabeth stood looking at the flowers. She turned away, and calculated whether there would be room to lay him on the floor, between the couch and the chiffonier. She pushed the chairs aside. There would be room to lay him down and to step round him. Then she fetched the old red tablecloth, and another old cloth, spreading them down to save her bit of carpet. She shivered on leaving the parlor; so, from the dresser drawer she took a clean shirt and put it at the fire to air. All the time her mother-in-law was rocking herself in the chair and moaning.

"You'll have to move from there, mother," said Elizabeth. "They'll be bringing him in. Come in the rocker."

---

7. Glass pendants around the edge of an ornamental vase.

The old mother rose mechanically, and seated herself by the fire, continuing to lament. Elizabeth went into the pantry for another candle, and there, in the little pent-house[8] under the naked tiles, she heard them coming. She stood still in the pantry doorway, listening. She heard them pass the end of the house, and come awkwardly down the three steps, a jumble of shuffling footsteps and muttering voices. The old woman was silent. The men were in the yard.

Then Elizabeth heard Matthews, the manager of the pit, say: "You go in first, Jim. Mind!"

The door came open, and the two women saw a collier backing into the room, holding one end of a stretcher, on which they could see the nailed pit-boots of the dead man. The two carriers halted, the man at the head stooping to the lintel of the door.

"Wheer will you have him?" asked the manager, a short, white-bearded man.

Elizabeth roused herself and came from the pantry carrying the unlighted candle.

"In the parlor," she said.

"In there, Jim!" pointed the manager, and the carriers backed round into the tiny room. The coat with which they had covered the body fell off as they awkwardly turned through the two doorways, and the women saw their man, naked to the waist, lying stripped for work. The old woman began to moan in a low voice of horror.

"Lay th' stretcher at th' side," snapped the manager, "an' put 'im on th' cloths. Mind now, mind! Look you now——!"

One of the men had knocked off a vase of chrysanthemums. He stared awkwardly, then they set down the stretcher. Elizabeth did not look at her husband. As soon as she could get in the room, she went and picked up the broken vase and the flowers.

"Wait a minute!" she said.

The three men waited in silence while she mopped up the water with a duster.

"Eh, what a job, what a job, to be sure!" the manager was saying, rubbing his brow with trouble and perplexity. "Never knew such a thing in my life, never! He'd no business to ha' been left. I never knew such a thing in my life! Fell over him clean as a whistle, an' shut him in. Not four foot of space, there wasn't—yet it scarce bruised him."

He looked down at the dead man, lying prone, half naked, all grimed with cold-dust.

"'Sphyxiated,' the doctor said. It *is* the most terrible job I've ever known. Seems as if it was done o' purpose. Clean over him, an' shut 'im in, like a mouse-trap"—he made a sharp, descending gesture with his hand.

The colliers standing by jerked aside their heads in hopeless comment.

The horror of the thing bristled upon them all.

Then they heard the girl's voice upstairs calling shrilly: "Mother, mother—who is it? Mother, who is it?"

Elizabeth hurried to the foot of the stairs and opened the door:

"Go to sleep!" she commanded sharply. "What are you shouting about? Go to sleep at once—there's nothing——"

---

8. Structure, usually with a sloping roof, attached to house.

Then she began to mount the stairs. They could hear her on the boards, and on the plaster floor of the little bedroom. They could hear her distinctly:

"What's the mater now?—what's the matter with you, silly thing?" —her voice was much agitated, with an unreal gentleness.

"I thought it was some men come," said the plaintive voice of the child. "Has he come?"

"Yes, they've brought him. There's nothing to make a fuss about. Go to sleep now, like a good child."

They could hear her voice in the bedroom, they waited whilst she covered the children under the bedclothes.

"Is he drunk?" asked the girl, timidly, faintly.

"No! No—he's not! He—he's asleep."

"Is he asleep downstairs?"

"Yes—and don't make a noise."

There was silence for a moment, then the men heard the frightened child again:

"What's that noise?"

"It's nothing, I tell you, what are you bothering for?"

The noise was the grandmother moaning. She was oblivious of everything, sitting on her chair rocking and moaning. The manager put his hand on her arm and bade her "Sh—sh!!"

The old woman opened her eyes and looked at him. She was shocked by this interruption, and seemed to wonder.

"What time is it?" the plaintive thin voice of the child, sinking back unhappily into sleep, asked this last question.

"Ten o'clock," answered the mother more softly. Then she must have bent down and kissed the children.

Matthews beckoned to the men to come away. They put on their caps and took up the stretcher. Stepping over the body, they tiptoed out of the house. None of them spoke till they were far from the wakeful children.

When Elizabeth came down she found her mother alone on the parlor floor, leaning over the dead man, the tears dropping on him.

"We must lay him out," the wife said. She put on the kettle, then returning knelt at the feet, and began to unfasten the knotted leather laces. The room was clammy and dim with only one candle, so that she had to bend her face almost to the floor. At last she got off the heavy boots and put them away.

"You must help me now," she whispered to the old woman. Together they stripped the man.

When they arose, saw him lying in the naïve dignity of death, the women stood arrested in fear and respect. For a few moments they remained still, looking down, the old mother whimpering. Elizabeth felt countermanded. She saw him, how utterly inviolable he lay in himself. She had nothing to do with him. She could not accept it. Stooping, she laid her hand on him, in claim. He was still warm, for the mine was hot where he had died. His mother had his face between her hands, and was murmuring incoherently. The old tears fell in succession as drops from wet leaves; the mother was not weeping, merely her tears flowed. Elizabeth embraced the body of her husband, with cheek and lips. She seemed to be listening, inquiring, trying to

get some connection. But she could not. She was driven away. He was impregnable.

She rose, went into the kitchen, where she poured warm water into a bowl, brought soap and flannel and a soft towel.

"I must wash him," she said.

Then the old mother rose stiffly, and watched Elizabeth as she carefully washed his face, carefully brushing the big blond moustache from his mouth with the flannel. She was afraid with a bottomless fear, so she ministered to him. The old woman, jealous, said:

"Let me wipe him!"—and she kneeled on the other side drying slowly as Elizabeth washed, her big black bonnet sometimes brushing the dark head of her daughter-in-law. They worked thus in silence for a long time. They never forgot it was death, and the touch of the man's dead body gave them strange emotions, different in each of the women; a great dread possessed them both, the mother felt the lie was given to her womb, she was denied; the wife felt the utter isolation of the human soul, the child within her was a weight apart from her.

At last it was finished. He was a man of handsome body, and his face showed no traces of drink. He was blond, full-fleshed, with fine limbs. But he was dead.

"Bless him," whispered his mother, looking always at his face, and speaking out of sheer terror. "Dear lad—bless him!" She spoke in a faint, sibilant ecstasy of fear and mother love.

Elizabeth sank down again to the floor, and put her face against his neck, and trembled and shuddered. But she had to draw away again. He was dead, and her living flesh had no place against his. A great dread and weariness held her: she was so unavailing. Her life was gone like this.

"White as milk he is, clear as a twelve-month baby, bless him, the darling!" the old mother murmured to herself. "Not a mark on him, clear and clean and white, beautiful as ever a child was made," she murmured with pride. Elizabeth kept her face hidden.

"He went peaceful, Lizzie—peaceful as sleep. Isn't he beautiful, the lamb? Ay—he must ha' made his peace, Lizzie. 'Appen he made it all right, Lizzie, shut in there. He'd have time. He wouldn't look like this if he hadn't made his peace. The lamb, the dear lamb. Eh, but he had a hearty laugh. I loved to hear it. He had the heartiest laugh, Lizzie, as a lad——"

Elizabeth looked up. The man's mouth was fallen back, slightly open under the cover of the moustache. The eyes, half shut, did not show glazed in the obscurity. Life with its smoky burning gone from him, had left him apart and utterly alien to her. And she knew what a stranger he was to her. In her womb was ice of fear, because of this separate stranger with whom she had been living as one flesh. Was this what it all meant—utter, intact separateness, obscured by heat of living? In dread she turned her face away. The fact was too deadly. There had been nothing between them, and yet they had come together, exchanging their nakedness repeatedly. Each time he had taken her, they had been two isolated beings, far apart as now. He was no more responsible than she. The child was like ice in her womb. For as she looked at the dead man, her mind, cold and detached, said clearly: "Who am I? What have I been doing? I have been fighting a husband who did not exist. *He* existed all the time. What wrong have I done? What was that I have been living with? There lies the reality, this

man." And her soul died in her for fear: she knew she had never seen him, he had never seen her, they had met in the dark and had fought in the dark, not knowing whom they met nor whom they fought. And now she saw, and turned silent in seeing. For she had been wrong. She had said he was something he was not; she had felt familiar with him. Whereas he was apart all the while, living as she never lived, feeling as she never felt.

In fear and shame she looked at his naked body, that she had known falsely. And he was the father of her children. Her soul was torn from her body and stood apart. She looked at his naked body and was ashamed, as if she had denied it. After all, it was itself. It seemed awful to her. She looked at his face, and she turned her own face to the wall. For his look was other than hers, his way was not her way. She had denied him what he was—she saw it now. She had refused him as himself. And this had been her life, and his life. She was grateful to death, which restored the truth. And she knew she was not dead.

And all the while her heart was bursting with grief and pity for him. What had he suffered? What stretch of horror for this helpless man! She was rigid with agony. She had not been able to help him. He had been cruelly injured, this naked man, this other being, and she could make no reparation. There were the children—but the children belonged to life. This dead man had nothing to do with them. He and she were only channels through which life had flowed to issue in the children. She was a mother—but how awful she knew it now to have been a wife. And he, dead now, how awful he must have felt it to be a husband. She felt that in the next world he would be a stranger to her. If they met there, in the beyond, they would only be ashamed of what had been before. The children had come, for some mysterious reason, out of both of them. But the children did not unite them. Now he was dead, she knew how eternally he was apart from her, how eternally he had nothing more to do with her. She saw this episode of her life closed. They had denied each other in life. Now he had withdrawn. An anguish came over her. It was finished then: it had become hopeless between them long before he died. Yet he had been her husband. But how little!

"Have you got his shirt, 'Lizabeth?"

Elizabeth turned without answering, though she strove to weep and behave as her mother-in-law expected. But she could not, she was silenced. She went into the kitchen and returned with the garment.

"It is aired," she said, grasping the cotton shirt here and there to try. She was almost ashamed to handle him; what right had she or anyone to lay hands on him; but her touch was humble on his body. It was hard work to clothe him. He was so heavy and inert. A terrible dread gripped her all the while: that he could be so heavy and utterly inert, unresponsive, apart. The horror of the distance between them was almost too much for her—it was so infinite a gap she must look across.

At last it was finished. They covered him with a sheet and left him lying, with his face bound. And she fastened the door of the little parlor, lest the children should see what was lying there. Then, with peace sunk heavy on her heart, she went about making tidy the kitchen. She knew she submitted to life, which was her immediate master. But from death, her ultimate master, she winced with fear and shame.

1914

D. H. LAWRENCE

The Blind Man

Isabel Pervin was listening for two sounds—for the sound of wheels on the drive outside and for the noise of her husband's footsteps in the hall. Her dearest and oldest friend, a man who seemed almost indispensable to her living, would drive up in the rainy dusk of the closing November day. The trap had gone to fetch him from the station. And her husband, who had been blinded in Flanders,[1] and who had a disfiguring mark on his brow, would be coming in from the out-houses.[2]

He had been home for a year now. He was totally blind. Yet they had been very happy. The Grange was Maurice's own place. The back was a farmstead, and the Wernhams, who occupied the rear premises, acted as farmers. Isabel lived with her husband in the handsome rooms in front. She and he had been almost entirely alone together since he was wounded. They talked and sang and read together in a wonderful and unspeakable intimacy. Then she reviewed books for a Scottish newspaper, carrying on her old interest, and he occupied himself a good deal with the farm. Sightless, he could still discuss everything with Wernham, and he could also do a good deal of work about the place—menial work, it is true, but it gave him satisfaction. He milked the cows, carried in the pails, turned the separator, attended to the pigs and horses. Life was still very full and strangely serene for the blind man, peaceful with the almost incomprehensible peace of immediate contact in darkness. With his wife he had a whole world, rich and real and invisible.

They were newly and remotely happy. He did not even regret the loss of his sight in these times of dark, palpable joy. A certain exultance swelled his soul.

But as time wore on, sometimes the rich glamour would leave them. Sometimes, after months of this intensity, a sense of burden overcame Isabel, a weariness, a terrible ennui, in that silent house approached between a colonnade of tall-shafted pines. Then she felt she would go mad, for she could not bear it. And sometimes he had devastating fits of depression, which seemed to lay waste his whole being. It was worse than depression—a black misery, when his own life was a torture to him, and when his presence was unbearable to his wife. The dread went down to the roots of her soul as these black days recurred. In a kind of panic she tried to wrap herself up still further in her husband. She forced the old spontaneous cheerfulness and joy to continue. But the effort it cost her was almost too much. She knew she could not keep it up. She felt she would scream with the strain, and would give anything, anything, to escape. She longed to possess her husband utterly; it gave her inordinate joy to have him entirely to herself. And yet, when again he was gone in a black and massive misery, she could not bear him, she could not bear herself; she wished she could be snatched away off the earth altogether, anything rather than live at this cost.

Dazed, she schemed for a way out. She invited friends, she tried

---

1. Now part of Belgium, scene of bloody fighting in World War I.

2. Buildings separate from the dwelling, such as barns, etc.

to give him some further connection with the outer world. But it was no good. After all their joy and suffering, after their dark, great year of blindness and solitude and unspeakable nearness, other people seemed to them both shallow, prattling, rather impertinent. Shallow prattle seemed presumptuous. He became impatient and irritated, she was wearied. And so they lapsed into their solitude again. For they preferred it.

But now, in a few weeks' time, her second baby would be born. The first had died, an infant, when her husband first went out to France. She looked with joy and relief to the coming of the second. It would be her salvation. But also she felt some anxiety. She was thirty years old, her husband was a year younger. They both wanted the child very much. Yet she could not help feeling afraid. She had her husband on her hands, a terrible joy to her, and a terrifying burden. The child would occupy her love and attention. And then, what of Maurice? What would he do? If only she could feel that he, too, would be at peace and happy when the child came! She did so want to luxuriate in a rich, physical satisfaction of maternity. But the man, what would he do? How could she provide for him, how avert those shattering black moods of his, which destroyed them both?

She sighed with fear. But at this time Bertie Reid wrote to Isabel. He was her old friend, a second or third cousin, a Scotsman, as she was a Scotswoman. They had been brought up near to one another, and all her life he had been her friend, like a brother, but better than her own brothers. She loved him—though not in the marrying sense. There was a sort of kinship between them, an affinity. They understood one another instinctively. But Isabel would never have thought of marrying Bertie. It would have seemed like marrying in her own family.

Bertie was a barrister and a man of letters, a Scotsman of the intellectual type, quick, ironical, sentimental, and on his knees before the women he adored but did not want to marry. Maurice Pervin was different. He came of a good old country family—the Grange was not a very great distance from Oxford. He was passionate, sensitive, perhaps over-sensitive, wincing—a big fellow with heavy limbs and a forehead that flushed painfully. For his mind was slow, as if drugged by the strong provincial blood that beat in his veins. He was very sensitive to his own mental slowness, his feelings being quick and acute. So that he was just the opposite to Bertie, whose mind was much quicker than his emotions, which were not so very fine.

From the first the two men did not like each other. Isabel felt that they *ought* to get on together. But they did not. She felt that if only each could have the clue to the other there would be such a rare understanding between them. It did not come off, however. Bertie adopted a slightly ironical attitude, very offensive to Maurice, who returned the Scotch irony with English resentment, a resentment which deepened sometimes into stupid hatred.

This was a little puzzling to Isabel. However, she accepted it in the course of things. Men were made freakish and unreasonable. Therefore, when Maurice was going out to France for the second time, she felt that, for her husband's sake, she must discontinue her friendship with Bertie. She wrote to the barrister to this effect. Bertram Reid simply replied that in this, as in all other matters, he must obey her wishes, if these were indeed her wishes.

For nearly two years nothing had passed between the two friends. Isabel rather gloried in the fact; she had no compunction. She had one great article of faith, which was, that husband and wife should be so important to one another, that the rest of the world simply did not count. She and Maurice were husband and wife. They loved one another. They would have children. Then let everybody and everything else fade into insignificance outside this connubial felicity. She professed herself quite happy and ready to receive Maurice's friends. She was happy and ready: the happy wife, the ready woman in possession. Without knowing why, the friends retired abashed, and came no more. Maurice, of course, took as much satisfaction in this connubial absorption as Isabel did.

He shared in Isabel's literary activities, she cultivated a real interest in agriculture and cattle-raising. For she, being at heart perhaps an emotional enthusiast, always cultivated the practical side of life, and prided herself on her mastery of practical affairs. Thus the husband and wife had spent the five years of their married life. The last had been one of blindness and unspeakable intimacy. And now Isabel felt a great indifference coming over her, a sort of lethargy. She wanted to be allowed to bear her child in peace, to nod by the fire and drift vaguely, physically, from day to day. Maurice was like an ominous thunder-cloud. She had to keep waking up to remember him.

When a little note came from Bertie, asking if he were to put up a tombstone to their dead friendship, and speaking of the real pain he felt on account of her husband's loss of sight, she felt a pang, a fluttering agitation of re-awakening. And she read the letter to Maurice.

"Ask him to come down," he said.

"Ask Bertie to come here!" she re-echoed.

"Yes—if he wants to."

Isabel paused for a few moments.

"I know he wants to—he'd only be too glad," she replied. "But what about you, Maurice? How would you like it?"

"I should like it."

"Well—in that case— But I thought you didn't care for him—"

"Oh, I don't know. I might think differently of him now," the blind man replied. It was rather abstruse to Isabel.

"Well, dear," she said, "if you're quite sure—"

"I'm sure enough. Let him come," said Maurice.

So Bertie was coming, coming this evening, in the November rain and darkness. Isabel was agitated, racked with her old restlessness and indecision. She had always suffered from this pain of doubt, just an agonizing sense of uncertainty. It had begun to pass off, in the lethargy of maternity. Now it returned, and she resented it. She struggled as usual to maintain her calm, composed, friendly bearing, a sort of mask she wore over all her body.

A woman had lighted a tall lamp beside the table, and spread the cloth. The long dining-room was dim, with its elegant but rather severe pieces of old furniture. Only the round table glowed softly under the light. It had a rich, beautiful effect. The white cloth glistened and dropped its heavy, pointed lace corners almost to the carpet, the china was old and handsome, creamy-yellow, with a blotched pattern of harsh red and deep blue, the cups large and bell-shaped, the teapot gallant. Isabel looked at it with superficial appreciation.

Her nerves were hurting her. She looked automatically again at the high, uncurtained windows. In the last dusk she could just perceive outside a huge fir tree swaying its boughs: it was as if she thought it rather than saw it. The rain came flying on the window panes. Ah, why had she no peace? These two men, why did they tear at her? Why did they not come—why was there this suspense?

She sat in a lassitude that was really suspense and irritation. Maurice, at least, might come in—there was nothing to keep him out. She rose to her feet. Catching sight of her reflection in a mirror, she glanced at herself with a slight smile of recognition, as if she were an old friend to herself. Her face was oval and calm, her nose a little arched. Her neck made a beautiful line down to her shoulder. With hair knotted loosely behind, she had something of a warm, maternal look. Thinking this of herself, she arched her eyebrows and her rather heavy eyelids, with a little flicker of a smile, and for a moment her gray eyes looked amused and wicked, a little sardonic, out of her transfigured Madonna face.

Then, resuming her air of womanly patience—she was really fatally self-determined—she went with a little jerk toward the door. Her eyes were slightly reddened.

She passed down the wide hall, and through a door at the end. Then she was in the farm premises. The scent of dairy, and of farm-kitchen, and of farmyard and of leather almost overcame her: but particularly the scent of dairy. They had been scalding out the pans. The flagged[3] passage in front of her was dark, puddled and wet. Light came out from the open kitchen door. She went forward and stood in the doorway. The farm-people were at tea, seated at a little distance from her, round a long, narrow table, in the center of which stood a white lamp. Ruddy faces, ruddy hands holding food, red mouths working, heads bent over the tea-cups: men, land-girls, boys: it was tea-time, feeding-time. Some faces caught sight of her. Mrs. Wernham, going round behind the chairs with a large black teapot, halting slightly in her walk, was not aware of her for a moment. Then she turned suddenly.

"Oh, is it Madam!" she exclaimed. "Come in, then, come in! We're at tea." And she dragged forward a chair.

"No, I won't come in," said Isabel. "I'm afraid I interrupt your meal."

"No—no—not likely, Madam, not likely."

"Hasn't Mr. Pervin come in, do you know?"

"I'm sure I couldn't say! Missed him, have you, Madam?"

"No, I only wanted him to come in," laughed Isabel, as if shyly.

"Wanted him, did ye? Get up, boy—get up, now—"

Mrs. Wernham knocked one of the boys on the shoulder. He began to scrape to his feet, chewing largely.

"I believe he's in top stable," said another face from the table.

"Ah! No, don't get up. I'm going myself," said Isabel.

"Don't you go out of a dirty night like this. Let the lad go. Get along wi' ye, boy," said Mrs. Wernham.

"No, no," said Isabel, with a decision that was always obeyed. "Go on with your tea, Tom. I'd like to go across to the stable, Mrs. Wernham."

"Did ever you hear tell!" exclaimed the woman.

3. Paved with flat stone.

"Isn't the trap late?" asked Isabel.

"Why, no," said Mrs. Wernham, peering into the distance at the tall, dim clock. "No, Madam—we can give it another quarter or twenty minutes yet, good—yes, every bit of a quarter."

"Ah! It seems late when darkness falls so early," said Isabel.

"It do, that it do. Bother the days, that they draw in so," answered Mrs. Wernham. "Proper[4] miserable!"

"They are," said Isabel, withdrawing.

She pulled on her overshoes, wrapped a large tartan shawl around her, put on a man's felt hat, and ventured out along the causeways of the first yard. It was very dark. The wind was roaring in the great elms behind the out-houses. When she came to the second yard the darkness seemed deeper. She was unsure of her footing. She wished she had brought a lantern. Rain blew against her. Half she liked it, half she felt unwilling to battle.

She reached at last the just visible door of the stable. There was no sign of a light anywhere. Opening the upper half, she looked in: into a simple well of darkness. The smell of horses, ammonia, and of warmth was startling to her, in that full night. She listened with all her ears, but could hear nothing save the night, and the stirring of a horse.

"Maurice!" she called, softly and musically, though she was afraid. "Maurice—are you there?"

Nothing came from the darkness. She knew the rain and wind blew in upon the horses, the hot animal life. Feeling it wrong, she entered the stable, and drew the lower half of the door shut, holding the upper part close. She did not stir, because she was aware of the presence of the dark hindquarters of the horses, though she could not see them, and she was afraid. Something wild stirred in her heart.

She listened intensely. Then she heard a small noise in the distance —far away, it seemed—the chink of a pan, and a man's voice speaking a brief word. It would be Maurice, in the other part of the stable. She stood motionless, waiting for him to come through the partition door. The horses were so terrifyingly near to her, in the invisible.

The loud jarring of the inner door-latch made her start; the door was opened. She could hear and feel her husband entering and invisibly passing among the horses near to her, in darkness as they were, actively intermingled. The rather low sound of his voice as he spoke to the horses came velvety to her nerves. How near he was, and how invisible! The darkness seemed to be in a strange swirl of violent life, just upon her. She turned giddy.

Her presence of mind made her call, quietly and musically:

"Maurice! Maurice—dea-ar!"

"Yes," he answered. "Isabel?"

She saw nothing, and the sound of his voice seemed to touch her.

"Hello!" she answered cheerfully, straining her eyes to see him. He was still busy, attending to the horses near her, but she saw only darkness. It made her almost desperate.

"Won't you come in, dear?" she said.

"Yes, I'm coming. Just half a minute. *Stand over—now!* Trap's not come, has it?"

"Not yet," said Isabel.

His voice was pleasant and ordinary, but it had a slight suggestion

4. Downright, thoroughly.

of the stable to her. She wished he would come away. While he was so utterly invisible she was afraid of him.

"How's the time?" he asked.

"Not yet six," she replied. She disliked to answer into the dark. Presently he came very near to her, and she retreated out of doors.

"The weather blows in here," he said, coming steadily forward, feeling for the doors. She shrank away. At last she could dimly see him.

"Bertie won't have much of a drive," he said, as he closed the doors.

"He won't indeed!" said Isabel calmly, watching the dark shape at the door.

"Give me your arm, dear," she said.

She pressed his arm close to her, as she went. But she longed to see him, to look at him. She was nervous. He walked erect, with face rather lifted, but with a curious tentative movement of his powerful, muscular legs. She could feel the clever, careful, strong contact of his feet with the earth, as she balanced against him. For a moment he was a tower of darkness to her, as if he rose out of the earth.

In the house-passage he wavered, and went cautiously, with a curious look of silence about him as he felt for the bench. Then he sat down heavily. He was a man with rather sloping shoulders, but with heavy limbs, powerful legs that seemed to know the earth. His head was small, usually carried high and light. As he bent down to unfasten his gaiters and boots he did not look blind. His hair was brown and crisp, his hands were large, reddish, intelligent, the veins stood out in the wrists; and his thighs and knees seemed massive. When he stood up his face and neck were surcharged with blood, the veins stood out on his temples. She did not look at his blindness.

Isabel was always glad when they had passed through the dividing door into their own regions of repose and beauty. She was a little afraid of him, out there in the animal grossness of the back. His bearing also changed, as he smelled the familiar, indefinable odor that pervaded his wife's surroundings, a delicate, refined scent, very faintly spicy. Perhaps it came from the potpourri bowls.

He stood at the foot of the stairs, arrested, listening. She watched him, and her heart sickened. He seemed to be listening to fate.

"He's not here yet," he said. "I'll go up and change."

"Maurice," she said, "you're not wishing he wouldn't come, are you?"

"I couldn't quite say," he answered. "I feel myself rather on the *qui vive*.[5]"

"I can see you are," she answered. And she reached up and kissed his cheek. She saw his mouth relax into a slow smile.

"What are you laughing at?" she said roguishly.

"You consoling me," he answered.

"Nay," she answered. "Why should I console you? You know we love each other—you know *how* married we are! What does anything else matter?"

"Nothing at all, my dear."

He felt for her face, and touched it, smiling.

"*You're* all right, aren't you?" he asked, anxiously.

"I'm wonderfully all right, love," she answered. "It's you I am a little troubled about, at times."

"Why me?" he said, touching her cheeks delicately with the tips of his fingers. The touch had an almost hyponotizing effect on her.

5. Alert.

He went away upstairs. She saw him mount into the darkness, unseeing and unchanging. He did not know that the lamps on the upper corridor were unlighted. He went on into the darkness with unchanging step. She heard him in the bathroom.

Pervin moved about almost unconsciously in his familiar surroundings, dark though everything was. He seemed to know the presence of objects before he touched them. It was a pleasure to him to rock thus through a world of things, carried on the flood in a sort of blood-prescience. He did not think much or trouble much. So long as he kept this sheer immediacy of blood-contact with the substantial world he was happy, he wanted no intervention of visual consciousness. In this state there was a certain rich positivity, bordering sometimes on rapture. Life seemed to move in him like a tide lapping, lapping, and advancing, enveloping all things darkly. It was a pleasure to stretch forth the hand and meet the unseen object, clasp it, and possess it in pure contact. He did not try to remember, to visualize. He did not want to. The new way of consciousness substituted itself in him.

The rich suffusion of this state generally kept him happy, reaching its culmination in the consuming passion for his wife. But at times the flow would seem to be checked and thrown back. Then it would beat inside him like a tangled sea, and he was tortured in the shattered chaos of his own blood. He grew to dread this arrest, this throw-back, this chaos inside himself, when he seemed merely at the mercy of his own powerful and conflicting elements. How to get some measure of control or surety, this was the question. And when the question rose maddening in him, he would clench his fists as if he would *compel* the whole universe to submit to him. But it was in vain. He could not even compel himself.

Tonight, however, he was still serene, though little tremors of unreasonable exasperation ran through him. He had to handle the razor very carefully, as he shaved, for it was not at one with him, he was afraid of it. His hearing also was too much sharpened. He heard the woman lighting the lamps on the corridor, and attending to the fire in the visitor's room. And then, as he went to his room he heard the trap arrive. Then came Isabel's voice, lifted and calling, like a bell ringing:

"Is it you, Bertie? Have you come?"

And a man's voice answered out of the wind:

"Hello, Isabel! There you are."

"Have you had a miserable drive? I'm so sorry we couldn't send a closed carriage. I can't see you at all, you know."

"I'm coming. No, I liked the drive—it was like Perthshire.[6] Well, how are you? You're looking fit as ever, as far as I can see."

"Oh, yes." said Isabel. "I'm wonderfully well. How are you? Rather thin, I think—"

"Worked to death—everybody's old cry. But I'm all right, Ciss. How's Pervin?—isn't he here?"

"Oh, yes, he's upstairs changing. Yes, he's awfully well. Take off your wet things; I'll send them to be dried."

"And how are you both, in spirits? He doesn't fret?"

"No—no, not at all. No, on the contrary, really. We've been wonderfully happy, incredibly. It's more than I can understand—so wonderful: the nearness, and the peace—"

6. County in central Scotland.

"Ah! Well, that's awfully good news—"

They moved away. Pervin heard no more. But a childish sense of desolation had come over him, as he heard their brisk voices. He seemed shut out—like a child that is left out. He was aimless and excluded, he did not know what to do with himself. The helpless desolation came over him. He fumbled nervously as he dressed himself, in a state almost of childishness. He disliked the Scotch accent in Bertie's speech, and the slight response it found on Isabel's tongue. He disliked the slight purr of complacency in the Scottish speech. He disliked intensely the glib way in which Isabel spoke of their happiness and nearness. It made him recoil. He was fretful and beside himself like a child, he had almost a childish nostalgia to be included in the life circle. And at the same time he was a man, dark and powerful and infuriated by his own weakness. By some fatal flaw, he could not be by himself, he had to depend on the support of another. And this very dependence enraged him. He hated Bertie Reid, and at the same time he knew the hatred was nonsense, he knew it was the outcome of his own weakness.

He went downstairs. Isabel was alone in the dining-room. She watched him enter, head erect, his feet tentative. He looked so strong-blooded and healthy, and, at the same time, cancelled. Cancelled—that was the word that flew across her mind. Perhaps it was his scars suggested it.

"You heard Bertie come, Maurice?" she said.

"Yes—isn't he here?"

"He's in his room. He looks very thin and worn."

"I suppose he works himself to death."

A woman came in with a tray—and after a few minutes Bertie came down. He was a little dark man, with a very big forehead, thin, wispy hair, and sad, large eyes. His expression was inordinately sad—almost funny. He had odd, short legs.

Isabel watched him hesitate under the door, and glance nervously at her husband. Pervin heard him and turned.

"Here you are, now," said Isabel. "Come, let us eat."

Bertie went across to Maurice.

"How are you, Pervin?" he said, as he advanced.

The blind man stuck his hand out into space, and Bertie took it.

"Very fit. Glad you've come," said Maurice.

Isabel glanced at them, and glanced away, as if she could not bear to see them.

"Come." she said. "Come to table. Aren't you both awfully hungry? I am, tremendously."

"I'm afraid you waited for me," said Bertie, as they sat down.

Maurice had a curious monolithic way of sitting in a chair, erect and distant. Isabel's heart always beat when she caught sight of him thus.

"No." she replied to Bertie. "We're very little later than usual. We're having a sort of high tea, not dinner. Do you mind? It gives us such a nice long evening uninterrupted."

"I like it." said Bertie.

Maurice was feeling, with curious little movements, almost like a cat kneading her bed, for his place, his knife and fork, his napkin. He was getting the whole geography of his cover[7] into his consciousness. He sat erect and inscrutable, remote-seeming. Bertie watched the static figure of the blind man, the delicate tactile discernment of the

7. Place setting.

large, ruddy hands, and the curious mindless silence of the brow, above the scar. With difficulty he looked away, and without knowing what he did, picked up a little crystal bowl of violets from the table, and held them to his nose.

"They are sweet-scented," he said. "Where do they come from?"

"From the garden—under the windows," said Isabel.

"So late in the year—and so fragrant! Do you remember the violets under Aunt Bell's south wall?"

The two friends looked at each other and exchanged a smile, Isabel's eyes lighting up.

"Don't I?" she replied. "*Wasn't* she queer!"

"A curious old girl," laughed Bertie. "There's a streak of freakishness in the family, Isabel."

"Ah—but not in you and me, Bertie," said Isabel. "Give them to Maurice, will you?" she added, as Bertie was putting down the flowers. "Have you smelled the violets, dear? Do!—they are so scented."

Maurice held out his hand, and Bertie placed the tiny bowl against his large, warm-looking fingers. Maurice's hand closed over the thin white fingers of the barrister. Bertie carefully extricated himself. Then the two watched the blind man smelling the violets. He bent his head and seemed to be thinking. Isabel waited.

"Aren't they sweet, Maurice?" she said at last, anxiously.

"Very," he said. And he held out the bowl. Bertie took it. Both he and Isabel were a little afraid, and deeply disturbed.

The meal continued. Isabel and Bertie chatted spasmodically. The blind man was silent. He touched his food repeatedly, with quick, delicate touches of his knife-point, then cut irregular bits. He could not bear to be helped. Both Isabel and Bertie suffered: Isabel wondered why. She did not suffer when she was alone with Maurice. Bertie made her conscious of a strangeness.

After the meal the three drew their chairs to the fire, and sat down to talk. The decanters were put on a table near at hand. Isabel knocked the logs on the fire, and clouds of brilliant sparks went up the chimney. Bertie noticed a slight weariness in her bearing.

"You will be glad when your child comes now, Isabel?" he said.

She looked up to him with a quick wan smile.

"Yes, I shall be glad," she answered. "It begins to seem long. Yes, I shall be very glad. So will you, Maurice, won't you?" she added.

"Yes, I shall," replied her husband.

"We are both looking forward so much to having it," she said.

"Yes, of course," said Bertie.

He was a bachelor, three or four years older than Isabel. He lived in beautiful rooms overlooking the river, guarded by a faithful Scottish manservant. And he had his friends among the fair sex—not lovers, friends. So long as he could avoid any danger of courtship or marriage, he adored a few good women with constant and unfailing homage, and he was chivalrously fond of quite a number. But if they seemed to encroach on him, he withdrew and detested them.

Isabel knew him very well, knew his beautiful constancy, and kindness, also his incurable weakness, which made him unable ever to enter into close contact of any sort. He was ashamed of himself, because he could not marry, could not approach women physically. He wanted to do so. But he could not. At the center of him he was afraid, helplessly and even brutally afraid. He had given up hope, had ceased to expect

any more that he could escape his own weakness. Hence he was a brilliant and successful barrister, also *littérateur* of high repute, a rich man, and a great social success. At the center he felt himself neuter, nothing.

Isabel knew him well. She despised him even while she admired him. She looked at his sad face, his little short legs, and felt contempt of him. She looked at his dark gray eyes, with their uncanny, almost child-like intuition, and she loved him. He understood amazingly—but she had no fear of his understanding. As a man she patronized him.

And she turned to the impassive, silent figure of her husband. He sat leaning back, with folded arms, and face a little uptilted. His knees were straight and massive. She sighed, picked up the poker, and again began to prod the fire, to rouse the clouds of soft, brilliant sparks.

"Isabel tells me," Bertie began suddenly, "that you have not suffered unbearably from the loss of sight."

Maurice straightened himself to attend, but kept his arms folded.

"No," he said, "not unbearably. Now and again one struggles against it, you know. But there are compensations."

"They say it is much worse to be stone deaf," said Isabel.

"I believe it is," said Bertie. "Are there compensations?" he added, to Maurice.

"Yes. You cease to bother about a great many things." Again Maurice stretched his figure, stretched the strong muscles of his back, and leaned backwards, with uplifted face.

"And that is a relief," said Bertie. "But what is there in place of the bothering? What replaces the activity?"

There was a pause. At length the blind man replied, as out of a negligent, unattentive thinking:

"Oh, I don't know. There's a good deal when you're not active."

"Is there?" said Bertie. "What, exactly? It always seems to me that when there is no thought and no action, there is nothing."

Again Maurice was slow in replying.

"There is something," he replied. "I couldn't tell you what it is."

And the talk lapsed once more, Isabel and Bertie chatting gossip and reminiscence, the blind man silent.

At length Maurice rose restlessly, a big, obtrusive figure. He felt tight and hampered. He wanted to go away.

"Do you mind," he said, "if I go and speak to Wernham?"

"No—go along, dear," said Isabel.

And he went out. A silence came over the two friends. At length Bertie said:

"Nevertheless, it is a great deprivation, Cissie."

"It is, Bertie. I know it is."

"Something lacking all the time," said Bertie.

"Yes, I know. And yet—and yet—Maurice is right. There is something else, something *there*, which you never knew was there, and which you can't express."

"What is there?" asked Bertie.

"I don't know—it's awfully hard to define it—but something strong and immediate. There's something strange in Maurice's presence—indefinable—but I couldn't do without it. I agree that it seems to put one's mind to sleep. But when we're alone I miss nothing; it seems awfully rich, almost splendid, you know."

"I'm afraid I don't follow," said Bertie.

They talked desultorily. The wind blew loudly outside, rain chattered on the window-panes, making a sharp drum-sound, because of the closed, mellow-golden shutters inside. The logs burned slowly, with hot, almost invisible small flames. Bertie seemed uneasy, there were dark circles round his eyes. Isabel, rich with her approaching maternity, leaned looking into the fire. Her hair curled in odd, loose strands, very pleasing to the man. But she had a curious feeling of old woe in her heart, old, timeless night-woe.

"I suppose we're all deficient somewhere," said Bertie.

"I suppose so," said Isabel wearily.

"Damned, sooner or later."

"I don't know," she said, rousing herself. "I feel quite all right, you know. The child coming seems to make me indifferent to everything, just placid. I can't feel that there's anything to trouble about, you know."

"A good thing, I should say," he replied slowly.

"Well, there it is. I suppose it's just Nature. If only I felt I needn't trouble about Maurice, I should be perfectly content—"

"But you feel you must trouble about him?"

"Well—I don't know—" She even resented this much effort.

The evening passed slowly. Isabel looked at the clock. "I say," she said. "It's nearly ten o'clock. Where can Maurice be? I'm sure they're all in bed at the back. Excuse me a moment."

She went out, returning almost immediately.

"It's all shut up and in darkness," she said. "I wonder where he is. He must have gone out to the farm—"

Bertie looked at her.

"I suppose he'll come in," he said.

"I suppose so," she said. "But it's unusual for him to be out now."

"Would you like me to go out and see?"

"Well—if you wouldn't mind. I'd go, but—" She did not want to make the physical effort.

Bertie put on an old overcoat and took a lantern. He went out from the side door. He shrank from the wet and roaring night. Such weather had a nervous effect on him: too much moisture everywhere made him feel almost imbecile. Unwilling, he went through it all. A dog barked violently at him. He peered in all the buildings. At last, as he opened the upper door of a sort of intermediate barn, he heard a grinding noise, and looking in, holding up his lantern, saw Maurice, in his shirt-sleeves, standing listening, holding the handle of a turnip-pulper. He had been pulping sweet roots, a pile of which lay dimly heaped in a corner behind him.

"That you, Wernham?" said Maurice, listening.

"No, it's me," said Bertie.

A large, half-wild gray cat was rubbing at Maurice's leg. The blind man stooped to rub its sides. Bertie watched the scene, then unconsciously entered and shut the door behind him. He was in a high sort of barn-place, from which, right and left, ran off the corridors in front of the stalled cattle. He watched the slow, stooping motion of the other man, as he caressed the great cat.

Maurice straightened himself.

"You came to look for me?" he said.

"Isabel was a little uneasy," said Bertie.

"I'll come in. I like messing about doing these jobs."

The cat had reared her sinister, feline length against his leg, clawing at his thigh affectionately. He lifted her claws out of his flesh.

"I hope I'm not in your way at all at the Grange here," said Bertie, rather shy and stiff.

"My way? No, not a bit. I'm glad Isabel has somebody to talk to. I'm afraid it's I who am in the way. I know I'm not very lively company. Isabel's all right, don't you think? She's not unhappy, is she?"

"I don't think so."

"What does she say?"

"She says she's very content—only a little troubled about you."

"Why me?"

"Perhaps afraid that you might brood," said Bertie cautiously.

"She needn't be afraid of that." He continued to caress the flattened gray head of the cat with his fingers. "What I am a bit afraid of," he resumed, "is that she'll find me a dead weight, always alone with me down here."

"I don't think you need think that," said Bertie, though this was what he feared himself.

"I don't know," said Maurice. "Sometimes I feel it isn't fair that she's saddled with me." Then he dropped his voice curiously. "I say," he asked, secretly struggling, "is my face much disfigured? Do you mind telling me?"

"There is the scar," said Bertie, wondering. "Yes, it is a disfigurement. But more pitiable than shocking."

"A pretty bad scar, though," said Maurice.

"Oh, yes."

There was a pause.

"Sometimes I feel I am horrible," said Maurice, in a low voice, talking as if to himself. And Bertie actually felt a quiver of horror.

"That's nonsense," he said.

Maurice again straightened himself, leaving the cat.

"There's no telling," he said. Then again, in an odd tone, he added: "I don't really know you, do I?"

"Probably not," said Bertie.

"Do you mind if I touch you?"

The lawyer shrank away instinctively. And yet, out of very philanthropy, he said, in a small voice: "Not at all."

But he suffered as the blind man stretched out a strong, naked hand to him. Maurice accidentally knocked off Bertie's hat.

"I thought you were taller," he said, starting. Then he laid his hand on Bertie Reid's head, closing the dome of the skull in a soft, firm grasp, gathering it, as it were; then, shifting his grasp and softly closing again, with a fine, close pressure, till he had covered the skull and the face of the smaller man, tracing the brows, and touching the full, closed eyes, touching the small nose and the nostrils, the rough, short moustache, the mouth, the rather strong chin. The hand of the blind man grasped the shoulder, the arm, the hand of the other man. He seemed to take him, in the soft, traveling grasp.

"You seem young," he said quietly, at last.

The lawyer stood almost annihilated, unable to answer.

"Your head seems tender, as if you were young," Maurice repeated. "So do your hands. Touch my eyes, will you?—touch my scar."

Now Bertie quivered with revulsion. Yet he was under the power of the blind man, as if hypnotized. He lifted his hand, and laid the

fingers on the scar, on the scarred eyes. Maurice suddenly covered them with his own hand, pressed the fingers of the other man upon his disfigured eye-sockets, trembling in every fiber, and rocking slightly, slowly, from side to side. He remained thus for a minute or more, whilst Bertie stood as if in a swoon, unconscious, imprisoned.

Then suddenly Maurice removed the hand of the other man from his brow, and stood holding it in his own.

"Oh, my God," he said, "we shall know each other now, shan't we? We shall know each other now."

Bertie could not answer. He gazed mute and terror-struck, overcome by his own weakness. He knew he could not answer. He had an unreasonable fear, lest the other man should suddenly destroy him. Whereas Maurice was actually filled with hot, poignant love, the passion of friendship. Perhaps it was this very passion of friendship which Bertie shrank from most.

"We're all right together now, aren't we?" said Maurice. "It's all right now, as long as we live, so far as we're concerned."

"Yes," said Bertie, trying by any means to escape.

Maurice stood with head lifted, as if listening. The new delicate fulfillment of mortal friendship had come as a revelation and surprise to him, something exquisite and unhoped-for. He seemed to be listening to hear if it were real.

Then he turned for his coat.

"Come," he said, "we'll go to Isabel."

Bertie took the lantern and opened the door. The cat disappeared. The two men went in silence along the causeways. Isabel, as they came, thought their footsteps sounded strange. She looked up pathetically and anxiously for their entrance. There seemed a curious elation about Maurice. Bertie was haggard, with sunken eyes.

"What is it?" she asked.

"We've become friends," said Maurice, standing with his feet apart, like a strange colossus.

"Friends!" re-echoed Isabel. And she looked again at Bertie. He met her eyes with a furtive, haggard look; his eyes were as if glazed with misery.

"I'm so glad," she said, in sheer perplexity.

"Yes," said Maurice.

He was indeed so glad. Isabel took his hand with both hers, and held it fast.

"You'll be happier now, dear," she said.

But she was watching Bertie. She knew that he had one desire—to escape from this intimacy, this friendship, which had been thrust upon him. He could not bear it that he had been touched by the blind man, his insane reserve broken in. He was like a mollusc whose shell is broken.

1922

D. H. LAWRENCE

The Rocking-Horse Winner

There was a woman who was beautiful, who started with all the advantages, yet she had no luck. She married for love, and the love

turned to dust. She had bonny children, yet she felt they had been thrust upon her, and she could not love them. They looked at her coldly, as if they were finding fault with her. And hurriedly she felt she must cover up some fault in herself. Yet what it was that she must cover up she never knew. Nevertheless, when her children were present, she always felt the center of her heart go hard. This troubled her, and in her manner she was all the more gentle and anxious for her children, as if she loved them very much. Only she herself knew that at the center of her heart was a hard little place that could not feel love, no, not for anybody. Everybody else said of her: "She is such a good mother. She adores her children." Only she herself, and her children themselves, knew it was not so. They read it in each other's eyes.

There were a boy and two little girls. They lived in a pleasant house, with a garden, and they had discreet servants, and felt themselves superior to anyone in the neighborhood.

Although they lived in style, they felt always an anxiety in the house. There was never enough money. The mother had a small income, and the father had a small income, but not nearly enough for the social position which they had to keep up. The father went into town to some office. But though he had good prospects, these prospects never materialized. There was always the grinding sense of the shortage of money, though the style was always kept up.

At last the mother said: "I will see if *I* can't make something." But she did not know where to begin. She racked her brains, and tried this thing and the other, but could not find anything successful. The failure made deep lines come into her face. Her children were growing up, they would have to go to school. There must be more money, there must be more money. The father, who was always very handsome and expensive in his tastes, seemed as if he never *would* be able to do anything worth doing. And the mother, who had a great belief in herself, did not succeed any better, and her tastes were just as expensive.

And so the house came to be haunted by the unspoken phrase: *There must be more money! There must be more money!* The children could hear it all the time, though nobody said it aloud. They heard it at Christmas, when the expensive and splendid toys filled the nursery. Behind the shining modern rocking-horse, behind the smart doll's house, a voice would start whispering: "There *must* be more money! There *must* be more money!" And the children would stop playing, to listen for a moment. They would look into each other's eyes, to see if they had all heard. And each one saw in the eyes of the other two that they too had heard. "There *must* be more money! There *must* be more money!"

It came whispering from the springs of the still-swaying rocking-horse, and even the horse, bending his wooden, champing head, heard it. The big doll, sitting so pink and smirking in her new pram,[1] could hear it quite plainly, and seemed to be smirking all the more self-consciously because of it. The foolish puppy, too, that took the place of the teddy bear, he was looking so extraordinarily foolish for no other reason but that he heard the secret whisper all over the house: "There *must* be more money!"

Yet nobody ever said it aloud. The whisper was everywhere, and therefore no one spoke it. Just as no one ever says: "We are breathing!" in spite of the fact that breath is coming and going all the time.

1. Baby carriage.

"Mother," said the boy Paul one day, "why don't we keep a car of our own? Why do we always use uncle's, or else a taxi?"

"Because we're the poor members of the family," said the mother.

"But why *are* we, mother?"

"Well—I suppose," she said slowly and bitterly, "it's because your father has no luck."

The boy was silent for some time.

"Is luck money, mother?" he asked, rather timidly.

"No, Paul. Not quite. It's what causes you to have money."

"Oh!" said Paul vaguely. "I thought when Uncle Oscar said *filthy lucker,* it meant money."

"*Filthy lucre* does mean money," said the mother. "But it's lucre, not luck."

"Oh!" said the boy. "Then what *is* luck, mother?"

"It's what causes you to have money. If you're lucky you have money. That's why it's better to be born lucky than rich. If you're rich, you may lose your money. But if you're lucky, you will always get more money."

"Oh! Will you? And is father not lucky?"

"Very unlucky, I should say," she said bitterly.

The boy watched her with unsure eyes.

"Why?" he asked.

"I don't know. Nobody ever knows why one person is lucky and another unlucky."

"Don't they? Nobody at all? Does *nobody* know?"

"Perhaps God. But He never tells."

"He ought to, then. And aren't you lucky either, mother?"

"I can't be, if I married an unlucky husband."

"But by yourself, aren't you?"

"I used to think I was, before I married. Now I think I am very unlucky indeed."

"Why?"

"Well—never mind! Perhaps I'm not really," she said.

The child looked at her to see if she meant it. But he saw, by the lines of her mouth, that she was only trying to hide something from him.

"Well, anyhow," he said stoutly, "I'm a lucky person."

"Why?" said his mother, with a sudden laugh.

He stared at her. He didn't even know why he had said it.

"God told me," he asserted, brazening it out.

"I hope He did, dear!" she said, again with a laugh, but rather bitter.

"He did, mother!"

"Excellent!" said the mother, using one of her husband's exclamations.

The boy saw she did not believe him; or rather, that she paid no attention to his assertion. This angered him somewhat, and made him want to compel her attention.

He went off by himself, vaguely, in a childish way, seeking for the clue to "luck." Absorbed, taking no heed of other people, he went about with a sort of stealth, seeking inwardly for luck. He wanted luck, he wanted it, he wanted it. When the two girls were playing dolls in the nursery, he would sit on his big rocking-horse, charging madly into space, with a frenzy that made the little girls peer at him uneasily.

Wildly the horse careered, the waving dark hair of the boy tossed, his eyes had a strange glare in them. The little girls dared not speak to him.

When he had ridden to the end of his mad little journey, he climbed down and stood in front of his rocking-horse, staring fixedly into its lowered face. Its red mouth was slightly open, its big eye was wide and glassy-bright.

"Now!" he would silently command the snorting steed. "Now, take me to where there is luck! Now take me!"

And he would slash the horse on the neck with the little whip he had asked Uncle Oscar for. He *knew* the horse could take him to where there was luck, if only he forced it. So he would mount again and start on his furious ride, hoping at last to get there. He knew he could get there.

"You'll break your horse, Paul!" said the nurse.

"He's always riding like that! I wish he'd leave off!" said his elder sister Joan.

But he only glared down on them in silence. Nurse gave him up. She could make nothing of him. Anyhow, he was growing beyond her.

One day his mother and his Uncle Oscar came in when he was on one of his furious rides. He did not speak to them.

"Hallo, you young jockey! Riding a winner?" said his uncle.

"Aren't you growing too big for a rocking-horse? You're not a very little boy any longer, you know," said his mother.

But Paul only gave a blue glare from his big, rather close-set eyes. He would speak to nobody when he was in full tilt. His mother watched him with an anxious expression on her face.

At last he suddenly stopped forcing his horse into the mechanical gallop and slid down.

"Well, I got there!" he announced fiercely, his blue eyes still flaring, and his sturdy long legs straddling apart.

"Where did you get to?" asked his mother.

"Where I wanted to go," he flared back at her.

"That's right, son!" said Uncle Oscar. "Don't you stop till you get there. What's the horse's name?"

"He doesn't have a name," said the boy.

"Gets on without all right?" asked the uncle.

"Well, he has different names. He was called Sansovino last week."

"Sansovino, eh? Won the Ascot. How did you know this name?"

"He always talks about horse-races with Bassett," said Joan.

The uncle was delighted to find that his small nephew was posted with all the racing news. Bassett, the young gardener, who had been wounded in the left foot in the war[2] and had got his present job through Oscar Cresswell, whose batman he had been, was a perfect blade[3] of the "turf." He lived in the racing events, and the small boy lived with him.

Oscar Cresswell got it all from Bassett.

"Master Paul comes and asks me, so I can't do more than tell him, sir," said Bassett, his face terribly serious, as if he were speaking of religious matters.

"And does he ever put anything on a horse he fancies?"

"Well—I don't want to give him away—he's a young sport, a fine

2. World War I, 1914–1918.   3. Dashing young man.

sport, sir. Would you mind asking him himself? He sort of takes a pleasure in it, and perhaps he'd feel I was giving him away, sir, if you don't mind."

Bassett was serious as a church.

The uncle went back to his nephew and took him off for a ride in the car.

"Say, Paul, old man, do you ever put anything on a horse?" the uncle asked.

The boy watched the handsome man closely.

"Why, do you think I ougntn't to?" he parried.

"Not a bit of it! I thought perhaps you might give me a tip for the Lincoln."[4]

The car sped on into the country, going down to Uncle Oscar's place in Hampshire.

"Honor bright?" said the nephew.

"Honor bright, son!" said the uncle.

"Well, then, Daffodil."

"Daffodil! I doubt it, sonny. What about Mirza?"

"I only know the winner," said the boy. "That's Daffodil."

"Daffodil, eh?"

There was a pause. Daffodil was an obscure horse comparatively.

"Uncle!"

"Yes, son?"

"You won't let it go any further, will you? I promised Bassett."

"Bassett be damned, old man! What's he got to do with it?"

"We're partners. We've been partners from the first. Uncle, he lent me my first five shillings,[5] which I lost. I promised him, honor bright, it was only between me and him; only you gave me that ten-shilling note I started winning with, so I thought you were lucky. You won't let it go any further, will you?"

The boy gazed at his uncle from those big, hot, blue eyes, set rather close together. The uncle stirred and laughed uneasily.

"Right you are, son! I'll keep your tip private. Daffodil, eh? How much are you putting on him?"

"All except twenty pounds," said the boy. "I keep that in reserve."

The uncle thought it a good joke.

"You keep twenty pounds in reserve, do you, you young romancer? What are you betting, then?"

"I'm betting three hundred," said the boy gravely. "But it's between you and me, Uncle Oscar! Honor bright?"

The uncle burst into a roar of laughter.

"It's between you and me all right, you young Nat Gould,"[6] he said, laughing. "But where's your three hundred?"

"Bassett keeps it for me. We're partners."

"You are, are you! And what is Bassett putting on Daffodil?"

"He won't go quite as high as I do, I expect. Perhaps he'll go a hundred and fifty."

4. Lincolnshire Handicap race then run at Lincoln Downs. Other races mentioned in the story include the St. Leger Stakes (the Leger) run at Doncaster; the Grand National Steeplechase run at Aintree, the most famous steeplechase in the world; the famous Derby, a mile-and-a-half race for three-year-olds run at Epsom Downs, and the Ascot (above) run at the course of that name in Berkshire.
5. Then just over a dollar. The English pound after World War I fluctuated considerably but was generally less than the $4.86 of the pre-War period and more than $4. There are 20 shillings to the pound.
6. Nathaniel Gould (1857–1919) novelist and journalist whose writings in both genres concerned horse-racing.

"What, pennies?" laughed the uncle.

"Pounds," said the child, with a surprised look at his uncle. "Bassett keeps a bigger reserve than I do."

Between wonder and amusement Uncle Oscar was silent. He pursued the matter no further, but he determined to take his nephew with him to the Lincoln races.

"Now, son," he said, "I'm putting twenty on Mirza, and I'll put five on for you on any horse you fancy. What's your pick?"

"Daffodil, uncle."

"No, not the fiver on Daffodil!"

"I should if it was my own fiver," said the child.

"Good! Good! Right you are! A fiver for me and a fiver for you on Daffodil."

The child had never been to a race-meeting before, and his eyes were blue fire. He pursed his mouth tight and watched. A Frenchman just in front had put his money on Lancelot. Wild with excitement, he flayed his arms up and down, yelling *"Lancelot! Lancelot!"* in his French accent.

Daffodil came in first, Lancelot second, Mirza third. The child, flushed and with eyes blazing, was curiously serene. His uncle brought him four five-pound notes, four to one.

"What am I to do with these?" he cried, waving them before the boy's eyes.

"I suppose we'll talk to Bassett," said the boy. "I expect I have fifteen hundred now; and twenty in reserve; and this twenty."

His uncle studied him for some moments.

"Look here, son!" he said. "You're not serious about Bassett and that fifteen hundred, are you?"

"Yes, I am. But it's between you and me, uncle. Honor bright?"

"Honor bright all right, son! But I must talk to Bassett."

"If you'd like to be a partner, uncle, with Bassett and me, we could all be partners. Only, you'd have to promise, honor bright, uncle, not to let it go beyond us three. Bassett and I are lucky, and you must be lucky, because it was your ten shillings I started winning with. . . ."

Uncle Oscar took both Bassett and Paul into Richmond Park for an afternoon, and there they talked.

"It's like this, you see, sir," Bassett said. "Master Paul would get me talking about racing events, spinning yarns, you know, sir. And he was always keen on knowing if I'd made or if I'd lost. It's about a year since, now, that I put five shillings on Blush of Dawn for him: and we lost. Then the luck turned, with that ten shillings he had from you: that we put on Singhalese. And since that time, it's been pretty steady, all things considering. What do you say, Master Paul?"

"We're all right when we're sure," said Paul. "It's when we're not quite sure that we go down."

"Oh, but we're careful then," said Bassett.

"But when are you *sure*?" smiled Uncle Oscar.

"It's Master Paul, sir," said Bassett in a secret, religious voice. "It's as if he had it from heaven. Like Daffodil, now, for the Lincoln. That was as sure as eggs."

"Did you put anything on Daffodil?" asked Oscar Cresswell.

"Yes, sir. I made my bit."

"And my nephew?"

Bassett was obstinately silent, looking at Paul.

"I made twelve hundred, didn't I, Bassett? I told uncle I was putting three hundred on Daffodil."

"That's right," said Bassett, nodding.

"But where's the money?" asked the uncle.

"I keep it safe locked up, sir. Master Paul he can have it any minute he likes to ask for it."

"What, fifteen hundred pounds?"

"And twenty! And *forty*, that is, with the twenty he made on the course."

"It's amazing!" said the uncle.

"If Master Paul offers you to be partners, sir, I would, if I were you: if you'll excuse me," said Bassett.

Oscar Cresswell thought about it.

"I'll see the money," he said.

They drove home again, and, sure enough, Bassett came round to the garden-house with fifteen hundred pounds in notes. The twenty pounds reserve was left with Joe Glee, in the Turf Commission deposit.

"You see, it's all right, uncle, when I'm *sure*! Then we go strong, for all we're worth. Don't we, Bassett?"

"We do that, Master Paul."

"And when are you sure?" said the uncle, laughing.

"Oh, well, sometimes I'm *absolutely* sure, like about Daffodil," said the boy; "and sometimes I have an idea; and sometimes I haven't even an idea, have I, Bassett? Then we're careful, because we mostly go down."

"You do, do you! And when you're sure, like about Daffodil, what makes you sure, sonny?"

"Oh, well, I don't know," said the boy uneasily. "I'm sure, you know, uncle; that's all."

"It's as if he had it from heaven, sir," Bassett reiterated.

"I should say so!" said the uncle.

But he became a partner. And when the Leger was coming on, Paul was "sure" about Lively Spark, which was a quite inconsiderable horse. The boy insisted on putting a thousand on the horse, Bassett went for five hundred, and Oscar Cresswell two hundred. Lively Spark came in first, and the betting had been ten to one against him. Paul had made ten thousand.

"You see," he said, "I was absolutely sure of him."

Even Oscar Cresswell had cleared two thousand.

"Look here, son," he said, "this sort of thing makes me nervous."

"It needn't, uncle! Perhaps I shan't be sure again for a long time."

"But what are you going to do with your money?" asked the uncle.

"Of course," said the boy, "I started it for mother. She said she had no luck, because father is unlucky, so I thought if *I* was lucky, it might stop whispering."

"What might stop whispering?"

"Our house. I *hate* our house for whispering."

"What does it whisper?"

"Why—why"—the boy fidgeted—"why, I don't know. But it's always short of money, you know, uncle."

"I know it, son, I know it."

"You know people send mother writs, don't you, uncle?"

"I'm afraid I do," said the uncle.

"And then the house whispers, like people laughing at you behind your back. It's awful, that is! I thought if I was lucky——"

"You might stop it," added the uncle.

The boy watched him with big blue eyes, that had an uncanny cold fire in them, and he said never a word.

"Well, then!" said the uncle. "What are we doing?"

"I shouldn't like mother to know I was lucky," said the boy.

"Why not, son?"

"She'd stop me."

"I don't think she would."

"Oh!"—and the boy writhed in an odd way—"I *don't* want her to know, uncle."

"All right, son! We'll manage it without her knowing."

They managed it very easily. Paul, at the other's suggestion, handed over five thousand pounds to his uncle, who deposited it with the family lawyer, who was then to inform Paul's mother that a relative had put five thousand pounds into his hands, which sum was to be paid out a thousand pounds at a time, on the mother's birthday, for the next five years.

"So she'll have a birthday present of a thousand pounds for five successive years," said Uncle Oscar. "I hope it won't make it all the harder for her later."

Paul's mother had her birthday in November. The house had been "whispering" worse than ever lately, and, even in spite of his luck, Paul could not bear up against it. He was very anxious to see the effect of the birthday letter, telling his mother about the thousand pounds.

When there were no visitors, Paul now took his meals with his parents, as he was beyond the nursery control. His mother went into town nearly every day. She had discovered that she had an odd knack of sketching furs and dress materials, so she worked secretly in the studio of a friend who was the chief "artist" for the leading drapers. She drew the figures of ladies in furs and ladies in silk and sequins for the newspaper advertisements. This young woman artist earned several thousand pounds a year, but Paul's mother only made several hundreds, and she was again dissatisfied. She so wanted to be first in something, and she did not succeed, even in making sketches for drapery advertisements.

She was down to breakfast on the morning of her birthday. Paul watched her face as she read her letters. He knew the lawyer's letter. As his mother read it, her face hardened and became more expressionless. Then a cold, determined look came on her mouth. She hid the letter under the pile of others, and said not a word about it.

"Didn't you have anything nice in the post for your birthday, mother?" said Paul.

"Quite moderately nice," she said, her voice cold and absent.

She went away to town without saying more.

But in the afternoon Uncle Oscar appeared. He said Paul's mother had had a long interview with the lawyer, asking if the whole five thousand could not be advanced at once, as she was in debt.

"What do you think, uncle?" said the boy.

"I leave it to you, son."

"Oh, let her have it, then! We can get some more with the other," said the boy.

"A bird in the hand is worth two in the bush, laddie!" said Uncle Oscar.

"But I'm sure to *know* for the Grand National; or the Lincolnshire; or else the Derby. I'm sure to know for one of them," said Paul.

So Uncle Oscar signed the agreement, and Paul's mother touched the whole five thousand. Then something very curious happened. The voices in the house suddenly went mad, like a chorus of frogs on a spring evening. There were certain new furnishings, and Paul had a tutor. He was *really* going to Eton, his father's school, in the following autumn. There were flowers in the winter, and a blossoming of the luxury Paul's mother had been used to. And yet the voices in the house, behind the sprays of mimosa and almond-blossom, and from under the piles of iridescent cushions, simply trilled and screamed in a sort of ecstasy: "There *must* be more money! Oh-h-h; there *must* be more money. Oh, now, now-w! Now-w-w—there *must* be more money! —more than ever! More than ever!"

It frightened Paul terribly. He studied away at his Latin and Greek with his tutor. But his intense hours were spent with Bassett. The Grand National had gone by: he had not "known," and had lost a hundred pounds. Summer was at hand. He was in agony for the Lincoln. But even for the Lincoln he didn't "know," and he lost fifty pounds. He became wild-eyed and strange, as if something were going to explode in him.

"Let it alone, son! Don't you bother about it!" urged Uncle Oscar. But it was as if the boy couldn't really hear what his uncle was saying.

"I've got to know for the Derby! I've got to know for the Derby!" the child reiterated, his big blue eyes blazing with a sort of madness.

His mother noticed how overwrought he was.

"You'd better go to the seaside. Wouldn't you like to go now to the seaside, instead of waiting? I think you'd better," she said, looking down at him anxiously, her heart curiously heavy because of him.

But the child lifted his uncanny blue eyes.

"I couldn't possibly go before the Derby, mother!" he said. "I couldn't possibly!"

"Why not?" she said, her voice becoming heavy when she was opposed. "Why not? You can still go from the seaside to see the Derby with your Uncle Oscar, if that's what you wish. No need for you to wait here. Besides, I think you care too much about these races. It's a bad sign. My family has been a gambling family, and you won't know till you grow up how much damage it has done. But it has done damage. I shall have to send Bassett away, and ask Uncle Oscar not to talk racing to you, unless you promise to be reasonable about it: go away to the seaside and forget it. You're all nerves!"

"I'll do what you like, mother, so long as you don't send me away till after the Derby," the boy said.

"Send you away from where? Just from this house?"

"Yes," he said, gazing at her.

"Why, you curious child, what makes you care about this house so much, suddenly? I never knew you loved it."

He gazed at her without speaking. He had a secret within a secret, something he had not divulged, even to Bassett or to his Uncle Oscar.

But his mother, after standing undecided and a little bit sullen for some moments, said:

"Very well, then! Don't go to the seaside till after the Derby, if you don't wish it. But promise me you won't let your nerves go to pieces. Promise you won't think so much about horse-racing and *events,* as you call them!"

"Oh, no," said the boy casually. "I won't think much about them, mother. You needn't worry. I wouldn't worry, mother, if I were you."

"If you were me and I were you," said his mother, "I wonder what we *should* do!"

"But you know you needn't worry, mother, don't you?" the boy repeated.

"I should be awfully glad to know it," she said wearily.

"Oh, well, you *can,* you know. I mean, you *ought* to know you needn't worry," he insisted.

"Ought I? Then I'll see about it," she said.

Paul's secret of secrets was his wooden horse, that which had no name. Since he was emancipated from a nurse and a nursery-governess, he had had his rocking-horse removed to his own bedroom at the top of the house.

"Surely you're too big for a rocking-horse!" his mother had remonstrated.

"Well, you see, mother, till I can have a *real* horse, I like to have *some* sort of animal about," had been his quaint answer.

"Do you feel he keeps you company?" she laughed.

"Oh, yes! He's very good, he always keeps me company, when I'm there," said Paul.

So the horse, rather shabby, stood in an arrested prance in the boy's bedroom.

The Derby was drawing near, and the boy grew more and more tense. He hardly heard what was spoken to him, he was very frail, and his eyes were really uncanny. His mother had sudden strange seizures of uneasiness about him. Sometimes, for half an hour, she would feel a sudden anxiety about him that was almost anguish. She wanted to rush to him at once, and know he was safe.

Two nights before the Derby, she was at a big party in town, when one of her rushes of anxiety about her boy, her first-born, gripped her heart till she could hardly speak. She fought with the feeling, might and main, for she believed in common sense. But it was too strong. She had to leave the dance and go downstairs to telephone to the country. The children's nursery-governess was terribly surprised and startled at being rung up in the night.

"Are the children all right, Miss Wilmot?"

"Oh, yes, they are quite all right."

"Master Paul? Is he all right?"

"He went to bed as right as a trivet. Shall I run up and look at him?"

"No," said Paul's mother reluctantly. "No! Don't trouble. It's all right. Don't sit up. We shall be home fairly soon." She did not want her son's privacy intruded upon.

"Very good," said the governess.

It was about one o'clock when Paul's mother and father drove up to their house. All was still. Paul's mother went to her room and slipped off her white fur cloak. She had told her maid not to wait up for her. She heard her husband downstairs, mixing a whisky and soda.

And then, because of the strange anxiety at her heart, she stole up-

stairs to her son's room. Noiselessly she went along the upper corridor. Was there a faint noise? What was it?

She stood, with arrested muscles, outside his door, listening. There was a strange, heavy, and yet not loud noise. Her heart stood still. It was a soundless noise, yet rushing and powerful. Something huge, in violent, hushed motion. What was it? What in God's name was it? She ought to know. She felt that she knew the noise. She knew what it was.

Yet she could not place it. She couldn't say what it was. And on and on it went, like a madness.

Softly, frozen with anxiety and fear, she turned the door-handle.

The room was dark. Yet in the space near the window, she heard and saw something plunging to and fro. She gazed in fear and amazement.

Then suddenly she switched on the light, and saw her son, in his green pajamas, madly surging on the rocking-horse. The blaze of light suddenly lit him up, as he urged the wooden horse, and lit her up, as she stood, blonde, in her dress of pale green and crystal, in the doorway.

"Paul!" she cried. "Whatever are you doing?"

"It's Malabar!" he screamed, in a powerful, strange voice. "It's Malabar!"

His eyes blazed at her for one strange and senseless second, as he ceased urging his wooden horse. Then he fell with a crash to the ground, and she, all her tormented motherhood flooding upon her, rushed to gather him up.

But he was unconscious, and unconscious he remained, with some brain-fever. He talked and tossed, and his mother sat stonily by his side.

"Malabar! It's Malabar! Bassett, Bassett, I *know*! It's Malabar!"

So the child cried, trying to get up and urge the rocking-horse that gave him his inspiration.

"What does he mean by Malabar?" asked the heart-frozen mother.

"I don't know," said the father stonily.

"What does he mean by Malabar?" she asked her brother Oscar.

"It's one of the horses running for the Derby," was the answer.

And, in spite of himself, Oscar Cresswell spoke to Bassett, and himself put a thousand on Malabar: at fourteen to one.

The third day of the illness was critical: they were waiting for a change. The boy, with his rather long, curly hair, was tossing ceaselessly on the pillow. He neither slept nor regained consciousness, and his eyes were like blue stones. His mother sat, feeling her heart had gone, turned actually into a stone.

In the evening, Oscar Cresswell did not come, but Bassett sent a message, saying could he come up for one moment, just one moment? Paul's mother was very angry at the intrusion, but on second thought she agreed. The boy was the same. Perhaps Bassett might bring him to consciousness.

The gardener, a shortish fellow with a little brown moustache and sharp little brown eyes, tiptoed into the room, touched his imaginary cap to Paul's mother, and stole to the bedside, staring with glittering, smallish eyes, at the tossing, dying child.

"Master Paul!" he whispered. "Master Paul! Malabar came in first all right, a clean win. I did as you told me. You've made over seventy

thousand pounds, you have; you've got over eighty thousand. Malabar came in all right, Master Paul."

"Malabar! Malabar! Did I say Malabar, mother? Did I say Malabar? Do you think I'm lucky, mother? I knew Malabar, didn't I? Over eighty thousand pounds! I call that lucky, don't you, mother? Over eighty thousand pounds! I knew, didn't I know I knew? Malabar came in all right. If I ride my horse till I'm sure, then I tell you, Bassett, you can go as high as you like. Did you go for all you were worth, Bassett?"

"I went a thousand on it, Master Paul."

"I never told you, mother, that if I can ride my horse, and *get there*, then I'm absolutely sure—oh, absolutely! Mother,, did I ever tell you? I *am* lucky!"

"No, you never did," said the mother.

But the boy died in the night.

And even as he lay dead, his mother heard her brother's voice saying to her: "My God, Hester, you're eighty-odd thousand to the good, and a poor devil of a son to the bad. But, poor devil, poor devil, he's best gone out of a life where he rides his rocking-horse to find a winner."

1932

NICOLAI GOGOL

The Nose*

1

A most extraordinary thing happened in Petersburg on the twenty-fifth of March. The barber, Ivan Yakovlevich,[1] who lives on the Voznessensky Avenue (his surname is lost, and even on his signboard, depicting a gentleman with a lathered face and bearing the inscription: "Also lets blood," no surname appears)—the barber Ivan Yakovlevich woke up rather early and inhaled the smell of hot bread. Raising himself a little in bed, he saw that his wife, a highly respectable lady who was very fond of a cup of coffee, was taking out of the oven some freshly baked bread.

"I won't have coffee today, my dear," said Ivan Yakovlevich. "Instead I'd like some hot bread with onions."

(That is to say, Ivan Yakovlevich would have liked both, but he knew that it was absolutely impossible to ask for two things at once; for his wife disliked such absurd whims.)

"Let the fool eat bread," his wife thought to herself. "All the better for me: there'll be an extra cup of coffee left." And she flung a loaf on the table.

After putting on, for propriety's sake, his frock coat over his shirt, Ivan Yakovlevich sat down at the table, sprinkled some salt, peeled two onions, picked up a knife, and, assuming a solemn expression, began cutting the bread. Having cut it in two, he had a look into the middle of one of the halves and, to his astonishment, noticed some white object there. Ivan Yakovlevich prodded it carefully with the knife and felt it with a finger. "It's solid," he said to himself. "What on earth can it be?"

---

* Translated by David Magarshack.
1. Russian middle names are patronymics, the father's name plus an ending that signifies either "son of" or "daughter of."

He dug his fingers into the bread and pulled out—a nose! Ivan Yakovlevich's heart sank: he rubbed his eyes and felt it again: a nose! There could be no doubt about it: it was a nose! And a familiar nose, too, apparently. Ivan Yakovlevich looked horrified. But his horror was nothing compared to the indignation with which his wife was overcome.

"Where have you cut off that nose, you monster?" she screamed angrily. "Blackguard! Drunkard! I shall inform the police against you myself. What a cutthroat! Three gentlemen have told me already that when you are shaving them you pull so violently at their noses that it is a wonder they still remain on their faces!"

But Ivan Yakovlevich was more dead than alive. He recognized the nose as belonging to no other person than the Collegiate Assessor[2] Kovalyov, whom he shaved every Wednesday and every Sunday.

"Wait, my dear, I'll wrap it in a rag and put it in a corner: let it stay there for a bit and then I'll take it out."

"I won't hear of it! What do you take me for? Keep a cutoff nose in my room? You heartless villain, you! All you know is to strop your razor. Soon you won't be fit to carry out your duties at all, you whoremonger, you scoundrel, you! You don't expect me to answer to the police for you, do you? Oh, you filthy wretch, you blockhead, you! Out with it! Out! Take it where you like, only don't let me see it here again!"

Ivan Yakovlevich stood there looking utterly crushed. He thought and thought and did not know what to think.

"Damned if I know how it happened," he said at last, scratching behind his ear. "Did I come home drunk last night? I'm sure I don't know. And yet the whole thing is quite impossible—it can't be true however you look at it: for bread is something you bake, and a nose is something quite different. Can't make head or tail of it!"

Ivan Yakovlevich fell silent. The thought that the police might find the nose at his place and charge him with having cut it off made him feel utterly dejected. He could already see the scarlet collar, beautifully embroidered with silver, the saber—and he trembled all over. At last he got his trousers and boots, pulled on these sorry objects, and, accompanied by his wife's execrations, wrapped the nose in a rag and went out into the street.

He wanted to shove it under something, either under the seat by the gates or drop it, as it were, by accident and then turn off into a side street. But as ill luck would have it, he kept coming across people he knew, who at once addressed him with the question: "Where are you off to?" or "Who are you going to shave so early in the morning?" —so that he could not find a right moment for getting rid of it. On one occasion he did succeed in dropping it, but a policeman shouted to him from the distance, pointing to it with his halberd:[3] "Hey, you, pick it up! You've dropped something!" And Ivan Yakovlevich had to pick up the nose and put it in his pocket. He was overcome by despair, particularly as the number of people in the streets was continually increasing with the opening of the stores and the small shops.

He decided to go to the Issakiyevsky Bridge, for it occurred to him

---

2. The eighth rank in the Russian civil service, equivalent to the army rank of major, though it was somewhat pretentious to use the military title for any civilian rank lower than that equivalent to general.

3. Apparently nightstick or its equivalent.

that he might be able to throw it into the Neva. But I'm afraid I am perhaps a little to blame for not having so far said something more about Ivan Yakovlevich, an estimable man in many respects.

Ivan Yakovlevich, like every other Russian working man, was a terrible drunkard. And though every day he shaved other people's chins, he never bothered to shave his own. Ivan Yakovlevich's frock coat (he never wore an ordinary coat) was piebald; that is to say, it was black, but covered all over with large brown, yellow, and gray spots; his collar was shiny; and instead of three buttons only bits of thread dangled from his coat. Ivan Yakovlevich was a great cynic, and every time the Collegiate Assessor Kovalyov said to him: "Your hands always stink, Ivan Yakovlevich," he would reply with the question: "Why should they stink, sir?" "I don't know why, my dear fellow," the Collegiate Assessor would say, "only they do stink." And after taking a pinch of snuff, Ivan Yakovlevich would lather him for that all over his cheeks, under the nose, behind his ears, and under his beard, in short, wherever he fancied.

This worthy citizen had in the meantime reached Issakiyevsky Bridge. First of all he looked round cautiously, then he leaned over the parapet, as though anxious to see whether there were a great many fishes swimming by, and as he did so he stealthily threw the rag with the nose into the river. He felt as though a heavy weight had been lifted from his shoulders: Ivan Yakovlevich even grinned. Instead of going to shave the chins of civil servants, he set off towards an establishment which bore the inscription: "Tea and Victuals," intending to ask for a glass of punch, when he suddenly noticed at the end of the bridge a police inspector of noble exterior, with large whiskers, with a three-cornered hat, and with a saber. He stood rooted to the spot; meanwhile the police officer beckoned to him and said: "Come here, my man!"

Knowing the rules, Ivan Yakovlevich took off his cap some way off and, coming up promptly, said: "I hope your honor is well."

"No, no, my good man, not 'your honor.' Tell me, what were you doing there on the bridge?"

"Why, sir, I was going to shave one of my customers and I just stopped to have a look how fast the current was running."

"You're lying, sir, you're lying! You won't get off with that. Answer my question, please!"

"I'm ready to shave you two or even three times a week, sir, with no conditions attached," replied Ivan Yakovlevich.

"No, my dear sir, that's nothing! I have three barbers who shave me and they consider it a great honor, too. You'd better tell me what you were doing there!"

Ivan Yakovlevich turned pale. . . . But here the incident is completely shrouded in a fog and absolutely nothing is known of what happened next.

2

Collegiate Assessor Kovalyov woke up fairly early and muttered, "Brrr . . ." with his lips, which he always did when he woke up, though he could not say himself why he did so. Kovalyov stretched and asked for the little looking glass standing on the table. He wanted to look at the pimple which had appeared on his nose the previous evening, but to his great astonishment, instead of his nose, he saw a

completely empty, flat place! Frightened, Kovalyov asked for some water and rubbed his eyes with a towel: there was no nose! He began feeling with his hand and pinched himself to see whether he was still asleep: no, he did not appear to be asleep. The Collegiate Assessor Kovalyov jumped out of bed and shook himself: he had no nose! He immediately told his servant to help him dress and rushed off straight to the Commissioner of Police.

Meanwhile we had better say something about Kovalyov so that the reader may see what sort of a person this Collegiate Assessor was. Collegiate Assessors who receive that title in consequence of their learned diplomas cannot be compared with those Collegiate Assessors who obtain this rank in the Caucasus. They are two quite different species. Learned Collegiate Assessors . . . But Russia is such a wonderful country that if you say something about one Collegiate Assessor, all the Collegiate Assessors, from Riga to Kamchatka, will most certainly think that you are referring to them. The same, of course, applies to all other callings and ranks. Kovalyov was a Caucasian Collegiate Assessor. He had obtained that rank only two years earlier and that was why he could not forget it for a moment; and to add to his own importance and dignity, he never described himself as a Collegiate Assessor, that is to say, a civil servant of the eighth rank, but always as a major, that is to say, by the corresponding rank in the army. "Look here, my good woman," he used to say when he met a peasant woman selling shirt fronts in the street, "you go to my house —I live on Sadovaya Street—and just ask: Does Major Kovalyov live here? Anyone will show you." But if he met some pretty little minx, he'd give her besides a secret instruction, adding: "You just ask for Major Kovalyov's apartment, darling." And that is why we, too, will in future refer to this Collegiate Assessor as Major Kovalyov.

Major Kovalyov was in the habit of taking a stroll on Nevsky Avenue every day. The collar of his shirt front was always extremely clean and well starched. His whiskers were such as one can still see nowadays on provincial district surveyors, architects, and army doctors, as well as on police officers performing various duties and, in general, on all gallant gentlemen who have full, ruddy cheeks and are very good at a game of boston:[4] these whiskers go right across the middle of the cheek and straight up to the nose. Major Kovalyov wore a great number of carnelian[5] seals, some with crests and others which had engraved on them: Wednesday, Thursday, Monday, and so on. Major Kovalyov came to Petersburg on business, to wit, to look for a post befitting his rank: if he were lucky, the post of a vice-governor, if not, one of an administrative clerk in some important department. Major Kovalyov was not averse to matrimony, either, but only if he could find a girl with a fortune of two hundred thousand.[6] The reader can, therefore, judge for himself the state in which the major was when he saw, instead of a fairly handsome nose of moderate size, a most idiotic, flat, smooth place.

As misfortune would have it, there was not a single cab to be seen in the street and he had to walk, wrapping himself in his cloak and

4. A card game similar to whist but usually played for high stakes in which a player gets to name trumps by bidding to take a certain number of tricks (thus, later in the story, his friend Yaryzhkin "always lost points when he went eight at boston"), the term "boston" itself meaning a bid to take five tricks.
5. A red quartz which, like onyx, has the luster of wax.
6. Rubles, then roughly equivalent to a dollar; one ruble contains 100 kopeks.

covering his face with a handkerchief, as though his nose were bleeding. "But perhaps I imagined it all," he thought. "It's impossible that I could have lost my nose without noticing it!" He went into a pastry cook's for the sole purpose of having a look at himself in a mirror. Fortunately, there was no one in the shop: the boys were sweeping the rooms and arranging the chairs; some of them, sleepy-eyed, were bringing in hot cream puffs on trays; yesterday's papers, stained with coffee, were lying about on tables and chairs. "Well, thank God, there's nobody here," he said. "Now I can have a look." He went timidly up to the mirror and looked. "Damn it," he said, disgusted, "the whole thing is too ridiculous for words! If only there'd be something instead of a nose, but there's just nothing!"

Biting his lips with vexation, Kovalyov went out of the pastry cook's and made up his mind, contrary to his usual practice, not to look or smile at anyone. Suddenly he stopped dead in his tracks at the front doors of a house; a most inexplicable thing happened before his very eyes: a carriage drew up before the entrance, the carriage door opened, and a gentleman in uniform jumped out and, stooping, rushed up the steps. Imagine the horror and, at the same time, amazement of Kovalyov when he recognized that this was his own nose! At this extraordinary sight everything went swimming before his eyes. He felt that he could hardly stand on his feet; but he made up his mind that, come what may, he would wait for the gentleman's return to the carriage. He was trembling all over as though in a fever. Two minutes later the nose really did come out. He wore a gold-embroidered uniform with a large stand-up collar, chamois-leather breeches, and a sword at his side. From his plumed hat it could be inferred that he was a State Councillor, a civil servant of the fifth rank. Everything showed that he was going somewhere to pay a visit. He looked round to the right and to the left, shouted to his driver, who had driven off a short distance, to come back, got into the carriage, and drove off.

Poor Kovalyov nearly went out of his mind. He did not know what to think of such a strange occurrence. And, indeed, how was it possible for a nose which had only the day before been on his face and which could neither walk nor drive—to be in a uniform! He ran after the carriage which, luckily, did not go far, stopping before the Kazan Cathedral.

He hastened into the cathedral, pushing his way through the crowd of beggarwomen with bandaged faces and only two slits for the eyes, at whom he used to laugh so much before, and went into the church. There were only a few worshipers inside the church; they were all standing near the entrance. Kovalyov felt so distraught that he was unable to pray and he kept searching with his eyes for the gentleman in the State Councillor's uniform. At last he saw him standing apart from the other worshipers. The nose was hiding his face completely in his large stand-up collar and was saying his prayers with the expression of the utmost piety.

"How am I to approach him?" thought Kovalyov. "It is clear from everything, from his uniform, from his hat, that he is a State Councillor. I'm damned if I know how to do it!"

He went up to him and began clearing his throat; but the nose did not change his devout attitude for a moment and carried on with his genuflections.

"Sir," said Kovalyov, inwardly forcing himself to take courage, "Sir—"

"What do you want?" answered the nose, turning round.

"I find it strange, sir, I—I believe you ought to know your proper place. And all of a sudden I find you in church of all places! You—you must admit that—"

"I'm sorry but I can't understand what you are talking about. . . . Explain yourself."

"How can I explain it to him?" thought Kovalyov and, plucking up courage, began: "Of course—er—you see—I—I am a major and—and you must admit that it isn't right for—er—a man of my rank to walk about without a nose. I mean—er—a tradeswoman selling peeled oranges on Voskressensky Bridge can sit there without a nose; but for a man like me who expects to obtain the post of a governor, which without a doubt he will obtain and—er—besides, being received in many houses by ladies of good position, such as Mrs. Chekhtaryov, the widow of a State Councillor, sir, and many others—er— Judge for yourself, sir, I mean, I—I don't know"—Major Kovalyov shrugged his shoulders—"I am sorry but if one were to look upon it according to the rules of honor and duty—er—you can understand yourself, sir—"

"I don't understand anything, sir," replied the nose. "Please explain yourself more clearly."

"Sir," said Kovalyov with a consciousness of his own dignity, "I don't know how to understand your words. It seems to me the whole thing is perfectly obvious. Or do you wish—I mean, you are my own nose, sir!"

The nose looked at the major and frowned slightly.

"You are mistaken, sir. I am *myself*. Besides, there can be no question of any intimate relationship beween us. I see, sir, from the buttons of your uniform that you are serving in a different department."

Having said this, the nose turned away and went on praying.

Kovalyov was utterly confounded, not knowing what to do or even what to think. At that moment he heard the agreeable rustle of a lady's dress; an elderly lady, her dress richly trimmed with lace, walked up to them, accompanied by a slim girl in a white dress, which looked very charming on her slender figure, and in a straw-colored hat, as light as a pastry puff. Behind them, opening a snuffbox, stood a tall flunkey with enormous whiskers and quite a dozen collars on his Cossack coat.

Kovalyov came nearer, pulled out the cambric collar of his shirt front, straightened the seals hanging on his gold watch chain and, turning his head this way and that and smiling, turned his attention to the ethereal young lady who, like a spring flower, bent forward a little, as she prayed, and put her little white hand with its semi-transparent fingers to her forehead to cross herself. The smile on Kovalyov's face distended a little more when he caught sight under her pretty hat of a chin of dazzling whiteness and part of her cheek, suffused with the color of the first spring rose. But suddenly he sprang back as though he had burned himself. He recollected that, instead of a nose, he had absolutely nothing on his face, and tears started to his eyes. He turned round, intending to tell the gentleman in uniform plainly that he was merely pretending to be a State Councillor, that he was a rogue and an impostor and nothing else than his own nose.

. . . But the nose was no longer there: he had managed to gallop off, no doubt to pay another visit. . . .

That plunged Kovalyov into despair. He left the church and stopped for a moment under the colonnade, carefully looking in all directions to see whether he could catch sight of the nose anywhere. He remembered very well that he wore a hat with a plume and a gold-embroidered uniform; but he had not noticed his cloak, nor the color of his carriage, nor his horses, nor even whether he had a footman behind him and, if so, in what livery. Besides, there were so many carriages careering backwards and forwards that it was difficult to distinguish one from another. But even if he had been able to distinguish any of them, there was no way of stopping it. It was a lovely, sunny day. There were hundreds of people on Nevsky Avenue. A whole flowery cascade of ladies was pouring all over the pavement from the Police Bridge to the Anichkin Bridge. There he saw coming a good acquaintance of his, a civil servant of the seventh rank, whom he always addressed as lieutenant colonel, especially in the presence of strangers. And there was Yaryzhkin, the head clerk in the Senate, a great friend of his, who always lost points when he went eight at boston. And here was another major, who had received the eighth rank of Collegiate Assessor in the Caucasus, waving to him to come up. . . .

"Oh, hell!" said Kovalyov. "Hey, cabby, take me straight to the Commissioner of Police!"

Kovalyov got into the cab and kept shouting to the driver: "Faster! Faster!"

"Is the Police Commissioner at home?" he asked, entering the hall.

"No, sir," replied the janitor. "He's just gone out."

"Well, of all things!"

"Yes, sir," the janitor added, "he's not been gone so long, but he's gone all right. If you'd come a minute earlier, you'd probably have found him at home."

Without taking his handkerchief off his face, Kovalyov got into the cab and shouted in an anguished voice:

"Drive on!"

"Where to, sir?" asked the cabman.

"Straight ahead!"

"Straight ahead, sir? But there's a turning here: to right or to left?"

This question stumped Kovalyov and made him think again. A man in his position ought first of all apply to the City Police Headquarters, not because they dealt with matters of this kind there, but because instructions coming from there might be complied with much more quickly than those coming from any other place; to seek satisfaction from the authorities of the department in which the nose claimed to be serving would have been unreasonable, for from the nose's replies he perceived that nothing was sacred to that individual and that he was quite capable of telling a lie just as he had lied in denying that he had ever seen him. Kovalyov was, therefore, about to tell the cabman to drive him to Police Headquarters, when it again occurred to him that this rogue and impostor, who had treated him in such a contumelious way, might take advantage of the first favorable opportunity and slip out of town, and then all his searches would be in vain or, which God forbid, might go on for a whole month. At last it seemed that Heaven itself had suggested a plan of action to him. He decided to

go straight to a newspaper office and, while there was still time, put in an advertisement with a circumstantial description of the nose so that anyone meeting it might bring it to him at once or, at any rate, let him know where it was. And so, having made up his mind, he told the cabman to drive him to the nearest newspaper office and all the way there he kept hitting the cabman on the back with his fist, repeating, "Faster, you rogue! Faster, you scoundrel!" "Good Lord, sir, what are you hitting me for?" said the cabman, shaking his head and flicking with the rein at the horse, whose coat was as long as a lap dog's. At last the cab came to a stop and Kovalyov ran panting into a small reception room where a gray-haired clerk, in an old frock coat and wearing spectacles, sat at a table, with a pen between his teeth, counting some coppers.

"Who receives advertisements here?" cried Kovalyov. "Oh, good morning!"

"How do you do?" said the clerk, raising his eyes for a moment and dropping them again on the carefully laid out heaps of coppers before him.

"I should like to insert—"

"One moment, sir, I must ask you to wait a little," said the clerk, writing down a figure on a piece of paper with one hand and moving two beads on his abacus with the other.

A footman with galloons on his livery and a personal appearance which showed that he came from an aristocratic house, was standing beside the clerk with a note in his hand. He thought it an opportune moment for displaying his knowledge of the world.

"Would you believe it, sir," he said, "the little bitch isn't worth eighty kopeks, and indeed I shouldn't give even eight kopeks for her, but the countess dotes on her, sir, she simply dotes on her, and that's why she's offering a hundred rubles to anyone who finds her! Now, to put it politely, sir, just as you and me are speaking now, you can never tell what people's tastes may be. What I mean is that if you are a sportsman, then keep a pointer or a poodle, don't mind spending five hundred or even a thousand rubles, so long as your dog is a good one."

The worthy clerk listened to this with a grave air and at the same time kept counting the number of letters in the advertisement the footman had brought. The room was full of old women, shop assistants, and house porters—all with bits of paper in their hands. In one a coachman of sober habits was advertised as being let out on hire; in another an almost new, secondhand carriage, brought from Paris in 1814, was offered for sale; in still others were offered for sale: a serf girl of nineteen, experienced in laundry work and suitable for other work, a well-built open carriage with only one spring broken, a young, dappled-gray, mettlesome horse of seventeen years of age, a new consignment of turnip and radish seed from London, a summer residence with all the conveniences, including two boxes for horses and a piece of land on which an excellent birchwood or pinewood could be planted; there was also an advertisement containing a challenge to those who wished to purchase old boot soles with an invitation to come to the auction rooms every day from eight o'clock in the morning to three o'clock in the afternoon. The room, in which all these people were crowded, was very small and the air extremely thick; but the Collegiate Assessor Kovalyov did not notice the bad

smell because he kept the handkerchief over his face and also because
his nose was at the time goodness knows where.

"Excuse me, sir," he said at last with impatience, "it's very
urgent. . . ."

Presently, presently," said the gray-haired gentleman, flinging their
notes back to the old women and the house porters. "Two rubles
forty kopeks! One moment, sir! One ruble sixty-four kopeks! What
can I do for you?" he said at last, turning to Kovalyov.

"Thank you, sir," said Kovalyov. "You see, I've been robbed or
swindled, I can't so far say which, but I should like you to put in an
advertisement that anyone who brings the scoundrel to me will receive
a handsome reward."

"What is your name, sir?"

"What do you want my name for? I'm sorry I can't give it to you.
I have a large circle of friends: Mrs. Chekhtaryov, the widow of a
State Councillor, Pelageya Grigoryevna Podtochin, the widow of a
first lieutenant. . . . God forbid that they should suddenly find out!
You can simply say: a Collegiate Assessor or, better still, a gentleman
of the rank of major."

"And is the runaway your house serf?"

"My house serf? Good Lord, no! That wouldn't have been so bad!
You see, it's my—er—nose that has run away from me. . . ."

"Dear me, what a strange name! And has this Mr. Nosov robbed
you of a large sum of money?"

"I said nose, sir, nose! You're thinking of something else! It is my
nose, my own nose that has disappeared I don't know where. The
devil himself must have played a joke on me!"

"But how did it disappear? I'm afraid I don't quite understand it."

"I can't tell you how it happened. The worst of it is that now it is
driving about all over the town under the guise of a State Councillor.
That's why I should like you to insert an advertisement that anyone
who catches him should bring him at once to me. You can see for
yourself, sir, that I cannot possibly carry on without such a conspicuous part of myself. It's not like some little toe which no one can see
whether it is missing or not once I'm wearing my boots. I call on
Thursdays on Mrs. Chekhtaryov, the widow of a State Councillor.
Mrs. Podtochin, the widow of a first lieutenant, and her pretty
daughter are also good friends of mine, and you can judge for yourself
the position I am in now. I can't go and see them now, can I?"

The clerk pursed his lips tightly which meant that he was thinking
hard.

"I'm sorry, sir," he said at last, after a long pause, "but I can't
possibly insert such an advertisement in the papers."

"What? Why not?"

"Well, you see, sir, the paper might lose its reputation. If everyone
were to write that his nose had run away, why—— As it is, people
are already saying that we are publishing a lot of absurd stories and
false rumors."

"But why is it so absurd? I don't see anything absurd in it."

"It only seems so to you. Last week, for instance, a similar thing
happened. A civil servant came to see me just as you have now. He
brought an advertisement, it came to two rubles and seventy-three
kopeks, but all it was about was that a poodle with a black coat had
run away. You wouldn't think there was anything in that, would you?

And yet it turned out to be a libelous statement. You see, the poodle was the treasurer of some institution or other. I don't remember which."

"But I am not asking you to publish an advertisement about a poodle, but about my own nose, which is the same as about myself."

"No, sir, I cannot possibly insert such an advertisement."

"Not even if my own nose really has disappeared?"

"If it's lost, then it's a matter for a doctor. I'm told there are people who can fit you with a nose of any shape you like. But I can't help observing, sir, that you are a gentleman of a merry disposition and are fond of pulling a person's leg."

"I swear to you by all that is holy! Why, if it has come to that, I don't mind showing you."

"Don't bother, sir," said the clerk, taking a pinch of snuff. "Still," he added, unable to suppress his curiosity, "if it's no bother, I'd like to have a look."

The Collegiate Assessor removed the handkerchief from his face.

"It is very strange, indeed!" said the clerk. "The place is perfectly flat, just like a pancake from a frying pan. Yes, quite incredibly flat."

"Well, you won't dispute it now, will you? You can see for yourself that you simply must insert it. I shall be infinitely grateful to you and very glad this incident has given me the pleasure of making your acquaintance. . . ."

It may be seen from that that the major decided to lay it on a bit thick this time.

"Well, of course, it's easy enough to insert an advertisement," said the clerk, "but I don't see that it will do you any good. If you really want to publish a thing like that, you'd better put it in the hands of someone skillful with his pen and let him describe it as a rare natural phenomenon and publish it in *The Northern Bee*"—here he took another pinch of snuff—"for the benefit of youth"—here he wiped his nose—"or just as a matter of general interest."

The Collegiate Assessor was utterly discouraged. He dropped his eyes and glanced at the bottom of the newspaper where the theatrical announcements were published; his face was ready to break into a smile as he read the name of a very pretty actress, and his hand went automatically to his pocket to feel whether he had a five-ruble note there, for, in Kovalyov's opinion, officers of the higher ranks ought to have a seat in the stalls[7]—but the thought of his nose spoiled it all!

The clerk himself appeared to be touched by Kovalyov's embarrassing position. Wishing to relieve his distress a little, he thought it proper to express his sympathy in a few words.

"I'm very sorry indeed, sir," he said, "that such a thing should have happened to you. Would you like a pinch of snuff? It relieves headaches, dispels melancholy moods, and it is even a good remedy against hemorrhoids."

Saying this, the clerk offered his snuffbox to Kovalyov, very deftly opening the lid with the portrait of a lady in a hat on it.

This unintentional action made Kovalyov lose his patience.

"I can't understand, sir," he said angrily, "how you can joke in a matter like this! Don't you see I haven't got the thing with which to take a pinch of snuff? To hell with your snuff! I can't bear the sight of

---

7. Seats in the orchestra of a theater near stage, separated from others by railings.

it now, and not only your rotten beresina brand, but even if you were to offer me rappee itself!"

Having said this, he walked out of the newspaper office, greatly vexed, and went to see the police inspector of his district, a man who had a great liking for sugar. At his home, the entire hall, which was also the dining room, was stacked with sugar loaves with which local tradesmen had presented him out of friendship. When Kovalyov arrived, the police inspector's cook was helping him off with his regulation top boots; his saber and the rest of his martial armor were already hung peaceably in the corners of the room, and his three-year-old son was playing with his awe-inspiring three-cornered hat. He himself was getting ready to partake of the pleasures of peace after his gallant, warlike exploits.

Kovalyov walked in at the time when he stretched, cleared his throat, and said: "Oh, for a couple of hours of sleep!" It could, therefore, be foreseen that the Collegiate Assessor could have hardly chosen a worse time to arrive; indeed, I am not sure whether he would have got a more cordial reception even if he had brought the police inspector several pounds of sugar or a piece of cloth. The inspector was a great patron of the arts and manufactures, but he preferred a bank note to everything else. "This is something," he used to say. "There is nothing better than that: it doesn't ask for food, it doesn't take up a lot of space, there's always room for it in the pocket, and when you drop it, it doesn't break."

The inspector received Kovalyov rather coldly and said that after dinner was not the time to carry out investigations and that nature herself had fixed it so that after a good meal a man had to take a nap (from which the Collegiate Assessor could deduce that the inspector was not unfamiliar with the sayings of the ancient sages), and that a respectable man would not have his nose pulled off.

A bull's eye! . . . It must be observed that Kovalyov was extremely quick to take offense. He could forgive anything people said about himself, but he could never forgive an insult to his rank or his calling. He was even of the opinion that any reference in plays to army officers or civil servants of low rank was admissible, but that the censorship ought not to pass any attack on persons of higher rank. The reception given him by the police inspector disconcerted him so much that he tossed his head and said with an air of dignity, with his hands slightly parted in a gesture of surprise: "I must say that after such offensive remarks, I have nothing more to say. . . ." and went out.

He arrived home hardly able to stand on his feet. By now it was dusk. After all these unsuccessful quests his rooms looked melancholy or rather extremely disgusting to him. On entering the hall, he saw his valet Ivan lying on his back on the dirty leather sofa and spitting on the ceiling and rather successfully aiming at the same spot. Such an indifference on the part of his servant maddened him; he hit him on the forehead with his hat, saying: "You pig, you're always doing something stupid!"

Ivan jumped up and rushed to help him off with his cloak.

On entering his room, the major, tired and dejected, threw himself into an armchair and, at last, after several sighs, said:

"Lord, oh Lord, why should I have such bad luck? If I had lost an arm or a leg, it would not be so bad; if I had lost my ears, it would be bad enough, but still bearable; but without a nose a man is goodness

knows what, neither fish, nor flesh, nor good red herring—he isn't a respectable citizen at all! He is simply something to take and chuck out of the window! If I had had it cut off in battle or in a duel or had been the cause of its loss myself, but to lose it without any reason whatever, for nothing, for absolutely nothing! . . . But no," he added after a brief reflection, "it can't be. It's inconceivable that a nose should be lost, absolutely inconceivable. I must be simply dreaming or just imagining it all. Perhaps by some mistake I drank, instead of water, the spirits which I rub on my face after shaving. Ivan, the blithering fool, did not take it away and I must have swallowed it by mistake."

To convince himself that he was not drunk, the major pinched himself so painfully that he cried out. The pain completely convinced him that he was fully awake and that everything had actually happened to him. He went up slowly to the looking glass and at first screwed up his eyes with the idea that perhaps he would see his nose in its proper place; but almost at the same moment he jumped back, saying: "What a horrible sight!"

And, indeed, the whole thing was quite inexplicable. If he had lost a button, a silver spoon, his watch, or something of the kind, but to lose—and in his own apartment, too! Taking all the circumstances into consideration, Major Kovalyov decided that he would not be far wrong in assuming that the whole thing was the fault of no other person than Mrs. Podtochin, who wanted him to marry her daughter. He was not himself averse to flirting with her, but he avoided a final decision. But when Mrs. Podtochin told him plainly that she would like her daughter to marry him, he quietly hung back with his compliments, declaring that he was still too young, that he had to serve another five years, as he had decided not to marry till he was exactly forty-two. That was why Mrs. Podtochin, out of revenge no doubt, had made up her mind to disfigure him and engaged some old witch to do the foul deed, for he simply refused to believe that his nose had been cut off: no one had entered his room, and his barber, Ivan Yakovlevich, had shaved him on Wednesday, and during the whole of that day and even on Thursday his nose was intact—he remembered that, he knew that for certain; besides, he would have felt pain and the wound could not possibly have healed so quickly and become as smooth as a pancake. He made all sorts of plans in his head: to issue a court summons against her or to go to see her and confront her with the undeniable proof of her crime. His thoughts were interrupted by a gleam of light through all the cracks of the door, which let him know that Ivan had lighted a candle in the hall. Soon Ivan himself appeared, carrying the candle in front of him and lighting the whole room brightly. Kovalyov instinctively seized his handkerchief and covered the place where his nose had been only the day before so that the stupid fellow should not stand there gaping, seeing his master so strangely transformed.

Ivan had scarcely had time to go back to his cubbyhole when an unfamiliar voice was heard in the hall, saying:

"Does the Collegiate Assessor Kovalyov live here?"

"Come in," said Kovalyov, jumping up quickly and opening the door. "Major Kovalyov is here."

A police officer of a handsome appearance, with whiskers that were neither too dark nor too light and with fairly full cheeks, came in.

It was, in fact, the same police officer who, at the beginning of this story, had been standing at the end of Issakiyevsky Bridge.

"Did you lose your nose, sir?"

"That's right."

"It's been found now."

"What are you saying?" cried Major Kovalyov.

He was bereft of speech with joy. He stared fixedly at the police officer who was standing before him and whose full lips and cheeks reflected the flickering light of the candle.

"How was it found?"

"By a most extraordinary piece of luck, sir. It was intercepted just before he was leaving town. It was about to get into the stagecoach and leave for Riga. He even had a passport made out in the name of a certain civil servant. And the funny thing is that at first I was myself inclined to take him for a gentleman. But luckily I was wearing my glasses at the time and I saw at once that it was a nose. You see, sir, I am shortsighted, and if you were to stand in front of me I would just see that you have a face, but would not be able to make out either your nose or your beard or anything else for that matter. My mother-in-law, that is to say, my wife's mother, can't see anything, either."

Kovalyov was beside himself with excitement.

"Where is it? Where? I'll go at once!"

"Don't trouble, sir. Realizing how much you must want it, I brought it with me. And the funny part about it is that the chief accomplice in this affair is the scoundrel of a barber on Voznessensky Avenue, who is now locked up in a cell at the police station. I've suspected him for a long time of theft and drunkenness and, as a matter of fact, he stole a dozen buttons from a shop only the other day. Your nose, sir, is just as it was."

At these words, the police officer put his hand in his pocket and pulled out the nose wrapped in a piece of paper.

"Yes, yes, it's my nose!" cried Kovalyov. "It's my nose all right! Won't you have a cup of tea with me, sir?"

"I'd be very glad to, sir, but I'm afraid I'm rather in a hurry. I have to go to the House of Correction from here. Food prices have risen a great deal, sir. . . . I have my mother-in-law, that is to say, my wife's mother, living with me and, of course, there are the children. My eldest, in particular, is a very promising lad, sir. A very clever boy he is, sir, but I haven't the means to provide a good education for him— none at all. . . ."

Kovalyov took the hint and, snatching up a ten-rouble note from the table, thrust it into the hand of the police officer, who bowed and left the room, and almost at the same moment Kovalyov heard his voice raised in the street, where he was boxing the ears of a foolish peasant who had happened to drive with his cart on to the boulevard.

After the departure of the police officer, the Collegiate Assessor remained for a time in a sort of daze, and it was only after several minutes that he was able to recover his senses, so overwhelmed was he by his joy at the unexpected recovery of his nose. He took the newly found nose very carefully in both his cupped hands and examined it attentively once more.

"Yes, it's my nose all right!" said Major Kovalyov. "There's the pimple on the left side which I only got the other day."

The major almost laughed with joy. But nothing lasts very long in the world, and that is why even joy is not so poignant after the first moment. A moment later it grows weaker still and at last it merges imperceptibly into one's ordinary mood, just as a circle made in the water by a pebble at last merges into its smooth surface. Kovalyov began to ponder and he realized that the matter was not at an end: the nose had been found, but it had still to be affixed, to be put back in its place.

"And what if it doesn't stick?"

At this question that he had put to himself the major turned pale.

With a feeling of indescribable panic he rushed up to the table and drew the looking glass closer to make sure that he did not stick his nose on crookedly. His hands trembled. Carefully and with the utmost circumspection he put it back on its former place. Oh horrror! The nose did not stick! . . . He put it to his mouth, breathed on it to warm it a little, and once more put it back on the smooth place between his two cheeks; but, try as he might, the nose refused to stick.

"Come on, come on! Stick, you idiot!" he kept saying to it.

But the nose, as though made of wood, kept falling down on the table with so strange a sound that it might have been cork. The major's face contorted spasmodically. "Won't it adhere?" he asked himself in a panic. But though he kept putting it back on its own place a great many times, his efforts were as unavailing as ever.

He called Ivan and sent him for the doctor, who occupied the best flat on the ground floor of the same house. The doctor was a fine figure of a man; he had wonderful pitch-black whiskers, a fresh, healthy wife, he ate fresh apples in the morning and kept his mouth quite extraordinarily clean, rinsing it every morning for nearly three quarters of an hour and brushing his teeth with five different kinds of toothbrushes. The doctor came at once. After asking how long it was since the accident, he lifted up Major Kovalyov's face by the chin and gave a fillip with his thumb, on the spot where the nose had been, with such force that the major threw back his head so violently that he hit the wall. The doctor said that it was nothing and, after advising him to move away from the wall a little, told him to bend his head to the right. After feeling the place where the nose had been, he said: "H'm!" Then he told him to bend his head to the left, and again said: "H'm!" In conclusion he gave him another fillip with the thumb so that the major tossed his head like a horse whose teeth are being examined. Having carried out this experiment, the doctor shook his head and said:

"No, I'm afraid it can't be done! You'd better remain like this, for it might be much worse. It is, of course, quite possible to affix your nose. In fact, I could do it right now. But I assure you that it might be the worse for you."

"How do you like that! How am I to remain without a nose?" said Kovalyov. "It can't possibly be worse than now. It's—it's goodness only knows what! How can I show myself with such a horrible face? I know lots of people of good social position. Why, today I have been invited to two parties. I have a large circle of friends: Mrs. Chekhtaryov, the widow of a State Councillor, Mrs. Podtochin, the widow of an army officer—though after what she did to me now I shall have no further dealings with her except through the police. Do me a favor, Doctor," said Kovalyov in an imploring voice. "Is there no way at all? Stick it on somehow. It may not be quite satisfactory, but so long as it sticks

I don't mind. I could even support it with a hand in an emergency. Besides, I don't dance, so that I could hardly do any harm to it by some inadvertent movement. As for my gratitude for your visits, you may be sure that I will recompense you as much as I can. . . ."

"Believe me, sir," said the doctor neither in too loud nor in too soft a voice, but in a very persuasive and magnetic one, "I never allow any selfish motives to interfere with the treatment of my patients. This is against my principles and my art. It is true I charge for my visits, but that is only because I hate to offend by my refusal. Of course, I could put your nose back, but I assure you on my honor, if you won't believe my words, that it will be much worse. You'd better leave it to nature. Wash it often with cold water, and I assure you that without a nose you will be as healthy as with one. As for your nose, I'd advise you to put it in a bottle of spirits or, better still, pour two spoonfuls of aqua fortis and warmed-up vinegar into the bottle, and you'd be able to get a lot of money for it. I might take it myself even, if you won't ask too much for it."

"No, no," cried the desperate Major Kovalyov, "I'd rather it rotted away!"

"I'm sorry," said the doctor, taking his leave, "I wish I could be of some help to you, but there's nothing I can do! At least you saw how anxious I was to help you."

Having said this, the doctor left the room with a dignified air. Kovalyov did not even notice his face, and in his profound impassivity only caught sight of the cuffs of his spotlessly clean white shirt peeping out of his black frock coat.

On the following day he decided, before lodging his complaint, to write to Mrs. Podtochin a letter with a request to return to him without a fight what she had taken away from him. The letter was as follows:

Dear Mrs. Podtochin,

I cannot understand your strange treatment of me. I assure you that, by acting like this, you will gain nothing and will certainly not force me to marry your daughter. Believe me, I know perfectly well what happened to my nose and that you, and no one else, are the chief instigator of this affair. Its sudden detachment from its place, its flight, and its disguise, first in the shape of a civil servant and then in its own shape, is nothing more than the result of witchcraft employed by you or by those who engage in the same honorable occupations as yourself. For my part, I deem it my duty to warn you that if the aforementioned nose is not back in its usual place today, I shall be forced to have recourse to the protection and the safeguard of the law.

However, I have the honor of remaining, madam, with the utmost respect

Your obedient servant,
Platon Kovalyov

Dear Platon Kuzmich,

Your letter has greatly surprised me. To be quite frank, I never expected it, particularly as regards your unjust reproaches. I wish to inform you that I have never received the civil servant you mention, neither in disguise nor in his own shape. It is true, Filipp Ivanovich Potachkin used to come to see me. And though he did ask me for my daughter's hand and is a man of good and sober habits and of great

learning, I have never held out any hopes to him. You also mention your nose. If you mean by that that I wished to put your nose out of joint, that is, to give you a formal refusal, I am surprised that you should speak of such a thing when, as you know perfectly well, I was quite of the contrary opinion and if you should now make a formal proposal to my daughter, I should be ready to satisfy you immediately, for that has always been my dearest wish, in the hope of which

I remain always at your service,
Pelageya Podtochin

"No," said Kovalyov, after he had read the letter, "she had certainly nothing to do with it. It's impossible! The letter is not written as a guilty person would have written it." The Collegiate Assessor was an expert on such things, for, while serving in the Caucasus, he had several times been under judicial examination. "How then, in what way, did it happen? The devil alone can sort it out!" he said at last, utterly discouraged.

Meanwhile the rumors about this extraordinary affair spread all over the town and, as usually happens, not without all sorts of embellishments. At that time people's minds were particularly susceptible to anything of an extraordinary nature: only a short time before everybody had shown a great interest in the experiments of magnetism.[8] Besides, the story of the dancing chairs in Konyushennaya Street was still fresh in people's minds, and it is therefore not surprising that people soon began talking about the Collegiate Assessor Kovalyov's nose which, it was alleged, was taking a walk on Nevsky Avenue at precisely three o'clock in the afternoon. Thousands of curious people thronged Nevsky Avenue every day. Someone said that the nose was in Junker's Stores, and such a crowd of people collected at the stores that the police had to be called to restore order. One enterprising, bewhiskered businessman of respectable appearance, who was selling all sorts of dry pasties[9] at the entrance to the theater, had purposely made beautiful wooden benches on which it was perfectly safe to stand and invited people to use them for eighty kopeks each. One highly estimable colonel, who had left his home earlier than usual so that he could see the nose, pushed his way through the crowd with great difficulty; but, to his great indignation, he saw in the window of the stores, instead of the nose, an ordinary woollen sweater and a lithograph of a girl pulling up her stocking and a dandy, with a small beard and an open waistcoat, peeping at her from behind a tree—a picture that had hung in the same place for over ten years. On stepping back from the window, he said with vexation: "One should not be allowed to create a disturbance among the common people by such stupid and improbable stories."

Then the rumor spread that Major Kovalyov's nose was not taking a walk on Nevsky Avenue but in Tavrichesky Gardens and that he had been there for a long time; in fact, that when the Persian Prince Khozrev Mirza had lived there he had greatly marveled at that curious freak of nature. A few students of the Surgical Academy set off there. One highly aristocratic lady wrote a letter to the head keeper of the gardens specially to ask him to show that rare phenomenon to her children and, if possible, with instructive and edifying explanations for young boys.

8. Hypnotism.   9. Meat pies.

All men about town, without whom no important social gathering is complete, who liked to amuse the ladies and whose stock of amusing stories had been entirely used up at the time, were extremely glad of all this affair. A small section of respectable and well-meaning people were highly dissatisfied. One gentleman declared indignantly that he failed to understand how in our enlightened age such absurd stories could be spread abroad and that he was surprised the government paid no attention to it. This gentleman evidently was one of those gentlemen who would like to involve the government in everything, even in his daily tiffs with his wife. After that—but here again a thick fog descends on the whole incident, and what happened afterward is completely unknown.

3

The world is full of all sorts of absurdities. Sometimes there is not even a semblance of truth: suddenly the very same nose, which had been driving about disguised as a State Councillor and had created such an uproar in town, found itself, as if nothing had happened, on its accustomed place again, namely, between the two cheeks of Major Kovalyov. This happened on the seventh of April. Waking up and looking quite accidentally into the mirror, he saw—his nose! He grabbed it with his hand—it was his nose all right! . . . "Aha!" said Kovalyov, and nearly went leaping barefoot all over the room in a roisterous dance in his joy. But Ivan, who entered just then, prevented him. He told Ivan to bring in some water for washing at once and, while washing, glanced once again into the mirror: he had a nose! While wiping himself with a towel, he again glanced into the mirror: he had a nose!

"Have a look, Ivan, there seems to be a pimple on my nose," he said, thinking to himself: "Won't it be awful if Ivan were to say, No, sir, there's no pimple and no nose, either!"

But Ivan said: "There's nothing, sir. I can't see no pimple. Nothing at all on your nose, sir."

"That's good, damn it!" said the major to himself, snapping his fingers.

At that moment the barber Ivan Yakovlevich poked his head through the door, but as timidly as a cat which had just been thrashed for the theft of suet.

"Tell me first of all—are your hands clean?" Kovalyov shouted to him from the other end of the room.

"They are clean, sir."

"You're lying!"

"I swear they are clean, sir!"

"Very well, they'd better be!"

Kovalyov sat down. Ivan Yakovlevich put a napkin round him and in a twinkling, with the aid of his brush alone, transformed his whole beard and part of his cheek into the sort of cream that is served in a merchant's home at a name-day party.

"Well, I never!" said Ivan Yakovlevich to himself as he glanced at the nose. Then he bent his head to the other side and looked at the nose sideways. "Well, I'm damned," he went on, looking at the nose for some considerable time. "Dear, oh dear, just think of it!" At last, gently and as cautiously as can only be imagined, he raised two fingers to grasp it by its end. Such was Ivan Yakovlevich's system.

"Mind, mind what you're doing!" cried Kovalyov.

Ivan Yakovlevich was utterly discouraged, perplexed, and confused as he had never been confused before. At last he began carefully titillating him with the razor under the beard, and though he found it difficult and not at all convenient to shave without holding on to the olfactory organ, he did at last overcome all the obstacles by pressing his rough thumb against the cheek and the lower jaw and finished shaving him.

When everything was ready, Kovalyov hastened to dress at once, took a cab, and drove straight to the nearest pastry cook's. On entering, he at once shouted to the boy at the other end of the shop: "Boy, a cup of chocolate!" and immediately went up to the looking glass: he had a nose all right! He turned round gaily and glanced ironically, screwing up one eye a little, at two military gentlemen, one of whom had a nose no bigger than a waistcoat button. After that he set off for the office of the department where he was trying to obtain the post of vice-governor or, if unsuccessful, of an administrative clerk. On passing through the reception room, he glanced into the looking glass: he had a nose all right! Then he went to see another Collegiate Assessor, a man who was very fond of sneering at people, to whom he often used to say in reply to his biting remarks: "Oh, away with you! I know you, Mr. Pinprick!" On the way he thought: "If the major does not split his sides with laughter when he sees me, it's a sure sign that everything is in its proper place." But the Collegiate Assessor showed no signs of merriment. "It's perfect, perfect, damn it!" thought Kovalyov to himself. On the way back he met Mrs. Podtochin and her daughter, greeted them, and was met with joyful exclamations, which again proved to him that there was nothing wrong with him. He talked a long time with them and, taking out his snuffbox deliberately, kept stuffing his nose with snuff at both entrances for a great while, saying to himself: "There, I'm putting on this show specially for you, stupid females! And I won't marry your daughter all the same. Flirt with her —by all means, but nothing more!" And Major Kovalyov took his walks after that as if nothing had happened. He was to be seen on Nevsky Avenue, in the theaters—everywhere. And his nose, too, just as if nothing had happened, remained on his face, without as much as a hint that he had been playing truant. And after that Major Kovalyov was always seen in the best of humor, smiling, running after all the pretty ladies, and once even stopping before a little shop in the Arcade and buying himself a ribbon of some order for some mysterious reason, for he had never been a member of any order.

So that is the sort of thing that happened in the northern capital of our far-flung Empire. Only now, on thinking it all over, we can see that there is a great deal that is improbable in it. Quite apart from the really strange fact of the supernatural displacement of the nose and its appearance in various parts of the town in the guise of a State Councillor, how did Kovalyov fail to realize that he could not advertise about his nose in a newspaper? I am not saying that because I think that advertisement rates are too high—that's nonsense, and I am not at all a mercenary person. But it's improper, awkward, not nice! And again —how did the nose come to be in a loaf of bread and what about Ivan Yakovlevich? No, that I cannot understand, I simply cannot understand it! But what is even stranger and more incomprehensible than anything is that authors should choose such subjects. I confess that is entirely beyond my comprehension. It's like—no, I simply don't understand it.

In the first place it's of no benefit whatever to our country, and in the second place—but even in the second place there's no benefit whatever. I simply don't know what to make of it. . . .

And yet, in spite of it all, though, of course, we may take for granted this and that and the other—may even— But then where do you not find all sorts of absurdities? All the same, on second thought, there really is something in it. Say what you like, but such things do happen —not often, but they do happen.

1835–36

FYODOR DOSTOEVSKY

The Crocodile*

AN EXTRAORDINARY INCIDENT[1]

A true story of how a gentleman of a certain age and of respectable appearance was swallowed by the crocodile in the Arcade, and of the consequences that followed.

> Ohé Lambert! Où est Lambert?
> As-tu vu Lambert?

1

On the thirteenth of January of this present year, 1865, at half-past twelve in the day, Elena Ivanovna, the wife of my cultured friend Ivan Matveitch, who is a colleague in the same department, and may be said to be a distant relation of mine, too, expressed the desire to see the crocodile now on view at a fixed charge in the Arcade. As Ivan Matveitch had already in his pocket his ticket for a tour abroad (not so much for the sake of his health as for the improvement of his mind), and was consequently free from his official duties and had nothing whatever to do that morning, he offered no objection to his wife's irresistible fancy, but was positively aflame with curiosity himself.

"A capital idea!" he said, with the utmost satisfaction. "We'll have a look at the crocodile! On the eve of visiting Europe it is as well to acquaint ourselves on the spot with its indigenous inhabitants." And with these words, taking his wife's arm, he set off with her at once for the Arcade. I joined them, as I usually do, being an intimate friend of the family. I have never seen Ivan Matveitch in a more agreeable frame of mind than he was on that memorable morning—how true it is that we know not beforehand the fate that awaits us! On entering the Arcade he was at once full of admiration for the splendors of the building, and when we reached the shop in which the monster lately arrived in Petersburg was being exhibited, he volunteered to pay the quarter-ruble[2] for me to the crocodile owner—a thing which had never hap-

* Translated by Constance Garnett.
1. When this story appeared in the February 1865 issue of *Epoch* it had a preface which read, in part: "I consider it my duty to state that if perchance this is all a lie, and not the truth, then a more incredible lie has not until now appeared in our literature, except perhaps that occurrence, familiar to everyone, when one fine morning a certain Major Kovalyov's own nose ran off from his face and then went walking about in a uniform and a plumed hat in the Tauride Garden and along Nevsky" (Konstantin Mochulsky, *Dostoevsky, His Life and Work*, trans. Michael A. Minihan [Princeton: Princeton University Press, 1967], p. 265).
The epigraph reads, "Oh Lambert! Where is Lambert? / Hast thou seen Lambert?" Source not identified.
2. A ruble in the 19th century was roughly equivalent to a dollar, a kopek to a cent.

pened before. Walking into a little room, we observed that besides the crocodile there were in it parrots of the species known as cockatoo, and also a group of monkeys in a special case in a recess. Near the entrance, along the left wall stood a big tin tank that looked like a bath covered with a thin iron grating, filled with water to the depth of two inches. In this shallow pool was kept a huge crocodile, which lay like a log absolutely motionless and apparently deprived of all its faculties by our damp climate, so inhospitable to foreign visitors. This monster at first aroused no special interest in any one of us.

"So this is the crocodile!" said Elena Ivanovna, with a pathetic cadence of regret. "Why, I thought it was . . . something different."

Most probably she thought it was made of diamonds. The owner of the crocodile, a German, came out and looked at us with an air of extraordinary pride.

"He has a right to be," Ivan Matveitch whispered to me, "he knows he is the only man in Russia exhibiting a crocodile."

This quite nonsensical observation I ascribe also to the extremely good-humored mood which had overtaken Ivan Matveitch, who was on other occasions of rather envious disposition.

"I fancy your crocodile is not alive," said Elena Ivanovna, piqued by the irresponsive stolidity of the proprietor, and addressing him with a charming smile in order to soften his churlishness—a maneuver so typically feminine.

"Oh, no, madam," the latter replied in broken Russian; and instantly moving the grating half off the tank, he poked the monster's head with a stick.

Then the treacherous monster, to show that it was alive, faintly stirred its paws and tail, raised its snout and emitted something like a prolonged snuffle.

"Come, don't be cross, Karlchen," said the German caressingly, gratified in his vanity.

"How horrid that crocodile is! I am really frightened," Elena Ivanovna twittered, still more coquettishly. "I know I shall dream of him now."

"But he won't bite you if you do dream of him," the German retorted gallantly, and was the first to laugh at his own jest, but none of us responded.

"Come, Semyon Semyonitch," said Elena Ivanovna, addressing me exclusively, "let us go and look at the monkeys. I am awfully fond of monkeys; they are such darlings . . . and the crocodile is horrid."

"Oh, don't be afraid, my dear!" Ivan Matveitch called after us, gallantly displaying his manly courage to his wife. "This drowsy denison of the realms of the Pharaohs will do us no harm." And he remained by the tank. What is more, he took his glove and began tickling the crocodile's nose with it, wishing, as he said afterwards, to induce him to snort. The proprietor showed his politeness to a lady by following Elena Ivanovna to the case of monkeys.

So everything was going well, and nothing could have been foreseen. Elena Ivanovna was quite skittish in her raptures over the monkeys, and seemed completely taken up with them. With shrieks of delight she was continually turning to me, as though determined not to notice the proprietor, and kept gushing with laughter at the resemblance she detected between these monkeys and her intimate friends and acquaintances. I too, was amused, for the resemblance was unmistakable. The

German did not know whether to laugh or not, and so at last was reduced to frowning. And it was at that moment that a terrible, I may
say unnatural, scream set the room vibrating. Not knowing what to
think, for the first moment I stood still, numb with horror, but noticing
that Elena Ivanovna was screaming too, I quickly turned round—and
what did I behold! I saw—oh, heavens!—I saw the luckless Ivan Matveitch in the terrible jaws of the crocodile, held by them round the
waist, lifted horizontally in the air and desperately kicking. Then—one
moment, and no trace remained of him. But I must describe it in detail,
for I stood all the while motionless, and had time to watch the whole
process taking place before me with an attention and interest such as
I never remember to have felt before. "What," I thought at that critical
moment, "what if all that had happened to me instead of to Ivan Matveitch—how unpleasant it would have been for me!"

But to return to my story. The crocodile began by turning the unhappy Ivan Matveitch in his terrible jaws so that he could swallow his
legs first; then bringing up Ivan Matveitch, who kept trying to jump
out and clutching at the sides of the tank, sucked him down again as
far as his waist. Then bringing him up again, gulped him down, and
so again and again. In this way Ivan Matveitch was visibly disappearing
before our eyes. At last, with a final gulp, the crocodile swallowed my
cultured friend entirely, this time leaving no trace of him. From the
outside of the crocodile we could see the protuberances of Ivan Matveitch's figure as he passed down the inside of the monster. I was on
the point of screaming again when destiny played another treacherous
trick upon us. The crocodile made a tremendous effort, probably oppressed by the magnitude of the object he had swallowed, once more
opened his terrible jaws, and with a final hiccup he suddenly let the
head of Ivan Matveitch pop out for a second, with an expression of
despair on his face. In that brief instant the spectacles dropped off his
nose to the bottom of the tank. It seemed as though that despairing
countenance had only popped out to cast one last look on the objects
around it, to take its last farewell of all earthly pleasures. But it had not
time to carry out its intention; the crocodile made another effort, gave
a gulp and instantly it vanished again—this time forever. This appearance and disappearance of a still living human head was so horrible,
but at the same time—either from its rapidity and unexpectedness or
from the dropping of the spectacles—there was something so comic
about it that I suddenly quite unexpectedly exploded with laughter.
But pulling myself together and realizing that to laugh at such a moment was not the thing for an old family friend, I turned at once to
Elena Ivanovna and said with a sympathetic air:

"Now it's all over with our friend Ivan Matveitch!"

I cannot even attempt to describe how violent was the agitation of
Elena Ivanovna during the whole process. After the first scream she
seemed rooted to the spot, and stared at the catastrophe with apparent
indifference, though her eyes looked as though they were starting out
of her head; then she suddenly went off into a heart-rending wail, but
I seized her hands. At this instant the proprietor, too, who had at first
been also petrified by horror, suddenly clasped his hands and cried,
gazing upwards:

"Oh, my crocodile! *Oh mein allerliebster Karlchen! Mutter, Mutter,
Mutter!*"[3]

---

3. "Oh my best-beloved little Karl! Mother, Mother, Mother!"

A door at the rear of the room opened at this cry, and the *Mutter,* a rosy-cheeked, elderly but disheveled woman in a cap made her appearance, and rushed with a shriek to her German.

A perfect Bedlam followed. Elena Ivanovna kept shrieking out the same phrase, as though in a frenzy, "Flay him! flay him!" apparently entreating them—probably in a moment of oblivion—to flay somebody for something. The proprietor and *Mutter* took no notice whatever of either of us; they were both bellowing like calves over the crocodile.

"He did for himself! He will burst himself at once, for he did swallow a *ganz*[4] official!" cried the proprietor.

"*Unser Karlchen, unser allerliebster Karlchen wird sterben,*"[5] howled his wife.

"We are bereaved and without bread!" chimed in the proprietor.

"Flay him! flay him! flay him!" clamored Elena Ivanovna, clutching at the German's coat.

"He did tease the crocodile. For what did your man tease the crocodile?" cried the German, pulling away from her. "You will if *Karlchen wird burst,* therefore pay, *das war mein Sohn, das war mein einziger Sohn.*"[6]

I must own I was intensely indignant at the sight of such egoism in the German and the cold-heartedness of his disheveled *Mutter;* at the same time Elena Ivanovna's reiterated shriek of "Flay him! flay him!" troubled me even more and absorbed at last my whole attention, positively alarming me. I may as well say straight off that I entirely misunderstood this strange exclamation: it seemed to me that Elena Ivanovna had for the moment taken leave of her senses, but nevertheless wishing to avenge the loss of her beloved Ivan Matveitch, was demanding by way of compensation that the crocodile should be severely thrashed, while she was meaning something quite different. Looking round at the door, not without embarrassment, I began to entreat Elena Ivanovna to calm herself, and above all not to use the shocking word "flay." For such a reactionary desire here, in the midst of the Arcade and of the most cultured society, not two paces from the hall where at this very minute Mr. Lavrov[7] was perhaps delivering a public lecture, was not only impossible but unthinkable, and might at any moment bring upon us the hisses of culture and the caricatures of Mr. Stepanov. To my horror I was immediately proved to be correct in my alarmed suspicions: the curtain that divided the crocodile room from the little entry where the quarter-roubles were taken suddenly parted, and in the opening there appeared a figure with moustaches and beard, carrying a cap, with the upper part of its body bent a long way forward, though the feet were scrupulously held beyond the threshold of the crocodile room in order to avoid the necessity of paying the entrance money.

"Such a reactionary desire, madam," said the stranger, trying to avoid falling over in our direction and to remain standing outside the room, "does no credit to your development, and is conditioned by lack of phosphorus in your brain. You will be promptly held up to shame in the *Chronicle of Progress* and in our satirical prints . . ."

But he could not complete his remarks; the proprietor coming to him-

---

4. Whole.
5. "Our little Karl, our best-loved little Karl will die."
6. ". . . he was my son, my only son."
7. Pytor Lavrovich Lavrov (1823–1900), positivist political thinker, early Russian disciple of Marx, who, though he did not participate in the radical activities of the 1860s, greatly influenced them, especially through the Populists, by his teachings. Stepanov, below, was the caricaturist of *Iskrá* (*Spark*), a radical journal whose popularity and effectiveness was weakened soon after 1866 by censorship prosecutions and the lessening of protests and other radical activities.

self, and seeing with horror that a man was talking in the crocodile room without having paid entrance money, rushed furiously at the progressive stranger and turned him out with a punch from each fist. For a moment both vanished from our sight behind a curtain, and only then I grasped that the whole uproar was about nothing. Elena Ivanovna turned out quite innocent; she had, as I have mentioned already, no idea whatever of subjecting the crocodile to a degrading corporal punishment, and had simply expressed the desire that he should be opened and her husband released from his interior.

"What! You wish that my crocodile be perished!" the proprietor yelled, running in again. "No! let your husband be perished first, before my crocodile! . . . *Mein Vater* showed crocodile, *mein Grossvater* showed crocodile, *mein Sohn*[8] will show crocodile, and I will show crocodile! All will show crocodile! I am known to *ganz Europa.* and you are not known to *ganz Europa,* and you must pay me a *strafe!*"[9]

"*Ja, ja,*" put in the vindictive German woman, "we shall not let you go. *Strafe,* since Karlchen is burst!"

"And, indeed, it's useless to flay the creature," I added calmly, anxious to get Elena Ivanovna away home as quickly as possible, "as our dear Ivan Matveitch is by now probably soaring somewhere in the empyrean."

"My dear"—we suddenly heard, to our intense amazement, the voice of Ivan Matveitch—"my dear, my advice is to apply direct to the superintendent's office, as without the assistance of the police the German will never be made to see reason."

These words, uttered with firmness and aplomb, and expressing an exceptional presence of mind, for the first minute so astounded us that we could not believe our ears. But, of course, we ran at once to the crocodile's tank, and with equal reverence and incredulity listened to the unhappy captive. His voice was muffled, thin and even squeaky, as though it came from a considerable distance. It reminded one of a jocose person who, covering his mouth with a pillow, shouts from an adjoining room, trying to mimic the sound of two peasants calling to one another in a deserted plain or across a wide ravine—a performance to which I once had the pleasure of listening in a friend's house at Christmas.

"Ivan Matveitch, my dear, and so you are alive!" faltered Elena Ivanovna.

"Alive and well," answered Ivan Matveitch, "and, thanks to the Almighty, swallowed without any damage whatever. I am only uneasy as to the view my superiors may take of the incident; for after getting a permit to go abroad I've got into a crocodile, which seems anything but clever."

"But, my dear, don't trouble your head about being clever; first of all we must somehow excavate you from where you are," Elena Ivanovna interrupted.

"Excavate!" cried the proprietor. "I will not let my crocodile be excavated. Now the *publicum* will come many more, and I will *fünfzig*[1] kopeks ask and Karlchen will cease to burst."

"*Gott sei dank!*"[2] put in his wife.

"They are right," Ivan Matveitch observed tranquilly; "the principles of economics before everything."

---

8. "My father . . . my grandfather . . . my son."
9. "all of Europe . . . compensation."

1. Fifty.
2. "Thank God."

"My dear! I will fly at once to the authorities and lodge a complaint, for I feel that we cannot settle this mess by ourselves."

"I think so too," observed Ivan Matveitch; "but in our age of industrial crisis it is not easy to rip open the belly of a crocodile without economic compensation, and meanwhile the inevitable question presents itself: What will the German take for his crocodile? And with it another: How will it be paid? For, as you know, I have no means . . ."

"Perhaps out of your salary . . ." I observed timidly, but the proprietor interrupted me at once.

"I will not the crocodile sell; I will for three thousand the crocodile sell! I will for four thousand the crocodile sell! Now the *publicum* will come very many. I will for five thousand the crocodile sell!"

In fact he gave himself insufferable airs. Covetousness and a revolting greed gleamed joyfully in his eyes.

"I am going!" I cried indignantly.

"And I! I too! I shall go to Andrey Osipitch himself. I will soften him with my tears," whined Elena Ivanovna.

"Don't do that, my dear," Ivan Matveitch hastened to interpose. He had long been jealous of Andrey Osipitch on his wife's account, and he knew she would enjoy going to weep before a gentleman of refinement, for tears suited her. "And I don't advise you to do so either, my friend," he added, addressing me. "It's no good plunging headlong in that slap-dash way; there's no knowing what it may lead to. You had much better go today to Timofey Semyonitch, as though to pay an ordinary visit; he is an old-fashioned and by no means brilliant man, but he is trustworthy, and what matters most of all, he is straightforward. Give him my greetings and describe the circumstances of the case. And since I owe him seven rubles over our last game of cards, take the opportunity to pay him the money; that will soften the stern old man. In any case his advice may serve as a guide for us. And meanwhile take Elena Ivanovna home. . . . Calm yourself, my dear," he continued, addressing her. "I am weary of these outcries and feminine squabblings, and should like a nap. It's soft and warm in here, though I have hardly had time to look around in this unexpected haven."

"Look round! Why, is it light in there?" cried Elena Ivanovna in a tone of relief.

"I am surrounded by impenetrable night," answered the poor captive, "but I can feel and, so to speak, have a look round with my hands. . . . Good-bye; set your mind at rest and don't deny yourself recreation and diversion. Till tomorrow! And you, Semyon Semyonitch, come to me in the evening, and as you are absent-minded and may forget it, tie a knot in your handkerchief."

I confess I was glad to get away, for I was overtired and somewhat bored. Hastening to offer my arm to the disconsolate Elena Ivanovna, whose charms were only enhanced by her agitation, I hurriedly led her out of the crocodile room.

"The charge will be another quarter-ruble in the evening," the proprietor called after us.

"Oh, dear, how greedy they are!" said Elena Ivanovna, looking at herself in every mirror on the walls of the Arcade, and evidently aware that she was looking prettier than usual.

"The principles of economics," I answered with some emotion, proud that passers-by should see the lady on my arm.

"The principles of economics," she drawled in a touching little voice.

"I did not in the least understand what Ivan Matveitch said about those horrid economics just now."

"I will explain to you," I answered, and began at once telling her of the beneficial effects of the introduction of foreign capital into our country, upon which I had read an article in the *Petersburg News* and the *Voice* that morning.

"How strange it is," she interrupted, after listening for some time. "But do leave off, you horrid man. What nonsense you are talking. . . . Tell me, do I look purple?"

"You look perfect, and not purple!" I observed, seizing the opportunity to pay her a compliment.

"Naughty man!" she said complacently. "Poor Ivan Matveitch," she added a minute later, putting her little head on one side coquettishly. "I am really sorry for him. Oh, dear!" she cried suddenly, "how is he going to have his dinner . . . and . . . and . . . what will he do . . . if he wants anything?"

"An unforeseen question," I answered, perplexed in my turn. To tell the truth, it had not entered my head, so much more practical are women than we men in the solution of the problems of daily life!

"Poor dear! how could he have got into such a mess . . . nothing to amuse him, and in the dark. . . . How vexing it is that I have no photograph of him. . . . And so now I am a sort of widow," she added, with a seductive smile, evidently interested in her new position. "Hm! . . . I am sorry for him, though."

It was, in short, the expression of the very natural and intelligible grief of a young and interesting wife for the loss of her husband. I took her home at last, soothed her, and after dining with her and drinking a cup of aromatic coffee, set off at six o'clock to Timofey Semyonitch, calculating that at that hour all married people of settled habits would be sitting or lying down at home.

Having written this first chapter in a style appropriate to the incident recorded, I intend to proceed in a language more natural though less elevated, and I beg to forewarn the reader of the fact.

2

The venerable Timofey Semyonitch met me rather nervously, as though somewhat embarrassed. He led me to his tiny study and shut the door carefully, "that the children may not hinder us," he added with evident uneasiness. There he made me sit down on a chair by the writing table, sat down himself in an easy chair, wrapped round him the skirts of his old wadded dressing-gown, and assumed an official and even severe air, in readiness for anything, though he was not my chief nor Ivan Matveitch's, and had hitherto been reckoned as a colleague and even a friend.

"First of all," he said, "take note that I am not a person in authority, but just such a subordinate official as you and Ivan Matveitch. . . . I have nothing to do with it, and do not intend to mix myself up in the affair."

I was surprised to find that he apparently knew all about it already. In spite of that I told him the whole story over in detail. I spoke with positive excitement, for I was at that moment fulfilling the obligations of a true friend. He listened without special surprise, but with evident signs of suspicion.

"Only fancy," he said, "I always believed that this would be sure to happen to him."

"Why, Timofey Semyonitch? It is a very unusual incident in itself . . ."

"I admit it. But Ivan Matveitch's whole career in the service was leading up to this end. He was flighty—conceited indeed. It was always 'progress' and ideas of all sorts, and this is what progress brings people to!"

"But this is a most unusual incident and cannot possibly serve as a general rule for all progressives."

"Yes, indeed it can. You see, it's the effect of overeducation, I assure you. For overeducation leads people to poke their noses into all sorts of places, especially where they are not invited. Though perhaps you know best," he added, as though offended. "I am an old man and not of much education. I began as a soldier's son, and this year has been the iubilee[3] of my service."

"Oh, no, Timofey Semyonitch, not at all. On the contrary, Ivan Matveitch is eager for your advice; he is eager for your guidance. He implores it, so to say, with tears."

"So to say, with tears! Hm! Those are crocodile's tears and one cannot quite believe in them. Tell me, what possessed him to want to go abroad? And how could he afford to go? Why, he has no private means!"

"He had saved the money from his last bonus," I answered plaintively. "He only wanted to go for three months—to Switzerland . . . to the land of William Tell."

"William Tell? Hm!"

"He wanted to meet the spring at Naples, to see the museums, the customs, the animals . . ."

"Hm! The animals! I think it was simply from pride. What animals? Animals, indeed! Haven't we animals enough? We have museums, menageries, camels. There are bears quite close to Petersburg! And here he's got inside a crocodile himself . . ."

"Oh, come, Timofey Semyonitch! The man is in trouble, the man appeals to you as to a friend, as to an older relation, craves for advice—and you reproach him. Have pity at least on the unfortunate Elena Ivanovna!"

"You are speaking of his wife? A charming little lady," said Timofey Semyonitch, visibly softening and taking a pinch of snuff with relish. "Particularly prepossessing. And so plump, and always putting her pretty little head on one side. . . . Very agreeable. Andrey Osipitch was speaking of her only the other day."

"Speaking of her?"

"Yes, and in very flattering terms. Such a bust, he said, such eyes, such hair. . . . A sugar-plum, he said, not a lady—and then he laughed. He is still a young man, of course." Timofey Semyonitch blew his nose with a loud noise. "And yet, young though he is, what a career he is making for himself."

"That's quite a different thing, Timofey Semyonitch."

"Of course, of course."

"Well, what do you say then, Timofey Semyonitch?"

"Why, what can I do?"

"Give advice, guidance, as a man of experience, a relative! What are we to do? What steps are we to take? Go to the authorities and . . ."

3. Fiftieth year.

"To the authorities? Certainly not," Timofey Semyonitch replied hurriedly. "If you ask my advice, you had better, above all, hush the matter up and act, so to speak, as a private person. It is a suspicious incident, quite unheard of. Unheard of, above all; there is no precedent for it, and it is far from creditable. . . . And so discretion above all. . . . Let him lie there a bit. We must wait and see . . . ."

"But how can we wait and see, Timofey Semyonitch? What if he is stifled there?"

"Why should he be? I think you told me that he made himself fairly comfortable there?"

I told him the whole story over again. Timofey Semyonitch pondered.

"Hm!" he said, twisting his snuff-box in his hands. "To my mind it's really a good thing he should lie there a bit, instead of going abroad. Let him reflect at his leisure. Of course he mustn't be stifled, and so he must take measures to preserve his health, avoiding a cough, for instance, and so on. . . . And as for the German, it's my personal opinion he is within his rights, and even more so than the other side, because it was the other party who got into *his* crocodile without asking permission, and not *he* who got into Ivan Matveitch's crocodile without asking permission, though, so far as I recollect, the latter has no crocodile. And a crocodile is private property, and so it is impossible to slit him open without compensation."

"For the saving of human life, Timofey Semyonitch."

"Oh, well, that's a matter for the police. You must go to them."

"But Ivan Matveitch may be needed in the department. He may be asked for."

"Ivan Matveitch needed? Ha-ha! Besides, he is on leave, so that we may ignore him—let him inspect the countries of Europe! It will be a different matter if he doesn't turn up when his leave is over. Then we shall ask for him and make inquiries."

"Three months! Timofey Semyonitch, for pity's sake!"

"It's his own fault. Nobody thrust him there. At this rate we should have to get a nurse to look after him at government expense, and that is not allowed for in the regulations. But the chief point is that the crocodile is private property, so that the principles of economics apply in this question. And the principles of economics are paramount. Only the other evening, at Luka Andreitch's, Ignaty Prokofyitch was saying so. Do you know Ignaty Prokofyitch? A capitalist, in a big way of business, and he speaks so fluently. 'We need industrial development,' he said; 'there is very little development among us. We must create it. We must create capital, so we must create a middle class, the so-called bourgeoisie. And as we haven't capital we must attract it from abroad. We must, in the first place, give facilities to foreign companies to buy up lands in Russia as is done now abroad. The communal holding of land is poison, is ruin.' And, you know, he spoke with such heat; well, that's all right for him—a wealthy man, and not in the service. 'With the communal system,' he said, 'there will be no improvement in industrial development or agriculture. Foreign companies,' he said, 'must as far as possible buy up the whole of our land in big lots, and then split it up, split it up, split it up, in the smallest parts possible'—and do you know he pronounced the words 'split it up' with such determination—'and then sell it as private property. Or rather, not sell it, but simply let it. When,' he said, 'all the land is in the hands of foreign companies they can fix any rent they like. And so the peasant will work three

times as much for his daily bread and he can be turned out at pleasure. So that he will feel it, will be submissive and industrious, and will work three times as much for the same wages. But as it is, with the commune, what does he care? He knows he won't die of hunger, so he is lazy and drunken. And meanwhile money will be attracted into Russia, capital will be created and the bourgeoisie will spring up. The English political and literary paper, *The Times*, in an article the other day on our finances stated that the reason our financial position was so unsatisfactory was that we had no middle class, no big fortunes, no accommodating proletariat.' Ignaty Prokofyitch speaks well. He is an orator. He wants to lay a report on the subject before the authorities, and then to get it published in the *News*. That's something very different from verses like Ivan Matveitch's . . ."

"But how about Ivan Matveitch?" I put in, after letting the old man babble on.

Timofey Semyonitch was sometimes fond of talking and showing that he was not behind the times, but knew all about things.

"How about Ivan Matveitch? Why, I am coming to that. Here we are, anxious to bring foreign capital into the country—and only consider: as soon as the capital of a foreigner, who has been attracted to Petersburg, has been doubled through Ivan Matveitch, instead of protecting the foreign capitalist, we are proposing to rip open the belly of his original capital—the crocodile. Is it consistent? To my mind, Ivan Matveitch, as the true son of his fatherland, ought to rejoice and to be proud that through him the value of a foreign crocodile has been doubled and possibly even trebled. That's just what is wanted to attract capital. If one man succeeds, mind you, another will come with a crocodile, and a third will bring two or three of them at once, and capital will grow up about them—there you have a bourgeoisie. It must be encouraged."

"Upon my word, Timofey Semyonitch!" I cried, "you are demanding almost supernatural self-sacrifice from poor Ivan Matveitch."

"I demand nothing, and I beg you, before everything—as I have said already—to remember that I am not a person in authority and so cannot demand anything of anyone. I am speaking as a son of the fatherland, that is, not as the *Son of the Fatherland*, but as a son of the fatherland. Again, what possessed him to get into the crocodile? A respectable man, a man of good grade in the service, lawfully married —and then to behave like that! Is it consistent?"

"But it was an accident."

"Who knows? And where is the money to compensate the owner to come from?"

"Perhaps out of his salary, Timofey Semyonitch?"

"Would that be enough?"

"No, it wouldn't, Timofey Semyonitch," I answered sadly. "The proprietor was at first alarmed that the crocodile would burst, but as soon as he was sure that it was all right, he began to bluster and was delighted to think that he could double the charge for entry."

"Treble and quadruple perhaps! The public will simply stampede the place now, and crocodile owners are smart people. Besides, it's not Lent yet, and people are keen on diversions, and so I say again, the great thing is that Ivan Matveitch should preserve his incognito, don't let him be in a hurry. Let everybody know, perhaps, that he is in the crocodile, but don't let them be officially informed of it. Ivan Matveitch is in particularly favorable circumstances for that, for he is reckoned to

be abroad. It will be said he is in the crocodile, and we will refuse to believe it. That is how it can be managed. The great thing is that he should wait; and why should he be in a hurry?"

"Well, but if . . ."

"Don't worry, he has a good constitution . . ."

"Well, and afterwards, when he has waited?"

"Well, I won't conceal from you that the case is exceptional in the highest degree. One doesn't know what to think of it, and the worst of it is there is no precedent. If we had a precedent we might have something to go by. But as it is, what is one to say? It will certainly take time to settle it."

A happy thought flashed upon my mind.

"Cannot we arrange," I said, "that if he is destined to remain in the entrails of the monster and it is the will of Providence that he should remain alive, that he should send in a petition to be reckoned as still serving?"

"Hm! . . . Possibly as on leave and without salary . . ."

"But couldn't it be with salary?"

"On what grounds?"

"As sent on a special commission."

"What commission and where?"

"Why, into the entrails of the crocodile. . . . So to speak, for exploration, for investigation of the facts on the spot. It would, of course, be a novelty, but that is progressive and would at the same time show zeal for enlightenment."

Timofey Semyonitch thought a little.

"To send a special official," he said at last, "to the inside of a crocodile to conduct a special inquiry is, in my personal opinion, an absurdity. It is not in the regulations. And what sort of special inquiry could there be there?"

"The scientific study of nature on the spot, in the living subject. The natural sciences are all the fashion nowadays, botany. . . . He could live there and report his observations. . . . For instance, concerning digestion or simply habits. For the sake of accumulating facts."

"You mean as statistics. Well, I am no great authority on that subject, indeed I am no philosopher at all. You say 'facts'—we are overwhelmed with facts as it is, and don't know what to do with them. Besides, statistics are a danger."

"In what way?"

"They are a danger. Moreover, you will admit he will report facts, so to speak, lying like a log. And, can one do one's official duties lying like a log? That would be another novelty and a dangerous one; and again, there is no precedent for it. If we had any sort of precedent for it, then, to my thinking, he might have been given the job."

"But no live crocodiles have been brought over hitherto, Timofey Semyonitch."

"Hm . . . yes," he reflected again. "Your objection is a just one, if you like, and might indeed serve as a ground for carrying the matter further; but consider again, that if with the arrival of living crocodiles government clerks begin to disappear, and then on the ground that they are warm and comfortable there, expect to receive the official sanction for their position, and then take their ease there . . . you must admit it would be a bad example. We should have everyone trying to go the same way to get a salary for nothing."

"Do your best for him, Timofey Semyonitch. By the way, Ivan

Matveitch asked me to give you seven rubles he had lost to you at cards."

"Ah, he lost that the other day at Nikifor Nikiforitch's. I remember. And how gay and amusing he was—and now!"

The old man was genuinely touched.

"Intercede for him, Timofey Semyonitch!"

"I will do my best. I will speak in my own name, as a private person, as though I were asking for information. And meanwhile, you find out indirectly, unofficially, how much would the proprietor consent to take for his crocodile?"

Timofey Semyonitch was visibly more friendly.

"Certainly," I answered. "And I will come back to you at once to report."

"And his wife . . . is she alone now? Is she depressed?"

"You should call on her, Timofey Semyonitch."

"I will. I thought of doing so before; it's a good opportunity. . . . And what on earth possessed him to go and look at the crocodile. Though, indeed, I should like to see it myself."

"Go and see the poor fellow, Timofey Semyonitch."

"I will. Of course, I don't want to raise his hopes by doing so. I shall go as a private person. . . . Well, good-bye, I am going to Nikifor Nikiforitch's again; shall you be there?"

"No, I am going to see the poor prisoner."

"Yes, now he is a prisoner! . . . Ah, that's what comes of thoughtlessness!"

I said good-bye to the old man. Ideas of all kinds were straying through my mind. A good-natured and most honest man, Timofey Semyonitch, yet, as I left him, I felt pleased at the thought that he had celebrated his fiftieth year of service, and that Timofey Semyonitchs are now a rarity among us. I flew at once, of course, to the Arcade to tell poor Ivan Matveitch all the news. And, indeed, I was moved by curiosity to know how he was getting on in the crocodile and how it was possible to live in a crocodile. And, indeed, was it possible to live in a crocodile at all? At times it really seemed to me as though it were all an outlandish, monstrous dream, especially as an outlandish monster was the chief figure in it.

3

And yet it was not a dream, but actual, indubitable fact. Should I be telling the story if it were not? But to continue.

It was late, about nine o'clock, before I reached the Arcade, and I had to go into the crocodile room by the back entrance, for the German had closed the shop earlier than usual that evening. Now in the seclusion of domesticity he was walking about in a greasy old frock coat, but he seemed three times as pleased as he had been in the morning. It was evidently that he had no apprehensions now, and that the public had been coming "many more." The *Mutter* came out later, evidently to keep an eye on me. The German and the *Mutter* frequently whispered together. Although the shop was closed he charged me a quarter-ruble. What unnecessary exactitude!

"You will every time pay; the public will one ruble, and you one quarter pay; for you are the good friend of your good friend; and I a friend respect . . ."

"Are you alive, are you alive, my cultured friend?" I cried, as I approached the crocodile, expecting my words to reach Ivan Matveitch from a distance and to flatter his vanity.

"Alive and well," he answered, as though from a long way off or from under the bed, though I was standing close beside him. "Alive and well; but of that later. . . . How are things going?"

As though purposely not hearing the question, I was just beginning with sympathetic haste to question him how he was, what it was like in the crocodile, and what, in fact, there was inside a crocodile. Both friendship and common civility demanded this. But with capricious annoyance he interrupted me.

"How are things going?" he shouted, in a shrill and on this occasion particularly revolting voice, addressing me peremptorily as usual.

I described to him my whole conversation with Timofey Semyonitch down to the smallest detail. As I told my story I tried to show my resentment in my voice.

"The old man is right," Ivan Matveitch pronounced as abruptly as usual in his conversation with me. "I like practical people, and can't endure sentimental milksops. I am ready to admit, however, that your idea about a special commission is not altogether absurd. I certainly have a great deal to report, both from a scientific and from an ethical point of view. But now all this has taken a new and unexpected aspect, and it is not worth while to trouble about mere salary. Listen attentively. Are you sitting down?"

"No, I am standing up."

"Sit down on the floor if there is nothing else, and listen attentively."

Resentfully I took a chair and put it down on the floor with a bang, in my anger.

"Listen," he began dictatorially. "The public came today in masses. There was no room left in the evening, and the police came in to keep order. At eight o'clock, that is, earlier than usual, the proprietor thought it necessary to close the shop and end the exhibition to count the money he had taken and prepare for tomorrow more conveniently. So I know there will be a regular fair tomorrow. So we may assume that all the most cultivated people in the capital, the ladies of the best society, the foreign ambassadors, the leading lawyers and so on, will all be present. What's more, people will be flowing here from the remotest provinces of our vast and interesting empire. The upshot of it is that I am the cynosure of all eyes, and though hidden to sight, I am eminent. I shall teach the idle crowd. Taught by experience, I shall be an example of greatness and resignation to fate! I shall be, so to say, a pulpit from which to instruct mankind. The mere biological details I can furnish about the monster I am inhabiting are of priceless value. And so, far from repining at what has happened, I confidently hope for the most brilliant of careers."

"You won't find it wearisome?" I asked sarcastically.

What irritated me more than anything was the extreme pomposity of his language. Nevertheless, it all rather disconcerted me. "What on earth, what, can this frivolous blockhead find to be so cocky about?" I muttered to myself. "He ought to be crying instead of being cocky."

"No!" he answered my observation sharply, "for I am full of great ideas, only now can I at leisure ponder over the amelioration of the lot of humanity. Truth and light will come forth now from the crocodile. I shall certainly develop a new economic theory of my own and I

shall be proud of it—which I have hitherto been prevented from doing by my official duties and by trivial distractions. I shall refute everything and be a new Fourier.[4] By the way, did you give Timofey Semyonitch the seven rubles?"

"Yes, out of my own pocket," I answered, trying to emphasize that fact in my voice.

"We will settle it," he answered superciliously. "I confidently expect my salary to be raised, for who should get a raise if not I? I am of the utmost service now. But to business. My wife?"

"You are, I suppose, inquiring after Elena Ivanovna?"

"My wife?" he shouted, this time in a positive squeal.

There was no help for it! Meekly, though gnashing my teeth, I told how I had left Elena Ivanovna. He did not even hear me out.

"I have special plans in regard to her," he began impatiently. "If I am celebrated *here*, I wish her to be celebrated *there*. Savants, poets, philosophers, foreign mineralogists, statesmen, after conversing in the morning with me, will visit her *salon* in the evening. From next week onwards she must have an 'At Home' every evening. With my salary doubled, we shall have the means for entertaining, and as the entertainment must not go beyond tea and hired footmen—that's settled. Both here and there they will talk of me. I have long thirsted for an opportunity for being talked about, but could not attain it, fettered by my humble position and low grade in the service. And now all this has been attained by a simple gulp on the part of the crocodile. Every word of mine will be listened to, every utterance will be thought over, repeated, printed. And I'll teach them what I am worth! They shall understand at last what alibities they have allowed to vanish in the entrails of a monster. 'This man might have been Foreign Minister or might have ruled a kingdom,' some will say. 'And that man did not rule a kingdom,' others will say. In what way am I inferior to a Garnier-Pagesishky[5] or whatever they are called? My wife must be a worthy second—I have brains, she has beauty and charm. 'She is beautiful, and that is why she is his wife,' some will say. 'She is beautiful *because* she is his wife,' others will amend. To be ready for anything let Elena Ivanovna buy tomorrow the Encyclopædia edited by Andrey Kraevsky,[6] that she may be able to converse on any topic. Above all, let her be sure to read the political leader in the *Petersburg News*, comparing it every day with the *Voice*. I imagine that the proprietor will consent to take me sometimes with the crocodile to my wife's brilliant *salon*. I will be in a tank in the middle of the magnificent drawing room, and I will scintillate with witticisms which I will prepare in the morning. To the statesman I will impart my projects; to the poet I will speak in rhyme; with the ladies I can be amusing and charming without impropriety, since I shall be no danger to their husbands' peace of mind. To all the rest I shall serve as a pattern of resignation to fate and the will of Providence. I shall make my wife a brilliant literary lady; I shall bring her forward and explain her to the

4. François Marie Fourier (1772–1837), French sociologist and major figure in 19th-century radical and liberal traditions, proposed reorganizing society into small communes.

5. Russianization of Louis Antoine Garnier-Pagès (1803–1878), French republican leader, member of provisional government of 1848, Minister of Finance and, during the Second Empire (1852–70),

leader of republican opposition to Napoleon III.

6. Andrey Alexandrovich Kraevsky (1810–1889), a rather hard-bargaining publisher with whom Dostoevsky had frequent, not always happy dealings; editor of *Fatherland Notes*, perhaps alluded to as *Son of the Fatherland* above, and at this time of *The Voice*, mentioned below; encyclopedia not identified.

public; as my wife she must be full of the most striking virtues; and if they are right in calling Andrey Alexandrovitch our Russian Alfred de Musset, they will be still more right in calling her our Russian Yevgenia Tour."[7]

I must confess that although this wild nonsense was rather in Ivan Matveitch's habitual style, it did occur to me that he was in a fever and delirious. It was the same, everyday Ivan Matveitch, but magnified twenty times.

"My friend," I asked him, "are you hoping for a long life? Tell me, in fact, are you well? How do you eat, how do you sleep, how do you breathe? I am your friend, and you must admit that the incident is most unnatural, and consequently my curiosity is most natural."

"Idle curiosity and nothing else," he pronounced sententiously, "but you shall be satisfied. You ask how I am managing in the entrails of the monster? To begin with, the crocodile, to my amusement, turns out to be perfectly empty. His inside consists of a sort of huge empty sack of gutta-percha, like the elastic goods sold in the Gorohovy Street, in the Morskaya, and, if I am not mistaken, in the Voznesensky Prospect. Otherwise, if you think of it, how could I find room?"

"Is it possible?" I cried, in a surprise that may well be understood. "Can the crocodile be perfectly empty?"

"Perfectly," Ivan Matveitch maintained sternly and impressively. "And in all probability, it is so constructed by the laws of Nature. The crocodile possesses nothing but jaws furnished with sharp teeth, and besides the jaws, a tail of considerable length—that is all, properly speaking. The middle part between these two extremities is an empty space enclosed by something of the nature of gutta-percha, probably really gutta-percha."

"But the ribs, the stomach, the intestines, the liver, the heart?" I interrupted quite angrily.

"There is nothing, absolutely nothing of all that, and probably there never has been. All that is the idle fancy of frivolous travelers. As one inflates an air-cushion, I am now with my person inflating the crocodile. He is incredibly elastic. Indeed, you might, as the friend of the family, get in with me if you were generous and self-sacrificing enough—and even with you here there would be room to spare. I even think that in the last resort I might send for Elena Ivanovna. However, this void, hollow formation of the crocodile is quite in keeping with the teachings of natural science. If, for instance, one had to construct a new crocodile, the question would naturally present itself. What is the fundamental characteristic of the crocodile? The answer is clear: to swallow human beings. How is one, in constructing the crocodile, to secure that he should swallow people? The answer is clearer still: construct him hollow. It was settled by physics long ago that Nature abhors a vacuum. Hence the inside of the crocodile must be hollow so that it may abhor the vacuum, and consequently swallow and so fill itself with anything it can come across. And that is the sole rational cause why every crocodile swallows men. It is not the same in the

---

7. Andrey Alexandrovich is Kraevsky (see note 6). Alfred de Musset (1810–1857), French Romantic poet, dandy, singer, lover of George Sand, whose best known works are the four lyric poems *Nuits* (*Nights*) which are dialogues between the poet and his muse concerning disappointed love and the autobiographical novel *Confession d'un enfant du siècle* (*Confession of a Child of the Century*) which maintains that love is the source of all art and typified for many the "malady" or "sickness" of the Romantic era of the 19th century. "Yevgenia Tour" (or "Tur") was the pseudonym of Countess Sal'yas (1810–1881), author of novels, criticism, and children's stories.

constitution of man: the emptier a man's head is, for instance, the less he feels the thirst to fill it, and that is the one exception to the general rule. It is all clear as day to me now. I have deduced it by my own observation and experience, being, so to say, in the very bowels of Nature, in its retort, listening to the throbbing of its pulse. Even etymology supports me, for the very word crocodile means voracity. Crocodile—*crocodillo*—is evidently an Italian word, dating perhaps from the Egyptian Pharaohs, and evidently derived from the French verb *croquer*, which means to eat, to devour, in general to absorb nourishment.[8] All these remarks I intend to deliver as my first lecture in Elena Ivanovna's *salon* when they take me there in the tank."

"My friend, oughtn't you at least to take some purgative?" I cried involuntarily.

"He is in a fever, a fever, he is feverish!" I repeated to myself in alarm.

"Nonsense!" he answered contemptuously. "Besides, in my present position it would be most inconvenient. I knew, though, you would be sure to talk of taking medicine."

"But, my friend, how . . . how do you take food now? Have you dined today?"

"No, but I am not hungry, and most likely I shall never take food again. And that, too, is quite natural; filling the whole interior of the crocodile I make him feel always full. Now he need not be fed for some years. On the other hand, nourished by me, he will naturally impart to me all the vital juices of his body; it is the same as with some accomplished coquettes who embed themselves and their whole persons for the night in raw steak, and then, after their morning bath, are fresh, supple, buxom and fascinating. In that way nourishing the crocodile, I myself obtain nourishment from him, consequently we mutually nourish one another. But as it is difficult even for a crocodile to digest a man like me, he must, no doubt, be conscious of a certain weight in his stomach—an organ which he does not, however, possess —and that is why, to avoid causing the creature suffering, I do not often turn over, and although I could turn over I do not do so from humanitarian motives. This is the one drawback of my present position, and in an allegorical sense Timofey Semyonitch was right in saying I was lying like a log. But I will prove that even lying like a log—nay, that only lying like a log—one can revolutionize the lot of mankind. All the great ideas and movements of our newspapers and magazines have evidently been the work of men who were lying like logs; that is why they call them divorced from the realities of life—but what does it matter, their saying that! I am constructing now a complete system of my own, and you wouldn't believe how easy it is! You have only to creep into a secluded corner or into a crocodile, to shut your eyes, and you immediately devise a perfect millennium for mankind. When you went away this afternoon I set to work at once and have already invented three systems, now I am preparing the fourth. It is true that at first one must refute everything that has gone before, but from the crocodile it is so easy to refute it; besides, it all becomes clearer, seen from the inside of the crocodile. . . . There are some drawbacks, though small ones, in my position, however; it is somewhat damp here and covered with a sort of slime; moreover, there is rather a smell of india-

---

8. False etymology; *crocodile* derives from two Greek words, *kroka* and *drilos* meaning *gravel* (apparently reference to the hide) and *worm*.

rubber exactly like the smell of my old galoshes. That is all, there are no other drawbacks."

"Ivan Matveitch," I interrupted, "all this is a miracle in which I can scarcely believe. And can you, can you intend never to dine again?"

"What trivial nonsense you are troubling about, you thoughtless, frivolous creature! I talk to you about great ideas, and you . . . Understand that I am sufficiently nourished by the great ideas which light up the darkness in which I am enveloped. The good-natured proprietor has, however, after consulting the kindly *Mutter*, decided with her that they will every morning insert into the monster's jaws a bent metal tube, something like a whistle pipe, by means of which I can absorb coffee or broth with bread soaked in it. The pipe has already been bespoken in the neighborhood, but I think this is superfluous luxury. I hope to live at least a thousand years, if it is true that crocodiles live so long, which, by the way—good thing I thought of it—you had better look up in some natural history tomorrow and tell me, for I may have been mistaken and have mixed it up with some excavated monster. There is only one reflection rather troubles me: as I am dressed in cloth and have boots on, the crocodile can obviously not digest me. Besides, I am alive, and so am opposing the process of digestion with my whole will power; for you can understand that I do not wish to be turned into what all nourishment turns into, for that would be too humiliating for me. But there is one thing I am afraid of: in a thousand years the cloth of my coat, unfortunately of Russian make, may decay, and then, left without clothing, I might perhaps, in spite of my indignation, begin to be digested; and though by day nothing would induce me to allow it, at night, in my sleep, when a man's will deserts him, I may be overtaken by the humiliating destiny of a potato, a pancake, or veal. Such an idea reduces me to fury. This alone is an argument for the revision of the tariff and the encouragement of the importation of English cloth, which is stronger and so will withstand Nature longer when one is swallowed by a crocodile. At the first opportunity I will impart this idea to some statesman and at the same time to the political writers on our Petersburg dailies. Let them publish it abroad. I trust this will not be the only idea they will borrow from me. I foresee that every morning a regular crowd of them, provided with quarter-rubles from the editorial office, will be flocking round me to seize my ideas on the telegrams of the previous day. In brief, the future presents itself to me in the rosiest light."

"Fever, fever!" I whispered to myself.

"My friend, and freedom?" I asked, wishing to learn his views thoroughly. "You are, so to speak, in prison, while every man has a right to the enjoyment of freedom."

"You are a fool," he answered. "Savages love independence, wise men love order; and if there is no order . . ."

"Ivan Matveitch, spare me, please!"

"Hold your tongue and listen!" he squealed, vexed at my interrupting him. "Never has my spirit soared as now. In my narrow refuge there is only one thing that I dread—the literary criticisms of the monthlies and the hiss of our satirical papers. I am afraid that thoughtless visitors, stupid and envious people and nihilists in general, may turn me into ridicule. But I will take measures. I am impatiently awaiting the response of the public tomorrow, and especially the opinion of the newspapers. You must tell me about the papers tomorrow."

"Very good; tomorrow I will bring a perfect pile of papers with me."

"Tomorrow it is too soon to expect reports in the newspapers, for it will take four days for it to be advertised. But from today come to me every evening by the back way through the yard. I am intending to employ you as my secretary. You shall read the newspapers and magazines to me, and I will dictate to you my ideas and give you commissions. Be particularly careful not to forget the foreign telegrams. Let all the European telegrams be here every day. But enough; most likely you are sleepy by now. Go home, and do not think of what I said just now about criticisms: I am not afraid of it, for the critics themselves are in a critical position. One has only to be wise and virtuous and one will certainly get onto a pedestal. If not Socrates, then Diogenes,[9] or perhaps both of them together—that is my future role among mankind."

So frivolously and boastfully did Ivan Matveitch hasten to express himself before me, like feverish weak-willed women who, as we are told by the proverb, cannot keep a secret. All that he told me about the crocodile struck me as most suspicious. How was it possible that the crocodile was absolutely hollow? I don't mind betting that he was bragging from vanity and partly to humiliate me. It is true that he was an invalid and one must make allowances for invalids; but I must frankly confess, I never could endure Ivan Matveitch. I have been trying all my life, from a child up, to escape from his tutelage and have not been able to! A thousand times over I have been tempted to break with him altogether, and every time I have been drawn to him again, as though I were still hoping to prove something to him or to revenge myself on him. A strange thing, this friendship! I can positively assert that nine-tenths of my friendship for him was made up of malice. On this occasion, however, we parted with genuine feeling.

"Your friend a very clever man!" the German said to me in an **under**tone as he moved to see me out; he had been listening all **the time** attentively to our conversation.

"À *propos*," I said, "while I think of it: how much would you ask for your crocodile in case anyone wanted to buy it?"

Ivan Matveitch, who heard the question, was waiting with curiosity for the answer; it was evident that he did not want the German to ask too little; anyway, he cleared his throat in a peculiar way on hearing my question.

At first the German would not listen—was positively angry.

"No one will dare my own crocodile to buy!" he cried furiously, and turned as red as a boiled lobster. "Me not want to sell the crocodile! I would not for the crocodile a million thalers[1] take. I took a hundred and thirty thalers from the public today, and I shall tomorrow ten thousand take, and then a hundred thousand every day I shall take. I will not him sell."

Ivan Matveitch positively chuckled with satisfaction. Controlling myself—for I felt it was a duty to my friend—I hinted coolly and reasonably to the crazy German that his calculations were not quite correct, that if he makes a hundred thousand every day, all Petersburg will have visited him in four days, and then there will be no one left

---

9. Greek Cynic philosopher (412?–323 B.C.) traditionally held to have searched unsuccessfully for an honest man and, appropriately, to have lived in a tub to show his austerity.

1. Dollar; coin of many German states in the 19th century with varying and wildly fluctuating value, but here apparently equivalent to a ruble.

to bring him rubles, that life and death are in God's hands, that the crocodile may burst or Ivan Matveitch may fall ill and die, and so on and so on.

The German grew pensive.

"I will him drops from the chemist's[2] get," he said, after pondering, "and will save your friend that he die not."

"Drops are all very well," I answered, "but consider, too, that the thing may get into the law courts. Ivan Matveitch's wife may demand the restitution of her lawful spouse. You are intending to get rich, but do you intend to give Elena Ivanovna a pension?"

"No, me not intend," said the German in stern decision.

"No, we not intend," said the *Mutter*, with positive malignancy.

"And so would it not be better for you to accept something now, at once, a secure and solid though moderate sum, than to leave things to chance? I ought to tell you that I am inquiring simply from curiosity."

The German drew the *Mutter* aside to consult with her in a corner where there stood a case with the largest and ugliest monkey of his collection.

"Well, you will see!" said Ivan Matveitch.

As for me, I was at that moment burning with the desire, first, to give the German a thrashing, next, to give the *Mutter* an even sounder one, and, thirdly, to give Ivan Matveitch the soundest thrashing of all for his boundless vanity. But all this paled beside the answer of the rapacious German.

After consultation with the *Mutter* he demanded for his crocodile fifty thousand rubles in bonds of the last Russian loan with lottery voucher attached, a brick house in Gorohovy Street with a chemist's shop attached, and in addition the rank of Russian colonel.

"You see!" Ivan Matveitch cried triumphantly. "I told you so! Apart from this last senseless desire for the rank of a colonel, he is perfectly right, for he fully understands the present value of the monster he is exhibiting. The economic principle before everything!"

"Upon my word!" I cried furiously to the German. "But what should you be made a colonel for? What exploit have you performed? What service have you done? In what way have you gained military glory? You are really crazy!"

"Crazy!" cried the German, offended. "No, a person very sensible, but you very stupid! I have a colonel deserved for that I have a crocodile shown and in him a live *hofrath*[3] sitting! And a Russian can a crocodile not show and a live *hofrath* in him sitting! Me extremely clever man and much wish colonel to be!"

"Well, good-bye, then, Ivan Matveitch!" I cried, shaking with fury, and I went out of the crocodile room almost at a run.

I felt that in another minute I could not have answered for myself. The unnatural expectations of these two blockheads were insupportable. The cold air refreshed me and somewhat moderated my indignation. At last, after spitting vigorously fifteen times on each side, I took a cab, got home, undressed and flung myself into bed. What vexed me more than anything was my having become his secretary. Now I was to die of boredom there every evening, doing the duty of a true friend! I was ready to beat myself for it, and I did, in fact, after putting out the candle and pulling up the bedclothes, punch myself several times on

2. Pharmacist's.
3. Privy Councillor, several ranks higher   than Ivan Matveitch's actual rank.

the head and various parts of my body. That somewhat relieved me, and at last I fell asleep fairly soundly, in fact, for I was very tired. All night long I could dream of nothing but monkeys, but toward morning I dreamed of Elena Ivanovna.

4

The monkeys I dreamed about, I surmise, because they were shut up in the case at the German's; but Elena Ivanovna was a different story.

I may as well say at once, I loved the lady, but I make haste—post-haste—to make a qualification. I loved her as a father, neither more nor less. I judge that because I often felt an irresistible desire to kiss her little head or her rosy cheek. And though I never carried out this inclination, I would not have refused even to kiss her lips. And not merely her lips, but her teeth, which always gleamed so charmingly like two rows of pretty, well-matched pearls when she laughed. She laughed extraordinarily often. Ivan Matveitch in demonstrative moments used to call her his "darling absurdity"—a name extremely happy and appropriate. She was a perfect sugar-plum, and that was all one could say of her. Therefore I am utterly at a loss to understand what possessed Ivan Matveitch to imagine his wife as a Russian Yevgenia Tour? Anyway, my dream, with the exception of the monkeys, left a most pleasant impression upon me, and going over all the incidents of the previous day as I drank my morning cup of tea, I resolved to go and see Elena Ivanovna at once on my way to the office—which, indeed, I was bound to do as the friend of the family.

In a tiny little room out of the bedroom—the so-called little drawing room, though their big drawing room was little too—Elena Ivanovna was sitting, in some half-transparent morning wrapper, on a smart little sofa before a little tea-table, drinking coffee out of a little cup in which she was dipping a minute biscuit. She was ravishingly pretty, but struck me as being at the same time rather pensive.

"Ah, that's you, naughty man!" she said, greeting me with an absent-minded smile. "Sit down, feather-head, have some coffee. Well, what were you doing yesterday? Were you at the masquerade?"

"Why, were you? I don't go. you know. Besides. yesterday I was visiting our captive. . . ." I sighed and assumed a pious expression as I took the coffee.

"Whom? . . . What captive? . . . Oh, yes! Poor fellow! Well, how is he—bored? Do you know . . . I wanted to ask you . . . I suppose I can ask for a divorce now?"

"A divorce!" I cried in indignation and almost spilled the coffee. "It's that swarthy fellow," I thought to myself bitterly.

There was a certain swarthy gentleman with little moustaches who was something in the architectural line, and who came far too often to see them, and was extremely skilful in amusing Elena Ivanovna. I must confess I hated him and there was no doubt that he had succeeded in seeing Elena Ivanovna yesterday either at the masquerade or even here, and putting all sorts of nonsense into her head.

"Why," Elena Ivanovna rattled off hurriedly, as though it were a lesson she had learned, "if he is going to stay on in the crocodile, perhaps not come back all his life, while I sit waiting for him here! A husband ought to live at home, and not in a crocodile. . . ."

"But this was an unforeseen occurrence," I was beginning, in very comprehensible agitation.

"Oh, no, don't talk to me, I won't listen, I won't listen," she cried,

suddenly getting quite cross. "You are always against me, you wretch! There's no doing anything with you, you will never give me any advice! Other people tell me that I can get a divorce because Ivan Matveitch will not get his salary now."

"Elena Ivanovna! is it you I hear!" I exclaimed pathetically. "What villain could have put such an idea into your head? And divorce on such a trivial ground as a salary is quite impossible. And poor Ivan Matveitch, poor Ivan Matveitch is, so to speak, burning with love for you even in the bowels of the monster. What's more, he is melting away with love like a lump of sugar. Yesterday while you were enjoying yourself at the masquerade, he was saying that he might in the last resort send for you as his lawful spouse to join him in the entrails of the monster, especially as it appears the crocodile is exceedingly roomy, not only able to accommodate two but even three persons. . . ."

And then I told her all that interesting part of my conversation the night before with Ivan Matveitch.

"What, what!" she cried, in surprise. "You want me to get into the monster too, to be with Ivan Matveitch? What an idea! And how am I to get in there, in my hat and crinoline? Heavens, what foolishness! And what should I look like while I was getting into it, and very likely there would be someone there to see me! It's absurd! And what should I have to eat there? And . . . and . . . and what should I do there when . . . Oh, my goodness, what will they think of next? . . . And what should I have to amuse me there? . . . You say there's a smell of gutta-percha? And what should I do if we quarreled—should we have to go on staying there side by side? Foo, how horrid!"

"I agree, I agree with all those arguments, my sweet Elena Ivanovna," I interrupted, striving to express myself with that natural enthusiasm which always overtakes a man when he feels the truth is on his side. "But one thing you have not appreciated in all this, you have not realized that he cannot live without you if he is inviting you there; that is a proof of love, passionate, faithful, ardent love. . . . You have thought too little of his love, dear Elena Ivanovna!"

"I won't, I won't, I won't hear anything about it!" waving me off with her pretty little hand with glistening pink nails that had just been washed and polished. "Horrid man! You will reduce me to tears! Get into it yourself, if you like the prospect. You are his friend, get in and keep him company, and spend your life discussing some tedious science. . . ."

"You are wrong to laugh at this suggestion"—I checked the frivolous woman with dignity—"Ivan Matveitch has invited me as it is. You, of course, are summoned there by duty; for me, it would be an act of generosity. But when Ivan Matveitch described to me last night the elasticity of the crocodile, he hinted very plainly that there would be room not only for you two, but for me also as a friend of the family, especially if I wished to join you, and therefore . . ."

"How so, the three of us!" cried Elena Ivanovna, looking at me in surprise. "Why, how should we . . . are we going to be all three there together? Ha-ha-ha! How silly you both are! Ha-ha-ha! I shall certainly pinch you all the time, you wretch! Ha-ha-ha! Ha-ha-ha!"

And falling back on the sofa, she laughed till she cried. All this—the tears and the laughter—were so fascinating that I could not resist rushing eagerly to kiss her hand, which she did not oppose, though she did pinch my ears lightly as a sign of reconciliation.

Then we both grew very cheerful, and I described to her in detail all Ivan Matveitch's plans. The thought of her evening receptions and her *salon* pleased her very much.

"Only I should need a great many new dresses," she observed, "and so Ivan Matveitch must send me as much of his salary as possible and as soon as possible. Only . . . only I don't know about that," she added thoughtfully. "How can he be brought here in the tank? That's very absurd. I don't want my husband to be carried about in a tank. I should feel quite ashamed for my visitors to see it. . . . I don't want that, no, I don't."

"By the way, while I think of it, was Timofey Semyonitch here yesterday?"

"Oh, yes, he was; he came to comfort me, and do you know, we played cards all the time. He played for sweetmeats, and if I lost he was to kiss my hands. What a wretch he is! And only fancy, he almost came to the masquerade with me, really!"

"He was carried away by his feelings!" I observed. "And who would not be with you, you charmer?"

"Oh, get along with your compliments! Stay, I'll give you a pinch as a parting present. I've learned to pinch awfully well lately. Well, what do you say to that? By the way, you say Ivan Matveitch spoke several times of me yesterday?"

"N-no, not exactly. . . . I must say he is thinking more now of the fate of humanity, and wants . . ."

"Oh, let him! You needn't go on! I am sure it's fearfully boring. I'll go and see him some time. I shall certainly go tomorrow. Only not today; I've got a headache, and besides, there will be such a lot of people there today. . . . They'll say, 'That's his wife,' and I shall feel ashamed. . . . Good-bye. You will be . . . there this evening, won't you?"

"To see him, yes. He asked me to go and take him the papers."

"That's capital. Go and read to him. But don't come and see me today. I am not well, and perhaps I may go and see someone. Good-bye, you naughty man."

"It's that swarthy fellow is going to see her this evening," I thought.

At the office, of course, I gave no sign of being consumed by these cares and anxieties. But soon I noticed some of the most progressive papers seemed to be passing particularly rapidly from hand to hand among my colleagues, and were being read with an extremely serious expression of face. The first one that reached me was the *News-sheet,* a paper of no particular party but humanitarian in general, for which it was regarded with contempt among us, though it was read. Not without surprise I read in it the following paragraph:

"Yesterday strange rumors were circulating among the spacious ways and sumptuous buildings of our vast metropolis. A certain well-known *bon-vivant* of the highest society, probably weary of the *cuisine* at Borel's and at the X. Club, went into the Arcade, into the place where an immense crocodile recently brought to the metropolis is being exhibited, and insisted on its being prepared for his dinner. After bargaining with the proprietor he at once set to work to devour him (that is, not the proprietor, a very meek and punctilious German, but his crocodile), cutting juicy morsels with his penknife from the living animal, and swallowing them with extraordinary rapidity. By degrees the whole crocodile disappeared into the vast recesses of his stomach, so

that he was even on the point of attacking an ichneumon,[4] constant companion of the crocodile, probably imagining that the latter would be as savory. We are by no means opposed to that new article of diet with which foreign *gourmands* have long been familiar. We have, indeed, predicted that it would come. English lords and travelers make up regular parties for catching crocodiles in Egypt, and consume the back of the monster cooked like beefsteak, with mustard, onions and potatoes. The French who followed in the train of Lesseps[5] prefer the paws baked in hot ashes, which they do, however, in opposition to the English, who laugh at them. Probably both ways would be appreciated among us. For our part, we are delighted at a new branch of industry, of which our great and varied fatherland stands preeminently in need. Probably before a year is out crocodiles will be brought in hundreds to replace this first one, lost in the stomach of a Petersburg *gourmand*. And why should not the crocodile be acclimatized among us in Russia? If the water of the Neva is too cold for these interesting strangers, there are ponds in the capital and rivers and lakes outside it. Why not breed crocodiles at Pargolovo, for instance, or at Pavlovsk, in the Presnensky Ponds and in Samoteka in Moscow? While providing agreeable, wholesome nourishment for our fastidious *gourmands,* they might at the same time entertain the ladies who walk about these ponds and instruct the children in natural history. The crocodile skin might be used for making jewel-cases, boxes, cigar-cases, pocketbooks, and possibly more than one thousand saved up in the greasy notes that are peculiarly beloved of merchants might be laid by in crocodile skin. We hope to return more than once to this interesting topic."

Though I had foreseen something of the sort, yet the reckless inaccuracy of the paragraph overwhelmed me. Finding no one with whom to share my impression, I turned to Prohor Savvitch who was sitting opposite to me, and noticed that the latter had been watching me for some time, while in his hand he held the *Voice* as though he were on the point of passing it to me. Without a word he took the *News-sheet* from me, and as he handed me the *Voice* he drew a line with his nail against an article to which he probably wished to call my attention. This Prohor Savvitch was a very queer man: a taciturn old bachelor, he was not on intimate terms with any of us, scarcely spoke to anyone in the office, always had an opinion of his own about everything, but could not bear to impart it to anyone. He lived alone. Hardly anyone among us had ever been in his lodging.

This was what I read in the *Voice.*

"Everyone knows that we are progressive and humanitarian and want to be on a level with Europe in this respect. But in spite of all our exertions and the efforts of our paper we are still far from maturity, as may be judged from the shocking incident which took place yesterday in the Arcade and which we predicted long ago. A foreigner arrives in the capital bringing with him a crocodile which he begins exhibiting in the Arcade. We immediately hasten to welcome a new branch of useful industry such as our powerful and varied fatherland stands in great need of. Suddenly yesterday at four o'clock in the afternoon a gentleman of exceptional stoutness enters the foreigner's shop in an intoxicated condition, pays his entrance money, and immediately

4. Mongoose.
5. Vicomte Ferdinand Marie de Lesseps   (1805–1894), builder of Suez Canal.

without any warning leaps into the jaws of the crocodile, who was forced, of course, to swallow him, if only from an instinct of self-preservation, to avoid being crushed. Tumbling into the inside of the crocodile, the stranger at once dropped asleep. Neither the shouts of the foreign proprietor, nor the lamentations of his terrified family, nor threats to send for the police made the slightest impression. Within the crocodile was heard nothing but laughter and a promise to flay him (*sic*), though the poor mammal, compelled to swallow such a mass, was vainly shedding tears. An uninvited guest is worse than a Tartar. But in spite of the proverb the insolent visitor would not leave. We do not know how to explain such barbarous incidents which prove our lack of culture and disgrace us in the eyes of foreigners. The recklessness of the Russian temperament has found a fresh outlet. It may be asked what was the object of the uninvited visitor? A warm and comfortable abode? But there are many excellent houses in the capital with very cheap and comfortable lodgings, with the Neva water laid on,[6] and a staircase lighted by gas, frequently with a hall-porter maintained by the proprietor. We would call our readers' attention to the barbarous treatment of domestic animals: it is difficult, of course, for the crocodile to digest such a mass all at once, and now he lies swollen out to the size of a mountain, awaiting death in insufferable agonies. In Europe persons guilty of inhumanity towards domestic animals have long been punished by law. But in spite of our European enlightenment, in spite of our European pavements, in spite of the European architecture of our houses, we are still far from shaking off our time-honored traditions.

Though the houses are new, the conventions are old.

"And, indeed, the houses are not new, at least the staircases in them are not. We have more than once in our paper alluded to the fact that in the Petersburg Side in the house of the merchant Lukyanov the steps of the wooden staircase have decayed, fallen away, and have long been a danger for Afimya Skapidarov, a soldier's wife who works in the house, and is often obliged to go up the stairs with water or armfuls of wood. At last our predictions have come true: yesterday evening at half-past eight Afimya Skapidarov fell down with a basin of soup and broke her leg. We do not know whether Lukyanov will mend his staircase now, Russians are often wise after the event, but the victim of Russian carelessness has by now been taken to the hospital. In the same way we shall never cease to maintain that the house-porters who clear away the mud from the wooden pavement in the Viborgsky Side ought not to spatter the legs of passers-by, but should throw the mud up into heaps as is done in Europe," and so on, and so on.

"What's this?" I asked in some perplexity, looking at Prohor Savvitch. "What's the meaning of it?"

"How do you mean?"

"Why, upon my word! Instead of pitying Ivan Matveitch, they pity the crocodile!"

"What of it? They have pity even for a beast, a *mammal*. We must be up to Europe, mustn't we? They have a very warm feeling for crocodiles there too. He-he-he!"

Saying this, queer old Prohor Savvitch dived into his papers and would not utter another word.

I stuffed the *Voice* and the *News-sheet* into my pocket and collected

6. Supplied, on tap.

as many old copies of the newspapers as I could find for Ivan Matveitch's diversion in the evening, and though the evening was far off, yet on this occasion I slipped away from the office early to go to the Arcade and look, if only from a distance, at what was going on there, and to listen to the various remarks and currents of opinion. I foresaw that there would be a regular crush there, and turned up the collar of my coat to meet it. I somehow felt rather shy—so unaccustomed are we to publicity. But I feel that I have no right to report my own prosaic feelings when faced with this remarkable and original incident.

p. 1865

THOMAS MANN

Disorder and Early Sorrow*

The principal dish at dinner had been croquettes made of turnip greens. So there follows a trifle, concocted out of one of those dessert powders we use nowadays, that taste like almond soap. Xaver, the youthful manservant, in his outgrown striped jacket, white woolen gloves, and yellow sandals, hands it round, and the "big folk" take this opportunity to remind their father, tactfully, that company is coming today.

The "big folk" are two, Ingrid and Bert. Ingrid is brown-eyed, eighteen, and perfectly delightful. She is on the eve of her exams, and will probably pass them, if only because she knows how to wind masters, and even headmasters, round her finger. She does not, however, mean to use her certificate once she gets it; having leanings toward the stage, on the ground of her ingratiating smile, her equally ingratiating voice, and a marked and irresistible talent for burlesque. Bert is blond and seventeen. He intends to get done with school somehow, anyhow, and fling himself into the arms of life. He will be a dancer, or a cabaret actor, possibly even a waiter—but not a waiter anywhere else save at the Cairo, the nightclub, whither he has once already taken flight, at five in the morning, and been brought back crestfallen. Bert bears a strong resemblance to the youthful manservant Xaver Kleinsgutl, of about the same age as himself; not because he looks common—in features he is strikingly like his father, Professor Cornelius—but by reason of an approximation of types, due in its turn to far-reaching compromises in matters of dress and bearing generally. Both lads wear their heavy hair very long on top, with a cursory parting in the middle, and give their heads the same characteristic toss to throw it off the forehead. When one of them leaves the house, by the garden gate, bareheaded in all weathers, in a blouse rakishly girt with a leather strap, and sheers off bent well over with his head on one side; or else mounts his push-bike—Xaver makes free with his employers', of both sexes, or even, in acutely irresponsible mood, with the Professor's own—Dr. Cornelius from his bedroom window cannot, for the life of him, tell whether he is looking at his son or his servant. Both, he thinks, look like young muzhiks. And both are impassioned cigarette smokers, though Bert has not the means to compete with Xaver, who smokes as many as thirty a day, of a brand named after a popular cinema star. The big folk call

---

* Translated by H. T. Lowe-Porter. Sociohistorical details will not be annotated.

their father and mother the "old folk"—not behind their backs, but as a form of address and in all affection: "Hullo, old folks," they will say; though Cornelius is only forty-seven years old and his wife eight years younger. And the Professor's parents, who lead in his household the humble and hesitant life of the really old, are on the big folk's lips the "ancients." As for the "little folk," Ellie and Snapper, who take their meals upstairs with blue-faced Ann—so-called because of her prevailing facial hue—Ellie and Snapper follow their mother's example and address their father by his first name, Abel. Unutterably comic it sounds, in its pert, confiding familiarity; particularly on the lips, in the sweet accents, of five-year-old Eleanor, who is the image of Frau Cornelius's baby pictures and whom the Professor loves above everything else in the world.

"Darling old thing," says Ingrid affably, laying her large but shapely hand on his, as he presides in proper middle-class style over the family table, with her on his left and the mother opposite: "Parent mine, may I ever so gently jog your memory, for you have probably forgotten: this is the afternoon we were to have our little jollification, our turkey-trot with eats to match. You haven't a thing to do but just bear up and not funk it; everything will be over by nine o'clock."

"Oh—ah!" says Cornelius, his face falling. "Good!" he goes on, and nods his head to show himself in harmony with the inevitable. "I only meant—is this really the day? Thursday, yes. How times flies! Well, what time are they coming?"

"Half-past four they'll be dropping in, I should say," answers Ingrid, to whom her brother leaves the major role in all dealings with the father. Upstairs, while he is resting, he will hear scarcely anything, and from seven to eight he takes his walk. He can slip out by the terrace if he likes.

"Tut!" says Cornelius deprecatingly, as who should say: "You exaggerate." But Bert puts in: "It's the one evening in the week Wanja doesn't have to play. Any other night he'd have to leave by half-past six, which would be painful for all concerned."

Wanja is Ivan Herzl, the celebrated young leading man at the Stadttheater. Bert and Ingrid are on intimate terms with him, they often visit him in his dressing-room and have tea. He is an artist of the modern school, who stands on the stage in strange and, to the Professor's mind, utterly affected dancing attitudes, and shrieks lamentably. To a professor of history, all highly repugnant; but Bert has entirely succumbed to Herzl's influence, blackens the lower rim of his eyelids—despite painful but fruitless scenes with the father—and with youthful carelessness of the ancestral anguish declares that not only will he take Herzl for his model if he becomes a dancer, but in case he turns out to be a waiter at the Cairo he means to walk precisely thus.

Cornelius slightly raises his brows and makes his son a little bow—indicative of the unassumingness and self-abnegation that befits his age. You could not call it a mocking bow or suggestive in any special sense. Bert may refer it to himself or equally to his so talented friend.

"Who else is coming?" next inquires the master of the house. They mention various people, names all more or less familiar, from the city, from the suburban colony, from Ingrid's school. They still have some telephoning to do, they say. They have to phone Max. This is Max Hergesell, an engineering student; Ingrid utters his name in the nasal drawl which according to her is the traditional intonation of all the

Hergesells. She goes on to parody it in the most abandonedly funny and lifelike way, and the parents laugh until they nearly choke over the wretched trifle. For even in these times when something funny happens people have to laugh.

From time to time the telephone bell rings in the Professor's study, and the big folk run across, knowing it is their affair. Many people had to give up their telephones the last time the price rose, but so far the Corneliuses have been able to keep theirs, just as they have kept their villa, which was built before the war, by dint of the salary Cornelius draws as professor of history—a million marks, and more or less adequate to the chances and changes of postwar life. The house is comfortable, even elegant, though sadly in need of repairs that cannot be made for lack of materials, and at present disfigured by iron stoves with long pipes. Even so, it is still the proper setting of the upper middle class, though they themselves look odd enough in it, with their worn and turned clothing and altered way of life. The children, of course, know nothing else; to them it is normal and regular, they belong by birth to the "villa proletariat." The problem of clothing troubles them not at all. They and their like have evolved a costume to fit the time, by poverty out of taste for innovation: in summer it consists of scarcely more than a belted linen smock and sandals. The middle-class parents find things rather more difficult.

The big folk's table-napkins hang over their chair-backs, they talk with their friends over the telephone. These friends are the invited guests who have rung up to accept or decline or arrange; and the conversation is carried on in the jargon of the clan, full of slang and high spirits, of which the old folk understand hardly a word. These consult together meantime about the hospitality to be offered to the impending guests. The Professor displays a middle-class ambitiousness: he wants to serve a sweet—or something that looks like a sweet—after the Italian salad and brown-bread sandwiches. But Frau Cornelius says that would be going too far. The guests would not expect it, she is sure—and the big folk, returning once more to their trifle, agree with her.

The mother of the family is of the same general type as Ingrid, though not so tall. She is languid; the fantastic difficulties of the housekeeping have broken and worn her. She really ought to go and take a cure, but feels incapable; the floor is always swaying under her feet, and everything seems upside down. She speaks of what is uppermost in her mind: the eggs, they simply must be bought today. Six thousand marks apiece they are, and just so many are to be had on this one day of the week at one single shop fifteen minutes' journey away. Whatever else they do, the big folk must go and fetch them immediately after luncheon, with Danny, their neighbor's son, who will soon be calling for them; and Xaver Kleinsgutl will don civilian garb and attend his young master and mistress. For no single household is allowed more than five eggs a week; therefore the young people will enter the shop singly, one after another, under assumed names, and thus wring twenty eggs from the shopkeeper for the Cornelius family. This enterprise is the sporting event of the week for all participants, not excepting the muzhik Kleinsgutl, and most of all for Ingrid and Bert, who delight in misleading and mystifying their fellowmen and would revel in the performance even if it did not achieve one single egg. They adore impersonating fictitious characters; they love to sit in a bus and carry on long lifelike conversations in a dialect which they otherwise never

speak, the most commonplace dialogue about politics and people and the price of food, while the whole bus listens open-mouthed to this incredibly ordinary prattle, though with a dark suspicion all the while that something is wrong somewhere. The conversation waxes ever more shameless, it enters into revolting detail about these people who do not exist. Ingrid can make her voice sound ever so common and twittering and shrill as she impersonates a shop-girl with an illegitimate child, said child being a son with sadistic tendencies, who lately out in the country treated a cow with such unnatural cruelty that no Christian could have borne to see it. Bert nearly explodes at her twittering, but restrains himself and displays a grisly sympathy; he and the unhappy shop-girl entering into a long, stupid, depraved, and shuddery conversation over the particular morbid cruelty involved; until an old gentleman opposite, sitting with his ticket folded between his index finger and his seal ring, can bear it no more and makes public protest against the nature of the themes these young folk are discussing with such particularity. He uses the Greek plural: "themata." Whereat Ingrid pretends to be dissolving in tears, and Bert behaves as though his wrath against the old gentleman was with difficulty being held in check and would probably burst out before long. He clenches his fists, he gnashes his teeth, he shakes from head to foot; and the unhappy old gentleman, whose intentions had been of the best, hastily leaves the bus at the next stop.

Such are the diversions of the big folk. The telephone plays a prominent part in them: they ring up any and everybody—members of government, opera singers, dignitaries of the Church—in the character of shop assistants, or perhaps as Lord or Lady Doolittle. They are only with difficulty persuaded that they have the wrong number. Once they emptied their parents' card-tray[1] and distributed its contents among the neighbors' letter boxes, wantonly, yet not without enough impish sense of the fitness of things to make it highly upsetting, God only knowing why certain people should have called where they did.

Xaver comes in to clear away, tossing the hair out of his eyes. Now that he has taken off his gloves you can see the yellow chain-ring on his left hand. And as the Professor finishes his watery eight-thousand-mark beer and lights a cigarette, the little folk can be heard scrambling down the stair, coming, by established custom, for their after-dinner call on Father and Mother. They storm the dining-room, after a struggle with the latch, clutched by both pairs of little hands at once; their clumsy small feet twinkle over the carpet, in red felt slippers with the socks falling down on them. With prattle and shoutings each makes for his own place: Snapper to Mother, to climb on her lap, boast of all he has eaten, and thump his fat little tum; Ellie to her Abel, so much hers because she is so very much his; because she consciously luxuriates in the deep tenderness—like all deep feeling, concealing a melancholy strain —with which he holds her small form embraced; in the love in his eyes as he kisses her little fairy hand or the sweet brow with its delicate tracery of tiny blue veins.

The little folk look like each other, with the strong undefined likeness of brother and sister. In clothing and haircut they are twins. Yet they are sharply distinguished after all, and quite on sex lines. It is a little Adam and a little Eve. Not only is Snapper the sturdier and more compact, he appears consciously to emphasize his four-year-old masculinity

1. Tray for calling-cards left by visitors.

in speech, manner, and carriage, lifting his shoulders and letting the little arms hang down quite like a young American athlete, drawing down his mouth when he talks and seeking to give his voice a gruff and forthright ring. But all this masculinity is the result of effort rather than natively his. Born and brought up in these desolate, distracted times, he has been endowed by them with an unstable and hypersensitive nervous system and suffers greatly under life's disharmonies. He is prone to sudden anger and outbursts of bitter tears, stamping his feet at every trifle; for this reason he is his mother's special nursling and care. His round, round eyes are chestnut brown and already inclined to squint, so that he will need glasses in the near future. His little nose is long, the mouth small—the father's nose and mouth they are, more plainly than ever since the Professor shaved his pointed beard and goes smooth-faced. The pointed beard had become impossible—even professors must make some concession to the changing times.

But the little daughter sits on her father's knee, his Eleanorchen,[2] his little Eve, so much more gracious a little being, so much sweeter-faced than her brother—and he holds his cigarette away from her while she fingers his glasses with her dainty wee hands. The lenses are divided for reading and distance, and each day they tease her curiosity afresh.

At bottom he suspects that his wife's partiality may have a firmer basis than his own: that Snapper's refractory masculinity perhaps is solider stuff than his own little girl's more explicit charm and grace. But the heart will not be commanded, that he knows; and once and for all his heart belongs to the little one, as it has since the day she came, since the first time he saw her. Almost always when he holds her in his arms he remembers that first time: remembers the sunny room in the Women's Hospital, where Ellie first saw the light, twelve years after Bert was born. He remembers how he drew near, the mother smiling the while, and cautiously put aside the canopy of the diminutive bed that stood beside the large one. There lay the little miracle among the pillows: so well formed, so encompassed, as it were, with the harmony of sweet proportions, with little hands that even then, though so much tinier, were beautiful as now; with wide-open eyes blue as the sky and brighter than the sunshine—and almost in that very second he felt himself captured and held fast. This was love at first sight, love ever-lasting: a feeling unknown, unhoped for, unexpected—in so far as it could be a matter of conscious awareness; it took entire possession of him, and he understood, with joyous amazement, that this was for life.

But he understood more. He knows, does Dr. Cornelius, that there is something not quite right about this feeling, so unaware, so undreamed of, so involuntary. He has a shrewd suspicion that it is not by accident it has so utterly mastered him and bound itself up with his existence; that he had—even subconsciously—been preparing for it, or, more precisely, been prepared for it. There is, in short, something in him which at a given moment was ready to issue in such a feeling; and this something, highly extraordinary to relate, is his essence and quality as a professor of history. Dr. Cornelius, however, does not actually say this, even to himself; he merely realizes it, at odd times, and smiles a private smile. He knows that history professors do not love history because it is something that comes to pass, but only because it is something that *has* come to pass; that they hate a revolution like the present one because they feel it is lawless, incoherent, irrelevant—in a word, unhis-

2. Little Eleanor.

toric; that their hearts belong to the coherent, disciplined, historic past. For the temper of timelessness, the temper of eternity—thus the scholar communes with himself when he takes his walk by the river before supper—that temper broods over the past; and it is a temper much better suited to the nervous system of a history professor than are the excesses of the present. The past is immortalized; that is to say, it is dead; and death is the root of all godliness and all abiding signifi- cance. Dr. Cornelius, walking alone in the dark, has a profound insight into this truth. It is this conservative instinct of his, his sense of the eter- nal, that has found in his love for his little daughter a way to save itself from the wounding inflicted by the times. For father love, and a little child on its mother's breast—are not these timeless, and thus very, very holy and beautiful? Yet Cornelius, pondering there in the dark, descries something not perfectly right and good in his love. Theoretically, in the interests of science, he admits it to himself. There is something ulterior about it, in the nature of it; that something is hostility, hostility against the history of today, which is still in the making and thus not history at all, in behalf of the genuine history that has already happened—that is to say, death. Yes, passing strange though all this is, yet it is true; true in a sense, that is. His devotion to this priceless little morsel of life and new growth has something to do with death, it clings to death as against life; and that is neither right nor beautiful—in a sense. Though only the most fanatical asceticism could be capable, on no other ground than such casual scientific perception, of tearing this purest and most precious of feelings out of his heart.

He holds his darling on his lap and her slim rosy legs hang down. He raises his brows as he talks to her, tenderly, with a half-teasing note of respect, and listens enchanted to her high, sweet little voice calling him Abel. He exchanges a look with the mother, who is caressing her Snapper and reading him a gentle lecture. He must be more reasonable, he must learn self-control; today again, under the manifold exaspera- tions of life, he has given way to rage and behaved like a howling der- vish. Cornelius casts a mistrustful glance at the big folk now and then, too; he thinks it not unlikely they are not unaware of those scientific preoccupations of his evening walks. If such be the case they do not show it. They stand there leaning their arms on their chair-backs and with a benevolence not untinctured with irony look on at the parental happiness.

The children's frocks are of a heavy, brick-red stuff, embroidered in modern "arty" style. They once belonged to Ingrid and Bert and are precisely alike, save that little knickers come out beneath Snapper's smock. And both have their hair bobbed. Snapper's is a streaky blond, inclined to turn dark. It is bristly and sticky and looks for all the world like a droll, badly fitting wig. But Ellie's is chestnut brown, glossy and fine as silk, as pleasing as her whole little personality. It covers her ears —and these ears are not a pair, one of them being the right size, the other distinctly too large. Her father will sometimes uncover this little abnormality and exclaim over it as though he had never noticed it be- fore, which both makes Ellie giggle and covers her with shame. Her eyes are now golden brown, set far apart and with sweet gleams in them—such a clear and lovely look! The brows above are blond; the nose still unformed, with thick nostrils and almost circular holes; the mouth large and expressive, with a beautifully arching and mobile upper lip. When she laughs, dimples come in her cheeks and she shows

her teeth like loosely strung pearls. So far she has lost but one tooth, which her father gently twisted out with his handkerchief after it had grown very wobbling. During this small operation she had paled and trembled very much. Her cheeks have the softness proper to her years, but they are not chubby; indeed, they are rather concave, due to her facial structure, with its somewhat prominent jaw. On one, close to the soft fall of her hair, is a downy freckle.

Ellie is not too well pleased with her looks—a sign that already she troubles about such things. Sadly she thinks it is best to admit it once for all, her face is "homely"; though the rest of her, "on the other hand," is not bad at all. She loves expressions like "on the other hand"; they sound choice and grown-up to her, and she likes to string them together, one after the other: "very likely," "probably," "after all." Snapper is self-critical too, though more in the moral sphere: he suffers from remorse for his attacks of rage and considers himself a tremendous sinner. He is quite certain that heaven is not for such as he; he is sure to go to "the bad place" when he dies, and no persuasions will convince him to the contrary—as that God sees the heart and gladly makes allowances. Obstinately he shakes his head, with the comic, crooked little peruke, and vows there is no place for him in heaven. When he has a cold he is immediately quite choked with mucus; rattles and rumbles from top to toe if you even look at him; his temperature flies up at once and he simply puffs. Nursy is pessimistic on the score of his constitution: such fat-blooded children as he might get a stroke any minute. Once she even thought she saw the moment at hand: Snapper had been in one of his berserker rages, and in the ensuing fit of penitence stood himself in the corner with his back to the room. Suddenly Nursy noticed that his face had gone all blue, far bluer, even, than her own. She raised the alarm, crying out that the child's all too rich blood had at length brought him to his final hour; and Snapper, to his vast astonishment, found himself, so far from being rebuked for evil-doing, encompassed in tenderness and anxiety—until it turned out that his color was not caused by apoplexy but by the distempering on the nursery wall, which had come off on his tear-wet face.

Nursy has come downstairs too, and stands by the door, sleek-haired, owl-eyed, with her hands folded over her white apron, and a severely dignified manner born of her limited intelligence. She is very proud of the care and training she gives her nurslings and declares that they are "enveloping wonderfully." She has had seventeen suppurated teeth lately removed from her jaws and been measured for a set of symmetrical yellow ones in dark rubber gums; these now embellish her peasant face. She is obsessed with the strange conviction that these teeth of hers are the subject of general conversation, that, as it were, the sparrows on the housetops chatter of them. "Everybody knows I've had a false set put in," she will say; "there has been a great deal of foolish talk about them." She is much given to dark hints and veiled innuendo: speaks, for instance, of a certain Dr. Bleifuss, whom every child knows, and "there are even some in the house who pretend to be him." All one can do with talk like this is charitably to pass it over in silence. But she teaches the children nursery rhymes: gems like:

> Puff, puff, here comes the train!
> Puff, puff, toot, toot,
> Away it goes again.

Or that gastronomical jingle, so suited, in its sparseness, to the times, and yet seemingly with a blitheness of its own:

> Monday we begin the week,
> Tuesday there's a bone to pick.
> Wednesday we're half way through,
> Thursday what a great to-do!
> Friday we eat what fish we're able,
> Saturday we dance round the table.
> Sunday brings us pork and greens—
> Here's a feast for kings and queens!

Also a certain four-line stanza with a romantic appeal, unutterable and unuttered:

> Open the gate, open the gate
> And let the carriage drive in.
> Who is it in the carriage sits?
> A lordly sir with golden hair.

Or, finally that ballad about golden-haired Marianne who sat on a, sat on a, sat on a stone, and combed out her, combed out her, combed out her hair; and about bloodthirsty Rudolph, who pulled out a, pulled out a, pulled out a knife—and his ensuing direful end. Ellie enunciates all these ballads charmingly, with her mobile little lips, and sings them in her sweet little voice—much better than Snapper. She does everything better than he does, and he pays her honest admiration and homage and obeys her in all things except when visited by one of his attacks. Sometimes she teaches him, instructs him upon the birds in the picture-book and tells him their proper names: "This is a chaffinch, Buddy, this is a bullfinch, this is a cowfinch." He has to repeat them after her. She gives him medical instruction too, teaches him the names of diseases, such as infammation of the lungs, infammation of the blood, infammation of the air. If he does not pay attention and cannot say the words after her, she stands him in the corner. Once she even boxed his ears, but was so ashamed that she stood herself in the corner for a long time. Yes, they are fast friends, two souls with but a single thought, and have all their adventures in common. They come home from a walk and relate as with one voice that they have seen two moollies and a teenty-weenty baby calf. They are on familiar terms with the kitchen, which consists of Xaver and the ladies Hinterhofer, two sisters once of the lower middle class who, in these evil days, are reduced to living *au pair* as the phrase goes and officiating as cook and housemaid for their board and keep. The little ones have a feeling that Xaver and the Hinterhofers are on much the same footing with their father and mother as they are themselves. At least sometimes, when they have been scolded, they go downstairs and announce that the master and mistress are cross. But playing with the servants lacks charm compared with the joys of playing upstairs. The kitchen could never rise to the height of the games their father can invent. For instance, there is "four gentlemen taking a walk." When they play it Abel will crook his knees until he is the same height with themselves and go walking with them, hand in hand. They never get enough of this sport; they could walk round and round the dining-room a whole day on end, five gentlemen in all, counting the diminished Abel.

Then there is the thrilling cushion game. One of the children, usually

Ellie, seats herself, unbeknownst to Abel, in his seat at table. Still as a mouse she awaits his coming. He draws near with his head in the air, descanting in loud, clear tones upon the surpassing comfort of his chair; and sits down on top of Ellie. "What's this, what's this?" says he. And bounces about, deaf to the smothered giggles exploding behind him. "Why have they put a cushion in my chair? And what a queer, hard, awkward-shaped cushion it is!" he goes on. "Frightfully uncomfortable to sit on!" And keeps pushing and bouncing about more and more on the astonishing cushion and clutching behind him into the rapturous giggling and squeaking, until at last he turns round, and the game ends with a magnificent climax of discovery and recognition. They might go through all this a hundred times without diminishing by an iota its power to thrill.

Today is no time for such joys. The imminent festivity disturbs the atmosphere, and besides there is work to be done, and, above all, the eggs to be got. Ellie has just time to recite "Puff, puff," and Cornelius to discover that her ears are not mates, when they are interrupted by the arrival of Danny, come to fetch Bert and Ingrid. Xaver, meantime, has exchanged his striped livery for an ordinary coat, in which he looks rather rough-and-ready, though as brisk and attractive as ever. So then Nursy and the children ascend to the upper regions, the Professor withdraws to his study to read, as always after dinner, and his wife bends her energies upon the sandwiches and salad that must be prepared. And she has another errand as well. Before the young people arrive she has to take her shopping-basket and dash into town on her bicycle, to turn into provisions a sum of money she has in hand, which she dares not keep lest it lose all value.

Cornelius reads, leaning back in his chair, with his cigar between his middle and index fingers. First he reads Macaulay[3] on the origin of the English public debt at the end of the seventeenth century; then an article in a French periodical on the rapid increase in the Spanish debt toward the end of the sixteenth. Both these for his lecture on the morrow. He intends to compare the astonishing prosperity which accompanied the phenomenon in England with its fatal effects a hundred years earlier in Spain, and to analyze the ethical and psychological grounds of the difference in results. For that will give him a chance to refer back from the England of William III, which is the actual subject in hand, to the time of Philip II[4] and the Counter-Reformation, which is his own special field. He has already written a valuable work on this period; it is much cited and got him his professorship. While his cigar burns down and gets strong, he excogitates a few pensive sentences in a key of gentle melancholy, to be delivered before his class next day: about the practically hopeless struggle carried on by the belated Philip against the whole trend of history: against the new, the kingdom-disrupting power of the Germanic ideal of freedom and individual liberty. And about the persistent, futile struggle of the aristocracy, condemned by God and rejected of man, against the forces of progress and change.

3. Thomas Babington Macaulay (1800–1859), author of the very popular *The History of England* (1847–59).
4. William III (1650–1702), better known as William of Orange, king of England 1689–1702, until 1694 reigning jointly with his wife, Mary II. Philip II (1529–1598) ruled Spain 1556–98, in 1554 married the Catholic Mary I of England, which nation, soon after he arrived, returned to the Roman Catholic Church; upon Mary's death he proposed to Elizabeth I. Though Philip had fought Pope Paul IV, he opposed Protestantism in both France and England. Under Philip, Spain was the most powerful country in Europe and the greatest colonial power, though even with colonial gold his treasury was drained by wars. His reign also saw the beginning of the Golden Age of literature in Spain.

He savors his sentences; keeps on polishing them while he puts back the books he has been using; then goes upstairs for the usual pause in his day's work, the hour with drawn blinds and closed eyes, which he so imperatively needs. But today, he recalls, he will rest under disturbed conditions, amid the bustle of preparations for the feast. He smiles to find his heart giving a mild flutter at the thought. Disjointed phrases on the theme of black-clad Philip and his times mingle with a confused consciousness that they will soon be dancing down below. For five minutes or so he falls asleep.

As he lies and rests he can hear the sound of the garden gate and the repeated ringing at the bell. Each time a little pang goes through him, of excitement and suspense, at the thought that the young people have begun to fill the floor below. And each time he smiles at himself again—though even his smile is slightly nervous, is tinged with the pleasurable anticipations people always feel before a party. At half-past four—it is already dark—he gets up and washes at the washstand. The basin has been out of repair for two years. It is supposed to tip, but has broken away from its socket on one side and cannot be mended because there is nobody to mend it; neither replaced because no shop can supply another. So it has to be hung up above the vent and emptied by lifting in both hands and pouring out the water. Cornelius shakes his head over this basin, as he does several times a day—whenever, in fact, he has occasion to use it. He finishes his toilet with care, standing under the ceiling light to polish his glasses till they shine. Then he goes downstairs.

On his way to the dining-room he hears the gramophone already going, and the sound of voices. He puts on a polite, society air; at his tongue's end is the phrase he means to utter: "Pray don't let me disturb you," as he passes directly into the dining-room for his tea. "Pray don't let me disturb you"—it seems to him precisely the *mot juste*,[5] towards the guests cordial and considerate, for himself a very bulwark.

The lower floor is lighted up, all the bulbs in the chandelier are burning save one that has burned out. Cornelius pauses on a lower step and surveys the entrance hall. It looks pleasant and cozy in the bright light, with its copy of Marées[6] over the brick chimney-piece, its wainscoted walls—wainscoted in soft wood—and red-carpeted floor, where the guests stand in groups, chatting, each with his teacup and slice of bread-and-butter spread with anchovy paste. There is a festal haze, faint scents of hair and clothing and human breath come to him across the room, it is all characteristic and familiar and highly evocative. The door into the dressing-room is open, guests are still arriving.

A large group of people is rather bewildering at first sight. The Professor takes in only the general scene. He does not see Ingrid, who is standing just at the foot of the steps, in a dark silk frock with a pleated collar falling softly over the shoulders, and bare arms. She smiles up at him, nodding and showing her lovely teeth.

"Rested?" she asks, for his private ear. With a quite unwarranted start he recognizes her, and she presents some of her friends.

"May I introduced Herr Zuber?" she says. "And this is Fräulein Plaichinger."

Herr Zuber is insignificant. But Fräulein Plaichinger is a perfect

---

5. The precisely appropriate word.
6. Hans Von Marées (1837–1887), German painter with two basic periods: the idyllic, full of dreamy beings; and the grandiose, full of monumental figures.

Germania, blond and voluptuous, arrayed in floating draperies. She has a snub nose, and answers the Professor's salutation in the high, shrill pipe so many stout women have.

"Delighted to meet you," he says. "How nice of you to come! A classmate of Ingrid's, I suppose?"

And Herr Zuber is a golfing partner of Ingrid's. He is in business; he works in his uncle's brewery. Cornelius makes a few jokes about the thinness of the beer and professes to believe that Herr Zuber could easily do something about the quality if he would. "But pray don't let me disturb you," he goes on, and turns towards the dining-room.

"There comes Max," says Ingrid. "Max, you sweep,[7] what do you mean by rolling up at this time of day?" For such is the way they talk to each other, offensively to an older ear; of social forms, of hospitable warmth, there is no faintest trace. They all call each other by their first names.

A young man comes up to them out of the dressing-room and makes his bow; he has an expanse of white shirt front and a little black string tie. He is as pretty as a picture, dark, with rosy cheeks, clean-shaven of course, but with just a sketch of side-whisker. Not a ridiculous or flashy beauty, not like a gypsy fiddler, but just charming to look at, in a winning, well-bred way, with kind dark eyes. He even wears his dinner jacket a little awkwardly.

"Please don't scold me, Cornelia," he says; "it's the idiotic lectures." And Ingrid presents him to her father as Herr Hergesell.

Well, and so this is Herr Hergesell. He knows his manners, does Herr Hergesell, and thanks the master of the house quite ingratiatingly for his invitation as they shake hands. "I certainly seem to have missed the bus," says he jocosely. "Of course I have lectures today up to four o'clock; I would have; and after that I had to go home to change." Then he talks about his pumps; with which he has just been struggling in the dressing-room.

"I brought them with me in a bag," he goes on. "Mustn't tramp all over the carpet in our brogues—it's not done. Well, I was ass enough not to fetch along a shoehorn, and I find I simply can't get in! What a sell![8] They are the tightest I've ever had, the numbers don't tell you a thing, and all the leather today is just cast iron. It's not leather at all. My poor finger"—he confidingly displays a reddened digit and once more characterizes the whole thing as a "sell," and a putrid sell into the bargain. He really does talk just as Ingrid said he did, with a peculiar nasal drawl, not affectedly in the least, but merely because that is the way of all the Hergesells.

Dr. Cornelius says it is very careless of them not to keep a shoehorn in the cloakroom and displays proper sympathy with the mangled finger. "But now you *really* must not let me disturb you any longer," he goes on. "*Auf wiedersehen!*" And he crosses the hall into the dining-room.

There are guests there too, drinking tea; the family table is pulled out. But the Professor goes at once to his own little upholstered corner with the electric light bulb above it—the nook where he usually drinks his tea. His wife is sitting there talking with Bert and two other young men, one of them Herzl, whom Cornelius knows and greets; the other a typical "Wandervogel"[9] named Möller, a youth who obviously neither

7. Scamp.
8. Bad deal.

9. Wanderer; the name of a group that started the German youth movement.

owns nor cares to own the correct evening dress of the middle classes (in fact, there is no such thing anymore), nor to ape the manners of a gentleman (and, in fact, there is no such thing anymore either). He has a wilderness of hair, horn spectacles, and a long neck, and wears golf stockings and a belted blouse. His regular occupation, the Professor learns, is banking, but he is by way of being an amateur folklorist and collects folksongs from all localities and in all languages. He sings them, too, and at Ingrid's command has brought his guitar; it is hanging in the dressing-room in an oilcloth case. Herzl, the actor, is small and slight, but he has a strong growth of black beard, as you can tell by the thick coat of powder on his cheeks. His eyes are larger than life, with a deep and melancholy glow. He has put on rouge besides the powder —those dull carmine highlights on the cheeks can be nothing but a cosmetic. "Queer," thinks the Professor. "You would think a man would be one thing or the other—not melancholic and use face paint at the same time. It's a psychological contradiction. How can a melancholy man rouge? But here we have a perfect illustration of the abnormality of the artist soul-form. It can make possible a contradiction like this— perhaps it even consists in the contradiction. All very interesting—and no reason whatever for not being polite to him. Politeness is a primitive convention—and legitimate. . . . Do take some lemon, Herr Hof-schauspieler!"[1]

Court actors and court theaters—there are no such things anymore, really. But Herzl relishes the sound of the title, notwithstanding he is a revolutionary artist. This must be another contradiction inherent in his soul-form; so, at least, the Professor assumes, and he is probably right. The flattery he is guilty of is a sort of atonement for his previous hard thoughts about the rouge.

"Thank you so much—it's really too good of you, sir," says Herzl, quite embarrassed. He is so overcome that he almost stammers; only his perfect enunciation saves him. His whole bearing toward his hostess and the master of the house is exaggeratedly polite. It is almost as though he had a bad conscience in respect of his rouge; as though an in-ward compulsion had driven him to put it on, but now, seeing it through the Professor's eyes, he disapproves of it himself, and thinks, by an air of humility toward the whole of unrouged society, to mitigate its effect.

They drink their tea and chat: about Möller's folksongs, about Basque folksongs and Spanish folksongs; from which they pass to the new production of *Don Carlos*[2] at the Stadttheater, in which Herzl plays the title role. He talks about his own rendering of the part and says he hopes his conception of the character has unity. They go on to criticize the rest of the cast, the setting, and the production as a whole; and Cornelius is struck, rather painfully, to find the conversation trend-ing toward his own special province, back to Spain and the Counter-Reformation. He has done nothing at all to give it this turn, he is perfectly innocent, and hopes it does not look as though he had sought an occasion to play the professor. He wonders, and falls silent, feeling relieved when the little folk come up to the table. Ellie and Snapper have on their blue velvet Sunday frocks; they are permitted to partake in the festivities up to bedtime. They look shy and large-eyed as they

---

1. Mr. Court-Theater Actor.   2. Play by Friedrich von Schiller (1759–1805).

say how-do-you-do to the strangers and, under pressure, repeat their names and ages. Herr Möller does nothing but gaze at them solemnly, but Herzl is simply ravished. He rolls his eyes up to heaven and puts his hands over his mouth; he positively blesses them. It all, no doubt, comes from his heart, but he is so addicted to theatrical methods of making an impression and getting an effect that both words and behavior ring frightfully false. And even his enthusiasm for the little folk looks too much like part of his general craving to make up for the rouge on his cheeks.

The tea-table has meanwhile emptied of guests, and dancing is going on in the hall. The children run off, the Professor prepares to retire. "Go and enjoy yourselves," he says to Möller and Herzl, who have sprung from their chairs as he rises from his. They shake hands and he withdraws into his study, his peaceful kingdom, where he lets down the blinds, turns on the desk lamp, and sits down to his work.

It is work which can be done, if necessary, under disturbed conditions: nothing but a few letters and a few notes. Of course, Cornelius's mind wanders. Vague impressions float through it: Herr Hergesell's refractory pumps, the high pipe in that plump body of the Plaichinger female. As he writes, or leans back in his chair and stares into space, his thoughts go back to Herr Möller's collection of Basque folksongs, to Herzl's posings and humility, to "his" Carlos and the court of Philip II. There is something strange, he thinks, about conversations. They are so ductile, they will flow of their own accord in the direction of one's dominating interest. Often and often he has seen this happen. And while he is thinking, he is listening to the sounds next door— rather subdued, he finds them. He hears only voices, no sound of footsteps. The dancers do not glide or circle round the room; they merely walk about over the carpet, which does not hamper their movements in the least. Their way of holding each other is quite different and strange, and they move to the strains of the gramophone, to the weird music of the new world. He concentrates on the music and makes out that it is a jazz-band record, with various percussion instruments and the clack and clatter of castanets, which, however, are not even faintly suggestive of Spain, but merely jazz like the rest. No, not Spain. . . . His thoughts are back at their old round.

Half an hour goes by. It occurs to him it would be no more than friendly to go and contribute a box of cigarettes to the festivities next door. Too bad to ask the young people to smoke their own—though they have probably never thought of it. He goes into the empty dining-room and takes a box from his supply in the cupboard: not the best ones, nor yet the brand he himself prefers, but a certain long, thin kind he is not averse to getting rid of—after all, they are nothing but youngsters. He takes the box into the hall, holds it up with a smile, and deposits it on the mantel shelf. After which he gives a look round and returns to his own room.

There comes a lull in dance and music. The guests stand about the room in groups or round the table at the window or are seated in a circle by the fireplace. Even the built-in-stairs, with their worn velvet carpet, are crowded with young folk as in an amphitheater: Max Hergesell is there, leaning back with one elbow on the step above and gesticulating with his free hand as he talks to the shrill, voluptuous Plaichinger. The floor of the hall is nearly empty, save just in the center:

there, directly beneath the chandelier, the two little ones in their blue velvet frocks clutch each other in an awkward embrace and twirl silently round and round, oblivious of all else. Cornelius, as he passes, strokes their hair, with a friendly word; it does not distract them from their small solemn preoccupation. But at his own door he turns to glance round and sees young Hergesell push himself off the stair by his elbow—probably because he noticed the Professor. He comes down into the arena, takes Ellie out of her brother's arms, and dances with her himself. It looks very comic, without the music, and he crouches down just as Cornelius does when he goes walking with the four gentlemen, holding the fluttered Ellie as though she were grown up and taking little "shimmying" steps. Everybody watches with huge enjoyment, the gramophone is put on again, dancing becomes general. The Professor stands and looks, with his hand on the doorknob. He nods and laughs; when he finally shuts himself into his study the mechanical smile still lingers on his lips.

Again he turns over pages by his desk lamp, takes notes, attends to a few simple matters. After a while he notices that the guests have forsaken the entrance hall for his wife's drawing-room, into which there is a door from his own study as well. He hears their voices and the sounds of a guitar being tuned. Herr Möller, it seems, is to sing—and does so. He twangs the strings of his instrument and sings in a powerful bass a ballad in a strange tongue, possibly Swedish. The Professor does not succeed in identifying it, though he listens attentively to the end, after which there is great applause. The sound is deadened by the portière that hangs over the dividing door. The young bank clerk begins another song. Cornelius goes softly in.

It is half-dark in the drawing-room; the only light is from the shaded standard lamp, beneath which Möller sits, on the divan, with his legs crossed, picking his strings. His audience is grouped easily about; as there are not enough seats, some stand, and more, among them many young ladies, are simply sitting on the floor with their hands clasped round their knees or even with their legs stretched out before them. Hergesell sits thus, in his dinner jacket, next to the piano, with Fräulein Plaichinger beside him. Frau Cornelius is holding both children on her lap as she sits in her easy chair opposite the singer. Snapper, the Bœotian, begins to talk loud and clear in the middle of the song and has to be intimidated with hushings and finger-shakings. Never, never would Ellie allow herself to be guilty of such conduct. She sits there daintily erect and still on her mother's knee. The Professor tries to catch her eye and exchange a private signal with his little girl; but she does not see him. Neither does she seem to be looking at the singer. Her gaze is directed lower down.

Möller sings the "joli tambour[3]":

> "*Sire, mon roi, donnez-moi votre*
> *fille—*"[4]

They are all enchanted. "How good!" Hergesell is heard to say, in the odd, nasally condescending Hergesell tone. The next one is a beggar ballad, to a tune composed by young Möller himself; it elicits a storm of applause:

---

3. Pretty tambourin, lively dance of Provence and its music.

4. "Sire, my king, give me your daughter. . . ."

Gypsy lassie a-goin' to the fair,
Huzza!
Gypsy laddie a-goin' to be there—
Huzza, diddlety umpty dido!

Laughter and high spirits, sheer reckless hilarity, reigns after this jovial ballad. "Frightfully good!" Hergesell comments again, as before. Follows another popular song, this time a Hungarian one; Möller sings it in its own outlandish tongue, and most effectively. The Professor applauds with ostentation. It warms his heart and does him good, this outcropping of artistic, historic, and cultural elements all among the shimmying. He goes up to young Möller and congratulates him, talks about the songs and their sources, and Möller promises to lend him a certain annotated book of folksongs. Cornelius is the more cordial because all the time, as fathers do, he has been comparing the parts and achievements of this young stranger with those of his own son, and being gnawed by envy and chagrin. This young Möller, he is thinking, is a capable bank clerk (though about Möller's capacity he knows nothing whatever) and has this special gift besides, which must have taken talent and energy to cultivate. "And here is my poor Bert, who knows nothing and can do nothing and thinks of nothing except playing the clown, without even talent for that!" He tries to be just; he tells himself that, after all, Bert has innate refinement; that probably there is a good deal more to him than there is to the successful Möller; that perhaps he has even something of the poet in him, and his dancing and table-waiting are due to mere boyish folly and the distraught times. But paternal envy and pessimism win the upper hand; when Möller begins another song, Dr. Cornelius goes back to his room.

He works as before, with divided attention, at this and that, while it gets on for seven o'clock. Then he remembers a letter he may just as well write, a short letter and not very important, but letter-writing is wonderful for the way it takes up the time, and it is almost half-past when he has finished. At half-past eight the Italian salad will be served; so now is the prescribed moment for the Professor to go out into the wintry darkness to post his letters and take his daily quantum of fresh air and exercise. They are dancing again, and he will have to pass through the hall to get his hat and coat; but they are used to him now, he need not stop and beg them not to be disturbed. He lays away his papers, takes up the letters he has written, and goes out. But he sees his wife sitting near the door of his room and pauses a little by her easy chair.

She is watching the dancing. Now and then the big folk or some of their guests stop to speak to her; the party is at its height, and there are more onlookers than these two: blue-faced Ann is standing at the bottom of the stairs, in all the dignity of her limitations. She is waiting for the children, who simply cannot get their fill of these unwonted festivities, and watching over Snapper, lest his all too rich blood be churned to the danger point by too much twirling round. And not only the nursery but the kitchen takes an interest: Xaver and the two ladies Hinterhofer are standing by the pantry door looking on with relish. Fräulein Walburga, the elder of the two sunken sisters (the culinary section—she objects to being called a cook), is a whimsical, good-natured sort, brown-eyed, wearing glasses with thick circular lenses; the nose-piece is wound with a bit of rag to keep it from pressing on

her nose. Fräulein Cecilia is younger, though not so precisely young either. Her bearing is as self-assertive as usual, this being her way of sustaining her dignity as a former member of the middle class. For Fräulein Cecilia feels acutely her descent into the ranks of domestic service. She positively declines to wear a cap or other badge of servitude, and her hardest trial is on the Wednesday evening when she has to serve the dinner while Xaver has his afternoon out. She hands the dishes with averted face and elevated nose—a fallen queen; and so distressing is it to behold her degradation that one evening when the little folk happened to be at table and saw her they both with one accord burst into tears. Such anguish is unknown to young Xaver. He enjoys serving and does it with an ease born of practice as well as talent, for he was once a "piccolo."[5] But otherwise he is a thorough-paced good-for-nothing and windbag—with quite distinct traits of character of his own, as his long-suffering employers are always ready to concede, but perfectly impossible and a bag of wind for all that. One must just take him as he is, they think, and not expect figs from thistles.[6] He is the child and product of the disrupted times, a perfect specimen of his generation, follower of the revolution, Bolshevist sympathizer. The Professor's name for him is the "minute-man," because he is always to be counted on in any sudden crisis, if only it address his sense of humor or love of novelty, and will display therein amazing readiness and resource. But he utterly lacks a sense of duty and can as little be trained to the performance of the daily round and common task as some kinds of dog can be taught to jump over a stick. It goes so plainly against the grain that criticism is disarmed. One becomes resigned. On grounds that appealed to him as unusual and amusing he would be ready to turn out of his bed at any hour of the night. But he simply cannot get up before eight in the morning, he cannot do it, he will not jump over the stick. Yet all day long the evidence of this free and un-trammeled existence, the sound of his mouth organ, his joyous whistle, or his raucous but expressive voice lifted in song, rises to the hearing of the world above-stairs; and the smoke of his cigarettes fills the pantry. While the Hinterhofer ladies work he stands and looks on. Of a morning while the Professor is breakfasting, he tears the leaf off the study calendar—but does not lift a finger to dust the room. Dr. Cornelius has often told him to leave the calendar alone, for he tends to tear off two leaves at a time and thus to add to the general confusion. But young Xaver appears to find joy in this activity, and will not be deprived of it.

Again, he is fond of children, a winning trait. He will throw himself into games with the little folk in the garden, make and mend their toys with great ingenuity, even read aloud from their books—and very droll it sounds in his thick-lipped pronunciation. With his whole soul he loves the cinema; after an evening spent there he inclines to melancholy and yearning and talking to himself. Vague hopes stir in him that some day he may make his fortune in that gay world and belong to it by rights—hopes based on his shock of hair and his physical agility and daring. He likes to climb the ash tree in the front garden, mounting branch by branch to the very top and frightening everybody to death who sees him. Once there he lights a cigarette and smokes it as he sways to and fro, keeping a lookout for a cinema director who might chance to come along and engage him.

5. Apprentice waiter or busboy.
6. See *Matthew* 7:16 (also *Luke* 6:44):   "Ye shall know them by their fruits. Do men gather grapes of thorns, or figs of thistles?"

If he changed his striped jacket for mufti, he might easily dance with the others and no one would notice the difference. For the big folk's friends are rather anomalous in their clothing: evening dress is worn by a few, but it is by no means the rule. There is quite a sprinkling of guests, both male and female, in the same general style as Möller the ballad-singer. The Professor is familiar with the circumstances of most of this young generation he is watching as he stands beside his wife's chair; he has heard them spoken of by name. They are students at the high school or at the School of Applied Art; they lead, at least the masculine portion, that precarious and scrambling existence which is purely the product of the time. There is a tall, pale, spindling youth, the son of a dentist, who lives by speculation. From all the Professor hears, he is a perfect Aladdin. He keeps a car, treats his friends to champagne suppers, and showers presents upon them on every occasion, costly little trifles in mother-of-pearl and gold. So today he has brought gifts to the young givers of the feast: for Bert a gold pencil, and for Ingrid a pair of earrings of barbaric size, great gold circlets that fortunately do not have to go through the little ear lobe, but are fastened over it by means of a clip. The big folk come laughing to their parents to display these trophies; and the parents shake their heads even while they admire—Aladdin bowing over and over from afar.

The young people appear to be absorbed in their dancing—if the performance they are carrying out with so much still concentration can be called dancing. They stride across the carpet, slowly, according to some unfathomable prescript, strangely embraced; in the newest attitude, tummy advanced and shoulders high, waggling the hips. They do not get tired, because nobody could. There is no such thing as heightened color or heaving bosoms. Two girls may dance together or two young men—it is all the same. They move to the exotic strains of the gramophone, played with the loudest needles to procure the maximum of sound: shimmies, foxtrots, one-steps, double foxes, African shimmies, Java dances, and Creole polkas, the wild musky melodies follow one another, now furious, now languishing, a monotonous Negro program in unfamiliar rhythm, to a clacking, clashing, and strumming orchestral accompaniment.

"What is that record?" Cornelius inquires of Ingrid, as she passes him by in the arms of the pale young speculator, with reference to the piece then playing, whose alternate languors and furies he finds comparatively pleasing and showing a certain resourcefulness in detail.

"*Prince of Pappenheim:* 'Console thee, dearest child,'" she answers, and smiles pleasantly back at him with her white teeth.

The cigarette smoke wreathes beneath the chandelier. The air is blue with a festal haze compact of sweet and thrilling ingredients that stir the blood with memories of green-sick pains and are particularly poignant to those whose youth—like the Professor's own—has been oversensitive. . . . The little folk are still on the floor. They are allowed to stay up until eight, so great is their delight in the party. The guests have got used to their presence; in their own way, they have their place in the doings of the evening. They have separated, anyhow: Snapper revolves all alone in the middle of the carpet, in his little blue velvet smock, while Ellie is running after one of the dancing couples, trying to hold the man fast by his coat. It is Max Hergesell and Fräulein Plaichinger. They dance well, it is a pleasure to watch them. One has to admit that these mad modern dances, when the right peo-

ple dance them, are not so bad after all—they have something quite taking. Young Hergesell is a capital leader, dances according to rule, yet with individuality. So it looks. With what aplomb can he walk backwards—when space permits! And he knows how to be graceful standing still in a crowd. And his partner supports him well, being unsuspectedly lithe and buoyant, as fat people often are. They look at each other, they are talking, paying no heed to Ellie, though others are smiling to see the child's persistence. Dr. Cornelius tries to catch up his little sweetheart as she passes and draw her to him. But Ellie eludes him, almost peevishly; her dear Abel is nothing to her now. She braces her little arms against his chest and turns her face away with a persecuted look. Then escapes to follow her fancy once more.

The Professor feels an involuntary twinge. Uppermost in his heart is hatred for this party, with its power to intoxicate and estrange his darling child. His love for her—that not quite disinterested, not quite unexceptionable love of his—is easily wounded. He wears a mechanical smile, but his eyes have clouded, and he stares fixedly at a point in the carpet, between the dancers' feet.

"The children ought to go to bed," he tells his wife. But she pleads for another quarter of an hour; she has promised already, and they do love it so! He smiles again and shakes his head, stands so a moment and then goes across to the cloakroom, which is full of coats and hats and scarves and overshoes. He has trouble in rummaging out his own coat, and Max Hergesell comes out of the hall, wiping his brow.

"Going out, sir?" he asks, in Hergesellian accents, dutifully helping the older man on with his coat. "Silly business this, with my pumps," he says. "They pinch like hell. The brutes are simply too tight for me, quite apart from the bad leather. They press just here on the ball of my great toe"—he stands on one foot and holds the other in his hand— "it's simply unbearable. There's nothing for it but to take them off; my brogues will have to do the business. . . . Oh, let me help you, sir."

"Thanks," says Cornelius. "Don't trouble. Get rid of your own tormentors. . . . Oh, thanks very much!" For Hergesell has gone on one knee to snap the fasteners of his snow-boots.

Once more the Professor expresses his gratitude; he is pleased and touched by so much sincere respect and youthful readiness to serve. "Go and enjoy yourself," he counsels. "Change your shoes and make up for what you have been suffering. Nobody can dance in shoes that pinch. Good-bye, I must be off to get a breath of fresh air."

"I'm going to dance with Ellie now," calls Hergesell after him. "She'll be a first-rate dancer when she grows up, and that I'll swear to."

"Think so?" Cornelius answers, already half out. "Well, you are a connoisseur, I'm sure. Don't get curvature of the spine with stooping."

He nods again and goes. "Fine lad," he thinks as he shuts the door. "Student of engineering. Knows what he's bound for, got a good clear head, and so well set up and pleasant too." And again paternal envy rises as he compares his poor Bert's status with this young man's, which he puts in the rosiest light that his son's may look the darker. Thus he sets out on his evening walk.

He goes up the avenue, crosses the bridge, and walks along the bank on the other side as far as the next bridge but one. The air is wet and cold, with a little snow now and then. He turns up his coat collar and slips the crook of his cane over the arm behind his back. Now and then he ventilates his lungs with a long deep breath of the night air. As

usual when he walks, his mind reverts to his professional preoccupations, he thinks about his lectures and the things he means to say tomorrow about Philip's struggle against the Germanic revolution, things steeped in melancholy and penetratingly just. Above all just, he thinks. For in one's dealings with the young it behooves one to display the scientific spirit, to exhibit the principles of enlightenment—not only for purposes of mental discipline, but on the human and individual side, in order not to wound them or indirectly offend their political sensibilities; particularly in these days, when there is so much tinder in the air, opinions are so frightfully split up and chaotic, and you may so easily incur attacks from one party or the other, or even give rise to scandal, by taking sides on a point of history. "And taking sides is unhistoric anyhow," so he muses. "Only justice, only impartiality is historic." And could not, properly considered, be otherwise. . . . For justice can have nothing of youthful fire and blithe, fresh, loyal conviction. It is by nature melancholy. And, being so, has secret affinity with the lost cause and the forlorn hope rather than with the fresh and blithe and loyal—perhaps this affinity is its very essence and without it it would not exist at all! . . . "And is there then no such thing as justice?" the Professor asks himself, and ponders the question so deeply that he absently posts his letters in the next box and turns round to go home. This thought of his is unsettling and disturbing to the scientific mind— but is it not after all itself scientific, psychological, conscientious, and therefore to be accepted without prejudice, no matter how upsetting? In the midst of which musings Dr. Cornelius finds himself back at his own door.

On the outer threshold stands Xaver, and seems to be looking for him.

"Herr Professor," says Xaver, tossing back his hair, "go upstairs to Ellie straight off. She's in a bad way."

"What's the matter?" asks Cornelius in alarm. "Is she ill?"

"No-o, not to say ill," answers Xaver. "She's just in a bad way and crying fit to bust her little heart. It's along o' that chap with the shirt front that danced with her—Herr Hergesell. She couldn't be got to go upstairs peaceably, not at no price at all, and she's b'en crying bucketfuls."

"Nonsense," says the Professor, who has entered and is tossing off his things in the cloakroom. He says no more; opens the glass door and without a glance at the guests turns swiftly to the stairs. Takes them two at a time, crosses the upper hall and the small room leading into the nursery. Xaver follows at his heels, but stops at the nursery door.

A bright light still burns within, showing the gay frieze that runs all round the room, the large row of shelves heaped with a confusion of toys, the rocking-horse on his swaying platform, with red-varnished nostrils and raised hoofs. On the linoleum lie other toys—building blocks, railway trains, a little trumpet. The two white cribs stand not far apart, Ellie's in the window corner, Snapper's out in the room.

Snapper is asleep. He has said his prayers in loud, ringing tones, prompted by Nurse, and gone off at once into vehement, profound, and rosy slumber—from which a cannonball fired at close range could not rouse him. He lies with both fists flung back on the pillows on either side of the tousled head with its funny crooked little slumber-tossed wig.

A circle of females surrounds Ellie's bed: not only blue-faced Ann

is there, but the Hinterhofer ladies too, talking to each other and to her. They make way as the Professor comes up and reveal the child sitting all pale among her pillows, sobbing and weeping more bitterly than he has ever seen her sob and weep in her life. Her lovely little hands lie on the coverlet in front of her, the nightgown with its narrow lace border has slipped down from her shoulder—such a thin, birdlike little shoulder—and the sweet head Cornelius loves so well, set on the neck like a flower on its stalk, her head is on one side, with the eyes rolled up to the corner between wall and ceiling above her head. For there she seems to envisage the anguish of her heart and even to nod to it— either on purpose or because her head wobbles as her body is shaken with the violence of her sobs. Her eyes rain down tears. The bow-shaped lips are parted, like a little *mater dolorosa*'s, and from them issue long, low wails that in nothing resemble the unnecessary and exasperating shrieks of a naughty child, but rise from the deep extremity of her heart and wake in the Professor's own a sympathy that is well-nigh intolerable. He has never seen his darling so before. His feelings find immediate vent in an attack on the ladies Hinterhofer.

"What about the supper?" he asks sharply. "There must be a great deal to do. Is my wife being left to do it alone?"

For the acute sensibilities of the former middle class this is quite enough. The ladies withdraw in righteous indignation, and Xaver Kleingutl jeers at them as they pass out. Having been born to low life instead of achieving it, he never loses a chance to mock at their fallen state.

"Childie, childie," murmurs Cornelius, and sitting down by the crib enfolds the anguished Ellie in his arms. "What is the trouble with my darling?"

She bedews his face with her tears.

"Abel . . . Abel . . ." she stammers between sobs. "Why—isn't Max —my brother? Max ought to be—my brother!"

Alas, alas! What mischance is this? Is this what the party has wrought, with its fatal atmosphere? Cornelius glances helplessly up at blue-faced Ann standing there in all the dignity of her limitations with her hands before her on her apron. She purses up her mouth and makes a long face. "It's pretty young," she says, "for the female instincts to be showing up."

"Hold your tongue," snaps Cornelius, in his agony. He has this much to be thankful for, that Ellie does not turn from him now; she does not push him away as she did downstairs, but clings to him in her need, while she reiterates her absurd, bewildered prayer that Max might be her brother, or with a fresh burst of desire demands to be taken downstairs so that he can dance with her again. But Max, of course, is dancing with Fräulein Plaichinger, that behemoth who is his rightful partner and has every claim upon him; whereas Ellie—never, thinks the Professor, his heart torn with the violence of his pity, never has she looked so tiny and birdlike as now, when she nestles to him shaken with sobs and all unaware of what is happening in her little soul. No, she does not know. She does not comprehend that her suffering is on account of Fräulein Plaichinger, fat, overgrown, and utterly within her rights in dancing with Max Hergesell, whereas Ellie may only do it once, by way of a joke, although she is incomparably the more charming of the two. Yet it would be quite mad to reproach young Hergesell with the state of affairs or to make fantastic demands upon him. No, Ellie's suffering

is without help or healing and must be covered up. Yet just as it is without understanding, so it is also without restraint—and that is what makes it so horribly painful. Xaver and blue-faced Ann do not feel this pain, it does not affect them—either because of native callousness or because they accept it as the way of nature. But the Professor's fatherly heart is quite torn by it, and by a distressful horror of this passion, so hopeless and so absurd.

Of no avail to hold forth to poor Ellie on the subject of the perfectly good little brother she already has. She only casts a distraught and scornful glance over at the other crib, where Snapper lies vehemently slumbering, and with fresh tears calls again for Max. Of no avail either the promise of a long, long walk tomorrow, all five gentlemen, round and round the dining-room table; or a dramatic description of the thrilling cushion games they will play. No, she will listen to none of all this, nor to lying down and going to sleep. She will not sleep, she will sit bolt upright and suffer. . . . But on a sudden they stop and listen, Abel and Ellie; listen to something miraculous that is coming to pass, that is approaching by strides, two strides, to the nursery door, that now overwhelmingly appears. . . .

It is Xaxer's work, not a doubt of that. He has not remained by the door where he stood to gloat over the ejection of the Hinterhofers. No, he has bestirred himself, taken a notion; likewise steps to carry it out. Downstairs he has gone, twitched Herr Hergesell's sleeve, and made a thick-lipped request. So here they both are. Xaver, having done his part, remains by the door; but Max Hergesell comes up to Ellie's crib; in his dinner jacket, with his sketchy side-whisker and charming black eyes; obviously quite pleased with his role of swan knight[7] and fairy prince, as one who should say: "See, here am I, now all losses are restored and sorrows end."

Cornelius is almost as much overcome as Ellie herself.

"Just look," he says feebly, "look who's here. This is uncommonly good of you, Herr Hergesell."

"Not a bit of it," says Hergesell. "Why shouldn't I come to say goodnight to my fair partner?"

And he approaches the bars of the crib, behind which Ellie sits struck mute. She smiles blissfully through her tears. A funny, high little note that is half a sigh of relief comes from her lips, then she looks dumbly up at her swan knight with her golden-brown eyes—tear-swollen though they are, so much more beautiful than the fat Plaichinger's. She does not put up her arms. Her joy, like her grief, is without understanding; but she does not do that. The lovely little hands lie quiet on the coverlet, and Max Hergesell stands with his arms leaning over the rail as on a balcony.

"And now," he says smartly, "she need not 'sit the livelong night and weep upon her bed'!" He looks at the Professor to make sure he is receiving due credit for the quotation. "Ha ha!" he laughs, "she's beginning young. 'Console thee, dearest child!' Never mind, you're all right! Just as you are you'll be wonderful! You've only got to grow up. . . . And you'll lie down and go to sleep like a good girl, now I've come to say goodnight? And not cry anymore, little Lorelei?"

Ellie looks up at him, transfigured. One birdlike shoulder is bare; the Professor draws the lace-trimmed nighty over it. There comes into

7. Lohengrin, the Knight of the Swan in the German Grail legends, is the deliverer of Elsa, Princess of Brabant.

his mind a sentimental story he once read about a dying child who longs to see a clown he had once, with unforgettable ecstasy, beheld in a circus. And they bring the clown to the bedside marvelously arrayed, embroidered before and behind with silver butterflies; and the child dies happy. Max Hergesell is not embroidered, and Ellie, thank God, is not going to die, she has only "been in a bad way." But, after all, the effect is the same. Young Hergesell leans over the bars of the crib and rattles on, more for the father's ear than the child's, but Ellie does not know that—and the father's feelings towards him are a most singular mixture of thankfulness, embarrassment, and hatred.

"Goodnight, little Lorelei," says Hergesell, and gives her his hand through the bars. Her pretty, soft, white little hand is swallowed up in the grasp of his big, strong, red one. "Sleep well," he says, "and sweet dreams! But don't dream about me—God forbid! Not at your age—ha ha!" And then the fairy clown's visit is at an end. Cornelius accompanies him to the door. "No, no, positively, no thanks called for, don't mention it," he large-heartedly protests; and Xaver goes downstairs with him, to help serve the Italian salad.

But Dr. Cornelius returns to Ellie, who is now lying down, with her cheek pressed into her flat little pillow.

"Well, wasn't that lovely?" he says as he smooths the covers. She nods, with one last little sob. For a quarter of an hour he sits beside her and watches while she falls asleep in her turn, beside the little brother who found the right way so much earlier than she. Her silky brown hair takes the enchanting fall it always does when she sleeps; deep, deep lie the lashes over the eyes that late so abundantly poured forth their sorrow; the angelic mouth with its bowed upper lip is peacefully relaxed and a little open. Only now and then comes a belated catch in her slow breathing.

And her small hands, like pink and white flowers, lie so quietly, one on the coverlet, the other on the pillow by her face—Dr. Cornelius, gazing, feels his heart melt with tenderness as with strong wine.

"How good," he thinks, "that she breathes in oblivion with every breath she draws! That in childhood each night is a deep, wide gulf between one day and the next. Tomorrow, beyond all doubt, young Hergesell will be a pale shadow, powerless to darken her little heart. Tomorrow, forgetful of all but present joy, she will walk with Abel and Snapper, all five gentlemen, round and round the table, will play the ever-thrilling cushion game."

Heaven be praised for that!

1925

HEINRICH BÖLL

Christmas Every Day*

Symptoms of decline have become evident in our family. For a time we were at pains to disregard them, but now we have resolved to face the danger. I dare not, as yet, use the word breakdown, but disturbing facts are piling up at such a rate as to constitute a menace and to com-

---

* Translated by Denver Lindley. Sociohistorical details will not be annotated.

pel me to report things that will sound disagreeable to my contemporaries; no one, however, can dispute their reality. The minute fungi of destruction have found lodgement beneath the hard, thick crust of respectability; colonies of deadly parasites that proclaim the end of a whole tribe's irreproachable correctness. Today we must deplore our disregard of Cousin Franz, who began long ago to warn us of the dreadful consequences that would result from an event that was harmless enough in itself. So insignificant indeed was the event that the disproportion of the consequences now terrifies us. Franz warned us betimes. Unfortunately he had too little standing. He had chosen a calling that no member of the family had ever followed before, and none ever should have: he was a boxer. Melancholy even in youth and possessed by a devoutness that was always described as "pious fiddle-faddle," he early adopted ways that worried my Uncle Franz, that good, kind man. He was wont to neglect his schoolwork to a quite abnormal degree. He used to meet disreputable companions in the thickets and deserted parks of the suburbs, and there practice the rough discipline of the prize fight, with no thought for his neglected humanistic heritage. These youngsters early revealed the vices of their generation, which, as has since become abundantly evident, is really worthless. The exciting spiritual combats of earlier centuries simply did not interest them; they were far too concerned with the dubious excitements of their own. At first I thought Franz's piety in contradiction to his systematic exercises in passive and active brutality. But today I begin to suspect a connection. This is a subject I shall have to return to.

And so it was Franz who warned us in good time, who refused above all to have anything to do with certain celebrations, calling the whole thing a folly and a disgrace, and later on declined to participate in those measures that proved necessary for the continuance of what he considered evil. But, as I have said, he had too little standing to get a hearing in the family circle.

Now, to be sure, things have gone so far that we stand helpless, not knowing how to call a halt.

Franz has long since become a famous boxer, but today he rejects the praises that the family lavishes on him with the same indifference he once showed toward their criticism.

His brother, however—my Cousin Johannes, a man for whom I would at any time have walked through fire, the successful lawyer and favorite son of my Uncle—Johannes is said to have struck up relations with the Communist Party, a rumor I stubbornly refuse to believe. My Cousin Lucie, hitherto a normal woman, is said to frequent disreputable nightclubs, accompanied by her helpless husband, and to engage in dances that I can only describe as existential. Even Uncle Franz, that good, kind man, is reported to have remarked that he is weary of life, he whom the whole family considered a paragon of vitality and the very model of what we were taught to call a Christian businessman.

Doctors' bills are piling up, psychiatrists and analysts are being called in. Only my Aunt Milla, who must be considered the cause of it all, enjoys the best of health, smiling, well and cheerful, as she has been almost all her life. Her liveliness and cheerfulness are slowly beginning to get on our nerves after our very serious concern about the state of her health. For there was a crisis in her life that threatened to be serious. It is just this that I must explain.

2

In retrospect it is easy enough to determine the source of a disquieting series of events, but only now, when I regard the matter dispassionately, do the things that have been taking place in our family for almost two years appear out of the ordinary.

We might have surmised earlier that something was not quite right. Something in fact was not, and if things ever were quite right—which I doubt—events are now taking place that fill me with consternation.

For a long time Aunt Milla has been famous in our family for her delight in decorating the Christmas tree, a harmless though particularized weakness which is fairly widespread in our country. This weakness of hers was indulgently smiled at by one and all, and the resistance that Franz showed from his earliest days to this "nonsense" was treated with indignation, especially since Franz was in other respects a disturbing young man. He refused to take part in the decoration of the tree. Up to a certain point all this was taken in stride. My aunt had become accustomed to Franz's staying away from the preparations at Advent and also from the celebration itself and only putting in an appearance for the meal. It was not even mentioned.

At the risk of making myself unpopular, I must here mention a fact in defense of which I can only say that it really is a fact. In the years 1939 to 1945 we were at war. In war there is singing, shooting, oratory, fighting, starvation and death—and bombs are dropped. These are thoroughly disagreeable subjects, and I have no desire to bore my contemporaries by dwelling on them. I must only mention them because the war had an influence on the story I am about to tell. For the war registered on my aunt simply as a force that, as early as Christmas 1939, began to threaten her Christmas tree. To be sure, this tree of hers was peculiarly sensitive.

As its principal attraction my Aunt Milla's Christmas tree was furnished with glass gnomes that held cork hammers in their upraised hands. At their feet were bell-shaped anvils, and under their feet candles were fastened. When the heat rose to a certain degree, a hidden mechanism went into operation, imparting a hectic movement to the gnomes' arms; a dozen in number, they beat like mad on the bell-shaped anvils with their cork hammers, thus producing a concerted, high-pitched, elfin tinkling. And at the top of the tree stood a red-cheeked angel, dressed in silver, who at certain intervals opened his lips and whispered "Peace, peace." The mechanical secret of the angel was strictly guarded, and I only learned about it later, when as it happened I had the opportunity of admiring it almost weekly. Naturally in addition to this my aunt's Christmas tree was decorated with sugar rings, cookies, angel hair, marzipan figures and, not to be forgotten, strands of tinsel. I still remember that the proper preparation of these varied decorations cost a good deal of trouble, demanding the help of all, and the whole family on Christmas Eve was too nervous to be hungry. The mood, as people say, was simply terrible, and the one exception was my Cousin Franz, who of course had taken no part in the preparations and was the only one to enjoy the roasts, asparagus, creams and ices. If after that we came for a call on the day after Christmas and ventured the bold conjecture that the secret of the speaking angel resided in the same sort of mechanism that makes certain dolls say "Mama" or "Papa," we were simply greeted by derisive laughter.

Now it is easy to understand that in the neighborhood of falling

bombs such a sensitive tree would be in great danger. There were terrible times when the gnomes pitched down from the tree, and once even the angel fell. My aunt was inconsolable. She went to endless pains to restore the tree completely after each air raid so as to preserve it at least through the Christmas holidays. But by 1940 it was out of the question. Once more at the risk of making myself unpopular I must briefly mention here that the number of air raids on our city was considerable, to say nothing of their severity. In any case my aunt's Christmas tree fell victim to the modern art of war (regulations forbid me to say anything about other victims); foreign ballistics experts temporarily extinguished it.

We all sympathized with our aunt, who was an amiable and charming woman, and pretty into the bargain. It pained us that she was compelled, after bitter struggles, endless disputes, scenes and tears, to agree to forego her tree for the duration.

Fortunately—or should I say unfortunately?—this was almost the only aspect of the war that was brought home to my aunt. The bunker my uncle built was really bombproof; in addition a car was always ready to whisk my Aunt Milla away to places where nothing was to be seen of the immediate effects of war. Everything was done to spare her the sight of the horrible ruins. My two cousins had the good fortune not to see military service in its harshest form. Johannes at once entered my uncle's firm, which played an essential part in the wholesale grocery business of our city. Besides, he suffered from gall bladder trouble. Franz on the other hand became a soldier, but he was only engaged in guarding prisoners, a post which he exploited to the extent of making himself unpopular with his military superiors by treating Russians and Poles like human beings. My Cousin Lucie was not yet married at that time and helped with the business. One afternoon a week she did voluntary war work, embroidering swastikas. But this is not the place to recite the political sins of my relations.

On the whole, then, there was no lack of money or food or reasonable safety, and my aunt's only sorrow was the absence of her tree. My Uncle Franz, that good, kind man, had for almost fifty years rendered invaluable service by purchasing oranges and lemons in tropical and subtropical countries and selling them at an appropriate profit. During the war he extended his business to less valuable fruits and to vegetables. After the war, however, the principal objects of his interest became popular once more under the name of citrus fruits and caused sharp competition in business circles. Here Uncle Franz succeeded once more in playing a decisive role by introducing the populace to a taste for vitamins and himself to a sizable fortune. He was almost seventy by that time, however, and wanted to retire and leave the business to his son-in-law. It was then that the event took place which made us smile at the time but which we now recognize as the cause of the whole affair.

My Aunt Milla began again with her Christmas tree. That was harmless in itself; even the tenacity with which she insisted that everything should be "as it used to be" only caused us to smile. At first there was really no reason to take the matter too seriously. To be sure, the war had caused much havoc which it was our duty to put right, but why—so we asked ourselves—deprive a charming old lady of this small joy?

Everyone knows how hard it was at that time to get butter and bacon. And even for my Uncle Franz, who had the best connections, it was

impossible in the year 1945 to procure marzipan figures and chocolate rings. It was not until 1946 that everything could be made ready. Fortunately a complete set of gnomes and anvils as well as an angel had been preserved.

I still clearly remember the day on which we were invited. It was in January '47 and it was cold outside. But at my uncle's it was warm and there was no lack of delicacies. When the lights were turned out and the candles lighted, when the gnomes began to hammer and the angel whispered "Peace, peace," I had a vivid feeling of being restored to a time that I had assumed was gone forever.

This experience, however, though surprising was not extraordinary. The extraordinary thing was what happened three months later. My mother—it was now the middle of March—sent me over to find out whether "there was anything doing" with Uncle Franz. She needed fruit. I wandered into the neighboring quarter—the air was mild and it was twilight. Unsuspecting, I walked past the overgrown piles of ruins and the untended parks, turned in at the gate to my uncle's garden and suddenly stopped in amazement. In the evening quiet I could distinctly hear someone singing in my uncle's living room. Singing is a good old German custom, and there are lots of spring songs—but here I clearly heard:

> *Unto us a child is born!*
> *The King of all creation . . .*

I must admit I was confused. Slowly I approached and waited for the end of the song. The curtains were drawn and so I bent down to the keyhole. At that moment the tinkling of the gnomes' bells reached my ear, and I distinctly heard the angel whispering.

I did not have the courage to intrude, and walked slowly home. My report caused general merriment in the family, and it was not until Franz turned up and told us the details that we discovered what had happened.

In our region Christmas trees are dismantled at Candlemas and are then thrown on the rubbish heap where good-for-nothing children pick them up, drag them through ashes and other debris and play all sorts of games with them. This was the time when the dreadful thing happened. On Candlemas Eve after the tree had been lighted for the last time, and Cousin Johannes began to unfasten the gnomes from their clamps, my aunt who had hitherto been so gentle set up a dreadful screaming, so loud and sudden that my cousin was startled, lost control of the swaying tree, and in an instant it was all over; there was a tinkling and ringing; gnomes and bells, anvils and angel, everything pitched down; and my aunt screamed.

She screamed for almost a week. Neurologists were summoned by telegram, psychiatrists came rushing up in taxicabs—but all of them, even the specialists, left with a shrug of the shoulders and a faint expression of dread.

No one could put an end to this shrill and maddening concert. Only the strongest drugs provided a few hours' rest, and the dose of Luminal that one can daily prescribe for a woman in her sixties without endangering her life is, alas, slight. But it is anguish to have a woman in the house screaming with all her might: on the second day the family was completely disorganized. Even the consolation of the priest, who was

accustomed to attend the celebration on Holy Eve, remained unavailing: my aunt screamed.

Franz made himself particularly unpopular by advising that a regular exorcism be performed. The minister rebuked him, the family was alarmed by his medieval views, and his reputation for brutality eclipsed for several weeks his reputation as a boxer.

Meanwhile everything was tried to cure my aunt's ailment. She refused nourishment, did not speak, did not sleep; cold water was tried, hot water, foot baths, alternate cold and hot baths; the doctors searched the lexicons for the name of this complex but could not find it. And my aunt screamed. She screamed until my Uncle Franz—that really kind, good man—hit on the idea of putting up a new Christmas tree.

3

The idea was excellent, but to carry it out proved extremely hard. It was now almost the middle of February, and to find a presentable fir tree in the market at that time is naturally difficult. The whole business world has long since turned with happy alacrity to other things. Carnival time is near: masks, pistols, cowboy hats and fanciful gypsy headgear fill the shop windows where angels and angel hair, candles and mangers, were formerly on view. In the candy stores Christmas items have long since gone back to the storeroom, while fireworks now adorn the windows. Nowhere in the regular market is a fir tree to be found.

Finally an expedition of rapacious grandchildren was fitted out with pocket money and a sharp hatchet. They rode to the state forest and came back toward evening, obviously in the best of spirits, with a silver fir. But meanwhile it was discovered that four gnomes, six bell-shaped anvils and the crowning angel had been completely destroyed. The marzipan figures and the cookies had fallen victim to the rapacious grandchildren. This coming generation, too, is worthless, and if any generation was ever of any worth—which I doubt—I am slowly coming to the belief that it was the generation of our fathers.

Although there was no lack of cash or the necessary connections, it took four days more before the decorations were complete. Meanwhile my aunt screamed uninterruptedly. Messages to the German centers of the toy business, which were just then resuming operations, were dispatched by wireless, hurried telephone conversations were carried on, packages were delivered in the night by heated young postal employees, an import license from Czechoslovakia was obtained, by bribery, without delay.

These days will stand out in the chronicle of my uncle's family by reason of the extraordinary consumption of coffee, cigarettes and nervous energy. Meanwhile my aunt fell into a decline: her round face became harsh and angular, her expression of kindliness changed to one of unalterable severity, she did not eat, she did not drink, she screamed constantly, she was attended by two nurses, and the dose of Luminal had to be increased daily.

Franz told us that the whole family was in the grip of a morbid tension when finally, on the twelfth of February, the decoration of the Christmas tree was at last completed. The candles were lighted, the curtains were drawn, my aunt was brought out from her sickroom, and in the family circle there was only the sound of sobs and giggles. My aunt's expression relaxed at the sight of the candles, and when the heat

had reached the proper point and the glass gnomes began to pound like mad and finally the angel, too, whispered "Peace, peace," a beautiful smile illuminated her face. Shortly thereafter everyone began to sing "O Tannenbaum." To complete the picture, they had invited the minister, whose custom it was to spend Christmas Eve at my Uncle Franz's; he, too, smiled, he too was relieved and joined in the singing.

What no test, no psychological opinion, no expert search for hidden traumas had succeeded in doing, my uncle's sympathetic heart had accomplished. This good, kind man's Christmas-tree therapy had saved the situation.

My aunt was reassured and almost—so they hoped at the time—cured. After more songs had been sung and several plates of cookies had been emptied, everyone was tired and went to bed. And, imagine, my aunt slept without sedatives. The two nurses were dismissed, the doctors shrugged their shoulders, and everything seemed in order. My aunt ate again, drank again, was once more kind and amiable.

But the following evening at twilight, when my uncle was reading his newspaper beside his wife under the tree, she suddenly touched him gently on the arm and said: "Now we will call the children for the celebration. I think it's time." My uncle admitted to us later that he was startled, but he got up and hastily summoned his children and grandchildren and dispatched a messenger for the minister. The latter appeared, somewhat distraught and amazed; the candles were lighted, the gnomes hammered away, the angel whispered, there was singing and eating—and everything seemed in order.

Now all vegetation is subject to certain biological laws, and fir trees torn from the soil have a well-known tendency to wilt and lose their needles, especially if they are kept in a warm room, and in my uncle's house it was warm. The life of the silver fir is somewhat longer than that of the common variety, as the well-known work *Abies Vulgaris and Abies Nobilis*[1] by Doctor Hergenring has shown. But even the life of the silver fir is not unlimited. As Carnival approached it became clear that my aunt would have to be prepared for a new sorrow: the tree was rapidly losing its needles, and at the evening singing a slight frown appeared on her forehead. On the advice of a really outstanding psychologist an attempt was made in light, casual conversation to warn her of the possible end of the Christmas season, especially as the trees outside were now covered with leaves, which is generally taken as a sign of approaching spring whereas in our latitudes the word Christmas connotes wintry scenes. My resourceful uncle proposed one evening that the songs "All the birds are now assembled" and "Come Lovely May" should be sung, but at the first verse of the former such a scowl appeared on my aunt's face that the singers quickly broke off and intoned "O Tannenbaum." Three days later my cousin Johannes was instructed to undertake a quiet dismantling operation, but as soon as he stretched out his hand and took the cork hammer from one of the gnomes my aunt broke into such violent screaming that the gnome was immediately given back his implement, the candles were lighted and somewhat hastily but very loudly everyone began to sing "Silent Night."

But the nights were no longer silent; groups of singing, youthful revelers streamed through the city with trumpets and drums, everything

---

1. *Common and Noble Fir Trees;* scarcely "well-known" and possibly fictional.

was covered with streamers and confetti, masked children crowded the streets, fired guns, screamed, some sang as well, and a private investigation showed that there were at least sixty thousand cowboys and forty thousand gypsy princesses in our city: in short it was Carnival, a holiday that is celebrated in our neighborhood with as much enthusiasm as Christmas or even more. But my aunt seemed blind and deaf: she deplored the carnival costumes that inevitably appeared at this time in the wardrobes of our household; in a sad voice she lamented the decline of morals that caused people even at Christmas to indulge in such disgraceful practices, and when she discovered a toy balloon in Lucie's bedroom, a balloon that had, to be sure, collapsed but nevertheless clearly showed a white fool's cap painted on it, she broke into tears and besought my uncle to put an end to these unholy activities.

They were forced to realize with horror that my aunt actually believed it was still Christmas Eve. My uncle called a family council, requested consideration for his wife in view of her extraordinary state of mind, and at once got together an expedition to insure that at least the evening celebration would be peacefully maintained.

While my aunt slept the decorations were taken down from the old tree and placed on a new one, and her state of health continued to be satisfactory.

Carnival, too, went by, spring came for fair; instead of "Come Lovely May" one might properly have sung "Lovely May, Thou Art Here." June arrived. Four Christmas trees had already been discarded and none of the newly summoned doctors could hold out hope of improvement. My aunt remained firm. Even that internationally famous authority, Doctor Bless, had returned to his study, shrugging his shoulders, after having pocketed an honorarium in the sum of 1365 marks, thereby demonstrating once more his complete unworldliness. A few tentative attempts to put an end to the celebration or to intermit it were greeted with such outcries from my aunt that these sacrileges had to be abandoned once and for all.

The dreadful thing was that my aunt insisted that all those closest to her must be present. Among these were the minister and the grandchildren. Even the members of the family could only be compelled by extreme severity to appear punctually; with the minister it was even more difficult. For some weeks he kept it up without protest, out of consideration for his aged pensioner, but then he attempted, clearing his throat in embarrassment, to make it clear to my uncle that this could not go on. The actual celebration was short—it lasted only about thirty-eight minutes—but even this brief ceremonial, the minister maintained, could not be kept up indefinitely. He had other obligations, evening conferences with his confratres, duties connected with his cure of souls, not to mention his regular Saturday confessional. He agreed, however, to some weeks' continuance; but toward the end of May, he began energetic attempts to escape. Franz stormed about, seeking accomplices in the family for his plan to have his mother put in an institution. Everyone turned him down.

And yet difficulties continued. One evening the minister was missing and could not be located either telephonically or by messenger, and it became evident that he had simply skipped out. My uncle swore horribly and took the occasion to describe the servants of the Church in words I must decline to repeat. In this extremity one of the chaplains,

a man of humble origin, was requested to help out. He did so, but behaved so abominably that it almost resulted in a catastrophe. However, one must bear in mind that it was June and therefore hot; nevertheless the curtains were drawn to give at least an illusion of wintry twilight and in addition the candles had been lighted. Then the celebration began. The chaplain had, to be sure, heard of this extraordinary event but had no proper idea of it. There was general apprehension when he was presented to my aunt as the minister's substitute. Unexpectedly she accepted this change in the program. Well then, the gnomes hammered, the angel whispered, "O Tannenbaum" was sung, then there was the eating of cookies, more singing, and suddenly the chaplain was overcome by a paroxysm of laughter. Later he admitted that it was the line ". . . in winter, too, when snow is falling" that had been too much for him to endure without laughing. He burst out with clerical tactlessness, left the room and was seen no more. All looked at my aunt apprehensively, but she only murmured resignedly something about "proletarians in priest's robes" and put a piece of marzipan in her mouth. We too deplored this event at the time—but today I am inclined to regard it as an outbreak of quite natural hilarity.

Here I must remark, if I am to be true to the facts, that my uncle exploited his connection with the highest Church authorities to lodge a complaint against both the minister and the chaplain. The matter was taken up with utmost correctness, proceedings were instituted on the grounds of neglect of pastoral duty, and in the first instance the two clergymen were exonerated. Further proceedings are in preparation.

Fortunately a pensioned prelate was found in the neighborhood. This charming old gentleman agreed, with amiable matter-of-factness, to hold himself in readiness daily for the evening celebration. But I am anticipating. My Uncle Franz, who was sensible enough to realize that no medical aid would be of avail and who stubbornly refused to try exorcism, was also a good enough businessman to plan economies for the long haul. First of all, by mid-June, the grandchildren's expeditions were stopped, because they proved too expensive. My resourceful Cousin Johannes, who was on good terms with all branches of the business world, discovered that Söderbaum and Company were in a position to provide fresh fir trees. For almost two years now this firm has done noble service in sparing my relations' nerves. At the end of six months Söderbaum and Company substantially reduced their charges and agreed to have the period of delivery determined most precisely by their conifer specialist Doctor Alfast, so that three days before the old tree became unpresentable a new one would be delivered and could be decorated at leisure. As an additional precaution two dozen gnomes and three crowning angels were kept constantly in reserve.

To this day the candles remain a sore point. They show a disturbing tendency to melt and drip down from the tree more quickly and completely than wax, at any rate in the summer months. Every effort to preserve them by carefully concealed refrigeration has thus far come to grief, as has a series of attempts to substitute artificial decorations. The family remains, however, gratefully receptive toward any proposal that might result in reducing the costs of this continuing festival.

4

Meanwhile the daily celebrations in my uncle's house have taken on an almost professional regularity. People assemble under the tree or

around the tree. My aunt comes in, the candles are lighted, the gnomes begin to hammer and the angel whispers "Peace, peace," songs are sung, cookies are nibbled, there is a little conversation and then everyone retires, yawning and murmuring "Merry Christmas to you, too." The young people turn to the forms of diversion dictated by the season, while my good, kind Uncle Franz goes to bed when Aunt Milla does. The smoke of the candles lingers in the room, there is the mild aroma of heated fir needles and the smell of spices. The gnomes, slightly phosphorescent, remain motionless in the darkness, their arms raised threateningly, and the angel can be seen in his silvery robes which are obviously phosphorescent too.

Perhaps it is superfluous to state that in our whole family circle the enjoyment of the real Christmas Eve has suffered a considerable diminution: we can, if we like, admire a classical Christmas tree at our uncle's at any time—and it often happens when we are sitting on the veranda in summertime after the toil and trouble of the day, pouring my uncle's mild orange punch down our throats, that the soft tinkling of glass bells comes to us and we can see in the twilight the gnomes hammering away like spry little devils while the angel whispers "Peace, peace." And it is still disconcerting to hear my uncle in midsummer suddenly whisper to his children: "Please light the tree, Mother will be right out." Then, usually on the dot, the prelate enters, a kindly old gentleman whom we have all taken to our hearts because he plays his role so admirably, if indeed he knows that he is playing one. But no matter: he plays it, white-haired, smiling, with the violet band beneath his collar giving his appearance the final touch of distinction. And it gives one an extraordinary feeling on a mild summer evening to hear the excited cry: "The snuffer, quick, where is the snuffer?" It has even happened during severe thunderstorms that the gnomes have been suddenly impelled to lift their arms without the agency of heat and swing them wildly as though giving a special performance—a phenomenon that people have tried, rather unimaginatively, to explain by the prosaic word "electricity."

A by no means inessential aspect of this arrangement is the financial one. Even though in general our family suffers no lack of cash, such extraordinary expenses upset all calculations. For naturally, despite precautions, the breakage of gnomes, anvils, and hammers is enormous, and the delicate mechanism that causes the angel to speak requires constant care and attention and must now and again be replaced. I have, incidentally, discovered its secret: the angel is connected by a cable with a microphone in the adjoining room, in front of whose metal snout there is a constantly rotating phonograph record which, at proper intervals, whispers "Peace, peace." All these things are the more costly because they are designed for use on only a few occasions during the year, whereas with us they are subjected to daily wear and tear. I was astounded when my uncle told me one day that the gnomes actually had to be replaced every three months, and that a complete set of them cost no less than 128 marks. He said he had requested an engineering friend of his to try strengthening them by a rubber covering without spoiling the beauty of the tone. This experiment was unsuccessful. The consumption of candles, butter-and-almond cookies, marzipan, the regular payments for the trees, doctor's bills and the quarterly honorarium that has to be given to the prelate, altogether, said my uncle, come to an average daily expense of 11 marks, not to mention the ner-

vous wear and tear and other disturbances of health that began to appear in the fall of the first year. These upsets were generally ascribed, at the time, to that autumnal sensibility that is always noticeable.

The real Christmas celebration went off quite normally. Something like a sigh of relief ran through my uncle's family when other families could be seen gathered under Christmas trees, others too had to sing and eat butter-and-almond cookies. But the relief lasted only as long as the Christmas holidays. By the middle of January my Cousin Lucie began to suffer from a strange ailment: at the sight of Christmas trees lying on the streets and on rubbish heaps she broke into hysterical sobs. Then she had a real attack of insanity which the family tried to discount as a nervous breakdown. At a coffee party in a friend's house she struck a dish out of her hostess' hand as the latter was smilingly offering her butter-and-almond cookies. My cousin is, to be sure, what is called a temperamental woman: and so she struck the dish from her friend's hand, went up to the Christmas tree, tore it from its stand and trampled on the glass balls, the artificial mushrooms, the candles and the stars, the while emitting a continuous roar. The assembled ladies fled, including the hostess. They let Lucie rage, and stood waiting for the doctor in the vestibule, forced to give ear to the sound of crashing china within. Painful though it is for me, I must report that Lucie was taken away in a straightjacket.

Sustained hypnotic treatment checked her illness, but the actual cure proceeded very slowly. Above all, release from the evening celebration, which the doctor demanded, seemed to do her visible good; after a few days she began to brighten. At the end of ten days the doctor could risk at least talking to her about butter-and-almond cookies, although she stubbornly persisted in refusing to eat them. The doctor then struck on the inspired idea of feeding her some sour pickles and offering her salads and nourishing meat dishes. That was poor Lucie's real salvation. She laughed once more and began to interject ironic observations into the endless therapeutic interview she had with her doctor.

To be sure, the vacancy caused by her absence from the evening celebration was painful to my aunt, but it was explained to her by a circumstance that is an adequate excuse in any woman's eyes—pregnancy.

But Lucie had created what is called a precedent: she had proved that although my aunt suffered when someone was absent, she did not immediately begin to scream, and now my Cousin Johannes and his brother-in-law Carl attempted to infringe on the severe regulations, giving sickness as excuse or business appointments or some other quite transparent pretext. But here my uncle remained astonishingly inflexible: with iron severity he decreed that only in exceptional cases upon presentation of acceptable evidence could very short leaves of absence be permitted. For my aunt noticed every further dereliction at once and broke into silent but continuing tears, which gave rise to the most serious apprehensions.

At the end of four weeks Lucie, too, returned and said she was ready to take part once more in the daily ceremony, but her doctor had insisted that a jar of pickles and a platter of nourishing sandwiches should be held in readiness, since her butter-and-almond trauma had proved incurable. Thus for a time, through my uncle's unexpected severity, all breaches of discipline were suppressed.

Shortly after the first anniversary of the daily Christmas celebration, disquieting rumors began to circulate: my Cousin Johannes was said to

have consulted a doctor friend of his about my aunt's life expectancy, a truly sinister rumor which throws a disturbing light on a peaceful family's evening gatherings. The doctor's opinion is said to have been crushing for Johannes. All my aunt's vital organs, which had always been sound, were in perfect condition; her father's age at the time of his death had been seventy-eight, and her mother's eighty-six. My aunt herself is sixty-two, and so there is no reason to prophesy an early passing. Still less reason, I consider, to wish for one. After this when my aunt fell ill in midsummer—the poor woman suffered from vomiting and diarrhea—it was hinted that she had been poisoned, but I expressly declare here and now that this rumor was simply the invention of evil-minded relations. The trouble was clearly shown to have been caused by an infection brought into the house by one of the grandchildren. Moreover, analyses that were made of my aunt's stools showed not the slightest traces of poison.

That same summer Johannes gave the first evidences of antisocial inclinations: he resigned from the singing circle and gave notice in writing that he planned to take no further part in the cultivation of the German song. It is only fair for me to add, however, that, despite the academic distinctions he had won, he was always an uncultivated man. For the "Virhymnia" the loss of his bass voice was a serious matter.

My brother-in-law Carl began secretly to consult travel agencies. The land of his dreams had to have unusual characteristics: no fir trees must grow there and their importation must be forbidden or rendered unfeasible by a high tariff; besides—on his wife's account—the secret of preparing butter-and-almond cookies must be unknown and the singing of German Christmas songs forbidden by law. Carl declared himself ready to undertake hard physical labor.

Since then he has been able to dispense with secrecy because of a complete and very sudden change which has taken place in my uncle. This happened at such a disagreeable level that we have really had cause to be disconcerted. The sober citizen, of whom it could be said that he was as stubborn as he was good and kind, was observed performing actions that are neither more nor less than immoral and will remain so as long as the world endures. Things became known about him, testified to by witnesses, that can only be described by the word adultery. And the most dreadful thing is that he no longer denies them, but claims for himself the right to live in circumstances and in relationships that make special legislation seem justifiable. Awkwardly enough, this sudden change became evident just at the time when the second hearing of the two parish priests was called. My Uncle Franz seems to have made such a deplorable impression as a witness, as disguised plaintiff indeed, that it must be ascribed to him alone that the second hearing turned out favorably for the two priests. But in the meantime all this had become a matter of indifference to Uncle Franz: his downfall is complete, already accomplished.

He too was the first to hit upon the shocking idea of having himself represented by an actor at the evening celebration. He had found an unemployed *bon vivant,* who for two weeks imitated him so admirably that not even his wife noticed the impersonation. Nor did his children notice it either. It was one of the grandchildren who, during a pause in the singing, suddenly shouted: "Grandpapa has on socks with rings," and triumphantly raised the *bon vivant's* trouser leg. This scene must have been terrifying for the poor artist; the family, too, was upset and

to avoid disaster struck up a song, as they had done so often before in critical situations. After my aunt had gone to bed, the identity of the artist was quickly established. It was the signal for almost complete collapse.

However one must bear in mind that a year and a half is a long time, and it was midsummer again, the time when participation in the play is hardest on my relations. Listless in the heat, they nibble at sand tarts and ginger cookies, smile vacantly while they crack dried-out nuts, listen to the indefatigable hammering of the gnomes and wince when the rosy-cheeked angel above their heads whispers "Peace, peace." But they carry on while, despite their summer clothing, sweat streams down their cheeks and necks and soaks their shirts. Or rather: they have carried on so far.

For the moment money plays no part—almost the reverse. People are beginning to whisper that Uncle Franz has adopted business methods, too, which can hardly be described as those of a "Christian businessman." He is determined not to allow any material lessening of the family fortune, a resolution that both calms and alarms us.

The unmasking of the *bon vivant* led to a regular mutiny, as a result of which a compromise was reached: Uncle Franz agreed to pay the expenses of a small theatrical troupe which would replace him, Johannes, my brother-in-law Carl, and Lucie, and it was further understood that one of the four would always take part in person in the evening celebration in order to keep the children in check. Up till now the prelate has not noticed this deception which can hardly be described as pious. Aside from my aunt and the children, he is the only original figure still in the play.

An exact schedule has been worked out which, in the family circle, is known as the operational program, and thanks to the provision that one of them is always present in person, the actors too are allowed certain vacations. Meanwhile it was observed that the latter were not averse to the celebration and were glad to earn some additional money; thus it was possible to reduce their wages, since fortunately there is no lack of unemployed actors. Carl tells me that there is reason to hope that these "salaries" can be reduced still more, especially as the actors are given a meal and it is well known that art becomes cheaper when food is involved.

I have already briefly mentioned Lucie's unhappy history: now she spends almost all her time in night spots and, on those days when she is compelled to take part in the household celebration, she is beside herself. She wears corduroy britches, colored pullovers, runs around in sandals and she has cut off her splendid hair in order to wear unbecoming bangs and a coiffure that I only recently discovered was once considered modern—it is known as a pony-tail. Although I have so far been unable to observe any overt immorality on her part, but only a kind of exultation, which she herself describes as existentialism, nevertheless I cannot regard this development as desirable; I prefer quiet women, who move decorously to the rhythm of the waltz, know how to recite agreeable verses and whose nourishment is not exclusively sour pickles and goulash seasoned with paprika. My brother-in-law Carl's plans to emigrate seem on the point of becoming a reality: he has found a country, not far from the equator, which seems to answer his requirements, and Lucie is full of enthusiasm; in this country people wear clothes not unlike hers, they love sharp spices and they dance to those rhythms

without which she maintains life is no longer possible for her. It is a little shocking that these two do not plan to obey the command "Abide in the land I have given you,"[2] but on the other hand I can understand their desire to flee.

Things are worse with Johannes. Unfortunately the evil rumor has proved true: he has become a Communist. He has broken off all relations with the family, pays no attention to anything and takes part in the evening celebration only in the person of his double. His eyes have taken on a fanatical expression, he makes public appearances behaving like a dervish at party meetings, neglects his practice and writes furious articles in the appropriate journals. Strangely enough he now sees more of Franz, who is vainly trying to convert him—and vice versa. Despite all their spiritual estrangement, they seem personally to have grown somewhat closer.

Franz I have not seen in a long time, but I have had news of him. He is said to have fallen into a profound depression, to spend his time in dim churches, and I believe that his piety can be fairly described as exaggerated. After the family misfortunes began he started to neglect his calling, and recently I saw on the wall of a ruined house a faded poster saying: "Last Battle of our Veteran Lenz against Lecoq. Lenz is Hanging up the Gloves." The date on the poster was March, and now we are well into August. Franz is said to have fallen on bad times. I believe he finds himself in a situation which has never before occurred in our family: he is poor. Fortunately he has remained single, and so the social consequences of his irresponsible piety harm only him. He has tried with amazing perseverance to have a guardian appointed for Lucie's children because he considers they are endangered by the daily celebration. But his efforts have remained fruitless; thank God, the children of wealthy people are not exposed to the interference of social institutions.

The one least removed from the rest of the family circle is, for all his deplorable actions, Uncle Franz. To be sure, despite his advanced years, he has a mistress. And his business practices, too, are of a sort that we admire, to be sure, but cannot at all approve. Recently he has appointed an unemployed stage manager to supervise the evening celebration and see that everything runs like clockwork. Everything does in fact run like clockwork.

5

Almost two years have now gone by—a long time. And I could not resist the temptation, during one of my evening strolls, to stop in at my uncle's house, where no true hospitality is any longer possible, since strange actors wander about every evening and the members of the family have devoted themselves to reprehensible pleasures. It was a mild summer evening, and as I turned into the avenue of chestnut trees I heard the verse:

The wintry woods are clad in snow . . .

A passing truck made the rest inaudible. Slowly and softly I approached the house and looked through a crack in the curtains. The similarity of

---

2. In *Deuteronomy* 3:19, Moses says, "But your wives, and your little ones, and your cattle (for I know that ye have much cattle) shall abide in your cities which I have given you"; in *Jeremiah* 42:10, Jeremiah reports God's response to the Israelites: "If ye will still abide in this land, then will I build you, and not pull you down, and I will plant you, and not pluck you up; for I repent me of the evil that I have done unto you."

the actors who were present to those of my relations whom they represented was so startling that for an instant I could not recognize which
one this evening was the superintendent, as they called him. I could not
see the gnomes but I could hear them. Their chirping tinkle has a wave
length that can penetrate any wall. The whispering of the angel was inaudible. My aunt seemed to be really happy: she was chatting with the
prelate, and it was only later that I recognized my brother-in-law as
the one real person present—if that is the right word. I recognized him
by the way he rounded and pointed his lips as he blew out a match.
Apparently there are unchangeable individual traits. This led me to
reflect that the actors, too, were obviously treated to cigars and wine—
in addition there was asparagus every evening. If their appetites were
shameless—and what artist's is not?—this meant a considerable additional expense for my uncle. The children were playing with dolls and
wooden wagons in a corner of the room. They looked pale and tired.
Perhaps one really ought to have some consideration for them. I was
struck by the idea that they might perhaps be replaced by wax dolls of
the kind one sees in the windows of drugstores as advertisements for
powdered milk and skin lotions. It seems to me those look quite natural.

As a matter of fact I intend to call the family's attention to the possible effect on the children's temperament of this unnatural daily excitement. Although a certain amount of discipline does no harm, it
seems to me that they are being subjected to excessive demands.

I left my observation post when the people inside began to sing:
"Silent Night." I simply could not bear the song. The air was so mild—
and for an instant I had the feeling that I was watching an assembly
of ghosts. Suddenly I had a craving for sour pickles and this gave me
some inkling of how very much Lucie must have suffered.

I have now succeeded in having the children replaced by wax dolls.
Their procurement was costly—Uncle Franz hesitated for some time—
but one really could not go on irresponsibly feeding the children on
marzipan every day and making them sing songs which in the long
run might cause them psychic injury. The procurement of the dolls
proved to be useful because Carl and Lucie really emigrated and
Johannes also withdrew his children from his father's household. I bade
farewell to Carl and Lucie and the children as they stood amid large
traveling trunks. They seemed happy, if a little worried. Johannes, too,
has left our town. Somewhere or other he is engaged in reorganizing a
Communist cell.

Uncle Franz is weary of life. Recently he complained to me that
people are always forgetting to dust off the dolls. His servants in particular cause him difficulties, and the actors seem inclined to be undisci-
plined. They drink more than they ought, and some of them have been
caught filling their pockets with cigars and cigarettes. I advised my
uncle to provide them with colored water and cardboard cigars.

The only reliable ones are my aunt and the prelate. They chat together about the good old times, giggle and seem to enjoy themselves,
interrupting their conversation only when a song is struck up.

In any event, the celebration goes on.

My cousin Franz has taken an amazing step. He has been accepted
as a lay brother in a nearby monastery. When I saw him for the first
time in a cowl I was startled: that large figure, with broken nose, thickened lips and melancholy expression, reminded me more of a prisoner

than a monk. He seemed almost to have read my thoughts. "Life is a prison sentence," he said softly. I followed him into the interview room. We conversed haltingly, and he was obviously relieved when the bell summoned him to the chapel for prayers. I remained behind, thoughtful, as he departed: he went in a great hurry, and his haste seemed genuine.

1957

The Elements of Fiction

"Action" is the primary element in drama, for a performed play exists only as an action or series of actions (including its words as actions), while in fiction action is only one of the primary elements; there is also the teller or **narrator.** The action of a story may be an external event or series of events, a change in a character's mind, a series of mental events' that lead to an external event or to the avoidance of an external event. There is always action of some sort, but there are always other things, some of which are described in other parts of this section. Something, external or internal, human or situational, "happens" in a story, but there is also somebody telling us about what happens or does not happen. A story told entirely in dialogue approaches the condition of a play; a story describing the feelings of the writer or narrator approaches the lyric poem.

"Action," as in drama, may refer to a single event or episode within a story or to the series of events that make up the whole story. The selection and arrangement of events within the story is usually called the **plot.** Selection is a matter of degree: it is scarcely conceivable that any diarist or chronicler could write down everything going on at any given moment in time even in a single place; a short story writer selects much more carefully from among all the relevancies called the universe those incidents that are appropriate to a more or less well defined purpose or meaning and then arranges them in an order that is in itself meaningful (even if the meaning is to express meaninglessness). The most common and, though significant, the least self-conscious or attention-calling order is the chronological; when events are juxtaposed in an order that is other than chronological, that order calls attention to itself as having a special purpose or meaning (see *A Preface to Fiction*).

Particularly crucial in ordering an action is the determination of the beginning and ending. It is clearly necessary to ignore what some might consider necessary preconditions or events to begin any chain of events, and even death of an individual is not a final ending. So a story of necessity begins in the middle of something or other—*in medias res*—and ends in the middle of something or other insofar as the whole universe is concerned. So beginnings and endings inevitably reveal something of the purpose of the ordering, or significance. The events in between beginning and end also are arranged, whether chronologically, causally, associatively, and that arrangement too reveals something of the purpose or significance of the story.

Even if the narrative returns to the same moment at which it began, or even if the end of the story is indecision or a nonhappening, the action involves **movement,** a change in events, in a character's mind, in

the reader's understanding, whatever. To make the story keep moving is one of the concerns of the art of fiction. This movement can be the resolution of a **conflict**: a clash between characters, between a character and his environment, within himself, a clash of forces in the universe, even a struggle for meaning on the part of the reader. Not all conflicts need to be resolved, however: there can be a **dilemma**, a situation in which there are two courses of action both of which are equally bad or equally impossible; or the conflict may be a condition of life within the story or within the world as the author sees it. The conflict is often the source of **suspense** for the reader: what will happen? who will win? will she marry the nasty rich man who holds the mortgage? Its resolution may surprise us, but to some extent it is prepared for— a good detective story, for example, while throwing us off the scent with false suspicions and misleading clues, also contains all the neces- sary clues for the solution. Such "clues" of things to come, whether at the end or earlier, are called **foreshadowings**. In some stories all the details are in a sense foreshadowings: if a gun is described as hanging on the wall at the beginning of a story, Chekhov has said, it must go off before the story ends. Such exhaustive use of detail is called **econ- omy** or **total relevance**.

2. CHARACTER

If there is action there must be someone to act, a character. In its most common usage with reference to literature, character simply means a person (or personified or anthropomorphized animal, object, or deity) who acts, appears, or is referred to in a work. In the aggregate the char- acters who appear in a work are called the **dramatis personae**, but most discussion of characters naturally concentrates on the "leading" charac- ters. The most common term for the leading male character is **hero**, but this term has connotations of high virtue or someone who is "larger than life," of almost godlike stature; he is the "good guy" who opposes the **villain** or "bad guy." Often, however, the leading character is a more ordinary and realistic character—like Gabriel Conroy in *The Dead* or the professor in *Disorder and Early Sorrow*—and he is referred to as the **anti-hero**, not because he is a villain, in opposition to a hero, but because he is ordinary, gigantic neither in stature nor in virtue, not necessarily a good guy wearing a white hat or a villain wearing a black one. Some critics, indeed, find the anti-hero characteristic of fiction, particularly the novel. An older and more general term for the leading character, one without quite so many implications of virtue, is **protag- onist**; his opponent is not called a villain but an **antagonist**. You might get into a long and pointless argument by calling Mr. Greenspahn in *Criers and Kibitzers* or Raskolnikov (in *Crime and Punishment*) or Bonnie's Clyde a hero, though the term may be used that way, so the apparently more neutral "protagonist" is useful.

The ambiguity in use of the term "hero"—essentially the question of whether the term is descriptive or evaluative—runs through much critical discussion of the element of character. At times the confusion

comes in distinguishing the moral from the esthetic. When we say someone is a "good" character, we can mean that if he were a real person he would be admirable, virtuous, a "good" guy; at other times we may mean that the fictional character is well drawn, "real" or "true to life" or "original" or both, though he may be repulsive. It is difficult to be consistent, but it may be well to try to speak of the esthetic aspect of character—the art, craft, method of presentation or creation of the fictional personages—as **characterization.**

E. M. Forster popularized a distinction between two kinds of characterization as that of **flat characters** and **round characters.** A flat character is one who has one or few dominant traits, who remains essentially consistent or two-dimensional, one who can usually be categorized or described in a sentence or two. These usually are minor characters. Dickens is generally considered a master of the flat character, and Lady Beldonald in *The Beldonald Holbein,* Ginger Nut and Turkey in *Bartleby,* and the characters in *The Lottery* may be considered "flat." "Round" characters tend to be more complex—Forster says they can "surprise convincingly." They are "more like real people." This descriptive distinction too readily but illegitimately becomes a value judgment —"flat" suggesting the artistically inferior. A further difficulty is inherent in this as in many other critical terms: we define and then spend a good deal of time trying to pigeonhole. Is Gurov, in *The Lady with the Dog,* a flat or round character? The definitions are useful as shorthand descriptions for extremes but wasteful if they lead to endless arguments about categories.

Some flat characters are **stereotypes:** the watermelon-eating, shuffling, happy, and childlike black; the avaricious Jewish moneylender; the gruff old man with the heart of gold, etc. Though a stereotype is almost always a flat character, not all flat characters are stereotypes— Lady Beldonald, for example, may be typical of certain kinds of aging beauties, but there is no literary tradition of such a character with a defined and fixed nature. There are fictional stereotypes, however: the hard-boiled or the coolly rational detective, for example, or the sensitive child who learns something, usually something distasteful, about adult life. There are types of characters, too, that may be defined by function. Henry James invented one that to some degree resembles the confidant in drama; he called it the *ficelle* or "thread," using the analogue of the stage magician's black threads that make things move but are invisible to the audience. Mrs. Munden in *The Beldonald Holbein* is such a character; she is useful primarily to allow the artist in the story to speak his mind so that we can hear, to supply him with information that takes place outside the range of the story, etc. Another type of recurrent fictional character is the **archetype,** one that recurs in literature and our mental lives as part of a mythic pattern (see STYLE). The **doppelgänger** (doubleganger), which, strictly speaking, is the supposed ghost of a living person, is archetypally any of the various kinds of doubles or "other selves" but especially the diabolic. Mr. Hyde is the evil *doppelgänger* of the good Dr. Jekyll. On the other hand, Sancho

Panza, though not diabolic, is considered by some a *doppelgänger,* the down-to-earth, anti-romantic half of a human character of which Don Quixote is the other and opposite half.

The term "character" which refers to a combination of qualities in a human being is also somewhat ambiguous. It usually has moral overtones, often favorable—"a man of character"; it is sometimes neutral but evaluative—"character reference." Judgment about character (not characterization, remember) usually involves moral terms like good and bad or strong and weak. **Personality** usually implies that which distinguishes or individualizes a person and the judgment called for is not so much moral as social—pleasing or displeasing. An older term, **nature**—it is his nature to be so or do such—usually implies something inherent or inborn, something fixed, and thus determined and predictable; the existential character implies the opposite; that is, whatever our past, our conditioning, our pattern of previous behavior, we can, by an act of will, change all that right this minute.

3. FOCUS OF NARRATION, POINT OF VIEW (See *A Preface to Fiction*)

There is sometimes in a short story a character who tells the story, usually in the first person, like the lawyer in *Bartleby* or the artist in *The Beldonald Holbein.* He is called the **narrator.** In neither *Bartleby* nor *The Beldonald Holbein* do we readily assume the "I" is the author, Herman Melville or Henry James. In *The Egg,* however, we may assume that the "I" is Sherwood Anderson—that is, when the first-person narrator is not identified in such a way as to be clearly distinct from the author or what we know about him, we sometimes leap to the conclusion that it is the author speaking. This can lead to difficulty. We can read the biography of the author and apply what we learn there to the character of the first-person narrator even though there is no evidence in the story that the narrator experienced what the author did or is a person like the author. Therefore many critics have resorted to the precaution of referring to this first-person narrator who is not distinguished from the author as the **persona** of the author.

Most often the first-person narrator, especially when he is also a character within the story, has a limited point of view. That is, he can tell you his thoughts and what he sees, thinks, and feels, but he cannot know what is happening when he is absent unless another character tells him, and he cannot tell what anyone else is thinking unless he is told. There is also a third-person limited point of view: a character whose thoughts and experiences we know to the exclusion of others' thoughts and actions but one who is not the narrator and is not referred to as "I." (*The Lady with the Dog, The Dead,* and many other stories in the collection use this point of view.) This device is called the **central** or **centered consciousness.**

There is, as well, an unlimited or less limited point of view, the **omniscient.** Here a narrator may refer to himself in the first person, but he seems miraculously empowered to know what anyone is thinking at any given time; he can know what is going on anywhere and can, in

effect, be in two or more places at the same time ("Meanwhile, back at the ranch . . ."). The omniscient point of view need have no apparent narrator, however; the focus of the story may simply shift in and out of different characters' minds, follow whom and what it will.

The focus of narration or point of view, then, is analogous to the camera in shooting a film: it can zoom in for a close-up (even so close as to get into a character's mind) or move back for a panoramic shot. It selects, frames, proportions, and emphasizes the action.

All fiction is mediated. Unlike drama, we do not only see characters act or hear them talk directly; something or someone intervenes, a mediator or narrator. Paradoxically, when the narrator speaks in the first-person and is a character in the story, there is less mediation. The action of the story is in a sense the act of the narrator telling the story (just as an actor on the stage can tell what happened offstage), and the action we see and hear is his telling. Such relatively unmediated narration is called **dramatic**. All first-person narration is dramatic in that sense, and the centered consciousness point of view is also relatively dramatic, the action being what that consciousness sees, thinks, and does.

4. FORM, STRUCTURE

Since where the camera is determines what we see and how we see it, focus of narration operates as an ordering or shaping device, and so it is an aspect of fictional form. The terms **form** and **structure** are really metaphors when applied to most literature, since they really denote shape, spatiality. These terms are often used interchangeably and are not often used by different people to mean the same thing.

Focus of narration, time and sequence (*A Preface to Fiction*), imagery and language (STYLE), are all aspects of form spoken of elsewhere; so here we will concentrate on another formal or structural concern, proportion.

There are no fixed forms in fiction as there are in poetry—sonnets, heroic couplets—or even in drama—five-act or three-act structures. Though there have been and are publishing conventions—three-volume novels, magazine serials—which have influenced the length and divisions of fiction, on the whole fiction is highly individualistic in form, each writer to some degree enabled or forced to create his own. He uses the ordinary devices of prose and typography: he can create units by sentence structure, paragraphs, skipping lines, or dividing his work into chapters or comparable units. *The Lady with the Dog*, for example, divides its action into four parts with the use of numbers which are to some extent the equivalents of chapters in a novel or acts in a play. Like acts, they often mark time gaps or changes of scene, but they also mark stages of the action; if you were to outline the story to show its structure or building units, you would probably use these four divisions as your main headings. Paying attention to such breaks, numbered or not, will often reveal the "bones" of a story's structure.

Such breaks do not have to be marked typographically, however.

In most stories there are the equivalents of dramatic scenes: two or more characters will be speaking in a fixed setting (or moving along the street or road by foot, carriage, or car) in a more or less continuous dialogue or action, or someone will be thinking uninterruptedly. When there is a break the scene will be ended. This can be followed immediately by another scene or by a bit of **summary narration:** "Several days passed, and I heard nothing more; and though I often felt a charitable prompting to call at the place and see poor Bartleby, yet a certain squeamishness of I know not what withheld me." Another form of summary narrative is the recounting of a habitual action: "I heard a lot of stories about the war and I used to draw pictures of them fighting with bayonets. . ." (*Train Whistle Guitar*). Inside or outside a scene there can also be **description**—of a person, place, thing—or **exposition**—an explanation of what has happened, identification of characters, etc.: "Arina was a servant at the hotel. She lived next to the main staircase, while Seryoga, the janitor's helper, lived over the back stairs. Between them there was shame" (*The Sin of Jesus*).

Like the focus of narration which selects and proportions, the actions that a story chooses to dwell on scenically as opposed to those which are passed over or mentioned briefly, what is described in scene or setting and what is not, what information is withheld and what and when information is released, how scenes are juxtaposed or divided— everything that has to do with selection and proportioning or emphasis is a matter of form or structure. Clearly, then, form and structure are not irrelevant or merely decorative but are important determinants of meaning (see THEME) and must be considered in any discussion of the significance or value of a work of fiction.

5. GENRE, KIND, TYPE

Literary criticism lacks the specific and agreed upon system of classification of biology, so that the terms here discussed are not so fixed as *phylum, genus, species,* even in the editors' own usage. As with other terms, the important thing to understand is the range of possibilities of the terms (and the necessity for clarifying your own usage). In general, we use the term **genre** for the largest, commonly agreed upon categories: *fiction, poetry, drama.* Since there are not enough terms to go around, we sometimes use **subgenre** for the classification of fiction, for example, into novel, novella, short story (as well as yarn, tale, etc.) or as the equivalent of **type** or **kind.** Northrop Frye has justifiably complained about the equating of fiction with the novel, and he adds the **romance,** the **confession,** and **Menippean satire** to the novel as subgenres of fiction: the novel, he says, deals with human character and society; the romance deals with more heroic characters, deals with them more personally and excludes to a degree the social dimension; the confession deals with characters or a character personally but in a more intellectual way, and the Menippean satire deals with characters less as people and more as representatives of mental attitudes. Admittedly, most fiction is a mixture of two or more of these. Most of the

stories here relate more closely to the novel than to other fictional forms.

Type and **kind** may be used interchangeably, but we use the more old-fashioned term "kind" because "type" suggests a greater fixity of form and subject than is generally the case throughout the genres of literature. A kind, then, is a species or subcategory within a genre. There are, for example, detective stories, horror stories, or—the example offered in the anthology—**initiation** stories. Initiation stories are those in which a character—often but not invariably a child or young person—first learns a truth about life, reality, the universe. The "truth" learned may be about the mixed nature of human beings (as in *The Basement Room*, for example) or about the possibilities of one's own imperfection or limitation (as in *O Yes*) or about the limitations of all life (as in *The Egg*). Once initiated, it is implied, the individual cannot return to his earlier state of innocence or ignorance, though he may retreat from knowledge and thus from life (as in *The Basement Room* or *The Artificial Nigger*).

Many critics resist timeless conceptions of genre and its subdivisions, and combine the notion of genres with historical literary periods— classical tragedy, the Gothic novel—so that the concept of genre or kind is not always separable from considerations of TRADITION.

6. STYLE

If **form, genre,** and **tradition** allow us to connect works by different authors, **style** is that which distinguishes or separates the work or works of an author from all others. It is the fingerprint or hallmark of the author. Though it may be necessary before discussing the style of a work or author to identify genre and kind, form and tradition, when we get to style itself we are usually talking about smaller though no less significant elements: **diction** (or choice of words), sentence structure, rhetorical **tropes** or figures of thought or speech, **imagery,** even rhythm. When a group of writers use comparable stylistic devices and devices uncommon to other groups, it is possible to speak of the "style of an age" or period or of a "movement," but ultimately style is unique: one famous nondefinition of style says that it is as individualized as is the author himself as a man—*le style, c'est l'homme.*

Perhaps because of the very uniqueness of style, the vocabulary for discussing stylistic elements is not very precise. We can broadly categorize *formal* or *informal* diction, or indicate *colloquial* as a level of informal language that approximates the speech of ordinary men, for example, but the more closely we approach the particular work the more difficult definition becomes.

The level of usage in areas of diction and sentence structure tends to be the same. Thus, in *Bartleby*, it is difficult to separate the formal choice of words from the formal sentence structure in a passage like this: "Yes, as before I had prospectively assumed that Bartleby would depart, so now I might retrospectively assume that departed he was"; or in this from *The Beldonald Holbein:* "It was a drama of small, smothered, intensely private things, and I knew of but one other person

in the secret; yet that person and I found it exquisitely unsusceptible of notation, followed it with an interest the mutual communication of which did much for our enjoyment, and were present with emotion at its touching catastrophe." Though both these passages are "formal," they are not identical or equivalent styles: the Melville passage is the more abstract and unemotional, the James passage almost exaggeratedly emotional ("smothered," "intensely," "exquisitely," "catastrophe"). And we must be cautious in attributing the style to the author and not the narrator: the style of *Bartleby* imitates the language of the lawyer who tells the story and that of *The Beldonald Holbein* that of the artist.

Diction and sentence structure contribute to the **tone** of a work, or the implied attitude or stance of the author toward the characters, events, etc., of his work and somewhat analogous to "tone of voice." When what is being said and the tone are consistent, it is difficult to separate one from the other; when there is or seems to be a discrepancy, we have some words that are useful to describe the difference. Thus if the language seems exaggerated, we call it **overstatement**: in the James passage "smothered," "exquisitely," and perhaps "catastrophe" seem stronger words than the events warrant. When Mr. Codrington, in *Raspberry Jam*, refers to Miss Dolly as "often a trifle naughty," he is indulging in a bit of obvious **understatement**, the phrase minimizing her awkward attempts at seduction. When a word or expression says virtually the opposite of what it intends, we have an example of **verbal irony**: when Arina tells Seryoga, in *The Sin of Jesus*, that she will put their illegitimate child up for adoption and marry an old man, "he took off his belt and beat her *like a hero*, right on the belly." There are also nonverbal forms of irony, the most common of which is **dramatic irony**, in which a character holds a position or has an expectation that is reversed or fulfilled in an unexpected way. Thus Rainsford's identification of himself as hunter and his callous attitude toward the hunted makes his becoming the hunted ironic.

Another and highly emphasized element of style is **imagery**. In its broadest sense imagery includes any sensory detail or evocation in a work, and it is important to note, for example, how much more imagery in that sense we find in *The Old People* than in, say, *The Lottery*. Imagery in this broad sense, however, is so prevalent in literature that it would take exhaustive statistics to differentiate styles by counting the number of sensory elements per hundred or thousand words, categorizing the images as primarily visual, tactile, etc. In a more restricted sense imagery refers to figurative language, particularly that which defines an abstraction or any emotional or psychological state with a sensory comparison. The opening paragraph of *Odour of Chrysanthemums* illustrates the broader definition of imagery, the final passage of *The Blind Man*—" . . . his insane reserve [was] broken in. He was like a mollusc whose shell is broken"—illustrates the latter. **Figurative language** involves the explicit or implicit comparing or merging of two unlike things. An explicit comparison—"like a mollusc" —is called a **simile**; an implicit comparison or identification of one thing with another unlike itself—"there was a boiling wave of dogs

about them" (*The Old People*)—is called a **metaphor,** though sometimes the latter term is used to include all such figures.

An **allegory** is like a metaphor in that one thing (usually nonrational, nonconcrete, abstract, or religious) is implicitly spoken of in terms of something that is concrete and usually sensuous, but the comparison in allegory is extended to include a whole work or a large portion of a work and is usually part of a whole system of equivalencies. *The Pilgrim's Progress* is probably the most famous prose allegory in English: its central character is named Christian; he was born in the City of Destruction and sets out for the Celestial City, passes through The Slough of Despond and Vanity Fair, meets men named Pliable and Obstinate, etc. A **symbol** can be as brief and local as a metaphor or as extended as an allegory, and like an allegory usually speaks in concrete terms of the non- or super-rational, the abstract, etc. Though some allegories can be complex, with many layers or "levels" of equivalency, and though some symbols can be very simple, with paraphrasable equivalencies, allegory usually refers to a one-to-one relationship (as the names from *The Pilgrim's Progress* imply) and literary symbols usually have highly complex or even inexpressible equivalencies. *The Lottery* may, for example, be considered a symbolic story, but precisely what it "stands for" is extremely difficult to express briefly and satisfactorily—New England Puritanism, man's cruelty to man, Original Sin, the dulling of human sensibility by ritualistic actions?

When an entire story is symbolic, it is sometimes called a **myth** or mythic. Myth originally meant a story of communal origin which provided an explanation or religious interpretation of man, nature, the universe, and the relation between them and, looked at from the vantage point of another culture or set of beliefs, usually implied that the story was false. We speak of classical myths, but Christians do not often speak of Christian myth. We also apply the term myth now to stories by individuals, sophisticated authors, but often there is still the implication that the mythic story relates to a communal or group experience whereas a symbolic story may be more personal or private. The line is difficult to draw firmly: *The Lottery* and *The Old People* seem to have clearly national, American implications, while *The Rocking-Horse Winner* may be a private Lawrencian symbol or a myth of modern bourgeois society. A plot or character element that recurs in cultural or cross-cultural myths, like stories or incidents or rebirth, or images of the devil or the *doppelgänger,* is now widely called an **archetype.**

7. THEME

When the central idea or thesis of a work can be paraphrased, it is called the **theme**: the theme of *Disorder and Early Sorrow* may be summarized as "Life is change and apparent disorder so that to try to hold on to the past, to order, to things as they are is to seek death and thus not to serve life." Theme is thus usually expressed at a fairly abstract level, and cannot always be stated in full sentences. The themes of symbolic or mythic (see STYLE) stories in particular are

difficult to paraphrase adequately. The **subject** of a story is more concrete and literal. The subject of *O Yes,* for example, is the breakup of
a childhood friendship between a black and a white girl; the theme
may be stated in terms of the class or group barriers society enforces
between individuals.

8. TRADITION

Most serious writers of fiction want to tell "the truth"—the truth
about God, the universe, man's life, the way it is or the way it was, the
view of some aspect of reality from the time and position of the author's
own life. It is tempting to see an author as an entirely free agent, with
reality "out there" and his own experiences and perceptions "in here"
and a blank sheet of paper in front of him. But the fact of the sheet of
paper, that fact that he is a writer, immediately limits his freedom: he
has chosen a communal act and medium and he is bound at least by
the limits of language in general and of his own language in particular.
The language itself has **conventions,** unrealistic devices that writers
and readers have agreed upon—words with parameters of meaning;
words and other signs (like punctuation marks) that establish relationships; word orders, syntax. These conventions extend into genre: prose
fiction will be set into type in blocks, poems will be set by lines, each
line beginning with a capital letter, etc. And conventions extend even
further, into types: the characteristics of the initiation story (see
GENRE) are actually conventions. Even were the writer to decide to
break these conventions, the fact that they exist for himself and his
audience creates a special effect in their rupture and limits how far
they can be broken and remain viable. Further, when he chooses to
write his truth in the form of a short story, all the short stories in his
culture—those that he has read, that his audience has or might have
read—define conventions or norms which he must observe or shatter
and, in shattering, take into account. All that has been done or a pattern
within what has been done in the genre, the subgenre, and the kind
form one or more traditions. Sometimes, indeed, the truth he wants to
tell is not just an experience or insight but a comparison between the
experience and the literary tradition with which he is familiar: no, that's
not the way it is; I'll show you. To some extent we can appreciate a
parody in which one work ridicules another through distorted imitation—"Deck us all with Boston Charley"—even if we do not know the
original, but knowing the original immeasurably increases the nature
and degree of our appreciation; all reading of literature is somewhat
like that—we can appreciate a work, but we appreciate it more and see
more in it when we know the tradition within which and against which
it is working. *The Crocodile* is a comically grotesque story with serious
intention, and we can understand both the humor and the attitude
without having read *The Nose.* Knowing the Gogol story, or many
Gogol stories, we can appreciate more fully Dostoevsky's adaptation
and extension of Gogol's serious grotesque, the kind of truth beyond
or other than Gogol's he expresses.

The short story does not have so long and rich a past as poetry and therefore does not have so defined and varied a tradition or traditions. One such tradition, which we associate with Edgar Allan Poe, is a development from the Gothic romances (complete with castles, ghosts, and other supernatural elements), stories of mystery or horror, which later branches off into the detective story on the one hand and the psychological or fantastic on the other. Another is associated with de Maupassant, the highly crafted, socially observant, ironic, and plotted story, a tradition that branches off into the adventure story, the story with the surprise twist at the end (like those of O. Henry), and the carrying forward of the realistic short story. **Realism** is no doubt the major tradition in the short story, as it is in the novel, for much of its short history. It is a broad term which covers the use of "ordinary"— low or middle class—everyday characters, everyday speech, and **verisimilitude** of detail—that is, a probable and acceptable representation of the way things really are. At times the demands of "realism" are used to justify the treatment of previously taboo subject matter such as sex. Realism is also a theory of form as well as subject matter, however: it minimizes coincidence and other manipulations of plot and sometimes gives the appearance of unselective reporting, of formlessness (as in some Chekhov stories and, for example, in *The Dead*). **Naturalism** is that branch of realism which assumes all that is real is in nature, that man is therefore primarily an animal as opposed to a soul, and that reality, including human reality, can be studied scientifically. In recent years there has been something of a reaction against the various realisms in favor of a search for truth through the extraordinary or the grotesque, and a tradition that in fiction includes Kafka, some of Faulkner, Dostoevsky, and Dickens.

List of Terms Defined

Poetry

EDITED BY
J. PAUL HUNTER

A Preface to Poetry

Reading a poem is one thing. Experiencing it is something else. And experiencing it fully depends not merely on a reader's willingness, but on his readiness to cope with a poem's richness, resonance, and complication. Look, for example, at this poem—one of the most famous in the English language:

To His Coy Mistress

Had we but world enough, and time,
This coyness, lady, were no crime.
We would sit down, and think which way
To walk, and pass our long love's day.
Thou by the Indian Ganges' side   5
Shouldst rubies find: I by the tide
Of Humber would complain. I would
Love you ten years before the Flood,
And you should if you please refuse
Till the conversion of the Jews.   10
My vegetable love should grow
Vaster than empires, and more slow;
An hundred years should go to praise
Thine eyes, and on thy forehead gaze;
Two hundred to adore each breast;   15
But thirty thousand to the rest.
An age at least to every part,
And the last age should show your heart.
For, lady, you deserve this state;
Nor would I love at lower rate.   20
    But at my back I always hear
Time's wingéd chariot hurrying near;
And yonder all before us lie
Deserts of vast eternity.
Thy beauty shall no more be found,   25
Nor, in thy marble vault, shall sound
My echoing song; then worms shall try
That long preserved virginity,
And your quaint honor turn to dust,
And into ashes all my lust: 30
The grave's a fine and private place,
But none, I think, do there embrace.
    Now therefore, while the youthful hue
Sits on thy skin like morning dew,
And while thy willing soul transpires   35
At every pore with instant fires,
Now let us sport us while we may,
And now, like am'rous birds of prey,

Rather at once our time devour,
Than languish in his slow-chapped pow'r.   40
Let us roll all our strength and all
Our sweetness up into one ball,
And tear our pleasures with rough strife
Thorough the iron gates of life.
Thus, though we cannot make our sun   45
Stand still, yet we will make him run.

The title suggests the situation—a man is speaking to his beloved—and before we are far into the poem we recognize his familiar argument: let's not wait, let's make love now. But much more is going on in the poem than this simple "message."

Seduction is a promising subject, but it is nearly as easy to be dull on this subject as on less fascinating ones, and the subject has inspired some very dreary poetry. The interest and power of this poem depend on more than the choice of subject, however useful that subject is in whetting a reader's expectations. No reader is likely to use the poem as a handbook for his own life, and few readers are likely to read it at a moment when their own lives parallel precisely the poem's situation. Its relevance is of a larger kind: it portrays vividly and forcefully a recognizable situation, saying something *about* that situation but (more important) making us react to the situation and feel something about it. Experiencing a poem involves not only knowing what it says but also feeling the pleasures provided by its clever management of our own ideas and emotions. All poems have a design on us—they try to make us feel certain things—and a full experience of a poem requires full recognition of the complexities of design so that we can feel specific emotions and pleasures—not only the general ones of contemplating seduction.

Let's begin at the beginning. What do you expect of a poem about a would-be seduction? One thing you can be almost certain of is that it will contain attractive images of physical enjoyment. The first verse-paragraph (lines 1–20) contains such images, and so does the third (especially lines 33–38). The first set of images suggest the languorous, lazy appeal of a timeless world where physical enjoyment seems to fill all time and all space. First are images of rich sensuousness; the leisurely contemplation of enjoyment, the timeless walks in exotic lands, the finding of precious stones, the luxury of delaying the supreme moment. Gradually sensuousness becomes sensuality, and the speaker imagines himself praising various parts of the girl's body. In line 33, the poem returns to sexual contemplation but with much more intensity. Now the girl seems to be not only a passive object of admiration but a live, breathing, perspiring, passionate respondent. And a moment later, the speaker projects the beauty and energy of the love act itself. He suggests something of his anticipation of supreme ecstasy by the vividness and intensity of the images and language he uses: from the languid, flowing, floating suggestions of the early lines through the breathless anticipation of lines 33–37 to the violence of lines 41–44

with their explicit visualization of the union, the rolling into one, of "strength" and "sweetness."

But not all the poem portrays glorious pleasure. The second verse paragraph (lines 21–32) contains some pretty grim stuff. Instead of the endless languor of unhurried walks and exotic places in the early lines, we have anxiety and consciousness of time—a hurrying chariot, moving up fast from behind. And instead of the centuries of body-worship, eternity consists of vast deserts. Grimmest of all is the image of a different kind of fall than the one the speaker desires; the carefully preserved virginity of the girl, the speaker imagines, will be tested and destroyed in the grave by worms. The speaker summarizes with gross understatement and macabre humor in lines 31–32:

> The grave's a fine and private place,
> But none, I think, do there embrace.

The contrast of all that grimness of future dryness and death emphasizes (first) the unreal romanticism of the timeless world which, according to the speaker, the girl seems to want, and (second) the vividly portrayed sensual pleasures of a potential moment right now. Such contrasts work for us as well as for the presumed girl; in fact, they are part of a carefully contrived argument that organizes the poem. We might well have expected, just from the title and the opening lines, that the poem would be organized as a formal argument. The first words of each paragraph clearly show the outlines: (1) "Had we . . . " (If we had no limits of time or space); (2) "But . . . " (But we do have such limits); (3) "Now, therefore . . . ." The poem is cast as a long, detailed hypothetical syllogism; it uses the form of a standard argument, with vivid examples and carefully contrived rhetoric, to suggest the urgency of enjoying the moment. It is a specious argument, of course, but real people have fallen for worse ones. But this isn't "real life"; the story doesn't even end. As in most other poems (and unlike most drama and fiction), the "plot" and its resolution have little to do with the final effect. Part of the point here is to notice the flaw in the argument. A good logician could show you that the speaker commits the fallacy of the "denied antecedent," that is, he proves what cannot happen but fails to prove what can. Seduction seldom, of course, gets worked out in purely logical terms, and so in one sense the logic of the argument doesn't matter—any more than whether the speaker finally seduces the girl. But in another sense it matters a great deal and contributes to our complex experience of the poem. For if we spot the illogic and find it amusing (since the argument is obviously an effective one, logical or not), we not only feel the accuracy of the poem's observation about seduction but we experience something important about the way words work. Often their effect is more far-reaching than what they say on a literal level, just as this poem reaches much further than any literal statement of its "message" or "meaning." Poetry often exploits the fact that words work in such mysterious ways; in fact, most poems, in one way or another, are concerned with the fact that

words may be used suggestively to open out on horizons beyond logical and syntactical categories.

Reading a poem about seduction is hardly the same thing as getting seduced, and only a very peculiar poet or reader would expect it to be, though some of the censorship controversies over the teaching of poems like this may sometimes imply that life and art are the same thing. Anyone who thinks they are is bound to be disappointed by a poem about seduction, or about anything else. One does not go to a poem instead of being seduced, or as a sublimation, or as a guide. A poem about anything does not intend to be the thing itself, or even to recreate it precisely. Poetry, like other literature, is an ordered imitation of perceived reality expressed in words. By definition, by intention, and by practice, poetry modifies life to its own artistic ends, "ordering" —that is, making meaningful—what is only a version in any case. What poetry offers us is not life itself, naked and available, but a perspective (*perceived* reality) on some recognizable situations or ideas; not Truth with a capital T, but interpretations and stances; not passion itself, but words that evoke associations and memories and feelings. A poem can provide an angle of vision which in "real life" is often blurred through our closeness to experience. And just as the poet fictionalizes—whether he begins with a real event or not—we as readers end with his version, which exists in tension with other things we know, about words, about poetry, about argument, about seduction, about everything. That tension tests not the "truth" of the poet's vision but the effects produced by the poem; the more we know, the richer these effects are likely to be.

Anyone with developed sensitivities and a modest amount of knowledge of the suggestiveness of words can find the crucial words that express and evoke the sensual appeal. The devices of contrast (the flowing Ganges flanked by rubies vs. vast deserts; the spacious wandering vs. the confinement of a marble vault; eternal adoration vs. those traditional symbols of mortality, ashes and dust) may be readily seen by anyone willing to look at the poem carefully. In short, much of the poem is readily available to almost any reader who looks carefully; much of its power is right there on the page, and a reader need make only a minimal effort to experience it.

But a number of things in the poem require special skill or knowledge. The poem's parody of a hypothetical syllogism is only available to those who can recognize a hypothetical syllogism and see the distortion in this one. Of course, not recognizing the syllogism is not too serious, as long as the reader "senses" the falsity of the argument and finds the incongruity in its effectiveness; he simply misses a joke which is part of the poem's complexity. But some other matters in the poem are more crucial, for lack of knowledge about them would not only drain the poem of some of its richness but might even force a misunderstanding of what the poem says on its most literal level.

Look, for instance, at the following words: "coy" (title) and "coyness" (line 2); "mistress" (title); "complain" (line 7); "vegetable" (line 11); "adore" (line 15). All of these words are common enough, but each offers a problem in interpretation because of changes in meaning. The

poem was written more than three hundred years ago, in the mid-17th century, and many words used in a specific way then have changed over the years. Words are, in a sense, alive and ever-changing; change is a part of the excitement of language as well as a potential frustration, and if we construe each of these words exactly as it is construed now we will be badly misled. The most obvious change in meaning is in the word "mistress," for to us it implies a specific sexual relationship, one that would make the elaborate seduction plea here seem a little late. The most common 17th-century meaning of "mistress" was simply "a woman who has command over a man's heart; a woman who is loved and courted by a man; a sweetheart, lady-love." This definition comes from the *Oxford English Dictionary*, a valuable reference guide that lists historical as well as modern meanings, with detailed examples of usages. The *OED* can also show us that the new meaning of "mistress" was coming into use when this poem was written, and perhaps the meanings are played off against each other, as a kind of false lead; such false leads are common in poetry, for poets often like to toy with our expectations and surprise us.

"Coy" and "coyness" offer a similar problem; in modern usage they usually suggest playful teasing, affectation, coquettishness. But originally they suggested shyness, modesty, reluctance, reserve, not simply the affectation of those things. Of course, we find out very little about the girl herself in this poem (except what we can infer from the things the speaker says to her and the way he says them), but we are not led to think of her as sly and affected in her hesitancy to receive her lover's advances.

"Complain" and "adore" are more technical. The former indicates a lover going through the ritual of composing a "complaint"—a poem which bewails his misery because of a lady's disdain. Thus, the speaker here self-deprecatingly (but comically) imagines himself (in the unreal, timeless world of the first verse paragraph) as a pining swain, while his love is luxuriating half-across the earth, oblivious to his pain. Obviously, the speaker wants no part of such sado-masochistic romantic nonsense; he prefers sexual pleasure to poetic posing. "Adore" technically means to worship as a deity; there is a certain irony in regarding the girl's body as an object of religious worship, but this speaker carries through his version of the girl's fantasy, modestly refusing to name those parts he wishes to devote thirty thousand years to, and regarding her "heart" (usually synonymous with soul in the Renaissance) as the ultimate conquest for the last age.

The term "vegetable" is even more complex, for it depends on a whole set of physiological/psychological doctrines in the Renaissance. According to those doctrines, the human soul was made up of three souls which corresponded to the different levels of living matter. The Vegetable Soul man possessed in common with plants and animals; the Sensible Soul he possessed in common with animals; the Rational Soul was possessed by man alone. The Vegetable Soul was the lowest and had only the powers of reproduction, nourishment, and growth. The sense, the passions, and the imagination were under the power of the

Sensible Soul. A "vegetable love" would be without feeling or passion, appropriate to the lowest forms of life. The speaker thus reduces the notion of timeless, romantic nonphysical love to what he considers its proper level—a subhuman, absurd one. He pictures love without physical involvement not as a higher spiritual attraction but rather as a lower, nonsentient one.

Several other parts of the poem similarly require historical knowledge. Lines 33–36 depend upon Renaissance love psychology which considered physiological reactions (the rosy skin, perspiration) to be stimulated by the release of "animal spirits" in the blood. This release happened when the emotions were heightened by sight of the beloved; phantasms from the eye descended to the soul and released the animal spirits. The soul was thus "present" in the physiological response (the animal spirits), and the speaker pictures it here as involved in the very moment of desire, trying to unite—through the body—with the soul of the beloved. This love psychology may seem somewhat naive, but it is a humbling experience to try to explain our modern notions of how eyes and emotions relate to bodily processes.

The final two lines of the poem depend heavily upon specific knowledge. First there is an allusion to Greek mythology—an allusion which actually began several lines before the end with the reference to Time's slow-chapped (i.e., slow-jawed) power. According to the myth, Chronos (Time) ate all his children except Zeus (who had been hidden by Rhea), and Zeus afterward seized Chronos' power as chief of the gods. Zeus later made the sun stand still to lengthen his love night with Alcmene. We cannot, the speaker says, make time stand still as Zeus did, but we can speed it up. His argument assumes the 17th-century belief that each sex act made a person's life one day shorter. The speaker keeps insisting that the coming of death—time's end—is easier to cope with if you have something interesting to do while you wait.

Up to now we have not even mentioned the man who wrote the poem, Andrew Marvell. Whether Marvell ever had such a coy friend as this poem implies is not very important to us (though it may have been very important to him). For us, the relevant point is the fiction of the poem—regardless of whether that fiction is based on actual fact. But some facts about authorship may be very useful to us as readers of the poem, as long as we *use* them to help us with the poem and do not simply engage in biographical speculation. In many cases, knowledge about the author is likely to help us recognize the poet's distinctive strategies, and reading other poems by him often reveals his attitudes or devices so that we can read any one poem with more clarity, security, and depth; the index can guide you to other poems by Marvell.

A reader may experience a poem in a satisfactory way without all of the special knowledge I have been describing, but additional knowledge and developed skill can heighten the experience of almost any poem. Poems do not "hide" their meaning, and good poets usually communicate rather quickly in some basic way. Rereadings, reconsiderations, and the application of additional knowledge allow us to hear resonances built into the poem, qualities that make it enjoyable to

experience again and again. We have really only begun to look closely at this particular poem, and if you were to continue to reread it carefully, you would very likely discover richnesses which this brief discussion has not even suggested. The route to meaning is often clear on first reading a poem, but the full possibilities of experience may require more time, energy, and knowledge of the right questions to ask.

Now look at this 20th-century poem:

(ponder,darling,these busted statues

(ponder,darling,these busted statues
of yon motheaten forum be aware
notice what hath remained
—the stone cringes
clinging to the stone, how obsolete   5

lips utter their extant smile. . . .
remark

a few deleted of texture
of meaning monuments and dolls

resist Them Greediest Paws of careful   10
time all of which is extremely
unimportant)whereas Life

matters if or

when the your-and-my-
idle vertical worthless   15
self unite in peculiarly
momentary

partnership (to instigate
constructive
        Horizontal
business. . . . even so, let us make haste   20
—consider well this ruined aqueduct

lady,
which used to lead something into somewhere)

Here are some questions about the poem:

1. In what ways is this poem easier to read after having analyzed *To His Coy Mistress?* What specific evidence can you find that the author of (*ponder,darling* had *Coy Mistress* in mind?

2. Why are the first and last parts of the poem in parentheses? In what way does the nonparenthesized section differ from the parenthesized sections? What other devices of contrast do you find?

3. Why are such formal and archaic words as "ponder" and "yon" juxtaposed with slang such as "busted" and "motheaten"?

4. How do the ravages of time in this poem differ from those in *Coy Mistress?*

5. The argument used in *Coy Mistress* is called the *carpe diem* argument; *carpe diem* is Latin for "seize the day," that is, live for the immediate moment. How does this poem vary from the basic *carpe diem* pattern? Could you tell, from the language of the poem itself, that it was not written in the 17th century, when the *carpe diem* motif flourished?

6. What is the setting of the poem? How is the setting important? How does the aqueduct unite the setting with the theme of the poem? Try to explain the speaker's habit of associating what he looks at with the argument he is trying to construct.

7. Why are the stanzas divided as they are?

8. Other poems by e.e. cummings (he insisted on spelling his own name without capitals) are *chanson innocente* (p. 551), *the season tis, my lovely lambs* (p. 540), *portrait* (p. 431), *l(a* (p. 617) and *anyone lived in a pretty how town* (p. 1147). Do you see any pattern in his uses of horizontal and vertical movement? Does the spacing affect the rhythm and pace as you read the poem?

The preceding discussion and questions may make it seem as if you need to know a lot to read a poem intelligently and experience it fully. You do. The more you know, the better a reader of poems you are likely to be; the more practice you have had in reading other poems, the more likely you are to be able to experience a poem new to you. But knowing facts is not by itself enough; willingness to discover something new is a crucial quality of mind for reading poems well, and being willing to let the poem itself dictate which questions to ask is important to locating the right facts and discovering the right way of putting them together. Most readers can find out what they need to know for most poems if they figure out what questions to ask.

Poetry reading has many hazards, and almost as many of them result from overeagerness as from apathy; many people who read poetry enthusiastically do not read it well, just as many poems that mean well do not mean much. The questions you ask of poetry should channel your enthusiasm and direct it toward meaningful experience, but they should not destroy it. Some people are rather protective about poetry, and think it shouldn't be analyzed lest it shrivel or collapse. But such an attitude toward the "poor little poem" is finally rather patronizing; good poems are hardy, and they won't disintegrate when confronted with difficult questions. The techniques of analysis mean to make you both tougher-minded (less subject to gimmicks and quackery) and more sensitive (to the nuances and depths of good poems), and they also aim to allow the poem to open itself to you.

No one can give you a method that will offer you total experience of all poems. But because many characteristics of an individual poem are characteristics that one poem shares with other poems, there are guidelines which can prompt you to ask the right questions. Here is a checklist of some things to remember:

1. *Identify the poem's situation.* What is said is often conditioned by where it is said and by whom. Identifying the speaker and his place in the situation puts what he says in perspective.

2. *Read the syntax literally.* What the words say literally in normal sentences is only a starting point, but it is the place to start. Not all poems use normal prose syntax, but most of them do, and you can save yourself embarrassment by paraphrasing accurately (that is, rephrasing what the poem literally says, in plain prose) and not simply free-associating from an isolated word or phrase.

3. *Articulate for yourself what the title, subject, and situation make you expect.* Poets often use false leads and try to surprise you by doing shocking things, but defining expectation lets you be conscious of where you are when you begin.

4. *Be willing to be surprised.* Things often happen in poems that turn them around. A poem may seem to suggest one thing at first, then persuade you to its opposite, or at least to a significant qualification or variation.

5. *Find out what is implied by the traditions behind the poem.* Verse forms, poetic kinds, and metrical patterns all have a frame of reference, traditions of the way they are usually used and for what. For example, the anapest is usually used for comic poems, and if a poet uses it "straight" he is aware of his "departure" and is probably making a point by doing it.

6. *Remember that poems exist in time, and times change.* Not only the meanings of words, but whole ways of looking at the universe and man's role vary in different ages. Consciousness of time works two ways: your knowledge of history provides a context for reading the poem, and the poem's *use* of a word or idea may modify your notion of a particular age.

7. *Bother the reference librarian.* Look up anything you don't understand: an unfamiliar word (or an ordinary word used in an unfamiliar way), a place, a person, a myth, an idea—anything the poem uses.

8. *Take a poem on its own terms.* Adjust to the poem; don't make the poem adjust to you. Be prepared to hear things you do not want to hear. Not all poems are about your ideas, nor will they always present emotions you want to feel. But be tolerant and listen to the poem's ideas, not only to your desire to revise them for yourself.

9. *Argue.* Discussion usually results in clarification and keeps you from being too dependent on personal biases and preoccupations which sometimes mislead even the best readers. Talking a poem over with someone else (especially someone very different) can expand the limits of a too narrow perspective.

10. *Assume there is a reason for everything.* Poets do make mistakes, but in poems that show some degree of verbal control it is usually safest to assume that the poet chose each word carefully; if the choice seems peculiar to us, it is usually *we* who are missing something. Craftsmanship obliges us to try to account for the specific choices and only settle

for conclusions of ineptitude if no hypothetical explanation will make sense.

These guidelines are built into the arrangement of this book so that it will be easier for you to ask the right questions. Most beginning readers have better instincts than they think they have and already know many things that can be useful in reading poetry; the arrangement is designed to begin where beginning readers are and make use of what they already have. Poems are arranged in groups so that you will find, side by side, poems that invite comparisons—because they treat the same subject in different ways, because they use the same device for different ends, because they share a form but have different content, different moods, etc. (Of course, any one poem may profitably be compared with other poems too, and many readers will want to construct their own groupings.)

The groups are progressive and cumulative too; the early groups invite questions that a beginning reader of poetry can readily handle, and the later groups assume some accretion of knowledge and sophistication. This does not mean that all the poems in the early groups are simple and all the later ones difficult; rather it means that the group—as group—invites questions which increasingly imply some familiarity with poetry. The early groupings are by subject matter; here you will find within an individual subject group widely different poems which invite you to find what artistic aims and choices brought the differences about. The groupings in Section II invite you to confront the many strategies and forms and inheritances that poets work from. The groupings in the last section suggest the problems of passing time and the questions these problems raise about the "present" of each poem—questions which are sometimes nearly as hard to answer for last week's poetry as for that of the Middle Ages. The groupings are identified in the Note on Arrangement, below. Many teachers and students will, of course, want to use the groups in a different order or ignore the grouping idea entirely; the editor does not claim to have discovered the best possible order for all possible readers or that any order or method will work for all students. And the book contains many more poems than most teachers would wish to assign in an introductory course; the groupings simply provide a suggestive framework for good teaching and good reading, and they are meant to stimulate questions and provoke discussion. At the end of the book are more conventional indices (by author, title, and first line) for users of the text who may wish to move from poem to poem in a different way.

The poems selected for this book are of many kinds, representing most of the major directions of poetry through the ages and including most of the classics usually taught in undergraduate courses. But I have placed more than the usual emphasis on new poems, especially by younger writers, for it seems to me that a knowledge of poetry demands not only a knowledge of what has been written but of what is being written now, and that the easiest access to older poems is, for students, often through the new. I have also tried to provide an appropriate context for much of this newness by choosing old poems that place

it in focus; the "Protest and Satire" selection reminds us, for example, that poems addressed to the moment have long been a part of the poetic tradition—that, in fact, "occasional" poetry is in the mainstream of the tradition. I have included some lyrics from popular songs (the Beatles, Paul Simon, Bob Dylan, Leonard Cohen), many poems by black poets (though not all on blackness itself), and poems based on non-Western traditions and forms. In short, experienced teachers of poetry will find most of their favorites here, but they will also find some surprises. Beginning readers will find enough variety to introduce them to most of the problems, and pleasures, they can find in poetry elsewhere.

The best way to learn about poetry is by reading poems. There is nothing magic about the arrangement of poems, or about any "method" in approaching them. At best, analysis is only a means to an end, not a value in itself. But careful attention to the issues suggested by arrangement and analysis is a way of getting access to poetry and what it offers. Having a finely developed skill may be a pleasure in itself, but the feel of it in action provides the real experience. And the best test of a method, or a course, or a textbook is what happens when its limits are transcended: if, when all is said and analyzed, you can experience more fully the next poem you read beyond the covers of this book, you will have begun to approach the worlds that offer themselves through poetry.

Note on Arrangement

The poems in this anthology are arranged in groups designed to suggest comparisons and stimulate classroom discussion. The groupings are of several kinds, gradually moving toward more difficult and complex questions. Those in Section I are by subject matter:

Love—from *They Flee from Me* through *Politics*
War—*There Died a Myriad* through *Kilroy*
Death—*A Litany in Time of Plague* through *Arrangements with Earth for Three Dead Friends*
Poetry and the Arts—*In Memory of W. B. Yeats* through *Lines on Brueghel's* Icarus
The Simple Life—*My Mind to Me a Kingdom Is* through *Not Leaving the House*
The Golden Age—*The Golden Age Was When the World Was Young* through *In California*
Sensuous and Sensual Experience—*After Great Pain* through *The Goose Fish*

Subject labels do justice to very few of the poems, of course, and one of the major values in reading poems grouped by subject is in recognizing how varied poems on traditional subjects may be: the poems here very often surprise the expectations readers bring to such subjects. The next group (beginning with *Auto Wreck*) contains poems on subjects which in some ages have been considered "unpoetic," but the poems themselves suggest that poetry's range is not to be circumscribed by artificial

limits of subject matter. The final group in Section I further tests such limits by presenting a series of attitudes sometimes thought to be "unpoetic"—even though poetry of satire and protest has flourished in almost all ages and cultures. Many of the groups contain subgroups (such as the poems describing Brueghel paintings) and "bridge" poems which connect different groups.

The groupings in Section II are more complex and raise a series of technical problems:

Speaker—*Channel Firing* through *A Widow in Wintertime*
Setting and Situation—*Sunday Morning* through *The Garden*
Connotation—*Still to Be Neat* through *Meditation on Statistical Method*
Metaphor and Symbolism—*That Time of Year* through *Disillusionment of Ten O'Clock*
Structure—*Frankie and Johnny* through *When Lilacs Last in the Dooryard Bloomed*

The poems in each group illustrate a range of possibilities and suggest the many different uses of poetic devices. The "structure" group, for example, contains subgroups structured by narrative, dramatic, and descriptive strategies, and the final few poems in the group suggest other varieties of structure and structural problems.

The next few groups suggest the various effects of different systems of belief and frames of reference, illustrating how individual poems make different degrees of demand:

Judeo-Christian Tradition—*The Windhover* through *The Ache of Marriage*
Classical History and Myth—*To Helen* through *chanson innocente*
Non-Western Cultural Traditions—*I Am a Cowboy in the Boat of Ra* through *Night in the House by the River*
Private Myth (example: Yeats)—*Easter 1916* through *Crazy Jane Talks with the Bishop*

The next group (from a Pope excerpt through *Opening the Cage*) presents a variety of stanza and verse forms, and the following one (beginning with Sidney) illustrates in detail one form, the sonnet. The poems from *The Lamb* to *At Barstow* illustrate some of the standard poetic kinds, and those from *You've Told Me, Maro* through *Parting in Wartime* present one kind (the epigram).

Coleridge's *Metrical Feet* exemplifies (and names) the most common poetic rhythms, and the poems which follow (from *The Secretary* through *Ah Sunflower*) demonstrate the varied tones possible within one meter, the anapest. The group beginning with Pope's famous "Sound and Sense" passage and ending with *To the Memory of Mr. Oldham* demonstrates various imitative sound effects, and the poems from *Break, Break, Break* to *Spring and Fall* exemplify other possibilities of pause, rhythm, and sound. The final group in Section II (from *Easter Wings* through *l(a)* suggests how visual effects are sometimes used.

Section III groups poems according to various problems of history

and context. The first group, from *To the Virgins, to Make Much of Time* to *(ponder,darling,these busted statues,* samples variations in *carpe diem* poetry from the Renaissance to modern times, and the next (beginning with *To Roses in the Bosom of Castara*) suggests some other traditional uses of the rose (the central symbol of *carpe diem* poetry). The next three groups exemplify various cultural assumptions about the idea of order and suggest how those assumptions relate to recurrent metaphors (the world as stage, for example). The group from *The Darkling Thrush* through *The Second-Best Bed* suggests a variety of problems in factual knowledge about context; the poems in this group have been left unannotated to emphasize informational demands that poems may make. The final two sections, illustrating problems and possibilities of interpreting an authorial context, present generous selections from two poets, John Keats and Adrienne Rich. Both groups are supplemented by prose passages in which the authors discuss their own work.

The groupings are, of course, merely for convenience of study; they are not relief maps of the poetic universe. Imaginative and sensible use of them may raise useful questions about poetry, as well as enrich one's experience of individual poems, but no arrangement (and no book) is an adequate substitute for a good teacher, and many teachers will think of other useful ways to approach the poems. Every classroom situation is unique in its demands and possibilities, and the aim of this book is to provide the teacher with a generous selection of poems from which to choose, a series of suggestive issues, and a convenient structure for moving toward increasingly complex critical problems. The arrangement assumes the need for close analysis and technical knowledge, but teachers will need to decide—on the basis of their own interests and the needs of individual classes—when and how to introduce specific problems and terms. Beyond the provocation of the groupings themselves, the book provides ten short essays ("The Elements of Poetry") which discuss technical problems and define terms. These essays may be used to introduce such topics as "Figurative Language" or "Prosody," or they may be consulted for definitions that, in context, provide a fuller sense of meaning than glossaries arranged in a series of isolated one-sentence units.

The texts of the poems have been carefully chosen and edited; poems which use older conventions of capitalization, spelling, and punctuation have been modernized except where (as in Emily Dickinson or Spenser's *The Faerie Queene*) unique authorial habits would have been obscured or (as in the passage from Chaucer) linguistic patterns distorted. Each poem is dated. Dates of publication appear below the poem on the right; the date is that of first volume publication (or, in the case of poems taken from plays, of performance), unless otherwise indicated. When periodical or anthology publication substantially preceded volume publication, that earlier date is given instead and preceded by a *p*. When the date of composition is known to differ substantially from the publication date, that date is given instead and appears on the *left*.

I

They Flee from Me

They flee from me, that sometime did me seek,
With naked foot stalking in my chamber.
I have seen them, gentle, tame, and meek,
That now are wild, and do not remember
That sometime they put themselves in danger 5
To take bread at my hand; and now they range,
Busily seeking with a continual change.

Thankéd be Fortune it hath been otherwise,
Twenty times better; but once in special,
In thin array, after a pleasant guise, 10
When her loose gown from her shoulders did fall,
And she me caught in her arms long and small.[1]
And therewith all sweetly did me kiss
And softly said, "Dear heart, how like you this?"

It was no dream, I lay broad waking. 15
But all is turned, thorough[2] my gentleness,
Into a strange fashion of forsaking;
And I have leave to go, of her goodness,
And she also to use newfangleness.[3]
But since that I so kindely[4] am servéd, 20
I fain[5] would know what she hath deservéd.

1557

EZRA POUND

A Virginal

No, no! Go from me. I have left her lately.
I will not spoil my sheath with lesser brightness,
For my surrounding air hath a new lightness;
Slight are her arms, yet they have bound me straitly
And left me cloaked as with a gauze of æther; 5
As with sweet leaves; as with a subtle clearness.
Oh, I have picked up magic in her nearness
To sheathe me half in half the things that sheathe her.
No, no! Go from me, I have still the flavor,
Soft as spring wind that's come from birchen bowers. 10
Green come the shoots, aye April in the branches,

1. Slender.
2. Through.
3. Fondness for novelty.

4. In a way natural to women.
5. Eagerly.

411

As winter's wound with her sleight hand she staunches,
Hath of the trees a likeness of the savor:
As white their bark, so white this lady's hours.

1912

WILLIAM SHAKESPEARE

Th' Expense of Spirit

Th' expense[1] of spirit in a waste[2] of shame
Is lust in action; and, till action, lust
Is perjured, murderous, bloody, full of blame,
Savage, extreme, rude, cruel, not to trust;
Enjoyed no sooner but despiséd straight: 5
Past reason hunted; and no sooner had,
Past reason hated, as a swallowed bait,
On purpose laid to make the taker mad:
Mad in pursuit, and in possession so;
Had, having, and in quest to have, extreme;   10
A bliss in proof;[3] and proved, a very woe;
Before, a joy proposed; behind, a dream.
All this the world well knows; yet none knows well
To shun the heaven that leads men to this hell.

1609

SIR PHILIP SIDNEY

Leave Me, O Love

Leave me, O Love, which reachest but to dust,
And thou, my mind, aspire to higher things;
Grow rich in that which never taketh rust:[1]
Whatever fades but fading pleasure brings.
   Draw in thy beams, and humble all thy might   5
To that sweet yoke where lasting freedoms be;
Which breaks the clouds and opens forth the light
That doth both shine and give us sight to see.
   O take fast hold; let that light be thy guide
In this small course which birth draws out to death,   10
And think how evil becometh him[2] to slide,
Who seeketh heav'n, and comes of heav'nly breath.
   Then farewell, world, thy uttermost I see;
   Eternal Love, maintain thy life in me.

1581

1. Expending.
2. Using up; also, desert.
3. In the act.
1. According to *Matthew* 6:19–20, the difference between heavenly and earthly treasures is that in heaven "neither moth nor rust doth corrupt, and . . . thieves do not break through nor steal."
2. How badly it suits him. (In the 16th century evil was usually pronounced as one syllable, e'il.)

DONALD J. LLOYD

Bridal Couch

Follows this a narrower bed,
Wood at feet, wood at head;
Follows this a sounder sleep,
Somewhat longer and too deep.

All too meanly and too soon   5
Waxes once and wanes our moon;
All too swiftly for each one
Falls to dark our winter sun.

Let us here then wrestle death,
Intermingled limb and breath,   10
Conscious both that we beget
End of rest, endless fret,

And come at last to permanence,
Tired dancers from a dance,
Yawning, and content to fall   15
Into any bed at all.

1956

JAMES DICKEY

Cherrylog Road

Off Highway 106[1]
At Cherrylog Road I entered
The '34 Ford without wheels,
Smothered in kudzu,[2]
With a seat pulled out to run   5
Corn whiskey down from the hills,

And then from the other side
Crept into an Essex
With a rumble seat of red leather
And then out again, aboard   10
A blue Chevrolet, releasing
The rust from its other color,

Reared up on three building blocks.
None had the same body heat;
I changed with them inward, toward   15
The weedy heart of the junkyard,
For I knew that Doris Holbrook
Would escape from her father at noon

---

1. The poem is set in the mountains of
North Georgia.
2. A rapidly growing vine, introduced
from Japan to combat erosion but now
covering whole fields and groves of trees.

And would come from the farm
To seek parts owned by the sun   20
Among the abandoned chassis,
Sitting in each in turn
As I did, leaning forward
As in a wild stock-car race

In the parking lot of the dead.   25
Time after time, I climbed in
And out the other side, like
An envoy or movie star
Met at the station by crickets.
A radiator cap raised its head,   30

Become a real toad or a kingsnake
As I neared the hub of the yard,
Passing through many states,
Many lives, to reach
Some grandmother's long Pierce-Arrow   35
Sending platters of blindness forth

From its nickel hubcaps
And spilling its tender upholstery
On sleepy roaches,
The glass panel in between   40
Lady and colored driver
Not all the way broken out,

The back-seat phone
Still on its hook.
I got in as though to exclaim,   45
"Let us go to the orphan asylum,
John; I have some old toys
For children who say their prayers."

I popped with sweat as I thought
I heard Doris Holbrook scrape   50
Like a mouse in the southern-state sun
That was eating the paint in blisters
From a hundred car tops and hoods.
She was tapping like code,

Loosening the screws,   55
Carrying off headlights,
Sparkplugs, bumpers,
Cracked mirrors and gear-knobs,
Getting ready, already,
To go back with something to show   60

Other than her lips' new trembling
I would hold to me soon, soon,
Where I sat in the ripped back seat
Talking over the interphone,

Praying for Doris Holbrook   65
To come from her father's farm

And to get back there
With no trace of me on her face
To be seen by her red-haired father
Who would change, in the squalling barn,   70
Her back's pale skin with a strop,
Then lay for me

In a bootlegger's roasting car
With a string-triggered 12-gauge shotgun
To blast the breath from the air.   75
Not cut by the jagged windshields,
Through the acres of wrecks she came
With a wrench in her hand,

Through dust where the blacksnake dies
Of boredom, and the beetle knows   80
The compost has no more life.
Someone outside would have seen
The oldest car's door inexplicably
Close from within:

I held her and held her and held her,   85
Convoyed at terrific speed
By the stalled, dreaming traffic around us,
So the blacksnake, stiff
With inaction, curved back
Into life, and hunted the mouse   90

With deadly overexcitement,
The beetles reclaimed their field
As we clung, glued together,
With the hooks of the seat springs
Working through to catch us red-handed   95
Amidst the gray breathless batting

That burst from the seat at our backs.
We left by separate doors
Into the changed, other bodies
Of cars, she down Cherrylog Road   100
And I to my motorcycle
Parked like the soul of the junkyard

Restored, a bicycle fleshed
With power, and tore off
Up Highway 106, continually   105
Drunk on the wind in my mouth,
Wringing the handlebar for speed,
Wild to be wreckage forever.

1964

JOHN ASHBERY

Civilization and Its Discontents[1]

A people chained to aurora[2]
I alone disarming you

Millions of facts of distributed light

Helping myself with some big boxes
Up the steps, then turning to no neighborhood;　　5
The child's psalm, slightly sung
In the hall rushing into the small room.
Such fire! leading away from destruction.
Somewhere in outer ether I glimpsed you
Coming at me, the solo barrier did it this time.　　10
Guessing us staying, true to be at the blue mark
Of the threshold. Tired of planning it again and again.
The cool boy distant, and the soaked-up
Afterthought, like so much rain, or roof.

The miracle took you in beside him.　　15
Leaves rushed the window, there was clear water and the sound of a lock.
Now I never see you much anymore.
The summers are much colder than they used to be
In that other time, when you and I were young.
I miss the human truth of your smile,　　20
The halfhearted gaze of your palms,
And all things together, but there is no comic reign
Only the facts you put to me. You must not, then,
Be very surprised if I am alone: it is all for you,
The night, and the stars, and the way we used to be.　　25

There is no longer any use in harping on
The incredible principle of daylong silence, the dark sunlight
As only the grass is beginning to know it,
The wreath of the north pole,
Festoons for the late return, the shy pensioners　　30
Agasp on the lamplit air. What is agreeable
Is to hold your hand. The gravel
Underfoot. The time is for coming close. Useless
Verbs shooting the other words far away.

I had already swallowed the poison　　35
And could only gaze into the distance at my life
Like a saint's with each day distinct.
No heaviness in the upland pastures. Nothing
In the forest. Only life under the huge trees
Like a coat that has grown too big, moving far away,　　40
Cutting swamps for men like lapdogs, holding its own,
Performing once again, for you and for me.

1965

---

1. The title of a book, by Freud, which deals with the demands of instinct and the restrictions of civilization.
2. Dawn.

ERNEST DOWSON

Non Sum Qualis Eram Bonae sub Regno Cynarae[1]

Last night, ah, yesternight, betwixt her lips and mine
There fell thy shadow, Cynara! thy breath was shed
Upon my soul between the kisses and the wine;
And I was desolate and sick of an old passion,
    Yea, I was desolate and bowed my head: 5
I have been faithful to thee, Cynara! in my fashion.

All night upon mine heart I felt her warm heart beat,
Night-long within mine arms in love and sleep she lay;
Surely the kisses of her bought red mouth were sweet;
But I was desolate and sick of an old passion,   10
    When I awoke and found the dawn was gray:
I have been faithful to thee, Cynara! in my fashion.

I have forgot much, Cynara! gone with the wind,
Flung roses, roses riotously with the throng,
Dancing, to put thy pale, lost lilies out of mind;   15
But I was desolate and sick of an old passion,
    Yea, all the time, because the dance was long:
I have been faithful to thee, Cynara! in my fashion.

I cried for madder music and for stronger wine,
But when the feast is finished and the lamps expire,   20
Then falls thy shadow, Cynara! the night is thine;
And I am desolate and sick of an old passion,
    Yea hungry for the lips of my desire:
I have been faithful to thee, Cynara! in my fashion.

                                        p. 1891

JOHN DRYDEN

Why Should a Foolish Marriage Vow[2]

Why should a foolish marriage vow,
    Which long ago was made,
Oblige us to each other now
    When passion is decayed?
We loved, and we loved, as long as we could,   5
    Till our love was loved out in us both;
But our marriage is dead when the pleasure is fled:
    'Twas pleasure first made it an oath.

If I have pleasures for a friend,
    And farther love in store,   10
What wrong has he whose joys did end,
    And who could give no more?

1. Horace, *Odes,* IV, i, lines 3–4: "I am not as I was under the reign of the kindly Cynara."

2. A song from Dryden's play, *Marriage a la Mode.*

'Tis a madness that he should be jealous of me,
    Or that I should bar him of another:
For all we can gain is to give ourselves pain,   15
    When neither can hinder the other.

1671

ANONYMOUS

Western Wind

Western wind, when wilt thou blow,
    The small rain down can rain?
Christ, if my love were in my arms
    And I in my bed again!

ca. 1300

W. B. YEATS

Politics

"In our time the destiny of man presents its meaning in political terms."
—THOMAS MANN

How can I, that girl standing there,
My attention fix
On Roman or on Russian
Or on Spanish politics?
Yet here's a traveled man that knows   5
What he talks about,
And there's a politician
That has read and thought,
And maybe what they say is true
Of war and war's alarms,   10
But O that I were young again
And held her in my arms!

1939

EZRA POUND

There Died a Myriad[1]

There died a myriad,
And of the best, among them,
For an old bitch gone in the teeth,
For a botched civilization,

Charm, smiling at the good mouth,   5
Quick eyes gone under earth's lid,

For two gross of broken statues,
For a few thousand battered books.

1920

1. Section V of "E. P. Ode pour L'Élection de Son Sépulcre."

HENRY REED

Lessons of the War

Judging Distances

Not only far away, but the way that you say it
Is very important. Perhaps you may never get
The knack of judging a distance, but at least you know
How to report on a landscape: the central sector,
The right of arc and that, which we had last Tuesday,   5
    And at least you know

That maps are of time, not place, so far as the army
Happens to be concerned—the reason being,
Is one which need not delay us. Again, you know
There are three kinds of tree, three only, the fir and the poplar,   10
And those which have bushy tops to; and lastly
    That things only seem to be things.

A barn is not called a barn, to put it more plainly,
Or a field in the distance, where sheep may be safely grazing.
You must never be over-sure. You must say, when reporting: 15
At five o'clock in the central sector is a dozen
Of what appear to be animals; whatever you do,
    Don't call the bleeders *sheep*.

I am sure that's quite clear; and suppose, for the sake of example,
The one at the end, asleep, endeavors to tell us   20
What he sees over there to the west, and how far away,
After first having come to attention. There to the west,
On the fields of summer the sun and the shadows bestow
    Vestments of purple and gold.

The still white dwellings are like a mirage in the heat,   25
And under the swaying elms a man and a woman
Lie gently together. Which is, perhaps, only to say
That there is a row of houses to the left of arc,
And that under some poplars a pair of what appear to be humans
    Appear to be loving.   30

Well that, for an answer, is what we might rightly call
Moderately satisfactory only, the reason being,
Is that two things have been omitted, and those are important.
The human beings, now: in what direction are they,
And how far away, would you say? And do not forget   35
    There may be dead ground in between.

There may be dead ground in between; and I may not have got
The knack of judging a distance; I will only venture
A guess that perhaps between me and the apparent lovers,
(Who, incidentally, appear by now to have finished,)   40
At seven o'clock from the houses, is roughly a distance
    Of about one year and a half.

1946

RICHARD LOVELACE

To Lucasta, Going to the Wars

Tell me not, sweet, I am unkind
    That from the nunnery
Of thy chaste breast and quiet mind,
    To war and arms I fly.

True, a new mistress now I chase,   5
    The first foe in the field;
And with a stronger faith embrace
    A sword, a horse, a shield.

Yet this inconstancy is such
    As you too shall adore;   10
I could not love thee, dear, so much,
    Loved I not Honor more.

                                1649

JOHN SCOTT

I Hate That Drum's Discordant Sound

I hate that drum's discordant sound,
Parading round, and round, and round:
To thoughtless youth it pleasure yields,
And lures from cities and from fields,
To sell their liberty for charms   5
Of tawdry lace, and glittering arms;
And when Ambition's voice commands,
To march, and fight, and fall, in foreign lands.

I hate that drum's discordant sound,
Parading round, and round, and round: 10
To me it talks of ravaged plains,
And burning towns, and ruined swains,[1]
And mangled limbs, and dying groans,
The widows' tears, and orphans' moans;
And all that Misery's hand bestows,   15
To fill the catalogue of human woes.

                                1782

DENISE LEVERTOV

What Were They Like?

1) Did the people of Viet Nam
   use lanterns of stone?
2) Did they hold ceremonies
   to reverence the opening of buds?
3) Were they inclined to rippling laughter?   5

1. Youths.

4) Did they use bone and ivory,
   jade and silver, for ornament?
5) Had they an epic poem?
6) Did they distinguish between speech and singing?

1) Sir, their light hearts turned to stone.   10
   It is not remembered whether in gardens
   stone lanterns illumined pleasant ways.
2) Perhaps they gathered once to delight in blossom,
   but after the children were killed
   there were no more buds.   15
3) Sir, laughter is bitter to the burned mouth.
4) A dream ago, perhaps. Ornament is for joy.
   All the bones were charred.
5) It is not remembered. Remember,
   most were peasants; their life   20
   was in rice and bamboo.
   When peaceful clouds were reflected in the paddies
   and the water buffalo stepped surely along terraces,
   maybe fathers told their sons old tales.
   When bombs smashed the mirrors   25
   there was time only to scream.
6) There is an echo yet, it is said,
   of their speech which was like a song.
   It is reported their singing resembled
   the flight of moths in moonlight.   30
   Who can say? It is silent now.

                                                                  1966

WILFRED OWEN

Dulce Et Decorum Est[1]

Bent double, like old beggars under sacks,
Knock-kneed, coughing like hags, we cursed through sludge,
Till on the haunting flares we turned our backs
And towards our distant rest began to trudge.
Men marched asleep. Many had lost their boots   5
But limped on, blood-shod. All went lame; all blind;
Drunk with fatigue; deaf even to the hoots
Of disappointed shells that dropped behind.

Gas! Gas! Quick, boys!—An ecstasy of fumbling,
Fitting the clumsy helmets just in time;   10
But someone still was yelling out and stumbling
And floundering like a man in fire or lime.—
Dim, through the misty panes and thick green light
As under a green sea, I saw him drowning.

In all my dreams, before my helpless sight,   15
He plunges at me, guttering, choking, drowning.

---

1. Part of a phrase from Horace, quoted in full in the last lines: "It is sweet and proper to die for one's country."

If in some smothering dreams you too could pace
Behind the wagon that we flung him in,
And watch the white eyes writhing in his face,
His hanging face, like a devil's sick of sin;   20
If you could hear, at every jolt, the blood
Come gargling from the froth-corrupted lungs,
Obscene as cancer, bitter as the cud
Of vile, incurable sores on innocent tongues,—
My friend, you would not tell with such high zest   25
To children ardent for some desperate glory,
The old Lie: Dulce et decorum est
Pro patria mori.

1917

A. E. HOUSMAN

Epitaph on an Army of Mercenaries

These, in the day when heaven was falling,
    The hour when earth's foundations fled,
Followed their mercenary calling
    And took their wages and are dead.

Their shoulders held the sky suspended;   5
    They stood, and earth's foundations stay;
What God abandoned, these defended,
    And saved the sum of things for pay.

p. 1917

RAYMOND R. PATTERSON

You Are the Brave

You are the brave who do not break
In the grip of the mob when the blow comes straight
To the shattered bone; when the sockets shriek;
When your arms lie twisted under your back.

Good men holding their courage slack   5
In their frightened pockets see how weak
The work that is done; and feel the weight
Of your blood on the ground for their spirits' sake;

And build their anger, stone on stone;
Each silently, but not alone.   10

1962

EDGAR A. GUEST

The Things that Make a Soldier Great

The things that make a soldier great and send him out to die,
To face the flaming cannon's mouth, nor ever question why,

Are lilacs by a little porch, the row of tulips red,
The peonies and pansies, too, the old petunia bed,
The grass plot where his children play, the roses on the wall: 5
'Tis these that make a soldier great. He's fighting for them all.

'Tis not the pomp and pride of kings that make a soldier brave;
'Tis not allegiance to the flag that over him may wave;
For soldiers never fight so well on land or on the foam
As when behind the cause they see the little place called home.   10
Endanger but that humble street whereon his children run—
You make a soldier of the man who never bore a gun.

What is it through the battle smoke the valiant soldier sees?
The little garden far away, the budding apple trees,
The little patch of ground back there, the children at their play,   15
Perhaps a tiny mound behind the simple church of gray.
The golden thread of courage isn't linked to castle dome
But to the spot, where'er it be—the humble spot called home.

And now the lilacs bud again and all is lovely there,
And homesick soldiers far away know spring is in the air;   20
The tulips come to bloom again, the grass once more is green,
And every man can see the spot where all his joys have been.
He sees his children smile at him, he hears the bugle call,
And only death can stop him now—he's fighting for them all.

1918

LARRY RUBIN

The Draft Dodger

The poets who are veterans of the wars
Know what to love: they have seen their lines
Crumble, and watched their ink run red from wells
Below the veins. The works of death bloom
In bursts above the trench; unchained from grief   5
This soldier's pen is splintered from the sword
He wields, a blade of blindness to protect
The poems unborn. Apocalypse glistens like peace
In his vision; past the void, the lines
Re-form. The bombardier goes home, and beauty   10
Suppurates[1] from wounds.
                                    My draft board
Was most kind, surmising, perhaps, an old
Embarrassment, the beauty of the guns,
The danger in the love of enemies.

1967

---

1. Festers.

RICHARD EBERHART

The Fury of Aerial Bombardment

You would think the fury of aerial bombardment
Would rouse God to relent; the infinite spaces
Are still silent. He looks on shock-pried faces.
History, even, does not know what is meant.

You would feel that after so many centuries   5
God would give man to repent; yet he can kill
As Cain could, but with multitudinous will,
No farther advanced than in his ancient furies.

Was man made stupid to see his own stupidity?
Is God by definition indifferent, beyond us all?   10
Is the eternal truth man's fighting soul
Wherein the Beast ravens in its own avidity?

Of Van Wettering I speak, and Averill,
Names on a list, whose faces I do not recall
But they are gone to early death, who late in school   15
Distinguished the belt feed lever from the belt holding pawl.[1]

                                                          1947

ANONYMOUS

The Soldier's Song

I sing the praise of honored wars,
The glory of well-gotten scars,
The bravery of glittering shields,
Of lusty hearts and famous fields;
For that is music worth the ear of Jove,   5
A sight for kings, and still the soldier's love.

  Look! Oh, methinks I see
  The grace of chivalry;
  The colors are displayed,
  The captains bright arrayed.   10
  See now the battle's ranged,
  Bullets now thick are 'changed.

  Hark! shots and wounds abound,
  The drums alarum sound.
  The captains cry: Za-za!   15
  The trumpets sound ta-ra!
Oh, this is music worth the ear of Jove,
A sight for kings, and still the soldier's love.

                                                          1605

1. Machine-gun parts.

RANDALL JARRELL

The Death of the Ball Turret Gunner[2]

From my mother's sleep I fell into the State,
And I hunched in its belly till my wet fur froze.
Six miles from earth, loosed from its dream of life,
I woke to black flak and the nightmare fighters.
When I died they washed me out of the turret with a hose.   5

1945

W. B. YEATS

On Being Asked for a War Poem

I think it better that in times like these
A poet's mouth be silent, for in truth
We have no gift to set a statesman right;
He has had enough of meddling who can please
A young girl in the indolence of her youth,   5
Or an old man upon a winter's night.

p. 1915

LI PO

Fighting South of the Ramparts[1]

Last year we were fighting at the source of the Sang-kan;[2]
This year we are fighting on the Onion River road.[3]
We have washed our swords in the surf of Parthian seas;
We have pastured our horses among the snows of the T'ien Shan,
The King's armies have grown grey and old   5
Fighting ten thousand leagues away from home.
The Huns have no trade but battle and carnage;
They have no fields or ploughlands,
But only wastes where white bones lie among yellow sands.
Where the House of Ch'in built the great wall that was to keep away
   the Tartars.   10
There, in its turn, the House of Han lit beacons of war.
The beacons are always alight, fighting and marching never stop.
Men die in the field, slashing sword to sword;
The horses of the conquered neigh piteously to Heaven.
Crows and hawks peck for human guts,   15
Carry them in their beaks and hang them on the branches of withered
   trees.

2. "A ball turret was a plexiglass sphere set into the belly of a B-17 or B-24 and inhabited by two .50 caliber machine-guns and one man, a short, small man. When this gunner tracked with his machine-guns a fighter attacking his bomber from below, he revolved with the turret; hunched upside-down in his little sphere, he looked like the foetus in the womb. The fighters which attacked him were armed with cannon firing explosive shells. The hose was a steam hose." (Jarrell's note)
1. Translated by Arthur Waley. All the notes to this poem are Waley's.
2. "Runs west to east through northern Shansi and Hopei, north of the Great Wall."
3. "The Kashgar-darya, in Turkestan."

Captains and soldiers are smeared on the bushes and grass;
The General schemed in vain.
Know therefore that the sword is a cursed thing
Which the wise man uses only if he must.[4]   20

ca. 750

EUGENE MCCARTHY

Kilroy[1]

Kilroy is gone,
the word is out,
absent without leave
from Vietnam.

Kilroy   5
who wrote his name
in every can
from Poland to Japan
and places in between
like Sheboygan and Racine   10
is gone
absent without leave
from Vietnam.

Kilroy
who kept the dice   15
and stole the ice
out of the BOQ[2]
Kilroy
whose name was good
on every IOU   20
in World War II
and even in Korea
is gone
absent without leave
from Vietnam.   25

Kilroy
the unknown soldier
who was the first to land
the last to leave,
with his own hand   30
has taken his good name
from all the walls
and toilet stalls.
Kilroy
whose name around the world   35

4. "Quotation from the *Tao Te Ching*."
1. A legendary "hero" of World War II.
American soldiers then and since scribbled
"Kilroy was here" everywhere—to suggest
that no task was too great nor place too
remote for American fighting spirit.
2. Bachelor Officers' Quarters.

was like the flag unfurled
has run it down
and left Saigon
and the Mekong
without a hero or a song   40
and gone
absent without leave
from Vietnam.

1968

THOMAS NASHE

A Litany in Time of Plague[1]

Adieu, farewell, earth's bliss;
This world uncertain is;
Fond[2] are life's lustful joys;
Death proves them all but toys;[3]
None from his darts can fly;   5
I am sick, I must die.
   Lord, have mercy on us!

Rich men, trust not in wealth,
Gold cannot buy you health;
Physic[4] himself must fade.   10
All things to end are made,
The plague full swift goes by;
I am sick, I must die.
   Lord, have mercy on us!

Beauty is but a flower   15
Which wrinkles will devour;
Brightness falls from the air;
Queens have died young and fair;
Dust hath closed Helen's[5] eye.
I am sick, I must die.   20
   Lord, have mercy on us!

Strength stoops unto the grave,
Worms feed on Hector[6] brave;
Swords may not fight with fate,
Earth still holds ope her gate.   25
"Come, come!" the bells[7] do cry.
I am sick, I must die.
   Lord, have mercy on us.

Wit with his wantonness
Tasteth death's bitterness;   30
Hell's executioner

1. England was ravaged by bubonic plague in 1592.
2. Foolish.
3. Trifles.
4. Restorative powers, personified.

5. Helen of Troy, a traditional type of beauty.
6. The bravest Trojan, a traditional type of strength.
7. Church bells which toll for deaths.

Hath no ears for to hear
What vain art can reply.
I am sick, I must die.
    Lord, have mercy on us.   35

Haste, therefore, each degree,
To welcome destiny;
Heaven is our heritage,
Earth but a player's stage;
Mount we unto the sky.   40
I am sick, I must die.
    Lord, have mercy on us.

1592

JOHN DONNE

Death Be Not Proud

Death be not proud, though some have calléd thee
Mighty and dreadful, for thou art not so;
For those whom thou think'st thou dost overthrow
Die not, poor Death, nor yet canst thou kill me.
From rest and sleep, which but thy pictures[1] be,   5
Much pleasure; then from thee much more must flow,
And soonest[2] our best men with thee do go,
Rest of their bones, and soul's delivery.[3]
Thou art slave to Fate, Chance, kings, and desperate men,
And dost with Poison, War, and Sickness dwell;   10
And poppy or charms can make us sleep as well,
And better than thy stroke; why swell'st[4] thou then?
One short sleep past, we wake eternally
And death shall be no more; Death, thou shalt die.

                                                1633

WILLIAM CARLOS WILLIAMS

Tract

I will teach you my townspeople
how to perform a funeral
for you have it over a troop
of artists—
unless one should scour the world—   5
you have the ground sense necessary.

See! the hearse leads.
I begin with a design for a hearse.
For Christ's sake not black—
nor white either—and not polished!   10
Let it be weathered—like a farm wagon—
with gilt wheels (this could be
applied fresh at small expense)

1. Likenesses.   3. Deliverance.
2. Most willingly.   4. Puff with pride.

or no wheels at all:
a rough dray to drag over the ground.   15

Knock the glass out!
My God—glass, my townspeople!
For what purpose? Is it for the dead
to look out or for us to see
how well he is housed or to see   20
the flowers or the lack of them—
or what?
To keep the rain and snow from him?
He will have a heavier rain soon:
pebbles and dirt and what not.   25
Let there be no glass—
and no upholstery, phew!
and no little brass rollers
and small easy wheels on the bottom—
my townspeople what are you thinking of?   30

A rough plain hearse then
with gilt wheels and no top at all.
On this the coffin lies
by its own weight.
                        No wreaths please—   35
especially no hot house flowers.
Some common memento is better,
something he prized and is known by:
his old clothes—a few books perhaps—
God knows what! You realize   40
how we are about these things
my townspeople—
something will be found—anything
even flowers if he had come to that.
So much for the hearse.   45

For heaven's sake though see to the driver!
Take off the silk hat! In fact
that's no place at all for him—
up there unceremoniously
dragging our friend out to his own dignity!   50
Bring him down—bring him down!
Low and inconspicuous! I'd not have him ride
on the wagon at all—damn him—
the undertaker's understrapper!
Let him hold the reins   55
and walk at the side
and inconspicuously too!

Then briefly as to yourselves:
Walk behind—as they do in France,
seventh class, or if you ride   60
Hell take curtains! Go with some show
of inconvenience; sit openly—
to the weather as to grief.

Or do you think you can shut grief in?
What—from us? We who have perhaps   65
nothing to lose? Share with us
share with us—it will be money
in your pockets.
                    Go now
I think you are ready.   70

1917

A. E. HOUSMAN

To an Athlete Dying Young

The time you won your town the race
We chaired[1] you through the marketplace;
Man and boy stood cheering by,
And home we brought you shoulder-high.

Today, the road all runners come,   5
Shoulder-high we bring you home,
And set you at your threshold down,
Townsman of a stiller town.

Smart lad, to slip betimes away
From fields where glory does not stay,   10
And early though the laurel[2] grows
It withers quicker than the rose.

Eyes the shady night has shut
Cannot see the record cut,
And silence sounds no worse than cheers   15
After earth has stopped the ears:

Now you will not swell the rout
Of lads that wore their honors out,
Runners whom renown outran
And the name died before the man.   20

So set, before its echoes fade,
The fleet foot on the sill of shade,
And hold to the low lintel[3] up
The still-defended challenge-cup.

And round that early-laureled head   25
Will flock to gaze the strengthless dead,
And find unwithered on its curls
The garland[4] briefer than a girl's.

1896

1. Carried aloft in triumph.   3. Upper part of a door frame.
2. Wreath of honor.   4. Wreath of flowers.

e. e. cummings

portrait

Buffalo Bill's
defunct
  who used to
  ride a watersmooth-silver
       stallion   5
and break onetwothreefourfive pigeonsjustlikethat
            Jesus
he was a handsome man
      and what i want to know is
how do you like your blueeyed boy   10
Mister Death

                1923

ETHERIDGE KNIGHT

For Malcolm, a Year After

Compose for Red[1] a proper verse;
Adhere to foot and strict iamb,[2]
Control the burst of angry words
Or they might boil and break the dam.
Or they might boil and overflow   5
And drench me, drown me, drive me mad.
So swear no oath, so shed no tear,
And sing no song blue Baptist sad.
Evoke no image, stir no flame,
And spin no yarn across the air.   10
Make empty anglo tea lace words—
Make them dead white and dry bone bare.

Compose a verse for Malcolm man,[3]
And make it rime and make it prim.
The verse will die—as all men do—   15
But not the memory of him!
Death might come singing sweet like C,
Or knocking like the old folk say,
The moon and stars may pass away,
But not the anger of that day.   20

1966

---

1. "Detroit Red" was one of the names of Malcolm X.
2. Metrical terms; see the glossary.
3. "No, I didn't mean for 'man' to be a vocative. Rather I meant for 'man' to be a term of endearment, an affectionate attachment to Malcolm. You know like 'ito & ita' is in Spanish? To me, 'man' & 'boy' serve the same purpose—like: Charlie boy, Sonny man, etc. Also, without the comma, the reader is less likely to make the mistake of thinking that I'm addressing him—which I am not. Further, 'man' simply for what it means literally and visually shows the inseparateness of the two, Malcolm & man." (Knight's note)

BEN JONSON

On My First Son

Farewell, thou child of my right hand,[1] and joy;
My sin was too much hope of thee, loved boy:
Seven years thou'wert lent to me, and I thee pay,
Exacted by thy fate, on the just[2] day.
O could I lose all father now! for why   5
Will man lament the state he should envý,
To have so soon 'scaped world's and flesh's rage,
And, if no other misery, yet age?
Rest in soft peace, and asked, say, "Here doth lie
Ben Jonson his[3] best piece of poetry."   10
For whose sake henceforth all his vows be such
As what he loves may never like too much.

1616

DYLAN THOMAS

A Refusal to Mourn the Death, by Fire, of a Child in London

Never until the mankind making
Bird beast and flower
Fathering and all humbling darkness
Tells with silence the last light breaking
And the still hour   5
Is come of the sea tumbling in harness

And I must enter again the round
Zion of the water bead
And the synagogue of the ear of corn
Shall I let pray the shadow of a sound   10
Or sow my salt seed
In the least valley of sackcloth to mourn

The majesty and burning of the child's death.
I shall not murder
The mankind of her going with a grave truth   15
Nor blaspheme down the stations of the breath
With any further
Elegy of innocence and youth.
Deep with the first dead lies London's daughter,
Robed in the long friends,   20
The grains beyond age, the dark veins of her mother,
Secret by the unmourning water
Of the riding Thames.
After the first death, there is no other.

1945

1. A literal translation of the son's name,
Benjamin.
   2. Exact; the son died on his seventh
birthday, in 1603.
   3. Ben Jonson's (a common Renaissance
form of the possessive).

JOHN CROWE RANSOM

Bells for John Whiteside's Daughter

There was such speed in her little body,
And such lightness in her footfall,
It is no wonder her brown study[1]
Astonishes us all.

Her wars were bruited in our high window.   5
We looked among orchard trees and beyond
Where she took arms against her shadow,
Or harried unto the pond

The lazy geese, like a snow cloud
Dripping their snow on the green grass,   10
Tricking and stopping, sleepy and proud,
Who cried in goose, Alas,

For the tireless heart within the little
Lady with rod that made them rise
From their noon apple-dreams and scuttle   15
Goose-fashion under the skies!

But now go the bells, and we are ready,
In one house we are sternly stopped
To say we are vexed at her brown study,
Lying so primly propped.   20

1924

MARK TWAIN

Ode to Stephen Dowling Bots, Dec'd[2]

And did young Stephen sicken,
    And did young Stephen die?
And did the sad hearts thicken,
    And did the mourners cry?

No; such was not the fate of   5
    Young Stephen Dowling Bots;
Though sad hearts round him thickened,
    'Twas not from sickness' shots.

No whooping-cough did rack his frame,
    Nor measles drear with spots;   10
Not these impaired the sacred name
    Of Stephen Dowling Bots.

1. Stillness, as if in meditation or deep thought.
2. The ode is supposedly written by Emmeline Grangerford, the 13-year-old daughter of one of the feuding families in *Huckleberry Finn*. Huck says, "She could write about anything you choose [sic] to give her to write about just so it was sadful. Every time a man died, or a woman died, or a child died, she would be on hand with her 'tribute' before he was cold."

Despised love struck not with woe
  That head of curly knots,
Nor stomach troubles laid him low,   15
  Young Stephen Dowling Bots.

O no. Then list with tearful eye,
  Whilst I his fate do tell.
His soul did from this cold world fly,
  By falling down a well.   20

They got him out and emptied him;
  Alas it was too late;
His spirit was gone for to sport aloft
  In the realms of the good and great.

1884

WILLIAM WORDSWORTH

A Slumber Did My Spirit Seal

A slumber did my spirit seal;
  I had no human fears:
She seemed a thing that could not feel
  The touch of earthly years.

No motion has she now, no force: 5
  She neither hears nor sees;
Rolled round in earth's diurnal[1] course,
  With rocks, and stones, and trees.

1800

SYLVIA PLATH

Lady Lazarus[2]

I have done it again.
One year in every ten
I manage it——

A sort of walking miracle, my skin
Bright as a Nazi lampshade,   5
My right foot

A paperweight,
My face a featureless, fine
Jew linen.

Peel off the napkin   10
O my enemy.
Do I terrify?——

---

1. Daily.
2. According to *John* 11, Jesus raised   Lazarus, the brother of Mary and Martha,
   from the dead.

The nose, the eye pits, the full set of teeth?
The sour breath
Will vanish in a day.   15

Soon, soon the flesh
The grave cave ate will be
At home on me

And I a smiling woman.
I am only thirty.   20
And like the cat I have nine times to die.

This is Number Three.
What a trash
To annihilate each decade.

What a million filaments.   25
The peanut-crunching crowd
Shoves in to see

Them unwrap me hand and foot——
The big strip tease.
Gentlemen, ladies   30

These are my hands
My knees.
I may be skin and bone,

Nevertheless, I am the same, identical woman.
The first time it happened I was ten.   35
It was an accident.

The second time I meant
To last it out and not come back at all.
I rocked shut

As a seashell.   40
They had to call and call
And pick the worms off me like sticky pearls.

Dying
Is an art, like everything else.
I do it exceptionally well.   45

I do it so it feels like hell.
I do it so it feels real.
I guess you could say I've a call.

It's easy enough to do it in a cell.
It's easy enough to do it and stay put.   50
It's the theatrical

Comeback in broad day
To the same place, the same face, the same brute
Amused shout:

"A miracle!"   55
That knocks me out.
There is a charge

For the eyeing of my scars, there is a charge
For the hearing of my heart——
It really goes.   60

And there is a charge, a very large charge
For a word or a touch
Or a bit of blood

Or a piece of my hair or my clothes.
So, so, Herr Doktor.   65
So, Herr Enemy.

I am your opus,
I am your valuable,
The pure gold baby

That melts to a shriek.   70
I turn and burn.
Do not think I underestimate your great concern.

Ash, ash—
You poke and stir.
Flesh, bone, there is nothing there——   75

A cake of soap,
A wedding ring,
A gold filling.

Herr God, Herr Lucifer
Beware   80
Beware.

Out of the ash
I rise with my red hair
And I eat men like air.

                                                              1965

EMILY DICKINSON

Because I Could Not Stop for Death

Because I could not stop for Death—
He kindly stopped for me—
The Carriage held but just Ourselves—
And Immortality.

We slowly drove—He knew no haste   5
And I had put away
My labor and my leisure too,
For His Civility—

We passed the School, where Children strove
At Recess—in the Ring—   10
We passed the Fields of Gazing Grain—
We passed the Setting Sun—

Or rather—He passed Us—
The Dews drew quivering and chill—
For only Gossamer,¹ my Gown—   15
My Tippet²—only Tulle³—

We paused before a House that seemed
A Swelling of the Ground—
The Roof was scarcely visible—
The Cornice—in the Ground—   20

Since then—'tis Centuries—and yet
Feels shorter than the Day
I first surmised the Horses' Heads
Were toward Eternity—

ca. 1863

JAMES WRIGHT

Arrangements with Earth for Three Dead Friends

Sweet earth, he ran and changed his shoes to go
Outside with other children through the fields.
He panted up the hills and swung from trees
Wild as a beast but for the human laughter
That tumbled like a cider down his cheeks.   5
Sweet earth, the summer has been gone for weeks,
And weary fish already sleeping under water
Below the banks where early acorns freeze.
Receive his flesh and keep it cured of colds.
Button his coat and scarf his throat from snow.   10

And now, bright earth, this other is out of place
In what, awake, we speak about as tombs.
He sang in houses when the birds were still
And friends of his were huddled round till dawn
After the many nights to hear him sing.   15
Bright earth, his friends remember how he sang
Voices of night away when wind was one.
Lonely the neighborhood beneath your hill
Where he is waved away through silent rooms.
Listen for music, earth, and human ways.   20

1. A soft sheer fabric.   3. A fine net fabric.
2. Scarf.

Dark earth, there is another gone away,
But she was not inclined to beg of you
Relief from water falling or the storm.
She was aware of scavengers in holes
Of stone, she knew the loosened stones that fell   25
Indifferently as pebbles plunging down a well
And broke for the sake of nothing human souls.
Earth, hide your face from her where dark is warm.
She does not beg for anything, who knew
The change of tone, the human hope gone gray.   30

1957

W. H. AUDEN

In Memory of W. B. Yeats

(d. January, 1939)

I

He disappeared in the dead of winter:
The brooks were frozen, the airports almost deserted,
And snow disfigured the public statues;
The mercury sank in the mouth of the dying day.
What instruments we have agree   5
The day of his death was a dark cold day.

Far from his illness
The wolves ran on through the evergreen forests,
The peasant river was untempted by the fashionable quays;
By mourning tongues   10
The death of the poet was kept from his poems.

But for him it was his last afternoon as himself,
An afternoon of nurses and rumors;
The provinces of his body revolted,
The squares of his mind were empty,   15
Silence invaded the suburbs,
The current of his feeling failed; he became his admirers.

Now he is scattered among a hundred cities
And wholly given over to unfamiliar affections,
To find his happiness in another kind of wood   20
And be punished under a foreign code of conscience.
The words of a dead man
Are modified in the guts of the living.

But in the importance and noise of tomorrow
When the brokers are roaring like beasts on the floor of the Bourse,[1]   25
And the poor have the sufferings to which they are fairly accustomed,
And each in the cell of himself is almost convinced of his freedom,
A few thousand will think of this day

As one thinks of a day when one did something slightly unusual.
What instruments we have agree   30
The day of his death was a dark cold day.

1. The Paris stock exchange.

II

You were silly like us; your gift survived it all:
The parish of rich women, physical decay,
Yourself. Mad Ireland hurt you into poetry.
Now Ireland has her madness and her weather still,   35
For poetry makes nothing happen: it survives
In the valley of its making where executives
Would never want to tamper, flows on south
From ranches of isolation and the busy griefs,
Raw towns that we believe and die in; it survives,   40
A way of happening, a mouth.

III

Earth, receive an honored guest:
William Yeats is laid to rest.
Let the Irish vessel lie
Emptied of its poetry.   45

In the nightmare of the dark
All the dogs of Europe bark,
And the living nations wait,
Each sequestered in its hate;

Intellectual disgrace   50
Stares from every human face,
And the seas of pity lie
Locked and frozen in each eye.

Follow, poet, follow right
To the bottom of the night,   55
With your unconstraining voice
Still persuade us to rejoice;

With the farming of a verse
Make a vineyard of the curse,
Sing of human unsuccess   60
In a rapture of distress;

In the deserts of the heart
Let the healing fountain start,
In the prison of his days
Teach the free man how to praise.   65

1939

A. E. HOUSMAN

Terence, This Is Stupid Stuff

"Terence,[1] this is stupid stuff:
You eat your victuals fast enough;

---

1. Housman originally titled the volume in which this poem appeared "The Poems of
Terence Hearsay."

There can't be much amiss, 'tis clear,
To see the rate you drink your beer.
But oh, good Lord, the verse you make,   5
It gives a chap the belly-ache.
The cow, the old cow, she is dead;
It sleeps well, the horned head:
We poor lads, 'tis our turn now
To hear such tunes as killed the cow.   10
Pretty friendship 'tis to rhyme
Your friends to death before their time
Moping melancholy mad:
Come, pipe a tune to dance to, lad."

Why, if 'tis dancing you would be,   15
There's brisker pipes than poetry.
Say, for what were hop-yards meant,
Or why was Burton built on Trent?[2]
Oh many a peer of England brews
Livelier liquor than the Muse,   20
And malt does more than Milton can
To justify God's ways to man.[3]
Ale, man, ale's the stuff to drink
For fellows whom it hurts to think:
Look into the pewter pot   25
To see the world as the world's not.
And faith, 'tis pleasant till 'tis past:
The mischief is that 'twill not last.
Oh I have been to Ludlow fair[4]
And left my necktie God knows where,   30
And carried half-way home, or near,
Pints and quarts of Ludlow beer:
Then the world seemed none so bad,
And I myself a sterling lad;
And down in lovely muck I've lain,   35
Happy till I woke again.
Then I saw the morning sky:
Heigho, the tale was all a lie;
The world, it was the old world yet,
I was I, my things were wet,   40
And nothing now remained to do
But begin the game anew.

Therefore, since the world has still
Much good, but much less good than ill,
And while the sun and moon endure   45
Luck's a chance, but trouble's sure,
I'd face it as a wise man would,
And train for ill and not for good.
'Tis true, the stuff I bring for sale

2. Burton was famous for its ales, originally brewed from special springs there.
3. Milton said his purpose in *Paradise Lost* was to "justify the ways of God to men."
4. Ludlow was a market town in Shropshire, and its town fair would be a social high point for a youth growing up in the county.

Is not so brisk a brew as ale:
Out of a stem that scored the hand
I wrung it in a weary land.
But take it: if the smack is sour,
The better for the embittered hour;
It should do good to heart and head   55
When your soul is in my soul's stead;
And I will friend you, if I may,
In the dark and cloudy day.

    There was a king reigned in the East:
There, when kings will sit to feast,   60
They get their fill before they think
With poisoned meat and poisoned drink.
He gathered all that springs to birth
From the many-venomed earth;
First a little, thence to more,   65
He sampled all her killing store;
And easy, smiling, seasoned sound,
Sate the king when healths went round.
They put arsenic in his meat
And stared aghast to watch him eat;   70
They poured strychnine in his cup
And shook to see him drink it up:
They shook, they stared as white's their shirt:
Them it was their poison hurt.
—I tell the tale that I heard told.   75
Mithridates,[5] he died old.

                        1896

MARIANNE MOORE

Poetry

I, too, dislike it: there are things that are important beyond all this
      fiddle.
  Reading it, however, with a perfect contempt for it, one discovers in
it after all, a place for the genuine.
      Hands that can grasp, eyes
        that can dilate, hair that can rise   5
          if it must, these things are important not because a

high-sounding interpretation can be put upon them but because they
      are
  useful. When they become so derivative as to become unintelligible,
the same thing may be said for all of us, that we
      do not admire what   10
      we cannot understand: the bat
        holding on upside down or in quest of something to

5. The king of Pontus, he was said to have developed a tolerance of poison by taking
gradually increasing quantities.

eat, elephants pushing, a wild horse taking a roll, a tireless wolf under
    a tree, the immovable critic twitching his skin like a horse that feels
        a flea, the base-
ball fan, the statistician—   15
    nor is it valid
        to discriminate against "business documents and

school-books"[1]; all these phenomena are important. One must make a
        distinction
    however: when dragged into prominence by half poets, the result is
        not poetry,
    nor till the poets among us can be   20
        "literalists of
        the imagination"[2]—above
            insolence and triviality and can present

for inspection, "imaginary gardens with real toads in them," shall we
        have
    it. In the meantime, if you demand on the one hand,   25
    the raw material of poetry in
        all its rawness and
        that which is on the other hand
            genuine, you are interested in poetry.

                                                                        1921

ARCHIBALD MACLEISH

Ars Poetica[1]

A poem should be palpable and mute
As a globed fruit,

Dumb
As old medallions to the thumb,

Silent as the sleeve-worn stone   5
Of casement ledges where the moss has grown—

A poem should be wordless
As the flight of birds.

A poem should be motionless in time
As the moon climbs,   10

---

1. *"Diary of Tolstoy,* p. 84: 'Where the boundary between prose and poetry lies, I shall never be able to understand. The question is raised in manuals of style, yet the answer to it lies beyond me. Poetry is verse: prose is not verse. Or else poetry is everything with the exception of business documents and school books.'" (Moore's note)
2. " 'Literalists of the imagination.' Yeats, *Ideas of Good and Evil* (A. H. Bullen, 1903), p. 182. 'The limitation of his view was from the very intensity of his vision; he was a too literal realist of imagination, as others are of nature; and because he believed that the figures seen by the mind's eye, when exalted by inspiration, were "eternal existences," symbols of divine essences, he hated every grace of style that might obscure their lineaments.' " (Moore's note)
1. "The Art of Poetry," title of a poetical treatise by the Roman poet Horace (65–8 B.C.).

Leaving, as the moon releases
Twig by twig the night-entangled trees,

Leaving, as the moon behind the winter leaves,
Memory by memory the mind—

A poem should be motionless in time   15
As the moon climbs.

A poem should be equal to:
Not true.

For all the history of grief
An empty doorway and a maple leaf.   20

For love
The leaning grasses and two lights above the sea—

A poem should not mean
But be.

                                                                    1926

ALEXANDER POPE

[Why Did I Write?][1]

Why did I write? what sin to me unknown   125
Dipped me in ink, my parents', or my own?
As yet a child, nor yet a fool to fame,
I lisped in numbers,[2] for the numbers came.
I left no calling for this idle trade,
No duty broke, no father disobeyed.   130
The Muse but served to ease some friend, not wife,
To help me through this long disease, my life,
To second, Arbuthnot! thy art and care,
And teach, the being you preserved, to bear.
But why then publish? Granville the polite,   135
And knowing Walsh, would tell me I could write;
Well-natured Garth inflamed with early praise,
And Congreve loved, and Swift endured my lays;
The courtly Talbot, Somers, Sheffield read,
Ev'n mitred Rochester would nod the head,   140
And St. John's self (great Dryden's friends before)[3]
With open arms received one poet more.
Happy my studies, when by these approved!
Happier their author, when by these beloved!
From these the world will judge of men and books,   145
Not from the Burnets, Oldmixons, and Cooks.[4]
    Soft were my numbers; who could take offense

---

1. From *An Epistle to Dr. Arbuthnot*, addressed to Pope's physician friend. The poem is Pope's "apologia" (explanation) for his poetic career.
2. Regular metrical units.

3. "All these were Patrons or Admirers of Mr. Dryden" (Pope's note), and early encouragers of Pope himself.
4. "Authors of secret and scandalous History." (Pope's note)

While pure description held the place of sense?
Like gentle Fanny's was my flow'ry theme,
A painted mistress, or a purling stream.   150
Yet then did Gildon[5] draw his venal quill;
I wished the man a dinner, and sate still:
Yet then did Dennis[6] rave in furious fret;
I never answered, I was not in debt:
If want provoked, or madness made them print,   155
I waged no war with Bedlam or the Mint.[7]
  Did some more sober critic come abroad?
If wrong, I smiled; if right, I kissed the rod.
Pains, reading, study, are their just pretense,
And all they want[8] is spirit, taste, and sense.   160
Commas and points they set exactly right,
And 'twere a sin to rob them of their mite.
Yet ne'er one sprig of laurel graced these ribalds,
From slashing Bentley down to pidling Tibalds.[9]

Each wight who reads not, and but scans and spells,   165
Each word-catcher that lives on syllables,
Ev'n such small critics some regard may claim,
Preserved in Milton's or in Shakespear's name.
Pretty! in amber[1] to observe the forms
Of hairs, or straws, or dirt, or grubs, or worms!   170
The things, we know, are neither rich nor rare,
But wonder how the devil they got there?
  Were others angry? I excused them too;
Well might they rage, I gave them but their due.
A man's true merit 'tis not hard to find,   175
But each man's secret standard in his mind,
That casting-weight[2] pride adds to emptiness,
This, who can gratify? for who can *guess*?
The bard whom pilfered pastorals renown,
Who turns[3] a Persian tale for half a crown,[4]   180
Just writes to make his barrenness appear,
And strains from hard-bound brains, eight lines a year;
He, who still wanting, though he lives on theft,
Steals much, spends little, yet has nothing left:
And he, who now to sense, now nonsense leaning,   185
Means not, but blunders round about a meaning:
And he, whose fustian's so sublimely bad,
It is not poetry, but prose run mad:
All these, my modest satire bade *translate*,
And owned that nine such poets made a Tate.[5]   190

5. Charles Gildon, a hack writer who frequently attacked Pope.
6. John Dennis, a talented but irascible critic with whom Pope quarreled often.
7. Bedlam is Bethlehem Hospital for the insane; the "Mint" was a "liberty" where fugitives could not be arrested. Many debtors lived there.
8. Lack.
9. Talented but pedantic scholars. Richard Bentley is "slashing" because of the many bracketed passages in his Milton edition, passages which Bentley thought Milton didn't write; Lewis Theobald (pronounced Tibald) fastidiously edited Shakespeare.
1. Small objects were often preserved in translucent amber.
2. A weight added to make the scales balance.
3. Translates.
4. "Ambrose Philips translated a book called the *Persian Tales*." (Pope's note)
5. Nahum Tate, poet laureate from 1692 to 1715.

How did they fume, and stamp, and roar, and chafe!
And swear, not Addison[6] himself was safe.

                                                    1735

WALLACE STEVENS

Of Modern Poetry

The poem of the mind in the act of finding
What will suffice. It has not always had
To find: the scene was set; it repeated what
Was in the script.
                        Then the theatre was changed   5
To something else. Its past was a souvenir.

It has to be living, to learn the speech of the place.
It has to face the men of the time and to meet
The women of the time. It has to think about war
And it has to find what will suffice. It has   10
To construct a new stage. It has to be on that stage
And, like an insatiable actor,   slowly   and
With meditation, speak words that in the ear,
In the delicatest ear of the mind,   repeat,
Exactly, that which it wants to hear, at the sound   15
Of which, an invisible audience listens,
Not to the play, but to itself, expressed
In an emotion as of two people, as of two
Emotions becoming one. The actor is
A metaphysician in the dark, twanging   20
An instrument, twanging a wiry string that gives
Sounds passing through sudden rightnesses, wholly
Containing the mind, below which it cannot descend,
Beyond which it has no will to rise.
                        It must   25
Be the finding of a satisfaction, and may
Be of a man skating, a woman dancing, a woman
Combing. The poem of the act of the mind.

                                              p. 1940

CHARLES OLSON

A B C s

The word forms
on the left: you must
stand in line. Speech
is as swift as synapse[1]
but the acquisition of same   5
is as long
as I am old

---

6. Joseph Addison, journalist and man
of letters who incurred Pope's displeasure
by comparing some of Pope's early poems
unfavorably with those of Ambrose Philips,
a justly neglected poet.
1. The junction between nerve cells.

rat   on the first floor landing of the three-decker
      (grey)
black   eat a peck of storage batteries 'fore   10
      I die
cabbage   my friend Cabbage, with whom to bake potatoes up
      Fisher's Hill

rust   in the bed of Beaver Brook—from the junk in it
      And the iris ("flags," we called 'em)   15
      And the turtle I was surprised by

up to last night's dream, the long brown body pleased
I kissed her buttock curve

Interiors,
and their registration   20

Words, form
but the extension of
content

Style, est verbum[2]

The word   25
is image, and the reverend reverse is
Eliot

Pound[3]
is verse

p. 1953

WILLIAM SHAKESPEARE

Not Marble, Nor the Gilded Monuments

Not marble, nor the gilded monuments
Of princes, shall outlive this powerful rhyme;
But you shall shine more bright in these conténts
Than unswept stone, besmeared with sluttish time.
When wasteful war shall statues overturn,   5
And broils root out the work of masonry,
Nor Mars his[1] sword nor war's quick fire shall burn
The living record of your memory.
'Gainst death and all-oblivious enmity
Shall you pace forth; your praise shall still find room   10
Even in the eyes of all posterity
That wear this world out to the ending doom.[2]

2. Is the Word.
3. T. S. Eliot and Ezra Pound, leading exponents of different kinds of modern poetry.

1. Mars's (a common Renaissance form of the possessive). "Nor . . . nor": neither . . . nor.
2. Judgment Day.

So, till the judgment that yourself arise,
You live in this, and dwell in lovers' eyes.

1609

ARCHIBALD MACLEISH

"Not Marble Nor the Gilded Monuments"

for Adele

The praisers of women in their proud and beautiful poems,
Naming the grave mouth and the hair and the eyes,
Boasted those they loved should be forever remembered:
These were lies.

The words sound but the face in the Istrian sun is forgotten.   5
The poet speaks but to her dead ears no more.
The sleek throat is gone—and the breast that was troubled to listen:
Shadow from door.

Therefore I will not praise your knees nor your fine walking
Telling you men shall remember your name as long   10
As lips move or breath is spent or the iron of English
Rings from a tongue.

I shall say you were young, and your arms straight, and your mouth
    scarlet:
I shall say you will die and none will remember you:
Your arms change, and none remember the swish of your garments,   15
Nor the click of your shoe.

Not with my hand's strength, not with difficult labor
Springing the obstinate words to the bones of your breast
And the stubborn line to your young stride and the breath to your
    breathing
And the beat to your haste   20
Shall I prevail on the hearts of unborn men to remember.

(What is a dead girl but a shadowy ghost
Or a dead man's voice but a distant and vain affirmation
Like dream words most)

Therefore I will not speak of the undying glory of women.   25
I will say you were young and straight and your skin fair
And you stood in the door and the sun was a shadow of leaves on your
    shoulders
And a leaf on your hair—

I will not speak of the famous beauty of dead women:
I will say the shape of a leaf lay once on your hair.   30
Till the world ends and the eyes are out and the mouths broken
Look! It is there!

1930

ROBINSON JEFFERS

To the Stone-Cutters

Stone-cutters fighting time with marble, you foredefeated
Challengers of oblivion
Eat cynical earnings, knowing rock splits, records fall down,
The square-limbed Roman letters
Scale in the thaws, wear in the rain. The poet as well   5
Builds his monument mockingly;
For the man will be blotted out, the blithe earth die, the brave sun
Die blind and blacken to the heart:
Yet stones have stood for a thousand years, and pained thoughts found
The honey of peace in old poems.   10

1924

W. H. AUDEN

Musée des Beaux Arts[1]

About suffering they were never wrong,
The Old Masters: how well they understood
Its human position; how it takes place
While someone else is eating or opening a window or just walking dully
    along;

How, when the aged are reverently, passionately waiting   5
For the miraculous birth, there always must be
Children who did not specially want it to happen, skating
On a pond at the edge of the wood:
They never forgot
That even the dreadful martyrdom must run its course   10
Anyhow in a corner, some untidy spot
Where the dogs go on with their doggy life and the torturer's horse
Scratches its innocent behind on a tree.

In Brueghel's *Icarus*,[2] for instance: how everything turns away
Quite leisurely from the disaster; the plowman may   15
Have heard the splash, the forsaken cry,
But for him it was not an important failure; the sun shone
As it had to on the white legs disappearing into the green
Water; and the expensive delicate ship that must have seen
Something amazing, a boy falling out of the sky,   20
Had somewhere to get to and sailed calmly on.

1938

---

1. The Museum of the Fine Arts, in Brussels.
2. "Landscape with the Fall of Icarus," by Pieter Brueghel the elder, located in the Brussels Museum. According to Greek myth, Daedalus and his son Icarus escaped from imprisonment by using home-made wings of wax; but Icarus flew too near the sun, the wax melted, and he drowned. In the Brueghel painting the central figure is a peasant plowing, and several other figures are more immediately noticeable than Icarus who, disappearing into the sea, is easy to miss in the lower right-hand corner. Equally ignored by the figures is a dead body in the woods.

WILLIAM CARLOS WILLIAMS

Landscape with the Fall of Icarus[1]

According to Brueghel
when Icarus fell
it was spring

a farmer was plowing
his field   5
the whole pageantry

of the year was
awake tingling
near

the edge of the sea   10
concerned
with itself

sweating in the sun
that melted
the wings' wax   15

unsignificantly
off the coast
there was

a splash quite unnoticed
this was   20
Icarus drowning

         1962

MICHAEL HAMBURGER

Lines on Brueghel's *Icarus*[2]

The plowman plows, the fisherman dreams of fish;
Aloft, the sailor through a world of ropes
Guides tangled meditations, feverish
With memories of girls forsaken, hopes
Of brief reunions, new discoveries,   5
Past rum consumed, rum promised, rum potential.
Sheep crop the grass, lift up their heads and gaze
Into a sheepish present: the essential,
Illimitable juiciness of things,
Greens, yellows, browns are what they see.   10
Churlish and slow, the shepherd, hearing wings—
Perhaps an eagle's—gapes uncertainly.

Too late. The worst had happened: lost to man
The angel, Icarus, for ever failed,

1. See the notes to the poem above.   2. See notes to Auden's "Musée des Beaux Arts."

Fallen with melted wings when, near the sun   15
He scorned the ordering planet, which prevailed
And, jeering, now slinks off, to rise once more.
But he—his damaged purpose drags him down—
Too far from his half-brothers on the shore,
Hardly conceivable, is left to drown.   20

1952

SIR EDWARD DYER

My Mind to Me a Kingdom Is

My mind to me a kingdom is;
   Such present joys therein I find
That it excels all other bliss
   That earth affords or grows by kind.[1]
Though much I want[2] which most would have,   5
Yet still my mind forbids to crave.

No princely pomp, no wealthy store,
   No force to win the victory,
No wily wit to salve a sore,
   No shape to feed a loving eye;   10
To none of these I yield as thrall.
For why[3] my mind doth serve for all.

I see how plenty suffers oft,
   And hasty climbers soon do fall;
I see that those which are aloft   15
   Mishap doth threaten most of all:
They get with toil, they keep with fear.
Such cares my mind could never bear.

Content I live, this is my stay;
   I seek no more than may suffice;   20
I press to bear no haughty sway;
   Look, what I lack my mind supplies;
Lo, thus I triumph like a king,
Content with that my mind doth bring.

Some have too much, yet still do crave;   25
   I little have, and seek no more.
They are but poor, though much they have,
   And I am rich with little store.
They poor, I rich; they beg, I give;
They lack, I leave; they pine, I live.   30

I laugh not at another's loss;
   I grudge not at another's gain;
No worldly waves my mind can toss;
   My state at one doth still remain.

1. Naturally.   3. Because.
2. Lack.

I fear no foe, I fawn no friend;   35
I loathe not life, nor dread my end.

Some weigh their pleasure by their lust,
  Their wisdom by their rage of will;
Their treasure is their only trust;
  A cloakéd craft their store of skill.   40
But all the pleasure that I find
Is to maintain a quiet mind.

My wealth is health and perfect ease;
  My conscience clear my choice defense;
I neither seek by bribes to please,   45
  Nor by deceit to breed offense.
Thus do I live; thus will I die.
Would all did so as well as I!

                                                                  1588

W. H. AUDEN

The Unknown Citizen

(To JS/07/M/378
This Marble Monument
Is Erected by the State)[1]

He was found by the Bureau of Statistics to be
One against whom there was no official complaint,
And all the reports on his conduct agree
That, in the modern sense of an old-fashioned word, he was a saint,
For in everything he did he served the Greater Community.   5
Except for the War till the day he retired
He worked in a factory and never got fired,
But satisfied his employers, Fudge Motors Inc.
Yet he wasn't a scab or odd in his views,
For his Union reports that he paid his dues,   10
(Our report on his Union shows it was sound)
And our Social Psychology workers found
That he was popular with his mates and liked a drink.
The Press are convinced that he bought a paper every day
And that his reactions to advertisements were normal in every way. 15
Policies taken out in his name prove that he was fully insured,
And his Health-card shows he was once in hospital but left it cured.
Both Producers Research and High-Grade Living declare
He was fully sensible to the advantages of the Installment Plan
And had everything necessary to the Modern Man,   20
A phonograph, a radio, a car and a frigidaire.
Our researchers into Public Opinion are content
That he held the proper opinions for the time of year;
When there was peace, he was for peace; when there was war, he
     went.
He was married and added five children to the population,   25

1. The title and subtitle parallel the inscription on the Tomb of the Unknown Soldier.

Which our Eugenist says was the right number for a parent of his
    generation,
And our teachers report that he never interfered with their education.
Was he free? Was he happy? The question is absurd:
Had anything been wrong, we should certainly have heard.

1940

MATTHEW ARNOLD

Lines Written in Kensington Gardens

In this lone, open glade I lie,
Screened by deep boughs on either hand;
And at its end, to stay the eye,
Those black-crowned, red-boled[1] pine-trees stand!

Birds here make song, each bird has his,   5
Across the girdling city's hum.
How green under the boughs it is!
How thick the tremulous sheep-cries come!

Sometimes a child will cross the glade
To take his nurse his broken toy;   10
Sometimes a thrush flit overhead
Deep in her unknown day's employ.

Here at my feet what wonders pass,
What endless, active life is here!
What blowing daisies, fragrant grass!   15
An air-stirred forest, fresh and clear.

Scarce fresher is the mountain-sod
Where the tired angler lies, stretched out,
And, eased of basket and of rod,
Counts his day's spoil, the spotted trout.   20

In the huge world, which roars hard by,
Be others happy if they can!
But in my helpless cradle I
Was breathed on by the rural Pan.[2]

I, on men's impious uproar hurled,   25
Think often, as I hear them rave,
That peace has left the upper world
And now keeps only in the grave.

Yet here is peace for ever new!
When I who watch them am away,   30
Still all things in this glade go through
The changes of their quiet day.

1. Red-trunked.   2. God of shepherds and huntsmen.

Then to their happy rest they pass!
The flowers upclose, the birds are fed,
The night comes down upon the grass,   35
The child sleeps warmly in his bed.

Calm soul of all things! make it mine
To feel, amid the city's jar,
That there abides a peace of thine,
Man did not make, and cannot mar.   40

The will to neither strive nor cry,
The power to feel with others give!
Calm, calm me more! nor let me die
Before I have begun to live.

                                                        1852

WILLIAM BLAKE

Song of Innocence[3]

Piping down the valleys wild,
Piping songs of pleasant glee,
On a cloud I saw a child,
And he laughing said to me:

"Pipe a song about a Lamb!"   5
So I piped with merry cheer.
"Piper, pipe that song again";
So I piped: he wept to hear.

"Drop thy pipe, thy happy pipe;
Sing thy songs of happy cheer!"   10
So I sung the same again,
While he wept with joy to hear.

"Piper, sit thee down and write
In a book that all may read."
So he vanished from my sight;   15
And I plucked a hollow reed,

And I made a rural pen,
And I stained the water clear,
And I wrote my happy songs
Every child may joy to hear.   20

                                                        1789

CHRISTOPHER MARLOWE

The Passionate Shepherd to His Love

Come live with me and be my love,
And we will all the pleasures prove[1]

---

3. The introductory poem in Blake's vol-   1. Try.
ume, *Songs of Innocence.*

That valleys, groves, hills, and fields,
Woods, or steepy mountain yields.

And we will sit upon the rocks,   5
Seeing the shepherds feed their flocks,
By shallow rivers to whose falls
Melodious birds sing madrigals.

And I will make thee beds of roses
And a thousand fragrant posies,   10
A cap of flowers, and a kirtle[2]
Embroidered all with leaves of myrtle;

A gown made of the finest wool
Which from our pretty lambs we pull;
Fair lined slippers for the cold,   15
With buckles of the purest gold;

A belt of straw and ivy buds,
With coral clasps and amber studs:
And if these pleasures may thee move,
Come live with me, and be my love.   20

The shepherd swains[3] shall dance and sing
For thy delight each May morning:
If these delights thy mind may move,
Then live with me and be my love.

1600

SIR WALTER RALEGH

The Nymph's Reply to the Shepherd

If all the world and love were young,
And truth in every shepherd's tongue,
These pretty pleasures might me move
To live with thee and be thy love.

Time drives the flocks from field to fold,   5
When rivers rage, and rocks grow cold,
And Philomel[1] becometh dumb;
The rest complain of cares to come.

The flowers do fade, and wanton fields
To wayward winter reckoning yields: 10
A honey tongue, a heart of gall,
Is fancy's spring, but sorrow's fall.

Thy gowns, thy shoes, they beds of roses,
Thy cap, thy kirtle, and thy posies
Soon break, soon wither, soon forgotten;   15
In folly ripe, in reason rotten.

2. Gown.   1. The nightingale.
3. Youths.

Thy belt of straw and ivy buds,
Thy coral clasps and amber studs,
All these in me no means can move
To come to thee and be thy love.   20

But could youth last, and love still breed,
Had joys no date,[2] nor age no need,
Then these delights my mind might move
To live with thee and be thy love.

1600

C. DAY LEWIS

Song

Come, live with me and be my love,
And we will all the pleasures prove
Of peace and plenty, bed and board,
That chance employment may afford.

I'll handle dainties on the docks   5
And thou shalt read of summer frocks:
At evening by the sour canals
We'll hope to hear some madrigals.

Care on thy maiden brow shall put
A wreath of wrinkles, and thy foot   10
Be shod with pain: not silken dress
But toil shall tire thy loveliness.

Hunger shall make thy modest zone
And cheat fond death of all but bone—
If these delights thy mind may move,   15
Then live with me and be my love.

1935

GARY SNYDER

Not Leaving the House

When Kai is born
I quit going out

Hang around the kitchen—make cornbread
Let nobody in.
Mail is flat.   5
    Masa lies on her side, Kai sighs,
    Non washes and sweeps
We sit and watch
    Masa nurse, and drink green tea.

Navajo turquoise beads over the bed   10
A peacock tail feather at the head

2. End.

A badger pelt from Nagano-ken
For a mattress; under the sheet;
A pot of yogurt setting
Under the blankets, at his feet.   15

Masa, Kai,
And Non, our friend
In the green garden light reflected in
Not leaving the house.
From dawn til late at night   20
        making a new world of ourselves
    around this life.

                                                          1970

FULKE GREVILLE, LORD BROOKE

The Golden Age Was When the World Was Young

The Golden Age was when the world was young,
Nature so rich, as earth did need no sowing,
Malice not known, the serpents had not stung,
Wit was but sweet affection's overflowing.

Desire was free, and Beauty's first-begotten;   5
Beauty then neither net,[1] nor made by art,
Words out of thoughts brought forth, and not forgotten,
The laws were inward that did rule the heart.

The Brazen Age[2] is now when earth is worn,
Beauty grown sick, Nature corrupt and nought,   10
Pleasure untimely dead as soon as born,
Both words and kindness[3] strangers to our thought:

If now this changing world do change her head,[4]
Caelica,[5] what have her new lords for to boast?
The old lord knows Desire is poorly fed,   15
And sorrows[6] not a wavering province lost,
Since in the gilt age Saturn ruled alone,
    And in this painted, planets every one.

ca. 1585

JONI MITCHELL

Woodstock[1]

I came upon a child of God
He was walking along the road
And I asked him, where are you going
And this he told me

---

1. Snare.
2. The age of war and violence, usually considered to follow the Golden and Silver Ages.
3. Natural affection.
4. Ruler.
5. The sequence of which this poem is a part is addressed to the lady Caelica.
6. Mourns.
1. Written after the rock festival there in 1969, celebrating not only the festival but what came to be called the "Woodstock Nation."

I'm going on down to Yasgur's farm 5
I'm going to join in a rock'n'roll band
I'm going to camp out on the land
And try an' get my soul free
    We are stardust
    We are golden 10
    And we've got to get ourselves
    Back to the garden

Then can I walk beside you
I have come here to lose the smog
And I feel to be a cog in something turning 15
Well maybe it is just the time of year
Or maybe it's the time of man
I don't know who I am
But life is for learning
    We are stardust 20
    We are golden
    And we've got to get ourselves
    Back to the garden

By the time we got to Woodstock
We were half a million strong 25
And everywhere there was song and celebration
And I dreamed I saw the bombers
Riding shotgun in the sky
And they were turning into butterflies
Above our nation 30
    We are stardust
    We are golden
    And we've got to get ourselves
    Back to the garden

                                                    1969

ROBERT FROST

Nothing Gold Can Stay

Nature's first green is gold,
Her hardest hue to hold.
Her early leaf's a flower;
But only so an hour.
Then leaf subsides to leaf. 5
So Eden sank to grief,
So dawn goes down to day.
Nothing gold can stay.

                                                    1923

ALAN DUGAN

Winter for an Untenable Situation

Outside it is cold. Inside,
although the fire has gone out

and all the furniture is burnt,
it is much warmer. Oh let
the white refrigerator car   5
of day go by in glacial thunder:
when it gets dark, and when
the branches of the tree outside
look wet because it is so dark,
oh we will burn the house itself   10
for warmth, the wet tree too,
you will burn me, I will burn you,
and when the last brick of the fireplace
has been cracked for its nut of warmth
and the last bone cracked for its coal   15
and the andirons themselves sucked cold,
we will move on!, remembering
the burning house, the burning tree,
the burning you, the burning me,
the ashes, the brick-dust, the bitter iron,   20
and the time when we were warm,
and say, "Those were the good old days."

1963

EDWIN ARLINGTON ROBINSON

Mr. Flood's Party

Old Eben Flood, climbing alone one night
Over the hill between the town below
And the forsaken upland hermitage
That held as much as he should ever know
On earth again of home, paused warily.   5
The road was his and not a native near;
And Eben, having leisure, said aloud,
For no man else in Tilbury Town to hear:

"Well, Mr. Flood, we have the harvest moon
Again, and we may not have many more;   10
The bird is on the wing, the poet says,[1]
And you and I have said it here before.
Drink to the bird." He raised up to the light
The jug that he had gone so far to fill,
And answered huskily: "Well, Mr. Flood,   15
Since you propose it, I believe I will."

Alone, as if enduring to the end
A valiant armor of scarred hopes outworn,
He stood there in the middle of the road
Like Roland's ghost winding a silent horn.[2]   20
Below him, in the town among the trees,
Where friends of other days had honored him,

1. Edward Fitzgerald, in "The Rubáiyat of Omar Khayyám," so describes the "Bird of Time."

2. In French legend, Roland's powerful ivory horn was used to warn his allies of impending attack.

A phantom salutation of the dead
Rang thinly till old Eben's eyes were dim.

Then, as a mother lays her sleeping child   25
Down tenderly, fearing it may awake,
He set the jug down slowly at his feet
With trembling care, knowing that most things break;
And only when assured that on firm earth
It stood, as the uncertain lives of men   30
Assuredly did not, he paced away,
And with his hand extended paused again:

"Well, Mr. Flood, we have not met like this
In a long time; and many a change has come
To both of us, I fear, since last it was   35
We had a drop together. Welcome home!"
Convivially returning with himself,
Again he raised the jug up to the light;
And with an acquiescent quaver said:
"Well, Mr. Flood, if you insist, I might.   40

"Only a very little, Mr. Flood—
For auld lang syne. No more, sir; that will do."
So, for the time, apparently it did,
And Eben evidently thought so too;
For soon amid the silver loneliness   45
Of night he lifted up his voice and sang,
Secure, with only two moons listening,
Until the whole harmonious landscape rang—

"For auld lang syne." The weary throat gave out,
The last word wavered, and the song was done.   50
He raised again the jug regretfully
And shook his head, and was again alone.
There was not much that was ahead of him,
And there was nothing in the town below—
Where strangers would have shut the many doors   55
That many friends had opened long ago.

                                                                            1921

D. H. LAWRENCE

Piano

Softly, in the dusk, a woman is singing to me;
Taking me back down the vista of years, till I see
A child sitting under the piano, in the boom of the tingling strings
And pressing the small, poised feet of a mother who smiles as she sings.

In spite of myself, the insidious mastery of song   5
Betrays me back, till the heart of me weeps to belong
To the old Sunday evenings at home, with winter outside
And hymns in the cozy parlor, the tinkling piano our guide.

So now it is vain for the singer to burst into clamor
With the great black piano appassionato. The glamour   10
Of childish days is upon me, my manhood is cast
Down in the flood of remembrance, I weep like a child for the past.

1918

W. B. YEATS

After Long Silence

Speech after long silence; it is right,
All other lovers being estranged or dead,
Unfriendly lamplight hid under its shade,
The curtains drawn upon unfriendly night,
That we descant and yet again descant   5
Upon the supreme theme of Art and Song:
Bodily decrepitude is wisdom; young
We loved each other and were ignorant.

1932

CLAUDE MC KAY

The Tropics in New York

Bananas ripe and green, and ginger-root,
    Cocoa in pods and alligator pears,
And tangerines and mangoes and grape fruit,
    Fit for the highest prize at parish fairs,

Set in the window, bringing memories   5
    Of fruit-trees laden by low-singing rills,
And dewy dawns, and mystical blue skies
    In benediction over nun-like hills.

My eyes grew dim, and I could no more gaze;
    A wave of longing through my body swept,   10
And, hungry for the old, familiar ways,
    I turned aside and bowed my head and wept.

1922

GEORGE BERKELEY

On the Prospect of Planting Arts and Learning in America

The Muse, disgusted at an age and clime
    Barren of every glorious theme,
In distant lands now waits a better time,
    Producing subjects worthy fame:

In happy climes where from the genial sun   5
    And virgin earth such scenes ensue,
The force of art by nature seems outdone,
    And fancied beauties by the true:

In happy climes, the seat of innocence,
    Where nature guides and virtue rules,   10
Where men shall not impose, for truth and sense,
    The pedantry of courts and schools:

There shall be sung another golden age,
    The rise of empire and of arts,
The good and great inspiring epic rage,   15
    The wisest heads and noblest hearts.

Not such as Europe breeds in her decay;
    Such as she bred when fresh and young,
When heavenly flame did animate her clay,
    By future poets shall be sung.   20

Westward the course of empire takes its way;
    The first four acts already past,
A fifth shall close the drama with the day;
    Time's noblest offspring is the last.

1752

LOUIS SIMPSON

In California

Here I am, troubling the dream coast
With my New York face,
Bearing among the realtors
And tennis-players my dark preoccupation.

There once was an epical clatter—   5
Voices and banjos, Tennessee, Ohio,
Rising like incense in the sight of heaven.
Today, there is an angel in the gate.

Lie back, Walt Whitman,[1]
There, on the fabulous raft with the King and the Duke![2]   10
For the white row of the Marina
Faces the Rock.[3] Turn round the wagons here.

Lie back! We cannot bear
The stars any more, those infinite spaces.
Let the realtors divide the mountain,   15
For they have already subdivided the valley.

Rectangular city blocks astonished
Herodotus in Babylon,[4]

1. Whitman's poetry often (as in "Facing West from California's Shores") celebrated the American dream.
2. Characters in *Huckleberry Finn* who capitalized on the ignorance and kindness of the people they met.
3. A nickname for the federal prison formerly located on Alcatraz Island in San Francisco Bay.
4. Herodotus, often called the "father of history," marveled at Babylonian accomplishments.

Cortez in Tenochtitlan,[5]
And here's the same old city-planner, death.   20

We cannot turn or stay.
For though we sleep, and let the reins fall slack,
The great cloud-wagons move
Outward still, dreaming of a Pacific.

1963

EMILY DICKINSON

After Great Pain

After great pain, a formal feeling comes—
The Nerves sit ceremonious, like Tombs—
The stiff Heart questions was it He, that bore,
And Yesterday, or Centuries before?

The Feet, mechanical, go round—   5
Of Ground, or Air, or Ought—
A Wooden way
Regardless grown,
A Quartz contentment, like a stone—

This is the Hour of Lead—   10
Remembered, if outlived,
As Freezing Persons recollect the Snow—
First—Chill—then Stupor—then the letting go—

ca. 1862

WILLIAM CARLOS WILLIAMS

The Red Wheelbarrow

so much depends
upon

a red wheel
barrow

glazed with rain   5
water

beside the white
chickens.

1923

5. The Aztec capital, taken by Cortez in 1519 after he was cordially received into the
city by Montezuma.

EZRA POUND

In a Station of the Metro[6]

The apparition of these faces in the crowd;
Petals on a wet, black bough.

p. 1913

JULIA FIELDS

Madness One Monday Evening

Late that mad Monday evening
I made mermaids come from the sea
As the block sky sat
Upon the waves
And night came   5
Creeping up to me

    (I tell you I made mermaids
    Come from the sea)

The green waves lulled and rolled
As I sat by the locust tree   10
And the bright glare of the neon world
Sent gas-words bursting free—
Their spewed splendor fell on the billows
And gaudy it grew to me
As I sat up upon the shore   15
And made mermaids come from the sea.

1964

RICHARD WILBUR

The Beautiful Changes

One wading a Fall meadow finds on all sides
The Queen Anne's Lace[1] lying like lilies
On water; it glides
So from the walker, it turns
Dry grass to a lake, as the slightest shade of you   5
Valleys my mind in fabulous blue Lucernes.[2]

The beautiful changes as a forest is changed
By a chameleon's tuning his skin to it;
As a mantis, arranged
On a green leaf, grows   10
Into it, makes the leaf leafier, and proves
Any greenness is deeper than anyone knows.

---

6. The Paris subway.
1. A delicate-looking plant, with finely divided leaves and flat clusters of small white flowers, sometimes called "wild carrot."

2. Alfalfa, a plant resembling clover, with small purple flowers. Lake Lucerne is famed for deep blue color and its picturesque Swiss setting amid limestone mountains.

Your hands hold roses always in a way that says
They are not only yours; the beautiful changes
In such kind ways,   15
Wishing ever to sunder
Things and things' selves for a second finding, to lose
For a moment all that it touches back to wonder.

                                                        1947

SAMUEL TAYLOR COLERIDGE

Kubla Khan: or, a Vision in a Dream[1]

In Xanadu did Kubla Khan
    A stately pleasure-dome decree:
Where Alph, the sacred river, ran
Through caverns measureless to man
    Down to a sunless sea.   5
So twice five miles of fertile ground
With walls and towers were girdled round:
And here were gardens bright with sinuous rills
Where blossomed many an incense-bearing tree;
And here were forests ancient as the hills,   10
Enfolding sunny spots of greenery.
But oh! that deep romantic chasm which slanted
Down the green hill athwart a cedarn cover![2]
A savage place! as holy and enchanted
As e'er beneath a waning moon was haunted   15
By woman wailing for her demon-lover![3]
And from this chasm, with ceaseless turmoil seething,
As if this earth in fast thick pants were breathing,
A mighty fountain momently was forced,
Amid whose swift half-intermitted burst   20
Huge fragments vaulted like rebounding hail,
Or chaffy grain beneath the thresher's flail:
And 'mid these dancing rocks at once and ever
It flung up momently the sacred river.
Five miles meandering with a mazy motion   25
Through wood and dale the sacred river ran,
Then reached the caverns measureless to man,
And sank in tumult to a lifeless ocean:
And 'mid this tumult Kubla heard from far
Ancestral voices prophesying war!   30

        The shadow of the dome of pleasure
        Floated midway on the waves;
        Where was heard the mingled measure
        From the fountain and the caves.
It was a miracle of rare device,   35
A sunny pleasure-dome with caves of ice!

---

1. Coleridge said he wrote this fragment immediately after waking from an opium dream and that after he was interrupted by a caller he was unable to finish the poem.
2. From side to side of a cover of cedar trees.

3. In a famous and often imitated German ballad, the lady Lenore is carried off on horseback by the specter of her lover and married to him at his grave.

A damsel with a dulcimer[4]
In a vision once I saw:
It was an Abyssinian maid,
And on her dulcimer she played,   40
Singing of Mount Abora.
Could I revive within me
Her symphony and song,
To such a deep delight 'twould win me,
That with music loud and long,   45
I would build that dome in air,
That sunny dome! those caves of ice!
And all who heard should see them there,
And all should cry, Beware! Beware!
His flashing eyes, his floating hair!   50
Weave a circle round him thrice,
And close your eyes with holy dread,
For he on honey-dew hath fed,
And drunk the milk of Paradise.

1798

THEODORE ROETHKE

I Knew a Woman

I knew a woman, lovely in her bones,
When small birds sighed, she would sigh back at them;
Ah, when she moved, she moved more ways than one:
The shapes a bright container can contain!
Of her choice virtues only gods should speak,   5
Or English poets who grew up on Greek
(I'd have them sing in chorus, cheek to cheek).

How well her wishes went! She stroked my chin,
She taught me Turn, and Counter-turn, and Stand;[1]
She taught me Touch, that undulant white skin;   10
I nibbled meekly from her proffered hand;
She was the sickle; I, poor I, the rake,
Coming behind her for her pretty sake
(But what prodigious mowing we did make).

Love likes a gander, and adores a goose: 15
Her full lips pursed, the errant note to seize;
She played it quick, she played it light and loose;
My eyes, they dazzled at her flowing knees;
Her several parts could keep a pure repose,
Or one hip quiver with a mobile nose   20
(She moved in circles, and those circles moved).

Let seed be grass, and grass turn into hay:
I'm martyr to a motion not my own;
What's freedom for? To know eternity.

---

4. A stringed instrument, prototype of the piano.

1. Literary terms for the parts of a Pindaric ode.

I swear she cast a shadow white as stone.   25
But who would count eternity in days?
These old bones live to learn her wanton ways:
(I measure time by how a body sways).

                                                    1958

JOHN DONNE

Batter My Heart

Batter my heart, three-personed God; for You
As yet but knock, breathe, shine, and seek to mend;
That I may rise and stand, o'erthrow me, and bend
Your force, to break, blow, burn, and make me new.
I, like an usurped town, to another due,   5
Labor to admit You, but Oh, to no end!
Reason, Your viceroy[1] in me, me should defend,
But is captived, and proves weak or untrue.
Yet dearly I love You, and would be loved fain.[2]
But am betrothed unto Your enemy: 10
Divorce me, untie, or break that knot again,
Take me to You, imprison me, for I,
Except You enthrall me, never shall be free,
Nor ever chaste, except You ravish me.

                                                    1633

X. J. KENNEDY

Nude Descending a Staircase[1]

Toe upon toe, a snowing flesh,
A gold of lemon, root and rind,
She sifts in sunlight down the stairs
With nothing on. Nor on her mind.

We spy beneath the banister   5
A constant thresh of thigh on thigh—
Her lips imprint the swinging air
That parts to let her parts go by.

One-woman waterfall, she wears
Her slow descent like a long cape   10
And pausing, on the final stair
Collects her motions into shape.

                                                    1961

1. One who rules as the representative   1. A celebrated cubist-futurist painting
of a higher power.   by Marcel Duchamp (1913).
2. Gladly.

ROBERT HERRICK

Upon Julia's Clothes

Whenas in silks my Julia goes
Then, then, methinks, how sweetly flows
That liquefaction of her clothes.

Next, when I cast mine eyes, and see
That brave[1] vibration, each way free,   5
O, how that glittering taketh me!

                                                    1648

EZRA POUND

The River-Merchant's Wife: A Letter

(after Rihaku[2])

While my hair was still cut straight across my forehead
I played about the front gate, pulling flowers.
You came by on bamboo stilts, playing horse,
You walked about my seat, playing with blue plums.
And we went on living in the village of Chokan: 5
Two small people, without dislike or suspicion.

At fourteen I married My Lord you.
I never laughed, being bashful.
Lowering my head, I looked at the wall.
Called to, a thousand times, I never looked back.   10

At fifteen I stopped scowling,
I desired my dust to be mingled with yours
For ever and for ever and for ever.
Why should I climb the look out?

At sixteen you departed,   15
You went into far Ku-to-yen, by the river of swirling eddies,
And you have been gone five months.
The monkeys make sorrowful noise overhead.

You dragged your feet when you went out.
By the gate now, the moss is grown, the different mosses,   20
Too deep to clear them away!
The leaves fall early this autumn, in wind.
The paired butterflies are already yellow with August
Over the grass in the West garden;
They hurt me. I grow older.   25
If you are coming down through the narrows of the river Kiang,
Please let me know beforehand,
And I will come out to meet you
        As far as Cho-fu-Sa.

                                                    1915

1. Handsome, showy.   2. The Japanese name for Li Po, an
                                   eighth-century Chinese poet.

HOWARD NEMEROV

The Goose Fish

On the long shore, lit by the moon
To show them properly alone,
Two lovers suddenly embraced
So that their shadows were as one.
The ordinary night was graced   5
For them by the swift tide of blood
That silently they took at flood,
And for a little time they prized
   Themselves emparadised.

Then, as if shaken by stage-fright   10
Beneath the hard moon's bony light,
They stood together on the sand
Embarrassed in each other's sight
But still conspiring hand in hand,
Until they saw, there underfoot,   15
As though the world had found them out,
The goose fish turning up, though dead,
   His hugely grinning head.

There in the china light he lay,
Most ancient and corrupt and gray   20
They hesitated at his smile,
Wondering what it seemed to say
To lovers who a little while
Before had thought to understand,
By violence upon the sand,   25
The only way that could be known
   To make a world their own.

It was a wide and moony grin
Together peaceful and obscene;
They knew not what he would express,   30
So finished a comedian
He might mean failure or success,
But took it for an emblem of
Their sudden, new and guilty love
To be observed by, when they kissed,   35
   That rigid optimist.

So he became their patriarch,
Dreadfully mild in the half-dark.
His throat that the sand seemed to choke,
His picket teeth, these left their mark   40
But never did explain the joke
That so amused him, lying there
While the moon went down to disappear
Along the still and tilted track
   That bears the zodiac.   45

1955

KARL SHAPIRO

Auto Wreck

Its quick soft silver bell beating, beating,
And down the dark one ruby flare
Pulsing out red light like an artery,
The ambulance at top speed floating down
Past beacons and illuminated clocks   5
Wings in a heavy curve, dips down,
And brakes speed, entering the crowd.
The doors leap open, emptying light;
Stretchers are laid out, the mangled lifted
And stowed into the little hospital.   10
Then the bell, breaking the hush, tolls once,
And the ambulance with its terrible cargo
Rocking, slightly rocking, moves away,
As the doors, an afterthought, are closed.

We are deranged, walking among the cops   15
Who sweep glass and are large and composed.
One is still making notes under the light.
One with a bucket douches ponds of blood
Into the street and gutter.
One hangs lanterns on the wrecks that cling,   20
Empty husks of locusts, to iron poles.

Our throats were tight as tourniquets,
Our feet were bound with splints, but now,
Like convalescents intimate and gauche,
We speak through sickly smiles and warn   25
With the stubborn saw of common sense,
The grim joke and the banal resolution.
The traffic moves around with care,
But we remain, touching a wound
That opens to our richest horror.   30
Already old, the question Who shall die?
Becomes unspoken Who is innocent?

For death in war is done by hands;
Suicide has cause and stillbirth, logic;
And cancer, simple as a flower, blooms.   35
But this invites the occult mind,
Cancels our physics with a sneer,
And spatters all we knew of denouement
Across the expedient and wicked stones.

1942

THEODORE ROETHKE

My Papa's Waltz

The whiskey on your breath
Could make a small boy dizzy;

But I hung on like death:
Such waltzing was not easy.

We romped until the pans   5
Slid from the kitchen shelf;
My mother's countenance
Could not unfrown itself.

The hand that held my wrist
Was battered on one knuckle;   10
At every step you missed
My right ear scraped a buckle.

You beat time on my head
With a palm caked hard by dirt,
Then waltzed me off to bed   15
Still clinging to your shirt.

1948

WALT WHITMAN

A Noiseless Patient Spider

A noiseless patient spider,
I marked where on a little promontory it stood isolated,
Marked how to explore the vacant vast surrounding,
It launched forth filament, filament, filament, out of itself,
Ever unreeling them, ever tirelessly speeding them.   5

And you O my soul where you stand,
Surrounded, detached, in measureless oceans of space,
Ceaselessly musing, venturing, throwing, seeking the spheres
       to connect them,
Till the bridge you will need be formed, till the ductile anchor hold,
Till the gossamer thread you fling catch somewhere, O my soul.   10

1881

ROBERT LOWELL

Mr. Edwards and the Spider[1]

I saw the spiders marching through the air,
Swimming from tree to tree that mildewed day
    In latter August when the hay
    Came creaking to the barn. But where
        The wind is westerly,   5
    Where gnarled November makes the spiders fly
    Into the apparitions of the sky,
        They purpose nothing but their ease and die
Urgently beating east to sunrise and the sea;

1. The speaker of the poem is Jonathan Edwards, from East Windsor, Conn. (line 28),
the early 19th-century Puritan preacher famous for his powerful rhetoric, sensuous
imagery, and vivid portraits of Hell. He is best known for his sermon, "Sinners in the
Hands of an Angry God" (line 10), but while only a boy of 11 he wrote a meticulous
account of the habits of the flying spider. His sermons often compare man to a spider—
in his cleverness and ultimate self-destruction.

What are we in the hands of the great God?   10
It was in vain you set up thorn and briar
     In battle array against the fire
     And treason crackling in your blood;
          For the wild thorns grow tame
And will do nothing to oppose the flame;   15
Your lacerations tell the losing game
You play against a sickness past your cure.
How will the hands be strong? How will the heart endure?

A very little thing, a little worm,
Or hourglass-blazoned spider, it is said,   20
     Can kill a tiger. Will the dead
     Hold up his mirror and affirm
          To the four winds the smell
And flash of his authority? It's well
If God who holds you to the pit of hell,   25
Much as one holds a spider, will destroy,
Baffle and dissipate your soul. As a small boy

On Windsor Marsh, I saw the spider die
When thrown into the bowels of fierce fire:
     There's no long struggle, no desire   30
     To get up on its feet and fly—
          It stretches out its feet
And dies. This is the sinner's last retreat;
Yes, and no strength exerted on the heat
Then sinews the abolished will, when sick   35
And full of burning, it will whistle on a brick.

But who can plumb the sinking of that soul?
Josiah Hawley,[2] picture yourself cast
     Into a brick-kiln where the blast
     Fans your quick vitals to a coal—   40
          If measured by a glass,
How long would it seem burning! Let there pass
A minute, ten, ten trillion; but the blaze
Is infinite, eternal: this is death,
To die and know it. This is the Black Widow, death.   45

                                                         1946

ROBERT FROST

Range-Finding

The battle rent a cobweb diamond-strung
And cut a flower beside a groundbird's nest
Before it stained a single human breast.
The stricken flower bent double and so hung.
And still the bird revisited her young.   5
A butterfly its fall had dispossessed,

---

2. Either Edwards' uncle, Joseph Hawley, Sr., who jeopardized his soul by committing suicide, or Major Joseph Hawley, Jr., Edwards' cousin, who was the leader of public proceedings which led to Edwards' dismissal from his pulpit. The images that follow (and much of the earlier phrasing) is from Edwards' sermon "The Future Punishment of the Wicked Unavoidable and Intolerable."

A moment sought in air his flower of rest,
Then lightly stooped to it and fluttering clung.
On the bare upland pasture there had spread
O'ernight 'twixt mullein[1] stalks a wheel of thread   10
And straining cables wet with silver dew.
A sudden passing bullet shook it dry.
The indwelling spider ran to greet the fly,
But finding nothing, sullenly withdrew.

1916

ROBERT FROST

Design

I found a dimpled spider, fat and white,
On a white heal-all,[2] holding up a moth
Like a white piece of rigid satin cloth—
Assorted characters of death and blight
Mixed ready to begin the morning right,   5
Like the ingredients of a witches' broth—
A snow-drop spider, a flower like a froth,
And dead wings carried like a paper kite.

What had that flower to do with being white,
The wayside blue and innocent heal-all?   10
What brought the kindred spider to that height,
Then steered the white moth thither in the night?
What but design of darkness to appall?—
If design govern in a thing so small.

1936

STEPHEN SPENDER

An Elementary School Classroom in a Slum

Far far from gusty waves these children's faces.
Like rootless weeds, the hair torn round their pallor.
The tall girl with her weighed-down head. The paper-
seeming boy, with rat's eyes. The stunted, unlucky heir
Of twisted bones, reciting a father's gnarled disease,   5
His lesson from his desk. At back of the dim class
One unnoted, sweet and young. His eyes live in a dream
Of squirrel's game, in tree room, other than this.
On sour cream walls, donations. Shakespeare's head,
Cloudless at dawn, civilized dome riding all cities.   10
Belled, flowery, Tyrolese valley.[1] Open-handed map
Awarding the world its world. And yet, for these
Children, these windows, not this world, are world,
Where all their future's painted with a fog,

1. Weed.
2. A plant, also called the "all-heal" and "self-heal," with tightly clustered violet-blue flowers.

1. A rich and beautiful section of Austria with many scenes like those in typical paintings of hamlets and picturesque countrysides.

A narrow street sealed in with a lead sky,
Far far from rivers, capes, and stars of words.

Surely, Shakespeare is wicked, the map a bad example
With ships and sun and love tempting them to steal—
For lives that slyly turn in their cramped holes
From fog to endless night? On their slag heap, these children   20
Wear skins peeped through by bones and spectacles of steel
With mended glass, like bottle bits on stones.
All of their time and space are foggy slum.
So blot their maps with slums as big as doom.

Unless, governor, teacher, inspector, visitor,   25
This map becomes their window and these windows
That shut upon their lives like catacombs,
Break O break open till they break the town
And show the children to green fields, and make their world
Run azure on gold sands, and let their tongues   30
Run naked into books, the white and green leaves open
History theirs whose language is the sun.

1939

CZESLAW MILOSZ

A Poor Christian Looks at the Ghetto[1]

Bees build around red liver,
Ants build around black bone.
It has begun: the tearing, the trampling on silks,
It has begun: the breaking of glass, wood, copper, nickel, silver, foam
Of gypsum, iron sheets, violin strings, trumpets, leaves, balls, crystals.   5
Poof! Phosphorescent fire from yellow walls
Engulfs animal and human hair.

Bees build around the honeycomb of lungs,
Ants build around white bone.
Torn is paper, rubber, linen, leather, flax,   10
Fiber, fabrics, cellulose, snakeskin, wire.
The roof and the wall collapse in flame and heat seizes the foundations.
Now there is only the earth, sandy, trodden down,
With one leafless tree.

Slowly, boring a tunnel, a guardian mole makes his way,   15
With a small red lamp fastened to his forehead.
He touches burned bodies, counts them, pushes on,
He distinguishes human ashes by their luminous vapor,
The ashes of each man by a different part of the spectrum.
Bees build around a red trace.   20
Ants build around the place left by my body.

I am afraid, so afraid of the guardian mole.
He has swollen eyelids, like a Patriarch

1. Translated from the Polish by the author.

Who has sat much in the light of candles
Reading the great book of the species.   25
What will I tell him, I, a Jew of the New Testament,
Waiting two thousand years for the second coming of Jesus?
My broken body will deliver me to his sight
And he will count me among the helpers of death:
The uncircumcised.   30

1943

JOHN LENNON AND PAUL MCCARTNEY

A Day in the Life

I read the news today oh boy
About a lucky man who made the grade
And though the news was rather sad
Well I just had to laugh
I saw the photograph.   5
He blew his mind out in a car
He didn't notice that the light had changed
A crowd of people stood and stared
They'd seen his face before
Nobody was really sure   10
If he was from the House of Lords.
I saw a film today oh boy
The English Army had just won the war
A crowd of people turned away   15
But I just had to look
Having read the book.
I'd love to turn you on

Woke up, fell out of bed,
Dragged a comb across my head   20
Found my way downstairs and drank a cup,
And looking up I noticed I was late.
Found my coat and grabbed my hat
Made the bus in seconds flat
Found my way upstairs and had a smoke,   25
Somebody spoke and I went into a dream.
I read the news today oh boy
Four thousand holes in Blackburn, Lancashire,
And though the holes were rather small
They had to count them all   30
Now they know how many holes it takes to fill the Albert Hall.[1]
I'd love to turn you on

1967

1. The Royal Albert Hall, a large oval amphitheater in London, has nightly concerts
that have included, for example, the Beatles.

LANGSTON HUGHES

Harlem

What happens to a dream deferred?

Does it dry up
like a raisin in the sun?
Or fester like a sore—
And then run?   5
Does it stink like rotten meat?
Or crust and sugar over—
like a syrupy sweet?

Maybe it just sags
like a heavy load.   10

Or does it explode?

1951

SAMUEL JOHNSON

from London

Could'st thou resign the park and play[1] content,   210
For the fair banks of Severn or of Trent;[2]
There might'st thou find some elegant retreat,
Some hireling senator's deserted seat;
And stretch thy prospects o'er the smiling land,
For less than rent the dungeons of the Strand;[3]   215
There prune thy walks, support thy drooping flow'rs,
Direct thy rivulets, and twine thy bow'rs;
And, while thy grounds a cheap repast afford,
Despise the dainties of a venal lord:
There ev'ry bush with nature's music rings,   220
There ev'ry breeze bears health upon its wings;
On all thy hours security shall smile,
And bless thine evening walk and morning toil.
    Prepare for death, if here at night you roam,
And sign your will before you sup from home.   225
Some fiery fop, with new commission[4] vain,
Who sleeps on brambles[5] till he kills his man;
Some frolic drunkard, reeling from a feast,
Provokes a broil,[6] and stabs you for a jest.
Yet ev'n these heroes, mischievously gay,   230
Lords of the street, and terrors of the way;
Flushed as they are with folly, youth and wine,

1. Promenading in the park and attending plays were popular and fashionable amusements, often attacked by 18th-century satirists.
2. In the country.
3. Cramped apartments on the busy street paralleling the River Thames near the center of the city.
4. Eighteenth-century London was plagued by clubs and gangs of men (often nobly born) who taunted each other · to violence just for sport.
5. Thorns.
6. Quarrel.

Their prudent insults to the poor confine;
Afar they mark the flambeau's bright approach,[7]
And shun the shining train, and golden coach.   235
    In vain, these dangers past, your doors you close,
And hope[8] the balmy blessings of repose:
Cruel with guilt, and daring with despair,
The midnight murd'rer bursts the faithless bar;
Invades the sacred hour of silent rest,   240
And leaves, unseen, a dagger in your breast.
    Scarce can our fields, such crowds at Tyburn[9] die,
With hemp the gallows and the fleet supply.
Propose your schemes, ye Senatorian band,
Whose Ways and Means[1] support the sinking land;   245
Lest ropes be wanting in the tempting spring,
To rig another convoy for the k——g.[2]
    A single jail, in Alfred's golden reign,[3]
Could half the nation's criminals contain;
Fair Justice then, without constraint adored,   250
Held high the steady scale, but dropped the sword;
No spies were paid, no special juries known,
Blest age! but ah! how diff'rent from our own!

                               1738

WILLIAM BLAKE

London

I wander through each chartered street,
Near where the chartered Thames does flow,
And mark in every face I meet
Marks of weakness, marks of woe.

In every cry of every man,   5
In every Infant's cry of fear,
In every voice, in every ban,
The mind-forged manacles I hear.

How the Chimney-sweeper's cry
Every black'ning Church appalls;   10
And the hapless Soldier's sigh
Runs in blood down Palace walls.

But most through midnight streets I hear
How the youthful Harlot's curse
Blasts the new-born Infant's tear,   15
And blights with plagues the Marriage hearse.

                               1794

7. See a torch indicating the approach of a well-attended group or a luxurious vehicle.
8. Wish for.
9. Until 1783, the place of public execution.
1. "A cant term in the House of Commons for methods of raising money." (Johnson's note)

2. King. It was common practice to omit letters (but usually not enough of them to obscure meaning) when attacking an office or person who might have legal redress.
3. Alfred the Great ruled the West Saxons, 871–899, and his reign had been glorified since the 12th century.

WILLIAM WORDSWORTH

London, 1802

Milton! thou should'st be living at this hour:
England hath need of thee: she is a fen[1]
Of stagnant waters: altar, sword, and pen,
Fireside, the heroic wealth of hall and bower,
Have forfeited their ancient English dower[2]   5
Of inward happiness. We are selfish men;
Oh! raise us up, return to us again;
And give us manners, virtue, freedom, power.
Thy soul was like a star, and dwelt apart:
Thou hadst a voice whose sound was like the sea: 10
Pure as the naked heavens, majestic, free,
So didst thou travel on life's common way,
In cheerful godliness; and yet thy heart
The lowliest duties on herself did lay.

1802

PERCY BYSSHE SHELLEY

England in 1819

An old, mad, blind, despised, and dying king[1]—
Princes, the dregs of their dull race, who flow
Through public scorn—mud from a muddy spring;
Rulers who neither see, nor feel, nor know,
But leechlike to their fainting country cling,   5
Till they drop, blind in blood, without a blow;
A people starved and stabbed in the untilled field—
An army, which liberticide and prey
Makes as a two-edged sword to all who wield;
Golden and sanguine[2] laws which tempt and slay;   10
Religion Christless, Godless—a book sealed;
A Senate—Time's worst statute[3] unrepealed—
Are graves, from which a glorious Phantom[4] may
Burst, to illumine our tempestuous day.

1819

EARLE BIRNEY

Irapuato[1]

For reasons any
          brigadier
                    could tell
this is a favorite nook for
                massacre   5

1. Marsh.
2. Inheritance.
1. George III, senile for many years, had ruled England since 1760. He died the year after the poem was written.
2. Motivated by greed, resulting in bloodshed.
3. A law discriminating against Catholics.
4. Revolution.
1. A city in central Mexico, northwest of Mexico City.

Toltex by Mixtex Mixtex by Aztex
Aztex by Spanishtex Spanishtex by
Mexitex by Mexitex by Mexitex by Texaco

So any farmer can see how the strawberries
are the biggest and reddest   10
    in the whole damn continent

but why
        when arranged under
                    the market flies

do they look like small clotting hearts?   15

1962

CLAUDE MC KAY

America

Although she feeds me bread of bitterness,
And sinks into my throat her tiger's tooth,
Stealing my breath of life, I will confess
I love this cultured hell that tests my youth!
Her vigor flows like tides into my blood,   5
Giving me strength erect against her hate.
Her bigness sweeps my being like a flood.
Yet as a rebel fronts a king in state,
I stand within her walls with not a shred
Of terror, malice, not a word of jeer.   10
Darkly I gaze into the days ahead,
And see her might and granite wonders there,
Beneath the touch of Time's unerring hand,
Like priceless treasures sinking in the sand.

1922

ROBERT FROST

U. S. 1946 King's X[1]

Having invented a new Holocaust,
And been the first with it to win a war,
How they make haste to cry with fingers crossed,
King's X—no fairs to use it any more!

p. 1946

1. Shortly after exploding the two atomic bombs that ended World War II, the United States proposed to share nuclear information with other countries in exchange for an agreement that the information would be used only for peaceful purposes. In children's games, time out is sometimes signaled by crossing fingers and saying "King's X."

CLAUDE MCKAY

The White House[2]

Your door is shut against my tightened face,
And I am sharp as steel with discontent;
But I possess the courage and the grace
To bear my anger proudly and unbent.
The pavement slabs burn loose beneath my feet,   5
And passion rends my vitals as I pass,
A chafing savage, down the decent street,
Where boldly shines your shuttered door of glass.
Oh, I must search for wisdom every hour,
Deep in my wrathful bosom sore and raw,   10
And find in it the superhuman power
To hold me to the letter of your law!
Oh, I must keep my heart inviolate
Against the poison of your deadly hate.

1937

RAY DUREM

Award

*A Gold Watch to the FBI
Man who has followed
me for 25 years.*

Well, old spy
looks like I
led you down some pretty blind alleys,
took you on several trips to Mexico,
fishing in the high Sierras,   5
jazz at the Philharmonic.[1]
You've watched me all your life,
I've clothed your wife,
put your two sons through college.
what good has it done?   10
the sun keeps rising every morning.
ever see me buy an Assistant President?
or close a school?
or lend money to Trujillo?[2]
ever catch me rigging airplane prices?   15
I bought some after-hours whiskey in L. A.
but the Chief got his pay.
I ain't killed no Koreans
or fourteen-year-old boys in Mississippi.
neither did I bomb Guatemala,   20

2. For many years this poem was anthologized as "White Houses" because the
first anthologist to include the poem, Alain
Locke, had changed the title against the
author's wishes. In his autobiography, *A
Long Way from Home* (1937), McKay
wrote: "My title . . . had no reference to
the official residence of the President of the
United States. . . . The title 'White Houses'
changed the whole symbolic intent and
meaning of the poem, making it appear as
if the burning ambition of the black mal-
content was to enter white houses in general."
1. A popular annual series of concerts at
Philharmonic Hall, Los Angeles, since the
mid 1940s.
2. Dictator of the Dominican Republic,
whose support by the U. S. was often
under attack.

or lend guns to shoot Algerians.
I admit I took a Negro child
to a white rest room in Texas,
but she was my daughter, only three,
who had to pee.   25

                                                                p. 1964

KENNETH KOCH

You Were Wearing

You were wearing your Edgar Allan Poe printed cotton blouse.
In each divided up square of the blouse was a picture of Edgar Allan
    Poe.
Your hair was blonde and you were cute. You asked me, "Do most boys
    think that most girls are bad?"
I smelled the mould of your seaside resort hotel bedroom on your hair
    held in place by a John Greenleaf Whittier clip.
"No," I said, "it's girls who think that boys are bad." Then we read
    Snowbound together   5
And ran around in an attic, so that a little of the blue enamel was
    scraped off my George Washington, Father of His Country, shoes.

Mother was walking in the living room, her Strauss Waltzes comb in
    her hair.
We waited for a time and then joined her, only to be served tea in cups
    painted with pictures of Herman Melville
As well as with illustrations from his book *Moby Dick* and from his
    novella, *Benito Cereno.*
Father came in wearing his Dick Tracy necktie: "How about a drink,
    everyone?"   10
I said, "Let's go outside a while." Then we went onto the porch and sat
    on the Abraham Lincoln swing.
You sat on the eyes, mouth, and beard part, and I sat on the knees.
In the yard across the street we saw a snowman holding a garbage can
    lid smashed into a likeness of the mad English king, George the
    Third.

                                                                1962

T. S. ELIOT

The Love Song of J. Alfred Prufrock

> *S'io credesse che mia risposta fosse*
> *A persona che mai tornasse al mondo,*
> *Questa fiamma staria senza piu scosse.*
> *Ma perciocche giammai di questo fondo*
> *Non torno vivo alcun, s'i'odo il vero,*
> *Senza tema d'infamia ti rispondo.*[1]

Let us go then, you and I,
When the evening is spread out against the sky

1. Dante's *Inferno*, XXVII, 61–66. In the Eighth Chasm, Dante and Vergil meet Count
Guido de Montefeltrano, one of the False Counselors. The spirits there are in the form of
flames, and Guido speaks from the trembling tip of the flame, responding to Dante's request that he tell his life story: "If I thought that my answer were to someone who would
ever go back to earth, this flame would be still, without any more movement. But because
no one has ever gone back alive from this chasm (if what I hear is true) I answer you
without fear of infamy."

Like a patient etherized upon a table;
Let us go, through certain half-deserted streets,
The muttering retreats   5
Of restless nights in one-night cheap hotels
And sawdust restaurants with oyster-shells:
Streets that follow like a tedious argument
Of insidious intent
To lead you to an overwhelming question . . .   10
Oh, do not ask, "What is it?"
Let us go and make our visit.

        In the room the women come and go
Talking of Michelangelo.

        The yellow fog that rubs its back upon the window-panes,   15
The yellow smoke that rubs its muzzle on the window-panes
Licked its tongue into the corners of the evening,
Lingered upon the pools that stand in drains,
Let fall upon its back the soot that falls from chimneys,
Slipped by the terrace, made a sudden leap,   20
And seeing that it was a soft October night,
Curled once about the house, and fell asleep.

        And indeed there will be time[2]
For the yellow smoke that slides along the street,
Rubbing its back upon the window-panes;   25
There will be time, there will be time
To prepare a face to meet the faces that you meet;
There will be time to murder and create,
And time for all the works and days[3] of hands
That lift and drop a question on your plate;   30
Time for you and time for me,
And time yet for a hundred indecisions,
And for a hundred visions and revisions,
Before the taking of a toast and tea.

        In the room the women come and go   35
Talking of Michelangelo.

        And indeed there will be time
To wonder, "Do I dare?" and, "Do I dare?"
Time to turn back and descend the stair,
With a bald spot in the middle of my hair—   40
(They will say: "How his hair is growing thin!")
My morning coat, my collar mounting firmly to the chin,
My necktie rich and modest, but asserted by a simple pin—
(They will say: "But how his arms and legs are thin!")
Do I dare   45
Disturb the universe?

2. See *Ecclesiastes* 3:1ff.: "To every-thing there is a season, and a time to every purpose under the heaven: A time to be born, and a time to die; a time to plant, and a time to pluck up that which is planted; A time to kill, and a time to heal. . . ." Also see Marvell's "To His Coy Mistress": "Had we but world enough and time. . . ."
3. Hesiod's ancient Greek didactic poem *Works and Days* prescribed in practical detail how to conduct one's life.

In a minute there is time
For decisions and revisions which a minute will reverse.

For I have known them all already, known them all:—
Have known the evenings, mornings, afternoons,   50
I have measured out my life with coffee spoons;
I know the voices dying with a dying fall
Beneath the music from a farther room.
  So how should I presume?

And I have known the eyes already, known them all—   55
The eyes that fix you in a formulated phrase,
And when I am formulated, sprawling on a pin,
When I am pinned and wriggling on the wall,
Then how should I begin
To spit out all the butt-ends of my days and ways?   60
  And how should I presume?

And I have known the arms already, known them all—
Arms that are braceleted and white and bare
(But in the lamplight, downed with light brown hair!)
Is it perfume from a dress   65
That makes me so digress?
Arms that lie along a table, or wrap about a shawl.
  And should I then presume?
  And how should I begin?

          .   .   .   .   .

Shall I say, I have gone at dusk through narrow streets   70
And watched the smoke that rises from the pipes
Of lonely men in shirt-sleeves, leaning out of windows? . . .

I should have been a pair of ragged claws
Scuttling across the floors of silent seas.

          .   .   .   .   .

And the afternoon, the evening, sleeps so peacefully!   75
Smoothed by long fingers,
Asleep . . . tired . . . or it malingers,
Stretched on the floor, here beside you and me.
Should I, after tea and cakes and ices,
Have the strength to force the moment to its crisis?   80
But though I have wept and fasted, wept and prayed,
Though I have seen my head (grown slightly bald) brought in upon
      a platter,[4]
I am no prophet—and here's no great matter;
I have seen the moment of my greatness flicker,
And I have seen the eternal Footman hold my coat, and snicker,   85
And in short, I was afraid.

And would it have been worth it, after all,
After the cups, the marmalade, the tea,
Among the porcelain, among some talk of you and me,
Would it have been worth while,   90

---

4. See *Matthew* 14:1–12 and *Mark* 6:17–29: John the Baptist was decapitated, upon
Salome's request and at Herod's command, and his head delivered on a platter.

To have bitten off the matter with a smile,
To have squeezed the universe into a ball[5]
To roll it toward some overwhelming question,
To say: "I am Lazarus,[6] come from the dead,
Come back to tell you all, I shall tell you all"——   95
If one, settling a pillow by her head,
    Should say: 'That is not what I meant at all.
    That is not it, at all."

    And would it have been worth it, after all,
Would it have been worth while,   100
After the sunsets and the dooryards and the sprinkled streets,
After the novels, after the teacups, after the skirts that trail along the
    floor——
And this, and so much more?——
It is impossible to say just what I mean!
But as if a magic lantern[7] threw the nerves in patterns on a screen: 105
Would it have been worth while
If one, settling a pillow or throwing off a shawl,
And turning toward the window, should say:
    "That is not it at all,
    That is not what I meant, at all."   110
                                    .   .   .   .   .

No! I am not Prince Hamlet, nor was meant to be;
Am an attendant lord,[8] one that will do
To swell a progress,[9] start a scene or two,
Advise the prince; no doubt, an easy tool,
Deferential, glad to be of use,   115
Politic, cautious, and meticulous;
Full of high sentence, but a bit obtuse;
At times, indeed, almost ridiculous——
Almost, at times, the Fool.

    I grow old . . . I grow old . . .   120
I shall wear the bottoms of my trousers rolled.

    Shall I part my hair behind? Do I dare to eat a peach?
I shall wear white flannel trousers, and walk upon the beach.
I have heard the mermaids singing, each to each.

    I do not think that they will sing to me.   125

    I have seen them riding seaward on the waves
Combing the white hair of the waves blown back
When the wind blows the water white and black.

    We have lingered in the chambers of the sea
By sea-girls wreathed with seaweed red and brown   130
Till human voices wake us, and we drown.

                                                                   1917

5. See Marvell's "To His Coy Mistress," lines 41–42: "Let us roll all our strength and all / our sweetness up into one ball. . . ."

6. One Lazarus was raised from the dead by Jesus (see *John* 1:1 to 2:2), and another (in the parable of the rich man Dives) is discussed in terms of returning from the dead to warn the living (*Luke* 16:19–31).

7. A nonelectric projector used as early as the 17th century.

8. Like Polonius in *Hamlet*, who is full of maxims ("high sentence," line 117).

9. Procession of state.

W. D. SNODGRASS

The Campus on the Hill

Up the reputable walks of old established trees
They stalk, children of the *nouveaux riches;* chimes
Of the tall Clock Tower drench their heads in blessing:
"I don't wanna play at your house;
I don't like you any more."   5
My house stands opposite, on the other hill,
Among meadows, with the orchard fences down and falling;
Deer come almost to the door.
You cannot see it, even in this clearest morning.
White birds hang in the air between   10
Over the garbage landfill and those homes thereto adjacent,
Hovering slowly, turning, settling down
Like the flakes sifting imperceptibly onto the little town
In a waterball of glass.
And yet, this morning, beyond this quiet scene,   15
The floating birds, the backyards of the poor,
Beyond the shopping plaza, the dead canal, the hillside lying tilted in
      the air,
Tomorrow has broken out today:
Riot in Algeria, in Cyprus, in Alabama;
Aged in wrong, the empires are declining,   20
And China gathers, soundlessly, like evidence.
What shall I say to the young on such a morning?—
Mind is the one salvation?—also grammar?—
No; my little ones lean not toward revolt. They
Are the Whites, the vaguely furiously driven, who resist   25
Their souls with such passivity
As would make Quakers swear. All day, dear Lord, all day
They wear their godhead lightly.
They look out from their hill and say,
To themselves, "We have nowhere to go but down;   30
The great destination is to stay."
Surely the nations will be reasonable;
They look at the world—don't they?—the world's way?
The clock just now has nothing more to say.

1959

ANDREI VOZNESENSKY

Antiworlds[1]

The clerk Bukashkin is our neighbor:
His face is grey as blotting-paper.

But like balloons of blue or red,
Bright Antiworlds
            float over his head!   5

---

1. Voznesensky uses, often playfully, the vocabulary and ideas of modern science. According to the concept of antimatter, particles of equal mass but with opposite magnetic value exist for all atoms. Translated from the Russian by Richard Wilbur.

On them reposes, prestidigitous,
Ruling the cosmos, a demon-magician,
Anti-Bukashkin the Academician,
Lapped in the arms of Lollobrigidas.

But Anti-Bukashkin's dreams are the color   10
Of blotting-paper, and couldn't be duller.

Long live Antiworlds! They rebut
With dreams the rat-race and the rut.
For some to be clever, some must be boring.
No deserts? No oases, then.   15

There are no women—
                    just anti-men.
In the forests, anti-machines are roaring.
There's the dirt of the earth, as well as the salt.
If the earth broke down, the sun would halt.   20

Ah, my critics; how I love them.
Upon the neck of the keenest of them,
Fragrant and bald as fresh-baked bread,
There shines a perfect anti-head . . .

. . . I sleep with windows open wide;   25
Somewhere a falling star invites,
And skyscrapers
                    like stalactites,
Hang from the planet's underside.
There, upside down   30
                    below me far,
Stuck like a fork into the earth,
Or perching like a carefree moth,
My little Antiworld,
                    there you are!   35

In the middle of the night, why is it
That Antiworlds are moved to visit?

Why do they sit together, gawking
At the television, and never talking?

Between them not one word has passed.   40
Their first strange meeting is their last.

Neither can manage the least *bon ton*.
Oh, how they'll blush for it, later on!

Their ears are burning like a pair
Of crimson butterflies, hovering there . . .   45

. . . A distinguished lecturer lately told me,
"Antiworlds are a total loss."

Still, my apartment-cell won't hold me;
I thrash in my sleep, I turn and toss.

And, radio-like, my cat lies curled   50
With his green eye tuned in to the world.

                                                              1962

ANONYMOUS

The Lady Fortune

The lady Fortune is bothe freend and fo.
Of poure she maketh riche, of riche poure also;
She turneth wo[1] al into wele,[2] and wele al into wo.
Ne truste no man to this wele, the wheel it turneth so.

ca. 1325

AMY LOWELL

Patterns

I walk down the garden-paths,
And all the daffodils
Are blowing, and the bright blue squills.[1]
I walk down the patterned garden-paths
In my stiff, brocaded gown.   5
With my powdered hair and jeweled fan,
I too am a rare
Pattern. As I wander down
The garden-paths.

My dress is richly figured,   10
And the train
Makes a pink and silver stain
On the gravel, and the thrift
Of the borders.
Just a plate of current fashion,   15
Tripping by in high-heeled, ribboned shoes.
Not a softness anywhere about me,
Only whalebone and brocade.
And I sink on a seat in the shade
Of a lime tree. For my passion   20
Wars against the stiff brocade.
The daffodils and squills
Flutter in the breeze
As they please.
And I weep;   25
For the lime-tree is in blossom
And one small flower has dropped upon my bosom.

And the plashing of waterdrops
In the marble fountain

1. Woe.   1. Bell-shaped flowers.
2. Weal: well-being, prosperity.

Comes down the garden-paths.   30
The dripping never stops.
Underneath my stiffened gown
Is the softness of a woman bathing in a marble basin,
A basin in the midst of hedges grown
So thick, she cannot see her lover hiding,   35
But she guesses he is near,
And the sliding of the water
Seems the stroking of a dear
Hand upon her.
What is Summer in a fine brocaded gown!   40
I should like to see it lying in a heap upon the ground.
All the pink and silver crumpled up on the ground.

I would be the pink and silver as I ran along the paths,
And he would stumble after,
Bewildered by my laughter.   45
I should see the sun flashing from his sword-hilt and the buckles on his
    shoes.
I would choose
To lead him in a maze along the patterned paths,
A bright and laughing maze for my heavy-booted lover.
Till he caught me in the shade,   50
And the buttons of his waistcoat bruised my body as he clasped me,
Aching, melting, unafraid.
With the shadows of the leaves and the sundrops
And the plopping of the waterdrops,
All about us in the open afternoon—   55
I am very like to swoon
With the weight of this brocade,
For the sun sifts through the shade.

Underneath the fallen blossom
In my bosom,   60
Is a letter I have hid.
It was brought to me this morning by a rider from the Duke.
"Madam, we regret to inform you that Lord Hartwell
Died in action Thursday se'nnight."[2]
As I read it in the white, morning sunlight,   65
The letters squirmed like snakes.
"Any answer, Madam?" said my footman.[3]
"No," I told him.
"See that the messenger takes some refreshment.
No, no answer."   70
And I walked into the garden,
Up and down the patterned paths,
In my stiff, correct brocade.
The blue and yellow flowers stood up proudly in the sun,
Each one.   75
I stood upright too,
Held rigid to the pattern
By the stiffness of my gown.

---

2. A week ago Thursday.   3. Servant.

Up and down I walked,
Up and down.   80

In a month he would have been my husband.
In a month, here, underneath this lime,
We would have broke the pattern;
He for me, and I for him,
He as Colonel, I as Lady,   85
On this shady seat.
He had a whim
That sunlight carried blessing.
And I answered, "It shall be as you have said."
Now he is dead.   90

In Summer and in Winter I shall walk
Up and down
The patterned garden-paths
In my stiff, brocaded gown.
The squills and daffodils   95
Will give place to pillared roses, and to asters, and to snow.
I shall go
Up and down,
In my gown.
Gorgeously arrayed,   100
Boned and stayed.
And the softness of my body will be guarded from embrace
By each button, hook, and lace.
For the man who should loose me is dead,
Fighting with the Duke in Flanders,   105
In a pattern called a war.
Christ! What are patterns for?

                                                                     1916

PAUL SIMON

Patterns

The night set softly
With the hush of falling leaves
Casting shivering shadows
On the houses through the trees
And light from a street lamp   5
Paints a pattern on my wall
Like the pieces of a puzzle
Or a child's uneven scrawl.

Up a narrow flight of stairs
In a narrow little room   10
As I lie upon my bed
In the early evening gloom.
Impaled on my wall
My eyes can dimly see
The pattern of my life   15
And the puzzle that is me.

From the moment of my birth
To the instant of my death
There are patterns I must follow
Just as I must breathe each breath.   20
Like a rat in a maze
The path before me lies
And the pattern never alters
Until the rat dies.

And the pattern still remains   25
On the wall where darkness fell
And it's fitting that it should
For in darkness I must dwell.
Like the color of my skin
Or the day that I grow old   30
My life is made of patterns
That can scarcely be controlled.

                                                       1965

ARTHUR HUGH CLOUGH

The Latest Decalogue

Thou shalt have one God only; who
Would be at the expense of two?
No graven images may be
Worshipped, except the currency.
Swear not at all; for, for thy curse   5
Thine enemy is none the worse.
At church on Sunday to attend
Will serve to keep the world thy friend.
Honor thy parents; that is, all
From whom advancement may befall.   10
Thou shalt not kill; but need'st not strive
Officiously to keep alive.
Do not adultery commit;
Advantage rarely comes of it.
Thou shalt not steal; an empty feat,   15
When it's so lucrative to cheat.
Bear not false witness; let the lie
Have time on its own wings to fly.
Thou shalt not covet; but tradition
Approves all forms of competition.   20

                                                       1862

DUDLEY RANDALL

Booker T. and W. E. B.[1]

"It seems to me," said Booker T.,
"It shows a mighty lot of cheek

1. Booker T. Washington (1856–1915), founder of Tuskegee Institute, who was willing to sacrifice the vote for economic power, and Dr. W[illiam] E[dward] B[urghardt] DuBois (1868–1963), sociologist, editor of *Crisis*, and a founder of the NAACP (1910).

To study chemistry and Greek
When Mister Charlie needs a hand
To hoe the cotton on his land,   5
And when Miss Ann looks for a cook,
Why stick your nose inside a book?"

"I don't agree," said W.E.B.
"If I should have the drive to seek
Knowledge of chemistry or Greek,   10
I'll do it. Charles and Miss can look
Another place for hand or cook.
Some men rejoice in skill of hand,
And some in cultivating land,
But there are others who maintain   15
The right to cultivate the brain."

"It seems to me," said Booker T.,
"That all you folks have missed the boat
Who shout about the right to vote,
And spend vain days and sleepless nights   20
In uproar over civil rights.
Just keep your mouths shut, do not grouse,
But work, and save, and buy a house."

"I don't agree," said W.E.B.,
"For what can property avail   25
If dignity and justice fail?
Unless you help to make the laws,
They'll steal your house with trumped-up clause.
A rope's as tight, a fire as hot,
No matter how much cash you've got.   30
Speak soft, and try your little plan,
But as for me, I'll be a man."

"It seems to me," said Booker T.—

"I don't agree,"
Said W.E.B.   35
                                                        1966

Commission[1]

Go, my songs, to the lonely and the unsatisfied,
Go also to the nerve-racked, go to the enslaved-by-convention,
Bear to them my contempt for their oppressors.
Go as a great wave of cool water,
Bear my contempt of oppressors.   5

Speak against unconscious oppression,
Speak against the tyranny of the unimaginative,

---

1. Poems or books of poems are sometimes sent into the world with an "envoi" or commission ("Go, little book . . .").

Speak against bonds.
Go to the bourgeoise who is dying of her ennuis,
Go to the women in suburbs.   10
Go to the hideously wedded,
Go to them whose failure is concealed,
Go to the unluckily mated,
Go to the bought wife,
Go to the woman entailed.[2]   15

Go to those who have delicate lust,
Go to those whose delicate desires are thwarted,
Go like a blight upon the dullness of the world;
Go with your edge against this,
Strengthen the subtle cords,   20
Bring confidence upon the algae and the tentacles of the soul.
Go in a friendly manner,
Go with an open speech.
Be eager to find new evils and new good,
Be against all forms of oppression.   25
Go to those who are thickened with middle age,
To those who have lost their interest.

Go to the adolescent who are smothered in family—
Oh how hideous it is
To see three generations of one house gathered together!   30
It is like an old tree with shoots,
And with some branches rotted and falling.

Go out and defy opinion,
Go against this vegetable bondage of the blood.
Be against all sorts of mortmain.[3]   35

p. 1913

2. Involuntarily committed. Property limited to a specific line of heirs is said to be entailed; the term is not usually applied to people.
3. Impersonal ownership.

II

THOMAS HARDY

Channel Firing[1]

That night your great guns, unawares,
Shook all our coffins as we lay,
And broke the chancel window squares,[2]
We thought it was the Judgment-day[3]

And sat upright. While drearisome   5
Arose the howl of wakened hounds:
The mouse let fall the altar-crumb,[4]
The worms drew back into the mounds,

The glebe cow[5] drooled. Till God called, "No;
It's gunnery practice out at sea   10
Just as before you went below;
The world is as it used to be:

"All nations striving strong to make
Red war yet redder. Mad as hatters
They do no more for Christés sake   15
Than you who are helpless in such matters.

"That this is not the judgment-hour
For some of them's a blessed thing,
For if it were they'd have to scour
Hell's floor for so much threatening . . .   20

"Ha, ha. It will be warmer when
I blow the trumpet (if indeed
I ever do; for you are men,
And rest eternal sorely need)."

So down we lay again. "I wonder,   25
Will the world ever saner be,"
Said one, "than when He sent us under
In our indifferent century!"

And many a skeleton shook his head.
"Instead of preaching forty year,"   30
My neighbor Parson Thirdly said,
"I wish I had stuck to pipes and beer."

1. Naval practice on the English Channel preceded the outbreak of World War I in the summer of 1914.
2. The windows near the altar in a church.
3. When, according to tradition, the dead will be awakened.
4. Breadcrumbs from the sacrament.
5. Parish cow pastured on the meadow next to the churchyard.

Again the guns disturbed the hour,
Roaring their readiness to avenge.
As far inland as Stourton Tower,   35
And Camelot, and starlit Stonehenge.[6]

April, 1914

EMILY DICKINSON

I Heard a Fly Buzz

I heard a Fly buzz—when I died—
The Stillness in the Room
Was like the Stillness in the Air—
Between the Heaves of Storm—

The Eyes around—had wrung them dry—   5
And Breaths were gathering firm
For that last Onset—when the King
Be witnessed—in the Room—

I willed my Keepsakes—Signed away
What portion of me be   10
Assignable—and then it was
There interposed a Fly—

With Blue—uncertain stumbling Buzz—
Between the light—and me—
And then the Windows failed—and then   15
I could not see to see—

ca. 1862

ROBERT BROWNING

Soliloquy of the Spanish Cloister[1]

Gr-r-r—there go, my heart's abhorrence!
    Water your damned flower-pots, do!
If hate killed men, Brother Lawrence,
    God's blood, would not mine kill you!
What? your myrtle-bush wants trimming?   5
    Oh, that rose has prior claims—
Needs its leaden vase filled brimming?
    Hell dry you up with its flames!

At the meal we sit together:
    Salve tibi![2] I must hear   10
Wise talk of the kind of weather,
    Sort of season, time of year:
Not a plenteous cork-crop: scarcely

---

6. Stourton Tower, built in the 18th century to commemorate King Alfred's ninth-century victory over the Danes, in Stourhead Park, Wiltshire. Camelot is the legendary site of King Arthur's court, said to have been in Cornwall or Somerset. Stonehenge, a circular formation of upright stones dating from about 1800 B.C., is on Salisbury Plain, Wiltshire; it is thought to have been a ceremonial site for political and religious occasions or an early scientific experiment in astronomy.
    1. Monastery.
    2. Hail to thee. Italics usually indicate the words of Brother Lawrence.

Dare we hope oak-galls,[3] *I doubt:*
What's the Latin name for "parsley"?   15
   What's the Greek name for Swine's Snout?

Whew! We'll have our platter burnished,
   Laid with care on our own shelf!
With a fire-new spoon we're furnished,
   And a goblet for ourself,   20
Rinsed like something sacrificial
   Ere 'tis fit to touch our chaps[4]—
Marked with L. for our initial!
   (He-he! There his lily snaps!)

Saint, forsooth! While brown Dolores   25
   Squats outside the Convent bank
With Sanchicha, telling stories,
   Steeping tresses in the tank,
Blue-black, lustrous, thick like horsehairs,
   —Can't I see his dead eye glow,   30
Bright as 'twere a Barbary corsair's?[5]
   (That is, if he'd let it show!)

When he finishes refection,[6]
   Knife and fork he never lays
Cross-wise, to my recollection,   35
   As do I, in Jesus praise.
I the Trinity illustrate,
   Drinking watered orange-pulp—
In three sips the Arian[7] frustrate;
   While he drains his at one gulp.   40

Oh, those melons? If he's able
   We're to have a feast! so nice!
One goes to the Abbot's table,
   All of us get each a slice.
How go on your flowers? None double?   45
   Not one fruit-sort can you spy?
Strange!—And I, too, at such trouble,
   Keep them close-nipped on the sly!

There's a great text in Galatians,[8]
   Once you trip on it, entails   50
Twenty-nine distinct damnations,
   One sure, if another fails:
If I trip him just a-dying,
   Sure of heaven as sure can be,
Spin him round and send him flying   55
   Off to hell, a Manichee?[9]

3. Abnormal growth on oak trees, used for tanning.
4. Jaws.
5. African pirate's.
6. A meal.
7. A heretical sect which denied the Trinity.
8. "Cursed is every one that continueth not in all things which are written in the book of law to do them," *Galatians* 3:10. *Galatians* 5:15–23 provides a long list of possible offenses, but they do not add up to 29.
9. A heretic. According to the Manichean heresy, the world was divided into the forces of good and evil, equally powerful.

Or, my scrofulous French novel
  On grey paper with blunt type!
Simply glance at it, you grovel
  Hand and foot in Belial's gripe: [1]   60
If I double down its pages
  At the woeful sixteenth print,
When he gathers his greengages,
  Ope a sieve and slip it in't?

Or, there's Satan!—one might venture   65
  Pledge one's soul to him, yet leave
Such a flaw in the indenture
  As he'd miss till, past retrieve,
Blasted lay that rose-acacia
  We're so proud of! *Hy, Zy, Hine* . . .[2]   70
'St, there's Vespers! *Plena gratiâ*
  Ave, Virgo.[3] Gr-r-r—you swine!

     1842

GEORGE HERBERT

The Collar

I struck the board[1] and cried, "No more;
    I will abroad!
What? shall I ever sigh and pine?
My lines[2] and life are free, free as the road,
Loose as the wind, as large as store.[3]   5
    Shall I be still in suit?[4]
Have I no harvest but a thorn
To let me blood, and not restore
What I have lost with cordial[5] fruit?
    Sure there was wine   10
Before my sighs did dry it; there was corn
  Before my tears did drown it.
Is the year only lost to me?
  Have I no bays[6] to crown it,
No flowers, no garlands gay? All blasted?   15
    All wasted?
Not so, my heart; but there is fruit,
    And thou hast hands.
Recover all thy sigh-blown age
On double pleasures: leave thy cold dispute   20
Of what is fit, and not. Forsake thy cage,
    Thy rope of sands,[7]
Which petty thoughts have made, and made to thee
Good cable, to enforce and draw,
    And be thy law,   25

1. In the clutches of Satan.
2. Possibly the beginning of an incantation or curse.
3. The opening words of the *Ave Maria*, but here reversed: "Full of grace, Hail, Virgin."
1. Table.

2. Lot.
3. A storehouse; i.e., in abundance.
4. In service to another.
5. Reviving, restorative.
6. Wreaths of triumph.
7. Moral restrictions.

While thou didst wink[8] and wouldst not see.
   Away! take heed;
   I will abroad.
Call in thy death's-head[9] there; tie up thy fears.
  He that forbears   30
To suit and serve his need,
   Deserves his load."
But as I raved and grew more fierce and wild
   At every word,
Methought I heard one calling, *Child!*   35
   And I replied, *My Lord.*

              1633

A. R. AMMONS

Needs

I want something suited to my special needs
I want chrome hubcaps, pin-on attachments
and year round use year after year
I want a workhorse with smooth uniform cut,
dozer blade and snow blade & deluxe steering 5
wheel
I want something to mow, throw snow, tow
and sow with
I want precision reel blades
I want a console styled dashboard   10
I want an easy spintype recoil starter
I want combination bevel and spur gears, 14
gauge stamped steel housing and
washable foam element air cleaner
I want a pivoting front axle and extrawide 15
turf tires
I want an inch of foam rubber inside a vinyl
covering
and especially if it's not too much, if I
can deserve it, even if I can't pay for it 20
I want to mow while riding.

              1970

SONIA SANCHEZ

221–1424

(San/francisco/suicide/number)

hello.
  are u the
suicide man? well
i'm callen to say
that i'm fixen to   5

---

8. I.e., close your eyes to the weaknesses of such restrictions. 9. *Memento mori*, a skull intended to remind men of their mortality.

hang it up.
            what's that man?
i mean i'm gonna do
myself in—i'm
checken out.
                                                    10
            what's that man?
yeh. that's right. i feel the
need to do away with myself.
why?
            ohhhh man. cuz   15
i'm blk. liven in a
wite/psychotic/neurotic
schizophrenic/society where
all honkies have been plannen
my death since . . .   20
                        what's that
u say? when did i first
feel that honkies?
                        yeh. honkies.
yeh. i'll spell it for u.   HONKIES . . .   25
were tryen to kill me?
                        well. man. it ain't
exactly my discovery.
                        but it's been happenen
for bout 400 yrs.   30
                        what's that?
can i au-then-ti-cate that?
                                how u
spell that man?   oh yeh?
now what that mean? oh yeh?   35
well that ain't one of my words.
but mannnn.
            don't u read the fucken papers?
don't u live?
            what's that? u say it's   40
all improven for us negroes.
                        what kind
of fool are u? what u? some kind of
wite/liberal/pacificist/jew?
                        all u   45
honkies are alike.
                        shit man u
ain't got no kind of understanding. hey.
                        what's that
funny sound like u belch/en or somethin?   50
oh u record/en the conversation.
                                i'm on a
sort of candid telephone.
                        what's that u say?
i sound better?   yeh.   55
                        matter of fact
i do.
    feel like go/en out and
do/en in a couple honkies.

yeh. honkies. hey. u still there?   60
yeh. well i'm gonna split.
hey. u know what?
                    u don't sound so gooood.
yehhhh if i wuz u
                    i'd hang it up mannnNN.   65
                    bye now!

                                                          1970

CAROLYN KIZER

A Widow in Wintertime

Last night a baby gargled in the throes
Of a fatal spasm. My children are all grown
Past infant strangles; so, reassured, I knew
Some other baby perished in the snow.
But no. The cat was making love again.   5

Later, I went down and let her in.
She hung her tail, flagging from her sins.
Though she'd eaten, I forked out another dinner,
Being myself hungry all ways, and thin
From metaphysic famines she knows nothing of,   10

The feckless beast! Even so, resemblances
Were on my mind: female and feline, though
She preens herself from satisfaction, and does
Not mind lying even in snow. She is
Lofty and bedraggled, without need to choose.   15

As an ex-animal, I look fondly on
Her excesses and simplicities, and would not return
To them; taking no marks for what I have become,
Merely that my nine lives peal in my ears again
And again, ring in these austerities,   20

These arbitrary disciplines of mine,
Most of them trivial: like covering
The children on my way to bed, and trying
To live well enough alone, and not to dream
Of grappling in the snow, claws plunged in fur,   25

Or waken in a caterwaul of dying.

                                                          1961

WALLACE STEVENS

Sunday Morning

I

Complacencies of the peignoir, and late
Coffee and oranges in a sunny chair,
And the green freedom of a cockatoo

Upon a rug mingle to dissipate
The holy hush of ancient sacrifice.   5
She dreams a little, and she feels the dark
Encroachment of that old catastrophe,[1]
As a calm darkens among water-lights.
The pungent oranges and bright, green wings
Seem things in some procession of the dead,   10
Winding across wide water, without sound.
The day is like wide water, without sound,
Stilled for the passing of her dreaming feet
Over the seas, to silent Palestine,
Dominion of the blood and sepulchre.   15

                              II

Why should she give her bounty to the dead?
What is divinity if it can come
Only in silent shadows and in dreams?
Shall she not find in comforts of the sun,
In pungent fruit and bright, green wings, or else   20
In any balm or beauty of the earth,
Things to be cherished like the thought of heaven?
Divinity must live within herself:
Passions of rain, or moods in falling snow;
Grievings in loneliness, or unsubdued   25
Elations when the forest blooms; gusty
Emotions on wet roads on autumn nights;
All pleasures and all pains, remembering
The bough of summer and the winter branch.
These are the measures destined for her soul.   30

                              III

Jove[2] in the clouds had his inhuman birth.
No mother suckled him, no sweet land gave
Large-mannered motions to his mythy mind
He moved among us, as a muttering king,
Magnificent, would move among his hinds,[3]   35
Until our blood, commingling, virginal,
With heaven, brought such requital to desire
The very hinds discerned it, in a star.[4]
Shall our blood fail? Or shall it come to be
The blood of paradise? And shall the earth   40
Seem all of paradise that we shall know?
The sky will be much friendlier then than now,
A part of labor and a part of pain,
And next in glory to enduring love,
Not this dividing and indifferent blue.   45

                              IV

She says, "I am content when wakened birds,
Before they fly, test the reality
Of misty fields, by their sweet questionings;

---

1. The Crucifixion.   3. Lowliest rural subjects.
2. Jupiter, the chief Roman god.   4. The star of Bethlehem.

But when the birds are gone, and their warm fields
Return no more, where, then, is paradise?"   50
There is not any haunt of prophecy,
Nor any old chimera of the grave,
Neither the golden underground, nor isle
Melodious, where spirits gat[5] them home,
Nor visionary south, nor cloudy palm   55
Remote on heaven's hill, that has endured
As April's green endures, or will endure
Like her remembrance of awakened birds,
Or her desire for June and evening, tipped
By the consummation of the swallow's wings.   60

V

She says, "But in contentment I still feel
The need of some imperishable bliss."
Death is the mother of beauty; hence from her,
Alone, shall come fulfillment to our dreams
And our desires. Although she strews the leaves   65
Of sure obliteration on our paths,
The path sick sorrow took, the many paths
Where triumph rang its brassy phrase, or love
Whispered a little out of tenderness,
She makes the willow shiver in the sun   70
For maidens who were wont to sit and gaze
Upon the grass, relinquished to their feet.
She causes boys to pile new plums and pears
On disregarded plate.[6] The maidens taste
And stray impassioned in the littering leaves.   75

VI

Is there no change of death in paradise?
Does ripe fruit never fall? Or do the boughs
Hang always heavy in that perfect sky,
Unchanging, yet so like our perishing earth,
With rivers like our own that seek for seas   80
They never find, the same receding shores
That never touch with inarticulate pang?
Why set the pear upon those river-banks
Or spice the shores with odors of the plum?
Alas, that they should wear our colors there,   85
The silken weavings of our afternoons,
And pick the strings of our insipid lutes!
Death is the mother of beauty, mystical,
Within whose burning bosom we devise
Our earthly mothers waiting, sleeplessly.   90

VII

Supple and turbulent, a ring of men
Shall chant in orgy[7] on a summer morn

---

5. Got.
6. "Plate is used in the sense of so-called family plate. Disregarded refers to the disuse into which things fall that have been possessed for a long time. I mean,

therefore, that death releases and renews. What the old have come to disregard. the young inherit and make use of" (*Letters of Wallace Stevens* [1966], pp. 183–184).
7. Ceremonial revelry.

Their boisterous devotion to the sun,
Not as a god, but as a god might be,
Naked among them, like a savage source.   95
Their chant shall be a chant of paradise,
Out of their blood, returning to the sky;
And in their chant shall enter, voice by voice,
The windy lake wherein their lord delights,
The trees, like serafin,[8] and echoing hills,   100
That choir among themselves long afterward.
They shall know well the heavenly fellowship
Of men that perish and of summer morn.
And whence they came and whither they shall go
The dew upon their feet shall manifest.   105

VIII

She hears, upon that water without sound,
A voice that cries, "The tomb in Palestine
Is not the porch of spirits lingering.
It is the grave of Jesus, where he lay."
We live in an old chaos of the sun,   110
Or old dependency of day and night,
Or island solitude, unsponsored, free,
Of that wide water, inescapable.
Deer walk upon our mountains, and the quail
Whistle about us their spontaneous cries;   115
Sweet berries ripen in the wilderness;
And, in the isolation of the sky,
At evening, casual flocks of pigeons make
Ambiguous undulations as they sink,
Downward to darkness, on extended wings.   120

1915

WILLIAM SHAKESPEARE

Hark, Hark! the Lark[1]

Hark, hark! the lark at heaven's gate sings,
    And Phoebus[2] 'gins arise,
His steeds to water at those springs
    On chaliced[3] flowers that lies;
And winking Mary-buds[4] begin   5
    To ope their golden eyes:
With every thing that pretty is,
    My lady sweet, arise!
    Arise, arise!

ca. 1610

---

8. Seraphim, the highest of the nine orders of angels.
1. From *Cymbeline*, Act II, sc. iii.

2. Apollo, the sun god.
3. Cup-shaped.
4. Buds of marigolds.

JOHN DONNE

The Sun Rising

Busy old fool, unruly sun,
    Why dost thou thus,
Through windows, and through curtains, call on us?
Must to thy motions lovers' seasons run?
        Saucy pedantic wretch, go chide   5
        Late schoolboys, and sour prentices,[1]
    Go tell court-huntsmen that the king will ride,
    Call country ants[2] to harvest offices;
Love, all alike, no season knows, nor clime,
Nor hours, days, months, which are the rags of time.   10

        Thy beams, so reverend and strong
        Why shouldst thou think?
I could eclipse and cloud them with a wink,
But that I would not lose her sight so long:
        If her eyes have not blinded thine,   15
        Look, and tomorrow late, tell me
    Whether both the Indias[3] of spice and mine
    Be where thou left'st them, or lie here with me.
Ask for those kings whom thou saw'st yesterday,
And thou shalt hear, all here in one bed lay.   20

        She is all states, and all princes I,
        Nothing else is.
Princes do but play us; compared to this,
All honor's mimic,[4] all wealth alchemy.[5]
        Thou, sun, art half as happy as we,   25
        In that the world's contracted thus;
    Thine age asks[6] ease, and since thy duties be
    To warm the world, that's done in warming us.
Shine here to us, and thou art every where;
This bed thy center[7] is, these walls thy sphere.   30

1633

LOUIS MAC NEICE

Aubade

Having bitten on life like a sharp apple
Or, playing it like a fish, been happy,

Having felt with fingers that the sky is blue,
What have we after that to look forward to?

Not the twilight of the gods but a precise dawn   5
Of sallow and grey bricks, and newsboys crying war.

1935

1. Apprentices.
2. Farmworkers.
3. The East and West Indies, commercial sources of spices and gold.
4. Hypocritical.
5. Imposture, like the "scientific" procedures for turning base metals into gold.
6. Requires.
7. Of orbit.

RICHARD WILBUR

Love Calls Us to the Things of This World[1]

The eyes open to a cry of pulleys,[2]
And spirited from sleep, the astounded soul
Hangs for a moment bodiless and simple
As false dawn.
            Outside the open window 5
The morning air is all awash with angels.

Some are in bed-sheets, some are in blouses,
Some are in smocks: but truly there they are.
Now they are rising together in calm swells
Of halcyon[3] feeling, filling whatever they wear 10
With the deep joy of their impersonal breathing;
       Now they are flying in place,[4] conveying
The terrible speed of their omnipresence, moving
And staying like white water; and now of a sudden
They swoon down into so rapt a quiet 15
That nobody seems to be there.
                 The soul shrinks

From all that it is about to remember,
From the punctual rape of every blesséd day,
And cries, 20
      "Oh, let there be nothing on earth but laundry,
Nothing but rosy hands in the rising steam
And clear dances done in the sight of heaven."

Yet, as the sun acknowledges
With a warm look the world's hunks and colors,
The soul descends once more in bitter love 25
To accept the waking body, saying now
In a changed voice as the man yawns and rises,

"Bring them down from their ruddy gallows;
Let there be clean linen for the backs of thieves; 30
Let lovers go fresh and sweet to be undone,
And the heaviest nuns walk in a pure floating
Of dark habits,
           keeping their difficult balance."

1956

JONATHAN SWIFT

A Description of the Morning

Now hardly[1] here and there a hackney-coach[2]
Appearing, showed the ruddy morn's approach.

---

1. A recurrent theme in St. Augustine's *Confessions*.
2. Laundry pulleys, designed so that clothes can be hung on the line inside and then sent outdoors to dry.

3. Serene.
4. Like planes in a formation.
1. Scarcely; i.e., they are just beginning to appear.
2. Hired coach.

Now Betty[3] from her master's bed had flown,
And softly stole to discompose her own.
The slip shod 'prentice from his master's door   5
Had pared the dirt, and sprinkled round the floor.
Now Moll had whirled her mop with dext'rous airs,
Prepared to scrub the entry and the stairs.
The youth with broomy stumps began to trace[4]
The kennel-edge[5] where wheels had worn the place.   10
The small-coal man[6] was heard with cadence deep,
Till drowned in shriller notes of chimney-sweep:
Duns[7] at his lordship's gate began to meet;
And brick-dust Moll had screamed through half the street.[8]
The turnkey now his flock returning sees,   15
Duly let out a-nights to steal for fees.[9]
The watchful bailiffs[1] take their silent stands,
And schoolboys lag with satchels in their hands.

p. 1709

BOB DYLAN

Mister Tambourine Man

Chorus

Hey, Mister Tambourine Man, play a song for me,
I'm not sleepy and there ain't no place I'm going to.
Hey, Mister Tambourine Man, play a song for me,
In the jingle, jangle morning I'll come followin' you.

I

Though I know that evenin's empire has returned into sand   5
Vanished from my hand,
Left me blindly here to stand
But still no sleepin'.
My weariness amazes me,
I'm branded on my feet,   10
I have no one to meet,
And the ancient empty street's
Too dead for dreamin'.
Chorus

II

Take me on a trip upon your magic swirlin' ship,
My senses have been stripped,   15
My hands can't feel to grip,
My toes too numb to step,
Wait only for my boot heels to be wanderin'.
I'm ready to go anywhere,

3. A stock name for a servant girl. Moll (lines 7, 14) is a frequent lower-class nickname.
4. "To find old Nails." (Swift's note)
5. Edge of the gutter which ran down the middle of the street.
6. A seller of coal and charcoal.
7. Bill collectors.

8. Selling powdered brick which was used to clean knives.
9. Jailers collected fees from prisoners for their keep and often let them out at night so they could steal to pay expenses.
1. Looking for those on their "wanted" lists.

I'm ready for to fade
Into my own parade.
Cast your dancin' spell my way,
I promise to go under it.
Chorus

III

Though you might hear laughin', spinnin', swingin' madly through the
  sun,
It's not aimed at anyone,   25
It's just escapin' on the run,
And but for the sky there are no fences facin'.
And if you hear vague traces
Of skippin' reels of rhyme
To your tambourine in time,   30
It's just a ragged clown behind,
I wouldn't pay it any mind,
It's just a shadow
You're seein' that he's chasin'.
Chorus

IV

Take me disappearin' through the smoke rings of my mind   35
Down the foggy ruins of time,
Far past the frozen leaves,
The haunted, frightened trees
Out to the windy beach
Far from the twisted reach of crazy sorrow.   40
Yes, to dance beneath the diamond sky
With one hand wavin' free,
Silhouetted by the sea,
Circled by the circus sands,
With memory and fate   45
Driven deep beneath the waves.
Let me forget about today until tomorrow.
Chorus

1964

MATTHEW ARNOLD

Dover Beach[1]

The sea is calm tonight.
The tide is full, the moon lies fair
Upon the straits; on the French coast the light
Gleams and is gone; the cliffs of England stand,
Glimmering and vast, out in the tranquil bay.   5
Come to the window, sweet is the night-air!
Only, from the long line of spray
Where the sea meets the moon-blanched land,
Listen! you hear the grating roar

---

1. At the narrowest point on the English Channel. The lights on the French coast
(lines 3–4) would be about 20 miles away.

Of pebbles which the waves draw back, and fling,   10
At their return, up the high strand,
Begin, and cease, and then again begin,
With tremulous cadence slow, and bring
The eternal note of sadness in.

Sophocles long ago   15
Heard it on the Aegean, and it brought
Into his mind the turbid ebb and flow
Of human misery;[2] we
Find also in the sound a thought,
Hearing it by this distant northern sea.   20

The Sea of Faith
Was once, too, at the full, and round earth's shore
Lay like the folds of a bright girdle furled.
But now I only hear
Its melancholy, long, withdrawing roar,   25
Retreating, to the breath
Of the night-wind, down the vast edges drear
And naked shingles[3] of the world.

Ah, love, let us be true
To one another! for the world, which seems   30
To lie before us like a land of dreams,
So various, so beautiful, so new,
Hath really neither joy, nor love, nor light,
Nor certitude, nor peace, nor help for pain;
And we are here as on a darkling plain   35
Swept with confused alarms of struggle and flight,
Where ignorant armies clash by night.

ca. 1851

ANDREW MARVELL

The Garden

How vainly men themselves amaze[1]
To win the palm, the oak, or bays,[2]
And their incessant labors see
Crowned from some single herb, or tree,
Whose short and narrow-vergéd[3] shade   5
Does prudently their toils upbraid;
While all flowers and all trees do close[4]
To weave the garlands of repose!

Fair Quiet, have I found thee here,
And Innocence, thy sister dear?   10

---

2. In *Antigone*, lines 583–91, the chorus
compares the fate of the house of Oedipus
to the waves of the sea.
3. Pebble-strewn beaches.
1. Become frenzied.

2. Awards for athletic, civic, and literary
achievements.
3. Narrowly cropped.
4. Unite.

Mistaken long, I sought you then
In busy companies of men.
Your sacred plants,[5] if here below,
Only among the plants will grow;
Society is all but rude[6]   15
To[7] this delicious solitude.

No white nor red was ever seen
So am'rous as this lovely green.
Fond lovers, cruel as their flame,
Cut in these trees their mistress' name: 20
Little, alas, they know, or heed
How far these beauties hers exceed!
Fair trees, wheresoe'er your barks I wound,
No name shall but your own be found.

When we have run our passion's heat,   25
Love hither makes his best retreat.
The gods, that mortal beauty chase,
Still in a tree did end their race:
Apollo hunted Daphne so,
Only that she might laurel grow;   30
And Pan did after Syrinx speed,
Not as a nymph, but for a reed.[8]

What wondrous life is this I lead!
Ripe apples drop about my head;
The luscious clusters of the vine   35
Upon my mouth do crush their wine;
The nectarine and curious[9] peach
Into my hands themselves do reach;
Stumbling on melons, as I pass,
Insnared with flowers, I fall on grass.   40

Meanwhile the mind, from pleasure less,
Withdraws into its happiness;[1]
The mind, that ocean where each kind
Does straight its own resemblance find;[2]
Yet it creates, transcending these,   45
Far other worlds and other seas,
Annihilating[3] all that's made
To a green thought in a green shade.

Here at the fountain's sliding foot,
Or at some fruit tree's mossy root,   50
Casting the body's vest[4] aside,
My soul into the boughs does glide:
There, like a bird, it sits and sings,

5. Cuttings.
6. Barbarous.
7. Compared to.
8. In Ovid's *Metamorphoses*, Daphne, pursued by Apollo, is turned into a laurel, and Syrinx, pursued by Pan, into a reed which Pan makes into a flute.
9. Exquisite.

1. I.e., the mind withdraws from lesser sense pleasure into contemplation.
2. All land creatures were supposed to have corresponding sea-creatures.
3. Reducing to nothing by comparison.
4. Vestment, clothing; the flesh is being considered as simply clothing for the soul.

Then whets[5] and combs its silver wings,
And, till prepared for longer flight,   55
Waves in its plumes the various[6] light.

Such was that happy garden-state,
While man there walked without a mate:
After a place so pure, and sweet,
What other help could yet be meet![7]   60
But 'twas beyond a mortal's share
To wander solitary there:
Two paradises 'twere in one
To live in paradise alone.

How well the skillful gardener drew   65
Of flowers and herbs this dial[8] new,
Where, from above, the milder sun
Does through a fragrant zodiac run;
And as it works, th' industrious bee
Computes its time as well as we!   70
How could such sweet and wholesome hours
Be reckoned but with herbs and flowers?

1681

BEN JONSON

Still to Be Neat[1]

Still[2] to be neat, still to be dressed,
As you were going to a feast;
Still to be powdered, still perfumed;
Lady, it is to be presumed,
Though art's hid causes are not found,   5
All is not sweet, all is not sound.

Give me a look, give me a face
That makes simplicity a grace;
Robes loosely flowing, hair as free;
Such sweet neglect more taketh me   10
Than all th' adulteries of art.
They strike mine eyes, but not my heart.

1609

ROBERT HERRICK

Delight in Disorder

A sweet disorder in the dress
Kindles in clothes a wantonness.
A lawn[1] about the shoulders thrown
Into a fine distractiön;

---

5. Preens.
6. Many-colored.
7. Appropriate.
8. A garden planted in the shape of a sundial, complete with zodiac.

1. A song from Jonson's play, *The Silent Woman.*
2. Continually.
1. Scarf of fine linen.

An erring lace, which here and there   5
Enthralls the crimson stomacher,[2]
A cuff neglectful, and thereby
Ribbands[3] to flow confusedly;
A winning wave, deserving note,
In the tempestuous petticoat;   10
A careless shoestring, in whose tie
I see a wild civility;
Do more bewitch me than when art
Is too precise[4] in every part.

                                                        1648

GERARD MANLEY HOPKINS

Pied Beauty[1]

Glory be to God for dappled things—
    For skies of couple-color as a brinded[2] cow;
        For rose-moles all in stipple[3] upon trout that swim;
Fresh-firecoal chestnut-falls;[4] finches' wings;
    Landscape plotted and pieced—fold, fallow, and plow;   5
        And all trades, their gear and tackle and trim.
All things counter, original, spare, strange;
    Whatever is fickle, freckled (who knows how?)
        With swift, slow; sweet, sour; adazzle, dim;
He fathers-forth whose beauty is past change: 10
                Praise him.

1877

YVOR WINTERS

At the San Francisco Airport

To my daughter, 1954

This is the terminal: the light
Gives perfect vision, false and hard;
The metal glitters, deep and bright.
Great planes are waiting in the yard—
They are already in the night.   5

And you are here beside me, small,
Contained and fragile, and intent
On things that I but half recall—
Yet going whither you are bent.
I am the past, and that is all.   10

But you and I in part are one:
The frightened brain, the nervous will,

2. Ornamental covering for the breasts.
3. Ribbons.
4. In the 16th and 17th centuries Puritans were often called Precisians because of their fastidiousness.
1. Particolored beauty: having patches or sections of more than one color.
2. Streaked or spotted.
3. Rose-colored dots or flecks.
4. Fallen chestnuts as red as burning coals.

The knowledge of what must be done,
The passion to acquire the skill
To face that which you dare not shun.   15

The rain of matter upon sense
Destroys me momently. The score:
There comes what will come. The expense
Is what one thought, and something more—
One's being and intelligence.   20

This is the terminal, the break.
Beyond this point, on lines of air,
You take the way that you must take;
And I remain in light and stare—
In light, and nothing else, awake.   25

1954

HELEN CHASIN

The Word *Plum*

The word *plum* is delicious

pout and push, luxury of
self-love, and savoring murmur

full in the mouth and falling
like fruit   5

taut skin
pierced, bitten, provoked into
juice, and tart flesh

question
and reply, lip and tongue   10
of pleasure.

1968

J. V. CUNNINGHAM

Meditation on Statistical Method

Plato,[1] despair!
We prove by norms
How numbers bear
Empiric[2] forms,

How random wrong   5
Will average right
If time be long
And error slight;

---

1. Whose philosophy assumed that all physical things pre-existed as forms in an Ideal world.   2. Empirical: observable.

But in our hearts
Hyperbole   10
Curves and departs
To infinity.

Error is boundless.
Nor hope nor doubt,
Though both be groundless,   15
Will average out.

                                                        1947

WILLIAM SHAKESPEARE

That Time of Year

That time of year thou mayst in me behold
When yellow leaves, or none, or few, do hang
Upon those boughs which shake against the cold,
Bare ruined choirs, where late the sweet birds sang.
In me thou see'st the twilight of such day   5
As after sunset fadeth in the west;
Which by and by[1] black night doth take away,
Death's second self,[2] that seals up all in rest.
In me thou see'st the glowing of such fire,
That on the ashes of his youth doth lie,   10
As the deathbed whereon it must expire,
Consumed with that which it was nourished by.
This thou perceiv'st, which makes thy love more strong,
To love that well which thou must leave ere long.

                                                        1609

EDWARD TAYLOR

Housewifery

Make me, O Lord, Thy spinning-wheel complete.[1]
    Thy holy Word my distaff make for me;
Make mine affections Thy swift flyers neat;
    And make my soul Thy holy spool to be;
    My conversation make to be Thy reel,   5
    And reel the yarn thereon spun of Thy wheel.

Make me Thy loom then; knit therein this twine;
    And make Thy Holy Spirit, Lord, wind quills;
Then weave the web Thyself. The yarn is fine.
    Thine ordinances make my fulling mills.   10
    Then dye the same in heavenly colors choice,
    All pinked[2] with varnished[3] flowers of paradise.

1. Shortly.
2. Sleep.
1. Stanzas 1 and 2 specify parts of the spinning wheel and loom: the distaff (line 2) holds the fibers, flyers (line 3) twist the fibers, the spool (line 4) receives the spun thread, and the reel (line 5) stores the thread; quills (line 8) are bobbins holding the thread in the shuttle of the loom, and in the fulling mills (line 10) the cloth is cleaned and thickened.
2. Decorated.
3. Shining.

Then clothe therewith mine understanding, will,
Affections,[4] judgment, conscience, memory,
My words and actions, that their shine may fill   15
My ways with glory and Thee glorify.
Then mine apparel shall display before Ye
That I am clothed in holy robes for glory.

ca. 1700

JEAN TOOMER

Song of the Son[1]

Pour O pour that parting soul in song,
O pour it in the sawdust glow of night,
Into the velvet pine-smoke air tonight,
And let the valley carry it along.
And let the valley carry it along.   5

O land and soil, red soil and sweet-gum tree,
So scant of grass, so profligate of pines,
Now just before an epoch's sun declines
Thy son, in time, I have returned to thee,
Thy son, I have in time returned to thee.   10

In time, for though the sun is setting on
A song-lit race of slaves, it has not set;
Though late, O soil, it is not too late yet
To catch thy plaintive soul, leaving, soon gone,
Leaving, to catch thy plaintive soul soon gone.   15

O Negro slaves, dark purple ripened plums,
Squeezed, and bursting in the pine-wood air,
Passing, before they strip the old tree bare
One plum was saved for me, one seed becomes

An everlasting song, a singing tree,   20
Caroling softly souls of slavery,
What they were, and what they are to me,
Caroling softly souls of slavery.

1923

JOHN LENNON AND PAUL MCCARTNEY

Lucy in the Sky with Diamonds

Picture yourself in a boat on a river,
With tangerine trees and marmalade skies
Somebody calls you, you answer quite slowly,
A girl with kaleidoscope eyes.
Cellophane flowers of yellow and green,   5
Towering over your head.
Look for the girl with the sun in her eyes,

---

4. Emotions.   1. From the novel *Cane.*

And she's gone.
Lucy in the sky with diamonds.

Follow her down to a bridge by a fountain   10
Where rocking horse people eat marshmallow pies,
Everyone smiles as you drift past the flowers,
That grow so incredibly high.
Newspaper taxis appear on the shore,
Waiting to take you away.   15
Climb in the back with your head in the clouds.
And you're gone.
Lucy in the sky with diamonds.

Picture yourself on a train in a station,
With plasticine[2] porters with looking glass ties,   20
Suddenly someone is there at the turnstile,
The girl with the kaleidoscope eyes.

1967

EDMUND SPENSER

Ye Tradeful Merchants

Ye tradeful merchants, that with weary toil
Do seek most precious things to make your gain;
And both the Indias[1] of their treasure spoil;
What needeth you to seek so far in vain?
For lo, my love doth in herself contain   5
All this world's riches that may far be found:
If sapphires, lo, her eyes be sapphires plain;
If rubies, lo, her lips be rubies sound;
If pearls, her teeth be pearls, both pure and round;
If ivory, her forehead ivory ween;[2]   10
If gold, her locks are finest gold on ground;
If silver, her fair hands are silver sheen;[3]
But that which fairest is, but few behold,
Her mind, adorned with virtues manifold.

1595

JOHN DONNE

The Canonization

For God's sake hold your tongue and let me love!
    Or chide my palsy or my gout,
My five grey hairs or ruined fortune flout;
With wealth your state, your mind with arts improve,
    Take you a course, get you a place,   5
    Observe his Honor or his Grace,
Or the king's real or his stampèd face[1]

2. Made of a plastic substitute for the
wax or clay ordinarily used in modeling.
    1. The East and West Indies, sources of
spices and precious metals.

2. Seems to be ivory.
3. Shining silver.
1. On coins.

Contemplate; what you will, approve,
    So you will let me love.

Alas, alas, who's injured by my love?   10
    What merchant's ships have my sighs drowned?
Who says my tears have overflowed his ground?
When did my colds a forward spring remove?
    When did the heats which my veins fill
    Add one man to the plaguy bill?[2]   15
Soldiers find wars, and lawyers find out still
    Litigious men which quarrels move,
        Though she and I do love.

Call us what you will, we are made such by love.
    Call her one, me another fly,   20
We're tapers[3] too, and at our own cost die;
And we in us find th' eagle and the dove.[4]
    The phoenix riddle[5] hath more wit[6]
    By us; we two, being one, are it.
So to one neutral thing both sexes fit,   25
    We die and rise the same, and prove
        Mysterious by this love.

We can die by it, if not live by love;
    And if unfit for tombs and hearse
Our legend be, it will be fit for verse;   30
And if no piece of chronicle we prove,[7]
    We'll build in sonnets[8] pretty rooms
    (As well a well-wrought urn becomes[9]
The greatest ashes, as half-acre tombs),
    And by these hymns all shall approve   35
        Us canonized for love.

And thus invoke us: "You whom reverent love
    Made one another's hermitage,
You to whom love was peace, that now is rage,
Who did the whole world's soul extract, and drove[1]   40
    Into the glasses of your eyes
    (So made such mirrors and such spies
That they did all to you epitomize)
    Countries, towns, courts; beg from above
        A pattern of your love!"   45

1633

---

2. List of plague victims.

3. Which consume themselves. To "die" is Renaissance slang for consummating the sexual act, which was popularly believed to shorten life by one day. "fly": a traditional symbol of transitory life.

4. Traditional symbols of strength and purity.

5. According to tradition, only one phoenix existed at a time, dying in a funeral pyre of its own making and being reborn from its own ashes. The bird's existence was thus a riddle akin to a religious mystery (line 27), and a symbol sometimes fused with Christian representations of immortality.

6. Meaning.

7. I.e., if we don't turn out to be an authenticated piece of historical narrative.

8. Love poems. In Italian, *stanza* means rooms.

9. Befits.

1. Compressed.

SIR PHILIP SIDNEY

With How Sad Steps, O Moon

With how sad steps, O Moon, thou climb'st the skies!
How silently, and with how wan a face!
What! may it be that even in heavenly place
That busy archer[2] his sharp arrows tries?
Sure, if that long-with-love-acquainted eyes   5
Can judge of love, thou feel'st a lover's case;
I read it in thy looks; thy languished grace[3]
To me, that feel the like, thy state descries.
Then, even of fellowship, O Moon, tell me,
Is constant love deemed there but want of wit?[4]   10
Are beauties[5] there as proud as here they be?
Do they above, love to be loved, and yet
Those lovers scorn whom that love doth possess?
Do they call virtue there ungratefulness?[6]

1582

DONALD JUSTICE

Here in Katmandu[1]

We have climbed the mountain,
There's nothing more to do.
It is terrible to come down
To the valley
Where, amidst many flowers,   5
One thinks of snow,

As, formerly, amidst snow,
Climbing the mountain,
One thought of flowers,
Tremulous, ruddy with dew,   10
In the valley.
One caught their scent coming down.

It is difficult to adjust, once down,
To the absence of snow.
Clear days, from the valley,   15
One looks up at the mountain.
What else is there to do?
Prayerwheels, flowers!

Let the flowers
Fade, the prayerwheels run down.   20
What have these to do
With us who have stood atop the snow
Atop the mountain,
Flags seen from the valley?

2. Cupid.
3. Manner.
4. Lack of imagination.
5. Beautiful women.

6. "Do they call ungratefulness there a virtue." (Charles Lamb)
1. The capital city of Nepal, about 100 miles west of Mt. Everest.

It might be possible to live in the valley,   25
To bury oneself among flowers,
If one could forget the mountain,
How, setting out before dawn,
Blinded with snow,
One knew what to do.   30

Meanwhile it is not easy here in Katmandu,
Especially when to the valley
That wind which means snow
Elsewhere, but here means flowers,
Comes down,   35
As soon it must, from the mountain.

                                                                    1960

WALLACE STEVENS

Disillusionment of Ten O'clock

The houses are haunted
By white night-gowns
None are green,
Or purple with green rings,
Or green with yellow rings,   5
Or yellow with blue rings.
None of them are strange,
With socks of lace
And beaded ceintures.[1]
People are not going   10
To dream of baboons and periwinkles.[2]
Only, here and there, an old sailor,
Drunk and asleep in his boots,
Catches tigers
In red weather.   15

                                                                    1923

ANONYMOUS

Frankie and Johnny

Frankie and Johnny were lovers,
    Lordy, how they could love,
Swore to be true to each other,
    True as the stars up above,
        He was her man, but he done her wrong.   5

Frankie went down to the corner,
    To buy her a bucket of beer,
Frankie says "Mister Bartender,
    Has my lovin' Johnny been here?
        He is my man, but he's doing me wrong."   10

1. Cinctures: belts, girdles.   2. Sea snails.

"I don't want to cause you no trouble
    Don't want to tell you no lie,
I saw your Johnny half-an-hour ago
    Making love to Nelly Bly.
        He is your man, but he's doing you wrong."   15

Frankie went down to the hotel
    Looked over the transom so high,
There she saw her lovin' Johnny
    Making love to Nelly Bly.
        He was her man; he was doing her wrong.   20

Frankie threw back her kimono,
    Pulled out her big forty-four;
Rooty-toot-toot: three times she shot
    Right through that hotel door,
        She shot her man, who was doing her wrong.   25

"Roll me over gently,
    Roll me over slow,
Roll me over on my right side,
    'Cause these bullets hurt me so,
        I was your man, but I done you wrong."   30

Bring all your rubber-tired hearses
    Bring all your rubber-tired hacks,
They're carrying poor Johnny to the burying ground
    And they ain't gonna bring him back,
        He was her man, but he done her wrong.   35

Frankie says to the sheriff,
    "What are they going to do?"
The sheriff he said to Frankie,
    "It's the 'lectric chair for you.
        He was your man, and he done you wrong."   40

"Put me in that dungeon,
    Put me in that cell,
Put me where the northeast wind
    Blows from the southeast corner of hell,
        I shot my man, 'cause he done me wrong."   45

                    (19th century)

ANONYMOUS

Lord Randal

"O where hae ye been, Lord Randal, my son?
O where hae ye been, my handsome young man?"
"I hae been to the wild wood; mother, make my bed soon,
For I'm weary wi' hunting, and fain wald[1] lie down."

1. Would like to.

"Where gat ye your dinner, Lord Randal, my son?   5
Where gat ye your dinner, my handsome young man?"
"I dined wi' my true-love; mother, make my bed soon,
For I'm weary wi' hunting, and fain wald lie down."

"What gat ye to your dinner, Lord Randal, my son?
What gat ye to your dinner, my handsome young man?"   10
"I gat eels boiled in broo; mother, make my bed soon,
For I'm weary wi' hunting, and fain wald lie down."

"What became of your bloodhounds, Lord Randal, my son?
What became of your bloodhounds, my handsome young man?"
"O they swelled and they died; mother, make my bed soon,   15
For I'm weary wi' hunting, and fain wald lie down."

"O I fear ye are poisoned, Lord Randal, my son!
O I fear ye are poisoned, my handsome young man!"
"O yes! I am poisoned; mother, make my bed soon,
For I'm sick at the heart, and I fain wald lie down."   20

(date of composition uncertain)

ANONYMOUS

Sir Patrick Spens

The king sits in Dumferling toune,[1]
  Drinking the blude-reid[2] wine:
"O whar will I get guid sailor,
  To sail this ship of mine?"

Up and spake an eldern knicht,   5
  Sat at the king's richt knee:
"Sir Patrick Spens is the best sailor
  That sails upon the sea."

The king has written a braid[3] letter
  And signed it wi' his hand,   10
And sent it to Sir Patrick Spens,
  Was walking on the sand.

The first line that Sir Patrick read,
  A loud lauch[4] lauched he;
The next line that Sir Patrick read,   15
  The tear blinded his ee.[5]

"O wha is this has done this deed,
  This il deed done to me,
To send me out this time o' the year,
  To sail upon the sea?   20

"Make haste, make haste, my merry men all,
  Our guid ship sails the morn."

1. Town.   4. Laugh.
2. Blood-red.   5. Eye.
3. Broad: explicit.

"O say na sae,[6] my master dear,
   For I fear a deadly storm.

"Late, late yestre'en I saw the new moon   25
   Wi' the auld moon in her arm,
And I fear, I fear, my dear mastér,
   That we will come to harm."

O our Scots nobles were richt laith[7]
   To weet their cork-heeled shoon,[8]   30
But lang owre a'[9] the play were played
   Their hats they swam aboon.[1]

O lang, lang, may their ladies sit,
   Wi' their fans into their hand,
Or ere they see Sir Patrick Spens   35
   Come sailing to the land.

O lang, lang, may the ladies stand
   Wi' their gold kems[2] in their hair,
Waiting for their ain[3] dear lords,
   For they'll see them na mair.   40

Half o'er, half o'er to Aberdour
   It's fifty fadom deep,
And there lies guid Sir Patrick Spens
   Wi' the Scots lords at his feet.

(probably 13th century)

ROBERT BROWNING

My Last Duchess

Ferrara[1]

That's my last Duchess painted on the wall,
Looking as if she were alive. I call
That piece a wonder, now: Frà Pandolf's hands[2]
Worked busily a day, and there she stands.
Will't please you sit and look at her? I said   5
"Frà Pandolf" by design, for never read
Strangers like you that pictured countenance,
The depth and passion of its earnest glance,
But to myself they turned (since none puts by
The curtain I have drawn for you, but I)   10
And seemed as they would ask me, if they durst,
How such a glance came there; so, not the first

---

6. Not so.
7. Right loath: very reluctant.
8. To wet their cork-heeled shoes. Cork was expensive, and therefore such shoes were a mark of wealth and status.
9. Before all.
1. Their hats swam above them.
2. Combs.
3. Own.
1. Alfonso II, Duke of Ferrara in Italy in the mid-16th century, is the presumed

speaker of the poem, which is loosely based on historical events. The Duke's first wife —whom he had married when she was 14 —died under suspicious circumstances at 17, and he then negotiated through an agent (to whom the poem is spoken) for the hand of the niece of the Count of Tyrol in Austria.
2. Frà Pandolf is, like Claus (line 56), fictitious.

Are you to turn and ask thus. Sir, 'twas not
Her husband's presence only, called that spot
Of joy into the Duchess' cheek: perhaps   15
Frà Pandolf chanced to say "Her mantle laps
Over my lady's wrist too much," or "Paint
Must never hope to reproduce the faint
Half-flush that dies along her throat": such stuff
Was courtesy, she thought, and cause enough   20
For calling up that spot of joy. She had
A heart—how shall I say?—too soon made glad,
Too easily impressed; she liked whate'er
She looked on, and her looks went everywhere.
Sir, 'twas all one! My favor at her breast,   25
The dropping of the daylight in the West,
The bough of cherries some officious fool
Broke in the orchard for her, the white mule
She rode with round the terrace—all and each
Would draw from her alike the approving speech,   30
Or blush, at least. She thanked men,—good! but thanked
Somehow—I know not how—as if she ranked
My gift of a nine-hundred-years-old name
With anybody's gift. Who'd stoop to blame
This sort of trifling? Even had you skill   35
In speech—which I have not—to make your will
Quite clear to such an one, and say, "Just this
Or that in you disgust me; here you miss,
Or there exceed the mark"—and if she let
Herself be lessoned so, nor plainly set   40
Her wits to yours, forsooth, and made excuse,
—E'en then would be some stooping; and I choose
Never to stoop. Oh sir, she smiled, no doubt,
Whene'er I passed her; but who passed without
Much the same smile? This grew; I gave commands   45
Then all smiles stopped together. There she stands
As if alive. Will't please you rise? We'll meet
The company below, then. I repeat,
The Count your master's known munificence
Is ample warrant that no just pretense   50
Of mine for dowry will be disallowed;
Though his fair daughter's self, as I avowed
At starting, is my object. Nay, we'll go
Together down, sir. Notice Neptune, though,
Taming a sea-horse, thought a rarity,   55
Which Claus of Innsbruck cast in bronze for me!

                                                        1842

X. J. KENNEDY

First Confession

Blood thudded in my ears. I scuffed,
   Steps stubborn, to the telltale booth
Beyond whose curtained portal coughed
   The robed repositor of truth.

The slat shot back. The universe   5
  Bowed down his cratered dome to hear
Enumerated my each curse,
  The sip snitched from my old man's beer,

My sloth pride envy lechery,
  The dime held back from Peter's Pence[1]   10
With which I'd bribed my girl to pee
  That I might spy her instruments.

Hovering scale-pans when I'd done
  Settled their balance slow as silt
While in the restless dark I burned   15
  Bright as a brimstone in my guilt

Until as one feeds birds he doled[2]
  Seven Our Fathers and a Hail
Which I to double-scrub my soul
  Intoned twice at the altar rail   20

Where Sunday in seraphic[3] light
  I knelt, as full of grace as most,
And stuck my tongue out at the priest:
  A fresh roost for the Holy Ghost.

                                                                    1961

PHILIP LARKIN

Church Going

Once I am sure there's nothing going on
I step inside, letting the door thud shut.
Another church: matting, seats, and stone,
And little books; sprawlings of flowers, cut
For Sunday, brownish now; some brass and stuff   5
Up at the holy end; the small neat organ;
And a tense, musty, unignorable silence,
Brewed God knows how long. Hatless, I take off
My cycle-clips in awkward reverence,
Move forward, run my hand around the font.[1]   10
From where I stand, the roof looks almost new—
Cleaned, or restored? Someone would know: I don't.
Mounting the lectern, I peruse a few
Hectoring[2] large-scale verses, and pronounce
"Here endeth" much more loudly than I'd meant.   15
The echoes snigger briefly. Back at the door
I sign the book, donate an Irish sixpence,
Reflect the place was not worth stopping for.

1. Hearth money: annual contributions
by Roman Catholic households for the support of the Holy See (Rome).
2. Set penance at.

3. Angelic.
1. A bowl for baptismal water, mounted
on a stone pedestal.
2. Intimidating.

Yet stop I did: in fact I often do,
And always end much at a loss like this,   20
Wondering what to look for; wondering, too,
When churches fall completely out of use
What we shall turn them into, if we shall keep
A few cathedrals chronically on show,
Their parchment, plate and pyx[3] in locked cases,   25
And let the rest rent-free to rain and sheep.
Shall we avoid them as unlucky places?

Or, after dark, will dubious women come
To make their children touch a particular stone;
Pick simples[4] for a cancer; or on some   30
Advised night see walking a dead one?
Power of some sort or other will go on
In games, in riddles, seemingly at random;
But superstition, like belief, must die,
And what remains when disbelief has gone?   35
Grass, weedy pavement, brambles, buttress, sky,

A shape less recognizable each week,
A purpose more obscure. I wonder who
Will be the last, the very last, to seek
This place for what it was; one of the crew   40
That tap and jot and know what rood-lofts[5] were?
Some ruin-bibber,[6] randy for antique,
Or Christmas-addict, counting on a whiff
Of gown-and-bands and organ-pipes and myrrh?
Or will he be my representative,   45

Bored, uninformed, knowing the ghostly silt
Dispersed, yet tending to this cross of ground
Through suburb scrub because it held unspilt
So long and equably what since is found
Only in separation—marriage, and birth,   50
And death, and thoughts of these—for whom was built
This special shell? For, though I've no idea
What this accoutered frowsty barn is worth,
It pleases me to stand in silence here;

A serious house on serious earth it is,   55
In whose blent air all our compulsions meet,
Are recognized, and robed as destinies.
And that much never can be obsolete,
Since someone will forever be surprising
A hunger in himself to be more serious,   60
And gravitating with it to this ground,
Which, he once heard, was proper to grow wise in,
If only that so many dead lie round.

                                                        1955

---

3. A container for the Eucharist.
4. Medicinal herbs.
5. Galleries atop the screens (on which crosses are mounted) which divide the naves or main bodies of churches from the choirs or chancels.
6. Literally, ruin-drinker: someone extremely attracted to antiquarian objects.

ROBERT FROST

Stopping by Woods on a Snowy Evening

Whose woods these are I think I know.
His house is in the village, though;
He will not see me stopping here
To watch his woods fill up with snow.

My little horse must think it queer   5
To stop without a farmhouse near
Between the woods and frozen lake
The darkest evening of the year.

He gives his harness bells a shake
To ask if there is some mistake.   10
The only other sound's the sweep
Of easy wind and downy flake.

The woods are lovely, dark, and deep,
But I have promises to keep,
And miles to go before I sleep,   15
And miles to go before I sleep.

1923

M. CARL HOLMAN

Three Brown Girls Singing

In the ribs of an ugly school building
Three rapt faces
Fuse one pure sound in a shaft of April light:
Three girls, choir robes over their arms, in a stairwell singing
Compose the irrelevancies of a halting typewriter,   5
Chalk dust and orange peel,
A French class drilling,
Into a shimmering column of flawed perfection;
Lasting as long
As their fresh, self-wondering voices climb to security;   10
Outlasting
The childbed death of one,
The alto's divorce,
The disease-raddled face of the third
Whose honey brown skin   15
Glows now in a nimbus[1] of dust motes,
But will be as estranged
As that faceless and voiceless typist
Who, unknown and unknowing, enters the limpid column,
Joins chalk, French verbs, the acrid perfume of oranges,   20
To mark the periphery
Of what shall be saved from calendars and decay.

p. 1963

1. Halo.

EDWIN ARLINGTON ROBINSON

Richard Cory

Whenever Richard Cory went down town,
We people on the pavement looked at him:
He was a gentleman from sole to crown,
Clean favored, and imperially slim.

And he was always quietly arrayed,   5
And he was always human when he talked;
But still he fluttered pulses when he said,
"Good-morning," and he glittered when he walked.

And he was rich—yes, richer than a king—
And admirably schooled in every grace: 10
In fine, we thought that he was everything
To make us wish that we were in his place.

So on we worked, and waited for the light,
And went without the meat, and cursed the bread;
And Richard Cory, one calm summer night,   15
Went home and put a bullet through his head.

1897

EZRA POUND

The Garden

En robe de parade.—Samain[1]

Like a skein of loose silk blown against a wall
She walks by the railing of a path in Kensington Gardens,[2]
And she is dying piece-meal
            of a sort of emotional anæmia.

And round about there is a rabble   5
Of the filthy, sturdy, unkillable infants of the very poor.
They shall inherit the earth.

In her is the end of breeding.
Her boredom is exquisite and excessive.
She would like some one to speak to her,   10
And is almost afraid that I
            will commit that indiscretion.

1916

1. Albert Samain, late 19th-century French poet. The phrase is from the first line of the prefatory poem in his first book of poems, *Au Jardin de l'Infante:* "Mon âme est une infante en robe de parade" ("My soul is an Infanta in ceremonial dress"). An "Infanta" is a daughter of the Spanish royal family which, long inbred, had for many years been afflicted with a real blood disease, hemophilia.
2. A fashionable park near the center of London.

JOHN BETJEMAN

In Westminster Abbey[1]

Let me take this other glove off
  As the *vox humana*[2] swells,
And the beauteous fields of Eden
  Bask beneath the Abbey bells.
Here, where England's statesmen lie,   5
Listen to a lady's cry.

Gracious Lord, oh bomb the Germans.
  Spare their women for Thy Sake,
And if that is not too easy
  We will pardon Thy Mistake.   10
But, gracious Lord, whate'er shall be,
Don't let anyone bomb me.

Keep our Empire undismembered
  Guide our Forces by Thy Hand,
Gallant blacks from far Jamaica,   15
  Honduras and Togoland;
Protect them Lord in all their fights,
And, even more, protect the whites.

Think of what our Nation stands for,
  Books from Boots[3] and country lanes,   20
Free speech, free passes, class distinction,
  Democracy and proper drains.
Lord, put beneath Thy special care
One-eighty-nine Cadogan Square.[4]

Although dear Lord I am a sinner,   25
  I have done no major crime;
Now I'll come to Evening Service
  Whensoever I have the time.
So, Lord, reserve for me a crown,
And do not let my shares go down.   30

I will labor for Thy Kingdom,
  Help our lads to win the war,
Send white feathers to the cowards[5]
  Join the Women's Army Corps,[6]
Then wash the Steps around Thy Throne   35
In the Eternal Safety Zone.

---

1. The famous Gothic church in London in which English monarchs are crowned and famous Englishmen are buried (see lines 5, 39–40).
2. Organ tones which resemble the human voice.
3. A chain of London pharmacies.
4. Presumably where the speaker lives, in a fairly fashionable area.

5. White feathers were sometimes given, or sent, to men not in uniform, to suggest that they were cowards and should join the armed forces.
6. The speaker uses the old World War I name (Women's Army Auxiliary Corps) of the Auxiliary Territorial Service, an organization which performed domestic (and some foreign) defense duties.

Now I feel a little better,
  What a treat to hear Thy Word
Where the bones of leading statesmen,
  Have so often been interred.   40
And now, dear Lord, I cannot wait
Because I have a luncheon date.

1940

SAMUEL ALLEN

To Satch[1]

Sometimes I feel like I will *never* stop
Just go on forever
Till one fine mornin'
I'm gonna reach up and grab me a handfulla stars
Throw out my long lean leg   5
And whip three hot strikes burnin' down the heavens
And look over at God and say
How about that!

p. 1963

LEONARD COHEN

Suzanne

Suzanne take you down
To her place by the river,
You can hear the boats go by
You can spend the night beside her,
And you know that she's half crazy,   5
And that's why you want to be there;
And she feeds you tea and oranges—
That come all the way from China;
And just when you mean to tell her
That you have no love to give her   10
She gets you on her wave length
And lets the river answer
That you've always been her lover,

And you want to travel with her,
And you want to travel blind,   15
And you know that you can trust her,
For you've touched her perfect body
With your mind.

And Jesus was a sailor
When He walked upon the water,   20

---

1. Leroy ("Satchell") Paige, legendary pitcher in the Negro American League for many years. No one knows exactly how old he was when he finally was allowed to pitch in the Major Leagues after World War II, but he dates back to the era of Babe Ruth and Lou Gehrig (he pitched effectively against them in exhibition games); he is generally agreed to have been past 40, the oldest "rookie" in the history of Organized Baseball. He continued to pitch effectively for several years and made a one-game "comeback" in 1965, pitching 3 scoreless innings at about 60 years of age. His witty proverbs and formulas for staying young are nearly as legendary as his pitching.

And He spent a long time watching
From a lonely wooden tower,
And when He knew for certain
Only drowning men could see Him
He said, "All men shall be brothers, then,   25
Until the sea shall free them,"
But He Himself was broken
Long before the sky would open,
Forsaken, almost human,
He sank beneath your wisdom   30
Like a stone.

And you want to travel with Him,
And you want to travel blind,
And you think you maybe trust Him,
For He's touched your perfect body,   35
With His mind.

Suzanne take your hand
And leads you to the river;
She's wearing rags and feathers
From Salvation Army counters.   40
And the sun pours down like honey
On our lady of the harbor;
And she shows you where to look
Amid the garbage and the flowers.
There are heroes in the seaweed,   45
There are children in the morning,
They are leaning out for love,
And they will lean that way forever,
While Suzanne holds the mirror.

And you want to travel with her,   50
And you want to travel blind,
And you think maybe you'll trust her,
For you've touched her perfect body,
With your mind.

1967

JONATHAN SWIFT

On Stella's Birthday, 1719

Stella this day is thirty-four,[1]
(We shan't dispute a year or more)
However Stella, be not troubled,
Although thy size and years are doubled,
Since first I saw thee at sixteen   5
The brightest virgin on the green,
So little is thy form declined
Made up so largely in thy mind.

1. Stella is Swift's pet name for Hester Johnson, a close friend for many years. She was actually 38.

Oh, would it please the gods to split
Thy beauty, size, and years, and wit,   10
No age could furnish out a pair
Of nymphs so graceful, wise and fair
With half the luster of your eyes,
With half your wit, your years and size:
And then before it grew too late,   15
How should I beg of gentle Fate,
(That either nymph might have her swain,[2])
To split my worship too in twain.

1719

JULIAN BOND

The Bishop of Atlanta: Ray Charles

The Bishop seduces the world with his voice
Sweat strangles mute eyes
As insinuations gush out through a hydrant of sorrow
Dreams, a world never seen
Moulded on Africa's anvil, tempered down home   5
Documented in cries and wails
Screaming to be ignored, crooning to be heard
Throbbing from the gutter
On Saturday night
Silver offering only   10
The Right Reverend's back in town
Don't it make you feel all right?

p. 1963

EMILY DICKINSON

A Narrow Fellow in the Grass

A narrow Fellow in the Grass
Occasionally rides—
You may have met Him—did you not
His notice sudden is—

The Grass divides as with a Comb—   5
A spotted shaft is seen—
And then it closes at your feet
And opens further on—

He likes a Boggy Acre
A Floor too cool for Corn—   10
Yet when a Boy, and Barefoot—
I more than once at Noon

Have passed, I thought, a Whip lash
Unbraiding in the Sun

2. Servant, admirer, lover.

When stooping to secure it   15
It wrinkled, and was gone—

Several of Nature's People
I know, and they know me—
I feel for them a transport
Of cordiality—   20

But never met this Fellow
Attended, or alone
Without a tighter breathing
And Zero at the Bone—

                                                            1866

DIANE WAKOSKI

The Buddha Inherits 6 Cars on His Birthday

I. *The Red Car*

I believe it was out of the red one that George Washington stepped,
or someone who looked like G. W.
The corridor was made of fibrous blood
and his feet sank in darkly
as teeth into a pear. Going past the service desk   5
he was paged by a man who had sitting in front of him a
tall jelly glass holding his false teeth. The gums,
false pink.
G. W. was in no mood for dalliance.
"Send all the seamstresses up at once," he said,   10
and when they got there he undressed them all,
picked the most voluptuous one
and gave her some cloth to
sew.

II. *The Blue Car*

It smelled like new rubber inside.   15
The man who drove it had no imagination.
"Will I turn into a machine," he thought,
but no
in a few days they found
a desert rat driving that new blue Ford.   20
And it seemed peculiar
but it's easier not to question things
these days.

III. *The Green Car*

Emily and James stepped out of their green car.
It was made of old metal melted down.   25
In your Lee corduroy dungarees and sweatshirt you
look so handsome.
I'm not particular
as long as you have money and style.
This money is easy to spend,   30

but if you tried to stuff dollars bills inside me you'd find
a yawning gap, hole
at the bottom where everything falls out
Oh pity
there is such an empty space   35
Oh pity
that the lives of some of us are
so vain.

IV. *The Yellow Car*
A very small man met a very large woman.
They were both in the teen-age section of the library.   40
They discovered they both liked the Mona Lisa. They
discovered they both listened to the 1812 Overture.
When true love comes,
        hallelujah
                you know it!   45

V. *The Two-Tone Car*
There are fish that change color for camouflage, but it is a fact that
blind ones never do. Experimentation follows it up. Scientists painted
a tank black at one end and white at the other. It was observed that a
certain fish would become grey as he got just in the middle at the
dividing line. This was the only time he showed up as a different color   50
from his surroundings, either black or white. Apparently, he could not
make an instantaneous change. At the dividing line he always turned
grey.

VI. *Old Cars*
In my car of crocodile teeth, in my
car of old candle wax, in   55
my car of tiger paws padding the waspy dust, in my car of
cat's teeth crushing the brittle insect wings, in my
car of leather straps, in my car of folded paper, silvery and pink,
in my car of Alpine tents, in my car of bits & braces,
in my car of fishing line, in my car at the bottom of a   60
violin, in my car as small as a flea hopping on the dog,
in my own car I want to drive
everywhere
every place there is to go.

                            1970

WILLIAM BLAKE

And Did Those Feet[1]

And did those feet in ancient time
    Walk upon England's mountains green?
And was the holy Lamb of God
    On England's pleasant pastures seen?

1. The prefatory poem to *Milton,* a long poem which asks for an art based on prophetic
inspiration and which attacks traditional art and poetry built on Greek and Roman models.
This prose passage introduces the poem:

And did the Countenance Divine   5
  Shine forth upon our clouded hills?
And was Jerusalem builded here
  Among these dark Satanic Mills?[2]

Bring me my Bow of burning gold!
  Bring me my Arrows of desire!   10
Bring me my Spear! O clouds, unfold!
  Bring me my Chariot of fire!

I will not cease from Mental Fight,
  Nor shall my Sword sleep in my hand,
Till we have built Jerusalem[3]   15
  In England's green and pleasant Land.

ca. 1805

WALT WHITMAN

When Lilacs Last in the Dooryard Bloomed[1]

1

When lilacs last in the dooryard bloomed,
And the great star early drooped in the western sky in the night,
I mourned, and yet shall mourn with ever-returning spring.

Ever-returning spring, trinity sure to me you bring,
Lilac blooming perennial and drooping star in the west,   5
And thought of him I love.

2

O powerful western fallen star!
O shades of night—O moody, tearful night!
O great star disappeared—O the black murk that hides the star!
O cruel hands that hold me powerless—O helpless soul of me!   10
O harsh surrounding cloud that will not free my soul.

3

In the dooryard fronting an old farm-house near the white-washed
   palings,

The stolen and perverted writings of Homer and Ovid, of Plato and Cicero, which all men ought to contemn, are set up by artifice against the sublime of the Bible; but when the New Age is at leisure to pronounce, all will be set right, and those grand works of the more ancient and consciously and professedly inspired men will hold their proper rank, and the daughters of memory shall become the daughters of inspiration. Shakespeare and Milton were both curbed by the general malady and infection from the silly Greek and Latin slaves of the sword.

Rouse up, O young men of the New Age! Set your foreheads against the ignorant hirelings! For we have hirelings in the camp, the court and the university, who would, if they could, forever depress mental and prolong corporeal war. Painters, on you I call! Sculptors! Architects! Suffer not the fashionable fools to depress your powers by the prices they pretend to give for contemptible works or the expensive advertising boasts that they make of such works; believe Christ and his apostles that there is a class of men whose whole delight is in destroying. We do not want either Greek or Roman models if we are but just and true to our own imaginations, those worlds of eternity in which we shall live forever, in Jesus our Lord.

2. In Blake's symbolic system, the unproductive, solipsistic activities of Urizen, an oppressive giver of abstract laws.

3. The New Jerusalem, described in *Revelation* 21.

1. The "occasion" of the poem is the assassination of Abraham Lincoln.

Stands the lilac-bush tall-growing with heart-shaped leaves of rich
    green,
With many a pointed blossom rising delicate, with the perfume strong
    I love,
With every leaf a miracle—and from this bush in the dooryard,   15
With delicate-colored blossoms and heart-shaped leaves of rich green,
A sprig with its flower I break.

4

In the swamp in secluded recesses,
A shy and hidden bird is warbling a song.

Solitary the thrush,   20
The hermit withdrawn to himself, avoiding the settlements,
Sings by himself a song.

Song of the bleeding throat,
Death's outlet song of life (for well dear brother I know,
If thou wast not granted to sing thou would'st surely die).   25

5

Over the breast of the spring, the land, amid cities,
Amid lanes and through old woods, where lately the violets peeped
    from the ground, spotting the gray debris,
Amid the grass in the fields each side of the lanes, passing the endless
    grass,
Passing the yellow-speared wheat, every grain from its shroud in the
    dark-brown fields uprisen,
Passing the apple-tree blows of white and pink in the orchards,   30
Carrying a corpse to where it shall rest in the grave,
Night and day journeys a coffin.

6

Coffin that passes through lanes and streets,[2]
Through day and night with the great cloud darkening the land,
With the pomp of the inlooped flags with the cities draped in black,   35
With the show of the States themselves as of crepe-veiled women
    standing,
With processions long and winding and the flambeaus of the night,
With the countless torches lit, with the silent sea of faces and the un-
    bared heads,
With the waiting depot, the arriving coffin, and the somber faces,
With dirges through the night, with the thousand voices rising strong
    and solemn,   40
With all the mournful voices of the dirges poured around the coffin,
The dim-lit churches and the shuddering organs—where amid these
    you journey,
With the tolling tolling bells' perpetual clang,
Here, coffin that slowly passes,
I give you my sprig of lilac.   45

7

(Nor for you, for one alone,
Blossoms and branches green to coffins all I bring,

2. The funeral cortège stopped at many towns between Washington and Springfield,
Illinois, where Lincoln was buried.

For fresh as the morning, thus would I chant a song for you O sane
    and sacred death.

All over bouquets of roses,
O death, I cover you over with roses and early lilies,   50
But mostly and now the lilac that blooms the first,
Copious I break, I break the sprigs from the bushes,
With loaded arms I come, pouring for you,
For you and the coffins all of you O death.)

8

O western orb sailing the heaven,   55
Now I know what you must have meant as a month since I walked,
As I walked in silence the transparent shadowy night,
As I saw you had something to tell as you bent to me night after night,
As you drooped from the sky low down as if to my side (while the
    other stars all looked on),
As we wandered together the solemn night (for something I know
    not what kept me from sleep),   60
As the night advanced, and I saw on the rim of the west how full you
    were of woe,
As I stood on the rising ground in the breeze in the cool transparent
    night,
As I watched where you passed and was lost in the netherward black
    of the night,
As my soul in its trouble dissatisfied sank, as where you sad orb,
Concluded, dropped in the night, and was gone.   65

9

Sing on there in the swamp,
O singer bashful and tender, I hear your notes, I hear your call,
I hear, I come presently, I understand you,
But a moment I linger, for the lustrous star has detained me,
The star my departing comrade holds and detains me.   70

10

O how shall I warble myself for the dead one there I loved?
And how shall I deck my song for the large sweet soul that has gone?
And what shall my perfume be for the grave of him I love?
Sea-winds blown from east and west,
Blown from the Eastern sea and blown from the Western sea, till there
    on the prairies meeting,   75
These and with these and the breath of my chant,
I'll perfume the grave of him I love.

11

O what shall I hang on the chamber walls?
And what shall the pictures be that I hang on the walls,
To adorn the burial-house of him I love?   80

Pictures of growing spring and farms and homes,
With the Fourth-month eve at sundown, and the gray smoke lucid and
    bright,

With floods of the yellow gold of the gorgeous, indolent, sinking sun,
    burning, expanding the air,
With the fresh sweet herbage under foot, and the pale green leaves of
    the trees prolific,
In the distance the flowing glaze, the breast of the river, with a wind-
    dapple here and there,   85
With ranging hills on the banks, with many a line against the sky, and
    shadows,
And the city at hand with dwellings so dense, and stacks of chimneys,
And all the scenes of life and the workshops, and the workmen home-
    ward returning.

12

Lo, body and soul—this land,
My own Manhattan with spires, and the sparkling and hurrying tides,
    and the ships,   90
The varied and ample land, the South and the North in the light,
    Ohio's shores and flashing Missouri,
And ever the far-spreading prairies covered with grass and corn.

Lo, the most excellent sun so calm and haughty,
The violet and purple morn with just-felt breezes,
The gentle soft-born measureless light,   95
The miracle spreading bathing all, the fulfilled noon,
The coming eve delicious, the welcome night and the stars,
Over my cities shining all, enveloping man and land.

13

Sing on, sing on you gray-brown bird,
Sing from the swamps, the recesses, pour your chant from the bushes, 100
Limitless out of the dusk, out of the cedars and pines.

Sing on dearest brother, warble your reedy song,
Loud human song, with voice of uttermost woe.
O liquid and free and tender!
O wild and loose to my soul—O wondrous singer!   105
You only I hear—yet the star holds me (but will soon depart),
Yet the lilac with mastering odor holds me.

14

Now while I sat in the day and looked forth,
In the close of the day with its light and the fields of spring, and the
    farmers preparing their crops,
In the large unconscious scenery of my land with its lakes and forests, 110
In the heavenly aerial beauty (after the perturbed winds and the
    storms),
Under the arching heavens of the afternoon swift passing, and the
    voices of children and women.
The many-moving sea-tides, and I saw the ships how they sailed,
And the summer approaching with richness, and the fields all busy
    with labor,
And the infinite separate houses, how they all went on, each with its
    meals and minutia of daily usages,   115
And the streets how their throbbings throbbed, and the cities pent—lo,
    then and there,

Falling upon them all and among them all, enveloping me with the rest,
Appeared the cloud, appeared the long black trail,
And I knew death, its thought, and the sacred knowledge of death.

Then with the knowledge of death as walking one side of me, 120
And the thought of death close-walking the other side of me,
And I in the middle as with companions, and as holding the hands of
    companions,
I fled forth to the hiding receiving night that talks not,
Down to the shores of the water, the path by the swamp in the dim-
    ness,
To the solemn shadowy cedars and ghostly pines so still. 125

And the singer so shy to the rest received me,
The gray-brown bird I know received us comrades three,
And he sang the carol of death, and a verse for him I love.

From deep secluded recesses,
From the fragrant cedars and the ghostly pines so still, 130
Came the carol of the bird.

And the charm of the carol rapt me,
As I held as if by their hands my comrades in the night,
And the voice of my spirit tallied the song of the bird.

Come lovely and soothing death, 135
Undulate round the world, serenely arriving, arriving,
In the day, in the night, to all, to each,
Sooner or later delicate death.

Praised be the fathomless universe,
For life and joy, and for objects and knowledge curious,
And for love, sweet love—but praise! praise! praise! 140
For the sure-enwinding arms of cool-enfolding death.

Dark mother always gliding near with soft feet,
Have none chanted for thee a chant of fullest welcome?
Then I chant it for thee, I glorify thee above all, 145
I bring thee a song that when thou must indeed come, come unfalter-
    ingly.

Approach strong deliveress,
When it is so, when thou hast taken them I joyously sing the dead,
Lost in the loving floating ocean of thee,
Laved in the flood of thy bliss O death. 150

From me to thee glad serenades,
Dances for thee I propose saluting thee, adornments and feastings for
    thee,
And the sights of the open landscape and the high-spread sky are
    fitting,
And life and the fields, and the huge and thoughtful night.

The night in silence under many a star, 155
The ocean shore and the husky whispering wave whose voice I know,

And the soul turning to thee O vast and well-veiled death,
And the body gratefully nestling close to thee.

Over the tree-tops I float thee a song,
Over the rising and sinking waves, over the myriad fields and the
*   prairies wide,*   160
Over the dense-packed cities all and the teeming wharves and ways,
I float this carol with joy, with joy to thee O death.

15

To the tally of my soul,
Loud and strong kept up the gray-brown bird,
With pure deliberate notes spreading filling the night.   165

Loud in the pines and cedars dim,
Clear in the freshness moist and the swamp-perfume,
And I with my comrades there in the night.

While my sight that was bound in my eyes unclosed,
As to long panoramas of visions.   170

And I saw askant[3] the armies,
I saw as in noiseless dreams hundreds of battle-flags,
Borne through the smoke of the battles and pierced with missiles I saw
    them,
And carried hither and yon through the smoke, and torn and bloody,
And at last but a few shreds left on the staffs (and all in silence), 175
And the staffs all splintered and broken.

I saw battle-corpses, myriads of them,
And the white skeletons of young men, I saw them,
I saw the debris and debris of all the slain soldiers of the war,
But I saw they were not as was thought,   180
They themselves were fully at rest, they suffered not,
The living remained and suffered, the mother suffered,
And the wife and the child and the musing comrade suffered,
And the armies that remained suffered.

16

Passing the visions, passing the night,   185
Passing, unloosing the hold of my comrades' hands,
Passing the song of the hermit bird and the tallying song of my soul,
Victorious song, death's outlet song, yet varying ever-altering song,
As low and wailing, yet clear the notes, rising and falling, flooding the
    night,
Sadly sinking and fainting, as warning and warning, and yet again
    bursting with joy,   190
Covering the earth and filling the spread of the heaven,
As that powerful psalm in the night I heard from recesses,
Passing, I leave thee lilac with heart-shaped leaves,
I leave thee there in the door-yard, blooming, returning with spring.

3. Askance: sideways.

I cease from my song for thee,   195
From my gaze on thee in the west, fronting the west, communing with
    thee,
O comrade lustrous with silver face in the night.

Yet each to keep and all, retrievements out of the night,
The song, the wondrous chant of the gray-brown bird,
And the tallying chant, the echo aroused in my soul,   200
With the lustrous and drooping star with the countenance full of woe,
With the holders holding my hand nearing the call of the bird,
Comrades mine and I in the midst, and their memory ever to keep, for
    the dead I loved so well,
For the sweetest, wisest soul of all my days and lands—and this for his
    dear sake,
Lilac and star and bird twined with the chant of my soul,   205
There in the fragrant pines and the cedars dusk and dim.
1865–66

GERARD MANLEY HOPKINS

The Windhover[1]

To Christ Our Lord

I caught this morning morning's minion,[2] king-
      dom of daylight's dauphin,[3] dapple-dawn-drawn Falcon, in his
      riding
    Of the rolling level underneath him steady air, and striding
High there, how he rung upon the rein of a wimpling[4] wing
In his ecstasy! then off, off forth on swing,   5
    As a skate's heel sweeps smooth on a bow-bend: the hurl and
      gliding
    Rebuffed the big wind. My heart in hiding
Stirred for a bird,—the achieve of, the mastery of the thing!

Brute beauty and valor and act, oh, air, pride, plume, here
    Buckle![5] AND the fire that breaks from thee then, a billion   10
Times told lovelier, more dangerous, O my chevalier![6]

    No wonder of it: sheér plód makes plow down sillion[7]
Shine, and blue-bleak embers, ah my dear,
    Fall, gall themselves, and gash gold-vermilion.
1877

1. A small hawk, the kestrel, which habitually hovers in the air, headed into the wind.
2. Favorite, beloved.
3. Heir to regal splendor.
4. Rippling.
5. Several meanings may apply: to join closely, to prepare for battle, to grapple with, to collapse.
6. Horseman, knight.
7. The narrow strip of land between furrows in an open field divided for separate cultivation.

GALWAY KINNELL

To Christ Our Lord

The legs of the elk punctured the snow's crust
And wolves floated lightfooted on the land
Hunting Christmas elk living and frozen;
Inside snow melted in a basin, and a woman basted
A bird spread over coals by its wings and head.   5

Snow had sealed the windows; candles lit
The Christmas meal. The Christmas grace chilled
The cooked bird, being long-winded and the room cold.
During the words a boy thought, it is fitting
To eat this creature killed on the wing?   10

He had killed it himself, climbing out
Alone on snowshoes in the Christmas dawn,
The fallen snow swirling and the snowfall gone,
Heard its throat scream as the rifle shouted,
Watched it drop, and fished from the snow the dead.   15

He had not wanted to shoot. The sound
Of wings beating into the hushed air
Had stirred his love, and his fingers
Froze in his gloves, and he wondered,
Famishing, could he fire? Then he fired.   20

Now the grace praised his wicked act. At its end
The bird on the plate
Stared at his stricken appetite.
There had been nothing to do but surrender,
To kill and to eat; he ate as he had killed, with wonder.   25

At night on snowshoes on the drifting field
He wondered again, for whom had love stirred?
The stars glittered on the snow and nothing answered.
Then the Swan spread her wings, cross of the cold north,
The pattern and mirror of the acts of earth.   30

1960

T. S. ELIOT

Journey of the Magi[1]

"A cold coming we had of it,
Just the worst time of the year
For a journey, and such a long journey:
The ways deep and the weather sharp,
The very dead of winter."[2]   5
And the camels galled, sore-footed, refractory,

---

1. The wise men who followed the star
of Bethlehem. See *Matthew* 2:1–12.

2. An adaptation of a passage from a
1622 sermon by Lancelot Andrewes.

Lying down in the melting snow.
There were times we regretted
The summer palaces on slopes, the terraces,
And the silken girls bringing sherbet.   10
Then the camel men cursing and grumbling
And running away, and wanting their liquor and women,
And the night-fires going out, and the lack of shelters,
And the cities hostile and the towns unfriendly
And the villages dirty and charging high prices: 15
A hard time we had of it.
At the end we preferred to travel all night,
Sleeping in snatches,
With the voices singing in our ears, saying
That this was all folly.   20

    Then at dawn we came down to a temperate valley,
Wet, below the snow line, smelling of vegetation;
With a running stream and a water-mill beating the darkness,
And three trees on the low sky,[3]
And an old white horse galloped away in the meadow.   25
Then we came to a tavern with vine-leaves over the lintel,
Six hands at an open door dicing for pieces of silver,
And feet kicking the empty wine-skins.
But there was no information, and so we continued
And arrived at evening, not a moment too soon   30
Finding the place; it was (you may say) satisfactory.

    All this was a long time ago, I remember,
And I would do it again, but set down
This set down
This: were we led all that way for   35
Birth or Death? There was a Birth, certainly,
We had evidence and no doubt. I had seen birth and death,
But had thought they were different; this Birth was
Hard and bitter agony for us, like Death, our death.
We returned to our places, these Kingdoms,[4]   40
But no longer at ease here, in the old dispensation,
With an alien people clutching their gods.
I should be glad of another death.

1927

W. B. YEATS

The Magi[1]

Now as at all times I can see in the mind's eye,
In their stiff, painted clothes, the pale unsatisfied ones

3. Suggestive of the three crosses of the Crucifixion (*Luke* 23:32–33). The Magi see several objects which suggest later events in Christ's life: pieces of silver (see *Matthew* 26:14–16), the dicing (see *Matthew* 27:35), the white horse (see *Revelation* 6:2 and 19:11–16), and the empty wine-skins (see *Matthew* 9:14–17, possibly relevant also to lines 41–42).
4. The Bible only identifies the wise men as "from the East," and subsequent tradition has made them kings. In Persia, Magi were members of an ancient priestly caste.

1. The three wise men who visited the Christ child at Bethlehem (see *Matthew* 2:1–12). Here they seem to be identified with the Magi of Persia, an ancient priestly class associated with magic and sorcery.

Appear and disappear in the blue depth of the sky
With all their ancient faces like rain-beaten stones,
And all their helms of silver hovering side by side,   5
And all their eyes still fixed, hoping to find once more,
Being by Calvary's turbulence[2] unsatisfied,
The uncontrollable mystery on the bestial floor.

                                                1914

e. e. cummings

the season 'tis, my lovely lambs

the season 'tis, my lovely lambs,

of Sumner Volstead Christ and Co.[1]
the epoch of Mann's righteousness
the age of dollars and no sense.
Which being quite beyond dispute   5

as prove from Troy (N. Y.) to Cairo
(Egypt) the luminous dithyrambs[2]
of large immaculate unmute
antibolshevistic gents
(each manufacturing word by word   10
his own unrivalled brand of pyro
-technic blurb anent[3] the (hic)
hero dead that gladly (sic)
in far lands perished of unheard
of maladies including flu)   15

my little darlings, let us now
passionately remember how—
braving the worst, of peril heedless,
each braver than the other, each
(a typewriter within his reach)   20
upon his fearless derrière
sturdily seated—Colonel Needless
To Name and General You know who
a string of pretty medals drew

(while messrs jack james john and jim   25
in token of their country's love
received my dears the order of
The Artificial Arm and Limb)

2. The Crucifixion. See *Luke* 23:33–45.
1. The Volstead Act (1919) gave the federal government power to enforce Prohibition. "Sumner": possibly, Charles Sumner, a late 19th-century U. S. senator who was considered the leading representative of the Puritan spirit in American politics, but more probably William Sumner, a late 19th and early 20th-century laissez-faire theorist who opposed laws regulating monopolies. The Mann Act (1910) made taking a woman across a state line "for immoral purposes" a federal offense.
2. Vehement expressions on neon signs.
3. In reference to (a somewhat affected term common in early businessese). "Hic" (line 12), Latin for "here," and "sic" (line 13), Latin for "thus," sometimes appear in similar incongruent contexts, ostensibly as shortcuts to saying "here is an example" or "it is correct as it stands," but often to show off. There are, of course, also puns on both terms.

—or, since bloodshed and kindred questions
inhibit unprepared digestions,   30
come: let us mildly contemplate
beginning with his wellfilled pants
earth's biggest grafter, nothing less;
the Honorable Mr. (guess)
who, breathing on the ear of fate,   35
landed a seat in the legislat-
ure whereas tommy so and so
(an erring child of circumstance
whom the bulls[4] nabbed at 33rd)

    pulled six months for selling snow[5]   40
                                                                1926

JOHN MILTON

[Before the Fall][1]

She as a veil down to the slender waist   304
Her unadorned golden tresses wore
Dishevelled, but in wanton[2] ringlets waved
As the vine curls her tendrils, which implied
Subjection,[3] but required with gentle sway,
And by her yielded, by him best received,
Yielded with coy[4] submission, modest pride,   310
And sweet reluctant amorous delay.
Nor those mysterious parts were then concealed,
Then was not guilty shame, dishonest shame
Of nature's works, honor dishonorable,
Sin-bred, how have ye troubled all mankind   315
With shows instead, mere shows of seeming pure,
And banished from man's life his happiest life,
Simplicity and spotless innocence.
So passed they naked on, nor shunned the sight
Of God or angel, for they thought no ill.   320
So hand in hand they passed, the loveliest pair
That ever since in love's embraces met,
Adam the goodliest man of men since born
His sons, the fairest of her daughters Eve.
Under a tuft of shade that on a green   325
Stood whispering soft, by a fresh fountain side
They sat them down, and after no more toil
Of their sweet gardening labor than sufficed
To recommend cool zephyr, and made ease
More easy, wholesome thirst and appetite   330
More grateful, to their supper fruits they fell,
Nectarine[5] fruits which the compliant boughs
Yielded them, sidelong as they sat recline

---

4. Police.
5. Cocaine, but also a reminder of the season.
1. From *Paradise Lost*, Book IV. For the Biblical description of Eden, see *Genesis* 2:8–25.

2. Luxuriant.
3. The idea derives from *Genesis* 3:16 and *I Corinthians* 11:9–10.
4. Shy.
5. Sweet as nectar, the traditional drink of the gods.

On the soft downy bank damasked[6] with flowers:
The savory pulp they chew, and in the rind   335
Still as they thirsted scoop the brimming stream;
Nor gentle purpose,[7] nor endearing smiles
Wanted,[8] nor youthful dalliance as beseems
Fair couple, linked in happy nuptial league,
Alone as they. About them frisking played   340
All beasts of the earth, since wild, and of all chase[9]
In wood or wilderness, forest or den;
Sporting the lion ramped, and in his paw
Dandled the kid; bears, tigers, ounces,[1] pards,
Gamboled before them, the unwieldy elephant   345
To make them mirth used all his might, and wreathed
His lithe proboscis; close the serpent sly
Insinuating, wove with Gordian[2] twine
His braided train, and of his fatal guile
Gave proof unheeded; others on the grass   350
Couched, and now filled with pasture gazing sat,
Or bedward ruminating: for the sun
Declined was hasting now with prone career
To the Ocean Isles,[3] and in the ascending scale
Of heaven the stars that usher evening rose.   355

1667

VASSAR MILLER

Adam's Footprint

Once as a child I loved to hop
On round plump bugs and make them stop
Before they crossed a certain crack.
My bantam brawn could turn them back,
My crooked step wrenched straight to kill   5
Live pods that then screwed tight and still.

Small sinner, stripping boughs of pears,
Shinnied past sweet and wholesome airs,
How could a tree be so unclean?
Nobody knows but Augustine.[1]   10
He nuzzled pears for dam-sin's dugs[2]—
And I scrunched roly-poly bugs.

No wolf's imprint or tiger's trace
Does Christ hunt down to catch with grace
In nets of love the devious preys   15
Whose feet go softly all their days:
The foot of Adam leaves the mark
Of some child scrabbling in the dark.

1956

6. Variegated.
7. Conversation. "Nor . . . nor": neither . . . nor (a common 17th-century construction).
8. Were lacking.
9. Tracts of land.
1. Lynxes. "pʳrds": leopards.
2. Like the Gordian knot, a legendary intricate knot, finally cut by Alexander the Great.

3. The Azores; i.e., westward.
1. In his *Confessions*, Book II, St. Augustine agonizes over his theft, from a nearby tree, of pears he did not really want and meditates on the human tendency to want what is forbidden.
2. I.e., as if they were the breasts of mother-sin (with, of course, more than one pun on "dam").

ROBERT FROST

Never Again Would Birds' Song Be the Same

He would declare and could himself believe
That the birds there in all the garden round
From having heard the daylong voice of Eve
Had added to their own an oversound,
Her tone of meaning but without the words.   5
Admittedly an eloquence so soft
Could only have had an influence on birds
When call or laughter carried it aloft.
Be that as may be, she was in their song.
Moreover her voice upon their voices crossed   10
Had now persisted in the woods so long
That probably it never would be lost.
Never again would birds' song be the same.
And to do that to birds was why she came.

1942

W. S. MERWIN

Noah's Raven[3]

Why should I have returned?
My knowledge would not fit into theirs.
I found untouched the desert of the unknown,
Big enough for my feet. It is my home.
It is always beyond them. The future   5
Splits the present with the echo of my voice.
Hoarse with fulfillment, I never made promises.

1963

DENISE LEVERTOV

The Ache of Marriage

The ache of marriage:

thigh and tongue, beloved,
are heavy with it,
it throbs in the teeth

We look for communion   5
and are turned away, beloved,
each and each

It is leviathan[1] and we
in its belly

3. According to *Genesis* 8:7, Noah sent a raven out a window of the ark when the Flood waters were partially abated, and the raven flew "to and fro" until the waters were dried up from the earth. A dove, by contrast (see *Genesis* 8:8–9), returned immediately because she "found no rest for the sole of her foot."
1. A sea monster (see *Job* 41:1), often identified with the "great fish" which swallowed Jonah and kept him in its belly for three days (see *Jonah* 1:17).

looking for joy, some joy   10
not to be known outside it

two by two in the ark[2] of
the ache of it.

1964

EDGAR ALLAN POE

To Helen[1]

Helen, thy beauty is to me
  Like those Nicéan[2] barks of yore,
That gently, o'er a perfumed sea,
  The weary, way-worn wanderer bore
  To his own native shore.   5

On desperate seas long wont to roam,
  Thy hyacinth hair, thy classic face,
Thy Naiad airs[3] have brought me home
  To the glory that was Greece
And the grandeur that was Rome.   10

Lo! in yon brilliant window-niche
  How statue-like I see thee stand,
  The agate lamp within thy hand!
Ah, Psyche,[4] from the regions which
  Are Holy Land![5]   15

1831

CHRISTOPHER MARLOWE

Was This the Face that Launched a Thousand Ships[1]

Was this the face that launched a thousand ships,
  And burnt the topless towers of Ilium?[2]
Sweet Helen, make me immortal with a kiss!
  Her lips suck forth my soul;[3] see where it flies.

2. According to *Genesis* 7:9, all beasts and creatures "went in two and two . . . into the ark, male and female," and their isolation lasted until the Flood ended civilization. Another kind of ark, a chest containing the Ten Commandments and later called the Ark of the Covenant of God, was carried everywhere on their wanderings by the ancient Hebrews as a symbol of God's presence (see, e.g., *I Kings* 8:1–11 and *II Samuel* 6); it was later built into the eastern wall of synagogues to symbolize the Holy of Holies of the Temple.
1. Helen of Troy, the traditional type of beauty. Hers was "the face that launched a thousand ships," and her elopement caused the siege and destruction of Troy described in Homer's *Iliad* and the first books of Vergil's *Aeneid*. After the war she returned to her husband.
2. The reference is uncertain: possibly, the island of Nysa (which Milton's *Paradise Lost* calls the "Nyseian Isle," IV, 275) in the river Triton in North Africa, where Bacchus was safely protected from Rhea; or

pertaining to the ancient city of Nicaea, a Byzantine seaport.
3. Graceful manners of a water nymph.
4. A beautiful maiden who, according to Apuleius's *Golden Ass*, was beloved by Cupid but deprived of him when she lit a lamp, disobeying his order that she never seek to know who he was. The word *psyche* in Greek means "soul."
5. In an 1836 review essay, Poe facetiously quotes a medieval monk who said that "Helen represents the Human Soul— Troy is Hell."
1. From Marlowe's play, *Dr. Faustus*. The title character overwhelmingly desires power through knowledge and sells his soul to the devil to gain it. In the last act, he conjures up Helen from the dead and speaks these lines.
2. Another name for Troy.
3. In Greek, the word for soul and breath were the same (*psuche* or *psyche*), and according to some philosophers the soul was present in breath.

Come, Helen, come, give me my soul again.   5
Here will I dwell, for heaven is in these lips,
And all is dross that is not Helena.
I will be Paris, and for love of thee
Instead of Troy shall Wittenberg[4] be sacked,
And I will combat with weak Menelaus,[5]   10
And wear thy colors on my pluméd crest.
Yea, I will wound Achilles in the heel,
And then return to Helen for a kiss.
O, thou art fairer than the evening's air,
Clad in the beauty of a thousand stars.   15
Brighter art thou than flaming Jupiter,
When he appeared to hapless Semele;[6]
More lovely than the monarch of the sky,
In wanton Arethusa's azured arms,[7]
And none but thou shalt be my paramour.   20

ca. 1588–92

H. D. (HILDA DOOLITTLE)

Helen

All Greece[1] hates
the still eyes in the white face,
the luster as of olives
where she stands,
and the white hands.   5

All Greece reviles
the wan face when she smiles,
hating it deeper still
when it grows wan and white,
remembering past enchantments   10
and past ills.

Greece sees unmoved
God's daughter, born of love,[2]
the beauty of cool feet
and slenderest of knees,   15
could love indeed the maid,
only if she were laid,
white ash amid funereal cypresses.

1924

---

4. The setting for Marlowe's play.
5. Helen's husband. Paris, Helen's abductor, later fought with Menelaus in single combat during the Trojan War and was badly beaten (*Iliad*, III). He later killed Achilles (line 12), however, when the gods directed his arrow so that it struck Achilles' only vulnerable part.
6. Jupiter (Zeus, Jove) was the father of Semele's child, Dionysus, but when she asked that he appear before her as the god of thunder, the lightning killed her.
7. In Greek mythology, Arethusa was a wood-nymph bathing in a river when

Alpheus, the god of the stream, began to pursue her. Diana helped her escape underground, and she later re-emerged as a fountain, but even so Alpheus finally caught her and his waters were mingled with hers. See Ovid's *Metamorphoses*, Book V. "Wanton": merciless, luxuriant.
1. Helen's husband, Menelaus, was King of Sparta; the Greeks attacked Troy to get her back from Paris, son of the Trojan king.
2. Helen was the daughter of Zeus, king of the gods, and Leda.

ALFRED, LORD TENNYSON

Ulysses[1]

It little profits that an idle king,
By this still hearth, among these barren crags,
Matched with an agéd wife,[2] I mete and dole
Unequal laws unto a savage race,
That hoard, and sleep, and feed, and know not me.   5

I cannot rest from travel; I will drink
Life to the lees.[3] All times I have enjoyed
Greatly, have suffered greatly, both with those
That loved me, and alone; on shore, and when
Through scudding drifts the rainy Hyades[4]   10
Vexed the dim sea. I am become a name;
For always roaming with a hungry heart
Much have I seen and known—cities of men
And manners, climates, councils, governments,
Myself not least, but honored of them all—   15
And drunk delight of battle with my peers,
Far on the ringing plains of windy Troy.
I am a part of all that I have met;
Yet all experience is an arch wherethrough
Gleams that untraveled world, whose margin fades   20
For ever and for ever when I move.
How dull it is to pause, to make an end,
To rust unburnished, not to shine in use!
As though to breathe were life. Life piled on life
Were all too little, and of one to me   25
Little remains; but every hour is saved
From that eternal silence, something more,
A bringer of new things; and vile it were
For some three suns to store and hoard myself,
And this gray spirit yearning in desire   30
To follow knowledge like a sinking star,
Beyond the utmost bound of human thought.

This is my son, mine own Telemachus,
To whom I leave the scepter and the isle—
Well-loved of me, discerning to fulfill   35
This labor by slow prudence to make mild
A rugged people, and through soft degrees
Subdue them to the useful and the good.
Most blameless is he, centered in the sphere
Of common duties, decent not to fail   40
In offices of tenderness, and pay
Meet adoration to my household gods,
When I am gone. He works his work, I mine.

1. After the end of the Trojan War, Ulysses (or Odysseus), King of Ithaca and one of the Greek heroes of the war, returned to his island home (line 34). Homer's account of the situation is in the *Odyssey*, Book XI, but Dante's account of Ulysses in *The Inferno*, XXVI, is the more immediate background of the poem.
2. Penelope.
3. All the way down to the bottom of the cup.
4. A group of stars which were supposed to predict rain when they rose at the same time as the sun.

There lies the port; the vessel puffs her sail:
There gloom the dark, broad seas. My mariners,   45
Souls that have toiled, and wrought, and thought with me—
That ever with a frolic welcome took
The thunder and the sunshine, and opposed
Free hearts, free foreheads—you and I are old;
Old age hath yet his honor and his toil.   50
Death closes all; but something ere the end,
Some work of noble note, may yet be done,
Not unbecoming men that strove with Gods.
The lights begin to twinkle from the rocks;
The long day wanes; the slow moon climbs; the deep   55
Moans round with many voices. Come, my friends.
'Tis not too late to seek a newer world.
Push off, and sitting well in order smite
The sounding furrows; for my purpose holds
To sail beyond the sunset, and the baths   60
Of all the western stars, until I die.
It may be that the gulfs will wash us down;[5]
It may be we shall touch the Happy Isles,[6]
And see the great Achilles, whom we knew.
Though much is taken, much abides; and though   65
We are not now that strength which in old days
Moved earth and heaven, that which we are, we are:
One equal temper of heroic hearts,
Made weak by time and fate, but strong in will
To strive, to seek, to find, and not to yield.   70

1833

PETER VIERECK

Kilroy[1]

Also Ulysses once—that other war.[2]
    (Is it because we find his scrawl
    Today on every privy door
    That we forget his ancient role?)
Also was there—he did it for the wages—   5
When a Cathay-drunk Genoese set sail.[3]
Whenever "longen folk to goon on pilgrimages,"[4]
Kilroy is there;
        he tells The Miller's Tale.

At times he seems a paranoiac king   10
Who stamps his crest on walls and says "My Own!"

---

5. Beyond the Gulf of Gibraltar was supposed to be a chasm that led to Hades.
6. Elysium, the Islands of the Blessed, where heroes like Achilles (line 64) abide after death.
1. A fictitious character in World War II who symbolized American daring and ingenuity; the phrase "Kilroy was here" was carved and scribbled everywhere, all over the world.
2. The Trojan War, in which Ulysses became a hero and a mythic symbol of the bold voyager who thrived on action and adventure.
3. When Columbus set sail from Genoa, he intended to find a new trade route to China (Cathay).
4. An early line in the "General Prologue" to Chaucer's *Canterbury Tales*, explaining the rationale for the journey on which the *Tales* are built. "The Miller's Tale" (line 9) is the bawdiest of the tales, and one of the most spirited.

But in the end he fades like a lost tune,
Tossed here and there, whom all the breezes sing.
"Kilroy was here"; these words sound wanly gay,
   Haughty yet tired with long marching.   15
He is Orestes[5]—guilty of what crime?—
   For whom the Furies still are searching;
   When they arrive, they find their prey
(Leaving his name to mock them) went away.
Sometimes he does not flee from them in time: 20
"*Kilroy was—*"
    (*with his blood a dying man*
    Wrote half the phrase out in Bataan.[6])

Kilroy, beware. "HOME" is the final trap
That lurks for you in many a wily shape: 25
In pipe-and-slippers plus a Loyal Hound
   Or fooling around, just fooling around.
Kind to the old (their warm Penelope[7])
But fierce to boys,
    thus "home" becomes that sea,   30
Horribly disguised, where you were always drowned—
   (How could suburban Crete[8] condone
The yarns you would have V-mailed[9] from the sun?)—
And folksy fishes sip Icarian tea.[1]
One stab of hopeless wings imprinted your   35
   Exultant Kilroy-signature
Upon sheer sky for all the world to stare:
   "*I was there! I was there! I was there!*"

God is like Kilroy. He, too, sees it all;
That's how He knows of every sparrow's fall;[2]   40
That's why we prayed each time the tightropes cracked
On which our loveliest clowns contrived their act.
The G. I. Faustus[3] who was
    everywhere
Strolled home again. "What was it like outside?"   45
Asked Can't, with his good neighbors Ought and But
And pale Perhaps and grave-eyed Better Not;
For "Kilroy" means: the world is very wide.
   He was there, he was there, he was there!

And in the suburbs Can't sat down and cried.   50
                 1948

---

5. The son of Agamemnon and Clytemnestra in Greek myth. After his mother killed his father, he avenged the death by killing her, and the Furies (line 17) pursued him from country to country.

6. The site, in the Philippine Islands, of two major battle campaigns in World War II.

7. Wife of Ulysses.

8. According to Pindar, the Cretans were incredible liars.

9. V-Mail was an overseas military mail system used in World War II. Letters were microfilmed, for compact transportation, and then re-enlarged before delivery.

1. Icarus, the son of Daedalus, flew with his father from Crete (line 32), but he strayed too near the sun, the wax which attached his wings melted, and he fell into the sea, which then became known as the Icarian Sea. "Icarian" once meant venturesome.

2. According to *Matthew* 10:29, even a sparrow "shall not fall on the ground" without God's knowledge of it.

3. The 16th-century astrologer and magician who became a symbol of man's desire to know everything regardless of the cost.

MATTHEW ARNOLD

Philomela[1]

Hark! ah, the nightingale—
The tawny-throated!
Hark, from that moonlit cedar what a burst!
What triumph! hark!—what pain!

O wanderer from a Grecian shore,   5
Still, after many years, in distant lands,
Still nourishing in thy bewildered brain
That wild, unquenched, deep-sunken, old-world pain—
Say, will it never heal?
And can this fragrant lawn   10
With its cool trees, and night,
And the sweet, tranquil Thames,
And moonshine, and the dew,
To thy racked heart and brain
Afford no balm?   15

Dost thou tonight behold,
Here, through the moonlight on this English grass,
The unfriendly palace in the Thracian wild?
Dost thou again peruse
With hot cheeks and seared eyes   20
The too clear web,[2] and thy dumb sister's shame?
Dost thou once more assay
Thy flight, and feel come over thee,
Poor fugitive, the feathery change
Once more, and once more seem to make resound   25
With love and hate, triumph and agony,
Lone Daulis, and the high Cephissian vale?[3]
Listen, Eugenia[4]—
How thick the bursts come crowding through the leaves!
Again—thou hearest?   30
Eternal passion!
Eternal pain!

1848

1. According to Greek legend, Philomela turned into a nightingale at Daulis (line 27) after a bizarre series of events and re- venges. Philomela's husband, King Tereus of Thrace, raped her sister, Procne, and cut out her tongue (see line 21) to prevent disclosure. But Procne wove a tapestry re- vealing the story and then killed Tereus' son in revenge and fed him the flesh. The gods turned Philomela into a nightingale and Procne into a swallow so that they could escape Tereus' wrath. In some ver- sions, the roles of the sisters are reversed; see, e.g., Swinburne's "When the Hounds of Spring."
2. The tapestry.
3. The home of Tereus.
4. An imaginary listener.

T. S. ELIOT

Sweeney Among the Nightingales

ὤμοι, πέπληγμαι καιρίαν\πληγὴν ἔσω.[1]

Apeneck Sweeney[2] spreads his knees
Letting his arms hang down to laugh,
The zebra stripes along his jaw
Swelling to maculate[3] giraffe.

The circles of the stormy moon   5
Slide westward toward the River Plate,[4]
Death and the Raven[5] drift above
And Sweeney guards the hornéd gate.[6]

Gloomy Orion and the Dog[7]
Are veiled; and hushed the shrunken seas;   10
The person in the Spanish cape
Tries to sit on Sweeney's knees

Slips and pulls the table cloth
Overturns a coffee-cup,
Reorganized upon the floor   15
She yawns and draws a stocking up;

The silent man in mocha brown
Sprawls at the window-sill and gapes;
The waiter brings in oranges
Bananas figs and hothouse grapes;   20

The silent vertebrate in brown
Contracts and concentrates, withdraws;
Rachel *née* Rabinovitch
Tears at the grapes with murderous paws;

She and the lady in the cape   25
Are suspect, thought to be in league;
Therefore the man with heavy eyes
Declines the gambit, shows fatigue,

Leaves the room and reappears
Outside the window, leaning in,   30
Branches of wistaria
Circumscribe a golden grin;

1. The cry of Agamemnon as he is stabbed by his wife Clytemnestra inside the palace: "Oh, I have been struck a mortal blow—within," Aeschylus, *Agamemnon*, line 1343. Agamemnon, the king of Mycenae in Greek legend, had just returned from the Trojan War, where he had been a leader and hero.
2. Eliot's respresentation, in several different poems, of modern vulgarity.
3. Spotted.

4. The Río de la Plata, an estuary between Uruguay and Argentina.
5. The constellation Corvus of the Southern Hemisphere.
6. The gate, according to Greek legend, through which true dreams come; false dreams come through the gates of ivory.
7. Sirius, the dog-star, and the constellation Orion, named (because of its appearance) for the giant hunter of Greek myth.

The host with someone indistinct
Converses at the door apart,
The nightingales are singing near
The Convent of the Sacred Heart,

        35

And sang within the bloody wood
When Agamemnon cried aloud,
And let their liquid siftings fall
To stain the stiff dishonored shroud.

        40

1920

e. e. cummings

chanson innocente

in Just-
spring   when the world is mud-
luscious the little
lame balloonman

whistles   far   and wee   5

and eddieandbill come
running from marbles and
piracies and it's
spring

when the world is puddle-wonderful   10

the queer
old balloonman whistles
far   and   wee
and bettyandisbel come dancing

from hop-scotch and jump-rope and   15

it's
spring
and
    the

        goat-footed   20

balloonMan   whistles
far
and
wee[3]

1923

3. Pan, whose Greek name means "everything," is traditionally represented with a syrinx (or the pipes of Pan). The upper half of his body is human, the lower half goat, and as the father of Silenus he is associated with the spring rites of Dionysus.

ISHMAEL REED

I Am a Cowboy in the Boat of Ra

"The devil must be forced to reveal any such physical evil (potions, charms, fetishes, etc.) still outside the body and these must be burned."—RITUALE ROMANUM, *published 1947, endorsed by the coat of arms and introduction letter from Francis Cardinal Spellman*

I am a cowboy in the boat of Ra,[1]
sidewinders in the saloons of fools
bit my forehead   like   O
the untrustworthiness of Egyptologists
Who do not know their trips. Who was that   5
dog-faced man? they asked, the day I rode
from town.

School marms with halitosis cannot see
the Nefertiti[2] fake chipped on the run by slick
germans, the hawk behind Sonny Rollins' head or   10
the ritual beard of his axe,[3] a longhorn winding
its bells thru the Field of Reeds.

I am a cowboy in the boat of Ra. I bedded
down with Isis,[4] Lady of the Boogaloo, dove
down deep in her horny, stuck up her Wells-Far-ago   15
in daring midday get away. "Start grabbing the
blue," i said from top of my double crown.

I am a cowboy in the boat of Ra. Ezzard Charles[5]
of the Chisholm Trail. Took up the bass but they
blew off my thumb. Alchemist in ringmanship but a   20
sucker for the right cross.

I am a cowboy in the boat of Ra. Vamoosed from
the temple i bide my time. The price on the wanted
poster was a-going down, outlaw alias copped my stance
and moody greenhorns were making me dance; while my mouth's   25
shooting iron got its chambers jammed.

I am a cowboy in the boat of Ra. Boning-up in
the ol West i bide my time. You should see
me pick off these tin cans whippersnappers. I
write the motown long plays for the comeback of   30
Osiris.[6] Make them up when stars stare at sleeping

1. The chief of the ancient Egyptian gods, the creator and protector of men and the vanquisher of evil. He was one of the many forms of the sun-god, and all the pharaohs are supposed to descend from him. Throughout, the poem draws heavily upon Egyptian mythology as well as upon American cowboy lore.
2. 14th-century B.C. Egyptian queen. The most famous bust of her (of painted limestone) was discovered and taken to Berlin in 1933. Elsewhere, Reed says that German scholars are responsible for the notion that her dynasty was white.
3. Musical instrument. Sonny Rollins was considered one of the most innovative young jazz musicians of the late 1950s and early 1960s, a modernizer of the tenor sax tradition established by Coleman Hawkins.
4. The principal goddess of ancient Egypt; cows were sacred to her.
5. World heavyweight boxing champion, 1949–51.
6. Husband of Isis and one of the major gods of Egyptian mythology. He is the constant foe of his brother Set (line 48), a pervasive fertility symbol, and he often represents the setting sun. He was also, according to legend, the mortal king who changed Egypt from a primitive society to a civilized one, teaching his people to grow corn and make wine from the grape. He died violently, tricked by Set, but later rose from the dead.

steer out here near the campfire. Women arrive
on the backs of goats and throw themselves on
my Bowie.[7]

I am a cowboy in the boat of Ra. Lord of the lash,   35
the Loup Garou[8] Kid. Half breed son of Pisces and
Aquarius. I hold the souls of men in my pot. I do
the dirty boogie with scorpions. I make the bulls
keep still and was the first swinger to grape the taste.

I am a cowboy in his boat. Pope Joan[9] of the   40
Ptah Ra.[1] C/mere a minute willya doll?
Be a good girl and
Bring me my Buffalo horn of black powder
Bring me my headdress of black feathers
Bring me my bones of Ju-Ju snake   45
Go get my eyelids of red paint.
Hand me my shadow
I'm going into town after Set[2]

I am a cowboy in the boat of Ra
look out Set   here i come Set   50
to get Set   to sunset Set
to unseat Set   to Set down Set
                  usurper of the Royal couch
                  imposter RAdio of Moses' bush[3]
                  party pooper O hater of dance   55
                  vampire outlaw of the milky way

                                                                    1969

DAVID DIOP

Africa[1]

Africa my Africa
Africa of proud warriors in ancestral savannahs[2]
Africa of whom my grandmother sings
On the banks of the distant river
I have never known you   5
But your blood flows in my veins[3]
Your beautiful black blood that irrigates the fields
The blood of your sweat
The sweat of your work

7. Heavy-sheathed hunting knife, more
than a foot long, named after James Bowie,
who died at the Alamo.
8. The leader of the giants in Rabelais'
Gargantua and Pantagruel, and a character
in Reed's novel, *Yellow Back Radio Broke-
down*. "Loup-garou" in French means
werewolf, and in voodoo it refers to a priest
who has run amuck or gone mad.
9. A mythical female pope, supposed to
have succeeded Leo IV to the papacy in
855.
1. The chief god of Memphis, the capital of ancient Egypt.
2. Brother of Osiris, usually portrayed
as the principle of evil itself, but sometimes as the protector of the sun-god's boat.
As ugly as his brother is beautiful, he is
associated with the opposite of Osiris' qualities and dominions; he is, e.g., connected
with deserts, as Osiris is with fertile land.
3. Which, according to *Exodus* 3:2,
burned but was not consumed and from
which Moses heard the voice of God telling
him to lead the Israelites out of Egypt.
1. Translated from the French by Gerard Moore and Ulli Beier.
2. Flat, treeless grasslands.
3. Diop was born in France of a Sene-
galese father and a Cameroonian mother;
during his childhood he traveled back and
forth to West Africa.

The work of your slavery   10
The slavery of your children
Africa tell me Africa
Is this you this back that is bent
This back that breaks under the weight of humiliation
This back trembling with red scars   15
And saying yes to the whip under the midday sun
But a grave voice answers me
Impetuous son that tree young and strong
That tree there
In splendid loneliness amidst white and faded flowers   20
That is Africa your Africa
That grows again patiently obstinately
And its fruit gradually acquire
The bitter taste of liberty.

                                                           1956

LANGSTON HUGHES

The Negro Speaks of Rivers

I've known rivers:
I've known rivers ancient as the world and older than the flow of human
    blood in human veins.

My soul has grown deep like the rivers.

I bathed in the Euphrates when dawns were young.
I built my hut near the Congo and it lulled me to sleep.   5

I looked upon the Nile and raised the pyramids above it.
I heard the singing of the Mississippi when Abe Lincoln went down
    to New Orleans, and I've seen its muddy bosom turn all golden in
    the sunset.

I've known rivers:
Ancient, dusky rivers.

My soul has grown deep like the rivers.   10

                                                           1926

JOHN PEALE BISHOP

Speaking of Poetry

The ceremony must be found
that will wed Desdemona to the huge Moor.[1]

It is not enough—
to win the approval of the Senator

1. Othello. In Shakespeare's play Desdemona is, of course, married to Othello, but the
ceremony was performed secretly and her father and the other Venetian senators are outraged nearly to the point of killing Othello. As a military leader, he is their hero, but he
is not their idea of an appropriate husband for a Venetian aristocrat.

or to outwit his disapproval; honest Iago[2]   5
can manage that: it is not enough. For then,
though she may pant again in his black arms
(his weight resilient as a Barbary stallion's)
she will be found
when the ambassadors of the Venetian state arrive   10
again smothered. These things have not been changed,
not in three hundred years.

        (Tupping is still tupping
though that particular word is obsolete.[3]
Naturally, the ritual would not be in Latin.)   15

For though Othello had his blood from kings
his ancestry was barbarous, his ways African,
his speech uncouth. It must be remembered
that though he valued an embroidery—
three mulberries proper on a silk like silver—   20
it was not for the subtlety of the stitches,
but for the magic in it. Whereas, Desdemona
once contrived to imitate in needlework
her father's shield, and plucked it out
three times, to begin again, each time   25
with diminished colors. This is a small point
but indicative.

        Desdemona was small and fair,
delicate as a grasshopper
at the tag-end of summer: a Venetian   30
to her noble finger tips.

        O, it is not enough
that they should meet, naked, at dead of night
in a small inn on a dark canal. Procurers
less expert than Iago can arrange as much.   35

The ceremony must be found

Traditional, with all its symbols
ancient as the metaphors in dreams;
strange, with never before heard music; continuous
until the torches deaden at the bedroom door.   40

1925

KENNETH HANSON

The Distance Anywhere

My neighbor, a lady from Fu-kien[1]
has rearranged her yard completely.

2. Othello often addresses the play's villain as "Honest Iago."
3. When he announces the elopement to Desdemona's father, Iago says that "an old black ram is tupping your white ewe" (Act I, sc. i, 88–89).
1. Province in southeastern China.

She has cut down the willow tree,
burning it, piecemeal, against a city
ordinance, and has put in its place   5
her garden of strange herbs.

I confess I resent the diligence
her side of the fence—the stink
of that oriental spinach she hangs
on the clothesline to dry, and the squawk   10
of the chicken I suspect she keeps,
against a city ordinance, shut up
in the white garage, eventual soup.

But when, across the rows of what-
ever she grows, she brings her   15
fabulous speech to bear, birds
in the trees, the very butterflies
unbend, acknowledging, to syllables
of that exacter scale, she'd make
the neighborhood, the unaccustomed   20
air, for all the world to see,
sight, sound and smell, Fu-kien,
beyond our ordinances, clear.

                                                       1954

KENNETH PATCHEN

Gautama in the Deer Park at Benares[1]

In a hut of mud and fire
Sits this single man—"Not to want
Money, to want a life in the world,
To want no trinkets on my name"—
And he was rich; his life lives where   5
Death cannot go; his honor stares
At the sun.

The fawn sleeps. The little winds
Ruffle the earth's green hair. It is
Wonderful to live. My sword rusts   10
In the pleasant rain. I shall not think
Anymore. I touch the face of my friend;
He shows his dirty teeth as he scratches
At a flea—and we grin. It is warm
And the rice stirs usefully in our bellies.   15

The fawn raises its head—the sun floods
Its soft eye with the kingdoms of life—
I think we should all go to sleep now,
And not care anymore.

                                                   1943

1. Where Gautama first preached after he reached the state of perfect illumination
(nirvana) and thereby became a Buddha ("the enlightened").

RALPH WALDO EMERSON

Brahma[1]

If the red slayer[2] think he slays,
　Or if the slain think he is slain,
They know not well the subtle ways
　I keep, and pass, and turn again.

Far or forgot to me is near;　　　　　　　　5
　Shadow and sunlight are the same;
The vanished gods to me appear;
　And one to me are shame and fame.

They reckon ill who leave me out;
　When me they fly, I am the wings;　　　　　10
I am the doubter and the doubt,
　And I the hymn the Brahmin sings.

The strong gods[3] pine for my abode,
　And pine in vain the sacred Seven;[4]
But thou, meek lover of the good!　　　　　　15
　Find me, and turn thy back on heaven.

1856

TU FU

Night in the House by the River[1]

It is late in the year;
Yin and Yang[2] struggle
In the brief sunlight.
On the desert mountains
Frost and snow　　　　　　　　　　　　5
Gleam in the freezing night.
Past midnight,
Drums and bugles ring out,
Violent, cutting the heart.
Over the Triple Gorge the Milky Way　　　　10
Pulsates between the stars.
The bitter cries of thousands of households
Can be heard above the noise of battle.
Everywhere the workers sing wild songs.
The great heroes and generals of old time　　15
Are yellow dust forever now.
Such are the affairs of men.
Poetry and letters
Persist in silence and solitude.

ca. 750

1. Both the supreme god of the Hindus and the absolute, unchanging, and impersonal reality which contrasts with the changing and illusory world of experience.
2. Siva the destroyer, with Brahma and Vishnu one of the persons of the Hindu Trimurti (trinity). He represents the destructive principle in life, but also the restorative principle.
3. Devas, similar to angels.
4. The highest Hindu saints.
1. Translated from the Chinese by Kenneth Rexroth.
2. The passive and active cosmic principles, always complementary, in Chinese dualistic philosophy.

W. B. YEATS

Easter 1916[1]

I have met them at close of day
Coming with vivid faces
From counter or desk among grey
Eighteenth-century houses.
I have passed with a nod of the head   5
Or polite meaningless words,
Or have lingered awhile and said
Polite meaningless words,
And thought before I had done
Of a mocking tale or a gibe   10
To please a companion
Around the fire at the club,
Being certain that they and I
But lived where motley[2] is worn:
All changed, changed utterly: 15
A terrible beauty is born.

That woman's[3] days were spent
In ignorant good-will,
Her nights in argument
Until her voice grew shrill.   20
What voice more sweet than hers
When, young and beautiful,
She rode to harriers?[4]
This man[5] had kept a school
And rode our wingéd horse;[6]   25
This other[7] his helper and friend
Was coming into his force;
He might have won fame in the end,
So sensitive his nature seemed,
So daring and sweet his thought.   30
This other man[8] I had dreamed
A drunken, vainglorious lout.
He had done most bitter wrong
To some who are near my heart,
Yet I number him in the song;   35
He, too, has resigned his part
In the casual comedy;

1. The famous Easter uprising began on Easter Monday when an Irish republic was proclaimed by nationalist leaders, but English military forces responded quickly; by April 29, some 300 people were dead and the Nationalists surrendered. Early in May, 15 leaders (including the four mentioned in lines 75–76) were executed, and more than 2,000 were held prisoners.
2. The particolored clothing of a professional fool or jester, at court or in a play.
3. Countess Constance Georgina Markiewicz, a beautiful and well-born young woman from County Sligo who became a vigorous and bitter nationalist. At first condemned to death, she later had her sentence commuted to life imprisonment, and she gained amnesty in 1917.
4. Hounds.
5. Patrick Pearse, who led the assault on the Dublin Post Office from which the proclamation of a republic was issued. A schoolmaster by profession, he had vigorously supported the restoration of the Gaelic language in Ireland and was an active political writer and poet.
6. Pegasus, the traditional symbol of poetic inspiration.
7. Thomas MacDonagh, also a writer and teacher.
8. Major John MacBride, who had married Yeats's beloved Maud Gonne in 1903 but separated from her two years later.

He, too, has been changed in his turn,
Transformed utterly:
A terrible beauty is born.   40

Hearts with one purpose alone
Through summer and winter seem
Enchanted to a stone
To trouble the living stream.
The horse that comes from the road,   45
The rider, the birds that range
From cloud to tumbling cloud,
Minute by minute they change;
A shadow of cloud on the stream
Changes minute by minute;   50
A horse-hoof slides on the brim,
And a horse plashes within it;
The long-legged moor-hens dive,
And hens to moor-cocks call;
Minute by minute they live: 55
The stone's in the midst of all.

Too long a sacrifice
Can make a stone of the heart.
O when may it suffice?
That is Heaven's part, our part   60
To murmur name upon name,
As a mother names her child
When sleep at last has come
On limbs that had run wild.
What is it but nightfall?   65
No, no, not night but death;
Was it needless death after all?
For England may keep faith[9]
For all that is done and said.
We know their dream; enough
To know they dreamed and are dead;   70
And what if excess of love
Bewildered them till they died?
I write it out in a verse—
MacDonagh and MacBride   75
And Connolly[1] and Pearse
Now and in time to be,
Wherever green is worn,
Are changed, changed utterly:
A terrible beauty is born.   80

1916

---

9. Before the uprising the English had promised eventual home rule to Ireland.

1. James Connolly, the leader of the Easter uprising.

W. B. YEATS

The Second Coming[1]

Turning and turning in the widening gyre[2]
The falcon cannot hear the falconer;
Things fall apart; the center cannot hold;
Mere anarchy is loosed upon the world,
The blood-dimmed tide is loosed, and everywhere   5
The ceremony of innocence is drowned;
The best lack all conviction, while the worst
Are full of passionate intensity.

Surely some revelation is at hand;
Surely the Second Coming is at hand.   10
The Second Coming! Hardly are those words out
When a vast image out of *Spiritus Mundi*[3]
Troubles my sight: somewhere in sands of the desert
A shape with lion body and the head of a man,
A gaze blank and pitiless as the sun,   15
Is moving its slow thighs, while all about it
Reel shadows of the indignant desert birds.[4]
The darkness drops again; but now I know
That twenty centuries of stony sleep
Were vexed to nightmare by a rocking cradle,   20
And what rough beast, its hour come round at last,
Slouches towards Bethlehem to be born?

p. 1920

W. B. YEATS

Leda and the Swan[1]

A sudden blow: the great wings beating still
Above the staggering girl, her thighs caressed
By the dark webs, her nape caught in his bill,
He holds her helpless breast upon his breast.

1. The Second Coming of Christ, according to *Matthew* 24:29–44, will come after a time of "tribulation." Disillusioned by Ireland's continued civil strife, Yeats saw his time as the end of another historical cycle. In *A Vision* (1937) Yeats describes his view of history as dependent on cycles of about 2000 years: the birth of Christ had ended the cycle of Greco-Roman civilization, and now the Christian cycle seemed near an end, to be followed by an antithetical cycle, ominous in its portents.
2. Literally, the widening spiral of a falcon's flight. "Gyre" is Yeats's term for a cycle of history, which he diagrammed in terms of a series of interpenetrating cones.
3. Or *Anima Mundi*, the spirit or soul of the world, a consciousness in which the individual participates. Yeats considered this universal consciousness or memory a fund from which poets drew their images and symbols. In *Per Amica Silentia Lunae* he wrote: "Before the mind's eye, whether in sleep or waking, came images that one was to discover presently in some book one

had never read, and after looking in vain for explanation . . . , I came to believe in a great memory passing on from generation to generation."
4. Yeats later writes of the "brazen winged beast . . . described in my poem *The Second Coming*" as "associated with laughing, ecstatic destruction." "Our civilization was about to reverse itself, or some new civilization about to be born from all that our age had rejected . . . ; because we had worshipped a single god it would worship many."
1. According to Greek myth, Zeus took the form of a swan to seduce Leda, who became the mother of Helen of Troy and also of Clytemnestra, Agamemnon's wife and murderer. Helen's abduction from her husband, Menelaus, brother of Agamemnon, began the Trojan War (line 10). Yeats described the visit of Zeus to Leda as an annunciation like that to Mary (see *Luke* 1:26–38): "I imagine the annunciation that founded Greece as made to Leda. . . ." (*A Vision*).

How can those terrified vague fingers push
The feathered glory from her loosening thighs?
And how can body, laid in that white rush,
But feel the strange heart beating where it lies?

A shudder in the loins engenders there
The broken wall, the burning roof and tower   10
And Agamemnon dead.
               Being so caught up,
So mastered by the brute blood of the air,
Did she put on his knowledge with his power
Before the indifferent beak could let her drop?

1923

W. B. YEATS

Sailing to Byzantium[1]

I

That[2] is no country for old men. The young
In one another's arms, birds in the trees
—Those dying generations—at their song,
The salmon-falls, the mackerel-crowded seas
Fish, flesh, or fowl, commend all summer long   5
Whatever is begotten, born, and dies.
Caught in that sensual music all neglect
Monuments of unaging intellect.

II

An aged man is but a paltry thing,
A tattered coat upon a stick, unless   10
Soul clap its hands and sing, and louder sing
For every tatter in its mortal dress,
Nor is there singing school but studying
Monuments of its own magnificence;
And therefore I have sailed the seas and come   15
To the holy city of Byzantium.

1. The ancient name of Istanbul, the capital and holy city of Eastern Christendom from the late fourth century until 1453. It was famous for its stylized and formal mosaics, its symbolic, nonnaturalistic art, and its highly developed intellectual life. Yeats repeatedly uses it to symbolize a world of artifice and timelessness, free from the decay and death of the natural and sensual world. In *A Vision*, Yeats wrote: "I think if I could be given a month of Antiquity and leave to spend it where I chose, I would spend it in Byzantium a little before Justinian opened St. Sophia and closed the Academy of Plato [about 535 A.D.]. I think I could find in some little wineshop some philosophical worker in mosaic who could answer all my questions, the supernatural descending nearer to him than to Plotinus even, for the pride of his delicate skill would make what was an instrument of power to princes and clerics, a murderous madness in the mob, show as a lovely flexible presence like that of a perfect human body. I think that in early Byzantium, maybe never before or since in recorded history, religious, aesthetic and practical life were one, that architect and artificers . . . spoke to the multitude and the few alike. The painter, the mosaic worker, the worker in gold and silver, the illuminator of sacred books, were almost impersonal, almost perhaps without the consciousness of individual design, absorbed in their subject-matter and that the vision of the whole people. They could . . . weave all into a vast design, the work of many that seemed the work of one, that made building, picture, metal-work or rail and lamp, seem but a single image. . . ."

2. Ireland, as an instance of the natural, temporal world.

III

O sages standing in God's holy fire
As in the gold mosaic of a wall,
Come from the holy fire, perne in a gyre,[3]
And be the singing-masters of my soul.   20
Consume my heart away; sick with desire
And fastened to a dying animal
It knows not what it is; and gather me
Into the artifice of eternity.

IV

Once out of nature I shall never take   25
My bodily form from any natural thing,
But such a form as Grecian goldsmiths make
Of hammered gold and gold enameling
To keep a drowsy Emperor awake;[4]
Or set upon a golden bough[5] to sing   30
To lords and ladies of Byzantium
Of what is past, or passing, or to come.

1927

W. B. YEATS

Two Songs from a Play[1]

I

I saw a staring virgin stand
Where holy Dionysus[2] died,
And tear the heart out of his side,
And lay the heart upon her hand
And bear that beating heart away;   5
And then did all the Muses sing
Of Magnus Annus[3] at the spring,
As though God's death were but a play.

Another Troy must rise and set,
Another lineage feed the crow,   10
Another Argo's[4] painted prow

3. I.e., whirl in a coiling motion, so that his soul may merge with its motion as the timeless world invades the cycles of history and nature. The gyre in "The Second Coming" moves in the opposite direction, up and out centripetally, so that "things fall apart." "Perne" is Yeats's coinage (from the noun "pirn"): to spin around in the kind of spiral pattern that thread makes as it comes off a bobbin or spool.
4. "I have read somewhere that in the Emperor's palace at Byzantium was a tree made of gold and silver, and artificial birds that sang." (Yeats's note)
5. In Book VI of *The Aeneid*, the sybil tells Aeneas that he must pluck a golden bough from a nearby tree in order to descend to Hades. There is only one such branch there, and when it is plucked an identical one takes its place.
1. "These songs are sung by the Chorus in a play [Yeats's *The Resurrection*] that

has for its theme Christ's first appearance to the Apostles after the Resurrection, a play intended for performance in a drawing-room or studio." (Yeats's note) The first song opens the play, the second ends it.
2. Who, according to Greek tradition, rose each year in the spring. The "staring virgin" is Athene (Minerva), the classical goddess of wisdom, parallel to "that fierce virgin" (Mary) in line 15. In the play, his followers pass in the street outside, celebrating his rebirth, while in the room are taking place events in the Christian cycle which is to destroy the Greco-Roman one.
3. The Great Year, a complete turning of the Great Wheel, a period of 26,000 years which encompasses 12 cycles in Yeats's system.
4. Argo was Jason's ship in which he sailed in search of the Golden Fleece.

Drive to a flashier bauble yet.
The Roman Empire stood appalled:
It dropped the reigns of peace and war
When that fierce virgin and her Star   15
Out of the fabulous darkness called.

II

In pity for man's darkening thought
He walked that room[5] and issued thence
In Galilean turbulence;
The Babylonian starlight brought   20
A fabulous, formless darkness in;
Odor of blood when Christ was slain
Made all Platonic tolerance vain
And vain all Doric discipline.

Everything that man esteems   25
Endures a moment or a day.
Love's pleasure drives his love away,
The painter's brush consumes his dreams;
The herald's cry, the soldier's tread
Exhaust his glory and his might: 30
Whatever flames upon the night
Man's own resinous heart has fed.

1927

W. B. YEATS

Among School Children

I

I walk through the long schoolroom questioning;
A kind old nun in a white hood replies;
The children learn to cipher and to sing,
To study reading-books and history,
To cut and sew, be neat in everything   5
In the best modern way—the children's eyes
In momentary wonder stare upon
A sixty-year-old smiling public man.[1]

II

I dream of a Ledaean body,[2] bent
Above a sinking fire, a tale that she   10
Told of a harsh reproof, or trivial event
That changed some childish day to tragedy—
Told, and it seemed that our two natures blent
Into a sphere from youthful sympathy,

5. Which is the play's setting. Near the end, Christ appears in the room, and his body is touched by a Greek who had earlier been skeptical of his risen reality.
1. At 60 (in 1925) Yeats had been a senator of the Irish Free State.
2. Like that of Helen of Troy, daughter of Leda. The memory dream is of Maud Gonne (see also lines 29–30), with whom Yeats had long been hopelessly in love.

Or else, to alter Plato's parable,   15
Into the yolk and white of the one shell.[3]

III

And thinking of that fit of grief or rage
I look upon one child or t'other there
And wonder if she stood so at that age—
For even daughters of the swan can share   20
Something of every paddler's heritage—
And had that color upon cheek or hair,
And thereupon my heart is driven wild:
She stands before me as a living child.

IV

Her present image floats into the mind—   25
Did Quattrocento finger[4] fashion it
Hollow of cheek as though it drank the wind
And took a mess of shadows for its meat?
And I though never of Ledaean kind
Had pretty plumage once—enough of that,   3c
Better to smile on all that smile, and show
There is a comfortable kind of old scarecrow.

V

What youthful mother, a shape upon her lap
Honey of generation[5] had betrayed,
And that must sleep, shriek, struggle to escape   35
As recollection or the drug decide,
Would think her son, did she but see that shape
With sixty or more winters on its head,
A compensation for the pang of his birth,
Or the uncertainty of his setting forth?   40

VI

Plato thought nature but a spume that plays
Upon a ghostly paradigm of things;[6]
Solider Aristotle played the taws
Upon the bottom of a king of kings;[7]

3. In Plato's *Symposium*, the origin of human love is explained by parable: Human beings were once spheres, but Zeus was fearful of their power and cut them in half; now each half longs to be reunited with its missing half. Helen and Pollux were hatched from one of two eggs born to Leda after her union with Zeus in the form of a swan; the other contained Castor and Clytemnestra. According to Yeats in *A Vision*, "from one of [Leda's] eggs came Love and from the other War."
4. Fifteenth-century artists, who fall within the 15th Phase of the Christian cycle. Yeats especially admired Botticelli, and in *A Vision* praises his "deliberate strangeness everywhere [which] gives one an emotion of mystery which is new to painting." Botticelli is grouped with those who make "intellect and emotion, *primary* curiosity and the *antithetical* dream . . . for the moment one."

5. "I have taken the 'honey of generation' from Porphyry's essay on 'The Cave of the Nymphs' [*Odyssey*, Book XIII], but find no warrant in Porphyry for considering it the 'drug' that destroys the 'recollection' of prenatal freedom. He blamed a cup of oblivion given in the zodiacal sign of Cancer." (Yeats's note) Porphyry, a third-century Greek scholar and neoplatonic philosopher, says "honey of generation" means the "pleasure arising from copulation" which draws souls "downward" to generation.
6. Plato considered the world of nature an imperfect and illusory copy of the ideal world.
7. Aristotle, the teacher of Alexander the Great, disciplined him with a strap ("taw," line 43). His philosophy, insisting on the interdependence of form and matter, took the world of nature far more seriously than did Plato's.

World-famous golden-thighed Pythagoras[8]   45
Fingered upon a fiddle-stick or strings
What a star sang and careless Muses heard:
Old clothes upon old sticks to scare a bird.

VII

Both nuns and mothers worship images,
But those the candles light are not as those   50
That animate a mother's reveries,
But keep a marble or a bronze repose.
And yet they too break hearts—O Presences
That passion, piety or affection knows,
And that all heavenly glory symbolize—   55
O self-born mockers of man's enterprise;

VIII

Labor is blossoming or dancing where
The body is not bruised to pleasure soul,
Nor beauty born out of its own despair,
Nor blear-eyed wisdom out of midnight oil.   60
O chestnut-tree, great-rooted blossomer,
Are you the leaf, the blossom or the bole?[9]
O body swayed to music, O brightening glance,
How can we know the dancer from the dance?

                                                        1927

W. B. YEATS

Byzantium[1]

The unpurged images of day recede;
The Emperor's drunken soldiery are abed;
Night resonance recedes, night-walkers' song
After great cathedral gong;
A starlit or a moonlit dome[2] disdains   5
All that man is,
All mere complexities,
The fury and the mire of human veins.

Before me floats an image, man or shade,
Shade more than man, more image than a shade;   10
For Hades' bobbin bound in mummy-cloth

---

8. Sixth-century B.C. Greek mathematician and philosopher, whose elaborate philosophical system included the doctrine of the harmony of the spheres. He was highly revered, and one legend describes his godlike golden thighs.

9. Trunk.

1. In his diary for April 30, 1930, Yeats sketched the following "Subject for a Poem": "Describe Byzantium as it is in the system towards the end of the first Christian millennium. A walking mummy. Flames at the street corners where the soul is purified, birds of hammered gold singing in the golden trees, in the harbor [dolphins], offering their backs to the wailing dead that they may carry them to paradise."

2. In *A Vision*, Yeats described the 28 phases of the moon in psychological terms related to his system. In Phase 1, only stars are visible ("starlit") and "body is completely absorbed in its supernatural environment." In its opposite, Phase 15, when the moon it full ("moonlit"), the mind is "completely absorbed in being."

May unwind the winding path;[3]
A mouth that has no moisture and no breath
Breathless mouths may summon;
I hail the superhuman;   15
I call it death-in-life and life-in-death.

Miracle, bird or golden handiwork,
More miracle than bird or handiwork,
Planted on the star-lit golden bough,
Can like the cocks of Hades crow,[4]   20
Or, by the moon embittered, scorn aloud
In glory of changeless metal
Common bird or petal
And all complexities of mire or blood.

At midnight on the Emperor's pavement flit   25
Flames that no fagot[5] feeds, nor steel has lit,
Nor storm disturbs, flames begotten of flame,
Where blood-begotten spirits come
And all complexities of fury leave,
Dying into a dance,   30
An agony of trance,
An agony of flame that cannot singe a sleeve.

Astraddle on the dolphin's mire and blood,[6]
Spirit after spirit! The smithies break the flood,
The golden smithies of the Emperor!   35
Marbles of the dancing floor
Break bitter furies of complexity,
Those images that yet
Fresh images beget,
That dolphin-torn, that gong-tormented sea.   40

                                                    1932

W. B. YEATS

Crazy Jane Talks with the Bishop[1]

I met the Bishop on the road
And much said he and I.
"Those breasts are flat and fallen now,

---

3. A volume in which "Byzantium" appeared, *The Winding Stair and Other Poems*, contains many similar images; of this volume Yeats wrote: "In this book and elsewhere I have used towers, and one tower in particular, as symbols and have compared their winding stairs to the philosophical gyres, but it is hardly necessary to interpret what comes from the main track of thought and expression. Shelley uses towers constantly as symbols, and there are gyres in Swedenborg, and in Thomas Aquinas and certain classical authors."
4. As the bird of dawn, the cock had from antiquity been a symbol of rebirth and resurrection.

5. Bundle of sticks.
6. In ancient art, dolphins symbolize the soul moving from one state to another, and sometimes they provide a vehicle for the dead. Palaemon, for example, in Greek tradition is often mounted on a dolphin.
1. Crazy Jane appears in a series of poems written in the early 1930s, usually juxtaposed with a rational figure who sees things in terms of antitheses while she sees them as paradoxes. Yeats said that she was "more or less founded upon an old woman who lives in a little cottage near Gort. She loves her flower-garden . . . and [has] an amazing power of audacious speech. She is the local satirist and a really terrible one."

Those veins must soon be dry;
Live in a heavenly mansion,   5
Not in some foul sty."

"Fair and foul are near of kin,
And fair needs foul," I cried.
"My friends are gone, but that's a truth
Nor grave nor bed denied,   10
Learned in bodily lowliness
And in the heart's pride.

"A woman can be proud and stiff
When on love intent;
But Love has pitched his mansion in   15
The place of excrement;
For nothing can be sole or whole
That has not been rent."

1933

ALEXANDER POPE

from Epistle to a Lady

Men, some to bus'ness, some to pleasure take;   215
But ev'ry woman is at heart a rake;
Men, some to quiet, some to public strife;
But ev'ry lady would be queen for life.
    Yet mark the fate of a whole sex of queens!
Pow'r all their end, but beauty all the means.   220
In youth they conquer with so wild a rage
As leaves them scarce a subject in their age:
For foreign glory, foreign joy, they roam;
No thought of peace or happiness at home.
But wisdom's triumph is well-timed retreat,   225
As hard a science to the fair as great!
Beauties, like tyrants, old and friendless grown,
Yet hate repose, and dread to be alone,
Worn out in public, weary ev'ry eye,
Nor leave one sigh behind them when they die.   230
    Pleasures the sex, as children birds, pursue,
Still out of reach, yet never out of view;
Sure, if they catch, to spoil the toy at most,
To covet flying, and regret when lost;
At last, to follies youth could scarce defend,   235
It grows their age's prudence to pretend;
Ashamed to own they gave delight before,
Reduced to feign it, when they give no more:
As hags hold sabbaths,[1] less for joy than spite,
So these their merry, miserable night;   240
Still round and round the ghosts of beauty glide,

---

1. Witches' sabbaths, late night meetings of witches and demons, characterized by wild
feasting and dancing.

And haunt the places where their honor died.
   See how the world its veterans rewards!
A youth of frolics, an old age of cards;
   Fair to no purpose, artful to no end,   245
Young without lovers, old without a friend;
A fop their passion, but their prize a sot,
Alive, ridiculous, and dead, forgot!

                                              1735

GEORGE GORDON, LORD BYRON

from Don Juan[1]

"Difficile est proprië communia dicere."[2]
                                    —Horace

"Dost thou think, because thou art virtuous, there shall be no more cakes and ale?
Yes, by Saint Anne, and ginger shall be hot i' the mouth, too!"—Shakespeare, *Twelfth
Night, or What You Will.*

Fragment

I would to heaven that I were so much clay,
   As I am blood, bone, marrow, passion, feeling—
Because at least the past were passed away—
   And for the future—(but I write this reeling,
Having got drunk exceedingly today,
   So that I seem to stand upon the ceiling)
I say—the future is a serious matter—
And so—for God's sake—hock[3] and soda-water!

from *Canto I*

1

I want a hero: an uncommon want,
   When every year and month sends forth a new one,
Till, after cloying the gazettes with cant,[4]
   The age discovers he is not the true one;
Of such as these I should not care to vaunt.   5
   I'll therefore take our ancient friend Don Juan—
We all have seen him, in the pantomime,[5]
Sent to the devil somewhat ere his time.

5

Brave men were living before Agamemnon[6]   33
   And since, exceeding valorous and sage,

---

1. The first stanza printed here is a manuscript fragment; the others are from Canto I.
2. Horace, *Ars Poetica*, line 128. Byron translated the line this way: " 'Tis no slight task to write on common things." More literally, "It is difficult to treat the universal in an original way." The context suggests that by "universal" Horace means the materials of epic.

3. *Hochheimer*: white German wine.
4. The fashionable language of the moment.
5. The legend of Don Juan, a 14th-century rake, was a frequent subject of plays, opera, and pantomime.
6. Who commanded the Greek forces in the Trojan War. Line 33 is directly translated from one of Horace's odes.

A good deal like him too, though quite the same none;
  But then they shone not on the poet's page,
And so have been forgotten—I condemn none,
  But can't find any in the present age
Fit for my poem (that is, for my new one);
So, as I said, I'll take my friend Don Juan.   40

6

Most epic poets plunge *"in medias res"*[7]
  (Horace makes this the heroic turnpike road),
And then your hero tells, whene'er you please,
  What went before—by way of episode,
While seated after dinner at his ease,   45
  Beside his mistress in some soft abode,
Palace, or garden, paradise, or cavern,
Which serves the happy couple for a tavern.

7

That is the usual method, but not mine—
  My way is to begin with the beginning;   50
The regularity of my design
  Forbids all wandering as the worst of sinning,
And therefore I shall open with a line
  (Although it cost me half an hour in spinning)
Narrating somewhat of Don Juan's father,   55
And also of his mother, if you'd rather.

1819

PERCY BYSSHE SHELLEY

Ode to the West Wind

I

O wild West Wind, thou breath of Autumn's being,
Thou, from whose unseen presence the leaves dead
Are driven, like ghosts from an enchanter fleeing,

Yellow, and black, and pale, and hectic red,
Pestilence-stricken multitudes: O thou,   5
Who chariotest to their dark wintry bed

The wingéd seeds, where they lie cold and low,
Each like a corpse within its grave, until
Thine azure sister of the Spring shall blow

Her clarion[1] o'er the dreaming earth, and fill   10
(Driving sweet buds like flocks to feed in air)
With living hues and odors plain and hill:

Wild Spirit, which art moving everywhere;
Destroyer and preserver; hear, oh, hear!

---

7. Into the middle of the subject.   1. Trumpet-call.

II

Thou on whose stream, mid the steep sky's commotion,   15
Loose clouds like earth's decaying leaves are shed,
Shook from the tangled boughs of Heaven and Ocean,

Angels[2] of rain and lightning: there are spread
On the blue surface of thine aëry surge,
Like the bright hair uplifted from the head   20

Of some fierce Maenad,[3] even from the dim verge
Of the horizon to the zenith's height,
The locks of the approaching storm. Thou dirge

Of the dying year, to which this closing night
Will be the dome of a vast sepulcher,   25
Vaulted with all thy congregated might

Of vapors, from whose solid atmosphere
Black rain, and fire, and hail will burst: oh, hear!

III

Thou who didst waken from his summer dreams
The blue Mediterranean, where he lay,   30
Lulled by the coil of his crystálline streams,

Beside a pumice isle in Baiae's bay,[4]
And saw in sleep old palaces and towers
Quivering within the wave's intenser day,

All overgrown with azure moss and flowers   35
So sweet, the sense faints picturing them! Thou
For whose path the Atlantic's level powers

Cleave themselves into chasms, while far below
The sea-blooms and the oozy woods which wear
The sapless foliage of the ocean, know   40

Thy voice, and suddenly grow gray with fear,
And tremble and despoil themselves:[5] oh, hear!

IV

If I were a dead leaf thou mightest bear;
If I were a swift cloud to fly with thee;
A wave to pant beneath thy power, and share   45

The impulse of thy strength, only less free
Than thou, O uncontrollable! If even
I were as in my boyhood, and could be

---

2. Messengers.
3. A frenzied female votary of Dionysus, the Greek god of vegetation and fertility who was supposed to die in the fall and rise again each spring.
4. Where Roman emperors had erected villas, west of Naples. "pumice": made of porous lava turned to stone.
5. "The vegetation at the bottom of the sea . . . sympathizes with that of the land in the change of seasons." (Shelley's note)

The comrade by thy wanderings over Heaven,
As then, when to outstrip thy skyey speed   50
Scarce seemed a vision; I would ne'er have striven

As thus with thee in prayer in my sore need.
Oh, lift me as a wave, a leaf, a cloud!
I fall upon the thorns of life! I bleed!

A heavy weight of hours has chained and bowed   55
One too like thee: tameless, and swift, and proud.

V

Make me thy lyre,[6] even as the forest is:
What if my leaves are falling like its own!
The tumult of thy mighty harmonies

My spirit! Be thou me, impetuous one!

Will take from both a deep, autumnal tone,   60
Sweet though in sadness. Be thou, Spirit fierce,
Drive my dead thoughts over the universe
Like withered leaves to quicken a new birth!
And, by the incantation of this verse,   65

Scatter, as from an unextinguished hearth
Ashes and sparks, my words among mankind!
Be through my lips to unawakened earth

The trumpet of a prophecy! O Wind,
If Winter comes, can Spring be far behind?   70

1820

WILLIAM WORDSWORTH

Lines Composed a Few Miles above Tintern Abbey on Revisiting the Banks of the Wye During a Tour, July 13, 1798[1]

Five years have passed; five summers, with the length
Of five long winters! and again I hear
These waters, rolling from their mountain-springs
With a soft inland murmur. Once again
Do I behold these steep and lofty cliffs,   5
That on a wild secluded scene impress
Thoughts of more deep seclusion; and connect
The landscape with the quiet of the sky.
The day is come when I again repose
Here, under this dark sycamore, and view   10

---

6. Aeolian lyre, a wind harp.
1. Wordsworth had first visited the Wye valley and the ruins of the medieval abbey there in 1793, while on a solitary walking tour. He was 23 then, 28 when he wrote this poem.

These plots of cottage-ground, these orchard tufts,
Which at this season, with their unripe fruits,
Are clad in one green hue, and lose themselves
'Mid groves and copses.[2] Once again I see
These hedge-rows, hardly hedge-rows, little lines   15
Of sportive wood run wild: these pastoral farms,
Green to the very door; and wreaths of smoke
Sent up, in silence, from among the trees!
With some uncertain notice, as might seem
Of vagrant dwellers in the houseless woods,   20
Or of some hermit's cave, where by his fire
The hermit sits alone.
                              These beauteous forms,
Through a long absence, have not been to me
As is a landscape to a blind man's eye;
But oft, in lonely rooms, and 'mid the din   25
Of towns and cities, I have owed to them,
In hours of weariness, sensations sweet,
Felt in the blood, and felt along the heart;
And passing even into my purer mind,
With tranquil restoration—feelings too   30
Of unremembered pleasure: such, perhaps,
As have no slight or trivial influence
On that best portion of a good man's life,
His little, nameless, unremembered acts
Of kindness and of love. Nor less, I trust,   35
To them I may have owed another gift,
Of aspect more sublime; that blessèd mood,
In which the burthen[3] of the mystery,
In which the heavy and the weary weight
Of all this unintelligible world,   40
Is lightened—that serene and blessèd mood,
In which the affections gently lead us on—
Until, the breath of this corporeal frame
And even the motion of our human blood
Almost suspended, we are laid asleep   45
In body, and become a living soul;
While with an eye made quiet by the power
Of harmony, and the deep power of joy,
We see into the life of things.
                              If this
Be but a vain belief, yet, oh! how oft—   50
In darkness and amid the many shapes
Of joyless daylight; when the fretful stir
Unprofitable, and the fever of the world,
Have hung upon the beatings of my heart—
How oft, in spirit, have I turned to thee,   55
O sylvan Wye! thou wanderer through the woods,
How often has my spirit turned to thee!

And now, with gleams of half-extinguished thought,
With many recognitions dim and faint,
And somewhat of a sad perplexity,   60

2. Thickets.   3. Burden.

The picture of the mind revives again;
While here I stand, not only with the sense
Of present pleasure, but with pleasing thoughts
That in this moment there is life and food
For future years. And so I dare to hope,   65
Though changed, no doubt, from what I was when first
I came among these hills; when like a roe
I bounded o'er the mountains, by the sides
Of the deep rivers, and the lonely streams,
Wherever nature led: more like a man   70
Flying from something that he dreads than one
Who sought the thing he loved. For nature then
(The coarser⁴ pleasures of my boyish days,
And their glad animal movements all gone by)
To me was all in all—I cannot paint   75
What then I was. The sounding cataract
Haunted me like a passion; the tall rock,
The mountain, and the deep and gloomy wood,
Their colors and their forms, were then to me
An appetite; a feeling and a love,   80
That had no need of a remoter charm,
By thought supplied, nor any interest
Unborrowed from the eye. That time is past,
And all its aching joys are now no more,
And all its dizzy raptures. Not for this   85
Faint I,⁵ nor mourn nor murmur; other gifts
Have followed; for such loss, I would believe,
Abundant recompense. For I have learned
To look on nature, not as in the hour
Of thoughtless youth; but hearing oftentimes   90
The still, sad music of humanity,
Nor harsh nor grating, though of ample power
To chasten and subdue. And I have felt
A presence that disturbs me with the joy
Of elevated thoughts; a sense sublime   95
Of something far more deeply interfused,
Whose dwelling is the light of setting suns,
And the round ocean and the living air,
And the blue sky, and in the mind of man:
A motion and a spirit, that impels   100
All thinking things, all objects of all thought,
And rolls through all things. Therefore am I still
A lover of the meadows and the woods
And mountains; and of all that we behold
From this green earth; of all the mighty world   105
Of eye, and ear—both what they half create,
And what perceive; well pleased to recognize
In nature and the language of the sense
The anchor of my purest thoughts, the nurse,
The guide, the guardian of my heart, and soul   110
Of all my moral being.
                           Nor perchance,
If I were not thus taught, should I the more

---

4. Physical.   5. Am I discouraged.

Suffer my genial spirits[6] to decay:
For thou art with me here upon the banks
Of this fair river; thou my dearest Friend,[7]   115
My dear, dear Friend; and in thy voice I catch
The language of my former heart, and read
My former pleasures in the shooting lights
Of thy wild eyes. Oh! yet a little while
May I behold in thee what I was once,   120
My dear, dear Sister! and this prayer I make,
Knowing that Nature never did betray
The heart that loved her; 'tis her privilege,
Through all the years of this our life, to lead
From joy to joy: for she can so inform   125
The mind that is within us, so impress
With quietness and beauty, and so feed
With lofty thoughts, that neither evil tongues,
Rash judgments, nor the sneers of selfish men,
Nor greetings where no kindness is, nor all   130
The dreary intercourse of daily life,
Shall e'er prevail against us, or disturb
Our cheerful faith that all which we behold
Is full of blessings. Therefore let the moon
Shine on thee in thy solitary walk;   135
And let the misty mountain-winds be free
To blow against thee: and, after years,
When these wild ecstasies shall be matured
Into a sober pleasure; when thy mind
Shall be a mansion for all lovely forms,   140
Thy memory be as a dwelling-place
For all sweet sounds and harmonies; oh! then,
If solitude, or fear, or pain, or grief,
Should be thy portion, with what healing thoughts
Of tender joy wilt thou remember me,   145
And these my exhortations! Nor, perchance—
If I should be where I no more can hear
Thy voice, nor catch from thy wild eyes these gleams
Of past existence—wilt thou then forget
That on the banks of this delightful stream   150
We stood together; and that I, so long
A worshiper of Nature, hither came
Unwearied in that service; rather say
With warmer love—oh! with far deeper zeal
Of holier love. Nor wilt thou then forget,   155
That after many wanderings, many years
Of absence, these steep woods and lofty cliffs,
And this green pastoral landscape, were to me
More dear, both for themselves and for thy sake!

                                                            1798

---

6. Natural disposition; i.e., the spirits   7. His sister Dorothy.
that are part of his individual genius.

MARIANNE MOORE

The Hero

Where there is personal liking we go.
  Where the ground is sour; where there are
  weeds of beanstalk height,
  snakes' hypodermic teeth, or
  the wind brings the "scarebabe voice"   5
  from the neglected yew set with
  the semi-precious cat's eyes of the owl—
awake, asleep, "raised ears extended to fine points," and so
on—love won't grow.

We do not like some things, and the hero   10
  doesn't; deviating head-stones
  and uncertainty;
  going where one does not wish
  to go; suffering and not
  saying so; standing and listening where something   15
  is hiding. The hero shrinks
as what it is flies out on muffled wings, with twin yellow
eyes—to and fro—

with quavering water-whistle note, low,
  high, in basso-falsetto chirps
  until the skin creeps.   20
  Jacob when a-dying, asked
  Joseph: Who are these? and blessed
  both sons, the younger most, vexing Joseph.[1] And
  Joseph was vexing to some.[2]   25
Cincinnatus[3] was: Regulus:[4] and some of our fellow
men have been, though

devout, like Pilgrim[5] having to go slow
  to find his roll; tired but hopeful—
  hope not being hope   30
  until all ground for hope has
  vanished; and lenient, looking
  upon a fellow creature's error with the
  feelings of a mother—a
woman or a cat. The decorous frock-coated Negro   35
by the grotto

  answers the fearless sightseeing hobo
    who asks the man she's with, what's this,

---

1. According to *Genesis* 48:1–14, Jacob gave Joseph's younger son the primary blessing. When he was young, Jacob had tricked his father (Isaac) into blessing him above his elder brother; see *Genesis* 27.
2. Potiphar's wife, for example; see *Genesis* 39.
3. A legendary Roman hero of the 5th century B.C. who left his plow to become dictator for 16 days.
4. Third-century B.C. Roman consul who defeated the Carthaginians and led the African campaign.
5. Christian, the hero of *Pilgrim's Progress*, carelessly leaves his "roll" (parchment scroll) behind in a fit of discouragement on the Hill Difficulty. The roll, given to him by Evangelist at his first setting out, is inscribed, "Fly from the wrath to come," and Christian considers it "the assurance of his life, and acceptance at the desired haven."

what's that, where's Martha
buried, "Gen-ral Washington   40
there; his lady, here"; speaking
as if in a play—not seeing her; with a
sense of human dignity
and reverence for mystery, standing like the shadow
of the willow.   45

Moses would not be grandson to Pharaoh.
It is not what I eat that is
my natural meat,
the hero says. He's not out
seeing a sight but the rock   50
crystal thing to see—the startling El Greco
brimming with inner light—that
covets nothing that it has let go. This then you may know
as the hero.

1935

WALT WHITMAN

Facing West from California's Shores

Facing west, from California's shores,
Inquiring, tireless, seeking what is yet unfound,
I, a child, very old, over waves, towards the house of maternity,[6] the
    land of migrations, look afar,
Look off the shores of my Western sea, the circle almost circled:
For starting westward from Hindustan, from the vales of Kashmere,   5
From Asia, from the north, from the God, the sage, and the hero,
From the south, from the flowery peninsulas and the spice islands,
Long having wandered since, round the earth having wandered,
Now I face home again, very pleased and joyous;
(But where is what I started for, so long ago?   10
And why is it yet unfound?)

1860

ALLEN GINSBERG

A Supermarket in California

What thoughts I have of you tonight, Walt Whitman,[1] for I
walked down the sidestreets under the trees with a headache self-conscious looking at the full moon.
    In my hungry fatigue, and shopping for images, I went into the
neon fruit supermarket, dreaming of your enumerations![2]
    What peaches and what penumbras! Whole families shopping at
night! Aisles full of husbands! Wives in the avocados, babies in the

6. Asia, as the supposed birthplace of
the human race.
    1. Whitman's free verse, strong indi-
vidualism, and passionate concern with
America as an idea have led many modern

poets to consider him the father of a new
poetry.
    2. Whitman's highly rhetorical poetry
often contains long lists or parallel con-
structions piled up for cumulative effect.

tomatoes!—and you, Garcia Lorca,[3] what were you doing down by the watermelons?

I saw you, Walt Whitman, childless, lonely old grubber, poking among the meats in the refrigerator and eyeing the grocery boys.

I heard you asking questions of each: Who killed the pork chops? 5
What price bananas? Are you my Angel?

I wandered in and out of the brilliant stacks of cans following you, and followed in my imagination by the store detective.

We strode down the open corridors together in our solitary fancy tasting artichokes, possessing every frozen delicacy, and never passing the cashier.

Where are we going, Walt Whitman? The doors close in an hour. Which way does your beard point tonight?

(I touch your book and dream of our odyssey in the supermarket and feel absurd.)

Will we walk all night through solitary streets? The trees add 10
shade to shade, lights out in the houses, we'll both be lonely.

Will we stroll dreaming of the lost America of love past blue automobiles in driveways, home to our silent cottage?

Ah, dear father, graybeard, lonely old courage-teacher, what America did you have when Charon quit poling his ferry and you got out on a smoking bank and stood watching the boat disappear on the black waters of Lethe?[4]

Berkeley 1955

WILLIAM EMPSON

Missing Dates

Slowly the poison the whole blood stream fills.
It is not the effort nor the failure tires.
The waste remains, the waste remains and kills.

It is not your system or clear sight that mills
Down small to the consequence a life requires;   5
Slowly the poison the whole blood stream fills.

They bled an old dog dry yet the exchange rills
Of young dog blood gave but a month's desires[1]
The waste remains, the waste remains and kills.

It is the Chinese tombs and the slag hills   10
Usurp the soil, and not the soil retires.
Slowly the poison the whole blood stream fills.

3. Early 20th-century Spanish poet and playwright, author of *Blood Wedding*. Murdered in 1936, at the beginning of the Spanish Civil War, his works were banned by the Franco government.

4. The River of Forgetfulness in Hades. Charon is the boatman who, according to classical myth, ferries souls to Hades.

1. "It is true about the old dog, at least I saw it reported somewhere, but the legend that a fifth or some such part of the soil of China is given up to ancestral tombs [lines 10–11] is (by the way) not true." (Empson's note)

Not to have fire is to be a skin that shrills.
The complete fire is death. From partial fires
The waste remains, the waste remains and kills.   15

It is the poems you have lost, the ills
From missing dates, at which the heart expires.
Slowly the poison the whole blood stream fills.
The waste remains, the waste remains and kills.

1940

EDWIN MORGAN

Opening the Cage: *14 variations on 14 words*

I have nothing to say and I am saying it and that is poetry. John Cage[2]

I have to say poetry and is that nothing and am I saying it
I am and I have poetry to say and is that nothing saying it
I am nothing and I have poetry to say and that is saying it
I that am saying poetry have nothing and it is I and to say
And I say that I am to have poetry and saying it is nothing   5
I am poetry and nothing and saying it is to say that I have
To have nothing is poetry and I am saying that and I say it
Poetry is saying I have nothing and I am to say that and it
Saying nothing I am poetry and I have to say that and it is
It is and I am and I have poetry saying say that to nothing   10
It is saying poetry to nothing and I say I have and am that
Poetry is saying I have it and I am nothing and to say that
And that nothing is poetry I am saying and I have to say it
Saying poetry is nothing and to that I say I am and have it

1968

SIR PHILIP SIDNEY

When Nature Made Her Chief Work, Stella's Eyes[1]

When Nature made her chief work, Stella's eyes,[2]
In color black[3] why wrapped she beams so bright?
Would she in beamy black, like painter wise,
Frame daintiest luster mixed of shades and light?
Or did she else that sober hue devise,   5
In object best to knit and strength our sight,
Lest if no veil those brave gleams did disguise,
They sunlike should more dazzle than delight?
Or would she her miraculous power show,
That, whereas black seems Beauty's contrary,   10

2. **Twentieth-century** American composer, noted for his startling experiments in sound and silence.
1. From Sidney's sonnet sequence, *Astrophel and Stella*, usually credited with having started the vogue of sonnet sequences in Elizabethan England.
2. Following Petrarch's lead, Sidney and other English sonneteers developed a series of exaggerated conventions to describe the physical features of the women they celebrated. The excessive brightness of the eyes—almost always compared favorably with the sun's brightness—was an expected feature.
3. Black was frequently used in the Renaissance to mean absence of light, and ugly or foul (see line 10).

She even in black doth make all beauties flow?
Both so and thus: she, minding[4] Love should be
Placed ever there, gave him this mourning weed
To honor all their deaths who for her bleed.

1582

HENRY CONSTABLE

My Lady's Presence Makes the Roses Red

My lady's presence makes the roses red
Because to see her lips they blush for shame.
The lily's leaves, for envy, pale became,
And her white hands in them this envy bred.
The marigold the leaves abroad doth spread   5
Because the sun's and her power is the same.
The violet of purple color came,
Dyed in the blood she made my heart to shed.
In brief, all flowers from her their virtue take;
From her sweet breath their sweet smells do proceed;   10
The living heat which her eyebeams doth make
Warmeth the ground and quickeneth the seed.
The rain wherewith she watereth the flowers
Falls from mine eyes, which she dissolves in showers.

1594

WILLIAM SHAKESPEARE

My Mistress' Eyes Are Nothing like the Sun[1]

My mistress' eyes are nothing like the sun;
Coral is far more red than her lips' red;
If snow be white, why then her breasts are dun;[2]
If hairs be wires, black wires grow on her head.[3]
I have seen roses damasked[4] red and white,   5
But no such roses see I in her cheeks;
And in some perfumes is there more delight
Than in the breath that from my mistress reeks.
I love to hear her speak, yet well I know
That music hath a far more pleasing sound;   10
I grant I never saw a goddess go;[5]
My mistress, when she walks, treads on the ground.
And yet, by heaven, I think my love as rare
As any she belied with false compare.

1609

4. Remembering that.
1. See Sidney's "When Nature Made
Her Chief Work, Stella's Eyes," and notes.
2. Mouse-colored.
3. Women in traditional sonnets have
hair of gold. Many poets who use the
Petrarchan conventions also wrote poems
which teased or deflated the conventions.
4. Variegated.
5. Walk.

HENRY CONSTABLE

Miracle of the World

Miracle of the world, I never will deny
That former poets praise the beauty of their days,
But all those beauties were but figures[1] of thy praise,
And all those poets did of thee but prophesy.
Thy coming to the world hath taught us to descry   5
What Petrarch's Laura[2] meant, for truth the lip bewrays.[3]
Lo, why th' Italians, yet which never saw thy rays,
To find out Petrarch's sense such forgéd glosses try:
The beauties, which he in a veil enclosed, beheld
But revelations were within his secret heart,[4]   10
By which in parables thy coming he foretold.
His songs were hymns of thee, which only now before
Thy image should be sung; for thou that goddess art
Which only we without idolatry adore.

1594

WILLIAM SHAKESPEARE

Let Me Not to the Marriage of True Minds

Let me not to the marriage of true minds
Admit impediments.[1] Love is not love
Which alters when it alteration finds,
Or bends with the remover to remove:
Oh, no! it is an ever-fixéd mark,   5
That looks on tempests and is never shaken;
It is the star to every wandering bark,
Whose worth's unknown, although his height be taken.[2]
Love's not Time's fool, though rosy lips and cheeks
Within his bending sickle's compass come;   10
Love alters not with his brief hours and weeks,
But bears it out even to the edge of doom.[3]
If this be error and upon me proved,
I never writ, nor no man ever loved.

1609

1. Prefigurations, like people in the Old Testament who, according to Christian typology, prefigured Christ.
2. The woman celebrated in Petrarch's 14th-century sonnets. Constable's sequence of sonnets is addressed to "Diana."
3. Reveals.
4. I.e., once the beauties are actually seen (in Diana), Petrarch's mysterious descriptions turn out to be private revelations of the future.

1. The Marriage Service contained this address to the observers: "If any of you know cause or just impediments why these persons should not be joined together . . . ."
2. I.e., measuring the altitude of stars (for purposes of navigation) is not a measurement of value.
3. End of the world.

WILLIAM SHAKESPEARE

When, in Disgrace with Fortune and Men's Eyes

When, in disgrace[1] with fortune and men's eyes,
I all alone beweep my outcast state,
And trouble deaf heaven with my bootless[2] cries,
And look upon myself and curse my fate,
Wishing me like to one more rich in hope,   5
Featured like him, like him with friends possessed,
Desiring this man's art, and that man's scope,
With what I most enjoy contented least;
Yet in these thoughts myself almost despising,
Haply[3] I think on thee, and then my state,   10
Like to the lark at break of day arising
From sullen[4] earth, sings hymns at heaven's gate;
For thy sweet love remembered such wealth brings
That then I scorn to change my state with kings.

1609

SIR PHILIP SIDNEY

What, Have I Thus Betrayed My Liberty?

What, have I thus betrayed my liberty?
Can those black beams such burning marks[1] engrave
In my free side? or am I born a slave,
Whose neck becomes[2] such yoke of tyranny?
Or want[3] I sense to feel my misery?   5
Or sprite,[4] disdain of such disdain to have?
Who for long faith, though daily help I crave,
May get no alms but scorn of beggary.[5]
Virtue, awake! Beauty but beauty is.
I may, I must, I can, I will, I do   10
Leave following that which it is gain to miss.
Let her go! Soft, but here she comes! Go to,
Unkind, I love you not! O me, that eye
Doth make my heart give to my tongue the lie!

1582

ELIZABETH BARRETT BROWNING

How Do I Love Thee?

How do I love thee? Let me count the ways.
I love thee to the depth and breadth and height
My soul can reach, when feeling out of sight

---

1. Disfavor.
2. Futile.
3. By chance.
4. Mournful.
1. Slaves had formerly been branded.

2. Befits.
3. Lack.
4. Spirit.
5. I.e., contempt for my beggarly condition.

For the ends of Being and ideal Grace.
I love thee to the level of every day's   5
Most quiet need, by sun and candlelight.
I love thee freely, as men strive for Right;
I love thee purely, as they turn from Praise;
I love thee with the passion put to use
In my old griefs, and with my childhood's faith.   10
I love thee with a love I seemed to lose
With my lost saints—I love thee with the breath,
Smiles, tears of all my life!—and, if God choose,
I shall but love thee better after death.

1850

JOHN MILTON

On the Late Massacre in Piedmont[1]

Avenge, O Lord, thy slaughtered saints, whose bones
Lie scattered on the Alpine mountains cold;
Ev'n them who kept thy truth so pure of old,
When all our fathers worshiped stocks and stones,
Forget not: in thy book record their groans   5
Who were thy sheep, and in their ancient fold
Slain by the bloody Piedmontese, that rolled
Mother with infant down the rocks. Their moans
The vales redoubled to the hills, and they
To Heav'n. Their martyred blood and ashes sow   10
O'er all th' Italian fields, where still doth sway
The triple Tyrant:[2] that from these may grow
A hundredfold who, having learnt thy way,
Early may fly the Babylonian woe.[3]

1655

PERCY BYSSHE SHELLEY

Ozymandias[1]

I met a traveler from an antique land
Who said: Two vast and trunkless legs of stone
Stand in the desert. . . . Near them, on the sand,
Half sunk, a shattered visage lies, whose frown,
And wrinkled lip, and sneer of cold command,   5
Tell that its sculptor well those passions read
Which yet survive, stamped on these lifeless things,

1. On Easter Sunday, 1655, the Duke of Savoy's forces massacred 1700 members of the Waldensian sect in the Piedmont in northwestern Italy. The sect, founded in 1170, existed at first within the Roman Catholic Church, but its vigorous condemnation of church rites and policies (especially of the use of icons—see line 4) led to a total break. Until the year of the massacre the group had been allowed freedom of worship.
2. The Pope's tiara has three crowns.
3. Protestants in Milton's day associated Catholicism with Babylonian decadence, called the church "the whore of Babylon," and read the prophecy of *Revelation* 17 and 18 as an allegory of its coming destruction.
1. The Greek name for Rameses II, 13th-century B.C. pharaoh of Egypt. According to a first century B.C. Greek historian, Diodorus Siculus, the largest statue in Egypt was inscribed: "I am Ozymandias, king of kings; if anyone wishes to know what I am and where I lie, let him surpass me in some of my exploits."

The hand that mocked them, and the heart that fed:
And on the pedestal these words appear:
"My name is Ozymandias, King of Kings: 10
Look on my works, ye Mighty, and despair!"
Nothing beside remains. Round the decay
Of that colossal wreck, boundless and bare
The lone and level sands stretch far away.

1818

e. e. cummings

a salesman

a salesman is an it that stinks Excuse

Me whether it's president of the you were say
or a jennelman name misder finger isn't
important whether it's millions of other punks
or just a handful absolutely doesn't   5
matter and whether it's in lonjewray

or shrouds is immaterial it stinks

a salesman is an it that stinks to please

but whether to please itself or someone else
makes no more difference than if it sells   10
hate condoms education snakeoil vac
uumcleaners terror strawberries democ
ra (caveat emptor[2]) cy superfluous hair

or Think We've Met subhuman rights Before

1944

JOHN KEATS

On First Looking into Chapman's Homer[1]

Much have I traveled in the realms of gold,
And many goodly states and kingdoms seen;
Round many western islands have I been
Which bards in fealty[2] to Apollo hold.
Oft of one wide expanse had I been told   5
That deep-browed Homer ruled as his demesne;[3]
Yet did I never breathe its pure serene[4]
Till I heard Chapman speak out loud and bold:
Then felt I like some watcher of the skies

2. Literally, "let the buyer beware": the principle that the seller is not responsible for a product unless he provides a formal guarantee.
1. Chapman's were among the most famous Renaissance translations; his *Iliad* was completed in 1611, *The Odyssey* in 1616. Keats wrote the sonnet after being led to Chapman by his former teacher and reading *The Iliad* all night long.
2. Literally, the loyalty owed by a vassal to his feudal lord. Apollo was the Greek and Roman god of poetry and music.
3. Estate, feudal possession.
4. Atmosphere.

When a new planet swims into his ken;[5]   10
Or like stout Cortez[6] when with eagle eyes
He stared at the Pacific—and all his men
Looked at each other with a wild surmise—
Silent, upon a peak in Darien.

1816

GEORGE STARBUCK

On First Looking in on Blodgett's *Keats's "Chapman's Homer"* (*Sum. ½C. M9–11*)

Mellifluous as bees, these brittle men
droning of Honeyed Homer give me hives.
I scratch, yawn like a bear, my arm arrives
at yours—oh, Honey, and we're back again,
me the Balboa, you the Darien,   5
lording the loud Pacific sands, our lives
as hazarded as when a petrel dives
to yank the dull sea's coverlet, or when,
breaking from me across the sand that's rink
and record of our weekend boning up   10
on *The Romantic Agony*,[1] you sink
John Keats a good surf-fisher's cast out—plump
in the sun's wake—and the parched pages drink
that great whales' blanket party hump and hump.

1960

HELEN CHASIN

Joy Sonnet in a Random Universe

Sometimes I'm happy: la la la la la la la
la la la la la la la la la la la la la la la la
la la la la. Tum tum ti tum. La la la la la la
la la la la la la la la la la la la la la la la.
Hey nonny nonny. La la la la la la la la   5
la la la la la la la la la la la. Vo do di o do.
Poo poo pi doo. La la la la la la la la la la
la la la la la la la la la la la la la la la la
la la. Whack a doo. La la la la la la la. Sh-
boom, sh-boom. La la la la la la la la la la   10
la la la la la la la la la la la la la la la la
la la. Dum di dum. La la la la la la la la la
la la la la la la la la la. Tra la la. Tra la la
la la la la la la la la la la. Yeah yeah yeah.

1968

---

5. Range of vision.
6. Actually, Balboa; he first viewed the Pacific from Darien, in Panama.

1. The title, conveniently enough, of a scholarly book about several writers, including Keats.

WILLIAM WORDSWORTH

Nuns Fret Not

Nuns fret not at their convent's narrow room;
And hermits are contented with their cells;
And students with their pensive citadels;
Maids at the wheel, the weaver at his loom,
Sit blithe and happy; bees that soar for bloom,   5
High as the highest Peak of Furness-fells,[1]
Will murmur by the hour in foxglove bells:[2]
In truth the prison, unto which we doom
Ourselves, no prison is: and hence for me,
In sundry moods, 'twas pastime to be bound   10
Within the sonnet's scanty plot of ground;
Pleased if some souls (for such there needs must be)
Who have felt the weight of too much liberty,
Should find brief solace there, as I have found.

1807

WILLIAM BLAKE

The Lamb

Little Lamb, who made thee?
Dost thou know who made thee?
Gave thee life, and bid thee feed
By the stream and o'er the mead;
Gave thee clothing of delight,   5
Softest clothing woolly bright;
Gave thee such a tender voice,
Making all the vales rejoice?
Little Lamb, who made thee?
Dost thou know who made thee?   10

Little Lamb, I'll tell thee!
Little Lamb, I'll tell thee:
He is calléd by thy name,
For he calls himself a Lamb,
He is meek and he is mild;   15
He became a little child.
I a child and thou a lamb,
We are calléd by his name,
Little Lamb, God bless thee!
Little Lamb, God bless thee!   20

1789

WILLIAM BLAKE

The Tiger

Tiger, Tiger, burning bright
In the forests of the night,

---

1. Mountains in England's Lake District, where Wordsworth lived.

2. Flowers from which digitalis (a heart medicine) began to be made in 1799.

What immortal hand or eye
Could frame thy fearful symmetry?

In what distant deeps or skies   5
Burnt the fire of thine eyes?
On what wings dare he aspire?
What the hand dare seize the fire?

And what shoulder and what art,
Could twist the sinews of thy heart?   10
And when thy heart began to beat,
What dread hand, and what dread feet?

What the hammer? What the chain?
In what furnace was thy brain?
What the anvil? What dread grasp   15
Dare its deadly terrors clasp?

When the stars threw down their spears
And watered heaven with their tears,
Did he smile his work to see?
Did he who made the Lamb make thee?   20

Tiger, Tiger, burning bright
In the forests of the night,
What immortal hand or eye
Dare frame thy fearful symmetry?

                                                                 1794

JOHN MILTON

from Paradise Lost[1]

I

Of man's first disobedience, and the fruit[2]
Of that forbidden tree whose mortal taste
Brought death into the world, and all our woe,
With loss of Eden, till one greater Man
Restore us, and regain the blissful seat,   5
Sing, Heav'nly Muse,[3] that, on the secret top
Of Oreb, or Sinai, didst inspire
That shepherd who first taught the chosen seed
In the beginning how the Heav'ns and Earth
Rose out of Chaos: or, if Sion hill   10

1. The opening lines of Books I and II and a short passage from Book III. The first passage states the poem's subject, and the second describes Satan's beginning address to the council of fallen angels meeting to discuss strategy; in the third, God is looking down from Heaven at his new human creation and watching Satan approach the Earth.
2. The apple, but also the consequences.
3. Addressing one of the muses and asking for aid is a convention for the opening lines of an epic; Milton complicates the standard procedure here by describing sources and circumstances of Judeo-Christian revelation rather than specifically invoking one of the nine classical muses. Sinai is the spur of Mount Oreb, where Moses ("That shepherd," line 8, who was traditionally regarded as author of the first five books of the Bible) received the Law; Sion hill and Siloa (lines 10–11), near Jerusalem, correspond to the traditional mountain (Helicon) and springs of classical tradition. Later, in Book VII, Milton calls upon Urania, the muse of astronomy, but he does not mention by name the muse of epic poetry, Calliope.

Delight thee more, and Siloa's brook that flowed
Fast[4] by the oracle of God, I thence
Invoke thy aid to my adventurous song,
That with no middle flight intends to soar
Above th' Aonian mount,[5] while it pursues   15
Things unattempted yet in prose or rhyme.
And chiefly thou, O Spirit,[6] that dost prefer
Before all temples th' upright heart and pure,
Instruct me, for thou know'st; thou from the first
Wast present, and, with mighty wings outspread,   20
Dovelike sat'st brooding on the vast abyss,
And mad'st it pregnant: what in me is dark
Illumine; what is low, raise and support;
That, to the height of this great argument,[7]
I may assert Eternal Providence,   25
And justify the ways of God to men.
    Say first (for Heav'n hides nothing from thy view,
Nor the deep tract of Hell), say first what cause
Moved our grand parents, in that happy state,
Favored of Heav'n so highly, to fall off   30
From their Creator, and transgress his will
For[8] one restraint, lords of the world besides?
Who first seduced them to that foul revolt?
Th' infernal serpent; he it was, whose guile,
Stirred up with envy and revenge, deceived   35
The mother of mankind, what time[9] his pride
Had cast him out from Heav'n, with all his host
Of rebel angels, by whose aid, aspiring
To set himself in glory above his peers,
He trusted to have equaled the Most High,   40
If he opposed; and with ambitious aim
Against the throne and monarchy of God,
Raised impious war in Heav'n and battle proud,
With vain attempt. Him the Almighty Power
Hurled headlong flaming from th' ethereal sky,   45
With hideous ruin and combustion down
To bottomless perdition, there to dwell
In adamantine chains and penal fire,
Who durst defy th' Omnipotent to arms.[1]

                    ✿   ✿   ✿

                         II
High on a throne of royal state, which far
Outshone the wealth of Ormus and of Ind,[2]
Or where the gorgeous East with richest hand

---

4. Close.
5. Mt. Helicon, home of the classical muses.
6. The divine voice that inspired the Hebrew prophets. *Genesis* 1:2 says that "the Spirit of God moved upon the face of the waters" as part of the process of the original creation; Milton follows tradition in making the inspirational and communicative function of God present in creation itself. The passage echoes and merges many Biblical references to divine creation and revelation.
7. Subject.
8. Because of. "besides": in all other respects.
9. When.
1. After invoking the muse and giving a brief summary of the poem's subject, an epic regularly begins *in medias res* (in the midst of things).
2. Hormuz, an island in the Persian Gulf, famous for pearls, and India.

Show'rs on her kings barbaric pearl and gold,
Satan exalted sat, by merit raised   5
To that bad eminence; and, from despair
Thus high uplifted beyond hope, aspires
Beyond thus high, insatiate to pursue
Vain war with Heav'n, and by success[3] untaught,
His proud imaginations thus displayed: 10
    "Powers and Dominions, Deities of Heav'n,
For since no deep within her gulf can hold
Immortal vigor, though oppressed and fall'n,
I give not Heav'n for lost. From this descent
Celestial virtues rising will appear   15
More glorious and more dread than from no fall,
And trust themselves to fear no second fate.
Me though just right and the fixed laws of Heav'n
Did first create your leader, next, free choice,
With what besides, in council or in fight,   20
Hath been achieved of merit, yet this loss,
Thus far at least recovered, hath much more
Established in a safe unenvied throne
Yielded with full consent. The happier state
In Heav'n, which follows dignity, might draw   25
Envy from each inferior; but who here
Will envy whom the highest place exposes
Foremost to stand against the Thunderer's aim
Your bulwark, and condemns to greatest share
Of endless pain? Where there is then no good   30
For which to strive, no strife can grow up there
From faction; for none sure will claim in hell
Precédence, none, whose portion is so small
Of present pain, that with ambitious mind
Will covet more. With this advantage then   35
To union, and firm faith, and firm accord,
More than can be in Heav'n, we now return
To claim our just inheritance of old,
Surer to prosper than prosperity
Could have assured us; and by what best way,   40
Whether of open war or covert guile,
We now debate; who can advise, may speak."

                        ❋   ❋   ❋

                          III

                        ❋   ❋   ❋

    Now had th' Almighty Father from above,   56
From the pure empyrean where he sits
High throned above all height, bent down his eye,
His own works and their works at once to view:
About him all the sanctities of Heav'n[4]   60
Stood thick as stars, and from his sight received
Beatitude past utterance; on his right
The radiant image of his glory sat,
His only Son. On earth he first beheld

---

3. Outcome, either good or bad.   4. The hierarchies of angels.

Our two first parents, yet the only two   65
Of mankind, in the happy garden placed,
Reaping immortal fruits of joy and love,
Uninterrupted joy, unrivaled love,
In blissful solitude. He then surveyed
Hell and the gulf between, and Satan there   70
Coasting the wall of Heav'n on this side Night
In the dun air sublime,[5] and ready now
To stoop[6] with wearied wings and willing feet
On the bare outside of this world, that seemed
Firm land embosomed without firmament,   75
Uncertain which, in ocean or in air.

1667

JONATHAN SWIFT

A Satirical Elegy

On the Death of a Late Famous General[1]

His Grace? impossible? what dead?
Of old age too, and in his bed?
And could that Mighty Warrior fall?
And so inglorious, after all!
Well, since he's gone, no matter how,   5
The last loud trump[2] must wake him now;
And, trust me, as the noise grows stronger,
He'd wish to sleep a little longer.

And could he be indeed so old
As by the newspapers we're told?[3]   10
Threescore, I think, is pretty high;
'Twas time in conscience he should die.
This world he cumbered long enough;
He burnt his candle to the snuff;
And that's the reason, some folks think,   15
He left behind *so great a stink.*

Behold his funeral appears,
Nor widow's sighs, nor orphan's tears,
Wont at such times each heart to pierce,
Attend the progress of his hearse.   20
But what of that, his friends may say,
He had those honors in his day;
True to his profit and his pride,
He made them weep before he died.

Come hither, all ye empty things,   25
Ye bubbles[4] raised by breath of Kings,

5. Aloft in the twilight atmosphere.
6. Swoop down, like a bird of prey.
1. John Churchill, the first Duke of
Marlborough, whose brilliant military exploits had made him an English hero. His
later pettiness and civilian politics tarnished, in the eyes of some, his earlier
glory, but the poem exaggerates his loss
of reputation.
2. On Judgment Day, when the dead are
supposed to be awakened.
3. Marlborough died at age 72.
4. Insubstantial things. Marlborough was
made a Duke in 1689, two days before
William became king, in a deal made during the succession crisis.

Who float upon the tide of state,
Come hither, and behold your fate.
Let pride be taught by this rebuke,
How very mean a thing's a Duke;   30
From all his ill-got honors flung,
Turned to that dirt from whence he sprung.

1722

JOHN MILTON

Lycidas[1]

In this monody the author bewails a learned friend, unfortunately drowned in his passage
from Chester on the Irish Seas, 1637.[2] And by occasion foretells the ruin of our corrupted
clergy then in their height.

Yet once more, O ye laurels, and once more
Ye myrtles brown, with ivy never sere,[3]
I come to pluck your berries harsh and crude,[4]
And with forced fingers rude,
Shatter your leaves before the mellowing year.   5
Bitter constraint, and sad occasion dear,[5]
Compels me to disturb your season due:
For Lycidas is dead, dead ere his prime,
Young Lycidas, and hath not left his peer.
Who would not sing for Lycidas? He knew   10
Himself to sing, and build the lofty rhyme.
He must not float upon his wat'ry bier
Unwept, and welter[6] to the parching wind,
Without the meed[7] of some melodious tear.
    Begin then, sisters of the sacred well,[8]   15
That from beneath the seat of Jove doth spring,
Begin, and somewhat loudly sweep the string.
Hence with denial vain and coy excuse;
So may some gentle muse[9]
With lucky words favor my destined urn,   20
And as he passes turn,
And bid fair peace be to my sable shroud.
For we were nursed upon the self-same hill,
Fed the same flock, by fountain, shade, and rill.
    Together both, ere the high lawns[1] appeared   25
Under the opening eyelids of the morn,
We drove afield, and both together heard
What time the gray-fly winds[2] her sultry horn,
Batt'ning[3] our flocks with the fresh dews of night,

1. The name of a shepherd in Vergil's
Eclogue III. Milton's elegy works from the
convention of treating the dead man as if
he were a shepherd and also transforms
other details to a pastoral setting and situation.
2. Edward King, a student with Milton
at Cambridge, and at the time of his death
a young clergyman. "monody": a song
sung by a single voice.
3. Withered. The laurel, myrtle, and ivy
were all materials used to construct traditional evergreen garlands signifying poetic

accomplishment. "brown": dusky, dark.
4. Unripe.
5. Dire.
6. Tumble about.
7. Tribute.
8. The muses, who lived on Mt. Helicon.
At the foot of the mountain were two
fountains, or wells, where the muses danced
around Jove's altar.
9. Poet.
1. Grasslands: pastures.
2. Blows; i.e., the insect hum of midday.
3. Fattening.

Oft till the star that rose, at ev'ning, bright,   30
Towards Heav'n's descent had sloped his westering wheel.
Meanwhile the rural ditties were not mute,
Tempered to the oaten flute;[4]
Rough satyrs danced, and fauns with clov'n heel,
From the glad sound would not be absent long,   35
And old Damaetas[5] loved to hear our song.
    But O the heavy change, now thou art gone,
Now thou art gone, and never must return!
Thee, shepherd, thee the woods and desert caves,
With wild thyme and the gadding[6] vine o'ergrown,   40
And all their echoes mourn.
The willows and the hazel copses[7] green
Shall now no more be seen,
Fanning their joyous leaves to thy soft lays.
As killing as the canker[8] to the rose,   45
Or taint-worm to the weanling herds that graze,
Or frost to flowers, that their gay wardrobe wear,
When first the white-thorn blows:[9]
Such, Lycidas, thy loss to shepherd's ear.
    Where were ye, nymphs,[1] when the remorseless deep   50
Closed o'er the head of your loved Lycidas?
For neither were ye playing on the steep,
Where your old Bards, the famous Druids, lie,
Nor on the shaggy top of Mona high,
Nor yet where Deva spreads her wizard stream:[2]   55
Ay me, I fondly[3] dream!
Had ye been there—for what could that have done?
What could the Muse[4] herself that Orpheus bore,
The Muse herself, for her enchanting[5] son
Whom universal nature did lament,   60
When by the rout that made the hideous roar,
His gory visage down the stream was sent,
Down the swift Hebrus to the Lesbian shore?
    Alas! What boots[6] it with uncessant care
To tend the homely slighted shepherd's trade,   65
And strictly meditate the thankless Muse?
Were it not better done, as others use,[7]
To sport with Amaryllis in the shade,
Or with the tangles of Neaera's hair?
Fame is the spur that the clear spirit doth raise   70
(That last infirmity of noble mind)
To scorn delights, and live laborious days;

4. Shepherds' pipes.
5. A traditional pastoral name, possibly referring here to a Cambridge tutor.
6. Wandering.
7. Thickets.
8. Cankerworm.
9. Blossoms.
1. Nature deities.
2. The River Dee, reputed to have prophetic powers. "Mona": the Isle of Anglesey. The steep (line 52) may be a burial ground, in northern Wales, for Druids, ancient priests and magicians; all three locations are near the place where King drowned.
3. Foolishly.

4. Calliope, the muse of epic poetry, whose son Orpheus was torn limb from limb by frenzied orgiasts. His head, thrown into the Hebrus (lines 62–63), floated into the sea and finally to Lesbos, where it was buried.
5. Orpheus was reputed to be able to charm even inanimate things with his music; he once persuaded Pluto to release his dead wife, Eurydice, from the infernal regions.
6. Profits.
7. Customarily do. Amaryllis (line 68) and Neaera (line 69) are stock names of women celebrated in pastoral love poetry.

But the fair guerdon[8] when we hope to find,
And think to burst out into sudden blaze,
Comes the blind Fury[9] with th' abhorréd shears,   75
And slits the thin-spun life. "But not the praise,"
Phoebus[1] replied, and touched my trembling ears:
"Fame is no plant that grows on mortal soil,
Nor in the glistering foil[2]
Set off to th' world, nor in broad rumor lies,   80
But lives and spreads aloft by those pure eyes
And perfect witness of all-judging Jove;
As he pronounces lastly on each deed,
Of so much fame in Heav'n expect thy meed."
    O fountain Arethuse,[3] and thou honored flood,   85
Smooth-sliding Mincius, crowned with vocal reeds,
That strain I heard was of a higher mood.
But now my oat[4] proceeds,
And listens to the herald of the sea,[5]
That came in Neptune's plea.   90
He asked the waves and asked the felon-winds,
What hard mishap hath doomed this gentle swain,[6]
And questioned every gust of rugged wings
That blows from off each beakéd promontory.
They knew not of his story,   95
And sage Hippotades[7] their answer brings:
That not a blast was from his dungeon strayed;
The air was calm, and on the level brine,
Sleek Panopë[8] with all her sisters played.
It was that fatal and perfidious bark   100
Built in th' eclipse, and rigged with curses dark,
That sunk so low that sacred head of thine.
    Next Camus,[9] reverend sire, went footing slow,
His mantle hairy, and his bonnet sedge,
Inwrought with figures dim, and on the edge   105
Like to that sanguine flower inscribed with woe.[1]
"Ah! who hath reft," quoth he, "my dearest pledge?"
Last came, and last did go,
The pilot of the Galilean Lake;[2]
Two massy keys he bore of metals twain   110
(The golden opes, the iron shuts amain).
He shook his mitered locks, and stern bespake:
"How well could I have spared for thee, young swain,

8. Reward.
9. Atropos, the Fate who cuts the threads of human life after they are spun and measured by her two sisters.
1. Apollo, god of poetic inspiration. In Roman tradition, touching the ears of one's hearers meant asking them to remember what they heard.
2. Flashy setting, used to make inferior gems glitter.
3. A Sicilian fountain, associated with the pastoral poetry of Theocritus. The River Mincius (line 86) is associated with Vergil's pastorals.
4. Oaten pipe: pastoral song.
5. Triton, who maintains the innocence of Neptune, the Roman god of the sea, in the death of Lycidas.

6. Youth, shepherd, poet.
7. Aeolus, god of the winds and son of Hippotas.
8. According to Vergil, the greatest of the Nereids (sea nymphs).
9. God of the River Cam, which flows through Cambridge.
1. The hyacinth, which was supposed to bear marks that meant "alas" because the flower was created by Phoebus from the blood of a youth he had killed accidentally.
2. St. Peter, a fisherman before he became a disciple. According to *Matthew* 16:19, Christ promised him "the keys of the kingdom of heaven"; he was traditionally regarded as the first head of the church, hence the bishop's miter in line 112.

Enow[3] of such as for their bellies' sake
Creep and intrude, and climb into the fold![4]   115
Of other care they little reck'ning make,
Than how to scramble at the shearers' feast,
And shove away the worthy bidden guest.
Blind mouths! that scarce themselves know how to hold
A sheep-hook,[5] or have learned aught else the least   120
That to the faithful herdman's art belongs!
What recks it[6] them? What need they? They are sped,[7]
And when they list,[8] their lean and flashy songs
Grate on their scrannel[9] pipes of wretched straw.
The hungry sheep look up and are not fed,   125
But swoln with wind, and the rank mist they draw,
Rot inwardly, and foul contagion spread,
Besides what the grim wolf with privy paw[1]
Daily devours apace, and nothing said;
But that two-handed engine[2] at the door   130
Stands ready to smite once, and smite no more."
     Return, Alpheus,[3] the dread voice is past,
That shrunk thy streams; return, Sicilian Muse,
And call the vales, and bid them hither cast
Their bells and flowrets of a thousand hues.   135
Ye valleys low, where the mild whispers use,[4]
Of shades and wanton winds and gushing brooks,
On whose fresh lap the swart star[5] sparely looks,
Throw hither all your quaint enameled eyes,
That on the green turf suck the honeyed showers,   140
And purple all the ground with vernal flowers.
Bring the rathe[6] primrose that forsaken dies,
The tufted crow-toe, and pale jessamine,
The white pink, and the pansy freaked[7] with jet,
The glowing violet,   145
The musk-rose, and the well-attired woodbine,
With cowslips wan that hang the pensive head,
And every flower that sad embroidery wears.
Bid amaranthus[8] all his beauty shed,
And daffodillies fill their cups with tears,   150
To strew the laureate hearse[9] where Lycid lies.
For so to interpose a little ease,
Let our frail thoughts dally with false surmise.
Ay me! Whilst thee the shores and sounding seas
Wash far away, where'er thy bones are hurled,   155

Whether beyond the stormy Hebrides,[1]
Where thou perhaps under the whelming tide
Visit'st the bottom of the monstrous world;[2]
Or whether thou to our moist vows denied,
Sleep'st by the fable of Bellerus old,[3]   160
Where the great vision of the guarded mount
Looks toward Namancos and Bayona's hold;
Look homeward, Angel, now, and melt with ruth.[4]
And, O ye dolphins,[5] waft the hapless youth.
　　Weep no more, woeful shepherds, weep no more,   165
For Lycidas your sorrow is not dead,
Sunk though he be beneath the wat'ry floor,
So sinks the day-star[6] in the ocean bed,
And yet anon repairs his drooping head,
And tricks[7] his beams, and with new-spangled ore   170
Flames in the forehead of the morning sky:
So Lycidas sunk low, but mounted high,
Through the dear might of him that walked the waves,[8]
Where, other groves and other streams along,
With nectar pure his oozy locks he laves,   175
And hears the unexpressive nuptial song,[9]
In the blest kingdoms meek of joy and love.
There entertain him all the saints above,
In solemn troops and sweet societies
That sing, and singing in their glory move,   180
And wipe the tears forever from his eyes.
Now, Lycidas, the shepherds weep no more;
Henceforth thou art the genius[1] of the shore,
In thy large recompense, and shalt be good
To all that wander in that perilous flood.   185
　　Thus sang the uncouth swain[2] to th' oaks and rills,
While the still morn went out with sandals gray;
He touched the tender stops of various quills,[3]
With eager thought warbling his Doric[4] lay.
And now the sun had stretched out all the hills,   190
And now was dropped into the western bay.
At last he rose, and twitched his mantle blue:
Tomorrow to fresh woods, and pastures new.

                                                  1637

NICHOLAS BRETON

The Plowman's Song

In the merry month of May,
In a morn by break of day,

1. Islands off Scotland, the northern edge of the sea where King drowned.
2. World where monsters live.
3. A legendary giant, supposedly buried at Land's End in Cornwall. At the tip of Land's End is St. Michael's Mount (line 161), from which the archangel is pictured looking south across the Atlantic toward Spanish (Catholic) strongholds ("Namancos and Bayona," line 162).
4. Pity.
5. According to Roman legend, dolphins brought the body of a drowned youth,

Melicertes, to land, where a temple was erected to him as the protector of sailors.
6. The sun.
7. Dresses.
8. Christ. See *Matthew* 14:25–26.
9. Sung at the "marriage of the Lamb," according to *Revelation* 19. "unexpressive": inexpressible.
1. Protecting deity.
2. Unlettered shepherd: i.e., Milton.
3. Reeds in the shepherd's pipes.
4. The Greek dialect of Theocritus, Bion, and Moschus, the first writers of pastoral.

Forth I walked by the wood side,
Whereas May was in his pride.
There I spied, all alone,   5
Phyllida and Corydon.[1]
Much ado there was, God wot,[2]
He would love and she would not.
She said, never man was true;
He said, none was false to you.   10
He said, he had loved her long;
She said, love should have no wrong.
Corydon would kiss her then;
She said, maids must kiss no men
Till they did for good and all.   15
Then she made the shepherd call
All the heavens to witness truth,
Never loved a truer youth.
Thus, with many a pretty oath,
Yea and nay, and faith and troth,   20
Such as silly[3] shepherds use
When they will not love abuse,
Love, which had been long deluded,
Was with kisses sweet concluded:
And Phyllida with garlands gay   25
Was made the Lady of the May.

1591

ROBERT LOWELL

Skunk Hour

(*For Elizabeth Bishop*)

Nautilus Island's hermit
heiress still lives through winter in her Spartan cottage;
her sheep still graze above the sea.
Her son's a bishop. Her farmer
is first selectman[1] in our village,   5
she's in her dotage.

Thirsting for
the hierarchic privacy
of Queen Victoria's century,
she buys up all   10
the eyesores facing her shore,
and lets them fall.

The season's ill—
we've lost our summer millionaire,
who seemed to leap from an L. L. Bean[2]   15
catalogue. His nine-knot yawl
was auctioned off to lobstermen.
A red fox stain covers Blue Hill.

---

1. Traditional pastoral names for a shepherdess and shepherd.
2. Knows.

3. Simple, unsophisticated, innocent.
1. An elected New England town official.
2. Famous old Maine sporting goods firm.

And now our fairy
decorator brightens his shop for fall,   20
his fishnet's filled with orange cork,
orange, his cobbler's bench and awl,
there is no money in his work,
he'd rather marry.

One dark night,   25
my Tudor Ford climbed the hill's skull,
I watched for love-cars. Lights turned down,
they lay together, hull to hull,
where the graveyard shelves on the town. . . .
My mind's not right.   30

A car radio bleats,
"Love, O careless Love. . . ."[3] I hear
my ill-spirit sob in each blood cell,
as if my hand were at its throat. . . .
I myself am hell;   35
nobody's here—

only skunks, that search
in the moonlight for a bite to eat.
They march on their soles up Main Street:
white stripes, moonstruck eyes' red fire   40
under the chalk-dry and spar spire
of the Trinitarian Church.

I stand on top
of our back steps and breathe the rich air—
a mother skunk with her column of kittens swills the garbage pail.   45
She jabs her wedge head in a cup
of sour cream, drops her ostrich tail,
and will not scare.

                                                                         1959

ETHERIDGE KNIGHT

Hard Rock Returns to Prison from the Hospital
for the Criminal Insane

Hard Rock was "known not to take no shit
From nobody," and he had the scars to prove it:
Split purple lips, lumped ears, welts above
His yellow eyes, and one long scar that cut
Across his temple and plowed through a thick   5
Canopy of kinky hair.

The WORD was that Hard Rock wasn't a mean nigger
Anymore, that the doctors had bored a hole in his head,
Cut out part of his brain, and shot electricity

3. A popular song.

Through the rest. When they brought Hard Rock back,   10
Handcuffed and chained, he was turned loose,
Like a freshly gelded stallion, to try his new status.
And we all waited and watched, like indians at a corral,
To see if the WORD was true.

As we waited we wrapped ourselves in the cloak   15
Of his exploits: "Man, the last time, it took eight
Screws[4] to put him in the Hole." "Yeah, remember when he
Smacked the captain with his dinner tray?" "He set
The record for time in the Hole—67 straight days!"
"Ol Hard Rock! man, that's one crazy nigger."   20
And then the jewel of a myth that Hard Rock had once bit
A screw on the thumb and poisoned him with syphilitic spit.

The testing came, to see if Hard Rock was really tame.
A hillbilly called him a black son of a bitch
And didn't lose his teeth, a screw who knew Hard Rock   25
From before shook him down and barked in his face.
And Hard Rock did *nothing*. Just grinned and looked silly,
His eyes empty like knot holes in a fence.

And even after we discovered that it took Hard Rock
Exactly 3 minutes to tell you his first name,   30
We told ourselves that he had just wised up,
Was being cool; but we could not fool ourselves for long,
And we turned away, our eyes on the ground. Crushed.
He had been our Destroyer, the doer of things
We dreamed of doing but could not bring ourselves to do,   35
The fears of years, like a biting whip,
Had cut grooves too deeply across our backs.

                                                                      1968

GEORGE HERBERT

The Windows[1]

Lord, how can man preach Thy eternal word?
          He is a brittle, crazy[2] glass:
Yet in Thy temple Thou dost him afford
          This glorious and transcendent place,
          To be a window, through Thy grace.   5

But when Thou dost anneal[3] in glass Thy story,
          Making Thy life to shine within
The holy Preachers; then the light and glory
          More rev'rend grows, and more doth win:
          Which else shows wat'rish, bleak, and thin.   10

4. Guards. "Hole": solitary confinement.
1. One of the lyrics from *The Temple*, a book of poems meditating on parts of the church, holy days, and aspects of Christian faith and practice.
2. Full of cracks.
3. Strengthen glass by heating.

Doctrine and life, colors and light, in one
        When they combine and mingle, bring
    A strong regard and awe: but speech alone
        Doth vanish like a flaring[4] thing,
        And in the ear, not conscience, ring.   15

1633

WALLACE STEVENS

The World as Meditation

J'ai passé trop de temps à travailler mon violon, à voyager. Mais l'exercice essentiel du compositeur—la méditation—rien ne l'a jamais suspendu en moi. . . . Je vis un rêve permanent, qui ne s'arrête ni nuit ni jour.

GEORGES ENESCO[1]

Is it Ulysses that approaches from the east,[2]
The interminable adventurer? The trees are mended.
That winter is washed away. Someone is moving

On the horizon and lifting himself up above it.
A form of fire approaches the cretonnes of Penelope,   5
Whose mere savage presence awakens the world in which she dwells.

She has composed, so long, a self with which to welcome him,
Companion to his self for her, which she imagined,
Two in a deep-founded sheltering, friend and dear friend.

The trees had been mended, as an essential exercise   10
In an inhuman meditation, larger than her own.
No winds like dogs watched over her at night.

She wanted nothing he could not bring her by coming alone.
She wanted no fetchings. His arms would be her necklace
And her belt, the final fortune of their desire.   15

But was it Ulysses? Or was it only the warmth of the sun
On her pillow? The thought kept beating in her like her heart.
The two kept beating together. It was only day.

It was Ulysses and it was not. Yet they had met,
Friend and dear friend and a planet's encouragement.   20
The barbarous strength within her would never fail.

She would talk a little to herself as she combed her hair,
Repeating his name with its patient syllables,
Never forgetting him that kept coming constantly so near.

1954

4. Unsteadily burning.
1. Rumanian violinist, conductor, and composer (1881–1955): "I have spent too much time working at my violin and traveling. But the essential exercise of the composer—meditation—nothing has ever kept me from that. I live a permanent dream which does not stop, night or day."
2. During Ulysses' absence to fight the Trojan War, Penelope remained at home for twenty years, besieged by suitors.

BEN JONSON

To Penshurst[1]

Thou art not, Penshurst, built to envious show,
Of touch[2] or marble; nor canst boast a row
Of polished pillars, or a roof of gold;
Thou hast no lantern[3] whereof tales are told,
Or stair, or courts; but stand'st an ancient pile,   5
And, these grudged at,[4] art reverenced the while.
Thou joy'st in better marks, of soil, of air,
Of wood, of water; therein thou art fair.
Thou hast thy walks for health, as well as sport;
Thy mount, to which the dryads[5] do resort,   10
Where Pan and Bacchus[6] their high feasts have made,
Beneath the broad beech and the chestnut shade,
That taller tree, which of a nut was set
At his great birth[7] where all the Muses met.
There in the writhéd bark are cut the names   15
Of many a sylvan, taken with his flames;[8]
And thence the ruddy satyrs oft provoke
The lighter fauns to reach thy Lady's Oak.[9]
Thy copse too, named of Gamage,[1] thou hast there,
That never fails to serve thee seasoned deer   20
When thou wouldst feast, or exercise, thy friends.
The lower land, that to the river bends,
Thy sheep, thy bullocks, kine, and calves do feed;
The middle grounds thy mares and horses breed.
Each bank doth yield thee conies;[2] and the tops,   25
Fertile of wood, Ashore and Sidney's copse,[3]
To crown thy open table, doth provide
The purpled pheasant with the speckled side;
The painted partridge lies in every field,
And for thy mess is willing to be killed.   30
And if the high-swollen Medway[4] fail thy dish,
Thou hast thy ponds that pay thee tribute fish,
Fat agéd carps that run into thy net,
And pikes, now weary their own kind to eat,
As loath the second draught[5] or cast to stay,   35
Officiously[6] at first themselves betray;
Bright eels that emulate them, and leap on land
Before the fisher, or into his hand.
Then hath thy orchard fruit, thy garden flowers,

---

1. The country seat (in Kent) of the Sidney family, owned by Sir Robert, brother of the poet, Sir Philip. Jonson's celebration of the estate is one of the earliest "house" poems and a prominent example of topographical or didactic-descriptive poetry.
2. Touchstone: basanite, a smooth dark stone similar to black marble.
3. A glassed or open tower or dome atop the roof.
4. I.e., although these (more pretentious structures) are envied. "the while": anyway.
5. Wood nymphs.
6. Ancient gods of nature and wine, both associated with spectacular feasting and celebration.
7. Sir Philip Sidney's, on November 30, 1554; the tree stood for nearly 150 years.
8. Inspired by Sidney's love poetry. "sylvan": forest dweller, rustic.
9. Where, according to legend, a former lady of the house (Lady Leicester) began labor pains. "satyrs": half-men, half-goats who participated in the rites of Bacchus.
1. The maiden name of the owner's wife. "copse": thicket.
2. Rabbits.
3. Two spinneys, or little woods.
4. A river bordering the estate.
5. Of a net. "stay": await.
6. Obligingly.

Fresh as the air, and new as are the hours.   40
The early cherry, with the later plum,
Fig, grape, and quince, each in his time doth come;
The blushing apricot and woolly peach
Hang on thy walls, that every child may reach.
And though thy walls be of the country stone,   45
They're reared with no man's ruin, no man's groan;
There's none that dwell about them wish them down,
But all come in, the farmer and the clown,[7]
And no one empty-handed, to salute
Thy lord and lady, though they have no suit.[8]   50
Some bring a capon, some a rural cake,
Some nuts, some apples; some that think they make
The better cheeses bring 'em, or else send
By their ripe daughters, whom they would commend
This way to husbands, and whose baskets bear   55
An emblem of themselves in plum or pear.
But what can this (more than express their love)
Add to thy free[9] provisions, far above
The need of such? whose liberal board doth flow
With all that hospitality doth know;   60
Where comes no guest but is allowed to eat,
Without his fear, and of thy lord's own meat;
Where the same beer and bread, and selfsame wine,
That is his lordship's shall be also mine.
And I not fain[1] to sit (as some this day   65
At great men's tables), and yet dine away.[2]
Here no man tells[3] my cups; nor, standing by,
A waiter doth my gluttony envý,
But gives me what I call, and lets me eat;
He knows below he shall find plenty of meat.   70
Thy tables hoard not up for the next day;
Nor, when I take my lodging, need I pray
For fire, or lights, or livery;[4] all is there,
As if thou then wert mine, or I reigned here:
There's nothing I can wish, for which I stay.   75
That found King James when, hunting late this way
With his brave son, the prince,[5] they saw thy fires
Shine bright on every hearth, as the desires
Of thy Penates[6] had been set on flame
To entertain them; or the country came   80
With all their zeal to warm their welcome here.
What (great I will not say, but) sudden cheer
Didst thou then make 'em! and what praise was heaped
On thy good lady then! who therein reaped
The just reward of her high housewifery;[7]   85
To have her linen, plate, and all things nigh,
When she was far; and not a room but dressed
As if it had expected such a guest!

7. Rustic, peasant.
8. Request for favors.
9. Generous.
1. Obliged.
2. Possibly, "elsewhere," because they do not get enough to eat; or "away" in the sense of far from the party of honor.
3. Counts.
4. Provisions (or, possibly, servants).
5. Prince Henry, who died in 1612.
6. Roman household gods who cared for the family's welfare.
7. Domestic economy.

These, Penshurst, are thy praise, and yet not all.
Thy lady's noble, fruitful, chaste withal.   90
His children thy great lord may call his own,
A fortune in this age but rarely known.
They are, and have been, taught religion; thence
Their gentler spirits have sucked innocence.
Each morn and even they are taught to pray,   95
With the whole household, and may, every day,
Read in their virtuous parents' noble parts
The mysteries of manners, arms, and arts.
Now, Penshurst, they that will proportion[8] thee
With other edifices, when they see   100
Those proud, ambitious heaps, and nothing else,
May say, their lords have built, but thy lord dwells.

1616

CHARLES TOMLINSON

At Barstow[1]

Nervy with neons, the main drag
was all there was. A placeless place.
A faint flavor of Mexico in the tacos
tasting of gasoline. Trucks refueled
before taking off through space. Someone lived   5
in the houses with their houseyards wired
like tiny Belsens.[2] The Götterdämmerung[3]
would be like this. No funeral pyres, no choirs
of lost trombones. An Untergand[4]
without a clang, without   10
a glimmer of gone glory
however dimmed. At the motel desk
was a photograph of Roy Rogers
signed. It was here
he made a stay. He did not   15
ride away on Trigger
through the high night, the tilted
Pleiades overhead, the polestar low, no
going off until
the eyes of beer-cans   20
had ceased to glint at him
and the desert darknesses
had quenched the neons. He was spent.
He was content. Down he lay.
The passing trucks patrolled his sleep,   25
the shifted gears contrived
a muffled fugue against the fading of his day
and his dustless, undishonored stetson rode
beside the bed,
glowed in the pulsating, never-final twilight   30
there, at that execrable conjunction
of gasoline and desert air.

1966

8. Compare.
1. The first town west of the desert on
the main highway into Southern California.

2. Nazi death camps.
3. End of the world.
4. Destruction, ruin.

MARTIAL

You've Told Me, Maro[1]

You've told me, Maro, whilst you live
You'd not a single penny give,
But that whene'er you chanced to die,
You'd leave a handsome legacy;
You must be mad beyond redress,   5
If my next wish you cannot guess.

ca. 100

PALLADAS (from the *Greek Anthology*[2])

This Life a Theater[3]

This life a theater we well may call,
    Where every actor must perform with art;
Or laugh it through and make a farce of all,
    Or learn to bear with grace his tragic part.

ca. 400

SAMUEL TAYLOR COLERIDGE

What Is an Epigram?

What is an epigram? a dwarfish whole,
Its body brevity, and wit its soul.

p. 1802

ANONYMOUS translation of a Latin distich

[Epigrams]

Three things must epigrams, like bees, have all,
A sting, and honey, and a body small.

BEN JONSON

Epitaph on Elizabeth, L. H.

Wouldst thou hear what man can say
In a little? Reader, stay.
Underneath this stone doth lie
As much beauty as could die;
Which in life did harbor give   5
To more virtue than doth live.
If at all she had a fault,

---

1. Translated from the Latin by F.
Lewis.
2. A collection of epigrams compiled
from earlier anthologies by a Byzantine
scholar, Cephalus, in the 10th century.
3. Translated from the Greek by Robert
Bland.

Leave it buried in this vault.
One name was Elizabeth;
Th' other, let it sleep with death: 10
Fitter, where it died, to tell,
Than that it lived at all. Farewell.

1616

JOHN GAY

My Own Epitaph

Life is a jest; and all things show it.
I thought so once; but now I know it.

ᶜ   1720

J. V. CUNNINGHAM

Here Lies My Wife

Here lies my wife. Eternal peace
Be to us both with her decease.

1959

X. J. KENNEDY

Epitaph for a Postal Clerk

Here lies wrapped up tight in sod
Henry Harkins c/o God.
On the day of Resurrection
May be opened for inspection.

1961

DOROTHY PARKER

Comment

Oh, life is a glorious cycle of song,
A medley of extemporanea;
And love is a thing that can never go wrong;
And I am Marie of Rumania.

1926

MATTHEW PRIOR

A True Maid

No, no; for my virginity,
    When I lose that, says Rose, I'll die:
Behind the elms, last night, cried Dick,
Rose, were you not extremely sick?

1718

THEODORE ROETHKE

Epigram: The Mistake

He left his pants upon a chair:
She was a widow, so she said:
But he was apprehended, bare,
By one who rose up from the dead.

p. 1957

WALTER DE LA MARE

Slim Cunning Hands

Slim cunning hands at rest, and cozening eyes—
Under this stone one loved too wildly lies;
How false she was, no granite could declare;
Nor all earth's flowers, how fair.

1950

SIR JOHN HARINGTON

Epigram: Of Treason

Treason doth never prosper, what's the reason?
For if it prosper, none dare call it treason.

1615

HENRY ALDRICH

Why I Drink

If on my theme I rightly think,
There are five reasons why I drink—
Good wine, a friend, because I'm dry,
Or lest I should be by and by,
Or any other reason why.

ca. 1690

COUNTEE CULLEN

For a Lady I Know

She even thinks that up in heaven
Her class lies late and snores,
While poor black cherubs rise at seven
To do celestial chores.

1925

J. V. CUNNINGHAM

All in Due Time

All in due time: love will emerge from hate,
And the due deference of truth from lies.
If not quite all things come to those who wait
They will not need them: in due time one dies.

1950

WALTER SAVAGE LANDOR

Various the Roads of Life

Various the roads of life; in one
    All terminate, one lonely way.
We go; and "Is he gone?"
    Is all our best friends say.

1846

FRANCIS QUARLES

Be Sad, My Heart

Be sad, my heart, deep dangers wait thy mirth:
Thy soul's waylaid by sea, by hell, by earth:
Hell has her hounds; earth, snares; the sea, a shelf;
But, most of all, my heart, beware thyself.

1635

FRANCES CORNFORD

Parting in Wartime

How long ago Hector[4] took off his plume,
Not wanting that his little son should cry,
Then kissed his sad Andromache good-bye—
And now we three in Euston[5] waiting-room.

1948

SAMUEL TAYLOR COLERIDGE

Metrical Feet

Lesson for a Boy

Trōchĕe trĭps frŏm lōng tŏ shōrt;[1]
From long to long in solemn sort
Slōw Spōndēe stālks; strŏng fōot! yet ill able
Ēvĕr tŏ cōme ŭp wĭth Dāctўl trĭsŷllăblĕ.

---

4. The noblest chieftain in ancient Troy.
5. A London railway station.
1. The long and short marks over syllables are Coleridge's; the kinds of metrical
feet named and exemplified here are defined in the glossary.

Ĭămbĭcs mārch frŏm shōrt tŏ lōng—   5
Wĭth ă lēap ănd ă bōund thĕ swĭft Ānăpĕsts thrōng;
One syllable long, with one short at each side,
Ămphĭbrăchy̆s hāstes wĭth ă stātĕly̆ stride—
Fīrst ănd lāst bēĭng lōng, mīddlĕ shŏrt, Ămphĭmācer
Strĭkes hĭs thūndērĭng hōofs līke ă prōud hīgh-brĕd Rācer.   10
If Derwent[2] be innocent, steady, and wise,
And delight in the things of earth, water, and skies;
Tender warmth at his heart, with these meters to show it,
With sound sense in his brains, may make Derwent a poet—
May crown him with fame, and must win him the love   15
Of his father on earth and his Father above.
          My dear, dear child!
Could you stand upon Skiddaw,[3] you would not from its whole ridge
See a man who so loves you as your fond s. t. coleridge.
1806

MATTHEW PRIOR

The Secretary

Written at The Hague, in the Year 1696[1]

While with labor assid'ous due pleasure I mix,
And in one day atone for the business of six,
In a little Dutch-chaise on a Saturday night,
On my left hand my Horace, a nymph on my right.
No memoir[2] to compose, and no post-boy[3] to move,   5
That on Sunday may hinder the softness of love;
For her, neither visits, nor parties of tea,
Nor the long-winded cant of a dull refugee.
This night and the next shall be hers, shall be mine,
To good or ill fortune the third we resign: 10
Thus scorning the world, and superior to fate,
I drive on my car in processional state;
So with Phia through Athens Pisistratus rode,
Men thought her Minerva, and him a new God.[4]
But why should I stories of Athens rehearse,   15
Where people knew love, and were partial to verse,
Since none can with justice my pleasures oppose,
In Holland half-drownded in int'rest[5] and prose:
By Greece and past ages, what need I be tried,
When the Hague and the present are both on my side,   20
And is it enough, for the joys of the day,
To think what Anacreon,[6] or Sappho would say.

2. Written originally for Coleridge's son Hartley, the poem was later adapted for his younger son, Derwent.
3. A mountain in the lake country of northern England (where Coleridge lived in his early years), near the town of Derwent.
1. Prior was then secretary to the English ambassador at The Hague.
2. Memorandum.
3. Letter carrier.

4. According to Herodotus, Pisistratus (an Athenian tyrant) was returned to power by a hoax; the beautiful Phia, disguised as the goddess Athene (Minerva), publicly proclaimed her wish that he be restored.
5. Political influence.
6. An ancient Greek poet who, like Sappho (of ancient Lesbos), wrote love lyrics.

When good Vandergoes, and his provident vrough,[7]
As they gaze on my triumph, do freely allow,
That search all the province, you'll find no man there is   25
So blessed as the *Englishen Heer Secretaris.*

1696

ANONYMOUS

Limericks

There once was a spinster of Ealing,
Endowed with such delicate feeling,
That she thought an armchair
Should not have its legs bare—
So she kept her eyes trained on the ceiling.

✿   ✿

I sat next to the Duchess at tea.
It was just as I thought it would be:
Her rumblings abdominal
Were simply phenomenal
And everyone thought it was me.

✿   ✿

A charming young woman named Pat
Would invite one to do this and that.
When speaking of this
She meant more than a kiss
So imagine her meaning of that.

✿   ✿

A staid schizophrenic named Struther,
When told of the death of his brother,
Said: "Yes, I am sad;
It makes me feel bad,
But then, I still have each other."

✿   ✿

There once was a pious young priest
Who lived almost wholly on yeast.
He said, "It's so plain
We must all rise again
That I'd like to get started at least."

GEORGE GORDON, LORD BYRON

The Destruction of Sennacherib[1]

The Assyrian came down like the wolf on the fold,
And his cohorts were gleaming in purple and gold;

7. Wife. "Vandergoes": a common Dutch surname.

1. King of Assyria who besieged Jerusalem during Hezekiah's reign as king of Judah. According to *II Kings* 18 and 19, Hezekiah paid ransom but refused to give up faith in his God, who promised that Jerusalem would not be taken. Hezekiah's loyalty was finally rewarded when "the angel of the lord went out, and smote in the camp of the Assyrians an hundred four score and five thousand." (*II Kings* 19:35)

And the sheen of their spears was like stars on the sea,
When the blue wave rolls nightly on deep Galilee.

Like the leaves of the forest when Summer is green,   5
That host with their banners at sunset were seen:
Like the leaves of the forest when Autumn hath blown,
That host on the morrow lay withered and strown.

For the Angel of Death spread his wings on the blast,
And breathed in the face of the foe as he passed;   10
And the eyes of the sleepers waxed deadly and chill,
And their hearts but once heaved, and for ever grew still!

And there lay the steed with his nostril all wide,
But through it there rolled not the breath of his pride;
And the foam of his gasping lay white on the turf,   15
And cold as the spray of the rock-beating surf.

And there lay the rider distorted and pale,
With the dew on his brow, and the rust on his mail:
And the tents were all silent, the banners alone,
The lances unlifted, the trumpet unblown.   20

And the widows of Ashur are loud in their wail,
And the idols are broke in the temple of Baal;[2]
And the might of the Gentile, unsmote by the sword,
Hath melted like snow in the glance of the Lord!

1815

WILLIAM BLAKE

Ah Sunflower

Ah Sunflower! weary of time,
Who countest the steps of the Sun,
Seeking after that sweet golden clime
Where the traveler's journey is done,

Where the Youth pined away with desire,   5
And the pale Virgin shrouded in snow,
Arise from their graves and aspire,
Where my Sunflower wishes to go.

1794

ALEXANDER POPE

[Sound and Sense][1]

But most by numbers[2] judge a poet's song,   337
And smooth or rough, with them, is right or wrong;

---

2. God of the Assyrians.
1. From *An Essay on Criticism*, Pope's poem on the art of poetry and the problems of literary criticism. The passage excerpted here follows a discussion of several common weaknesses of critics: failure to regard an author's intention, for example, or over-emphasis on clever metaphors and ornate style.
2. Meter, rhythm, sound.

In the bright muse though thousand charms conspire,[3]
Her voice is all these tuneful fools admire,   340
Who haunt Parnassus[4] but to please their ear,
Not mend their minds; as some to church repair,
Not for the doctrine, but the music there.
These, equal syllables[5] alone require,
Though oft the ear the open vowels tire,   345
While expletives[6] their feeble aid do join,
And ten low words oft creep in one dull line,
While they ring round the same unvaried chimes,
With sure returns of still expected rhymes.
Where'er you find "the cooling western breeze,"   350
In the next line, it "whispers through the trees";
If crystal streams "with pleasing murmurs creep,"
The reader's threatened (not in vain) with "sleep."
Then, at the last and only couplet fraught
With some unmeaning thing they call a thought,   355
A needless Alexandrine[7] ends the song,
That, like a wounded snake, drags its slow length along.
Leave such to tune their own dull rhymes, and know
What's roundly smooth, or languishingly slow;
And praise the easy vigor of a line,   360
Where Denham's strength and Waller's[8] sweetness join.
True ease in writing comes from art, not chance,
As those move easiest who have learned to dance.
'Tis not enough no harshness gives offense,
The sound must seem an echo to the sense:
Soft is the strain when Zephyr[9] gently blows,
And the smooth stream in smoother numbers flows;
But when loud surges lash the sounding shore,
The hoarse, rough verse should like the torrent roar.
When Ajax[1] strives, some rock's vast weight to throw,   370
The line too labors, and the words move slow;
Not so, when swift Camilla[2] scours the plain,
Flies o'er th' unbending corn, and skims along the main.
Hear how Timotheus'[3] varied lays surprise,
And bid alternate passions fall and rise!   375
While, at each change, the son of Libyan Jove[4]
Now burns with glory, and then melts with love;
Now his fierce eyes with sparkling fury glow,
Now sighs steal out, and tears begin to flow:
Persians and Greeks like turns of nature[5] found,   380
And the world's victor stood subdued by sound!

3. Unite.
4. A mountain in Greece, traditionally associated with the muses and considered the seat of poetry and music.
5. Regular accents.
6. Filler words, such as "do."
7. A six-foot line, sometimes used in pentameter poems to vary the pace mechanically. Line 357 is an alexandrine.
8. Sir John Denham and Edmund Waller, 17th-century poets credited with perfecting the heroic couplet.
9. The west wind.
1. A Greek hero of the Trojan War, noted for his strength.
2. A woman warrior in *The Aeneid*.
3. The court-musician of Alexander the Great, celebrated in a famous poem by Dryden (see line 383) for the power of his music over Alexander's emotions.
4. In Greek tradition, the chief god of any people was often given the name Zeus (Jove), and the chief god of Libya (the Greek name for all of Africa) was called Zeus Ammon. Alexander visited his oracle and was proclaimed son of the god.
5. Similar alternations of emotion.

The pow'r of music all our hearts allow,
And what Timotheus was, is DRYDEN now.

1711

WILLIAM SHAKESPEARE

Like as the Waves

Like as the waves make towards the pebbled shore,
So do our minutes hasten to their end,
Each changing place with that which goes before,
In sequent[1] toil all forwards do contend.[2]
Nativity,[3] once in the main[4] of light,   5
Crawls to maturity, wherewith being crowned,
Crooked[5] eclipses 'gainst his glory fight,
And Time that gave doth now his gift confound.[6]
Time doth transfix[7] the flourish set on youth
And delves the parallels[8] in beauty's brow,   10
Feeds on the rarities of nature's truth,
And nothing stands but for his scythe to mow.
And yet to times in hope[9] my verse shall stand,
Praising thy worth, despite his cruel hand.

1609

ROBERT BURNS

Afton Water

Flow gently, sweet Afton,[1] among thy green braes,[2]
Flow gently, I'll sing thee a song in thy praise;
My Mary's asleep by thy murmuring stream,
Flow gently, sweet Afton, disturb not her dream.

Thou stock dove whose echo resounds through the glen,   5
Ye wild whistling blackbirds in yon thorny den,
Thou green-crested lapwing thy screaming forbear,
I charge you disturb not my slumbering fair.

How lofty, sweet Afton, thy neighboring hills,
Far marked with the courses of clear, winding rills;   10
There daily I wander as noon rises high,
My flocks and my Mary's sweet cot[3] in my eye.

How pleasant thy banks and green valleys below,
Where wild in the woodlands the primroses blow;
There oft as mild evening weeps over the lea,   15
The sweet-scented birk[4] shades my Mary and me.

1. Successive.
2. Struggle.
3. New-born life.
4. High seas.
5. Perverse.
6. Bring to nothing.
7. Pierce.

8. Lines, wrinkles.
9. In the future.
1. A small river in Ayrshire, Scotland.
2. Hillsides.
3. Cottage.
4. Birch.

Thy crystal stream, Afton, how lovely it glides,
And winds by the cot where my Mary resides;
How wanton thy waters her snowy feet lave,
As gathering sweet flowerets she stems thy clear wave.   20

Flow gently, sweet Afton, among thy green braes,
Flow gently, sweet river, the theme of my lays;
My Mary's asleep by thy murmuring stream,
Flow gently, sweet Afton, disturb not her dream.

1792

JAMES MERRILL

Watching the Dance

1. BALANCHINE'S[1]

Poor savage, doubting that a river flows
But for the myriad eddies made
By unseen powers twirling on their toes,

Here in this darkness it would seem
You had already died, and were afraid.   5
Be still. Observe the powers. Infer the stream.

2. DISCOTHÈQUE

Having survived entirely your own youth,
Last of your generation, purple gloom
Investing you, sit, Jonah,[2] beyond speech,

And let towards the brute volume VOOM whale mouth   10
VAM pounding viscera VAM VOOM
A teenage plankton luminously twitch.

1967

HART CRANE

from The Bridge[1]

The nasal whine of power whips a new universe . . .   63
Where spouting pillars spoor the evening sky,
Under the looming stacks of the gigantic power house
Stars prick the eyes with sharp ammoniac proverbs,
New verities, new inklings in the velvet hummed
Of dynamos, where hearing's leash is strummed . . .
Power's script—wound, bobbin-bound, refined—
Is stropped to the slap of belts on booming spools, spurred   70
Into the bulging bouillon, harnessed jelly of the stars.
Towards what? The forked crash of split thunder parts

1. George Balanchine, Russian-born
(1894) ballet choreographer and teacher.
2. According to *Jonah* 4, Jonah sat in
gloom near Nineveh after its residents re-
pented and God decided to spare the city
from destruction.
1. From "Cape Hatteras," Section IV of
The Bridge, Crane's epic about the history
of America.

Our hearing momentwise; but fast in whirling armatures,
As bright as frogs' eyes, giggling in the girth
Of steely gizzards—axle-bound, confined   75
In coiled precision, bunched in mutual glee
The bearings glint—O murmurless and shined
In oilrinsed circles of blind ecstasy!

1930

JOHN DRYDEN

A Song for St. Cecilia's Day[1]

I

From harmony, from heav'nly harmony
        This universal frame began:
        When Nature[2] underneath a heap
            Of jarring atoms lay,
            And could not heave her head,   5
The tuneful voice was heard from high:
            "Arise, ye more than dead."
Then cold, and hot, and moist, and dry,
        In order to their stations leap,
            And Music's pow'r obey.   10
From harmony, from heav'nly harmony
        This universal frame began:
            From harmony to harmony
Through all the compass of the notes it ran,
The diapason closing full in man.[3]   15

II

What passion cannot Music raise and quell!
        When Jubal[4] struck the chorded shell,
        His list'ning brethren stood around,
        And, wond'ring, on their faces fell
        To worship that celestial sound.   20
Less than a god they thought there could not dwell
            Within the hollow of that shell
            That spoke so sweetly and so well.
What passion cannot Music raise and quell!

III

        The TRUMPET's loud clangor   25
            Excites us to arms

1. St. Cecilia, a third-century Roman who became a Christian martyr and the patron saint of music, is said to be the inventor of the organ. In late 17th-century England her festival day (November 22) was elaborately celebrated with concerts, religious services, and the commissioning of original compositions like this ode, which was first set to music by Giovanni Baptiste Draghi and later by Handel.
2. The created world, ordered by the Divine Word, according to *Genesis* 1. According to Epicurean physics, atoms of the four elements (earth, fire, water, air [line 8]) were discordant and at war ("jarring," line 4), and Dryden follows traditional Judeo-Christian thought in describing the elements being put into place ("stations," line 9) by divine power. The tradition that the world moves according to harmonious musical principles—and that an unheard "music of the spheres" represents that harmony—goes back to Pythagoras, a sixth-century B.C. Greek philosopher and mathematician.
3. Total concord, which culminates in man, the highest earthly creation in the Chain of Being.
4. "The father of all such as handle the harp and organ." (*Genesis* 4:21)

With shrill notes of anger,
    And mortal alarms.
The double double double beat
    Of the thundering DRUM   30
Cries: "Hark! the foes come;
Charge, charge, 'tis too late to retreat."

IV

The soft complaining FLUTE
    In dying notes discovers
    The woes of hopeless lovers,   35
Whose dirge is whispered by the warbling LUTE.

V

Sharp VIOLINS proclaim
Their jealous pangs, and desperation,
Fury, frantic indignation,
Depth of pains, and height of passion,   40
    For the fair, disdainful dame.

VI

But O! what art can teach,
    What human voice can reach,
The sacred ORGAN's praise?
    Notes inspiring holy love,   45
Notes that wing their heav'nly ways
    To mend the choirs above.

VII

Orpheus[5] could lead the savage race;
And trees unrooted left their place,
    Sequacious of[6] the lyre.   50
But bright Cecilia raised the wonder higher:
When to her ORGAN vocal breath was given,
An angel heard, and straight appeared,
    Mistaking earth for heaven.

GRAND CHORUS

As from the power of sacred lays   55
*   The spheres began to move,*
And sung the great Creator's praise
*   To all the blest above;*
So, when the last and dreadful hour
This crumbling pageant[7] shall devour,   60
The TRUMPET shall be heard on high,[8]
The dead shall live, the living die,
And Music shall untune the sky.

1687

---

5. Whose music was supposed to be so powerful that he could control even inanimate objects.
6. Made slavish by.
7. The world as stage.

8. According to *I Corinthians* 15:52, "the trumpet shall sound and the dead shall be raised incorruptible" on Judgment Day.

A. B. SPELLMAN

John Coltrane[9]

An Impartial Review

may he have new life like the fall
fallen tree, wet moist rotten enough
to see shoots stalks branches & green
leaves (& may the roots) grow into his side.

around the back of the mind, in its closet   5
is a string, i think, a coil around things.
listen to *summertime,* think of spring, negroes
cats in the closet, anything that makes a rock

of your eye. imagine you steal. you are frightened
you want help. you are sorry you are born with ears   10

p. 1964

JOHN DRYDEN

To the Memory of Mr. Oldham[1]

Farewell, too little, and too lately known,
Whom I began to think and call my own;
For sure our souls were near allied, and thine
Cast in the same poetic mold with mine.
One common note on either lyre did strike,   5
And knaves and fools we both abhorred alike.
To the same goal did both our studies drive;
The last set out the soonest did arrive.
Thus Nisus fell upon the slippery place,
While his young friend performed and won the race.[2]   10
O early ripe! to thy abundant store
What could advancing age have added more?
It might (what nature never gives the young)
Have taught the numbers[3] of thy native tongue.
But satire needs not those, and wit will shine   15
Through the harsh cadence of a rugged line.[4]
A noble error, and but seldom made,
When poets are by too much force betrayed.
Thy generous fruits, though gathered ere their prime,
Still showed a quickness; and maturing time   20
But mellows what we write to the dull sweets of rhyme.
Once more, hail and farewell; farewell, thou young,

9. Controversial jazz musician (1926–
67), whose tenor sax style finally came to
be recognized as the most innovative in
modern jazz.
    1. John Oldham (1653–83), who like
Dryden (see lines 3–6) wrote satiric poetry.
    2. In Vergil's *Aeneid* (Book V), Nisus

(who is leading the race) falls and then
trips the second runner so that his friend
Euryalus can win.
    3. Rhythms.
    4. In Dryden's time, R's were pro-
nounced with a harsh, trilling sound.

But ah too short, Marcellus[5] of our tongue;
Thy brows with ivy, and with laurels bound;
But fate and gloomy night encompass thee around.   25

1684

ALFRED, LORD TENNYSON

Break, Break, Break

Break, break, break,
  On thy cold gray stones, O Sea!
And I would that my tongue could utter
  The thoughts that arise in me.

O well for the fisherman's boy,   5
  That he shouts with his sister at play!
O well for the sailor lad,
  That he sings in his boat on the bay!
And the stately ships go on
  To their haven under the hill;   10
But O for the touch of a vanished hand,
  And the sound of a voice that is still!

Break, break, break,
  At the foot of thy crags, O Sea!
But the tender grace of a day that is dead   15
  Will never come back to me.

ca. 1834

BEN JONSON

Slow, Slow, Fresh Fount[1]

Slow, slow, fresh fount, keep time with my salt tears;
  Yet slower, yet, O faintly gentle springs!
List to the heavy part the music bears,
  Woe weeps out her division,[2] when she sings.
    Droop herbs, and flowers;   5
    Fall grief in showers;
    Our beauties are not ours:
      O, I could still
(Like melting snow upon some craggy hill)
    Drop, drop, drop, drop,   10
Since nature's pride is now a withered daffodil.

1600

5. The nephew of the Roman emperor
Augustus; he died at 20, and Vergil celebrated him in *The Aeneid*, Book VI.
1. A song from *Cynthia's Revels*, a satiric comedy. In the play, Echo sings the
song for Narcissus, who had seen his reflection in a fountain, become entranced by
it, and been transformed into a flower
(line 11).
2. Portion. "Division," in musical terminology, also means "variation on a
theme."

THOMAS NASHE

Spring, the Sweet Spring

Spring, the sweet spring, is the year's pleasant king,
Then blooms each thing, then maids dance in a ring,
Cold doth not sting, the pretty birds do sing:
    Cuckoo, jug-jug, pu-we, to-witta-woo![1]

The palm and may make country houses gay,   5
Lambs frisk and play, the shepherds pipe all day,
And we hear aye birds tune this merry lay:
    Cuckoo, jug-jug, pu-we, to-witta-woo!

The fields breathe sweet, the daisies kiss our feet,
Young lovers meet, old wives a-sunning sit,   10
In every street these tunes our ears do greet:
    Cuckoo, jug-jug, pu-we, to-witta-woo!
      Spring, the sweet spring!

                                    1592

DONALD JUSTICE

Counting the Mad

This one was put in a jacket,
This one was sent home,
This one was given bread and meat
But would eat none,
And this one cried No No No No   5
All day long.

This one looked at the window
As though it were a wall,
This one saw things that were not there,
This one things that were,   10
And this one cried No No No No
All day long.

This one thought himself a bird,
This one a dog,
And this one thought himself a man,   15
An ordinary man,
And cried and cried No No No No
All day long.

                                      1960

---

1. The calls of the cuckoo, nightingale, lapwing, and owl, respectively.

GERARD MANLEY HOPKINS

Spring and Fall:

To a Young Child

Márgarét áre you gríeving
Over Goldengrove unleaving?
Leáves, líke the things of man, you
With your fresh thoughts care for, can you?
Áh! ás the heart grows older   5
It will come to such sights colder
By and by, nor spare a sigh
Though worlds of wanwood[1] leafmeal lie;
And yet you wíll weep and know why.
Now no matter, child, the name: 10
Sórrow's spríngs áre the same.
Nor mouth had, no nor mind, expressed
What heart heard of, ghost[2] guessed:
It ís the blight man was born for,
It is Margaret you mourn for.   15

1880

e. e. cummings

l(a

l(a

le
af
fa

ll   5

s)
one
l

iness

1958

1. Pale, gloomy woods. "leafmeal": broken up, leaf by leaf, (analogous to "piecemeal").
2. Soul.

ROBERT HOLLANDER

You Too? Me Too—Why Not?
Soda Pop

<pre>
           I am
           look
           ing at
           the Co
           caCola
           bottle
           which is
           green wi
           th ridges
           just   like
         c   c   c
         o   o   o
         l   l   l
         u   u   u
         m   m   m
         n   n   n
         s   s   s
    and on itself it says
</pre>

COCA-COLA
reg.u.s.pat.off.

exactly like an art pop
statue of that kind of
bottle but not so green
that the juice inside
gives other than the co
lor it has when I pour
it out in a clear glass
glass on this table top
(It's making me thirsty
all this winking and
beading of Hippocrene
please let me pause
drinking the fluid in)
ah! it is enticing how
each color is the same
brown in green bottle
brown in uplifted glass
making each utensil on
the table laid a brown
fork in a brown shade
making me long to watch
them harvesting the crop
which makes the deep-aged
rich brown wine of America
that is to say which makes
soda   pop

p. 1968

EDWIN MORGAN

The Computer's First Christmas Card

```
            jollymerry
            hollyberry
            jollyberry
            merryholly
            happyjolly                      5
            jollyjelly
            jellybelly
            bellymerry
            hollyheppy
            jollyMolly                      10
            marryJerry
            merryHarry
            hoppyBarry
            heppyJarry
            boppyheppy                      15
            berryjorry
            jorryjolly
            moppyjelly
            Mollymerry
            Jerryjolly                      20
            bellyboppy
            jorryhoppy
            hollymoppy
            Barrymerry
            Jarryhappy                      25
            happyboppy
            boppyjolly
            jollymerry
            merrymerry
            merrymerry                      30
            merryChris
            ammerryasa
            Chrismerry
            aSMERRYCHR
            YSANTHEMUM                      35
```

1968

RICHARD KOSTELANETZ

Tribute to Henry Ford

TRIBUTE TO HENRY FORD 1

TRIBUTE TO HENRY FORD 2

TRIBUTE TO HENRY FORD 3

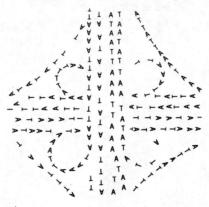

p. 1969

GEORGE HERBERT

Easter Wings

Lord, who createdst man in wealth and store,[1]
Though foolishly he lost the same,
Decaying more and more,
Till he became
Most poor:
With thee
O let me rise
As larks,[2] harmoniously,
And sing this day thy victories:
Then shall the fall further the flight in me.

My tender age in sorrow did begin;
And still with sicknesses and shame
Thou didst so punish sin,
That I became
Most thin.
With thee
Let me combine,
And feel this day thy victory;
For, if I imp[3] my wing on thine,
Affliction shall advance the flight in me.

1633

ROBERT HERRICK

The Pillar of Fame

Fame's pillar here, at last, we set,
Out-during *Marble, Brass,* or *Jet,*[1]
Charmed and enchanted so,
As to withstand the blow
Of   overthrow:
Nor shall the seas,
Or   OUTRAGES
Of storms o'erbear
What we up-rear,
Tho Kingdoms fall,
This   pillar   never   shall
Decline   or   waste   at   all;
But stand for ever by his own
Firm and well fixed foundation.

1648

---

1. In plenty.
2. Which herald the morning.
3. Engraft. In falconry, to engraft feathers in a damaged wing, so as to restore the powers of flight (OED).
1. Black lignite or black marble. "Out-during": out-lasting.

III

ROBERT HERRICK

To the Virgins, to Make Much of Time

Gather ye rosebuds while ye may,
Old time is still a-flying;
And this same flower that smiles today
Tomorow will be dying.

The glorious lamp of heaven, the sun,   5
The higher he's a-getting,
The sooner will his race be run,
And nearer he's to setting.

That age is best which is the first,
When youth and blood are warmer;   10
But being spent, the worse, and worst
Times still succeed the former.

Then be not coy, but use your time,
And, while ye may, go marry;
For, having lost but once your prime,   15
You may forever tarry.

1648

EDMUND WALLER

Song

Go, lovely rose!
Tell her that wastes her time and me
That now she knows,
When I resemble[1] her to thee,
How sweet and fair she seems to be.   5

Tell her that's young,
And shuns to have her graces spied,
That hadst thou sprung
In deserts, where no men abide,
Thou must have uncommended died.   10

Small is the worth
Of beauty from the light retired;
Bid her come forth,
Suffer herself to be desired,
And not blush so to be admired.   15

1. Compare.

Then die! that she
The common fate of all things rare
May read in thee;
How small a part of time they share
That are so wondrous sweet and fair! 20

1645

JOHN DONNE

The Flea

Mark but this flea, and mark in this[1]
How little that which thou deny'st me is;
It sucked me first, and now sucks thee,
And in this flea our two bloods mingled be;
Thou know'st that this cannot be said 5
A sin, nor shame, nor loss of maidenhead,
  Yet this enjoys before it woo,
  And pampered[2] swells with one blood made of two,
  And this, alas, is more than we would do.[3]

Oh stay, three lives in one flea spare, 10
Where we almost, yea more than, married are.
This flea is you and I, and this
Our marriage bed, and marriage temple is;
Though parents grudge, and you, we're met
And cloistered in these living walls of jet. 15
  Though use[4] make you apt to kill me,
  Let not to that, self-murder added be,
  And sacrilege, three sins in killing three.

Cruel and sudden, hast thou since
Purpled thy nail in blood of innocence? 20
Wherein could this flea guilty be,
Except in that drop which it sucked from thee?
Yet thou triumph'st, and say'st that thou
Find'st not thyself, nor me, the weaker now;
  'Tis true; then learn how false, fears be; 25
  Just so much honor, when thou yield'st to me,
  Will waste, as this flea's death took life from thee.

1633

ROBERT HERRICK

Corinna's Going A-Maying

Get up, get up, for shame! the blooming morn
Upon her wings presents the god unshorn.[1]

1. Medieval preachers and rhetoricians asked their hearers to "mark" (look at) an object which illustrated a moral or philosophical lesson they wished to emphasize.
2. Fed luxuriously.
3. According to contemporary medical theory, conception involved the literal mingling of the lovers' blood.
4. Habit.
1. Apollo, the sun god, whose golden hair represents the sun's rays.

See how Aurora[2] throws her fair
Fresh-quilted[3] colors through the air:
   Get up, sweet slug-a-bed, and see   5
   The dew bespangling herb and tree.
Each flower has wept, and bowéd toward the east,
Above an hour since; yet you not dressed,
   Nay, not so much as out of bed?
   When all the birds have matins[4] said,   10
   And sung their thankful hymns, 'tis sin,
   Nay, profanation to keep in,
Whenas a thousand virgins on this day
Spring, sooner than the lark, to fetch in May.[5]

Rise, and put on your foliage, and be seen   15
To come forth, like the springtime, fresh and green,
   And sweet as Flora.[6] Take no care
   For jewels for your gown, or hair;
   Fear not; the leaves will strew
   Gems in abundance upon you;   20
Besides, the childhood of the day has kept,
Against[7] you come, some orient[8] pearls unwept;
   Come, and receive them while the light
   Hangs on the dew-locks of the night,
   And Titan[9] on the eastern hill   25
   Retires himself, or else stands still,
Till you come forth. Wash, dress, be brief in praying:
Few beads[1] are best when once we go a-Maying.

Come, my Corinna, come; and, coming, mark
How each field turns[2] a street, each street a park   30
   Made green and trimmed with trees; see how
   Devotion gives each house a bough
   Or branch: each porch, each door, ere this,
   An ark, a tabernacle is,
Made up of whitethorn neatly interwove,   35
As if here were those cooler shades of love.
   Can such delights be in the street,
   And open fields, and we not see 't?
   Come, we'll abroad; and let's obey
   The proclamation made for May,   40
And sin no more, as we have done, by staying;
But, my Corinna, come, let's go a-Maying.

There's not a budding boy or girl this day
But is got up, and gone to bring in May;
   A deal of youth, ere this, is come   45
   Back, and with whitethorn laden home.

2. Goddess of the dawn.
3. Mingled.
4. Morning prayers.
5. The traditional celebration of May Day morning included the gathering of white hawthorn blossoms and boughs to decorate houses and streets.
6. Goddess of flowers.
7. Until.
8. Shining.
9. The sun.
1. Prayers.
2. Turns into.

Some have dispatched their cakes and cream
Before that we have left to dream;
And some have wept, and wooed, and plighted troth,
And chose their priest, ere we can cast off sloth.   50
  Many a green-gown[3] has been given,
  Many a kiss, both odd and even,
  Many a glance, too, has been sent
  From out the eye, love's firmament;
Many a jest told of the keys betraying   55
This night, and locks picked; yet we're not a-Maying.

Come, let us go while we are in our prime,
And take the harmless folly of the time.
  We shall grow old apace, and die
  Before we know our liberty.   60
  Our life is short, and our days run
  As fast away as does the sun;
And as a vapor, or a drop of rain,
Once lost, can ne'er be found again:
  So when or you or[4] I are made   65
  A fable, song, or fleeting shade,
  All love, all liking, all delight
  Lies drowned with us in endless night.
Then while time serves, and we are but decaying,
Come, my Corinna, come, let's go a-Maying.   70

                                    1648

BEN JONSON

Come, My Celia[1]

Come, my Celia, let us prove,[2]
While we can, the sports of love;
Time will not be ours forever:
He at length our good will sever.
Spend not, then, his gifts in vain;   5
Suns that set may rise again,
But if once we lose this light,
'Tis with us perpetual night.
Why should we defer our joys?
Fame and rumor are but toys.   10
Cannot we delude the eyes
Of a few poor household spies?
Or his easier ears beguile,
Thus removéd by our wile?
'Tis no sin love's fruits to steal,   15
But the sweet thefts to reveal;
To be taken, to be seen,
These have crimes accounted been.

                                    1606

3. Grass-stained gown.
4. Either . . . or.
1. A song from *Volpone*, sung by the play's villain and would-be seducer. Part of the poem paraphrases Catullus, V, "Vivamus, mea Lesbia, atque amemus."
2. Try.

ALFRED, LORD TENNYSON

Now Sleeps the Crimson Petal[1]

Now sleeps the crimson petal, now the white;
Nor waves the cypress in the palace walk;
Nor winks the gold fin in the porphyry font;[2]
The firefly wakens; waken thou with me.

Now droops the milk-white peacock like a ghost,   5
And like a ghost she glimmers on to me.

Now lies the Earth all Danaë[3] to the stars,
And all thy heart lies open unto me.

Now slides the silent meteor on, and leaves
A shining furrow, as thy thoughts in me.   10

Now folds the lily all her sweetness up,
And slips into the bosom of the lake;
So fold thyself, my dearest, thou, and slip
Into my bosom and be lost in me.

                                                1847

X. J. KENNEDY

In a Prominent Bar in Secaucus One Day

*To the tune of "The Old Orange Flute" or
the tune of "Sweet Betsy from Pike"*

In a prominent bar in Secaucus[1] one day
Rose a lady in skunk with a topheavy sway,
Raised a knobby red finger—all turned from their beer—
While with eyes bright as snowcrust she sang high and clear:

"Now who of you'd think from an eyeload of me   5
That I once was a lady as proud as could be?
Oh I'd never sit down by a tumbledown drunk
If it wasn't, my dears, for the high cost of junk.

"All the gents used to swear that the white of my calf
Beat the down of a swan by a length and a half.   10
In the kerchief of linen I caught to my nose
Ah, there never fell snot, but a little gold rose.

"I had seven gold teeth and a toothpick of gold,
My Virginia cheroot was a leaf of it rolled
And I'd light it each time with a thousand in cash—   15
Why the bums used to fight if I flicked them an ash.

1. A song from *The Princess*, in the form
of a ghazal.
2. Stone fishbowl. "porphyry": a red
stone containing fine white crystals.
3. A princess, confined in a tower, seduced by Zeus after he became a shower of
gold in order to gain access to her.
1. A small, smoggy town on the Hack-
ensack River in New Jersey, a few miles
west of Manhattan.

"Once the toast of the Biltmore,[2] the belle of the Taft,
I would drink bottle beer at the Drake, never draft,
And dine at the Astor on Salisbury steak
With a clean tablecloth for each bite I did take.   20

"In a car like the Roxy[3] I'd roll to the track,
A steel-guitar trio, a bar in the back,
And the wheels made no noise, they turned over so fast,
Still it took you ten minutes to see me go past.

"When the horses bowed down to me that I might choose,   25
I bet on them all, for I hated to lose.
Now I'm saddled each night for my butter and eggs
And the broken threads race down the backs of my legs.

"Let you hold in mind, girls, that your beauty must pass
Like a lovely white clover that rusts with its grass.   30
Keep your bottoms off barstools and marry you young
Or be left—an old barrel with many a bung.

"For when time takes you out for a spin in his car
You'll be hard-pressed to stop him from going too far
And be left by the roadside, for all your good deeds,   35
Two toadstools for tits and a face full of weeds."

All the house raised a cheer, but the man at the bar
Made a phonecall and up pulled a red patrol car
And she blew us a kiss as they copped her away
From that prominent bar in Secaucus, N.J.   40

1961

ANDREW MARVELL

To His Coy Mistress

Had we but world enough, and time,
This coyness,[1] lady, were no crime.
We would sit down, and think which way
To walk, and pass our long love's day.
Thou by the Indian Ganges' side   5
Shouldst rubies[2] find: I by the tide
Of Humber[3] would complain. I would
Love you ten years before the Flood,
And you should if you please refuse
Till the conversion of the Jews.[4]   10
My vegetable love[5] should grow

---

2. Like the Taft, Drake, and Astor, a once fashionable New York hotel.
3. A luxurious old New York theater and movie house, the site of many "World Premieres" in the heyday of Hollywood.
1. Hesitancy, modesty (not necessarily suggesting calculation).
2. Talismans which are supposed to preserve virginity.
3. A small river which flows through Marvell's home town, Hull. "complain":

write love complaints, conventional songs lamenting the cruelty of love.
4. Which, according to popular Christian belief, will occur just before the end of the world.
5. Which is capable only of passive growth, not of consciousness. The "Vegetable Soul" is lower than the other two divisions of the Soul, "Animal" and "Rational."

Vaster than empires, and more slow;
An hundred years should go to praise
Thine eyes, and on thy forehead gaze;
Two hundred to adore each breast,   15
But thirty thousand to the rest.
An age at least to every part,
And the last age should show your heart.
For, lady, you deserve this state;[6]
Nor would I love at lower rate.   20
    But at my back I always hear
Time's wingéd chariot hurrying near;
And yonder all before us lie
Deserts of vast eternity.
Thy beauty shall no more be found,   25
Nor, in thy marble vault, shall sound
My echoing song; then worms shall try
That long preserved virginity,
And your quaint honor turn to dust,
And into ashes all my lust: 30
The grave's a fine and private place,
But none, I think, do there embrace.
    Now therefore, while the youthful hue
Sits on thy skin like morning dew,[7]
And while thy willing soul transpires[8]   35
At every pore with instant fires,
Now let us sport us while we may,
And now, like am'rous birds of prey,
Rather at once our time devour
Than languish in his slow-chapped[9] pow'r.   40
Let us roll all our strength and all
Our sweetness up into one ball,
And tear our pleasures with rough strife
Thorough[1] the iron gates of life.
Thus, though we cannot make our sun   45
Stand still,[2] yet we will make him run.[3]

1681

e. e. cummings

(ponder,darling,these busted statues

(ponder,darling,these busted statues
of yon motheaten forum be aware
notice what hath remained
—the stone cringes
clinging to the stone,how obsolete   5

6. Dignity.
7. The text reads "glew." "Lew" (warmth) has also been suggested as an emendation.
8. Breathes forth.
9. Slow-jawed. Chronos (Time), ruler of the world in early Greek myth, devoured all of his children except Zeus, who was hidden. Later, Zeus seized power (see line 46 and note).
1. Through.
2. To lengthen his night of love with Alcmene, Zeus made the sun stand still.
3. Each sex act was believed to shorten life by one day.

lips utter their extant smile . . . .
remark

a few deleted of texture
or meaning monuments and dolls

resist Them Greediest Paws of careful   10
time[4] all of which is extremely
unimportant)whereas Life

matters if or

when the your- and my-
idle vertical worthless   15
self unite in a peculiarly
momentary

partnership(to instigate
constructive
        Horizontal   20
business . . . . even so,let us make haste
—consider well this ruined aqueduct

lady,
which used to lead something into somewhere)

            1926

WILLIAM HABINGTON

To Roses in the Bosom of Castara

Ye blushing virgins happy are
In the chaste nunn'ry of her breasts,
For he'd profane so chaste a fair,[1]
Whoe'er should call them Cupid's nests.

Transplanted thus, how bright ye grow,   5
How rich a perfume do ye yield.
In some close garden, cowslips so
Are sweeter than i' th' open field.

In those white cloisters live secure
From the rude blasts of wanton breath,   10
Each hour more innocent and pure,
Till you shall wither into death.

Then that which living gave you room,
Your glorious sepulcher shall be;
There wants[2] no marble for a tomb,   15
Whose breast hath marble been to me.

            1634

4. See "To His Coy Mistress," above,   1. Beautiful woman.
especially lines 39–40.   2. Lacks.

ROBERT BURNS

A Red, Red Rose

O, my luve's like a red, red rose
That's newly sprung in June.
O, my luve is like the melodie
That's sweetly played in tune.

As fair art thou, my bonnie lass,   5
So deep in luve am I;
And I will luve thee still, my dear,
Till a' the seas gang[1] dry.

Till a' the seas gang dry, my dear,
And the rocks melt wi' the sun;   10
And I will luve thee still, my dear,
While the sands o' life shall run.

And fare thee weel, my only luve,
And fare thee weel a while!
And I will come again, my luve,   15
Though it were ten thousand mile.

1796

ROBERT FROST

The Rose Family[2]

The rose is a rose,
And was always a rose.
But the theory now goes
That the apple's a rose,
And the pear is, and so's   5
The plum, I suppose.
The dear only knows
What will next prove a rose.
You, of course, are a rose—
But were always a rose.   10

1928

WILLIAM BLAKE

The Sick Rose[1]

O rose, thou art sick.
The invisible worm
That flies in the night
In the howling storm

---

1. Go.
2. A response to Gertrude Stein's famous line, "A rose is a rose is a rose."
1. In Renaissance emblem books, the scarab beetle, worm, and rose are closely associated: The beetle feeds on dung, and the smell of the rose is fatal to it.

Has found out thy bed   5
Of crimson joy,
And his dark secret love
Does thy life destroy.

1794

DONALD JUSTICE

Southern Gothic

(*for W.E.B. & P.R.*)

Something of how the homing bee at dusk
Seems to inquire, perplexed, how there can be
No flowers here, not even withered stalks of flowers,
Conjures a garden where no garden is
And trellises too frail almost to bear   5
The memory of a rose, much less a rose.
Great oaks, more monumentally great oaks now
Than ever when the living rose was new,
Cast shade that is the more completely shade
Upon a house of broken windows merely   10
And empty nests up under broken eaves.
No damask any more prevents the moon,
But it unravels, peeling from a wall,
Red roses within roses within roses.

1960

WILLIAM CARLOS WILLIAMS

Poem

The rose fades
and is renewed again
by its seed, naturally
but where

save in the poem   5
shall it go
to suffer no diminution
of its splendor

1962

WILLIAM SHAKESPEARE

All the World's a Stage[1]

All the world's a stage,   139
And all the men and women merely players.
They have their exits and their entrances,

---

1. A speech by Jaques in *As You Like It*, Act II, sc. vii. The metaphor of the world as
stage (and the stage as a little world) dates from classical antiquity, and the motto of the
newly opened Globe Theater (where *As You Like It* was played) was "Totus mundus agit
histrionem": "All the world plays the actor."

And one man in his time plays many parts,
His acts being seven ages. At first, the infant,
Mewling and puking in the nurse's arms.
Then the whining schoolboy, with his satchel   145
And shining morning face, creeping like snail
Unwillingly to school. And then the lover,
Sighing like furnace, with a woeful ballad[2]
Made to his mistress' eyebrow. Then a soldier,
Full of strange oaths and bearded like the pard,[3]   150
Jealous in honor,[4] sudden and quick in quarrel,
Seeking the bubble reputation
Even in the cannon's mouth. And then the justice,
In fair round belly with good capon lined,[5]
With eyes severe and beard of formal cut,   155
Full of wise saws[6] and modern instances;
And so he plays his part. The sixth age shifts
Into the lean and slippered pantaloon,[7]
With spectacles on nose and pouch on side;
His youthful hose, well saved, a world too wide   160
For his shrunk shank, and his big manly voice,
Turning again toward childish treble, pipes
And whistles in his sound. Last scene of all,
That ends this strange eventful history,
Is second childishness and mere oblivion,   165
Sans teeth, sans eyes, sans taste, sans everything.

ca. 1599

FRANCIS QUARLES

My Soul, Sit Thou a Patient Looker-on[8]

My soul, sit thou a patient looker-on;
Judge not the play before the play is done.
Her plot has many changes: every day
Speaks a new scene. The last act crowns the play.

1635

JOHN DONNE

This Is My Play's Last Scene

This is my play's last scene, here heavens appoint
My pilgrimage's last mile; and my race,
Idly yet quickly run, hath this last pace,
My span's[1] last inch, my minute's last point;
And gluttonous death will instantly unjoint   5
My body and soul, and I shall sleep a space;

2. Verse, song.
3. Leopard.
4. Zealous in pursuing fame; sensitive about his good name.
5. Well fed with presents (from those who seek his favorable judgment).
6. Sayings: maxims.
7. A ridiculous old man in Italian comedy.

8. The concluding epigram to Quarles' *Emblem XV*, depicting and then meditating upon a scene presided over by Satan, who has usurped God's throne.
1. Literally, a "span" is the distance from the tip of the thumb to the tip of the little finger; traditionally, a representation of the shortness of human life.

But my ever-waking part shall see that face
Whose fear[2] already shakes my every joint.
Then, as my soul to heaven, her first seat, takes flight,
And earth-born body in the earth shall dwell,   10
So, fall my sins, that all may have their right,
To where they're bred, and would press me, to hell.
Impute me righteous, thus purged of evil,
For thus I leave the world, the flesh, the devil.[3]

1633

GEOFFREY CHAUCER

Whan that Aprill with His Shoures Soote[1]

Whan that Aprill with his shoures soote[2]
The droghte[3] of March hath perced to the roote,
And bathed every veyne[4] in swich licour,
Of which vertu[5] engendred is the flour;
Whan Zephyrus[6] eek with his sweete breeth   5
Inspired hath in every holt and heeth[7]
The tendre croppes, and the yonge sonne[8]
Hath in the Ram his halfe cours yronne,
And smale foweles[9] maken melodye
That slepen[1] al the nyght with open yë—   10
So priketh hem[2] Nature in hir corages—
Thanne longen[3] folk to goon on pilgrimages,
And palmeres[4] for to seken straunge strondes
To ferne halwes, kowthe[5] in sondry londes;
And specially from every shires[6] ende   15
Of Engelond to Caunterbury they wende,[7]
The holy blisful martir for to seke
That hem hath holpen[8] whan that they were seeke.

ca. 1386

DYLAN THOMAS

The Force that Through the Green Fuse Drives the Flower

The force that through the green fuse drives the flower
Drives my green age; that blasts the roots of trees

2. The fear of whom.
3. The traditional Three Temptations.
1. The opening lines of the "General Prologue" to *The Canterbury Tales*, a series of stories told by pilgrims going to Canterbury.
2. Sweet showers.
3. Drought. "perced": pierced.
4. Vein: vessel of sap. "swich licour": such liquid.
5. By the power ("vertu") of which. "flour": flower.
6. The west wind, traditionally the spring wind which renews life. "eek": also.
7. Woods and field.
8. Sun: "young" because it has run only halfway (line 8) through its course in Aries (the Ram), the first sign of the

zodiac in the solar year. "croppes": shoots, sprouts.
9. Fowls: birds.
1. Sleep. "yë": eye.
2. Them. "hir corages": their hearts.
3. Long: desire. "goon": go.
4. Pilgrims who range widely to far-off shrines ("ferne halwes") on the foreign shores of the Holy Land ("straunge strondes").
5. Known.
6. Shire's: county's.
7. Go. At Canterbury was the shrine of St. Thomas à Becket ("the holy blisful martir"), murdered in Canterbury Cathedral in 1170.
8. Helped. "seeke": sick.

Is my destroyer.
And I am dumb to tell the crooked rose
My youth is bent by the same wintry fever.   5

The force that drives the water through the rocks
Drives my red blood; that dries the mouthing streams
Turns mine to wax.
And I am dumb to mouth unto my veins
How at the mountain spring the same mouth sucks.   10

The hand that whirls the water in the pool
Stirs the quicksand; that ropes the blowing wind
Hauls my shroud sail.
And I am dumb to tell the hanging man
How of my clay is made the hangman's lime.   15

The lips of time leech to the fountain head;
Love drips and gathers, but the fallen blood
Shall calm her sores.
And I am dumb to tell a weather's wind
How time has ticked a heaven round the stars.   20

And I am dumb to tell the lover's tomb
How at my sheet goes the same crooked worm.

                                                      1934

JOSEPH ADDISON

The Spacious Firmament on High[1]

The spacious firmament on high,
With all the blue ethereal sky,
And spangled heav'ns, a shining frame,
Their great Original proclaim:
Th' unwearied sun, from day to day,   5
Does his Creator's power display,
And publishes to ev'ry land
The work of an Almighty Hand.

Soon as the ev'ning shades prevail,
The moon takes up the wondrous tale,   10
And nightly to the list'ning earth
Repeats the story of her birth:
Whilst all the stars that round her burn,
And all the planets, in their turn,
Confirm the tidings as they roll,   15
And spread the truth from pole to pole.

1. In an essay accompanying this poem on its first publication in *The Spectator*, Addison cites *Psalm* 19 ("The heavens declare the glory of God; and the firmament showeth his handiwork") and writes: "The Supreme Being has made the best arguments for his own existence, in the formation of the heaven and the earth, and these are arguments which a man of sense cannot forbear attending to, who is out of the noise and hurry of human affairs."

What though, in solemn silence, all
Move round the dark terrestrial ball?
What though nor real voice nor sound
Amid their radiant orbs be found? 20
In reason's ear they all rejoice,
And utter forth a glorious voice,
Forever singing, as they shine,
"The Hand that made us is divine."

p. 1712

WILLIAM SHAKESPEARE

[Order and Degree][1]

The heavens themselves, the planets, and this center[2] 85
Observe degree, priority, and place,
Insisture,[3] course, proportion, season, form,
Office, and custom, in all line of order.
And therefore is the glorious planet Sol[4]
In noble eminence enthroned and sphered 90
Amidst the other,[5] whose med'cinable eye
Corrects the influence[6] of evil planets,
And posts, like the commandment of a king,
Sans check to good and bad. But when the planets
In evil mixture to disorder wander, 95
What plagues, and what portents, what mutiny,
What raging of the sea, shaking of earth,
Commotion in the winds, frights, changes, horrors,
Divert and crack, rend and deracinate,
The unity and married calm of states 100
Quite from their fixure[7]? O, when degree is shaked,
Which is the ladder of all high designs,
The enterprise is sick. How could communities,
Degrees in schools, and brotherhoods in cities,
Peaceful commerce from dividable shores, 105
The primogenity[8] and due of birth,
Prerogative of age, crowns, scepters, laurels,
But by degree, stand in authentic place?
Take but degree away, untune that string,
And hark what discord follows. Each thing meets 110
In mere oppugnancy.[9] The bounded waters
Should lift their bosoms higher than the shores
And make a sop[1] of all this solid globe;
Strength should be lord of imbecility,[2]
And the rude son should strike his father dead; 115
Force should be right, or rather, right and wrong,
Between whose endless jar[3] justice resides,
Should lose their names, and so should justice too;

1. A speech by Ulysses to other Greek
leaders in *Troilus and Cressida*, Act I,
sc. iii.
2. Earth.
3. Regularity.
4. The sun.
5. Others.

6. Astrological effect.
7. Fixed place, stability.
8. Rights of the first-born son.
9. Total war.
1. Sponge.
2. Weakness.
3. Conflict.

Then everything include itself in power,
Power into will, will into appetite,   120
And appetite, an universal wolf,
So doubly seconded with will and power,
Must make perforce an universal prey,
And last eat up himself. Great Agamemnon,[4]
This chaos, when degree is suffocate,   125
Follows the choking.
And this neglection of degree it is
That by a pace goes backward with a purpose
It hath to climb. The general's disdained
By him one step below, he by the next,   130
That next by him beneath; so every step,
Exampled by the first pace[5] that is sick
Of his superior, grows to an envious fever
Of pale and bloodless emulation.

ca. 1601

WALLACE STEVENS

The Idea of Order at Key West

She sang beyond the genius of the sea.
The water never formed to mind or voice,
Like a body wholly body, fluttering
Its empty sleeves; and yet its mimic motion
Made constant cry, caused constantly a cry,   5
That was not ours although we understood,
Inhuman, of the veritable ocean.

The sea was not a mask. No more was she.
The song and water were not medleyed sound
Even if what she sang was what she heard,   10
Since what she sang was uttered word by word.
It may be that in all her phrases stirred
The grinding water and the gasping wind;
But it was she and not the sea we heard.

For she was the maker of the song she sang.   15
The ever-hooded, tragic-gestured sea
Was merely a place by which she walked to sing.
Whose spirit is this? we said, because we knew
It was the spirit that we sought and knew
That we should ask this often as she sang.   20

If it was only the dark voice of the sea
That rose, or even colored by many waves;
If it was only the outer voice of sky
And cloud, of the sunken coral water-walled,
However clear, it would have been deep air,   25
The heaving speech of air, a summer sound

---

4. One of the leaders addressed by
Ulysses.

5. Step of another rebel.

Repeated in a summer without end
And sound alone. But it was more than that,
More even than her voice, and ours, among
The meaningless plungings of water and the wind,   30
Theatrical distances, bronze shadows heaped
On high horizons, mountainous atmospheres
Of sky and sea.
     It was her voice that made
The sky acutest at its vanishing.
She measured to the hour its solitude.   35
She was the single artificer of the world
In which she sang. And when she sang, the sea,
Whatever self it had, became the self
That was her song, for she was the maker. Then we,
As we beheld her striding there alone,   40
Knew that there never was a world for her
Except the one she sang and, singing, made.

Ramon Fernandez,[1] tell me, if you know,
Why, when the singing ended and we turned
Toward the town, tell why the glassy lights,   45
The lights in the fishing boats at anchor there,
As the night descended, tilting in the air,
Mastered the night and portioned out the sea,
Fixing emblazoned zones and fiery poles,
Arranging, deepening, enchanting night.   50

Oh! Blessed rage for order, pale Ramon,
The maker's rage to order words of the sea,
Words of the fragrant portals, dimly-starred,
And of ourselves and of our origins,
In ghostlier demarcations, keener sounds.   55

                 1935

THOMAS HARDY

Hap[2]

If but some vengeful god would call to me
From up the sky, and laugh: "Thou suffering thing,
Know that thy sorrow is my ecstasy,
That thy love's loss is my hate's profiting!"

Then would I bear it, clench myself, and die,   5
Steeled by the sense of ire unmerited;
Half-eased in that a Powerfuller than I
Had willed and meted me the tears I shed.

---

1. French classicist and critic, 1894–1944, who emphasized the ordering role of a writer's consciousness upon the materials he used. Stevens denied that he had Fernandez in mind, saying that he combined a Spanish first name and surname at random: "I knew of Ramon Fernandez, the critic, and had read some of his criticisms, but I did not have him in mind." (*Letters* [New York: Knopf, 1960], p. 798) Later, Stevens wrote to another correspondent that he did not have the critic "consciously" in mind. (*Letters*, p. 823)
2. Chance.

But not so. How arrives it[2] joy lies slain,
And why unblooms the best hope ever sown?   10
—Crass Casualty[3] obstructs the sun and rain,
And dicing Time for gladness casts a moan. . . .
These purblind Doomsters[4] had as readily strown
Blisses about my pilgrimage as pain.

1866

JULIAN BOND

Rotation

Like plump green floor plans
the pool tables squat
Among fawning mahogany Buddhas with felt heads.
Like clubwomen blessed with adultery
The balls dart to kiss   5
and tumble erring members into silent oblivion.
Right-angled over the verdant barbered turf
Sharks point long fingers at the multi-colored worlds
and play at percussion
Sounding cheap plastic clicks   10
in an 8-ball universe built for ivory.

p. 1964

TURNER CASSITY

Calvin in the Casino[1]

(*He apostrophizes a roulette ball*)

Sphere of pure chance, free agent of no cause,
Your progress is a motion without laws.

Let every casuist henceforth rejoice
To cite your amoralities of choice,

By whose autonomy one apprehends   5
The limits where predestination ends;

Where the Eternal Will divides its see[2]
In latitudes of probability,

And the divine election is obscured
Through being momently and long endured.   10

It is obscured and is rejustified,
That stands fulfilled in being here denied,

2. How does it happen that.
3. Chance.
4. Those who decide one's fate.
1. John Calvin (1509–1564), a French theologian best known for his doctrine of predestination.
2. Area of jurisdiction (usually used to describe the power of bishops).

Lest its caprice should lead the mind to curse
A biased and encircling universe,

Or its vagaries urge us to reject   15
That one same Will which chooses the elect.

                                                                    1966

A. R. AMMONS

Cascadilla Falls

I went down by Cascadilla
Falls this
evening, the
stream below the falls,
and picked up a   5
handsized stone
kidney-shaped, testicular, and

thought all its motions into it,
the 800 mph earth spin,
the 190-million-mile yearly   10
displacement around the sun,
the overriding
grand
haul

of the galaxy with the 30,000   15
mph of where
the sun's going:
thought all the interweaving
motions
into myself: dropped   20

the stone to dead rest:
the stream from other motions
broke
rushing over it:
shelterless,   25
I turned

to the sky and stood still:
oh
I do
not know where I am going   30
that I can live my life
by this single creek.

                                                                    1970

WALLACE STEVENS

Anecdote of the Jar

I placed a jar in Tennessee,
And round it was, upon a hill.

It made the slovenly wilderness
Surround that hill.

The wilderness rose up to it,   5
And sprawled around, no longer wild.
The jar was round upon the ground
And tall and of a port in air.

It took dominion everywhere.
The jar was gray and bare.   10
It did not give of bird or bush,
Like nothing else in Tennessee.

1923

ARTHUR GUITERMAN

On the Vanity of Earthly Greatness

The tusks that clashed in mighty brawls
Of mastodons, are billiard balls.

The sword of Charlemagne the Just
Is ferric oxide known as rust.

The grizzly bear whose potent hug   5
Was feared by all, is now a rug.

Great Caesar's bust in on the shelf,
And I don't feel so well myself!

1930

RICHARD ARMOUR

Hiding Place

A speaker at a meeting of the New York State Frozen Food Locker Association
declared that the best hiding place in event of an atomic explosion is a frozen-
food locker, where "radiation will not penetrate."[1]   NEWS ITEM.

Move over, ham
And quartered cow,
My Geiger[2] says
The time is now.

Yes, now I lay me   5
Down to sleep,
And if I die,
At least I'll keep.

1954

1. Before home freezers became popular, many Americans rented lockers in specially equipped commercial buildings.   2. Geiger counter: used to detect radiation.

SYLVIA PLATH

The Hanging Man

By the roots of my hair some god got hold of me.
I sizzled in his blue volts like a desert prophet.

The nights snapped out of sight like a lizard's eyelid:
A world of bald white days in a shadeless socket.

A vulturous boredom pinned me in this tree.   5
If he were I, he would do what I did.

1966

THOM GUNN

On the Move

"Man, you gotta Go."

The blue jay scuffling in the bushes follows
Some hidden purpose, and the gust of birds
That spurts across the field, the wheeling swallows,
Have nested in the trees and undergrowth.
Seeking their instinct, or their poise, or both,   5
One moves with an uncertain violence
Under the dust thrown by a baffled sense
Or the dull thunder of approximate words.

On motorcycles, up the road, they come:
Small, black, as flies hanging in heat, the Boys,   10
Until the distance throws them forth, their hum
Bulges to thunder held by calf and thigh.
In goggles, donned impersonality,
In gleaming jackets trophied with the dust,
They strap in doubt—by hiding it, robust—   15
And almost hear a meaning in their noise.

Exact conclusion of their hardiness
Has no shape yet, but from known whereabouts
They ride, direction where the tires press.
They scare a flight of birds across the field: 20
Much that is natural, to the will must yield.
Men manufacture both machine and soul,
And use what they imperfectly control
To dare a future from the taken routes.

It is a part solution, after all.   25
One is not necessarily discord
On earth; or damned because, half animal,
One lacks direct instinct, because one wakes
Afloat on movement that divides and breaks.
One joins the movement in a valueless world,   30
Choosing it, till, both hurler and the hurled,
One moves as well, always toward, toward.

A minute holds them, who have come to go:
The self-defined, astride the created will
They burst away; the towns they travel through   35
Are home for neither bird nor holiness,
For birds and saints complete their purposes.
At worst, one is in motion; and at best,
Reaching no absolute, in which to rest,
One is always nearer by not keeping still.   40
California, 1957

MARK STRAND

Keeping Things Whole

In a field
I am the absence
of field.
This is
always the case.   5
Wherever I am
I am what is missing.

When I walk
I part the air
and always   10
the air moves in
to fill the spaces
where my body's been.

We all have reasons
for moving.   15
I move
to keep things whole.

1968

THOMAS HARDY

The Darkling Thrush[1]

I leant upon a coppice gate
    When Frost was specter gray,
And Winter's dregs made desolate
    The weakening eye of day.
The tangled bine-stems scored the sky   5
    Like strings of broken lyres,
And all mankind that haunted nigh
    Had sought their household fires.

The land's sharp features seemed to be
    The Century's corpse outleant,   10
His crypt the cloudy canopy,
    The wind his death-lament.

---

1. The following group of poems (to p. 652) is not annotated. See the Note on Arrangement in "A Preface to Poetry."

The ancient pulse of germ and birth
  Was shrunken hard and dry,
And every spirit upon earth   15
  Seemed fervorless as I.

At once a voice arose among
  The bleak twigs overhead
In a full-hearted evensong
  Of joy illimited;   20
An aged thrush, frail, gaunt, and small,
  In blast-beruffled plume,
Had chosen thus to fling his soul
  Upon the growing gloom.

So little cause for carolings   25
  Of such ecstatic sound
Was written on terrestrial things
  Afar or nigh around,
That I could think there trembled through
  His happy good-night air   30
Some blessed Hope, whereof he knew
  And I was unaware.

December 31, 1900

JOHN MILTON

On the New Forcers of Conscience
under the Long Parliament

Because you have thrown off your prelate lord,
And with stiff vows renounced his liturgy
To seize the widowed whore Plurality
From them whose sin ye envied, not abhorred,
Dare ye for this adjure the civil sword   5
To force our consciences that Christ set free,
And ride us with a classic hierarchy
Taught ye by mere A. S. and Rutherford?
Men whose life, learning, faith, and pure intent
Would have been held in high esteem with Paul   10
Must now be named and printed heretics
By shallow Edwards and Scotch what-d'ye-call:
But we do hope to find out all your tricks,
Your plots and packing worse than those of Trent,
That so the Parliament   15
May with their wholesome and preventive shears
Clip your phylacteries, though balk your ears,
And succor our just fears
When they shall read this clearly on your charge:
New presbyter is but *old priest* writ large.   20

ca. 1646

ANONYMOUS "NURSERY RHYMES"

Wee Willie Winkie

Wee Willie Winkie runs through the town,
Upstairs and downstairs in his night-gown,
Rapping at the window, crying through the lock,
Are the children all in bed, for now it's eight o'clock?

Georgie Porgie

Georgie Porgie, pudding and pie,
Kissed the girls and made them cry;
When the boys came out to play,
Georgie Porgie ran away.

e. e. cummings

poem, or beauty hurts mr. vinal

take it from me kiddo
believe me
my country, 'tis of

you, land of the Cluett
Shirt Boston Garter and Spearmint   5
Girl With The Wrigley Eyes (of you
land of the Arrow Ide
and Earl &
Wilson
Collars) of you i   10
sing:land of Abraham Lincoln and Lydia E. Pinkham,
land above all of Just Add Hot Water And Serve—
from every B. V. D.

let freedom ring

amen. i do however protest, anent the un   15
-spontaneous and otherwise scented merde which
greets one (Everywhere Why) as divine poesy per
that and this radically defunct periodical. i would
suggest that certain ideas gestures
rhymes, like Gillette Razor Blades   20
having been used and reused
to the mystical moment of dullness emphatically are
Not To Be Resharpened. (Case in point

if we are to believe these gently O sweetly
melancholy trillers amid the thrillers   25
these crepuscular violinists among my and your
skyscrapers—Helen & Cleopatra were Just Too Lovely,
The Snail's On The Thorn enter Morn and God's
In His andsoforth

do you get me?) according   30
to such supposedly indigenous
throstles Art is O World O Life
a formula:example, Turn Your Shirttails Into
Drawers and If It Isn't An Eastman It Isn't A
Kodak therefore my friends let   35
us now sing each and all fortissimo A-
mer
i

ca, I
love,   40
You. And there're a
hun-dred-mil-lion-oth-ers, like
all of you successfully if
delicately gelded (or spaded)
gentlemen (and ladies)—pretty   45

littleliverpill-
hearted-Nujolneeding-There's-A-Reason
americans (who tensetendoned and with
upward vacant eyes, painfully
perpetually crouched, quivering, upon the   50
sternly allotted sandpile
—how silently
emit a tiny violetflavoured nuisance:Odor?

ono.
comes out like a ribbon lies flat on the brush   55

                 1926

AMIRI BARAKA (LE ROI JONES)

In Memory of Radio

Who has ever stopped to think of the divinity of Lamont Cranston?
(Only Jack Kerouac, that I know of: & me.
The rest of you probably had on WCBS and Kate Smith,
Or something equally unattractive.)

What can I say?   5
It is better to have loved and lost
Than to put linoleum in your living rooms?

Am I a sage or something?
Mandrake's hypnotic gesture of the week?
(Remember, I do not have the healing powers of Oral Roberts . . .   10
I cannot, like F. J. Sheen, tell you how to get saved & *rich!*
I cannot even order you to gaschamber satori like Hitler or Goody Knight
& Love is an evil word.
Turn it backwards/see, what I mean?
An evol word. & besides   15
Who understands it?
I certainly wouldn't like to go out on that kind of limb.

Saturday mornings we listened to *Red Lantern* & his undersea folk.
At 11, *Let's Pretend*/& we did/& I, the poet, still do, Thank God!

What was it he used to say (after the transformation, when he was safe 20
& invisible & the unbelievers couldn't throw stones?) "Heh, heh, heh,
Who knows what evil lurks in the hearts of men? The Shadow knows."

O, yes he does
O, yes he does.
An evil word it is,   25
This Love.

                                                                1961

ALLEN GINSBERG

Howl (Part I)

(*for Carl Solomon*)

I saw the best minds of my generation destroyed by madness, starving
    hysterical naked,
dragging themselves through the negro streets at dawn looking for an
    angry fix,
angelheaded hipsters burning for the ancient heavenly connection to
    the starry dynamo in the machinery of night,
who poverty and tatters and hollow-eyed and high sat up smoking in
    the supernatural darkness of cold-water flats floating across the
    tops of cities contemplating jazz,
who bared their brains to Heaven under the El and saw Mohammedan
    angels staggering on tenement roofs illuminated,   5
who passed through universities with radiant cool eyes hallucinating
    Arkansas and Blake-light tragedy among the scholars of war,
who were expelled from the academies for crazy & publishing obscene
    odes on the windows of the skull,
who cowered in unshaven rooms in underwear, burning their money in
    wastebaskets and listening to the Terror through the wall,
who got busted in their pubic beards returning through Laredo with
    a belt of marijuana for New York,
who ate fire in paint hotels or drank turpentine in Paradise Alley, death,
    or purgatoried their torsos night after night   10
with dreams, with drugs, with waking nightmares, alcohol and cock
    and endless balls,
incomparable blind streets of shuddering cloud and lightning in the
    mind leaping toward poles of Canada & Paterson, illuminating
    all the motionless world of Time between,
Peyote solidities of halls, backyard green tree cemetery dawns, wine
    drunkenness over the rooftops, storefront boroughs of teahead
    joyride neon blinking traffic light, sun and moon and tree
    vibrations in the roaring winter dusks of Brooklyn, ashcan
    rantings and kind king light of mind,
who chained themselves to subways for the endless ride from Battery
    to holy Bronx on benzedrine until the noise of wheels and
    children brought them down shuddering mouth-wracked and

battered bleak of brain all drained of brilliance in the drear
light of Zoo,
who sank all night in submarine light of Bickford's floated out and sat
through the stale beer afternoon in desolate Fugazzi's, listening
to the crack of doom on the hydrogen jukebox, 15
who talked continuously seventy hours from park to pad to bar to
Bellevue to museum to the Brooklyn Bridge,
a lost battalion of platonic conversationalists jumping down the stoops
off fire escapes off windowsills off Empire State out of the moon,
yacketayakking screaming vomiting whispering facts and memories
and anecdotes and eyeball kicks and shocks of hospitals and
jails and wars,
whole intellects disgorged in total recall for seven days and nights with
brilliant eyes, meat for the Synagogue cast on the pavement,
who vanished into nowhere Zen New Jersey leaving a trail of ambiguous
picture postcards of Atlantic City Hall, 20
suffering Eastern sweats and Tangerian bone-grindings and migraines
of China under junk-withdrawal in Newark's bleak furnished
room,
who wandered around and around at midnight in the railroad yard
wondering where to go, and went, leaving no broken hearts,
who lit cigarettes in boxcars boxcars boxcars racketing through snow
toward lonesome farms in grandfather night,
who studied Plotinus Poe St. John of the Cross telepathy and bop
kaballa because the cosmos instinctively vibrated at their feet
in Kansas,
who loned it through the streets of Idaho seeking visionary indian
angels who were visionary indian angels, 25
who thought they were only mad when Baltimore gleamed in supernatural ecstasy,
who jumped in limousines with the Chinaman of Oklahoma on the
impulse of winter midnight streetlight smalltown rain,
who lounged hungry and lonesome through Houston seeking jazz or sex
or soup, and followed the brilliant Spaniard to converse about
America and Eternity, a hopeless task, and so took ship to Africa,
who disappeared into the volcanoes of Mexico leaving behind nothing
but the shadow of dungarees and the lava and ash of poetry
scattered in fireplace Chicago,
who reappeared on the West Coast investigating the F.B.I. in beards
and shorts with big pacifist eyes sexy in their dark skin passing
out incomprehensible leaflets, 30
who burned cigarette holes in their arms protesting the narcotic
tobacco haze of Capitalism,
who distributed Supercommunist pamphlets in Union Square weeping
and undressing while the sirens of Los Alamos wailed them
down, and wailed down Wall, and the Staten Island Ferry also
wailed,
who broke down crying in white gymnasiums naked and trembling
before the machinery of other skeletons,
who bit detectives in the neck and shrieked with delight in policecars
for committing no crime but their own wild cooking pederasty
and intoxication,
who howled on their knees in the subway and were dragged off the
roof waving genitals and manuscripts, 35

who let themselves be fucked in the ass by saintly motorcyclists, and
    screamed with joy,
who blew and were blown by those human seraphim, the sailors,
    caresses of Atlantic and Caribbean love,
who balled in the morning in the evenings in rosegardens and the grass
    of public parks and cemeteries scattering their semen freely to
    whomever come who may,
who hiccupped endlessly trying to giggle but wound up with a sob
    behind a partition in a Turkish Bath when the blonde & naked
    angel came to pierce them with a sword,
who lost their loveboys to the three old shrews of fate the one eyed
    shrew of the heterosexual dollar the one eyed shrew that winks
    out of the womb and the one eyed shrew that does nothing but
    sit on her ass and snip the intellectual golden threads of the
    craftsman's loom,   40
who copulated ecstatic and insatiate with a bottle of beer a sweetheart
    a package of cigarettes a candle and fell off the bed, and con-
    tinued along the floor and down the hall and ended fainting on
    the wall with a vision of ultimate cunt and come eluding the
    last gyzym of consciousness,
who sweetened the snatches of a million girls trembling in the sunset,
    and were red eyed in the morning but prepared to sweeten the
    snatch of the sunrise, flashing buttocks under barns and naked
    in the lake,
who went out whoring through Colorado in myriad stolen night-cars,
    N.C., secret hero of these poems, cocksman and Adonis of
    Denver—joy to the memory of his innumerable lays of girls in
    empty lots & diner backyards, moviehouses' rickety rows, on
    mountaintops in caves or with gaunt waitresses in familiar
    roadside lonely petticoat upliftings & especially secret gas-station
    solipsisms of johns, & hometown alleys too,
who faded out in vast sordid movies, were shifted in dreams, woke on a
    sudden Manhattan, and picked themselves up out of basements
    hungover with heartless Tokay and horrors of Third Avenue
    iron dreams & stumbled to unemployment offices,
who walked all night with their shoes full of blood on the snowbank
    docks waiting for a door in the East River to open to a room
    full of steamheat and opium,   45
who created great suicidal dramas on the apartment cliff-banks of the
    Hudson under the wartime blue floodlight of the moon & their
    heads shall be crowned with laurel in oblivion,
who ate the lamb stew of the imagination or digested the crab at the
    muddy bottom of the rivers of Bowery,
who wept at the romance of the streets with their pushcarts full of
    onions and bad music,
who sat in boxes breathing in the darkness under the bridge, and rose
    up to build harpsichords in their lofts,
who coughed on the sixth floor of Harlem crowned with flame under
    the tubercular sky surrounded by orange crates of theology,   50
who scribbled all night rocking and rolling over lofty incantations which
    in the yellow morning were stanzas of gibberish,
who cooked rotten animals lung heart feet tail borsht & tortillas dream-
    ing of the pure vegetable kingdom,
who plunged themselves under meat trucks looking for an egg,

who threw their watches off the roof to cast their ballot for Eternity
 outside of Time, & alarm clocks fell on their heads every day
 for the next decade,

who cut their wrists three times successively unsuccessfully, gave up
 and were forced to open antique stores where they thought they
 were growing old and cried,   55

who were burned alive in their innocent flannel suits on Madison
 Avenue amid blasts of leaden verse & the tanked-up clatter of
 the iron regiments of fashion & the nitroglycerine shrieks of the
 fairies of advertising & the mustard gas of sinister intelligent
 editors, or were run down by the drunken taxicabs of Absolute
 Reality,

who jumped off the Brooklyn Bridge this actually happened and walked
 away unknown and forgotten into the ghostly daze of China-
 town soup alleyways & firetrucks, not even one free beer,

who sang out of their windows in despair, fell out of the subway window, jumped in the filthy Passaic, leaped on negroes, cried all
 over the street, danced on broken wineglasses barefoot smashed
 phonograph records of nostalgic European 1930's German jazz
 finished the whiskey and threw up groaning into the bloody
 toilet, moans in their ears and the blast of colossal steamwhistles,

who barreled down the highways of the past journeying to each other's
 hotrod-Golgotha jail-solitude watch or Birmingham jazz incarnation,

who drove crosscountry seventytwo hours to find out if I had a vision
 or you had a vision or he had a vision to find out Eternity,   60

who journeyed to Denver, who died in Denver, who came back to
 Denver & waited in vain, who watched over Denver & brooded
 & loned in Denver and finally went away to find out the Time, &
 now Denver is lonesome for her heroes,

who fell on their knees in hopeless cathedrals praying for each other's
 salvation and light and breasts, until the soul illuminated its
 hair for a second,

who crashed through their minds in jail waiting for impossible criminals with golden heads and the charm of reality in their hearts
 who sang sweet blues to Alcatraz,

who retired to Mexico to cultivate a habit, or Rocky Mount to tender
 Buddha or Tangiers to boys or Southern Pacific to the black
 locomotive or Harvard to Narcissus to Woodlawn to the daisy-
 chain or grave,

who demanded sanity trials accusing the radio of hypnotism & were
 left with their insanity & their hands & a hung jury,   65

who threw potato salad at CCNY lecturers on Dadaism and subse-
 quently presented themselves on the granite steps of the madhouse with shaven heads and harlequin speech of suicide,
 demanding instantaneous lobotomy,

and who were given instead the concrete void of insulin metrasol
 electricity hydrotherapy psychotherapy occupational therapy
 pingpong & amnesia,

who in humorless protest overturned only one symbolic pingpong table,
 resting briefly in catatonia,

returning years later truly bald except for a wig of blood, and tears and
 fingers, to the visible madman doom of the wards of the mad-
 towns of the East,

Pilgrim State's Rockland's and Greystone's foetid halls, bickering with
the echoes of the soul, rocking and rolling in the midnight
solitude-bench dolmen-realms of love, dream of life a nightmare, bodies turned to stone as heavy as the moon,   70
with mother finally******, and the last fantastic book flung out of the
tenement window, and the last door closed at 4 AM and the last
telephone slammed at the wall in reply and the last furnished
room emptied down to the last piece of mental furniture, a
yellow paper rose twisted on a wire hanger in the closet, and
even that imaginary, nothing but a hopeful little bit of hallu-
cination—
ah, Carl, while you are not safe I am not safe, and now you're really
in the total animal soup of time—
and who therefore ran through the icy streets obsessed with a sudden
flash of the alchemy of the use of the ellipse the catalog the
meter & the vibrating plane,
who dreamt and made incarnate gaps in Time & Space through images
juxtaposed, and trapped the archangel of the soul between 2
visual images and joined the elemental verbs and set the noun
and dash of consciousness together jumping with sensation of
Pater Omnipotens Aeterna Deus
to recreate the syntax and measure of poor human prose and stand
before you speechless and intelligent and shaking with shame,
rejected yet confessing out the soul to conform to the rhythm of
thought in his naked and endless head,   75
the madman bum and angel beat in Time, unknown, yet putting down
here what might be left to say in time come after death,
and rose reincarnate in the ghostly clothes of jazz in the goldhorn
shadow of the band and blew the suffering of America's naked
mind for love into an eli eli lamma lamma sabacthani saxophone
cry that shivered the cities down to the last radio
with the absolute heart of the poem of life butchered out of their own
bodies good to eat a thousand years.

1955

HOWARD NEMEROV

The Second-Best Bed

Consider now that Troy has burned
—Priam is dead, and Hector dead,
And great Aeneas long since turned
Away seaward with his gods
To find, found or founder, against frightful odds.   5

And figure to yourselves the clown
Who comes with educated word
To illustrate in mask and gown
King Priam's most illustrious son
And figure forth his figure with many another one   10

Of that most ceremented time
In times have been or are to be
Inhearsed in military rime;

And will recite of royal fates
Until, infamonized among those potentates   15

By a messenger from nearer home,
His comedy is compromised
And he must leave both Greece and Rome
Abuilding but not half begun,
To play the honest Troyan to a girl far gone.   20

The wench lived on, if the son died—
All Denmark wounded in one bed
Cried vengeance on the lusty bride,
Who could not care that there would follow,
After the words of Mercury, songs of Apollo.   25

1950

JOHN KEATS
On the Grasshopper and the Cricket

The poetry of earth is never dead:
When all the birds are faint with the hot sun,
And hide in cooling trees, a voice will run
From hedge to hedge about the new-mown mead;
That is the grasshopper's—he takes the lead   5
In summer luxury—he has never done
With his delights; for when tired out with fun
He rests at ease beneath some pleasant weed.
The poetry of earth is ceasing never:
On a lone winter evening, when the frost   10
Has wrought a silence, from the stove there shrills
The cricket's song, in warmth increasing ever,
And seems to one in drowsiness half lost,
The grasshopper's among some grassy hills.

December 30, 1816

from Endymion (Book I)[1]

A thing of beauty is a joy for ever:
Its loveliness increases; it will never
Pass into nothingness; but still will keep
A bower quiet for us, and a sleep
Full of sweet dreams, and health, and quiet breathing.   5
Therefore, on every morrow, are we wreathing
A flowery band to bind us to the earth,
Spite of despondence, of the inhuman dearth
Of noble natures, of the gloomy days,
Of all the unhealthy and o'er-darkened ways   10
Made for our searching: yes, in spite of all,
Some shape of beauty moves away the pall
From our dark spirits. Such the sun, the moon,
Trees old, and young sprouting a shady boon
For simple sheep; and such are daffodils   15
With the green world they live in; and clear rills
That for themselves a cooling covert make
'Gainst the hot season; the mid forest brake,[2]
Rich with a sprinkling of fair musk-rose blooms:
And such too is the grandeur of the dooms[3]   20
We have imagined for the mighty dead;
All lovely tales that we have heard or read:
An endless fountain of immortal drink,
Pouring unto us from the heaven's brink.
    Nor do we merely feel these essences   25
For one short hour; no, even as the trees
That whisper round a temple become soon
Dear as the temple's self, so does the moon,

1. Keats's long poem about the myth of   2. Thicket.
a mortal (Endymion) loved by the goddess   3. Judgments.
of the moon.

The passion poesy, glories infinite,
Haunt us till they become a cheering light   30
Unto our souls, and bound to us so fast,
That, whether there be shine, or gloom o'ercast,
They always must be with us, or we die.

1817

When I Have Fears

When I have fears that I may cease to be
Before my pen has gleaned my teeming brain,
Before high-piléd books, in charact'ry,
Hold like rich garners the full-ripened grain;
When I behold, upon the night's starred face,   5
Huge cloudy symbols of a high romance,
And think that I may never live to trace
Their shadows, with the magic hand of chance;
And when I feel, fair creature of an hour!
That I shall never look upon thee more,   10
Never have relish in the faery power
Of unreflecting love!—then on the shore
Of the wide world I stand alone, and think
Till Love and Fame to nothingness do sink.

1818

Bright Star

Bright star! would I were steadfast as thou art—
    Not in lone splendor hung aloft the night
And watching, with eternal lids apart,
    Like nature's patient, sleepless Eremite,[1]
The moving waters at their priestlike task   5
    Of pure ablution round earth's human shores,
Or gazing on the new soft fallen mask
    Of snow upon the mountains and the moors—
No—yet still steadfast, still unchangeable,
    Pillowed upon my fair love's ripening breast,   10
To feel for ever its soft fall and swell,
    Awake for ever in a sweet unrest,
Still, still to hear her tender-taken breath,
And so live ever—or else swoon to death.

1819

1. Religious hermit.

The Eve of St. Agnes[1]

I

St. Agnes' Eve—Ah, bitter chill it was!
The owl, for all his feathers, was a-cold;
The hare limped trembling through the frozen grass,
And silent was the flock in woolly fold:
Numb were the Beadsman's[2] fingers, while he told   5
His rosary, and while his frosted breath,
Like pious incense from a censer old,
Seemed taking flight for heaven, without a death,
Past the sweet Virgin's picture, while his prayer he saith.

II

His prayer he saith, this patient, holy man;   10
Then takes his lamp, and riseth from his knees,
And back returneth, meager, barefoot, wan,
Along the chapel aisle by slow degrees:
The sculptured dead, on each side, seem to freeze,
Emprisoned in black, purgatorial rails: 15
Knights, ladies, praying in dumb orat'ries,[3]
He passeth by; and his weak spirit fails
To think[4] how they may ache in icy hoods and mails.

III

Northward he turneth through a little door,
And scarce three steps, ere Music's golden tongue   20
Flattered[5] to tears this aged man and poor;
But no—already had his deathbell rung:
The joys of all his life were said and sung:
His was harsh penance on St. Agnes' Eve:
Another way he went, and soon among   25
Rough ashes sat he for his soul's reprieve,
And all night kept awake, for sinners' sake to grieve.

IV

That ancient Beadsman heard the prelude soft;
And so it chanced, for many a door was wide,
From hurry to and fro. Soon, up aloft,   30
The silver, snarling trumpets 'gan to chide:
The level chambers, ready with their pride,[6]
Were glowing to receive a thousand guests:
The carvéd angels, ever eager-eyed,
Stared, where upon their heads the cornice rests,   35
With hair blown back, and wings put cross-wise on their breasts.

V

At length burst in the argent revelry,[7]
With plume, tiara, and all rich array,

---

1. Martyred early in the fourth century at the age of 13, St. Agnes became the patron saint of virgins. According to popular belief, if a virgin performed the proper ritual on St. Agnes' Eve (January 20), she would dream of her future husband.
2. Someone paid to pray for the soul of another. "told": counted his beads.
3. Silent chapels inside the larger chapel.
4. When he thinks. "mails": suits of armor.
5. Coaxed, beguiled.
6. Splendor.
7. Silver-clad revelers.

Numerous as shadows haunting fairily
The brain, new stuffed, in youth, with triumphs gay   40
Of old romance. These let us wish away,
And turn, sole-thoughted, to one Lady there,
Whose heart had brooded, all that wintry day,
On love, and winged St. Agnes' saintly care,
As she had heard old dames full many times declare.   45

VI
They told her how, upon St. Agnes' Eve,
Young virgins might have visions of delight,
And soft adorings from their loves receive
Upon the honeyed middle of the night,
If ceremonies due they did aright;   50
As, supperless to bed they must retire,
And couch supine their beauties, lily white;
Nor look behind, nor sideways, but require
Of Heaven with upward eyes for all that they desire.

VII
Full of this whim was thoughtful Madeline: 55
The music, yearning like a God in pain,
She scarcely heard: her maiden eyes divine,
Fixed on the floor, saw many a sweeping train
Pass by—she heeded not at all: in vain
Came many a tiptoe, amorous cavalier,   60
And back retired; not cooled by high disdain,
But she saw not: her heart was otherwhere:
She sighed for Agnes' dreams, the sweetest of the year.

VIII
She danced along with vague, regardless eyes,
Anxious her lips, her breathing quick and short: 65
The hallowed hour was near at hand: she sighs
Amid the timbrels,[8] and the thronged resort
Of whisperers in anger, or in sport;
'Mid looks of love, defiance, hate, and scorn,
Hoodwinked with faery fancy; all amort,[9]   70
Save to St. Agnes and her lambs unshorn,[1]
And all the bliss to be before tomorrow morn.

IX
So, purposing each moment to retire,
She lingered still. Meantime, across the moors,
Had come young Porphyro, with heart on fire   75
For Madeline. Beside the portal doors,
Buttressed[2] from moonlight, stands he, and implores
All saints to give him sight of Madeline,
But for one moment in the tedious hours,
That he might gaze and worship all unseen;   80
Perchance speak, kneel, touch, kiss—in sooth such things have been.

8. Small hand drums or tambourines.
9. Deadened: oblivious.
1. At the feast of St. Agnes the next day, lamb's wool was traditionally offered; later, nuns wove it into cloth (lines 115–17).
2. Shaded by the wall supports.

X

He ventures in: let no buzzed whisper tell:
All eyes be muffled, or a hundred swords
Will storm his heart, Love's fev'rous citadel:
For him, those chambers held barbarian hordes,   85
Hyena foemen, and hot-blooded lords,
Whose very dogs would execrations howl
Against his lineage:[3] not one breast affords
Him any mercy, in that mansion foul,
Save one old beldame,[4] weak in body and in soul.   90

XI

Ah, happy chance! the aged creature came,
Shuffling along with ivory-headed wand,[5]
To where he stood, hid from the torch's flame,
Behind a broad hall-pillar, far beyond
The sound of merriment and chorus bland:[6]   95
He startled her; but soon she knew his face,
And grasped his fingers in her palsied hand,
Saying, "Mercy, Porphyro! hie thee from this place;
They are all here tonight, the whole blood-thirsty race!

XII

Get hence! get hence! there's dwarfish Hildebrand;   100
He had a fever late, and in the fit
He curséd thee and thine, both house and land:
Then there's that old Lord Maurice, not a whit
More tame for his gray hairs—Alas me! flit!
Flit like a ghost away."—"Ah, Gossip[7] dear,   105
We're safe enough; here in this arm-chair sit,
And tell me how"—"Good Saints! not here, not here;
Follow me, child, or else these stones will be thy bier."

XIII

He followed through a lowly archéd way,
Brushing the cobwebs with his lofty plume,   110
And as she muttered "Well-a—well-a-day!"
He found him in a little moonlight room,
Pale, latticed, chill, and silent as a tomb.
"Now tell me where is Madeline," said he,
"O tell me, Angela, by the holy loom   115
Which none but secret sisterhood may see,
When they St. Agnes' wool are weaving piously."

XIV

"St. Agnes! Ah! it is St. Agnes' Eve—
Yet men will murder upon holy days:
Thou must hold water in a witch's sieve,   120
And be liege-lord of all the Elves and Fays,
To venture so:[8] it fills me with amaze

3. Because of the feud between his family and Madeline's.
4. Old, usually ugly, woman.
5. Walking stick, cane.
6. Soothing.
7. Old friend.
8. I.e., Porphyro would need to be a magician to take such chances.

To see thee, Porphyro!—St. Agnes' Eve!
God's help! my lady fair the conjuror plays[9]
This very night: good angels her deceive!   125
But let me laugh awhile, I've mickle[1] time to grieve."

XV

Feebly she laugheth in the languid moon,
While Porphyro upon her face doth look,
Like puzzled urchin on an aged crone
Who keepeth closed a wond'rous riddle-book,   130
As spectacled she sits in chimney nook.
But soon his eyes grew brilliant, when she told
His lady's purpose; and he scarce could brook[2]
Tears, at the thought of those enchantments cold
And Madeline asleep in lap of legends old.   135

XVI

Sudden a thought came like a full-blown rose,
Flushing his brow, and in his painéd heart
Made purple riot: then doth he propose
A stratagem, that makes the beldame start:
"A cruel man and impious thou art: 140
Sweet lady, let her pray, and sleep, and dream
Alone with her good angels, far apart
From wicked men like thee. Go, go!—I deem
Thou canst not surely be the same that thou didst seem."

XVII

"I will not harm her, by all saints I swear,"   145
Quoth Porphyro: "O may I ne'er find grace
When my weak voice shall whisper its last prayer,
If one of her soft ringlets I displace,
Or look with ruffian passion in her face:
Good Angela, believe me by these tears;   150
Or I will, even in a moment's space,
Awake, with horrid shout, my foemen's ears,
And beard[3] them, though they be more fanged than wolves and bears."

XVIII

"Ah! why wilt thou affright a feeble soul?
A poor, weak, palsy-stricken, churchyard thing,   155
Whose passing-bell[4] may ere the midnight toll;
Whose prayers for thee, each morn and evening,
Were never missed."—Thus plaining,[5] doth she bring
A gentler speech from burning Porphyro;
So woeful, and of such deep sorrowing,   160
That Angela gives promise she will do
Whatever he shall wish, betide her weal or woe.[6]

---

9. In trying to evoke the image of her lover.
1. Plenty of.
2. Hold back.
3. Defy, affront.

4. Bell that rings for death.
5. Complaining.
6. Whatever happens to her, good or bad.

XIX

Which was, to lead him, in close secrecy,
Even to Madeline's chamber, and there hide
Him in a closet, of such privacy   165
That he might see her beauty unespied,
And win perhaps that night a peerless bride,
While legioned fairies paced the coverlet,
And pale enchantment held her sleepy-eyed.
Never on such a night have lovers met,   170
Since Merlin paid his Demon all the monstrous debt.[7]

XX

"It shall be as thou wishest," said the Dame:
"All cates[8] and dainties shall be storéd there
Quickly on this feast-night: by the tambour frame[9]
Her own lute thou wilt see: no time to spare,   175
For I am slow and feeble, and scarce dare
On such a catering trust my dizzy head.
Wait here, my child, with patience; kneel in prayer
The while: Ah! thou must needs the lady wed,
Or may I never leave my grave among the dead."   180

XXI

So saying, she hobbled off with busy fear.
The lover's endless minutes slowly passed;
The dame returned, and whispered in his ear
To follow her; with agéd eyes aghast
From fright of dim espial. Safe at last,   185
Through many a dusky gallery, they gain
The maiden's chamber, silken, hushed, and chaste;
Where Porphyro took covert, pleased amain.[1]
His poor guide hurried back with agues in her brain.

XXII

Her falt'ring hand upon the balustrade,   190
Old Angela was feeling for the stair,
When Madeline, St. Agnes' charméd maid,
Rose, like a missioned spirit,[2] unaware:
With silver taper's light, and pious care,
She turned, and down the agéd gossip led   195
To a safe level matting. Now prepare,
Young Porphyro, for gazing on that bed;
She comes, she comes again, like ring dove frayed[3] and fled.

XXIII

Out went the taper as she hurried in;
Its little smoke, in pallid moonshine, died: 200
She closed the door, she panted, all akin
To spirits of the air, and visions wide:
No uttered syllable, or, woe betide!

---

7. Merlin was a powerful magician in
the Arthurian legends; the incident referred
to here has not been identified.
8. Delicacies.

9. Embroidery frame.
1. Greatly.
2. Angel on a mission.
3. Frightened.

But to her heart, her heart was voluble,
Paining with eloquence her balmy side;   205
As though a tongueless nightingale should swell
Her throat in vain, and die, heart-stifled, in her dell.

XXIV

A casement[4] high and triple-arched there was,
All garlanded with carven imag'ries
Of fruits, and flowers, and bunches of knot-grass,   210
And diamonded with panes of quaint device,
Innumerable of stains and splendid dyes,
As are the tiger moth's deep-damasked wings;
And in the midst, 'mong thousand heraldries,
And twilight saints, and dim emblazonings,   215
A shielded scutcheon blushed with blood of queens and kings.

XXV

Full on this casement shone the wintry moon,
And threw warm gules[5] on Madeline's fair breast,
As down she knelt for heaven's grace and boon;[6]
Rose-bloom fell on her hands, together pressed,   220
And on her silver cross soft amethyst,

And on her hair a glory,[7] like a saint:
She seemed a splendid angel, newly dressed,
Save wings, for heaven—Porphyro grew faint:
She knelt, so pure a thing, so free from mortal taint.   225

XXVI

Anon his heart revives: her vespers done,
Of all its wreathéd pearls her hair she frees;
Unclasps her warméd jewels one by one;
Loosens her fragrant bodice; by degrees
Her rich attire creeps rustling to her knees: 230
Half-hidden, like a mermaid in sea-weed,
Pensive awhile she dreams awake, and sees,
In fancy, fair St. Agnes in her bed,
But dares not look behind, or all the charm is fled.

XXVII

Soon, trembling in her soft and chilly nest,   235
In sort of wakeful swoon, perplexed she lay,
Until the poppied warmth of sleep oppressed
Her soothéd limbs, and soul fatigued away;
Flown, like a thought, until the morrow-day;
Blissfully havened both from joy and pain;   240
Clasped like a missal where swart Paynims[8] pray;
Blinded alike from sunshine and from rain,
As though a rose should shut, and be a bud again.

---

4. Window, in which are stained-glass   6. Gift, blessing.
representations of many kinds, including a   7. Halo.
royal coat of arms (line 216).   8. Pagans.
   5. Heraldic red.

XXVIII

Stol'n to this paradise, and so entranced,
Porphyro gazed upon her empty dress,   245
And listened to her breathing, if it chanced
To wake into a slumberous tenderness;
Which when he heard, that minute did he bless,
And breathed himself: then from the closet crept,
Noiseless as fear in a wide wilderness,   250
And over the hushed carpet, silent, stepped,
And 'tween the curtains peeped, where, lo!—how fast she slept.

XXIX

Then by the bedside, where the faded moon
Made a dim, silver twilight, soft he set
A table, and, half anguished, threw thereon   255
A cloth of woven crimson, gold, and jet—
O for some drowsy Morphean amulet!⁹
The boisterous, midnight, festive clarion,¹
The kettledrum, and far-heard clarinet,
Affray his ears, though but in dying tone—   260
The hall door shuts again, and all the noise is gone.

XXX

And still she slept an azure-lidded sleep,
In blanchéd linen, smooth, and lavendered,
While he from forth the closet brought a heap
Of candied apple, quince, and plum, and gourd;   265
With jellies soother than the creamy curd,
And lucent syrups, tinct with cinnamon;
Manna² and dates, in argosy³ transferred
From Fez; and spicéd dainties, every one,
From silken Samarcand to cedared Lebanon.   270

XXXI

These delicates he heaped with glowing hand
On golden dishes and in baskets bright
Of wreathéd silver: sumptuous they stand
In the retired quiet of the night,
Filling the chilly room with perfume light.   275
"And now, my love, my seraph⁴ fair, awake!
Thou art my heaven, and I thine eremite:
Open thine eyes, for meek St. Agnes' sake,
Or I shall drowse beside thee, so my soul doth ache."

XXXII

Thus whispering, his warm, unnervéd arm   280
Sank in her pillow. Shaded was her dream
By the dusk curtains:—'twas a midnight charm
Impossible to melt as icéd stream:

9. A charm of Morpheus, god of sleep.   Lebanon are in Morocco, central Asia, and
1. Trumpet.   the Levant, respectively.
2. Sweet gum.   4. The highest order of angel. "eremite":
3. Merchant ships. Fez, Samarcand, and devotee.

The lustrous salvers in the moonlight gleam;
Broad golden fringe upon the carpet lies: 285
It seemed he never, never could redeem
From such a steadfast spell his lady's eyes;
So mused awhile, entoiled[5] in wooféd fantasies.

XXXIII

Awakening up, he took her hollow lute—
Tumultuous—and, in chords that tenderest be,   290
He played an ancient ditty, long since mute,
In Provence called, "La belle dame sans merci":[6]
Close to her ear touching the melody—
Wherewith disturbed, she uttered a soft moan.
He ceased—she panted quick—and suddenly   295
Her blue affrayéd eyes wide open shone:
Upon his knees he sank, pale as smooth-sculptured stone.

XXXIV

Her eyes were open, but she still beheld,
Now wide awake, the vision of her sleep:
There was a painful change, that nigh expelled   300
The blisses of her dream so pure and deep,
At which fair Madeline began to weep,
And moan forth witless words with many a sigh;
While still her gaze on Porphyro would keep;

Who knelt, with joinéd hands and piteous eye,   305
Fearing to move or speak, she looked so dreamingly.

XXXV

"Ah, Porphyro!" said she, "but even now
Thy voice was at sweet tremble in mine ear,
Made tunable with every sweetest vow;
And those sad eyes were spiritual and clear: 310
How changed thou art! how pallid, chill, and drear!
Give me that voice again, my Porphyro,
Those looks immortal, those complainings dear!
Oh leave me not in this eternal woe,
For if thou diest, my Love, I know not where to go."   315

XXXVI

Beyond a mortal man impassioned far
At these voluptuous accents, he arose,
Ethereal, flushed, and like a throbbing star
Seen mid the sapphire heaven's deep repose
Into her dream he melted, as the rose   320
Blendeth its odor with the violet—
Solution sweet: meantime the frost-wind blows
Like Love's alarum pattering the sharp sleet
Against the windowpanes; St. Agnes' moon hath set.

---

5. Entangled. "wooféd": woven.
6. "The beautiful lady without pity,"
the kind of love song played or sung in
medieval Provence.

XXXVII

'Tis dark: quick pattereth the flaw-blown[7] sleet: 325
"This is no dream, my bride, my Madeline!"
'Tis dark: the icéd gusts still rave and beat:
"No dream, alas! alas! and woe is mine!
Porphyro will leave me here to fade and pine.
Cruel! what traitor could thee hither bring?   330
I curse not, for my heart is lost in thine,
Though thou forsakest a deceivéd thing—
A dove forlorn and lost with sick unprunéd wing."

XXXVIII

"My Madeline! sweet dreamer! lovely bride!
Say, may I be for aye[8] thy vassal blest?   335
Thy beauty's shield, heart-shaped and vermeil[9] dyed?
Ah, silver shrine, here will I take my rest
After so many hours of toil and quest,
A famished pilgrim—saved by miracle.
Though I have found, I will not rob thy nest   340
Saving of thy sweet self; if thou think'st well
To trust, fair Madeline, to no rude infidel.

XXXIX

"Hark! 'tis an elfin-storm from faery land,
Of haggard[1] seeming, but a boon indeed:
Arise—arise! the morning is at hand—   345
The bloated wassailers[2] will never heed—
Let us away, my love, with happy speed;
There are no ears to hear, or eyes to see—
Drowned all in Rhenish and the sleepy mead:[3]
Awake! arise! my love, and fearless be,   350
For o'er the southern moors I have a home for thee."

XL

She hurried at his words, beset with fears,
For there were sleeping dragons all around,
At glaring watch, perhaps, with ready spears—
Down the wide stairs a darkling way they found.   355
In all the house was heard no human sound.
A chain-drooped lamp was flickering by each door;
The arras,[4] rich with horseman, hawk, and hound,
Fluttered in the besieging wind's uproar;
And the long carpets rose along the gusty floor.   360

XLI

They glide, like phantoms, into the wide hall;
Like phantoms, to the iron porch, they glide;
Where lay the Porter, in uneasy sprawl,
With a huge empty flagon by his side:
The wakeful bloodhound rose, and shook his hide,   365

---

7. Gust-blown.
8. Forever.
9. Vermilion: bright red.
1. Wild.

2. Drunken revelers.
3. Liquor made from honey. "Rhenish":
rhine wine.
4. Tapestry.

But his sagacious eye an inmate[5] owns:
By one, and one, the bolts full easy slide—
The chains lie silent on the footworn stones—
The key turns, and the door upon its hinges groans.

XLII

And they are gone: ay, ages long ago 370
These lovers fled away into the storm.
That night the Baron dreamt of many a woe,
And all his warrior-guests, with shade and form
Of witch, and demon, and large coffin-worm,
Were long be-nightmared. Angela the old 375
Died palsy-twitched, with meager face deform;
The Beadsman, after thousand aves[6] told,
For aye unsought for slept among his ashes cold.

1819

La Belle Dame sans Merci[1]

A Ballad
(original version)

O what can ail thee, knight-at-arms,
    Alone and palely loitering?
The sedge has withered from the lake,
    And no birds sing.

O what can ail thee, knight-at-arms, 5
    So haggard and so woe-begone?
The squirrel's granary is full,
    And the harvest's done.

I see a lily on thy brow,
    With anguish moist and fever dew, 10
And on thy cheeks a fading rose
    Fast withereth too.

I met a lady in the meads,[2]
    Full beautiful—a faery's child,
Her hair was long, her foot was light, 15
    And her eyes were wild.

I made a garland for her head,
    And bracelets too, and fragrant zone;[3]
She looked at me as she did love,
    And made sweet moan. 20

I set her on my pacing steed,
    And nothing else saw all day long,

5. Member of the household. "owns": recognizes.
6. Ave Maria's: Hail Mary's.
1. "The beautiful lady without pity." The title (but not the subject matter) de-rives from a medieval poem by Alain Chartier.
2. Meadows.
3. Girdle.

For sidelong would she bend, and sing
    A faery's song.

She found me roots of relish sweet,   25
    And honey wild, and manna dew,
And sure in language strange she said,
    "I love thee true."

She took me to her elfin grot,
    And there she wept, and sighed full sore,   30
And there I shut her wild wild eyes
    With kisses four.

And there she lulléd me asleep,
    And there I dreamed—Ah! woe betide!
The latest[4] dream I ever dreamed   35
    On the cold hill side.

I saw pale kings and princes too,
    Pale warriors, death-pale were they all;
They cried—"La Belle Dame sans Merci
    Hath thee in thrall!"   40

I saw their starved lips in the gloam,
    With horrid warning gapéd wide,
And I awoke and found me here,
    On the cold hill's side.

And this is why I sojourn here,   45
    Alone and palely loitering,
Though the sedge has withered from the lake,
    And no birds sing.

April, 1819

To Sleep

O soft embalmer of the still midnight,
Shutting, with careful fingers and benign,
Our gloom-pleased eyes, embowered from the light,
Enshaded in forgetfulness divine;
O soothest[1] Sleep! if so it please thee, close,   5
In midst of this thine hymn, my willing eyes,
Or wait the amen, ere thy poppy[2] throws
Around my bed its lulling charities;
Then save me, or the passéd day will shine
Upon my pillow, breeding many woes;   10
Save me from curious[3] conscience, that still lords
Its strength for darkness, burrowing like a mole;
Turn the key deftly in the oiléd wards,[4]
And seal the hushéd casket of my soul.

April, 1819

---

4. Last.
1. Softest.
2. Because opium derives from it, the
poppy was associated with sleep.

3. Scrupulous. "lords": marshals.
4. Ridges in a lock that distinguish
proper from improper keys.

Ode to a Nightingale

I

My heart aches, and a drowsy numbness pains
  My sense, as though of hemlock[1] I had drunk,
Or emptied some dull opiate to the drains
  One minute past, and Lethe-wards[2] had sunk:
'Tis not through envy of thy happy lot,   5
  But being too happy in thine happiness,
    That thou, light-wingéd Dryad[3] of the trees,
      In some melodious plot
  Of beechen green, and shadows numberless,
  Singest of summer in full-throated ease.   10

II

O, for a draught of vintage! that hath been
  Cooled a long age in the deep-delvéd earth,
Tasting of Flora[4] and the country green,
  Dance, and Provençal song,[5] and sunburnt mirth!
O for a beaker full of the warm South,   15
  Full of the true, the blushful Hippocrene,[6]
    With beaded bubbles winking at the brim,
      And purple-stainéd mouth;
  That I might drink, and leave the world unseen,
  And with thee fade away into the forest dim: 20

III

Fade far away, dissolve, and quite forget
  What thou among the leaves hast never known,
The weariness, the fever, and the fret
  Here, where men sit and hear each other groan;
Where palsy shakes a few, sad, last gray hairs,   25
  Where youth grows pale, and specter-thin, and dies;
    Where but to think is to be full of sorrow
      And leaden-eyed despairs,
  Where Beauty cannot keep her lustrous eyes,
  Or new Love pine at them beyond tomorrow.   30

IV

Away! away! for I will fly to thee,
  Not charioted by Bacchus and his pards,[7]
But on the viewless wings of Poesy,
  Though the dull brain perplexes and retards:
Already with thee! tender is the night,   35
  And haply the Queen-Moon is on her throne,
    Clustered around by all her starry Fays;[8]
      But here there is no light,

---

1. A poisonous drug.
2. Toward the river of forgetfulness (Lethe) in Hades.
3. Wood nymph.
4. Roman goddess of flowers.
5. The medieval troubadors of Provence (in southern France) were famous for their love songs.
6. The fountain of the Muses on Mt. Helicon, whose waters bring poetic inspiration.
7. The Roman god of wine was sometimes portrayed in a chariot drawn by leopards. "viewless": invisible.
8. Fairies.

Save what from heaven is with the breezes blown
  Through verdurous glooms and winding mossy ways.   40

V

I cannot see what flowers are at my feet,
  Nor what soft incense hangs upon the boughs,
But, in embalmèd⁹ darkness, guess each sweet
  Wherewith the seasonable month endows
The grass, the thicket, and the fruit-tree wild;   45
  White hawthorn, and the pastoral eglantine;¹
    Fast fading violets covered up in leaves;
      And mid-May's eldest child,
  The coming musk-rose, full of dewy wine,
    The murmurous haunt of flies on summer eves.   50

VI

Darkling² I listen; and, for many a time
  I have been half in love with easeful Death,
Called him soft names in many a musèd rhyme,
  To take into the air my quiet breath;
Now more than ever seems it rich to die,   55
  To cease upon the midnight with no pain,
    While thou art pouring forth thy soul abroad
      In such an ecstasy!
  Still wouldst thou sing, and I have ears in vain—
    To thy high requiem become a sod.   60

VII

Thou wast not born for death, immortal Bird!
  No hungry generations tread thee down;
The voice I hear this passing night was heard
  In ancient days by emperor and clown:
Perhaps the selfsame song that found a path   65
  Through the sad heart of Ruth,³ when, sick for home,
    She stood in tears amid the alien corn;
      The same that ofttimes hath
  Charmed magic casements, opening on the foam
    Of perilous seas, in faery lands forlorn.   70

VIII

Forlorn! the very word is like a bell
  To toll me back from thee to my sole self!
Adieu! the fancy cannot cheat so well
  As she is famed to do, deceiving elf.
Adieu! adieu! thy plaintive anthem fades   75
  Past the near meadows, over the still stream,
    Up the hillside; and now 'tis buried deep
      In the next valley-glades:
  Was it a vision, or a waking dream?
    Fled is that music:—Do I wake or sleep?   80

May, 1819

9. Fragrant, aromatic.
1. Sweetbriar or honeysuckle.
2. In the dark.
3. A virtuous Moabite widow who, ac-

cording to the Old Testament *Book of Ruth*,
found a husband while gleaning in the
wheat fields of Judah.

Ode on a Grecian Urn

I

Thou still unravished bride of quietness,
   Thou foster-child of silence and slow time,
Sylvan[1] historian, who canst thus express
   A flowery tale more sweetly than our rhyme:
What leaf-fringed legend haunts about thy shape   5
   Of deities or mortals, or of both,
      In Tempe or the dales of Arcady?[2]
What men or gods are these? What maidens loath?
   What mad pursuit? What struggle to escape?
      What pipes and timbrels? What wild ecstasy?   10

II

Heard melodies are sweet, but those unheard
   Are sweeter; therefore, ye soft pipes, play on;
Not to the sensual[3] ear, but, more endeared,
   Pipe to the spirit ditties of no tone:
Fair youth, beneath the trees, thou canst not leave   15
   Thy song, nor ever can those trees be bare;
      Bold Lover, never, never canst thou kiss,
Though winning near the goal—yet, do not grieve;
   She cannot fade, though thou hast not thy bliss,
      For ever wilt thou love, and she be fair!   20

III

Ah, happy, happy boughs! that cannot shed
   Your leaves, nor ever bid the Spring adieu;
And, happy melodist, unweariéd,
   For ever piping songs for ever new;
More happy love! more happy, happy love!   25
   For ever warm and still to be enjoyed,
      For ever panting, and for ever young;
All breathing human passion far above,
   That leaves a heart high-sorrowful and cloyed,
      A burning forehead, and a parching tongue.   30

IV

Who are these coming to the sacrifice?
   To what green altar, O mysterious priest,
Lead'st thou that heifer lowing at the skies,
   And all her silken flanks with garlands dressed?
What little town by river or sea shore,   35
   Or mountain-built with peaceful citadel,
      Is emptied of this folk, this pious morn?
And, little town, thy streets for evermore
   Will silent be; and not a soul to tell
      Why thou art desolate, can e'er return.   40

---

1. Rustic. The urn depicts a woodland scene.
2. Arcadia. Tempe is a beautiful valley near Mt. Olympus in Greece, and the valley ("dales") of Arcadia a picturesque section of the Peloponnesus; both came to be associated with the pastoral ideal.
3. Of the senses, as distinguished from the "ear" of the spirit or imagination.

V

O Attic[4] shape! Fair attitude! with brede[5]
    Of marble men and maidens overwrought,
With forest branches and the trodden weed;
    Thou, silent form, dost tease us out of thought
As doth eternity: Cold Pastoral!   45
    When old age shall this generation waste,
        Thou shalt remain, in midst of other woe
Than ours, a friend to man, to whom thou say'st,
    Beauty is truth, truth beauty[6]—that is all
        Ye know on earth, and all ye need to know.   50

May, 1819

Ode on Melancholy

I

No, no, go not to Lethe,[1] neither twist
    Wolfsbane, tight-rooted, for its poisonous wine;[2]
Nor suffer thy pale forehead to be kissed
    By nightshade, ruby grape of Proserpine;
Make not your rosary of yew-berries,[3]   5
    Nor let the beetle, nor the death-moth be
        Your mournful Psyche,[4] nor the downy owl
A partner in your sorrow's mysteries;
    For shade to shade will come too drowsily,
        And drown the wakeful anguish of the soul.   10

II

But when the melancholy fit shall fall
    Sudden from heaven like a weeping cloud,
That fosters the droop-headed flowers all,
    And hides the green hill in an April shroud;
Then glut thy sorrow on a morning rose,   15
    Or on the rainbow of the salt sand-wave,
        Or on the wealth of globéd peonies;
Or if thy mistress some rich anger shows,
    Emprison her soft hand, and let her rave,
        And feed deep, deep upon her peerless eyes.   20

III

She[5] dwells with Beauty—Beauty that must die;
    And Joy, whose hand is ever at his lips
Bidding adieu; and aching Pleasure nigh,
    Turning to poison while the bee-mouth sips:

---

4. Attica was the district of ancient Greece surrounding Athens.
5. Woven pattern. "overwrought": ornamented all over.
6. In some texts of the poem "Beauty is truth, truth beauty" is in quotation marks and in some texts it is not, leading to critical disagreements about whether the last line and a half are also inscribed on the urn or spoken by the poet.
1. The river of forgetfulness in Hades.
2. Like nightshade (line 4), wolfsbane

is a poisonous plant. "Proserpine": Queen of Hades.
3. Which often grow in cemeteries and which are traditionally associated with death.
4. *Psyche* means both "soul" and "breath," and sometimes it was anciently represented by a moth leaving the mouth at death. Owls and beetles were also traditionally associated with darkness and death.
5. The goddess Melancholy, whose chief place of worship ("shrine") is described in lines 25–26.

Ay, in the very temple of Delight 25
 Veiled Melancholy has her sov'reign shrine,
  Though seen of none save him whose strenuous tongue
Can burst Joy's grape against his palate fine;[6]
 His soul shall taste the sadness of her might,
  And be among her cloudy trophies hung.[7] 30

May, 1819

To Autumn

I

Season of mists and mellow fruitfulness,
 Close bosom-friend of the maturing sun;
Conspiring with him how to load and bless
 With fruit the vines that round the thatch-eves run;
To bend with apples the mossed cottage-trees, 5
 And fill all fruit with ripeness to the core;
  To swell the gourd, and plump the hazel shells
With a sweet kernel; to set budding more,
 And still more, later flowers for the bees,
 Until they think warm days will never cease, 10
  For Summer has o'er-brimmed their clammy cells.

II

Who hath not seen thee oft amid thy store?
 Sometimes whoever seeks abroad may find
Thee sitting careless on a granary floor,
 Thy hair soft-lifted by the winnowing wind;[1] 15
Or on a half-reaped furrow sound asleep,
 Drowsed with the fume of poppies, while thy hook[2]
  Spares the next swath and all its twinéd flowers:
And sometimes like a gleaner thou dost keep
 Steady thy laden head across a brook; 20
 Or by a cider-press, with patient look,
  Thou watchest the last oozings hours by hours.

III

Where are the songs of Spring? Ay, where are they?
 Think not of them, thou hast thy music too—
While barréd clouds bloom the soft-dying day, 25
 And touch the stubble-plains with rosy hue;
Then in a wailful choir the small gnats mourn
 Among the river sallows,[3] borne aloft
  Or sinking as the light wind lives or dies;
And full-grown lambs loud bleat from hilly bourn;[4] 30
 Hedge-crickets sing; and now with treble soft
 The red-breast whistles from a garden-croft;[5]
  And gathering swallows twitter in the skies.

September 19, 1819

6. Sensitive, discriminating.
7. The ancient Greeks and Romans hung trophies in their gods' temples.
1. Which sifts the grain from the chaff.

2. Scythe or sickle.
3. Willows.
4. Domain.
5. An enclosed garden near a house.

from Letter to Benjamin Bailey, November 22, 1817[1]

* * * I am certain of nothing but of the holiness of the Heart's affections and the truth of Imagination—What the imagination seizes as Beauty must be truth—whether it existed before or not—for I have the same Idea of all our Passions as of Love they are all in their sublime, creative of essential Beauty * * * The Imagination may be compared to Adam's dream[2]—he awoke and found it truth. I am the more zealous in this affair, because I have never yet been able to perceive how any thing can be known for truth by consequitive reasoning—and yet it must be—Can it be that even the greatest Philosopher ever ~~when~~ arrived at his goal without putting aside numerous objections—However it may be, O for a Life of Sensations rather than of Thoughts! It is "a Vision in the form of Youth" a Shadow of reality to come—and this consideration has further conv[i]nced me for it has come as auxiliary to another favorite Speculation of mine, that we shall enjoy ourselves here after by having what we called happiness on Earth repeated in a finer tone and so repeated—And yet such a fate can only befall those who delight in sensation rather than hunger as you do after Truth—Adam's dream will do here and seems to be a conviction that Imagination and its empyreal reflection is the same as human Life and its spiritual repetition. But as I was saying—the simple imaginative Mind may have its rewards in the repeti[ti]on of its own silent Working coming continually on the spirit with a fine suddenness—to compare great things with small—have you never by being surprised with an old Melody—in a delicious place—by a delicious voice, fe[l]t over again your very speculations and surmises at the time it first operated on your soul—do you not remember forming to yourself the singer's face more beautiful that [for than] it was possible and yet with the elevation of the Moment you did not think so—even then you were mounted on the Wings of Imagination so high—that the Prototype must be here after—that delicious face you will see—What a time! I am continually running away from the subject—sure this cannot be exactly the case with a complex Mind—one that is imaginative and at the same time careful of its fruits—who would exist partly on sensation partly on thought—to whom it is necessary that years should bring the philosophic Mind—such an one I consider your's and therefore it is necessary to your eternal Happiness that you not only have drink this old Wine of Heaven which I shall call the redigestion of our most ethereal Musings on Earth; but also increase in knowledge and know all things. * * *

from Letter to George and Thomas Keats,
December 21, 1817

* * * I spent Friday evening with Wells[1] & went the next morning to see *Death on the Pale horse.*[2] It is a wonderful picture, when West's age is considered; But there is nothing to be intense upon; no women one feels mad to kiss, no face swelling into reality. the excellence of every Art is its intensity, capable of making all disagreeables evapo-

1. Keats's private letters, often carelessly written, are reprinted uncorrected.
2. In *Paradise Lost*, VIII, 460–90.
1. Charles Wells (1800–1879), an author.

2. By Benjamin West (1738–1820), American painter and president of the Royal Academy; "Christ Rejected" (mentioned below) is also by West.

rate, from their being in close relationship with Beauty & Truth—
Examine King Lear & you will find this examplified throughout; but
in this picture we have unpleasantness without any momentous depth
of speculation excited, in which to bury its repulsiveness—The picture
is larger than Christ rejected—I dined with Haydon the sunday after
you left, & had a very pleasant day, I dined too (for I have been out
too much lately) with Horace Smith & met his two Brothers with Hill
& Kingston & one Du Bois,[3] they only served to convince me, how
superior humour is to wit in respect to enjoyment—These men say
things which make one start, without making one feel, they are all
alike; their manners are alike; they all know fashionables; they have a
mannerism in their very eating & drinking, in their mere handling a
Decanter—They talked of Kean[4] & his low company—Would I were
with that company instead of yours said I to myself! I know such like
acquaintance will never do for me & yet I am going to Reynolds, on
wednesday—Brown & Dilke walked with me & back from the Christmas pantomime. I had not a dispute but a disquisition with Dilke, on
various subjects; several things dovetailed in my mind, & at once it
struck me, what quality went to form a Man of Achievement especially
in Literature & which Shakespeare posessed so enormously—I mean
Negative Capability, that is when man is capable of being in uncer-
tainties, Mysteries, doubts, without any irritable reaching after fact &
reason—Coleridge, for instance, would let go by a fine isolated verisimilitude caught from the Penetralium of mystery, from being incapable of remaining content with half knowledge. This pursued
through Volumes would perhaps take us no further than this, that with
a great poet the sense of Beauty overcomes every other consideration,
or rather obliterates all consideration.

Letter to John Hamilton Reynolds,
February 19, 1818

I have an idea that a Man might pass a very pleasant life in this
manner—let him on any certain day read a certain Page of full Poesy
or distilled Prose and let him wander with it, and muse upon it, and
reflect from it, and bring home to it, and prophesy upon it, and dream
upon it—untill it becomes stale—but when will it do so? Never—
When Man has arrived at a certain ripeness in intellect any one grand
and spiritual passage serves him as a starting post towards all "the two-
and-thirty Pallaces"[1] How happy is such a "voyage of conception,"
what delicious diligent Indolence! A doze upon a Sofa does not hinder
it, and a nap upon Clover engenders ethereal finger-pointings—the
prattle of a child gives it wings, and the converse of middle age a
strength to beat them—a strain of musick conducts to "an odd angle of
the Isle",[2] and when the leaves whisper it puts a "girdle round the
earth",[3] Nor will this sparing touch of noble Books be any irreverance
to their Writers—for perhaps the honors paid by Man to Man are trifles
in comparison to the Benefit done by great Works to the "Spirit and
pulse of good" by their mere passive existence. Memory should not be

---

3. Thomas Hill (1760–1840), a book
collector, and Edward duBois (1774–1850),
a journalist.
4. Edmund Kean, a famous Shakespearean actor.

1. "Places of delight" in Buddhism.
2. *The Tempest,* Act I, sc. ii, 223.
3. The phrase is from *Midsummer
Night's Dream,* Act II, sc. i, 175.

called knowledge—Many have original minds who do not think it—
they are led away by Custom—Now it appears to me that almost any
Man may like the Spider spin from his own inwards his own airy
Citadel—the points of leaves and twigs on which the Spider begins
her work are few and she fills the Air with a beautiful circuiting: man
should be content with as few points to tip with the fine Webb of his
Soul and weave a tapestry empyrean—full of Symbols for his spiritual
eye, of softness for his spiritual touch, of space for his wandering of
distinctness for his Luxury—But the Minds of Mortals are so different
and bent on such diverse Journeys that it may at first appear impossible
for any common taste and fellowship to exist ~~bettween~~ between two
or three under these suppositions—It is however quite the contrary—
Minds would leave each other in contrary directions, traverse each
other in Numberless points, and all [*for* at] last greet each other at the
Journeys end—An old Man and a child would talk together and the old
Man be led on his Path, and the child left thinking—Man should not
dispute or assert but whisper results to his neighbor, and thus by every
germ of Spirit sucking the Sap from mould ethereal every human might
become great, and Humanity instead of being a wide heath of Furse[4]
and Briars with here and there a remote Oak or Pine, would become a
grand democracy of Forest Trees. It has been an old Comparison for
our urging on—the Bee hive—however it seems to me that we should
rather be the flower than the Bee—for it is a false notion that more is
gained by receiving than giving—no, the receiver and the giver are
equal in their benefits—The f[l]ower I doubt not receives a fair guerdon from the Bee—its leaves blush deeper in the next spring—and
who shall say between Man and Woman which is the most delighted?
Now it is more noble to sit like Jove that [*for* than] to fly like Mercury—let us not therefore go hurrying about and collecting honey bee
like, buzzing here and there impatiently from a knowledge of what is
to be arrived at; but let us open our leaves like a flower and be passive
and receptive—budding patiently under the eye of Apollo and taking
hints from every noble insect that favors us with a visit—sap will be
given us for Meat and dew for drink—I was led into these thoughts,
my dear Reynolds, by the beauty of the morning operating on a sense
of Idleness—I have not read any Books—the Morning said I was right
—I had no Idea but of the Morning, and the Thrush said I was right—
seeming to say—

> O thou whose face hath felt the Winter's wind,
> Whose eye has seen the snow-clouds hung in mist,
> And the black elm tops 'mong the freezing stars,
> To thee the spring will be a harvest-time.
> O thou, whose only book has been the light
> Of supreme darkness which thou feddest on
> Night after night when Phœbus was away,
> To thee the spring shall be a triple morn.
> O fret not after knowledge—I have none,
> And yet my song comes native with the warmth.
> O fret not after knowledge—I have none,
> And yet the Evening listens. He who saddens
> At thought of idleness cannot be idle,
> And he's awake who thinks himself asleep.

4. *The Tempest*, Act I, sc. i, 68–69.

Now I am sensible all this is a mere sophistication, however it may neighbor to any truths, to excuse my own indolence—so I will not deceive myself that Man should be equal with jove—but think himself very well off as a sort of scullion-Mercury, or even a humble Bee—It is not [*for no*] matter whether I am right or wrong either one way or another, if there is sufficient to lift a little time from your Shoulders.

from Letter to John Taylor, February 27, 1818

* * * It is a sorry thing for me that any one should have to overcome Prejudices in reading my Verses—that affects me more than any hypercriticism on any particular Passage. In *Endymion* I have most likely but moved into the Go-cart from the leading strings. In Poetry I have a few Axioms, and you will see how far I am from their Centre. 1st I think Poetry should surprise by a fine excess and not by Singularity—it should strike the Reader as a wording of his own highest thoughts, and appear almost a Remembrance—2nd Its touches of Beauty should never be half way therby making the reader breathless instead of content: the rise, the progress, the setting of imagery should like the Sun come natural natural too him—shine over him and set soberly although in magnificence leaving him in the Luxury of twilight—but it is easier to think what Poetry should be than to write it—and this leads me on to another axiom. That if Poetry comes not as naturally as the Leaves to a tree it had better not come at all. However it may be with me I cannot help looking into new countries with "O for a Muse of fire to ascend!"[1]—If Endymion serves me as a Pioneer perhaps I ought to be content. I have great reason to be content, for thank God I can read and perhaps understand Shakspeare to his depths, and I have I am sure many friends, who, if I fail, will attribute any change in my Life and Temper to Humbleness rather than to Pride—to a cowering under the Wings of great Poets rather than to a Bitterness that I am not appreciated. I am anxious to get Endymion printed that I may forget it and proceed. * * *

from the Preface to *Endymion*, dated April 10, 1818

The imagination of a boy is healthy, and the mature imagination of a man is healthy; but there is a space of life between, in which the soul is in a ferment, the character undecided, the way of life uncertain, the ambition thick-sighted: thence proceeds mawkishness, and all the thousand bitters which those men I speak of must necessarily taste in going over the following pages.

I hope I have not in too late a day touched the beautiful mythology of Greece, and dulled its brightness: for I wish to try once more, before I bid it farewell.

from Letter to James Augustus Hessey, October 8, 1818

* * * Praise or blame has but a momentary effect on the man whose love of beauty in the abstract makes him a severe critic on his own

---

1. Shakespeare, *Henry V*, Prologue, 1.

Works. My own domestic criticism has given me pain without comparison beyond what Blackwood or the ~~Edinburgh~~ Quarterly[1] could possibly inflict. and also when I feel I am right, no external praise can give me such a glow as my own solitary reperception & ratification of what is fine. J. S.[2] is perfectly right in regard to the slip-shod Endymion. That it is so is no fault of mine.—No!—though it may sound a little paradoxical. It is as good as I had power to make it—by myself—Had I been nervous about its being a perfect piece, & with that view asked advice, & trembled over every page, it would not have been written; for it is not in my nature to fumble—I will write independantly.—I have written independently *without Judgment.*—I may write independently & *with judgment* hereafter.—The Genius of Poetry must work out its own salvation in a man: It cannot be matured by law & precept, but by sensation & watchfulness in itself—That which is creative must create itself—In Endymion, I leaped headlong into the Sea, and thereby have become better acquainted with the Soundings, the quicksands & the rocks, than if I had ~~stayed~~ stayed upon the green shore, and piped a silly pipe, and took tea & comfortable advice.—I was never afraid of failure; for I would sooner fail than not be among the greatest—But I am nigh getting into a rant. * * *

1. *Endymion* was violently attacked by reviewers in *Blackwood's Edinburgh Magazine* and *The Quarterly Review.*

2. Whose letter to the *Morning Chronicle* defended Keats.

ADRIENNE RICH

A Clock in the Square

This handless clock stares blindly from its tower,
Refusing to acknowledge any hour.
But what can one clock do to stop the game
When others go on striking just the same?
Whatever mite of truth the gesture held,   5
Time may be silenced but will not be stilled,
Nor we absolved by any one's withdrawing
From all the restless ways we must be going
And all the rings in which we're spun and swirled,
Whether around a clockface or a world.   10

1951

Aunt Jennifer's Tigers

Aunt Jennifer's tigers prance across a screen,
Bright topaz denizens of a world of green.
They do not fear the men beneath the tree;
They pace in sleek chivalric certainty.

Aunt Jennifer's fingers fluttering through her wool   5
Find even the ivory needle hard to pull.
The massive weight of Uncle's wedding band
Sits heavily upon Aunt Jennifer's hand.

When Aunt is dead, her terrified hands will lie
Still ringed with ordeals she was mastered by.   10
The tigers in the panel that she made
Will go on prancing, proud and unafraid.

1951

[*In* When We Dead Awaken: Writing as Re-Vision, *a talk*[1] *given in December, 1971, the author said of* Aunt Jennifer's Tigers: "In writing this poem, composed and apparently cool as it is, I thought I was creating a portrait of an imaginary woman. But this woman suffers from the opposition of her imagination, worked out in tapestry, and her life style, 'ringed with ordeals she was mastered by.' It was important to me that Aunt Jennifer was a person as distinct from myself as possible—distanced by the formalism of the poem, by its objective, observant tone— even by putting the woman in a different generation. In those years formalism was part of the strategy—like asbestos gloves, it allowed me to handle materials I couldn't pick up bare-handed."]

Storm Warnings

The glass has been falling all the afternoon,
And knowing better than the instrument

---

1. At the Women's Forum of the Modern Language Association.

What winds are walking overhead, what zone
Of gray unrest is moving across the land,
I leave the book upon a pillowed chair   5
And walk from window to closed window, watching
Boughs strain against the sky

And think again, as often when the air
Moves inward toward a silent core of waiting,
How with a single purpose time has traveled   10
By secret currents of the undiscerned
Into this polar realm. Weather abroad
And weather in the heart alike come on
Regardless of prediction.

Between foreseeing and averting change   15
Lies all the mastery of elements
Which clocks and weatherglasses cannot alter.
Time in the hand is not control of time,
Nor shattered fragments of an instrument
A proof against the wind; the wind will rise,   20
We can only close the shutters.

I draw the curtains as the sky goes black
And set a match to candles sheathed in glass
Against the keyhole draught, the insistent whine
Of weather through the unsealed aperture.   25
This is our sole defense against the season;
These are the things that we have learned to do
Who live in troubled regions.

                                                    1951

The Diamond Cutters

However legendary,
The stone is still a stone,
Though it had once resisted
The weight of Africa,
The hammer-blows of time   5
That wear to bits of powder
The mountain and the pebble—
But not this coldest one.

Now, you intelligence
So late dredged up from dark   10
Upon whose smoky walls
Bison took fumbling form
Or flint was edged on flint—
Now, careful arriviste,[1]
Delineate at will   15
Incisions in the ice.

1. Opportunist, upstart.

Be serious, because
The stone may have contempt
For too-familiar hands,
And because all you do   20
Loses or gains by this:
Respect the adversary,
Meet it with tools refined,
And thereby set your price.

Be hard of heart, because   25
The stone must leave your hand.
Although you liberate
Pure and expensive fires
Fit to enamour Shebas,
Keep your desire apart.   30
Love only what you do,
And not what you have done.

Be proud, when you have set
The final spoke of flame
In that prismatic wheel,   35
And nothing's left this day
Except to see the sun
Shine on the false and the true,
And know that Africa
Will yield you more to do.   40

                                                          1955

Snapshots of a Daughter-in-Law

1

You, once a belle in Shreveport,
with henna-colored hair, skin like a peachbud,
still have your dresses copied from that time,
and play a Chopin prelude
called by Cortot: "*Delicious recollections*   5
float like perfume through the memory."

Your mind now, mouldering like wedding-cake,
heavy with useless experience, rich
with suspicion, rumor, fantasy,
crumbling to pieces under the knife-edge   10
of mere fact. In the prime of your life.

Nervy, glowering, your daughter
wipes the teaspoons, grows another way.

2

Banging the coffee-pot into the sink
she hears the angels chiding, and looks out   15
past the raked gardens to the sloppy sky.
Only a week since They said: *Have no patience.*

The next time it was: *Be insatiable.*
Then: *Save yourself; others you cannot save.*[1]
Sometimes she's let the tapstream scald her arm,   20
a match burn to her thumbnail,

or held her hand above the kettle's snout
right in the woolly steam. They are probably angels,
since nothing hurts her any more, except
each morning's grit blowing into her eyes.   25

3

A thinking woman sleeps with monsters.
The beak that grips her, she becomes. And Nature,
that sprung-lidded, still commodious
steamer-trunk of *tempora* and *mores*[2]
gets stuffed with it all: the mildewed orange-flowers,   30
the female pills, the terrible breasts
of Boadicea[3] beneath flat foxes' heads and orchids.

Two handsome women, gripped in argument,
each proud, acute, subtle, I hear scream
across the cut glass and majolica   35
like Furies[4] cornered from their prey:
The argument *ad feminam*,[5] all the old knives
that have rusted in my back, I drive in yours,
ma semblable, ma soeur![6]

4

Knowing themselves too well in one another: 40
their gifts no pure fruition, but a thorn,
the prick filed sharp against a hint of scorn . . .
Reading while waiting
for the iron to heat,
writing, *My Life had stood—a Loaded Gun—*[7]   45
in that Amherst pantry while the jellies boil and scum,
or, more often,
iron-eyed and beaked and purposed as a bird,
dusting everything on the whatnot every day of life.

5

Dulce ridens, dulce loquens,[8]   50
she shaves her legs until they gleam
like petrified mammoth-tusk.

1. According to *Matthew* 27:42, the chief priests, scribes, and elders mocked the crucified Jesus by saying, "He saved others; himself he cannot save."
2. Times and customs.
3. Queen of the ancient Britons. When her husband died, the Romans seized the territory he ruled and scourged Boadicea; she then led a heroic but ultimately unsuccessful revolt.
4. In Roman mythology, the three sisters were the avenging spirits of retributive justice.
5. The *argumentum ad hominem* (literally, argument to the man) is (in logic) an argument aimed at a person's individual prejudices or special interests.
6. "My mirror-image (or 'double'), my sister." Baudelaire, in the prefatory poem to *Les Fleurs du Mal*, addresses (and attacks) his "hypocrite reader" as "mon semblable, mon frère" (my double, my brother).
7. "'My Life had stood—a Loaded Gun' [Poem No. 754], Emily Dickinson, *Complete Poems*, ed. T. H. Johnson, 1960, p. 369." (Rich's note)
8. "Sweet (or winsome) laughter, sweet chatter." The phrase concludes Horace's *Ode*, 1, 22, describing the appeal of a mistress.

6

When to her lute Corinna sings[9]
neither words nor music are her own;
only the long hair dipping
over her check, only the song
of silk against her knees
and these
adjusted in reflections of an eye.

55

Poised, trembling and unsatisfied, before
an unlocked door, that cage of cages,
tell us, you bird, you tragical machine—
is this *fertilisante douleur?*[1] Pinned down
by love, for you the only natural action,
are you edged more keen
to prise the secrets of the vault? has Nature shown
her household books to you, daughter-in-law,
that her sons never saw?

60

65

7

"To have in this uncertain world some stay
which cannot be undermined, is
of the utmost consequence."[2]
            Thus wrote
a woman, partly brave and partly good,
who fought with what she partly understood.
Few men about her would or could do more,
hence she was labeled harpy, shrew and whore.

70

75

8

"You all die at fifteen," said Diderot,[3]
and turn part legend, part convention.
Still, eyes inaccurately dream
behind closed windows blankening with steam.
Deliciously, all that we might have been,
all that we were—fire, tears,
wit, taste, martyred ambition—
stirs like the memory of refused adultery
the drained and flagging bosom of our middle years.

80

9

Not that it is done well, but
that it is done at all?[4] Yes, think
of the odds! or shrug them off forever.
This luxury of the precocious child,

85

---

9. The opening line of a famous Elizabethan lyric (by Thomas Campion) in which Corinna's music is said to control totally the poet's happiness or despair.
1. Enriching pain.
2. " '. . . is of the utmost consequence,' from Mary Wollstonecraft, *Thoughts on the Education of Daughters*, London, 1787." (Rich's note)
3. " 'Vous mourez toutes à quinze ans,' from the *Lettres à Sophie Volland*, quoted by Simone de Beauvoir in *Le Deuxième Sexe*, vol. II, pp. 123–4." (Rich's note)

Editor of the *Encyclopédie* (the central document of the French Enlightenment), Diderot became disillusioned with the traditional education of women and undertook an experimental education for his own daughter.
4. Samuel Johnson's comment on women preachers: "Sir, a woman's preaching is like a dog's walking on his hinder legs. It is not done well, but you are surprised to find it done at all." (Boswell's *Life of Johnson*, ed. Birbeck-Hill, I, 463)

Time's precious chronic invalid,—
would we, darlings, resign it if we could?   90
Our blight has been our sinecure:
mere talent was enough for us—
glitter in fragments and rough drafts.

Sigh no more, ladies.
                    Time is male
and in his cups drinks to the fair.   95
Bemused by gallantry, we hear
our mediocrities over-praised,
indolence read as abnegation,
slattern thought styled intuition,
every lapse forgiven, our crime   100
only to cast too bold a shadow
or smash the mould straight off.

For that, solitary confinement,
tear gas, attrition shelling.
Few applicants for that honor.

                    10
                    Well,   105
she's long about her coming, who must be
more merciless to herself than history.[5]
Her mind full to the wind, I see her plunge
breasted and glancing through the currents,
taking the light upon her   110
at least as beautiful as any boy
or helicopter,
                    poised, still coming,
her fine blades making the air wince

but her cargo
no promise then: 115
delivered
palpable
ours.
1958–60

[*In* When We Dead Awaken, *Rich described her consciousness during the time she was writing this poem:* "Over two years I wrote a
10-part poem called 'Snapshots of A Daughter-in-Law,' in a longer,
looser mode than I've ever trusted myself with before. It was an extraordinary relief to write that poem. It strikes me now as too literary, too
dependent on allusion; I hadn't found the courage yet to do without
authorities, or even to use the pronoun 'I'—the woman in the poem is
always 'she.' One section of it, #2, concerns a woman who thinks she
is going mad; she is haunted by voices telling her to resist and rebel,
voices which she can hear but not obey."]

5. "Cf. *Le Deuxième Sexe*, vol. II, p. 574: '. . . elle arrive du fond des ages, de Thèbes,
de Minos, de Chichen Itza; et elle est aussi le totem planté au coeur de la brousse afri-
caine; c'est un helicoptère et c'est un oiseau; et voilà la plus grande merveille: sous ses
cheveux peints le bruissement des feuillages devient une pensée et des paroles s'échap-
pent de ses seins.' " (Rich's note)

Necessities of Life

Piece by piece I seem
to re-enter the world: I first began

a small, fixed dot, still see
that old myself, a dark-blue thumbtack

pushed into the scene,   5
a hard little head protruding

from the pointillist's[1] buzz and bloom.
After a time the dot

begins to ooze. Certain heats
melt it.
        Now I was hurriedly   10
blurring into ranges
of burnt red, burning green,

whole biographies swam up and
swallowed me like Jonah.

Jonah! I was Wittgenstein,[2]   15
Mary Wollstonecraft, the soul

of Louis Jouvet, dead
in a blown-up photograph.

Till, wolfed almost to shreds,
I learned to make myself   20

unappetizing. Scaly as a dry bulb
thrown into a cellar

I used myself, let nothing use me.
Like being on a private dole,

sometimes more like kneading bricks in Egypt.[3]   25
What life was there, was mine,

now and again to lay
one hand on a warm brick

and touch the sun's ghost
with economical joy,   30

---

1. Post-impressionist painters (Seurat, for example) who fused small dots of paint with brush strokes.
2. Ludwig Wittgenstein (1889–1951), Austrian-born philosopher. His early thought heavily influenced logical positivism, and his later work expressed such strong skepticism about the reliability of language that he ultimately resigned his chair of philosophy lest his ideas be misunderstood or misinterpreted. Mary Wollstonecraft, an early feminist, wrote *Vindication of the Rights of Women* (1792). Louis Jouvet (1887–1951), innovative French actor and producer.
3. According to *Exodus* 5, one of the most oppressive tasks imposed on the Israelites during their Egyptian bondage was the making of bricks.

now and again to name
over the bare necessities.

So much for those days. Soon
practice may make me middling-perfect, I'll

dare inhabit the world   35
trenchant in motion as an eel, solid

as a cabbage-head. I have invitations:
a curl of mist steams upward

from a field, visible as my breath,
houses along a road stand waiting   40

like old women knitting, breathless
to tell their tales.

1962

Orion

Far back when I went zig-zagging
through tamarack pastures
you were my genius, you
my cast-iron Viking, my helmed
lion-heart king in prison.   5
Years later now you're young

my fierce half-brother, staring
down from that simplified west
your breast open, your belt dragged down
by an oldfashioned thing, a sword   10
the last bravado you won't give over
though it weighs you down as you stride

and the stars in it are dim
and maybe have stopped burning.
But you burn, and I know it;   15
as I throw back my head to take you in
an old transfusion happens again:
divine astronomy is nothing to it.

Indoors I bruise and blunder,
break faith, leave ill enough   20
alone, a dead child born in the dark.
Night cracks up over the chimney,
pieces of time, frozen geodes
come showering down in the grate.

A man reaches behind my eyes   25
and finds them empty
a woman's head turns away
from my head in the mirror

children are dying my death
and eating crumbs of my life.   30

Pity is not your forte.
Calmly you ache up there
pinned aloft in your crow's nest,
my speechless pirate!
You take it all for granted   35
and when I look you back

it's with a starlike eye
shooting its cold and egotistical spear
where it can do least damage.
Breathe deep! No hurt, no pardon   40
out here in the cold with you
you with your back to the wall.

1965

[*In* When We Dead Awaken, *Rich described* Orion *as* "a poem of re-construction with a part of myself I had felt I was losing—the active principle, the energetic imagination, the 'half-brother' whom I projected, as I had for many years, into the constellation Orion. It's no accident that the words 'cold and egotistical' appear in this poem, and are applied to myself. The choice still seemed to be between 'love'—womanly, maternal love, altruistic love—a love defined and ruled by the weight of an entire culture—and egotism—a force directed by men into creation, achievement, ambition, often at the expense of others, but justifiably so. For weren't they men, and wasn't that their destiny as womanly love was ours? I know now that the alternatives are false ones—that the word 'love' is itself in need of re-vision."]

Planetarium

(*Thinking of Caroline Herschel, 1750–1848,*
astronomer, sister of William; and others)

A woman in the shape of a monster
a monster in the shape of a woman
the skies are full of them

a woman   "in the snow
among the Clocks and instruments   5
or measuring the ground with poles"

in her 98 years to discover
8 comets

she whom the moon ruled
like us   10
levitating into the night sky
riding the polished lenses

Galaxies of women, there
doing penance for impetuousness
ribs chilled   15
in those spaces   of the mind

An eye,
        "virile, precise and absolutely certain"
        from the mad webs of Uranisborg
                              encountering the NOVA

every impulse of light exploding   20
from the core
as life flies out of us

        Tycho[1] whispering at last
        "Let me not seem to have lived in vain"

What we see, we see   25
and seeing is changing

the light that shrivels a mountain
and leaves a man alive

Heartbeat of the pulsar
heart sweating through my body   30

The radio impulse
pouring in from Taurus
        I am bombarded yet   I stand

I have been standing all my life in the
direct path of a battery of signals   35
the most accurately transmitted most
untranslatable language in the universe
I am a galactic cloud so deep   so invo-
luted that a light wave could take 15
years to travel through me   And has   40
taken   I am an instrument in the shape
of a woman trying to translate pulsations
into images   for the relief of the body
and the reconstruction of the mind.

1968

[*Rich described this poem, in* When We Dead Awaken, *as a* "companion poem to 'Orion,' " *above:* "at last the woman in the poem and
the woman writing the poem become the same person. . . . It was written after a visit to a real planetarium, where I read an account of the
work of Caroline Herschel, the astronomer, who worked with her
brother William, but whose name remained obscure, as his did not."]

1. Tycho Brahe (1546–1601), Danish astronomer whose cosmology tried to fuse the
Ptolemaic and Copernican systems. He discovered and described (*De Nova Stella,* 1573)
a new star in what had previously been considered a fixed star-system. Uraniborg (line
19) was Tycho's famous and elaborate palace-laboratory-observatory.

I Dream I'm the Death of Orpheus[1]

I am walking rapidly through striations of light and dark thrown under
    an arcade.
I am a woman in the prime of life, with certain powers
and those powers severely limited
by authorities whose faces I rarely see.
I am a woman in the prime of life   5
driving her dead poet in a black Rolls-Royce
through a landscape of twilight and thorns.
A woman with a certain mission
which if obeyed to the letter will leave her intact.
A woman with the nerves of a panther   10
a woman with contacts among Hell's Angels
a woman feeling the fullness of her powers
at the precise moment when she must not use them
a woman sworn to lucidity
who sees through the mayhem, the smoky fires   15
of these underground streets
her dead poet learning to walk backward against the wind
on the wrong side of the mirror
1968

Leaflets

1

    The big star, and that other
lonely on black glass
overgrown with frozen
lesions, endless night
the Coal Sack gaping   5
black veins of ice on the pane
spelling a word:
                Insomnia
not manic but ordinary
to start out of sleep
turning off and on   10
this seasick neon
vision, this
division

the head clears of sweet smoke
and poison gas   15

life without caution
the only worth living

---

1. A legendary Greek poet whose music could charm even inanimate objects and who
once briefly secured—by the power of his music—the release of his wife, Eurydice, from
Hades. But when she returned to Hades, he was overcome with grief, and his prolonged
wailing enraged Bacchanalian orgiasts, who tore him to pieces. Later the fragments of
his body, except for the head, were collected by the Muses and buried at the foot of
Mt. Olympus. The poem derives from Cocteau's version of the myth in his film *Orphée;*
in this version a modern poet goes to the underworld (which looks like a bombed-out
city) and confronts Death, a handsome middle-aged lady whose car is escorted by two
men on motorcycles (see line 11). Rich points out that the poem assumes the perspective of Death who, in the film, comes and goes through a mirror.

love for a man
love for a woman
love for the facts   20
protectless

that self-defense be not
the arm's first motion

memory not only
cards of identity   25

that I can live half a year
as I have never lived up to this time—[1]

Chekhov coughing up blood almost daily
the steamer edging in toward the penal colony

chained men dozing on deck   30
five forest fires lighting the island

lifelong that glare, waiting.

                            2
Your face
            stretched like a mask
                        begins to tear
as you speak of Che Guevara[2]
Bolivia, Nanterre   35
I'm too young to be your mother
you're too young to be my brother

your tears are not political
they are real water, burning
as the tears of Telemachus   40
burned

Over Spanish Harlem the moon
swells up, a fire balloon
fire gnawing the edge   45
of this crushed-up newspaper

                        now
the bodies come whirling
coal-black, ash-white
out of torn windows
and the death columns blacken
                whispering   50
Who'd choose this life?

---

1. Quoted from a letter by Anton Chekhov to I. L. Scheglov, March 22, 1890, explaining his forthcoming visit to Saghalien, an island penal colony. Chekhov (1860–1904), the Russian playwright and short story writer, had contracted tuberculosis at age 23 (see line 28).
2. Cuban revolutionary theorist and an early leader in the Castro regime. Guevara was killed in the abortive Bolivian revolution in 1967. Nanterre: site of the French student uprising.

We're fighting for a slash of recognition,
a piercing to the pierced heart.
Tell me what you are going through—[3]

but the attention flickers   55
   and will flicker
a matchflame in poison air
a thread, a hair of light
    sum of all answer
to the *Know that I exist!* of all existing things.   60

3

If, says the Dahomeyan devil,[4]
someone has courage to enter the fire
the young man will be restored to life.

If, the girl whispers,
I do not go into the fire   65
I will not be able to live with my soul.

(Her face calm and dark as amber
under the dyed butterfly turban
her back scarified in ostrich-skin patterns.)

4

Crusaders' wind glinting   70
off linked scales of sea
ripping the ghostflags
galloping at the fortress
Acre, bloodcaked, lionhearted
raw vomit curdling in the sun   75
gray walkers walking
straying with a curbed intentness
in and out the inclosures
the gallows, the photographs
of dead Jewish terrorists, aged 15   80
their fading faces wide-eyed
and out in the crusading sunlight
gray strayers still straying
dusty paths
the mad who live in the dried-up moat   85
of the War Museum

what are we coming to
what wants these things of us
who wants them

5

The strain of being born   90
  over and over has torn your smile into pieces
 Often I have seen it broken

---

3. "Simone Weil: 'The love of a fellow-creature in all its fullness consists simply in the ability to say to him: "What are you going through" '—*Waiting for God.*" (Rich's note)

4. Legba the trickster.

and then re-membered
and wondered how a beauty
    so anarch, so ungelded   95
will be cared for in this world.
    I want to hand you this
leaflet streaming with rain or tears
    but the words coming clear
something you might find crushed into your hand   100
    after passing a barricade
and stuff in your raincoat pocket.
    I want this to reach you
who told me once that poetry is nothing sacred
    —no more sacred that is   105
than other things in your life—
    to answer yes, if life is uncorrupted
no better poetry is wanted.

    I want this to be yours
in the sense that if you find and read it   110
    it will be there in you already
and the leaflet then merely something
    to leave behind, a little leaf
in the drawer of a sublet room.
    What else does it come down to   115
but handing on scraps of paper
    little figurines or phials
no stronger than the dry clay they are baked in
    yet more than dry clay or paper
because the imagination crouches in them.   120
    If we needed fire to remind us
that all true images
    were scooped out of the mud
where our bodies curse and flounder
    then perhaps that fire is coming   125
to sponge away the scribes and time-servers
    and much that you would have loved will be lost as well
before you could handle it and know it
    just as we almost miss each other
in the ill cloud of mistrust, who might have touched   130
    hands quickly, shared food or given blood
for each other. I am thinking how we can use what we have
    to invent what we need.
Winter–Spring 1968

Trying to Talk with a Man

Perhaps my life is nothing but an image of this kind; perhaps I am doomed to retrace my
steps under the illusion that I am exploring, doomed to try and learn what I should
simply recognize, learning a mere fraction of what I have forgotten.
                                            —ANDRE BRETON, *Nadja*[1]

Out in this desert we are testing bombs,

that's why we came here.

1. Breton (1896–1968), a French poet and critic, was one of the founders of both
Dadaism and Surrealism. His novel *Nadja* was published in 1928.

Sometimes I feel an underground river
forcing its way between deformed cliffs
an acute angle of understanding   5
moving itself like a locus of the sun
into this condemned scenery.

What we've had to give up to get here—
Whole LP collections, films we starred in
playing in the neighborhoods, bakery windows   10
full of dry, chocolate-filled Jewish cookies,
the language of love-letters, of suicide notes,
afternoons on the riverbank
pretending to be children

Coming out to this desert   15
we meant to change the face of
driving among dull green succulents
walking at noon in the ghost-town
surrounded by a silence

that sounds like the silence of the place   20
except that it came with us
and is familiar
and everything we were saying until now
was an effort to blot it out—
Coming out here we are up against it   25

Out here I feel more helpless
with you than without you
You mention the danger
and list the equipment
we talk of people caring for each other   30
in emergencies—laceration, thirst—
but you look at me like an emergency

Your dry heat feels like power
your eyes are stars of a different magnitude
they reflect lights that spell out: EXIT   35
when you get up and pace the floor

talking of the danger
as if it were not ourselves
as if we were testing anything else.

                                                        p. 1971

Diving into the Wreck

First having read the book of myths,
and loaded the camera,
and checked the edge of the knife-blade,
I put on
the body-armor of black rubber   5
the absurd flippers
the grave and awkward mask.

I am having to do this
not like Cousteau with his
assiduous team   10
aboard the sun-flooded schooner
but here alone.

There is a ladder.
The ladder is always there
hanging innocently   15
close to the side of the schooner.
We know what it is for,
we who have used it.
Otherwise
it's a piece of maritime floss   20
some sundry equipment.

I go down.
Rung after rung and still
the oxygen immerses me
the blue light   25
the clear atoms
of our human air.
I go down.
My flippers cripple me,
I crawl like an insect down the ladder   30
and there is no one
to tell me when the ocean
will begin.

First the air is blue and then
it is bluer and then green and then   35
black I am blacking out and yet
my mask is powerful
it pumps my blood with power
the sea is another story
the sea is not a question of power   40
I have to learn alone
to turn my body without force
in the deep element.

And now: it is easy to forget
what I came for   45
among so many who have always
lived here
swaying their crenellated fans
between the reefs
and besides   50
you breathe differently down here.

I came to explore the wreck.
The words are purposes.
The words are maps.
I came to see the damage that was done   55
and the treasures that prevail.

I stroke the beam of my lamp
slowly along the flank
of something more permanent
than fish or weed   60

the thing I came for:
the wreck and not the story of the wreck
the thing itself and not the myth
the drowned face always staring
toward the sun   65
the evidence of damage
worn by salt and sway into this threadbare beauty
the ribs of the disaster
curving their assertion
among the tentative haunters.   70

This is the place.
And I am here, the mermaid whose dark hair
streams black, the merman in his armored body
We circle silently
about the wreck   75
we dive into the hold.
I am she: I am he

whose drowned face sleeps with open eyes
whose breasts still bear the stress
whose silver, copper, vermeil cargo lies   80
obscurely inside barrels
half-wedged and left to rot
we are the half-destroyed instruments
that once held to a course
the water-eaten log   85
the fouled compass

We are, I am, you are
by cowardice or courage
the one who find our way
back to this scene   90
carrying a knife, a camera
a book of myths
in which
our names do not appear.

                                                        p. 1972

from Talking with Adrienne Rich[1]

* * * I think of myself as using poetry as a chief means of self-exploration—one of several means, of which maybe another would be dreams, really thinking about, paying attention to dreams, but the poem, like the dream, does this through images and it is in the images

1. A transcript of a conversation recorded March 9, 1971, and printed in *The Ohio Review,* Fall, 1971.

of my poems that I feel I am finding out more about my own experience, my sense of things. But I don't think of myself as having a position or a self-description which I'm then going to present in the poem.

❊   ❊   ❊

When I started writing poetry I was tremendously conscious of, and very much in need of, a formal structure that could be obtained from outside, into which I could pour whatever I had, whatever I thought I had to express. But I think that was a part of a whole thing that I see, now as a teacher, very much with young writers, of using language more as a kind of façade than as either self-revelation or as a probe into one's own consciousness. I think I would attribute a lot of the change in my poetry simply to the fact of growing older, undergoing certain kinds of experiences, realizing that formal metrics were not going to suffice me in dealing with those experiences, realizing that experience itself is much more fragmentary, much more sort of battering, much ruder than these structures would allow, and it had to find its own form.

❊   ❊   ❊

I have a very strong sense about the existence of poetry in daily life and poetry being part of the world as it is, and that the attempt to reduce poetry to what is indited on a page just limits you terribly. . . . The poem is the poetry of things lodged in the innate shape of the experience. My saying "The moment of change is the only poem" is the kind of extreme statement you feel the need to make at certain times if only to force someone to say, "But I always thought a poem is something written on a piece of paper," you know, and to say: "But look, how did those words get on that piece of paper." There had to be a mind; there had to be an experience; the mind had to go through certain shocks, certain stresses, certain strains, and if you're going to carry the poem back to its real beginnings it's that moment of change. I feel that we are always writing.

❊   ❊   ❊

When I was in my twenties ❊ ❊ ❊ I was going through a very sort of female thing—of trying to distinguish between the ego that is capable of writing poems, and then this other kind of being that you're asked to be if you're a woman, who is, in a sense, denying that ego. I had great feelings of split about that for many years actually, and there are a lot of poems I couldn't write even, because I didn't want to confess to having that much aggression, that much ego, that much sense of myself. I had always thought of my first book as being a book of very well-tooled poems of a sort of very bright student, which I was at that time, but poems in which the unconscious things never got to the surface. But there's a poem in that book about a woman who sews a tapestry and the tapestry has figures of tigers on it. But the woman is represented as being completely—her hand is burdened by the weight of the wedding band, and she's meek, and she's fearful, and the only way in which she can express any other side of her nature is in embroidering these tigers. Well, I thought of that as almost a formal exercise, but when I go back and look at that poem I really think it's saying something about what I was going through. And now that's lessened a great deal for all sorts of reasons—that split.

from An Interview with Adrienne Rich[1]

I would have said ten or fifteen years ago that I would not even want to identify myself as a woman poet. That term *has* been used pejoratively; I just don't think it can be at this point. You know, for a woman the act of creation is prototypically to produce children, while the act of creating with language—I'm not saying that women writers haven't been accepted; certainly, more have been accepted than women lawyers or doctors. Still, a woman writer feels, she is going against the grain—or there has been this sense until very recently (if there isn't still). Okay, it's all right to be a young thing and write verse. But a friend of mine was telling me about meeting a noted poet at a cocktail party. She'd sent him a manuscript for a contest he was judging. She went up to him and asked him about it, and he looked at her and said, "Young girls *are* poems; they shouldn't write them." This attitude toward women poets manifests itself so strongly that you are made to feel you are becoming the thing you are not.

❋   ❋   ❋

If a man is writing, he's gone through all the nonsense and said "Okay, I am a poet and I'm still a man. They don't cancel each other out or, if they do, then I'll opt to be a poet." He's not writing for a hostile sex, a breed of critics who by virtue of their sex are going to look at his language and pass judgment on it. That does happen to a woman. I don't know why the woman poet has been slower than the woman novelist in taking risks though I'm very grateful that this is no longer so. I feel that I dare to think further than I would have dared to think ten years ago—and *that* certainly is going to affect my writing. And I now dare to entertain thoughts and speculations that then would have seemed unthinkable.

❋   ❋   ❋

Many of the male writers whom I very much admire—Galway Kinnell, James Wright, W. S. Merwin—are writing poetry of such great desolation. They come from different backgrounds, write in different ways, and yet all seem to write out of a sense of doom, as if we were fated to carry on these terribly flawed relationships. I think it's expressive of a feeling that "we, the masters, have created a world that's impossible to live in and that probably may not be livable in, in a very literal sense. What we thought, what we'd been given to think is our privilege, our right, and our sexual prerogative has led to this, to our doom." I guess a lot of women—if not a lot of women poets— are feeling that there has to be some other way, that human life is messed-up but that it doesn't have to be *this* desolate.

❋   ❋   ❋

Today, much poetry by women is charged with anger and uses voices of rage and anger that I don't think were ever used in poetry before. In poets like Sylvia Plath and Diane Wakoski, say, those voices are so convincing that it is impossible to describe them by using those favorite adjectives of phallic criticism—shrill and hysterical. Well, Sylvia Plath is dead. I always maintained from the first time I read

1. By David Kalstone, in *The Saturday Review*, April 22, 1972.

her last poems that her suicide was not necessary, that she could have gone on and written poems that would have given us even more insight into the states of anger and willfulness, even of self-destructiveness, that women experience. She didn't need literally to destroy herself in order to reflect and express those things. Diane Wakoski is a young woman. She's changing a lot and will continue to change. What I admire in her, besides her energy and dynamism and quite a beautiful gift for snatching the image that she wants out of the air, is her honesty. No woman has written before about her face and said she hated it, that it had served her ill, that she wished she could throw acid in it. That's very shocking. But I think all women, even the most beautiful women, at times have felt that in a kind of self-hatred. Because the *face* is supposed to be the *woman*.

*   *   *

A lot of poetry is becoming more oral. Certainly, it's true of women and black poets. Reading black poetry on the printed page gives no sense of the poem, if you're going to look at that poetry the way you look at poems by Richard Wilbur. Yet you can hear these poets read and realize it's the oldest kind of poetry.

*   *   *

I think the energy of language comes somewhat from the pressure and need and unbearableness of what's being done to you. It's not the same energy you find in the blues. The blues are a grief language, a lost language, and a cry of pain, usually in a woman's voice, which is interesting. For a long time you sing the blues, and then you begin to say, "I'm tired of singing the blues. I want something else." And that's what you're hearing now. There seems to be a connection between an oppressed condition and having access to certain kinds of energy, vitality, and subjectivity. For women as well as blacks. Though I don't feel there is a necessary cause-and-effect relationship; what seems to happen is that being on top, being in a powerful position leads to a divorce between one's unruly, chaotic, revolutionary sensitivity and one's reason, sense of order and of maintaining a hold. And, therefore, you have at the bottom of the pile, so to speak, a kind of churning energy that gets lost up there among the administrators.

*   *   *

I don't know how or whether poetry changes anything. But neither do I know how or whether bombing or even community organizing changes anything when we are pitted against a massive patriarchal system armed with supertechnology. I believe in subjectivity—that a lot of male Left leaders have turned into Omnipotent Administrators, because their "masculinity" forced them to deny their subjectivity. I believe in dreams and visions and "the madness of art." And at moments I can conceive of a women's movement that will show the way to humanizing technology and fusing dreams and skills and visions and reason to begin the healing of the human race. But I don't want women to take over the world and run it the way men have, or to take on—yet again!—the burden of carrying the subjectivity of the race. Women are a vanguard now, and I believe will increasingly become so, because we have—Western women, Third World women, all women—

known and felt the pain of the human condition most consistently. But in the end it can't be women alone.

from When We Dead Awaken: Writing as Re-Vision

Most, if not all, human lives are full of fantasy—passive daydreaming which need not be acted on. But to write poetry or fiction, or even to think well, is not to fantasize or to put fantasies on paper. For a poem to coalesce, for a character or an action to take shape, there has to be an imaginative transformation of reality which is in no way passive. And a certain freedom of the mind is needed—freedom to press on, to enter the currents of your thought like a glider pilot, knowing that your motion can be sustained, that the buoyancy of your attention will not be suddenly snatched away. Moreover, if the imagination is to transcend and transform experience it has to question, to challenge, to conceive of alternatives, perhaps to the very life you are living at that moment. You have to be free to play around with the notion that day might be night, love might be hate; nothing can be too sacred for the imagination to turn into its opposite or to call experimentally by another name. For writing is re-naming.

Now, to be maternally with small children all day in the old way, to be with a man in the old way of marriage, requires a holding back, a putting aside of that imaginative activity, and seems to demand instead a kind of conservatism. I want to make it clear that I am *not* saying that in order to write well, or think well, it is necessary to become unavailable to others, or to become a devouring ego. This has been the myth of the masculine artist and thinker; and, I repeat, I do not accept it. But to be a female human being trying to fulfill traditional female functions in a traditional way *is* in direct conflict with the subversive function of the imagination. The word "traditional" is important here. There must be ways, and we will be finding out more and more about them, in which the energy of creation and the energy of relation can be united. But in those earlier years I always felt the conflict as a failure of love in myself. I had thought I was choosing a full life: the life available to most men, in which sexuality, work and parenthood could coexist. But I felt, at 29, guilt toward the people closest to me, and guilty toward my own being.

I wanted, then, more than anything, the one thing of which there was never enough: time to think, time to write. The '50s and early '60s were years of rapid revelations: the sit-ins and marches in the South, the Bay of Pigs, the early antiwar movement, raised large questions—questions for which the masculine world of the academy around me seemed to have expert and fluent answers. But I needed desperately to think for myself—about pacifism and dissent and violence, about poetry and society, and about my own relationship to all these things. For about ten years I was reading in fierce snatches, scribbling in notebooks, writing poetry in fragments; I was looking desperately for clues, because if there were no clues then I thought I might be insane. I wrote in a notebook about this time:

Paralyzed by the sense that there exists a mesh of relationships —e.g. between my anger at the children, my sensual life, pacifism,

sex (I mean sex in its broadest significance, not merely sexual desire)—an interconnectedness which, if I could see it, make it valid,
would give me back myself, make it possible to function lucidly
and passionately. Yet I grope in and out among these dark webs.

I think I began at this point to feel that politics was not something
"out there" but something "in here" and of the essence of my condition.

In the late '50s I was able to write, for the first time, directly about
experiencing myself as a woman. The poem was jotted in fragments
during children's naps, brief hours in a library, or at 3 A.M. after rising
with a wakeful child. I despaired of doing any continuous work at this
time. Yet I began to feel that my fragments and scraps had a common
consciousness and a common theme, one which I would have been
very unwilling to put on paper at an earlier time because I had been
taught that poetry should be "universal," which meant, of course, non-
female. Until then I had tried very much *not* to identify myself as a
female poet.

The Elements of Poetry

1. ARGUMENT, MEANING, AND THEME

Most readers would agree with Archibald MacLeish that "a poem should not mean but be," but discovering what a poem "is" often involves identifying what it contains. Poets often used to provide an **argument** for their poems, a prose summary of what "happens"; now they seldom provide such a convenience, but to begin interpretation and experience of a poem readers often find it useful to **paraphrase,** put into prose exactly what the poem says, line by line, in words that are different but as nearly equivalent as possible. Such a method will usually clarify the situation and setting of the poem and help to characterize the speaker (see §3), leading to a definition of a poem's attitude toward its subject and to more careful distinctions about its ideas. A poem's **meaning** involves more than the **statement** it makes, more than a prose summary of its idea or ideas. Recognizing the ideas and seeing how they are articulated in the poem is an important early step toward experiencing the poem in its full meaning, which includes the implications of its statement.

Some of the terms used to describe a poem's ideas are often used interchangeably, but it is useful to distinguish among them. The **subject,** or **topic,** of a poem is its general or specific area of concern, usually something categorical such as death (or the death of a particular person), war (or a specific war, or specific battle), suffering, love, rejection, or the simple life. Most poems make statements about a subject and define the degree and kind of their interest in it; a poem about war, for example, may ultimately be more concerned to say something about the nature of man or about honor or about peace than about war itself. Subjects offer a great variety of **themes:** that death is a release from pain, or a gateway to immortality, that war is senseless, or brutal, or a necessary evil, or a heroic quest for justice. A poem's theme is the statement it makes about its subject; summarizing a paraphrase in one or two sentences often yields the theme. A poem also may be said to use a **motif** (plural, motifs or motives): a recurrent device, formula, or situation which deliberately connects the poem with common patterns of previous thought. One common motif, occurring in such poems as Waller's "Go, lovely rose" (p. 622) or Marvell's *To His Coy Mistress* (p. 627), is that of **carpe diem.** The phrase literally means "seize the day," and *carpe diem* poems inevitably remind us of the shortness of life and beauty and the necessity to take advantage of the present. Such recurring situations as temptations in the garden are also motifs; one might speak of the "garden motif" or "temptation motif" in Milton's *Paradise Lost* (p. 586) or the journey motif in Tennyson's *Ulysses* (p. 546).

697

The **meaning** of every poem, like the "being" of the poem, is finally unique, but a poem's subject, theme, and motif relate it to other poems with similar ideas and attitudes. An **explication**, or **exegesis**, explains how all of the elements in an individual poem or passage work; in explication, a critic analyzes the various component parts in order to interpret the poem's statement. Explication takes a step beyond paraphrase in attempting to discover a poem's meaning. The terms **message** and **moral**, once used to summarize the poem's meaning, are now usually considered outmoded and misleading because they tend to oversimplify and confuse statement with meaning. Similarly objectionable to many is the term **hidden meaning**, which implies that a poem is a puzzle or that the author is deliberately obscuring his or her point; a poem may use complicated methods to achieve its clarity and emotional impact, but a good poem does not value obscurity or even difficulty purely for its own sake. **Meaning** is the poem's combination of motifs, themes, and statements about a subject or series of subjects *and* the emotions that it artfully evokes toward them by means of poetic devices and strategies. But meaning—however well defined and articulated—is never the precise equivalent of the poem itself.

2. AUDIENCE

Even poems which seem personal, confessional, and private are influenced by a poet's sense of who he or she is writing for and who will ultimately read the poem. Because poems are meant to be read and experienced by someone besides the poet, they are more than simple records of an event, or idea, or state of mind. Poets fictionalize or imagine circumstances and reflections, and they usually try to communicate by evoking in the reader a particular attitude or emotion.

The means by which poems generate an effect are usually called **poetic** (or **artistic**) **devices** or **strategies**. Even when the precise effect of a poem is difficult to determine (as it often is, unless one uses a purely mechanical criterion), the efforts to obtain an effect can usually be isolated. Almost everything in a poem is in some sense (but not a bad sense) a device: the choice of one word rather than another one, the use of metaphor, of certain sounds and rhythms, of allusions, conventions, forms—all contribute to a total effect. Most poets depend upon some version of the poetic tradition (§9) and use standard poetic conventions as short cuts for projecting an attitude or gaining an impact; even highly unusual or eccentric poems use strategies that have proved effective in the past or invent new strategies which will produce a predictable response. Often poets depend upon a reader's recognition of a tradition, conventions, or standard poetic devices to produce a knowing response, but often too there is a kind of friendly deception involved, an attempt to persuade by using some means which will move readers without their consent, or even against their will. The **rhetoric** of a poem is the sum of the persuasive devices used to affect readers, with or without their consent.

Many of the most important **rhetorical devices** (or **rhetorical figures**) date from classical antiquity, and some of these are so common in

ordinary life that we scarcely recognize them as devices, even in a poem. **Comparison** and **contrast** may clarify the identity and properties of a person, place, or thing, but persuasive values may also be built in, depending on what is being compared with what. Acceptance by association is as common as guilt by association; naming admired names may lull a reader into easy submission or be part of a complex web of interrelationships in which an author places his or her values among things certain to be admired, or expected to be admired among readers of a certain kind. Or vice versa. Ginsberg's *Howl* (p. 646) achieves many of its most persuasive effects by listing cultural villains his audience is likely to agree about, and then inserting in the list forces that to most of his audience might ordinarily seem neutral. An **allusion** is a reference to something outside the poem (in history, perhaps, or in another poem) which has built-in emotional associations; in *Sunday Morning* (p. 498) Stevens alludes to the Crucifixion to suggest a tradition of use of Sunday mornings, and in *The Love Song of J. Alfred Prufrock* (p. 480) Eliot alludes to Polonius (in *Hamlet*) to help establish the manner of his "hero." **Example** is simply the giving of a specific instance to back up a generalization, and many whole poems are built upon the principle, directly or indirectly; sometimes, as in Pound's *The Garden* (p. 524), the whole poem presents the example, and the generalization for which the example stands is left unstated.

Several classic figures of speech, though not restricted to poetry, are often found in poems. **Hyperbole** (or extravagant **exaggeration**) may be serious or comic or both at the same time, pushing something so far toward absurdity that its ordinary manifestation may seem normal and acceptable, as in Marvell's *To His Coy Mistress*. **Meiosis** (or **understatement**) consciously underrates something or portrays it as lesser than it is usually thought to be; its psychology is to bring the reader instinctively to the defense of the thing being undervalued. It is closely related to **irony** (§3), especially in one of its forms, **litotes**, which affirms something by denying its opposite, as in colloquial expressions such as "He's no Einstein." **Periphrasis** (or **circumlocution**) is deliberate avoidance of the obvious, writing which circles its subject and refuses to take the simplest route toward clear meaning. **Synechdoche** is using a part of something to signify the whole (as in "hired hands" for "workmen"), and **metonymy** is naming something associated with what is being talked about rather than the thing itself, as in the use of "crown" for "king." **Hyperbaton** is the rearrangement of sentence elements for special effects; Milton, in *Paradise Lost*, for example, often uses extreme instances of the figure, as in the sentence beginning in line 44 of Book I (p. 587). **Prolepsis** is the **foreshadowing** of a future event as if it were already influencing the present, as in Eliot's *Journey of the Magi* (p. 538) when the wise men on their way to Bethlehem see objects suggestive of the Crucifixion.

Some writers, especially during the Renaissance and 18th century, have deliberately used these rhetorical devices and hosts of others, but even more common is use of them without deliberation, for the terms

themselves try to describe and categorize standard ways in which words may affect psychological processes. Many kinds of attempts to persuade—sermons, political speeches, TV commercials, informal conversations—use some version of such devices, though often in more simple and less subtle ways than good poetry. Identifying the devices is only a way of discovering what a poem advocates, how it tries to develop emotional energy, and whether its methods are effective. Being able to identify the devices is useful but only as a means to a more important end.

Poems which openly and directly advocate a particular ideology, argue for a specific cause, or try to teach us something are called **didactic** poems. Critics sometimes distinguish between didactic poems and **mimetic** (or **imaginative**) poems, which are more concerned to present than to persuade. But the distinction is one of degree, for most poems mean at the very least to make their attitudes, their vision, their presentation of reality plausible and attractive. Poems which openly and explicitly have designs upon their readers have been out of fashion since the 18th century, and some modern critics use the term "didactic" pejoratively to suggest that an author is too blatant, unsubtle, and moralistic in approach. The term **propaganda** is almost always used pejoratively, to suggest that a writer's main aim is to arouse readers toward immediate action in a specific situation; poems so specifically and narrowly directed are usually assumed to be ephemeral, though good "occasional poems" and "satires" (see §6 and §10) often transcend their occasions.

3. AUTHOR, SPEAKER, AND TONE

It has become traditional to distinguish between the person who wrote the poem and the person who speaks in a poem, for an author often deliberately chooses to speak through a **character** quite different from his real self. Poets thus sometimes create a fictional person as a **speaker,** just as playwrights create a character who is then obliged to say things in a characteristic way, that is, a way appropriate to the character as created. In Robert Browning's *Soliloquy of the Spanish Cloister* (p. 493), for example, the speaker is a disagreeable, vindictive monk pursuing a vendetta against a fellow monk, and he is not much like Browning, who was not a monk and not necessarily disagreeable and vindictive; Browning allows the character to reveal himself through his own words and in doing so to clarify what Browning thinks of such attitudes. In many poems the speaker is very like the author himself, or very like what the author wishes to think he or she is like. Between the speaker who is a fully distinct character and the author speaking honestly and directly are many degrees of detachment. Many critics and teachers prefer that the person speaking the words of a poem always be called a speaker, but others find it unnecessary to make the distinction when the author is clearly speaking in his own person; the difficulty usually lies in deciding what "clearly" means.

The term **persona** is often used synonymously with speaker, especially in satire, where the author usually speaks in a voice very like his

own except that he often pretends to be more innocent, more earnest, and more pure than he knows himself to be. Such a **pose** (or **posture**, or **mask**) is not really dishonest any more than the creation of a character in a play or story is dishonest; it is part of the author's strategy of making a point effectively and persuasively. It is often useful to compare several poems by the same author; such a procedure helps identify the speaker in individual poems and points up similarities in attitude and strategy that run through an author's work.

Defining the attitude which a poem takes toward a certain subject or theme or situation is often a matter of being clear about the poem's speaker, situation, and setting. In poems that tell a story or present a clearly defined dramatic situation, the circumstances under which someone speaks affect the way we receive and interpret what is being said. **Setting** (either as place or time) may also affect interpretation, just as in a story or play—as, for example, in Arnold's *Dover Beach* or Stevens' *Sunday Morning*.

When the author's attitude is different from that of the speaker (as in Browning's *Soliloquy*) the poem is said to be ironic, though the term **irony** also means several other things. Irony is not only saying one thing and meaning its opposite; it is also any manner of being oblique rather than straightforward and often involves exaggeration or understatement. A whole poem may be said to be ironic (or to have **structural irony**) when its total effect is to reverse the attitude presented by the speaker, but poems which are not wholly ironic may use ironic words and phrases (**verbal irony**) to generate a more complex statement or attitude. When irony is stark, simple, snide, exactly inverted—that is, when what is said is exactly the opposite of what is meant—it is called **sarcasm**. The term "irony," qualified in various ways, may indicate almost any kind of discrepancy between what is apparent in a literary work and what someone else knows to be so. **Dramatic irony** (which may be used in a poem as well as in a play) occurs when the speaker is unaware of something about himself or his situation but the reader is not, as in Henry Reed's *Lessons of the War* (p. 419) or Jonson's *Come, My Celia* (p. 625). In **socratic irony**, the speaker poses as an innocent and ignorant person who then provokes a revelation through his apparently naive assumptions or questions, as in Chaucer's *Canterbury Tales* and many satires.

The terms **tone** and **voice** represent attempts to be still more precise about the author's attitude toward what his or her poem literally says. Descriptions of tone try to characterize the way the words of the poem are (or should be) spoken when one sensitively reads the poem aloud. The concept of tone recognizes that meaning is often adjusted in human speech by the way one says words, for by subtle modulation one can change the meaning of words completely, and by stress, rhythm, and volume, one regulates emphases which the syntax may not by itself make clear. Tone literally tries to describe the vocal sounds which a poem seems to demand, and one may speak of the tone of an individual word or phrase, of a longer passage, or of a whole poem. Words such as "ironic," "comic," "playful," "sincere," and "straight-

forward" may sometimes accurately describe tone, as may more particular adjectives such as "boisterous," "boastful," "taunting," "apologetic," "plaintive," or "bemused." Sometimes, when the speaker's attitude toward what he says is different from that of the author, the term "voice" is used to describe the prevailing sense of the author's presence. In Browning's *Soliloquy of the Spanish Cloister*, for example, the speaker's tone may be described as "gruff," "resentful," "vindictive," "sadistic," but the voice disapproves of these tones. The interrelationship between voice and tone is sometimes called **mood**, that total **atmosphere** which pervades the work and gives the reader a sense of what to expect. In some poems, of course, the tone, voice, and mood may be identical, but the reader is always well advised to examine the situation and speaker carefully as a means of testing the emotional charge of words, phrases, and larger units of expression.

4. FIGURATIVE LANGUAGE

Most nouns, verbs, adjectives, and adverbs not only **denote** a thing, action, or attribute, but also **connote** feelings and associations suggested by it. A horse is literally a four-legged, whinnying, rideable, workable animal, but the word "horse" connotes to most people strength, vitality, vigor. To speak of a horse that is not strong and vigorous, one either qualifies the term in some way ("drawhorse" or "bedraggled horse" or "sorry horse") or uses a synonym such as "nag"—which literally denotes the same animal but which implies (connotes) different qualities. To be even more emphatic about its vigor and strength and to imply wildness as well, one might call it a steed or stallion. To the extent that the **connotations** of a word are generally agreed on, a writer may use the word to indicate a whole range of attitudes. In *Still to Be Neat* (p. 508) Ben Jonson uses words with heavily moral connotations ("sound," "adulteries") to question the fears behind a woman's fastidiousness and to help create a preference for women who are more casually dressed and made up, less powdered and more natural; in *Delight in Disorder* (p. 508) Robert Herrick expresses the same preference, but the praising words he uses are joyous and carefree, suggesting that the preference is based on sensual, not moral grounds—even implying that the carefree, informally clad woman is apt not to be chaste.

Not all words have clear, universally accepted connotations built into them, and writers often use the more elaborate devices of metaphor and symbolism to build a specific set of associations and values into the words and combinations of words that they use. By building visual patterns or self-contained systems out of individual words, a poet may control more accurately and more complexly the emotional value and suggestion of individual words and develop a more satisfying total effect. How this is done in an individual poem depends upon the particular requirements of the subject and theme as well as upon the talents, style, and artistic choices of an individual poet; one can, however, distinguish among different kinds of methods, and it is useful to have a set of distinguishing terms firmly in mind. Many of

the most popular terms are used differently by different critics; uniformity of terminology—even if considered ideal—is not really possible, but all readers of poetry should take care that they themselves use whatever terms they use consistently, carefully, and unambiguously.

Imagery is used by different critics to mean three related but distinct things: (1) the mental pictures suggested by the verbal descriptions in a poem; (2) the visual descriptions in the poem itself; or (3) the figurative language (including metaphors, similes, and analogies) in the poem. In all three uses, imagery is technically a visual term, though other sense impressions are sometimes included under its large umbrella; imagery which mingles different sense impressions (sound or touch, for example, with sight, as in Roethke's *I Knew a Woman,* p. 465) is said to be **synesthetic imagery**.

The first definition of imagery is the least precise one, for it tries to describe the effect of the poem in the reader; effects may be predicated generally, but because each reader's response is likely to be a little different from every other reader's, critics usually find it safer and more precise to articulate the poem's efforts to create the effect; the second and third definitions of imagery are attempts to describe these efforts, the *means* of bringing about a certain effect. The third definition is the most common one, and it has the advantage of greater precision in describing different indirect ways that a poem may use to translate words into less abstract sense experience. Critics who use the term "imagery" in this third way may refer to nonfigurative description simply as description and to the presumed effect on the reader of both description and imagery as **visual impressions** or **sense impressions**. Imagery is the collective term for a group of individual **images**. One may speak of an **image cluster** (a group of similar images concentrated in a short passage), of a **controlling image** (when a single image seems to dominate a passage or even a whole poem, making other images subservient to it), or of an **image pattern** (when one or more images recur in a passage or poem). Sometimes it is convenient to speak of **kinds of imagery** ("animal imagery" or "architectural imagery") as well as to define individual images in greater detail.

Imagery defined in the third way includes the use of simile, metaphor, analogy, and personification. A **simile** is a direct, explicit comparison of one thing to another and usually uses "like" or "as" in drawing the connection. In *A Red, Red Rose* (p. 630) Burns explicitly compares his friend to a rose, detailing in the poem itself in what different ways she is like a rose. A simile may **extend** throughout a poem and be elaborated (it is then called an **analogy**) or be used to make a brief comparison in only one specified sense.

A **metaphor** pretends that one thing is something else, thus making an implicit comparison between the things. Even more than similes, metaphors are often **extended** because, in describing a thing in terms of something else, a metaphor often implies a detailed and complex resemblance between the two, one which may not be obvious at first glance. When a metaphor compares things which seem radically unlike, but which can be developed into a striking parallel, it is called a

conceit; the "metaphysical poets" of the 17th century specialized in finding surprising likenesses in things usually considered unlike, and their poems often elaborate a single **metaphysical conceit,** as in Donne's *The Flea* (p. 623) or Herbert's *The Collar* (p. 495). The terms **tenor** and **vehicle** are often used to distinguish the primary object of attention from the thing being used to clarify that object. In Shakespeare's *That Time of Year* (p. 511) the primary object of attention (**tenor**) is the aging speaker, and late autumn is the **vehicle** which in the first few lines clarifies his aging. Metaphors are often said to be **extended metaphors** or **controlling metaphors** (in the same sense I have described above for images) when they dominate or organize a passage or poem. Because the central thrust of metaphor is to provide a new experience of something by letting us see it in terms of something else, metaphor is often said to be the soul of poetry itself, and whole poems are sometimes said to be metaphors for an action, or feeling, or state of mind which they attempt to explore and communicate.

A **mixed metaphor** is one in which terms from one metaphor are incorporated into another one, usually by mistake. A **dead metaphor** is one that has passed into such common usage as to have obscured its origins: we speak of a "leg" of a chair or the "heart" of the problem without remembering that the terms are metaphors implying a comparison to living bodies. When language, metaphorical or not, becomes unnecessarily specialized and self-consciously unavailable to an outsider, it is **jargon.** When such language is used mindlessly, it is called **cant.** When it is slangy and lives the short life of fashion among a select in-group, it is called **argot.** A **cliché** is any expression or idea which, through repeated use, has become commonplace, tiresome, and trite.

Personification (or **prosopopeia**) is the strategy of giving human qualities to abstract concepts or inanimate things: Beauty, Honor, Cruelty, Death, flowers and various aspects of the natural landscape have been personified in various ages, but the strategy has been largely out of favor except for specialized and comic uses in the 20th century. Closely related is the **pathetic fallacy,** the strategy of ascribing to nature emotions which reflect human happenings, as when "universal Nature did lament" the death of Milton's Lycidas.

A **symbol** is many things to many people, and often it means no more than that the person using the term is dealing with something he doesn't know how to describe or think about precisely. The term is difficult to define and be precise about, but it can be used quite sensibly. A symbol is, put simply, something which stands for something else. The everyday world is full of simple examples; a flag, a peace sign, a star, or a skull and crossbones all suggest things beyond themselves, and everyone is likely to understand what their display is meant to signify, even though the viewer may not necessarily share the commitment which the object represents. In common usage a prison is a symbol of confinement, constriction, and loss of freedom, and in specialized traditional usage a cross may symbolize oppression, cruelty,

suffering, death, resurrection, triumph, or the intersection of two separate things, traditions, ideas, etc. The specific symbolic significance is controlled by the context; a reader may often decide by looking at contiguous details in the poem and by examining the poem's attitude toward a particular tradition or body of beliefs; a star means one kind of thing to a Jewish poet and something else to a Christian poet, still something else to a Nazi or to someone whose religion is surfing. Too easy categorization, though, is dangerous, for a Christian poet may use the star of David in a traditional Jewish way (as in Marianne Moore's *The Hero*, p. 575), and a nonbeliever may draw upon the fund of traditional symbolic values without implying commitment to a particular religious system that lies behind them.

In a very literal sense, words themselves are all symbols (they stand for an object, action, or quality, not just for letters or sounds), but symbols in poetry are said to be those words and groups of words which have a range of reference beyond their literal denotation. The word "rose" simply denotes a kind of flower, but in poetry over the years it has come to symbolize youth, beauty, perfection, and shortness of youth and life. When a poem pervasively uses symbols as a major strategy and when the poem is more committed to the things which the symbols represent than to everyday reality, it is called a **symbolic poem** and is said to use **symbolism**. Poems, like everyday conversation, may use symbols occasionally and casually without being called symbolic.

Allegory is another slippery term closely related to symbol. In allegory, the action of the poem consistently and systematically describes another order of things beyond the obvious one. Spenser's *The Faerie Queene* is allegorical on several levels at the same time; the narrative action makes literal sense as a story, but the characters and actions also stand for political happenings, religious events, and moral values. *The Faerie Queene* is thus said to be a political, religious, and moral allegory. Allegory need not however, operate on more than one level beyond the literal one.

Poets sometimes develop a highly specialized and personal set of **private symbols**—words, objects, and phrases which take on specific meanings as a result of repeated use by the poet in poem after poem. Yeats, for example, developed a highly complex symbolic system, and so did Blake; their poems are largely accessible without specialized knowledge of their "systems," but the experienced reader of each soon discovers that the meanings of individual poems resonate in the context of other poems and in the reader's expanding knowledge of special symbols.

At the opposite extreme from private symbols are those which are universally shared within a defined culture. The framework of such shared symbols is called a **myth,** and the myth may include characters, events, and recurrent patterns of experience which the culture recognizes as, on some deep level, true. Poets often draw heavily upon the myth or myths of their culture; poets such as Milton or Eliot draw as heavily upon the Christian myth as ancient Greek and Roman poets

upon classical myth. Poets sometimes too use particulars of a myth no longer literally or generally accepted; many English poets, for example, allude to classical myths in which neither they nor their audience believe in a truly mythic sense, but the wide recognition of standard myths allows writers to employ examples either in or out of their full mythic context. In recent years, critics have been heavily influenced by **myth criticism**, which may mean a great many things but which usually signifies an attempt to discover **archetypes**, patterns of experience and action which are similar in different nations and cultures. In this sense, myth is not restricted to a single system, but rather attempts to transcend the particulars of time and place and locate fundamental recurrent patterns in human nature and human history. Myth is also sometimes used in a very general sense to include a closed or self-defining system; in this sense, Yoknapatawpha County in Faulkner's novels is a myth, the ideals and goals of a culture (the American dream or frontierism or progress) are myths, and the framework which supports an individual poet's private symbols may be called his private or personal myth.

5. FORM AND STRUCTURE

The terms **form** and **structure** are among the most frequently used and abused in literary criticism. Almost everyone agrees that both terms describe organizing principles in a literary work and that meaning is finally inseparable from form and structure, but the particular values associated with each term vary widely. It is useful, though, to distinguish between the two, taking advantage of the spatial basis of the terms.

The **form** of a poem has to do with its appearance, just as does the form of a building, and one can describe that form in many different ways, just as a description of the form of a building depends upon the angle of vision (from the ground or from the air), the distance of the viewer, and to what other buildings the building is being compared. The simplest sense of poetic form involves the literal appearance on the page, the poem's shape seen physically, conceived literally. On the page most traditional poems look regular—that is, they are either divided into regular "stanzas" (§8) or they flow continually down the page in lines of more or less equal length. The breaks between stanzas, when they occur, usually reinforce divisions of meaning, much as do paragraph breaks in prose, though sometimes the break in meaning and break in form contradict each other, or operate in tension, for a particular purpose. Modern poems tend to be less regular and thus to look more scattered and fragmented on the page, reflecting a general modern attitude that poetic meaning accumulates in a less regular and less programmed way. Sometimes the appearance on the page reflects a visual attempt to capture oral patterns or speech rhythms (in the alternately bunched and scattered words of cummings's *chanson innocente*, p. 259, or *portrait*, p. 431); sometimes the appearance tries to reflect the action described (as in cummings's *l(a* in which the fall of a leaf is described and depicted). Occasionally the words are even shaped

like a particular object, as in Renaissance **emblem poetry** (or **carmen figuratum** or **shaped verse**) such as Herbert's *Easter Wings* (p. 621) or recent **concrete poetry** such as Richard Kostelanetz's *Tribute to Henry Ford* (p. 620) or Robert Hollander's *You Too? Me Too—Why Not* (p. 618) which resemble a freeway and a Coke bottle, respectively. Concrete poetry involves experiments with eye appeal, attempting to supplement (or replace) verbal meanings with devices from painting and sculpture. The idea is an old one; Theodoric in ancient Greece is credited with inventing **technopaegnia**—that is, constructing poems with visual appeal. The **acrostic**, a crossword-puzzle type of poem in which the first letter of each line spells words when read down as well as across, similarly counts on visual impact. Such experimentation was once thought to have mystical significance, but it now survives only as playful exercise.

More enduring, more significant, and more complex senses of form involve less easily seeable ways of classifying external characteristics. Poetry is itself a sort of **formal** classification as distinguished from drama or fiction, and one can also distinguish between kinds of poetry (elegy, for example, or epigram) on the basis of subject matter, tone, conventions, etc. (see §6). Stanza varieties and rhythmic patterns (see §8 and §7) are also formal matters, for each involves external patterns which may be described relative to other poems. If one diagrams such matters as rhyme and accent, the patterns are readily visible, though the unpracticed eye might not discover them without help, just as casual viewers may need to have the Doric or Attic lines of a building pointed out to them.

As in a building, **structure** supports form and makes it possible. Many organizational elements enter into considerations of structure, and there are countless ways to speak of structure. The order and arrangement of all of a poem's constituent parts—words, images, figures of speech, ideas, everything—involve structure, and the ways of discussing the relationship between parts vary from matters of word arrangement (grammar, syntax) to the development and presentation of ideas. Structure enables the form; the planning and craft of poetry are all, finally, structural matters.

The distinction I have made between form and structure corresponds to distinctions that some critics make between **external** and **internal** form (or external and internal structure). Another frequent distinction is that between **organic** structure or form and **architechtonic** structure or form (those who make this distinction do not necessarily use the terms "form" and "structure" as they have been explained above). Things organic are said to take their shape from natural forces, like living organisms, and things architechtonic to have shape artificially imposed upon them from without; a strong bias is usually implied toward the former, for the distinction implies the livingness, wholeness, and uniqueness of an individual poem.

Some works are shaped by other works which they **imitate** or **parody**. An **imitation** which makes fun of another work is a **burlesque** or **parody** of it, exaggerating its distinctive features and holding them up to ridi-

cule; it is a parody if its attitude is one of gentle teasing, a burlesque if it is harsh and vicious. Imitation may also be a kind of flattery, honoring the methods, values, and meanings of another work and expropriating them into the new one. Imitation is sometimes considered an inferior, unoriginal way of constructing a poem, but many great poems have their basis in imitation (*The Aeneid,* for example, imitates *The Iliad*), and a good imitation—even though it may borrow major features from its original—is never a simple copy, and it often derives major effects from its similarities to and differences from the original.

Finally, questions of form and structure are related to questions about the integrity and autonomy of individual poems. For many years, critics were reluctant to deal with **parts** of a poem, insisting that as self-existent **wholes** poems deserved to be dealt with **holistically,** as creations having their own laws. More recently, criticism has dealt more directly with parts of poems, admitting that they too have organizational principles and facing squarely the difficulty that knowing whether a poem is whole or not is, even for the author, very nearly a mystical matter. Besides, an individual poem is often part of a larger **sequence** or **cycle**—that is, a group of poems which have significant features in common: they may be about a similar subject, tell a story progressively, or be calculated to produce a particular effect. Some ages have emphasized the possibilities of such sequences (see §10), and in the early 17th century poets such as Herbert and Herrick arranged poems in their volumes very carefully toward a total effect; and some poets (Stevens and Ammons, for example) have insisted that all their poems are really only parts of the larger poem which is their total work or even their life. Almost all poets themselves arrange the poems in their individual volumes, and it is often useful and revealing to read individual poems in the context of these volumes.

6. GENRES AND KINDS

The word **genre** signifies an attempt to classify literary works in a way similar to biological classification, but there has never been a very precise agreement as to how that classification should be done. Different poems are said to belong to different groups, classified according to subject matter, level of language, mode of presentation, shape of plot, prose or verse form, etc., and often all of these ways of classifying are lumped together as **genre** classifications. But it is useful to distinguish among different ways of classifying literary works; here we use the term **genre** to indicate the traditional classroom distinction between fiction, poetry, and drama. Other less inclusive terms may then be used for subdividing genres and for different ways of classifying literary works according to characteristics they have in common.

A **mode** is, literally, a way of doing something; as a literary term it may most usefully be employed to indicate basic literary patterns of organizing experience. The **narrative mode** tells a story and organizes experience along a time continuum. The **dramatic mode** presents a change, usually an abrupt one, and organizes experience emotionally according to the rise and fall of someone's fortunes. The **lyric mode**

reflects upon an experience or an idea and organizes experience irrespective of time and space, though it may describe a particular time or specific place. These traditional modes represent basic ways of viewing experience and have been around for a very long time. They obviously influenced the development of genres, which represent a somewhat artificial stiffening or rigidification of the narrative, dramatic, and lyric modes.

One may also think of modes in terms of the conclusions they draw about experience or the dominant emotions they arouse in their presentations of experience. Such a use of the term "mode" also has the sanction of time, and four such divisions are popularly used. **Tragedy,** or the **tragic mode,** describes someone's downfall, usually in stately language; and tragedy may exist in poetry (see, for example, *Sir Patrick Spens,* p. 518) as well as in drama. **Comedy,** or the **comic mode,** describes in more common language someone's triumph or the successful emergence of some order which encompasses and mutes all disorderly forces. **Romance,** or the **romantic mode,** describes the ideal, or what ought to be, often in terms of nostalgia or fantasy or longing. **Satire,** or the **satiric mode,** attacks the way things are and usually distributes the blame. In *The Anatomy of Criticism,* Northrup Frye argues that these modes correspond to the **myths** of the four seasons (comedy—spring; romance—summer; tragedy—autumn; satire—winter) and thus considers them universal ways of organizing experience.

Poetry considered as a genre may also be subdivided into **kinds** (or **types,** or **subgenres**). In the 17th century, French neoclassical critics believed poetry to consist of specific kinds that corresponded to absolute categories in the nature of things, though they never agreed on exactly what the kinds were. Even if one does not believe in kinds as such absolutes, knowing the characteristics of major kinds can be useful to readers in letting them know what to expect of a poem which consciously defines itself as of a certain kind. Over the years there has been general agreement about some of these kinds and their characteristics. The **epic,** or **heroic poetry,** was traditionally regarded as the highest in a hierarchy of kinds because it described the great deeds of mighty heroes and heroines, usually in founding a nation or developing a distinctive culture, and used elevated language and a grand, high style. **Pastoral poetry,** on the other hand, describes the simple life of country folk, usually shepherds who live a timeless, painless (and sheepless) life in a world that is full of beauty, music, and love, and that remains forever green. (Most pastoral poetry was, of course, written by city poets who used the kind nostalgically and self-consciously as fantasy; see, for example, Ralegh's *Nymph's Reply* to Marlowe's *Passionate Shepherd to His Love,* p. 454). The pastoral poem is also sometimes called an **eclogue,** a **bucolic,** or an **idyll.** The **elegy** was, in classical times, a poem on any subject written in "elegiac" meter, but since the Renaissance the term has usually indicated a formal lament for the death of a particular person; a **dirge,** or **threnody,** is similar but less formal and is supposed to be sung. A dirge or elegy supposed to be sung by one person is called a **monody.** Many elegies are **pastoral**

elegies in which the dead person is imagined to be a shepherd (as in Milton's *Lycidas*); many of the conventions of pastoral carry over to the pastoral elegy, except that here time and death have invaded the simple world and destroyed its joyful, carefree spirit. An **epigram** was originally any poem carved in stone (on tombstones, buildings, gates, etc.), but in modern usage it denotes a very short, usually witty verse with a quick turn at the end; it is often, but not always, comic, as the group of epigrams in this anthology demonstrates. Two epigrams on page 602 attempt to define the kind. The **epitaph** is a variety of epigram in which the poem is supposed to be carved on someone's tombstone, but many epitaphs are comic, written about people not yet dead, and of course not really intended for engraving.

A **verse epistle** is ostensibly a letter from the poet to someone, usually a friend, and it uses the tone of a familiar letter; its themes are usually the joys of friendship and the pleasures of civilized conversation, but sometimes (as in Pope's *Epistle to Dr. Arbuthnot*, p. 443) the traditional materials are turned to satiric use. A **georgic**, or **didactic-descriptive poem**, is a how-to-do-it poem, often mixing moral instruction with practical advice about homely matters; georgics often contain long descriptive passages about natural phenomena or processes. If a georgic describes a particular place in detail, it is called **topographical poetry**, which has several variations. **House poems**, very popular in the Renaissance, describe the residence and estate of someone who is directly characterized by the account of his tastes in ambience (Jonson's *To Penshurst*, for example, p. 599). **Prospect poems** describe in receding detail toward infinity the land visible from some specific vista, and they often unite a temporal (historical) with a spatial description of the place. (Some of the changes in topographical poetry over the years may be seen by comparing Jonson's poem with Tomlinson's *At Barstow*, p. 601).

A **mock poem** uses the conventions of one of the standard kinds in order to attack something; the thing attacked may be the kind itself, the artificiality of its conventions, or a real situation which does not measure up to the quality of life usually represented in the kind. **Mock-epic**, or **mock-heroic**, poems (*The Dunciad*, for example) commonly attack conditions in the present which do not measure up to the presumed heroism in epical accounts of the past.

A **lyric** is a short poem in which a speaker expresses intense personal emotion rather than telling a story or anecdote; Blake's *The Lamb* (p. 585) and *The Tiger* (p. 585), Roethke's *My Papa's Waltz* (p. 469), Wordsworth's *Tintern Abbey* (p. 571), and Elizabeth Barrett Browning's *How Do I Love Thee* (p. 581) suggest the range of poems which are properly called lyrics, and sometimes the term is used even more broadly for *any* short poem. The lyric is considered by many to be the essence of poetry itself as distinguished from the other genres (note its relation to the term "lyrical mode"). Originally the term "lyric" designated poems meant to be sung to the accompaniment of the lyre, and the names of several other kinds also specify their original connection with music. Many **songs** (whose words are usually called lyrics) are

poems which have been set to music. During the Renaissance music and poetry were especially closely related. Many of the best Renaissance short poems were written specifically for music or were later set to music by professional musicians, and in recent years an increasing number of song writers are serious poets whose lyrics are poems of some quality. A **ballad** is a narrative poem which is, or originally was, meant to be sung (*Sir Patrick Spens,* for example). Characterized by much repetition and often by a repeated **refrain** (recurrent phrase or series of phrases), ballads were originally a folk creation, transmitted orally from person to person and age to age. Once **folk ballads** began to be written down (in the 18th century), **literary ballads** in imitation of folk ballads began to be created by individual authors. A **hymn** is a song of praise, usually in praise of God but sometimes of abstract qualities. A **chanson** (which in French simply means "song") was originally a song written in "couplets" (§8), but the term now describes any simple song; poems such as cummings' *chanson innocente* or Blake's *Song of Innocence* (p. 453) make use of the expectations aroused by the claim to simplicity. The **madrigal**, a short poem, usually about love, set to music for unaccompanied voices, was very popular in Renaissance England. A **rhapsody**, like its counterpart in music, is a medley of extravagant utterances, usually in praise of something. An **epithalamium** or **epithalamion** is a marriage song or a song in praise of the bride. An **aubade** is a morning song in which the coming of dawn is either celebrated or denounced as a nuisance (Donne's *The Sun Rising*, p. 502, for example). An **aube** is a more rigidly defined morning poem; the speaker of an aube is the woman in a love triangle, and she expresses regret that dawn is coming so that she and her lover must part. In a **complaint** a lover bemoans his sad condition as a result of neglect by his mistress (the speaker in Marvell's *To His Coy Mistress* mentions such a complaint, line 7). A **litany** (Nashe's *A Litany in Time of Plague*, p. 427) is a ritualistic invocational prayer, related to responsive readings in church liturgy. The **debate** is an old medieval kind in which two allegorical figures dispute; Randall's *Booker T. and W.E.B.* (p. 489) is a modern example of the debate kind. In a **palinode**, an author recants his previous attitude toward something, often apologizing for his earlier poetry, which he now claims to have been trifling. The **confessional poem** is a relatively new (or at least only recently defined) kind in which the speaker describes his confused chaotic state, which becomes a metaphor for the state of the world around him (as in Robert Lowell's *Skunk Hour*, p. 595). A **meditation** is a contemplation of some physical object as a way of reflecting upon some larger truth, often (but not necessarily) a spiritual one; Herbert's *The Windows* and Stevens' *The World as Meditation* are traditional and modern examples.

Many other ways of grouping poetry are less categorical, and some of them consciously overlap with other groupings. Debates are, for example, **dialogues** (that is, they have two speakers); and many of the kinds (confessional, complaint, aube, and many others) are traditionally **monologues** (one clearly distinguishable speaker does all the

speaking). Monologues are sometimes called **interior monologues** (as in fiction) if the speaker seems to be thinking thoughts rather than speaking to someone. A monologue set in a specific situation and spoken to someone (but not necessarily anyone in particular) is often called a **soliloquy** or **dramatic monologue** (Browning's *Soliloquy of the Spanish Cloister* and *My Last Duchess*, p. 519). **Light verse** encompasses many poems in many kinds; it is not necessarily trivial, but its speaker takes or affects a whimsical, twitting attitude toward his or her subject, as in most epigrams or poems such as Armour's *Hiding Place* (p. 640). Light verse that deals with the manners and mores of polite society is called **vers de société**. And some terms which properly describe a kind also properly describe some other sort of grouping. If satire, for example, is in one sense a mode, it is also a kind, for there is **formal verse satire** which attacks a specific vice in the manner of a verse essay. And the term "satire" also describes an attitude toward experience and a tone; as the opposite of **panegyric** (poetry praising something) satire attacks something, usually by analyzing, specifying, and naming names. Satire which is mild, civilized, and gentle is called **Horatian satire** (named after the Roman poet Horace); vicious, violent, loud satire is **Juvenalian satire** (named after Juvenal), or **invective**; **Menippean satire** (named after Menippus) mixes poetry and prose (Wakoski's *The Buddha Inherits 6 Cars on His Birthday*, p. 529, is a modern instance of this tradition). A satire which attacks a specific person is a **lampoon**.

It is also difficult to distinguish certain poetic kinds from stanza forms. The **sonnet**, for example, is in a sense a kind, for it has certain conventions and usually treats specified subjects in a traditional way. But its conventions include a specified stanza, metrical pattern, and rhyme scheme, and I have described it (as well as the **ode** and **haiku**) under "Stanza and Verse Forms" (§8). The sonnet, ode, and haiku may properly be called either kinds or verse forms.

7. PROSODY

Prosody is the study of sound and rhythm in poetry. It is not a very exact science, but properly used it can be an aid to reading and *hearing* poems more fully. Poetry is more than a collection of sounds in a particular sequence, but poetry has a historical and primal relationship to music, and the audial aspects of poetry are basic to more complex matters involving words and arrangement. The sounds of poetry often clarify meaning, sometimes extend it, and nearly always provide tonal controls and gauges. A careful student of prosody may discover nuances and subtleties unavailable to a more casual hearer and may often gain insights into a poet's craft, but the most important function of prosody for most readers is to develop a sense of how poetry should be read aloud and, when it is read aloud, heard in its full subtlety and resonance.

The **rhythm** of a passage—in prose or poetry—is the pattern of sound pulsations in the voice as one reads it. Almost all spoken language has some kind of rhythm, however irregular, and simply listening to a human voice reciting, reading, or talking informally reveals

recurrent systems of **stress** or **accent**. Stress is a relative matter (and this fact is a major difficulty for prosodic analysis), but in listening to the human voice we can always hear that some words and syllables are **stressed** (**accented**), and that others are, relatively, **unstressed** (**unaccented**). When the stress recurs at quite regular intervals—that is, when the rhythm has a pattern—the result is **meter**. The systematic analysis of patterns of stress, syllable by syllable, sound unit by sound unit, is called **scansion**; a reader who can **scan** a poem will discern the poem's basic rhythmic pattern (meter) and may then notice variations in the pattern or departures from it. These variations are often the most interesting metrical characteristics of the poem (and it is here that prosody is the least dull). But to discover variations one must see how patterns are formed and what the basic ones are.

According to pronouncing dictionaries, all words bear a stress on one or more syllables, and it is this syllable stress that forms the basis of any meter. But when words are put together into a sentence, or even a phrase, other regulators of stress are added. Monosyllabic words (words of one syllable) all have, according to a pronouncing dictionary, the same stress, but in a sentence or phrase the sameness of stress disappears; nouns and verbs generally receive stress while prepositions, articles, and conjunctions do not, but meaning governs where the stresses fall. In the sentence,

Throw the ball to me

stresses "naturally" fall on "throw," "ball," and "me," but another context of meaning might considerably alter the stress pattern:

I said, throw the ball to me, not over my head.

Stress here would likely fall on "to," and there might be some other "unusual" stresses, provided by the demands of meaning in particular instances or by particular speakers. When a sentence or phrase appears in a certain rhythmic context (in, for example, a poem written in a certain meter), the sound context also affects it, tending to bend it (or "wrench" it) toward the basic pattern in the surrounding passage. There are, then, three factors which determine stress: (1) the "natural" stress or stresses of each word; (2) meaning and emphasis in a sentence or phrase; and (3) the patterns of stress in the surrounding context.

Meter is measured in feet; a **foot** normally consists of a stressed syllable and one or more unstressed syllables. In the following line, in which stressed syllables are marked "‐" and unstressed syllables "◡," the division into five feet is indicated by a **virgule**, or **slash mark** (/):

A lit/tle lear/ning is/ a dang/'rous thing

Each of its feet is an **iambic** foot—that is, it has an unstressed syllable followed by a stressed one. Iambic meter is the most common one in English poetry, but three other meters are of some importance:

Trochaic (a stressed syllable followed by an unstressed one):

Tĕll mĕ/ nŏt ĭn/ moŭrn fŭl/ nŭm bĕrs

Anapestic (two unstressed syllables followed by a stressed one):

'Twăs thĕ nīght/ bĕ fŏre Chrīst/ măs ănd āll/ thrŏugh thĕ hoūse

Dactylic (a stressed syllable followed by two unstressed ones):

Hīg glĕ dў/ pīg glĕ dў/ Āl frĕd Lŏrd/ Tēn nў sŏn.

Most English poems use one of these meters as their basic meter, but not with absolute regularity. An iambic poem will often contain trochaic feet (for emphasis, perhaps, or just for change), and some variation is almost a requirement if a poem is not to lull the ear into total dull deafness. Besides the standard meters, there are special feet used for variations.

Here is a table of the basic metrical feet and the most frequent variations:

ADJECTIVAL FORM OF THE NAME	NOUN FORM	PATTERN
iambic	*iamb* (or *iambus*)	˘ ¯
trochaic	*trochee*	¯ ˘
anapestic	*anapest*	˘ ˘ ¯
dactylic	*dactyl*	¯ ˘ ˘
spondaic	*spondee*	¯ ¯
pyrrhic	*pyrrhic*	˘ ˘
amphibrachic	*amphibrach* (or *amphibrachys* or *rocking foot*)	˘ ¯ ˘
amphimacric	*amphimacer* (or *amphimac* or *cretic*)	¯ ˘ ¯

Coleridge's *Metrical Feet* (p. 605) exemplifies most of them.

The most common line length in English poetry is pentameter, five feet. Here is a table of the most common line lengths:

monometer	one foot
dimeter	two feet
trimeter	three feet
tetrameter	four feet
pentameter	five feet
hexameter	six feet
heptameter	seven feet
octameter	eight feet

Iambic and anapestic meters are sometimes called **rising rhythms** (or **rising meters**) because their basic movement is from unstressed to stressed syllables; and trochaic and dactylic meters are called **falling rhythms** (or **falling meters**). When a foot lacks a syllable it is called **catalectic**; the first foot of anapestic lines is often catalectic, and the final foot of most trochaic lines is catalectic because lines that end with an unstressed syllable are usually thought to "sound funny"; such lines usually occur only in comic poetry. Lines that rhyme by using an unstressed final syllable are said to have **feminine rhyme**. Certain meters are also said to incline toward comic effects; anapestic rhythm tends to produce comic effects, though the examples on pages 605–608 demonstrate that anapests may also produce serious, even lofty, tones. Iambic tetrameter also seems more liable than most meters to comic effects, though it also has been used (as in Marvell's *To His Coy Mistress*) for great varieties of tone. The number and length of pauses in a line affect the speed with which the line is read and, indirectly, the tone in any meter, for a slow-paced line seems less emphatic in its rhythm than a rapid-paced one. Almost all lines contain one or more natural pauses, some very short and some fairly long; any significant pause within a line is called a **caesura**, and in scansion it is indicated by a double virgule (//).

I have been pretending that metrical matters can be dealt with categorically and with great certainty, but the whole question is much more approximate (and often uncertain) than I have let on. The distinction between stressed and unstressed is, for example, not a very precise one, for many degrees of stress are possible, and even an untrained ear can usually hear great variety of stress in the reading of a single line from a single poem. Division into feet is sometimes arbitrary, for there is often more than one way to count the number of feet, even assuming that the stresses are all accurately marked. Students often get bogged down in the technicalities of such matters and lose sight of the point of metrical analysis—which is to *hear* poems more accurately and notice those surprising places when the poem departs from its basic pattern. Often (but not always) a sharp departure from rhythmic expectations which the poem builds up signals something special going on. Note, for example, the variations from the basic iambic pattern in Dryden's *To the Memory of Mr. Oldham* (p. 614); some are for emphasis, others indicate structural breaks, and some mimic or echo the action or sounds of action which the poem describes.

Not all English poetry uses meter in the traditional senses I have described. Much modern poetry is in **free verse**, which avoids regularized meter and has no significant recurrent stress rhythms, though it may use other repetitive patterns—of words, phrases, structures—as Whitman often does. (**Free verse** should not be confused with **blank verse**, which is unrhymed but is by definition written in iambic pentameter.) So-called **prose poems** (such as Ginsberg's *A Supermarket in California*, p. 576) avoid even the appearance of traditional line divisions and lengths. Many modern poems that may appear unpatterned are, however, very tightly controlled metrically; the absence of rhyme does not mean the absence of metrical pattern, and many un-

traditional-looking modern poems use traditional meter in traditional ways. Many poems, old as well as new, experiment with meter too, trying odd combinations within the definitions I have given or using different principles altogether. The **sprung rhythm** used by Gerard Manley Hopkins avoids the usual distinctions about kinds of feet and only counts the numbers of stressed syllables; each foot begins with a stressed syllable, but any number of unstressed syllables may follow before the next foot begins, so that traditional scansion would make the pattern seem unpatterned. **Quantitative verse,** imitating the metrical principles used by Latin and Greek poets, has been attempted in almost every age, but seldom with success. Unlike stress meters of any kind, quantitative verse determines pattern by the duration of sounds and sets up various meters in combinations of long and short syllables. Some modern experimenters have fused quantitative and stress patterns, and still others have tried patterns based on the number of sounds (see the discussion of syllabic verse in §8), on the kind of sounds used rather than either duration or stress, or on attempts at precise distinctions in the *amount* of stress in stressed syllables.

Until recently **rhyme** has been nearly as important as meter to most poetry, and there are still some poets and critics who regard rhyme as a requirement for poetry. Robert Frost, paraphrasing a 17th-century French poet, used to say that writing a poem without rhyme was like playing tennis without a net. Proponents of rhyme usually argue along similar lines, emphasizing craft and discipline; opponents insist that rhyme requirements wrench and distort natural, effective expression.

Rhyme is based on the duplication of the vowel sound and all sounds after the vowel in the relevant words. Most rhyme is **end-rhyme** (that is, the near-duplication of sound takes place at the ends of the lines), but other patterns are possible. **Internal rhyme** involves rhyming sounds within the same line; in **beginning rhyme,** the first word or syllable rhymes in two or more lines. Not-quite rhyme is often used to vary strict rhyme schemes; the most common form is **slant rhyme** (or **half rhyme**) in which the relevant words have similar but not exactly rhyming sounds because either the vowel or consonant varies slightly (as in backs/box, bent/want, or web/step). **Visual** (or **eye**) **rhyme** uses words with identical endings but different pronunciations (bead/ tread), and **rime riche** uses words that sound exactly the same but have different spellings and meanings (knight/night; lead/led; him/ hymn). The variations of rhyme possibility are many, and it is surprising how many of the possibilities have actually been given names—on the basis of whether the vowel or consonant varies, which vowel or consonant sounds are used, how many syllables are rhymed, and whether a word is partly carried over into another line so that rhyme will work. Most of the more extreme variations are used for comic effect, though almost all have been used seriously at one time or another. In poetry of earlier ages, one needs to watch, too, for **historical rhyme**—rhyme that was perfect when the poem was written but, because of historical changes in pronunciation, is no longer so; tea/day and join/divine were once good rhymes in the easiest and simplest sense.

Sound effects not involving rhyme continue to be important to poetry, and many of them are (like rhyme and meter) based on the ordering principle of **repetition**. **Alliteration** is the repetition of sounds in nearby words; usually alliteration involves the initial consonant sounds of words (and sometimes internal consonants in stressed syllables). Such insistence of a single sound may reinforce meaning or imitate a sound relevant to what the words are describing; sometimes, too, alliteration is used to link certain words within a line or in close-by lines, implying connections not strictly logical. Satirists, for example, often invent damaging alliterative patterns for their objects of attack. **Assonance** is a repetition of vowel sounds in a line or series of lines; assonance often affects pace (by unbalancing short and long vowel patterns) and the way words included in the pattern tend to seem underscored. **Consonance** involves a repeated sequence of consonants but with varied vowels (as in stop/step, rope/reap, or hip/hop).

Onomatopoeia is the attempt to imitate or echo sounds being described. Some words are in themselves **onomatopoeic** (buzz, fizz, murmur), and others suggest action or qualities related to their literal meaning (slippery, lull). Passages may use rhythms and vocal sounds for onomatopoeic purposes, as in Shakespeare's *Like as the Waves* (p. 610) or Hart Crane's "The Nasal Whine of Power" (p. 611). Sometimes the term onomatopoeia is used rather loosely to describe any sound effects correlated to the meaning of the poem; the famous "Sound and Sense" passage by Pope exemplifies many of the possibilities of sound to produce imitative, harmonious, or cacophonous effects.

8. STANZA AND VERSE FORMS

Most poems of more than a few lines are divided into **stanzas**, groups of lines with a specific cogency of their own and usually set off from one another by a space. Traditionally, stanzas are linked by a common **rhyme scheme** (pattern of rhyme words) or by a common pattern of rhythms; modern poems which are divided into stanzas often, however, lack such patterns. Stanza lengths vary considerably, and so do the patterns and complexity of rhyme. Poets often invent distinctive patterns of their own—sometimes for novelty, sometimes to generate a particular effect—but over the years some stanza patterns have proved quite durable.

The **ballad stanza** is one of the oldest; it consists of four lines, the second and fourth of which are iambic trimeter and rhyme with each other. The first and third lines, in iambic tetrameter, do not rhyme. Letters of the alphabet are usually used to indicate the rhyme scheme, as in this stanza from *Sir Patrick Spens*:

> The king sits in Dumferling toune,   a
> Drinking the blude-reid wine: b
> "O where will I get guid sailor   c
> To sail this ship of mine?"   b

The ballad stanza moves quickly, and combines some rhyme with relative structural freedom; it is easy to memorize (an important quality in folk poetry, which was transmitted orally), for both the simplicity and

the rhyme are **mnemonic** (memory) devices. Rhyme, repetition, and other memorable sound combinations are almost always features of primitive poetry.

The **elegiac stanza** consists of four lines of iambic pentameter, rhymed abab; it takes its name from the use of it in Gray's once famous and influential *Elegy Written in a Country Churchyard.* **Terza rima** is the three-line stanza in which Dante wrote *The Divine Comedy;* each iambic pentameter stanza (aba) interlocks with the next (bcb, cdc, ded, etc.), and English poets (even those translating Dante) have generally found its rhyme needs too demanding for English, which is usually regarded as a "rhyme-poor" language because of its wholesale adoption of words from many languages rather than home growth of parallel endings. Still, some important poems, such as Shelley's *Ode to the West Wind* (p. 569), have used terza rima. Among longer stanza forms are **rime royal,** seven iambic pentameter lines which rhyme ababbcc, used by Chaucer and Shakespeare and revived in the 19th century; **ottava rima,** an Italian form adapted to English as eight lines of iambic pentameter rhyming abababcc and used especially by Byron (in *Don Juan,* for example); and the **Spenserian stanza,** the nine-line form Spenser invented for his *Faerie Queene* (eight lines of iambic pentameter and a ninth line of iambic hexameter, called an **alexandrine,** rhymed ababbcbcc). There are, of course, many varieties possible in the rhythms, lengths of lines, and rhymes in stanzas of all lengths, and many popular combinations have remained nameless. Stanzas with no official names are simply designated by the number of lines; a three-line stanza is called a **tristich, triplet,** or **tercet** (the latter is also a term for part of the sonnet—see the discussion below); a four-line stanza is a **quatrain;** a five-line stanza is a **quintain** or **quintet;** a six-line stanza is a **sextain** or **sixain.**

The modern rebellion against rhyme and traditional meters has brought many experiments with new ways of generating and justifying breaks within poems. Many modern poems are divided according to breaks in syntax, meaning, or tone, and the individual characteristics of a particular poem may dictate such breaks; some spatial breaks produce a special effect; some breaks represent merely capriciousness or convenience. Some experiments have also produced patterns as demanding in their own way as rhyme-based stanzas. **Syllabic verse,** for example, requires that the number of syllables in each line of the first stanza be duplicated in each subsequent stanza; stanzas (and lines within them) may thus be of any length, but the poet commits himself to a pattern in the first stanza and thereafter sticks to it. Many early- to mid-20th-century poets worked seriously in the form; see, for example, Marianne Moore's *The Hero* (p. 575). In a **rhopalic stanza,** which may theoretically be of any length, each line has one more (or one less) foot than the preceding line, and in a **rhopalic poem** each stanza has one more (or less) line than the preceding one.

The **couplet** is a rather special case among stanza forms. It consists of two lines (of any specifiable length or rhythm) which rhyme with one another, and seldom is one couplet divided by space from another one. Larger divisions within couplet verse are usually indicated (as in blank verse) by indentation, and the units are called **verse paragraphs,**

which may or may not be separated by space. The **heroic couplet,** rhyming lines of iambic pentameter, has been the most popular and durable of couplet forms; it dominated English poetry during much of the 17th and 18th centuries and has been used successfully by many earlier and later poets. When the syntax of one couplet carries over into the next couplet, the couplets are said to be **open** or **enjambed; enjambment** is the continuation of syntax beyond the borders of a single couplet. **Closed** (or **end-stopped**) **couplets** are—as far as the technicalities of syntax are concerned—complete in themselves. Couplets written in iambic tetrameter tend to be used for comic effect because of the emphatic regularity of the rhythms and the abrupt underscoring of the rhyme. Not to be confused with the couplet is the **distich,** a two-line unit of verse in which both lines are structurally similar but do not rhyme. The **ghazal,** an Eastern stanza form, contains at least five couplets unified imagistically or associationally.

In some stanza forms (most notably the **sonnet** and **ode**) the overlapping with poetic kind (§6) is obvious. A sonnet is a poetic kind in the sense that it usually deals with certain subjects, bears a tradition of attitudes and tones, and has many conventions; but it also (unlike most poetic kinds) makes specific rhythmic and rhyme demands. A **sonnet** is a 14-line poem in iambic pentameter; its divisions and rhyme scheme depend upon whether it is an **Italian sonnet** or an **English sonnet.** An Italian sonnet has a two-part division; the first eight lines, or **octave** (sometimes divided into two four-line sections or **quatrains**) forms one unit of meaning. The octave's statement or question is qualified, balanced, or answered in the second, six-line part, or **sestet** (sometimes divided into two three-line sections called **tercets**). The Italian sonnet (it is also sometimes called a **Petrarchan sonnet**) is especially suited to dramatic contrasts; its rhyme scheme is usually abbaabba cdecde, but that of the sestet sometimes varies widely. The English sonnet (sometimes called the **Shakespearean sonnet** after its most famous practitioner but not because he invented it) is divided into three four-line sections (quatrains) and a final couplet; its rhyme scheme is abab cdcd efef gg. Usually the English sonnet contains a progression by steps in an argument or situation, and the couplet summarizes (or sometimes reverses) what has developed or what has been proved. Both Italian and English sonnets traditionally deal with love and private emotions, but their compact, tight form and the resulting intensity have sometimes made them attractive to satirists and political poets. As a form (and kind), the sonnet is very demanding, but many poets have found its rigidities useful for discipline, for organizing and controlling intense feelings, and for discussing themes of limitation and confinement (as in Wordsworth's *Nuns Fret Not,* p. 585).

The **ode** is an ancient and dignified kind; it treats an exalted theme in an elevated style and usually praises something or somebody. Its stanzaic demands result from the traditional following of two ancient models, Pindar and Horace. The **Pindaric ode** consists of an indefinite number of three-stanza units. Each unit contains a **strophe** (or **turn**), an **antistrophe** (**counterturn**), and **epode** (**stand**); the strophe and

antistrophe are equal in length, for the Pindaric ode was originally an attempt to imitate the chorus in Greek drama (the strophe was to be chanted as the chorus moved to the left, the antistrophe as they returned, and the epode as they stood still). The **Horatian ode** consists of a series of **homostrophic** (regular) stanzas. The **irregular ode,** introduced in the 17th century, is closer to Pindar, but its often complex stanzas have no rigid pattern; the form resulted from a lack of understanding of Pindar's principles.

Several **fixed poetic forms** (which contain a certain number of stanzas organized in a determined way) have been popular, from time to time, with English poets. Most of them were introduced by French troubadours in Provence, some of them as early as the 12th century. The **villanelle** contains five three-line stanzas and a final four-line stanza; only two rhymes are permitted, and the first and third lines of the first stanza are repeated, alternately, as the third line of subsequent stanzas throughout the poem until the last stanza. In the last stanza the repeating lines become the final two lines of the poem, as in Empson's *Missing Dates* (p. 577). The **sestina** is even more complex; it contains six six-line stanzas and a final three-line stanza, all unrhymed; but the final word in each line of the first stanza then becomes the final word in other stanzas (but in a different specified pattern); the final stanza uses these words again in a specified way, one in each half line. Justice's *Here in Katmandu* (p. 515) is a modern example which exemplifies the pattern (and difficulty) of the form and uses several innovative puns. Some poets have even written **double** and **triple sestinas,** in which the demands increase geometrically. The **rondel** contains two four-line stanzas and a final five-line stanza and has only two rhymes. Like the villanelle it also repeats whole lines in a specified way, as indicated here by capital letters: ABba abAB abbaA; sometimes a 14th line is added, repeating the second (B) line. Repetition (probably originally for mnemonic purposes) is a major feature in each of these forms and in other fixed forms: the **rondeau,** the **virelay,** the **pantoum,** the **triolet,** the **chant royal,** and the **ballade** (not to be confused with the ballad). Many fixed poetic froms conclude with an **envoi,** or postscript stanza, which may summarize the poem, imply a wider significance, dedicate the poem to someone, or send it into the world with a specific commission or set of directions. An envoi, or **commission,** may also be appended to any poem or book of poems, sometimes assuming a length and form quite different from what precedes it. An **epigraph** (or **motto**) is a brief quotation which prefaces a poem, often to set up its subject or tone.

Several single-stanza forms also exist. They include the **limerick,** five lines in anapestic rhythms (the first, second, and fifth lines in trimeter, the third and fourth in dimeter), rhymed aabba, always comic, often obscene, and usually purporting to present the exploits of a fictional person; the **haiku,** a three-line poem with five syllables each in the first and third lines and seven syllables in the middle line, used primarily to describe a momentary sensation or impression which

seems to characterize a specific season of the year; and several other highly technical forms (including the tanka and double dactyl) not exemplified in this anthology.

9. TRADITION AND CONVENTION

Tradition is seldom listed or defined in glossaries of literary terms, perhaps because it is so pervasive, persistent, complex, and controversial. In its most inclusive sense, **tradition** is the influence—deliberate or not—of any previous event, technique, or consciousness upon subsequent ways of thought and action. Poetic tradition may involve an influence in ideas, or style, or both. Poets may deliberately seek to follow, refine, or respond to previous thinkers and poets, or they may find themselves conditioned by the past in ways over which they have no control. An awareness of continuity (from one time to another or from one poet to another) is essential to tradition, but the continuity need not be obvious to the persons and times involved; sometimes the awareness of continuity is only available to observers after the fact, when the tradition is no longer operable. But often poets write with a **sense of tradition**; that is, they deliberately attempt to confront the past and turn it to their own purposes. Such a sense may involve the accumulated characteristics of a whole culture or, more narrowly, the expectations of a poetic kind, a verse form, or any particular literary device.

Poetry, perhaps more than drama or fiction, is subject to the characteristic habits and limitations of a particular language, and it is common practice to speak of **the English tradition** (or **the English poetic tradition,** or simply **the tradition**), meaning all of the recurrent tendencies over the years, including many which oppose, modify, or contradict other tendencies. The poetry of Pound or cummings, for example, is as surely a part of the tradition as that of Milton or Tennyson, for the tradition is not something which once and for all defines itself but rather consists of a continuity marked by continual modification. Participation in the tradition is not always easy to recognize or predict, for some of the English tradition's brightest lights (Shakespeare, Swift, Shelley, and Eliot are examples) at first seemed to their contemporaries most untraditional—in the sense of the tradition then understood. Tradition continually redefines itself to comprehend rebellious sons and daughters born into its line and intent on the old rituals of father-killing and mansion-burning. Sometimes the tradition is defined as if it were already complete, but it is more useful to consider it a living, changing thing which will, by definition, ultimately render any definition incomplete. Much (perhaps most) of what seems new and innovative does not, of course, last long enough in the public memory or evoke a substantial enough response in its audience to become part of the tradition. Contemporary with Shakespeare, for example, were many poets whose innovations did not "catch on" or whose distinctive appeal did not prove to be permanent; it is so in every age, and the process of developing a tradition is a perpetual matter of experimenting and sorting.

Within a language tradition are **national** and **regional traditions** as well; one may speak, for example, of a Canadian tradition, an Irish tradition, or a New England tradition. Such divisions have partly to do with local variations in linguistic usage, but they also relate to ideological concerns, cultural assumptions, and social, political, and economic movements. The same sort of division may be broadened, reaching beyond language barriers to comprehend the **European tradition** or the **Western tradition**. The latter term is often used nearly synonymously with the English tradition; such usage is not entirely precise, but many of the most characteristic features of English poetry do have origins or counterparts in ancient Greece or Rome or in more recent Continental cultures, especially those of France, Italy, and Germany.

Besides definitions based on linguistic, national, and cultural boundaries, there are other, more narrow senses of tradition in common use. Tradition may describe the history and accumulated characteristics of a literary kind or a stanza form (one might speak of the epic tradition, the sonnet tradition, the couplet tradition, or the tradition of free verse), the recurrent appearances of a motif or theme (the **carpe diem** tradition), the characteristics of a thought or value pattern (the Puritan tradition or the metaphysical tradition), or characteristics associated with a particular time or age (the Elizabethan tradition). Any device that recurs (metaphor, alliteration, a particular rhyme scheme or rhythmic pattern) tends to develop a tradition of usage that affects every new user. All of these senses represent a tendency for a poet to do things in a way related to how they have been done before, and they all represent a series of expectations he can count on in his readers. Readers who have read many sonnets have an idea of what to expect in a new one; they will know the conventions (see below), the ranges of possibility, the presumed limits. A new sonneteer may not stay within the presumed limits and may actually extend the range of possibility, but having the tradition to begin from offers a firm sense of where the frontiers are and provides an initial common ground with the reader.

Tradition may, of course, be an enemy as well as a friend, and many poets feel hostile toward the limitations which they believe tradition places upon them, and others feel intimidated by past accomplishments which seem to crowd present possibilities. Some of the uses and liabilities of tradition are not necessarily deliberate or conscious; there is an important sense in which poets are stuck with their traditions just as they are stuck with their genes, their bodies, and, after a while, with their personal habits and mannerisms. Few poets learn a new language well enough to make it their own for poetry, and perhaps even fewer fully become part of a new culture, with other institutions, histories, and expectations—though they may use information from another culture and try to translate values from it. The most deliberate uses of traditions—whether to praise, denounce, or modify them—may be said to involve awareness of one's own hereditary plight within them. Recent attempts by black poets to recover a part of their past

in Africa—even though removed from it by generations, centuries, and attempts to suppress mere memory of it—suggest the deep attraction to felt lineage. And the recurrent attempts by many Westerners to engraft new life from the East finally comes down to a sense of strengths and weaknesses, real or imaginary, in one's own traditions.

A **convention** is any characteristic which over a period of time has come to be expected in poetry or in a poem of a certain sort. There are conventions of subject matter and conventional ways of using the standard poetic devices, but conventions are especially associated with the older poetic kinds. In pastoral, for example, it is a convention that shepherds sing and are happy and cheerful; this does not mean that the poet thinks that all shepherds are musical and jolly—or that *any* are, or that the poet knows anything about real shepherds—but simply that the poet, wishing to accomplish something in pastoral poetry or through it, has followed the conventions of his chosen poetic kind. Following the standard conventions is usually less significant than not following them; when a poem ignores or contradicts a convention, a reader can be pretty sure that the convention is missing or altered for a specific reason. Conventions at their best are shortcuts in communication; they tell a reader what to look for and establish a beginning rapport between poet and reader; what happens as the expectations are satisfied or surprised is then up to the poet.

The function of conventions is, of course, lost on the reader who does not know the conventions, and sometimes, too, conventions diminish their own effects by overuse or by continued mechanical use after their function has disappeared. Most conventions originated in the doctrine of **decorum**, which insists on appropriateness in all things: every poetic kind, for example, was assumed to require a certain level of language and persons and incidents of a specific level of dignity. Conventions almost always begin in a need to accomplish a specific thing in a specific way; pastorals contain happy shepherds because writers of pastoral were consciously creating a never-never land as a contrast to the worlds they themselves lived in, and they meant to project imaginatively what it would be like to live in a world without time pressures, death, disharmony, failures, and disappointments—a world which lacked the stench, pollution, and crowding of the city and in which no one felt winter cold or lacked the ability to carry a tune. New poetic kinds have conventions too, but they are more difficult to see because they seem, in the beginning, to be "natural" characteristics. Confessional poems, for example, are written in the first person, express a sense of personal disorientation, and describe a perception which links individual experience with a larger social or cosmic disorder. But many of the classic confessional poems imaginatively participate in such situations and strategies rather than deriving from a specific real experience; they assume the posture of the first person and use the conventions of the kind. As a kind takes shape, becomes known, and gets defined, it channels (for better or worse) subject matter and strategies into conventional molds, some useful, some not. Most conventions begin in necessity, flourish when

they are recognizable to a large number of readers, and linger on simply as decoration, a memory of past needs. When specific conventions totally lose their use and force, they become merely ornamental, and sometimes seem amusing or absurd. This is why mechanical repetition of what is expected is often said to be "conventional" (or "merely conventional") in a negative sense. Sensible use of conventions involves taking advantage of the technical solutions and shortcuts they provide, but it involves too the personalized touch of an individual poet. No great poet leaves a convention exactly as he found it.

A list of even the major conventions would exhaust the reader before it exhausted the possibilities. Here instead are brief definitions of some of the major conventions of one poetic kind, the epic; the passage from Milton's *Paradise Lost* uses and illustrates most of them. The **invocation of the muse,** at the beginning of an epic poem, asks for supernatural help for the poet, usually from one of the nine muses which classical poets celebrated as the source of poetic inspiration; Calliope, the muse of heroic poetry, is usually the muse invoked in epics. The action of an epic traditionally begins **in medias res—** that is, in the middle of things; rather than beginning with a careful exposition of the situation, epics move quickly to action and conflict and save background explanations for later. **Epic similes** are lengthy and detailed comparisons of a person, place, or thing to something else; in epic they are frequent and likely to occur even at the height of the action. **Epic epithets** are descriptive phrases repeatedly used to recall the traits of a particular character; **epic catalogues** give long lists of things often peripheral to the action, providing a sense of detail, completeness, and range of involvement. The **epic hero** is usually many times life-size and seems superhuman in his power and strength of character; his majesty and grandeur match the huge scope or **magnitude** of the action (which usually involves the history and destiny of a whole people) and the **grand style** considered appropriate to the recounting of great actions. It is also conventional in epic to have supernatural interventions, gigantic battles, and a clearly defined **theme** which involves universal human issues.

In the hands of a shrewd craftsman, tradition and convention may be innovative and exciting; in the hands of a mindless ape of the past, they are nearly always dull and deadly. There are, of course, poets and critics who take a far more uncompromising view. Some say that any attempt to engage or use tradition in any way dooms originality and creativity, others that any departures from the tried ways of the past deprive poetry of shared values and leave a poet undernourished, incomplete, and alone. The two writers whose poems are grouped at the end of this book—Keats and Rich—by no means represent these extremes, but they do provide a strong contrast in their attitudes toward the uses of tradition.

10. WIDER CONTEXTS

No poem is altogether self-existent. In a sense, every poem creates a world all its own, but every poem also reflects aspects of a larger

world from which it derives. Often it is important—and sometimes it is crucial—for a reader to recognize **context**, the circumstances that surrounded the making of the poem. The most obvious and compelling contexts are in poems that refer explicitly to some historical event or situation; poems such as Milton's *On the New Forcers of Conscience under the Long Parliament* (p. 643) or Joni Mitchell's *Woodstock* (p. 456) require knowledge of the central event they describe and of the whole cultural ambience surrounding and influencing that event. A poem written about a specific event or occasion is called an **occasional poem**; the occasion may be a well known public one (as in Yeats' *Easter 1916* (p. 558) or a private one as in Swift's *On Stella's Birthday, 1719* (p. 527) or Rich's *Planetarium* (p. 683). In poems which celebrate, attack, or reflect upon an event likely to seem obscure to most readers, editors often provide footnotes as a guide to the context, but footnotes are at best a pathetic attempt to mention facts about the context, and they can only begin to suggest the complex of emotions and attitudes from which a poem may begin. In Shelley's *England in 1819* (p. 477), for example, the political facts, though important, are only a small part of the total context; also important, but less easily specified, are the surrounding climate of political and cultural opinion, the tide of antimonarchic feeling, the frustration of reformers, the winds of change on the continent, the weight of English tradition, and Romantic ideas about poetry and its relation to public and political issues. All of these matters make up the referential context of the poem; they specify and explain the events and situations to which the poem refers. Such matters are easier to recover for newer poems, but the poems themselves may be just as demanding contextually. Ginsberg's *Howl* (p. 646), for example, requires a sense of the 1950s as much as specific facts about people, places, and terminology; Snodgrass's *Campus on the Hill* (p. 484) and Knight's *For Malcolm* (p. 431) make similar demands. Often, of course, a reader may be able to share the poem's intensity of feeling without substantial factual knowledge (as in Milton's *On the Late Massacre in Piedmont*, p. 582), and contextual knowledge may explain details and extend the range of effects.

Even when they do not refer to a specific event or situation, poems are very much influenced by the times and circumstances in which they were written. All poems, even those that may seem "timeless" or "universal", have a **historical present**—that is, they depend upon the ideological and esthetic resources available to the poet in his or her society. Linguistic patterns and tendencies, philosophical and social assumptions, and ideas about practically everything change from age to age, and how poets write—as well as what they write about—is to an extent dependent on the when and where of their lives. All matters of time and circumstance that might affect either the conception or execution are part of the poem's **historical** or **cultural context**. It is not always easy to determine exactly which factors are relevant to a poem and which are not; deciding just what information is necessary

and how to use it once acquired is one of the most delicate tasks in good interpretation. The needs of historical context vary from minute details to broad generalizations about a nation or an era; to read Snyder's *Not Leaving the House* (p. 455) accurately one needs to know a great deal about American social patterns and the youth culture of the late 1960s and early 1970s, but for Shakespeare's *All the World's a Stage* (p. 631) and Stevens' *Anecdote of the Jar* (p. 639) one needs the larger cultural assumptions about order in the Renaissance and the 20th century.

Literary historians often designate **periods** in which cultural and esthetic assumptions are more or less shared, speaking for example of the Elizabethan period (literally, 1558–1603, the reign of Queen Elizabeth in England) or the Romantic period (approximately 1790–1830) to describe certain common tendencies in a given historical era. The terminal dates in such periods are not meant to be taken too literally, and poets who outlive a period or whose lives span two or more periods continually offer problems in placement that may affect the interpretation of individual poems. Sensibly applied, period designations may provide convenient shortcuts for contextual description, but they always run the risk of oversimplifying and stereotyping, and like any generalizations they have limited applications.

Another kind of context involves individual traits of the authors themselves. Reading a group of poems by an author usually clarifies every individual poem, for the reader can develop a sense of the poet's distinctive style, strategies, and ideas. The total work of an author is called a **canon;** one may speak of the Milton canon or the Eliot canon. But even a sampling of a poet's work often leads a reader to expect certain procedures and attitudes, enabling a more exact and intense response. In its broadest sense, the **authorial context** may include biographical detail, psychological analysis, and specific facts about the conditions under which a poem was created, as well as dominant characteristics or tendencies in poems by a certain author. Like other contexts, the authorial context needs to be applied to interpretation with care and good sense; a poet is not necessarily always concerned with immortality or revolutionary politics just because several poems show that concern. And poets do change their techniques as well as their ideas. Still, intensive reading of an author often isolates characteristics not visible (or not so easily visible) in an individual poem, and the use of such authorial contexts may clarify or intensify an experience of an individual poem.

Closely related to the authorial context is the problem of **parts and wholes.** Many short poems are actually parts of larger wholes (songs in a play, for example) or part of a sequence of poems. Very popular in the Elizabethan period were **sonnet sequences,** groups of a hundred or more sonnets which, when read consecutively, told a kind of story which supplemented the effects of individual poems. When a poem is part of some larger work, the **internal context** of the larger work (that is, the situation, action, and tone in the surrounding passages) influences the meaning of the poem. Jonson's *Come, My Celia* (p. 625), for

example, is sung by a villain in the play in which it appears, and most of Sidney's sonnets are from a sonnet sequence in which the speaker is portrayed as ignorant, awkward, bumbling—the very antithesis of the courtier Sir Philip Sidney. Questions of completeness and integrity become very difficult in cases where the poet has conceived the poem doubly, both as a part of a larger unit of meaning and as a whole in itself. Reading passages from a long poem is a similar but not identical problem, for here it is the reader (or editor) who asserts the ability of the passage to stand alone. Some critics adamantly insist that no work should be excerpted or considered in part, but they still have to face the difficult question of how to construe those poems which are wholes and parts at the same time. When a poem is part of something larger— a play, a novel, a long poem, a sequence or cycle of poems, or even a book of poems put together by the author—it is best to consider that larger internal context when interpreting the poem.

What kind of contextual knowledge and how much of it a poem requires varies, of course, from poem to poem; many poems are readily accessible without deliberate pursuit of historical, intellectual, or authorial background, but the range and intensity of experience available through a poem is almost always enhanced by more knowledge. The group of poems on pages 642–652 has been left unannotated so that readers may test for themselves various kinds of contextual problems and textual needs. Some of these poems need footnotes only to supplement fundamental clarity or to explain a small point, but a poem such as Nemerov's *The Second-Best Bed* (p. 650) is not likely to make any sense at all to a reader who does not know that Shakespeare, in his will, bequeathed the "second-best bed" to his wife.

List of Terms Defined

Drama

EDITED BY
CARL E. BAIN

A Preface to Drama

A play is written to be performed on a stage before an audience. That audience is a group of people collected together in the same place and at the same time for the purpose of sharing the experience of the theater. Such collective behavior as the theater and similar activities persists in human societies. At different times and places the particular form may vary from the gatherings of primitive tribes to the rock festivals of our own day. Participation in such collective behavior often involves a certain amount of inconvenience and discomfort, yet communal experience persists. In some cases, indeed, the stated object can be attained more perfectly under private conditions, as is true of a rock festival. People do go to a rock festival to hear the music, but they also go to share the experience with others, to become a part of the group. Man needs to mingle his individual experiences with others in which he functions as a part of a larger body, in church, at the stadium, in the theater, or at a rock festival.

Because there are many diverse forms of collective behavior, no audience or group is a random assembly of individuals; rather the audience is a group of people who are like-minded enough to have made the same choice. The average man, however unarticulated his expectation, goes to the theater, the stadium, or the rock festival because he expects the satisfaction of experiencing the performance and the satisfaction of sharing that experience with others. Only drama critics and other masochists do not expect to like what they see. This likeness of intent may express itself in similarities of dress or age, but whatever the differences the individuals gather at the appointed time and place. Traditionally in the theater the new identity as a member of the group is expressed as a seat number, and as the individuals are seated, the house lights are dimmed. Individuality is for a time surrendered.

Among the members of the audience, behavior is largely controlled by the group. Anyone who has laughed at the wrong time in a theater or cheered for the visiting team among the home fans can testify to his own embarrassment and the disapproval of others that attend acting as an individual. When the sense of participation is strong enough, the members of the group will act in ways none of them would act as an individual. This group-controlled behavior also involves certain elements of ritual, the exact repetition of a series of actions. Individual performances occur at different times and places, involve different participants, and include individual variations at optional points, but the pattern of the ritual elements remains the same. The playing of the national anthem and the seventh-inning "stretch" at a baseball game are ritual actions in one kind of collective activity, just as intermissions

735

and curtain calls are ritual actions in the theater. These activities are not so highly ritualized as the Mass, but collective behavior does involve elements of ritual.

The theatrical performance itself is also a ritual. Although no two performances of a play can be precisely the same, exact repetition is an implied goal, the aim of the series of rehearsals which precede the performance. The nature of the play as dramatic ritual is overtly expressed in several modern plays, such as Thornton Wilder's *The Skin of Our Teeth* and Jean Genet's *The Balcony*. At the end of both plays a character dismisses the audience and says that the players must start the dramatic sequence over and repeat it again and again.

The audience also exercises an influence on the content of a performance. Plays are the most public form of literature, and the playwright writes for the group rather than the individual. As Prince Hamlet put it, the drama shows "the very age and body of the time his form and pressure." The subjects treated by a play must have some relevance to its society. The play intended only to entertain will gain its relevance by endorsing the values of its society. Many popular comedies, for example, reflect the attitudes of the society toward marriage. Plays may also reflect historical events as well as values and attitudes. Most of Shakespeare's great tragedies concern the succession to a throne or position of leadership. At the time they are believed to have been written, Elizabeth I was an aging queen without prospect of issue. For two centuries England had been subjected to war and destruction brought on by crises of succession. Stories about succession might well fascinate Shakespeare as well as his audiences. Such contemporary problems are only a part of the relation to society that a classic play has. *The Wild Duck*, for example, deals with a particular reformer, but it speaks also to the dangers inescapable in any attempt to change people and their situations.

Another way in which the audience affects the content of the play is that in the theater certain representations are taboo. The exact area of taboo will vary at different periods. The Greeks, for example, eschewed violence on stage. In *The Bacchae* the death of Pentheus must take place offstage and be reported by a messenger. In Shakespeare's time, however, the audience loved violence on stage as can be seen in the final scene of *Hamlet*. In our time the use of racial stereotypes is offensive to audiences. In modern productions of Shakespeare's *The Merchant of Venice* we see therefore a different Shylock from the one that Shakespeare's contemporaries saw. Today another area of taboo, nudity and sexual activity, is losing its forbidden character.

In addition to the contemporary appeal, a play may affect an audience by the use of timeless myth. A myth is a narrative which has a group significance. The first appeal of myth was religious, but the basic narrative sequence of a myth retains an appeal even when the religious significance is lost. The story of Venus and Adonis, a form of the myth of the death and rebirth of the young god, retains an appeal even when we no longer believe that the seasons are caused by

that death and rebirth. Certain kinds of drama have strong mythical affinities. Melodrama has a basic narrative pattern in which good and evil are struggling, evil seems about to triumph, and good finally wins out. The popularity of melodrama attests to the appeal of the myth.

The first three plays in this collection illustrate a different way in which the drama uses myth. The scapegoat was originally a victim sacrificed for the redemption of the tribe by being driven into the wilderness. In *The Bacchae* Pentheus is a scapegoat who still has religious significance. He goes out into the wilderness, here Mount Cithaeron, and by his death purges the guilt of Thebes for its failure to recognize the new god Dionysus. In *Hamlet* the myth is used politically. Claudius sends Hamlet to England to die in order to restore the health of his kingdom. Hamlet acquiesces in Claudius' plan to the extent that he leaves without struggle, although he suspects Claudius' intentions, and then he provides substitute victims in Rosencrantz and Guildenstern. In a more personal way, Gregers Werle has gone to the wilderness of Højdal because of his father's guilt, and he encourages Hedvig to sacrifice the duck in his wilderness in the attic to atone for the guilts in her family. She chooses rather to be the scapegoat herself and dies in the attic. The treatment of the scapegoat is vastly different in each of these plays, but the basic mythical pattern is there to lend its appeal.

The theater has emerged twice in Western culture, each time from relatively sophisticated societies and each time in connection with religious rituals in those societies. In Athens the festivals of Dionysus gave birth to the classical drama, and in the later Middle Ages the services of the Christian church produced its own form of drama. These two religious systems share a number of characteristics; an important one is their emphasis on rebirth and on ritual which signifies that the worshipper has become a new creature by virtue of his religious experience.

The literary counterpart of rebirth is peripety (or peripeteia), a sudden reversal of the character of a situation as a result of a particular event. The first play of modern times, the *Quem Quaeritis Trope*, provides an example of peripety, or dramatic event. This play was a dramatization by the participating priests of a part of the liturgy. It occurs in several forms, including the minimal one given here. The scene is the tomb of Jesus on Easter morning as the women approach and find the angel there.

ANGEL   Whom do you seek in this sepulchre, Christians?
WOMEN   Jesus of Nazareth, who was crucified, heavenly one.
ANGEL   He is not here; he is risen as he foretold. Go, announce that he is risen from the grave.

The single dramatic event, the angel's announcement that "he is risen," reverses the emotional tone of the situation and the direction of the action.

Conflict is basic to drama, of course, but a conflict without peripety or the possibility of peripety is not truly dramatic. A struggle whose outcome is never in doubt may have other kinds of interest, but it makes a dull play or a dull football game in dramatic terms. If, however, the opposing forces are matched so that neither can control the situation for any considerable period, or the weaker force can mount a credible threat to the stronger, or the apparently weaker can overcome the stronger, then there is drama. In *Hamlet,* for example, the power of the conflict between Hamlet and Claudius depends on their being evenly matched. Claudius has the throne and the Queen, but Hamlet has his relation to the last king and his popularity among the people. Early in the play Claudius has the upper hand, but he realizes that he has underestimated Hamlet and he overreacts. Until he stops the play-within-a-play, the King seems firmly in command, the expected outcome of the action seems to favor him. From that point on Hamlet more and more takes command and ultimately restores the kingdom to the order which Claudius' kingship had disturbed.

The King's outburst is an example of a specific kind of peripety called a climax, the dramatic event about which the typical structure of a play is built. Like the myth of the scapegoat, this typical dramatic structure is realized in many ways in actual practice and with varying degrees of completeness. The structure is useful in interpreting and understanding only if it is used with flexibility and intelligence. This typical dramatic structure consists of five parts: (1) the exposition, the presentation and definition of the established situation from which the play takes rise; (2) the rising action, in which new factors complicate the original situation; (3) the climax or turning point, which reverses the emotional tone and direction of the action; (4) the falling action, in which the various complications begin to find their resolution; and (5) the conclusion, which establishes a new stable situation to end the play. Ibsen's treatment of the exposition in *The Wild Duck* can show us how flexible the parts of the typical structure can be. The play opens with a short scene of pure exposition between Pettersen and the hired waiters, but much of the expository material, including the state of Werle's health and Hedvig's and the circumstances of Hjalmar's marriage to Gina, is presented later in the play.

In addition to the climax or central peripety, a play may include many other instances of sudden, dramatic reverses. The scene at Ophelia's grave can illustrate. When Hamlet enters, he is confident and happy, joking with the First Clown about mortality. Then he learns that the skull he is holding and joking about is the skull of Yorick, and he passes into a mood of nostalgia and reflection. When his reflections reach the use of cosmetics, he falls into a jesting, cynical mood, which is interrupted by the appearance of the cortege. His emotion changes first to curiosity about the identity of the dead lady, then to sorrow when he learns that it is Ophelia. When Laertes jumps into the open grave, Hamlet reacts with violent, impulsive action and rhetoric. Much of the power and tension of the scene comes from this series of reverses of emotional tone.

Peripety renders conflict dramatic, serves as the basis of the typical dramatic structure, and gives power to individual scenes of the play. It is a basic element of drama.

A play is performed on a stage, as mentioned above, and the character of that stage and the conventions which govern it vary from age to age. In French 17th-century theater the audience was seated on three sides of the playing area, whereas Ibsen worked within a proscenium, with the audience seated on only one side of the action from which they were separated by an invisible fourth wall. This difference has its effect on the convention of place in the two theaters. For example, in Molière's *The Misanthrope* the action takes place in and around the house of Célimène and Éliante, but no action depends on a particular location. The whole play can be presented in a single, rather generalized setting. By contrast the action of *The Wild Duck* is closely related to specific places. The first act takes place in a room of the elder Werle's house, which has three entrances, one to the office, one to the dining room, and one to the drawing room and the outside. All of these doors are necessary if the crucial scene in which Hjalmar ignores his father is to work. Doors in Ibsen lead to specific places. If there is not an actual door, then the different entrances must be somehow distinguished. The first act of *The Misanthrope* requires only one door, although more may be used, since nothing in the action depends on the number or positioning of doors.

Both these plays share the convention that the nature of the place represented may be changed by some conventional means, most obviously the lowering and raising of a front curtain. Between acts, if there is a change of place, the objects on stage may be removed and replaced by others more suitable to the new milieu. In cases where there is no curtain, this can be done in full view of spectators who have chosen to remain in their seats during the intermission. They do not "see" the change because the convention requires that they are not "present." Alternatively, the lights may be dimmed during the change, or the change might be accomplished, as in the Chinese theater, by men dressed in black (and therefore invisible).

Greek tragedies were performed in broad daylight without a curtain or other conventional means of changing the place. In consequence almost all the extant Greek tragedies occur in a single place. The action took place in an open semicircular area with a stage building, the *skene*, at the back. In *The Bacchae* the *skene* represented the palace of Pentheus, and the acting area represented a square or public area before the palace which included the tomb of Semele. Shakespeare's plays were also performed in broad daylight, but the acting area was more complex, including a recessed area at the back of the stage and a raised area above. Such areas were easily adapted to serve as the Queen's chamber in *Hamlet*, a cave in *The Tempest*, or a balcony in *Romeo and Juliet*. Because his stage was so flexible, in Shakespeare's plays place becomes a function of character. When the stage is emptied, the characters, in a sense, take the "place" with them, and a

new place is established by the appearance of a new character or group of characters.

Convention governs equally the treatment of time on stage. Only rarely can playing time and elapsed time of the action coincide. The choral odes in *The Bacchae* provide an example of one such convention. Each of them represents a span of time between the two scenes it separates, or joins, since it does both. There is no correlation between the length of the ode and the elapsed time it represents; the elapsed time is determined by the necessities of the action. The earlier odes represent relatively short periods of time, whereas the ode spoken between the departure of Pentheus and Dionysus and the reappearance of the messenger with the report of Pentheus' death represents several hours at the least. Although there is no such formal device, the time difference between scenes in *Hamlet* varies even more greatly. Only a few moments elapse between Hamlet's departure to see his mother at the end of Act 3, Scene 2, and the scene of the King's prayer which follows. By contrast, several weeks must elapse between Scenes 4 and 5 of Act 4 to allow time for the news of Polonius' death to reach Paris and for Laertes' subsequent return to Elsinore. *The Wild Duck*, in comparison with *Hamlet*, has a restricted time span and a careful definition of the temporal relation of the acts.

Another area of convention involves the actors. Although early Greek plays were written for a single actor plus a chorus, plays like *The Bacchae* (a relatively late tragedy of the surviving ones) were written for three actors plus a chorus. Individual actors (all men) would of necessity play several roles during the course of such a play, and the actor had to be able, first, to play all kinds of roles without regard to physical suitability and, second, to move quickly from one role to another. On the assumption that a given role was played by a single actor whenever possible, we can see how Euripides used the convention to reinforce the esthetic design in *The Bacchae*. One actor would play Pentheus and Agauë, thus calling attention to the relation between mother and son. A second actor would play the god Dionysus and the seer Teiresias, the two figures who represent the holy in the play. The other parts can be played by the third actor without difficulty.

The conditions of Euripides' theater probably precluded any prior knowledge by the author of the particular actors who would perform his play. Shakespeare, on the other hand, worked with a company of players whose abilities and weaknesses he knew. The role of Polonius suggests that Shakespeare was writing for an actor who was particularly good at portraying sententious old men. The scene with Reynaldo, for example, serves no necessary dramatic function and merely reinforces the characterization established in the earlier scene between Polonius and Laertes. Shakespeare seems to have written the scene to take advantage of the particular abilities of the actor who was to portray Polonius. His acting company was restricted because the female roles were assumed by pre-pubescent boys. Only occasionally, as with Lady Macbeth and Cleopatra, did Shakespeare write complex female parts for his boy actors.

By the time of Ibsen, theater had become international. Plays were no longer written for performance at a specific time by a specific group of actors. A play which had a success in London would be performed in Paris, Vienna, or New York. To accommodate this trend, acting companies were composed of specialists in certain "lines," such as leading man, leading lady, juveniles (ingénues) of both sexes, heavies, and character actors. The role of Hedvig is written for an ingénue rather than for a particular actress. In this, as in time and place, the stage convention of the period will exercise an influence on the writing of the play.

Every play has two manifestations: it is a literary work, an order of words on a page to be read, and it is a performance, an order of speeches and visual effects (or gestures) presented on a stage. As a literary work the play is subject to the same canons of literary criticism as other forms, including the canon of internal complexity (or organic unity) which has dominated recent criticism. Many of the same kinds of internal complexity which are found in poems, novels, and short stories can be found in plays.

One kind of internal complexity involving plot structure can be seen in the parallel structures of *The Bacchae*. A series of events in the rising action occurs in the same order as a like series of events in the falling action. When Teiresias and Cadmus appear dressed in Bacchic costumes, they are upbraided for doing so by Pentheus, but later on Pentheus himself, after he has given in to Dionysus, appears dressed as a female worshipper of Bacchus. Shortly after his encounter with Teiresias and Cadmus, Pentheus has a scene with Dionysus in which he cuts Dionysus' hair, takes away his thyrsus, and imprisons him. This sequence gives ironic power to the scene in which Dionysus straightens Pentheus' wig, teaches him to carry his thyrsus properly, and leads him away to his death on the mountain, a more than figurative prisoner. A final set of parallels is provided by the accounts of the mountainside activities of Agaüe and her fellow devotees. Each of the messengers describes them first in repose and then in Bacchic frenzy, the first telling how they killed cattle barehanded and the second describing the slaughter of Pentheus.

Another type of complex plotting can be seen in Pirandello's *Six Characters in Search of an Author*. Here two quite different stories are presented in a highly sophisticated blend. The apparent plot of the play, the "outer" story, concerns a group of actors, their director or manager, and others who are needed to present a play. They are interrupted in their rehearsal by a group of six "characters"; these characters are not "real" people, but the persons of a play imagined by an author but not committed to words on a page. The characters try to persuade the manager and the actors to give their story the life its creator refused it, but the attempt is a complete fiasco. The story that the characters tell is the "inner" plot of the play, and by contrast to the outer plot it is a lurid, melodramatic tale of infidelity, suicide, prostitution, and other things. This story is told in fragments and out

of chronological order. Parts of it are pieced together from the scenes between the characters on stage, from other scenes they re-enact, and from narration. The method of presentation means that the "inner" story can be used to illustrate ideas rather than merely to titillate the audience.

Another common device in literature to give complexity is allusion, a reference to something which recalls some other work or idea. This can work in the drama, as the use of the number thirteen in *The Wild Duck* will illustrate. A careful reading of the play will reveal several references to thirteen, particularly thirteen at the table. Thus when Gregers says at the end of the play that his destiny is "To be the thirteenth man at the table," the speech is more than obscurantism. One notable example of thirteen people at a meal is the final Passover meal of Jesus and his twelve disciples. This allusion may help us to understand Gregers' enigmatic remark.

Another device which lends internal complexity to other forms of literature and which functions in the drama is a recurring pattern of images. Throughout *Hamlet*, for example, images dealing with the body are used as a metaphor of the state as the body politic. Studying the play with this in mind will reveal dozens of such references. To give only one example, when the Ghost tells Hamlet that his death was falsely reported, his choice of words is significant: "So the whole ear of Denmark / Is by a forged process of my death / Rankly abused." This image becomes even more significant when he tells Hamlet the precise manner of his death. He was killed when his brother "in the porches of my ear did pour / The leperous distilment." The knowledge that the king is the "head" of the state and that Hamlet believes the wrong man is king may throw some light on his "madness." The understanding of the play can be greatly increased by watching for such image patterns.

The title of *The Wild Duck* might also suggest that the image of the wild duck is an important one for the reader of the play. Here the image is used symbolically; that means, among other things, that we cannot draw up a simple metaphorical equation between the image and what it represents. The wild duck itself, the method of its capture, the dog that actually captured it, and its life in the attic are used in many ways throughout the play. At one point, for example, Werle tells Gregers that old Ekdal is one of the "people in this world who sink to the bottom the minute they get a couple of slugs in them, and they never come up." Again a careful reading of the play will reveal many other uses of the image of the wild duck.

Yet another kind of internal complexity can result from the use of language. The dialogue of the various plays in this collection illustrates various degrees of attempting to reproduce actual speech. The kind of imitation of speech has much to do with the character of a play. Within a given play a writer may choose to give one or more characters individual speech patterns—for example, Hamlet's tendency to repeat the final phrase of a speech, Gina's malapropism, and Madame Pace's peculiar mixture of English and Italian.

Other examples of devices which induce internal complexity might be presented, for as literature the drama has precisely the same kinds of resources as other literary forms. None of these methods is peculiar to the drama.

The play on stage is different from the play as literature, not only because of its transience but also because every performance is a unique expression of the collaborative energies which make up the totality of the performance. In part this is due to the thousands of discrete elements which make up a performance. An actor may forget a line or the technician responsible for the lights may miss the speech which should tell him to change the lighting. Either of these or one of a thousand other possible accidents will make the performance unique. Another factor which makes every performance unique is that no two audiences are quite the same. Some audiences respond with warmth and enthusiasm; others are cold and unresponsive. The character of the audience on a given night invariably affects the performance. A warm, responsive audience brings out the best in the performers, as any actor can testify. No performance can exactly duplicate another.

Among the collaborators in a performance, the actors are the most visible. The actual control of a performance, however, varies in different times and places. In the 19th century performances were often dominated by the star actor-manager who played the lead and controlled the other persons involved. In the American theater in recent years the director has been the person most responsible for the collaborative effort. The stage direction may call for a sofa, but the director and the stage designer must provide a sofa of a particular style and color. In *Six Characters* the Stepdaughter expresses her dismay at their choice thus: "No, no! Green won't do! It was yellow, ornamented with flowers—very large! and most comfortable!"

Before a performance takes place the director and his colleagues must make hundreds of such decisions in such relatively unimportant matters as well as in more substantive ones. The selection of an actress to play Gertrude in *Hamlet* can serve as an example of a substantive choice. One possible interpretation of the play maintains that Hamlet suffers from an Oedipus complex. If the actress chosen to play Gertrude is young enough and physically attractive enough to be a suitable sexual partner for the actor playing Hamlet, then this Freudian interpretation of the play will seem more plausible. A less substantive but still important decision can be seen in Act 3 of Molière's *Tartuffe*. After two acts in which the question whether the title character is or is not a hypocrite has been discussed, Tartuffe makes his appearance and immediately places a handkerchief over the bosom of Dorine, the maid, in order to remove the temptation caused by the sight of her bosom. The director must decide where the neckline is to be. If the neckline is high, then Tartuffe is immediately recognizable as a hypocrite. If it is low, he may be merely a man with a mammary fixation. In other cases the dialogue more explicitly affects the staging. When, for example, in Act 1, Scene 2 of *Hamlet,* the Queen asks

Hamlet to "cast thy nighted color off," Hamlet should obviously be dressed in black.

Hamlet's appearance dressed in black in this scene is an example of how an author can imagine or invent a striking stage effect. Hamlet enters at the beginning of the scene with the King, the Queen, and the courtiers. Throughout the scenes with the ambassadors to Norway and then with Laertes, he is on stage but silent and isolated from the other figures by his dress. The stage picture has an effect which can be imagined in reading the scene but which is even more striking in performance. Another kind of striking stage effect can be seen in the entrance of Madame Pace in *Six Characters*. On stage the Father is bustling about, collecting hats and coats from the unwilling actresses and placing the garments on the prop forms provided for them. The audience's attention is forced toward the stage, allowing the actress playing Madame Pace to enter from the back of the seating area without being observed. As he moves about the Father says, "Who knows if, by arranging the stage for her, she does not come here herself, attracted by the very articles of her trade?" At this point the actor playing the Father will turn and point toward her, the spotlight will hit her, and some members of the audience will gasp with surprise.

There are other ways in which a stage-wise playwright can create moments of dramatic power on stage. When Hamlet says of the dead Polonius, "I'll lug the guts into the neighbor room," the ugliness and vulgarity of the language and the sentiments they express must startle the viewer as well as the reader. The entrance of the Mother in the brothel scene in *Six Characters* is carefully prepared for. The audience has been given the information necessary to be powerfully affected by the scene. The violence of the final scene of *Hamlet* is made more graphic by the relatively quiet scene between Hamlet and Horatio, including the comic moments with Osric. The audience has had a chance to relax after the confrontation at Ophelia's grave, and the lull makes the storm which follows more terrible.

At its best the drama establishes a tension between language and gesture which provides a supreme dramatic event. The great recognition scene in *Six Characters* shows how the two can work together. The Father, as *raisonneur*, propounds several ideas in the play which are presented dramatically in the scene. First, he says that the representation on stage of a scene is limited and impermanent and therefore inferior to the "form" or idea of it. Second, he points out that in art the true (that is, the probable) occurs necessarily. After the exit of Madame Pace in Act 2, the Father and the Stepdaughter begin to play the scene for the Manager and the Actors. Speaking outside the character in the scene, she tells him to make his entrance, but very quickly the reality of the story overcomes both of them and they are trapped in the action. *"The Father does as he is told, looking troubled and perplexed at first. But as soon as he begins to move, the reality of the action affects him, and he begins to smile and be more natural."* The

effect makes the Father's second point, using the very means he decries, the interpretive skill of the actor. Once the scene has begun, the Father and the Stepdaughter proceed without noticing the others. The Mother cries, "Oh, my God, my God!" L'Ingénue attempts to interrupt and the Manager scolds her. The Manager tells the Stepdaughter to "Begin again, please!" but the participants in the scene have no choice but to continue. The scene is the reality of art, and it must fulfill itself in that probable world, regardless of distractions. Finally a determined effort by the Manager stops them, although the Stepdaughter pleads to continue: "The best's coming now. Why can't we go on?"

Now the Leading Man and the Leading Lady prepare to play the scene. In spite of the Stepdaughter's objection that the scene will not work because the Leading Lady "isn't dressed in black," the actors begin. "*The rendering of the scene by the Actors from the very first word is seen to be quite a different thing, though it has not in any way the air of parody. . . . The Leading Lady and the Leading Man . . . deliver their words in different tones and with a different psychology.*" The effect cannot fail to work, as Pirandello knew, for no two pairs of actors can perform a scene in exactly the same way. Any interpretation is only one of the partial ways of realizing the words, and the difference between the pairs of actors represents the difference between the ideal of the scene contained in the words and any particular realization of it. Before the scene has proceeded very far, the Father interrupts, objecting to the reading of the first line by the Leading Man. The Actors, unlike the Father and the Stepdaughter, can allow themselves to be interrupted and can step out of character, as the Leading Man does to defend his reading. "If I've got to represent an old fellow who's coming into a house of an equivocal character . . . ," he begins. The Manager calms him and tells the Actors to start over. Unlike the characters in the same situation, because they are not "living" it, they can and do begin again. It is acting, not the reality of art, and they are not swept along by the force of probability. The Manager interrupts several times to give them line readings, but they are not disturbed. The Father and the Stepdaughter also interrupt to comment on the "truth" of the performance until it becomes impossible to continue, and the Manager stops the scene. "Well then, let's have no more of it! We'll have the rehearsals by ourselves afterward in the ordinary way." Throughout the scene the visual, gestural resources of the stage reinforce the language and ideas of the play.

So far this introduction has dealt largely with individual plays, but groups of plays have several important relations to one another. One such relation involves plays by a single author, for every art work bears to some extent the imprint of the artist's personality, his education, and his experiences. Where a substantial body of work by a given artist exists, meaningful relations between the separate works can illuminate individual works. In Shakespeare's plays, for example, the issue of orderly succession is examined again and again in the

histories and tragedies. Furthermore, the character of Hamlet combines important elements of earlier Shakespearean heroes such as
Richard II, Brutus, and Prince Hal.

To illustrate this kind of relation, a play of George Bernard Shaw
is included in this volume; for among playwrights other than Shakespeare who write in English, Shaw is probably the most frequently
performed and the one who has more plays which are still viable on
stage. Some ten or twelve of his plays are still frequently performed
and as many more are played occasionally. Although he was almost
forty when he began writing for the theater, Shaw wrote over sixty
plays, ranging from vaudeville sketches to his "Metabiological Pen-
tateuch," *Back to Methuselah*. Before he began writing plays, he had
been a would-be novelist, a notable reviewer of music and drama for
periodicals, and a crowd-pleasing lecturer, particularly on economics.
His cogent analyses of the plays and operas performed in London
while he was a reviewer and of the performances themselves stood him
in good stead as a dramatist. As a lecturer, he learned to please and
hold an audience. "I first caught the ear of the British public on a
cart in Hyde Park, to the blaring of brass bands, and this not at all as
a reluctant sacrifice of instincts of privacy to political necessity, but
because, like all dramatists and mimes of genuine vocation, I am a
natural-born mountebank." This piece of self-deprecation ignores the
other side of Shaw's character, the polemical moralist and social philosopher. He left the platform for the stage, at least in part, because he
believed that in his plays and the series of prefaces which he wrote
for some of them, he would find a more effective vehicle for propa-
gandizing his ideas about economics and education, about vegetarian-
ism and spelling reform, about "Creative Evolution" and marriage and
the legal status of women. His plays would bring their audience to a
new and better understanding of themselves and their society.

Shaw's characteristic method in his plays is satiric, for he exhibits
the evils of society rather than the way things ought to be. The plays
diagnose the ills; the prefaces prescribe the remedies. Shaw consistently
deals with the hypocrisies of society, and the central figures of his plays
are strong, powerful, and attractive not because they try to reform
the world but because they are not deceived by its hypocrisies. They
observe what people do, not what they say. The method can be illustrated by the treatment of economics. Shaw was a Fabian socialist,
but he does not describe a socialist Utopia in his plays. He concentrates on an analysis of the materialistic, capitalistic society which he
sees around him—a society dominated by economic values, whatever
people say. An exchange from each of the plays in this collection makes
the point. In *Major Barbara* Stephen believes that politicians govern,
but his father, the munitions maker Andrew Undershaft, voices Shaw's
criticism. "Government of your country! Be off with you, my boy, and
play with your caucuses and leading articles and historic parties and
great leaders and burning questions and the rest of your toys. *I* am
going back to my countinghouse to pay the piper and call the tune."

In structuring his plays, Shaw used a parodistic method, based on his knowledge of the stage gained as a drama critic. He described it thus: "I have always cast my plays in the ordinary practical comedy form in use at all the theatres." The first act of *Major Barbara* and the first part of the third act are in the tradition of the comedy of manners, as exemplified in Shaw's own time by Oscar Wilde's *The Importance of Being Earnest*. Although Wilde moved the setting of his play from the city to the country, he never really left the drawing room, as Shaw did in his visits to the Salvation Army shelter and the munitions factory.

Another characteristically Shavian feature of the play is the concern with a teacher-student relation between an older man and a young woman. In several of Shaw's plays such a relation replaces the traditional romantic intrigue of comedy. In *Major Barbara* although Barbara "loves" Cusins in the conventional way, the passion between Barbara and her father is stronger. Cusins says: "A father's love for a grown-up daughter is the most dangerous of all infatuations. I apologize for mentioning my own pale, coy, mistrustful fancy in the same breath with it." The same pattern of an intellectual passion between an older man and a younger woman can be seen in such plays as *Pygmalion, Caesar and Cleopatra,* and *Heartbreak House.*

Shaw's tendency to downgrade sexual relationships often makes the theoretical heroes and heroines of his plays into rather bland figures like Cusins, but he achieves greater success with his strong, aware figures such as Undershaft, as well as with a series of stereotypes adapted from earlier dramatic forms. Lady Britomart in *Major Barbara,* for example, is Shaw's version of the middle-aged, dominating society matron exemplified by such characters as Lady Wishfort in Congreve's *The Way of the World* and Lady Bracknell in Wilde's *The Importance of Being Earnest.* Other characters, like Bill Walker and Britannus, are in the comedy of humors tradition, especially as that tradition was used by Dickens. The strongest and most vital characters in the plays, however, are those like Undershaft who see the world as clearly as Shaw did and who act on their insights to control and manipulate others.

Because Shaw did not have Pirandello's gift for devising actions to exemplify his ideas, his plays sometimes seem "talky." The scene between Undershaft, Barbara, and Cusins near the end of *Major Barbara* is an example of a scene where the real action is in the play of ideas. However, he was capable of the flashing comic line such as Lady Britomart's assertion that "[I] believe in liberty. Let snobbish people say what they please; Barbara shall marry, not the man they like, but the man *I* like." At other times, the wit lies in the structure of the speeches, using the rhetorical tricks Shaw had learned on the lecture platform. "When you vote, you only change the names of the cabinet. When you shoot, you pull down governments, inaugurate new epochs, abolish old orders and set up new."

In his best work Shaw presented a witty and elegant expression of his unique vision. He saw a society where people lived for money and

power but talked of romance and religion, of charity and honor. He attacked the hypocrisies of such a society, many of which are still present in our lives. As long as they are, his plays will be an important part of our dramatic heritage.

Another means of understanding plays in relation to one another is the study of dramatic kinds (or genres). The dramatic kind that has been studied most frequently is tragedy, the subject of Aristotle's *Poetics* and numerous works of later critics. Sophocles' *Oedipus Tyrannus* is close to being the perfect exemplar of Aristotle's definition of tragedy. Tragedy describes the fall from prosperity to adversity of a great individual because he has transgressed against the great moral principles which govern the universe. In his adversity he comes to understand himself and his situation, blessed with enlightenment even though he may be dying. At the beginning of the play Oedipus is prosperous and happy, enjoying the confidence and love of his subjects and the pleasures of warm personal relations. But Oedipus believes that he can save the city, that he can control Fate. He did it once before, when he fled from Corinth to avoid carrying out the destiny assigned him. Oedipus is wrong in his belief, for Fate will carry the day. His attempt to avoid his fate led directly to his carrying it out, to the murder of his own father and the marriage with his mother. At the end of the play, having lost both his kingdom and his eyes, he understands. His final appearance radiates a serene and dignified resignation to his destiny, an enlightenment gained at a terrible price.

Several of the other plays in this collection share some characteristic features of tragedy with *Oedipus Tyrannus*, particularly *Hamlet* and *The Bacchae*. Neither is quite like *Oedipus Tyrannus* in every regard, and examining them at the points of dissimilarity can provide one approach to our understanding of them. For example, what kind of Fate or destiny is involved in each of them? What moral principles are at stake in them, and how does the author describe these principles? Although Sophocles and Euripides were closely contemporary, the plays seem to show different attitudes toward the destiny that governs mankind.

Another opening into the plays can be seen in the characters of their beginnings and endings. Oedipus was prosperous and happy, sure of himself and of his happy future. To what extent is this true of Hamlet and of Pentheus? At the end of the play Oedipus, though in terrible circumstances, wins through to enlightenment. What do Hamlet's final speeches tell us about his state of mind as he dies? In *The Bacchae* what are we to make of Pentheus' leaving the stage two-thirds of the way through the play and not returning? We do not witness him in his adversity, and we do not know whether he reached enlightenment. All of these are questions which arise from our knowledge of tragedy.

Most of the serious plays of the contemporary theater have not attempted to be tragedies. One reason for this is that none of the value

systems available to the modern dramatist—and here "available" means acceptable to and understandable by his audience—provides a suitable framework for tragedy. Rather than focusing on man's relation to a universal order of some kind, playwrights like Ibsen, Chekhov, and others have turned to depicting man's life on this earth and the ways he finds to deal with it. Transcendent values have tended either to disappear or to become eroded to the point where they cannot be used for dramatic purposes. Only a naive man like Hjalmar Ekdal in *The Wild Duck* can believe that old Werle's loss of eyesight is a punishment; only an old man with a failing mind like Old Ekdal can believe that the forests will have their revenge. The Prozorovs in *Three Sisters* watch helplessly while the forces of social and economic change destroy the lovely world of the past and replace it with a newer and uglier present. Death without enlightenment is the ending which waits patiently at the end of a road marked by failing powers and compromises with life. Hedvig dies; Tusenbach dies. They are the lucky ones, for the others are compelled to begin another day, to repeat yesterday's routines. Hjalmar will recover from Hedvig's death, just as Irina will recover from Tusenbach's because life goes on. The dramatic event represents only a moment in an otherwise humdrum life. The vivid recognition scene in *Six Characters* is an exceptional experience, but the Actors cannot even recognize that they have been touched by the truth of art. Instead they regret the wasted day and look forward only to returning to the treadmill of their ordinary rehearsals tomorrow. Plays like these are the most typical form of our serious drama, so much a part of our consciousness that we have no name for this dramatic kind.

Here, as in tragedy, the resemblances call our attention to the differences. In Ibsen, for example, the emphasis is on the individual and his fate. For Hjalmar life has been a series of disappointments and compromises which have produced the Hjalmar we see. In Chekhov, by contrast, the emphasis is on the society. The three sisters and their brother personify various ways in which the gleam has been lost; our concern is not with any of them as individuals, but as representatives of a class and a society that is dying.

A third way of studying groups of plays is to examine those written during a certain period of time. The drama is the most social of literary forms, and dramatic styles vary widely even in different decades. The last two plays in this collection are examples of the new dramatic style of the 1960s in America. One obvious characteristic of this style is the use of language. Writers as diverse as Lewis Carroll and Gertrude Stein heralded a breakdown of confidence in the reliability of language, and Pirandello observed that each of us uses words in terms of his own experience and that therefore no two of us use them in the same way. Samuel Beckett, Eugene Ionesco, and other writers of the Theater of the Absurd during the 1950s presented the problems of language in dramatic terms. Real communication between people is impossible because of the dangers of language. Clichés serve a real purpose, for

though they mean little (or because they mean little), they are less likely to be misunderstood than more complex utterances. The effect in more recent playwrights is threefold: (1) avoidance of anything that sounds like "literature" or "fine writing," (2) the use of cliché in dialogue, and (3) the use of nonsense and of regular speech treated as nonsense, passages in which words are treated as music or sound effects.

Another feature of this style is its concern with the communal and ritual aspects of the theater. Many of the plays begin in theatrical workshops or performing groups in which the playwright is only one of the members of the group. The playwright develops the play in collaboration with the group until a performing script is ready for public presentation. Rewriting parts of a play prior to public performance is a common practice in the commercial theater, but the method and purpose are quite different. The groups from which the new dramatic style springs are more closely knit than had been the case in the recent past, and the members of the group often share a mystique of communality. In some instances this mystique acquires an intense, quasi-religious character (generally with little or no theological content). It is not religious in the traditional sense, but its emotional tone is almost religious. The performances can become theatrical rituals at which the actors are the priests and acolytes and the audience the members of this secular congregation. Accounts of the activities and performances of a group like the Living Theater illustrate this tendency.

A third common feature of this style is the way in which it exposes its theatricality. In the last hundred years the dominant tradition of the drama has been to turn the stage into as perfect a representation of reality as possible. There have been other less illusive styles, but generally a stage living room looks as much as possible like a real living room. In the new style the barriers between the acting area and the auditorium are broken down; movement from one to the other is frequently used. The acting area itself is a part of a total theatrical environment. Sets may imitate by suggesting rather than by copying the real place being represented. The treatment of time in both plays involves little attempt to make stage time imitate real time. Character too makes little attempt to imitate realistically. In *A Son, Come Home,* for example, the Boy and the Girl each play a number of different roles without any attempt to change their appearance and thus increase the illusion. All of the visual means are presented so that the audience is aware that it is watching actors on a stage at all times. Rather than an illusive representation of something outside, the play in performance becomes a theatrical event, governed by its own laws and experience for its own sake. Even plot participates in this theatricality, for a different notion of plot animates the plays; plot as the blueprint for a theatrical performance. Emphasis is on performance, and the plot is not constructed to imitate life but to provide effective means for using the theatrical resources to make the ideal theatrical experience.

The features of this new dramatic style are not really new, for they can be found in earlier plays and traditions of performance. Their combination into a new dramatic style, however, is a significant part of our culture today.

Note on Arrangement

The first three plays in this selection are chosen from different times and places to illustrate the common features of all drama in works of widely diverse styles. Thematically they are similar in that they deal with the conflict between the individual and his society, although the actual conflict in each is different from the others.

The play in Section II illuminates the relation between the drama as a literary form and as a public performance. It and the Shaw play which opens Section III also deal with a common theme—the relationship between a younger woman and an older man.

The plays by Shaw and Chekhov may be interestingly compared as "comedies" and also for their generic affinities with the serious modern play. The last two are American plays of the 1960s, which illustrate the relationship of the play to its historic and social contexts.

The dates following each play are those of first performance.

I

EURIPIDES

The Bacchae*

CHARACTERS

DIONYSUS
CHORUS, *of Oriental women, devotees of Dionysus*
TEIRESIAS, *a blind Seer*
CADMUS, *founder of Thebes, and formerly king*[1]

PENTHEUS, *his grandson, now king of Thebes*
A GUARD, *attending Pentheus*
A HERDSMAN
A MESSENGER
AGAUË, *daughter of Cadmus and mother of Pentheus*

THE SCENE. *Before the palace of Pentheus in Thebes. At one side of the stage is the monument of Semele; above it burns a low flame, and around it are the remains of ruined and blackened masonry.*

DIONYSUS *enters on stage right. He has a crown of ivy, a thyrsus in his hand, and a fawnskin draped over his body.*[2] *He has long flowing hair and a youthful, almost feminine beauty.*

DIONYSUS   I am Dionysus, son of Zeus. My mother was
Semele, Cadmus' daughter. From her womb the fire
Of a lightning-flash delivered me. I have come here
To Thebes and her two rivers, Dirce and Ismenus,
Veiling my godhead in a mortal shape. I see   5
Here near the palace my mother's monument, that records
Her death by lightning. Here her house stood; and its ruins
Smoulder with the still living flame of Zeus's fire—
The immortal cruelty Hera wreaked upon my mother.[3]
Cadmus does well to keep this ground inviolable,   10
A precinct consecrated in his daughter's name;
And I have decked it round with sprays of young vine-leaves.
From the fields of Lydia and Phrygia, fertile in gold,
I traveled first to the sun-smitten Persian plains,
The walled cities of Bactria, the harsh Median country,   15
Wealthy Arabia, and the whole tract of the Asian coast
Where mingled swarms of Greeks and Orientals live
In vast magnificent cities; and before reaching this,
The first city of Hellas I have visited,
I had already, in all those regions of the east,   20

---

* Translated by Philip Vellacott.
1. See the note on Thebes and the House of Cadmus, p. 785.
2. The traditional attributes of Dionysus included a crown of ivy, a fawnskin, and the *thyrsus*, a staff of fennel wrapped with ivy or vine leaves.
3. Hera, as chief goddess of the Greeks and consort of Zeus, the chief god, felt a not unnatural aversion to the mortal girls who were the objects of his frequent adulteries.

Performed my dances and set forth my ritual
To make my godhead manifest to mortal men.[4]

The reason why I have chosen Thebes as the first place
To raise my Bacchic shout, and clothe all who respond
In fawnskin habits, and put my thyrsus in their hands—   25
The weapon wreathed with ivy-shoots—my reason is this:
My mother's sisters said—what they should have been the last
To say—that I, Dionysus, was not Zeus's son;
That Semele, being with child—they said—by some mortal,
Obeyed her father's prompting, and ascribed to Zeus   30
The loss of her virginity; and they loudly claimed
That this lie was the sin for which Zeus took her life.

Therefore I have driven those same sisters mad, turned them
All frantic out of doors; their home now is the mountain;
Their wits are gone. I have made them bear the emblem of   35
My mysteries; the whole female population of Thebes,
To the last woman, I have sent raving from their homes.
Now, side by side with Cadmus' daughters, one and all
Sit roofless on the rocks under the silver pines.
For Thebes, albeit reluctantly, must learn in full   40
This lesson, that my Bacchic worship is a matter
As yet beyond her knowledge and experience;
And I must vindicate my mother Semele
By manifesting myself before the human race
As the divine son whom she bore to immortal Zeus.   45

Now Cadmus has made over his throne and kingly honors
To Pentheus, son of his eldest daughter Agauë. He
Is a fighter against gods, defies me, excludes me from
Libations, never names me in prayers. Therefore I will
Demonstrate to him, and to all Thebes, that I am a god.   50

When I have set all in order here, I will pass on
To another place, and manifest myself. Meanwhile
If Thebes in anger tries to bring the Bacchants home
By force from the mountain, I myself will join that army
Of women possessed and lead them to battle. That is why   55
I have changed my form and taken the likeness of a man.

Come, my band of worshippers, women whom I have brought
From lands of the east, from Tmolus, bastion of Lydia,
To be with me and share my travels! Raise the music
Of your own country, the Phrygian drums invented by   60
Rhea the Great Mother and by me.[5] Fill Pentheus' palace
With a noise to make the city of Cadmus turn and look!
—And I will go to the folds of Mount Cithaeron, where
The Bacchants are, and join them in their holy dance.

---

4. Hellas was another name for Greece, and the people of Greece were also called Hellenes. The other places mentioned by Dionysus are in Asia Minor or Asia proper.

5. Tmolus is a mountain in Asia Minor. Rhea was a Greek name for the earth goddess responsible for the fertility of the soil, or the Great Mother.

DIONYSUS *goes out toward the mountain. The* CHORUS *enter where* DIONYSUS *entered, from the road by which they have traveled.*

CHORUS

From far-off lands of Asia,   *Strophe 1*   65
From Tmolus the holy mountain,
We run with the god of laughter;
Labor is joy and weariness is sweet,
And our song resounds to Bacchus!

Who stands in our path?   *Antistrophe 1*   70
Make way, make way!
Who in the house? Close every lip,
Keep holy silence, while we sing
The appointed hymn to Bacchus!

Blest is the happy man   *Strophe 2*   75
Who knows the mysteries the gods ordain,
And sanctifies his life,
Joins soul with soul in mystic unity,
And, by due ritual made pure,
Enters the ecstasy of mountain solitudes;   80
Who observes the mystic rites
Made lawful by Cybele[6] the Great Mother;
Who crowns his head with ivy,
And shakes aloft his wand in worship of Dionysus.
On, on! Run, dance, delirious, possessed!   85
Dionysus comes to his own;
Bring from the Phrygian hills to the broad streets of Hellas
The god, child of a god,
Spirit of revel and rapture, Dionysus!

Once, on the womb that held him   *Antistrophe 2*   90
The fire-bolt flew from the hand of Zeus;
And pains of childbirth bound his mother fast,
And she cast him forth untimely,
And under the lightning's lash relinquished life;
And Zeus the son of Cronos   95
Ensconced him instantly in a secret womb
Chambered within his thigh,
And with golden pins closed him from Hera's sight.
So, when the Fates had made him ripe for birth,
Zeus bore the bull-horned god   100
And wreathed his head with wreaths of writhing snakes;
Which is why the Maenads catch
Wild snakes, nurse them and twine them round their hair.

O Thebes, old nurse that cradled Semele,   *Strophe 3*
Be ivy-garlanded, burst into flower   105

6. Cybele was another name for the Great Mother, especially as a goddess of Asia Minor.

With wreaths of lush bright-berried bryony,
Bring sprays of fir, green branches torn from oaks,
Fill soul and flesh with Bacchus' mystic power;
Fringe and bedeck your dappled fawnskin cloaks
With woolly tufts and locks of purest white.   110
There's a brute wildness in the fennel-wands—
Reverence it well. Soon the whole land will dance
    When the god with ecstatic shout
    Leads his companies out
    To the mountain's mounting height   115
    Swarming with riotous bands
    Of Theban women leaving
    Their spinning and their weaving
    Stung with the maddening trance
        Of Dionysus!   120

O secret chamber the Curetes knew!   *Antistrophe 3*
O holy cavern in the Cretan glade
Where Zeus was cradled, where for our delight
The triple-crested Corybantes drew
Tight the round drum-skin, till its wild beat made   125
Rapturous rhythm to the breathing sweetness
Of Phrygian flutes! Then divine Rhea found
The drum could give her Bacchic airs completeness;
    From her, the Mother of all,
    The crazy Satyrs soon,   130
    In their dancing festival
    When the second year comes round,
    Seized on the timbrel's tune
    To play the leading part
    In feasts that delight the heart   135
        Of Dionysus.[7]

O what delight is in the mountains!   *Epode*
There the celebrant, wrapped in his sacred fawnskin,
Flings himself on the ground surrendered,
While the swift-footed company streams on;   140
There he hunts for blood, and rapturously
Eats the raw flesh of the slaughtered goat,
Hurrying on to the Phrygian or Lydian mountain heights.
Possessed, ecstatic, he leads their happy cries;
The earth flows with milk, flows with wine,   145
Flows with nectar of bees;
The air is thick with a scent of Syrian myrrh.
The celebrant runs entranced, whirling the torch
That blazes red from the fennel-wand in his grasp,
And with shouts he rouses the scattered bands,   150
Sets their feet dancing,

---

7. The Curetes were Cretan spirits who saved the life of the infant Zeus by dancing
and shouting so frenziedly that his cries could not be heard. He had been hidden on
Crete by his mother Rhea because his father Cronos, or Saturn, had the unpleasant habit
of eating his newborn children. The Corybantes were male attendants of Cybele, also
known for their frenzied revels. The Satyrs were woodland figures, men from the waist
up and goats from the waist down, associated with Pan and Dionysus and known for
their exuberance.

As he shakes his delicate locks to the wild wind.
And amidst the frenzy of song he shouts like thunder:
"On, on! Run, dance, delirious, possessed!
You, the beauty and grace of golden Tmolus,   155
Sing to the rattle of thunderous drums,
Sing for joy,
Praise Dionysus, god of joy!
Shout like Phrygians, sing out the tunes you know,
While the sacred pure-toned flute   160
Vibrates the air with holy merriment,
In time with the pulse of the feet that flock
To the mountains, to the mountains!"
And, like a foal with its mother at pasture,
Runs and leaps for joy every daughter of Bacchus.   165

     Enter TEIRESIAS. *Though blind, he makes his way unaided to the door, and knocks.*

TEIRESIAS   Who keeps the gate? Call Cadmus out, Agenor's son,
Who came from Sidon here to build these walls of Thebes.
Go, someone, say Teiresias is looking for him.
He knows why; I'm an old man, and he's older still—
But we agreed to equip ourselves with Bacchic wands   170
And fawnskin cloaks, and put on wreaths of ivy-shoots.

     Enter CADMUS.

CADMUS   Dear friend, I knew your voice, although I was indoors,
As soon as I heard it—the wise voice of a wise man.
I am ready. See, I have all that the god prescribes.
He is my daughter's son; we must do all we can   175
To exalt and honor him. Where shall we go to dance
And take our stand with others, tossing our grey heads?
You tell me what to do, Teiresias. We're both old,
But you're the expert. [*He stumps about, beating his thyrsus on the ground.*] I could drum the ground all night
And all day too, without being tired. What joy it is   180
To forget one's age!
TEIRESIAS   I feel exactly the same way,
Bursting with youth! I'll try it—I'll dance with the rest.
CADMUS   You don't think we should go to the mountain in a coach?
TEIRESIAS   No, no. That would not show the god the same respect.   185
CADMUS   I'll take you there myself then—old as we both are.
TEIRESIAS   The god will guide us there, and without weariness.
CADMUS   Are we the only Thebans who will dance to him?
TEIRESIAS   We see things clearly; all the others are perverse.
CADMUS   We're wasting time; come, take my hand.   190
TEIRESIAS   Here, then; hold tight.
CADMUS   I don't despise religion. I'm a mortal man.
TEIRESIAS   We have no use for theological subtleties.
The beliefs we have inherited, as old as time,
Cannot be overthrown by any argument,   195
Not by the most inventive ingenuity.
It will be said, I lack the dignity of my age,

To wear this ivy-wreath and set off for the dance.
Not so; the god draws no distinction between young
And old, to tell us which should dance and which should not.   200
He desires equal worship from all men; his claim
To glory is universal; no one is exempt.

CADMUS   Teiresias, I shall be your prophet, since you are blind.
Pentheus, to whom I have resigned my rule in Thebes,
Is hurrying here toward the palace. He appears   205
Extremely agitated. What news will he bring?

> *Enter* PENTHEUS. *He addresses the audience, without at first
> noticing* CADMUS *and* TEIRESIAS, *who stand at the opposite side
> of the stage.*

PENTHEUS   I happen to have been away from Thebes; reports
Of this astounding scandal have just been brought to me.
Our women, it seems, have left their homes on some pretense
Of Bacchic worship, and now are gadding about   210
On the wooded mountain slopes, dancing in honor of
This upstart god Dionysus, whoever he may be.
Amidst these groups of worshippers, they tell me, stand
Bowls full of wine; and our women go creeping off
This way and that to lonely places and give themselves   215
To lecherous men. They are Maenad priestesses, if you please!
Aphrodite supplants Bacchus in their ritual.[8]
Well, those I've caught, my guards are keeping safe; we've tied
Their hands, and lodged them at state expense. Those still at large
On the mountain I am going to hunt out; and that   220
Includes my own mother Agaüe and her sisters
Ino and Autonoe. Once they're fast in iron fetters,
I'll put a stop to this outrageous Bacchism.

They tell me, too, some oriental conjurer
Has come from Lydia, a magician with golden hair   225
Flowing in scented ringlets, his face flushed with wine,
His eyes lit with the charm of Aphrodite; and he
Entices young girls with his Bacchic mysteries,
Spends days and nights consorting with them. Once let me
Get that fellow inside my walls—I'll cut his head   230
From his shoulders; that will stop him drumming with his thyrsus,
Tossing his long hair. *He's* the one—this foreigner—
Who says Dionysus is a god; who says he was
Sewn up in Zeus's thigh. The truth about Dionysus
Is that he's dead, burned to a cinder by lightning   235
Along with his mother, because she said Zeus lay with her.
Whoever the man may be, is not his arrogance
An outrage? Has he not earned a rope around his neck?

> PENTHEUS *turns to go, and sees* CADMUS *and* TEIRESIAS.

Why, look! Another miracle! Here's Teiresias
The prophet—in a fawnskin; and my mother's father—   240

---

8. Aphrodite (Roman name, Venus) was the goddess of love and beauty. Bacchus was
one of the many names used for Dionysus. The women who made up Dionysus' train or
participated in his rites were called "Bacchantes" or "Maenads."

A Bacchant with a fennel-wand! Well, there's a sight
For laughter! [*But he is raging, not laughing.*]

Sir, I am ashamed to see two men
Of your age with so little sense of decency.
Come, you're my grandfather: throw down that ivy-wreath,   245
Get rid of that thyrsus! *You* persuaded him to this,
Teiresias. By introducing a new god, you hope
To advance your augurer's business, to collect more fees
For inspecting sacrifices. Listen: your gray hairs
Are your protection; otherwise you'd be sitting now   250
In prison with all these crazy females, for promoting
Pernicious practices. As for women, I tell you this:
Wherever the sparkle of sweet wine adorns their feasts,
No good will follow from such Bacchic ceremonies.
CHORUS   Have you no reverence, Sir, no piety? Do you mock   255
Cadmus, who sowed the dragon-seed of earth-born men?
Do you, Echion's son, dishonor your own race?
TEIRESIAS   When a good speaker has a sound case to present,
Then eloquence is no great feat. Your fluent tongue
Promises wisdom; but the content of your speech   260
Is ignorant. Power and eloquence in a headstrong man
Spell folly; such a man is a peril to the state.

This new god, whom you ridicule—no words of mine
Could well express the ascendancy he will achieve
In Hellas. There are two powers, young man, which are supreme   265
In human affairs: first, Demeter[9]—the same goddess
Is also Earth; give her which name you please—and she
Supplies mankind with solid food. After her came
Dionysus, Semele's son; the blessing he procured
And gave to men is counterpart to that of bread: 270
The clear juice of the grape. When mortals drink their fill
Of wine, the sufferings of our unhappy race
Are banished, each day's troubles are forgotten in sleep.
There is no other cure for sorrow. Dionysus,
Himself a god, is thus poured out in offering   275
To the gods, so that through him come blessings on mankind.
And do you scorn this legend, that he was sewn up
In Zeus's thigh? I will explain the truth to you.
When Zeus snatched Dionysus from the lightning-flame
And took the child up to Olympus as a god,   280
Hera resolved to cast him out of heaven. But Zeus
Found such means to prevent her as a god will find.
He took a fragment of the ether that surrounds
The earth, fashioned it like a child, presented it
To Hera as a pledge to soothe her jealousy,   285
And saved Dionysus from her. Thus, in time, because
The ancient words for "pledge" and "thigh" are similar,
People confused them, and the "pledge" Zeus gave to Hera
Became transformed, as time went on, into the tale
That Dionysus was sewn up in Zeus's thigh.   290

9. Demeter (Roman name, Ceres) was a goddess of the harvest and of grain. Here she
and Dionysus are used by metonymy for bread and wine.

And this god is a prophet; the Bacchic ecstasy
And frenzy hold a strong prophetic element.
When he fills irresistibly a human body
He gives those so possessed power to foretell the future.
In Ares' province too Dionysus has his share;   295
Sometimes an army, weaponed and drawn up for battle,
Has fled in wild panic before a spear was raised.
This too is an insanity sent by Dionysus.

Ay, and the day will come when, on the very crags
Of Delphi, you shall see him leaping, amidst the blaze   300
Of torches, over the twin-peaked ridge, waving aloft
And brandishing his Bacchic staff, while all Hellas
Exalts him. Pentheus, pay heed to my words. You rely
On force; but it is not force that governs human affairs.
Do not mistake for wisdom that opinion which   305
May rise from a sick mind. Welcome this god to Thebes,
Offer libations to him, celebrate his rites,
Put on his garland. Dionysus will not compel
Women to be chaste, since in all matters self-control
Resides in our own natures. You should consider this;   310
For in the Bacchic ritual, as elsewhere, a woman
Will be safe from corruption if her mind is chaste.

Think of this too: when crowds stand at the city gates
And Thebes extols the name of Pentheus, you rejoice;
So too, I think, the god is glad to receive honor.   315
Well, I at least, and Cadmus, whom you mock, will wear
The ivy-wreath and join the dancing—we are a pair
Of gray heads, but this is our duty; and no words
Of yours shall lure me into fighting against gods.
For a most cruel insanity has warped your mind;   320
While drugs may well have caused it, they can bring no cure.
CHORUS   What you have said, Teiresias, shows no disrespect
To Apollo; at the same time you prove your judgment sound
In honoring Dionysus as a mighty god.[1]
CADMUS   My dear son, Teiresias has given you good advice.   325
Don't stray beyond pious tradition; live with us.
Your wits have flown to the winds, your sense is foolishness.
Even if, as you say, Dionysus is no god,
Let him have *your* acknowledgement; lie royally,
That Semele may get honor as having borne a god,   330
And credit come to us and to all our family.

Remember, too, Actaeon's miserable fate—[2]
Torn and devoured by hounds which he himself had bred,
Because he filled the mountains with the boast that he

---

1. Apollo was the Greek sun god. He was also associated with such activities as poetry, healing, and divination. As a god of divination and prophecy, his most famous shrine was at Delphi.
2. Actaeon was a cousin of Pentheus. There are several accounts of his tragic end. The one more customary than that used here by Euripides was that one day while hunting, he accidentally saw Artemis, the moon goddess but also a patroness of hunting, bathing in a forest pool. The goddess, renowned for her modesty and chastity, was not amused and caused Actaeon to be turned into a stag and to be killed by his own hounds.

Was a more skilful hunter than Artemis herself.   335
Don't share his fate, my son! Come, let me crown your head
With a wreath of ivy; join us in worshipping this god.
PENTHEUS   Keep your hands off! Go to your Bacchic rites, and don't
Wipe off your crazy folly on me. But I will punish
This man who has been your instructor in lunacy.   340
Go, someone, quickly to his seat of augury,
Smash it with crowbars, topple the walls, throw all his things
In wild confusion, turn the whole place upside down,
Fling out his holy fripperies to the hurricane winds!
This sacrilege will sting him more than anything else.   345
The rest of you—go, comb the country and track down
That effeminate foreigner, who plagues our women with
This new disease, fouls the whole land with lechery;
And once you catch him, tie him up and bring him here
To me; I'll deal with him. He shall be stoned to death.   350
He'll wish he'd never brought his Bacchic rites to Thebes.

Exit PENTHEUS.

TEIRESIAS   Foolhardy man! You do not know what you have said.
Before, you were unbalanced; now you are insane.
Come, Cadmus; let us go and pray both for this man,
Brutish as he is, and for our city, and beg the god   355
To show forbearance. Come, now, take your ivy staff
And let us go. Try to support me; we will help
Each other. It would be scandalous for two old men
To fall; still, we must go, and pay our due service
To Dionysus, son of Zeus. Cadmus, the name   360
Pentheus means *sorrow*. God grant he may not bring sorrow
Upon your house. Do not take that as prophecy;
I judge his acts. Such foolish words bespeak a fool.

Exeunt TEIRESIAS *and* CADMUS.

CHORUS

Holiness, Queen of heaven,   *Strophe 1*
Holiness, golden-winged ranging the earth,   365
Do you hear his blasphemy?
Pentheus dares—do you hear?—to revile the god of joy,
The son of Semele, who when the gay-crowned feast is set
Is named among gods the chief;
Whose gifts are joy and union of soul in dancing,   370
Joy in music of flutes,
Joy when sparkling wine at feasts of the gods
Soothes the sore regret,
Banishes every grief,
When the reveler rests, enfolded deep   375
In the cool shade of ivy-shoots,
On wine's soft pillow of sleep.

The brash, unbridled tongue,   *Antistrophe 1*
The lawless folly of fools, will end in pain.
But the life of wise content   380
Is blest with quietness, escapes the storm
And keeps its house secure.

Though blessed gods dwell in the distant skies,
They watch the ways of men.
To know much is not to be wise.   385
Pride more than mortal hastens life to its end;
And they who in pride pretend
Beyond man's limit, will lose what lay
Close to their hand and sure.
I count it madness, and know no cure can mend   390
The evil man and his evil way.

O to set foot on Aphrodite's island,   *Strophe 2*
On Cyprus, haunted by the Loves, who enchant
Brief life with sweetness; or in that strange land
Whose fertile river carves a hundred channels   395
To enrich her rainless sand;
Or where the sacred pastures of Olympus slant
Down to Pieria, where the Muses dwell—
Take me, O Bromius, take me and inspire
Laughter and worship! There our holy spell   400
And ecstasy are welcome; there the gentle band
Of Graces have their home, and sweet Desire.[3]

Dionysus, son of Zeus, delights in banquets;   *Antistrophe 2*
And his dear love is Peace, giver of wealth,
Savior of young men's lives—a goddess rare!   405
In wine, his gift that charms all griefs away,
Alike both rich and poor may have their part.
His enemy is the man who has no care
To pass his years in happiness and health,
His days in quiet and his nights in joy,   410
Watchful to keep aloof both mind and heart
From men whose pride claims more than mortals may.
The life that wins the poor man's common voice,
His creed, his practice—this shall be my choice.

> *Some of the guards whom* PENTHEUS *sent to arrest* DIONYSUS
> *now enter with their prisoner.* PENTHEUS *enters from the palace.*

GUARD   Pentheus, we've brought the prey you sent us out to catch;   415
We hunted him, and here he is. But, Sir, we found
The beast was gentle; made no attempt to run away,
Just held his hands out to be tied; didn't turn pale,
But kept his florid color, smiling, telling us
To tie him up and run him in; gave us no trouble   420
At all, just waited for us. Naturally I felt
A bit embarrassed. "You'll excuse me, Sir," I said,
"I don't want to arrest you; it's the king's command."

Another thing, Sir—those women you rounded up
And put in fetters in the prison, those Bacchants;   425
Well, they're all gone, turned loose to the glens; and there they are,

---

3. The island of Cyprus was associated with the goddess Aphrodite. Pieria was a
region near Mount Olympus associated with the Muses, minor goddesses related to learning and the arts. Loves, Graces, and Desire are figured as minor goddesses attendant on
Aphrodite.

Frisking about, calling on Bromius their god.
The fetters simply opened and fell off their feet;
The bolts shot back, untouched by mortal hand; the doors
Flew wide. Master, this man has come here with a load   430
Of miracles. Well, what happens next is your concern.
PENTHEUS   Untie this man's hands. [*The* GUARD *does so.*] He's securely
   in the trap.
He's not so nimble-footed as to escape me now.
Well, friend: your shape is not unhandsome—for the pursuit
Of women, which is the purpose of your presence here.   435
You are no wrestler, I can tell from these long curls
Cascading most seductively over your cheek.
Your skin, too, shows a whiteness carefully preserved;
You keep away from the sun's heat, walk in the shade,
So hunting Aphrodite with your lovely face.   440

Ah, well; first tell me who you are. What is your birth?
DIONYSUS   Your question's easily answered, it is no secret.
Perhaps you have heard of Tmolus, a mountain decked with flowers.
PENTHEUS   A range that curves round Sardis? Yes, I know of it.
DIONYSUS   That is my home. I am a Lydian by birth.   445
PENTHEUS   How comes it that you bring these rituals to Hellas?
DIONYSUS   Dionysus, son of Zeus, himself instructed me.
PENTHEUS   Is there a Lydian Zeus, then, who begets new gods?
DIONYSUS   I speak of Zeus who wedded Semele here in Thebes.
PENTHEUS   Did he possess you in a dream, or visibly?   450
DIONYSUS   Yes, face to face; he gave these mysteries to me.
PENTHEUS   These mysteries you speak of: what form do they take?
DIONYSUS   To the uninitiated that must not be told.
PENTHEUS   And those who worship—what advantage do they gain?
DIONYSUS   It is not for you to learn; yet it is worth knowing.   455
PENTHEUS   You bait your answer well, to arouse my eagerness.
DIONYSUS   His rituals abhor a man of impious life.
PENTHEUS   You say you saw him face to face: what was he like?
DIONYSUS   Such as he chose to be. I had no say in that.
PENTHEUS   Still you sidetrack my question with an empty phrase.   460
DIONYSUS   Just so. A prudent speech sleeps in a foolish ear.
PENTHEUS   Is Thebes the first place where you have introduced this
   god?
DIONYSUS   No; every eastern land dances these mysteries.
PENTHEUS   No doubt. Their moral standards fall far below ours.
DIONYSUS   In this they are superior; but their customs differ.   465
PENTHEUS   Do you perform these mysteries by night or day?
DIONYSUS   Chiefly by night. Darkness promotes religious awe.
PENTHEUS   For women darkness is deceptive and impure.
DIONYSUS   Impurity can be pursued by daylight too.
PENTHEUS   You must be punished for your foul and slippery tongue.   470
DIONYSUS   And you for blindness and impiety to the god.
PENTHEUS   How bold this Bacchant is! A practiced pleader too.
DIONYSUS   Tell me my sentence. What dread pain will you inflict?
PENTHEUS   I'll start by cutting of your delicate long hair.
DIONYSUS   My hair is sacred; I preserve it for the god.   475
PENTHEUS   And next, that thyrsus in your hand—give it to me.
DIONYSUS   Take it from me yourself; it is the god's emblem.

PENTHEUS   I'll lock you up in prison and keep you there.

DIONYSUS   The god
     Himself, whenever I desire, will set me free.

PENTHEUS   Of course—when you, with all your Bacchants, call to him! 480

DIONYSUS   He is close at hand here, and sees what is done to me.

PENTHEUS   Indeed? Where is he, then? Not visible to my eyes.

DIONYSUS   Beside me. You, being a blasphemer, see nothing.

PENTHEUS   [*to the* GUARDS]   Get hold of him; he's mocking me and the
     whole city.

DIONYSUS   [*to the* GUARDS]   Don't bind me, I warn you. [*To* PEN-
     THEUS.] I am sane, and you are mad.   485

PENTHEUS   My word overrules yours. [*To the* GUARDS.] I tell you, bind
     him fast.

DIONYSUS   You know not what you are saying, what you do, nor who
     You are.

PENTHEUS   Who? Pentheus, son of Echion and Agaüe.

DIONYSUS   Your name points to calamity. It fits you well.   490

PENTHEUS   Take him away and shut him in my stables, where
     He can stay staring at darkness.—You can dance in there!
     As for these women you've brought as your accomplices,
     I'll either send them to the slave-market to be sold,
     Or keep them in my own household to work the looms;   495
     And that will stop their fingers drumming on tambourines!

DIONYSUS   I'll go. Nothing can touch me that is not ordained.
     But I warn you: Dionysus, who you say is dead,
     Will come in swift pursuit to avenge this sacrilege.
     You are putting *him* in prison when you lay hands on me.   500

          GUARDS *take* DIONYSUS *away to the stables;* PENTHEUS *follows.*

CHORUS
     Dirce sweet and holy maid,[4]   *Strophe*
     Acheloüs' Theban daughter,
     Once the child of Zeus was made
     Welcome in your welling water,
     When the lord of earth and sky   505
     Snatched him from the undying flame,
     Laid him safe within his thigh,
     Calling loud the infant's name:
     "Twice-born Dithyrambus![5] Come,
     Enter here your father's womb;   510
     Bacchic child, I now proclaim
     This in Thebes shall be your name."
     Now, divine Dirce, when my head is crowned
     And my feet dance in Bacchus' revelry—
     Now you reject me from your holy ground.   515
     Why should you fear me? By the purple fruit
     That glows in glory on Dionysus' tree,
     His dread name yet shall haunt your memory!

4. The stream of Dirce in Thebes was associated with a queen of Thebes who was changed into a stream by Dionysus after she had mistreated her husband's niece and been killed by being tied to a bull by that lady's son. According to that legend she had been a worshipper of Dionysus and was changed therefore to a stream as a re-ward. Euripides here seems to be dealing with an earlier myth in which the river nymph Dirce, daughter of the river god Acheloüs, gave sanctuary to the infant Dionysus.
5. Dithyrambus (twice-born) was another name for Dionysus.

Oh, what anger lies beneath   *Antistrophe*
Pentheus' voice and sullen face—   520
Offspring of the dragon's teeth,
And Echion's earth-born race,
Brute with bloody jaws agape,
God-defying, gross and grim,
Slander of his human shape!   525
Soon he'll chain us limb to limb—
Bacchus' servants! Yes, and more:
Even now our comrade lies
Deep on his dark prison floor.
Dionysus! do your eyes   530
See us? O son of Zeus, the oppressor's rod
Falls on your worshippers; come, mighty god,
Brandish your golden thyrsus and descend
From great Olympus; touch this murderous man,
And bring his violence to a sudden end!   535

Where are you, Dionysus? Leading your dancing bands   *Epode*
Over the mountain slopes, past many a wild beast's lair,
Or on Corycian crags,[6] with the thyrsus in their hands?
Or in the wooded coverts, maybe, of Olympus, where
Orpheus once gathered the trees and mountain beasts,   540
Gathered them with his lyre, and sang an enchanting air.
Happy vale of Pieria! Bacchus delights in you;
He will cross the flood and foam of the Axius river, and there
He will bring his whirling Maenads, with dancing and with feasts—
Cross the father of waters, Lydias, generous giver   545
Of wealth and luck, they say, to the land he wanders through,
Whose famous horses graze by the rich and lovely river.

> *Suddenly a shout is heard from inside the building—the voice of* DIONYSUS.

DIONYSUS   Io, Io! Do you know my voice, do you hear?
   Worshippers of Bacchus! Io, Io![7]
CHORUS   Who is that? Where is he?   550
   The shout of Dionysus is calling us!
DIONYSUS   Io, Io! hear me again:
   I am the son of Semele, the son of Zeus!
CHORUS   Io, Io, our lord, our lord!
   Come, then, come to our company, lord of joy!   555
DIONYSUS   O dreadful earthquake, shake the floor of the world!
CHORUS [*with a scream of terror*]   Pentheus' palace is falling, crumbling
   in pieces! [*They continue severally.*]
   —Dionysus stands in the palace; bow before him!
   —We bow before him.—See how the roof and pillars
   Plunge to the ground!—Bromius is with us,   560
   He shouts from prison the shout of victory!

> *The flame on Semele's tomb grows and brightens.*

---

6. Corycia was a nymph associated with   meaning used by worshippers in praise or
Mt. Parnassus.   supplication.
7. "Io" was a cry of rather generalized

DIONYSUS   Fan to a blaze the flame the lightning lit;
  Kindle the conflagration of Pentheus' palace!
CHORUS   Look, look, look!
  Do you see, do you see the flame of Semele's tomb,   565
  The flame that lived when she died of the lightning-stroke?

  A noise of crashing masonry is heard.

  Down, trembling Maenads! Hurl yourselves to the ground.
  Your god is wrecking the palace, roof to floor;
  He heard our cry—he is coming, the son of Zeus!

  The doors open and DIONYSUS *appears.*

DIONYSUS   Women of Asia, why do you cower thus, prostrate and
    terrified?   570
  Surely you could hear Dionysus shattering Pentheus' palace? Come,
  Lift yourselves up, take good courage, stop this trembling of your
    limbs!
CHORUS   We are saved! Oh, what a joy to hear your Bacchic call ring
    out!
  We were all alone, deserted; you have come, and we rejoice.
DIONYSUS   Were you comfortless, despondent, when I was escorted in,   575
  Helpless, sentenced to be cast in Pentheus' murky prison cell?
CHORUS   Who could help it? What protector had we, once deprived
    of you?
  Tell us now how you escaped the clutches of this wicked man.
DIONYSUS   I alone, at once, unaided, effortlessly freed myself.
CHORUS   How could that be? Did not Pentheus bind your arms with
    knotted ropes?   580
DIONYSUS   There I made a mockery of him. He thought he was bind-
    ing me;
  But he neither held nor touched me, save in his deluded mind.
  Near the mangers where he meant to tie me up, he found a bull;
  And he tied his rope round the bull's knees and hooves, panting with
    rage,
  Dripping sweat, biting his lips, while I sat quietly by and watched. 585
  It was then that Dionysus shook the building, made the flame
  On his mother's tomb flare up. When Pentheus saw this, he supposed
  The whole place was burning. He rushed this way, that way, calling
    out
  To the servants to bring water; every slave about the place
  Was engaged upon this futile task. He left it presently,   590
  Thinking I had escaped; snatched up his murderous sword, darted
    indoors.
  Thereupon Dionysus—as it seemed to me; I merely guess—
  Made a phantom hover in the courtyard. Pentheus flew at it,
  Stabbing at the empty sunlight, thinking he was killing *me*.
  Yet a further humiliation Bacchus next contrived for him: 595
  He destroyed the stable buildings. Pentheus sees my prison now
  Lying there, a heap of rubble; and the picture grieves his heart.
  Now he's dazed and helpless with exhaustion. He has dropped his
    sword.
  He, a man, dared to take arms against a god. I quietly walked
  Out of the palace here to join you, giving Pentheus not a thought.   600
  But I hear his heavy tread inside the palace. Soon, I think,

He'll be out here in the forecourt. After what has happened now,
What will he have to say? For all his rage, he shall not ruffle *me*.
It's a wise man's part to practice a smooth-tempered self-control.

Enter PENTHEUS.

PENTHEUS   This is outrageous. He has escaped—that foreigner.   605
Only just now I had him locked up and in chains.

He sees DIONYSUS *and gives an excited shout.*

He's there! Well, what's going on now? How did you get out?
How dare you show your face here at my very door?
DIONYSUS   Stay where you are. You àre angry; now control yourself.
PENTHEUS   You were tied up inside there. How did you escape?   610
DIONYSUS   I said—did you not hear?—that I should be set free—
PENTHEUS   By whom? You're always finding something new to say.
DIONYSUS   By him who plants for mortals the rich-clustered vine.
PENTHEUS   The god who frees his worshippers from every law.
DIONYSUS   Your insult to Dionysus is a compliment.   615
PENTHEUS   [*to attendant* GUARDS]   Go round the walls and tell them to
close every gate.
DIONYSUS   And why? Or cannot gods pass even over walls?
PENTHEUS   Oh, you know everything—save what you ought to know.
DIONYSUS   The things most needful to be known, those things I know.
But listen first to what this man has to report;   620
He comes from the mountain, and he has some news for you.
I will stay here; I promise not to run away.

Enter a HERDSMAN.

HERDSMAN   Pentheus, great king of Thebes! I come from Mount
Cithaeron,
Whose slopes are never free from dazzling shafts of snow.
PENTHEUS   And what comes next? What urgent message do you bring?   625
HERDSMAN   I have seen the holy Bacchae, who like a flight of spears
Went streaming bare-limbed, frantic, out of the city gate.
I have come with the intention of telling you, my lord,
And the city, of their strange and terrible doings—things
Beyond all wonder. But first I would learn whether   630
I may speak freely of what is going on there, or
If I should trim my words. I fear your hastiness,
My lord, your anger, your too potent royalty.
PENTHEUS   From me fear nothing. Say all that you have to say;
Anger should not grow hot against the innocent.   635
The more dreadful your story of these Bacchic rites,
The heavier punishment I will inflict upon
This man who enticed our women to their evil ways.
HERDSMAN   At dawn today, when first the sun's rays warmed the earth,
My herd of cattle was slowly climbing up toward   640
The high pastures; and there I saw three separate
Companies of women. The leader of one company
Was Autonoe; your mother Agauë was at the head
Of the second, Ino of the third; and they all lay
Relaxed and quietly sleeping. Some rested on beds   645
Of pine-needles, others had pillows of oak-leaves.
They lay just as they had thrown themselves down on the ground,

But modestly, not—as you told us—drunk with wine
Or flute-music, seeking the solitary woods
For the pursuit of love.   650
When your mother Agaüe
Heard the horned cattle bellowing, she stood upright
Among the Bacchae, and called to them to stir themselves
From sleep; and they shook off the strong sleep from their eyes
And leaped to their feet. They were a sight to marvel at   655
For modest comeliness; women both old and young,
Girls still unmarried. First they let their hair fall free
Over their shoulders; some tied up the fastenings
Of fawnskins they had loosened; round the dappled fur
Curled snakes that licked their cheeks. Some would have in their arms 660
A young gazelle, or wild wolf-cubs, to which they gave
Their own white milk—those of them who had left at home
Young children newly born, so that their breasts were full.
And they wore wreaths of ivy-leaves, or oak, or flowers
Of bryony. One would strike her thyrsus on a rock,   665
And from the rock a limpid stream of water sprang.
Another dug her wand into the earth, and there
The god sent up a fountain of wine. Those who desired
Milk had only to scratch the earth with fingertips,
And there was the white stream flowing for them to drink,   670
While from the thyrsus a sweet ooze of honey dripped.
Oh! if you had been there and seen all this, you would
Have offered prayers to this god whom you now condemn.
We herdsmen, then, and shepherds gathered to exchange
Rival reports of these strange and extraordinary   675
Performances; and one, who had knocked about the town,
And had a ready tongue, addressed us: "You who live
On the holy mountain heights," he said, "shall we hunt down
Agaüe, Pentheus' mother, and bring her back from these
Rituals, and gratify the king? What do you say?"   680
This seemed a good suggestion; so we hid ourselves
In the leafy bushes, waiting. When the set time came,
The women began brandishing their wands, preparing
To dance, calling in unison on the son of Zeus,
"Iacchus! Bromius!"[8] And with them the whole mountain,   685
And all the creatures there, joined in the mystic rite
Of Dionysus, and with their motion all things moved.

Now, Agaüe as she danced passed close to me; and I
At once leaped out from hiding, bent on capturing her.
But she called out, "Oh, my swift-footed hounds, these men   690
Are hunting us. Come, follow me! Each one of you
Arm herself with the holy thyrsus, and follow me!"

So we fled, and escaped being torn in pieces by
Those possessed women. But our cattle were there, cropping
The fresh grass; and the women attacked them, with their bare
    hands.   695
You could see one take a full-uddered bellowing young heifer

8. "Iacchus" and "Bromius" were names of Dionysus.

And hold it by the legs with her two arms stretched wide;
Others seized on our cows and tore them limb from limb;
You'd see some ribs, or a cleft hoof, tossed high and low;
And rags of flesh hung from pine-branches, dripping blood.   700
Bulls, which one moment felt proud rage hot in their horns,
The next were thrown bodily to the ground, dragged down
By hands of girls in thousands; and they stripped the flesh
From the bodies faster than you could wink your royal eyes.
Then, skimming bird-like over the surface of the ground,   705
They scoured the plain which stretches by Asopus' banks
And yields rich crops for Thebes; and like an enemy force
They fell on Hysiae and Erythrae, two villages
On the low slopes of Cithaeron, and ransacked them both;
Snatched babies out of the houses; any plunder which   710
They carried on their shoulders stayed there without straps—
Nothing fell to the ground, not bronze or iron; they carried
Fire on their heads, and yet their soft hair was not burned.
The villagers, enraged at being so plundered, armed
Themselves to resist; and then, my lord, an amazing sight   715
Was to be seen. The spears those men were throwing drew
No blood; but the women, hurling a thyrsus like a spear,
Dealt wounds; in short, those women turned the men to flight.
There was the power of a god in that. Then they went back
To the place where they had started from, to those fountains   720
The god had caused to flow for them. And they washed off
The blood; and snakes licked clean the stains, till their cheeks shone.

So, master, whoever this divinity may be,
Receive him in this land. His powers are manifold;
But chiefly, as I hear, he gave to men the vine   725
To cure their sorrows, and without wine, neither love
Nor any other pleasure would be left for us.
CHORUS   I shrink from speaking freely before the king; yet I
Will say it: there is no greater god than Dionysus.
PENTHEUS   This Bacchic arrogance advances on us like   730
A spreading fire, disgracing us before all Hellas.
We must act now. [*To the* HERDSMAN.] Go quickly to the Electran
gate;[9]
Tell all my men who carry shields, heavy or light,
All riders on fast horses, all my archers with
Their twanging bows, to meet me there in readiness   735
For an onslaught on these maniacs. This is beyond
All bearing, if we must let women so defy us.
DIONYSUS   You refuse, Pentheus, to give heed to what I say
Or change your ways. Yet still, despite your wrongs to me,
I warn you: stay here quietly; do not take up arms   740
Against a god. Dionysus will not tolerate
Attempts to drive his worshippers from their holy hills.
PENTHEUS   I'll not have you instruct me. You have escaped your
chains;
Now be content—or must I punish you again?
DIONYSUS   I would control my rage and sacrifice to him   745

9. One of the seven gates of Thebes.

If I were you, rather than kick against the goad.
Can you, a mortal, measure your strength with a god's?
PENTHEUS   I'll sacrifice, yes—blood of women, massacred
Wholesale, as they deserve, among Cithaeron's glens.
DIONYSUS   Your army will be put to flight. What a disgrace   750
For bronze shields to be routed by those women's wands!
PENTHEUS   How can I deal with this impossible foreigner?
In prison or out, nothing will make him hold his tongue.
DIONYSUS   My friend, a happy settlement may still be found.
PENTHEUS   How? must I be a slave to my own slave-women?   755
DIONYSUS   I will, using no weapons, bring those women here.
PENTHEUS   Hear that, for the gods' sake! You're playing me some trick.
DIONYSUS   What trick?—if I am ready to save you by my skill.
PENTHEUS   You've planned this with them, so that the rituals can go
on.
DIONYSUS   Indeed I have planned this—not with them, but with the
god.   760
PENTHESUS   Bring out my armor, there!—That is enough from you.
DIONYSUS [*with an authoritative shout*]   Wait! [*Then quietly.*] Do you
want *to see*
Those women, where they sit together, up in the hills?
PENTHEUS   Why, yes; for that, I'd give a weighty sum of gold.
DIONYSUS   What made you fall into this great desire to see?   765
PENTHEUS   It would cause me distress to see them drunk with wine.
DIONYSUS   Yet you would gladly witness this distressing sight?
PENTHEUS   Of course—if I could quietly sit under the pines.
DIONYSUS   They'll track you down, even if you go there secretly.
PENTHEUS   Openly, then. Yes, what you say is very true.   770
DIONYSUS   Then shall I lead you? You will undertake to go?
PENTHEUS   Yes, lead me there at once; I am impatient.
DIONYSUS   Then,
You must first dress yourself in a fine linen gown.
PENTHEUS   Why in a linen gown? Must I then change my sex?   775
DIONYSUS   In case they kill you, if you are seen there as a man.
PENTHEUS   Again you are quite right. How you think of everything!
DIONYSUS   It was Dionysus who inspired me with that thought.
PENTHEUS   Then how can your suggestion best be carried out?
DIONYSUS   I'll come indoors with you myself and dress you.   780
PENTHEUS   What?
Dress me? In woman's clothes? But I would be ashamed.
DIONYSUS   Do you want to watch the Maenads? Are you less eager
now?
PENTHEUS   What kind of dress did you say you would put on me?
DIONYSUS   First I'll adorn your head with locks of flowing hair.   785
PENTHEUS   And after that? What style of costume shall I have?
DIONYSUS   A full-length robe; and on your head shall be a snood.
PENTHEUS   Besides these, is there anything else you'll put on me?
DIONYSUS   A dappled fawnskin round you, a thyrsus in your hand.
PENTHEUS   I could not bear to dress myself in woman's clothes.   790
DIONYSUS   If you join battle with the Maenads, blood will flow.
PENTHEUS   You are right; I must first go to spy on them.
DIONYSUS   That way
Is better than inviting force by using it.
PENTHEUS   And how shall I get through the town without being seen? 795

DIONYSUS   We'll go by empty streets; I will show you the way.
PENTHEUS   The Maenads must not mock me; better anything
   Than that. Now I'll go in, and think how best to act.
DIONYSUS   You may do so. My preparations are all made.
PENTHEUS   I'll go in, then; and either I'll set forth at the head   800
   Of my armed men—or else I'll follow your advice.

Exit PENTHEUS.

DIONYSUS   Women, this man is walking into the net. He will
   Visit the Bacchae; and there death shall punish him.

Dionysus!—for you are not far distant—all is now
In your hands. Let us be revenged on him! And first   805
Fill him with wild delusions, drive him out of his mind.
While sane, he'll not consent to put on woman's clothes;
Once free from the curb of reason, he will put them on.
I long to set Thebes laughing at him, as he walks
In female garb through all the streets; to humble him   810
From the arrogance he showed when first he threatened me.
Now I will go, to array Pentheus in the dress
Which he will take down with him to the house of Death,
Slaughtered by his own mother's hands. And he shall know
Dionysus, son of Zeus, in his full nature God,   815
Most terrible, although most gentle, to mankind.

   DIONYSUS *follows* PENTHEUS *into the palace.*

CHORUS
   O for long nights of worship, gay   *Strophe*
   With the pale gleam of dancing feet,
   With head tossed high to the dewy air—
   Pleasure mysterious and sweet!   820
   O for the joy of a fawn at play
   In the fragrant meadow's green delight,
   Who has leaped out free from the woven snare,
   Away from the terror of chase and flight,
   And the huntsman's shout, and the straining pack,   825
   And skims the sand by the river's brim
   With the speed of wind in each aching limb,
   To the blessed lonely forest where
   The soil's unmarked by a human track,
   And leaves hang thick and the shades are dim.   830

   What prayer should we call wise?   *Refrain*
   What gift of Heaven should man
   Count a more noble prize,
   A prayer more prudent, than
   To stretch a conquering arm   835
   Over the fallen crest
   Of those who wished us harm?
   And what is noble every heart loves best.

   Slow, yet unfailing, move the Powers   *Antistrophe*
   Of Heaven with the moving hours.   840
   When mind runs mad, dishonors God,

And worships self and senseless pride,
Then Law eternal wields the rod.
Still Heaven hunts down the impious man,
Though divine subtlety may hide   845
Time's creeping foot. No mortal ought
To challenge Time—to overbear
Custom in act, or age in thought.
All men, at little cost, may share
The blessing of a pious creed;   850
Truths more than mortal, which began
In the beginning, and belong
To very nature—these indeed
Reign in our world, are fixed and strong.

What prayer should we call wise?   *Refrain* 855
What gift of Heaven should man
Count a more noble prize,
A prayer more prudent, than
To stretch a conquering arm
Over the fallen crest   860
Of those who wished us harm?
And what is noble every heart loves best.

Blest is the man who cheats the stormy sea   *Epode*
And safely moors beside the sheltering quay;
So, blest is he who triumphs over trial.   865
One man, by various means, in wealth or strength
Outdoes his neighbor; hope in a thousand hearts
Colors a thousand different dreams; at length
Some find a dear fulfillment, some denial.
    But this I say,   870
    That he who best
    Enjoys each passing day
    Is truly blest.

    Enter DIONYSUS. *He turns to call* PENTHEUS.

DIONYSUS   Come, perverse man, greedy for sights you should not see,
  Eager for deeds you should not do—Pentheus! Come out   875
Before the palace and show yourself to me, wearing
The garb of a frenzied Bacchic woman, and prepared
To spy on your mother and all her Bacchic company.

    Enter PENTHEUS *dressed as a Bacchic devotee. He is dazed and
    entirely subservient to* DIONYSUS.

You are the very image of one of Cadmus' daughters.
PENTHEUS   Why now! I seem to see two suns; a double Thebes;   880
Our city's wall with seven gates appears double.

    DIONYSUS *takes* PENTHEUS *by the hand and leads him forward.*

You are a bull I see leading me forward now;
A pair of horns seems to have grown upon your head.
Were you a beast before? You have become a bull.

DIONYSUS   The god then did not favor us; he is with us now,   885
We have made our peace with him; you see as you should see.
PENTHEUS   How do I look? Tell me, is not the way I stand
Like the way Ino stands, or like my mother Agauë?
DIONYSUS   Looking at you, I think I see them both. Wait, now;
Here is a curl has slipped out of its proper place,   890
Not as I tucked it carefully below your snood.
PENTHEUS   Indoors, as I was tossing my head up and down
Like a Bacchic dancer, I dislodged it from its place.
DIONYSUS   Come, then; I am the one who should look after you.
I'll fix it in its place again. There; lift your head.   895
PENTHEUS   You dress me, please; I have put myself in your hands now.
DIONYSUS   Your girdle has come loose; and now your dress does not
Hang, as it should, in even pleats down to the ankle.
PENTHEUS   That's true, I think—at least by the right leg, on this side;
But on the other side the gown hangs well to the heel.   900
DIONYSUS   You'll surely count me chief among your friends, when you
Witness the Maenads' unexpected modesty.
PENTHEUS   Ought I to hold my thyrsus in the right hand—so,
Or in the left, to look more like a Bacchanal?
DIONYSUS   In the right hand; and raise it at the same time as   905
Your right foot. I am glad you are so changed in mind.
PENTHEUS   Could I lift up on my own shoulders the whole weight
Of Mount Cithaeron, and all the women dancing there?
DIONYSUS   You could, if you so wished. The mind you had before
Was sickly; now your mind is just as it should be.   910
PENTHEUS   Shall we take crowbars? Or shall I put my shoulder under
The rocks, and heave the mountain up with my two arms?
DIONYSUS   Oh, come, now! Don't destroy the dwellings of the nymphs,
And the quiet places where Pan sits to play his pipes.
PENTHEUS   You are right. We ought not to use force to overcome   915
Those women. I will hide myself among the pines.
DIONYSUS   Hide—yes, you'll hide, and find the proper hiding place
For one who comes by stealth to spy on Bacchic rites.
PENTHEUS   Why, yes! I think they are there now in their hidden nests,
Like birds, all clasped close in the sweet prison of love.   920
DIONYSUS   What you are going to watch for is this very thing!
Perhaps you will catch them—if you are not first caught yourself.
PENTHEUS   Now take me through the central streets of Thebes; for I
Am the one man among them all that dares do this.
DIONYSUS   One man alone, you agonize for Thebes; therefore   925
It is your destined ordeal that awaits you now.
Come with me; I will bring you safely to the place;
Another shall conduct you back.
PENTHEUS   My mother—yes?
DIONYSUS   A sight for all to witness.   930
PENTHEUS   To this end I go.
DIONYSUS   You will return borne high—
PENTHEUS   Royal magnificence!
DIONYSUS   In your own mother's arms.
PENTHEUS   You insist that I be spoiled.   935
DIONYSUS   One kind of spoiling.
PENTHEUS   Yet I win what I deserve.

Exit PENTHEUS.

DIONYSUS   Pentheus, you are a man to make men fear; fearful
Will be your end—an end that shall lift up your fame
To the height of heaven.   940
Agauë, and you her sisters, daughters of Cadmus,
Stretch out your hands! See, I am bringing this young man
To his great battle; and I and Bromius shall be
Victors. What more shall happen, the event will show.

Exit DIONYSUS.

CHORUS
Hounds of Madness, fly to the mountain, fly   *Strophe* 945
Where Cadmus' daughters are dancing in ecstasy!
Madden them like a frenzied herd stampeding,
Against the madman hiding in woman's clothes
To spy on the Maenad's rapture!
First his mother shall see him craning his neck   950
Down from a rounded rock or a sharp crag,
And shout to the Maenads, "Who is the man, you Bacchae,
Who has come to the mountain, come to the mountain spying
On the swift wild mountain dances of Cadmus' daughters?
Which of you is his mother?   955
No, that lad never lay in a woman's womb;
A lioness gave him suck, or a Libyan Gorgon!"[1]

Justice, now be revealed! Now let your sword   *Refrain*
Thrust—through and through—to sever the throat
Of the godless, lawless, shameless son of Echion,   960
Who sprang from the womb of Earth!

See! With contempt of right, with a reckless rage   *Antistrophe*
To combat your and your mother's mysteries, Bacchus,
With maniac fury out he goes, stark mad,
For a trial of strength against *your* invincible arm!   965
His proud purposes death shall discipline.
He who unquestioning gives the gods their due,
And knows that his days are as dust, shall live untouched.
I have no wish to grudge the wise their wisdom;
But the joys *I* seek are greater, outshine all others,   970
And lead our life to goodness and loveliness:
The joy of the holy heart
That night and day is bent to honor the gods
And disown all custom that breaks the bounds of right.

Justice, now be revealed! Now let your sword   *Refrain* 975
Thrust—through and through—to sever the throat
Of the godless, lawless, shameless son of Echion,
Who sprang from the womb of Earth!

*Then with growing excitement, shouting in unison, and dancing
to the rhythm of their words.*

1. The Gorgons were three monstrous sisters who had live snakes on their heads instead
of hair. Their other features were hardly more beautiful, and they were therefore believed
to be capable of turning to stone anyone who gazed on them. One of them, Medusa, was
slain by the hero Perseus.

Come, Dionysus!   *Epode*
Come, and appear to us!   980
Come like a bull or a
Hundred-headed serpent,
Come like a lion snorting
Flame from your nostrils!
Swoop down, Bacchus, on the   985
Hunter of the Bacchae;
Smile at him and snare him;
Then let the stampeding
Herd of the Maenads
Throw him and throttle him,   990
Catch, trip, trample him to death!

Enter a MESSENGER.

MESSENGER   O house that once shone glorious throughout Hellas, home
Of the old Sidonian king who planted in this soil
The dragon's earth-born harvest! How I weep for you!
Slave though I am, I suffer with my master's fate.   995
CHORUS   Are you from the mountain, from the Bacchic rites? What
news?
MESSENGER   Pentheus, son of Echion, is dead.
CHORUS   Bromius, lord! Your divine power is revealed!
MESSENGER   What, woman? What was that you said? Do you exult
When such a cruel fate has overtaken the king?   1000
CHORUS   I am no Greek.
I sing my joy in a foreign tune.
Not any more do I cower in terror of prison!
MESSENGER   Do you think Thebes has no men left who can take com-
mand?
CHORUS   Dionysus commands *me;*   1005
Not Thebes, but Dionysus.
MESSENGER   Allowance must be made for you; yet, to rejoice
At the accomplishment of horrors is not right.
CHORUS   Tell us everything, then: this tyrant king
Bent on cruelty—how did he die?   1010
MESSENGER   When we had left behind the outlying parts of Thebes
And crossed the river Asopus, we began to climb
Toward the uplands of Cithaeron, Pentheus and I—
I went as his attendant—and the foreigner
Who was our guide to the spectacle we were to see.   1015
Well, first we sat down in a grassy glade. We kept
Our footsteps and our talk as quiet as possible,
So as to see without being seen. We found ourselves
In a valley full of streams, with cliffs on either side.
There, under the close shade of branching pines, the Maenads   1020
Were sitting, their hands busy at their happy tasks;
Some of them twining a fresh crown of ivy-leaves
For a stripped thyrsus; others, gay as fillies loosed
From painted yokes, were singing holy Bacchic songs,
Each answering other. But the ill-fated Pentheus saw   1025
None of this; and he said, "My friend, from where we stand
My eyes cannot make out these so-called worshippers;
But if I climbed a towering pine-tree on the cliff

I would have a clear view of their shameful practices."
And then I saw that foreigner do an amazing thing.   1030
He took hold of a pine-tree's soaring, topmost branch,
And dragged it down, down, down to the dark earth. It was bent
In a circle as a bow is bent, as a wheel's curve,
Drawn with a compass, bends the rim to its own shape;
The foreigner took that mountain pine in his two hands   1035
And bent it down—a thing no mortal man could do.
Then seating Pentheus on a high branch, he began
To let the tree spring upright, slipping it through his hands
Steadily, taking care he should not be flung off.
The pine trunk, straightened, soared into the soaring sky,   1040
Bearing my master seated astride, so that he was
More visible to the Maenads than they were to him.
He was just coming into view on his high perch
When out of the sky a voice—Dionysus, I suppose;
That foreigner was nowhere to be seen—pealed forth: 1045
"Women, here is the man who made a mock of you,
And me, and of my holy rites. Now punish him."
And in the very moment the voice spoke, a flash
Of dreadful fire stretched between earth and high heaven.

The air fell still. The wooded glade held every leaf   1050
Still. You could hear no cry of any beast. The women,
Not having caught distinctly what the voice uttered,
Stood up and gazed around. Then came a second word
Of command. As soon as Cadmus' daughters recognized
The clear bidding of Bacchus, with the speed of doves   1055
They darted forward, and all the Bacchae after them.
Through the torrent-filled valley, over the rocks, possessed
By the very breath of Bacchus they went leaping on.
Then, when they saw my master crouched high in the pine,
At first they climbed the cliff which towered opposite,   1060
And violently flung at him pieces of rocks, or boughs
Of pine trees which they hurled as javelins; and some
Aimed with the thyrsus; through the high air all around
Their wretched target missiles flew. Yet every aim
Fell short, the tree's height baffled all their eagerness;   1065
While Pentheus, helpless in this pitiful trap, sat there.
Then, with a force like lightning, they tore down branches
Of oak, and with these tried to prize up the tree's roots.
When all their struggles met with no success, Agauë
Cried out, "Come, Maenads, stand in a circle round the tree   1070
And take hold of it. We must catch this climbing beast,
Or he'll disclose the secret dances of Dionysus."
They came; a thousand hands gripped on the pine and tore it
Out of the ground. Then from his high perch plunging, crashing
To the earth Pentheus fell, with one incessant scream   1075
As he understood what end was near.

His mother first,
As priestess, led the rite of death, and fell upon him.
He tore the headband from his hair, that his wretched mother
Might recognize him and not kill him. "Mother," he cried,   1080

Touching her cheek, "it is I, your own son Pentheus, whom
You bore to Echion. Mother, have mercy; I have sinned,
But I am still your own son. Do not take my life!"

Agauë was foaming at the mouth; her rolling eyes
Were wild, she was not in her right mind, but possessed   1085
By Bacchus, and she paid no heed to him. She grasped
His right arm between wrist and elbow, set her foot
Against his ribs, and tore his arm off by the shoulder.
It was no strength of hers that did it, but the god
Filled her, and made it easy. On the other side   1090
Ino was at him, tearing at his flesh; and now
Autonoe joined them, and the whole maniacal horde.
A single and continuous yell arose—Pentheus
Shrieking as long as life was left in him, the women
Howling in triumph. One of them carried off an arm,   1095
Another a foot, the boot still laced on it. The ribs
Were stripped, clawed clean; and women's hands, thick red with
      blood,
Were tossing, catching, like a plaything, Pentheus' flesh.
His body lies—no easy task to find—scattered
Under hard rocks, or in the green woods. His poor head—   1100
His mother carries it, fixed on her thyrsus-point,
Openly over Cithaeron's pastures, thinking it
The head of a young mountain lion. She has left her sisters
Dancing among the Maenads, and herself comes here
Inside the walls, exulting in her hideous prey,   1105
Shouting to Bacchus, calling him her fellow hunter,
Her partner in the kill, comrade in victory.
But Bacchus gives her bitter tears for her reward.

Now I will go. I must find some place far away
From this horror, before Agauë returns home.   1110
A sound and humble heart that reverences the gods
Is man's noblest possession; and the same virtue
Is wisest too, I think, for those who practice it.

                                   Exit the MESSENGER.

CHORUS
Let us dance a dance to Bacchus, shout and sing
For the fall of Pentheus, heir of the dragon's seed,   1115
Who hid his beard in a woman's gown,
And sealed his death with the holy sign
Of ivy wreathing a fennel reed,
When bull led man to the ritual slaughter ring.
Frenzied daughters of Cadmus, what renown   1120
Your victory wins you—such a song
As groans must stifle, tears must drown!

Emblem of conquest, brave and fine!
A mother's hand, defiled
With blood and dripping red   1125
Caresses the torn head
Of her own murdered child!

But look! I see her—there, running toward the palace—
Agauë, Pentheus' mother, her eyes wildly rolling.
Come, welcome them—Dionysus' holy company.   1130

> AGAUË *appears, frenzied and panting, with* PENTHEUS' *head held
> in her hand. The rest of her band of devotees, whom the* CHORUS
> *saw approaching with her, do not enter; but a few are seen
> standing by the entrance, where they wait until the end of
> the play.*

AGAUË   Women of Asia! Worshippers of Bacchus!

> AGAUË *tries to show them* PENTHEUS' *head; they shrink from it.*

CHORUS   Why do you urge me? Oh!
AGAUË   I am bringing home from the mountains
A vine branch freshly cut,
For the gods have blessed our hunting.   1135
CHORUS   We see it . . . and welcome you in fellowship.
AGAUË   I caught him without a trap,
A lion cub, young and wild.
Look, you may see him—there!
CHORUS   Where was it?   1140
AGAUË   On Cithaeron;
The wild and empty mountain—
CHORUS   Cithaeron!
AGAUË   . . . spilled his life-blood.
CHORUS   Who shot him?   1145
AGAUË   I was first;
All the women are singing,
"Honor to great Agauë!"
CHORUS   And then—who next?
AGAUË   Why, Cadmus' . . .   1150
CHORUS   What—Cadmus?
AGAUË   Yes, his daughters—
But after me, after me—
Laid their hands to the kill.
Today was a splendid hunt!   1155
Come now, join in the feast!
CHORUS   What, wretched woman? *Feast?*
AGAUË   [*tenderly stroking the head as she holds it*] This calf is young:
how thickly
The new-grown hair goes crisping
Up to his delicate crest!   1160
CHORUS   Indeed, his long hair makes him
Look like some wild creature.
AGAUË   The god is a skilled hunter;
And he poised his hunting women,
And hurled them at the quarry.   1165
CHORUS   True, our god is a hunter.
AGAUË   Do you praise me?
CHORUS   Yes, we praise you.
AGAUË   So will the sons of Cadmus . . .
CHORUS   And Pentheus too, Agauë?   1170
AGAUË   Yes, he will praise his mother
For the lion cub she killed.

CHORUS   Oh, fearful!
AGAUË   Ay, fearful!
CHORUS   You are happy? 1175
AGAUË   I am enraptured;
    Great in the eyes of the world,
    Great are the deeds I've done,
    And the hunt that I hunted there!
CHORUS   Then show it, poor Agauë—this triumphant spoil 1180
    You've brought home; show it to all the citizens of Thebes.
AGAUË   Come, all you Thebans living within these towered walls,
    Come, see the beast we, Cadmus' daughters, caught and killed;
    Caught not with nets or thonged Thessalian[2] javelins,
    But with our own bare arms and fingers. After this 1185
    Should huntsmen glory in their exploits, who must buy
    Their needless tools from armorers? We with our hands
    Hunted and took this beast, then tore it limb from limb.

    Where is my father? Let old Cadmus come. And where
    Is my son Pentheus? Let him climb a strong ladder 1190
    And nail up on the cornice of the palace wall
    This lion's head that I have hunted and brought home.

       Enter CADMUS *with attendants bearing the body of* PENTHEUS.

CADMUS   Come, men, bring your sad burden that was Pentheus. Come,
    Set him at his own door. By weary, endless search
    I found his body's remnants scattered far and wide 1195
    About Cithaeron's glens, or hidden in thick woods.
    I gathered them and brought them here.

       I had already
    Returned with old Teiresias from the Bacchic dance,
    And was inside the walls, when news was brought me of 1200
    My daughters' terrible deed. I turned straight back; and now
    Return, bringing my grandson, whom the Maenads killed.
    I saw Autonoe, who bore Actaeon to Aristaeus,
    And Ino with her, there among the trees, still rapt
    In their unhappy frenzy; but I understood 1205
    That Agauë had come dancing on her way to Thebes—
    And there indeed she is, a sight for misery!
AGAUË   Father! Now you may boast as loudly as you will
    That you have sired the noblest daughters of this age!
    I speak of all three, but myself especially. 1210
    I have left weaving at the loom for greater things,
    For hunting wild beasts with my bare hands. See this prize,
    Here in my arms; I won it, and it shall be hung
    On your palace wall. There, father, take it in your hands.
    Be proud of my hunting; call your friends to a feast; let them 1215
    Bless you and envy you for the splendor of my deed.
CADMUS   Oh, misery unmeasured, sight intolerable!
    Oh, bloody deed enacted by most pitiful hands!
    What noble prize is this you lay at the gods' feet,

---

2. Thessaly is the northeastern section of the Greek peninsula, just south of Macedonia.
It was regarded as less civilized than the other sections of Greece.

Calling the city, and me, to a banquet? Your wretchedness   1220
Demands the bitterest tears; but mine is next to yours.
Dionysus has dealt justly, but pursued justice
Too far; born of my blood, he has destroyed my house.

AGAUË   What an ill-tempered creature an old man is! How full
Of scowls! I wish my son were a great hunter like   1225
His mother, hunting beasts with the young men of Thebes;
But *he* can only fight with gods. Father, you must
Correct him.—Will not someone go and call him here
To see me, and to share in my great happiness?

CADMUS   Alas, my daughters! If you come to understand   1230
What you have done, how terrible your pain will be!
If you remain as you are now, though you could not
Be happy, at least you will not feel your wretchedness.

AGAUË   Why not happy? What cause have I for wretchedness?

CADMUS   Come here. First turn your eyes this way. Look at the sky.   1235

AGAUË   I am looking. Why should you want me to look at it?

CADMUS   Does it appear the same to you, or is it changed?

AGAUË   Yes, it is clearer than before, more luminous.

CADMUS   And this disturbance of your mind—is it still there?

AGAUË   I don't know what you mean; but—yes, I feel a change;   1240
My mind is somehow clearer than it was before.

CADMUS   Could you now listen to me and give a clear reply?

AGAUË   Yes, father. I have forgotten what we said just now.

CADMUS   When you were married, whose house did you go to then?

AGAUË   You gave me to Echion, of the sown race, they said.   1245

CADMUS   Echion had a son born to him. Who was he?

AGAUË   Pentheus. His father lay with me; I bore a son.

CADMUS   Yes; and whose head is that you are holding in your arms?

AGAUË   A lion's—so the women said who hunted it.

CADMUS   Then look straight at it. Come, to look is no great task.   1250

AGAUË *looks; and suddenly screams.*

AGAUË   What am I looking at? What is this in my hands?

CADMUS   Look at it steadily; come closer to the truth.

AGAUË   I see—O gods, what horror! Oh, what misery!

CADMUS   Does this appear to you to be a lion's head?

AGAUË   No! I hold Pentheus' head in my accursed hand.   1255

CADMUS   It is so. Tears have been shed for him, before you knew.

AGAUË   But who killed him? How did he come into my hands?

CADMUS   O cruel hour that brings a bitter truth to light!

AGAUË   Tell me—my heart is bursting, I must know the rest.

CADMUS   It was you, Agauë, and your sisters. You killed him.   1260

AGAUË   Where was it done? Here in the palace? Or where else?

CADMUS   Where, long ago, Actaeon was devoured by hounds.

AGAUË   Cithaeron. But what evil fate took Pentheus there?

CADMUS   He went to mock Dionysus and your Bacchic rites.

AGAUË   Why were we on Cithaeron? What had brought us there?   1265

CADMUS   You were possessed. All Thebes was in a Bacchic trance.

AGAUË   Dionysus has destroyed us. Now I understand.

CADMUS   He was insulted. You refused to call him god.

AGAUË   Father, where is the beloved body of my son?

CADMUS   Here. It was I who brought it, after painful search.   1270

AGAUË   And are his limbs now decently composed?

CADMUS   Not yet.
We came back to the city with all possible haste.
AGAUË   How could I touch his body with these guilty hands?
CADMUS   Your guilt, my daughter, was not heavier than his.   1275
AGAUË   What part did Pentheus have, then, in my insanity?
CADMUS   He sinned like you, refusing reverence to a god.
Therefore the god has joined all in one ruin—you,
Your sisters, Pentheus—to destroy my house and me.
I have no son; and now, my unhappy child, I see   1280
This son of yours dead by a shameful, hideous death.
You were the new hope of our house, its bond of strength,
Dear grandson. And Thebes feared you; no one dared insult
Your old grandfather if he saw you near; you would
Teach him his lesson. But now I shall live exiled,   1285
Dishonored—I, Cadmus the great, who planted here,
And reaped, that glorious harvest of the Theban race.

O dearest son—yes, even in death you shall be held
Most dear—you will never touch my beard again, and call
Me Grandfather, and put your arm round me and say,   1290
"Who has wronged you or insulted you? Who is unkind,
Or vexes or disturbs you? Tell me, Grandfather,
That I may punish him." Never again. For me
All that remains is pain; for you, the pity of death;
For your mother, tears; torment for our whole family.   1295

If any man derides the unseen world, let him
Ponder the death of Pentheus, and believe in gods.

CHORUS   I grieve for your fate, Cadmus; though your grandson's death
Was justly merited, it falls cruelly on you.
AGAUË   Father, you see how one disastrous day has shattered   1300
My whole life . . .

> [At this point the two MSS on which the text of this play de-
> pends show a lacuna of considerable extent; it covers the end of
> this scene, in which Agauë mourns over Pentheus' body, and the
> appearance of Dionysus manifested as a god. The MSS resume
> in the middle of a speech by Dionysus. A number of quotations
> by ancient authors, together with less than 20 lines from *Christus
> Patiens* (an anonymous 4th-century A.D. work consisting largely
> of lines adapted from Greek tragedies) make it possible to at-
> tempt a guess at the content of the missing lines. Since this play
> is often performed, it seems worthwhile to provide here a usable
> text. In the lines that follow, the words printed in italics are
> mere conjecture, and have no value except as a credible com-
> pletion of the probable sense; while those in Roman type repre-
> sent the sources available from *Christus Patiens* and elsewhere.]

. . . my whole life, *turned my pride to shame, my happiness*
To horror. Now my only wish is to compose
My son's body for burial, and lament for him;
And then die. But this is not lawful; for my hands
Are filthy with pollution of their own making.   1305
When I have spilled the blood I bore, and torn the flesh

That grew in my own womb, how can I after this
Enfold him to my breast, or chant his ritual dirge?
And yet, I beg you, pity me, and let me touch
My son, and say farewell to that dear body which   1310
I cherished, and destroyed unknowing. It is right
That you should pity, for your hands are innocent.

CADMUS   *My daughter, you and I and our whole house are crushed*
And broken by the anger of this powerful god.
It is not for me to keep you from your son. Only   1315
Be resolute, and steel your heart against a sight
Which must be fearful to any eyes, but most of all
To a mother's. [To attendants.] *Men, put down your burden on the*
ground
Before Agauë, and remove the covering.
AGAUË   *Dear child, how cruel, how unnatural are these tears,*   1320
Which should have fallen from your eyes on my dead face.
Now I shall die with none to mourn me. This is just;
For in my pride I did not recognize the god,
Nor understand the things I ought to have understood.
You too are punished for the same impiety;   1325
But which is the more terrible, your fate or mine,
I cannot tell. Since you have suffered too, you will
Forgive both what I did, not knowing what I did,
And what I do now, touching you with unholy hands—
At once your cruelest enemy and your dearest friend.   1330

I place your limbs as they should lie; I kiss the flesh
That my own body nourished and my own care reared
To manhood. Help me, father; lay his poor head here.
Make all exact and seemly, with what care we can.
O dearest face, O young fresh cheek! O kingly eyes,   1335
Your light now darkened! O my son! See, with this veil
I now cover your head, your torn and bloodstained limbs.
Take him up, carry him to burial, a king
Lured to a shameful death by the anger of a god.

          Enter DIONYSUS.

CHORUS   *But look! Who is this, rising above the palace door?*   1340
It is he—Dionysus comes himself, no more disguised
As mortal, but in the glory of his divinity!
DIONYSUS   *Behold me, a god great and powerful, Dionysus,*
The son whom Theban Semele bore to immortal Zeus.
I come to the city of seven gates, to famous Thebes,   1345
Whose people slighted me, denied my divinity,
Refused my ritual dances. Now they reap the fruit
Of impious folly. The royal house is overthrown;
The city's streets tremble in guilt, as every Theban
Repents too late his blindness and his blasphemy.   1350
Foremost in sin was Pentheus, who not only scorned
My claims, but put me in fetters and insulted me.
Therefore death came to him in the most shameful way,
At his own mother's hands. This fate he justly earned;
No god can see his worship scorned, and hear his name   1355

Profaned, and not take vengeance to the utmost limit.
Thus men may learn that gods are more powerful than they.

Agauë and her sisters must immediately
Depart from Thebes; their exile will be just penance
For the pollution which this blood has brought on them.   1360
Never again shall they enjoy their native land;
That such defilement ever should appear before
The city's altars, is an offense to piety.

Now, Cadmus, hear what suffering Fate appoints for you.

[Here the MSS resume.]

You shall transmute your nature and become a serpent.   1365
Your wife Harmonia, whom her father Ares gave
To you, a mortal, likewise shall assume the nature
Of beasts, and live a snake. The oracle of Zeus
Foretells that you, at the head of a barbaric horde,
Shall with your wife drive forth a pair of heifers yoked,   1370
And with your countless army destroy many cities;
But when they plunder Loxias' oracle, they shall find
A miserable homecoming. However, Ares shall
At last deliver both you and Harmonia,
And grant you immortal life among the blessed gods.   1375
I who pronounce these fates am Dionysus, begotten
Not by a mortal father, but by Zeus. If you
Had chosen wisdom, when you would not, you would have lived
In wealth and safety, having the son of Zeus your friend.
CADMUS   Have mercy on us, Dionysus. We have sinned.   1380
DIONYSUS   You know too late. You did not know me when you should.
CADMUS   We acknowledge this; but your revenge is merciless.
DIONYSUS   And rightly; I am a god, and you insulted me.
CADMUS   Gods should not be like mortals in vindictiveness.
DIONYSUS   All this my father Zeus ordained from the beginning.   1385
AGAUË   No hope, father. Our harsh fate is decreed: exile.
DIONYSUS   Then why put off a fate which is inevitable?

Exit DIONYSUS.

CADMUS   Dear child, what misery has overtaken us all—
You, and your sisters, and your old unhappy father!
I must set forth from home and live in barbarous lands;   1390
Further than that, it is foretold that I shall lead
A mixed barbarian horde to Hellas. And my wife,
Harmonia, Ares' daughter, and I too, must take
The brutish form of serpents; and I am to lead her thus
At the head of an armed force, to desecrate the tombs   1395
And temples of our native land. I am to reach
No respite from this curse; I may not even cross
The downward stream of Acheron[3] to find peace in death.
AGAUË   And I in exile, father, shall live far from you.
CADMUS   Poor child, why do you cling to me, as the young swan   1400
Clings fondly to the old, helpless and white with age?

_____
3. One of the rivers in the classical underworld.

AGAUË   Where can I turn for comfort, homeless and exiled?
CADMUS   I do not know. Your father is little help to you.
AGAUË   Farewell, my home; farewell the land I know.
    Exiled, accursed, and wretched, now I go   1405
    Forth from this door where first I came a bride.
CADMUS   Go, daughter; find some secret place to hide
    Your shame and sorrow.
AGAUË   Father, I weep for you.
CADMUS   I for your suffering, and your sisters' too.   1410
AGAUË   There is strange tyranny in the god who sent
    Against your house this cruel punishment.
CADMUS   Not strange: our citizens despised his claim,
    And you, and they, put him to open shame.
AGAUË   Father, farewell.   1415
CADMUS   Poor child! I cannot tell
    How you can *fare well;* yet I say, Farewell.
AGAUË   I go to lead my sisters by the hand
    To share my wretchedness in a foreign land.

> *She turns to the Theban women who have been waiting at the edge of the stage.*

Come, see me forth.   1420
Gods, lead me to some place
Where loath'd Cithaeron may not see my face,
Nor I Cithaeron. I have had my fill
Of mountain-ecstasy; now take who will
My holy ivy-wreath, my thyrsus rod,   1425
All that reminds me how I served this god!

> *Exit, followed by* CADMUS.

CHORUS
Gods manifest themselves in many forms,
Bring many matters to surprising ends;
The things we thought would happen do not happen;
The unexpected God makes possible: 1430
And that is what has happened here today.

> *Exeunt.*

406–5 B.C.

Thebes and the House of Cadmus

Many of the principal myths of the Greeks centered about royal families who seemed particularly susceptible to sensational crimes and punishments. Few families had more lurid histories than that of Cadmus, the founder of Thebes.

When Cadmus' sister Europa was stolen by Zeus, in the form of a white bull, his father, Agenor of Sidon, sent Cadmus and his brothers forth to search for her. After various adventures, Cadmus, led by Athena, set out to establish a city. Led by a cow chosen by the goddess, he came to a spring where he was to establish the city. When most of his men were killed by a serpent who lived there, Cadmus killed the serpent and, again following the instructions of the goddess, sowed its teeth. From the teeth sprang up armed men who began fighting among themselves until Cadmus stopped them by throwing a stone into their midst. These "Sown Men" and their descendants were the great families of Thebes. Among them were Echion, the father of Pentheus, and an ancestor of Menoeceus, the father of Jocasta and Creon.

The chart below shows the relations of the members of the house of Cadmus who are mentioned in *The Bacchae* and *Oedipus Tyrannus*. A number of their relatives with equally spectacular destinies are omitted to make the chart more useful to readers of these two plays.

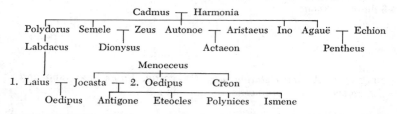

Although *The Bacchae* and *Oedipus Tyrannus* occur in different generations, the figure of Teiresias, the blind prophet, occurs in both. The name may have designated an office rather than an individual.

Thebes was the principal city of Boeotia, a district to the northwest of Attica in which Athens was located. This may help to explain its prominence in the Athenian drama. The two plays here considered make frequent reference to some of the features of the city, including its seven gates (where *The Seven Against Thebes* fought), the great mountain Cithaeron, which was nearby, the streams Ismenus, Dirce, and Asopus, and the neighboring villages of Hysiae and Erythrae.

Hamlet

CHARACTERS

CLAUDIUS, *King of Denmark*
HAMLET, *son of the former and*
  nephew to the present King
POLONIUS, *Lord Chamberlain*
HORATIO, *friend of Hamlet*
LAERTES, *son of Polonius*
VOLTEMAND ⎫
CORNELIUS ⎪
ROSENCRANTZ ⎬ *courtiers*
GUILDENSTERN ⎪
OSRIC ⎪
A GENTLEMAN ⎭
A PRIEST

MARCELLUS ⎫ *officers*
BERNARDO ⎭
FRANCISCO, *a soldier*
REYNALDO, *servant to Polonius*
PLAYERS
TWO CLOWNS, *gravediggers*
FORTINBRAS, *Prince of Norway*
A NORWEGIAN CAPTAIN
ENGLISH AMBASSADORS
GERTRUDE, *Queen of Denmark, and*
  mother of Hamlet
OPHELIA, *daughter of Polonius*
GHOST OF HAMLET'S FATHER

LORDS, LADIES, OFFICERS, SOLDIERS, SAILORS, MESSENGERS, *and*
  ATTENDANTS

SCENE: *The action takes place in or near the royal castle of Denmark at Elsinore.*

Act 1

SCENE 1: *A guard station atop the castle. Enter* BERNARDO *and* FRANCISCO, *two sentinels.*

BERNARDO Who's there?
FRANCISCO Nay, answer me. Stand and unfold yourself.
BERNARDO Long live the king!
FRANCISCO Bernardo?
BERNARDO He. 5
FRANCISCO You come most carefully upon your hour.
BERNARDO 'Tis now struck twelve. Get thee to bed, Francisco.
FRANCISCO For this relief much thanks. 'Tis bitter cold,
And I am sick at heart.
BERNARDO Have you had quiet guard?
FRANCISCO   Not a mouse stirring. 10
BERNARDO Well, good night.
If you do meet Horatio and Marcellus,
The rivals[1] of my watch, bid them make haste.

Enter HORATIO *and* MARCELLUS.

FRANCISCO I think I hear them. Stand, ho! Who is there?
HORATIO Friends to this ground.
MARCELLUS   And liegemen to the Dane.[2] 15

1. companions
2. The "Dane" is the King of Denmark, who is also called "Denmark," as in line 48 of this scene. In line 61 the same figure is used for the King of Norway.

FRANCISCO   Give you good night.

MARCELLUS   O, farewell, honest soldier!
Who hath relieved you?

FRANCISCO   Bernardo hath my place.
Give you good night.   *Exit* FRANCISCO.

MARCELLUS   Holla, Bernardo!

BERNARDO   Say—
What, is Horatio there?

HORATIO   A piece of him.

BERNARDO   Welcome, Horatio. Welcome, good Marcellus.   20

HORATIO   What, has this thing appeared again tonight?

BERNARDO   I have seen nothing.

MARCELLUS   Horatio says 'tis but our fantasy,
And will not let belief take hold of him
Touching this dreaded sight twice seen of us.   25
Therefore I have entreated him along
With us to watch the minutes of this night,
That if again this apparition come,
He may approve[3] our eyes and speak to it.

HORATIO   Tush, tush, 'twill not appear.

BERNARDO   Sit down awhile,   30
And let us once again assail your ears,
That are so fortified against our story,
What we have two nights seen.

HORATIO   Well, sit we down,
And let us hear Bernardo speak of this.

BERNARDO   Last night of all,   35
When yond same star that's westward from the pole[4]
Had made his course t' illume that part of heaven
Where now it burns, Marcellus and myself,
The bell then beating one—

Enter GHOST.

MARCELLUS   Peace, break thee off. Look where it comes again.   40

BERNARDO   In the same figure like the king that's dead.

MARCELLUS   Thou art a scholar; speak to it, Horatio.

BERNARDO   Looks 'a[5] not like the king? Mark it, Horatio.

HORATIO   Most like. It harrows me with fear and wonder.

BERNARDO   It would be spoke to.

MARCELLUS   Speak to it, Horatio.   45

HORATIO   What art thou that usurp'st this time of night
Together with that fair and warlike form
In which the majesty of buried Denmark
Did sometimes march? By heaven I charge thee, speak.

MARCELLUS   It is offended.

BERNARDO   See, it stalks away.   50

HORATIO   Stay. Speak, speak. I charge thee, speak.   *Exit* GHOST.

MARCELLUS   'Tis gone and will not answer.

BERNARDO   How now, Horatio! You tremble and look pale.
Is not this something more than fantasy?
What think you on't?   55

HORATIO   Before my God, I might not this believe

3. confirm the testimony of   5. he
4. polestar

Without the sensible[6] and true avouch
Of mine own eyes.
MARCELLUS   Is it not like the king?
HORATIO   As thou art to thyself.
Such was the very armor he had on   60
When he the ambitious Norway combated.
So frowned he once when, in an angry parle,[7]
He smote the sledded Polacks on the ice.
'Tis strange.
MARCELLUS   Thus twice before, and jump[8] at this dead hour,   65
With martial stalk hath he gone by our watch.
HORATIO   In what particular thought to work I know not,
But in the gross and scope of mine opinion,
This bodes some strange eruption to our state.
MARCELLUS   Good now, sit down, and tell me he that knows,   70
Why this same strict and most observant watch
So nightly toils the subject[9] of the land,
And why such daily cast of brazen cannon
And foreign mart for implements of war;
Why such impress of shipwrights, whose sore task   75
Does not divide the Sunday from the week.
What might be toward that this sweaty haste
Doth make the night joint-laborer with the day?
Who is't that can inform me?
HORATIO   That can I.
At least, the whisper goes so. Our last king,   80
Whose image even but now appeared to us,
Was as you know by Fortinbras of Norway,
Thereto pricked on by a most emulate pride,
Dared to the combat; in which our valiant Hamlet
(For so this side of our known world esteemed him)   85
Did slay this Fortinbras; who by a sealed compact
Well ratified by law and heraldry,
Did forfeit, with his life, all those his lands
Which he stood seized of,[1] to the conqueror;
Against the which a moiety competent[2]   90
Was gagéd[3] by our king; which had returned
To the inheritance of Fortinbras,
Had he been vanquisher; as, by the same covenant
And carriage of the article designed,
His fell to Hamlet. Now, sir, young Fortinbras,   95
Of unimprovéd mettle hot and full,
Hath in the skirts of Norway here and there
Sharked up a list of lawless resolutes
For food and diet to some enterprise
That hath a stomach in't; which is no other,   100
As it doth well appear unto our state,
But to recover of us by strong hand
And terms compulsatory, those foresaid lands
So by his father lost; and this, I take it,

6. of the senses   1. possessed
7. parley   2. portion of similar value
8. precisely   3. pledged
9. people

Is the main motive of our preparations,   105
The source of this our watch, and the chief head
Of this post-haste and romage[4] in the land.
BERNARDO   I think it be no other but e'en so.
Well may it sort[5] that this portentous figure
Comes arméd through our watch so like the king   110
That was and is the question of these wars.
HORATIO   A mote[6] it is to trouble the mind's eye.
In the most high and palmy state of Rome,
A little ere the mightiest Julius fell,
The graves stood tenantless, and the sheeted dead   115
Did squeak and gibber in the Roman streets;
As stars with trains of fire, and dews of blood,
Disasters in the sun; and the moist star,
Upon whose influence Neptune's empire stands,[7]
Was sick almost to doomsday with eclipse.   120
And even the like precurse[8] of feared events,
As harbingers preceding still the fates
And prologue to the omen coming on,
Have heaven and earth together demonstrated
Unto our climatures[9] and countrymen.   125

> *Enter* GHOST.

But soft, behold, lo where it comes again!
I'll cross it[1] though it blast me.—Stay, illusion.

> *It spreads [its] arms.*

If thou hast any sound or use of voice,
Speak to me.
If there be any good thing to be done,   130
That may to thee do ease, and grace to me,
Speak to me.
If thou art privy to thy country's fate,
Which happily foreknowing may avoid,
O, speak!   135
Or if thou hast uphoarded in thy life
Extorted treasure in the womb of earth,
For which, they say, you spirits oft walk in death,

> *The cock crows.*

Speak of it. Stay, and speak. Stop it, Marcellus.
MARCELLUS   Shall I strike at it with my partisan[2]?   140
HORATIO   Do, if it will not stand.
BERNARDO   'Tis here.
HORATIO   'Tis here.
MARCELLUS   'Tis gone.   *Exit* GHOST.
We do it wrong, being so majestical,
To offer it the show of violence;
For it is as the air, invulnerable,   145

---

4. stir
5. chance
6. speck of dust
7. Neptune was the Roman sea god; the "moist star" is the moon.
8. precursor
9. regions
1. Horatio means either that he will

move across the Ghost's path in order to stop him or that he will make the sign of the cross to gain power over him. The stage direction which follows is somewhat ambiguous. "It" seems to refer to the Ghost, but the movement would be appropriate to Horatio.
2. halberd

And our vain blows malicious mockery.
BERNARDO   It was about to speak when the cock crew.
HORATIO   And then it started like a guilty thing
Upon a fearful summons. I have heard
The cock, that is the trumpet to the morn,   150
Doth with his lofty and shrill-sounding throat
Awake the god of day, and at his warning,
Whether in sea or fire, in earth or air,
Th' extravagant and erring[3] spirit hies
To his confine; and of the truth herein   155
This present object made probation.[4]
MARCELLUS   It faded on the crowing of the cock.
Some say that ever 'gainst that season comes
Wherein our Savior's birth is celebrated,
This bird of dawning singeth all night long,   160
And then, they say, no spirit dare stir abroad,
The nights are wholesome, then no planets strike,
No fairy takes,[5] nor witch hath power to charm,
So hallowed and so gracious is that time.
HORATIO   So have I heard and do in part believe it.   165
But look, the morn in russet mantle clad
Walks o'er the dew of yon high eastward hill.
Break we our watch up, and by my advice
Let us impart what we have seen tonight
Unto young Hamlet, for upon my life   170
This spirit, dumb to us, will speak to him.
Do you consent we shall acquaint him with it,
As needful in our loves, fitting our duty?
MARCELLUS   Let's do't, I pray, and I this morning know
Where we shall find him most convenient.   *Exeunt.* 175

SCENE 2: *A chamber of state. Enter* KING CLAUDIUS, QUEEN GER-
TRUDE, HAMLET, POLONIUS, LAERTES, OPHELIA, VOLTEMAND, COR-
NELIUS *and other members of the court.*

KING   Though yet of Hamlet our dear brother's death
The memory be green, and that it us befitted
To bear our hearts in grief, and our whole kingdom
To be contracted in one brow of woe,
Yet so far hath discretion fought with nature   5
That we with wisest sorrow think on him,
Together with remembrance of ourselves.
Therefore our sometime sister, now our queen,
Th' imperial jointress[6] to this warlike state,
Have we, as 'twere with a defeated joy,   10
With an auspicious and a dropping eye,
With mirth in funeral, and with dirge in marriage,
In equal scale weighing delight and dole,
Taken to wife; nor have we herein barred
Your better wisdoms, which have freely gone   15
With this affair along. For all, our thanks.

---

3. wandering out of bounds   6. A "jointress" is a widow who holds a
4. proof   *jointure* or life interest in the estate of her
5. enchants   deceased husband.

Now follows that you know young Fortinbras,
Holding a weak supposal of our worth,
Or thinking by our late dear brother's death
Our state to be disjoint and out of frame, 20
Colleaguéd with this dream of his advantage,
He hath not failed to pester us with message
Importing the surrender of those lands
Lost by his father, with all bands of law,
To our most valiant brother. So much for him. 25
Now for ourself, and for this time of meeting,
Thus much the business is: we have here writ
To Norway, uncle of young Fortinbras—
Who, impotent and bedrid, scarcely hears
Of this his nephew's purpose—to suppress 30
His further gait[7] herein, in that the levies,
The lists, and full proportions are all made
Out of his subject; and we here dispatch
You, good Cornelius, and you, Voltemand,
For bearers of this greeting to old Norway, 35
Giving to you no further personal power
To business with the king, more than the scope
Of these dilated[8] articles allow.
Farewell, and let your haste commend your duty.

CORNELIUS ⎱
VOLTEMAND ⎰ In that, and all things will we show our duty. 40

KING   We doubt it nothing, heartily farewell.

Exeunt VOLTEMAND *and* CORNELIUS.

And now, Laertes, what's the news with you?
You told us of some suit. What is't, Laertes?
You cannot speak of reason to the Dane
And lose your voice. What wouldst thou beg, Laertes, 45
That shall not be my offer, not thy asking?
The head is not more native to the heart,
The hand more instrumental[9] to the mouth,
Than is the throne of Denmark to thy father.
What wouldst thou have, Laertes?

LAERTES   My dread lord, 50
Your leave and favor to return to France,
From whence, though willingly, I came to Denmark
To show my duty in your coronation,
Yet now I must confess, that duty done,
My thoughts and wishes bend again toward France, 55
And bow them to your gracious leave and pardon.

KING   Have you your father's leave? What says Polonius?

POLONIUS   He hath, my lord, wrung from me my slow leave
By laborsome petition, and at last
Upon his will I sealed my hard consent. 60
I do beseech you give him leave to go.

KING   Take thy fair hour, Laertes. Time be thine,
And thy best graces spend it at thy will.

7. progress
8. fully expressed   9. serviceable

But now, my cousin[1] Hamlet, and my son—
HAMLET [*aside*]   A little more than kin, and less than kind.   65
KING   How is it that the clouds still hang on you?
HAMLET   Not so, my lord. I am too much in the sun.
QUEEN   Good Hamlet, cast thy nighted color off,
And let thine eye look like a friend on Denmark.
Do not for ever with thy vailéd lids[2]   70
Seek for thy noble father in the dust.
Thou know'st 'tis common—all that lives must die,
Passing through nature to eternity.
HAMLET   Ay, madam, it is common.
QUEEN   If it be,
Why seems it so particular with thee?   75
HAMLET   Seems, madam? Nay, it is. I know not "seems."
'Tis not alone my inky cloak, good mother,
Nor customary suits of solemn black,
Nor windy suspiration of forced breath,
No, nor the fruitful river in the eye,   80
Nor the dejected havior[3] of the visage,
Together with all forms, moods, shapes of grief,
That can denote me truly. These indeed seem,
For they are actions that a man might play,
But I have that within which passes show—   85
These but the trappings and the suits of woe.
KING   'Tis sweet and commendable in your nature, Hamlet,
To give these mourning duties to your father,
But you must know your father lost a father,
That father lost, lost his, and the survivor bound   90
In filial obligation for some term
To do obsequious[4] sorrow. But to persever
In obstinate condolement is a course
Of impious stubbornness. 'Tis unmanly grief.
It shows a will most incorrect to[5] heaven,   95
A heart unfortified, a mind impatient,
An understanding simple and unschooled.
For what we know must be, and is as common
As any the most vulgar thing to sense,
Why should we in our peevish opposition   100
Take it to heart? Fie, 'tis a fault to heaven,
A fault against the dead, a fault to nature,
To reason most absurd, whose common theme
Is death of fathers, and who still hath cried,
From the first corse[6] till he that died today,   105
"This must be so." We pray you throw to earth
This unprevailing woe, and think of us
As of a father, for let the world take note
You are the most immediate[7] to our throne,
And with no less nobility of love   110
Than that which dearest father bears his son
Do I impart toward you. For your intent

---

1. "Cousin" is used here as a general term of kinship.
2. lowered eyes
3. appearance
4. suited for funeral obsequies
5. uncorrected toward
6. corpse
7. next in line

In going back to school in Wittenberg,
It is most retrograde[8] to our desire,
And we beseech you, bend you to remain   115
Here in the cheer and comfort of our eye,
Our chiefest courtier, cousin, and our son.
QUEEN   Let not thy mother lose her prayers, Hamlet.
I pray thee stay with us, go not to Wittenberg.
HAMLET   I shall in all my best obey you, madam.   120
KING   Why, 'tis a loving and a fair reply.
Be as ourself in Denmark. Madam, come.
This gentle and unforced accord of Hamlet
Sits smiling to my heart, in grace whereof,
No jocund health that Denmark drinks today   125
But the great cannon to the clouds shall tell,
And the king's rouse[9] the heaven shall bruit[1] again,
Respeaking earthly thunder. Come away.

Flourish. Exeunt all but HAMLET.

HAMLET   O, that this too too solid flesh would melt,
Thaw, and resolve itself into a dew,   130
Or that the Everlasting had not fixed
His canon[2] 'gainst self-slaughter. O God, God,
How weary, stale, flat, and unprofitable
Seem to me all the uses of this world!
Fie on't, ah, fie, 'tis an unweeded garden   135
That grows to seed. Things rank and gross in nature
Possess it merely.[3] That it should come to this,
But two months dead, nay, not so much, not two.
So excellent a king, that was to this
Hyperion to a satyr,[4] so loving to my mother,   140
That he might not beteem[5] the winds of heaven
Visit her face too roughly. Heaven and earth,
Must I remember? Why, she would hang on him
As if increase of appetite had grown
By what it fed on, and yet, within a month—   145
Let me not think on't. Frailty, thy name is woman—
A little month, or ere those shoes were old
With which she followed my poor father's body
Like Niobe,[6] all tears, why she, even she—
O God, a beast that wants discourse of reason   150
Would have mourned longer—married with my uncle,
My father's brother, but no more like my father
Than I to Hercules.[7] Within a month,
Ere yet the salt of most unrighteous tears
Had left the flushing in her galléd eyes,   155
She married. O, most wicked speed, to post
With such dexterity to incestuous sheets!

8. contrary
9. carousal
1. echo
2. law
3. entirely
4. Hyperion, a sun god, stands here for
beauty in contrast to the monstrous satyr,
a lecherous creature, half man and half
goat.

5. permit
6. In Greek mythology Niobe was turned
to stone after a tremendous fit of weeping
over the death of her fourteen children, a
misfortune brought about by her boasting
over her fertility.
7. The demigod Hercules was noted for
his strength and the series of spectacular
labors which it allowed him to accomplish.

It is not, nor it cannot come to good.
But break my heart, for I must hold my tongue.

Enter HORATIO, MARCELLUS, *and* BERNARDO.

HORATIO   Hail to your lordship!
HAMLET   I am glad to see you well.   160
Horatio—or I do forget myself.
HORATIO   The same, my lord, and your poor servant ever.
HAMLET   Sir, my good friend, I'll change[8] that name with you.
And what make you from Wittenberg, Horatio?
Marcellus?   165
MARCELLUS   My good lord!
HAMLET   I am very glad to see you. [*To* BERNARDO.] Good even, sir.—
But what, in faith, make you from Wittenberg?
HORATIO   A truant disposition, good my lord.
HAMLET   I would not hear your enemy say so,   170
Nor shall you do my ear that violence
To make it truster of your own report
Against yourself. I know you are no truant.
But what is your affair in Elsinore?
We'll teach you to drink deep ere you depart.   175
HORATIO   My lord, I came to see your father's funeral.
HAMLET   I prithee do not mock me, fellow-student,
I think it was to see my mother's wedding.
HORATIO   Indeed, my lord, it followed hard upon.
HAMLET   Thrift, thrift, Horatio. The funeral-baked meats   180
Did coldly furnish forth the marriage tables.
Would I had met my dearest[9] foe in heaven
Or ever I had seen that day, Horatio!
My father—methinks I see my father.
HORATIO   Where, my lord?
HAMLET   In my mind's eye, Horatio.   185
HORATIO   I saw him once, 'a was a goodly king.
HAMLET   'A was a man, take him for all in all,
I shall not look upon his like again.
HORATIO   My lord, I think I saw him yesternight.
HAMLET   Saw who?   190
HORATIO   My lord, the king your father.
HAMLET   The king my father?
HORATIO   Season[1] your admiration[2] for a while
With an attent[3] ear till I may deliver[4]
Upon the witness of these gentlemen
This marvel to you.
HAMLET   For God's love, let me hear!   195
HORATIO   Two nights together had these gentlemen,
Marcellus and Bernardo, on their watch
In the dead waste and middle of the night
Been thus encountered. A figure like your father,
Armed at point exactly,[5] cap-a-pe,[6]   200
Appears before them, and with solemn march

---

8. exchange
9. bitterest
1. moderate
2. wonder

3. attentive
4. relate
5. completely
6. from head to toe

Goes slow and stately by them. Thrice he walked
By their oppressed and fear-surprisèd eyes
Within his truncheon's[7] length, whilst they, distilled
Almost to jelly with the act of fear,   205
Stand dumb and speak not to him. This to me
In dreadful secrecy impart they did,
And I with them the third night kept the watch,
Where, as they had delivered, both in time,
Form of the thing, each word made true and good,   210
The apparition comes. I knew your father.
These hands are not more like.
HAMLET   But where was this?
MARCELLUS   My lord, upon the platform where we watch.
HAMLET   Did you not speak to it?
HORATIO   My lord, I did,
But answer made it none. Yet once methought   215
It lifted up it head and did address
Itself to motion, like as it would speak;
But even then the morning cock crew loud,
And at the sound it shrunk in haste away
And vanished from our sight.
HAMLET   'Tis very strange.   220
HORATIO   As I do live, my honored lord, 'tis true,
And we did think it writ down in our duty
To let you know of it.
HAMLET   Indeed, sirs, but
This troubles me. Hold you the watch tonight?
ALL   We do, my lord.
HAMLET   Armed, say you?
ALL   Armed, my lord.   225
HAMLET   From top to toe?
ALL   My lord, from head to foot.
HAMLET   Then saw you not his face.
HORATIO   O yes, my lord, he wore his beaver[8] up.
HAMLET   What, looked he frowningly?
HORATIO   A countenance more in sorrow than in anger.   230
HAMLET   Pale or red?
HORATIO   Nay, very pale.
HAMLET   And fixed his eyes upon you?
HORATIO   Most constantly.
HAMLET   I would I had been there.
HORATIO   It would have much amazed you.
HAMLET   Very like.
Stayed it long?   235
HORATIO   While one with moderate haste might tell a hundred.
BOTH   Longer, longer.
HORATIO   Not when I saw't.
HAMLET   His beard was grizzled, no?
HORATIO   It was as I have seen it in his life,
A sable silvered.
HAMLET   I will watch tonight.   240
Perchance 'twill walk again.

---

7. baton of office   8. movable face protector

HORATIO   I warr'nt it will.
HAMLET   If it assume my noble father's person,
I'll speak to it though hell itself should gape[9]
And bid me hold my peace. I pray you all,
If you have hitherto concealed this sight,   245
Let it be tenable[1] in your silence still,
And whatsomever else shall hap tonight,
Give it an understanding but no tongue.
I will requite your loves. So fare you well.
Upon the platform 'twixt eleven and twelve   250
I'll visit you.
ALL   Our duty to your honor.
HAMLET   Your loves, as mine to you. Farewell.

                              Exeunt all but HAMLET.

My father's spirit in arms? All is not well.
I doubt[2] some foul play. Would the night were come!
Till then sit still, my soul. Foul deeds will rise,   255
Though all the earth o'erwhelm them, to men's eyes.   *Exit.*

SCENE 3: *The dwelling of* POLONIUS. *Enter* LAERTES *and* OPHELIA.

LAERTES   My necessaries are embarked. Farewell.
And, sister, as the winds give benefit
And convoy[3] is assistant,[4] do not sleep,
But let me hear from you.
OPHELIA   Do you doubt that?
LAERTES   For Hamlet, and the trifling of his favor,   5
Hold it a fashion and a toy in blood,
A violet in the youth of primy[5] nature,
Forward, not permanent, sweet, not lasting,
The perfume and suppliance of a minute,
No more.
OPHELIA   No more but so?
LAERTES   Think it no more.   10
For nature crescent[6] does not grow alone
In thews and bulk, but as this temple[7] waxes
The inward service of the mind and soul
Grows wide withal. Perhaps he loves you now,
And now no soil nor cautel[8] doth besmirch   15
The virtue of his will, but you must fear,
His greatness weighed,[9] his will is not his own,
For he himself is subject to his birth.
He may not, as unvalued persons do,
Carve for himself, for on his choice depends   20
The safety and health of this whole state,
And therefore must his choice be circumscribed
Unto the voice[1] and yielding of that body
Whereof he is the head. Then if he says he loves you,

9. open (its mouth) wide
1. held
2. suspect
3. means of transport
4. available
5. of the spring

6. growing
7. body
8. deceit
9. rank considered
1. assent

It fits your wisdom so far to believe it   25
As he in his particular act and place
May give his saying deed, which is no further
Than the main voice of Denmark goes withal.
Then weigh what loss your honor may sustain
If with too credent[2] ear you list[3] his songs,   30
Or lose your heart, or your chaste treasure open
To his unmastered importunity.
Fear it, Ophelia, fear it, my dear sister,
And keep you in the rear of your affection,
Out of the shot and danger of desire.   35
The chariest[4] maid is prodigal enough
If she unmask her beauty to the moon.
Virtue itself scapes not calumnious strokes.
The canker[5] galls the infants of the spring
Too oft before their buttons[6] be disclosed,   40
And in the morn and liquid dew of youth
Contagious blastments[7] are most imminent.
Be wary then; best safety lies in fear.
Youth to itself rebels, though none else near.
OPHELIA   I shall the effect of this good lesson keep   45
As watchman to my heart. But, good my brother,
Do not as some ungracious pastors do,
Show me the steep and thorny way to heaven,
Whiles like a puffed and reckless libertine
Himself the primrose path of dalliance treads   50
And recks[8] not his own rede.[9]
LAERTES   O, fear me not.

Enter POLONIUS.

I stay too long. But here my father comes.
A double blessing is a double grace;
Occasion smiles upon a second leave.
POLONIUS   Yet here, Laertes? Aboard, aboard, for shame!   55
The wind sits in the shoulder of your sail,
And you are stayed for. There—my blessing with thee,
And these few precepts in thy memory
Look thou character.[1] Give thy thoughts no tongue,
Nor any unproportioned thought his act.   60
Be thou familiar, but by no means vulgar.
Those friends thou hast, and their adoption tried,
Grapple them unto thy soul with hoops of steel;
But do not dull[2] thy palm with entertainment
Of each new-hatched, unfledged comrade. Beware   65
Of entrance to a quarrel, but being in,
Bear't[3] that th' opposéd[4] may beware of thee.
Give every man thy ear, but few thy voice;[5]
Take each man's censure, but reserve thy judgment.

2. credulous
3. listen to
4. most circumspect
5. rose caterpillar
6. buds
7. blights
8. heeds

9. advice
1. write
2. make callous
3. conduct it
4. opponent
5. approval

Costly thy habit as thy purse can buy,   70
But not expressed in fancy; rich not gaudy,
For the apparel oft proclaims the man,
And they in France of the best rank and station
Are of a most select and generous chief⁶ in that.
Neither a borrower nor a lender be,   75
For loan oft loses both itself and friend,
And borrowing dulls th' edge of husbandry.
This above all, to thine own self be true,
And it must follow as the night the day
Thou canst not then be false to any man.   80
Farewell. My blessing season this in thee!

LAERTES   Most humbly do I take my leave, my lord.
POLONIUS   The time invites you. Go, your servants tend.⁷
LAERTES   Farewell, Ophelia, and remember well
  What I have said to you.
OPHELIA   'Tis in my memory locked,   85
  And you yourself shall keep the key of it.
LAERTES   Farewell.   *Exit* LAERTES.
POLONIUS   What is't, Ophelia, he hath said to you?
OPHELIA   So please you, something touching the Lord Hamlet.
POLONIUS   Marry, well bethought.   90
  'Tis told me he hath very oft of late
  Given private time to you, and you yourself
  Have of your audience been most free and bounteous.
  If it be so—as so 'tis put on me,
  And that in way of caution—I must tell you,   95
  You do not understand yourself so clearly
  As it behooves my daughter and your honor.
  What is between you? Give me up the truth.
OPHELIA   He hath, my lord, of late made many tenders
  Of his affection to me.   100
POLONIUS   Affection? Pooh! You speak like a green girl,
  Unsifted in such perilous circumstance.
  Do you believe his tenders, as you call them?
OPHELIA   I do not know, my lord, what I should think.
POLONIUS   Marry, I will teach you. Think yourself a baby   105
  That you have ta'en these tenders for true pay
  Which are not sterling. Tender yourself more dearly,
  Or (not to crack the wind of the poor phrase,
  Running it thus) you'll tender me a fool.
OPHELIA   My lord, he hath importuned me with love   110
  In honorable fashion.
POLONIUS   Ay, fashion you may call it. Go to, go to.
OPHELIA   And hath given countenance⁸ to his speech, my lord,
  With almost all the holy vows of heaven.
POLONIUS   Ay, springes⁹ to catch woodcocks. I do know,   115
  When the blood burns, how prodigal the soul
  Lends the tongue vows. These blazes, daughter,
  Giving more light than heat, extinct in both
  Even in their promise, as it is a-making,
  You must not take for fire. From this time   120

6. eminence   8. confirmation
7. await   9. snares

Be something scanter of your maiden presence.
Set your entreatments[1] at a higher rate
Than a command to parle. For Lord Hamlet,
Believe so much in him that he is young,
And with a larger tether may he walk   125
Than may be given you. In few, Ophelia,
Do not believe his vows, for they are brokers,[2]
Not of that dye which their investments[3] show,
But mere implorators[4] of unholy suits,
Breathing like sanctified and pious bawds,   130
The better to beguile. This is for all:
I would not, in plain terms, from this time forth
Have you so slander any moment leisure
As to give words or talk with the Lord Hamlet.
Look to't, I charge you. Come your ways.   135
OPHELIA   I shall obey, my lord.   *Exeunt.*

SCENE 4: *The guard station. Enter* HAMLET, HORATIO *and*
MARCELLUS.

HAMLET   The air bites shrewdly[5]; it is very cold.
HORATIO   It is a nipping and an eager[6] air.
HAMLET   What hour now?
HORATIO   I think it lacks of twelve.
MARCELLUS   No, it is struck.
HORATIO   Indeed? I heard it not. It then draws near the season   5
Wherein the spirit held his wont to walk.
      A flourish of trumpets, and two pieces go off.
What does this mean, my lord?
HAMLET   The king doth wake tonight and takes his rouse,
Keeps wassail, and the swagg'ring up-spring[7] reels,
And as he drains his draughts of Rhenish down,   10
The kettledrum and trumpet thus bray out
The triumph of his pledge.
HORATIO   Is it a custom?
HAMLET   Ay, marry, is't,
But to my mind, though I am native here
And to the manner born, it is a custom   15
More honored in the breach than the observance.
This heavy-headed revel east and west
Makes us traduced and taxed of other nations.
They clepe[8] us drunkards, and with swinish phrase
Soil our addition,[9] and indeed it takes   20
From our achievements, though performed at height,
The pith and marrow of our attribute.[1]
So oft it chances in particular men,
That for some vicious mole of nature in them,
As in their birth, wherein they are not guilty   25
(Since nature cannot choose his origin),

1. negotiations before a surrender
2. panders
3. garments
4. solicitors
5. sharply

6. keen
7. a German dance
8. call
9. reputation
1. honor

By the o'ergrowth of some complexion,
Oft breaking down the pales[2] and forts of reason,
Or by some habit that too much o'er-leavens
The form of plausive[3] manners—that these men,   30
Carrying, I say, the stamp of one defect,
Being nature's livery or fortune's star,
His virtues else, be they as pure as grace,
As infinite as man may undergo,
Shall in the general censure take corruption   35
From that particular fault. The dram of evil
Doth all the noble substance often doubt[4]
To his own scandal.

Enter GHOST.

HORATIO   Look, my lord, it comes.
HAMLET   Angels and ministers of grace defend us!
Be thou a spirit of health or goblin damned,   40
Bring with thee airs from heaven or blasts from hell,
Be thy intents wicked or charitable,
Thou com'st in such a questionable[5] shape
That I will speak to thee. I'll call thee Hamlet,
King, father, royal Dane. O, answer me!   45
Let me not burst in ignorance, but tell
Why thy canonized[6] bones, hearséd in death,
Have burst their cerements[7]; why the sepulchre
Wherein we saw thee quietly interred
Hath oped his ponderous and marble jaws   50
To cast thee up again. What may this mean
That thou, dead corse, again in complete steel[8]
Revisits thus the glimpses of the moon,
Making night hideous, and we fools of nature
So horridly to shake our disposition   55
With thoughts beyond the reaches of our souls?
Say, why is this? wherefore? What should we do?

GHOST *beckons.*

HORATIO   It beckons you to go away it,
As if it some impartment[9] did desire
To you alone.
MARCELLUS   Look with what courteous action   60
It waves[1] you to a more removéd[2] ground.
But do not go with it.
HORATIO   No, by no means.
HAMLET   It will not speak; then I will follow it.
HORATIO   Do not, my lord.
HAMLET   Why, what should be the fear?
I do not set my life at a pin's fee,[3]   65
And for my soul, what can it do to that,
Being a thing immortal as itself?

2. barriers
3. pleasing
4. put out
5. prompting question
6. buried in accordance with church
canons

7. gravecloths
8. armor
9. communication
1. beckons
2. distant
3. price

It waves me forth again. I'll follow it.
HORATIO   What if it tempt you toward the flood, my lord,
Or to the dreadful summit of the cliff   70
That beetles⁴ o'er his base into the sea,
And there assume some other horrible form,
Which might deprive⁵ your sovereignty of reason⁶
And draw you into madness? Think of it.
The very place puts toys of desperation,⁷   75
Without more motive, into every brain
That looks so many fathoms to the sea
And hears it roar beneath.
HAMLET   It waves me still.
Go on. I'll follow thee.
MARCELLUS   You shall not go, my lord.
HAMLET   Hold off your hands.   80
HORATIO   Be ruled. You shall not go.
HAMLET   My fate cries out
And makes each petty artere in this body
As hardy as the Nemean lion's nerve.⁸
Still am I called. Unhand me, gentlemen.
By heaven, I'll make a ghost of him that lets⁹ me.   85
I say, away! Go on. I'll follow thee.

Exeunt GHOST *and* HAMLET.

HORATIO   He waxes desperate with imagination.
MARCELLUS   Let's follow. 'Tis not fit thus to obey him.
HORATIO   Have after. To what issue will this come?
MARCELLUS   Something is rotten in the state of Denmark.   90
HORATIO   Heaven will direct it.
MARCELLUS   Nay, let's follow him.   *Exeunt.*

SCENE 5: *Near the guard station. Enter* GHOST *and* HAMLET.

HAMLET   Whither wilt thou lead me? Speak. I'll go no further.
GHOST   Mark me.
HAMLET   I will.
GHOST   My hour is almost come,
When I to sulph'rous and tormenting flames
Must render up myself.
HAMLET   Alas, poor ghost!
GHOST   Pity me not, but lend thy serious hearing   5
To what I shall unfold.
HAMLET   Speak. I am bound to hear.
GHOST   So art thou to revenge, when thou shalt hear.
HAMLET   What?
GHOST   I am thy father's spirit,
Doomed for a certain term to walk the night,   10
And for the day confined to fast in fires,
Till the foul crimes done in my days of nature¹
Are burnt and purged away. But that I am forbid

---

4. juts out
5. take away
6. rational power
7. desperate fancies
8. The Nemean lion was a mythological

monster slain by Hercules as one of his twelve labors.
9. hinders
1. i.e., while I was alive

To tell the secrets of my prison house,
I could a tale unfold whose lightest word 15
Would harrow up thy soul, freeze thy young blood,
Make thy two eyes like stars start from their spheres,
Thy knotted and combinéd² locks to part,
And each particular hair to stand an end,
Like quills upon the fretful porpentine.³ 20
But this eternal blazon⁴ must not be
To ears of flesh and blood. List, list, O, list!
If thou didst ever thy dear father love—

HAMLET   O God!

GHOST   Revenge his foul and most unnatural murder. 25

HAMLET   Murder!

GHOST   Murder most foul, as in the best it is,
But this most foul, strange, and unnatural.

HAMLET   Haste me to know't, that I, with wings as swift
As meditation or the thoughts of love, 30
May sweep to my revenge.

GHOST   I find thee apt,
And duller shouldst thou be than the fat weed
That rots itself in ease on Lethe⁵ wharf,—
Wouldst thou not stir in this. Now, Hamlet, hear.
'Tis given out that, sleeping in my orchard, 35
A serpent stung me. So the whole ear of Denmark
Is by a forgéd process⁶ of my death
Rankly abused. But know, thou noble youth,
The serpent that did sting thy father's life
Now wears his crown.

HAMLET   O my prophetic soul! 40
My uncle!

GHOST   Ay, that incestuous, that adulterate beast,
With witchcraft of his wits, with traitorous gifts—
O wicked wit and gifts that have the power
So to seduce!—won to his shameful lust 45
The will of my most seeming virtuous queen.
O Hamlet, what a falling off was there,
From me, whose love was of that dignity
That it went hand in hand even with the vow
I made to her in marriage, and to decline⁷ 50
Upon a wretch whose natural gifts were poor
To those of mine!
But virtue, as it never will be moved,
Though lewdness court it in a shape of heaven,
So lust, though to a radiant angel linked, 55
Will sate itself in a celestial bed
And prey on garbage.
But soft, methinks I scent the morning air.
Brief let me be. Sleeping within my orchard,
My custom always of the afternoon, 60
Upon my secure hour thy uncle stole,

2. tangled
3. porcupine
4. description of eternity
5. The Lethe was one of the rivers of the classical underworld. Its specific im-

portance was that its waters when drunk induced forgetfulness. The "fat weed" is the asphodel which grew there.
6. false report
7. sink

With juice of cursed hebona[8] in a vial,
And in the porches of my ears did pour
The leperous distilment, whose effect
Holds such an enmity with blood of man   65
That swift as quicksilver it courses through
The natural gates and alleys of the body,
And with a sudden vigor it doth posset[9]
And curd,[1] like eager[2] droppings into milk,
The thin and wholesome blood. So did it mine,   70
And a most instant tetter[3] barked about[4]
Most lazar-like[5] with vile and loathsome crust
All my smooth body.
Thus was I sleeping by a brother's hand
Of life, of crown, of queen at once dispatched,   75
Cut off even in the blossoms of my sin,
Unhouseled, disappointed, unaneled,[6]
No reck'ning made, but sent to my account
With all my imperfections on my head.
O, horrible! O, horrible! most horrible!   80
If thou hast nature in thee, bear it not.
Let not the royal bed of Denmark be
A couch for luxury[7] and damnéd incest.
But howsomever thou pursues this act,
Taint not thy mind, nor let thy soul contrive   85
Against thy mother aught. Leave her to heaven,
And to those thorns that in her bosom lodge
To prick and sting her. Fare thee well at once.
The glowworm shows the matin[8] to be near,
And gins to pale his uneffectual fire.   90
Adieu, adieu, adieu. Remember me.   *Exit.*
HAMLET   O all you host of heaven! O earth! What else?
And shall I couple hell? O, fie! Hold, hold, my heart,
And you, my sinews, grow not instant old,
But bear me stiffly up. Remember thee?   95
Ay, thou poor ghost, whiles memory holds a seat
In this distracted globe.[9] Remember thee?
Yea, from the table[1] of my memory
I'll wipe away all trivial fond[2] records,
All saws of books, all forms, all pressures past   100
That youth and observation copied there,
And thy commandment all alone shall live
Within the book and volume of my brain,
Unmixed with baser matter. Yes, by heaven!
O most pernicious woman!   105
O villain, villain, smiling, damnéd villain!
My tables—meet it is I set it down
That one may smile, and smile, and be a villain.
At least I am sure it may be so in Denmark.

8. a poison
9. coagulate
1. curdle
2. acid
3. a skin disease
4. covered like bark
5. leper-like
6. The Ghost means that he died with-

out the customary rites of the church, that is, without receiving the sacrament, without confession, and without extreme unction.
7. lust
8. morning
9. skull
1. writing tablet
2. foolish

So, uncle, there you are. Now to my word[3]:   110
It is "Adieu, adieu. Remember me."
I have sworn't.

      Enter HORATIO *and* MARCELLUS.

HORATIO   My lord, my lord!
MARCELLUS   Lord Hamlet!
HORATIO   Heavens secure him!
HAMLET   So be it!
MARCELLUS   Illo, ho, ho, my lord!   115
HAMLET   Hillo, ho, ho, boy![4] Come, bird, come.
MARCELLUS   How is't, my noble lord?
HORATIO   What news, my lord?
HAMLET   O, wonderful!
HORATIO   Good my lord, tell it.
HAMLET   No, you will reveal it.
HORATIO   Not I, my lord, by heaven.
MARCELLUS   Nor I, my lord.   120
HAMLET   How say you then, would heart of man once think it?
But you'll be secret?
BOTH   Ay, by heaven, my lord.
HAMLET   There's never a villain dwelling in all Denmark
But he's an arrant knave.
HORATIO   There needs no ghost, my lord, come from the grave   125
To tell us this.
HAMLET   Why, right, you are in the right,
And so without more circumstance at all
I hold it fit that we shake hands and part,
You, as your business and desire shall point you,
For every man hath business and desire   130
Such as it is, and for my own poor part,
I will go pray.
HORATIO   These are but wild and whirling words, my lord.
HAMLET   I am sorry they offend you, heartily;
Yes, faith, heartily.
HORATIO   There's no offence, my lord.   135
HAMLET   Yes, by Saint Patrick, but there is, Horatio,
And much offence too. Touching this vision here,
It is an honest ghost, that let me tell you.
For your desire to know what is between us,
O'ermaster't as you may. And now, good friends,   140
As you are friends, scholars, and soldiers,
Give me one poor request.
HORATIO   What is't, my lord? We will.
HAMLET   Never make known what you have seen tonight.
BOTH   My lord, we will not.
HAMLET   Nay, but swear't.
HORATIO   In faith,   145
My lord, not I.
MARCELLUS   Nor I, my lord, in faith.
HAMLET   Upon my sword.
MARCELLUS   We have sworn, my lord, already.

---

3. for my motto   4. a falconer's cry

HAMLET   Indeed, upon my sword, indeed.

GHOST *cries under the stage.*

GHOST   Swear.
HAMLET   Ha, ha, boy, say'st thou so? Art thou there, truepenny⁵?
Come on. You hear this fellow in the cellarage.⁶   150
Consent to swear.
HORATIO   Propose the oath, my lord.
HAMLET   Never to speak of this that you have seen,
Swear by my sword.
GHOST [*beneath*]   Swear.
HAMLET   Hic et ubique?⁷ Then we'll shift our ground.   155
Come hither, gentlemen,
And lay your hands again upon my sword.
Swear by my sword
Never to speak of this that you have heard.
GHOST [*beneath*]   Swear by his sword.   160
HAMLET   Well said, old mole! Canst work i' th' earth so fast?
A worthy pioneer!⁸ Once more remove, good friends.
HORATIO   O day and night, but this is wondrous strange!
HAMLET   And therefore as a stranger give it welcome.
There are more things in heaven and earth, Horatio,   165
Than are dreamt of in your philosophy.
But come.
Here as before, never, so help you mercy,
How strange or odd some'er I bear myself
(As I perchance hereafter shall think meet   170
To put an antic⁹ disposition on),
That you, at such times, seeing me, never shall,
With arms encumbered¹ thus, or this head-shake,
Or by pronouncing of some doubtful phrase,
As "Well, well, we know," or "We could, and if we would"   175
Or "If we list to speak," or "There be, and if they might"
Or such ambiguous giving out, to note
That you know aught of me—this do swear,
So grace and mercy at your most need help you.
GHOST [*beneath*]   Swear.   *They swear.* 180
HAMLET   Rest, rest, perturbéd spirit! So, gentlemen,
With all my love I do commend me to you,
And what so poor a man as Hamlet is
May do t'express his love and friending² to you,
God willing, shall not lack. Let us go in together,   185
And still your fingers on your lips, I pray.
The time is out of joint. O curséd spite
That ever I was born to set it right!
Nay, come, let's go together.   *Exeunt.*

5. old fellow
6. below
7. here and everywhere
8. soldier who digs trenches

9. mad
1. folded
2. friendship

Act 2

SCENE 1: *The dwelling of* POLONIUS. *Enter* POLONIUS
and REYNALDO.

POLONIUS   Give him this money and these notes, Reynaldo.
REYNALDO   I will, my lord.
POLONIUS   You shall do marvellous wisely, good Reynaldo,
Before you visit him, to make inquire[3]
Of his behavior.
REYNALDO   My lord, I did intend it.   5
POLONIUS   Marry, well said, very well said. Look you, sir.
Enquire me first what Danskers[4] are in Paris,
And how, and who, what means, and where they keep,[5]
What company, at what expense; and finding
By this encompassment[6] and drift of question   10
That they do know my son, come you more nearer
Than your particular demands[7] will touch it.
Take you as 'twere some distant knowledge of him,
As thus, "I know his father and his friends,
And in part him." Do you mark this, Reynaldo?   15
REYNALDO   Ay, very well, my lord.
POLONIUS   "And in part him, but," you may say, "not well,
But if't be he I mean, he's very wild,
Addicted so and so." And there put on him
What forgeries[8] you please; marry, none so rank[9]   20
As may dishonor him. Take heed of that.
But, sir, such wanton, wild, and usual slips
As are companions noted and most known
To youth and liberty.
REYNALDO   As gaming, my lord.
POLONIUS   Ay, or drinking, fencing, swearing, quarrelling,   25
Drabbing[1]—you may go so far.
REYNALDO   My lord, that would dishonor him.
POLONIUS   Faith, no, as you may season it in the charge.[2]
You must not put another scandal on him,
That he is open to incontinency.[3]   30
That's not my meaning. But breathe his faults so quaintly[4]
That they may seem the taints of liberty,[5]
The flash and outbreak of a fiery mind,
A savageness in unreclaiméd[6] blood,
Of general assault.[7]
REYNALDO   But, my good lord—   35
POLONIUS   Wherefore should you do this?
REYNALDO   Ay, my lord,
I would know that.
POLONIUS   Marry, sir, here's my drift,

3. inquiry
4. Danes
5. live
6. indirect means
7. direct questions
8. lies
9. foul

1. whoring
2. soften the accusation
3. sexual excess
4. with delicacy
5. faults of freedom
6. untamed
7. touching everyone

And I believe it is a fetch of warrant.[8]
You laying these slight sullies on my son,
As 'twere a thing a little soiled i' th' working, 40
Mark you,
Your party in converse,[9] him you would sound,
Having ever seen in the prenominate[1] crimes
The youth you breathe[2] of guilty, be assured
He closes with you in this consequence, 45
"Good sir," or so, or "friend," or "gentleman,"
According to the phrase or the addition
Of man and country.

REYNALDO   Very good, my lord.

POLONIUS   And then, sir, does 'a this—'a does—What was I about to
    say? 50
By the mass, I was about to say something.
    Where did I leave?

REYNALDO   At "closes in the consequence."

POLONIUS   At "closes in the consequence"—ay, marry,
He closes thus: "I know the gentleman. 55
I saw him yesterday, or th' other day,
Or then, or then, with such, or such, and as you say,
There was 'a gaming, there o'ertook in's rouse,
There falling out at tennis," or perchance
"I saw him enter such a house of sale," 60
Videlicet,[3] a brothel, or so forth.
See you, now—
Your bait of falsehood takes this carp of truth,
And thus do we of wisdom and of reach,[4]
With windlasses and with assays of bias,[5] 65
By indirections find directions out;
So by my former lecture and advice
Shall you my son. You have me, have you not?

REYNALDO   My lord, I have.

POLONIUS   God b'wi' ye; fare ye well.

REYNALDO   Good my lord. 70

POLONIUS   Observe his inclination in yourself.

REYNALDO   I shall, my lord.

POLONIUS   And let him ply[6] his music.

REYNALDO   Well, my lord.

POLONIUS   Farewell.   *Exit* REYNALDO.

Enter OPHELIA.

                 How now, Ophelia, what's the matter?

OPHELIA   O my lord, my lord, I have been so affrighted! 75

POLONIUS   With what, i' th' name of God?

OPHELIA   My lord, as I was sewing in my closet,[7]
Lord Hamlet with his doublet[8] all unbraced,[9]
No hat upon his head, his stockings fouled,
Ungartered and down-gyvéd[1] to his ankle, 80

8. permissible trick
9. conversation
1. already named
2. speak
3. namely
4. ability

5. indirect tests
6. practice
7. chamber
8. jacket
9. unlaced
1. fallen down like fetters

Pale as his shirt, his knees knocking each other,
And with a look so piteous in purport
As if he had been loosèd out of hell
To speak of horrors—he comes before me.
POLONIUS   Mad for thy love?
OPHELIA   My lord, I do not know,   85
But truly I do fear it.
POLONIUS   What said he?
OPHELIA   He took me by the wrist, and held me hard,
Then goes he to the length of all his arm,
And with his other hand thus o'er his brow,
He falls to such perusal of my face   90
As 'a would draw it. Long stayed he so.
At last, a little shaking of mine arm,
And thrice his head thus waving up and down,
He raised a sigh so piteous and profound
As it did seem to shatter all his bulk,[2]   95
And end his being. That done, he lets me go,
And with his head over his shoulder turned
He seemed to find his way without his eyes,
For out adoors he went without their helps,
And to the last bended[3] their light on me.   100
POLONIUS   Come, go with me. I will go seek the king.
This is the very ecstasy of love,
Whose violent property[4] fordoes[5] itself,
And leads the will to desperate undertakings
As oft as any passion under heaven   105
That does afflict our natures. I am sorry.
What, have you given him any hard words of late?
OPHELIA   No, my good lord, but as you did command
I did repel[6] his letters, and denied
His access to me.
POLONIUS   That hath made him mad.   110
I am sorry that with better heed and judgment
I had not quoted[7] him. I feared he did but trifle,
And meant to wrack[8] thee; but beshrew my jealousy.
By heaven, it is as proper to our age
To cast beyond ourselves in our opinions   115
As it is common for the younger sort
To lack discretion. Come, go we to the king.
This must be known, which being kept close, might move
More grief to hide than hate to utter love.
Come.   *Exeunt.* 120

SCENE 2: *A public room.* Enter KING, QUEEN, ROSENCRANTZ
and GUILDENSTERN.

KING   Welcome, dear Rosencrantz and Guildenstern.
Moreover that[9] we much did long to see you,
The need we have to use you did provoke

---

2. body
3. directed
4. character
5. destroys

6. refuse
7. observed
8. harm
9. in addition to the fact that

Our hasty sending. Something have you heard
Of Hamlet's transformation—so call it,   5
Sith[1] nor th' exterior nor the inward man
Resembles that it was. What it should be,
More than his father's death, that thus hath put him
So much from th' understanding of himself,
I cannot deem of. I entreat you both   10
That, being of so young days[2] brought up with him,
And sith so neighbored[3] to his youth and havior,
That you vouchsafe your rest here in our court
Some little time, so by your companies
To draw him on to pleasures, and to gather   15
So much as from occasion you may glean,
Whether aught to us unknown afflicts him thus,
That opened lies within our remedy.

QUEEN   Good gentlemen, he hath much talked of you,
And sure I am two men there are not living   20
To whom he more adheres. If it will please you
To show us so much gentry[4] and good will
As to expend your time with us awhile
For the supply and profit of our hope,
Your visitation shall receive such thanks   25
As fits a king's remembrance.

ROSENCRANTZ   Both your majesties
Might, by the sovereign power you have of us,
Put your dread pleasures more into command
Than to entreaty.

GUILDENSTERN   But we both obey,
And here give up ourselves in the full bent[5]   30
To lay our service freely at your feet,
To be commanded.

KING   Thanks, Rosencrantz and gentle Guildenstern.

QUEEN   Thanks, Guildenstern and gentle Rosencrantz.
And I beseech you instantly to visit   35
My too much changed son. Go, some of you,
And bring these gentlemen where Hamlet is.

GUILDENSTERN   Heavens make our presence and our practices
Pleasant and helpful to him!

QUEEN   Ay, amen!

Exeunt ROSENCRANTZ *and* GUILDENSTERN.

Enter POLONIUS.

POLONIUS   Th' ambassadors from Norway, my good lord,   40
Are joyfully returned.

KING   Thou still[6] hast been the father of good news.

POLONIUS   Have I, my lord? I assure you, my good liege,
I hold my duty as I hold my soul,
Both to my God and to my gracious king;   45
And I do think—or else this brain of mine
Hunts not the trail of policy[7] so sure

---

1. since
2. from childhood
3. closely allied
4. courtesy

5. completely
6. ever
7. statecraft

As it hath used to do—that I have found
The very cause of Hamlet's lunacy.
KING   O, speak of that, that do I long to hear.   50
POLONIUS   Give first admittance to th' ambassadors.
My news shall be the fruit[8] to that great feast.
KING   Thyself do grace to them, and bring them in.

Exit POLONIUS.

He tells me, my dear Gertrude, he hath found
The head and source of all your son's distemper.   55
QUEEN   I doubt it is no other but the main,
His father's death and our o'erhasty marriage.
KING   Well, we shall sift[9] him.

Enter Ambassadors (VOLTEMAND *and* CORNELIUS) *with*
POLONIUS.
                                                Welcome, my good friends,
Say, Voltemand, what from our brother Norway?
VOLTEMAND   Most fair return of greetings and desires.   60
Upon our first,[1] he sent out to suppress
His nephew's levies, which to him appeared
To be a preparation 'gainst the Polack,
But better looked into, he truly found
It was against your highness, whereat grieved,   65
That so his sickness, age, and impotence
Was falsely borne in hand,[2] sends out arrests[3]
On Fortinbras, which he in brief obeys,
Receives rebuke from Norway, and in fine,
Makes vow before his uncle never more   70
To give th' assay[4] of arms against your majesty.
Whereon old Norway, overcome with joy,
Gives him threescore thousand crowns in annual fee,
And his commission to employ those soldiers,
So levied as before, against the Polack,   75
With an entreaty, herein further shown,   *Gives* CLAUDIUS *a paper.*
That it might please you to give quiet pass[5]
Through your dominions for this enterprise,
On such regards of safety and allowance
As therein are set down.
KING   It likes[6] us well,   80
And at our more considered time[7] we'll read,
Answer, and think upon this business.
Meantime we thank you for your well-took[8] labor.
Go to your rest; at night we'll feast together.
Most welcome home!   *Exeunt* AMBASSADORS.
POLONIUS   This business is well ended.   85
My liege and madam, to expostulate[9]
What majesty should be, what duty is,
Why day is day, night night, and time is time,

---

8. dessert
9. examine
1. i.e., first appearance
2. deceived
3. orders to stop
4. trial

5. safe conduct
6. pleases
7. time for more consideration
8. successful
9. discuss

Were nothing but to waste night, day, and time.
Therefore, since brevity is the soul of wit,   90
And tediousness the limbs and outward flourishes,[1]
I will be brief. Your noble son is mad.
Mad call I it, for to define true madness,
What is't but to be nothing else but mad?
But let that go.
QUEEN   More matter with less art.   95
POLONIUS   Madam, I swear I use no art at all.
That he is mad, 'tis true: 'tis true 'tis pity,
And pity 'tis 'tis true. A foolish figure,
But farewell it, for I will use no art.
Mad let us grant him, then, and now remains   100
That we find out the cause of this effect,
Or rather say the cause of this defect,
For this effect defective comes by cause.
Thus it remains, and the remainder thus.
Perpend.[2]   105
I have a daughter—have while she is mine—
Who in her duty and obedience, mark,
Hath given me this. Now gather, and surmise.
      "To the celestial, and my soul's idol, the most beautified
Ophelia."—That's an ill phrase, a vile phrase, "beautified" is a   110
vile phrase. But you shall hear. Thus:
      "In her excellent white bosom, these, etc."
QUEEN   Came this from Hamlet to her?
POLONIUS   Good madam, stay awhile. I will be faithful.

            "Doubt thou the stars are fire,   115
              Doubt that the sun doth move;
            Doubt truth to be a liar;
              But never doubt I love.

      O dear Ophelia, I am ill at these numbers.[3]
I have not art to reckon my groans, but that I love thee best, O   120
most best, believe it. Adieu.
                        Thine evermore, most dear lady, whilst
                              this machine[4] is to him, HAMLET."
This in obedience hath my daughter shown me,
And more above, hath his solicitings,   125
As they fell out by time, by means, and place,
All given to mine ear.
KING   But how hath she
Received his love?
POLONIUS   What do you think of me?
KING   As of a man faithful and honorable.
POLONIUS   I would fain prove so. But what might you think,   130
When I had seen this hot love on the wing,
(As I perceived it, I must tell you that,
Before my daughter told me), what might you,
Or my dear majesty your queen here, think,
If I had played the desk or table-book,   135
Or given my heart a winking, mute and dumb,

---

1. adornments   3. verses
2. consider   4. body

Or looked upon this love with idle sight,[5]
What might you think? No, I went round[6] to work,
And my young mistress thus I did bespeak:
"Lord Hamlet is a prince out of thy star.[7]   140
This must not be." And then I prescripts[8] gave her,
That she should lock herself from his resort,
Admit no messengers, receive no tokens.
Which done, she took[9] the fruits of my advice;
And he repelled, a short tale to make,   145
Fell into a sadness, then into a fast,
Thence to a watch, thence into a weakness,
Thence to a lightness, and by this declension,
Into the madness wherein now he raves,
And all we mourn for.

KING   Do you think 'tis this?   150
QUEEN   It may be, very like.
POLONIUS   Hath there been such a time—I would fain know that—
That I have positively said "Tis so,"
When it proved otherwise?
KING   Not that I know.
POLONIUS [*pointing to his head and shoulder*]   Take this from this, if
this be otherwise.   155
If circumstances lead me, I will find
Where truth is hid, though it were hid indeed
Within the centre.[1]
KING   How may we try it further?
POLONIUS   You know sometimes he walks four hours together
Here in the lobby.
QUEEN   So he does, indeed.   160
POLONIUS   At such a time I'll loose[2] my daughter to him.
Be you and I behind an arras[3] then.
Mark the encounter. If he love her not,
And be not from his reason fall'n thereon,
Let me be no assistant for a state,   165
But keep a farm and carters.
KING   We will try it.

Enter HAMLET *reading a book.*

QUEEN   But look where sadly the poor wretch comes reading.
POLONIUS   Away, I do beseech you both away,
I'll board[4] him presently.

                                        Exeunt KING *and* QUEEN.

                    O, give me leave.
How does my good Lord Hamlet?   170
HAMLET   Well, God-a-mercy.
POLONIUS   Do you know me, my lord?
HAMLET   Excellent well, you are a fishmonger.

---

5. Polonius means that he would have been at fault if, having seen Hamlet's attention to Ophelia, he had winked at it or not paid attention, an "idle sight," and if he had remained silent and kept the information to himself, as if it were written in a "desk" or "table-book."
6. directly

7. beyond your sphere
8. orders
9. followed
1. of the earth
2. let loose
3. tapestry
4. accost

POLONIUS   Not I, my lord.

HAMLET   Then I would you were so honest a man.   175

POLONIUS   Honest, my lord?

HAMLET   Ay, sir, to be honest as this world goes, is to be one man picked out of ten thousand.

POLONIUS   That's very true, my lord.

HAMLET   For if the sun breed maggots in a dead dog, being a god 180 kissing carrion[5]—Have you a daughter?

POLONIUS   I have, my lord.

HAMLET   Let her not walk i' th' sun. Conception is a blessing, but as your daughter may conceive—friend, look to't.

POLONIUS   How say you by that? [*Aside.*] Still harping on my daughter. 185 Yet he knew me not at first. 'A said I was a fishmonger. 'A is far gone. And truly in my youth I suffered much extremity for love. Very near this. I'll speak to him again.—What do you read, my lord?

HAMLET   Words, words, words.

POLONIUS   What is the matter, my lord?   190

HAMLET   Between who?

POLONIUS   I mean the matter that you read, my lord.

HAMLET   Slanders, sir; for the satirical rogue says here that old men have grey beards, that their faces are wrinkled, their eyes purging thick amber and plum-tree gum, and that they have a plentiful lack 195 of wit, together with most weak hams[6]—all which, sir, though I most powerfully and potently believe, yet I hold it not honesty to have it thus set down, for yourself, sir, shall grow old as I am, if like a crab you could go backward.

POLONIUS [*aside*]   Though this be madness, yet there is method in't. 200 —Will you walk out of the air, my lord?

HAMLET   Into my grave?

POLONIUS [*aside*]   Indeed, that's out of the air. How pregnant sometime his replies are! a happiness that often madness hits on, which reason and sanity could not so prosperously be delivered of. I will 205 leave him, and suddenly contrive the means of meeting between him and my daughter.—My lord. I will take my leave of you.

HAMLET   You cannot take from me anything that I will more willingly part withal—except my life, except my life, except my life.

Enter GUILDENSTERN *and* ROSENCRANTZ.

POLONIUS   Fare you well, my lord.   210

HAMLET   These tedious old fools!

POLONIUS   You go to seek the Lord Hamlet. There he is.

ROSENCRANTZ [*to* POLONIUS]   God save you, sir!   *Exit* POLONIUS.

GUILDENSTERN   My honored lord!

ROSENCRANTZ   My most dear lord!   215

HAMLET   My excellent good friends! How dost thou, Guildenstern? Ah, Rosencrantz! Good lads, how do you both?

ROSENCRANTZ   As the indifferent[7] children of the earth.

GUILDENSTERN   Happy in that we are not over-happy; On Fortune's cap we are not the very button.[8]   220

HAMLET   Nor the soles of her shoe?

ROSENCRANTZ   Neither, my lord.

---

5. A reference to the belief of the period that maggots were produced spontaneously by the action of sunshine on carrion.

6. limbs
7. ordinary
8. i.e., on top

HAMLET   Then you live about her waist, or in the middle of her favors.

GUILDENSTERN   Faith, her privates we.

HAMLET   In the secret parts of Fortune? O, most true, she is a 225
strumpet.[9] What news?

ROSENCRANTZ   None, my lord, but that the world's grown honest.

HAMLET   Then is doomsday near. But your news is not true. Let me
question more in particular. What have you, my good friends, deserved at the hands of Fortune, that she sends you to prison hither? 230

GUILDENSTERN   Prison, my lord?

HAMLET   Denmark's a prison.

ROSENCRANTZ   Then is the world one.

HAMLET   A goodly one, in which there are many confines, wards,[1] and
dungeons, Denmark being one o' th' worst.   235

ROSENCRANTZ   We think not so, my lord.

HAMLET   Why then 'tis none to you; for there is nothing either good
or bad, but thinking makes it so. To me it is a prison.

ROSENCRANTZ   Why then your ambition makes it one. 'Tis too narrow
for your mind.   240

HAMLET   O God, I could be bounded in a nutshell and count myself
a king of infinite space, were it not that I have bad dreams.

GUILDENSTERN   Which dreams indeed are ambition; for the very substance of the ambitious is merely the shadow of a dream.

HAMLET   A dream itself is but a shadow.   245

ROSENCRANTZ   Truly, and I hold ambition of so airy and light a quality
that it is but a shadow's shadow.

HAMLET   Then are our beggars bodies, and our monarchs and outstretched heroes the beggars' shadows. Shall we to th' court? for,
by my fay,[2] I cannot reason.   250

BOTH   We'll wait upon you.

HAMLET   No such matter. I will not sort[3] you with the rest of my
servants; for to speak to you like an honest man, I am most dreadfully attended. But in the beaten way of friendship, what make you
at Elsinore?   255

ROSENCRANTZ   To visit you, my lord; no other occasion.

HAMLET   Beggar that I am, I am even poor in thanks, but I thank
you; and sure, dear friends, my thanks are too dear a halfpenny.[4]
Were you not sent for? Is it your own inclining? Is it a free visitation? Come, come, deal justly with me. Come, come, nay speak.   260

GUILDENSTERN   What should we say, my lord?

HAMLET   Why anything but to th' purpose. You were sent for, and
there is a kind of confession in your looks, which your modesties
have not craft enough to color. I know the good king and queen
have sent for you.   265

ROSENCRANTZ   To what end, my lord?

HAMLET   That you must teach me. But let me conjure you by the
rights of our fellowship, by the consonancy of our youth, by the
obligation of our ever-preserved love, and by what more dear a
better proposer can charge you withal, be even and direct[5] with me 270
whether you were sent for or no.

---

9. Hamlet is indulging in characteristic
ribaldry. Guildenstern means that they are
"privates" = ordinary citizens, but Hamlet
takes him to mean "privates" = sexual organs and "middle of her favors" = waist =
sexual organs.

1. cells
2. faith
3. include
4. not worth a halfpenny
5. straightforward

ROSENCRANTZ [*aside to* GUILDENSTERN] What say you?

HAMLET [*aside*] Nay, then, I have an eye of you.—If you love me, hold not off.

GUILDENSTERN My lord, we were sent for. 275

HAMLET I will tell you why; so shall my anticipation prevent your discovery,[6] and your secrecy to the king and queen moult no feather. I have of late—but wherefore I know not—lost all my mirth, forgone all custom of exercises; and indeed it goes so heavily with my disposition, that this goodly frame the earth seems to me 280 a sterile promontory, this most excellent canopy the air, look you, this brave o'er-hanging firmament, this majestical roof fretted[7] with golden fire, why it appeareth nothing to me but a foul and pestilent congregation of vapors. What a piece of work is a man, how noble in reason, how infinite in faculties, in form and moving, how express[8] 285 and admirable in action, how like an angel in apprehension, how like a god: the beauty of the world, the paragon of animals. And yet to me, what is this quintessence of dust? Man delights not me, nor woman neither, though by your smiling you seem to say so.

ROSENCRANTZ My lord, there was no such stuff in my thoughts. 290

HAMLET Why did ye laugh, then, when I said "Man delights not me"?

ROSENCRANTZ To think, my lord, if you delight not in man, what lenten[9] entertainment the players shall receive from you. We coted[1] them on the way, and hither are they coming to offer you service.

HAMLET He that plays the king shall be welcome—his majesty shall 295 have tribute on me; the adventurous knight shall use his foil and target[2]; the lover shall not sigh gratis; the humorous[3] man shall end his part in peace; the clown shall make those laugh whose lungs are tickle o' th' sere[4]; and the lady shall say her mind freely, or the blank verse shall halt for't. What players are they? 300

ROSENCRANTZ Even those you were wont to take such delight in, the tragedians of the city.

HAMLET How chances it they travel? Their residence, both in reputation and profit, was better both ways.

ROSENCRANTZ I think their inhibition comes by the means of the late 305 innovation.

HAMLET Do they hold the same estimation they did when I was in the city? Are they so followed?

ROSENCRANTZ No, indeed, are they not.

HAMLET How comes it? Do they grow rusty? 310

ROSENCRANTZ Nay, their endeavor keeps in the wonted pace; but there is, sir, an eyrie of children, little eyases,[5] that cry out on the top of question,[6] and are most tyrannically clapped for't. These are now the fashion, and so berattle the common stages (so they call them) that many wearing rapiers are afraid of goose quills[7] and 315 dare scarce come thither.[8]

HAMLET What, are they children? Who maintains 'em? How are they

6. disclosure
7. ornamented with fretwork
8. well built
9. scanty
1. passed
2. sword and shield
3. eccentric
4. easily set off
5. little hawks
6. with a loud, high delivery
7. pens of satirical writers

8. The passage refers to the emergence at the time of the play of theatrical companies made up of children from London choir schools. Their performances became fashionable and hurt the business of the established companies. Hamlet says that if they continue to act, "pursue the quality," when they are grown, they will find that they have been damaging their own future careers.

escoted[9]? Will they pursue the quality no longer than they can sing?
Will they not say afterwards, if they should grow themselves to
common players (as it is most like, if their means are no better), 320
their writers do them wrong to make them exclaim against their
own succession[1]?

ROSENCRANTZ   Faith, there has been much to do on both sides; and
the nation holds it no sin to tarre[2] them to controversy. There was
for a while no money bid for argument,[3] unless the poet and the 325
player went to cuffs[4] in the question.

HAMLET   Is't possible?

GUILDENSTERN   O, there has been much throwing about of brains.

HAMLET   Do the boys carry it away?

ROSENCRANTZ   Ay, that they do, my lord, Hercules and his load too.[5] 330

HAMLET   It is not very strange, for my uncle is King of Denmark, and
those that would make mouths[6] at him while my father lived give
twenty, forty, fifty, a hundred ducats apiece for his picture in little.[7]
'Sblood, there is something in this more than natural, if philosophy
could find it out.   *A flourish.* 335

GUILDENSTERN   There are the players.

HAMLET   Gentlemen, you are welcome to Elsinore. Your hands. Come
then, th' appurtenance of welcome is fashion and ceremony. Let me
comply with[8] you in this garb, lest my extent[9] to the players, which
I tell you must show fairly outwards, should more appear like enter- 340
tainment[1] than yours. You are welcome. But my uncle-father and
aunt-mother are deceived.

GUILDENSTERN   In what, my dear lord?

HAMLET   I am but mad north-north-west; when the wind is southerly
I know a hawk from a handsaw.[2]   345

Enter POLONIUS.

POLONIUS   Well be with you, gentlemen.

HAMLET   Hark you, Guildenstern—and you too—at each ear a hearer.
That great baby you see there is not yet out of his swaddling clouts.[3]

ROSENCRANTZ   Happily he is the second time come to them, for they
say an old man is twice a child.   350

HAMLET   I will prophesy he comes to tell me of the players. Mark it.
—You say right, sir, a Monday morning, 'twas then indeed.

POLONIUS   My lord, I have news to tell you.

HAMLET   My lord, I have news to tell you.
When Roscius was an actor in Rome—[4]   355

POLONIUS   The actors are come hither, my lord.

HAMLET   Buzz, buzz.

POLONIUS   Upon my honor—

HAMLET   Then came each actor on his ass—

POLONIUS   The best actors in the world, either for tragedy, comedy, 360

9. supported
1. future careers
2. urge
3. paid for a play plot
4. blows
5. During one of his labors Hercules assumed for a time the burden of the Titan
Atlas, who supported the heavens on his
shoulder. Also a reference to the effect on
business at Shakespeare's theater, the
Globe.

6. sneer
7. miniature
8. welcome
9. fashion
1. cordiality
2. A "hawk" is a plasterer's tool; Hamlet may also be using "handsaw" = hern-
shaw = heron.
3. wrappings for an infant
4. Roscius was the most famous actor of
classical Rome.

history, pastoral, pastoral-comical, historical-pastoral, tragical-historical, tragical-comical-historical-pastoral, scene individable, or poem unlimited. Seneca cannot be too heavy nor Plautus too light. For the law of writ and the liberty, these are the only men.[5]

HAMLET   O Jephtha, judge of Israel, what a treasure hadst thou![6] 365
POLONIUS   What a treasure had he, my lord?
HAMLET   Why—

"One fair daughter, and no more,
The which he loved passing well."

POLONIUS [*aside*]   Still on my daughter.   370
HAMLET   Am I not i' th' right, old Jephtha?
POLONIUS   If you call me Jephtha, my lord, I have a daughter that I love passing well.
HAMLET   Nay, that follows not.
POLONIUS   What follows then, my lord?   375
HAMLET   Why—

"As by lot, God wot"

and then, you know,

"It came to pass, as most like it was."

The first row[7] of the pious chanson[8] will show you more, for look 380 where my abridgement[9] comes.

Enter the PLAYERS.

You are welcome, masters; welcome, all.—I am glad to see thee well.—Welcome, good friends.—O, old friend! Why thy face is valanced[1] since I saw thee last. Com'st thou to beard me in Denmark?—What, my young lady and mistress? By'r lady, your ladyship 385 is nearer to heaven than when I saw you last by the altitude of a chopine.[2] Pray God your voice, like a piece of uncurrent gold, be not cracked within the ring.—Masters, you are all welcome. We'll e'en to't like French falconers, fly at anything we see. We'll have a speech straight. Come give us a taste of your quality,[3] come a passionate 390 speech.
FIRST PLAYER   What speech, my good lord?
HAMLET   I heard thee speak me a speech once, but it was never acted, or if it was, not above once, for the play, I remember, pleased not the million; 'twas caviary[4] to the general.[5] But it was—as I received 395

5. Seneca and Plautus were Roman writers of tragedy and comedy, respectively. The "law of writ" refers to plays written according to such rules as the three unities; the "liberty" to those written otherwise.
6. To insure victory, Jephtha promised to sacrifice the first creature to meet him on his return. Unfortunately, his only daughter outstripped his dog and was the victim of his vow. The Biblical story is told in *Judges* 11.
7. stanza
8. song
9. that which cuts short by interrupting

1. fringed (with a beard)
2. A reference to the contemporary theatrical practice of using boys to play women's parts. The company's "lady" has grown in height by the size of a woman's thick-soled shoe, "chopine," since Hamlet saw him last. The next sentence refers to the possibility, suggested by his growth, that the young actor's voice may soon begin to change.
3. trade
4. caviar
5. masses

it, and others whose judgments in such matters cried in the top of[6] mine—an excellent play, well digested[7] in the scenes, set down with as much modesty as cunning. I remember one said there were no sallets[8] in the lines to make the matter savory, nor no matter in the phrase that might indict the author of affectation, but called it an 400 honest method, as wholesome as sweet, and by very much more handsome than fine. One speech in't I chiefly loved. 'Twas Æneas' tale to Dido, and thereabout of it especially where he speaks of Priam's slaughter.[9] If it live in your memory, begin at this line—let me see, let me see: 405

"The rugged Pyrrhus, like th' Hyrcanian beast"[1]—

'tis not so; it begins with Pyrrhus—

"The rugged Pyrrhus, he whose sable arms,
Black as his purpose, did the night resemble
When he lay couchéd in th' ominous horse,[2]   410
Hath now this dread and black complexion smeared
With heraldry more dismal; head to foot
Now is he total gules,[3] horridly tricked[4]
With blood of fathers, mothers, daughters, sons,
Baked and impasted[5] with the parching[6] streets,   415
That lend a tyrannous and a damnéd light
To their lord's murder. Roasted in wrath and fire,
And thus o'er-sizéd[7] with coagulate[8] gore,
With eyes like carbuncles, the hellish Pyrrhus
Old grandsire Priam seeks."   420

So proceed you.

POLONIUS   Fore God, my lord, well spoken, with good accent and good
    discretion.
FIRST PLAYER   "Anon he[9] finds him[1]
    Striking too short at Greeks. His antique[2] sword,   425
    Rebellious[3] to his arm, lies where it falls,
    Repugnant to command. Unequal matched,
    Pyrrhus at Priam drives, in rage strikes wide.
    But with the whiff and wind of his fell sword
    Th' unnervéd father falls. Then senseless[4] Ilium,   430
    Seeming to feel this blow, with flaming top
    Stoops[5] to his base, and with a hideous crash
    Takes prisoner Pyrrhus' ear. For, lo! his sword,
    Which was declining[6] on the milky head
    Of reverend Priam, seemed i' th' air to stick.   435

6. were weightier than
7. arranged
8. spicy passages
9. Aeneas, fleeing with his band from fallen Troy (Ilium), arrives in Carthage, where he tells Dido, the Queen of Carthage, of the fall of Troy. Here he is describing the death of Priam, the aged king of Troy, at the hands of Pyrrhus, the son of the slain Achilles.
    1. tiger
    2. i.e., the Trojan horse
    3. completely red

4. adorned
5. crusted
6. burning
7. glued over
8. clotted,
9. Pyrrhus
1. Priam
2. which he used when young
3. refractory
4. without feeling
5. falls
6. about to fall

So as a painted tyrant Pyrrhus stood,
And like a neutral to his will and matter,[7]
Did nothing.
But as we often see, against some storm,
A silence in the heavens, the rack[8] stand still,   440
The bold winds speechless, and the orb below
As hush as death, anon the dreadful thunder
Doth rend the region; so, after Pyrrhus' pause,
A rouséd vengeance sets him new awork,[9]
And never did the Cyclops' hammers fall   445
On Mars's armor, forged for proof eterne,[1]
With less remorse than Pyrrhus' bleeding sword
Now falls on Priam.
Out, out, thou strumpet, Fortune! All you gods,
In general synod take away her power,   450
Break all the spokes and fellies[2] from her wheel,
And bowl[3] the round nave[4] down the hill of heaven
As low as to the fiends."

POLONIUS   This is too long.

HAMLET   It shall to the barber's with your beard.—Prithee say on. 455
He's for a jig,[5] or a tale of bawdry, or he sleeps. Say on; come to
Hecuba.[6]

FIRST PLAYER   "But who, ah woe! had seen the mobled[7] queen—"

HAMLET   "The mobled queen"?

POLONIUS   That's good. "Mobled queen" is good.   460

FIRST PLAYER   "Run barefoot up and down, threat'ning the flames
With bisson rheum,[8] a clout[9] upon that head
Where late the diadem stood, and for a robe,
About her lank and all o'er-teeméd loins,
A blanket, in the alarm of fear caught up—   465
Who this had seen, with tongue in venom steeped,
'Gainst Fortune's state[1] would treason have pronounced.
But if the gods themselves did see her then,
When she saw Pyrrhus make malicious sport
In mincing[2] with his sword her husband's limbs,   470
The instant burst of clamor that she made,
Unless things mortal move them not at all,
Would have made milch[3] the burning eyes of heaven,
And passion in the gods."

POLONIUS   Look whe'r[4] he has not turned his color, and has tears in's 475
eyes. Prithee no more.

HAMLET   'Tis well. I'll have thee speak out the rest of this soon.—
Good my lord, will you see the players well bestowed?[5] Do you
hear, let them be well used, for they are the abstract[6] and brief

---

7. between his will and the fulfillment
of it
8. clouds
9. to work
1. Mars, as befits a Roman war god, had
armor made for him by the blacksmith god
Vulcan and his assistants, the Cyclops. It
was suitably impenetrable, of "proof
eterne."
2. parts of the rim
3. roll
4. hub
5. a comic act
6. Hecuba was the wife of Priam and

Queen of Troy. Her "loins" are described
below as "o'erteemed" because of her unusual fertility. The number of her children
varies in different accounts. but twenty is
a safe minimum.
7. muffled (in a hood)
8. blinding tears
9. cloth
1. government
2. cutting up
3. tearful (*lit.* milk-giving)
4. whether
5. provided for
6. summary

chronicles of the time; after your death you were better have a bad ⁴⁸⁰
epitaph than their ill report while you live.

POLONIUS   My lord, I will use them according to their desert.

HAMLET   God's bodkin, man, much better. Use every man after his
desert, and who shall 'scape whipping? Use them after your own
honor and dignity. The less they deserve, the more merit is in your ⁴⁸⁵
bounty. Take them in.

POLONIUS   Come, sirs.

HAMLET   Follow him, friends. We'll hear a play tomorrow. [*Aside to*
FIRST PLAYER.] Dost thou hear me, old friend, can you play "The
Murder of Gonzago"?   ⁴⁹⁰

FIRST PLAYER   Ay, my lord.

HAMLET   We'll ha't tomorrow night. You could for a need study a
speech of some dozen or sixteen lines which I would set down and
insert in't, could you not?

FIRST PLAYER   Ay, my lord.   ⁴⁹⁵

HAMLET   Very well. Follow that lord, and look you mock him not.

Exeunt POLONIUS *and* PLAYERS.

My good friends, I'll leave you till night. You are welcome to
Elsinore.

ROSENCRANTZ   Good my lord.

Exeunt ROSENCRANTZ *and* GUILDENSTERN.

HAMLET   Ay, so God b'wi'ye. Now I am alone.   ⁵⁰⁰
O, what a rogue and peasant slave am I!
Is it not monstrous that this player here,
But in a fiction, in a dream of passion,
Could force his soul so to his own conceit⁷
That from her working all his visage wanned;⁸   ⁵⁰⁵
Tears in his eyes, distraction in his aspect,⁹
A broken voice, and his whole function suiting
With forms to his conceit? And all for nothing,
For Hecuba!
What's Hecuba to him or he to Hecuba,   ⁵¹⁰
That he should weep for her? What would he do
Had he the motive and the cue for passion
That I have? He would drown the stage with tears,
And cleave the general ear with horrid speech,
Make mad the guilty, and appal the free,   ⁵¹⁵
Confound the ignorant, and amaze indeed
The very faculties of eyes and ears.
Yet I,
A dull and muddy-mettled¹ rascal, peak²
Like John-a-dreams,³ unpregnant⁴ of my cause,   ⁵²⁰
And can say nothing; no, not for a king
Upon whose property and most dear life
A damned defeat was made. Am I a coward?
Who calls me villain, breaks my pate across,
Plucks off my beard and blows it in my face,   ⁵²⁵

---

7. imagination   2. mope
8. grew pale   3. a man dreaming
9. face   4. not quickened by
1. dull-spirited

Tweaks me by the nose, gives me the lie i' th' throat
As deep as to the lungs? Who does me this?
Ha, 'swounds, I should take it; for it cannot be
But I am pigeon-livered and lack gall[5]
To make oppression bitter, or ere this   530
I should 'a fatted all the region kites[6]
With this slave's offal. Bloody, bawdy villain!
Remorseless, treacherous, lecherous, kindless[7] villain!
Why, what an ass am I! This is most brave,
That I, the son of a dear father murdered,   535
Prompted to my revenge by heaven and hell,
Must like a whore unpack[8] my heart with words,
And fall a-cursing like a very drab,
A scullion![9] Fie upon't! foh!
About, my brains. Hum—I have heard   540
That guilty creatures sitting at a play,
Have by the very cunning of the scene
Been struck so to the soul that presently
They have proclaimed[1] their malefactions;
For murder, though it have no tongue, will speak   545
With most miraculous organ. I'll have these players
Play something like the murder of my father
Before mine uncle. I'll observe his looks.
I'll tent[2] him to the quick. If 'a do blench,[3]
I know my course. The spirit that I have seen   550
May be a devil, and the devil hath power
T' assume a pleasing shape, yea, and perhaps
Out of my weakness and my melancholy,
As he is very potent with such spirits,
Abuses me to damn me. I'll have grounds   555
More relative[4] than this. The play's the thing
Wherein I'll catch the conscience of the king.   *Exit.*

Act 3

SCENE 1: *A room in the castle. Enter* KING, QUEEN, POLONIUS,
OPHELIA, ROSENCRANTZ *and* GUILDENSTERN.

KING   And can you by no drift of conference[5]
Get from him why he puts on this confusion,
Grating so harshly all his days of quiet
With turbulent[6] and dangerous lunacy?
ROSENCRANTZ   He does confess he feels himself distracted,   5
But from what cause 'a will by no means speak.
GUILDENSTERN   Nor do we find him forward[7] to be sounded,[8]
But with a crafty madness keeps aloof

5. bitterness
6. birds of prey of the area
7. unnatural
8. relieve
9. In some versions of the play, the word "stallion," a slang term for a prostitute, appears in place of "scullion."
1. admitted

2. try
3. turn pale
4. conclusive
5. line of conversation
6. disturbing
7. eager
8. questioned

When we would bring him on to some confession
Of his true state.

QUEEN   Did he receive you well?   10

ROSENCRANTZ   Most like a gentleman.

GUILDENSTERN   But with much forcing of his disposition.[9]

ROSENCRANTZ   Niggard of question, but of our demands[1]
Most free in his reply.

QUEEN   Did you assay[2] him
To any pastime?   15

ROSENCRANTZ   Madam, it so fell out that certain players
We o'er-raught[3] on the way. Of these we told him,
And there did seem in him a kind of joy
To hear of it. They are here about the court,
And as I think, they have already order   20
This night to play before him.

POLONIUS   'Tis most true,
And he beseeched me to entreat your majesties
To hear and see the matter.[4]

KING   With all my heart, and it doth much content me
To hear him so inclined.   25
Good gentlemen, give him a further edge,
And drive his purpose[5] into these delights.

ROSENCRANTZ   We shall, my lord.

> *Exeunt* ROSENCRANTZ *and* GUILDENSTERN.

KING   Sweet Gertrude, leave us too,
For we have closely sent for Hamlet hither,
That he, as 'twere by accident, may here   30
Affront[6] Ophelia.
Her father and myself (lawful espials[7])
Will so bestow ourselves that, seeing unseen,
We may of their encounter frankly judge,
And gather by him, as he is behaved,   35
If't be th' affliction of his love or no
That thus he suffers for.

QUEEN   I shall obey you.—
And for your part, Ophelia, I do wish
That your good beauties be the happy cause
Of Hamlet's wildness. So shall I hope your virtues   40
Will bring him to his wonted[8] way again,
To both your honors.

OPHELIA   Madam, I wish it may.   *Exit* QUEEN.

POLONIUS   Ophelia, walk you here.—Gracious,[9] so please you,
We will bestow ourselves.—[*To* OPHELIA.] Read on this book,
That show of such an exercise[1] may color[2]   45
Your loneliness.—We are oft to blame in this,
'Tis too much proved, that with devotion's visage
And pious action we do sugar o'er
The devil himself.

9. conversation
1. to our questions
2. tempt
3. passed
4. performance
5. sharpen his intention

6. confront
7. justified spies
8. usual
9. Majesty
1. act of devotion
2. explain

KING [*aside*]   O, 'tis too true.

How smart a lash that speech doth give my conscience!   50
The harlot's cheek, beautied with plast'ring[3] art,
Is not more ugly to the thing that helps it
Than is my deed to my most painted word.
O heavy burden!

POLONIUS   I hear him coming. Let's withdraw, my lord.   55

Exeunt KING *and* POLONIUS.

Enter HAMLET.

HAMLET   To be, or not to be, that is the question:
Whether 'tis nobler in the mind to suffer
The slings and arrows of outrageous fortune,
Or to take arms against a sea of troubles,
And by opposing end them. To die, to sleep—   60
No more; and by a sleep to say we end
The heartache, and the thousand natural shocks
That flesh is heir to. 'Tis a consummation
Devoutly to be wished—to die, to sleep—
To sleep, perchance to dream, ay there's the rub;   65
For in that sleep of death what dreams may come
When we have shuffled off this mortal coil[4]
Must give us pause—there's the respect[5]
That makes calamity of so long life.
For who would bear the whips and scorns of time,   70
Th' oppressor's wrong, the proud man's contumely,[6]
The pangs of despised love, the law's delay,
The insolence of office, and the spurns[7]
That patient merit of th' unworthy takes,
When he himself might his quietus[8] make   75
With a bare bodkin?[9] Who would fardels[1] bear,
To grunt and sweat under a weary life,
But that the dread of something after death,
The undiscovered country, from whose bourn[2]
No traveller returns, puzzles the will,   80
And makes us rather bear those ills we have
Than fly to others that we know not of?
Thus conscience does make cowards of us all;
And thus the native[3] hue of resolution
Is sicklied o'er with the pale cast of thought,   85
And enterprises of great pitch[4] and moment[5]
With this regard their currents turn awry
And lose the name of action.—Soft you now,
The fair Ophelia.—Nymph, in thy orisons[6]
Be all my sins remembered.

OPHELIA   Good my lord,   90
How does your honor for this many a day?

HAMLET   I humbly thank you, well, well, well.

3. thickly painted	1. burdens
4. turmoil	2. boundary
5. consideration	3. natural
6. insulting behavior	4. height
7. rejections	5. importance
8. settlement	6. prayers
9. dagger	

OPHELIA   My lord, I have remembrances of yours
That I have longed long to re-deliver.
I pray you now receive them.
HAMLET   No, not I,   95
I never gave you aught.
OPHELIA   My honored lord, you know right well you did,
And with them words of so sweet breath composed
As made the things more rich. Their perfume lost,
Take these again, for to the noble mind   100
Rich gifts wax[7] poor when givers prove unkind.
There, my lord.
HAMLET   Ha, ha! are you honest?[8]
OPHELIA   My lord?
HAMLET   Are you fair?   105
OPHELIA   What means your lordship?
HAMLET   That if you be honest and fair, your honesty should admit
no discourse to your beauty.
OPHELIA   Could beauty, my lord, have better commerce[9] than with
honesty?   110
HAMLET   Ay, truly, for the power of beauty will sooner transform
honesty from what it is to a bawd than the force of honesty can
translate beauty into his likeness. This was sometime a paradox, but
now the time gives it proof. I did love you once.
OPHELIA   Indeed, my lord, you made me believe so.   115
HAMLET   You should not have believed me, for virtue cannot so in-
oculate[1] our old stock but we shall relish of it. I loved you not.
OPHELIA   I was the more deceived.
HAMLET   Get thee to a nunnery.[2] Why wouldst thou be a breeder of
sinners? I am myself indifferent[3] honest, but yet I could accuse me 120
of such things that it were better my mother had not borne me: I
am very proud, revengeful, ambitious, with more offences at my
beck[4] than I have thoughts to put them in, imagination to give them
shape, or time to act them in. What should such fellows as I do
crawling between earth and heaven? We are arrant[5] knaves all; be- 125
lieve none of us. Go thy ways to a nunnery. Where's your father?
OPHELIA   At home, my lord.
HAMLET   Let the doors be shut upon him, that he may play the fool
nowhere but in's own house. Farewell.
OPHELIA   O, help him, you sweet heavens!   130
HAMLET   If thou dost marry, I'll give thee this plague for thy dowry:
be thou as chaste as ice, as pure as snow, thou shalt not escape
calumny. Get thee to a nunnery, farewell. Or if thou wilt needs
marry, marry a fool, for wise men know well enough what monsters[6]
you make of them. To a nunnery, go, and quickly too. Farewell.   135
OPHELIA   Heavenly powers, restore him!
HAMLET   I have heard of your paintings well enough. God hath given
you one face, and you make yourselves another. You jig, you amble,
and you lisp;[7] you nickname God's creatures, and make your wantonness your ignorance.[8] Go to, I'll no more on't, it hath made me mad. 140

7. become
8. chaste
9. intercourse
1. change by grafting
2. With typical ribaldry Hamlet uses
"nunnery" in two senses, the second as a
slang term for brothel.
3. moderately

4. command
5. thorough
6. horned because cuckolded
7. walk and talk affectedly
8. Hamlet means that women call things
by pet names and then blame the affectation on ignorance.

I say we will have no more marriage. Those that are married already, all but one, shall live. The rest shall keep as they are. To a nunnery, go.   *Exit.*

OPHELIA   O, what a noble mind is here o'erthrown!
The courtier's, soldier's, scholar's, eye, tongue, sword,   145
Th' expectancy⁹ and rose¹ of the fair state,
The glass² of fashion and the mould³ of form,
Th' observed of all observers, quite quite down!
And I of ladies most deject and wretched,
That sucked the honey of his music⁴ vows,   150
Now see that noble and most sovereign reason
Like sweet bells jangled, out of time and harsh;
That unmatched form and feature of blown⁵ youth
Blasted with ecstasy. O, woe is me
T' have seen what I have seen, see what I see!   155

Enter KING *and* POLONIUS.

KING   Love! His affections do not that way tend,
Nor what he spake, though it lacked form a little,
Was not like madness. There's something in his soul
O'er which his melancholy sits on brood,⁶
And I do doubt⁷ the hatch and the disclose⁸   160
Will be some danger; which to prevent,
I have in quick determination
Thus set it down: he shall with speed to England
For the demand of our neglected tribute.
Haply the seas and countries different,   165
With variable objects, shall expel
This something-settled matter in his heart
Whereon his brains still beating puts him thus
From fashion of himself. What think you on't?
POLONIUS   It shall do well. But yet do I believe   170
The origin and commencement of his grief
Sprung from neglected love.—How now, Ophelia?
You need not tell us what Lord Hamlet said,
We heard it all.—My lord, do as you please,
But if you hold it fit, after the play   175
Let his queen-mother all alone entreat him
To show his grief. Let her be round⁹ with him,
And I'll be placed, so please you, in the ear¹
Of all their conference. If she find him not,²
To England send him; or confine him where   180
Your wisdom best shall think.
KING   It shall be so.
Madness in great ones must not unwatched go.   *Exeunt.*

SCENE 2: *A public room in the castle. Enter* HAMLET *and three of the* PLAYERS.

HAMLET   Speak the speech, I pray you, as I pronounced it to you, trippingly on the tongue; but if you mouth it as many of our players do,

9. hope	4. musical	8. result
1. ornament	5. full-blown	9. direct
2. mirror	6. i.e., like a hen	1. hearing
3. model	7. fear	2. discover his problem

I had as lief the town-crier spoke my lines. Nor do not saw the air too much with your hand thus, but use all gently, for in the very torrent, tempest, and as I may say, whirlwind of your passion, you must 5 acquire and beget a temperance that may give it smoothness. O, it offends me to the soul to hear a robustious[3] periwig-pated[4] fellow tear a passion to tatters, to very rags, to split the ears of the groundlings,[5] who for the most part are capable of[6] nothing but inexplicable dumb shows and noise. I would have such a fellow whipped for 10 o'erdoing Termagant. It out-herods Herod.[7] Pray you avoid it.

FIRST PLAYER   I warrant your honor.

HAMLET   Be not too tame neither, but let your own discretion be your tutor. Suit the action to the word, the word to the action, with this special observance, that you o'erstep not the modesty of nature; 15 for anything so o'erdone is from[8] the purpose of playing, whose end both at the first, and now, was and is, to hold as 'twere the mirror up to nature, to show virtue her own feature, scorn her own image, and the very age and body of the time his form and pressure.[9] Now this overdone, or come tardy off, though it makes the unskilful[1] laugh, 20 cannot but make the judicious grieve, the censure[2] of the which one must in your allowance o'erweigh a whole theatre of others. O, there be players that I have seen play—and heard others praise, and that highly—not to speak it profanely, that neither having th' accent of Christians, nor the gait of Christian, pagan, nor man, have so strut- 25 ted and bellowed that I have thought some of nature's journeymen[3] had made men, and not made them well, they imitated humanity so abominably.

FIRST PLAYER   I hope we have reformed that indifferently[4] with us.

HAMLET   O, reform it altogether. And let those that play your clowns 30 speak no more than is set down for them, for there be of them that will themselves laugh, to set on some quantity of barren[5] spectators to laugh too, though in the meantime some necessary question of the play be then to be considered. That's villainous, and shows a most pitiful ambition in the fool that uses it. Go, make you ready. 35

Exeunt PLAYERS.

Enter POLONIUS, GUILDENSTERN, *and* ROSENCRANTZ.

How now, my lord? Will the king hear this piece of work?

POLONIUS   And the queen too, and that presently.

HAMLET   Bid the players make haste.   *Exit* POLONIUS.
Will you two help to hasten them?

ROSENCRANTZ   Ay, my lord.   *Exeunt they two.* 40

HAMLET   What, ho, Horatio!

Enter HORATIO.

HORATIO   Here, sweet lord, at your service.

HAMLET   Horatio, thou art e'en as just a man
As e'er my conversation coped[6] withal.

---

3. noisy
4. bewigged
5. the spectators who paid least
6. i.e., capable of understanding
7. Termagant, a "Saracen" deity, and the Biblical Herod were stock characters in popular drama noted for the excesses of sound and fury used by their interpreters.

8. contrary to
9. shape
1. ignorant
2. judgment
3. inferior craftsmen
4. somewhat
5. dull-witted
6. encountered

HORATIO   O my dear lord!

HAMLET   Nay, do not think I flatter,   45
For what advancement may I hope from thee,
That no revenue hast but thy good spirits
To feed and clothe thee? Why should the poor be flattered?
No, let the candied tongue lick absurd pomp,
And crook the pregnant⁷ hinges of the knee   50
Where thrift⁸ may follow fawning. Dost thou hear?
Since my dear soul was mistress of her choice
And could of men distinguish her election,
S'hath sealed thee for herself, for thou hast been
As one in suff'ring all that suffers nothing,   55
A man that Fortune's buffets and rewards
Hast ta'en with equal thanks; and blest are those
Whose blood and judgment are so well commingled
That they are not a pipe⁹ for Fortune's finger
To sound¹ what stop² she please. Give me that man   60
That is not passion's slave, and I will wear him
In my heart's core, ay, in my heart of heart,
As I do thee. Something too much of this.
There is a play tonight before the king.
One scene of it comes near the circumstance   65
Which I have told thee of my father's death.
I prithee, when thou seest that act afoot,
Even with the very comment³ of thy soul
Observe my uncle. If his occulted⁴ guilt
Do not itself unkennel⁵ in one speech,   70
It is a damnéd ghost that we have seen,
And my imaginations are as foul
As Vulcan's stithy.⁶ Give him heedful note,⁷
For I mine eyes will rivet to his face,
And after we will both our judgments join   75
In censure of his seeming.⁸

HORATIO   Well, my lord.
If 'a steal aught the whilst this play is playing,
And 'scape detecting, I will pay⁹ the theft.

Enter Trumpets and Kettledrums, KING, QUEEN, POLONIUS,
OPHELIA, ROSENCRANTZ, GUILDENSTERN, *and other* LORDS *attendant.*

HAMLET   They are coming to the play. I must be idle.
Get you a place.   80

KING   How fares our cousin Hamlet?

HAMLET   Excellent, i' faith, of the chameleon's dish.¹ I eat the air,
promise-crammed. You cannot feed capons so.

7. quick to bend
8. profit
9. musical instrument
1. play
2. note
3. keenest observation
4. hidden
5. break loose

6. smithy
7. careful attention
8. manner
9. repay
1. A reference to a popular belies that the chameleon subsisted on a diet of air. Hamlet has deliberately misunderstood the King's question.

KING   I have nothing with this answer, Hamlet. These words are not
mine.   85

HAMLET   No, nor mine now. [*To* POLONIUS.] My lord, you played once
i' th' university, you say?

POLONIUS   That did I, my lord, and was accounted a good actor.

HAMLET   What did you enact?

POLONIUS   I did enact Julius Cæsar. I was killed i' th' Capitol; Brutus   90
killed me.[2]

HAMLET   It was a brute part of him to kill so capital a calf there. Be
the players ready?

ROSENCRANTZ   Ay, my lord, they stay[3] upon your patience.[4]

QUEEN   Come hither, my dear Hamlet, sit by me.   95

HAMLET   No, good mother, here's metal more attractive.

POLONIUS [*to the* KING]   O, ho! do you mark that?

HAMLET   Lady, shall I lie in your lap?

Lying down at OPHELIA's *feet.*

OPHELIA   No, my lord.

HAMLET   I mean, my head upon your lap?   100

OPHELIA   Ay, my lord.

HAMLET   Do you think I meant country matters?[5]

OPHELIA   I think nothing, my lord.

HAMLET   That's a fair thought to lie between maids' legs.

OPHELIA   What is, my lord?   105

HAMLET   Nothing.

OPHELIA   You are merry, my lord.

HAMLET   Who, I?

OPHELIA   Ay, my lord.

HAMLET   O God, your only jig-maker![6] What should a man do but be   110
merry? For look you how cheerfully my mother looks, and my father
died within's two hours.

OPHELIA   Nay, 'tis twice two months, my lord.

HAMLET   So long? Nay then, let the devil wear black, for I'll have a
suit of sables. O heavens! die two months ago, and not forgotten   115
yet? Then there's hope a great man's memory may outlive his life
half a year, but by'r lady 'a must build churches then, or else shall
'a suffer not thinking on, with the hobby-horse, whose epitaph is
"For O, for O, the hobby-horse is forgot!"[7]

The trumpets sound. Dumb Show follows. Enter a KING *and a*
QUEEN *very lovingly; the* QUEEN *embracing him and he her.*
She kneels, and makes show of protestation unto him. He takes
her up, and declines[8] his head upon her neck. He lies him down
upon a bank of flowers; she, seeing him asleep, leaves him.
Anon come in another man, takes off his crown, kisses it, pours
poison in the sleeper's ears, and leaves him. The QUEEN *returns,*
finds the KING *dead, makes passionate action. The* POISONER
with some three or four come in again, seem to condole with
her. The dead body is carried away. The POISONER *woos the*

2. The assassination of Julius Caesar by
Brutus and others is the subject of another
play by Shakespeare.
3. wait
4. leisure
5. Presumably, rustic misbehavior, but
here and elsewhere in this exchange Hamlet treats Ophelia to some ribald double
meanings.
6. writer of comic scenes
7. In traditional games and dances one
of the characters was a man represented as
riding a horse. The horse was made of
something like cardboard and was worn
about the "rider's" waist.
8. lays

QUEEN *with gifts; she seems harsh awhile, but in the end accepts* *love.* *Exeunt.*

OPHELIA   What means this, my lord?   120
HAMLET   Marry, this is miching mallecho;[9] it means mischief.
OPHELIA   Belike this show imports[1] the argument[2] of the play.

Enter PROLOGUE.

HAMLET   We shall know by this fellow. The players cannot keep
counsel; they'll tell all.
OPHELIA   Will 'a tell us what this show meant?   125
HAMLET   Ay, or any show that you will show him. Be not you ashamed
to show, he'll not shame to tell you what it means.
OPHELIA   You are naught,[3] you are naught. I'll mark[4] the play.
PROLOGUE *For us, and for our tragedy,*
          Here stooping to your clemency,   130
          We beg your hearing patiently. *Exit.*
HAMLET   Is this a prologue, or the posy[5] of a ring?
OPHELIA   'Tis brief, my lord.
HAMLET   As woman's love.

Enter the PLAYER KING *and* QUEEN.

PLAYER KING   *Full thirty times hath Phœbus' cart gone round*   135
Neptune's salt wash and Tellus' orbéd ground,
And thirty dozen moons with borrowed sheen[6]
About the world have times twelve thirties been,
Since love our hearts and Hymen did our hands
Unite comutual[7] in most sacred bands.[8]   140
PLAYER QUEEN   *So many journeys may the sun and moon*
Make us again count o'er ere love be done!
But woe is me, you are so sick of late,
So far from cheer and from your former state,
That I distrust[9] you. Yet though I distrust,   145
Discomfort you, my lord, it nothing must.
For women's fear and love hold quantity,[1]
In neither aught, or in extremity.[2]
Now what my love is proof hath made you know,
And as my love is sized,[3] my fear is so.   150
Where love is great, the littlest doubts are fear;
Where little fears grow great, great love grows there.
PLAYER KING   *Faith, I must leave thee, love, and shortly too;*
My operant powers[4] their functions leave[5] to do.
And thou shalt live in this fair world behind,   155
Honored, beloved, and haply one as kind
For husband shalt thou—

---

9. sneaking crime
1. explains
2. plot
3. obscene
4. attend to
5. motto engraved inside
6. light
7. mutually
8. The speech contains several mythological references. "Phoebus" was a sun
god, and his chariot or "cart" the sun.

The "salt wash" of Neptune is the ocean;
"Tellus" was an earth goddess, and her
"orbed ground" is the earth, or globe.
Hymen was the god of marriage.
9. fear for
1. agree in weight
2. The lady means without regard to
too much or too little.
3. in size
4. active forces
5. cease

PLAYER QUEEN   *O, confound the rest!*
Such love must needs be treason in my breast.
In second husband let me be accurst!
None wed the second but who killed the first.[6]   160
HAMLET   That's wormwood.
PLAYER QUEEN   *The instances[7] that second marriage move*
Are base respects[8] of thrift, but none of love.
A second time I kill my husband dead,
When second husband kisses me in bed.   165
PLAYER KING   *I do believe you think what now you speak,*
But what we do determine oft we break.
Purpose is but the slave to memory,
Of violent birth, but poor validity;
Which now, like fruit unripe, sticks on the tree,   170
But fall unshaken when they mellow be.
Most necessary 'tis that we forget
To pay ourselves what to ourselves is debt.
What to ourselves in passion we propose,
The passion ending, doth the purpose lose.   175
The violence of either grief or joy
Their own enactures[9] with themselves destroy.
Where joy most revels, grief doth most lament;
Grief joys, joy grieves, on slender accident.
This world is not for aye,[1] nor 'tis not strange   180
That even our loves should with our fortunes change;
For 'tis a question left us yet to prove,
Whether love lead fortune, or else fortune love.
The great man down, you mark his favorite flies;
The poor advanced makes friends of enemies;   185
And hitherto doth love on fortune tend,
For who not needs shall never lack a friend,
And who in want a hollow[2] friend doth try,
Directly seasons him[3] his enemy.
But orderly to end where I begun,   190
Our wills and fates do so contrary run
That our devices[4] still are overthrown;
Our thoughts are ours, their ends none of our own.
So think thou wilt no second husband wed,
But die thy thoughts when thy first lord is dead.   195
PLAYER QUEEN   *Nor earth to me give food, nor heaven light,*
Sport and repose lock from me day and night,
To desperation turn my trust and hope,
An anchor's cheer[5] in prison be my scope,
Each opposite that blanks[6] the face of joy   200
Meet what I would have well, and it destroy,
Both here and hence[7] pursue me lasting strife,
If once a widow, ever I be wife!
HAMLET   If she should break it now!

---

6. Though there is some ambiguity, she
seems to mean that the only kind of woman
who would remarry is one who has killed
or would kill her first husband.
   7. causes
   8. concerns
   9. actions

1. eternal
2. false
3. ripens him into
4. plans
5. anchorite's food
6. blanches
7. in the next world

PLAYER KING   'Tis deeply sworn. Sweet, leave me here awhile.   205
My spirits grow dull, and fain I would beguile
The tedious day with sleep.   Sleeps.
PLAYER QUEEN   Sleep rock thy brain,
And never come mischance between us twain!   Exit.
HAMLET   Madam, how like you this play?
QUEEN   The lady doth protest too much, methinks.   210
HAMLET   O, but she'll keep her word.
KING   Have you heard the argument? Is there no offence in't?
HAMLET   No, no, they do but jest, poison in jest; no offence i' th'
world.
KING   What do you call the play?   215
HAMLET   "The Mouse-trap." Marry, how? Tropically.[8] This play is the
image of a murder done in Vienna. Gonzago is the duke's name; his
wife, Baptista. You shall see anon. 'Tis a knavish piece of work, but
what of that? Your majesty, and we that have free souls, it touches
us not. Let the galled jade wince, our withers are unwrung.[9]   220

    Enter LUCIANUS.

This is one Lucianus, nephew to the king.
OPHELIA   You are as good as a chorus, my lord.
HAMLET   I could interpret between you and your love, if I could see
the puppets dallying.
OPHELIA   You are keen, my lord, you are keen.   225
HAMLET   It would cost you a groaning to take off mine edge.
OPHELIA   Still better, and worse.
HAMLET   So you mis-take your husbands.—Begin, murderer. Leave
thy damnable faces and begin. Come, the croaking raven doth bel-
low for revenge.   230
LUCIANUS   Thoughts black, hands apt, drugs fit, and time agreeing,
Confederate season,[1] else no creature seeing,
Thou mixture rank, of midnight weeds collected,
With Hecate's ban thrice blasted, thrice infected,[2]
Thy natural magic[3] and dire property   235
On wholesome life usurps immediately.
                            Pours the poison in his ears.
HAMLET   'A poisons him i' th' garden for his estate. His name's Gon-
zago. The story is extant, and written in very choice Italian. You
shall see anon how the murderer gets the love of Gonzago's wife.
OPHELIA   The king rises.   240
HAMLET   What, frighted with false fire?
QUEEN   How fares my lord?
POLONIUS   Give o'er the play.
KING   Give me some light. Away!
POLONIUS   Lights, lights, lights!   245

    Exeunt all but HAMLET *and* HORATIO.

HAMLET   Why, let the strucken deer go weep,
                The hart ungalléd[4] play.
        For some must watch while some must sleep;
            Thus runs the world away.

8. figuratively
9. A "galled jade" is a horse, particularly one of poor quality, with a sore
back. The "withers" are the ridge between
a horse's shoulders; "unwrung withers" are
not chafed by the harness.

1. a helpful time for the crime
2. Hecate was a classical goddess of
witchcraft.
3. native power
4. uninjured

Would not this, sir, and a forest of feathers[5]—if the rest of my for- 250
tunes turn Turk with me—with two Provincial roses on my razed
shoes, get me a fellowship in a cry[6] of players?[7]
HORATIO   Half a share.
HAMLET   A whole one, I.

> For thou dost know, O Damon dear,[8]   255
> This realm dismantled was
> Of Jove himself, and now reigns here
> A very, very—peacock.

HORATIO   You might have rhymed.
HAMLET   O good Horatio, I'll take the ghost's word for a thousand 260
pound. Didst perceive?
HORATIO   Very well, my lord.
HAMLET   Upon the talk of the poisoning.
HORATIO   I did very well note[9] him.
HAMLET   Ah, ha! Come, some music. Come, the recorders.[1]   265
For if the king like not the comedy,
Why then, belike he likes it not, perdy.[2]
Come, some music.

Enter ROSENCRANTZ *and* GUILDENSTERN.

GUILDENSTERN   Good my lord, vouchsafe me a word with you.
HAMLET   Sir, a whole history.   270
GUILDENSTERN   The king, sir—
HAMLET   Ay, sir, what of him?
GUILDENSTERN   Is in his retirement[3] marvellous distempered.[4]
HAMLET   With drink, sir?
GUILDENSTERN   No, my lord, with choler.[5]   275
HAMLET   Your wisdom should show itself more richer to signify this
to the doctor, for for me to put him to his purgation[6] would perhaps
plunge him into more choler.
GUILDENSTERN   Good my lord, put your discourse[7] into some frame,[8]
and start not so wildly from my affair.   280
HAMLET   I am tame, sir. Pronounce.
GUILDENSTERN   The queen your mother, in most great affliction of
spirit, hath sent me to you.
HAMLET   You are welcome.
GUILDENSTERN   Nay, good my lord, this courtesy is not of the right 285
breed. If it shall please you to make me a wholesome[9] answer, I will
do your mother's commandment. If not, your pardon and my return[1]
shall be the end of my business.
HAMLET   Sir, I cannot.
ROSENCRANTZ   What, my lord?   290

---

5. plumes
6. company
7. Hamlet asks Horatio if "this" recitation, accompanied with a player's costume, including plumes and rosettes on shoes which have been slashed for decorative effect, might not entitle him to become a shareholder in a theatrical company in the event that Fortune goes against him, "turn Turk."
8. Damon was a common name for a young man or a shepherd in lyric, especially pastoral poetry. Jove was the chief god of the Romans. The Reader may sup-

ply for himself the rhyme referred to by Horatio.
9. observe
1. wooden end-blown flutes
2. *par Dieu* (by God)
3. place to which he has retired
4. vexed
5. bile
6. treatment with a laxative
7. speech
8. order
9. reasonable
1. i.e., to the Queen

HAMLET   Make you a wholesome answer; my wit's diseased. But, sir, such answer as I can make, you shall command, or rather, as you say, my mother. Therefore no more, but to the matter. My mother, you say—

ROSENCRANTZ   Then thus she says: your behavior hath struck her into 295 amazement and admiration.[2]

HAMLET   O wonderful son, that can so stonish a mother! But is there no sequel at the heels of this mother's admiration? Impart.[3]

ROSENCRANTZ   She desires to speak with you in her closet[4] ere you go to bed. 300

HAMLET   We shall obey, were she ten times our mother. Have you any further trade[5] with us?

ROSENCRANTZ   My lord, you once did love me.

HAMLET   And do still, by these pickers and stealers.[6]

ROSENCRANTZ   Good my lord, what is your cause of distemper? You 305 do surely bar the door upon your own liberty, if you deny your griefs to your friend.

HAMLET   Sir, I lack advancement.

ROSENCRANTZ   How can that be, when you have the voice of the king himself for your succession in Denmark? 310

HAMLET   Ay, sir, but "while the grass grows"—the proverb[7] is something musty.

Enter the PLAYERS *with recorders.*

O, the recorders! Let me see one. To withdraw with you[8]—why do you go about to recover the wind of me, as if you would drive me into a toil?[9] 315

GUILDENSTERN   O my lord, if my duty be too bold, my love is too unmannerly.

HAMLET   I do not well understand that. Will you play upon this pipe?[1]

GUILDENSTERN   My lord, I cannot.

HAMLET   I pray you. 320

GUILDENSTERN   Believe me, I cannot.

HAMLET   I do beseech you.

GUILDENSTERN   I know no touch of it,[2] my lord.

HAMLET   It is as easy as lying. Govern[3] these ventages[4] with your fingers and thumb, give it breath with your mouth, and it will 325 discourse most eloquent music. Look you, these are the stops.[5]

GUILDENSTERN   But these cannot I command to any utt'rance of harmony. I have not the skill.

HAMLET   Why, look you now, how unworthy a thing you make of me! You would play upon me, you would seem to know my stops, you 330 would pluck out the heart of my mystery, you would sound[6] me from my lowest note to the top of my compass[7]; and there is much music, excellent voice, in this little organ, yet cannot you make it speak. 'Sblood, do you think I am easier to be played on than a pipe?

2. wonder
3. tell me
4. bedroom
5. business
6. hands
7. The proverb ends "the horse starves."
8. let me step aside
9. The figure is from hunting. "You will approach me with the wind blowing from me toward you in order to drive me into the net."
1. recorder
2. have no ability
3. cover and uncover
4. holes
5. wind-holes
6. play
7. range

Call me what instrument you will, though you can fret[8] me, you 335
cannot play upon me.

Enter POLONIUS.

God bless you, sir!
POLONIUS   My lord, the queen would speak with you, and presently.[9]
HAMLET   Do you see yonder cloud that's almost in shape of a camel?
POLONIUS   By th' mass, and 'tis like a camel indeed.   340
HAMLET   Methinks it is like a weasel.
POLONIUS   It is backed like a weasel.
HAMLET   Or like a whale.
POLONIUS   Very like a whale.
HAMLET   Then I will come to my mother by and by. [*Aside.*] They 345
fool me to the top of my bent.[1]—I will come by and by.
POLONIUS   I will say so.   *Exit* POLONIUS.
HAMLET   "By and by" is easily said. Leave me, friends.

Exeunt all but HAMLET.

'Tis now the very witching time of night,
When churchyards yawn, and hell itself breathes out   350
Contagion to this world. Now could I drink hot blood,
And do such bitter business as the day
Would quake to look on. Soft, now to my mother.
O heart, lose not thy nature; let not ever
The soul of Nero[2] enter this firm bosom.   355
Let me be cruel, not unnatural;
I will speak daggers to her, but use none.
My tongue and soul in this be hypocrites—
How in my words somever she be shent,[3]
To give them seals[4] never, my soul, consent!   *Exit.* 360

SCENE 3: *A room in the castle. Enter* KING, ROSENCRANTZ
and GUILDENSTERN.

KING   I like him not,[5] nor stands it safe with us
To let his madness range.[6] Therefore prepare you.
I your commission will forthwith dispatch,
And he to England shall along with you.
The terms of our estate[7] may not endure   5
Hazard so near's as doth hourly grow
Out of his brows.
GUILDENSTERN   We will ourselves provide.[8]
Most holy and religious fear it is
To keep those many many bodies safe
That live and feed upon your majesty.   10
ROSENCRANTZ   The single and peculiar[9] life is bound
With all the strength and armor of the mind

---

8. "Fret" is used in a double sense, to
annoy and to play a guitar or similar instrument using the "frets" or small bars on
the neck.
  9. at once
  1. treat me as an utter fool
  2. The Emperor Nero, known for his
excesses, was believed to have been re-

sponsible for the death of his mother.
  3. shamed
  4. fulfillment in action
  5. distrust him
  6. roam freely
  7. condition of the state
  8. equip (for the journey)
  9. individual

To keep itelf from noyance,[1] but much more
That spirit upon whose weal[2] depends and rests
The lives of many. The cess[3] of majesty   15
Dies not alone, but like a gulf[4] doth draw
What's near it with it. It is a massy[5] wheel
Fixed on the summit of the highest mount,
To whose huge spokes ten thousand lesser things
Are mortised and adjoined,[6] which when it falls,   20
Each small annexment, petty consequence,
Attends[7] the boist'rous ruin. Never alone
Did the king sigh, but with a general groan.

KING   Arm you, I pray you, to this speedy voyage,
For we will fetters put about this fear,   25
Which now goes too free-footed.

ROSENCRANTZ   We will haste us.

     Exeunt ROSENCRANTZ *and* GUILDENSTERN.

  Enter POLONIUS.

POLONIUS   My lord, he's going to his mother's closet.
Behind the arras I'll convey[8] myself
To hear the process.[9] I'll warrant she'll tax him home,[1]
And as you said, and wisely was it said,   30
'Tis meet that some more audience than a mother,
Since nature makes them partial, should o'erhear
The speech, of vantage.[2] Fare you well, my liege.
I'll call upon you ere you go to bed,
And tell you what I know.

KING   Thanks, dear my lord.   35

       Exit POLONIUS.

O, my offence is rank, it smells to heaven;
It hath the primal eldest curse[3] upon't,
A brother's murder. Pray can I not,
Though inclination be as sharp as will.
My stronger guilt defeats my strong intent,   40
And like a man to double business[4] bound,
I stand in pause where I shall first begin,
And both neglect. What if this curséd hand
Were thicker than itself with brothers' blood,
Is there not rain enough in the sweet heavens   45
To wash it white as snow? Whereto serves mercy
But to confront the visage of offence?
And what's in prayer but this twofold force,
To be forestalléd[5] ere we come to fall,
Or pardoned being down[6]? Then I'll look up.   50
My fault is past. But, O, what form of prayer
Can serve my turn? "Forgive me my foul murder"?
That cannot be, since I am still possessed

---

1. harm
2. welfare
3. cessation
4. whirlpool
5. massive
6. attached
7. joins in
8. station

9. proceedings
1. sharply
2. from a position of vantage
3. i.e., of Cain
4. two mutually opposed interests
5. prevented (from sin)
6. having sinned

Of those effects[7] for which I did the murder—
My crown, mine own ambition, and my queen.   55
May one be pardoned and retain th' offence[8]?
In the corrupted currents of this world
Offence's gilded[9] hand may shove by justice,
And oft 'tis seen the wicked prize itself
Buys out the law. But 'tis not so above.   60
There is no shuffling; there the action[1] lies
In his true nature, and we ourselves compelled,
Even to the teeth and forehead of[2] our faults,
To give in evidence. What then? What rests[3]?
Try what repentance can. What can it not?   65
Yet what can it when one can not repent?
O wretched state! O bosom black as death!
O liméd[4] soul, that struggling to be free
Art more engaged! Help, angels! Make assay.
Bow, stubborn knees, and heart with strings of steel,   70
Be soft as sinews of the new-born babe.
All may be well.   *He kneels.*

Enter HAMLET.

HAMLET   Now might I do it pat,[5] now 'a is a-praying,
And now I'll do't—and so 'a goes to heaven,
And so am I revenged. That would be scanned.[6]   75
A villain kills my father, and for that,
I, his sole son, do this same villain send
To heaven.
Why, this is hire and salary, not revenge.
'A took my father grossly, full of bread,[7]   80
With all his crimes broad blown,[8] as flush[9] as May;
And how his audit stands who knows save heaven?
But in our circumstance and course of thought
'Tis heavy with him; and am I then revenged
To take him in the purging of his soul,   85
When he is fit and seasoned[1] for his passage?
No.
Up, sword, and know thou a more horrid hent.[2]
When he is drunk, asleep, or in his rage,
Or in th' incestuous pleasure of his bed,   90
At game a-swearing, or about some act
That has no relish[3] of salvation in't—
Then trip him, that his heels may kick at heaven,
And that his soul may be as damned and black
As hell, whereto it goes. My mother stays.   95
This physic[4] but prolongs thy sickly days.   *Exit.*
KING [*rising*]   My words fly up, my thoughts remain below.
Words without thoughts never to heaven go.   *Exit.*

7. gains
8. i.e., benefits of the offence
9. bearing gold as a bribe
1. case at law
2. face-to-face with
3. remains
4. caught as with bird-lime
5. easily

6. deserves consideration
7. in a state of sin and without fasting
8. full-blown
9. vigorous
1. ready
2. opportunity
3. flavor
4. medicine

SCENE 4: *The Queen's chamber. Enter* QUEEN *and* POLONIUS.

POLONIUS   'A will come straight. Look you lay home to⁵ him.
Tell him his pranks have been too broad⁶ to bear with,
And that your grace hath screen'd⁷ and stood between
Much heat and him. I'll silence me even here.
Pray you be round.
QUEEN   I'll warrant you. Fear⁸ me not.   5
Withdraw, I hear him coming.

                              POLONIUS *goes behind the arras.*

    Enter HAMLET.

HAMLET   Now, mother, what's the matter?
QUEEN   Hamlet, thou hast thy father much offended.
HAMLET   Mother, you have my father much offended.
QUEEN   Come, come, you answer with an idle tongue.   10
HAMLET   Go, go, you question with a wicked tongue.
QUEEN   Why, how now, Hamlet?
HAMLET   What's the matter now?
QUEEN   Have you forgot me?
HAMLET   No, by the rood,⁹ not so.
You are the queen, your husband's brother's wife,
And would it were not so, you are my mother.   15
QUEEN   Nay, then I'll set those to you that can speak.
HAMLET   Come, come, and sit you down. You shall not budge.
You go not till I set you up a glass¹
Where you may see the inmost part of you.
QUEEN   What wilt thou do? Thou wilt not murder me?   20
Help, ho!
POLONIUS [*behind*]   What, ho! help!
HAMLET [*draws*]   How now, a rat?
Dead for a ducat, dead!

    Kills POLONIUS *with a pass through the arras.*

POLONIUS [*behind*]   O, I am slain!   25
QUEEN   O me, what hast thou done?
HAMLET   Nay, I know not.
Is it the king?
QUEEN   O, what a rash and bloody deed is this!
HAMLET   A bloody deed!—almost as bad, good mother,
As kill a king and marry with his brother.   30
QUEEN   As kill a king?
HAMLET   Ay, lady, it was my word.

    Parting the arras.

Thou wretched, rash, intruding fool, farewell!
I took thee for thy better. Take thy fortune.
Thou find'st to be too busy² is some danger.—
Leave wringing of your hands. Peace, sit you down   35
And let me wring your heart, for so I shall
If it be made of penetrable stuff,

5. be sharp with
6. outrageous
7. acted as a fire screen
8. doubt

9. cross
1. mirror
2. officious

If damnéd custom have not brazed it[3] so
That it be proof[4] and bulwark against sense.[5]
QUEEN   What have I done that thou dar'st wag thy tongue   40
  In noise so rude against me?
HAMLET   Such an act
  That blurs the grace and blush of modesty,
  Calls virtue hypocrite, takes off the rose
  From the fair forehead of an innocent love,
  And sets a blister[6] there, makes marriage-vows   45
  As false as dicers' oaths. O, such a deed
  As from the body of contraction[7] plucks
  The very soul, and sweet religion makes
  A rhapsody of words. Heaven's face does glow
  And this solidity and compound mass[8]   50
  With heated visage, as against the doom[9]—
  Is thought-sick at the act.
QUEEN   Ay me, what act,
  That roars so loud and thunders in the index[1]?
HAMLET   Look here upon this picture[2] and on this,
  The counterfeit presentment of two brothers.   55
  See what a grace was seated on this brow:
  Hyperion's curls, the front[3] of Jove himself,
  An eye like Mars, to threaten and command,
  A station[4] like the herald Mercury[5]
  New lighted[6] on a heaven-kissing hill—   60
  A combination and a form indeed
  Where every god did seem to set his seal,[7]
  To give the world assurance of a man.
  This was your husband. Look you now what follows.
  Here is your husband, like a mildewed ear   65
  Blasting his wholesome brother. Have you eyes?
  Could you on this fair mountain leave to feed,
  And batten[8] on this moor? Ha! have you eyes?
  You cannot call it love, for at your age
  The heyday in the blood is tame, it's humble,   70
  And waits upon the judgment, and what judgment
  Would step from this to this? Sense sure you have,
  Else could you not have motion, but sure that sense
  Is apoplexed[9] for madness would not err,
  Nor sense to ecstasy was ne'er so thralled   75
  But it reserved some quantity[1] of choice
  To serve in such a difference. What devil was't
  That thus hath cozened[2] you at hoodman-blind[3]?
  Eyes without feeling, feeling without sight,
  Ears without hands or eyes, smelling sans[4] all,   80
  Or but a sickly part of one true sense
  Could not so mope.[5] O shame! where is thy blush?

3. plated it with brass
4. armor
5. feeling
6. brand
7. the marriage contract
8. meaningless mass (Earth)
9. Judgment Day
1. table of contents
2. portrait
3. forehead
4. bearing

5. Mercury was a Roman god who served as the messenger of the gods.
6. newly alighted
7. mark of approval
8. feed greedily
9. paralyzed
1. power
2. cheated
3. blindman's buff
4. without
5. be stupid

Rebellious hell,
If thou canst mutine[6] in a matron's bones,
To flaming youth let virtue be as wax   85
And melt in her own fire. Proclaim no shame
When the compulsive ardor gives the charge,[7]
Since frost itself as actively doth burn,
And reason panders[8] will.

QUEEN   O Hamlet, speak no more!
Thou turn'st my eyes into my very soul;   90
And there I see such black and grainéd[9] spots
As will not leave their tinct.[1]

HAMLET   Nay, but to live
In the rank sweat of an enseaméd[2] bed,
Stewed in corruption, honeying and making love
Over the nasty sty—

QUEEN   O, speak to me no more!   95
These words like daggers enter in my ears;
No more, sweet Hamlet.

HAMLET   A murderer and a villain,
A slave that is not twentieth part the tithe[3]
Of your precedent lord,[4] a vice of kings,[5]
A cutpurse[6] of the empire and the rule,   100
That from a shelf the precious diadem stole
And put it in his pocket—

QUEEN   No more.

        Enter GHOST.

HAMLET   A king of shreds and patches—
Save me and hover o'er me with your wings,   105
You heavenly guards! What would your gracious figure?

QUEEN   Alas, he's mad.

HAMLET   Do you not come your tardy[7] son to chide,
That lapsed in time and passion lets go by
Th' important acting of your dread command?   110
O, say!

GHOST   Do not forget. This visitation
Is but to whet thy almost blunted purpose.
But look, amazement on thy mother sits.
O, step between her and her fighting soul!   115
Conceit[8] in weakest bodies strongest works.
Speak to her, Hamlet.

HAMLET   How is it with you, lady?

QUEEN   Alas, how is't with you,
That you do bend[9] your eye on vacancy,
And with th' incorporal air do hold discourse?   120
Forth at your eyes your spirits wildly peep,
And as the sleeping soldiers in th' alarm,
Your bedded hairs like life in excrements[1]

6. commit mutiny
7. attacks
8. pimps for
9. ingrained
1. lose their color
2. greasy
3. one-tenth
4. first husband

5. The "Vice," a common figure in the popular drama, was a clown or buffoon.
6. pickpocket
7. slow to act
8. imagination
9. turn
1. nails and hair

Start up and stand an end. O gentle son,
Upon the heat and flame of thy distemper   125
Sprinkle cool patience. Whereon do you look?
HAMLET   On him, on him! Look you how pale he glares.
His form and cause conjoined,[2] preaching to stones,
Would make them capable.[3]—Do not look upon me,
Lest with piteous action you convert   130
My stern effects.[4] Then what I have to do
Will want true color—tears perchance for blood.
QUEEN   To whom do you speak this?
HAMLET   Do you see nothing there?
QUEEN   Nothing at all, yet all that is I see.   135
HAMLET   Nor did you nothing hear?
QUEEN   No, nothing but ourselves.
HAMLET   Why, look you there. Look how it steals away.
My father, in his habit[5] as he lived!
Look where he goes even now out at the portal.   *Exit* GHOST. 140
QUEEN   This is the very coinage[6] of your brain.
This bodiless creation ecstasy[7]
Is very cunning[8] in.
HAMLET   My pulse as yours doth temperately keep time,
And makes as healthful music. It is not madness   145
That I have uttered. Bring me to the test,
And I the matter will re-word, which madness
Would gambol[9] from. Mother, for love of grace,
Lay not that flattering unction[1] to your soul,
That not your trespass but my madness speaks.   150
It will but skin and film the ulcerous place
Whiles rank corruption, mining[2] all within,
Infects unseen. Confess yourself to heaven,
Repent what's past, avoid what is to come,
And do not spread the compost on the weeds,   155
To make them ranker. Forgive me this my virtue,
For in the fatness of these pursy[3] times
Virtue itself of vice must pardon beg,
Yea, curb[4] and woo for leave to do him good.
QUEEN   O Hamlet, thou hast cleft my heart in twain.   160
HAMLET   O, throw away the worser part of it,
And live the purer with the other half.
Good night—but go not to my uncle's bed.
Assume a virtue, if you have it not.
That monster custom[5] who all sense doth eat   165
Of habits evil, is angel yet in this,
That to the use of actions fair and good
He likewise gives a frock or livery
That aptly[6] is put on. Refrain tonight,
And that shall lend a kind of easiness   170
To the next abstinence; the next more easy;
For use almost can change the stamp of nature,

2. working together	9. shy away
3. of responding	1. ointment
4. deeds	2. undermining
5. costume	3. bloated
6. invention	4. bow
7. madness	5. habit
8. skilled	6. easily

And either curb the devil, or throw him out
With wondrous potency. Once more, good night,
And when you are desirous to be blest,   175
I'll blessing beg of you. For this same lord
I do repent; but heaven hath pleased it so,
To punish me with this, and this with me,
That I must be their scourge and minister.
I will bestow[7] him and will answer well   180
The death I gave him. So, again, good night.
I must be cruel only to be kind.
Thus bad begins and worse remains behind.
One word more, good lady.
QUEEN   What shall I do?
HAMLET   Not this, by no means, that I bid you do: 185
Let the bloat[8] king tempt you again to bed,
Pinch wanton[9] on your cheek, call you his mouse,
And let him, for a pair of reechy[1] kisses,
Or paddling in your neck with his damned fingers,
Make you to ravel[2] all this matter out,   190
That I essentially am not in madness,
But mad in craft. 'Twere good you let him know,
For who that's but a queen, fair, sober, wise,
Would from a paddock,[3] from a bat, a gib,[4]
Such dear concernings hide? Who would so do?   195
No, in despite of sense and secrecy,
Unpeg the basket on the house's top,
Let the birds fly, and like the famous ape,
To try conclusions, in the basket creep
And break your own neck down.[5]   200
QUEEN   Be thou assured, if words be made of breath
And breath of life, I have no life to breathe
What thou hast said to me.
HAMLET   I must to England; you know that?
QUEEN   Alack,
I had forgot. 'Tis so concluded on.   205
HAMLET   There's letters sealed, and my two school-fellows,
Whom I will trust as I will adders fanged,
They bear the mandate[6]; they must sweep[7] my way
And marshal me to knavery. Let it work,
For 'tis the sport to have the enginer   210
Hoist with his own petar; and't shall go hard
But I will delve[8] one yard below their mines
And blow them at the moon. O, 'tis most sweet
When in one line two crafts directly meet.[9]

---

7. dispose of
8. bloated
9. lewdly
1. foul
2. reveal
3. toad
4. tomcat
5. Apparently a reference to a now lost fable in which an ape, finding a basket containing a cage of birds on a housetop, opens the cage. The birds fly away. The ape, thinking that if he were in the basket he too could fly, enters, jumps out, and breaks his neck.

6. command
7. prepare
8. dig
9. The "enginer" or engineer is a military man who is here described as being blown up by a bomb of his own construction, "hoist with his own petar." The military figure continues in the succeeding lines where Hamlet describes himself as digging a countermine or tunnel beneath the one Claudius is digging to defeat Hamlet. In line 214 the two tunnels unexpectedly meet.

This man shall set me packing.   215
I'll lug the guts into the neighbor room.
Mother, good night. Indeed, this counsellor
Is now most still, most secret, and most grave,
Who was in life a foolish prating knave,
Come sir, to draw toward an end with you.   220
Good night, mother.

> *Exit the* QUEEN. *Then exit* HAMLET *tugging* POLONIUS.

Act 4

SCENE 1: *A room in the castle. Enter* KING, QUEEN, ROSENCRANTZ *and* GUILDENSTERN.

KING   There's matter in these sighs, these profound heaves,
You must translate[1]; 'tis fit we understand them.
Where is your son?
QUEEN   Bestow this place on us a little while.

> *Exeunt* ROSENCRANTZ *and* GUILDENSTERN.

Ah, mine own lord, what have I seen tonight!   5
KING   What, Gertrude? How does Hamlet?
QUEEN   Mad as the sea and wind when both contend
Which is the mightier. In his lawless fit,
Behind the arras hearing something stir,
Whips out his rapier, cries "A rat, a rat!"   10
And in this brainish apprehension[2] kills
The unseen good old man.
KING   O heavy deed!
It had been so with us had we been there.
His liberty is full of threats to all—
To you yourself, to us, to every one.   15
Alas, how shall this bloody deed be answered?
It will be laid to us, whose providence[3]
Should have kept short, restrained, and out of haunt,[4]
This mad young man. But so much was our love,
We would not understand what was most fit;   20
But, like the owner of a foul disease,
To keep it from divulging, let it feed
Even on the pith of life. Where is he gone?
QUEEN   To draw apart the body he hath killed,
O'er whom his very madness, like some ore   25
Among a mineral of metals base,
Shows itself pure: 'a weeps for what is done.
KING   O Gertrude, come away!
The sun no sooner shall the mountains touch
But we will ship him hence, and this vile deed   30
We must with all our majesty and skill
Both countenance and excuse. Ho, Guildenstern!

Enter ROSENCRANTZ *and* GUILDENSTERN.

Friends both, go join you with some further aid.

1. explain
2. insane notion
3. prudence
4. away from court

Hamlet in madness hath Polonius slain,
And from his mother's closet hath he dragged him.   35
Go seek him out; speak fair, and bring the body
Into the chapel. I pray you haste in this.

Exeunt ROSENCRANTZ *and* GUILDENSTERN.

Come, Gertrude, we'll call up our wisest friends
And let them know both what we mean to do
And what's untimely done;   40
Whose whisper o'er the world's diameter,
As level[5] as the cannon to his blank,[6]
Transports his poisoned shot—may miss our name,
And hit the woundless air. O, come away!
My soul is full of discord and dismay.   *Exeunt.* 45

SCENE 2: *A passageway. Enter* HAMLET.

HAMLET   Safely stowed.—But soft, what noise? Who calls on Hamlet?
O, here they come.

Enter ROSENCRANTZ, GUILDENSTERN, *and* OTHERS.

ROSENCRANTZ   What have you done, my lord, with the dead body?
HAMLET   Compounded it with dust, whereto 'tis kin.
ROSENCRANTZ   Tell us where 'tis, that we may take it thence   5
And bear it to the chapel.
HAMLET   Do not believe it.
ROSENCRANTZ   Believe what?
HAMLET   That I can keep your counsel and not mine own. Besides, to
be demanded of[7] a sponge—what replication[8] should be made by   10
the son of a king?
ROSENCRANTZ   Take you me for a sponge, my lord?
HAMLET   Ay, sir, that soaks up the king's countenance,[9] his rewards,
his authorities. But such officers do the king best service in the end.
He keeps them like an apple in the corner of his jaw, first mouthed 15
to be last swallowed. When he needs what you have gleaned, it is
but squeezing you and, sponge, you shall be dry again.
ROSENCRANTZ   I understand you not, my lord.
HAMLET   I am glad of it. A knavish speech sleeps in a foolish ear.
ROSENCRANTZ   My lord, you must tell us where the body is, and go   20
with us to the king.
HAMLET   The body is with the king, but the king is not with the body.
The king is a thing—
GUILDENSTERN   A thing, my lord!
HAMLET   Of nothing. Bring me to him. Hide fox, and all after.[1]   25

Exeunt.

SCENE 3: *A room in the castle. Enter* KING.

KING   I have sent to seek him, and to find the body.
How dangerous is it that this man goes loose!

---

5. direct
6. mark
7. questioned by
8. answer

9. favor
1. Apparently a reference to a children's
game like hide-and-seek.

Yet must not we put the strong law on him.
He's loved of the distracted[2] multitude,
Who like not in their judgment but their eyes,   5
And where 'tis so, th' offender's scourge[3] is weighed,
But never the offence. To bear all smooth and even,
This sudden sending him away must seem
Deliberate pause.[4] Diseases desperate grown
By desperate appliance are relieved,   10
Or not at all.

Enter ROSENCRANTZ, GUILDENSTERN, *and all the rest.*

How now! what hath befall'n?
ROSENCRANTZ   Where the dead body is bestowed, my lord,
We cannot get from him.
KING   But where is he?
ROSENCRANTZ   Without,[5] my lord; guarded, to know[6] your pleasure.
KING   Bring him before us.
ROSENCRANTZ   Ho! bring in the lord.   15

They enter with HAMLET.

KING   Now, Hamlet, where's Polonius?
HAMLET   At supper.
KING   At supper? Where?
HAMLET   Not where he eats, but where 'a is eaten. A certain convoca-
tion[7] of politic[8] worms are e'en at him. Your worm is your only   20
emperor for diet. We fat all creatures else to fat us, and we fat
ourselves for maggots. Your fat king and your lean beggar is but
variable service—two dishes, but to one table. That's the end.
KING   Alas, alas!
HAMLET   A man may fish with the worm that hath eat of a king, and   25
eat of the fish that hath fed of that worm.
KING   What dost thou mean by this?
HAMLET   Nothing but to show you how a king may go a progress
through the guts of a beggar.
KING   Where is Polonius?   30
HAMLET   In heaven. Send thither to see. If your messenger find him
not there, seek him i' th' other place yourself. But if, indeed, you find
him not within this month, you shall nose[9] him as you go up the
stairs into the lobby.
KING *[to* ATTENDANTS*]*   Go seek him there.   35
HAMLET   'A will stay till you come.   *Exeunt* ATTENDANTS.
KING   Hamlet, this deed, for thine especial safety—
Which we do tender,[1] as we dearly[2] grieve
For that which thou hast done—must send thee hence
With fiery quickness. Therefore prepare thyself.   40
The bark is ready, and the wind at help,
Th' associates tend, and everything is bent
For England.
HAMLET   For England?
KING   Ay, Hamlet.

2. confused
3. punishment
4. i.e., not an impulse
5. outside
6. await

7. gathering
8. statesmanlike
9. smell
1. consider
2. deeply

HAMLET   Good.

KING   So it is, if thou knew'st our purposes.

HAMLET   I see a cherub that sees them. But come, for England!   45
Farewell, dear mother.

KING   Thy loving father, Hamlet.

HAMLET   My mother. Father and mother is man and wife, man and
wife is one flesh. So, my mother. Come, for England.   *Exit.*

KING   Follow him at foot[3]; tempt him with speed aboard.   50
Delay it not; I'll have him hence tonight.
Away! for everything is sealed and done
That else leans on th' affair. Pray you make haste.

Exeunt all but the KING.

And, England, if my love thou hold'st at aught—
As my great power thereof may give thee sense,[4]   55
Since yet thy cicatrice[5] looks raw and red
After the Danish sword, and thy free awe
Pays homage to us—thou mayst not coldly set[6]
Our sovereign process,[7] which imports at full
By letters congruing[8] to that effect   60
The present death of Hamlet. Do it, England,
For like the hectic[9] in my blood he rages,
And thou must cure me. Till I know 'tis done,
Howe'er my haps, my joys were ne'er begun.   *Exit.*

SCENE 4: *Near Elsinore. Enter* FORTINBRAS *with his army.*

FORTINBRAS   Go, captain, from me greet the Danish king.
Tell him that by his license Fortinbras
Craves the conveyance[1] of a promised march
Over his kingdom. You know the rendezvous.
If that his majesty would aught with us,   5
We shall express our duty in his eye,[2]
And let him know so.

CAPTAIN   I will do't, my lord.

FORTINBRAS   Go softly on.   *Exeunt all but the* CAPTAIN.

Enter HAMLET, ROSENCRANTZ, GUILDENSTERN, *and* OTHERS.

HAMLET   Good sir, whose powers are these?

CAPTAIN   They are of Norway, sir.   10

HAMLET   How purposed, sir, I pray you?

CAPTAIN   Against some part of Poland.

HAMLET   Who commands them, sir?

CAPTAIN   The nephew to old Norway, Fortinbras.

HAMLET   Goes it against the main[3] of Poland, sir,   15
Or for some frontier?

CAPTAIN   Truly to speak, and with no addition,[4]
We go to gain a little patch of ground
That hath in it no profit but the name.

3. closely,
4. of its value
5. wound scar
6. set aside
7. mandate
8. agreeing

9. chronic fever
1. escort
2. presence
3. central part
4. exaggeration

To pay five ducats,[5] five, I would not farm it;   20
Nor will it yield to Norway or the Pole
A ranker[6] rate should it be sold in fee.[7]
HAMLET   Why, then the Polack never will defend it.
CAPTAIN   Yes, it is already garrisoned.
HAMLET   Two thousand souls and twenty thousand ducats   25
Will not debate the question of this straw.
This is th' imposthume[8] of much wealth and peace,
That inward breaks, and shows no cause without
Why the man dies. I humbly thank you, sir.
CAPTAIN   God b'wi'ye, sir.   *Exit.*
ROSENCRANTZ   Will't please you go, my lord?   30
HAMLET   I'll be with you straight. Go a little before.

Exeunt all but HAMLET.

How all occasions do inform against me,
And spur my dull revenge! What is a man,
If his chief good and market[9] of his time
Be but to sleep and feed? A beast, no more.   35
Sure he that made us with such large discourse,[1]
Looking before and after, gave us not
That capability and godlike reason
To fust[2] in us unused. Now, whether it be
Bestial oblivion, or some craven scruple   40
Of thinking too precisely on th' event[3]—
A thought which, quartered, hath but one part wisdom
And ever three parts coward—I do not know
Why yet I live to say "This thing's to do,"
Sith[4] I have cause, and will, and strength, and means, 45
To do't. Examples gross as earth exhort me.
Witness this army of such mass and charge,[5]
Led by a delicate and tender prince,
Whose spirit, with divine ambition puffed,
Makes mouths at[6] the invisible event,   50
Exposing what is mortal and unsure
To all that fortune, death, and danger dare,
Even for an eggshell. Rightly to be great
Is not to stir without great argument,
But greatly to find quarrel in a straw   55
When honor's at the stake. How stand I then,
That have a father killed, a mother stained,
Excitements of my reason and my blood,
And let all sleep, while to my shame I see
The imminent death of twenty thousand men   60
That for a fantasy and trick of fame
Go to their graves like beds, fight for a plot
Whereon the numbers cannot try the cause,
Which is not tomb enough and continent

---

5. i.e., in rent
6. higher
7. outright
8. abscess
9. occupation
1. ample reasoning power

2. grow musty
3. outcome
4. since
5. expense
6. scorns

To hide the slain?[7] O, from this time forth,   65
My thoughts be bloody, or be nothing worth!   *Exit.*

SCENE 5: *A room in the castle. Enter* QUEEN, HORATIO *and a*
GENTLEMAN.

QUEEN   I will not speak with her.
GENTLEMAN   She is importunate, indeed distract.
    Her mood will needs be pitied.
QUEEN   What would she have?
GENTLEMAN   She speaks much of her father, says she hears
    There's tricks i' th' world, and hems, and beats her heart,   5
    Spurns enviously at straws,[8] speaks things in doubt
    That carry but half sense. Her speech is nothing,
    Yet the unshaped use of it doth move
    The hearers to collection[9]; they yawn at it,
    And botch the words up fit to their own thoughts,   10
    Which, as her winks and nods and gestures yield them,
    Indeed would make one think there might be thought,
    Though nothing sure, yet much unhappily.
HORATIO   'Twere good she were spoken with, for she may strew
    Dangerous conjectures in ill-breeding minds.   15
QUEEN   Let her come in.   *Exit* GENTLEMAN.
    [*Aside.*] To my sick soul, as sin's true nature is,
    Each toy[1] seems prologue to some great amiss.[2]
    So full of artless jealousy is guilt,
    It spills itself in fearing to be spilt.   20

    Enter OPHELIA *distracted.*

OPHELIA   Where is the beauteous majesty of Denmark?
QUEEN   How now, Ophelia!
OPHELIA   How should I your true love know   *She sings.*
                From another one?
                By his cockle hat and staff,[3]   25
                And his sandal shoon.[4]
QUEEN   Alas, sweet lady, what imports this song?
OPHELIA   Say you? Nay, pray you mark.

                He is dead and gone, lady,
                He is dead and gone;   30
                At his head a grass-green turf,
                At his heels a stone.

    O, ho!
QUEEN   Nay, but, Ophelia—
OPHELIA   Pray you mark.
                White his shroud as the mountain snow—   35

    Enter KING.

QUEEN   Alas, look here, my lord.

---

7. The plot of ground involved is so
small that it cannot contain the number of
men involved in fighting nor furnish burial
space for the number of those who will die.
8. takes offense at trifles
9. an attempt to order
1. trifle

2. catastrophe
3. A "cockle hat," one decorated with a
shell, indicated that the wearer had made a
pilgrimage to the shrine of St. James at
Compostela in Spain. The staff also marked
the carrier as a pilgrim.
4. shoes

OPHELIA   Larded all with sweet flowers;
                Which bewept to the grave did not go
                    With true-love showers.

KING   How do you, pretty lady?   40

OPHELIA   Well, God dild[5] you! They say the owl was a baker's daughter. Lord, we know what we are, but know not what we may be.
God be at your table!

KING   Conceit[6] upon her father.

OPHELIA   Pray let's have no words of this, but when they ask you   45
what it means, say you this:

                Tomorrow is Saint Valentine's day,
                    All in the morning betime,
                And I a maid at your window,
                    To be your Valentine.   50
                Then up he rose, and donn'd his clo'es,
                    And dupped[7] the chamber-door,
                Let in the maid, that out a maid
                    Never departed more.

KING   Pretty Ophelia!   55

OPHELIA   Indeed, without an oath, I'll make an end on't.

                By Gis[8] and by Saint Charity,
                    Alack, and fie for shame!
                Young men will do't, if they come to't;
                    By Cock,[9] they are to blame.   60
                Quoth she "Before you tumbled me,
                    You promised me to wed."

He answers:

                "So would I 'a done, by yonder sun,
                    An thou hadst not come to my bed."   65

KING   How long hath she been thus?

OPHELIA   I hope all will be well. We must be patient, but I cannot
choose but weep to think they would lay him i' th' cold ground. My
brother shall know of it, and so I thank you for your good counsel.
Come, my coach! Good night, ladies, good night. Sweet ladies, good   70
night, good night.   *Exit.*

KING   Follow her close; give her good watch, I pray you.

                        Exeunt HORATIO *and* GENTLEMAN.

O, this is the poison of deep grief; it springs
All from her father's death, and now behold!
O Gertrude, Gertrude!   75
When sorrows come, they come not single spies,
But in battalions: first, her father slain;
Next, your son gone, and he most violent author
Of his own just remove; the people muddied,[1]
Thick and unwholesome in their thoughts and whispers   80
For good Polonius' death; and we have done but greenly[2]
In hugger-mugger[3] to inter him; poor Ophelia

---

5. yield   9. God
6. thought   1. disturbed
7. opened   2. without judgment
8. Jesus   3. haste

Divided from herself and her fair judgment,
Without the which we are pictures, or mere beasts;
Last, and as much containing as all these,   85
Her brother is in secret come from France,
Feeds on his wonder, keeps himself in clouds,
And wants not buzzers to infect his ear
With pestilent speeches of his father's death,
Wherein necessity, of matter beggared,[4]   90
Will nothing stick[5] our person to arraign[6]
In ear and ear.[7] O my dear Gertrude, this,
Like to a murd'ring piece,[8] in many places
Gives me superfluous death. Attend,   *A noise within.*

    Enter a MESSENGER.

Where are my Switzers[9]? Let them guard the door.   95
What is the matter?
MESSENGER   Save yourself, my lord.
The ocean, overpeering of his list,[1]
Eats not the flats with more impiteous[2] haste
Than young Laertes, in a riotous head,[3]
O'erbears your officers. The rabble call him lord,   100
And as the world were now but to begin,
Antiquity forgot, custom not known,
The ratifiers and props of every word,
They cry "Choose we, Laertes shall be king."
Caps, hands, and tongues, applaud it to the clouds,   105
"Laertes shall be king, Laertes king."
QUEEN   How cheerfully on the false trail they cry[4]! *A noise within.*
O, this is counter,[5] you false Danish dogs!
KING   The doors are broke.

    Enter LAERTES, *with* OTHERS.

LAERTES   Where is this king?—Sirs, stand you all without.   110
ALL   No, let's come in.
LAERTES   I pray you give me leave.
ALL   We will, we will.   *Exeunt his followers.*
LAERTES   I thank you. Keep[6] the door.—O thou vile king,
Give me my father!
QUEEN   Calmly, good Laertes.
LAERTES   That drop of blood that's calm proclaims me bastard,   115
Cries cuckold to my father, brands the harlot
Even here between the chaste unsmirchéd brow
Of my true mother.
KING   What is the cause, Laertes,
That thy rebellion looks so giant-like?
Let him go, Gertrude. Do not fear[7] our person.   120
There's such divinity doth hedge a king
That treason can but peep to[8] what it would,
Acts little of his will. Tell me, Laertes,

4. short on facts
5. hesitate
6. accuse
7. from both sides
8. a weapon designed to scatter its shot
9. Swiss guards
1. towering above its limits

2. pitiless
3. with an armed band
4. as if following the scent
5. backward
6. guard
7. fear for
8. look at over or through a barrier

Why thou art thus incensed. Let him go, Gertrude.
Speak, man.
LAERTES   Where is my father?
KING   Dead.   125
QUEEN   But not by him.
KING   Let him demand[9] his fill.
LAERTES   How came he dead? I'll not be juggled with.
To hell allegiance, vows to the blackest devil,
Conscience and grace to the profoundest pit!
I dare damnation. To this point I stand,   130
That both the worlds[1] I give to negligence,[2]
Let come what comes, only I'll be revenged
Most throughly for my father.
KING   Who shall stay you?
LAERTES   My will, not all the world's.
And for my means, I'll husband[3] them so well   135
They shall go far with little.
KING   Good Laertes,
If you desire to know the certainty
Of your dear father, is't writ in your revenge
That, swoopstake,[4] you will draw both friend and foe,
Winner and loser?
LAERTES   None but his enemies.   140
KING   Will you know them, then?
LAERTES   To his good friends thus wide I'll ope my arms,
And like the kind life-rend'ring pelican,[5]
Repast them with my blood.
KING   Why, now you speak
Like a good child and a true gentleman.   145
That I am guiltless of your father's death,
And am most sensibly in grief for it,
It shall as level[6] to your judgment 'pear
As day does to your eye.

A noise within: "Let her come in."

LAERTES   How now? What noise is that?   150

Enter OPHELIA.

O, heat dry up my brains! tears seven times salt
Burn out the sense[7] and virtue[8] of mine eye!
By heaven, thy madness shall be paid with weight
Till our scale turn the beam. O rose of May,
Dear maid, kind sister, sweet Ophelia!   155
O heavens! is't possible a young maid's wits
Should be as mortal as an old man's life?
Nature is fine[9] in love, and where 'tis fine
It sends some precious instance of itself
After the thing it loves.[1]   160
OPHELIA   They bore him barefac'd on the bier;

9. question
1. i.e., this and the next
2. disregard
3. manage
4. sweeping the board
5. The pelican was believed to feed her young with her own blood.

6. plain
7. feeling
8. function
9. refined
1. Laertes means that Ophelia, because of her love for her father, gave up her sanity as a token of grief at his death.

Hey non nonny, nonny, hey nonny;
And in his grave rain'd many a tear—

Fare you well, my dove!

LAERTES   Hadst thou thy wits, and didst persuade revenge,   165
It could not move thus.

OPHELIA   You must sing "A-down, a-down, and you call him a-down-
a." O, how the wheel becomes it! It is the false steward, that stole his
master's daughter.[2]

LAERTES   This nothing's more than matter.   170

OPHELIA   There's rosemary, that's for remembrance. Pray you, love,
remember. And there is pansies, that's for thoughts.

LAERTES   A document[3] in madness, thoughts and remembrance fitted.

OPHELIA   There's fennel for you, and columbines. There's rue for you,
and here's some for me. We may call it herb of grace a Sundays. O,   175
you must wear your rue with a difference. There's a daisy. I would
give you some violets, but they withered all when my father died.
They say 'a made a good end.

[*Sings.*]   For bonny sweet Robin is all my joy.

LAERTES   Thought and affliction, passion, hell itself,   180
She turns to favor[4] and to prettiness.

OPHELIA   And will 'a not come again?
And will 'a not come again?
No, no, he is dead,
Go to thy death-bed,   185
He never will come again.

His beard was as white as snow,
All flaxen was his poll[5];
He is gone, he is gone,
And we cast away moan: 190
God-a-mercy on his soul!

And of all Christian souls, I pray God. God b'wi'you.   *Exit.*

LAERTES   Do you see this, O God?

KING   Laertes, I must commune with your grief,
Or you deny me right. Go but apart,   195
Make choice of whom your wisest friends you will,
And they shall hear and judge 'twixt you and me.
If by direct or by collateral[6] hand
They find us touched,[7] we will our kingdom give,
Our crown, our life, and all that we call ours,   200
To you in satisfaction; but if not,
Be you content to lend your patience to us,
And we shall jointly labor with your soul
To give it due content.

LAERTES   Let this be so.

---

2. The "wheel" refers to the *burden* or refrain of a song, in this case "A-down, a-down, and you call him a-down-a." The ballad to which she refers was about a false steward. Others have suggested that the "wheel" is the Wheel of Fortune, a spinning wheel to whose rhythm such a song might have been sung or a kind of dance movement performed by Ophelia as she sings.
3. lesson
4. beauty
5. head
6. indirect
7. by guilt

His means of death, his obscure funeral—   205
No trophy, sword, nor hatchment,[8] o'er his bones,
No noble rite nor formal ostentation[9]—
Cry to be heard, as 'twere from heaven to earth,
That I must call't in question.
KING   So you shall;
And where th' offence is, let the great axe fall.   210
I pray you go with me.   *Exeunt.*

SCENE 6: *Another room in the castle. Enter* HORATIO *and*
a GENTLEMAN.

HORATIO   What are they that would speak with me?
GENTLEMAN   Sea-faring men, sir. They say they have letters for you.
HORATIO   Let them come in.   *Exit* GENTLEMAN.
   I do not know from what part of the world
   I should be greeted, if not from Lord Hamlet.   5

   Enter SAILORS.

SAILOR   God bless you, sir.
HORATIO   Let him bless thee too.
SAILOR   'A shall, sir, an't please him. There's a letter for you, sir—it
   came from th' ambassador that was bound for England—if your
   name be Horatio, as I am let to know[1] it is.   10
HORATIO   [*reads*]   "Horatio, when thou shalt have overlooked[2] this,
   give these fellows some means[3] to the king. They have letters for
   him. Ere we were two days old at sea, a pirate of very warlike appointment[4] gave us chase. Finding ourselves too slow of sail, we put
   on a compelled valor, and in the grapple I boarded them. On the in-   15
   stant they got clear of our ship, so I alone became their prisoner.
   They have dealt with me like thieves of mercy, but they knew what
   they did; I am to do a good turn for them. Let the king have the
   letters I have sent, and repair thou to me with as much speed as thou
   wouldest fly death. I have words to speak in thine ear will make   20
   thee dumb; yet are they much too light for the bore of the matter.[5]
   These good fellows will bring thee where I am. Rosencrantz and
   Guildenstern hold their course for England. Of them I have much to
   tell thee. Farewell.
                   He that thou knowest thine, HAMLET."
   Come, I will give you way[6] for these your letters,   25
   And do't the speedier that you may direct me
   To him from whom you brought them.   *Exeunt.*

SCENE 7: *Another room in the castle. Enter* KING *and* LAERTES.

KING   Now must your conscience my acquittance seal,[7]
   And you must put me in your heart for friend,
   Sith you have heard, and with a knowing ear,
   That he which hath your noble father slain

---

8. coat of arms
9. pomp
1. informed
2. read through
3. access
4. equipment

5. A figure from gunnery, referring to
shot which is too small for the size of the
weapon to be fired.
6. means of delivery
7. grant me innocent

Pursued my life.

LAERTES   It well appears. But tell me   5
Why you proceeded not against these feats,
So criminal and so capital in nature,
As by your safety, greatness, wisdom, all things else,
You mainly were stirred up.

KING   O, for two special reasons,
Which may to you, perhaps, seem much unsinewed,[8]   10
But yet to me th' are strong. The queen his mother
Lives almost by his looks, and for myself—
My virtue or my plague, be it either which—
She is so conjunctive[9] to my life and soul
That, as the star moves not but in his sphere,[1]   15
I could not but by her. The other motive,
Why to a public count[2] I might not go,
Is the great love the general gender[3] bear him,
Who, dipping all his faults in their affection,
Work like the spring that turneth wood to stone,[4]   20
Convert his gyves[5] to graces; so that my arrows,
Too slightly timbered[6] for so loud a wind,
Would have reverted to my bow again,
But not where I have aimed them.

LAERTES   And so have I a noble father lost,   25
A sister driven into desp'rate terms,
Whose worth, if praises may go back again,
Stood challenger on mount of all the age
For her perfections. But my revenge will come.

KING   Break not your sleeps for that. You must not think   30
That we are made of stuff so flat and dull
That we can let our beard be shook with danger,
And think it pastime. You shortly shall hear more.
I loved your father, and we love our self,
And that, I hope, will teach you to imagine—   35

Enter a MESSENGER *with letters.*

MESSENGER   These to your majesty; this to the queen.
KING   From Hamlet! Who brought them?
MESSENGER   Sailors, my lord, they say. I saw them not.
They were given me by Claudio; he received them
Of him that brought them.

KING   Laertes, you shall hear them.—   40
Leave us.   *Exit* MESSENGER.
    [*Reads.*] "High and mighty, you shall know I am set naked on
your kingdom. Tomorrow shall I beg leave to see your kingly eyes;
when I shall, first asking your pardon thereunto, recount the occasion
of my sudden and more strange return.   45
                              HAMLET."
What should this mean? Are all the rest come back?

----

8. weak
9. closely joined
1. A reference to the Ptolemaic cosmology in which planets and stars were believed to revolve about the earth in crystal-
line spheres concentric with the earth.
2. reckoning

3. common people
4. Certain English springs contain so
much lime in the water that a lime covering will be deposited on a log placed in
one of them for a length of time.
5. fetters
6. shafted

Or is it some abuse,[7] and no such thing?

LAERTES   Know you the hand?

KING   'Tis Hamlet's character.[8] "Naked"!   50
And in a postscript here, he says "alone."
Can you devise[9] me?

LAERTES   I am lost in it, my lord. But let him come.
It warms the very sickness in my heart
That I shall live and tell him to his teeth   55
"Thus didest thou."

KING   If it be so, Laertes—
As how should it be so, how otherwise?—
Will you be ruled by me?

LAERTES   Ay, my lord
So you will not o'errule me to a peace.

KING   To thine own peace. If he be now returned,   60
As checking at[1] his voyage, and that he means
No more to undertake it, I will work him
To an exploit now ripe in my device,
Under the which he shall not choose but fall;
And for his death no wind of blame shall breathe   65
But even his mother shall uncharge[2] the practice
And call it accident.

LAERTES   My lord, I will be ruled;
The rather if you could devise it so
That I might be the organ.[3]

KING   It falls right.
You have been talked of since your travel much,   70
And that in Hamlet's hearing, for a quality
Wherein they say you shine. Your sum of parts
Did not together pluck such envy from him
As did that one, and that, in my regard,
Of the unworthiest siege.[4]

LAERTES   What part is that, my lord?   75

KING   A very riband in the cap of youth,
Yet needful too, for youth no less becomes
The light and careless livery that it wears
Than settled age his sables and his weeds,[5]
Importing health and graveness. Two months since   80
Here was a gentleman of Normandy.
I have seen myself, and served against, the French,
And they can[6] well on horseback, but this gallant
Had witchcraft in't. He grew unto his seat,
And to such wondrous doing brought his horse,   85
As had he been incorpsed and demi-natured
With the brave beast. So far he topped my thought
That I, in forgery[7] of shapes and tricks,
Come short of what he did.[8]

7. trick
8. handwriting
9. explain it to
1. turning aside from
2. not accuse
3. instrument
4. rank
5. dignified clothing
6. perform

7. imagination
8. The gentleman referred to was so skilled in horsemanship that he seemed to share one body with the horse, "incorpsed." The King further extends the compliment by saying that he appeared like the mythical centaur, a creature who was man from the waist up and horse from the waist down, therefore "demi-natured."

LAERTES   A Norman was't?
KING   A Norman.   90
LAERTES   Upon my life, Lamord.
KING   The very same.
LAERTES   I know him well. He is the brooch indeed
    And gem of all the nation.
KING   He made confession[9] of you,
    And gave you such a masterly report   95
    For art and exercise in your defence,[1]
    And for your rapier most especial,
    That he cried out 'twould be a sight indeed
    If one could match you. The scrimers[2] of their nation
    He swore had neither motion, guard, nor eye,   100
    If you opposed them. Sir, this report of his
    Did Hamlet so envenom with his envy
    That he could nothing do but wish and beg
    Your sudden coming o'er, to play with you.
    Now out of this—
LAERTES   What out of this, my lord?   105
KING   Laertes, was your father dear to you?
    Or are you like the painting of a sorrow,
    A face without a heart?
LAERTES   Why ask you this?
KING   Not that I think you did not love your father,
    But that I know love is begun by time,   110
    And that I see in passages of proof,[3]
    Time qualifies the spark and fire of it.
    There lives within the very flame of love
    A kind of wick or snuff that will abate it,
    And nothing is at a like goodness still,   115
    For goodness, growing to a plurisy,[4]
    Dies in his own too much.[5] That we would do,
    We should do when we would; for this "would" changes,
    And hath abatements and delays as many
    As there are tongues, are hands, are accidents,   120
    And then this "should" is like a spendthrift's sigh
    That hurts by easing. But to the quick of th' ulcer—
    Hamlet comes back; what would you undertake
    To show yourself in deed your father's son
    More than in words?
LAERTES   To cut his throat i' th' church.   125
KING   No place indeed should murder sanctuarize[6];
    Revenge should have no bounds. But, good Laertes,
    Will you do this? Keep close within your chamber.
    Hamlet returned shall know you are come home.
    We'll put on those shall praise your excellence,   130
    And set a double varnish[7] on the fame
    The Frenchman gave you, bring you in fine[8] together,
    And wager on your heads. He, being remiss,[9]
    Most generous, and free from all contriving,

9. gave a report
1. skill in fencing
2. fencers
3. tests of experience
4. fullness

5. excess
6. provide sanctuary for murder
7. gloss
8. in short
9. careless

Will not peruse[1] the foils, so that with ease,   135
Or with a little shuffling, you may choose
A sword unbated,[2] and in a pass of practice
Requite him for your father.
LAERTES   I will do't,
And for that purpose I'll anoint my sword.
I bought an unction of a mountebank,   140
So mortal that but dip a knife in it,
Where it draws blood no cataplasm[3] so rare,
Collected from all simples[4] that have virtue
Under the moon, can save the thing from death
That is but scratched withal. I'll touch my point   145
With this contagion, that if I gall[5] him slightly,
It may be death.
KING   Let's further think of this,
Weigh what convenience both of time and means
May fit us to our shape. If this should fail,
And that our drift look[6] through our bad performance,   150
'Twere better not assayed. Therefore this project
Should have a back or second that might hold
If this did blast in proof.[7] Soft, let me see.
We'll make a solemn wager on your cunnings—
I ha't.   155
When in your motion you are hot and dry—
As make your bouts more violent to that end—
And that he calls for drink, I'll have preferred him
A chalice for the nonce, whereon but sipping,
If he by chance escape your venomed stuck,[8]   160
Our purpose may hold there.—But stay, what noise?

        Enter QUEEN.

QUEEN   One woe doth tread upon another's heel,
So fast they follow. Your sister's drowned, Laertes.
LAERTES   Drowned? O, where?
QUEEN   There is a willow grows aslant the brook   165
That shows his hoar leaves in the glassy stream.
Therewith fantastic garlands did she make
Of crowflowers, nettles, daisies, and long purples
That liberal[9] shepherds give a grosser[1] name,
But our cold[2] maids do dead men's fingers call them.   170
There on the pendent boughs her coronet weeds
Clamb'ring to hang, an envious[3] sliver broke,
When down her weedy trophies and herself
Fell in the weeping brook. Her clothes spread wide,
And mermaid-like awhile they bore her up,   175
Which time she chanted snatches of old tunes,
As one incapable[4] of her own distress,
Or like a creature native and indued[5]
Unto that element. But long it could not be

---

1. examine   8. thrust
2. not blunted   9. vulgar
3. poultice   1. coarser
4. herbs   2. chaste
5. scratch   3. malicious
6. intent become obvious   4. unaware
7. fail when tried   5. habituated

Till that her garments, heavy with their drink,   180
Pulled the poor wretch from her melodious lay
To muddy death.
LAERTES   Alas, then she is drowned?
QUEEN   Drowned, drowned.
LAERTES   Too much of water hast thou, poor Ophelia,
And therefore I forbid my tears; but yet   185
It is our trick; nature her custom holds,
Let shame say what it will. When these are gone,
The woman will be out. Adieu, my lord.
I have a speech o' fire that fain would blaze
But that this folly drowns it.   *Exit.*
KING   Let's follow, Gertrude.   190
How much I had to do to calm his rage!
Now fear I this will give it start again;
Therefore let's follow.   *Exeunt.*

Act 5

SCENE 1: *A churchyard. Enter two* CLOWNS.[6]

CLOWN   Is she to be buried in Christian burial when she wilfully
seeks her own salvation?
OTHER   I tell thee she is. Therefore make her grave straight. The
crowner[7] hath sat on her,[8] and finds it Christian burial.
CLOWN   How can that be, unless she drowned herself in her own de-   5
fence?
OTHER   Why, 'tis found so.
CLOWN   It must be "se offendendo";[9] it cannot be else. For here lies
the point: if I drown myself wittingly, it argues an act, and an act
hath three branches—it is to act, to do, to perform; argal,[1] she   10
drowned herself wittingly.
OTHER   Nay, but hear you, Goodman Delver.
CLOWN   Give me leave. Here lies the water; good. Here stands the
man; good. If the man go to this water and drown himself, it is, will
he, nill he, he goes—mark you that. But if the water come to him   15
and drown him, he drowns not himself. Argal, he that is not guilty
of his own death shortens not his own life.
OTHER   But is this law?
CLOWN   Ay, marry, is't; crowner's quest[2] law.
OTHER   Will you ha' the truth on't? If this had not been a gentle-   20
woman, she should have been buried out o' Christian burial.
CLOWN   Why, there thou say'st. And the more pity that great folk
should have count'nance[3] in this world to drown or hang themselves
more than their even-Christen.[4] Come, my spade. There is no ancient
gentlemen but gard'ners, ditchers, and grave-makers. They hold up   25
Adam's profession.
OTHER   Was he a gentleman?
CLOWN   'A was the first that ever bore arms.

6. rustics
7. coroner
8. held an inquest
9. an error for *se defendendo,* in self-defense

1. therefore
2. inquest
3. approval
4. fellow Christians

OTHER   Why, he had none.

CLOWN   What, art a heathen? How dost thou understand the Scrip- 30
ture? The Scripture says Adam digged. Could he dig without arms?
I'll put another question to thee. If thou answerest me not to the
purpose, confess thyself—

OTHER   Go to.

CLOWN   What is he that builds stronger than either the mason, the 35
shipwright, or the carpenter?

OTHER   The gallows-maker, for that frame outlives a thousand tenants.

CLOWN   I like thy wit well, in good faith. The gallows does well. But
how does it well? It does well to those that do ill. Now thou dost ill
to say the gallows is built stronger than the church. Argal, the gal- 40
lows may do well to thee. To't again,⁵ come.

OTHER   Who builds stronger than a mason, a shipwright, or a carpenter?

CLOWN   Ay tell me that, and unyoke.⁶

OTHER   Marry, now I can tell.   45

CLOWN   To't.

OTHER   Mass, I cannot tell.

CLOWN   Cudgel thy brains no more about it, for your dull ass will not
mend his pace with beating. And when you are asked this question
next, say "a grave-maker." The houses he makes lasts till doomsday. 50
Go, get thee in, and fetch me a stoup⁷ of liquor. *Exit* OTHER CLOWN.

Enter HAMLET *and* HORATIO *as* CLOWN *digs and sings.*

> In youth, when I did love, did love,
>   Methought it was very sweet,
> To contract⁸ the time for-a my behove,⁹
>   O, methought there-a was nothing-a meet.¹   55

HAMLET   Has this fellow no feeling of his business, that 'a sings in
grave-making?

HORATIO   Custom hath made it in him a property of easiness.

HAMLET   'Tis e'en so. The hand of little employment hath the daintier
sense.   60

CLOWN
> But age, with his stealing steps,
>   Hath clawed me in his clutch,
> And hath shipped me into the land,
>   As if I had never been such.

Throws up a skull.

HAMLET   That skull had a tongue in it, and could sing once. How the 65
knave jowls² it to the ground, as if 'twere Cain's jawbone, that did
the first murder! This might be the pate of a politician, which this
ass now o'erreaches³; one that would circumvent God, might it not?

HORATIO   It might, my lord.

HAMLET   Or of a courtier, which could say "Good morrow, sweet lord! 70
How dost thou, sweet lord?" This might be my Lord Such-a-one,
that praised my Lord Such-a-one's horse, when 'a meant to beg it,
might it not?

---

5. guess again
6. finish the matter
7. mug
8. shorten
9. advantage

1. The gravedigger's song is a free version of "The aged lover renounceth love"
by Thomas, Lord Vaux, published in *Tot-
tel's Miscellany*, 1557.
2. hurls
3. gets the better of

HORATIO Ay, my lord.

HAMLET Why, e'en so, and now my Lady Worm's, chapless,[4] and 75
knock'd abut the mazzard[5] with a sexton's spade. Here's fine revolution,[6] an we had the trick to see't. Did these bones cost no more the
breeding but to play at loggets with them?[7] Mine ache to think on't.

CLOWN   A pick-axe and a spade, a spade,
                    For and a shrouding sheet: 80
                    O, a pit of clay for to be made
                    For such a guest is meet.

    Throws up another skull.

HAMLET There's another. Why may not that be the skull of a lawyer?
Where be his quiddities now, his quillets, his cases, his tenures, and
his tricks? Why does he suffer this mad knave now to knock him 85
about the sconce[8] with a dirty shovel, and will not tell him of his
action of battery? Hum! This fellow might be in's time a great buyer
of land, with his statutes, his recognizances, his fines, his double
vouchers, his recoveries. Is this the fine[9] of his fines, and the recovery
of his recoveries, to have his fine pate full of fine dirt? Will his vouch- 90
ers vouch him no more of his purchases, and double ones too, than
the length and breadth of a pair of indentures[1]? The very convey-
ances of his lands will scarcely lie in this box, and must th' inheritor
himself have no more, ha?[2]

HORATIO Not a jot more, my lord.   95

HAMLET Is not parchment made of sheepskins?

HORATIO Ay, my lord, and of calves' skins too.

HAMLET They are sheep and calves which seek out assurance in that.
I will speak to this fellow. Whose grave's this, sirrah?

CLOWN Mine, sir.   100

    [*Sings.*] O, a pit of clay for to be made—

HAMLET I think it be thine indeed, for thou liest in't.

CLOWN You lie out on't, sir, and therefore 'tis not yours. For my part,
I do not lie in't, yet it is mine.

HAMLET Thou dost lie in't, to be in't and say it is thine. 'Tis for the 105
dead, not for the quick[3]; therefore thou liest.

CLOWN 'Tis a quick lie, sir; 'twill away again from me to you.

HAMLET What man dost thou dig it for?

CLOWN For no man, sir.

HAMLET What woman, then?   110

CLOWN For none neither.

HAMLET Who is to be buried in't?

CLOWN One that was a woman, sir; but, rest her soul, she's dead.

HAMLET How absolute[4] the knave is! We must speak by the card,[5] or
equivocation will undo us. By the Lord, Horatio, this three years I 115
have took note of it, the age is grown so picked[6] that the toe of the
peasant comes so near the heel of the courtier, he galls his kibe.[7]
How long hast thou been a grave-maker?

4. lacking a lower jaw
5. head
6. skill
7. "Loggets" were small pieces of wood
thrown as part of a game.
8. head
9. end
1. contracts

2. In this speech Hamlet reels off a list
of legal terms relating to property trans-
actions.
3. living
4. precise
5. exactly
6. refined
7. rubs a blister on his heel

CLOWN   Of all the days i' th' year, I came to't that day that our last
King Hamlet overcame Fortinbras.   120
HAMLET   How long is that since?
CLOWN   Cannot you tell that? Every fool can tell that. It was that
very day that young Hamlet was born—he that is mad, and sent
into England.
HAMLET   Ay, marry, why was he sent into England?   125
CLOWN   Why, because 'a was mad. 'A shall recover his wits there; or,
if 'a do not, 'tis no great matter there.
HAMLET   Why?
CLOWN   'Twill not be seen in him there. There the men are as mad
as he.   130
HAMLET   How came he mad?
CLOWN   Very strangely, they say.
HAMLET   How strangely?
CLOWN   Faith, e'en with losing his wits.
HAMLET   Upon what ground?   135
CLOWN   Why, here in Denmark. I have been sexton here, man and
boy, thirty years.
HAMLET   How long will a man lie i' th' earth ere he rot?
CLOWN   Faith, if 'a be not rotten before 'a die—as we have many
pocky[8] corses now-a-days that will scarce hold the laying in—'a will   140
last you some eight year or nine year. A tanner will last you nine
year.
HAMLET   Why he more than another?
CLOWN   Why, sir, his hide is so tanned with his trade that 'a will keep
out water a great while; and your water is a sore decayer of your   145
whoreson[9] dead body. Here's a skull now hath lien[1] you i' th' earth
three and twenty years.
HAMLET   Whose was it?
CLOWN   A whoreson mad fellow's it was. Whose do you think it was?
HAMLET   Nay, I know not.   150
CLOWN   A pestilence on him for a mad rogue! 'A poured a flagon of
Rhenish on my head once. This same skull, sir, was, sir, Yorick's
skull, the king's jester.
HAMLET   [*takes the skull*]   This?
CLOWN   E'en that.   155
HAMLET   Alas, poor Yorick! I knew him, Horatio—a fellow of infinite
jest, of most excellent fancy. He hath bore me on his back a thousand
times, and now how abhorred in my imagination it is! My gorge[2]
rises at it. Here hung those lips that I have kissed I know not how
oft. Where be your gibes now, your gambols, your songs, your flashes   160
of merriment that were wont to set the table on a roar? Not one now
to mock your own grinning? Quite chap-fall'n[3]? Now get you to my
lady's chamber, and tell her, let her paint an inch thick, to this favor[4]
she must come. Make her laugh at that. Prithee, Horatio, tell me one
thing.   165
HORATIO   What's that, my lord?
HAMLET   Dost thou think Alexander looked o' this fashion i' th' earth?
HORATIO   E'en so.
HAMLET   And smelt so? Pah!   *Throws down the skull.*

---

8. corrupted by syphilis   2. throat
9. bastard (not literally)   3. lacking a lower jaw
1. lain   4. appearance

HORATIO   E'en so, my lord.   170

HAMLET   To what base uses we may return, Horatio! Why may not imagination trace the noble dust of Alexander till 'a find it stopping a bung-hole?

HORATIO   'Twere to consider too curiously[5] to consider so.

HAMLET   No, faith, not a jot, but to follow him thither with modesty[6] 175 enough, and likelihood to lead it. Alexander died, Alexander was buried, Alexander returneth to dust; the dust is earth; of earth we make loam; and why of that loam whereto he was converted might they not stop a beer-barrel?

> Imperious Cæsar, dead and turned to clay,   180
> Might stop a hole to keep the wind away.
> O, that that earth which kept the world in awe
> Should patch a wall t'expel the winter's flaw![7]

But soft, but soft awhile! Here comes the king,
The queen, the courtiers.

Enter KING, QUEEN, LAERTES, *and the Corse with a* PRIEST *and* LORDS *attendant.*

Who is this they follow?   185
And with such maiméd[8] rites? This doth betoken
The corse they follow did with desperate hand
Fordo[9] it own life. 'Twas of some estate.[1]
Couch[2] we awhile and mark.   *Retires with* HORATIO.

LAERTES   What ceremony else[3]?   190

HAMLET   That is Laertes, a very noble youth. Mark.

LAERTES   What ceremony else?

PRIEST   Her obsequies have been as far enlarged[4]
As we have warranty. Her death was doubtful,
And but that great command o'ersways the order,[5]   195
She should in ground unsanctified been lodged
Till the last trumpet. For charitable prayers,
Shards, flints, and pebbles, should be thrown on her.
Yet here she is allowed her virgin crants,[6]
Her maiden strewments,[7] and the bringing home   200
Of bell and burial.

LAERTES   Must there no more be done?

PRIEST   No more be done.
We should profane the service of the dead
To sing a requiem and such rest to her
As to peace-parted souls.

LAERTES   Lay her i' th' earth,   205
And from her fair and unpolluted flesh
May violets spring! I tell thee, churlish priest,
A minist'ring angel shall my sister be
When thou liest howling.[8]

HAMLET   What, the fair Ophelia!

QUEEN   Sweets to the sweet. Farewell!   *Scatters flowers.* 210

---

5. precisely
6. moderation
7. gusty wind
8. cut short
9. destroy
1. rank
2. conceal ourselves

3. more
4. extended
5. usual rules
6. wreaths
7. flowers strewn on the grave
8. in Hell

I hoped thou shouldst have been my Hamlet's wife.
I thought thy bride-bed to have decked, sweet maid,
And not have strewed thy grave.
LAERTES   O, treble woe
Fall ten times treble on that curséd head
Whose wicked deed thy most ingenious sense[9]   215
Deprived thee of! Hold off the earth awhile,
Till I have caught her once more in mine arms.

                                          Leaps into the grave.

Now pile your dust upon the quick and dead,
Till of this flat a mountain you have made
T' o'er-top old Pelion or the skyish head   220
Of blue Olympus.[1]
HAMLET [*coming forward*]   What is he whose grief
Bears such an emphasis, whose phrase of sorrow
Conjures[2] the wand'ring stars, and makes them stand
Like wonder-wounded hearers? This is I,
Hamlet the Dane.   225

          HAMLET *leaps into the grave and they grapple.*

LAERTES   The devil take thy soul!
HAMLET   Thou pray'st not well.
I prithee take thy fingers from my throat,
For though I am not splenitive[3] and rash,
Yet have I in me something dangerous,
Which let thy wisdom fear. Hold off thy hand.   230
KING   Pluck them asunder.
QUEEN   Hamlet! Hamlet!
ALL   Gentlemen!
HORATIO   Good my lord, be quiet.

     The ATTENDANTS *part them, and they come out of the grave.*

HAMLET   Why, I will fight with him upon this theme   235
Until my eyelids will no longer wag.[4]
QUEEN   O my son, what theme?
HAMLET   I loved Ophelia. Forty thousand brothers
Could not with all their quantity of love
Make up my sum. What wilt thou do for her?   240
KING   O, he is mad, Laertes.
QUEEN   For love of God, forbear[5] him.
HAMLET   'Swounds, show me what th'owt do.
Woo't[6] weep, woo't fight, woo't fast, woo't tear thyself,
Woo't drink up eisel,[7] eat a crocodile?   245
I'll do't. Dost come here to whine?
To outface[8] me with leaping in her grave?
Be buried quick with her, and so will I.
And if thou prate of mountains, let them throw

---

9. lively mind
1. The rivalry between Laertes and Hamlet in this scene extends even to their rhetoric. Pelion and Olympus, mentioned here by Laertes, and Ossa, mentioned below by Hamlet, were Greek mountains noted in mythology for their height. Olympus was the reputed home of the gods, and the other two were piled one on top of the other by the Giants in an attempt to reach the top of Olympus and overthrow the gods.
2. casts a spell on
3. hot-tempered
4. move
5. bear with
6. will you
7. vinegar
8. get the best of

Millions of acres on us, till our ground,   250
Singeing his pate against the burning zone,⁹
Make Ossa like a wart! Nay, an thou'lt mouth,
I'll rant as well as thou.
QUEEN   This is mere madness;
And thus awhile the fit will work on him.
Anon, as patient as the female dove   255
When that her golden couplets¹ are disclosed,
His silence will sit drooping.
HAMLET   Hear you, sir.
What is the reason that you use me thus?
I loved you ever. But it is no matter.
Let Hercules himself do what he may,   260
The cat will mew, and dog will have his day.
KING   I pray thee, good Horatio, wait upon² him.
                                        Exeunt HAMLET *and* HORATIO.
[*To* LAERTES.] Strengthen your patience in our last night's speech.
We'll put the matter to the present push.³—
Good Gertrude, set some watch over your son.—   265
This grave shall have a living monument.
An hour of quiet shortly shall we see;
Till then in patience our proceeding be.   *Exeunt.*

SCENE 2: *A hall or public room. Enter* HAMLET *and* HORATIO.

HAMLET   So much for this, sir; now shall you see the other.
You do remember all the circumstance?
HORATIO   Remember it, my lord!
HAMLET   Sir, in my heart there was a kind of fighting
That would not let me sleep. Methought I lay   5
Worse than the mutines⁴ in the bilboes.⁵ Rashly,
And praised be rashness for it—let us know,
Our indiscretion sometime serves us well,
When our deep plots do pall; and that should learn⁶ us
There's a divinity that shapes our ends,   10
Rough-hew them how we will—
HORATIO   That is most certain.
HAMLET   Up from my cabin,
My sea-gown scarfed⁷ about me, in the dark
Groped I to find out them, had my desire,
Fingered⁸ their packet, and in fine⁹ withdrew   15
To mine own room again, making so bold,
My fears forgetting manners, to unseal
Their grand commission; where I found, Horatio—
Ah, royal knavery!—an exact¹ command,
Larded² with many several sorts of reasons,   20
Importing Denmark's health, and England's too,
With, ho! such bugs and goblins in my life,³
That on the supervise,⁴ no leisure bated,

---

9. sky in the torrid zone   7. wrapped
1. pair of eggs   8. stole
2. attend   9. quickly
3. immediate trial   1. precisely stated
4. mutineers   2. garnished
5. stocks   3. such dangers if I remained alive
6. teach   4. as soon as the commission was read

No, not to stay the grinding of the axe,
My head should be struck off.
HORATIO   Is't possible?   25
HAMLET   Here's the commission; read it at more leisure.
But wilt thou hear now how I did proceed?
HORATIO   I beseech you.
HAMLET   Being thus benetted[5] round with villainies,
Or I could make a prologue to my brains,   30
They had begun the play. I sat me down,
Devised[6] a new commission, wrote it fair.[7]
I once did hold it, as our statists[8] do,
A baseness to write fair, and labored much   35
How to forget that learning; but sir, now
It did me yeoman's service. Wilt thou know
Th' effect[9] of what I wrote?
HORATIO   Ay, good my lord.
HAMLET   An earnest conjuration from the king,
As England was his faithful tributary,[1]
As love between them like the palm might flourish,   40
As peace should still her wheaten garland wear
And stand a comma 'tween their amities,[2]
And many such like as's of great charge,[3]
That on the view and knowing of these contents,
Without debatement[4] further more or less,   45
He should those bearers put to sudden death,
Not shriving-time allowed.[5]
HORATIO   How was this sealed?
HAMLET   Why, even in that was heaven ordinant,[6]
I had my father's signet in my purse,
Which was the model of that Danish seal,   50
Folded the writ up in the form of th' other,
Subscribed it, gave't th' impression,[7] placed it safely,
The changeling[8] never known. Now, the next day
Was our sea-fight, and what to this was sequent[9]
Thou knowest already.   55
HORATIO   So Guildenstern and Rosencrantz go to't.
HAMLET   Why, man, they did make love to this employment.
They are not near[1] my conscience; their defeat[2]
Does by their own insinuation grow.
'Tis dangerous when the baser nature comes   60
Between the pass[3] and fell[4] incenséd points
Of mighty opposites.
HORATIO   Why, what a king is this!
HAMLET   Does it not, think thee, stand me now upon—
He that hath killed my king and whored my mother,
Popped in between th' election and my hopes,   65
Thrown out his angle[5] for my proper life,

---

5. caught in a net
6. made
7. legibly
8. politicians
9. contents
1. vassal
2. link friendships
3. import
4. consideration
5. without time for confession

6. operative
7. of the seal
8. alteration
9. followed
1. do not touch
2. death
3. thrust
4. cruel
5. fishhook

And with such coz'nage[6]—is't not perfect conscience
To quit[7] him with this arm? And is't not to be damned
To let this canker of our nature come
In further evil? 70
HORATIO It must be shortly known to him from England
What is the issue[8] of the business there.
HAMLET It will be short[9]; the interim is mine.
And a man's life's no more than to say "one."
But I am very sorry, good Horatio, 75
That to Laertes I forgot myself;
For by the image of my cause I see
The portraiture of his. I'll court his favors.
But sure the bravery[1] of his grief did put me
Into a tow'ring passion.
HORATIO   Peace; who comes here? 80

Enter OSRIC.

OSRIC Your lordship is right welcome back to Denmark.
HAMLET I humbly thank you, sir. [*Aside to* HORATIO.] Dost know
this water-fly?
HORATIO [*aside to* HAMLET] No, my good lord.
HAMLET [*aside to* HORATIO] Thy state is the more gracious, for 'tis a 85
vice to know him. He hath much land, and fertile. Let a beast be
lord of beasts, and his crib shall stand at the king's mess. 'Tis a
chough,[2] but as I say, spacious in the possession of dirt.
OSRIC Sweet lord, if your lordship were at leisure, I should impart a
thing to you from his majesty. 90
HAMLET I will receive it, sir, with all diligence of spirit. Put your
bonnet to his right use. 'Tis for the head.
OSRIC I thank your lordship, it is very hot.
HAMLET No, believe me, 'tis very cold; the wind is northerly.
OSRIC It is indifferent[3] cold, my lord, indeed. 95
HAMLET But yet methinks it is very sultry and hot for my com-
plexion.[4]
OSRIC Exceedingly, my lord; it is very sultry, as 'twere—I cannot tell
how. My lord, his majesty bade me signify to you that 'a has laid
a great wager on your head. Sir, this is the matter— 100
HAMLET I beseech you, remember.

HAMLET *moves him to put on his hat.*

OSRIC Nay, good my lord; for my ease, in good faith. Sir, here is
newly come to court Laertes; believe me, an absolute[5] gentleman,
full of most excellent differences,[6] of very soft society and great
showing.[7] Indeed, to speak feelingly of him, he is the card or cal- 105
endar[8] of gentry, for you shall find in him the continent[9] of what
part a gentleman would see.
HAMLET Sir, his definement[1] suffers no perdition in you, though I
know to divide him inventorially[2] would dozy[3] th' arithmetic of

6. trickery
7. repay
8. outcome
9. soon
1. exaggerated display
2. jackdaw
3. moderately
4. temperament

5. perfect
6. qualities
7. good manners
8. measure
9. sum total
1. description
2. examine bit by bit
3. daze

memory, and yet but yaw[4] neither in respect of his quick sail. But [110] in the verity of extolment, I take him to be a soul of great article,[5] and his infusion[6] of such dearth and rareness as, to make true diction[7] of him, his semblage[8] is his mirror, and who else would trace[9] him, his umbrage,[1] nothing more.

OSRIC   Your lordship speaks most infallibly of him.   [115]

HAMLET   The concernancy[2] sir? Why do we wrap the gentleman in our more rawer breath?[3]

OSRIC   Sir?

HORATIO   Is't not possible to understand in another tongue? You will to't, sir, really.   [120]

HAMLET   What imports the nomination[4] of this gentleman?

OSRIC   Of Laertes?

HORATIO   [*aside*]   His purse is empty already. All's golden words are spent.

HAMLET   Of him, sir.   [125]

OSRIC   I know you are not ignorant—

HAMLET   I would you did, sir; yet, in faith, if you did, it would not much approve me. Well, sir.

OSRIC   You are not ignorant of what excellence Laertes is—

HAMLET   I dare not confess that, lest I should compare[5] with him in [130] excellence; but to know a man well were to know himself.

OSRIC   I mean, sir, for his weapon; but in the imputation[6] laid on him by them, in his meed he's unfellowed.[7]

HAMLET   What's his weapon?

OSRIC   Rapier and dagger.   [135]

HAMLET   That's two of his weapons—but well.

OSRIC   The king, sir, hath wagered with him six Barbary horses, against the which he has impawned,[8] as I take it, six French rapiers and poniards, with their assigns,[9] as girdle, hangers, and so. Three of the carriages, in faith, are very dear to fancy,[1] very responsive to [140] the hilts, most delicate[2] carriages, and of very liberal conceit.[3]

HAMLET   What call you the carriages?

HORATIO   [*aside to* HAMLET]   I knew you must be edified by the margent[4] ere you had done.

OSRIC   The carriages, sir, are the hangers.   [145]

HAMLET   The phrase would be more germane to the matter if we could carry a cannon by our sides. I would it might be hangers till then. But on! Six Barbary horses against six French swords, their assigns, and three liberal conceited carriages; that's the French bet against the Danish. Why is this all impawned, as you call it?   [150]

OSRIC   The king, sir, hath laid, sir, that in a dozen passes between yourself and him he shall not exceed you three hits; he hath laid on twelve for nine, and it would come to immediate trial if your lordship would vouchsafe the answer.

HAMLET   How if I answer no?   [155]

OSRIC   I mean, my lord, the opposition of your person in trial.

4. steer wildly
5. scope
6. nature
7. telling
8. rival
9. keep pace with
1. shadow
2. meaning
3. cruder words
4. naming

5. i.e., compare myself
6. reputation
7. unequaled in his excellence
8. staked
9. appurtenances
1. finely designed
2. well adjusted
3. elegant design
4. marginal gloss

HAMLET   Sir, I will walk here in the hall. If it please his majesty, it is the breathing time[5] of day with me. Let the foils be brought, the gentleman willing, and the king hold his purpose; I will win for him an I can. If not, I will gain nothing but my shame and the 160 odd hits.

OSRIC   Shall I deliver you so?

HAMLET   To this effect, sir, after what flourish your nature will.

OSRIC   I commend my duty to your lordship.

HAMLET   Yours, yours. [*Exit* OSRIC.] He does well to commend it 165 himself; there are no tongues else for's turn.

HORATIO   This lapwing runs away with the shell on his head.[6]

HAMLET   'A did comply,[7] sir, with his dug[8] before 'a sucked it. Thus has he, and many more of the same bevy that I know the drossy age dotes on, only got the tune of the time; and out of an habit of en- 170 counter, a kind of yesty[9] collection which carries them through and through the most fanned and winnowed opinions; and do but blow them to their trial, the bubbles are out.

   Enter a LORD.

LORD   My lord, his majesty commended him to you by young Osric, who brings back to him that you attend[1] him in the hall. He sends 175 to know if your pleasure hold to play with Laertes, or that you will take longer time.

HAMLET   I am constant to my purposes; they follow the king's pleasure. If his fitness speaks, mine is ready; now or whensoever, provided I be so able as now.   180

LORD   The king and queen and all are coming down.

HAMLET   In happy time.

LORD   The queen desires you to use some gentle entertainment[2] to Laertes before you fall to play.

HAMLET   She well instructs me.   *Exit* LORD. 185

HORATIO   You will lose this wager, my lord.

HAMLET   I do not think so. Since he went into France I have been in continual practice. I shall win at the odds. But thou wouldst not think how ill[3] all's here about my heart. But it is no matter.

HORATIO   Nay, good my lord—   190

HAMLET   It is but foolery, but it is such a kind of gaingiving[4] as would perhaps trouble a woman.

HORATIO   If your mind dislike anything, obey it. I will forestall their repair[5] hither, and say you are not fit.

HAMLET   Not a whit, we defy augury. There is special providence in 195 the fall of a sparrow. If it be now, 'tis not to come; if it be not to come, it will be now; if it be not now, yet it will come. The readiness is all. Since no man of aught he leaves knows, what is't to leave betimes? Let be.

   A table prepared. Enter TRUMPETS, DRUMS, *and* OFFICERS *with cushions;* KING, QUEEN, OSRIC *and* ATTENDANTS *with foils, daggers, and* LAERTES.

---

5. time for exercise
6. The lapwing was thought to be so precocious that it could run immediately after being hatched, even as here with bits of the shell still on its head.
7. deal formally
8. mother's breast

9. yeasty
1. await
2. cordiality
3. uneasy
4. misgiving
5. coming

KING   Come, Hamlet, come and take this hand from me.   200

    The KING *puts* LAERTES' *hand into* HAMLET'*s.*

HAMLET   Give me your pardon, sir. I have done you wrong,
But pardon 't as you are a gentleman.
This presence[6] knows, and you must needs have heard,
How I am punished with a sore distraction.
What I have done   205
That might your nature, honor, and exception,[7]
Roughly awake, I here proclaim was madness.
Was 't Hamlet wronged Laertes? Never Hamlet.
If Hamlet from himself be ta'en away,
And when he's not himself does wrong Laertes,   210
Then Hamlet does it not, Hamlet denies it.
Who does it then? His madness. If't be so,
Hamlet is of the faction that is wronged;
His madness is poor Hamlet's enemy.
Sir, in this audience,   215
Let my disclaiming from[8] a purposed evil
Free[9] me so far in your most generous thoughts
That I have shot my arrow o'er the house
And hurt my brother.
LAERTES   I am satisfied in nature,
Whose motive in this case should stir me most   220
To my revenge. But in my terms of honor
I stand aloof, and will no reconcilement
Till by some elder masters of known honor
I have a voice[1] and precedent of peace
To keep my name ungored.[2] But till that time   225
I do receive your offered love like love,
And will not wrong it.
HAMLET   I embrace it freely,
And will this brother's wager frankly[3] play.
Give us the foils.
LAERTES   Come, one for me.
HAMLET   I'll be your foil, Laertes. In mine ignorance   230
Your skill shall, like a star i' th' darkest night,
Stick fiery off[4] indeed.
LAERTES   You mock me, sir.
HAMLET   No, by this hand.
KING   Give them the foils, young Osric. Cousin Hamlet,
You know the wager?
HAMLET   Very well, my lord;   235
Your Grace has laid the odds o' th' weaker side.
KING   I do not fear it, I have seen you both;
But since he is bettered,[5] we have therefore odds.
LAERTES   This is too heavy; let me see another.
HAMLET   This likes[6] me well. These foils have all a[7] length?   240

    They prepare to play.

6. company
7. resentment
8. denying of
9. absolve
1. authority
2. unshamed

3. without rancor
4. shine brightly
5. reported better
6. suits
7. the same

OSRIC Ay, my good lord.
KING Set me the stoups of wine upon that table.
  If Hamlet give the first or second hit,
  Or quit in answer of[8] the third exchange,
  Let all the battlements their ordnance fire.   245
  The king shall drink to Hamlet's better breath,
  And in the cup an union[9] shall he throw,
  Richer than that which four successive kings
  In Denmark's crown have worn. Give me the cups,
  And let the kettle[1] to the trumpet speak,   250
  The trumpet to the cannoneer without,
  The cannons to the heavens, the heaven to earth,
  "Now the king drinks to Hamlet." Come, begin——

  Trumpets the while.

  And you, the judges, bear a wary eye.
HAMLET Come on, sir.
LAERTES   Come, my lord.   *They play.*
HAMLET   One.
LAERTES   No.
HAMLET   Judgment?   255
OSRIC A hit, a very palpable hit.

  Drums, trumpets, and shot. Flourish; a piece goes off.

LAERTES Well, again.
KING Stay, give me drink. Hamlet, this pearl is thine.
  Here's to thy health. Give him the cup.
HAMLET I'll play this bout first; set it by awhile.   260
  Come.   *They play.*
  Another hit; what say you?
LAERTES I do confess't.
KING Our son shall win.
QUEEN   He's fat,[2] and scant of breath.
  Here, Hamlet, take my napkin, rub thy brows.   265
  The queen carouses to thy fortune, Hamlet.
HAMLET Good madam!
KING Gertrude, do not drink.
QUEEN I will, my lord; I pray you pardon me.
KING [*aside*] It is the poisoned cup; it is too late.   270
HAMLET I dare not drink yet, madam; by and by.
QUEEN Come, let me wipe thy face.
LAERTES My lord, I'll hit him now.
KING   I do not think't.
LAERTES [*aside*] And yet it is almost against my conscience.
HAMLET Come, for the third, Laertes. You do but dally.   275
  I pray you pass[3] with your best violence;
  I am afeard you make a wanton of me.[4]
LAERTES Say you so? Come on.   *They play.*
OSRIC Nothing, neither way.
LAERTES Have at you now!   280

8. repay
9. pearl
1. kettledrum

2. out of shape
3. attack
4. trifle with me

LAERTES *wounds* HAMLET: *then, in scuffling, they change rapiers, and* HAMLET *wounds* LAERTES.

KING   Part them. They are incensed.
HAMLET   Nay, come again.   *The* QUEEN *falls.*
OSRIC   Look to the queen there, ho!
HORATIO   They bleed on both sides. How is it, my lord?
OSRIC   How is't, Laertes?   285
LAERTES   Why, as a woodcock to mine own springe,[5] Osric.
    I am justly killed with mine own treachery.
HAMLET   How does the queen?
KING   She swoons to see them bleed.
QUEEN   No, no, the drink, the drink! O my dear Hamlet!
    The drink, the drink! I am poisoned.   *Dies.* 290
HAMLET   O, villainy! Ho! let the door be locked.
    Treachery! seek it out.
LAERTES   It is here, Hamlet. Hamlet, thou art slain;
    No med'cine in the world can do thee good.
    In thee there is not half an hour's life.   295
    The treacherous instrument is in thy hand,
    Unbated[6] and envenomed. The foul practice
    Hath turned itself on me. Lo, here I lie,
    Never to rise again. Thy mother's poisoned.
    I can no more. The king, the king's to blame.   300
HAMLET   The point envenomed too?
    Then, venom, to thy work.   *Hurts the* KING.
ALL   Treason! treason!
KING   O, yet defend me, friends. I am but hurt.[7]
HAMLET   Here, thou incestuous, murd'rous, damnéd Dane,   305
    Drink off this potion. Is thy union here?
    Follow my mother.   *The* KING *dies.*
LAERTES   He is justly served.
    It is a poison tempered[8] by himself.
    Exchange forgiveness with me, noble Hamlet.
    Mine and my father's death come not upon thee,   310
    Nor thine on me!   *Dies.*
HAMLET   Heaven make thee free of[9] it! I follow thee.
    I am dead, Horatio. Wretched queen, adieu!
    You that look pale and tremble at this chance,[1]
    That are but mutes or audience to this act,   315
    Had I but time, as this fell sergeant Death
    Is strict in his arrest,[2] O, I could tell you—
    But let it be. Horatio, I am dead:
    Thou livest; report me and my cause aright
    To the unsatisfied.[3]
HORATIO   Never believe it.   320
    I am more an antique Roman than a Dane.
    Here's yet some liquor left.
HAMLET   As th'art a man,
    Give me the cup. Let go. By heaven, I'll ha't.

5. snare
6. unblunted
7. wounded
8. mixed

9. forgive
1. circumstance
2. summons to court
3. uninformed

O God, Horatio, what a wounded name,
Things standing thus unknown, shall live behind me!　　　325
If thou didst ever hold me in thy heart,
Absent thee from felicity awhile,
And in this harsh world draw thy breath in pain,
To tell my story.　　　　　　　　　　　*A march afar off.*
　　　　　　What warlike noise is this?
OSRIC　Young Fortinbras, with conquest come from Poland,　　330
To th' ambassadors of England gives
This warlike volley.[4]
HAMLET　　　　　　　O, I die, Horatio!
The potent poison quite o'er-crows[5] my spirit.
I cannot live to hear the news from England,
But I do prophesy th' election lights　　　　　　　335
On Fortinbras. He has my dying voice.[6]
So tell him, with th' occurrents,[7] more and less,
Which have solicited[8]—the rest is silence.　　　*Dies.*
HORATIO　Now cracks a noble heart. Good night, sweet prince,
And flights of angels sing thee to thy rest!　　*March within.* 340
Why does the drum come hither?

　　　Enter FORTINBRAS, *with the* AMBASSADORS *and with drum,*
　　　colors, and ATTENDANTS.

FORTINBRAS　Where is this sight?
HORATIO　　　　　　　　What is it you would see?
If aught of woe or wonder, cease your search.
FORTINBRAS　This quarry cries on havoc.[9] O proud death,
What feast is toward[1] in thine eternal cell　　　　345
That thou so many princes at a shot
So bloodily hast struck?
AMBASSADORS　　　　　　The sight is dismal;
And our affairs from England come too late.
The ears are senseless[2] that should give us hearing
To tell him his commandment is fulfilled,　　　　　350
That Rosencrantz and Guildenstern are dead.
Where should we have our thanks?
HORATIO　　　　　　　　Not from his mouth,
Had it th' ability of life to thank you.
He never gave commandment for their death.
But since, so jump[3] upon this bloody question,　　　355
You from the Polack wars, and you from England,
Are here arrived, give orders that these bodies
High on a stage be placéd to the view,
And let me speak to th' yet unknowing world
How these things came about. So shall you hear　　　360
Of carnal, bloody, and unnatural acts;

---

4. The staging presents some difficulties here. If Osric is not clairvoyant, he must have left the stage at some point and returned. One possibility is that he might have left to carry out Hamlet's order to lock the door (line 291) and returned when the sound of the distant march is heard.
5. overcomes
6. support
7. circumstances
8. brought about this scene
9. The game killed in the hunt proclaims a slaughter.
1. in preparation
2. without sense of hearing
3. exactly

Of accidental judgments, casual[4] slaughters;
Of deaths put on by cunning and forced cause;
And, in this upshot,[5] purposes mistook
Fall'n on th' inventors' heads. All this can I   365
Truly deliver.
FORTINBRAS   Let us haste to hear it,
And call the noblest to the audience.[6]
For me, with sorrow I embrace my fortune.
I have some rights of memory[7] in this kingdom,
Which now to claim my vantage[8] doth invite me.   370
HORATIO   Of that I shall have also cause to speak,
And from his mouth whose voice will draw on more.
But let this same be presently performed,
Even while men's minds are wild, lest more mischance
On plots and errors happen.
FORTINBRAS   Let four captains   375
Bear Hamlet like a soldier to the stage,
For he was likely, had he been put on,[9]
To have proved most royal; and for his passage
The soldier's music and the rite of war
Speak loudly for him.   380
Take up the bodies. Such a sight as this
Becomes the field, but here shows much amiss.
Go, bid the soldiers shoot.

                        Exeunt marching. A peal of ordnance shot off.

                                            ca. 1600

---

4. brought about by apparent accident   7. succession
5. result   8. position
6. hearing   9. elected king

HENRIK IBSEN

The Wild Duck*

CHARACTERS

HÅKON WERLE, *businessman, industrialist, etc.*
GREGERS WERLE, *his son*
OLD EKDAL
HJALMAR EKDAL, *his son, a photographer*
GINA EKDAL, *Hjalmar's wife*
HEDVIG, *their fourteen-year-old daughter*
MRS. SØRBY, *housekeeper to Håkon Werle*
RELLING, *a doctor*

MOLVIK, *a one-time theological student*
PETTERSEN, *Håkon Werle's servant*
GRÅBERG, *Håkon Werle's bookkeeper*
JENSEN, *a hired waiter*
A FLABBY GENTLEMAN
A THIN-HAIRED GENTLEMAN
A NEARSIGHTED GENTLEMAN
SIX OTHER GENTLEMEN, *Håkon Werle's guests*
SEVERAL HIRED SERVANTS

The first act takes place at the home of HÅKON WERLE; *the four following acts at* HJALMAR EKDAL's.

Act 1

At HÅKON WERLE's *house. The study, expensively and comfortably appointed; bookcases and upholstered furniture; in the middle of the room a desk with papers and documents; subdued lighting from lamps with green shades. In the rear, open folding doors with portières drawn back reveal a large, elegant drawing room, brilliantly lit by lamps and candelabra. Front right in study, a small baize-covered door to the office wing. Front left, a fireplace with glowing coal fire. Farther back on left wall, double doors to the dining room.*

*   PETTERSEN, WERLE's *servant, in livery, and the hired waiter* JENSEN, *in black, are putting the study in order. In the drawing room, two or three other hired waiters are busy arranging for the guests and lighting more candles. The hum of conversation and the laughter of many voices can be heard from the dining room. Somebody taps his wine glass with a knife to signal he is about to make a speech; silence follows; a toast is proposed; cheers, and again the hum of conversation.*

PETTERSEN [*lights a lamp on mantlepiece and sets shade on*]   Say, just listen to them, Jensen. That's the old man on his feet now, making a long toast to Mrs. Sørby.

JENSEN [*moving an armchair forward*]   Do you think it's true, what they're saying—that there's something between them?

PETTERSEN   Devil knows.

JENSEN   I guess he must've been quite a guy in his day.

PETTERSEN   Could be.

JENSEN   They say he's giving this dinner for his son.

PETTERSEN   That's right. His son came home yesterday.

---

* Translated by Dounia Christiani.

873

JENSEN   I never even knew old Werle had a son.

PETTERSEN   Oh, yes, he's got a son all right. But you can't budge him from the works up at Højdal. He's never once been to town in all the years I've worked in this house.

A HIRED WAITER [*in doorway to drawing room*]   Say, Pettersen, there's an old fellow here . . .

PETTERSEN [*grumbling*]   Oh damn. Who'd want to come at this time!

> OLD EKDAL *appears from the right in drawing room. He is dressed in a shabby overcoat with high collar, and woolen mittens. He has a stick and a fur cap in his hand; a parcel wrapped in brown paper under his arm. Wears a dirty reddish-brown wig and has a little gray mustache.*

PETTERSEN [*going toward him*]   Good God! What are you doing here?

EKDAL [*in doorway*]   Absolutely must get into the office, Pettersen.

PETTERSEN   The office closed an hour ago, and . . .

EKDAL   They told me that at the gate, old man. But Gråberg's still in there. Be a good sport, Pettersen, and let me slip in through here. [*Points to baize door.*] Been this way before.

PETTERSEN   Well, all right then, go ahead. [*Opens door.*] But just be sure you go out the right way. We've got company.

EKDAL   Know that—hm! Thanks, Pettersen, old chap! Good old friend. Thanks. [*Mutters to himself.*] Ass! [*Exit into office.* PETTERSEN *shuts door after him.*]

JENSEN   Does he work in the office?

PETTERSEN   No, they just give him some copying to do at home when they're rushed. Not that he hasn't been a somebody in his day, old Ekdal.

JENSEN   Yes, he looked like there's something about him.

PETTERSEN   Yes, indeed. I want you to know he was once a lieutenant.[1]

JENSEN   Go on—him a lieutenant!

PETTERSEN   So help me, he was. But then he switched over to the timber business, or whatever it was. They say he's supposed to have played a dirty low-down trick on Mr. Werle once. The two of them were in on the Højdal works together then, you see. Oh, I know old Ekdal well, I do. Many's the time we've had a bitters and beer together down at Ma Eriksen's place.

JENSEN   Him? He sure can't have much money to throw around?

PETTERSEN   Lord, Jensen, no. It's me that stands treat, naturally. Seems to me we owe a little respect to them that's come down in the world.

JENSEN   Oh, so he went bankrupt?

PETTERSEN   Worse than that. He was sentenced to hard labor.

JENSEN   Hard labor!

PETTERSEN   Anyway, he went to jail . . . [*Listening.*] Sh! They're getting up from the table now.

> *The dining room doors are thrown open from within by two servants.* MRS. SØRBY *comes out, in conversation with two gentlemen. The rest of the party, among them* HÅKON WERLE, *follow shortly thereafter. Last come* HJALMAR EKDAL *and* GREGERS WERLE.

1. See the note on European titles, p. 939.

MRS. SØRBY [*to the servant, in passing*]   Pettersen, will you have the coffee served in the music room, please.

PETTERSEN   Very good, Mrs. Sørby.

She and the two gentlemen exit into drawing room and thence off to right. PETTERSEN *and* JENSEN *exit the same way.*

A FLABBY GENTLEMAN [*to a* THIN-HAIRED ONE]   Whew! What a dinner! *That* was something to tuck away!

THE THIN-HAIRED GENTLEMAN   Oh, with a little good will it's incredible what one can manage in three hours' time.

THE FLABBY GENTLEMAN   Yes, but afterwards, my dear sir, afterwards!

A THIRD GENTLEMAN   I hear the coffee and liqueurs are being served in the music room.

THE FLABBY GENTLEMAN   Splendid! Then perhaps Mrs. Sørby will play something for us.

THE THIN-HAIRED GENTLEMAN [*in an undertone*]   As long as Mrs. Sørby doesn't play something *on* us, one of these days.

THE FLABBY GENTLEMAN   Oh, Berta wouldn't do that. She isn't the type to cast off her old friends. [*They laugh and exit into drawing room.*]

WERLE [*in a low, depressed tone*]   I don't think anybody noticed, Gregers.

GREGERS [*looks at him*]   Noticed what?

WERLE   Didn't you notice either?

GREGERS   What was I supposed to notice?

WERLE   We were thirteen at table.

GREGERS   Really? Were there thirteen?

WERLE [*with a glance toward* HJALMAR EKDAL]   As a rule we are always twelve. [*To the others.*] In here if you please, Gentlemen!

He and the remaining guests, except HJALMAR *and* GREGERS, *exit rear right.*

HJALMAR [*who had heard what was said*]   You shouldn't have sent me that invitation, Gregers.

GREGERS   What! This party is supposed to be for *me*. And I'm not to invite my best, my only friend?

HJALMAR   But I don't think your father approves. I never come to this house any other time.

GREGERS   So I hear. But I had to see you and have a talk with you. Because I expect to be leaving again soon.—Yes, we two old school chums, we've certainly drifted far apart, haven't we. It must be sixteen-seventeen years since we saw each other.

HJALMAR   Is it as long as all that?

GREGERS   It is indeed. Well now, how are you getting along? You look fine. You've put on weight, you're even a bit stout.

HJALMAR   Hm, stout is hardly the word. But I suppose I do look a bit more of a man than I did in the old days.

GREGERS   Yes, you do. Outwardly you don't seem to have suffered much harm.

HJALMAR [*in a gloomy voice*]   But inwardly, Gregers! That's a different story, believe me. You know, of course, how terribly everything collapsed for me and mine since we last saw each other.

GREGERS [*more softly*]   How are things now with your father?

HJALMAR   Ah, let's not go into that. Naturally, my poor unfortunate

father makes his home with me. He hasn't anyone else in the world to turn to. But look, it's so desperately hard for me to talk about this. —Tell me instead how you've been, up there at the works.

GREGERS   Delightfully lonely, that's how I've been. Plenty of opportunity to think about all sorts of things.—Come over here; let's make ourselves comfortable.

He sits down in an armchair by the fireplace and draws HJALMAR *into another beside him.*

HJALMAR   [*with sentiment*]   I do want to thank you, all the same, Gregers, for asking me to your father's party. Because now I can see you don't have anything against me anymore.

GREGERS   [*in surprise*]   Whatever gave you the idea I had anything against you?

HJALMAR   Why, you did have, you know, the first few years.

GREGERS   What first few years?

HJALMAR   After the great disaster. And it was only natural that you should. After all, it was only by a hair that your father himself missed being dragged into that . . . oh, that terrible business!

GREGERS   And because of that I'm supposed to have a grudge against you? Whoever gave you that idea?

HJALMAR   I *know* you did, Gregers. Your father told me himself.

GREGERS   [*startled*]   My father! Oh, I see. Hm.—Was that the reason I never heard from you afterwards—not a single word?

HJALMAR   Yes.

GREGERS   Not even when you went and became a photographer.

HJALMAR   Your father said it would be better not to write you about anything at all.

GREGERS   [*absently*]   Well, well, maybe he was right, at that.—But tell me, Hjalmar—are you pretty well satisfied now with things as they are?

HJALMAR   [*with a light sigh*]   Why, yes, on the whole I can't complain, really. At first, as you can imagine, it was all pretty strange. My whole world shot to pieces. But then, so was everything else. That terrible calamity of Father's—the shame and disgrace, Gregers . . .

GREGERS   [*shaken*]   I know, I know.

HJALMAR   Of course I couldn't possibly think of continuing my studies. There wasn't a penny left. On the contrary, there were debts—mostly to your father, I believe.

GREGERS   Hm . . .

HJALMAR   Well, so I thought it best to make a clean break, you know—drop my old life and all my connections. It was your father especially who advised me to do that; and since he put himself out to be so helpful to me . . .

GREGERS   My father did?

HJALMAR   Yes, surely you know that? Where could *I* have got the money to learn photography and equip a studio and set up in business? Things like that are expensive, let me tell you.

GREGERS   And my *father* paid for it all?

HJALMAR   Why, of course, didn't you know? I understood him to say he'd written and told you.

GREGERS   Not a word about its being *him.* He must have forgotten. We've never exchanged anything but business letters. So it was my *father* . . . !

HJALMAR   It certainly was. He never wanted it to get around, but

it was him, all right. And of course it was also he who put me in a position to get married. Or maybe you didn't know about that either?

GREGERS   No, I certainly did not. [*Clapping him on the arm.*] But my dear Hjalmar, I can't tell you how delighted I am to hear all this—and remorseful too. I may have been unjust to my father after all—on a few points. Because this does reveal a kind heart, doesn't it. It's as if, in a way, he had a conscience . . .

HJALMAR   A conscience . . . ?

GREGERS   Well, well, whatever you want to call it, then. No, I really can't tell you how glad I am to hear this about my father.—So you're a married man, Hjalmar. That's more than I'm ever likely to be. Well, I trust you are happy in your marriage?

HJALMAR   Yes, indeed I am. She's as capable and fine a wife as any man could ask for. And she's by no means without culture.

GREGERS   [*a little surprised*]   Why no, I don't suppose she is.

HJALMAR   Life itself is an education, you see. Her daily contact with me . . . besides which there's a couple of very intelligent fellows we see regularly. I assure you, you wouldn't know Gina now.

GREGERS   Gina?

HJALMAR   Why yes, don't you remember her name is Gina?

GREGERS   Whose name is Gina? I haven't the faintest idea what . . .

HJALMAR   But don't you remember she was employed here in this house for a time?

GREGERS   [*looking at him*]   You mean Gina Hansen . . . ?

HJALMAR   Yes, of course I mean Gina Hansen.

GREGERS   . . . who kept house for us the last year of my mother's illness?

HJALMAR   Well of course. But my dear fellow, I know for a fact that your father wrote and told you I had got married.

GREGERS   [*who has risen*]   Yes, he did that, all right. But not that . . . [*Pacing floor.*] Wait a minute—perhaps after all—now that I think about it. But my father always writes me such short letters. [*Sits on arm of chair.*] Listen, Hjalmar, tell me—this is interesting— how did you happen to meet Gina—your wife, that is?

HJALMAR   Oh, quite simply. Gina didn't stay very long here in this house. There was so much trouble here at the time, what with your mother's illness . . . Gina couldn't take all that, so she gave notice and left. That was the year before your mother died—or maybe it was the same year.

GREGERS   It was the same year. I was up at the works at the time. But afterwards?

HJALMAR   Well, Gina went to live with her mother, a Mrs. Hansen, a most capable and hard-working woman who ran a little eating place. She also had a room for rent, a really nice, comfortable room.

GREGERS   And you, I suppose, were lucky enough to find it?

HJALMAR   Yes, as a matter of fact it was your father who gave me the lead. And it was there—you see—that's where I really got to know Gina.

GREGERS   And so you got engaged?

HJALMAR   Yes. You know how easily young people get to care for each other—Hm . . .

GREGERS   [*rises and walks around*]   Tell me—when you had got engaged—was it then that my father got you to . . . I mean—was it then that you started to take up photography?

HJALMAR   Yes, exactly. Because I did so want to get settled and have a home of my own, the sooner the better. And both your father and I felt that this photography business was the best idea. And Gina thought so too. Oh yes, there was another reason as well. It so happened that Gina had just taken up retouching.

GREGERS   *That* fitted in marvelously well.

HJALMAR   [*pleased, rises*]   Yes, didn't it though? It *did* fit in marvelously well, don't you think?

GREGERS   Yes, I must say. Why, my father seems to have been a kind of Providence for you.

HJALMAR   [*moved*]   He did not forsake his old friend's son in the hour of need. For he's a man with *heart,* you see.

MRS. SØRBY   [*entering arm in arm with* HÅKON WERLE]   Not another word, my dear Mr. Werle. You must not stay in there any longer staring at all those lights. It's not good for you.

WERLE   [*letting go her arm and passing his hand over his eyes*]   I rather think you are right.

PETTERSEN *and* JENSEN, *the hired waiter, enter with trays.*

MRS. SØRBY   [*to guests in other room*]   Punch is served, Gentlemen. If anybody wants some he'll have to come in here and get it.

THE FLABBY GENTLEMAN   [*walking over to* MRS. SØRBY]   Good heavens, it is true you've abrogated our precious right to smoke?

MRS. SØRBY   Yes, my dear Chamberlain, here in Mr. Werle's private domain it is forbidden.

THE THIN-HAIRED GENTLEMAN   And when did you introduce this harsh restriction into our cigar regulations, Mrs. Sørby?

MRS. SØRBY   After our last dinner, Chamberlain. I'm afraid certain persons allowed themselves to overstep the bounds.

THE THIN-HAIRED GENTLEMAN   And is one not allowed to overstep the bounds just a little, Madame Berta? Not even the least little bit?

MRS. SØRBY   Under no circumstances, Chamberlain Balle.

Most of the guests are now assembled in WERLE's *study; the waiters hand around glasses of punch.*

WERLE   [*to* HJALMAR, *standing over by a table*]   What's that you're so engrossed in, Ekdal?

HJALMAR   It's just an album, Mr. Werle.

THE THIN-HAIRED GENTLEMAN   [*drifting about*]   Ah yes, photographs! That's in your line, of course.

THE FLABBY GENTLEMAN   [*in an armchair*]   Haven't you brought along any of your own?

HJALMAR   No, I haven't.

THE FLABBY GENTLEMAN   You should have. It's so good for the digestion, don't you know, to sit and look at pictures.

THE THIN-HAIRED GENTLEMAN   Besides contributing a mite to the general entertainment, you know.

A NEARSIGHTED GENTLEMAN   And all contributions are gratefully accepted.

MRS. SØRBY   The gentlemen mean, when you're invited out, you're expected to work a little for your dinner, Ekdal.

THE FLABBY GENTLEMAN   With a cuisine like this, *that* is an absolute pleasure.

THE THIN-HAIRED GENTLEMAN   Good Lord, if it's a question of the struggle for existence . . .

MRS. SØRBY   You're so right!

They continue the conversation, laughing and joking.

GREGERS [*quietly*]   You must join in, Hjalmar.

HJALMAR [*with a squirm*]   What am I to talk about?

THE FLABBY GENTLEMAN   Don't you agree, Mr. Werle, that Tokay may be regarded as a relatively healthy wine for the stomach?

WERLE [*by the fireplace*]   I can vouch for the Tokay you had today, at any rate; it is one of the very finest vintages. But of course you must have noticed that yourself.

THE FLABBY GENTLEMAN   Yes, it had a remarkably delicate bouquet.

HJALMAR [*uncertainly*]   Does the vintage make a difference?

THE FLABBY GENTLEMAN [*laughs*]   That's a good one!

WERLE [*smiling*]   There's certainly no point in putting a noble wine in front of *you*.

THE THIN-HAIRED GENTLEMAN   It's the same with Tokay as with photographs, Mr. Ekdal. Both must have sunlight. Or am I mistaken?

HJALMAR   Oh no. In photography, the light is everything.

MRS. SØRBY   Why, its exactly the same with chamberlains. They also depend on sunshine, as the saying goes—royal sunshine.

THE THIN-HAIRED GENTLEMAN   Ouch! That's a tired old joke.

THE NEARSIGHTED GENTLEMAN   The lady is in great form . . .

THE FLABBY GENTLEMAN   . . . and at our expense, too. [*Wagging his finger.*] Madame Berta! Madame Berta!

MRS. SØRBY   Well, but it *is* perfectly true that vintages can differ enormously. The old vintages are the best.

THE NEARSIGHTED GENTLEMAN   Do you count *me* among the old ones?

MRS. SØRBY   Oh, far from it.

THE THIN-HAIRED GENTLEMAN   Listen to that! But what about *me*, dear Mrs. Sørby?

THE FLABBY GENTLEMAN   Yes, and me! Where do you put us?

MRS. SØRBY   You, among the sweet vintages, Gentlemen.

She sips a glass of punch; the chamberlains laugh and flirt with her.

WERLE   Mrs. Sørby always finds a way out—when she wants to. But Gentlemen, you aren't drinking! Pettersen, see to . . . ! Gregers, I think we might take a glass together. [GREGERS *does not move.*] Won't you join us, Ekdal? I didn't get a chance to have a toast with you at table.

GRÅBERG, *the bookkeeper, looks in at baize door.*

GRÅBERG   Excuse me, Mr. Werle, but I can't get out.

WERLE   What, have they locked you in again?

GRÅBERG   Yes, and Flakstad's gone home with the keys . . .

WERLE   Well, just come through here, then.

GRÅBERG   But there's somebody else . . .

WERLE   Come on, come on, both of you. Don't be shy.

GRÅBERG *and* OLD EKDAL *enter from the office.*

WERLE [*involuntarily*]   What the . . . !

Laughter and chatter of guests die down. HJALMAR *gives a start at the sight of his father, puts down his glass, and turns away toward the fireplace.*

EKDAL [*does not look up, but makes quick little bows to both sides as he crosses, mumbling*]   Beg pardon. Came the wrong way. Gate's locked . . . gate's locked. Beg pardon.

He and GRÅBERG *go off, rear right.*

WERLE [*between his teeth*]   Damn that Gråberg!

GREGERS [*staring open-mouthed, to* HJALMAR]   Don't tell me that was . . . !

THE FLABBY GENTLEMAN   What's going on? Who was that?

GREGERS   Oh, nobody. Just the bookkeeper and another man.

THE NEARSIGHTED GENTLEMAN [*to* HJALMAR]   Did you know the man?

HJALMAR   I don't know . . . I didn't notice . . .

THE FLABBY GENTLEMAN [*getting up*]   What the devil's the matter, anyway? [*He walks over to some of the others, who are talking in lowered voices.*]

MRS. SØRBY [*whispers to the servant*]   Slip him something outside, something *really* good.

PETTERSEN [*nods his head*]   I'll do that. [*Goes out.*]

GREGERS [*in a low, shocked voice, to* HJALMAR]   Then it really was he!

HJALMAR   Yes.

GREGERS   And you stood here and denied you knew him!

HJALMAR [*whispers vehemently*]   But how *could* I . . . ?

GREGERS   . . . acknowledge your own father?

HJALMAR [*bitterly*]   Oh, if you were in my place, maybe . . .

The conversation among the guests, which has been conducted in low voices, now changes to forced gaiety.

THE THIN-HAIRED GENTLEMAN [*approaching* HJALMAR *and* GREGERS *in a friendly manner*]   Ah, are we reminiscing about old student days, Gentlemen? Eh? Don't you smoke, Mr. Ekdal? Can I give you a light? Oh, no, that's right. We are not allowed . . .

HJALMAR   Thank you, I don't smoke.

THE FLABBY GENTLEMAN   Don't you have some nice bit of poetry you could recite for us, Mr. Ekdal? You used to do that so charmingly.

HJALMAR   I'm afraid I can't remember any.

THE FLABBY GENTLEMAN   Oh, what a pity. Well, Balle, what shall we do now?

Both men cross and go into the drawing room.

HJALMAR [*gloomily*]   Gregers—I'm going! You see, when once a man has felt the crushing blow of fate . . . Say good-bye to your father for me.

GREGERS   Yes, of course. Are you going straight home?

HJALMAR   Yes. Why?

GREGERS   I thought I might drop in later on.

HJALMAR   No, don't do that. Not at my home. My house is a sad place, Gregers—especially after a brilliant banquet like this. We can always meet somewhere in town.

MRS. SØRBY [*has come up to them; in a low voice*]   Are you leaving, Mr. Ekdal?

HJALMAR   Yes.

MRS. SØRBY   Give my best to Gina.

HJALMAR   Thanks.

MRS. SØRBY   And tell her I'll be up to see her one of these days.

HJALMAR   Thanks, I'll do that. [*To* GREGERS.] Don't bother to see me out. I want to slip away unnoticed. [*He crosses room, then into drawing room, and goes off, right.*]

MRS. SØRBY [*softly to the servant, who has returned*]   Well, did you give the old man something?

PETTERSEN   Oh yes; I slipped him a bottle of brandy.

MRS. SØRBY   Oh, you might have thought of something better than that.

PETTERSEN   Not at all, Mrs. Sørby. There's nothing he likes better than brandy.

THE FLABBY GENTLEMAN [*in the doorway, with a sheet of music in his hand*]   What do you say we play something together, Mrs. Sørby?

MRS. SØRBY   Yes, let's do that.

GUESTS   Bravo! Bravo!

She and all the guests cross room and go off, right. GREGERS *remains standing by fireplace.* WERLE *searches for something on the desk and seems to wish* GREGERS *to leave. As* GREGERS *does not move,* WERLE *starts toward the drawing room door.*

GREGERS   Father, do you have a moment?

WERLE [*stops*]   What is it?

GREGERS   I'd like a word with you.

WERLE   Can't it wait till we're alone?

GREGERS   No, it can't. Because we might very well never be alone.

WERLE [*coming closer*]   And what is that supposed to mean?

During the following, the sound of a piano is distantly heard from the music room.

GREGERS   How could people here let that family go to the dogs like that?

WERLE   I suppose you mean the Ekdals?

GREGERS   Yes, I mean the Ekdals. After all, Lieutenant Ekdal was once your close friend.

WERLE   Alas, yes—all too close. Years and years I had to smart for it. He's the one I can thank for the fact that my good name and reputation were blemished in a way, mine too.

GREGERS [*quietly*]   Was he in fact the only guilty one?

WERLE   Who else do you think!

GREGERS   After all, you and he were both in that big timber deal together . . .

WERLE   But was it not Ekdal who drew up the survey map of the area —that fraudulent map? He was the one who did all that illegal felling of timber on State property. In fact, he was in charge of the entire operation up there. I had no idea what Lieutenant Ekdal was up to.

GREGERS   I doubt Lieutenant Ekdal himself knew what he was doing.

WERLE   Maybe so. But the fact remains that he was found guilty and I was acquitted.

GREGERS   Yes, I'm well aware there was no evidence.

WERLE   Acquittal is acquittal. Why do you have to rake up all that miserable old business that turned my hair gray before its time? Is this the sort of stuff you've gone and brooded over all those years up there? I can assure you, Gregers, here in town that whole story was forgotten ages ago—as far as it concerns me.

GREGERS   But what about the poor Ekdals!

WERLE   What exactly do you want me to do for those people? When Ekdal was released he was a broken man, altogether beyond help. There are people in this world who sink to the bottom the minute they get a couple of slugs in them, and they never come up again. You can take my word for it, Gregers, I've put myself out as far as I possibly could, short of encouraging all kinds of talk and suspicion . . .

GREGERS   Suspicion? Oh, I see.

WERLE   I have given Ekdal copying to do for the office, and I pay him far, far more for his work than it is worth . . .

GREGERS   [*without looking at him*]   Hm; I don't doubt *that.*

WERLE   What's the joke? Don't you think I'm telling you the truth? Naturally, you won't find anything about it in my books. I never enter expenses like that.

GREGERS   [*with a cold smile*]   No, I daresay certain expenses are best not accounted for.

WERLE   [*starts*]   What do you mean by *that?*

GREGERS   [*with forced courage*]   Did you enter what it cost you to have Hjalmar Ekdal learn photography?

WERLE   I? What do you mean—enter?

GREGERS   I know now it was you who paid for it. And I also know it was you who set him up so cozily.

WERLE   There, and still I'm supposed to have done nothing for the Ekdals! I assure you, those people have certainly put me to enough expense.

GREGERS   Have you entered any of those expenses?

WERLE   Why do you keep asking that?

GREGERS   Oh, I have my reasons. Look, tell me—that time, when you took such a warm interest in your old friend's son—wasn't it exactly when he was about to get married?

WERLE   What the devil—how can I remember, after all these years . . . ?

GREGERS   You wrote me a letter at the time—a business letter, naturally—and in a postscript it said, nothing more, that Hjalmar Ekdal had married a Miss Hansen.

WERLE   That's right. That was her name.

GREGERS   But you neglected to mention that this Miss Hansen was Gina Hansen—our former maid.

WERLE   [*with a scornful but forced laugh*]   No, because it certainly never occurred to me that you were particularly interested in our former maid.

GREGERS   I wasn't. But—[*lowers his voice*] there were others in this house who *were.*

WERLE   What do you mean by *that?* [*Flaring up.*] Don't tell me you're referring to *me!*

GREGERS   [*quietly but firmly*]   Yes, I'm referring to you.

WERLE   And you dare . . . ! You have the insolence to . . . ! And that ingrate, that, that—photographer! How dare he come here with such accusations!

GREGERS   Hjalmar never said a word about this. I don't think he has the slightest suspicion of anything of the kind.

WERLE   Then where have you got it from? Whoever could have said a thing like that?

GREGERS   My poor, unhappy mother said it. The last time I saw her.

WERLE   Your mother! I might have guessed as much. You and she—— you always stuck together. It was she that turned you against me from the start.

GREGERS   No, it was all the things she had to bear, till at last she gave way and went to pieces.

WERLE   Oh, she didn't have anything to bear! No more than plenty of others do, anyway. But there's no way of getting along with morbid, neurotic people—that's a lesson *I* learned, all right. And now here you are, nursing a suspicion like that—mixing up in all kinds of ancient rumors and slander against your own father. Listen here, Gregers, I honestly think that at your age you could find something more useful to do.

GREGERS   Yes, perhaps it is about time.

WERLE   Then maybe you wouldn't take things so seriously as you seem to do now. What's the point in your sitting up there at the works year in year out, slaving away like a common office clerk, refusing to draw a cent more than the standard wage? It's plain silly.

GREGERS   I wish I were so sure about that.

WERLE   Not that I don't understand you. You want to be independent, want to be under no obligation to me. Well, here is your chance to get your independence, to be your own master in everything.

GREGERS   Really? And in what way . . . ?

WERLE   When I wrote you it was urgent that you come to town at once—hm . . .

GREGERS   Yes, what exactly is it you want me for? I have been waiting all day to hear.

WERLE   I propose that you become a partner in the firm.

GREGERS   Me? A partner in your firm?

WERLE   Yes. It needn't mean we'd have to be together all the time. You could take over the business here in town, and I would move up to the works.

GREGERS   *You* would?

WERLE   Well, you see, I don't have the capacity for work that I once had. I've got to go easy on my eyes, Gregers; they've started to get a bit weak.

GREGERS   They've always been that way.

WERLE   Not like now. And besides . . . circumstances might perhaps make it desirable for me to live up there—at any rate for a time.

GREGERS   I never dreamed of anything like that.

WERLE   Look, Gregers—I know we differ on a great many things. But after all, we *are* father and son. Surely we ought to be able to reach some sort of understanding.

GREGERS   To all outward appearances, I take it you mean?

WERLE   Well, even that would be something. Think it over, Gregers. Don't you think it could be done? Eh?

GREGERS   [*looks at him coldly*]   There's something behind all this.

WERLE   What do you mean?

GREGERS   There must be something you want to use me for.

WERLE   In a relationship as close as ours surely one can always be of use to the other.

GREGERS   Yes, so they say.

WERLE   I should like to have you home now for a while. I'm a lonely man, Gregers; I've always felt lonely, all my life, but especially now that I'm getting along in years. I need somebody around me.

GREGERS   You've got Mrs. Sørby.

WERLE   Yes, so I have. And she's become just about indispensable to me. She's bright, she's easygoing, she livens up the house—and that I need pretty badly.

GREGERS   Well, then. In that case you've got just what you want.

WERLE   Yes, but I'm afraid it can't last. A woman in this kind of situation can easily have her position misconstrued. For that matter, it doesn't do the man much good either.

GREGERS   Oh, when a man gives such dinner parties as you do, I daresay he can take quite a few risks.

WERLE   Yes, but what about *her,* Gregers? I'm afraid she won't put up with it much longer. And even if she did—even if, out of devotion to me, she ignored the gossip and the aspersions and such . . . ? Do you really feel, Gregers, you with your strong sense of justice . . .

GREGERS   [*interrupts him*]   Get to the point. Are you thinking of marrying her?

WERLE   Supposing I were? What then?

GREGERS   Yes, that's what I'm asking, too. What then?

WERLE   Would you be so dead set against it?

GREGERS   No, not at all. By no means.

WERLE   You see, I didn't know if perhaps, out of regard for the memory of your mother . . .

GREGERS   I am not neurotic.

WERLE   Well, whatever you may or may not be, you've taken a great load off my mind. I can't tell you how glad I am that I can count on your support in this matter.

GREGERS   [*looks fixedly at him*]   Now I see what you want to use me for.

WERLE   Use you for? What an expression!

GREGERS   Oh, let's not be so particular in our choice of words—not when we are alone, at any rate. [*Short laugh.*] So that's it! That's why I had to make a personal appearance in town, come hell or high water. To put up a show of family life in this house for Mrs. Sørby's sake. Touching little tableau between father and son! *That* would be something new!

WERLE   How dare you talk like that!

GREGERS   When was there ever any family life around here? Never as long as I can remember! But now, all of a sudden, we could use a touch of home-sweet-home. Just think, the fine effect when it can be reported how the son hastened home—on wings of filial piety—to the aging father's wedding feast. *Then* what remains of all the rumors about what the poor dead wife had to put up with? Not a breath. Why, her own son snuffs them out.

WERLE   Gregers—I don't think there's a man on earth you hate as much as me.

GREGERS   [*quietly*]   I've seen you too close up.

WERLE   You have seen me through your mother's eyes. [*Drops his voice a little.*] But don't forget that those eyes were—clouded, now and then.

GREGERS   [*with trembling voice*]   I know what you're getting at. But who's to blame for Mother's tragic failing? *You,* and all those . . . ! The last of them was that female you palmed off on Hjalmar Ekdal when you yourself no longer . . . ugh!

WERLE   [*shrugs his shoulders*]   Word for word as though it were your mother talking.

GREGERS [*paying no attention*] . . . And there he is now, that great trusting, childlike soul, engulfed in treachery—living under the same roof with such a creature. With no idea that what he calls his home is founded on a lie! [*Comes a step closer.*] When I look back upon your long career, it's as if I saw a battlefield strewn at every turn with shattered lives.

WERLE I almost think the gulf between us is too wide.

GREGERS [*bows stiffly*] So I have observed. Therefore I'll take my hat and go.

WERLE Go? Leave the house?

GREGERS Yes. For now at last I see an objective to live for.

WERLE What objective is that?

GREGERS You'd only laugh if I told you.

WERLE Laughter doesn't come so easily to a lonely man, Gregers.

GREGERS [*pointing to the rear*] Look, Father—your guests are playing Blind Man's Buff with Mrs. Sørby. Goodnight and good-bye.

> *He goes off, rear right. Laughter and banter are heard from the party, which comes into view in the drawing room.*

WERLE [*mutters contemptuously after* GREGERS] Huh! Poor devil. And he says he's not neurotic!

Act 2

> HJALMAR EKDAL's *studio. The room, which is quite large, is apparently part of an attic. On the right is a pitched roof with a big skylight, half covered by a blue curtain. In the right corner at the rear is the entrance door; downstage on the same side, a door to the living room. On the left there are likewise two doors, with an iron stove between them. In the rear wall, wide double sliding doors. The studio is cheaply but comfortably furnished and arranged. Between the doors on the right and a little out from the wall stand a sofa and table and some chairs; on the table, a lighted lamp with shade; near the stove, an old armchair. Various pieces of photographic equipment here and there about the room. In the rear, left of the sliding doors, a bookcase containing a few books, some boxes and bottles of chemicals, various instruments, tools, and other objects. Photographs and small items such as brushes, paper, and the like are lying on the table.*
>
> GINA EKDAL *is sitting at the table, sewing.* HEDVIG *is sitting on the sofa reading a book, her hands shading her eyes, her thumbs plugging her ears.*

GINA [*after glancing at her several times as if with suppressed anxiety*] Hedvig! [HEDVIG *does not hear.*]

GINA [*louder*] Hedvig!

HEDVIG [*takes away her hands and looks up*] Yes, Mother?

GINA Hedvig, darling, you mustn't sit and read so long.

HEDVIG Oh, please, Mother, can't I read a little more? Just a little!

GINA No, no. Now you put that book away. Your father doesn't like it; he never reads at night himself.

HEDVIG [*shuts the book*] No, Father doesn't care much for reading.

GINA [*puts her sewing aside and picks up a pencil and a small note-*

book from the table]   Can you remember how much we paid for the butter today?

HEDVIG   It was one crown sixty-five.[2]

GINA   That's right. [*Writes it down.*] The amount of butter we go through in this house! Then there was the sausage and the cheese . . . let me see . . . [*makes a note*] . . . and then the ham . . . hm . . . [*Adding up.*] Yes, that already comes to . . .

HEDVIG   And the beer.

GINA   That's right, of course. [*Notes it down.*] It does mount up. But what can you do.

HEDVIG   But then you and I didn't need anything hot for dinner, since Father was going to be out.

GINA   Yes, that was a help. And besides I did take in eight crowns fifty for the pictures.

HEDVIG   My! As much as that?

GINA   Eight crowns fifty exactly.

Silence. GINA *takes up her sewing again.* HEDVIG *takes paper and pencil and starts to draw, her left hand shading her eyes.*

HEDVIG   Isn't it nice to think that Father's at a big dinner party at Mr. Werle's?

GINA   You can't say he's at Mr. Werle's, really. It was the son that invited him. [*Short pause.*] We've got nothing to do with old Mr. Werle.

HEDVIG   I can't wait till Father comes home. He promised to ask Mrs. Sørby for something good for me.

GINA   Oh yes, there's plenty of good things in *that* house, all right.

HEDVIG [*still drawing*]   Besides, I am just a bit hungry.

OLD EKDAL *enters right rear, a bundle of papers under his arm and another parcel in his coat pocket.*

GINA   How late you are tonight, Grandpa.

EKDAL   They had locked up the office. Had to wait in Gråberg's room. Then I had to go through . . . hm.

HEDVIG   Did they give you any more copying to do, Grandfather?

EKDAL   This whole bundle. Just look.

GINA   Well, that's nice.

HEDVIG   And you've got another bundle in your pocket.

EKDAL   What? Nonsense, that isn't anything. [*Stands his walking stick away in the corner.*] This will keep me busy a long time, Gina. [*Draws one of the sliding doors in the rear wall a little to one side.*] Shhh! [*Peeks into the attic a while, then carefully slides the door to.*] Heh-heh! They're sound asleep, the whole lot of 'em. And she has settled in the basket by herself. Heh-heh!

HEDVIG   Are you sure she won't be cold in that basket, Grandfather?

EKDAL   Cold? What an idea! In all that straw? [*Walks toward rear door on left.*] Any matches in my room?

2. Statements about the comparative purchasing power are difficult to make accurately, but at the time of the play one American dollar was worth three crowns, seventy-five öre, approximately (one crown = 100 öre). At that time in America, the New York *Times* could be purchased for two cents daily (three cents on Sundays), and theater tickets ran as high as $1.50. Room and board in a college rooming home was two dollars a week, and first-class steamship passage from New York to Liverpool ranged from $60 to $100. In Act 4, Hedvig's legacy of 100 crowns a month was worth less than $27, but a dollar had considerably more purchasing power than it does today.

GINA On the dresser.

EKDAL *goes into his room.*

HEDVIG Isn't it nice Grandfather got all that copying to do.

GINA Yes, poor old thing. Now he can make himself a little pocket money.

HEDVIG Besides, he won't be able to sit all morning in that nasty café of Mrs. Eriksen's.

GINA Yes, that's another thing.

A short silence.

HEDVIG Do you think they're still sitting at the table?

GINA Lord knows. I guess they could be, though.

HEDVIG Just think, all the delicious things Father must be having! I'm sure he'll be in a good mood when he gets home. Don't you think so, Mother?

GINA Oh yes. Now, if only we could tell him we got the room rented.

HEDVIG But we don't need that tonight.

GINA Oh, it would come in very handy, you know. It's no use to us just standing there empty.

HEDVIG No, I mean it's not necessary because Father will be in a good mood tonight anyway. It's better to have the news about the room for another time.

GINA [*looks across at her*] You like having something nice to tell your father when he gets home evenings?

HEDVIG Certainly, it makes things more cheerful.

GINA [*thinking this over*] Why yes, I guess there's something in that.

OLD EKDAL *enters from his room and makes for the door on front left.*

GINA [*turning half around in her chair*] Do you want something in the kitchen, Grandpa?

EKDAL Yes. Don't get up. [*Goes out.*]

GINA I hope he's not messing with the fire out there! [*Waits a moment.*] Hedvig, go see what he's up to.

EKDAL *returns with a little mug of steaming water.*

HEDVIG Are you getting hot water, Grandfather?

EKDAL Yes, I am. Need it for something. I've got writing to do, and the ink's gone as thick as mud—hm.

GINA But you ought to eat your supper first, Grandpa. It's all set out for you.

EKDAL Can't be bothered with supper, Gina. Terribly busy, I tell you. I don't want anybody coming into my room. Not anybody—hm.

He goes into his room. GINA *and* HEDVIG *look at each other.*

GINA [*in a low voice*] Where on earth do you suppose he got the money?

HEDVIG I guess from Gråberg.

GINA No, impossible. Gråberg always sends the money to me.

HEDVIG Then he must have got a bottle on credit somewhere.

GINA Poor old soul. Who'd give *him* anything on credit?

HJALMAR EKDAL, *in topcoat and gray felt hat, enters right.*

GINA [*throws down her sewing and gets up*]   Why, Hjalmar, you're back already!

HEDVIG [*simultaneously jumping up*]   Father, what a surprise!

HJALMAR [*lays down his hat*]   Most of them seemed to be leaving.

HEDVIG   So early?

HJALMAR   Well, it was a dinner party, you know. [*About to take off his topcoat.*]

GINA   Let me help you.

HEDVIG   Me too.

> *They help him off with his coat.* GINA *hangs it up on the rear wall.*

HEDVIG   Were there many there, Father?

HJALMAR   Not too many. There were about twelve or fourteen of us at table.

GINA   Did you get to talk to everybody?

HJALMAR   Oh yes, a little. But actually Gregers monopolized me most of the evening.

GINA   Is Gregers as ugly as ever?

HJALMAR   Well, he isn't exactly a beauty. Hasn't the old man come home?

HEDVIG   Yes, Grandfather's in his room writing.

HJALMAR   Did he say anything?

GINA   No, what about?

HJALMAR   He didn't mention anything about . . . ? I thought I heard he'd been to see Gråberg. I think I'll go in and see him a moment.

GINA   No, no, I wouldn't do that . . .

HJALMAR   Why not? Did he say he didn't want to see me?

GINA   I guess he doesn't want *anybody* in there this evening . . .

HEDVIG [*making signs*]   Ahem—ahem!

GINA [*not noticing*]   . . . he's been out and got himself some hot water.

HJALMAR   Aha, is he sitting and . . . ?

GINA   Yes, that's probably it.

HJALMAR   Dear me—my poor old white-haired father!—Well, let him be, let him get what pleasure he can out of life.

> OLD EKDAL, *in dressing gown and with lighted pipe, enters from his room.*

EKDAL   You back? *Thought* it was you I heard talking.

HJALMAR   I just got in this minute.

EKDAL   Guess you didn't see me, did you?

HJALMAR   No. But they said you'd gone through—so I thought I'd catch up with you.

EKDAL   Hm, good of you, Hjalmar. Who were they, all those people?

HJALMAR   Oh, different ones. There was Chamberlain Flor and Chamberlain Balle and Chamberlain Kaspersen and Chamberlain this-that-and-the-other; I don't know . . .

EKDAL [*nodding his head*]   Hear that, Gina? He's been hobnobbing with nothing but chamberlains.

GINA   Yes, I guess they're mighty high-toned in that house now.

HEDVIG   Did the chamberlains sing, Father? Or give recitations?

HJALMAR   No, they just talked nonsense. They did try to get me to recite something for them, but they couldn't make me.

EKDAL   They couldn't make you, eh?

GINA   Seems to me you could just as well have done it.

HJALMAR   No. One should not be at everybody's beck and call. [*Taking a turn about the room.*] I, at any rate, am not.

EKDAL   No, no. *Hjalmar's* not that obliging.

HJALMAR   I don't see why *I* should be expected to provide the entertainment the one evening I'm out. Let the others exert themselves. Those fellows do nothing but go from one spread to the next, feasting and drinking day in and day out. Let *them* do something in return for all the good food they get.

GINA   I hope you didn't tell them that?

HJALMAR   [*humming*]   Hm . . . hm . . . hm . . . Well, they were told a thing or two.

EKDAL   What, the chamberlains!

HJALMAR   And why not? [*Casually.*] Then we had a little controversy over Tokay.

EKDAL   Tokay, eh? Say, that's a grand wine.

HJALMAR   [*pauses*]   It *can* be. But let me tell you, not all vintages are equally fine. It all depends on how much sunshine the grapes have had.

GINA   Why, Hjalmar, if you don't know just about everything!

EKDAL   They started arguing about that?

HJALMAR   They tried to. But then they were given to understand that it's exactly the same with chamberlains. Not all vintages are equally good in their case either—it was pointed out.

GINA   Honest, the things you come up with!

EKDAL   Heh-heh! So they had to put *that* in their pipes and smoke it!

HJALMAR   They got it straight in the face.

EKDAL   Hear that, Gina? He said it straight to the chamberlains' faces.

GINA   Imagine, straight in their face.

HJALMAR   Yes, but I don't want it talked about. You don't repeat this kind of thing. Besides, the whole thing went off in the friendliest possible manner, of course. They were all decent, warm-hearted people—why should I hurt their feelings? No!

EKDAL   Still, straight in the face . . .

HEDVIG   [*ingratiatingly*]   How nice it is to see you all dressed up, Father. You do look nice in a tailcoat.

HJALMAR   Yes, don't you think so? And this one really doesn't fit too badly. It could almost have been made to order for me—a trifle tight in the armholes, maybe . . . Give me a hand, Hedvig. [*Takes the tailcoat off.*] I'll put on my jacket instead. Where'd you put my jacket, Gina?

GINA   Here it is. [*Brings the jacket and helps him on with it.*]

HJALMAR   There we are! Now don't forget to let Molvik have the tails back first thing in the morning.

GINA   [*putting tailcoat aside*]   I'll take care of it.

HJALMAR   [*stretching*]   Aaahh, that's more like it. And this type of loose-fitting casual house jacket really suits my style better. Don't you think so, Hedvig?

HEDVIG   Oh yes, Father!

HJALMAR   And if I pull out my tie like this into two flowing ends . . . look! Eh?

HEDVIG   Yes, it goes so well with your mustache and your thick curly hair.

HJALMAR   I wouldn't exactly call my hair curly. Wavy, rather.

HEDVIG   Yes, because the curls are so big.

HJALMAR   Waves, actually.

HEDVIG [*after a moment, tugs at his jacket*]   Father!

HJALMAR   Well, what is it?

HEDVIG   Oh, you know as well as I.

HJALMAR   Why no, I certainly don't.

HEDVIG [*half-laughing, half-whimpering*]   Oh yes you do, Daddy! Stop teasing!

HJALMAR   But what is it?

HEDVIG [*shaking him*]   Come on, give it to me, Daddy. You know, the good things you promised me.

HJALMAR   Oh, dear. Imagine, I completely forgot!

HEDVIG   Now you're just trying to fool me, Daddy! That's not very nice! Where did you hide it?

HJALMAR   No, honest, I really did forget. But wait a minute! I've got something else for you, Hedvig. [*Goes across and searches his coat pockets.*]

HEDVIG [*jumping and clapping her hands*]   Oh Mother, Mother!

GINA   See? If you just give him time . . .

HJALMAR [*with a sheet of paper*]   Look, here it is.

HEDVIG   That? It's just a piece of paper.

HJALMAR   It's the menu, Hedvig, the entire menu. Look, they had it specially printed.

HEDVIG   Haven't you got anything else?

HJALMAR   I forgot the rest, I tell you. But take my word for it, it's no great treat all that fancy stuff. Now, why don't you sit down at the table and read the menu, and later on I'll tell you what the different courses taste like. Here you are, Hedvig.

HEDVIG [*swallowing her tears*]   Thanks.

> *She sits down but does not read.* GINA *makes signs to her, which* HJALMAR *notices.*

HJALMAR [*pacing the floor*]   It's really incredible the things a family man is expected to keep in mind. And just let him forget the least little thing—right away he gets a lot of sour looks. Oh well, that's another thing you get used to. [*Stops by the stove, where* OLD EKDAL *is sitting.*] Have you looked in there this evening, Father?

EKDAL   You bet I have. She's asleep in her basket.

HJALMAR   No, really? In her basket! She's beginning to get used to it, then.

EKDAL   Sure, I told you she would. But now, you know, there are still one or two other little things . . .

HJALMAR   Improvements, yes.

EKDAL   They've got to be done, you know.

HJALMAR   Yes, let's have a little chat about these improvements, Father. Come over here and we'll sit down on the sofa.

EKDAL   Right! Hm, think I'll just fill my pipe first . . . Got to clean it, too. Hm. [*Goes into his room.*]

GINA [*smiles to* HJALMAR]   Clean his pipe—I'll bet.

HJALMAR   Oh well, Gina, let him be—poor shipwrecked old man. —Yes, those improvements—we'd better get them out of the way tomorrow.

GINA   You won't have time tomorrow, Hjalmar.

HEDVIG [*interrupting*]   Yes he will, Mother!

GINA   Don't forget those prints that need to be retouched. They keep coming around for them.

HJALMAR   What! Those prints again? Don't worry, they'll be ready. Any new orders come in?

GINA   No, worse luck. Tomorrow I've got nothing but that double sitting I told you about.

HJALMAR   Is that all? Well, of course, if one doesn't make an effort . . .

GINA   But what more can I do? I'm advertising in the papers as much as we can afford, seems to me.

HJALMAR   Oh, the papers, the papers—you see for yourself what good *they* are. And I suppose there hasn't been anybody to look at the room, either?

GINA   No, not yet.

HJALMAR   That was only to be expected. If people don't show any initiative, well . . . ! One's got to make a determined effort, Gina!

HEDVIG [*going toward him*]   Couldn't I bring you your flute, Father?

HJALMAR   No, no flute for me. *I* need no pleasures in this world. [*Pacing about.*] All right, you'll see how I'll get down to work tomorrow, don't you worry. You can be sure I shall work as long as my strength holds out . . .

GINA   But, Hjalmar dear, I didn't mean it that way.

HEDVIG   Father, how about a bottle of beer?

HJALMAR   No, certainly not. I don't need anything . . . [*Stops.*] Beer? Was it beer you said?

HEDVIG [*gaily*]   Yes, Father, nice cold beer.

HJALMAR   Well—if you insist, you might bring in a bottle.

GINA   Yes, do that. That'll be nice and cozy.

> HEDVIG *runs toward the kitchen door.* HJALMAR, *by the stove, stops her, looks at her, takes her face between his hands, and presses her to him.*

HJALMAR   Hedvig! Hedvig!

HEDVIG [*happy and in tears*]   Daddy darling!

HJALMAR   No, don't call me that. There I sat indulging myself at the rich man's table—sat and gorged myself at the groaning board—and I couldn't even . . . !

GINA [*seated by the table*]   Oh, don't talk nonsense, Hjalmar.

HJALMAR   No, it's the truth. But you mustn't judge me too harshly. You know I love you, all the same.

HEDVIG [*throwing her arms around him*]   And we love you too, Daddy —so much!

HJALMAR   And if I *am* unreasonable once in a while, well—heavens above—remember I am a man beset by a host of cares. Ah, well! [*Drying his eyes.*] No beer, no, not at such a moment. Give me my flute.

> HEDVIG *runs to the bookcase and fetches it.*

HJALMAR   Thanks! That's right, yes. With flute in hand and you two at my side—ah!

> HEDVIG *sits down at the table beside* GINA. HJALMAR *walks up and down and begins a Bohemian folk dance, playing it with vigor but in a slow elegiac tempo and with sentimental interpretation.*

HJALMAR [*breaks off the tune, holds out his left hand to* GINA, *and says with strong emotion*] What if this place *is* cramped and shoddy, Gina. It's still our home. And this I will say: here is my heart's abode.

> *He starts to play again. Soon after, there is a knock on the hall door.*

GINA [*getting up*] Shhh, Hjalmar—I think somebody's coming.
HJALMAR [*putting the flute on the shelf*] Wouldn't you just know!

> GINA *walks over and opens the door.*

GREGERS WERLE [*out in the hall*] I beg your pardon . . .
GINA [*recoiling slightly*] Oh!
GREGERS   . . . isn't this where Mr. Ekdal the photographer lives?
GINA   Yes, it is.
HJALMAR [*going toward the door*] Gregers! You came after all? Well, come in then.
GREGERS [*entering*] I told you I would drop in to see you.
HJALMAR   But tonight . . . ? You left the party?
GREGERS   Both the party and my father's house. —Good evening, Mrs. Ekdal. I don't suppose you recognize me.
GINA   Oh yes. You're not so hard to recognize, Mr. Werle.
GREGERS   No, I resemble my mother, of course. And no doubt you remember her.
HJALMAR   Did I hear you say you left the house?
GREGERS   Yes, I've taken a room at a hotel.
HJALMAR   Really? Well, as long as you're here, take off your coat and sit down.
GREGERS   Thanks. [*Removes his overcoat. He has changed into a plain gray country suit.*]
HJALMAR   Here, on the sofa. Make yourself comfortable.

> GREGERS *sits down on the sofa,* HJALMAR *on a chair by the table.*

GREGERS   So this is where you keep yourself, Hjalmar. This is your place.
HJALMAR   This is the studio, as you can see . . .
GINA   But it's roomier in here, so this is mostly where we stay.
HJALMAR   We had a nicer place before, but this apartment has one great advantage—there's such a lot of splendid extra space.
GINA   And then we've got a room across the hall that we can rent out.
GREGERS [*to* HJALMAR] Well, well—so you've got roomers besides.
HJALMAR   No, not yet. It's not so easily done as all that, you know; it calls for initiative. [*To* HEDVIG.] What about that beer?

> HEDVIG *nods and goes out to the kitchen.*

GREGERS   Your daughter, I take it?
HJALMAR   Yes, that's Hedvig.
GREGERS   Your only child?
HJALMAR   Our only one, yes. She is our greatest joy in the world, and—[*lowers his voice*] she's also our deepest sorrow, Gregers.
GREGERS   What are you saying!
HJALMAR   Yes, Gregers. She's in grave danger of losing her eyesight.
GREGERS   Going blind!
HJALMAR   Yes. So far, there are only the first signs, and things may

still be all right for some time yet. But the doctor has warned us. It's inevitable.

GREGERS   But this is a terrible misfortune. How did she get like that?

HJALMAR [*sighs*]   Heredity, most likely.

GREGERS [*with a start*]   Heredity?

GINA   Yes, Hjalmar's mother also had bad eyesight.

HJALMAR   That's what Father says. I can't remember her myself.

GREGERS   Poor child. How does she take it?

HJALMAR   Oh, as you can imagine, we don't have the heart to tell her. She doesn't suspect a thing. Happy and carefree, chirping like a little bird, she is fluttering into life's eternal night. [*Overcome.*] Oh, Gregers, it's heartbreaking for me.

HEDVIG *enters carrying a tray with beer and glasses, which she sets down on the table.*

HJALMAR [*stroking her head*]   Thank you, thank you, Hedvig.

HEDVIG *puts her arms around his neck and whispers in his ear.*

HJALMAR   No, no sandwiches just now. [*Looks across.*] That is, unless Gregers would care for some?

GREGERS [*declining*]   No, no thanks.

HJALMAR [*with continued pathos*]   Oh well, perhaps you might bring in a few, after all. A crust would be nice, if you happen to have one. Just make sure there's plenty of butter on it.

HEDVIG *nods delightedly and goes out again to the kitchen.*

GREGERS [*who has followed her with his eyes*]   She looks strong and healthy enough to me in all other respects.

GINA   Yes, thank God. Otherwise there's nothing the matter with her.

GREGERS   She's going to look like you in time, Mrs. Ekdal. How old might she be now?

GINA   Hedvig's just fourteen; it's her birthday the day after tomorrow.

GREGERS   A big girl for her age.

GINA   Yes, she certainly shot up this last year.

GREGERS   The young ones growing up make us realize how old we ourselves are getting.—How long is it now you've been married?

GINA   We've been married already fifteen years—just about.

GREGERS   Imagine, is it that long!

GINA [*becomes attentive; looks at him*]   Yes, that's what it is, all right.

HJALMAR   Yes, it must be all of that. Fifteen years, give or take a couple of months. [*Changing the subject.*] They must have been long years for you, Gregers, up there at the works.

GREGERS   They seemed long while I was living through them—now, looking back, I hardly know where all that time went.

OLD EKDAL *enters from his room, without his pipe, but with his old-fashioned lieutenant's cap on his head. His gait is a bit unsteady.*

EKDAL   All right, Hjalmar, now we can sit down and talk about that . . . hm . . . What was it again?

HJALMAR [*going toward him*]   Father, there's somebody here. Gregers Werle . . . I don't know if you remember him.

EKDAL [*looks at* GREGERS, *who has risen*]   Werle? Is that the son? What does he want with me?

HJALMAR   Nothing. It's me he's come to see.

EKDAL   Oh. So there's nothing the matter?

HJALMAR   No, of course not.

EKDAL   [*swinging his arm*]   Not that I care, you know. I'm not scared . . .

GREGERS   [*goes up to him*]   I just wanted to bring you greetings from your old hunting grounds, Lieutenant Ekdal.

EKDAL   Hunting grounds?

GREGERS   Yes, up there around the Højdal works.

EKDAL   Oh, up there. Oh yes, I used to know my way around up there at one time.

GREGERS   You were a mighty hunter in those days.

EKDAL   So I was. True enough. You're looking at my officer's cap. I don't ask anybody's permission to wear it here in the house. Just as long as I don't go outside with it . . .

HEDVIG *brings a plate of open-faced sandwiches, which she sets on the table.*

HJALMAR   Come sit down now, Father, and have a glass of beer. Help yourself, Gregers.

EKDAL *mutters and hobbles over to the sofa.* GREGERS *sits down on the chair nearest him,* HJALMAR *on the other side of* GREGERS. GINA *sits a little away from the table, sewing;* HEDVIG *stands beside her father.*

GREGERS   Do you remember, Lieutenant Ekdal, how Hjalmar and I used to come up and visit you summers and at Christmas?

EKDAL   Did you? No, no, no, that I can't recollect. But I *was* a crack shot, if I do say so myself. Even used to shoot bears. Got nine of 'em, no less.

GREGERS   [*looking sympathetically at him*]   And now your hunting days are over.

EKDAL   Oh, I wouldn't say *that*, old chap. Still manage a bit of shooting now and then. Of course, not in the old way. Because the forest, you know . . . the forest, the forest . . . ! [*Drinks.*] Is the forest in good shape up there now?

GREGERS   Not so fine as in your day. There's been a lot of cutting down.

EKDAL   Cutting down? [*Lowers his voice as if afraid.*] That's risky business, that. You don't get away with it. The forest takes revenge.

HJALMAR   [*filling his glass*]   Here, Father, have a little more.

GREGERS   How can a man like you—such a lover of the great outdoors —how can you live in the middle of a stuffy city, shut in here by four walls?

EKDAL   [*gives a little laugh and glances at* HJALMAR]   Oh, it's not so bad here. Not so bad at all.

GREGERS   But all those things that were once so much a part of you— the cool sweeping breeze, the free life in the forest and on the moors, among birds and beasts . . . ?

EKDAL   [*smiling*]   Hjalmar, shall we show it to him?

HJALMAR   [*quickly, a little embarrassed*]   No, no, Father. Not tonight.

GREGERS   What does he want to show me?

HJALMAR   Oh, it's only a kind of . . . You can see it another time.

GREGERS   [*continues to the old man*]   Well, let me tell you what I had

in mind, Lieutenant Ekdal. Why don't you come up to Højdal with me. I'll probably be going back soon. You could easily get some copying to do up there as well. While here you don't have a thing in the world to liven you up or amuse you.

EKDAL [*staring at him in astonishment*]   Me? Not a thing in the world to . . . !

GREGERS   Of course, you have Hjalmar. But then he has his own family. And a man like you, who has always been drawn to what is free and untamed . . .

EKDAL [*strikes the table*]   Hjalmar, he's *got* to see it now!

HJALMAR   But, Father, do you really think so? It's dark . . .

EKDAL   Nonsense! It's moonlight. [*Gets up.*] I tell you he's got to see it. Let me pass. Come on and help me, Hjalmar!

HEDVIG   Oh yes, go on, Father!

HJALMAR [*gets up*]   Well, all right.

GREGERS [*to* GINA]   What is it?

GINA   Oh, don't expect anything special.

> EKDAL *and* HJALMAR *have gone to the rear wall and each slides one of the double doors aside.* HEDVIG *helps the old man;* GREGERS *remains standing by the sofa;* GINA *sits unconcerned, sewing. Through the open doors can be seen a long, irregular-shaped attic with nooks and crannies and a couple of free-standing chimneys. Bright moonlight falls through skylights on some parts of the attic, while others are in deep shadow.*

EKDAL [*to* GREGERS]   You're welcome to come right up close.

GREGERS [*goes up to them*]   But what *is* it?

EKDAL   Look and see. Hm.

HJALMAR [*somewhat embarrassed*]   All this belongs to Father, you understand.

GREGERS [*at the door, looking into the attic*]   Why, Lieutenant Ekdal, you keep poultry!

EKDAL   Should hope to say we keep poultry. They're roosting now. But you ought to see this poultry by daylight!

HEDVIG   And then there's . . .

EKDAL   Sh! Sh! Don't say anything yet.

GREGERS   And I see you've got pigeons, too.

EKDAL   Yes indeed, we've got pigeons all right! They have their nesting boxes up under the eaves, they do. Pigeons like to roost high, you see.

HJALMAR   They aren't all of them just ordinary pigeons.

EKDAL   Ordinary! Should say not! We've got tumblers, and a couple of pouters, too. But come over here! Do you see that hutch over there by the wall?

GREGERS   Yes. What do you use that for?

EKDAL   That's where the rabbits sleep at night, old chap.

GREGERS   Oh, so you have rabbits too?

EKDAL   You're damn right we have rabbits! He wants to know if we've got rabbits, Hjalmar! Hm! But now we come to the *real* thing! Now it comes! Move, Hedvig. Come and stand here; that's right! Now, look down there.—Can you see a basket with straw in it?

GREGERS   Why yes. And I see there's a bird sitting in the basket.

EKDAL   Hm—"a bird" . . .

GREGERS   Isn't it a duck?

EKDAL [*offended*]   Well, obviously it's a duck.

HJALMAR   But what *kind* of duck do you suppose it is?

HEDVIG   It's no common ordinary duck . . .

EKDAL   Hush!

GREGERS   And it's not a muscovy duck either.

EKDAL   No, Mr.—Werle, it's not a muscovy duck. It's a wild duck.

GREGERS   What, is it really? A wild duck?

EKDAL   Yessir, that's what it is. That "bird," as you called it—that's the wild duck. Our wild duck, old chap.

HEDVIG   My wild duck. It belongs to me.

GREGERS   And it can really live here in the attic? And thrive?

EKDAL   Of course, you understand, she's got a trough of water to splash around in.

HJALMAR   Fresh water every other day.

GINA [*turning to* HJALMAR]   Hjalmar, please, it's getting freezing cold in here.

EKDAL   Hm, let's shut the door then. Better not to disturb them when they're settled for the night, anyhow. Hedvig, lend a hand.

   HJALMAR *and* HEDVIG *slide the attic door shut.*

EKDAL   You can take a good look at her some other time. [*Sits down in the armchair by the stove.*] Oh, they're most remarkable, let me tell you, these wild ducks.

GREGERS   But how did you ever catch it, Lieutenant Ekdal?

EKDAL   Wasn't me that caught it. There's a certain man here in town we have to thank for her.

GREGERS [*struck by a thought*]   That man wouldn't happen to be my father, would he?

EKDAL   Oh yes indeed. Precisely your father. Hm.

HJALMAR   Funny you should guess that, Gregers.

GREGERS   Well, you told me before that you owed such a lot to my father, so it occurred to me that . . .

GINA   But we didn't get the duck from Mr. Werle personally . . .

EKDAL   It's Håkon Werle we have to thank for her just the same, Gina. [*To* GREGERS.] He was out in a boat, you see, and took a shot at her. But it happens his sight isn't so good anymore, your father's. Hm. So she was only winged.

GREGERS   I see. She got some shot in her.

HJALMAR   Yes, a few.

HEDVIG   It was in the wing, so she couldn't fly.

GREGERS   So she dived to the bottom, I suppose?

EKDAL [*sleepily, his voice thick*]   Goes without saying. Always do that, wild ducks. Plunge to the bottom—as deep as they can get, old chap —bite themselves fast in the weeds and tangle—and all the other damn mess down there. And never come up again.

GREGERS   But, Lieutenant Ekdal, *your* wild duck did come up again.

EKDAL   He had such an absurdly clever dog, your father . . . And that dog—it dived after and fetched the duck up again.

GREGERS [*turning to* HJALMAR]   And so you brought it here?

HJALMAR   Not right away. First it was taken to your father's house. But it didn't seem to thrive there, so Pettersen was told to do away with it . . .

EKDAL [*half asleep*]   Hm . . . yes, Pettersen . . . Ass . . .

HJALMAR [*lowering his voice*]   That was how we got it, you see.

Father knows Pettersen slightly, and when he heard all this about the wild duck, he managed to get it turned over to him.

GREGERS   And now it's thriving perfectly well there in the attic.

HJALMAR   Yes, incredibly well. It's got quite plump. Of course, it's been in there so long now, it's forgotten what real wild life is like. That's the whole secret.

GREGERS   You're probably right, Hjalmar. Just don't ever let it catch sight of sea or sky . . . But I mustn't stay any longer, I think your father's asleep.

HJALMAR   Oh, don't worry about that . . .

GREGERS   But incidentally—didn't you say you had a room for rent— a vacant room?

HJALMAR   Yes, why? Do you happen to know somebody . . . ?

GREGERS   May I have that room?

HJALMAR   You?

GINA   You, Mr. Werle?

GREGERS   May I have the room? I could move in first thing tomorrow morning.

HJALMAR   Sure, with the greatest pleasure . . .

GINA   No, really, Mr. Werle, it's not in the least no room for you.

HJALMAR   Why Gina, how can you say that?

GINA   Well, that room's neither big enough or light enough, and . . .

GREGERS   That doesn't matter too much, Mrs. Ekdal.

HJALMAR   I think it's quite a nice room, myself, and not so badly furnished, either.

GINA   But don't forget those two downstairs.

GREGERS   Who are they?

GINA   Oh, there's one that used to be a private tutor . . .

HJALMAR   That's Molvik. He studied to be a pastor, once.

GINA   . . . And then there's a doctor called Relling.

GREGERS   Relling? I know him slightly; he practiced for a while up at Højdal.

GINA   They're a couple of characters, those two. Out on a binge as often as not, and then they come home all hours of the night, and they're not always what you'd call . . .

GREGERS   One soon gets accustomed to things like that. I hope I shall be like the wild duck . . .

GINA   Hm. I think you'd better sleep on it, all the same.

GREGERS   You certainly don't seem anxious to have me in the house, Mrs. Ekdal.

GINA   For heaven's sake, whatever gives you *that* idea?

HJALMAR   Yes, Gina, you really are being strange. [*To* GREGERS.] But tell me, does this mean you'll be staying in town for a while?

GREGERS [*putting on his overcoat*]   Yes, now I think I'll stay.

HJALMAR   But not at your father's? What do you intend to do?

GREGERS   Ah, if only I knew that, Hjalmar—it wouldn't be so bad. But when you're cursed with a name like Gregers . . . ! "Gregers"— and then "Werle" on top of that! Have you ever heard anything so ghastly?

HJALMAR   Why, I don't think so at all.

GREGERS   Ugh! Phew! I could spit on a man with a name like that. But since it's my cross in life to be Gregers Werle—such as I am . . .

HJALMAR [*laughing*]   Ha-ha! Suppose you weren't Gregers Werle, what would you choose to be?

GREGERS   If I had the choice, I'd like most of all to be a clever dog.

GINA   A dog!

HEDVIG [*involuntarily*]   Oh no!

GREGERS   Yes, a really absurdly clever dog. The kind that goes in after ducks when they plunge and fasten themselves in the weeds and the tangle in the mud.

HJALMAR   Honestly now, Gregers—what *are* you talking about.

GREGERS   Oh well, it probably doesn't make much sense. Well then, first thing tomorrow morning—I'm moving in. [*To* GINA.] I won't be any trouble to you; I do everything for myself. [*To* HJALMAR.] The rest we'll talk about tomorrow.—Goodnight, Mrs. Ekdal. [*Nods to* HEDVIG.] Goodnight.

GINA   Goodnight, Mr. Werle.

HEDVIG   Goodnight.

HJALMAR [*who has lit a candle*]   Wait a minute, I'd better see you down, it's sure to be dark on the stairs.

GREGERS *and* HJALMAR *leave by the hall door.*

GINA [*gazing ahead, her sewing on her lap*]   Wasn't that crazy talk, wanting to be a dog?

HEDVIG   You know what, Mother—I think he meant something else.

GINA   What else could he mean?

HEDVIG   Oh, I don't know. But it was just as though he meant something different from what he was saying—the whole time.

GINA   You think so? Well, it sure was queer though.

HJALMAR [*returning*]   The light was still on. [*Blows out candle and puts it down.*] Ah, at last a man can get a bite to eat. [*Starts on the sandwiches.*] Well, there you see, Gina—if only you keep your eyes open . . .

GINA   What do you mean, keep your eyes open?

HJALMAR   Well, wasn't it lucky we finally got the room rented? And then imagine, to somebody like Gregers—a dear old friend.

GINA   Well, I don't know what to say, myself.

HEDVIG   Oh, Mother, it will be nice, you'll see.

HJALMAR   You *are* funny, you know. First you were so set on getting it rented, and now you don't like it.

GINA   Well, Hjalmar, if only it had been somebody else. . . . What do you think Mr. Werle's going to say?

HJALMAR   Old Werle? It's none of his business.

GINA   But can't you see there's something the matter between them again, since the young one is moving out? You know what those two are like with each other.

HJALMAR   Yes, that could be, but . . .

GINA   And now maybe Mr. Werle will think you were behind it . . .

HJALMAR   Let him think what he wants! Mr. Werle has done a great deal for me—God knows, I'm the first to admit it. But that doesn't mean I've got to be under his thumb all my life.

GINA   But Hjalmar, dear, he could take it out on Grandpa. Suppose he loses the little money he makes working for Gråberg.

HJALMAR   I almost wish he would! Isn't it rather humiliating for a man like me to see his poor old white-haired father treated like dirt? But now the fullness of time is at hand, I feel. [*Helps himself to another sandwich.*] As sure as I have a mission in life, I shall fulfill it!

HEDVIG   Oh yes, Father, do!

GINA Shhh! Don't wake him up.

HJALMAR [*in a lower voice*] I shall fulfill it, I tell you. The day will come, when . . . That's why it's such a good thing we got the room rented; it puts me in a more independent position. And independent is one thing a man with a mission in life has got to be. [*Over by the armchair, with feeling.*] My poor old white-haired Father . . . Trust in your Hjalmar! He has broad shoulders—strong shoulders, anyway. One fine day you'll wake up and . . . [*To* GINA.] Maybe you don't believe that?

GINA [*getting up*] Sure, I believe it. But let's see about getting him to bed first.

HJALMAR Yes, let's.

They carefully lift the old man.

Act 3

HJALMAR EKDAL'*s studio. It is morning; light is coming through the large window in the sloping roof; the curtain is drawn back.*

  HJALMAR *is sitting at the table, busy retouching a photograph; several more pictures are lying in front of him. After a while,* GINA, *in coat and hat, enters by the hall door; she has a covered basket on her arm.*

HJALMAR Back already, Gina?

GINA Oh, yes. I've got no time to waste. [*Puts the basket on a chair and takes off her outdoor things.*]

HJALMAR Did you look in on Gregers?

GINA I sure did. And a fine sight it is in there. He certainly fixed the place up the minute he moved in.

HJALMAR Oh?

GINA Yes, he wanted to manage for himself, he said. So he decides to light the fire, and what does he do but turn down the damper so the whole room gets filled with smoke. Phew, there's a smell in there like . . .

HJALMAR Oh dear.

GINA And that's not the worst of it. Next he wants to put out the fire, so he goes and dumps all the water from the washbasin into the stove, so the whole floor's a stinking mess.

HJALMAR What a nuisance.

GINA I got the janitor's wife to clean up after him, the pig, but the place won't be fit to go into again till this afternoon.

HJALMAR What's he doing with himself meanwhile?

GINA He's going out for a while, he said.

HJALMAR I also dropped in on him for a minute—while you were gone.

GINA So I heard. You've gone and invited him to lunch.

HJALMAR Just for a little snack, that's all. After all, it's his first day—we can hardly do less. You must have something in the house.

GINA I'd better see what I can find.

HJALMAR Make sure there's plenty, though. Because I think Relling and Molvik are also coming up. I happened to run into Relling on the stairs, you see, so of course I had to . . .

GINA Well, so we've got to have those two besides?

HJALMAR   Good Lord—one more or less, what difference does that make?

OLD EKDAL [*opens his door and looks in*] I say, Hjalmar . . . [*Notices* GINA.] Never mind.

GINA   Is there something you want, Grandpa?

EKDAL No, no, it doesn't matter. Hm! [*Goes back inside his room.*]

GINA [*takes the basket*] Make sure you keep an eye on him, so he don't go out.

HJALMAR   All right, all right, I will.—Say, Gina, a little herring salad would be very nice. Because I suspect Relling and Molvik were out on a binge last night.

GINA   If only they don't barge in before I can . . .

HJALMAR   No, of course they won't. Take your time.

GINA   Well, all right. Meantime you can get a little work done.

HJALMAR   I *am* working, can't you see? I'm working as hard as I can!

GINA   That way you'll get that off your hands, that's all I meant. [*She goes into the kitchen, with the basket.*]

> HJALMAR *sits a while, working on the photograph with a brush, laboring slowly and with distaste.*

EKDAL [*peeps in, looks around the studio, and says in a low voice*] You busy, Hjalmar?

HJALMAR   Yes, can't you see I'm sitting here struggling with these pictures?

EKDAL   All right, all right. Goodness' sake, if you're all that busy—hm! [*Goes back inside his room; the door remains open.*]

HJALMAR [*continues working in silence for a while, then puts down his brush and walks over to the door*] Are *you* busy, Father?

EKDAL [*grumbling, inside his room*] If you're so busy, then I'm busy too. Hm!

HJALMAR   Oh, all right. [*Returns to his work.*]

EKDAL [*after a while, appears again at his door*] Hm, look, Hjalmar, I'm not really as busy as all *that.*

HJALMAR   I thought you were writing.

EKDAL   What the hell, that Gråberg can wait a day or two, can't he? I don't suppose it's a matter of life and death.

HJALMAR   Of course not. And besides, you're not a slave.

EKDAL   And then there was this other thing in there . . .

HJALMAR   That's just what I was thinking. Do you want to go in? Shall I open the door for you?

EKDAL   Wouldn't really be such a bad idea.

HJALMAR [*getting up*] Then we'd have *that* off our hands.

EKDAL   Yes, exactly. It was supposed to be ready first thing tomorrow. It *is* tomorrow, isn't it? Hm?

HJALMAR   Oh, yes, it's tomorrow, all right.

> HJALMAR *and* EKDAL *each pull aside one of the double doors. The morning sun is shining in through the skylights. A few pigeons are flying back and forth; others are cooing on the rafters; from farther back in the attic, now and then, can be heard the clucking of hens.*

HJALMAR   There, now you can go ahead with it, Father.

EKDAL [*going in*] Aren't you coming along?

HJALMAR   Well, you know—I rather think . . . [*Sees* GINA *at the*

kitchen door.] Who, me? No, I have no time, I've got work to do.
—Now, how about this contraption of ours . . .

*He pulls a cord, and inside the door a curtain comes down. Its
lower part consists of a strip of old canvas, its upper part of a
piece of fishing net stretched taut. The attic floor is thus no
longer visible.*

HJALMAR [*going across to the table*]   There. Maybe now I can have a
few minutes' peace.

GINA   Does he have to go messing around in there again?

HJALMAR   I suppose you'd rather see him running down to Ma Eriksen's place? [*Sitting down.*] Do you want something? I thought you
said . . .

GINA   I was only going to ask if you think we could set the table in
here.

HJALMAR   Why not? I don't suppose there are any appointments this
early?

GINA   No, I'm only expecting that engaged couple that want to be
taken together.

HJALMAR   Damn! Couldn't they be taken together some other day!

GINA   But, Hjalmar, dear, I especially booked them for this afternoon,
while you're taking your nap.

HJALMAR   Oh, that's all right then. Yes, let's eat in here.

GINA   All right. But there's no rush about setting the table, you can go
on using it for a while yet.

HJALMAR   Well, can't you see I *am* using it for all I'm worth?

GINA   Then you'll be free later on, you see. [*Returns to the kitchen.*]

Short pause.

EKDAL [*in the attic door, behind the net*]   Hjalmar!

HJALMAR   What?

EKDAL   Afraid we'll have to move the water trough after all.

HJALMAR   Well, that's just what I've been saying all along.

EKDAL   Hm . . . hm . . . hm . . . [*Disappears inside again.*]

HJALMAR *works a little while, glances toward the attic, and
half gets up.* HEDVIG *enters from the kitchen.*

HJALMAR [*sits down again quickly*]   What is it you want?

HEDVIG   I only wanted to be with you, Father.

HJALMAR [*after a while*]   I have a feeling you're kind of snooping
around. Were you told to check up on me by any chance?

HEDVIG   No, of course not.

HJALMAR   What's your mother doing out there?

HEDVIG   Oh, she's busy making the herring salad. [*Walks over to the
table.*] Isn't there some little thing I could help you with, Father?

HJALMAR   No, no. It's best I do it all myself—so long as my strength
holds out. There's no need, Hedvig; so long as your father manages
to preserve his health . . .

HEDVIG   Oh, come on, Daddy, you mustn't say such awful things.

*She wanders around a little, stops by the opening to the attic,
and looks inside.*

HJALMAR   What's he doing, Hedvig?

HEDVIG   Looks like he's making a new path up to the water trough.

HJALMAR   He'll never manage that by himself, never in the world! And here am I, condemned to sit here . . . !

HEDVIG [*going up to him*]   Let me have the brush, Father; I can do it.

HJALMAR   Nonsense; you'll only ruin your eyes.

HEDVIG   No I won't. Come on, give me the brush.

HJALMAR [*getting up*]   Well, it shouldn't take more than a minute or two.

HEDVIG   Pooh, take your time. [*Takes the brush.*] There. [*Sits down.*] And here's one I can copy from.

HJALMAR   But don't you dare strain your eyes! You hear? I'm not taking any responsibility; you'll have to take the responsibility yourself. I'm just telling you.

HEDVIG [*retouching*]   Yes, yes, of course I will.

HJALMAR   My, you're good at it, Hedvig. Just for a couple of minutes, you understand.

> *He sneaks past the edge of the curtain into the attic,* HEDVIG *sits at her work.* HJALMAR *and* EKDAL *are heard debating inside.*

HJALMAR [*appears behind the netting*]   Oh, Hedvig, hand me those pliers on the shelf, will you? And the chisel, please. [*Turns to face into attic.*] Now you'll see, Father. Just give me a chance first to show you what I have in mind. [HEDVIG *fetches the tools he wanted from the shelf and reaches them in to him.*] That's it, thanks. Well, it certainly was a good thing I came.

> *He moves away from the opening. They can be heard carpentering and chatting within.* HEDVIG *stands watching them. Presently there is a knock on the hall door; she does not notice it.* GREGERS WERLE *enters and stands by the door a moment; he is bareheaded and without overcoat.*

GREGERS   Ahem . . . !

HEDVIG [*turns and goes toward him*]   Good morning. Please, come right in.

GREGERS   Thank you. [*Looks toward the attic.*] Sounds like you've got workmen in the house.

HEDVIG   No, it's only Father and Grandfather. I'll tell them you're here.

GREGERS   No, no, don't do that; I'd rather wait a while. [*Sits down on the sofa.*]

HEDVIG   Everything is in such a mess . . . [*Starting to clear away the photographs.*]

GREGERS   Oh, just leave it. Are those photographs that have to be finished?

HEDVIG   Yes, a little job I'm helping Father with.

GREGERS   Please don't let me disturb you.

HEDVIG   Not a bit.

> *She moves the things back into her reach and settles down to work.* GREGERS *watches her in silence.*

GREGERS   Did the wild duck sleep well last night?

HEDVIG   Yes, thank you, I think so.

GREGERS [*turning toward the attic*]   It looks quite different by day from what it did last night by moonlight.

HEDVIG   Yes, it can change such a lot. In the morning it looks differ-

ent than in the afternoon, and when it's raining it looks different from when it's sunny.

GREGERS   Have you noticed that?

HEDVIG   Sure, anybody can see it.

GREGERS   Do you like to stay in there with the wild duck too?

HEDVIG   Yes, whenever I can.

GREGERS   I don't suppose you have much spare time, though. You go to school, of course?

HEDVIG   No, not any more. Father's afraid I'll hurt my eyes reading.

GREGERS   Oh, so he gives you lessons himself, then.

HEDVIG   He promised he would, but he hasn't had the time yet.

GREGERS   But isn't there anybody else to help you a little?

HEDVIG   Well, there's Mr. Molvik. But he isn't always, you know . . . er . . .

GREGERS   You mean he drinks? ·

HEDVIG   I guess so.

GREGERS   Well, in that case you've got time for all sorts of things. And in there, it must be like a world all its own—I imagine.

HEDVIG   Absolutely all of its own. And there are such a lot of strange things in there.

GREGERS   Really?

HEDVIG   Yes, big cases with books in them, and lots of the books have pictures.

GREGERS   Aha!

HEDVIG   Then there's an old writing desk with drawers and secret compartments, and a big clock with figures that are supposed to pop out on the hour. Only the clock doesn't work any more.

GREGERS   So time has stopped in there—in the wild duck's domain.

HEDVIG   Yes. And then there are old paint-boxes and things like that. And all those books.

GREGERS   And do you ever read the books?

HEDVIG   Oh yes, whenever I get the chance. But most of them are in English, and I can't read that. But then I look at the pictures. There's a great big book called *Harrison's History of London;* it must be a hundred years old, and there's an enormous lot of pictures in it. In front there's a picture of Death with an hourglass, and a girl. I think that's horrible. But then there's all the other pictures of churches and castles and streets and big ships sailing on the sea.

GREGERS   But tell me, where did all those wonderful things come from?

HEDVIG   Oh, an old sea captain used to live here once, and he brought them back with him. They called him "The Flying Dutchman." That's funny, because he wasn't a Dutchman at all.

GREGERS   He wasn't?

HEDVIG   No. But finally he didn't come back, and everything just stayed here.

GREGERS   Tell me something . . . When you sit in there looking at pictures, don't you wish you could go abroad and see the real wide world itself?

HEDVIG   Not at all! I want to stay here at home always and help my father and mother.

GREGERS   Retouching photographs?

HEDVIG   Well, not only that. Most of all I'd like to learn how to engrave pictures like the ones in the English books.

GREGERS   Hm. What does your father say to that?

HEDVIG   I don't think Father likes the idea. He's funny about things like that. Imagine, he talks about me learning basket-weaving and braiding straw! I certainly don't think much of that.

GREGERS   No, neither do I.

HEDVIG   Still, he's right when he says that if I'd learned basket-weaving I could have made the new basket for the wild duck.

GREGERS   You could have, true. And of course you'd have been just the right person for the job.

HEDVIG   Because it's *my* wild duck.

GREGERS   Of course it is.

HEDVIG   Oh yes. I own it. But Daddy and Grandfather can borrow it as often as they like.

GREGERS   I see. What do they do with it?

HEDVIG   Oh, they look after it and build things for it, and things like that.

GREGERS   I understand. Because the wild duck must be the most important creature in there.

HEDVIG   Of course, because she's a *real* wild bird. And besides, it's such a pity for her, poor thing. She's got nobody at all to keep her company.

GREGERS   No family, like the rabbits . . .

HEDVIG   No. The chickens also have plenty of others they grew up together with from the time they were baby chicks. But she's completely cut off from her own kind, poor thing. Everything's so strange about the wild duck, too. Nobody knows her and nobody knows where she comes from, either.

GREGERS   And then she has been down in the depths of the sea.

HEDVIG   [*glances quickly at him, suppresses a smile, and asks*]   Why do you say "the depths of the sea"?

GREGERS   Why, what *should* I say?

HEDVIG   You could say "the bottom of the sea"—or "the sea bottom."

GREGERS   Can't I just as well say "the depths of the sea"?

HEDVIG   Yes, But it sounds so strange to hear other people say "the depths of the sea."

GREGERS   Why is that? Tell me.

HEDVIG   No, I won't. It's something silly.

GREGERS   Oh, I'm sure it isn't. Come on, tell me why you smiled.

HEDVIG   Well, it's because every time I happen to think about the way it is in there—when it kind of comes in a flash through my mind—it always seems to me that the whole room and everything in it is called "the depths of the sea." But that's just silly.

GREGERS   I wouldn't say so at all.

HEDVIG   Well, it's only an attic.

GREGERS   [*looking intently at her*]   Are you so sure of that?

HEDVIG   [*astonished*]   That it's an attic?

GREGERS   Yes, do you know that for sure?

> HEDVIG *is silent, looking at him open-mouthed.* GINA *enters from the kitchen with a tablecloth and silverware.*

GREGERS   [*getting up*]   I'm afraid I've descended on you too early.

GINA   Oh well, you got to be someplace. Anyhow, everything's just about ready. Clear the table, Hedvig.

HEDVIG *clears up; she and* GINA *lay the table during the following dialogue.* GREGERS *sits down in the armchair and starts leafing through an album of photographs.*

GREGERS   I hear you know how to do retouching, Mrs. Ekdal.

GINA [*with a sidelong glance*]   Yes, I know how.

GREGERS   That was indeed most fortunate.

GINA   How do you mean—"fortunate"?

GREGERS   Seeing that Hjalmar became a photographer, I mean.

HEDVIG   Mother knows how to take pictures, too.

GINA   Oh yes, I managed to pick that up, all right.

GREGERS   So perhaps it is really you that carries on the business?

GINA   Well, when Hjalmar hasn't got the time himself . . .

GREGERS   He's very much taken up with his old father, I would imagine.

GINA   Yes. Besides it's no job for a man like Hjalmar, taking pictures of every Tom, Dick and Harry that comes along.

GREGERS   I quite agree. Still, once he's gone in for that line of work, shouldn't he . . .

GINA   Sure, Mr. Werle, you don't imagine Hjalmar is just a common ordinary photographer.

GREGERS   True enough. Nevertheless . . . [*A shot is fired inside the attic.*]

GREGERS [*jumps up*]   What was that!

GINA   Ugh, they're shooting again!

GREGERS   Do they *shoot* in there?

HEDVIG   They go hunting.

GREGERS   What on earth . . . ! [*Over by the door into the attic.*] Are you hunting, Hjalmar?

HJALMAR [*behind the netting*]   Oh, you're here? I had no idea, I was so busy . . . [*To* HEDVIG.] You might let a person know! [*Enters studio.*]

GREGERS   You go around shooting in the attic?

HJALMAR [*showing him a double-barreled pistol*]   Oh, only with this thing.

GINA   Yes, one of these days you and Grandpa's going to have an accident yet, with that pissle.

HJALMAR [*annoyed*]   I believe I have told you that a firearm such as this is called a pis*tol.*

GINA   Well, I can't see it makes it any safer, whatever you call it.

GREGERS   So you too have taken up hunting, Hjalmar?

HJALMAR   Only a bit of rabbit shooting now and then. Mostly for Father's sake, you understand.

GINA   Ain't men the limit—always got to have *some*thing to detract theirself with.

HJALMAR [*grimly*]   Yes, yes, we always have to distract ourselves with something.

GINA   That's just what I said.

HJALMAR   Hm. Oh well . . . [*To* GREGERS.] Yes, as I was about to say, by a lucky chance the attic is so situated that nobody can hear us shoot. [*Places the pistol on the top shelf.*] Don't touch the pistol, Hedvig! One of the barrels is loaded, remember that.

GREGERS [*looking in through the net*]   You have a hunting rifle too, I see.

HJALMAR   That's Father's old rifle. It's no good anymore, something's gone wrong with the lock. Still, it's fun to have around; we take it apart and clean it once in a while and grease it and put it together again. Of course, it's mostly Father that plays around with that sort of thing.

HEDVIG [*standing by* GREGERS]   Now you can really see the wild duck.

GREGERS   Yes, I was just looking at it. One of her wings droops a bit, it seems to me.

HJALMAR   Well, that's not so strange. After all, she was hit.

GREGERS   And she's dragging one foot slightly. Or am I mistaken?

HJALMAR   Perhaps, just a wee bit.

HEDVIG   Yes, that's the foot the dog got hold of.

HJALMAR   But aside from that there's not a thing the matter with her —which is really remarkable, considering she's got a charge of shot in her and that she's been between the teeth of a dog . . .

GREGERS [*with a glance at* HEDVIG]   . . . and has been in "the depths of the sea"—for so long.

HEDVIG [*smiles*]   Yes.

GINA [*busy at the table*]   My goodness, that blessed wild duck. You sure make a fuss over her.

HJALMAR   Hm.—Lunch ready soon?

GINA   Yes, right away. Hedvig, come give me a hand.

GINA *and* HEDVIG *go out to the kitchen.*

HJALMAR [*in an undertone*]   I don't think you'd better stand there watching Father. He doesn't like it.

GREGERS *moves from attic door.*

HJALMAR   Maybe I ought to close this door anyhow, before the others get here. [*Clapping his hand to scare the birds.*] Shoo, shoo—beat it! [*Lifting the curtain and pulling the doors together.*] This gadget here is my own invention. It's really quite amusing to have something like this to putter around with and fix up when it gets out of order. Besides which, of course, it's absolutely necessary; Gina doesn't want rabbits and chickens running around in the studio.

GREGERS   No, of course not. And I suppose it's your wife who's in charge here?

HJALMAR   As a rule I leave the routine business to her. That way I can retire to the living room and think about more important things.

GREGERS   What things actually, Hjalmar? Tell me.

HJALMAR   I wonder you didn't ask that sooner. Or maybe you haven't heard about the invention?

GREGERS   Invention? No.

HJALMAR   Really? You haven't? Well, of course, up there in the wilderness . . .

GREGERS   So you've made an invention!

HJALMAR   Not quite *made,* just yet—but I'm busy on it. As you can imagine, when I decided to devote myself to photography it was not merely in order to take pictures of a lot of nobodies . . .

GREGERS   Of course not. Your wife was just saying the same thing.

HJALMAR   I vowed that if I was going to dedicate my powers to this calling, I would raise it so high that it would become both a science and an art. And so I decided to work on this remarkable invention.

GREGERS   What does the invention consist of? What is it going to do?

HJALMAR   Come, come, my dear Gregers, you mustn't ask for details yet. It takes time, you know. Another thing—don't imagine it's vanity that spurs me on. I'm certainly not working for my own sake. Oh no, it is my life's mission that stands before me night and day.

GREGERS   What mission?

HJALMAR   Have you forgotten the silver-haired old man?

GREGERS   Your poor father, yes. But what can you actually do for him?

HJALMAR   I can restore his self-respect by raising the name of Ekdal once again to honor and dignity.

GREGERS   So that is your life's mission.

HJALMAR   Yes, I will rescue the shipwrecked old man. For shipwrecked he was, the moment the storm broke over him. By the time of that terrible investigation he was no longer himself. That pistol there, Gregers—the one we use to shoot rabbits—that has played a role in the tragedy of the House of Ekdal.

GREGERS   The pistol? Really?

HJALMAR   When sentence had been pronounced and he was to be imprisoned—he took that pistol in his hand . . .

GREGERS   He meant to . . . !

HJALMAR   Yes—but didn't dare. Lost his nerve. So broken, so demoralized was he already then. Oh, can you conceive it! He, an army officer, a man who had shot nine bears. He, who was descended from two lieutenant colonels—one after the other, naturally—. Can you conceive it, Gregers?

GREGERS   Yes, very well.

HJALMAR   Not I. Then, once again, the pistol figured in our family chronicle. When he had put on the gray prison uniform and sat behind bars . . . Oh, that was a terrible time for me, let me tell you. I kept the shades down on both my windows. When I peeped out, there was the sun, shining as usual. I couldn't grasp it. I saw people walking in the street, laughing and chatting about trivialities. I could not grasp it. It seemed to me that the whole of existence ought to come to a standstill, like an eclipse.

GREGERS   That's just how I felt, when my mother died.

HJALMAR   In such an hour did Hjalmar Ekdal point the pistol at his own breast.

GREGERS   You also thought of . . . !

HJALMAR   Yes.

GREGERS   But you did not fire.

HJALMAR   No. In the decisive moment I won the victory over myself. I chose to live. And believe me, it takes courage to choose life under those circumstances.

GREGERS   Well, that depends on how you look at it.

HJALMAR   No, my friend, no doubt about it. But it was all for the best. Because now I'll soon perfect my invention, and then Dr. Relling thinks, just as I do, that Father will be allowed to wear his uniform again. I will demand that as my sole reward.

GREGERS   So it's about wearing the uniform that he . . . ?

HJALMAR   Yes, that's what he yearns and pines for most of all. You have no idea how my heart bleeds for him. Every time we celebrate some little family occasion—like Gina's and my wedding anniversary,

or whatever it may be—in trots the old man wearing his uniform of happier days. But just let him hear so much as a knock on the door—because he doesn't dare show himself like that in front of strangers, you see—back into his room he scurries as fast as his old legs will carry him. Think, Gregers, how heart-rending it is for a son to see such things!

GREGERS   About how soon do you think the invention will be perfected?

HJALMAR   Good lord, you mustn't ask me for details like dates. An invention is not a thing entirely under one's control. It's largely a matter of inspiration—of a sudden insight—and it's next to impossible to figure out in advance just when that may come.

GREGERS   But you *are* making progress?

HJALMAR   Of course I'm making progress. I grapple every single day with the invention, I'm filled with it. Every afternoon, right after dinner, I shut myself in the living room, where I can concentrate in peace. But I simply must not be rushed; that doesn't do a bit of good. That's what Relling says, too.

GREGERS   And you don't think all this business in the attic there draws you away from your work, and distracts you too much?

HJALMAR   No, no, no. Quite the reverse. You mustn't say such things. After all, I can't go around day in day out everlastingly poring over the same exhausting problems. I must have something to occupy me during the waiting period. The inspiration, the intuition—look, when it's ready to come, it will come, and that's all.

GREGERS   My dear Hjalmar, I almost think there is something of the wild duck in you.

HJALMAR   The wild duck? How do you mean?

GREGERS   You have dived down and bitten yourself fast into the undergrowth.

HJALMAR   Are you by any chance alluding to the all but fatal shot that maimed my father—and me as well?

GREGERS   Not exactly. I wouldn't say that you are maimed. But you have landed in a poisonous swamp, Hjalmar; an insidious blight has got hold of you, and you have sunk down to the depths to die in darkness.

HJALMAR   I? Die in darkness! Now look here, Gregers, you'd really better quit talking such nonsense.

GREGERS   Don't worry, I'll get you up again. You see, I too have got a mission in life now. I found it yesterday.

HJALMAR   That's all very well, but just you leave me out of it. I can assure you that—apart from my understandable melancholy, of course—I am as content as any man could wish to be.

GREGERS   The fact that you are content is itself a result of the poison.

HJALMAR   Look, my dear Gregers, will you please cut out all this rot about blight and poison. I am not at all used to that sort of talk; in my house nobody ever talks to me about unpleasant things.

GREGERS   That I can well believe.

HJALMAR   No, because it's not good for me. And there are no swamp vapors here, as you put it. The roof may be low in the poor photographer's home, that I know—and my means are slender. But I am an inventor, man—and a breadwinner as well. That raises me above my humble circumstances . . . Ah, here comes our lunch!

GINA *and* HEDVIG *enter with bottles of beer, a decanter of schnapps, glasses, and other things for the lunch. At the same time,* RELLING *and* MOLVIK *enter from the hallway, both without hat or overcoat.* MOLVIK *is dressed in black.*

GINA [*setting things on table*]   Well, here they come right on the dot.

RELLING   Once Molvik got the idea he could smell herring salad, there was no holding him.—Good morning again, Ekdal.

HJALMAR   Gregers, may I present Mr. Molvik; Dr. . . . that's right, you know Relling, don't you?

GREGERS   Slightly.

RELLING   Oh, it's Mr. Werle junior. Yes indeed, we once had a couple of skirmishes up at the Højdal works. You just moved in?

GREGERS   This morning.

RELLING   Molvik and I live on the floor below, so you're not far from doctor or parson, should you have need of either.

GREGERS   Thanks, it's not unlikely I may—yesterday we were thirteen at table.

HJALMAR   Oh, don't start on that creepy talk again!

RELLING   Relax, Ekdal. You can be damn sure it won't be you.

HJALMAR   I hope not, for my family's sake. Well, come sit down and let's eat, drink, and be merry.

GREGERS   Aren't we going to wait for your father?

HJALMAR   No, he'll have a bite later on in his room. Do sit down!

The men sit down at the table, and eat and drink. GINA *and* HEDVIG *go in and out, waiting on them.*

RELLING   Molvik really tied one on last night, Mrs. Ekdal.

GINA   Yeah? Again?

RELLING   Didn't you hear him when I brought him home?

GINA   No, I can't say I did.

RELLING   That's good—because last night Molvik really was awful.

GINA   Is it true, Molvik?

MOLVIK   Let us draw a veil over last night's proceedings. Such episodes are totally foreign to my better self.

RELLING [*to* GREGERS]   It comes over him like a sort of possession, so I am obliged to take him out on a binge. Because Mr. Molvik, you see, is dæmonic.

GREGERS   Dæmonic?

RELLING   Molvik is dæmonic, yes.

GREGERS   Hm.

RELLING   And dæmonic natures are not made for the straight and narrow; they've got to kick over the traces once in a while.—Well, so you're still sticking it out up there at those ghastly dark works?

GREGERS   I have till now.

RELLING   Say, did you ever collect on that claim you used to go around with?

GREGERS   Claim? [*Grasps his meaning.*] Oh, that.

HJALMAR   Were you a bill collector, Gregers?

GREGERS   Oh, nonsense.

RELLING   He certainly was. He used to go around to all the workmen's shacks presenting something he called "the claim of the ideal."

GREGERS   I was young in those days.

RELLING   You bet you were. Mighty young. And that claim of the ideal—you never did get it honored as long as I was up there.

GREGERS   Nor afterwards, either.

RELLING   Well, then I imagine you've got the sense by now to knock a little off the bill.

GREGERS   Never—not when I'm dealing with an authentic human being.

HJALMAR   Well, that sounds reasonable enough.—Some butter, Gina.

RELLING   And a slice of pork for Molvik.

MOLVIK   Ugh, not pork!

Knocking inside the attic door.

HJALMAR   Open up, Hedvig; Father wants to come out.

HEDVIG *goes and opens the door a little;* OLD EKDAL *enters, carrying a fresly flayed rabbit skin; she closes the door after him.*

EKDAL   Good morning, Gentlemen! Good hunting today. Bagged a beauty.

HJALMAR   And you went and skinned it without waiting for me!

EKDAL   Salted it down, too. Good tender meat, rabbit. Sweet, too, tastes like sugar. Hearty appetite, Gentlemen! [*Goes into his room.*]

MOLVIK [*rising*]   Excuse me . . . I can't . . . I must get downstairs at once . . .

RELLING   Drink some soda water, man!

MOLVIK [*hurrying*]   Uh . . . uh! [*Exit through the hall door.*]

RELLING [*to* HJALMAR]   Let us drain a glass to the old Nimrod.[3]

HJALMAR [*clinks glasses with him*]   Yes, to the sportsman on the brink of the grave.

RELLING   To the gray-headed . . . [*Drinks.*] By the way—is it gray hair he's got, or is it white?

HJALMAR   Sort of betwixt and between, I'd say. As a matter of fact, not much of either any more.

RELLING   Oh well, life can be good enough under a toupee. Yes, Ekdal, when you come right down to it, you are a lucky man. You have your beautiful goal to strive for . . .

HJALMAR   And I do strive, believe me.

RELLING   And then you've got your excellent wife, waddling so cozily in and out in her felt slippers, swaying her hips and making everything nice and comfortable for you.

HJALMAR   Yes, Gina . . . [*nods to her*] you are a good companion to have on life's journey.

GINA   Oh, don't sit there bisecting me.

RELLING   And then your Hedvig, Ekdal, what?

HJALMAR [*moved*]   The child, yes! First and foremost, the child. Hedvig, come here to me. [*Stroking her hair.*] What day is it tomorrow, eh?

HEDVIG [*shaking him*]   Oh, don't say anything about that, Father.

HJALMAR   It pierces me to the heart to think how little we can do— only a little celebration in the attic . . .

HEDVIG   Oh, but that'll be just lovely!

RELLING   And wait till the marvelous invention comes out, Hedvig!

---

3. Nimrod is described in *Genesis* 10:9 as "a mighty hunter before the Lord."

HJALMAR   Yes indeed—*then* you shall see! Hedvig, I am resolved to secure your future. You shall want for nothing as long as you live. For you, I shall demand . . . something or other. That will be the poor inventor's sole reward.

HEDVIG   [*whispers, her arms around his neck*]   Oh you dear, dear Daddy!

RELLING   [*to* GREGERS]   Well, now, don't you think it's nice, for a change, to sit at a well-laid table in a happy family circle?

HJALMAR   Yes, I really appreciate these meal-times.

GREGERS   I, for my part, do not thrive in swamp vapors.

RELLING   Swamp vapors?

HJALMAR   Oh, don't start on *that* again!

GINA   God knows there's no swamp vapors around here, Mr. Werle. I air the house out every blessed day.

GREGERS   [*leaving the table*]   The stench I have in mind, you can hardly air out.

HJALMAR   Stench!

GINA   Yes, Hjalmar, how do you like that!

RELLING   Pardon me—I don't suppose it could be yourself that brought the stink with you from the pits up north?

GREGERS   It's just like you to call what I bring to this house a stink.

RELLING   [*goes up to him*]   Listen here, Mr. Werle junior, I have a strong suspicion you are still carrying around that "claim of the ideal" unabridged in your back pocket.

GREGERS   I carry it in my heart.

RELLING   Well wherever the hell you carry it, I advise you not to play bill collector here as long as *I'm* around.

GREGERS   And suppose I do?

RELLING   You'll be sent head first down the stairs. Now you know.

HJALMAR   [*rising*]   No, Relling, really . . . !

GREGERS   Go ahead, throw me out . . .

GINA   [*interposing*]   You can't do that, Relling. But I must say, Mr. Werle, you've got a nerve to talk to *me* about smells, after the mess you made with your stove.

There is a knock on the hall door.

HEDVIG   Mother, somebody's knocking.

HJALMAR   Darn! Now all we need is customers barging in.

GINA   I'll go . . . [*Goes and opens the door; gives a start; draws back.*] Oh! What the . . . !

HÅKON WERLE, *in a fur coat, takes a step into the room.*

WERLE   I beg your pardon, but I believe my son is staying here.

GINA   [*gulping*]   Yes.

HJALMAR   [*coming forward*]   Sir, won't you do us the honor to . . . ?

WERLE   Thanks, I just want a word with my son.

GREGERS   Yes, what is it? Here I am.

WERLE   I wish to talk with you in your room.

GREGERS   In my room—all right . . . [*About to go.*]

GINA   God, no. It's not fit in there for . . .

WERLE   Very well, out in the hall, then. I want to talk to you in private.

HJALMAR   You can do it right here, Mr. Werle. Relling, come into the living room.

HJALMAR *and* RELLING *exit right.* GINA *takes* HEDVIG *off with her to the kitchen.*

GREGERS [*after a brief pause*]   Well, now we are alone.

WERLE   You let drop certain remarks last night . . . And in view of the fact that you've gone and moved in with the Ekdals, I can only assume that you have something or other in mind against me.

GREGERS   I intend to open Hjalmar Ekdal's eyes. He must see his position for what it is—that's all.

WERLE   Is that the objective in life you spoke of yesterday?

GREGERS   Yes. You have left me no other.

WERLE   Is it I, then, who twisted your mind, Gregers?

GREGERS   You've twisted my whole life. I'm not thinking of all that concerning Mother . . . But it's you I have to thank that I am forever driven and tormented by a guilty conscience.

WERLE   Aha, your conscience! So that's your trouble.

GREGERS   I should have stood up to you that time the trap was laid for Lieutenant Ekdal. I should have warned him—for I suspected well enough how it was all going to end.

WERLE   Yes, in that case you certainly ought to have spoken out.

GREGERS   I didn't dare. That's what a frightened coward I was. I was so unspeakably afraid of you—not only then but long after.

WERLE   You've got over that fear now, it appears.

GREGERS   Yes, fortunately. The crime committed against old Ekdal, both by myself and by—others—that can never be redeemed. But Hjalmar I can still rescue from all the lies and deceit that threaten to destroy him.

WERLE   Do you think you'll be doing him a favor?

GREGERS   I *know* it.

WERLE   I suppose you think our good photographer is the kind of man to thank you for such a friendly service?

GREGERS   Yes! He certainly is.

WERLE   Hm . . . we'll see.

GREGERS   And besides . . . if I am to go on living, I must find some cure for my sick conscience.

WERLE   It will never be well. Your conscience has been sickly right from childhood. It is a legacy from your mother, Gregers—the only thing she ever left you.

GREGERS [*with a contemptuous half-smile*]   So you still haven't swallowed your disappointment that she didn't bring you the dowry you counted on?

WERLE   Let us keep to the point.—Are you quite resolved to set young Ekdal on what you assume to be the right track?

GREGERS   Yes, quite resolved.

WERLE   Well, in that case I could have saved myself the trouble of coming up here. Then I suppose it's no use asking you to come back home?

GREGERS   No.

WERLE   And you won't join the firm, either?

GREGERS   No.

WERLE   Very well. But since I intend to marry again, your share of my estate will be turned over to you at once.[4]

---

4. As a widower, the elder Werle coud not remarry without securing some part of his estate to surviving children of his previous marriage.

GREGERS [*quickly*]   No, I don't want that.

WERLE   You don't want it?

GREGERS   No, I don't dare. My conscience won't let me.

WERLE [*after a pause*]   Are you going up to the works again?

GREGERS   No, I consider myself released from your service.

WERLE   But what are you going to do?

GREGERS   Accomplish my mission. That's all.

WERLE   All right, but afterwards? What are you going to live on?

GREGERS   I've put aside a little of my salary.

WERLE   Yes, but how long will *that* last!

GREGERS   I think it will last out my time.

WERLE   What's that supposed to mean?

GREGERS   I'm answering no more questions.

WERLE   Good-bye, then, Gregers.

GREGERS   Good-bye.

> HÅKON WERLE *goes.*

HJALMAR [*peeping in*]   Has he gone?

GREGERS   Yes.

> HJALMAR *and* RELLING *enter; also* GINA *and* HEDVIG, *from the kitchen.*

RELLING   Well, that fixed *that* lunch.

GREGERS   Put on your things, Hjalmar. You're coming with me for a long walk.

HJALMAR   Gladly. What did your father want? Anything to do with me?

GREGERS   Just come. We must have a little talk. I'll go get my coat. [*Goes out by the hall door.*]

GINA   You shouldn't go with him, Hjalmar.

RELLING   No, don't you do it, old man. Stay where you are.

HJALMAR [*getting his coat and hat*]   What! When an old friend feels the need to open his heart to me in private . . . !

RELLING   But damn it!—can't you see the fellow is mad, cracked, off his rocker!

GINA   There, what did I tell you? His mother used to get these here fits and conniptions too.

HJALMAR   All the more reason he needs a friend's watchful eye. [*To* GINA.] Be sure and have dinner ready on time. So long. [*Goes out by the hall door.*]

RELLING   What a calamity that fellow didn't go straight to hell down one of the Højdal pits.

GINA   Good God!—what makes you say that?

RELLING [*muttering*]   Oh, I have my reasons.

GINA   Do you think young Werle is really crazy?

RELLING   No, worse luck; he's no more crazy than most. But there's one bug he certainly has got in his system.

GINA   What's the matter with him, anyway?

RELLING   Well, I'll tell you, Mrs. Ekdal. He's got a severe case of inflamed integrity.

GINA   Inflamed integrity?

HEDVIG   Is that a kind of disease?

RELLING   Oh yes. It's a national disease. But it only breaks out sporadically. [*Nods to* GINA.] Thanks for lunch!

> He goes out by the hall door.

GINA [*pacing the floor, disturbed*]   Ugh, that Gregers Werle—he always *was* a queer fish.

HEDVIG [*standing by the table and looking searchingly at her*]   I think this is all so strange.

Act 4

HJALMAR EKDAL's *studio. Photographs have apparently just been taken; a camera covered with a cloth, a stand, two chairs, a console, and other portrait materials are set out in the middle of the room. Afternoon light; the sun is about to set; after a while it begins to get dark.*

GINA *is standing at the open hall door with a dark slide and a wet photographic plate in her hand. She is speaking to somebody outside.*

GINA   Yes, positively. When I make a promise, I keep it. The first dozen will be ready on Monday.—Good-bye now, good-bye!

Footsteps can be heard going down the stairs. GINA *shuts the door, puts the plate in the slide, and inserts the slide in the covered camera.*

HEDVIG [*entering from the kitchen*]   Did they leave?

GINA [*tidying up*]   Yes, thank goodness. I finally got rid of them.

HEDVIG   Can you understand why Father isn't back yet?

GINA   You're sure he's not down at Relling's?

HEDVIG   No, he's not there. I just went down the back stairs and asked.

GINA   And his dinner standing there getting cold.

HEDVIG   Imagine! And Father's always so punctual about dinner.

GINA   Well, he'll be here soon, don't worry.

HEDVIG   Oh, I wish he'd come. Everything seems so strange.

GINA [*calls out*]   There he is!

HJALMAR EKDAL *comes in through the hall door.*

HEDVIG [*up to him*]   Father! We've been waiting and waiting for you!

GINA [*glancing across*]   You sure have been out a long time, Hjalmar.

HJALMAR [*without looking at her*]   I suppose I have, yes. [*He takes off his overcoat.* GINA *and* HEDVIG *try to help him; he waves them aside.*]

GINA   Maybe you ate someplace with Werle?

HJALMAR [*hanging up his coat*]   No.

GINA [*going toward the kitchen door*]   Then I'll go get your dinner.

HJALMAR   No, never mind. I don't want anything now.

HEDVIG [*coming closer*]   Aren't you feeling well, Father?

HJALMAR   Feeling well? Oh yes, tolerably. We had a tiring walk together, Gregers and I.

GINA   You shouldn't do that, Hjalmar, you're not used to it.

HJALMAR   Hm. There are lots of things a man must get used to in this world. [*Paces up and down.*] Did anybody come while I was out?

GINA   Only the engaged couple.

HJALMAR   No new orders?

GINA   No, not today.

HEDVIG   There'll be some tomorrow, Father, you'll see.

HJALMAR   I hope you're right, because tomorrow I mean to get down to work in real earnest.

HEDVIG   Tomorrow! Don't you remember what day it is tomorrow?

HJALMAR   Oh, that's right . . . Well, the day after tomorrow, then. From now on I intend to do everything myself; I want to do all the work entirely on my own.

GINA   What on earth for, Hjalmar? You'd only make your life a misery. I can still manage the photography; you go on with the invention.

HEDVIG   And what about the wild duck—and all the chickens and rabbits . . .

HJALMAR   Don't talk to me about that junk! I'm never setting foot in that attic again.

HEDVIG   But Father, you promised me there'd be a party tomorrow . . .

HJALMAR   Hm, that's right. Well, starting the day after tomorrow, then. That damn wild duck, I'd like to wring its neck!

HEDVIG [*cries out*]   The wild duck!

GINA   Well, I never!

HEDVIG [*shaking him*]   But Father, it's *my* wild duck!

HJALMAR   That's the only thing that stops me. I haven't the heart—for your sake, Hedvig, I haven't got the heart. But deep down I feel I ought to do it. I ought not tolerate under my roof any creature that has been in that man's hands.

GINA   Goodness sake, just because Grandpa got it off that good-for-nothing Pettersen . . .

HJALMAR [*walking up and down*]   There are certain demands . . . what shall I call them? Let us say—demands of the ideal—certain claims that a man cannot disregard without peril to his soul.

HEDVIG [*following him about*]   But think, the wild duck—that poor wild duck!

HJALMAR [*halts*]   I *told* you I'll spare it—for your sake. Not a hair of its head shall be . . . hm. As I said, I shall spare it. I have more important things to think about now. But now you ought to go for a little walk, Hedvig; the twilight is just right for you.

HEDVIG   I don't care to go out now.

HJALMAR   Yes, go on. Seems to me you're blinking your eyes a lot. It's not good for you, all these fumes in here. The air is close under this roof.

HEDVIG   Well, all right, I'll run down the kitchen way and walk around a little. My hat and coat . . . ? That's right, they're in my room. Father—promise you won't do anything to the wild duck while I'm gone.

HJALMAR   Not a feather of its head shall be touched. [*Presses her to him.*] You and I, Hedvig—we two . . . ! Well, run along now.

HEDVIG *nods to her parents and goes out through the kitchen.*

HJALMAR [*walks up and down without looking up*]   Gina.

GINA   Yes?

HJALMAR   As of tomorrow . . . or, let us say as of the day after tomorrow—I wish to keep the household accounts myself.

GINA   You want to keep the accounts also?

HJALMAR   Yes, keep track of what we take in, at any rate.

GINA   Oh, God help us, *that's* soon done.

HJALMAR   I wonder. It seems to me you make the money go a remarkably long way. [*Halts and looks at her.*] How do you do it?

GINA   That's because Hedvig and I need so little.

HJALMAR   Is it true that Father is highly paid for the copying he does
for Mr. Werle?

GINA   I don't know if it's all that high. I don't know what the rates are
for things like that.

HJALMAR   Well, roughly what *does* he get? I want to know.

GINA   It differs. I guess it comes to about what he costs us, and a little
pocket money.

HJALMAR   What he *costs* us! You never told me that before!

GINA   No, how could I. It made you so happy to think he got everything from you.

HJALMAR   And in fact it comes from Mr. Werle!

GINA   Oh, don't worry. He can afford it.

HJALMAR   Light me the lamp!

GINA [*lighting the lamp*]   Besides, how can we tell if it actually comes
from him; it could easily be Gråberg . . .

HJALMAR   Why do you suddenly drag Gråberg into this?

GINA   Well, I don't know, I just thought . . .

HJALMAR   Hm!

GINA   Anyway, it wasn't me that got Grandpa the copying to do. You
know yourself it was Berta, the time she took service there.

HJALMAR   It seems to me your voice is trembling.

GINA [*putting the shade on the lamp*]   Is it?

HJALMAR   And your hands are shaking. Aren't they?

GINA [*firmly*]   Say it straight out, Hjalmar. What's he gone and told
you about me?

HJALMAR   Is it true—*can* it be true—that there was something between you and Mr. Werle while you were working in his house?

GINA   It's not true. Not then, there wasn't. He was after me all right,
that I will say. And the Missus thought there was something going
on, and she made such a fuss and a hullaballoo about it and went
for me tooth and nail. She sure did.—So I quit.

HJALMAR   But then, afterwards . . . !

GINA   Well, *you* know, I went home. And my mother . . . she wasn't
exactly as straight as you thought she was, Hjalmar. Anyway, she
got after me about this, that, and the other. Because by that time
Werle was a widower.

HJALMAR   All right! And then?

GINA   Well, I guess you might as well know it. He wouldn't give up
till he had his way.

HJALMAR [*striking his hands together*]   And this is the mother of my
child! How could you keep a thing like that from me!

GINA   Yes, I know it was wrong. I should've told you long ago, I guess.

HJALMAR   Right at the *start* you should have told me—then I'd have
known the sort of woman you were.

GINA   But would you have married me, just the same?

HJALMAR   What do *you* think?

GINA   There you are, that's why I didn't dare tell you at the time. You
know how much I'd come to care for you. So how could I go and
make my own life a misery?

HJALMAR [*pacing about*]   And this is my Hedvig's mother! And to
realize that everything I lay my eyes on . . . [*kicks a chair*] . . . my

entire home . . . I owe to a favored predecessor! Oh, that old lecher!

GINA   Do you regret the fourteen-fifteen years we've had together?

HJALMAR   [*fronting her*]   Tell me, have you not—every day, every hour—regretted this web of deceit you've spun around me, like a spider? Answer me! Have you really gone around here and not suffered agonies of remorse and shame?

GINA   Bless you, Hjalmar, I've had enough to think about just running the house and everything . . .

HJALMAR   You mean you never even give a thought to your past?

GINA   No, God knows I'd just about forgotten that old business.

HJALMAR   Oh, this dull, apathetic calm! That's what I find so outrageous. Imagine—not even a twinge of remorse!

GINA   But just tell me, Hjalmar—what would've become of you, if you hadn't had a wife like me?

HJALMAR   Like you!

GINA   Well, you've got to admit I've always been kind of more practical and with my feet on the ground than you. Well, of course I *am* a couple of years older.

HJALMAR   What would have become of me!

GINA   Because you weren't exactly living right when you first met me; you can't deny that.

HJALMAR   Is that what you call not living right? Oh, what would you know about a man's feelings when he falls into grief and despair— especially a man of my fiery temperament.

GINA   All right, all right, have it your way. Anyhow, I don't want to make no song and dance about it. Because you certainly turned out to be a real good man, once you got your own home and family. And now we'd got things so nice and comfortable here, and Hedvig and me was just thinking that soon we could spend a little on ourselves in the way of food and clothes.

HJALMAR   In this swamp of deceit, yes.

GINA   Oh, why did that nasty creature have to come poking his nose in here for!

HJALMAR   I, too, thought our home a happy one. What a delusion! And now where am I to find the inner force I need in order to bring forth my invention? Perhaps it will die with me. And then it will have been your past, Gina, that killed it.

GINA   [*about to weep*]   Please, Hjalmar, you mustn't say a thing like that. When all my days I only tried to make everything the best for you!

HJALMAR   I ask you—what happens now to the breadwinner's dream? As I would lie there on the sofa, pondering the invention, I suspected full well that it would drain the last drop of my strength. Well I knew that the day I held the patent in my hands, that day would mark my—final hour. And so it was my dream that you would be left the well-to-do widow of the late inventor.

GINA   [*drying her tears*]   Hjalmar, don't talk like that. God forbid I should ever live to see the day I'm left a widow!

HJALMAR   Oh well, what's the difference. It's all over now, anyway. All over!

GREGERS WERLE *cautiously opens the hall door and looks in.*

GREGERS   May I come in?

HJALMAR   Yes, come in.

GREGERS [*advances, his face radiant with joy, and reaches out his hands to them*]   Well, you two dear people . . . ! [*Looks from the one to the other and whispers to* HJALMAR.] You haven't done it yet?

HJALMAR [*aloud*]   It is done.

GREGERS   It is?

HJALMAR   I have lived through the bitterest hour of my life.

GREGERS   But also, I trust, the most sublime.

HJALMAR   Anyway, for the time being it's done and over with.

GINA   God forgive you, Mr. Werle.

GREGERS [*in great amazement*]   But I don't understand this.

HJALMAR   What don't you understand?

GREGERS   So great an accounting—an accounting that a whole new way of life is to be founded on—a way of life, a partnership in truth, free of all deception . . .

HJALMAR   Yes, yes, I know. I know all that.

GREGERS   I was absolutely confident that when I came through that door I would be met by a radiance of transfiguration shining from the faces of both husband and wife. And all I see is this dull, heavy, gloomy . . .

GINA   Is that it. [*Takes the shade off the lamp.*]

GREGERS   You're not trying to understand me, Mrs. Ekdal. Well, well, I suppose you'll need time . . . But *you*, now, Hjalmar? Surely *you* must feel exalted by this great reckoning.

HJALMAR   Yes, naturally I do. That is—in a kind of way.

GREGERS   For surely nothing in the world can compare to finding forgiveness in one's heart for one who has erred, and raising her up to you with love.

HJALMAR   Do you think a man so easily gets over the bitter cup I just drained?

GREGERS   No, not an ordinary man, perhaps. But a man like *you* . . . !

HJALMAR   All right, I know, I know. But don't push me, Gregers. It takes time.

GREGERS   There is much of the wild duck in you, Hjalmar.

RELLING *has entered by the hall door.*

RELLING   What's this? Are we back to the wild duck again?

HJALMAR   Yes. The damaged trophy of Mr. Werle's sport.

RELLING   Werle senior? Is it him you're talking about?

HJALMAR   Him and . . . the rest of us.

RELLING [*to* GREGERS, *under his breath*]   Damn you to hell!

HJALMAR   What's that you're saying?

RELLING   I was expressing the fervent wish that this quack here would take himself off where he belongs. If he stays around here much longer, he's quite capable of messing you both up.

GREGERS   These two are not going to be "messed up," Mr. Relling. I need not speak for Hjalmar. Him we know. But she too must surely have, deep down inside, something worthy of trust, something of integrity . . .

GINA [*on the point of tears*]   Then why couldn't you leave me be like I was.

RELLING [*to* GREGERS]   Would it be impertinent to ask what it is exactly you want in this house?

GREGERS   I want to lay the foundation for a true marriage.

RELLING   So you don't think the Ekdals' marriage is good enough as it is?

GREGERS   It's probably as good a marriage as most, I regret to say. But a true marriage it has yet to become.

HJALMAR   You never did have an eye for the claim of the ideal, Relling.

RELLING   Nonsense, my boy!—Begging your pardon, Mr. Werle, but how many—at a rough guess—how many true marriages have you seen in your life?

GREGERS   Hardly a single one.

RELLING   Neither have I.

GREGERS   But I *have* seen innumerable marriages of the opposite sort. And I had occasion to observe at close quarters the havoc such a marriage can wreak on both partners.

HJALMAR   A man's whole moral foundation can crumble under his feet; that's the terrible thing.

RELLING   Well, of course I've never been exactly married myself, so I can't judge about that. But this I do know, that the child is part of a marriage too. And you had better leave the child in peace.

HJALMAR   Oh—Hedvig! My poor Hedvig!

RELLING   Yes, see to it you keep Hedvig out of this. You two are grown people. In God's name, go ahead and muck up your own affairs to your heart's content. But I'm warning you—go easy with Hedvig, or you may end by doing her serious injury.

HJALMAR   Injury!

RELLING   Yes, or else she might do herself one—and maybe not only to herself.

GINA   How can you tell a thing like that, Relling?

HJALMAR   There's no immediate danger to her eyes, is there?

RELLING   This has nothing to do with her eyes. But Hedvig is at a difficult age. There's no telling *what* wild ideas she can get into her head.

GINA   Say, that's right! Lately she's started to fool around in such a peculiar way with the stove out in the kitchen. "Playing house on fire," she calls it. Sometimes I'm scared she *will* burn down the house.

RELLING   There you are; I knew it.

GREGERS [*to* RELLING]   But how do you explain a thing like that?

RELLING [*sullenly*]   Puberty, man.

HJALMAR   As long as the child has me! As long as I'm above the ground . . . !

There is a knock on the door.

GINA   Shhh, Hjalmar, there's somebody outside. [*Calls.*] Come in!

Enter MRS. SØRBY, *in outdoor clothes.*

MRS. SØRBY   Good evening!

GINA [*going toward her*]   Why, Berta, it's *you!*

MRS. SØRBY   It certainly is. Have I come at an inconvenient time?

HJALMAR   Gracious, no—a messenger from that house . . .

MRS. SØRBY [*to* GINA]   To tell the truth I hoped I wouldn't find your menfolk at home this time of day. So I dropped in to have a little chat with you and say good-bye.

GINA   Oh? Why? Are you going away?

MRS. SØRBY   Yes, tomorrow early—up to Højdal. Mr. Werle left this afternoon. [*Casually, to* GREGERS.] He send his regards.

GINA   Imagine!

HJALMAR   So Mr. Werle has left? And you're following him?

MRS. SØRBY   Yes, Ekdal, what do you say to that?

HJALMAR   I say—beware!

GREGERS   Let me explain. My father is marrying Mrs. Sørby.

HJALMAR   Marrying her!

GINA   Oh, Berta—finally!

RELLING [*his voice trembling slightly*]   Surely this can't be true?

MRS. SØRBY   Yes, my dear Relling, it's quite true.

RELLING   You are going to get married again?

MRS. SØRBY   It looks like it. Werle has got a special license, and we're going to have a quiet wedding up at the works.

GREGERS   Then I suppose I must wish you joy, like a good stepson.

MRS. SØRBY   Thank you, if you really mean it. I do hope it will lead to happiness for both Werle and myself.

RELLING   You have every reason for hope. Mr. Werle never gets drunk —at least not to my knowledge. And I doubt he's in the habit of beating his wives, either, like the late lamented horse-doctor.

MRS SØRBY   Oh, come now, let Sørby rest in peace. He had his good points too.

RELLING   Mr. Werle has better ones, I'm sure.

MRS. SØRBY   At any rate he didn't go and throw away the best that was in him. The man who does that must take the consequences.

RELLING   Tonight I will go out with Molvik.

MRS. SØRBY   Don't do that, Relling. Don't—for my sake.

RELLING   Can't be helped. [*To* HJALMAR.] Come along too, if you like.

GINA   No, thanks. Hjalmar don't go on such disserpations.

HJALMAR [*angrily, in an undertone*]   Oh, be still!

RELLING   Good-bye, Mrs.—Werle. [*Exit through hall door.*]

GREGERS [*to* MRS. SØRBY]   It appears that you and Dr. Relling are rather intimately acquainted.

MRS. SØRBY   Yes, we've known each other a good many years. As a matter of fact, at one time something or other might have even come of it.

GREGERS   It was certainly lucky for you it didn't.

MRS. SØRBY   You may well say that. But I have always been careful not to act on impulse. After all, a woman can't afford to throw herself away.

GREGERS   Aren't you the least bit afraid I might drop a hint to my father about this old friendship?

MRS. SØRBY   You may be quite sure I told him myself.

GREGERS   Oh?

MRS. SØRBY   Your father knows every last thing that anyone could possibly say about me with any truth. I've told him everything of that kind. It was the first thing I did when I realized what he had in mind.

GREGERS   Then I'd say you are exceptionally frank.

MRS. SØRBY   I have always been frank. For us women it's the best policy.

HJALMAR   What do you say to that, Gina?

GINA   Oh, us women can't all be the same. Some's made one way and some another.

MRS. SØRBY   Well, Gina, I do think it's best to go about things as I did. And Werle hasn't kept back anything about himself, either. You know, that's mainly what brought us together. With me he can sit and talk as openly as a child. He never got a chance to do that before. Imagine, a healthy, vigorous man like him, listening all his youth and the best years of his life to nothing but hell-fire sermons. And many a time sermons about completely imaginary offenses—to judge by what I've heard.

GINA   That's God's truth, all right.

GREGERS   If you ladies are going to embark on that topic, you'll have to excuse me.

MRS. SØRBY   There's no need to go on that account. I won't say another word. But I wanted you to know that I haven't hushed up a thing or done anything underhanded. People may say I'm making quite a catch—and so I am, in a way. But still, I don't think I'm getting any more than I'm giving. I will never let him down. And I can look after him and help him as nobody else can, now that he'll soon be helpless.

HJALMAR   Soon be helpless?

GREGERS   [*to* MRS. SØRBY]   All right, all right, don't talk about it here.

MRS. SØRBY   It's no use trying to hide it any more, much as he'd like to. He's going blind.

HJALMAR   [*struck*]   Going blind? But how extraordinary. He too?

GINA   Well, lots of people do.

MRS. SØRBY   And you can imagine what that means for a businessman. Well, I'll try to use my eyes for him as best I can. But now I really must be going, I've got a thousand things to do.—Oh yes, Ekdal, I was to tell you that if there's anything at all Mr. Werle can do for you, just get in touch with Gråberg.

GREGERS   That offer you may be sure Hjalmar Ekdal will decline with thanks.

MRS. SØRBY   Really? I didn't have the impression in the past . . .

GINA   No, Berta, Hjalmar don't need anything more from Mr. Werle.

HJALMAR   [*slowly and with emphasis*]   Will you pay my respects to your intended husband and tell him that in the very near future I propose to call on Gråberg . . .

GREGERS   What! You want to do *that!*

HJALMAR   . . . to call on Gråberg, I repeat, and demand an account of what I owe his employer. I will pay that debt of honor . . . Ha-ha-ha, "debt of honor," that's a good joke! But enough of that. I will pay it all, with five per cent interest.

GINA   But Hjalmar, dear, God knows we haven't got the money for that.

HJALMAR   Will you inform your intended that I am working indefatigably on my invention. Tell him that what sustains me in that exhausting labor is the wish to free myself from a painful burden of debt. This is my motive for the invention. The entire proceeds shall be used to release me from my pecuniary obligations to your future spouse.

MRS. SØRBY   Something has happened in this house.

HJALMAR   Yes, so it has.

MRS. SØRBY   Well, good-bye then. I still had something I wanted to talk to you about, Gina, but it will have to wait for another time. Good-bye.

HJALMAR *and* GREGERS *bow silently;* GINA *follows* MRS. SØRBY *to the door.*

HJALMAR   Not a step beyond the threshold, Gina!

MRS. SØRBY *leaves;* GINA *shuts the door after her.*

HJALMAR   There, Gregers; now I've got that load of debt off my mind.

GREGERS   Soon, anyway.

HJALMAR   I believe my attitude may be called correct.

GREGERS   You are the man I always took you for.

HJALMAR   In certain cases it is impossible to disregard the claim of the ideal. As provider for my family, naturally I'm bound to writhe and groan. Believe me, it's no joke for a man without private means to pay off a debt of many years' standing—a debt over which, so to speak, the dust of oblivion had already settled. But never mind. My human dignity also demands its rights.

GREGERS [*laying his hand on his shoulder*]   Dear Hjalmar—wasn't it a good thing that I came?

HJALMAR   Yes.

GREGERS   Getting your whole situation clarified—wasn't that a good thing?

HJALMAR [*a bit impatiently*]   Yes, of course it was. But there's one thing that outrages my sense of justice.

GREGERS   And what is that?

HJALMAR   It's this, that . . . Well, I don't know if I ought to speak so freely about your father.

GREGERS   Don't hesitate in the least on *my* account.

HJALMAR   Well, then. Can't you see . . . I think it's absolutely outrageous, to realize it turns out that it's not I but *he* who will achieve the true marriage.

GREGERS   How can you say such a thing!

HJALMAR   Because it's so. Aren't your father and Mrs. Sørby entering upon a marriage built on full confidence, built on complete and unconditional frankness on both sides? They sweep nothing under the carpet, nothing is hushed up between them. There has been declared between them, if I may so put it, mutual forgiveness of sin.

GREGERS   All right, what about it?

HJALMAR   Well—then it's all *there*. You said yourself this was the difficulty in founding the true marriage.

GREGERS   But Hjalmar, that's entirely different. Surely you're not going to compare either yourself or her with those two . . . ? Oh, *you* know what I mean.

HJALMAR   All the same, I can't get over the fact that there's something in all this that offends my sense of justice. Why, it looks exactly as if there were no divine Providence in the world.

GINA   For God's sake, Hjalmar, don't talk like that.

GREGERS   Hm; let's not get involved in those questions.

HJALMAR   Though on the other hand, I think I'm beginning to make out the hand of fate after all. He *is* going blind.

GINA   Oh, maybe it's not so certain.

HJALMAR   There's no doubt about it. At least we *ought* not to doubt it, because precisely in that fact lies the proof of just retribution. He blinded the eyes of a trusting fellow being once.

GREGERS   Alas, he has blinded many.

HJALMAR   And now comes Nemesis, mysterious and inexorable, and demands the man's own eyes.[5]

GINA   Don't say such awful things! It scares me.

HJALMAR   It profits a man to immerse himself, once in a while, in the dark side of existence.

> HEDVIG, *in her hat and coat, comes in through the hall door, happy and breathless.*

GINA   Are you back already?

HEDVIG   Yes, I didn't feel like walking any more. It was lucky, too, because I just met somebody outside the house.

HJALMAR   That Mrs. Sørby, I suppose.

HEDVIG   Yes.

HJALMAR   [*pacing the floor*]   I hope you have seen her for the last time.

> Silence. HEDVIG *looks timidly from one to the other as though trying to gauge their mood.*

HEDVIG   [*approaching* HJALMAR, *ingratiatingly*]   Daddy . . . ?

HJALMAR   Well—what is it, Hedvig?

HEDVIG   Mrs. Sørby brought something for me.

HJALMAR   [*halts*]   For you?

HEDVIG   Yes. It's something for tomorrow.

GINA   Berta always brings some little thing for your birthday.

HJALMAR   What is it?

HEDVIG   No, you're not supposed to find out yet. Mother is to bring it to me in bed first thing in the morning.

HJALMAR   All these intrigues; all these secrets . . . !

HEDVIG   [*hastily*]   Oh, you can see it if you want. It's a big letter. [*Takes the letter out of her coat pocket.*]

HJALMAR   A letter too?

HEDVIG   The letter is all there is. The other thing is coming later on, I guess. But imagine—a letter! I never got a letter before. And it says "Miss" on the outside. [*Reads.*] "Miss Hedvig Ekdal." Imagine —that's me!

HJALMAR   Let me see that letter.

HEDVIG   [*handing it to him*]   There, you see?

HJALMAR   It's Mr. Werle's handwriting.

GINA   Are you sure, Hjalmar?

HJALMAR   See for yourself.

GINA   What would *I* know about it?

HJALMAR   Hedvig, may I open the letter—and read it?

HEDVIG   Yes, of course you may, if you want to.

GINA   Not tonight, Hjalmar. You know it's meant for tomorrow.

HEDVIG   [*in a low voice*]   Oh, why not let him read it! It's bound to be something nice, then he'll be glad and everything will be all right again.

HJALMAR   I may open it, then?

HEDVIG   Yes, please do, Father. It will be fun to find out what it is.

HJALMAR   Very well. [*Opens the letter, reads it, and appears bewildered.*]   What *is* this . . . ?

GINA   Why, what does it say?

---

5. Nemesis was the Greek goddess of revenge, and the term is used still, as here, for providential retribution.

HEDVIG   Please, Father—tell us!

HJALMAR   Be quiet. [*Reads it through again. He has turned pale, but speaks with control.*] It's a bequest, Hedvig, a deed of gift.

HEDVIG   Really? What do I get?

HJALMAR   Read it yourself.

HEDVIG *goes over to the lamp and reads.*

HJALMAR   [*in an undertone, clenching his fists*]   The eyes! The eyes— and now this letter!

HEDVIG   [*interrupts her reading*]   Yes, but it looks to me like it's Grand- father who's getting it.

HJALMAR   [*takes the letter from her*]   You, Gina—can you understand this?

GINA   I don't know the first thing about it. Why don't you just *tell* me?

HJALMAR   Mr. Werle writes to Hedvig that her old grandfather need not trouble himself any more about the copying but that from now on he can draw a hundred crowns every month from the office . . .

GREGERS   Aha!

HEDVIG   A hundred crowns, Mother! I read that part.

GINA   That will be nice for Grandpa.

HJALMAR   . . . one hundred crowns, for as long as he needs it— naturally that means till he passes on.

GINA   Well, that's him provided for, poor old soul.

HJALMAR   But then it comes. You didn't read far enough, Hedvig. Afterwards, the gift passes to you.

HEDVIG   To me? All of it?

HJALMAR   You are assured the same amount for the rest of your life, he writes. Do you hear that, Gina?

GINA   Yes, I hear.

HEDVIG   Imagine—all the money I'm going to get! [*Shaking him.*] Father, Father, aren't you glad?

HJALMAR   [*disengages himself from her*]   Glad! [*Walking about.*] Oh, what vistas, what perspectives open up before me! It's Hedvig— *she's* the one he's providing for so amply!

GINA   Naturally. She's the one with the birthday . . .

HEDVIG   Oh, but you'll get it anyway, Father! Don't you know I'll give it all to you and Mother?

HJALMAR   To your mother, yes! There we have it.

GREGERS   Hjalmar, this is a trap that's being set for you.

HJALMAR   Another trap, you think?

GREGERS   When he was here this morning, he said: "Hjalmar Ekdal is not the man you think he is."

HJALMAR   Not the man . . . !

GREGERS   "Just wait, you'll see," he said.

HJALMAR   See that I would let myself be bought off with a bribe . . . !

HEDVIG   Mother, what *is* this all about?

GINA   Go and take off your things.

HEDVIG, *about to cry, goes out by the kitchen door.*

GREGERS   Yes, Hjalmar, now we see who is right—he or I.

HJALMAR   [*slowly tears the letter in two and lays the pieces on the table*]   Here is my answer.

GREGERS   Just as I thought.

HJALMAR   [*goes over to* GINA, *who is standing by the stove, and speaks*

in a low voice]   Now, I want the whole truth. If everything was over between you and him when you—"got to care" for me, as you call it—why did he arrange things so we could afford to get married?

GINA   I guess he thought he'd be able to come and go here as he liked.

HJALMAR   Only that? Wasn't he afraid of a certain possibility?

GINA   I don't know what you mean.

HJALMAR   I want to know if—your child has the right to live under my roof.

GINA [*drawing herself up, her eyes flashing*]   You ask me that!

HJALMAR   I want a straight answer. Is Hedvig mine—or . . . Well?

GINA [*looks at him with cold defiance*]   I don't know.

HJALMAR [*quavering*]   You don't know!

GINA   How should *I* know? A woman like me . . .

HJALMAR [*quietly, turning away from her*]   Then I have nothing more to do in this house.

GREGERS   Think well what you're doing, Hjalmar!

HJALMAR [*putting on his overcoat*]   There's nothing to think about, for a man like me.

GREGERS   On the contrary, there's everything in the world to think about. You three must stay together if you are to win through to the sublime spirit of sacrifice and forgiveness.

HJALMAR   I don't *want* to! Never! Never! My hat! [*Takes his hat.*] My house lies in ruins about me. [*Bursts into tears.*] Gregers, I have no child!

HEDVIG [*who has opened the kitchen door*]   What are you saying! [*Up to him.*] Father! Father!

GINA   *Now* look what you did!

HJALMAR   Don't come near me, Hedvig. Get away from me. I can't bear to look at you. Oh, those eyes . . . ! Good-bye. [*He makes for the door.*]

HEDVIG [*clinging to him, cries out*]   No! No! Don't leave me!

GINA [*shouts*]   Look at the child, Hjalmar! Look at the child!

HJALMAR   I won't! I can't! I must get out—away from all this. [*He tears himself loose from* HEDVIG *and goes.*]

HEDVIG [*despair in her eyes*]   He's leaving us, Mother! He's leaving us! He'll never come back any more!

GINA   Don't you cry, Hedvig. Your father's coming back, you'll see.

HEDVIG [*throws herself sobbing on the sofa*]   No, no, he's never coming back to us again.

GREGERS   You do believe I meant it all for the best, Mrs. Ekdal?

GINA   Yes, I imagine you did. But God forgive you all the same.

HEDVIG [*on the sofa*]   Oh, I just want to die! What did I do to him! Mother, you've got to get him home again!

GINA   Yes, yes, yes. Just calm down and I'll go out and look for him. [*Putting on her coat.*] Maybe he's gone down to Relling. But you mustn't lie there bawling like that. Promise?

HEDVIG [*sobbing convulsively*]   All right, I'll stop. If only Father comes back.

GREGERS [*to* GINA, *who is about to leave*]   Wouldn't it perhaps be better if you first let him go through his ordeal?

GINA   Oh, he can do that after. First of all we have to get the child quieted down. [*Goes out by hall door.*]

HEDVIG [*sitting up, drying her tears*]   Now you've got to tell me what's the matter. Why doesn't my father want me any more?

GREGERS   You're not to ask that till you're all grown up.

HEDVIG [*with little catches in her breath*]   But I can't go on feeling so awful all the time till I'm grown up.—I know what it is. Maybe I'm not really Father's child.

GREGERS [*uneasily*]   How could that be?

HEDVIG   Mother could have found me somewhere. And now maybe Father got to know about it. I've read about things like that.

GREGERS   Well, even in that case . . .

HEDVIG   You'd think he could care for me just the same. Even more, almost. After all, we got the wild duck as a present too, and look how much I love her.

GREGERS [*glad to change the subject*]   Yes, that's right, the wild duck. Let's talk a little about the wild duck, Hedvig.

HEDVIG   That poor wild duck. He can't stand the sight of her either, any more. Imagine, he wanted to wring her neck!

GREGERS   Oh, he wouldn't do that.

HEDVIG   No, but he *said* it. And I think it's an awful thing to say, because I pray for the wild duck every night, that she should be safe from death and everything bad.

GREGERS [*looking at her*]   Do you say your prayers every night?

HEDVIG   Oh yes.

GREGERS   Who taught you that?

HEDVIG   Myself. One time when Father was terribly sick and had leeches on his neck, and he said he was lying at death's door.

GREGERS   Really?

HEDVIG   So I prayed for him when I went to bed. And I've kept it up ever since.

GREGERS   And now you pray for the wild duck too?

HEDVIG   I thought I'd better include her, because she was so sick in the beginning.

GREGERS   Do you also say your prayers in the morning?

HEDVIG   Of course not.

GREGERS   Why *not* in the morning, as well?

HEDVIG   Why, it's light in the morning, so what's there to be afraid of.

GREGERS   And that wild duck you love so much, your father wanted to wring its neck . . .

HEDVIG   No, he said he *ought* to do it, but that he would spare her for my sake. That was nice of him.

GREGERS [*drawing closer to her*]   But supposing now that you of your own free will sacrificed the wild duck for *his* sake?

HEDVIG [*rising*]   The wild duck!

GREGERS   Supposing you were ready to sacrifice for him the most precious thing you have in the world?

HEDVIG   Do you think that would help?

GREGERS   Try it, Hedvig.

HEDVIG [*softly, with eyes shining*]   Yes—I will.

GREGERS   Have you will power enough for that, do you think?

HEDVIG   I'll ask Grandfather to shoot her for me.

GREGERS   Yes, do that. But not a word about this to your mother!

HEDVIG   Why not?

GREGERS   She doesn't understand us.

HEDVIG   The wild duck . . . ? I'll do it in the morning!

GINA *enters by the hall door.*

HEDVIG [*up to her*]   Did you find him, Mother?

GINA   No, but I heard he'd been down to Relling and gone out with him.

GREGERS   Are you sure?

GINA   Yes, the janitor's wife said so. Molvik went with them too, she said.

GREGERS   At a time like this, when his soul so desperately needs to struggle in solitude . . . !

GINA [*taking off her coat*]   Yes, men sure are something. God only knows where Relling dragged him off to. I ran across to Ma Eriksen's, but they're not there.

HEDVIG [*fighting back her tears*]   What if he never comes back!

GREGERS   *He'll* come back. I shall get word to him in the morning, and then you'll *see* how he comes back. You can count on that. Sleep well, Hedvig. Goodnight. [*Goes out by hall door.*]

HEDVIG [*throws her arms around* GINA's *neck, sobbing*]   Mother! Mother!

GINA [*patting her back, sighing*]   Ah, yes. Relling knew what he was talking about, all right. This is what you get when these here maniacs get after you with their "claim of the ordeal."

Act 5

HJALMAR EKDAL's *studio in the cold gray light of morning. There is wet snow on the big panes of the skylight.*

GINA, *aproned and carrying a broom and dust cloth, enters from the kitchen and goes toward the living room door. At the same moment,* HEDVIG *rushes in from the hall.*

GINA [*stops*]   Well?

HEDVIG   Yes, Mother, I think he is down at Relling's . . .

GINA   What did I tell you!

HEDVIG   . . . because the janitor's wife said she heard Relling bring home two others when he came back last night.

GINA   I thought as much.

HEDVIG   But what good does it do, if he won't come up to us.

GINA   Well, at least I can go down and talk to him.

OLD EKDAL, *in dressing gown and slippers and smoking his pipe, appears at the door of his room.*

EKDAL   Say, Hjalmar . . . Isn't Hjalmar home?

GINA   No, he's gone out.

EKDAL   So early? In this blizzard? All right, suit yourself, I can do the morning tour without you.

He slides the attic door open. HEDVIG *helps him. He goes in, and she closes the door after him.*

HEDVIG [*in a low voice*]   Mother, just think, when poor Grandfather finds out that Father wants to leave us.

GINA   Silly! Grandpa mustn't hear anything about it. What a godsend he wasn't home yesterday in all that hullaballoo.

HEDVIG   Yes, but . . .

GREGERS *enters through the hall door.*

GREGERS   Well? Any trace of him?

GINA   He's downstairs at Relling's, from what I hear.

GREGERS   At Relling's! Has he really been out with those two?

GINA   Looks like it.

GREGERS   How *could* he—just when he desperately needed to be alone and really pull himself together . . . !

GINA   You can say *that* again.

RELLING *enters from the hall.*

HEDVIG [*up to him*]   Is Father with you?

GINA [*at the same time*]   Is he there?

RELLING   Yes, he's there all right.

HEDVIG   And you never told us!

RELLING   I know, I'm a bea-east. But first I had to look after that other bea-east, the dæmonic one, I mean. And then I dropped off into such a heavy sleep that . . .

GINA   What's Hjalmar got to say today?

RELLING   Not a thing.

HEDVIG   Isn't he talking at all?

RELLING   Not a blessed word.

GREGERS   Ah, no. I understand that so well.

GINA   What's he doing with himself then?

RELLING   He's lying on the sofa, snoring.

GINA   Oh? Yes, Hjalmar snores something terrific.

HEDVIG   He's asleep? Can he sleep now?

RELLING   Looks damn well like it.

GREGERS   It's understandable, after the spiritual upheaval he's been through . . .

GINA   And him not used to gallivantin' nights, either.

HEDVIG   Maybe it's a good thing he's getting some sleep, Mother.

GINA   That's what I'm thinking too. But in that case we'd better not wake him up too soon. Thanks a lot, Relling. Well, first I'll get the house cleaned and straightened up, and then . . . Come and help me, Hedvig.

GINA *and* HEDVIG *go into the living room.*

GREGERS [*turns to* RELLING]   How would you describe the spiritual turmoil going on in Hjalmar Ekdal?

RELLING   I'm damned if I've noticed any spiritual turmoil in him.

GREGERS   What! At such a turning point, when his whole life has acquired a new foundation . . . ! How can you imagine that with a character like Hjalmar's . . . ?

RELLING   Character! *Him?* If he ever had a tendency to anything as abnormal as you mean by "character," I assure you it was cleared out of him root and branch while he was still a boy.

GREGERS   That would indeed be strange—considering the tender upbringing he enjoyed.

RELLING   By those two crackpot, hysterical maiden aunts of his, you mean?

GREGERS   Let me tell you, *there* were women who never lost sight of the claim of the ideal . . . all right, now I suppose you'll start being funny again.

RELLING   No, I'm not in the mood. Besides, I know what I'm talking about, he has certainly spouted enough rhetoric about those "twin

soul-mothers" of his. Personally, I don't think he has much to thank them for. Ekdal's misfortune is that in his own little circle he has always been taken for a shining light . . .

GREGERS   And you don't think he is? Deep down inside, I mean.

RELLING   I never noticed anything of the kind. That his father thought so—that doesn't mean a thing. The old Lieutenant always *was* a bit simple.

GREGERS   He's always been a man with the innocence of a child. That's what you don't understand.

RELLING   All right, all right. But then when our dear sweet Hjalmar managed to get into the University—after a fashion—right away he became the light of the future for his fellow students too. Of course, he was good-looking, the rascal—pink and white—just the type the girls fall for. And as he had that easy sentimentality and that appealing something in his voice, and a pretty knack for declaiming other people's poetry and other people's ideas . . .

GREGERS   [*indignantly*]   Is it Hjalmar Ekdal you're talking about like this?

RELLING   Yes, with your permission. For that's what he looks like inside, this idol you are groveling to.

GREGERS   I hardly think I'm as blind as all that.

RELLING   Well, you're not far from it. You see, you are a sick man, too.

GREGERS   There you are right.

RELLING   Yes indeed. Yours is a complicated case. First there's this pesky fever of integrity you suffer from. And then, what's even worse, you're forever going around in a delirium of adoration—forever butting in where you don't belong, looking for something to admire.

GREGERS   Well, I certainly won't find anything of the sort where I do belong.

RELLING   The trouble is, you're so shockingly mistaken about those fabulous beings you dream up around you. Here you are at it again, coming to a tenement with your claim of the ideal. Nobody in this house is solvent.

GREGERS   If that's all you think of Hjalmar Ekdal, how can you take pleasure in being everlastingly in his company?

RELLING   Good Lord, I'm supposed to be a doctor of sorts, though I'm ashamed to say it. The least I can do is look after the sick I live in the same house with.

GREGERS   Really! Is Hjalmar Ekdal sick too?

RELLING   Pretty nearly everybody is sick, I'm afraid.

GREGERS   And what treatment are you giving Hjalmar?

RELLING   The usual. I see to it that his life-lie is kept going.

GREGERS   Life—lie? Did I hear you right . . . ?

RELLING   That's right, I said life-lie. You see, the life-lie is the stimulating principle.

GREGERS   May I ask what life-lie you're injecting into Hjalmar?

RELLING   Sorry, I don't betray professional secrets to quacks. You'd be in a position to mess him up for me even worse than you have. But the method is tried and true. I've used it on Molvik as well. Him I made "dæmonic"—that's *his* shot in the arm.

GREGERS   Then he's *not* dæmonic?

RELLING   What the devil does it mean, to be dæmonic? It's just some nonsense I hit on to keep life in him. If I hadn't done that, the poor

harmless slob would have succumbed to self-contempt and despair
years ago. Same with the old Lieutenant. Though he managed to find
his treatment by himself.

GREGERS   Lieutenant Ekdal? What about him?

RELLING   Well, what do *you* think? He, the great bear-hunter, stalking
rabbits in that dark attic. And there's not a happier sportsman alive
than that old man when he's playing around in there with all that
rubbish. The four or five dried-up Christmas trees he saved up, to
him they're the same as the whole great living Højdal forest. The
rooster and chickens, why, they're wild fowl in the treetops; and
the rabbits bumping around underfoot, they are bears he grapples
with, the lusty old Nimrod.

GREGERS   Poor, unfortunate old Lieutenant Ekdal—yes. He has certainly had to renounce the ideals of his youth.

RELLING   While I think of it, Mr. Werle junior—don't use this fancy
word "ideals." We have a perfectly good plain one: lies.

GREGERS   Are you trying to say the two things are related?

RELLING   Yes, about like typhus and typhoid fever.

GREGERS   Dr. Relling, I won't give up till I have rescued Hjalmar from
your clutches!

RELLING   So much the worse for him. Take away the life-lie from the
average person, and you take his happiness along with it. [*To*
HEDVIG, *who enters from the living room.*] Well, little duck-mother,
I'll go down and see if Papa is still lying there pondering on that
remarkable invention. [*Goes out by the hall door.*]

GREGERS   [*approaching* HEDVIG]   I can see by your look that it's not yet
accomplished.

HEDVIG   What? Oh, about the wild duck. No.

GREGERS   Your courage failed you, I suppose, when it came to the
point.

HEDVIG   No, it's not that. But when I woke up this morning and remembered what we had talked about, it seemed so queer.

GREGERS   Queer?

HEDVIG   Yes, I don't know . . . Last night, right when you said it, I
thought there was something so lovely about the idea; but after I
slept and it all came back to me again, it didn't seem like anything
much.

GREGERS   Ah no, you could hardly be expected to grow up in this
house without being the worse for it in some way.

HEDVIG   I don't care anything about that. If only my father would
come back . . .

GREGERS   Ah, had your eyes but been opened to what really makes
life worthwhile—had you the true, joyful, courageous spirit of sacrifice, then you would see how fast he'd come back to you.—But I
still have faith in you, Hedvig. [*He goes out through hall door.*]

> HEDVIG *wanders about the room. She is about to go into the*
> *kitchen, when there is a knocking from within the attic.* HEDVIG
> *goes and opens the door a little way.* OLD EKDAL *comes out;*
> *she pushes the door to again.*

EKDAL   Hm, not much fun going for your morning walk by yourself.

HEDVIG   Wouldn't you like to go hunting, Grandfather?

EKDAL   It's not hunting weather today. So *dark.* You can hardly see
in front of you.

HEDVIG   Don't you ever feel like shooting something besides rabbits?

EKDAL   Why, aren't the rabbits good enough, maybe?

HEDVIG   Yes, but how about the wild duck?

EKDAL   Ho, ho, so you're scared I'll go and shoot your wild duck? Never in the world, child. Never.

HEDVIG   No, I guess you couldn't. It's supposed to be very hard to shoot wild ducks.

EKDAL   Couldn't I? Should hope to say I could.

HEDVIG   How would you go about it, Grandfather?—I don't mean with *my* wild duck, but with some other one.

EKDAL   Would aim to get the shot in just below the breast, you know. That's the surest. And then you've got to shoot *against* the lie of the feathers, see, not *with*.

HEDVIG   Do they die then, Grandfather?

EKDAL   Damn right they die—if you shoot 'em properly. Well, got to go and spruce up. Hm . . . you know why . . . hm. [*Goes into his room.*]

> HEDVIG *waits a moment, glances toward the living room door, goes to the bookcase, and, standing on tiptoe, takes the double-barreled pistol down off the shelf and looks at it.* GINA, *with broom and dust cloth, enters from the living room.* HEDVIG *hastily puts back the pistol, without* GINA *noticing.*

GINA   Don't go fooling with your father's things, Hedvig.

HEDVIG [*moving away from the bookcase*]   I only wanted to straighten up a little.

GINA   Why don't you go in the kitchen and see if the coffee is still hot, I'm taking a tray down to him when I go.

> HEDVIG *goes out.* GINA *begins to clear the studio. Presently the hall door is hesitantly opened, and* HJALMAR EKDAL *looks in. He has his overcoat on, but no hat. He looks unwashed and unkempt; his eyes are sleepy and dull.*

GINA [*stops in the midst of sweeping and looks at him*]   Bless me, Hjalmar—are you back after all?

HJALMAR [*enters, answers in a dull voice*]   I come—only to depart at once.

GINA   Yes, yes, I imagine. But, gosh sakes! Don't you look a sight!

HJALMAR   A sight?

GINA   And just look at your good wintercoat! Well, that's had it.

HEDVIG [*at the kitchen door*]   Mother, do you want me . . . [*Sees* HJALMAR, *gives a shout of joy and runs toward him.*] Father! Father!

HJALMAR [*turns aside and waves her away*]   Go away! Go away! [*To* GINA.] Get her away from me, I tell you!

GINA [*in a low voice*]   Go in the living room, Hedvig.

> HEDVIG *goes in silently.*

HJALMAR [*busy, pulling out the table drawer*]   I must have my books with me. Where are my books?

GINA   What books?

HJALMAR   My scientific works, naturally—the technical journals I use for my invention.

GINA [*looking in the bookcase*]   Is it these here that there's no covers on?

HJALMAR   Yes, of course.

GINA [*puts a pile of unbound volumes on the table*]   Shouldn't I get Hedvig to cut the pages for you?

HJALMAR   Nobody needs to cut pages for me.

Short silence.

GINA   So you've made up your mind to leave us, Hjalmar?

HJALMAR [*rummaging among the books*]   That goes without saying, I should think.

GINA   All right.

HJALMAR [*vehemently*]   You expect me to stay around here and have a knife twisted in my heart every minute of the day?

GINA   God forgive you for thinking I could be that bad.

HJALMAR   Prove to me . . . !

GINA   Seems to me *you're* the one that's got something to prove.

HJALMAR   With a past like yours? There are certain claims . . . I am tempted to call them claims of the ideal . . .

GINA   And what about Grandpa? What's to become of *him,* poor old thing?

HJALMAR   I know my duty. The helpless old man comes with me. I must go into town and make the necessary arrangements . . . Hm . . . [*Hesitantly.*] Has anybody found my hat on the stairs?

GINA   No. Did you lose your hat?

HJALMAR   Of course I had it on when I came back last night, there's no doubt about that. But now I can't find it.

GINA   Gosh sakes, wherever did you go with them two rowdies?

HJALMAR   Oh, don't bother me with trivialities. Do you think I'm in a mood to remember details?

GINA   I only hope you didn't catch a cold, Hjalmar. [*Goes into kitchen.*]

HJALMAR [*talking angrily to himself in a low voice as he empties the drawer*]   You're a scoundrel, Relling!—A villain is what you are! You rotten traitor!—If I could just get somebody to murder you!

He puts some old letters to one side, finds the torn gift document of the day before, picks it up and looks at the pieces. As GINA *enters, he quickly puts them down again.*

GINA [*setting a laden coffee tray on the table*]   Here's a drop of something hot, in case you'd like it. And some cold cuts.

HJALMAR [*glances at the tray*]   Cold cuts? Never again, under this roof! True, I've taken no solid nourishment for nearly twenty-four hours, but never mind.—My notes! The beginning of my memoirs! Where have you put my diary and all my important papers? [*Opens the door to the living room, but draws back.*] There she is again!

GINA   For God's sake, Hjalmar, the child's got to be *some*place.

HJALMAR   Get out.

He stands back. HEDVIG, *terrified, comes into the studio.*

HJALMAR [*his hand on the doorknob, to* GINA]   As I spend these last moments in what was once my home, I wish to be spared the presence of intruders . . . [*Goes into the living room.*]

HEDVIG [*darting towards her mother, asks in a low and trembling voice*]   Does he mean me?

GINA   Stay in the kitchen, Hedvig. Or no—better go to your own room.

[*To* HJALMAR, *as she goes in to him.*] Wait a minute, Hjalmar, don't mess up the whole bureau. I know where everything is.

HEDVIG [*stands motionless for a moment, in terror and confusion, biting her lips to keep from crying. Then she clenches her hands convulsively and says softly*] The wild duck!

> She steals across and takes the pistol from the shelf, opens the attic door a little, slips in and pulls it shut after her. HJALMAR *and* GINA *begin arguing in the living room.*

HJALMAR [*appears with some notebooks and a pile of old sheets of paper, which he puts on the table*] Oh, what good will the valise do! There are a thousand things I've got to drag along with me.

GINA [*follows with the valise*] Well, leave the rest for the time being, just take a clean shirt and some underwear.

HJALMAR Phew! All these exhausting preparations! [*Takes off his overcoat and throws it on the sofa.*]

GINA Meantime your coffee's standing there getting cold.

HJALMAR Hm. [*Without thinking, he takes a mouthful, and then another.*]

GINA [*dusting the backs of the chairs*] Your worst job will be finding another attic big enough for the rabbits.

HJALMAR What! Am I expected to drag along all those rabbits too?

GINA Well, Grandpa can't do without his rabbits, you know that.

HJALMAR He'll just have to get used to it. There are more important things in life than rabbits that I have to give up.

GINA [*dusting the bookcase*] Should I put your flute in the bag for you?

HJALMAR No. No flute for me. But give me the pistol.

GINA You want to take that old gun with you?

HJALMAR Yes. My loaded pistol.

GINA [*looking for it*] It's gone. He must have taken it in with him.

HJALMAR Is he in the attic?

GINA Sure he's in the attic.

HJALMAR Hm. Poor lonely old man. [*He eats an open-face sandwich, finishes his cup of coffee.*]

GINA If only we hadn't rented out the room, you could've moved in there.

HJALMAR And stay under the same roof as . . . ! Never! Never!

GINA But couldn't you move into the living room for a day or two? There you could have everything all to yourself.

HJALMAR Never, within these walls!

GINA Well, how about moving in with Relling and Molvik, then?

HJALMAR Don't mention their names to me! I get sick just thinking about them. Oh no, I must out into the storm and the snowdrifts— go from house to house seeking shelter for my father and myself.

GINA But Hjalmar, you haven't got a hat! You lost your hat, remember?

HJALMAR Oh, that despicable pair, those depraved villains! A hat must be procured. [*Takes another sandwich.*] Arrangements must be made. After all, I don't propose to catch my death of cold. [*Looks for something on the tray.*]

GINA What are you looking for?

HJALMAR Butter.

GINA In a minute. [*Goes into the kitchen.*]

HJALMAR [*calls after her*]   Oh, don't bother. Dry bread is good enough for me.

GINA [*bringing a butter dish*]   Here you are. It's fresh churned, they told me.

> *She pours him another cup of coffee. He sits down on the sofa, spreads more butter on his bread, eats and drinks in silence for a while.*

HJALMAR   Could I, without being interfered with by anyone—and I mean *anyone*—stay in the living room a day or two, do you suppose?

GINA   Sure you could, if you wanted.

HJALMAR   Because I don't see much likelihood of moving all of Father's things in such a rush.

GINA   And another thing, too. First you'll have to tell him you're not going to live with us others no more.

HJALMAR [*pushes his cup away*]   That too, yes. To have to go into all these complicated matters all over again . . . I must consider ways and means. I must have breathing space. I can't take on all these burdens in a single day.

GINA   No, and in such rotten weather, too.

HJALMAR [*moving Werle's letter*]   I see this paper is still lying around.

GINA   Yes, *I* didn't touch it.

HJALMAR   Not that that scrap of paper concerns me . . .

GINA   Well, *I* certainly don't intend to use it.

HJALMAR   . . . still, I don't suppose we should just let it get destroyed. In all the confusion while I'm moving out it could easily . . .

GINA   I'll take care of it, Hjalmar.

HJALMAR   After all, the letter belongs to Father in the first place; it's his business whether he wants to make use of it or not.

GINA [*sighing*]   Yes, poor old Father . . .

HJALMAR   Just to be on the safe side . . . Where will I find some paste?

GINA [*goes to the bookshelf*]   Here's the paste.

HJALMAR   And a brush?

GINA   The brush is here too. [*Brings him the things.*]

HJALMAR [*picks up a pair of scissors*]   Just a strip of paper along the back . . . [*Cutting and pasting.*] Far be it from me to lay hands on somebody else's property—least of all a penniless old man's. —Well, or on—the other person's, either . . . There we are. Let it stay there a while. And when it's dry—remove it. I don't wish to lay eyes on that document again. Ever!

> GREGERS WERLE *enters from the hall.*

GREGERS [*a little surprised*]   What—you sitting here, Hjalmar?

HJALMAR [*gets up quickly*]   I sank down from sheer exhaustion.

GREGERS   I see you've had breakfast, though.

HJALMAR   The body, too, makes claims on us occasionally.

GREGERS   What have you decided to do?

HJALMAR   For a man like myself there is but one way open. I am in the process of gathering together my most important possessions. But you realize it takes time.

GINA [*a bit impatient*]   Well, do I get the room ready for you, or do I pack the bag?

HJALMAR [*after an irritated glance at* GREGERS] Pack—and get the room ready.

GINA [*takes the valise*] All right. I'll put in the shirt and the other things, then. [*Goes into the living room and shuts the door behind her.*]

GREGERS [*after a short pause*] I never dreamed it would end like this. Is it really necessary for you to leave house and home?

HJALMAR [*paces restlessly up and down*] What do you expect me to do?—I'm not made for unhappiness, Gregers. I must have things nice and secure and peaceful around me.

GREGERS But *can't* you stay? Just try. To my mind you now have a firm foundation to build on—so start all over again. And remember, you have your invention to live for, besides.

HJALMAR Oh, don't talk about the invention. It may be a long way off yet.

GREGERS Really?

HJALMAR For God's sake, what do you expect me to invent, anyway? They've already invented just about everything. It gets to be more difficult every day . . .

GREGERS After all the work you've put into it . . . !

HJALMAR It was that dissolute Relling who got me into it.

GREGERS Relling?

HJALMAR Yes, he was the one who first called attention to my talent for making some marvelous invention or other in photography.

GREGERS Aha! . . . It was Relling!

HJALMAR Oh, what deep satisfaction I got out of that thing. Not so much the invention itself, but because Hedvig believed in it—believed with all the faith and fervor of a child . . . that is, like a fool I went around imagining she believed in it.

GREGERS Can you really think that Hedvig deceived you!

HJALMAR I'm ready to think anything now. It's Hedvig that stands in the way. She'll end up shutting the sun out of my life forever.

GREGERS Hedvig! You mean Hedvig? How could *she* do anything like that?

HJALMAR [*without answering*] It's beyond words, how I loved that child. Beyond words, how happy I was every time I came home to my humble rooms and she would run to greet me, with her sweet blinking eyes. Oh, credulous fool that I was! I loved her so unutterably—and so I persuaded myself of the fiction that she loved me the same.

GREGERS Are you saying it wasn't true?

HJALMAR How can I tell? Gina I can't get a word out of. And anyway she has absolutely no conception of the principles involved in the situation. But I do feel the need to unburden myself to you, Gregers. It's this terrible doubt . . . Maybe Hedvig never really loved me at all.

GREGERS You may yet have proof that she did. [*Listening.*] What's that? The wild duck's cry?

HJALMAR She's quacking. Father's in there.

GREGERS Is he! [*Joy lights up his face.*] I tell you, you may yet have proof that your poor misunderstood Hedvig loves you!

HJALMAR Oh, what proof can she give me! I don't dare believe in any assurance from *that* quarter.

GREGERS   Surely Hedvig is incapable of deception.

HJALMAR   Oh, Gregers, that's just what isn't so certain. Who knows what Gina and that Mrs. Sørby have sat here whispering and tittle-tattling about? And nothing escapes Hedvig, believe me. It could even be that the birthday gift wasn't such a surprise. As a matter of fact, I thought I noticed something of the kind.

GREGERS   What on earth has got into you!

HJALMAR   My eyes have been opened. Just you watch—you'll see, the gift is only a beginning. Mrs. Sørby always did have a great liking for Hedvig, and now of course she's in a position to do whatever she wants for the child. They can take her away from me any time they like.

GREGERS   Hedvig would never leave you. Never.

HJALMAR   Don't be too sure. With them standing and beckoning to her with full hands? And I who have loved her so unutterably . . . ! I, whose greatest joy it would have been to take her gently by the hand and lead her, as one leads a child that's afraid of the dark through a great empty room! —I feel it now with painful certainty— the poor photographer in his attic apartment never really meant anything to her. She was just shrewd enough to play along with him till the time was ripe.

GREGERS   Hjalmar, you don't believe that yourself.

HJALMAR   The terrible thing is just that I don't know what to believe —that I can *never* know. But do you really doubt that I'm right? Hoho, my dear Gregers, you count too much on the claim of the ideal! Just let the others come with overflowing hands and call to the child: Leave him; life awaits you here with us . . .

GREGERS   [*quickly*]   Yes, what then, do you think?

HJALMAR   If I asked her then: Hedvig, are you willing to turn your back on life for me? [*Laughs scornfully.*] Thanks a lot—you'd soon hear the answer I'd get!

A pistol shot is heard from within the attic.

GREGERS   [*shouts with joy*]   Hjalmar!

HJALMAR   Damn! He *would* have to go hunting now!

GINA   [*entering*]   Ugh, Hjalmar, it sounds like the old man's banging away in there by himself.

HJALMAR   I'll go have a look . . .

GREGERS   [*quickly, excitedly*]   Wait! Do you know what that was?

HJALMAR   Of course I know.

GREGERS   No, you don't. But *I* know. That was the proof!

HJALMAR   What proof?

GREGERS   It was a child's act of sacrifice. She's got your father to shoot the wild duck.

HJALMAR   Shoot the wild duck!

GINA   Imagine . . . !

HJALMAR   Whatever for?

GREGERS   She wanted to sacrifice to you the most precious thing she had in the world. Because then, she thought, you would be sure to love her again.

HJALMAR   [*softly, with emotion*]   Oh, that child!

GINA   The things she'll think of!

GREGERS   All she wanted was to have your love again, Hjalmar. She felt she couldn't live without it.

GINA [*fighting back her tears*]   There you see, Hjalmar.

HJALMAR   Gina, where is she?

GINA [*sniffling*]   Poor little thing, sitting out in the kitchen, I guess.

HJALMAR [*crosses, and throws open the kitchen door*]   Hedvig— come! Come to me! [*Looks around.*] No, she's not in here.

GINA   Then she must be in her little room. [HJALMAR *walks out.*]

HJALMAR [*offstage*]   No, she's not here either. [*Re-enters the studio.*] She must have gone out.

GINA   Well, you wouldn't let her stay anyplace in the house.

HJALMAR   Oh, if only she'd come home soon—so I can tell her . . . Everything will be all right now, Gregers. Now I really believe we can start life over again.

GREGERS [*quietly*]   I knew it. Redemption would come through the child.

> OLD EKDAL *appears at the door of his room. He is in full uni-form, and is busy trying to buckle on his saber.*

HJALMAR [*astonished*]   Father! You *there?*

GINA   You were shooting in your *room?*

EKDAL [*approaches indignantly*]   So, now you go hunting without me, do you, Hjalmar?

HJALMAR [*tense, bewildered*]   You mean it wasn't you that fired the shot in the attic?

EKDAL   Me? Hm!

GREGERS [*calls out to* HJALMAR]   She has shot the wild duck herself!

HJALMAR   What *is* all this? [*Rushes to the attic door, tears it open, looks in, and screams.*] Hedvig!

GINA [*running to the door*]   My God, what is it?

HJALMAR [*going inside*]   She's lying on the floor!

GREGERS   Hedvig? On the floor? [*Follows* HJALMAR *in.*]

GINA [*at the same time*]   Hedvig! [*Enters the attic.*] No! No! No!

EKDAL   Ho-ho, so *she's* taken to hunting too, now.

> HJALMAR, GINA, *and* GREGERS *carry* HEDVIG *into the studio. Her right hand hangs down, the fingers still gripping the pistol.*

HJALMAR [*dazed*]   The pistol went off. She's been hit. Call for help! Help!

GINA [*runs out into the hall and shouts down*]   Relling! Relling! Dr. Relling, come up here quick!

> HJALMAR *and* GREGERS *lay* HEDVIG *down on the sofa.*

EKDAL [*quietly*]   The forest's revenge.

HJALMAR [*on his knees beside* HEDVIG]   She'll come to, right away. She's coming to—yes, yes, yes.

GINA [*having returned*]   Where is she hit? I can't see a thing . . .

> RELLING *hurries in, followed closely by* MOLVIK. *The latter is without vest or collar, and his jacket is unbuttoned.*

RELLING   What's going on here?

GINA   They say Hedvig shot herself.

HJALMAR   Come here and help!

RELLING   Shot herself! [*He pushes the table aside and starts to examine her.*]

HJALMAR [*still kneeling, looking anxiously up at him*]   Surely it can't

be serious? What, Relling? She's hardly bleeding at all. Surely it can't be serious?

RELLING   How did this happen?

HJALMAR   Oh, how do I know . . .

GINA   She wanted to shoot the wild duck.

RELLING   The wild duck?

HJALMAR   The pistol must have gone off by itself.

RELLING   Hm. Indeed.

EKDAL   The forest's revenge. Still, I'm not afraid. [*Goes into the attic and shuts himself in.*]

HJALMAR   Well, Relling . . . why don't you *say* something?

RELLING   The bullet entered the chest.

HJALMAR   Yes, but she's coming to!

RELLING   Can't you see? Hedvig is dead.

GINA [*bursts into tears*]   Oh, my baby! My baby!

GREGERS [*huskily*]   In the depths of the sea . . .

HJALMAR [*springing up*]   No, no, she's *got* to live! Oh dear God, Relling—just for a moment—just long enough so I can tell her how unutterably I loved her the whole time!

RELLING   The heart's been hit. Internal hemorrhage. She died instantly.

HJALMAR   And I drove her away from me like an animal! And in terror she crept into the attic and died for love of me. [*Sobbing.*] Never to be able to make up for it! Never to be able to tell her . . . ! [*Clenches his hands and cries to heaven.*] Oh, Thou above . . . ! If Thou *art* there! Why hast Thou done this thing to me . . .

GINA   Hush, hush, you mustn't carry on like this. I guess maybe we didn't have the right to keep her.

MOLVIK   The child is not dead. She but sleeps.

RELLING   Nonsense.

HJALMAR [*quiets down, goes over to the sofa, folds his arms, and looks at* HEDVIG]   There she lies, so stiff and still.

RELLING [*trying to free the pistol*]   It's so tight, so tight.

GINA   No, no, Relling, don't hurt her fingers. Leave the gun be.

HJALMAR   She shall take it with her.

GINA   Yes, let her. But the child's not going to lie out here for a show. She'll go into her own little room, that's what. Give me a hand, Hjalmar.

HJALMAR *and* GINA *take* HEDVIG *between them.*

HJALMAR [*as they carry her out*]   Oh, Gina, Gina, can you bear this!

GINA   We'll have to help each other. Now she's as much yours as mine.

MOLVIK [*stretching forth his arms and mumbling*]   Praised be the name of the Lord. Dust unto dust . . . dust unto dust . . .

RELLING [*whispers*]   Shut up, man! You're drunk.

HJALMAR *and* GINA *carry the body out by the kitchen door.* RELLING *shuts it after them.* MOLVIK *slinks out into the hall.*

RELLING [*crosses to* GREGERS]   No one will ever persuade me that this was an accident.

GREGERS [*who has stood horror-stricken, twitching convulsively*]   Who can say how this terrible thing happened.

RELLING   There were powder burns on her dress. She must have pressed the muzzle right against her chest and fired.

GREGERS   Hedvig has not died in vain. Did you see how this sorrow brought out all the nobility in him?

RELLING   Most people become noble when they stand in the presence of death. But how long do you think this glory of his will last?

GREGERS   Surely it will last and flourish for the rest of his life!

RELLING   Before the year is out little Hedvig will be nothing more to him than a theme for pretty declamations.

GREGERS   You dare say that about Hjalmar Ekdal!

RELLING   We'll talk about it again when the first grass has withered on her grave. *Then* listen to the vomit about "the child untimely torn from its father's breast," *then* watch him wallow in sentimentality and self-admiration and self-pity. Just you wait!

GREGERS   If *you* are right, and *I* am wrong, then life's not worth living.

RELLING   Oh, life wouldn't be too bad if it weren't for these blessed bill collectors who come pestering us poor folk with their claims of the ideal.

GREGERS   [*staring into space*]   In that case, I'm glad my destiny is what it is.

RELLING   And may I ask—what *is* your destiny?

GREGERS   [*on the point of leaving*]   To be the thirteenth man at the table.

RELLING   The devil it is.

1885

EUROPEAN TITLES

In reading a play like *The Wild Duck,* one should remember that certain titles or forms of address carried a different implication for the nineteenth-century European than they would for twentieth-century Americans. Three used in the play require some elucidation.

When Pettersen tells the hired servant that old Ekdal was once a lieutenant, the response of the hired servant depends on the fact that the title indicated other than the kind of callow incompetent implied in our familiar term "shavetail." Officers of all ranks were generally members of distinguished and well-to-do families, sometimes younger sons who were destined for the army from birth. Understanding this about old Ekdal, we can better appreciate Hjalmar's sense of disgrace in the fallen fortunes of his family and his comments to Gregers about Gina, which imply that he had married beneath him.

At this period titles of nobility had been abolished in Norway, but the title "chamberlain" (*Kammerherr*) was used to indicate officers of the royal court, in many cases certainly honorary officers.

The term "Miss" (*Frøken*), which Hedvig is pleased to find before her name on the letter containing the deed of gift, implied not only that she was growing up but also a certain amount of social status, as the same term implies in the title of Strindberg's *Fröken Julie* (variously translated "Miss Julie" or "Lady Julia").

II

LUIGI PIRANDELLO

Six Characters in Search of an Author *

A COMEDY IN THE MAKING

CHARACTERS OF THE COMEDY IN THE MAKING

THE FATHER
THE MOTHER
THE STEPDAUGHTER
THE SON

THE BOY
THE CHILD
(*The last two do not speak.*)
MADAME PACE

ACTORS OF THE COMPANY

THE MANAGER
LEADING LADY
LEADING MAN
SECOND LADY LEAD
L'INGÉNUE
JUVENILE LEAD
OTHER ACTORS AND ACTRESSES

PROPERTY MAN
PROMPTER
MACHINIST
MANAGER'S SECRETARY
DOORKEEPER
SCENE-SHIFTERS

SCENE: *Daytime. The stage of a theater.*

N. B. *The Comedy is without acts or scenes. The performance is interrupted once, without the curtain being lowered, when the manager and the chief characters withdraw to arrange the scenario. A second interruption of the action takes place when, by mistake, the stage hands let the curtain down.*

Act 1

The spectators will find the curtain raised and the stage as it usually is during the day time. It will be half dark, and empty, so that from the beginning the public may have the impression of an impromptu performance.

Prompter's box and a small table and chair for the MANAGER. *Two other small tables and several chairs scattered about as during rehearsals.*

The ACTORS *and* ACTRESSES *of the company enter from the back of the stage: first one, then another, then two together; nine or ten in all. They are about to rehearse a Pirandello play: Mixing It Up.[1] Some of the company move off towards their dressing rooms. The* PROMPTER, *who has the "book" under his arm, is waiting for the* MANAGER *in order to begin the rehearsal.*

---

* Translated by Edward Storer.

1. The play referred to is Pirandello's *Il Giuoco delle Parti* (1918).

The ACTORS *and* ACTRESSES, *some standing, some sitting, chat and smoke. One perhaps reads a paper; another cons his part.*

Finally, the MANAGER *enters and goes to the table prepared for him. His* SECRETARY *brings him his mail, through which he glances. The* PROMPTER *takes his seat, turns on a light, and opens the "book."*

THE MANAGER [*throwing a letter down on the table*] I can't see. [*To* PROPERTY MAN.] Let's have a little light, please!

PROPERTY MAN Yes sir, yes, at once. [*A light comes down on to the stage.*]

THE MANAGER [*clapping his hands*] Come along! Come along! Second act of "Mixing It Up." [*Sits down.*]

The ACTORS *and* ACTRESSES *go from the front of the stage to the wings, all except the three who are to begin the rehearsal.*

THE PROMPTER [*reading the "book"*] "Leo Gala's house. A curious room serving as dining-room and study."

THE MANAGER [*to* PROPERTY MAN] Fix up the old red room.

PROPERTY MAN [*noting it down*] Red set. All right!

THE PROMPTER [*continuing to read from the "book"*] "Table already laid and writing desk with books and papers. Book-shelves. Exit rear to Leo's bedroom. Exit left to kitchen. Principal exit to right."

THE MANAGER [*energetically*] Well, you understand: The principal exit over there; here, the kitchen. [*Turning to actor who is to play the part of* SOCRATES.] You make your entrances and exits here. [*To* PROPERTY MAN.] The baize doors at the rear, and curtains.

PROPERTY MAN [*noting it down*] Right!

PROMPTER [*reading as before*] "When the curtain rises, Leo Gala, dressed in cook's cap and apron, is busy beating an egg in a cup. Philip, also dressed as a cook, is beating another egg. Guido Venanzi is seated and listening."

LEADING MAN [*to* MANAGER] Excuse me, but must I absolutely wear a cook's cap?

THE MANAGER [*annoyed*] I imagine so. It says so there anyway. [*Pointing to the "book."*]

LEADING MAN But it's ridiculous!

THE MANAGER [*jumping up in a rage*] Ridiculous? Ridiculous? Is it my fault if France won't send us any more good comedies, and we are reduced to putting on Pirandello's works, where nobody understands anything, and where the author plays the fool with us all? [*The* ACTORS *grin. The* MANAGER *goes to* LEADING MAN *and shouts.*] Yes sir, you put on the cook's cap and beat eggs. Do you suppose that with all this egg-beating business you are on an ordinary stage? Get that out of your head. You represent the shell of the eggs you are beating! [*Laughter and comments among the* ACTORS.] Silence! and listen to my explanations, please! [*To* LEADING MAN.] "The empty form of reason without the fullness of instinct, which is blind."—You stand for reason, your wife is instinct. It's a mixing up of the parts, according to which you who act your own part become the puppet of yourself. Do you understand?

LEADING MAN I'm hanged if I do.

THE MANAGER Neither do I. But let's get on with it. It's sure to be a

glorious failure anyway. [*Confidentially.*] But I say, please face three-quarters. Otherwise, what with the abstruseness of the dialogue, and the public that won't be able to hear you, the whole thing will go to hell. Come on! come on!

PROMPTER Pardon sir, may I get into my box? There's a bit of a draught.

THE MANAGER Yes, yes, of course!

At this point, the DOORKEEPER *has entered from the stage door and advances towards the* MANAGER's *table, taking off his braided cap. During this maneuver, the* SIX CHARACTERS *enter, and stop by the door at back of stage, so that when the* DOOR-KEEPER *is about to announce their coming to the* MANAGER, *they are already on the stage. A tenuous light surrounds them, almost as if irradiated by them—the faint breath of their fantastic reality.*

This light will disappear when they come forward toward the actors. They preserve, however, something of the dream lightness in which they seem almost suspended; but this does not detract from the essential reality of their forms and expressions.

He who is known as the FATHER *is a man of about 50: hair, reddish in color, thin at the temples; he is not bald, however; thick mustaches, falling over his still fresh mouth, which often opens in an empty and uncertain smile. He is fattish, pale; with an especially wide forehead. He has blue, oval-shaped eyes, very clear and piercing. Wears light trousers and a dark jacket. He is alternatively mellifluous and violent in his manner.*

The MOTHER *seems crushed and terrified as if by an intolerable weight of shame and abasement. She is dressed in modest black and wears a thick widow's veil of crêpe. When she lifts this, she reveals a wax-like face. She always keeps her eyes downcast.*

The STEPDAUGHTER *is dashing, almost impudent, beautiful. She wears mourning too, but with great elegance. She shows contempt for the timid half-frightened manner of the wretched* BOY (14 *years old, and also dressed in black*); *on the other hand, she displays a lively tenderness for her little sister, the* CHILD (*about four*), *who is dressed in white, with a black silk sash at the waist.*

The SON (22) *tall, severe in his attitude of contempt for the* FATHER, *supercilious and indifferent to the* MOTHER. *He looks as if he had come on the stage against his will.*

DOORKEEPER [*cap in hand*] Excuse me, sir . . .

THE MANAGER [*rudely*] Eh? What is it?

DOORKEEPER [*timidly*] These people are asking for you, sir.

THE MANAGER [*furious*] I am rehearsing, and you know perfectly well no one's allowed to come in during rehearsals! [*Turning to the* CHAR-ACTERS.] Who are you, please? What do you want?

THE FATHER [*coming forward a little, followed by the others who seem embarrassed*] As a matter of fact . . . we have come here in search of an author . . .

THE MANAGER [*half angry, half amazed*] An author? What author?

THE FATHER Any author, sir.

THE MANAGER   But there's no author here. We are not rehearsing a new piece.

THE STEPDAUGHTER [*vivaciously*]   So much the better, so much the better! We can be your new piece.

AN ACTOR [*coming forward from the others*]   Oh, do you hear that?

THE FATHER [*to* STEPDAUGHTER]   Yes, but if the author isn't here . . . [*to* MANAGER] unless you would be willing . . .

THE MANAGER   You are trying to be funny.

THE FATHER   No, for Heaven's sake, what are you saying? We bring you a drama, sir.

THE STEPDAUGHTER   We may be your fortune.

THE MANAGER   Will you oblige me by going away? We haven't time to waste with mad people.

THE FATHER [*mellifluously*]   Oh sir, you know well that life is full of infinite absurdities, which, strangely enough, do not even need to appear plausible, since they are true.

THE MANAGER   What the devil is he talking about?

THE FATHER   I say that to reverse the ordinary process may well be considered a madness: that is, to create credible situations, in order that they may appear true. But permit me to observe that if this be madness, it is the sole *raison d'être*[2] of your profession, gentlemen. [*The* ACTORS *look hurt and perplexed.*]

THE MANAGER [*getting up and looking at him*]   So our profession seems to you one worthy of madmen then?

THE FATHER   Well, to make seem true that which isn't true . . . without any need . . . for a joke as it were . . . Isn't that your mission, gentlemen: to give life to fantastic characters on the stage?

THE MANAGER [*interpreting the rising anger of the* COMPANY]   But I would beg you to believe, my dear sir, that the profession of the comedian is a noble one. If today, as things go, the playwrights give us stupid comedies to play and puppets to represent instead of men, remember we are proud to have given life to immortal works here on these very boards! [*The* ACTORS, *satisfied, applaud their* MANAGER.]

THE FATHER [*interrupting furiously*]   Exactly, perfectly, to living beings more alive than those who breathe and wear clothes: beings less real perhaps, but truer! I agree with you entirely. [*The* ACTORS *look at one another in amazement.*]

THE MANAGER   But what do you mean? Before, you said . . .

THE FATHER   No, excuse me, I meant it for you, sir, who were crying out that you had no time to lose with madmen, while no one better than yourself knows that nature uses the instrument of human fantasy in order to pursue her high creative purpose.

THE MANAGER   Very well,—but where does all this take us?

THE FATHER   Nowhere! It is merely to show you that one is born to life in many forms, in many shapes, as tree, or as stone, as water, as butterfly, or as woman. So one may also be born a character in a play.

THE MANAGER [*with feigned comic dismay*]   So you and these other friends of yours have been born characters?

THE FATHER   Exactly, and alive as you see! [MANAGER *and* ACTORS *burst out laughing.*]

---

2. French expression meaning justification; literally, reason to be.

THE FATHER [*hurt*]   I am sorry you laugh, because we carry in us a drama, as you can guess from this woman here veiled in black.

THE MANAGER [*losing patience at last and almost indignant*]   Oh, chuck it! Get away please! Clear out of here! [*To* PROPERTY MAN.] For Heaven's sake, turn them out!

THE FATHER [*resisting*]   No, no, look here, we . . .

THE MANAGER [*roaring*]   We come here to work, you know.

LEADING ACTOR   One cannot let oneself be made such a fool of.

THE FATHER [*determined, coming forward*]   I marvel at your incredulity, gentlemen. Are you not accustomed to see the characters created by an author spring to life in yourselves and face each other? Just because there is no "book" [*pointing to the* PROMPTER'S *box*] which contains us, you refuse to believe . . .

THE STEPDAUGHTER [*advances towards* MANAGER, *smiling and coquettish*]   Believe me, we are really six most interesting characters, sir; side-tracked however.

THE FATHER   Yes, that is the word! [*To* MANAGER *all at once.*] In the sense, that is, that the author who created us alive no longer wished, or was no longer able, materially to put us into a work of art. And this was a real crime, sir; because he who has had the luck to be born a character can laugh even at death. He cannot die. The man, the writer, the instrument of the creation will die, but his creation does not die. And to live for ever, it does not need to have extraordinary gifts or to be able to work wonders. Who was Sancho Panza? Who was Don Abbondio?[3] Yet they live eternally because—live germs as they were—they had the fortune to find a fecundating matrix, a fantasy which could raise and nourish them: make them live forever!

THE MANAGER   That is quite all right. But what do you want here, all of you?

THE FATHER   We want to live.

THE MANAGER [*ironically*]   For eternity?

THE FATHER   No, sir, only for a moment . . . in you.

AN ACTOR   Just listen to him!

LEADING LADY   They want to live, in us. . . .

JUVENILE LEAD [*pointing to the* STEPDAUGHTER]   I've no objection, as far as that one is concerned!

THE FATHER   Look here! look here! The comedy has to be made. [*To the* MANAGER.] But if you and your actors are willing, we can soon concert it among ourselves.

THE MANAGER [*annoyed*]   But what do you want to concert? We don't go in for concerts here. Here we play dramas and comedies!

THE FATHER   Exactly! That is just why we have come to you.

THE MANAGER   And where is the "book"?

THE FATHER   It is in us! [*The* ACTORS *laugh.*] The drama is in us, and we are the drama. We are impatient to play it. Our inner passion drives us on to this.

THE STEPDAUGHTER [*disdainful, alluring, treacherous, full of impudence*]   My passion, sir! Ah, if you only knew! My passion for him! [*Points to the* FATHER *and makes a pretense of embracing him. Then she breaks out into a loud laugh.*]

---

3. Sancho Panza is Don Quixote's squire in Cervantes' famous novel. Don Abbondio is a priest in Manzoni's *I Promessi Sposi* (The Fiancés), one of the most famous works of Italian literature.

THE FATHER [*angrily*]   Behave yourself! And please don't laugh in that fashion.

THE STEPDAUGHTER   With your permission, gentlemen, I, who am a two months' orphan, will show you how I can dance and sing. [*Sings and then dances* Prends garde à Tchou-Tchin-Tchou.][4]

> Les chinois sont un peuple malin,
> De Shangaî à Pékin,
> Ils ont mis des écriteaux partout:
> Prenez garde à Tchou-Tchin-Tchou.

ACTORS *and* ACTRESSES   Bravo! Well done! Tip-top!

THE MANAGER   Silence! This isn't a café concert, you know! [*Turning to the* FATHER *in consternation.*] Is she mad?

THE FATHER   Mad? No, she's worse than mad.

THE STEPDAUGHTER [*to* MANAGER]   Worse? Worse? Listen! Stage this drama for us at once! Then you will see that at a certain moment I . . . when this little darling here. . . . [*Takes the* CHILD *by the hand and leads her to the* MANAGER.] Isn't she a dear? [*Takes her up and kisses her.*] Darling! Darling! [*Puts her down again and adds feelingly.*] Well, when God suddenly takes this dear little child away from that poor mother there; and this imbecile here [*seizing hold of the* BOY *roughly and pushing him forward*] does the stupidest things, like the fool he is, you will see me run away. Yes, gentlemen, I shall be off. But the moment hasn't arrived yet. After what has taken place between him and me [*indicates the* FATHER *with a horrible wink*] I can't remain any longer in this society, to have to witness the anguish of this mother here for that fool. . . . [*Indicates the* SON.] Look at him! Look at him! See how indifferent, how frigid he is, because he is the legitimate son. He despises me, despises him [*pointing to the* BOY], despises this baby here; because . . . we are bastards. [*Goes to the* MOTHER *and embraces her.*] And he doesn't want to recognize her as his mother—she who is the common mother of us all. He looks down upon her as if she were only the mother of us three bastards. Wretch! [*She says all this very rapidly, excitedly. At the word "bastards" she raises her voice, and almost spits out the final "Wretch!"*]

THE MOTHER [*to the* MANAGER, *in anguish*]   In the name of these two little children, I beg you. . . . [*She grows faint and is about to fall.*] Oh God!

THE FATHER [*coming forward to support her as do some of the* ACTORS]   Quick, a chair, a chair for this poor widow!

THE ACTORS   Is it true? Has she really fainted?

THE MANAGER   Quick, a chair! Here!

> *One of the* ACTORS *brings a chair, the* OTHERS *proffer assistance. The* MOTHER *tries to prevent the* FATHER *from lifting the veil which covers her face.*

THE FATHER   Look at her! Look at her!

THE MOTHER   No, no; stop it please!

THE FATHER [*raising her veil*]   Let them see you!

---

4. The French words of this song mean "The Chinese are a wicked people, from Shanghai to Peking, they have put up posters everywhere: 'Watch out for Tchou-Tchin-Tchou.'" This is a French adaptation of a song called "Chu-Chin-Chow," music by Dave Stamper and words by Gene Buck, which first appeared in the Ziegfeld Follies of 1917.

THE MOTHER [*rising and covering her face with her hands, in desperation*]   I beg you, sir, to prevent this man from carrying out his plan which is loathsome to me.

THE MANAGER [*dumbfounded*]   I don't understand at all. What is the situation? Is this lady your wife? [*To the* FATHER.]

THE FATHER   Yes, gentlemen: my wife!

THE MANAGER   But how can she be a widow if you are alive? [*The* ACTORS *find relief for their astonishment in a loud laugh.*]

THE FATHER   Don't laugh! Don't laugh like that, for Heaven's sake. Her drama lies just here in this: she has had a lover, a man who ought to be here.

THE MOTHER [*with a cry*]   No! No!

THE STEPDAUGHTER   Fortunately for her, he is dead. Two months ago as I said. We are in mourning, as you see.

THE FATHER   He isn't here, you see, not because he is dead. He isn't here—look at her a moment and you will understand—because her drama isn't a drama of the love of two men for whom she was incapable of feeling anything except possibly a little gratitude—gratitude not for me but for the other. She isn't a woman, she is a mother, and her drama—powerful, sir, I assure you—lies, as a matter of fact, all in these four children she has had by two men.

THE MOTHER   I had them? Have you got the courage to say that I wanted them? [*To the* COMPANY.] It was his doing. It was he who gave me to that other man, who forced me to go away with him.

THE STEPDAUGHTER   It isn't true.

THE MOTHER [*startled*]   Not true, isn't it?

THE STEPDAUGHTER   No, it isn't true, it just isn't true.

THE MOTHER   And what can you know about it?

THE STEPDAUGHTER   It isn't true. Don't believe it. [*To* MANAGER.] Do you know why she says so? For that fellow there. [*Indicates the* SON.] She tortures herself, destroys herself on account of the neglect of that son there; and she wants him to believe that if she abandoned him when he was only two years old, it was because he [*indicates the* FATHER] made her do so.

THE MOTHER [*vigorously*]   He forced me to it, and I call God to witness it. [*To the* MANAGER.] Ask him [*indicates* HUSBAND] if it isn't true. Let him speak. You [*to* DAUGHTER] are not in a position to know anything about it.

THE STEPDAUGHTER   I know you lived in peace and happiness with my father while he lived. Can you deny it?

THE MOTHER   No, I don't deny it. . . .

THE STEPDAUGHTER   He was always full of affection and kindness for you. [*To the* BOY, *angrily.*] It's true, isn't it? Tell them! Why don't you speak, you little fool?

THE MOTHER   Leave the poor boy alone. Why do you want to make me appear ungrateful, daughter? I don't want to offend your father. I have answered him that I didn't abandon my house and my son through any fault of mine, nor from any wilful passion.

THE FATHER   It is true. It was my doing.

LEADING MAN [*to the* COMPANY]   What a spectacle!

LEADING LADY   We are the audience this time.

JUVENILE LEAD   For once, in a way.

THE MANAGER [*beginning to get really interested*]   Let's hear them out. Listen!

THE SON Oh yes, you're going to hear a fine bit now. He will talk to you of the Demon of Experiment.

THE FATHER You are a cynical imbecile. I've told you so already a hundred times. [*To the* MANAGER.] He tries to make fun of me on account of this expression which I have found to excuse myself with.

THE SON [*with disgust*] Yes, phrases! phrases!

THE FATHER Phrases! Isn't everyone consoled when faced with a trouble or fact he doesn't understand, by a word, some simple word, which tells us nothing and yet calms us?

THE STEPDAUGHTER Even in the case of remorse. In fact, especially then.

THE FATHER Remorse? No, that isn't true. I've done more than use words to quiet the remorse in me.

THE STEPDAUGHTER Yes, there was a bit of money too. Yes, yes, a bit of money. There were the hundred lire he was about to offer me in payment, gentlemen. . . . [*Sensation of horror among the* ACTORS.]

THE SON [*to the* STEPDAUGHTER] This is vile.

THE STEPDAUGHTER Vile? There they were in a pale blue envelope on a little mahogany table in the back of Madame Pace's shop. You know Madame Pace—one of those ladies who attract poor girls of good family into their ateliers, under the pretext of their selling *robes et manteaux*.⁵

THE SON And she thinks she has bought the right to tyrannize over us all with those hundred lire he was going to pay; but which, fortunately—note this, gentlemen—he had no chance of paying.

THE STEPDAUGHTER It was a near thing, though, you know! [*Laughs ironically.*]

THE MOTHER [*protesting*] Shame, my daughter, shame!

THE STEPDAUGHTER Shame indeed! This is my revenge! I am dying to live that scene. . . . The room . . . I see it. . . . Here is the window with the cloaks on display, there the divan, the looking-glass, a screen, there in front of the window the little mahogany table with the blue envelope containing one hundred lire. I see it. I see it. I could take hold of it. . . . But you, gentlemen, you ought to turn your backs now: I am almost nude, you know. But I don't blush: I leave that to him. [*Indicating* FATHER.]

THE MANAGER I don't understand this at all.

THE FATHER Naturally enough. I would ask you, sir, to exercise your authority a little here, and let me speak before you believe all she is trying to blame me with. Let me explain.

THE STEPDAUGHTER Ah yes, explain it in your own way.

THE FATHER But don't you see that the whole trouble lies here? In words, words. Each one of us has within him a whole world of things, each man of us his own special world. And how can we ever come to an understanding if I put in the words I utter the sense and value of things as I see them; while you who listen to me must inevitably translate them according to the conception of things each one of you has within himself. We think we understand each other, but we never really do. Look here! This woman [*indicating the* MOTHER] takes all my pity for her as a specially ferocious form of cruelty.

THE MOTHER But you drove me away.

---

5. French for "dresses and coats (or capes)."

THE FATHER   Do you hear her? I drove her away! She believes I really sent her away.

THE MOTHER   You know how to talk, and I don't; but, believe me, sir [*to* MANAGER], after he had married me . . . who knows why? . . . I was a poor insignificant woman. . . .

THE FATHER   But, good Heavens! it was just for your humility that I married you. I loved this simplicity in you. [*He stops when he sees she makes signs to contradict him, opens his arms wide in sign of desperation seeing how hopeless it is to make himself understood.*] You see she denies it. Her mental deafness, believe me, is phenomenal, the limit: [*touches his forehead*] deaf, deaf, mentally deaf! She has plenty of feeling. Oh yes, a good heart for the children; but the brain—deaf, to the point of desperation—!

THE STEPDAUGHTER   Yes, but ask him how his intelligence has helped us.

THE FATHER   If we could see all the evil that may spring from good, what should we do? [*At this point the* LEADING LADY, *who is biting her lips with rage at seeing the* LEADING MAN *flirting with the* STEP-DAUGHTER, *comes forward and speaks to the* MANAGER.]

LEADING LADY   Excuse me, but are we going to rehearse today?

MANAGER   Of course, of course; but let's hear them out.

JUVENILE LEAD   This is something quite new.

L'INGÉNUE   Most interesting!

LEADING LADY   Yes, for the people who like that kind of thing. [*Casts a glance at* LEADING MAN.]

THE MANAGER [*to* FATHER]   You must please explain yourself quite clearly. [*Sits down.*]

THE FATHER   Very well then: listen! I had in my service a poor man, a clerk, a secretary of mine, full of devotion, who became friends with her. [*Indicating the* MOTHER.] They understood one another, were kindred souls in fact, without, however, the least suspicion of any evil existing. They were incapable even of thinking of it.

THE STEPDAUGHTER   So he thought of it—for them!

THE FATHER   That's not true. I meant to do good to them—and to myself, I confess, at the same time. Things had come to the point that I could not say a word to either of them without their making a mute appeal, one to the other, with their eyes. I could see them silently asking each other how I was to be kept in countenance, how I was to be kept quiet. And this, believe me, was just about enough of itself to keep me in a constant rage, to exasperate me beyond measure.

THE MANAGER   And why didn't you send him away then—this secretary of yours?

THE FATHER   Precisely what I did, sir. And then I had to watch this poor woman drifting forlornly about the house like an animal without a master like an animal one has taken in out of pity.

THE MOTHER   Ah yes . . . !

THE FATHER [*suddenly turning to the* MOTHER]   It's true about the son anyway, isn't it?

THE MOTHER   He took my son away from me first of all.

THE FATHER   But not from cruelty. I did it so that he should grow up healthy and strong by living in the country.

THE STEPDAUGHTER [*pointing to him ironically*]   As one can see.

THE FATHER [*quickly*]   Is it my fault if he has grown up like this?

I sent him to a wet nurse in the country, a peasant, as *she* did not seem to me strong enough, though she is of humble origin. That was, anyway, the reason I married her. Unpleasant all this may be, but how can it be helped? My mistake possibly, but there we are! All my life I have had these confounded aspirations towards a certain solid moral sanity. [*At this point, the* STEPDAUGHTER *bursts into a noisy laugh.*] Oh, stop it! Stop it! I can't stand it.

THE MANAGER   Yes, please stop it, for Heaven's sake.

THE STEPDAUGHTER   But imagine moral sanity from him, if you please —the client of certain ateliers like that of Madame Pace!

THE FATHER   Fool! That is the proof that I am a man! This seeming contradiction, gentlemen, is the strongest proof that I stand here a live man before you. Why, it is just for this very incongruity in my nature that I have had to suffer what I have. I could not live by the side of that woman [*indicating the* MOTHER] any longer; but not so much for the boredom she inspired me with as for the pity I felt for her.

THE MOTHER   And so he turned me out—.

THE FATHER   —well provided for! Yes, I sent her to that man, gentlemen . . . to let her go free of me.

THE MOTHER   And to free himself.

THE FATHER   Yes, I admit it. It was also a liberation for me. But great evil has come of it. I meant well when I did it; and I did it more for her sake than mine. I swear it. [*Crosses his arms on his chest; then turns suddenly to the* MOTHER.] Did I ever lose sight of you until that other man carried you off to another town, like the angry fool he was? And on account of my pure interest in you . . . my pure interest, I repeat, that had no base motive in it. . . . I watched with the tenderest concern the new family that grew up around her. She can bear witness to this. [*Points to the* STEPDAUGHTER.]

THE STEPDAUGHTER   Oh yes, that's true enough. When I was a kiddie, so so high, you know, with plaits over my shoulders and panties longer than my skirts, I used to see him waiting outside the school for me to come out. He came to see how I was growing up.

THE FATHER   This is infamous, shameful!

THE STEPDAUGHTER   No. Why?

THE FATHER   Infamous! infamous! [*Then excitedly to* MANAGER *explaining.*] After she [*indicating* MOTHER] went away, my house seemed suddenly empty. She was my incubus, but she filled my house. I was like a dazed fly alone in the empty rooms. This boy here [*indicating the* SON] was educated away from home, and when he came back, he seemed to me to be no more mine. With no mother to stand between him and me, he grew up entirely for himself, on his own, apart, with no tie of intellect or affection binding him to me. And then—strange but true—I was driven, by curiosity at first and then by some tender sentiment, towards her family, which had come into being through my will. The thought of her began gradually to fill up the emptiness I felt all around me. I wanted to know if she were happy in living out the simple daily duties of life. I wanted to think of her as fortunate and happy because far away from the complicated torments of my spirit. And so, to have proof of this, I used to watch that child coming out of school.

THE STEPDAUGHTER   Yes, yes. True. He used to follow me in the street and smiled at me, waved his hand, like this. I would look at him with

interest, wondering who he might be. I told my mother, who guessed at once. [*The* MOTHER *agrees with a nod.*] Then she didn't want to send me to school for some days; and when I finally went back, there he was again—looking so ridiculous—with a paper parcel in his hands. He came close to me, caressed me, and drew out a fine straw hat from the parcel, with a bouquet of flowers—all for me!

THE MANAGER   A bit discursive this, you know!

THE SON [*contemptuously*]   Literature! Literature!

THE FATHER   Literature indeed! This is life, this is passion!

THE MANAGER   It may be, but it won't act.

THE FATHER   I agree. This is only the part leading up. I don't suggest this should be staged. She [*pointing to the* STEPDAUGHTER], as you see, is no longer a little girl with plaits down her back—.

THE STEPDAUGHTER   —and the panties showing below the skirt!

THE FATHER   The drama is coming now, sir; something new, complex, most interesting.

THE STEPDAUGHTER   As soon as my father died . . .

THE FATHER   —there was absolute misery for them. They came back here, unknown to me. Through her stupidity! [*Pointing to the* MOTHER.] It is true she can barely write her own name; but she could anyhow have got her daughter to write to me that they were in need . . .

THE MOTHER   And how was I to divine all this sentiment in him?

THE FATHER   That is exactly your mistake, never to have guessed any of my sentiments.

THE MOTHER   After so many years apart, and all that had happened . . .

THE FATHER   Was it my fault if that fellow carried you away? It happened quite suddenly; for after he had obtained some job or other, I could find no trace of them; and so, not unnaturally, my interest in them dwindled. But the drama culminated unforeseen and violent on their return, when I was impelled by my miserable flesh that still lives. . . . Ah! what misery, what wretchedness is that of the man who is alone and disdains debasing *liaisons!* Not old enough to do without women, and not young enough to go and look for one without shame. Misery? It's worse than misery; it's a horror; for no woman can any longer give him love; and when a man feels this. . . . One ought to do without, you say? Yes, yes, I know. Each of us when he appears before his fellows is clothed in a certain dignity. But every man knows what unconfessable things pass within the secrecy of his own heart. One gives way to the temptation, only to rise from it again, afterwards, with a great eagerness to re-establish one's dignity, as if it were a tombstone to place on the grave of one's shame, and a monument to hide and sign the memory of our weaknesses. Everybody's in the same case. Some folks haven't the courage to say certain things, that's all!

THE STEPDAUGHTER   All appear to have the courage to do them though.

THE FATHER   Yes, but in secret. Therefore, you want more courage to say these things. Let a man but speak these things out, and folks at once label him a cynic. But it isn't true. He is like all the others, better indeed, because he isn't afraid to reveal with the light of the intelligence the red shame of human bestiality on which most men close their eyes so as not to see it.

Woman—for example, look at her case! She turns tantalizing

inviting glances on you. You seize her. No sooner does she feel herself in your grasp than she closes her eyes. It is the sign of her mission, the sign by which she says to man: "Blind yourself, for I am blind."

THE STEPDAUGHTER Sometimes she can close them no more: when she no longer feels the need of hiding her shame to herself, but dry-eyed and dispassionately, sees only that of the man who has blinded himself without love. Oh, all these intellectual complications make me sick, disgust me—all this philosophy that uncovers the beast in man, and then seeks to save him, excuse him . . . I can't stand it, sir. When a man seeks to "simplify" life bestially, throwing aside every relic of humanity, every chaste aspiration, every pure feeling, all sense of ideality, duty, modesty, shame . . . then nothing is more revolting and nauseous than a certain kind of remorse—crocodiles' tears, that's what it is.

THE MANAGER Let's come to the point. This is only discussion.

THE FATHER Very good, sir! But a fact is like a sack which won't stand up when it is empty. In order that it may stand up, one has to put into it the reason and sentiment which have caused it to exist. I couldn't possibly know that after the death of that man, they had decided to return here, that they were in misery, and that she [*pointing to the* MOTHER] had gone to work as a modiste, and at a shop of the type of that of Madame Pace.

THE STEPDAUGHTER A real high-class modiste, you must know, gentlemen. In appearance, she works for the leaders of the best society; but she arranges matters so that these elegant ladies serve her purpose . . . without prejudice to other ladies who are . . . well . . . only so so.

THE MOTHER You will believe me, gentlemen, that it never entered my mind that the old hag offered me work because she had her eye on my daughter.

THE STEPDAUGHTER Poor mamma! Do you know, sir, what that woman did when I brought her back the work my mother had finished? She would point out to me that I had torn one of my frocks, and she would give it back to my mother to mend. It was I who paid for it, always I; while this poor creature here believed she was sacrificing herself for me and these two children here, sitting up at night sewing Madame Pace's gowns.

THE MANAGER And one day you met there . . .

THE STEPDAUGHTER Him, him. Yes sir, an old client. There's a scene for you to play! Superb!

THE FATHER She, the Mother arrived just then . . .

THE STEPDAUGHTER [*treacherously*] Almost in time!

THE FATHER [*crying out*] No, in time! in time! Fortunately I recognized her . . . in time. And I took them back home with me to my house. You can imagine now her position and mine; she, as you see her; and I who cannot look her in the face.

THE STEPDAUGHTER Absurd! How can I possibly be expected—after that—to be a modest young miss, a fit person to go with his confounded aspirations for "a solid moral sanity"?

THE FATHER For the drama lies all in this—in the conscience that I have, that each one of us has. We believe this conscience to be a single thing, but it is many-sided. There is one for this person, and another for that. Diverse consciences. So we have this illusion of being one person for all, of having a personality that is unique

in all our acts. But it isn't true. We perceive this when, tragically perhaps, in something we do, we are as it were, suspended, caught up in the air on a kind of hook. Then we perceive that all of us was not in that act, and that it would be an atrocious injustice to judge us by that action alone, as if all our existence were summed up in that one deed. Now do you understand the perfidy of this girl? She surprised me in a place, where she ought not to have known me, just as I could not exist for her; and she now seeks to attach to me a reality such as I could never suppose I should have to assume for her in a shameful and fleeting moment of my life. I feel this above all else. And the drama, you will see, acquires a tremendous value from this point. Then there is the position of the others . . . his. . . . [*Indicating the* SON.]

THE SON [*shrugging his shoulders scornfully*]   Leave me alone! I don't come into this.

THE FATHER   What? You don't come into this?

THE SON   I've got nothing to do with it, and don't want to have; because you know well enough I wasn't made to be mixed up in all this with the rest of you.

THE STEPDAUGHTER   We are only vulgar folk! He is the fine gentleman. You may have noticed, Mr. Manager, that I fix him now and again with a look of scorn while he lowers his eyes—for he knows the evil he has done me.

THE SON [*scarcely looking at her*]   I?

THE STEPDAUGHTER   You! you! I owe my life on the streets to you. Did you or did you not deny us, with your behavior, I won't say the intimacy of home, but even that mere hospitality which makes guests feel at their ease? We were intruders who had come to disturb the kingdom of your legitimacy. I should like to have you witness, Mr. Manager, certain scenes between him and me. He says I have tyrannized over everyone. But it was just his behavior which made me insist on the reason for which I had come into the house— this reason he calls "vile"—into his house, with my mother who is his mother too. And I came as mistress of the house.

THE SON   It's easy for them to put me always in the wrong. But imagine, gentlemen, the position of a son, whose fate it is to see arrive one day at his home a young woman of impudent bearing, a young woman who inquires for his father, with whom who knows what business she has. This young man has then to witness her return bolder than ever, accompanied by that child there. He is obliged to watch her treat his father in an equivocal and confidential manner. She asks money of him in a way that lets one suppose he must give it to her, *must*, do you understand, because he has every obligation to do so.

THE FATHER   But I have, as a matter of fact, this obligation. I owe it to your mother.

THE SON   How should I know? When had I ever seen or heard of her? One day there arrive with her [*indicating* STEPDAUGHTER] that lad and this baby here. I am told: "This is *your* mother too, you know." I divine from her manner [*indicating* STEPDAUGHTER *again*] why it is they have come home. I had rather not say what I feel and think about it. I shouldn't even care to confess to myself. No action can therefore be hoped for from me in this affair. Believe me, Mr. Manager, I am an "unrealized" character, dramatically speaking; and I

find myself not at all at ease in their company. Leave me out of it, I beg you.

THE FATHER   What? It is just because you are so that . . .

THE SON   How do you know what I am like? When did you ever bother your head about me?

THE FATHER   I admit it. I admit it. But isn't that a situation in itself? This aloofness of yours which is so cruel to me and to your mother, who returns home and sees you almost for the first time grown up, who doesn't recognize you but knows you are her son . . . [*Pointing out the* MOTHER *to the* MANAGER.] See, she's crying!

THE STEPDAUGHTER   [*angrily, stamping her foot*]   Like a fool!

THE FATHER   [*indicating* STEPDAUGHTER]   She can't stand him, you know. [*Then referring again to the* SON.] He says he doesn't come into the affair, whereas he is really the hinge of the whole action. Look at that lad who is always clinging to his mother, frightened and humiliated. It is on account of this fellow here. Possibly his situation is the most painful of all. He feels himself a stranger more than the others. The poor little chap feels mortified, humiliated at being brought into a home out of charity as it were. [*In confidence.*] He is the image of his father. Hardly talks at all. Humble and quiet.

THE MANAGER   Oh, we'll cut him out. You've no notion what a nuisance boys are on the stage. . . .

THE FATHER   He disappears soon, you know. And the baby too. She is the first to vanish from the scene. The drama consists finally in this: when that mother re-enters my house, her family born outside of it, and shall we say superimposed on the original, ends with the death of the little girl, the tragedy of the boy and the flight of the elder daughter. It cannot go on, because it is foreign to its surroundings. So after much torment, we three remain: I, the mother, that son. Then, owing to the disappearance of that extraneous family, we too find ourselves strange to one another. We find we are living in an atmosphere of mortal desolation which is the revenge, as he [*indicating* SON] scornfully said of the Demon of Experiment, that unfortunately hides in me. Thus, sir, you see when faith is lacking, it becomes impossible to create certain states of happiness, for we lack the necessary humility. Vaingloriously, we try to substitute ourselves for this faith, creating thus for the rest of the world a reality which we believe after their fashion, while, actually, it doesn't exist. For each one of us has his own reality to be respected before God, even when it is harmful to one's very self.

THE MANAGER   There is something in what you say. I assure you all this interests me very much. I begin to think there's the stuff for a drama in all this, and not a bad drama either.

THE STEPDAUGHTER   [*coming forward*]   When you've got a character like me.

THE FATHER   [*shutting her up, all excited to learn the decision of the* MANAGER]   You be quiet!

THE MANAGER   [*reflecting, heedless of interruption*]   It's new . . . hem . . . yes. . . .

THE FATHER   Absolutely new!

THE MANAGER   You've got a nerve though, I must say, to come here and fling it at me like this. . . .

THE FATHER   You will understand, sir, born as we are for the stage . . .

THE MANAGER   Are you amateur actors then?

THE FATHER   No. I say born for the stage, because . . .

THE MANAGER   Oh, nonsense. You're an old hand, you know.

THE FATHER   No sir, no. We act that role for which we have been cast, that role which we are given in life. And in my own case, passion itself, as usually happens, becomes a trifle theatrical when it is exalted.

THE MANAGER   Well, well, that will do. But you see, without an author . . . I could give you the address of an author if you like. . . .

THE FATHER   No, no. Look here! You must be the author.

THE MANAGER   I? What are you talking about?

THE FATHER   Yes, you, you! Why not?

THE MANAGER   Because I have never been an author: that's why.

THE FATHER   Then why not turn author now? Everybody does it. You don't want any special qualities. Your task is made much easier by the fact that we are all here alive before you. . . .

THE MANAGER   It won't do.

THE FATHER   What? When you see us live our drama . . .

THE MANAGER   Yes, that's all right. But you want someone to write it.

THE FATHER   No, no. Someone to take it down, possibly, while we play it, scene by scene! It will be enough to sketch it out at first, and then try it over.

THE MANAGER   Well . . . I am almost tempted. It's a bit of an idea. One might have a shot at it.

THE FATHER   Of course. You'll see what scenes will come out of it. I can give you one, at once . . .

THE MANAGER   By Jove, it tempts me. I'd like to have a go at it. Let's try it out. Come with me to my office. [*Turning to the* ACTORS.] You are at liberty for a bit, but don't step out of the theatre for long. In a quarter of an hour, twenty minutes, all back here again! [*To the* FATHER.] We'll see what can be done. Who knows if we don't get something really extraordinary out of it?

THE FATHER   There's no doubt about it. They [*indicating the* CHARACTERS] had better come with us too, hadn't they?

THE MANAGER   Yes, yes. Come on! come on! [*Moves away and then turning to the* ACTORS.] Be punctual, please! [MANAGER *and the* SIX CHARACTERS *cross the stage and go off. The other* ACTORS *remain, looking at one another in astonishment.*]

LEADING MAN   Is he serious? What the devil does he want to do?

JUVENILE LEAD   This is rank madness.

THIRD ACTOR   Does he expect to knock off a drama in five minutes?

JUVENILE LEAD   Like the improvisers!

LEADING LADY   If he thinks that I'm going to take part in a joke like this . . .

JUVENILE LEAD   I'm out of it anyway.

FOURTH ACTOR   I should like to know who they are. [*Alludes to* CHARACTERS.]

THIRD ACTOR   What do you suppose? Madmen or rascals!

JUVENILE LEAD   And he takes them seriously!

L'INGÉNUE   Vanity! He fancies himself as an author now.

LEADING MAN   It's absolutely unheard of. If the stage has come to this . . . well I'm . . .

FIFTH ACTOR   It's rather a joke.

THIRD ACTOR   Well, we'll see what's going to happen next.

Thus talking, the ACTORS *leave the stage; some going out by the little door at the back; others retiring to their dressing-rooms. The curtain remains up. The action of the play is suspended for twenty minutes.*

Act 2

The stage call-bells ring to warn the company that the play is about to begin again.

The STEPDAUGHTER *comes out of the* MANAGER's *office along with the* CHILD *and the* BOY. *As she comes out of the office, she cries:*

THE STEPDAUGHTER   Nonsense! nonsense! Do it yourselves! I'm not going to mix myself up in this mess. [*Turning to the* CHILD *and coming quickly with her on to the stage.*] Come on, Rosetta, let's run!

The BOY *follows them slowly, remaining a little behind and seeming perplexed.*

THE STEPDAUGHTER [*stops, bends over the* CHILD *and takes the latter's face between her hands*]   My little darling! You're frightened, aren't you? You don't know where we are, do you? [*Pretending to reply to a question of the* CHILD.] What is the stage? It's a place, baby, you know, where people play at being serious, a place where they act comedies. We've got to act a comedy now, dead serious, you know; and you're in it also, little one. [*Embraces her, pressing the little head to her breast, and rocking the* CHILD *for a moment.*] Oh darling, darling, what a horrid comedy you've got to play! What a wretched part they've found for you! A garden . . . a fountain . . . look . . . just suppose, kiddie, it's here. Where, you say? Why, right here in the middle. It's all pretense you know. That's the trouble, my pet: it's all make-believe here. It's better to imagine it though, because if they fix it up for you, it'll only be painted cardboard, painted cardboard for the rockery, the water, the plants. . . . Ah, but I think a baby like this one would sooner have a make-believe fountain than a real one, so she could play with it. What a joke it'll be for the others! But for you, alas! not quite such a joke: you who are real, baby dear, and really play by a real fountain that is big and green and beautiful, with ever so many bamboos around it that are reflected in the water, and a whole lot of little ducks swimming about. . . . No, Rosetta, no, your mother doesn't bother about you on account of that wretch of a son there. I'm in the devil of a temper, and as for that lad . . . [*Seizes* BOY *by the arm to force him to take one of his hands out of his pockets.*] What have you got there? What are you hiding? [*Pulls his hand out of his pocket, looks into it and catches the glint of a revolver.*] Ah! where did you get this? [*The* BOY, *very pale in the face, looks at her, but does not answer.*] Idiot! If I'd been in your place, instead of killing myself, I'd have shot one of those two, or both of them: father and son.

The FATHER *enters from the office, all excited from his work. The* MANAGER *follows him.*

THE FATHER   Come on, come on dear! Come here for a minute! We've arranged everything. It's all fixed up.

THE MANAGER [*also excited*]   If you please, young lady, there are one or two points to settle still. Will you come along?

THE STEPDAUGHTER [*following him towards the office*]   Ouff! what's the good, if you've arranged everything.

> *The* FATHER, MANAGER, *and* STEPDAUGHTER *go back into the office again for a moment. At the same time, the* SON, *followed by the* MOTHER, *comes out.*

THE SON [*looking at the three entering office*]   Oh this is fine, fine! And to think I can't even get away!

> *The* MOTHER *attempts to look at him, but lowers her eyes immediately when he turns away from her. She then sits down. The* BOY *and the* CHILD *approach her. She casts a glance again at the* SON, *and speaks with humble tones, trying to draw him into conversation.*

THE MOTHER   And isn't my punishment the worst of all? [*Then seeing from the* SON's *manner that he will not bother himself about her.*] My God! Why are you so cruel? Isn't it enough for one person to support all this torment? Must you then insist on others seeing it also?

THE SON [*half to himself, meaning the* MOTHER *to hear, however*]   And they want to put it on the stage! If there was at least a reason for it! He thinks he has got at the meaning of it all. Just as if each one of us in every circumstance of life couldn't find his own explanation of it! [*Pauses.*] He complains he was discovered in a place where he ought not to have been seen, in a moment of his life which ought to have remained hidden and kept out of the reach of that convention which he has to maintain for other people. And what about my case? Haven't I had to reveal what no son ought ever to reveal: how father and mother live and are man and wife for themselves quite apart from that idea of father and mother which we give them? When this idea is revealed, our life is then linked at one point only to that man and that woman; and as such it should shame them, shouldn't it?

> *The* MOTHER *hides her face in her hands. From the dressing-rooms and the little door at the back of the stage the* ACTORS *and* STAGE MANAGER *return, followed by the* PROPERTY MAN, *and the* PROMPTER. *At the same moment, the* MANAGER *comes out of his office, accompanied by the* FATHER *and the* STEP-DAUGHTER.

THE MANAGER   Come on, come on, ladies and gentlemen! Heh! you there, machinist!

MACHINIST   Yes sir?

THE MANAGER   Fix up the white parlor with the floral decorations. Two wings and a drop with a door will do. Hurry up!

> *The* MACHINIST *runs off at once to prepare the scene, and arranges it while the* MANAGER *talks with the* STAGE MANAGER, *the* PROPERTY MAN, *and the* PROMPTER *on matters of detail.*

THE MANAGER [*to* PROPERTY MAN]   Just have a look, and see if there isn't a sofa or divan in the wardrobe . . .

PROPERTY MAN   There's the green one.

THE STEPDAUGHTER   No no! Green won't do. It was yellow, orna-
mented with flowers—very large! and most comfortable!
PROPERTY MAN   There isn't one like that.
THE MANAGER   It doesn't matter. Use the one we've got.
THE STEPDAUGHTER   Doesn't matter? It's most important!
THE MANAGER   We're only trying it now. Please don't interfere. [*To*
PROPERTY MAN.] See if we've got a shop window—long and nar-
rowish.
THE STEPDAUGHTER   And the little table! The little mahogany table
for the pale blue envelope!
PROPERTY MAN [*to* MANAGER]   There's that little gilt one.
THE MANAGER   That'll do fine.
THE FATHER   A mirror.
THE STEPDAUGHTER   And the screen! We must have a screen. Other-
wise how can I manage?
PROPERTY MAN   That's all right, Miss. We've got any amount of them.
THE MANAGER [*to the* STEPDAUGHTER]   We want some clothes pegs
too, don't we?
THE STEPDAUGHTER   Yes, several, several!
THE MANAGER   See how many we've got and bring them all.
PROPERTY MAN   All right!

> *The* PROPERTY MAN *hurries off to obey his orders. While he is
> putting the things in their places, the* MANAGER *talks to the*
> PROMPTER *and then with the* CHARACTERS *and the* ACTORS.

THE MANAGER [*to* PROMPTER]   Take your seat. Look here: this is the
outline of the scenes, act by act. [*Hands him some sheets of paper.*]
And now I'm going to ask you to do something out of the ordinary.
PROMPTER   Take it down in shorthand?
THE MANAGER [*pleasantly surprised*]   Exactly! Can you do shorthand?
PROMPTER   Yes, a little.
THE MANAGER   Good! [*Turning to a* STAGE HAND.] Go and get some
paper from my office, plenty, as much as you can find.

> *The* STAGE HAND *goes off, and soon returns with a handful of
> paper which he gives to the* PROMPTER.

THE MANAGER [*to* PROMPTER]   You follow the scenes as we play them,
and try and get the points down, at any rate the most important
ones. [*Then addressing the* ACTORS.] Clear the stage, ladies and
gentlemen! Come over here [*pointing to the left*] and listen attentively.
LEADING LADY   But, excuse me, we . . .
THE MANAGER [*guessing her thought*]   Don't worry! You won't have
to improvise.
LEADING MAN   What have we to do then?
THE MANAGER   Nothing. For the moment you just watch and listen.
Everybody will get his part written out afterwards. At present we're
going to try the thing as best we can. They're going to act now.
THE FATHER [*as if fallen from the clouds into the confusion of the
stage*]   We? What do you mean, if you please, by a rehearsal?
THE MANAGER   A rehearsal for them. [*Points to the* ACTORS.]
THE FATHER   But since we are the characters . . .
THE MANAGER   All right: "characters" then, if you insist on calling
yourselves such. But here, my dear sir, the characters don't act. Here

the actors do the acting. The characters are there, in the "book" [*pointing towards* PROMPTER'S *box*]—when there is a "book"!

THE FATHER   I won't contradict you; but excuse me, the actors aren't the characters. They want to be, they pretend to be, don't they? Now if these gentlemen here are fortunate enough to have us alive before them . . .

THE MANAGER   Oh this is grand! You want to come before the public yourselves then?

THE FATHER   As we are. . . .

THE MANAGER   I can assure you it would be a magnificent spectacle!

LEADING MAN   What's the use of us here anyway then?

THE MANAGER   You're not going to pretend that you can act? It makes me laugh! [*The* ACTORS *laugh.*] There, you see, they are laughing at the notion. But, by the way, I must cast the parts. That won't be difficult. They cast themselves. [*To the* SECOND LADY LEAD.] You play the Mother. [*To the* FATHER.] We must find her a name.

THE FATHER   Amalia, sir.

THE MANAGER   But that is the real name of your wife. We don't want to call her by her real name.

THE FATHER   Why ever not, if it is her name? . . . Still, perhaps, if that lady must. . . . [*Makes a slight motion of the hand to indicate the* SECOND LADY LEAD.] I see this woman here [*means the* MOTHER] as Amalia. But do as you like. [*Gets more and more confused.*] I don't know what to say to you. Already, I begin to hear my own words ring false, as if they had another sound. . . .

THE MANAGER   Don't you worry about it. It'll be our job to find the right tones. And as for her name, if you want her Amalia, Amalia it shall be; and if you don't like it, we'll find another! For the moment though, we'll call the characters in this way. [*To* JUVENILE LEAD.] You are the Son. [*To the* LEADING LADY.] You naturally are the Stepdaughter. . . .

THE STEPDAUGHTER   [*excitedly*]   What? what? I, that woman there? [*Bursts out laughing.*]

THE MANAGER   [*angry*]   What is there to laugh at?

LEADING LADY   [*indignant*]   Nobody has ever dared to laugh at me. I insist on being treated with respect; otherwise I go away.

THE STEPDAUGHTER   No, no, excuse me . . . I am not laughing at you. . . .

THE MANAGER   [*to* STEPDAUGHTER]   You ought to feel honored to be played by . . .

LEADING LADY   [*at once, contemptuously*]   "That woman there" . . .

THE STEPDAUGHTER   But I wasn't speaking of you, you know. I was speaking of myself—whom I can't see at all in you! That is all. I don't know . . . but . . . you . . . aren't in the least like me. . . .

THE FATHER   True. Here's the point. Look here, sir, our temperaments, our souls . . .

THE MANAGER   Temperament, soul, be hanged! Do you suppose the spirit of the piece is in you? Nothing of the kind!

THE FATHER   What, haven't we our own temperaments, our own souls?

THE MANAGER   Not at all. Your soul or whatever you like to call it takes shape here. The actors give body and form to it, voice and gesture. And my actors—I may tell you—have given expression to much more lofty material than this little drama of yours, which may

or may not hold up on the stage. But if it does, the merit of it, believe me, will be due to my actors.

THE FATHER   I don't dare contradict you, sir; but, believe me, it is a terrible suffering for us who are as we are, with these bodies of ours, these features to see . . .

THE MANAGER [*cutting him short and out of patience*]   Good heavens! The make-up will remedy all that, man, the make-up. . . .

THE FATHER   Maybe. But the voice, the gestures . . .

THE MANAGER Now, look here! On the stage, you as yourself, cannot exist. The actor here acts you, and that's an end to it!

THE FATHER   I understand. And now I think I see why our author who conceived us as we are, all alive, didn't want to put us on the stage after all. I haven't the least desire to offend your actors. Far from it! But when I think that I am to be acted by . . . I don't know by whom. . . .

LEADING MAN [*on his dignity*]   By me, if you've no objection!

THE FATHER [*humbly, mellifluously*]   Honored, I assure you, sir. [*Bows.*] Still, I must say that try as this gentleman may, with all his good will and wonderful art, to absorb me into himself . . .

LEADING MAN Oh chuck it! "Wonderful art!" Withdraw that, please!

THE FATHER   The performance he will give, even doing his best with make-up to look like me . . .

LEADING MAN It will certainly be a bit difficult! [*The* ACTORS *laugh.*]

THE FATHER   Exactly! It will be difficult to act me as I really am. The effect will be rather—apart from the make-up—according as to how he supposes I am, as he senses me—if he does sense me—and not as I inside of myself feel myself to be. It seems to me then that account should be taken of this by everyone whose duty it may become to criticize us. . . .

THE MANAGER Heavens! The man's starting to think about the critics now! Let them say what they like. It's up to us to put on the play if we can. [*Looking around.*] Come on! come on! Is the stage set? [*To the* ACTORS *and* CHARACTERS.] Stand back—stand back! Let me see, and don't let's lose any more time! [*To the* STEPDAUGHTER.] Is it all right as it is now?

THE STEPDAUGHTER Well, to tell the truth, I don't recognize the scene.

THE MANAGER My dear lady, you can't possibly suppose that we can construct that shop of Madame Pace piece by piece here? [*To the* FATHER.] You said a white room with flowered wall paper, didn't you?

THE FATHER Yes.

THE MANAGER Well then. We've got the furniture right more or less. Bring that little table a bit further forward. [*The* STAGE HANDS *obey the order. To* PROPERTY MAN.] You go and find an envelope, if possible, a pale blue one; and give it to that gentleman. [*Indicates* FATHER.]

PROPERTY MAN An ordinary envelope?

MANAGER *and* FATHER Yes, yes, an ordinary envelope.

PROPERTY MAN At once, sir. [*Exit.*]

THE MANAGER Ready, everyone! First scene—the Young Lady. [*The* LEADING LADY *comes forward.*] No, no, you must wait. I meant her. [*Indicating the* STEPDAUGHTER.] You just watch—

THE STEPDAUGHTER [*adding at once*]   How I shall play it, how I shall live it! . . .

LEADING LADY [*offended*]   I shall live it also, you may be sure, as soon as I begin!

THE MANAGER [*with his hands to his head*]   Ladies and gentlemen, if you please! No more useless discussions! Scene I: the young lady with Madame Pace: Oh! [*Looks around as if lost.*] And this Madame Pace, where is she?

THE FATHER   She isn't with us, sir.

THE MANAGER   Then what the devil's to be done?

THE FATHER   But she is alive too.

THE MANAGER   Yes, but where is she?

THE FATHER   One minute. Let me speak! [*Turning to the* ACTRESSES.] If these ladies would be so good as to give me their hats for a moment. . . .

THE ACTRESSES [*half surprised, half laughing, in chorus*]   What? Why? Our hats? What does he say?

THE MANAGER   What are you going to do with the ladies' hats? [*The* ACTORS *laugh.*]

THE FATHER   Oh nothing. I just want to put them on these pegs for a moment. And one of the ladies will be so kind as to take off her cloak. . . .

THE ACTORS   Oh, what d'you think of that? Only the cloak? He must be mad.

SOME ACTRESSES   But why? Cloaks as well?

THE FATHER   To hang them up here for a moment. Please be so kind, will you?

THE ACTRESSES [*taking off their hats, one or two also their cloaks, and going to hang them on the racks*]   After all, why not? There you are! This is really funny. We've got to put them on show.

THE FATHER   Exactly; just like that, on show.

THE MANAGER   May we know why?

THE FATHER   I'll tell you. Who knows if, by arranging the stage for her, she does not come here herself, attracted by the very articles of her trade? [*Inviting the* ACTORS *to look towards the exit at back of stage.*] Look! Look!

> *The door at the back of stage opens and* MADAME PACE *enters and takes a few steps forward. She is a fat, oldish woman with crudely dyed hair. She is rouged and powdered, dressed with a comical elegance in black silk. Round her waist is a long silver chain from which hangs a pair of scissors. The* STEPDAUGHTER *runs over to her at once amid the stupor of the* ACTORS.

THE STEPDAUGHTER [*turning towards her*]   There she is! There she is!

THE FATHER [*radiant*]   It's she! I said so, didn't I? There she is!

THE MANAGER [*conquering his surprise, and then becoming indignant*]   What sort of a trick is this?

LEADING MAN [*almost at the same time*]   What's going to happen next?

JUVENILE LEAD   Where does *she* come from?

L'INGÉNUE   They've been holding her in reserve, I guess.

LEADING LADY   A vulgar trick!

THE FATHER [*dominating the protests*]   Excuse me, all of you! Why are you so anxious to destroy in the name of a vulgar, commonplace sense of truth, this reality which comes to birth attracted and formed by the magic of the stage itself, which has indeed more right to live

here than you, since it is much truer than you—if you don't mind my saying so? Which is the actress among you who is to play Madame Pace? Well, here is Madame Pace herself. And you will allow, I fancy, that the actress who acts her will be less true than this woman here, who is herself in person. You see my daughter recognized her and went over to her at once. Now you're going to witness the scene!

> But the scene between the STEPDAUGHTER *and* MADAME PACE *has already begun despite the protest of the actors and the reply of the* FATHER. *It has begun quietly, naturally, in a manner impossible for the stage. So when the* ACTORS, *called to attention by the* FATHER, *turn round and see* MADAME PACE, *who has placed one hand under the* STEPDAUGHTER's *chin to raise her head, they observe her at first with great attention, but hearing her speak in an unintelligible manner their interest begins to wane.*

THE MANAGER   Well? well?

LEADING MAN   What does she say?

LEADING LADY   One can't hear a word.

JUVENILE LEAD   Louder! Louder please!

THE STEPDAUGHTER [*leaving* MADAME PACE, *who smiles a Sphinxlike smile, and advancing towards the* ACTORS] Louder? Louder? What are you talking about? These aren't matters which can be shouted at the top of one's voice. If I have spoken them out loud, it was to shame him and have my revenge. [*Indicates* FATHER.] But for Madame it's quite a different matter.

THE MANAGER   Indeed? indeed? But here, you know, people have got to make themselves heard, my dear. Even we who are on the stage can't hear you. What will it be when the public's in the theatre? And anyway, you can very well speak up now among yourselves, since we shan't be present to listen to you as we are now. You've got to pretend to be alone in a room at the back of a shop where no one can hear you.

> *The* STEPDAUGHTER *coquettishly and with a touch of malice makes a sign of disagreement two or three times with her finger.*

THE MANAGER   What do you mean by no?

THE STEPDAUGHTER [*sotto voce, mysteriously*] There's someone who will hear us if she [*indicating* MADAME PACE] speaks out loud.

THE MANAGER [*in consternation*] What? Have you got someone else to spring on us now? [*The* ACTORS *burst out laughing.*]

THE FATHER   No, no sir. She is alluding to me. I've got to be here— there behind that door, in waiting; and Madame Pace knows it. In fact, if you will allow me, I'll go there at once, so I can be quite ready. [*Moves away.*]

THE MANAGER [*stopping him*] No! Wait! wait! We must observe the conventions of the theatre. Before you are ready . . .

THE STEPDAUGHTER [*interrupting him*] No, get on with it at once! I'm just dying, I tell you, to act this scene. If he's ready, I'm more than ready.

THE MANAGER [*shouting*] But, my dear young lady, first of all, we must have the scene between you and this lady. . . . [*Indicates* MADAME PACE.] Do you understand? . . .

THE STEPDAUGHTER   Good Heavens! She's been telling me what you

know already: that mamma's work is badly done again, that the material's ruined; and that if I want her to continue to help us in our misery I must be patient. . . .

MADAME PACE [*coming forward with an air of great importance*]   Yes indeed, sir, I no wanta take advantage of her, I no wanta be hard. . . .

> *Note.* MADAME PACE *is supposed to talk in a jargon half Italian, half English.*

THE MANAGER [*alarmed*]   What? What? She talks like that? [*The* ACTORS *burst out laughing again.*]

THE STEPDAUGHTER [*also laughing*]   Yes yes, that's the way she talks, half English, half Italian! Most comical it is!

MADAME PACE   Itta seem not verra polite gentlemen laugha atta me eeff I trya best speaka English.

THE MANAGER   *Diamine!*[6] Of course! Of course! Let her talk like that! Just what we want. Talk just like that, Madame, if you please! The effect will be certain. Exactly what was wanted to put a little comic relief into the crudity of the situation. Of course she talks like that! Magnificent!

THE STEPDAUGHTER   Magnificent? Certainly! When certain suggestions are made to one in language of that kind, the effect is certain, since it seems almost a joke. One feels inclined to laugh when one hears her talk about an "old signore" "who wanta talka nicely with you." Nice old signore,[7] eh, Madame?

MADAME PACE   Not so old my dear, not so old! And even if you no lika him, he won't make any scandal!

THE MOTHER [*jumping up amid the amazement and consternation of the* ACTORS *who had not been noticing her. They move to restrain her*]   You old devil! You murderess!

THE STEPDAUGHTER [*running over to calm her* MOTHER]   Calm yourself, Mother, calm yourself! Please don't. . . .

THE FATHER [*going to her also at the same time*]   Calm yourself! Don't get excited! Sit down now!

THE MOTHER   Well then, take that woman away out of my sight!

THE STEPDAUGHTER [*to* MANAGER]   It is impossible for my mother to remain here.

THE FATHER [*to* MANAGER]   They can't be here together. And for this reason, you see: that woman there was not with us when we came. . . . If they are on together, the whole thing is given away inevitably, as you see.

THE MANAGER   It doesn't matter. This is only a first rough sketch— just to get an idea of the various points of the scene, even confusedly. . . . [*Turning to the* MOTHER *and leading her to her chair.*] Come along, my dear lady, sit down now, and let's get on with the scene. . . .

> *Meanwhile, the* STEPDAUGHTER, *coming forward again, turns to* MADAME PACE.

THE STEPDAUGHTER   Come on, Madame, come on!

MADAME PACE [*offended*]   No, no, *grazie.*[8] I not do anything witha your mother present.

---

6. An Italian exclamation, equivalent to "The deuce!" or "The devil!"

7. "Signore" is Italian for "gentleman."

8. Italian for "Thank you" or "Thanks."

THE STEPDAUGHTER   Nonsense! Introduce this "old signore" who wants to talk nicely to me. [*Addressing the* COMPANY *imperiously.*] We've got to do this scene one way or another, haven't we? Come on! [*To* MADAME PACE.] You can go!

MADAME PACE   Ah yes! I go'way! I go'way! Certainly! [*Exits furious.*]

THE STEPDAUGHTER [*to the* FATHER]   Now you make your entry. No, you needn't go over there. Come here. Let's suppose you've already come in. Like that, yes! I'm here with bowed head, modest like. Come on! Out with your voice! Say "Good morning, Miss" in that peculiar tone, that special tone. . . .

THE MANAGER   Excuse me, but are you the Manager, or am I? [*To the* FATHER, *who looks undecided and perplexed.*] Get on with it, man! Go down there to the back of the stage. You needn't go off. Then come right forward here.

> The FATHER *does as he is told, looking troubled and perplexed at first. But as soon as he begins to move, the reality of the action affects him, and he begins to smile and to be more natural. The* ACTORS *watch intently.*

THE MANAGER [*sotto voce, quickly to the* PROMPTER *in his box*]   Ready! ready? Get ready to write now.

THE FATHER [*coming forward and speaking in a different tone*]   Good afternoon, Miss!

THE STEPDAUGHTER [*head bowed down slightly, with restrained disgust*]   Good afternoon!

THE FATHER [*looks under her hat which partly covers her face. Perceiving she is very young, he makes an exclamation, partly of surprise, partly of fear lest he compromise himself in a risky adventure*]   Ah . . . but . . . ah . . . I say . . . this is not the first time that you have come here, is it?

THE STEPDAUGHTER [*modestly*]   No sir.

THE FATHER   You've been here before, eh? [*Then seeing her nod agreement.*] More than once? [*Waits for her to answer, looks under her hat, smiles, and then says.*] Well then, there's no need to be so shy, is there? May I take off your hat?

THE STEPDAUGHTER [*anticipating him and with veiled disgust*]   No sir . . . I'll do it myself. [*Takes it off quickly.*]

> The MOTHER, *who watches the progress of the scene with the* SON *and the other two children who cling to her, is on thorns; and follows with varying expressions of sorrow, indignation, anxiety, and horror the words and actions of the other two. From time to time she hides her face in her hands and sobs.*

THE MOTHER   Oh, my God, my God!

THE FATHER [*playing his part with a touch of gallantry*]   Give it to me! I'll put it down. [*Takes hat from her hands.*] But a dear little head like yours ought to have a smarter hat. Come and help me choose one from the stock, won't you?

L'INGÉNUE [*interrupting*]   I say . . . those are our hats you know.

THE MANAGER [*furious*]   Silence! silence! Don't try and be funny, if you please. . . . We're playing the scene now I'd have you notice. [*To the* STEPDAUGHTER.] Begin again, please!

THE STEPDAUGHTER [*continuing*]   No thank you, sir.

THE FATHER   Oh, come now. Don't talk like that. You must take it.

I shall be upset if you don't. There are some lovely little hats here;
and then—Madame will be pleased. She expects it, anyway, you
know.

THE STEPDAUGHTER   No, no! I couldn't wear it!

THE FATHER   Oh, you're thinking about what they'd say at home if
they saw you come in with a new hat? My dear girl, there's always
a way round these little matters, you know.

THE STEPDAUGHTER [*all keyed up*]   No, it's not that. I couldn't wear
it because I am . . . as you see . . . you might have noticed . . .
[*Showing her black dress.*]

THE FATHER   . . . in mourning! Of course: I beg your pardon: I'm
frightfully sorry. . . .

THE STEPDAUGHTER [*forcing herself to conquer her indignation and
nausea*]   Stop! Stop! It's I who must thank you. There's no need
for you to feel mortified or specially sorry. Don't think any more of
what I've said. [*Tries to smile.*] I must forget that I am dressed
so. . . .

THE MANAGER [*interrupting and turning to the* PROMPTER]   Stop a
minute! Stop! Don't write that down. Cut out that last bit. [*Then
to the* FATHER *and* STEPDAUGHTER.] Fine! it's going fine! [*To the*
FATHER *only.*] And now you can go on as we arranged. [*To the*
ACTORS.] Pretty good that scene, where he offers her the hat, eh?

THE STEPDAUGHTER   The best's coming now. Why can't we go on?

THE MANAGER   Have a little patience! [*To the* ACTORS.] Of course, it
must be treated rather lightly.

LEADING MAN   Still, with a bit of go in it!

LEADING LADY   Of course! It's easy enough! [*To* LEADING MAN.] Shall
you and I try it now?

LEADING MAN   Why, yes! I'll prepare my entrance. [*Exit in order to
make his entrance.*]

THE MANAGER [*to* LEADING LADY]   See here! The scene between you
and Madame Pace is finished. I'll have it written out properly after.
You remain here . . . oh, where are you going?

LEADING LADY   One minute. I want to put my hat on again. [*Goes
over to hat-rack and puts her hat on her head.*]

THE MANAGER   Good! You stay here with your head bowed down a bit.

THE STEPDAUGHTER   But she isn't dressed in black.

LEADING LADY   But I shall be, and much more effectively than you.

THE MANAGER [*to* STEPDAUGHTER]   Be quiet please, and watch! You'll
be able too learn something. [*Clapping his hands.*] Come on! come
on! Entrance, please!

The door at rear of stage opens, and the LEADING MAN *enters
with the lively manner of an old gallant. The rendering of the
scene by the* ACTORS *from the very first words is seen to be
quite a different thing, though it has not in any way the air of
a parody. Naturally, the* STEPDAUGHTER *and the* FATHER, *not
being able to recognize themselves in the* LEADING LADY *and
the* LEADING MAN, *who deliver their words in different tones
and with a different psychology, express, sometimes with smiles,
sometimes with gestures, the impression they receive.*

LEADING MAN   Good afternoon, Miss. . . .

THE FATHER [*at once unable to contain himself*]   No! no!

The STEPDAUGHTER, *noticing the way the* LEADING MAN *enters, bursts out laughing.*

THE MANAGER [*furious*]   Silence! And you please just stop that laughing. If we go on like this, we shall never finish.

THE STEPDAUGHTER   Forgive me, sir, but it's natural enough. This lady [*indicating* LEADING LADY] stands there still; but if she is supposed to be me, I can assure you that if I heard anyone say "Good afternoon" in that manner and in that tone, I should burst out laughing as I did.

THE FATHER   Yes, yes, the manner, the tone. . . .

THE MANAGER   Nonsense! Rubbish! Stand aside and let me see the action.

LEADING MAN   If I've got to represent an old fellow who's coming into a house of an equivocal character . . .

THE MANAGER   Don't listen to them, for Heaven's sake! Do it again! It goes fine. [*Waiting for the* ACTORS *to begin again.*] Well?

LEADING MAN   Good afternoon, Miss.

LEADING LADY   Good afternoon.

LEADING MAN [*imitating the gesture of the* FATHER *when he looked under the hat, and then expressing quite clearly first satisfaction and then fear*]   Ah, but . . . I say . . . this is not the first time that you have come here, is it?

THE MANAGER   Good, but not quite so heavily. Like this. [*Acts himself.*] "This isn't the first time that you have come here." . . . [*To* LEADING LADY.]   And you say: "No, sir."

LEADING LADY   No, sir.

LEADING MAN   You've been here before, more than once.

THE MANAGER   No, no, stop! Let her nod "yes" first. "You've been here before, eh?" [*The* LEADING LADY *lifts up her head slightly and closes her eyes as though in disgust. Then she inclines her head twice.*]

THE STEPDAUGHTER [*unable to contain herself*]   Oh my God! [*Puts a hand to her mouth to prevent herself from laughing.*]

THE MANAGER [*turning round*]   What's the matter?

THE STEPDAUGHTER   Nothing, nothing!

THE MANAGER [*to* LEADING MAN]   Go on!

LEADING MAN   You've been here before, eh? Well then, there's no need to be so shy, is there? May I take off your hat?

The LEADING MAN *says this last speech in such a tone and with such gestures that the* STEPDAUGHTER, *though she has her hand to her mouth, cannot keep from laughing.*

LEADING LADY [*indignant*]   I'm not going to stop here to be made a fool of by that woman there.

LEADING MAN   Neither am I! I'm through with it!

THE MANAGER [*shouting to* STEPDAUGHTER]   Silence! for once and all, I tell you!

THE STEPDAUGHTER   Forgive me! forgive me!

THE MANAGER   You haven't any manners: that's what it is! You go too far.

THE FATHER [*endeavoring to intervene*]   Yes, it's true, but excuse her. . . .

THE MANAGER   Excuse what? It's absolutely disgusting.

THE FATHER   Yes, sir, but believe me, it has such a strange effect when . . .

THE MANAGER   Strange? Why strange? Where is it strange?

THE FATHER   No, sir; I admire your actors—this gentleman here, this lady; but they are certainly not us!

THE MANAGER   I should hope not. Evidently they cannot be you, if they are actors.

THE FATHER   Just so: actors! Both of them act our parts exceedingly well. But, believe me, it produces quite a different effect on us. They want to be us, but they aren't, all the same.

THE MANAGER   What is it then anyway?

THE FATHER   Something that is . . . that is theirs—and no longer ours . . .

THE MANAGER   But naturally, inevitably. I've told you so already.

THE FATHER   Yes, I understand . . . I understand. . . .

THE MANAGER   Well then, let's have no more of it! [*Turning to the* ACTORS.] We'll have the rehearsals by ourselves, afterwards, in the ordinary way. I never could stand rehearsing with the author present. He's never satisfied! [*Turning to* FATHER *and* STEPDAUGHTER.] Come on! Let's get on with it again; and try and see if you can't keep from laughing.

THE STEPDAUGHTER   Oh, I shan't laugh any more. There's a nice little bit coming for me now: you'll see.

THE MANAGER   Well then: when she says "Don't think any more of what I've said, I must forget, etc.," you [*addressing the* FATHER] come in sharp with "I understand, I understand"; and then you ask her . . .

THE STEPDAUGHTER [*interrupting*]   What?

THE MANAGER   Why she is in mourning.

THE STEPDAUGHTER   Not at all! See here: when I told him that it was useless for me to be thinking about my wearing mourning, do you know how he answered me? "Ah well," he said, "then let's take off this little frock."

THE MANAGER   Great! Just what we want, to make a riot in the theatre!

THE STEPDAUGHTER   But it's the truth!

THE MANAGER   What does that matter? Acting is our business here. Truth up to a certain point, but no further.

THE STEPDAUGHTER   What do you want to do then?

THE MANAGER   You'll see, you'll see! Leave it to me.

THE STEPDAUGHTER   No sir! What you want to do is to piece together a little romantic sentimental scene out of my disgust, out of all the reasons, each more cruel and viler than the other, why I am what I am. He is to ask me why I'm in mourning; and I'm to answer with tears in my eyes, that it is just two months since papa died. No sir, no! He's got to say to me; as he did say: "Well, let's take off this little dress at once." And I, with my two months' mourning in my heart, went there behind that screen, and with these fingers tingling with shame . . .

THE MANAGER [*running his hands through his hair*]   For Heaven's sake! What are you saying?

THE STEPDAUGHTER [*crying out excitedly*]   The truth! The truth!

THE MANAGER   It may be. I don't deny it, and I can understand all your horror; but you must surely see that you can't have this kind of thing on the stage. It won't go.

THE STEPDAUGHTER   Not possible, eh? Very well! I'm much obliged to you—but I'm off!

THE MANAGER   Now be reasonable! Don't lose your temper!

THE STEPDAUGHTER   I won't stop here! I won't! I can see you've fixed it all up with him in your office. All this talk about what is possible for the stage . . . I understand! He wants to get at his complicated "cerebral drama," to have his famous remorses and torments acted; but I want to act my part, *my part!*

THE MANAGER [*annoyed, shaking his shoulders*]   Ah! Just *your* part! But, if you will pardon me, there are other parts than yours: His [*indicating the* FATHER] and hers! [*Indicating the* MOTHER.] On the stage you can't have a character becoming too prominent and overshadowing all the others. The thing is to pack them all into a neat little framework and then act what is actable. I am aware of the fact that everyone has his own interior life which he wants very much to put forward. But the difficulty lies in this fact: to set out just so much as is necessary for the stage, taking the other characters into consideration, and at the same time hint at the unrevealed interior life of each. I am willing to admit, my dear young lady, that from your point of view it would be a fine idea if each character could tell the public all his troubles in a nice monologue or a regular one hour lecture. [*Good humoredly.*] You must restrain yourself, my dear, and in your own interest, too; because this fury of yours, this exaggerated disgust you show, may make a bad impression, you know. After you have confessed to me that there were others before him at Madame Pace's and more than once . . .

THE STEPDAUGHTER [*bowing her head, impressed*]   It's true. But remember those others mean him for me all the same.

THE MANAGER [*not understanding*]   What? The others? What do you mean?

THE STEPDAUGHTER   For one who has gone wrong, sir, he who was responsible for the first fault is responsible for all that follow. He is responsible for my faults, was, even before I was born. Look at him, and see if it isn't true!

THE MANAGER   Well, well! And does the weight of so much responsibility seem nothing to you? Give him a chance to act it, to get it over!

THE STEPDAUGHTER   How? How can he act all his "noble remorses," all his "moral torments," if you want to spare him the horror of being discovered one day—after he had asked her what he did ask her—in the arms of her, that already fallen woman, that child, sir, that child he used to watch come out of school? [*She is moved.*]

> The MOTHER *at this point is overcome with emotion, and breaks out into a fit of crying. All are touched. A long pause.*

THE STEPDAUGHTER [*as soon as the* MOTHER *becomes a little quieter, adds resolutely and gravely*]   At present, we are unknown to the public. Tomorrow, you will act us as you wish, treating us in your own manner. But do you really want to see drama, do you want to see it flash out as it really did?

THE MANAGER   Of course! That's just what I do want, so I can use as much of it as is possible.

THE STEPDAUGHTER   Well then, ask that Mother there to leave us.

THE MOTHER [*changing her low plaint into a sharp cry*]   No! No! Don't permit it, sir, don't permit it!

THE MANAGER   But it's only to try it.

THE MOTHER   I can't bear it. I can't.

THE MANAGER   But since it has happened already . . . I don't understand!

THE MOTHER   It's taking place now. It happens all the time. My torment isn't a pretended one. I live and feel every minute of my torture. Those two children there—have you heard them speak? They can't speak any more. They cling to me to keep up my torment actual and vivid for me. But for themselves, they do not exist, they aren't any more. And she [*indicating the* STEPDAUGHTER] has run away, she has left me, and is lost. If I now see her here before me, it is only to renew for me the tortures I have suffered for her too.

THE FATHER   The eternal moment! She [*indicating the* STEPDAUGHTER] is here to catch me, fix me, and hold me eternally in the stocks for that one fleeting and shameful moment of my life. She can't give it up! And you sir, cannot either fairly spare me it.

THE MANAGER   I never said I didn't want to act it. It will form, as a matter of fact, the nucleus of the whole first act right up to her surprise. [*Indicates the* MOTHER.]

THE FATHER   Just so! This is my punishment: the passion in all of us that must culminate in her final cry.

THE STEPDAUGHTER   I can hear it still in my ears. It's driven me mad, that cry!—You can put me on as you like; it doesn't matter. Fully dressed, if you like—provided I have at least the arm bare; because, standing like this [*she goes close to the* FATHER *and leans her head on his breast*] with my head so, and my arms round his neck, I saw a vein pulsing in my arm here; and then, as if that live vein had awakened disgust in me, I closed my eyes like this, and let my head sink on his breast. [*Turning to the* MOTHER.] Cry out, mother! Cry out! [*Buries head in* FATHER's *breast, and with her shoulders raised as if to prevent her hearing the cry, adds in tones of intense emotion.*] Cry out as you did then!

THE MOTHER   [*coming forward to separate them*]   No! My daughter, my daughter! [*And after having pulled her away from him.*] You brute! you brute! She is my daughter! Don't you see she's my daughter?

THE MANAGER   [*walking backwards towards footlights*]   Fine! fine! Damned good! And then, of course—curtain!

THE FATHER   [*going towards him excitedly*]   Yes, of course, because that's the way it really happened.

THE MANAGER   [*convinced and pleased*]   Oh, yes, no doubt about it. Curtain here, curtain!

> *At the reiterated cry of the* MANAGER, *the* MACHINIST *lets the curtain down, leaving the* MANAGER *and the* FATHER *in front of it before the footlights.*

THE MANAGER   The darned idiot! I said "curtain" to show the act should end there, and he goes and lets it down in earnest. [*To the* FATHER, *while he pulls the curtain back to go on to the stage again.*] Yes, yes, it's all right. Effect certain! That's the right ending. I'll guarantee the first act at any rate.

Act 3

When the curtain goes up again, it is seen that the stage hands have shifted the bit of scenery used in the last part, and have rigged up instead at the back of the stage a drop, with some trees, and one or two wings. A portion of a fountain basin is visible. The MOTHER *is sitting on the right with the two children by her side. The* SON *is on the same side, but away from the others. He seems bored, angry, and full of shame. The* FATHER *and the* STEPDAUGHTER *are also seated toward the right front. On the other side (left) are the* ACTORS, *much in the positions they occupied before the curtain was lowered. Only the* MANAGER *is standing up in the middle of the stage, with his hand closed over his mouth in the act of meditating.*

THE MANAGER [*shaking his shoulders after a brief pause*] Ah yes: the second act! Leave it to me, leave it all to me as we arranged, and you'll see! It'll go fine!

THE STEPDAUGHTER Our entry into his house [*indicates* FATHER] in spite of him. . . . [*Indicates the* SON.]

THE MANAGER [*out of patience*] Leave it to me, I tell you!

THE STEPDAUGHTER Do let it be clear, at any rate, that it is in spite of my wishes.

THE MOTHER [*from her corner, shaking her head*] For all the good that's come of it. . . .

THE STEPDAUGHTER [*turning toward her quickly*] It doesn't matter. The more harm done us, the more remorse for him.

THE MANAGER [*impatiently*] I understand! Good Heavens! I understand! I'm taking it into account.

THE MOTHER [*supplicatingly*] I beg you, sir, to let it appear quite plain that for conscience' sake I did try in every way . . .

THE STEPDAUGHTER [*interrupting indignantly and continuing for the* MOTHER] . . . to pacify me, to dissuade me from spiting him. [*To* MANAGER.] Do as she wants: satisfy her, because it is true! I enjoy it immensely. Anyhow, as you can see, the meeker she is, the more she tries to get at his heart, the more distant and aloof does he become.

THE MANAGER Are we going to begin this second act or not?

THE STEPDAUGHTER I'm not going to talk any more now. But I must tell you this: you can't have the whole action take place in the garden, as you suggest. It isn't possible!

THE MANAGER Why not?

THE STEPDAUGHTER Because he [*indicates the* SON *again*] is always shut up alone in his room. And then there's all the part of that poor dazed-looking boy there which takes place indoors.

THE MANAGER Maybe! On the other hand, you will understand—we can't change scenes three or four times in one act.

THE LEADING MAN They used to once.

THE MANAGER Yes, when the public was up to the level of that child there.

THE LEADING LADY It makes the illusion easier.

THE FATHER [*irritated*] The illusion! For Heaven's sake, don't say illusion. Please don't use that word, which is particularly painful for us.

THE MANAGER [*astounded*]   And why, if you please?

THE FATHER   It's painful, cruel, really cruel; and you ought to understand that.

THE MANAGER   But why? What ought we to say then? The illusion, I tell you, sir, which we've got to create for the audience. . . .

THE LEADING MAN   With our acting.

THE MANAGER   The illusion of a reality.

THE FATHER   I understand; but you, perhaps, do not understand us. Forgive me! You see . . . here for you and your actors, the thing is only—and rightly so . . . a kind of game. . . .

THE LEADING LADY [*interrupting indignantly*]   A game! We're not children here, if you please! We are serious actors.

THE FATHER   I don't deny it. What I mean is the game, or play, of your art, which has to give, as the gentleman says, a perfect illusion of reality.

THE MANAGER   Precisely—!

THE FATHER   Now, if you consider the fact that we [*indicates himself and the other five* CHARACTERS], as we are, have no other reality outside of this illusion. . . .

THE MANAGER [*astonished, looking at his* ACTORS, *who are also amazed*] And what does that mean?

THE FATHER [*after watching them for a moment with a wan smile*]   As I say, sir, that which is a game of art for you is our sole reality. [*Brief pause. He goes a step or two nearer the* MANAGER *and adds.*] But not only for us, you know, by the way. Just you think it over well. [*Looks him in the eyes.*] Can you tell me who you are?

THE MANAGER [*perplexed, half smiling*]   What? Who am I? I am myself.

THE FATHER   And if I were to tell you that that isn't true, because you and I . . . ?

THE MANAGER   I should say you were mad—! [*The* ACTORS *laugh.*]

THE FATHER   You're quite right to laugh: because we are all making believe here. [*To* MANAGER.] And you can therefore object that it's only for a joke that that gentleman there [*indicates the* LEADING MAN], who naturally is himself, has to be me, who am on the contrary myself—this thing you see here. You see I've caught you in a trap! [*The* ACTORS *laugh.*]

THE MANAGER [*annoyed*]   But we've had all this over once before. Do you want to begin again?

THE FATHER   No, no! That wasn't my meaning! In fact, I should like to request you to abandon this game of art [*looking at the* LEADING LADY *as if anticipating her*] which you are accustomed to play here with your actors, and to ask you seriously once again: who are you?

THE MANAGER [*astonished and irritated, turning to his* ACTORS]   If this fellow here hasn't got a nerve! A man who calls himself a character comes and asks me who I am!

THE FATHER [*with dignity, but not offended*]   A character, sir, may always ask a man who he is. Because a character has really a life of his own, marked with his especial characteristics; for which reason he is always "somebody." But a man—I'm not speaking of you now—may very well be "nobody."

THE MANAGER   Yes, but you are asking these questions of me, the boss, the manager! Do you understand?

THE FATHER   But only in order to know if you, as you really are now,

see yourself as you once were with all the illusions that were yours then, with all the things both inside and outside of you as they seemed to you—as they were then indeed for you. Well, sir, if you think of all those illusions that mean nothing to you now, of all those things which don't even *seem* to you to exist any more, while once they *were* for you, don't you feel that—I won't say these boards—but the very earth under your feet is sinking away from you when you reflect that in the same way this *you* as you feel it to-day—all this present reality of yours—is fated to seem a mere illusion to you tomorrow?

THE MANAGER [*without having understood much, but astonished by the specious argument*]   Well, well! And where does all this take us anyway?

THE FATHER   Oh, nowhere! It's only to show you that if we [*indicating the* CHARACTERS] have no other reality beyond the illusion, you too must not count overmuch on your reality as you feel it today, since, like that of yesterday, it may prove an illusion for you tomorrow.

THE MANAGER [*determining to make fun of him*]   Ah, excellent! Then you'll be saying next that you, with this comedy of yours that you brought here to act, are truer and more real than I am.

THE FATHER [*with the greatest seriousness*]   But of course; without doubt!

THE MANAGER   Ah, really?

THE FATHER   Why, I thought you'd understand that from the beginning.

THE MANAGER   More real than I?

THE FATHER   If your reality can change from one day to another. . .

THE MANAGER   But everyone knows it can change. It is always changing, the same as anyone else's.

THE FATHER [*with a cry*]   No, sir, not ours! Look here! That is the very difference! Our reality doesn't change: it can't change! It can't be other than what it is, because it is already fixed for ever. It's terrible. Ours is an immutable reality which should make you shudder when you approach us if you are really conscious of the fact that your reality is a mere transitory and fleeting illusion, taking this form today and that tomorrow, according to the conditions, according to your will, your sentiments, which in turn are controlled by an intellect that shows them to you today in one manner and to-morrow. . . . Who knows how? . . . Illusions of reality represented in this fatuous comedy of life that never ends, nor can ever end! Because if tomorrow it were to end . . . then why, all would be finished.

THE MANAGER   Oh for God's sake, will you *at least* finish with this philosophizing and let us try and shape this comedy which you yourself have brought me here? You argue and philosophize a bit too much, my dear sir. You know you seem to me almost, almost. . . . [*Stops and looks him over from head to foot.*] Ah, by the way, I think you introduced yourself to me as a—what shall . . . we say—a "character," created by an author who did not afterward care to make a drama of his own creations.

THE FATHER   It is the simple truth, sir.

THE MANAGER   Nonsense! Cut that out, please! None of us believes it, because it isn't a thing, as you must recognize yourself, which one can believe seriously. If you want to know, it seems to me you are trying to imitate the manner of a certain author whom I heartily

detest—I warn you—although I have unfortunately bound myself to put on one of his works.[9] As a matter of fact, I was just starting to rehearse it, when you arrived. [*Turning to the* ACTORS.] And this is what we've gained—out of the frying-pan into the fire!

THE FATHER   I don't know to what author you may be alluding, but believe me I feel what I think; and I seem to be philosophizing only for those who do not think what they feel, because they blind themselves with their own sentiment. I know that for many people this self-blinding seems much more "human"; but the contrary is really true. For man never reasons so much and becomes so introspective as when he suffers; since he is anxious to get at the cause of his sufferings, to learn who has produced them, and whether it is just or unjust that he should have to bear them. On the other hand, when he is happy, he takes his happiness as it comes and doesn't analyze it, just as if happiness were his right. The animals suffer without reasoning about their sufferings. But take the case of a man who suffers and begins to reason about it. Oh no! it can't be allowed! Let him suffer like an animal, and then—ah yet, he is "human"!

THE MANAGER   Look here! Look here! You're off again, philosophizing worse than ever.

THE FATHER   Because I suffer, sir! I'm not philosophizing: I'm crying aloud the reason of my sufferings.

THE MANAGER   [*makes brusque movement as he is taken with a new idea*]   I should like to know if anyone has ever heard of a character who gets right out of his part and perorates and speechifies as you do. Have you ever heard of a case? I haven't.

THE FATHER   You have never met such a case, sir, because authors, as a rule, hide the labor of their creations. When the characters are really alive before their author, the latter does nothing but follow them in their action, in their words, in the situations which they suggest to him; and he has to will them the way they will themselves—for there's trouble if he doesn't. When a character is born, he acquires at once such an independence, even of his own author, that he can be imagined by everybody even in many other situations where the author never dreamed of placing him; and so he acquires for himself a meaning which the author never thought of giving him.

THE MANAGER   Yes, yes, I know this.

THE FATHER   What is there then to marvel at in us? Imagine such a misfortune for characters as I have described to you: to be born of an author's fantasy, and be denied life by him; and then answer me if these characters left alive, and yet without life, weren't right in doing what they did do and are doing now, after they have attempted everything in their power to persuade him to give them their stage life. We've all tried him in turn, I, she [*indicating the* STEPDAUGHTER] and she. [*Indicating the* MOTHER.]

THE STEPDAUGHTER   It's true. I too have sought to tempt him, many, many times, when he has been sitting at his writing table, feeling a bit melancholy, at the twilight hour. He would sit in his arm-chair too lazy to switch on the light, and all the shadows that crept into his room were full of our presence coming to tempt him. [*As if she saw herself still there by the writing table, and was annoyed*

---

9. The "certain author" is Pirandello himself.

by the presence of the ACTORS.] Oh, if you would only go away,
go away and leave us alone—mother here with that son of hers—
I with that child—that boy there always alone—and then I
with him [*just hints at the* FATHER]—and then I alone, alone . . .
in those shadows! [*Makes a sudden movement as if in the vision she
has of herself illuminating those shadows she wanted to seize hold
of herself.*] Ah! my life! my life! Oh, what scenes we proposed to him
—and I tempted him more than any of the others!

THE FATHER   Maybe. But perhaps it was your fault that he refused to
give us life: because you were too insistent, too troublesome.

THE STEPDAUGHTER   Nonsense! Didn't he make me so himself? [*Goes
close to the* MANAGER *to tell him as if in confidence.*] In my opinion
he abandoned us in a fit of depression, of disgust for the ordinary
theatre as the public knows it and likes it.

THE SON   Exactly what it was, sir; exactly that!

THE FATHER   Not at all! Don't believe it for a minute. Listen to me!
You'll be doing quite right to modify, as you suggest, the excesses
both of this girl here, who wants to do too much, and of this young
man, who won't do anything at all.

THE SON   No, nothing!

THE MANAGER   You too get over the mark occasionally, my dear sir, if
I may say so.

THE FATHER   I? When? Where?

THE MANAGER   Always! Continuously! Then there's this insistence of
yours in trying to make us believe you are a character. And then too,
you must really argue and philosophize less, you know, much less.

THE FATHER   Well, if you want to take away from me the possibility
of representing the torment of my spirit which never gives me peace,
you will be suppressing me: that's all. Every true man, sir, who is a
little above the level of the beasts and plants does not live for the
sake of living, without knowing how to live; but he lives so as to give
a meaning and a value of his own to life. For me this is *everything*.
I cannot give up this, just to represent a mere fact as she [*indicating
the* STEPDAUGHTER] wants. It's all very well for her, since her "vendetta" lies in the "fact." I'm not going to do it. It destroys my *raison
d'être.*

THE MANAGER   Your *raison d'être!* Oh, we're going ahead fine! First
she starts off, and then you jump in. At this rate, we'll never finish.

THE FATHER   Now, don't be offended! Have it your own way—provided, however, that within the limits of the parts you assign us each
one's sacrifice isn't too great.

THE MANAGER   You've got to understand that you can't go on arguing
at your own pleasure. Drama is action, sir, action and not confounded philosophy.

THE FATHER   All right. I'll do just as much arguing and philosophizing
as everybody does when he is considering his own torments.

THE MANAGER   If the drama permits! But for Heaven's sake, man,
let's get along and come to the scene.

THE STEPDAUGHTER   It seems to me we've got too much action with
our coming into his house. [*Indicating* FATHER.] You said, before,
you couldn't change the scene every five minutes.

THE MANAGER   Of course not. What we've got to do is to combine
and group up all the facts in one simultaneous, close-knit, action.
We can't have it as you want, with your little brother wandering

like a ghost from room to room, hiding behind doors and meditating a project which—what did you say it did to him?

THE STEPDAUGHTER   Consumes him, sir, wastes him away!

THE MANAGER   Well, it may be. And then at the same time, you want the little girl there to be playing in the garden . . . one in the house, and the other in the garden: isn't that it?

THE STEPDAUGHTER   Yes, in the sun, in the sun! That is my only pleasure: to see her happy and careless in the garden after the misery and squalor of the horrible room where we all four slept together. And I had to sleep with her—I, do you understand?—with my vile contaminated body next to hers; with her folding me fast in her loving little arms. In the garden, whenever she spied me, she would run to take me by the hand. She didn't care for the big flowers, only the little ones; and she loved to show me them and pet me.

THE MANAGER   Well then, we'll have it in the garden. Everything shall happen in the garden; and we'll group the other scenes there. [*Calls a* STAGE HAND.] Here, a backcloth with trees and something to do as a fountain basin. [*Turning round to look at the back of the stage.*] Ah, you've fixed it up. Good! [*To* STEPDAUGHTER.] This is just to give an idea, of course. The Boy, instead of hiding behind the doors, will wander about here in the garden, hiding behind the trees. But it's going to be rather difficult to find a child to do that scene with you where she shows you the flowers. [*Turning to the* BOY.] Come forward a little, will you please? Let's try it now! Come along! come along! [*Then seeing him come shyly forward, full of fear and looking lost.*] It's a nice business, this lad here. What's the matter with him? We'll have to give him a word or two to say. [*Goes close to him, puts a hand on his shoulders, and leads him behind one of the trees.*] Come on! come on! Let me see you a little! Hide here . . . yes, like that. Try and show your head just a little as if you were looking for someone. . . . [*Goes back to observe the effect, when the* BOY *at once goes through the action.*] Excellent! fine! [*Turning to* STEPDAUGHTER.] Suppose the little girl there were to surprise him as he looks round, and run over to him, so we could give him a word or two to say?

THE STEPDAUGHTER   It's useless to hope he will speak, as long as that fellow there is here. . . . [*Indicates the* SON.] You must send him away first.

THE SON   [*jumping up*]   Delighted! Delighted! I don't ask for anything better. [*Begins to move away.*]

THE MANAGER   [*at once stopping him*]   No! No! Where are you going? Wait a bit!

> The MOTHER *gets up alarmed and terrified at the thought that he is really about to go away. Instinctively she lifts her arms to prevent him, without, however, leaving her seat.*

THE SON   [*to* MANAGER *who stops him*]   I've got nothing to do with this affair. Let me go please! Let me go!

THE MANAGER   What do you mean by saying you've got nothing to do with this?

THE STEPDAUGHTER   [*calmly, with irony*]   Don't bother to stop him: he won't go away.

THE FATHER   He has to act the terrible scene in the garden with his mother.

THE SON [*suddenly resolute and with dignity*] I shall act nothing at all. I've said so from the very beginning. [*To the* MANAGER.] Let me go!

THE STEPDAUGHTER [*going over to the* MANAGER] Allow me? [*Puts down the* MANAGER's *arm which is restraining the* SON.] Well, go away then, if you want to! [*The* SON *looks at her with contempt and hatred. She laughs and says.*] You see, he can't, he can't go away! He is obliged to stay here, indissolubly bound to the chain. If I, who fly off when that happens which has to happen, because I can't bear him—if I am still here and support that face and expression of his, you can well imagine that he is unable to move. He has to remain here, has to stop with that nice father of his, and that mother whose only son he is. [*Turning to the* MOTHER.] Come on, mother, come along! [*Turning to* MANAGER *to indicate her.*] You see, she was getting up to keep him back. [*To the* MOTHER, *beckoning her with her hand.*] Come on! come on! [*Then to* MANAGER.] You can imagine how little she wants to show these actors of yours what she really feels; but so eager is she to get near him that. . . . There, you see? She is willing to act her part. [*And in fact, the* MOTHER *approaches him; and as soon as the* STEPDAUGHTER *has finished speaking, opens her arms to signify that she consents.*]

THE SON [*suddenly*] No! no! If I can't go away, then I'll stop here; but I repeat: I act nothing!

THE FATHER [*to* MANAGER *excitedly*] You can force him, sir.

THE SON Nobody can force me.

THE FATHER I can.

THE STEPDAUGHTER Wait a minute, wait. . . . First of all, the baby has to go to the fountain. . . . [*Runs to take the* CHILD *and leads her to the fountain.*]

THE MANAGER Yes, yes of course; that's it. Both at the same time.

> The SECOND LADY LEAD *and the* JUVENILE LEAD *at this point separate themselves from the group of* ACTORS. *One watches the* MOTHER *attentively; the other moves about studying the movements and manner of the* SON *whom he will have to act.*

THE SON [*to* MANAGER] What do you mean by both at the same time? It isn't right. There was no scene between me and her. [*Indicates the* MOTHER.] Ask her how it was!

THE MOTHER Yes, it's true. I had come into his room. . . .

THE SON Into my room, do you understand? Nothing to do with the garden.

THE MANAGER It doesn't matter. Haven't I told you we've got to group the action?

THE SON [*observing the* JUVENILE LEAD *studying him*] What do you want?

THE JUVENILE LEAD Nothing! I was just looking at you.

THE SON [*turning toward the* SECOND LADY LEAD] Ah! she's at it too: to re-act her part! [*Indicating the* MOTHER.]

THE MANAGER Exactly! And it seems to me that you ought to be grateful to them for their interest.

THE SON Yes, but haven't you yet perceived that it isn't possible to live in front of a mirror which not only freezes us with the image of ourselves, but throws our likeness back at us with a horrible grimace?

THE FATHER That is true, absolutely true. You must see that.

THE MANAGER [*to* SECOND LADY LEAD *and* JUVENILE LEAD]   He's right!
Move away from them!

THE SON   Do as you like. I'm out of this!

THE MANAGER   Be quiet, you, will you? And let me hear your mother!
[*To* MOTHER.] You were saying you had entered. . . .

THE MOTHER   Yes, into his room, because I couldn't stand it any
longer. I went to empty my heart to him of all the anguish that tortures me. . . . But as soon as he saw me come in. . . .

THE SON   Nothing happened! There was no scene. I went away, that's
all! I don't care for scenes!

THE MOTHER   It's true, true. That's how it was.

THE MANAGER   Well now, we've got to do this bit between you and
him. It's indispensable.

THE MOTHER   I'm ready . . . when you are ready. If you could only
find a chance for me to tell him what I feel here in my heart.

THE FATHER [*going to* SON *in a great rage*]   You'll do this for your
mother, for your mother, do you understand?

THE SON [*quite determined*]   I do nothing!

THE FATHER [*taking hold of him and shaking him*]   For God's sake, do
as I tell you! Don't you hear your mother asking you for a favor?
Haven't you even got the guts to be a son?

THE SON [*taking hold of the* FATHER]   No! No! And for God's sake
stop it, or else. . . . [*General agitation. The* MOTHER, *frightened, tries
to separate them.*]

THE MOTHER [*pleading*]   Please! please!

THE FATHER [*not leaving hold of the* SON]   You've got to obey, do you
hear?

THE SON [*almost crying from rage*]   What does it mean, this madness
you've got? [*They separate.*] Have you no decency, that you insist on
showing everyone our shame? I won't do it! I won't! And I stand for
the will of our author in this. He didn't want to put us on the stage,
after all!

THE MANAGER   Man alive! You came here . . .

THE SON [*indicating* FATHER]   *He* did! I didn't!

THE MANAGER   Aren't you here now?

THE SON   It was his wish, and he dragged us along with him. He's
told you not only the things that did happen, but also things that
have never happened at all.

THE MANAGER   Well, tell me then what did happen. You went out of
your room without saying a word?

THE SON   Without a word, so as to avoid a scene!

THE MANAGER   And then what did you do?

THE SON   Nothing . . . walking in the garden. . . . [*Hesitates for a
moment with expression of gloom.*]

THE MANAGER [*coming closer to him, interested by his extraordinary
reserve*]   Well, well . . . walking in the garden. . . .

THE SON [*exasperated*]   Why on earth do you insist? It's horrible!

The MOTHER *trembles, sobs, and looks towards the fountain.*

THE MANAGER [*slowly observing the glance and turning toward the
SON *with increasing apprehension*]   The baby?

THE SON   There in the fountain. . . .

THE FATHER [*pointing with tender pity to the* MOTHER]   She was following him at the moment. . . .

THE MANAGER [*to the* SON *anxiously*] And then you. . . .

THE SON I ran over to her; I was jumping in to drag her out when I saw something that froze my blood . . . the boy standing stock still, with eyes like a madman's, watching his little drowned sister, in the fountain! [*The* STEPDAUGHTER *bends over the fountain to hide the* CHILD. *She sobs.*] Then. . . . [*A revolver shot rings out behind the trees where the* BOY *is hidden.*]

THE MOTHER [*with a cry of terror runs over in that direction together with several of the* ACTORS *amid general confusion*] My son! My son! [*Then amid the cries and exclamations one hears her voice.*] Help! Help!

THE MANAGER [*pushing the* ACTORS *aside while they lift up the* BOY *and carry him off*] Is he really wounded?

SOME ACTORS He's dead! dead!

OTHER ACTORS No, no, it's only make-believe, it's only pretense!

THE FATHER [*with a terrible cry*] Pretense? Reality, sir, reality!

THE MANAGER Pretense? Reality? To hell with it all! Never in my life has such a thing happened to me. I've lost a whole day over these people, a whole day!

1921

III

GEORGE BERNARD SHAW

Major Barbara

CHARACTERS

ANDREW UNDERSHAFT, *a munitions manufacturer*

LADY BRITOMART, *his wife, from whom he lives apart*[1]

STEPHEN ⎫
BARBARA ⎬ *their children*
SARAH ⎭

ADOLPHUS CUSINS, *a Professor of Greek, in love with Barbara*

CHARLES LOMAX, *a scion of the upper classes, in love with Sarah*

MORRISON, *Lady Britomart's butler*

ROMOLA (RUMMY) MITCHENS ⎫
BRONTERRE O'BRIEN (SNOBBY) ⎬
   PRICE ⎭
habitués of the West Ham Shelter of the Salvation Army

JENNY HILL, *a young Salvation Army girl*

PETER SHIRLEY, *an older man who has lost his job*

BILL WALKER, *an intruder at the Shelter*

MRS. BAINES, *a senior officer in the Salvation Army*

BILTON, *a foreman at Undershaft's munitions works*

Act 1

It is after dinner in January 1906, in the library in LADY BRITOMART UNDERSHAFT'S *house in Wilton Crescent.*[2] *A large and comfortable settee is in the middle of the room, upholstered in dark leather. A person sitting on it (it is vacant at present) would have, on his right,* LADY BRITOMART'S *writing table, with the lady herself busy at it; a smaller writing table behind him on his left; the door behind him on* LADY BRITOMART'S *side; and a window with a window seat directly on his left. Near the window is an armchair.*

LADY BRITOMART *is a woman of fifty or thereabouts, well dressed and yet careless of her dress, well bred and quite reckless of her breeding, well mannered and yet appallingly outspoken and indifferent to the opinion of her interlocutors, amiable and yet peremptory, arbitrary, and high-tempered to the last bearable degree, and withal a very typical managing matron of the upper class, treated as a naughty child until she grew into a scolding mother, and finally settling down with plenty of practical ability and worldly experience, limited in the oddest way with domestic and class limitations, conceiving the universe exactly as if it were a large house in Wilton Crescent, though handling her corner of it very effec-*

---

1. As the daughter of an earl, Lady Britomart retains her title after her marriage although neither her husband nor children share it.

2. Wilton Crescent is located near Hyde Park Corner in the fashionable section of London called Belgravia.

978

*tively on that assumption, and being quite enlightened and liberal
as to the books in the library, the pictures on the walls, the music
in the portfolios, and the articles in the papers.*

Her son, STEPHEN, *comes in. He is a gravely correct young man
under 25, taking himself very seriously, but still in some awe of his
mother, from childish habit and bachelor shyness rather than from
any weakness of character.*

STEPHEN   Whats the matter?

LADY BRITOMART   Presently, Stephen.

> STEPHEN *submissively walks to the settee and sits down. He
> takes up a Liberal weekly called The Speaker.*[3]

LADY BRITOMART   Dont begin to read, Stephen. I shall require all
your attention.

STEPHEN   It was only while I was waiting—

LADY BRITOMART   Dont make excuses, Stephen. [*He puts down The
Speaker.*] Now! [*She finishes her writing; rises; and comes to the
settee.*] I have not kept you waiting v e r y long, I think.

STEPHEN   Not at all, mother.

LADY BRITOMART   Bring me my cushion. [*He takes the cushion from
the chair at the desk and arranges it for her as she sits down on the
settee.*] Sit down. [*He sits down and fingers his tie nervously.*] Dont
fiddle with your tie, Stephen: there is nothing the matter with it.

STEPHEN   I beg your pardon. [*He fiddles with his watch chain instead.*]

LADY BRITOMART   Now are you attending to me, Stephen?

STEPHEN   Of course, mother.

LADY BRITOMART   No: it's n o t of course. I want something much
more than your everyday matter-of-course attention. I am going to
speak to you very seriously, Stephen. I wish you would let that chain
alone.

STEPHEN [*hastily relinquishing the chain*]   Have I done anything to annoy you, mother? If so, it was quite unintentional.

LADY BRITOMART [*astonished*]   Nonsense! [*With some remorse.*] My
poor boy, did you think I was angry with you?

STEPHEN   What is it, then, mother? You are making me very uneasy.

LADY BRITOMART [*squaring herself at him rather aggressively*]   Stephen: may I ask how soon you intend to realize that you are a
grown-up man, and that I am only a woman?

STEPHEN [*amazed*]   Only a—

LADY BRITOMART   Dont repeat my words, please: it is a most aggravating habit. You must learn to face life seriously, Stephen. I really
cannot bear the whole burden of our family affairs any longer. You
must advise me; you must assume the responsibility.

STEPHEN   I!

LADY BRITOMART   Yes, you, of course. You were 24 last June. Youve
been at Harrow and Cambridge. Youve been to India and Japan.
You must know a lot of things, now; unless you have wasted your
time most scandalously. Well, a d v i s e me.

---

3. *The Speaker* first appeared in 1890 and was a left-wing review of politics, letters,
science, and the arts. In 1907 it became *The Nation*. In 1931 it merged with *The New
Statesman,* founded two decades earlier by Shaw and his Socialist friends, the Webbs.
For a time the merged publication was called *The New Statesman and the Nation,* but
since 1957 the name *The New Statesman* has been used.

STEPHEN [*much perplexed*]　You know I have never interfered in the household—

LADY BRITOMART　No: I should think not. I dont want you to order the dinner.

STEPHEN　I mean in our family affairs.

LADY BRITOMART　Well, you must interfere now; for they are getting quite beyond me.

STEPHEN [*troubled*]　I have thought sometimes that perhaps I ought; but really, mother, I know so little about them; and what I do know is so painful! it is so impossible to mention some things to you—[*He stops, ashamed.*]

LADY BRITOMART　I suppose you mean your father.

STEPHEN [*almost inaudibly*]　Yes.

LADY BRITOMART　My dear: we cant go on all our lives not mentioning him. Of course you were quite right not to open the subject until I asked you to; but you are old enough now to be taken into my confidence, and to help me to deal with him about the girls.

STEPHEN　But the girls are all right. They are engaged.

LADY BRITOMART [*complacently*]　Yes: I have made a very good match for Sarah. Charles Lomax will be a millionaire at 35. But that is ten years ahead; and in the meantime his trustees cannot under the terms of his father's will allow him more than £800 a year.[4]

STEPHEN　But the will says also that if he increases his income by his own exertions, they may double the increase.

LADY BRITOMART　Charles Lomax's exertions are much more likely to decrease his income than to increase it. Sarah will have to find at least another £800 a year for the next ten years; and even then they will be as poor as church mice. And what about Barbara? I thought Barbara was going to make the most brilliant career of all of you. And what does she do? Joins the Salvation Army; discharges her maid; lives on a pound a week; and walks in one evening with a professor of Greek whom she has picked up in the street, and who pretends to be a Salvationist, and actually plays the big drum for her in public because he has fallen head over ears in love with her.

STEPHEN　I was certainly rather taken aback when I heard they were engaged. Cusins is a very nice fellow, certainly: nobody would ever guess that he was born in Australia; but—

LADY BRITOMART　Oh, Adolphus Cusins will make a very good husband. After all, nobody can say a word against Greek: it stamps a man at once as an educated gentleman. And my family, thank Heaven, is not a pig-headed Tory one. We are Whigs, and believe in liberty.[5] Let snobbish people say what they please: Barbara shall marry, not the man they like, but the man *I* like.

STEPHEN　Of course I was thinking only of his income. However, he is not likely to be extravagant.

4. At the time of the play and until recently, the units of British currency were the penny (*pl.* pence), the shilling, and the pound or pound sterling. The pound contained 20 shillings, each worth 12 pence. Other terms used to describe British money are guinea (21 shillings), sovereign (a coin worth one pound), crown (five shillings), half crown (coin worth two and one-half shillings), florin (coin worth two shillings), groat (four pence) and farthing (one-fourth of a penny). In some cases, like the farthing, the term remained in the language long after the coin had ceased to circulate. At the time of the play the pound was worth about $4.90 in American money. Some prices of the period: one cent for the daily *New York Times* in the metropolitan area (two cents elsewhere) and five cents on Sunday; coffee sold for 16 to 40 cents per pound, a man's dress shirt for a dollar, and theater tickets from 25 cents to $1.50.

5. Lady Britomart is somewhat out of date politically. The terms "Whig" and "Tory" were generally replaced by Liberal and Conservative after the passage of the First Reform Bill in 1832, almost 75 years prior to the date of the play's action.

LADY BRITOMART   Dont be too sure of that, Stephen. I know your
quiet, simple, refined, poetic people like Adolphus: quite content
with the best of everything! They cost more than your extravagant
people, who are always as mean as they are second rate. No: Barbara will need at least £2000 a year. You see it means two additional households. Besides, my dear, y o u must marry soon. I dont
approve of the present fashion of philandering bachelors and late
marriages; and I am trying to arange something for you.

STEPHEN   It's very good of you, mother; but perhaps I had better arrange that for myself.

LADY BRITOMAT   Nonsense! you are much too young to begin match-
making: you would be taken in by some pretty little nobody. Of
course I dont mean that you are not to be consulted: you know that
as well as I do. [STEPHEN *closes his lips and is silent.*] Now dont sulk,
Stephen.

STEPHEN   I am not sulking, mother. What has all this got to do with—
with—with my father?

LADY BRITOMART   My dear Stephen: where is the money to come
from? It is easy enough for you and the other children to live on my
income as long as we are in the same house; but I cant keep four
families in four separate houses. You know how poor my father is:
he has barely seven thousand a year now; and really, if he were not
the Earl of Stevenage, he would have to give up society. He can do
nothing for us. He says, naturally enough, that it is absurd that he
should be asked to provide for the children of a man who is rolling in
money. You see, Stephen, your father must be fabulously wealthy,
because there is always a war going on somewhere.

STEPHEN   You need not remind me of that, mother. I have hardly
ever opened a newspaper in my life without seeing our name in it.
The Undershaft torpedo! The Undershaft quick firers! The Undershaft ten inch! The Undershaft disappearing rampart gun! The Undershaft submarine! and now the Undershaft aerial battleship! At
Harrow they called me the Woolwich Infant. At Cambridge it was
the same. A little brute at King's who was always trying to get up
revivals, spoilt my Bible—your first birthday present to me—by writing under my name, "Son and heir to Undershaft and Lazarus, Death
and Destruction Dealers: address, Christendom and Judea." But that
was not so bad as the way I was kowtowed to everywhere because
my father was making millions by selling cannons.

LADY BRITOMART   It is not only the cannons, but the war loans that
Lazarus arranges under cover of giving credit for the cannons. You
know, Stephen, it's perfectly scandalous. Those two men, Andrew
Undershaft and Lazarus, positively have Europe under their thumbs.
That is why your father is able to behave as he does. He is above
the law. Do you think Bismarck or Gladstone or Disraeli could have
openly defied every social and moral obligation all their lives as your
father has?[6] They simply wouldnt have dared. I asked Gladstone to
take it up. I asked The Times to take it up. I asked the Lord Chamberlain to take it up.[7] But it was just like asking them to declare war

---

6. Prince Otto von Bismarck (1815–
1898), William Ewart Gladstone (1809–
1898) and Benjamin Disraeli (1804–
1881) were among the most distinguished
statemen of the nineteenth century.
7. The Lord Chamberlain, chief officer
of the royal household, would have exerted
little political power. Shaw despised the
office because the Lord Chamberlain was
charged with precensoring plays. Shaw
fought the law, but it remained in force
until 1968. The first play produced without precensorship was the American musical *Hair*.

on the Sultan. They w o u l d n t. They said they couldnt touch
him. I believe they were afraid.

STEPHEN   What could they do? He does not actually break the law.

LADY BRITOMART   Not break the law! He is always breaking the law.
He broke the law when he was born: his parents were not married.

STEPHEN   Mother! Is that true?

LADY BRITOMART   Of course it's true: that was why we separated.

STEPHEN   He married without letting you know this!

LADY BRITOMART [*rather taken aback by this inference*]   Oh no. To
do Andrew justice, that was not the sort of thing he did. Besides,
you know the Undershaft motto: Unashamed. Everybody knew.

STEPHEN   But you said that was why you separated.

LADY BRITOMART   Yes, because he was not content with being a
foundling himself: he wanted to disinherit you for another foundling. That was what I couldnt stand.

STEPHEN [*ashamed*]   Do you mean for—for—for—

LADY BRITOMART   Dont stammer, Stephen. Speak distinctly.

STEPHEN   But this is so frightful to me, mother. To have to speak to
you about such things!

LADY BRITOMART   It's not pleasant for me, either, especially if you are
still so childish that you must make it worse by a display of embarrassment. It is only in the middle classes, Stephen, that people get
into a state of dumb helpless horror when they find that there are
wicked people in the world. In our class, we have to decide what is
to be done with wicked people; and nothing should disturb our self-
possession. Now ask your question properly.

STEPHEN   Mother: have you no consideration for me? For Heaven's
sake either treat me as a child, as you always do, and tell me nothing at all; or tell me everything and let me take it as best I can.

LADY BRITOMART   Treat you as a child! What do you mean? It is most
unkind and ungrateful of you to say such a thing. You know I have
never treated any of you as children. I have always made you my
companions and friends, and allowed you perfect freedom to do and
say whatever you liked, so long as you liked what I could approve of.

STEPHEN [*desperately*]   I daresay we have been the very imperfect
children of a very perfect mother; but I do beg you to let me alone
for once, and tell me about this horrible business of my father wanting to set me aside for another son.

LADY BRITOMART [*amazed*]   Another son! I never said anything of the
kind. I never dreamt of such a thing. This is what comes of interrupting me.

STEPHEN   But you said—

LADY BRITOMART [*cutting him short*]   Now be a good boy, Stephen,
and listen to me patiently. The Undershafts are descended from a
foundling in the parish of St Andrew Undershaft in the city. That
was long ago, in the reign of James the First. Well, this foundling
was adopted by an armorer and gun-maker. In the course of time
the foundling succeeded to the business; and from some notion of
gratitude, or some vow or something, he adopted another foundling,
and left the business to him. And that foundling did the same. Ever
since that, the cannon business has always been left to an adopted
foundling named Andrew Undershaft.

STEPHEN   But did they never marry? Were there no legitimate sons?

LADY BRITOMART   Oh yes: they married just as your father did; and

they were rich enough to buy land for their own children and leave them well provided for. But they always adopted and trained some foundling to succeed them in the business; and of course they always quarrelled with their wives furiously over it. Your father was adopted in that way; and he pretends to consider himself bound to keep up the tradition and adopt somebody to leave the business to. Of course I was not going to stand that. There may have been some reason for it when the Undershafts could only marry women in their own class, whose sons were not fit to govern great estates. But there could be no excuse for passing over m y son.

STEPHEN [*dubiously*]   I am afraid I should make a poor hand of managing a cannon foundry.

LADY BRITOMART   Nonsense! you could easily get a manager and pay him a salary.

STEPHEN   My father evidently had no great opinion of my capacity.

LADY BRITOMART   Stuff, child! you were only a baby: it had nothing to do with your capacity. Andrew did it on principle, just as he did every perverse and wicked thing on principle. When my father remonstrated, Andrew actually told him to his face that history tells us of only two successful institutions: one the Undershaft firm, and the other the Roman Empire under the Antonines.[8] That was because the Antonine emperors all adopted their successors. Such rubbish! The Stevenages are as good as the Antonines, I hope; and you are a Stevenage. But that was Andrew all over. There you have the man! Always clever and unanswerable when he was defending nonsense and wickedness: always awkward and sullen when he had to behave sensibly and decently!

STEPHEN   Then it was on my account that your home life was broken up, mother. I am sorry.

LADY BRITOMART   Well, dear, there were other differences. I really cannot bear an immoral man. I am not a Pharisee, I hope; and I should not have minded his merely d o i n g wrong things: we are none of us perfect. But your father didnt exactly d o wrong things: he said them and thought them: that was what was so dreadful. He really had a sort of religion of wrongness. Just as one doesnt mind men practising immorality so long as they own that they are in the wrong by preaching morality; so I couldnt forgive Andrew for preaching immorality while he practised morality. You would all have grown up without principles, without any knowledge of right and wrong, if he had been in the house. You know, my dear, your father was a very attractive man in some ways. Children did not dislike him; and he took advantage of it to put the wickedest ideas into their heads, and make them quite unmanageable. I did not dislike him myself: very far from it; but nothing can bridge over moral disagreement.

STEPHEN   All this simply bewilders me, mother. People may differ about matters of opinion, or even about religion; but how can they differ about right and wrong? Right is right; and wrong is wrong; and if a man cannot distinguish them properly, he is either a fool or a rascal: thats all.

8. From 96 A.D. to 180 A.D. the Roman emperors, the so-called Five Good Emperors, were succeeded by persons they had adopted. The five were Nerva (96–98), Trajan (98–117), Hadrian (117–138), Antoninus Pius (138–161), from whose name the term "Antonines" is derived, and Marcus Aurelius (161–180). Commodus, the son and successor of Marcus Aurelius, did not live up to the reputation of his predecessors.

LADY BRITOMART [*touched*]   Thats my own boy! [*She pats his cheek.*] Your father never could answer that: he used to laugh and get out of it under cover of some affectionate nonsense. And now that you understand the situation, what do you advise me to do?

STEPHEN   Well, what c a n you do?

LADY BRITOMART   I must get the money somehow.

STEPHEN   We cannot take money from him. I had rather go and live in some cheap place like Bedford Square or even Hampstead than take a farthing of his money.[9]

LADY BRITOMART   But after all, Stephen, our present income comes from Andrew.

STEPHEN [*shocked*]   I never knew that.

LADY BRITOMART   Well, you surely didnt suppose your grandfather had anything to give me. The Stevenages could not do everything for you. We gave you social position. Andrew had to contribute s o m e t h i n g. He had a very good bargain, I think.

STEPHEN [*bitterly*]   We are utterly dependent on him and his cannons, then?

LADY BRITOMART   Certainly not: the money is settled. But he provided it. So you see it is not a question of taking money from him or not: it is simply a question of how much. I dont want any more for myself.

STEPHEN   Nor do I.

LADY BRITOMART   But Sarah does; and Barbara does. That is, Charles Lomax and Adolphus Cusins will cost them more. So I must put my pride in my pocket and ask for it, I suppose. That is your advice, Stephen, is it not?

STEPHEN   No.

LADY BRITOMART [*sharply*]   Stephen!

STEPHEN   Of course if you are determined—

LADY BRITOMART   I am not determined: I ask your advice; and I am waiting for it. I will not have all the responsibility thrown on my shoulders.

STEPHEN [*obstinately*]   I would die sooner than ask him for another penny.

LADY BRITOMART [*resignedly*]   You mean that *I* must ask him. Very well, Stephen: it shall be as you wish. You will be glad to know that your grandfather concurs. But he thinks I ought to ask Andrew to come here and see the girls. After all, he must have some natural affection for them.

STEPHEN   Ask him here!!!

LADY BRITOMART   Do n o t repeat my words, Stephen. Where else can I ask him?

STEPHEN   I never expected you to ask him at all.

LADY BRITOMART   Now dont tease, Stephen. Come! you see that it is necessary that he should pay us a visit, dont you?

STEPHEN [*reluctantly*]   I suppose so, if the girls cannot do without his money.

LADY BRITOMART   Thank you, Stephen: I knew you would give me the

---

9. Hampstead, about four miles northwest of the center of London, and Bloomsbury, which includes Bedford Square as well as the British Museum and the University of London, were less fashionable than Belgravia but hardly poor districts. Many writers and theatrical personalities have been associated with both districts. Shaw is mocking Stephen's anti-intellectualism.

right advice when it was properly explained to you. I have asked
your father to come this evening. [STEPHEN *bounds from his seat.*]
Dont jump, Stephen: it fidgets me.

STEPHEN [*in utter consternation*]   Do you mean to say that my father
is coming here tonight—that he may be here at any moment?

LADY BRITOMART [*looking at her watch*]   I said nine. [*He gasps. She
rises.*] Ring the bell, please. [STEPHEN *goes to the smaller writing
table; presses a button on it; and sits at it with his elbows on the table
and his head in his hands, outwitted and overwhelmed.*] It is ten
minutes to nine yet; and I have to prepare the girls. I asked Charles
Lomax and Adolphus to dinner on purpose that they might be here.
Andrew had better see them in case he should cherish any delusions
as to their being capable of supporting their wives. [*The butler enters:* LADY BRITOMART *goes behind the settee to speak to him.*] Morrison: go up to the drawing room and tell everybody to come down
here at once. [MORRISON *withdraws.* LADY BRITOMART *turns to* STE-
PHEN.] Now remember, Stephen: I shall need all your countenance
and authority. [*He rises and tries to recover some vestige of these
attributes.*] Give me a chair, dear. [*He pushes a chair forward from
the wall to where she stands, near the smaller writing table. She sits
down; and he goes to the armchair, into which he throws himself.*]
I dont know how Barbara will take it. Ever since they made her a
major in the Salvation Army she has developed a propensity to have
her own way and order people about which quite cows me sometimes. It's not ladylike: I'm sure I dont know where she picked it up.
Anyhow, Barbara shant bully m e; but still it's just as well that your
father should be here before she has time to refuse to meet him or
make a fuss. Dont look nervous, Stephen: it will only encourage Barbara to make difficulties. *I* am nervous enough, goodness knows; but
I dont shew it.

SARAH *and* BARBARA *come in with their respective young men,*
CHARLES LOMAX *and* ADOLPHUS CUSINS. SARAH *is slender, bored,
and mundane.* BARBARA *is robuster, jollier, much more energetic.*
SARAH *is fashionably dressed:* BARBARA *is in Salvation Army uniform.* LOMAX, *a young man about town, is like many other
young men about town. He is afflicted with a frivolous sense of
humor which plunges him at the most inopportune moments
into paroxysms of imperfectly suppressed laughter.* CUSINS *is a
spectacled student, slight, thin haired, and sweet voiced, with
a more complex form of* LOMAX's *complaint. His sense of humor is intellectual and subtle, and is complicated by an appalling temper. The lifelong struggle of a benevolent temperament and a high conscience against impulses of inhuman ridicule
and fierce impatience has set up a chronic strain which has visibly wrecked his constitution. He is a most implacable, determined, tenacious, intolerant person who by mere force of character presents himself as—and indeed actually is—considerate,
gentle, explanatory, even mild and apologetic, capable possibly
of murder, but not of cruelty or coarseness. By the operation of
some instinct which is not merciful enough to blind him with
the illusions of love, he is obstinately bent on marrying* BAR-
BARA. LOMAX *likes* SARAH *and thinks it will be rather a lark to
marry her. Consequently, he has not attempted to resist* LADY*

BRITOMART'S *arrangements to that end.*
All four look as if they had been having a good deal of fun in the drawing room. The girls enter first, leaving the swains outside. SARAH *comes to the settee.* BARBARA *comes in after her and stops at the door.*

BARBARA   Are Cholly and Dolly to come in?
LADY BRITOMART [*forcibly*]   Barbara: I will not have Charles called Cholly: the vulgarity of it positively makes me ill.
BARBARA   It's all right, mother: Cholly is quite correct nowadays. Are they to come in?
LADY BRITOMART   Yes, if they will behave themselves.
BARBARA [*through the door*]   Come in, Dolly; and behave yourself.

BARBARA *comes to her mother's writing table.* CUSINS *enters smiling, and wanders towards* LADY BRITOMART.

SARAH [*calling*]   Come in, Cholly. [LOMAX *enters, controlling his features very imperfectly, and places himself vaguely between* SARAH *and* BARBARA.]
LADY BRITOMART [*peremptorily*]   Sit down, all of you. [*They sit.* CUSINS *crosses to the window and seats himself there.* LOMAX *takes a chair.* BARBARA *sits at the writing table and* SARAH *on the settee.*] I dont in the least know what you are laughing at, Adolphus. I am surprised at you, though I expected nothing better from Charles Lomax.
CUSINS [*in a remarkably gentle voice*]   Barbara has been trying to teach me the West Ham Salvation March.[1]
LADY BRITOMART   I see nothing to laugh at in that; nor should you if you are really converted.
CUSINS [*sweetly*]   You were not present. It was really funny, I believe.
LOMAX   Ripping.
LADY BRITOMART   Be quiet, Charles. Now listen to me, children. Your father is coming here this evening.

General stupefaction. LOMAX, SARAH, *and* BARBARA *rise:* SARAH *scared, and* BARBARA *amused and expectant.*

LOMAX [*remonstrating*]   Oh I say!
LADY BRITOMART   You are not called on to say anything, Charles.
SARAH   Are you serious, mother?
LADY BRITOMART   Of course I am serious. It is on your account, Sarah, and also on Charles's. [*Silence.* SARAH *sits, with a shrug.* CHARLES *looks painfully unworthy.*] I hope you are not going to object, Barbara.
BARBARA   I! why should I? My father has a soul to be saved like anybody else. He's quite welcome as far as I am concerned. [*She sits on the table, and softly whistles 'Onward, Christian Soldiers.'*]
LOMAX [*still remonstrant*]   But really, dont you know! Oh I say!
LADY BRITOMART [*frigidly*]   What do you wish to convey, Charles?
LOMAX   Well, you must admit that this is a bit thick.
LADY BRITOMART [*turning with ominous suavity to* CUSINS]   Adolphus: you are a professor of Greek. Can you translate Charles Lomax's remarks into reputable English for us?

---

1. West Ham is a poor section in the East End of London and the site of Barbara's good works.

CUSINS [*cautiously*]   If I may say so, Lady Brit, I think Charles has rather happily expressed what we all feel. Homer, speaking of Auto-lycus, uses the same phrase.   πυκινὸν δόμον ἐλθεῖν ² means a bit thick.

LOMAX [*handsomely*]   Not that I mind, you know, if Sarah dont. [*He sits.*]

LADY BRITOMART [*crushingly*]   Thank you. Have I y o u r permission, Adolphus, to invite my own husband to my own house?

CUSINS [*gallantly*]   You have my unhesitating support in everything you do.

LADY BRITOMART   Tush! Sarah: have you nothing to say?

SARAH   Do you mean that he is coming regularly to live here?

LADY BRITOMART   Certainly not. The spare room is ready for him if he likes to stay for a day or two and see a little more of you; but there are limits.

SARAH   Well, he cant eat us, I suppose. *I* dont mind.

LOMAX [*chuckling*]   I wonder how the old man will take it.

LADY BRITOMART   Much as the old woman will, no doubt, Charles.

LOMAX [*abashed*]   I didnt mean—at least—

LADY BRITOMART   You didnt t h i n k, Charles. You never do; and the result is, you never mean anything. And now please attend to me, children. Your father will be quite a stranger to us.

LOMAX   I suppose he hasnt seen Sarah since she was a little kid.

LADY BRITOMART   Not since she was a little kid, Charles, as you ex-press it with that elegance of diction and refinement of thought that seem never to desert you. Accordingly—er— [*Impatiently.*] Now I have forgotten what I was going to say. That comes of your provok-ing me to be sarcastic, Charles. Adolphus: will you kindly tell me where I was.

CUSINS [*sweetly*]   You were saying that as Mr Undershaft has not seen his children since they were babies, he will form his opinion of the way you have brought them up from their behavior tonight, and that therefore you wish us all to be particularly careful to conduct our-selves well, especially Charles.

LADY BRITOMART [*with emphatic approval*]   Precisely.

LOMAX   Look here, Dolly: Lady Brit didnt say that.

LADY BRITOMART [*vehemently*]   I did, Charles. Adolphus's recollec-tion is perfectly correct. It is most important that you should be good; and I do beg you for once not to pair off into opposite corners and giggle and whisper while I am speaking to your father.

BARBARA   All right, mother. We'll do you credit. [*She comes off the table, and sits in her chair with ladylike elegance.*]

LADY BRITOMART   Remember, Charles, that Sarah will want to feel proud of you instead of ashamed of you.

LOMAX   Oh I say! theres nothing to be exactly proud of, dont you know.

LADY BRITOMART   Well, try and look as if there was.

MORRISON, *pale and dismayed, breaks into the room in uncon-cealed disorder.*

---

2. The Greek phrase was supplied to Shaw by Gilbert Murray, the Greek scholar to whom the play was dedicated and who was the model for Cusins. The Greek original actually reads πυκινὸν δόμον αντιτορήσας.

MORRISON   Might I speak a word to you, my lady?

LADY BRITOMART   Nonsense! Shew him up.

MORRISON   Yes, my lady. [*He goes.*]

LOMAX   Does Morrison know who it is?

LADY BRITOMART   Of course. Morrison has always been with us.

LOMAX   It must be a regular corker for him, dont you know.

LADY BRITOMART   Is this a moment to get on my nerves, Charles, with your outrageous expressions?

LOMAX   But this is something out of the ordinary, really—

MORRISON   [*at the door*]   The—er—Mr Undershaft. [*He retreats in confusion.*]

> ANDREW UNDERSHAFT *comes in. All rise.* LADY BRITOMART *meets him in the middle of the room behind the settee.*
>
> ANDREW *is, on the surface, a stoutish, easygoing elderly man, with kindly patient manners, and an engaging simplicity of character. But he has a watchful, deliberate, waiting, listening face, and formidable reserves of power, both bodily and mental, in his capacious chest and long head. His gentleness is partly that of a strong man who has learnt by experience that his natural grip hurts ordinary people unless he handles them very carefully, and partly the mellowness of age and success. He is also a little shy in his present very delicate situation.*

LADY BRITOMART   Good evening, Andrew.

UNDERSHAFT   How d'ye do, my dear.

LADY BRITOMART   You look a good deal older.

UNDERSHAFT   [*apologetically*]   I a m somewhat older. [*Taking her hand with a touch of courtship.*] Time has stood still with you.

LADY BRITOMART   [*throwing away his hand*]   Rubbish! This is your family.

UNDERSHAFT   [*surprised*]   Is it so large? I am sorry to say my memory is failing very badly in some things. [*He offers his hand with paternal kindness to* LOMAX.]

LOMAX   [*jerkily shaking his hand*]   Ahdedoo.

UNDERSHAFT   I can see you are my eldest. I am very glad to meet you again, my boy.

LOMAX   [*remonstrating*]   No, but look here dont you know—[*Overcome.*] Oh I say!

LADY BRITOMART   [*recovering from momentary speechlessness*]   Andrew: do you mean to say that you dont remember how many children you have?

UNDERSHAFT   Well, I am afraid I—. They have grown so much—er. Am I making any ridiculous mistake? I may as well confess: I recollect only one son. But so many things have happened since, of course —er—

LADY BRITOMART   [*decisively*]   Andrew: you are talking nonsense. Of course you have only one son.

UNDERSHAFT   Perhaps you will be good enough to introduce me, my dear.

LADY BRITOMART   That is Charles Lomax, who is engaged to Sarah.

UNDERSHAFT   My dear sir, I beg your pardon.

LOMAX   Notatall. Delighted, I assure you.

LADY BRITOMART   This is Stephen.

UNDERSHAFT   [*bowing*]   Happy to make your acquaintance, Mr Ste-

phen. Then [*going to* CUSINS] y o u must be my son. [*Taking* CUSINS' *hands in his.*] How are you, my young friend? [*To* LADY BRITOMART.] He is very like you, my love.

CUSINS   You flatter me, Mr Undershaft. My name is Cusins: engaged to Barbara. [*Very explicitly.*] That is Major Barbara Undershaft, of the Salvation Army. That is Sarah, your second daughter. This is Stephen Undershaft, your son.

UNDERSHAFT   My dear Stephen, I b e g your pardon.

STEPHEN   Not at all.

UNDERSHAFT   Mr Cusins: I am much indebted to you for explaining so precisely. [*Turning to* SARAH.] Barbara, my dear—

SARAH [*prompting him*]   Sarah.

UNDERSHAFT   Sarah, of course. [*They shake hands. He goes over to* BARBARA.] Barbara—I am right this time, I hope?

BARBARA   Quite right. [*They shake hands.*]

LADY BRITOMART [*resuming command*]   Sit down, all of you. Sit down, Andrew. [*She comes forward and sits on the settee.* CUSINS *also brings his chair forward on her left.* BARBARA *and* STEPHEN *resume their seats.* LOMAX *gives his chair to* SARAH *and goes for another.*]

UNDERSHAFT   Thank you, my love.

LOMAX [*conversationally, as he brings a chair forward between the writing table and the settee, and offers it to* UNDERSHAFT]   Takes you some time to find out exactly where you are, dont it?

UNDERSHAFT [*accepting the chair, but remaining standing*]   That is not what embarrasses me, Mr Lomax. My difficulty is that if I play the part of a father, I shall produce the effect of an intrusive stranger; and if I play the part of a discreet stranger, I may appear a callous father.

LADY BRITOMART   There is no need for you to play any part at all, Andrew. You had much better be sincere and natural.

UNDERSHAFT [*submissively*]   Yes, my dear: I daresay that will be best. [*He sits down comfortably.*] Well, here I am. Now what can I do for you all?

LADY BRITOMART   You need not do anything, Andrew. You are one of the family. You can sit with us and enjoy yourself.

A painfully conscious pause. BARBARA *makes a face at* LOMAX, *whose too long suppressed mirth immediately explodes in agonized neighings.*

LADY BRITOMART [*outraged*]   Charles Lomax: if you can behave yourself, behave yourself. If not, leave the room.

LOMAX   I'm awfully sorry, Lady Brit; but really you know, upon my soul! [*He sits on the settee between* LADY BRITOMART *and* UNDERSHAFT, *quite overcome.*]

BARBARA   Why dont you laugh if you want to, Cholly? It's good for your inside.

LADY BRITOMART   Barbara: you have had the education of a lady. Please let your father see that; and dont talk like a street girl.

UNDERSHAFT   Never mind me, my dear. As you know, I am not a gentleman; and I was never educated.

LOMAX [*encouragingly*]   Nobody'd know it, I assure you. You look all right, you know.

CUSINS   Let me advise you to study Greek, Mr Undershaft. Greek scholars are privileged men. Few of them know Greek; and none of

them know anything else; but their position is unchallengeable. Other languages are the qualifications of waiters and commercial travellers: Greek is to a man of position what the hallmark is to silver.

BARBARA   Dolly: dont be insincere. Cholly: fetch your concertina and play something for us.

LOMAX [*jumps up eagerly, but checks himself to remark doubtfully to* UNDERSHAFT]   Perhaps that sort of thing isnt in your line, eh?

UNDERSHAFT   I am particularly fond of music.

LOMAX [*delighted*]   Are you? Then I'll get it. [*He goes upstairs for the instrument.*]

UNDERSHAFT   Do you play, Barbara?

BARBARA   Only the tambourine. But Cholly's teaching me the concertina.

UNDERSHAFT   Is Cholly also a member of the Salvation Army?

BARBARA   No: he says it's bad form to be a dissenter.[3] But I dont despair of Cholly. I made him come yesterday to a meeting at the dock gates, and take the collection in his hat.

UNDERSHAFT [*looks whimsically at his wife*]!!!

LADY BRITOMART   It is not my doing, Andrew. Barbara is old enough to take her own way. She has no father to advise her.

BARBARA   Oh yes she has. There are no orphans in the Salvation Army.

UNDERSHAFT   Your father there has a great many children and plenty of experience, eh?

BARBARA [*looking at him with quick interest and nodding*]   Just so. How did y o u come to understand that? [LOMAX *is heard at the door trying the concertina.*]

LADY BRITOMART   Come in, Charles. Play us something at once.

LOMAX   Righto! [*He sits down in his former place, and preludes.*]

UNDERSHAFT   One moment, Mr Lomax. I am rather interested in the Salvation Army. Its motto might be my own: Blood and Fire.

LOMAX [*shocked*]   But not your sort of blood and fire, you know.

UNDERSHAFT   My sort of blood cleanses: my sort of fire purifies.

BARBARA   So do ours. Come down tomorrow to my shelter—the West Ham shelter—and see what we're doing. We're going to march to a great meeting in the Assembly Hall at Mile End.[4] Come and see the shelter and then march with us: it will do you a lot of good. Can you play anything?

UNDERSHAFT   In my youth I earned pennies, and even shillings occasionally, in the streets and in public house parlors by my natural talent for stepdancing.[5] Later on, I became a member of the Undershaft orchestral society, and performed passably on the tenor trombone.

LOMAX [*scandalized—putting down the concertina*]   Oh I say!

BARBARA   Many a sinner has played himself into heaven on the trombone, thanks to the Army.

LOMAX [*to* BARBARA, *still rather shocked*]   Yes; but what about the cannon business, dont you know? [*To* UNDERSHAFT.] Getting into heaven is not exactly in your line, is it?

---

3. A "dissenter" is a Protestant who worships outside the established Anglican church.
    4. Mile End is a poor section in the East End of London. Mile End Road is a continuation of Whitechapel Road, beginning one mile to the east of the old City wall. The section is associated with the Salvation Army which began there with outdoor services conducted by William Booth in 1865.
    5. Stepdancing is a form intended to display the performer's skill by the use of special steps.

LADY BRITOMART   Charles!!!

LOMAX   Well; but it stands to reason, dont it? The cannon business may be necessary and all that: we cant get on without cannons; but it isnt right, you know. On the other hand, there may be a certain amount of tosh[6] about the Salvation Army—I belong to the Established Church myself—but still you cant deny that it's religion; and you cant go against religion, can you? At least unless youre downright immoral, dont you know.

UNDERSHAFT   You hardly appreciate my position, Mr Lomax—

LOMAX   [*hastily*]   I'm not saying anything against you personally—

UNDERSHAFT   Quite so, quite so. But consider for a moment. Here I am, a profiteer in mutilation and murder. I find myself in a specially amiable humor just now because, this morning, down at the foundry, we blew twenty-seven dummy soldiers into fragments with a gun which formerly destroyed only thirteen.

LOMAX   [*leniently*]   Well, the more destructive war becomes, the sooner it will be abolished, eh?

UNDERSHAFT   Not at all. The more destructive war becomes the more fascinating we find it. No, Mr Lomax: I am obliged to you for making the usual excuse for my trade; but I am not ashamed of it. I am not one of those men who keep their morals and their business in water-tight compartments. All the spare money my trade rivals spend on hospitals, cathedrals, and other receptacles for conscience money, I devote to experiments and researches in improved methods of destroying life and property. I have always done so; and I always shall. Therefore your Christmas card moralities of peace on earth and goodwill among men are of no use to me. Your Christianity, which enjoins you to resist not evil, and to turn the other cheek, would make me a bankrupt. M y morality—m y religion—must have a place for cannons and torpedoes in it.

STEPHEN   [*coldly—almost sullenly*]   You speak as if there were half a dozen moralities and religions to choose from, instead of one true morality and one true religion.

UNDERSHAFT   For me there is only one true morality; but it might not fit you, as you do not manufacture aerial battleships. There is only one true morality for every man; but every man has not the same true morality.

LOMAX   [*overtaxed*]   Would you mind saying that again? I didnt quite follow it.

CUSINS   It's quite simple. As Euripides says, one man's meat is another man's poison morally as well as physically.[7]

UNDERSHAFT   Precisely.

LOMAX   Oh, t h a t ! Yes, yes, yes. True. True.

STEPHEN   In other words, some men are honest and some are scoundrels.

BARBARA   Bosh! There are no scoundrels.

UNDERSHAFT   Indeed? Are there any good men?

---

6. Pretension or nonsense.
7. In his dedication to the play Shaw expressed his admiration for Gilbert Murray's translation of *The Bacchae* of Euripides. If Cusins is referring to a specific passage, he may mean the following from that translation: "For strangely graven / Is the orb of life, that one and another / In gold and power may outpass his brother. / And men in their millions float and flow / And seethe with a million hopes as leaven; / And they win their Will, or they miss their Will, / And the hopes are dead or are pined for still; / But whoe'er can know, / As the long days go, / That to Live is happy, hath found his Heaven!" The passage is quoted with some alterations in Act 2 of this play.

BARBARA   No. Not one. There are neither good men nor scoundrels: there are just children of one Father; and the sooner they stop calling one another names the better. You neednt talk to me: I know them. Ive had scores of them through my hands: scoundrels, criminals, infidels, philanthropists, missionaries, county councillors, all sorts. Theyre all just the same sort of sinner; and theres the same salvation ready for them all.

UNDERSHAFT   May I ask have you ever saved a maker of cannons?

BARBARA   No. Will you let me try?

UNDERSHAFT   Well, I will make a bargain with you. If I go to see you tomorrow in your Salvation Shelter, will you come the day after to see me in my cannon works?

BARBARA   Take care. It may end in your giving up the cannons for the sake of the Salvation Army.

UNDERSHAFT   Are you sure it will not end in your giving up the Salvation Army for the sake of the cannons?

BARBARA   I will take my chance of that.

UNDERSHAFT   And I will take my chance of the other. [*They shake hands on it.*] Where is your shelter?

BARBARA   In West Ham. At the sign of the cross. Ask anybody in Canning Town.[8] Where are your works?

UNDERSHAFT   In Perivale St Andrews. At the sign of the sword. Ask anybody in Europe.

LOMAX   Hadnt I better play something?

BARBARA   Yes. Give us Onward, Christian Soldiers.

LOMAX   Well, thats rather a strong order to begin with, dont you know. Suppose I sing Thourt passing hence, my brother. It's much the same tune.

BARBARA   It's too melancholy. You get saved, Cholly; and youll pass hence, my brother, without making such a fuss about it.

LADY BRITOMART   Really, Barbara, you go on as if religion were a pleasant subject. Do have some sense of propriety.

UNDERSHAFT   I do not find it an unpleasant subject, my dear. It is the only one that capable people really care for.

LADY BRITOMART [*looking at her watch*]   Well, if you are determined to have it, I insist on having it in a proper and respectable way. Charles: ring for prayers.

General amazement. STEPHEN *rises in dismay.*

LOMAX [*rising*]   Oh I say!

UNDERSHAFT [*rising*]   I am afraid I must be going.

LADY BRITOMART   You cannot go now, Andrew: it would be most improper. Sit down. What will the servants think?

UNDERSHAFT   My dear: I have conscientious scruples. May I suggest a compromise? If Barbara will conduct a little service in the drawing room, with Mr Lomax as organist, I will attend it willingly. I will even take part, if a trombone can be procured.

LADY BRITOMART   Dont mock, Andrew.

UNDERSHAFT [*shocked—to* BARBARA]   You dont think I am mocking, my love, I hope.

BARBARA   No, of course not; and it wouldnt matter if you were: half the Army came to their first meeting for a lark. [*Rising.*] Come along.

---

8. Canning Town is a poor area in the East End of London, near the East India docks.

[*She throws her arm round her father and sweeps him out, calling to the others from the threshold.*] Come, Dolly. Come, Cholly.

CUSINS *rises.*

LADY BRITOMART   I will not be disobeyed by everybody. Adolphus: sit down. [*He does not.*] Charles: you may go. You are not fit for prayers: you cannot keep your countenance.

LOMAX   Oh I say! [*He goes out.*]

LADY BRITOMART [*continuing*]   But you, Adolphus, can behave yourself if you choose to. I insist on your staying.

CUSINS   My dear Lady Brit: there are things in the family prayer book that I couldnt bear to hear you say.

LADY BRITOMART   What things, pray?

CUSINS   Well, you would have to say before all the servants that we have done things we ought not to have done, and left undone things we ought to have done, and that there is no health in us. I cannot bear to hear you doing yourself such an injustice, and Barbara such an injustice. As for myself, I flatly deny it: I have done my best. I shouldnt dare to marry Barbara—I couldnt look you in the face—if it were true. So I must go to the drawing room.

LADY BRITOMART [*offended*]   Well, go. [*He starts for the door.*] And remember this, Adolphus: [*He turns to listen.*] I have a very strong suspicion that you went to the Salvation Army to worship Barbara and nothing else. And I quite appreciate the very clever way in which you systematically humbug me. I have found you out. Take care Barbara doesnt. Thats all.

CUSINS [*with unruffled sweetness*]   Dont tell on me. [*He steals out.*]

LADY BRITOMART   Sarah: if you want to go, go. Anything's better than to sit there as if you wished you were a thousand miles away.

SARAH [*languidly*]   Very well, mamma. [*She goes.*]

LADY BRITOMART, *with a sudden flounce, gives way to a little gust of tears.*

STEPHEN [*going to her*]   Mother: whats the matter?

LADY BRITOMART [*swishing away her tears with her handkerchief*] Nothing. Foolishness. You can go with him, too, if you like, and leave me with the servants.

STEPHEN   Oh, you mustnt think that, mother. I—I dont like him.

LADY BRITOMART   The others do. That is the injustice of a woman's lot. A woman has to bring up her children; and that means to restrain them, to deny them things they want, to set them tasks, to punish them when they do wrong, to do all the unpleasant things. And then the father, who has nothing to do but pet them and spoil them, comes in when all her work is done and steals their affection from her.

STEPHEN   He has not stolen our affection from you. It is only curiosity.

LADY BRITOMART [*violently*]   I wont be consoled, Stephen. There is nothing the matter with me. [*She rises and goes towards the door.*]

STEPHEN   Where are you going, mother?

LADY BRITOMART   To the drawing room, of course. [*She goes out. Onward, Christian Soldiers, on the concertina, with tambourine accompaniment, is heard when the door opens.*] Are you coming, Stephen?

STEPHEN   No. Certainly not. [*She goes. He sits down on the settee, with compressed lips and an expression of strong dislike.*]

Act 2

*The yard of the West Ham shelter of the Salvation Army is a
cold place on a January morning. The building itself, an old ware-
house, is newly whitewashed. Its gabled end projects into the yard
in the middle, with a door on the ground floor, and another in the
loft above it without any balcony or ladder, but with a pulley
rigged over it for hoisting sacks. Those who come from this central
gable end into the yard have the gateway leading to the street on
their left, with a stone horse-trough just beyond it, and, on the
right, a penthouse shielding a table from the weather. There are
forms at the table; and on them are seated a man and a woman,
both much down on their luck, finishing a meal of bread (one
thick slice each, with margarine and golden syrup) and diluted
milk.*

*The man, a workman out of employment, is young, agile, a
talker, a poser, sharp enough to be capable of anything in reason
except honesty or altruistic considerations of any kind. The woman
is a commonplace old bundle of poverty and hard-worn humanity.
She looks sixty and probably is forty-five. If they were rich people,
gloved and muffed and well wrapped up in furs and overcoats,
they would be numbed and miserable; for it is a grindingly cold
raw January day; and a glance at the background of grimy ware-
houses and leaden sky visible over the whitewashed walls of the
yard would drive any idle rich person straight to the Mediterranean. But these two, being no more troubled with visions of the
Mediterranean than of the moon, and being compelled to keep
more of their clothes in the pawnshop, and less on their persons, in
winter than in summer, are not depressed by the cold: rather are
they stung into vivacity, to which their meal has just now given an
almost jolly turn. The man takes a pull at his mug, and then gets
up and moves about the yard with his hands deep in his pockets,
occasionally breaking into a stepdance.*

THE WOMAN   Feel better arter your meal, sir?[9]

THE MAN   No. Call that a meal! Good enough for you, praps; but wot
is it to me, an intelligent workin man.

THE WOMAN   Workin man! Wot are you?

THE MAN   Painter.

THE WOMAN [*sceptically*]   Yus, I dessay.

THE MAN   Yus, you dessay! I know. Every loafer that cant do nothink calls isself a painter. Well, I'm a real painter: grainer, finisher,
thirty-eight bob a week when I can get it.[1]

THE WOMAN   Then why dont you go and get it?

THE MAN   I'll tell you why. Fust: I'm intelligent—fffff! it's rotten cold
here [*he dances a step or two*]—yes: intelligent beyond the station
o life into which it has pleased the capitalists to call me; and they
dont like a man that sees through em. Second, an intelligent bein
needs a doo share of appiness; so I drink somethink cruel when I
get the chawnce. Third, I stand by my class and do as little as I can
so's to leave arf the job for me fellow workers. Fourth, I'm fly enough

9. See note on Shaw's spelling, p. 1044.
1. A "grainer" is a craftsman who paints
an imitation of the grain of wood or the
streaks of marble in inferior materials. A
"finisher" puts the final touches on the
paint job.

to know wots inside the law and wots outside it;[2] and inside it I do as the capitalists do: pinch wot I can lay me ands on. In a proper state of society I am sober, industrious and honest: in Rome, so to speak, I do as the Romans do. Wots the consequence? When trade is bad—and it's rotten bad just now—and the employers az to sack arf their men, they generally start on me.

THE WOMAN   Whats your name?

THE MAN   Price. Bronterre O'Brien Price. Usually called Snobby Price, for short.

THE WOMAN   Snobby's a carpenter, aint it? You said you was a painter.

PRICE   Not that kind of snob, but the genteel sort. I'm too uppish, owing to my intelligence, and my father being a Chartist[3] and a reading, thinking man: a stationer, too. I'm none of your common hewers of wood and drawers of water; and dont you forget it. [*He returns to his seat at the table, and takes up his mug.*] Wots y o u r name?

THE WOMAN   Rummy Mitchens, sir.

PRICE [*quaffing the remains of his milk to her*]   Your elth, Miss Mitchens.

RUMMY [*correcting him*]   Missis Mitchens.

PRICE   Wot! Oh Rummy, Rummy! Respectable married woman, Rummy, gittin rescued by the Salvation Army by pretendin to be a bad un. Same old game!

RUMMY   What am I to do? I cant starve. Them Salvation lasses is dear good girls; but the better you are, the worse they likes to think you were before they rescued you. Why shouldnt they av a bit o credit, poor loves? theyre worn to rags by their work. And where would they get the money to rescue us if we was to let on we're no worse than other people? You know what ladies and gentlemen are.

PRICE   Thievin swine! Wish I ad their job, Rummy, all the same. Wot does Rummy stand for? Pet name praps?

RUMMY   Short for Romola.[4]

PRICE   For wot!?

RUMMY   Romola. It was out of a new book. Somebody me mother wanted me to grow up like.

PRICE   We're companions in misfortune, Rummy. Both on us got names that nobody cawnt pronounce. Consequently I'm Snobby and youre Rummy because Bill and Sally wasnt good enough for our parents. Such is life!

RUMMY   Who saved you, Mr Price? Was it Major Barbara?

PRICE   No: I come here on my own. I'm goin to be Bronterre O'Brien Price, the converted painter. I know wot they like. I'll tell em how I blasphemed and gambled and wopped my poor old mother—

RUMMY [*shocked*]   Used you to beat your mother?

PRICE   Not likely. She used to beat me. No matter: you come and listen to the converted painter, and youll hear how she was a pious woman that taught me me prayers at er knee, an how I used to come home drunk and drag her out o bed be er snow white airs, an lam into er with the poker.

RUMMY   That whats so unfair to us women. Your confessions is just as big lies as ours: you dont tell what you really done no more than us;

---

2. "Fly" is a slang word meaning knowing or aware.

3. Chartism was a political movement concerned with electoral and parliamentary reform. It arose in the 1830s and continued with varying success until 1848.

4. The heroine and title character of George Eliot's historical novel about Savonarola, published in 1863.

but you men can tell your lies right out at the meetins and be made much of for it; while the sort o confessions we az to make az to be wispered to one lady at a time. It aint right, spite of all their piety.

PRICE   Right! Do you spose the Army'd be allowed if it went and did right? Not much. It combs our air and makes us good little blokes to be robbed and put upon. But I'll play the game as good as any of em. I'll see somebody struck by lightnin, or hear a voice sayin "Snobby Price: where will you spend eternity?" I'll av a time of it, I tell you.

RUMMY   You wont be let drink, though.

PRICE   I'll take it out in gorspellin, then. I dont want to drink if I can get fun enough any other way.

> JENNY HILL, *a pale, overwrought, pretty Salvation lass of 18, comes in through the yard gate, leading* PETER SHIRLEY, *a half hardened, half worn-out elderly man, weak with hunger.*

JENNY [*supporting him*]   Come! pluck up. I'll get you something to eat. Youll be all right then.

PRICE [*rising and hurrying officiously to take the old man off* JENNY'S *hands*]   Poor old man! Cheer up, brother: youll find rest and peace and appiness ere. Hurry up with the food, miss: e's fair done. [JENNY *hurries into the shelter.*] Ere, buck up, daddy! shes fetchin y'a thick slice o breadn treacle, an a mug o skyblue.[5] [*He seats him at the corner of the table.*]

RUMMY [*gaily*]   Keep up your old art! Never say die!

SHIRLEY   I'm not an old man. I'm only 46. I'm as good as ever I was. The grey patch come in my hair before I was thirty. All it wants is three pennorth o hair dye: am I to be turned on the streets to starve for it? Holy God! Ive worked ten to twelve hours a day since I was thirteen, and paid my way all through; and now am I to be thrown into the gutter and my job given to a young man that can do it no better than me because Ive black hair that goes white at the first change?

PRICE [*cheerfully*]   No good jawrin about it. Youre ony a jumped-up, jerked-off, orspittle-turned-out incurable of an ole workin man: who cares about you? Eh? Make the thievin swine give you a meal: theyve stole many a one from you. Get a bit o your own back. [JENNY *returns with the usual meal.*] There you are, brother. Awsk a blessin an tuck that into you.

SHIRLEY [*looking at it ravenously but not touching it, and crying like a child*]   I never took anything before.

JENNY [*petting him*]   Come, come! the Lord sends it to you: he wasnt above taking bread from his friends; and why should you be? Besides, when we find you a job you can pay us for it if you like.

SHIRLEY [*eagerly*]   Yes, yes: thats true. I can pay you back: its only a loan. [*Shivering.*] Oh Lord! oh Lord! [*He turns to the table and attacks the meal ravenously.*]

JENNY   Well, Rummy, are you more comfortable now?

RUMMY   God bless you, lovey! youve fed my body and saved my soul, havnt you? [JENNY, *touched, kisses her.*] Sit down and rest a bit: you must be ready to drop.

JENNY   Ive been going hard since morning. But theres more work than we can do. I mustnt stop.

---

5. "Treacle" is roughly molasses. "Skyblue" is a name for thin or watery milk.

RUMMY   Try a prayer for just two minutes. Youll work all the better after.

JENNY [*her eyes lighting up*]   Oh isnt it wonderful how a few minutes prayer revives you! I was quite lightheaded at twelve o'clock, I was so tired; but Major Barbara just sent me to pray for five minutes; and I was able to go on as if I had only just begun. [*To* PRICE.] Did you have a piece of bread?

PRICE [*with unction*]   Yes, miss; but Ive got the piece that I value more; and thats the peace that passeth hall hannerstennin.

RUMMY [*fervently*]   Glory Hallelujah!

BILL WALKER, *a rough customer of about 25, appears at the yard gate and looks malevolently at* JENNY.

JENNY   That makes me so happy. When you say that, I feel wicked for loitering here. I must get to work again.

She is hurrying to the shelter, when the new-comer moves quickly up to the door and intercepts her. His manner is so threatening that she retreats as he comes at her truculently, driving her down the yard.

BILL   Aw knaow you. Youre the one that took awy maw girl. Youre the one that set er agen me. Well, I'm gowin to ev er aht. Not that Aw care a carse for er or you: see? Bat Aw'll let er knaow; and Aw'll let y o u knaow. Aw'm gowing to give her a doin thatll teach er to cat awy from me. Nah in wiv you and tell er to cam aht afore Aw cam in and kick er aht. Tell er Bill Walker wants er. She'll knaow wot thet means; and if she keeps me witin itll be worse. You stop to jawr beck at me; and Aw'll stawt on you: d'ye eah? Theres your wy. In you gow. [*He takes her by the arm and slings her towards the door of the shelter. She falls on her hand and knee.* RUMMY *helps her up again.*]

PRICE [*rising, and venturing irresolutely towards* BILL]   Easy there, mate. She aint doin you no arm.

BILL   Oo are you callin mite? [*Standing over him threateningly.*] Youre gowin to stend ap for er, aw yer? Put ap your ends.

RUMMY [*running indignantly to him to scold him*]   Oh, you great brute—[*He instantly swings his left hand back against her face. She screams and reels back to the trough, where she sits down, covering her bruised face with her hands and rocking herself and moaning with pain.*]

JENNY [*going to her*]   Oh, God forgive you! How could you strike an old woman like that?

BILL [*seizing her by the hair so violently that she also screams, and tearing her away from the old woman*]   You Gawd forgimme again an Aw'll Gawd forgive you one on the jawr thetll stop you pryin for a week. [*Holding her and turning fiercely on* PRICE.] Ev you ennything to sy agen it?

PRICE [*intimidated*]   No, matey: she aint anything to do with me.

BILL   Good job for you! Aw'd pat two meals into you and fawt you with one finger arter, you stawved cur. [*To* JENNY.] Nah are you gowin to fetch aht Mog Ebbijem;[6] or em Aw to knock your fice off you and fetch her meself?

JENNY [*writhing in his grasp*]   Oh please someone go in and tell Major

_____

6. Bill's young lady must have been named Margaret (Mag) Habberjam or Habbijam.

Barbara—[*She screams again as he wrenches her head down; and*
PRICE *and* RUMMY *flee into the shelter.*]

BILL   You want to gow in and tell your Mijor of me, do you?

JENNY   Oh please dont drag my hair. Let me go.

BILL   Do you or downt you? [*She stifles a scream.*] Yus or nao?

JENNY   God give me strength—

BILL   [*striking her with his fist in the face*]   Gow an shaow her thet,
and tell her if she wants one lawk it to cam and interfere with me.
[JENNY, *crying with pain, goes into the shed. He goes to the form and
addresses the old man.*] Eah: finish your mess; an git aht o maw wy.

SHIRLEY   [*springing up and facing him fiercely, with the mug in his
hand*]   You take a liberty with me, and I'll smash you over the face
with the mug and cut your eye out. Aint you satisfied—young whelps
like you—with takin the bread out o the mouths of your elders that
have brought you up and slaved for you, but you must come shovin
and cheekin and bullyin in here, where the bread o charity is sick-
enin in our stummicks?

BILL   [*contemptuously, but backing a little*]   Wot good are you, you
aold palsy mag?[7] Wot good are you?

SHIRLEY   As good as you and better. I'll do a day's work agen you or
any fat young soaker of your age. Go and take my job at Horrockses,
where I worked for ten year. They want young men there: they cant
afford to keep men over forty-five. Theyre very sorry—give you a
character and happy to help you to get anything suited to your years
—sure a steady man wont be long out of a job. Well, let em try
y o u. Theyll find the differ. What do y o u know? Not as much as
how to beeyave yourself—layin your dirty fist across the mouth of a
respectable woman!

BILL   Downt provowk me to ly it acrost yours: d'ye eah?

SHIRLEY   [*with blighting contempt*]   Yes: you like an old man to hit,
dont you, when youve finished with the women. I aint seen you hit a
young one yet.

BILL   [*stung*]   You loy, you aold soupkitchener, you. There was a yang
menn eah. Did Aw offer to itt him or did Aw not?

SHIRLEY   Was he starvin or was he not? Was he a man or only a cross-
eyed thief an a loafer? Would you hit my son-in-law's brother?

BILL   Oo's ee?

SHIRLEY   Todger Fairmile o Balls Pond. Him that won £20 off the
Japanese wrastler at the music hall by standin out 17 minutes 4
seconds agen him.

BILL   [*sullenly*]   Aw'm nao music awl wrastler. Ken he box?

SHIRLEY   Yes: an you cant.

BILL   Wot! Aw cawnt, cawnt Aw? Wots thet you sy? [*Threatening
him.*]

SHIRLEY   [*not budging an inch*]   Will you box Todger Fairmile if I put
him on to you? Say the word.

BILL   [*subsiding with a slouch*]   Aw'll stend ap to enny menn alawv,
if he was ten Todger Fairmawls. But Aw dont set ap to be a per-
feshnal.

SHIRLEY   [*looking down on him with unfathomable disdain*]   Y o u
box! Slap an old woman with the back o your hand! You hadnt even
the sense to hit her where a magistrate couldnt see the mark of it,

7. Literally, a palsied, old chatterer (from magpie), but used here as a general term of
contempt.

you silly young lump of conceit and ignorance. Hit a girl in the jaw
and ony make her cry! If Todger Fairmile'd done it, she wouldnt a
got up inside o ten minutes, no more than you would if he got on to
you. Yah! I'd set about you myself if I had a week's feedin in me instead o two months' starvation. [*He turns his back on him and sits
down moodily at the table.*]

BILL [*following him and stooping over him to drive the taunt in*]   You
loy! youve the bread and treacle in you that you cam eah to beg.

SHIRLEY [*bursting into tears*]   Oh God! it's true: I'm only an old pauper on the scrap heap. [*Furiously.*] But youll come to it yourself; and
then youll know. Youll come to it sooner than a teetotaller like me,
fillin yourself with gin at this hour o the mornin!

BILL   Aw'm nao gin drinker, you oald lawr; bat wen Aw want to give
my girl a bloomin good awdin Aw lawk to ev a bit o devil in me:
see? An eah Aw emm, talkin to a rotten aold blawter like you sted o
givin her wot for. [*Working himself into a rage.*] Aw'm gowin in
there to fetch her aht. [*He makes vengefully for the shelter door.*]

SHIRLEY   Youre goin to the station on a stretcher, more likely; and
theyll take the gin and the devil out of you there when they get you
inside. You mind what youre about: the major here is the Earl o
Stevenage's granddaughter.

BILL [*checked*]   Garn![8]

SHIRLEY   Youll see.

BILL [*his resolution oozing*]   Well, Aw aint dan nathin to er.

SHIRLEY   Spose she said you did! who'd believe you?

BILL [*very uneasy, skulking back to the corner of the penthouse[9]*]
Gawd! theres no jastice in this cantry. To think wot them people can
do! Aw'm as good as er.

SHIRLEY   Tell her so. It's just what a fool like you would do.

BARBARA, *brisk and businesslike, comes from the shelter with a
note book, and addresses herself to* SHIRLEY. BILL, *cowed, sits
down in the corner on a form, and turns his back on them.*

BARBARA   Good morning.

SHIRLEY [*standing up and taking off his hat*]   Good morning, miss.

BARBARA   Sit down: make yourself at home. [*He hesitates; but she
puts a friendly hand on his shoulder and makes him obey.*] Now
then! since youve made friends with us, we want to know all about
you. Names and addresses and trades.

SHIRLEY   Peter Shirley. Fitter. Chucked out two months ago because
I was too old.

BARBARA [*not at all surprised*]   Youd pass still. Why didnt you dye
your hair?

SHIRLEY   I did. Me age come out at a coroner's inquest on me daughter.

BARBARA   Steady?

SHIRLEY   Teetotaller. Never out of a job before. Good worker. And
sent to the knackers like an old horse![1]

BARBARA   No matter: if you did your part God will do his.

SHIRLEY [*suddenly stubborn*]   My religion's no concern of anybody
but myself.

8. A colloquial expression, used by the
lower classes, meaning something like "get
away with you."
9. A shed or secondary building, usually
with a sloping roof and attached to the

main structure.
1. A "knacker" bought old or diseased
horses and slaughtered them for their hides
and hooves and for meat to be used in dog
food.

BARBARA [*guessing*]   *I* know. Secularist?[2]

SHIRLEY [*hotly*]   Did I offer to deny it?

BARBARA   Why should you? My own father's a Secularist, I think. Our Father—yours and mine—fulfils himself in many ways; and I daresay he knew what he was about when he made a Secularist of you. So buck up, Peter! we can always find a job for a steady man like you. [SHIRLEY, *disarmed and a little bewildered, touches his hat. She turns from him to* BILL.] Whats y o u r name?

BILL [*insolently*]   Wots thet to you?

BARBARA [*calmly making a note*]   Afraid to give his name. Any trade?

BILL   Oo's afride to give is nime? [*Doggedly, with a sense of heroically defying the House of Lords in the person of Lord Stevenage.*] If you want to bring a chawge agen me, bring it. [*She waits, unruffled.*] Moy nime's Bill Walker.

BARBARA [*as if the name were familiar: trying to remember how*]   Bill Walker? [*Recollecting.*] Oh, I know: youre the man that Jenny Hill was praying for inside just now. [*She enters his name in her note book.*]

BILL   Oo's Jenny Ill? And wot call as she to pry for me?

BARBARA   I dont know. Perhaps it was you that cut her lip.

BILL [*defiantly*]   Yus, it w a s me that cat her lip. Aw aint afride o y o u.

BARBARA   How could you be, since youre not afraid of God? Youre a brave man, Mr Walker. It takes some pluck to do o u r work here; but none of us dare lift our hand against a girl like that, for fear of her father in heaven.

BILL [*sullenly*]   I want nan o your kentin jawr. I spowse you think Aw cam eah to beg from you, like this demmiged lot eah. Not me. Aw downt want your bread and scripe and ketlep.[3] Aw dont blieve in your Gawd, no more than you do yourself.

BARBARA [*sunnily apologetic and ladylike, as on a new footing with him*]   Oh, I beg your pardon for putting your name down, Mr Walker. I didnt understand. I'll strike it out.

BILL [*taking this as a slight, and deeply wounded by it*]   Eah! you let maw nime alown. Aint it good enaff to be in your book?

BARBARA [*considering*]   Well, you see, theres no use putting down your name unless I can do something for you, is there? Whats your trade?

BILL [*still smarting*]   Thets nao concern o yours.

BARBARA   Just so. [*Very businesslike.*] I'll put you down as [*writing*] the man who—struck—poor little Jenny Hill—in the mouth.

BILL [*rising threateningly*]   See eah. Awve ed enaff o this.

BARBARA [*quite sunny and fearless*]   What did you come to us for?

BILL   Aw cam for maw gel, see? Aw cam to tike her aht o this and to brike er jawr for er.

BARBARA [*complacently*]   You see I was right about your trade. [BILL, *on the point of retorting furiously, finds himself, to his great shame and terror, in danger of crying instead. He sits down again suddenly.*] Whats her name?

BILL [*dogged*]   Er nime's Mog Ebbijem: thets wot her nime is.

---

2. Secularism as a formal movement dates from about 1850 and the teachings of G. J. Holyoake. It taught that man should order and interpret his life in terms of this world, without recourse to a belief in God or the afterlife.

3. "Scripe" (i.e., scrape) is a thin spreading (of butter) on bread. "Ketlep" (i.e., catlap) is tea or some other weak drink fit only for a cat to lap up.

BARBARA   Mog Habbijam! Oh, she's gone to Canning Town, to our barracks there.

BILL [*fortified by his resentment of Mog's perfidy*]   Is she? [*Vindictively.*] Then Aw'm gowin to Kennintahn arter her. [*He crosses to the gate; hesitates; finally comes back at* BARBARA.] Are you loyin to me to git shat o me?

BARBARA   I dont want to get shut of you. I want to keep you here and save your soul. Youd better stay: youre going to have a bad time to-day, Bill.

BILL   Oo's gowin to give it to me? Y o u, preps?

BARBARA   Someone you dont believe in. But youll be glad afterwards.

BILL [*slinking off*]   Aw'll gow to Kennintahn to be aht o reach o your tangue. [*Suddenly turning on her with intense malice.*] And if Aw downt fawnd Mog there, Aw'll cam beck and do two years for you, selp me Gawd if Aw downt!

BARBARA [*a shade kindlier, if possible*]   It's no use, Bill. She's got another bloke.

BILL   Wot!

BARBARA   One of her own converts. He fell in love with her when he saw her with her soul saved, and her face clean, and her hair washed.

BILL [*surprised*]   Wottud she wash it for, the carroty slat? It's red.

BARBARA   It's quite lovely now, because she wears a new look in her eyes with it. It's a pity youre too late. The new bloke has put your nose out of joint, Bill.

BILL   Aw'll put his nowse aht o joint for him. Not that Aw care a carse for er, mawnd thet. But Aw'll teach her to drop me as if Aw was dirt. And Aw'll teach him to meddle with maw judy. Wots iz bleedin nime?

BARBARA   Sergeant Todger Fairmile.

SHIRLEY [*rising with grim joy*]   I'll go with him, miss. I want to see them two meet. I'll take him to the infirmary when it's over.

BILL [*to* SHIRLEY, *with undissembled misgiving*]   Is thet im you was speakin on?

SHIRLEY   Thats him.

BILL   Im that wrastled in the music awl?

SHIRLEY   The competitions at the National Sportin Club was worth nigh a hundred a year to him. He's gev em up now for religion; so he's a bit fresh for want of the exercise he was accustomed to. He'll be glad to see you. Come along.

BILL   Wots is wight?

SHIRLEY   Thirteen four.[4] [BILL's *last hope expires.*]

BARBARA   Go and talk to him, Bill. He'll convert you.

SHIRLEY   He'll convert your head into a mashed potato.

BILL [*sullenly*]   Aw aint afride of im. Aw aint afride of ennybody. Bat e can lick me. She's dan me. [*He sits down moodily on the edge of the horse-trough.*]

SHIRLEY   You aint goin. I thought not. [*He resumes his seat.*]

BARBARA [*calling*]   Jenny!

JENNY [*appearing at the shelter door with a plaster on the corner of her mouth*]   Yes, Major.

BARBARA   Send Rummy Mitchens out to clear away here.

4. In England the weight of human beings is frequently given in terms of the *stone*, a measure equal to fourteen pounds. The Sergeant weighs 186 pounds.

JENNY   I think she's afraid.

BARBARA [*her resemblance to her mother flashing out for a moment*] Nonsense! she must do as she's told.

JENNY [*calling into the shelter*]   Rummy: the Major says you must come.

> JENNY *comes to* BARBARA, *purposely keeping on the side next* BILL, *lest he should suppose that she shrank from him or bore malice.*

BARBARA   Poor little Jenny! Are you tired? [*Looking at the wounded cheek.*] Does it hurt?

JENNY   No: it's all right now. It was nothing.

BARBABA [*critically*]   It was as hard as he could hit, I expect. Poor Bill! You dont feel angry with him, do you?

JENNY   Oh no, no, no: indeed I dont, Major, bless his poor heart!

> BARBARA *kisses her; and she runs away merrily into the shelter.* BILL *writhes with an agonizing return of his new and alarming symptoms, but says nothing.* RUMMY MITCHENS *comes from the shelter.*

BARBARA [*going to meet* RUMMY]   Now Rummy, bustle. Take in those mugs and plates to be washed; and throw the crumbs about for the birds.

> RUMMY *takes the three plates and mugs; but* SHIRLEY *takes back his mug from her, as there is still some milk left in it.*

RUMMY   There aint any crumbs. This aint a time to waste good bread on birds.

PRICE [*appearing at the shelter door*]   Gentleman come to see the shelter, Major. Says he's your father.

BARBARA   All right. Coming. [SNOBBY *goes back into the shelter, followed by* BARBARA.]

RUMMY [*stealing across to* BILL *and addressing him in a subdued voice, but with intense conviction*]   I'd av the lor of you, you flat eared pignosed potwalloper,[5] if she'd let me. Youre no gentleman, to hit a lady in the face. [BILL, *with greater things moving in him, takes no notice.*]

SHIRLEY [*following her*]   Here! in with you and dont get yourself into more trouble by talking.

RUMMY [*with hauteur*]   I aint ad the pleasure o being hintroduced to you, as I can remember. [*She goes into the shelter with the plates.*]

SHIRLEY   Thats the—

BILL [*savagely*]   Downt you talk to me, d'ye eah? You lea me alown, or Aw'll do you a mischief. Aw'm not dirt under y o u r feet, ennywy.

SHIRLEY [*calmly*]   Dont you be afeerd. You aint such prime company that you need expect to be sought after. [*He is about to go into the shelter when* BARBARA *comes out, with* UNDERSHAFT *on her right.*]

BARBARA   Oh, there you are, Mr Shirley! [*Between them.*] This is my father: I told you he was a Secularist, didnt I? Perhaps youll be able to comfort one another.

UNDERSHAFT [*startled*]   A Secularist! Not the least in the world: on the contrary, a confirmed mystic.

---

5. A "potwalloper," originally "potwaller," was a householder, who was therefore eligible to vote in Parliamentary elections. The word began to be used as a term of contempt early in the nineteenth century.

BARBARA Sorry, I'm sure. By the way, papa, what i s your religion? in case I have to introduce you again.

UNDERSHAFT My religion? Well, my dear, I am a Millionaire. That is my religion.

BARBARA Then I'm afraid you and Mr Shirley wont be able to comfort one another after all. Youre not a Millionaire, are you, Peter?

SHIRLEY No; and proud of it.

UNDERSHAFT [*gravely*] Poverty, my friend, is not a thing to be proud of.

SHIRLEY [*angrily*] Who made your millions for you? Me and my like. Whats kep us poor? Keepin you rich. I wouldnt have your conscience, not for all your income.

UNDERSHAFT I wouldnt have your income, not for all your conscience, Mr Shirley. [*He goes to the penthouse and sits down on a form.*]

BARBARA [*stopping* SHIRLEY *adroitly as he is about to retort*] You wouldnt think he was my father, would you, Peter? Will you go into the shelter and lend the lasses a hand for a while: we're worked off our feet.

SHIRLEY [*bitterly*] Yes: I'm in their debt for a meal, aint I?

BARBARA Oh, not because youre in their debt, but for love of them, Peter, for love of them. [*He cannot understand, and is rather scandalized.*] There! dont stare at me. In with you; and give that conscience of yours a holiday. [*Bustling him into the shelter.*]

SHIRLEY [*as he goes in*] Ah! it's a pity you never was trained to use your reason, miss. Youd have been a very taking lecturer on Secularism.

BARBARA *turns to her father.*

UNDERSHAFT Never mind me, my dear. Go about your work; and let me watch it for a while.

BARBARA All right.

UNDERSHAFT For instance, whats the matter with that out-patient over there?

BARBARA [*looking at* BILL, *whose attitude has never changed, and whose expression of brooding wrath has deepened*] Oh, we shall cure him in no time. Just watch. [*She goes over to* BILL *and waits. He glances up at her and casts his eyes down again, uneasy, but grimmer than ever.*] It w o u l d be nice to just stamp on Mog Habbijam's face, wouldnt it, Bill?

BILL [*starting up from the trough in consternation*] It's a loy: Aw never said so. [*She shakes her head.*] Oo taold you wot was in moy mawnd?

BARBARA Only your new friend.

BILL Wot new friend?

BARBARA The devil, Bill. When he gets round people they get miserable, just like you.

BILL [*with a heartbreaking attempt at devil-may-care cheerfulness*] Aw aint miserable. [*He sits down again, and stretches his legs in an attempt to seem indifferent.*]

BARBARA Well, if youre happy, why dont you look happy, as we do?

BILL [*his legs curling back in spite of him*] Aw'm eppy enaff, Aw tell you. Woy cawnt you lea me alown? Wot ev I dan to y o u? Aw aint smashed y o u r fice, ev Aw?

BARBARA [*softly: wooing his soul*]   It's not me thats getting at you, Bill.

BILL   Oo else is it?

BARBARA   Somebody that doesn't intend you to smash women's faces, I suppose. Somebody or something that wants to make a man of you.

BILL [*blustering*]   Mike a menn o m e! Aint Aw a menn? eh? Oo sez Aw'm not a menn?

BARBARA   Theres a man in you somewhere, I suppose. But why did he let you hit poor little Jenny Hill? That wasnt very manly of him, was it?

BILL [*tormented*]   Ev dan wiv it, Aw tell you. Chack it. Aw'm sick o your Jenny Ill and er silly little fice.

BARBARA   Then why do you keep thinking about it? Why does it keep coming up against you in your mind? Youre not getting converted, are you?

BILL [*with conviction*]   Not ME. Not lawkly.

BARBARA   Thats right, Bill. Hold out against it. Put out your strength. Dont lets get you cheap. Todger Fairmile said he wrestled for three nights against his salvation harder than he ever wrestled with the Jap at the music hall. He gave in to the Jap when his arm was going to break. But he didnt give in to his salvation until his heart was going to break. Perhaps youll escape that. You havnt any heart, have you?

BILL   Wot d'ye mean? Woy aint Aw got a awt the sime as ennybody else?

BARBARA   A man with a heart wouldnt have bashed poor little Jenny's face, would he?

BILL [*almost crying*]   Ow, w i l l you lea me alown? Ev Aw ever offered to meddle with y o u, that you cam neggin and provowkin me lawk this? [*He writhes convulsively from his eyes to his toes.*]

BARBARA [*with a steady soothing hand on his arm and a gentle voice that never lets him go*]   It's your soul thats hurting you, Bill, and not me. Weve been through it all ourselves. Come with us, Bill. [*He looks wildly round.*] To brave manhood on earth and eternal glory in heaven. [*He is on the point of breaking down.*] Come. [*A drum is heard in the shelter; and* BILL, *with a gasp, escapes from the spell as* BARBARA *turns quickly.* ADOLPHUS *enters from the shelter with a big drum.*] Oh! there you are, Dolly. Let me introduce a new friend of mine, Mr Bill Walker. This is my bloke, Bill: Mr Cusins. [CUSINS *salutes with his drumstick.*]

BILL   Gowin to merry im?

BARBARA   Yes.

BILL [*fervently*]   Gawd elp im! Gaw-aw-aw-awd elp im!

BARBARA   Why? Do you think he wont be happy with me?

BILL   Awve aony ed to stend it for a mawnin: e'll ev to stend it for a lawftawm.

CUSINS   That is a frightful reflection, Mr Walker. But I cant tear myself away from her.

BILL   Well, Aw ken. [*To* BARBARA.] Eah! do you knaow where Aw'm gowin to, and wot Aw'm gowin to do?

BARBARA   Yes: youre going to heaven; and youre coming back here before the week's out to tell me so.

BILL   You loy. Aw'm gowin to Kennintahn, to spit in Todger Fairmawl's eye. Aw beshed Jenny Ill's fice; an nar Aw'll git me aown fice

beshed and cam beck and shaow it to er. Ee'll itt me ardern Aw itt er. Thatll mike us square. [*To* ADOLPHUS.] Is thet fair or is it not? Youre a genlmn: you oughter knaow.

BARBARA   Two black eyes wont make one white one, Bill.

BILL   Aw didnt awst y o u. Cawnt you never keep your mahth shat? Oy awst the genlmn.

CUSINS [*reflectively*]   Yes: I think youre right, Mr Walker. Yes: I should do it. It's curious: it's exactly what an ancient Greek would have done.

BARBARA   But what good will it do?

CUSINS   Well, it will give Mr Fairmile some exercise; and it will satisfy Mr. Walker's soul.

BILL   Rot! there aint nao sach a thing as a saoul. Ah kin you tell wevver Awve a saoul or not? You never seen it.

BARBARA   Ive seen it hurting you when you went against it.

BILL [*with compressed aggravation*]   If you was maw gel and took the word aht o me mahth lawk thet, Aw'd give you sathink youd feel urtin, Aw would. [*To* ADOLPHUS.] You tike maw tip, mite. Stop er jawr; or youll doy afoah your tawn. [*With intense expression.*] Wore aht: thets wot youll be: wore aht. [*He goes away through the gate.*]

CUSINS [*looking after him*]   I wonder!

BARBARA   Dolly! [*Indignant, in her mother's manner.*]

CUSINS   Yes, my dear, it's very wearing to be in love with you. If it lasts, I quite think I shall die young.

BARBARA   Should you mind?

CUSINS   Not at all. [*He is suddenly softened, and kisses her over the drum, evidently not for the first time, as people cannot kiss over a big drum without practice.* UNDERSHAFT *coughs.*]

BARBARA   It's all right, papa, weve not forgotten you. Dolly: explain the place to papa: I havnt time. [*She goes busily into the shelter.*]

> UNDERSHAFT *and* ADOLPHUS *now have the yard to themselves.* UNDERSHAFT, *seated on a form, and still keenly attentive, looks hard at* ADOLPHUS. ADOLPHUS *looks hard at him.*

UNDERSHAFT   I fancy you guess something of what is in my mind, Mr Cusins. [CUSINS *flourishes his drumsticks as if in the act of beating a lively rataplan, but makes no sound.*]   Exactly so. But suppose Barbara finds you out!

CUSINS   You know, I do not admit that I am imposing on Barbara. I am quite genuinely interested in the views of the Salvation Army. The fact is, I am a sort of collector of religions; and the curious thing is that I find I can believe them all. By the way, have you any religion?

UNDERSHAFT   Yes.

CUSINS   Anything out of the common?

UNDERSHAFT   Only that there are two things necessary to Salvation.

CUSINS [*disappointed, but polite*]   Ah, the Church Catechism. Charles Lomax also belongs to the Established Church.

UNDERSHAFT   The two things are—

CUSINS   Baptism and—

UNDERSHAFT   No. Money and gunpowder.

CUSINS [*surprised, but interested*]   That is the general opinion of our governing classes. The novelty is in hearing any man confess it.

UNDERSHAFT   Just so.

CUSINS   Exuse me: is there any place in your religion for honor, justice, truth, love, mercy and so forth?

UNDERSHAFT   Yes: they are the graces and luxuries of a rich, strong, and safe life.

CUSINS   Suppose one is forced to choose between them and money or gunpowder?

UNDERSHAFT   Choose money a n d gunpowder; for without enough of both you cannot afford the others.

CUSINS   That is your religion?

UNDERSHAFT   Yes.

The cadence of this reply makes a full close in the conversation. CUSINS *twists his face dubiously and contemplates* UNDERSHAFT. UNDERSHAFT *contemplates him.*

CUSINS   Barbara wont stand that. You will have to choose between your religion and Barbara.

UNDERSHAFT   So will you, my friend. She will find out that that drum of yours is hollow.

CUSINS   Father Undershaft: you are mistaken: I am a sincere Salvationist. You do not understand the Salvation Army. It is the army of joy, of love, of courage: it has banished the fear and remorse and despair of the old hell-ridden evangelical sects: it marches to fight the devil with trumpet and drum, with music and dancing, with banner and palm, as becomes a sally from heaven by its happy garrison. It picks the waster out of the public house and makes a man of him: it finds a worm wriggling in a back kitchen, and lo! a woman! Men and women of rank too, sons and daughters of the Highest. It takes the poor professor of Greek, the most artificial and self-suppressed of human creatures, from his meal of roots, and lets loose the rhapsodist in him; reveals the true worship of Dionysos to him; sends him down the public street drumming dithyrambs. [*He plays a thundering flourish on the drum.*]

UNDERSHAFT   You will alarm the shelter.

CUSINS   Oh, they are accustomed to these sudden ecstasies. However, if the drum worries you—[*He pockets the drumsticks; unhooks the drum; and stands it on the ground opposite the gateway.*]

UNDERSHAFT   Thank you.

CUSINS   You remember what Euripides says about your money and gunpowder?

UNDERSHAFT   No.

CUSINS [*declaiming*]

>   One and another
>   In money and guns may outpass his brother;
>   And men in their millions float and flow
>   And seethe with a million hopes as leaven;
>   And they win their will; or they miss their will;
>   And their hopes are dead or are pined for still;
>   But whoe'er can know
>   As the long days go
>   That to live is happy, has found h i s heaven.

My translation: what do you think of it?

UNDERSHAFT   I think, my friend, that if you wish to know, as the long days go, that to live is happy, you must first acquire money enough for a decent life, and power enough to be your own master.

CUSINS   You are damnably discouraging. [*He resumes his declamation.*]

> Is it so hard a thing to see
> That the spirit of God—whate'er it be—
> The law that abides and changes not, ages long,
> The Eternal and Nature-born: t h e s e things be strong?
> What else is Wisdom? What of Man's endeavor,
> Or God's high grace so lovely and so great?
> To stand from fear set free? to breathe and wait?
> To hold a hand uplifted over Fate?
> And shall not Barbara be loved for ever?[6]

UNDERSHAFT   Euripides mentions Barbara, does he?

CUSINS   It is a fair translation. The word means Loveliness.

UNDERSHAFT   May I ask—as Barbara's father—how much a year she is to be loved for ever on?

CUSINS   As Barbara's father, that is more your affair than mine. I can feed her by teaching Greek: that is about all.

UNDERSHAFT   Do you consider it a good match for her?

CUSINS [*with polite obstinacy*]   Mr Undershaft: I am in many ways a weak, timid, ineffectual person; and my health is far from satisfactory. But whenever I feel that I must have anything, I get it, sooner or later. I feel that way about Barbara. I dont like marriage: I feel intensely afraid of it; and I dont know what I shall do with Barbara or what she will do with me. But I feel that I and nobody else must marry her. Please regard that as settled.—Not that I wish to be arbitrary; but why should I waste your time in discussing what is inevitable?

UNDERSHAFT   You mean that you will stick at nothing: not even the conversion of the Salvation Army to the worship of Dionysos.[7]

CUSINS   The business of the Salvation Army is to save, not to wrangle about the name of the pathfinder. Dionysos or another: what does it matter?

UNDERSHAFT [*rising and approaching him*]   Professor Cusins: you are a young man after my own heart.

CUSINS   Mr Undershaft: you are, as far as I am able to gather, a most infernal old rascal; but you appeal very strongly to my sense of ironic humor.

> UNDERSHAFT *mutely offers his hand. They shake.*

UNDERSHAFT [*suddenly concentrating himself*]   And now to business.

CUSINS   Pardon me. We are discussing religion. Why go back to such an uninteresting and unimportant subject as business?

UNDERSHAFT   Religion is our business at present, because it is through religion alone that we can win Barbara.

CUSINS   Have you, too, fallen in love with Barbara?

UNDERSHAFT   Yes, with a father's love.

CUSINS   A father's love for a grown-up daughter is the most dangerous

---

6. Both quotations are freely adapted from Gilbert Murray's translation of *The Bacchae.* In the first, Shaw substitutes "money and guns" for "gold and power," and in the second, "Fate" for "Hate" and "Barbara" for "Loveliness."

7. Dionysos, or Dionysus, the Greek god of wine, was associated with a form of worship more ecstatic and emotional than that of the Olympians, which was regarded as an intrusion on the religious scene (as in *The Bacchae*). Some scholars believe that the worship of Dionysus, in fact, represents an older stage of religion.

of all infatuations. I apologize for mentioning my own pale, coy, mistrustful fancy in the same breath with it.

UNDERSHAFT   Keep to the point. We have to win her; and we are neither of us Methodists.

CUSINS   That doesnt matter. The power Barbara wields here—the power that wields Barbara herself—is not Calvinism, not Presbyterianism, not Methodism—[8]

UNDERSHAFT   Not Greek Paganism either, eh?

CUSINS   I admit that. Barbara is quite original in her religion.

UNDERSHAFT [*triumphantly*]   Aha! Barbara Undershaft would be. Her inspiration comes from within herself.

CUSINS   How do you suppose it got there?

UNDERSHAFT [*in towering excitement*]   It is the Undershaft inheritance. I shall hand on my torch to my daughter. She shall make my converts and preach my gospel—

CUSINS   What! Money and gunpowder!

UNDERSHAFT   Yes, money and gunpowder. Freedom and power. Command of life and command of death.

CUSINS [*urbanely: trying to bring him down to earth*]   This is extremely interesting, Mr Undershaft. Of course you know that you are mad.

UNDERSHAFT [*with redoubled force*]   And you?

CUSINS   Oh, mad as a hatter. You are welcome to my secret since I have discovered yours. But I am astonished. Can a madman make cannons?

UNDERSHAFT   Would anyone else than a madman make them? And now [*with surging energy*] question for question. Can a sane man translate Euripides?

CUSINS   No.

UNDERSHAFT [*seizing him by the shoulder*]   Can a sane woman make a man of a waster or a woman of a worm?

CUSINS [*reeling before the storm*]   Father Colossus—Mammoth Millionaire—

UNDERSHAFT [*pressing him*]   Are there two mad people or three in this Salvation shelter today?

CUSINS   You mean Barbara is as mad as we are?

UNDERSHAFT [*pushing him lightly off and resuming his equanimity suddenly and completely*]   Pooh, Professor! let us call things by their proper names. I am a millionaire; you are a poet; Barbara is a savior of souls. What have we three to do with the common mob of slaves and idolaters? [*He sits down again with a shrug of contempt for the mob.*]

CUSINS   Take care! Barbara is in love with the common people. So am I. Have you never felt the romance of that love?

UNDERSHAFT [*cold and sardonic*]   Have you ever been in love with Poverty, like St Francis? Have you ever been in love with Dirt, like St Simeon![9] Have you ever been in love with disease and suffering, like our nurses and philanthropists? Such passions are not virtues,

---

8. Calvinism refers to the theological teachings of John Calvin (1509–1564), Presbyterianism is a movement, traditionally Calvinistic, which sprang up in the 16th century and which rejected traditional forms of church government. Methodism was a nonconformist movement which began at Oxford in 1729 with preaching of John Wesley, his brother Charles, and others who had been within the established Anglican church.

9. St. Francis of Assisi (1181–1226), the founder of the Franciscan order, and Saint Simeon Stylites the Elder (c. 388–459), who lived atop a column for 36 years and conditioned himself to remain standing throughout Lent, were famous ascetics.

but the most unnatural of all the vices. This love of the common people may please an earl's granddaughter and a university professor; but I have been a common man and a poor man; and it has no romance for me. Leave it to the poor to pretend that poverty is a blessing: leave it to the coward to make a religion of his cowardice by preaching humility: we know better than that. We three must stand together above the common people: how else can we help their children to climb up beside us? Barbara must belong to us, not to the Salvation Army.

CUSINS   Well, I can only say that if you think you will get her away from the Salvation Army by talking to her as you have been talking to me, you dont know Barbara.

UNDERSHAFT   My friend: I never ask for what I can buy.

CUSINS [*in a white fury*]   Do I understand you to imply that you can buy Barbara?

UNDERSHAFT   No; but I can buy the Salvation Army.

CUSINS   Quite impossible.

UNDERSHAFT   You shall see. All religious organizations exist by selling themselves to the rich.

CUSINS   Not the Army. That is the Church of the poor.

UNDERSHAFT   All the more reason for buying it.

CUSINS   I dont think you quite know what the Army does for the poor.

UNDERSHAFT   Oh yes I do. It draws their teeth: that is enough for me as a man of business.

CUSINS   Nonsense! It makes them sober—

UNDERSHAFT   I prefer sober workmen. The profits are larger.

CUSINS   —honest—

UNDERSHAFT   Honest workmen are the most economical.

CUSINS   —attached to their homes—

UNDERSHAFT   So much the better: they will put up with anything sooner than change their shop.

CUSINS   —happy—

UNDERSHAFT   An invaluable safeguard against revolution.

CUSINS   —unselfish—

UNDERSHAFT   Indifferent to their own interests, which suits me exactly.

CUSINS   —with their thoughts on heavenly things—

UNDERSHAFT [*rising*]   And not on Trade Unionism nor Socialism. Excellent.

CUSINS [*revolted*]   You really are an infernal old rascal.

UNDERSHAFT [*indicating* PETER SHIRLEY, *who has just come from the shelter and strolled dejectedly down the yard between them*]   And this is an honest man!

SHIRLEY   Yes; and what av I got by it? [*He passes on bitterly and sits on the form, in the corner of the penthouse.*]

SNOBBY PRICE, *beaming sanctimoniously, and* JENNY HILL *with a tambourine full of coppers, come from the shelter and go to the drum, on which* JENNY *begins to count the money.*

UNDERSHAFT [*replying to* SHIRLEY]   Oh, your employers must have got a good deal by it from first to last. [*He sits on the table, with one foot on the side form.* CUSINS, *overwhelmed, sits down on the same form nearer the shelter.* BARBARA *comes from the shelter to the middle of the yard. She is excited and a little overwrought.*]

BARBARA   Weve just had a splendid experience meeting at the other

gate in Cripps's Lane. Ive hardly ever seen them so much moved as they were by your confession, Mr Price.

PRICE   I could almost be glad of my past wickedness if I could believe that it would elp to keep hathers stright.

BARBARA   So it will, Snobby. How much, Jenny?

JENNY   Four and tenpence, Major.

BARBARA   Oh Snobby, if you had given your poor mother just one more kick, we should have got the whole five shillings!

PRICE   If she heard you say that, miss, she'd be sorry I didnt. But I'm glad. Oh what a joy it will be to her when she hears I'm saved!

UNDERSHAFT   Shall I contribute the odd twopence, Barbara? The millionaire's mite, eh? [*He takes a couple of pennies from his pocket.*]

BARBARA   How did you make that twopence?

UNDERSHAFT   As usual. By selling cannons, torpedoes, submarines, and my new patent Grand Duke hand grenade.

BARBARA   Put it back in your pocket. You cant buy your salvation here for two pence: you must work it out.

UNDERSHAFT   Is twopence not enough? I can afford a little more, if you press me.

BARBARA   Two million millions would not be enough. There is bad blood on your hands; and nothing but good blood can cleanse them. Money is no use. Take it away. [*She turns to* CUSINS.] Dolly: you must write another letter for me to the papers. [*He makes a wry face.*] Yes: I know you dont like it; but it must be done. The starvation this winter is beating us: everybody is unemployed. The General says we must close this shelter if we cant get more money. I force the collections at the meetings until I am ashamed: dont I, Snobby?

PRICE   It's a fair treat to see you work it, miss. The way you got them up from three-and-six to four-and-ten with that hymn, penny by penny and verse by verse, was a caution. Not a Cheap Jack on Mile End Waste could touch you at it.[1]

BARBARA   Yes; but I wish we could do without it. I am getting at last to think more of the collection than of the people's souls. And what are those hatfuls of pence and halfpence? We want thousands! tens of thousands! hundreds of thousands! I want to convert people, not to be always begging for the Army in a way I'd die sooner than beg for myself.

UNDERSHAFT   [*in profound irony*]   Genuine unselfishness is capable of anything, my dear.

BARBARA   [*unsuspectingly, as she turns away to take the money from the drum and put it in a bag she carries*]   Yes, isnt it? [UNDERSHAFT *looks sardonically at* CUSINS.]

CUSINS   [*aside to* UNDERSHAFT]   Mephistopheles! Machiavelli![2]

BARBARA   [*tears coming into her eyes as she ties the bag and pockets it*]   How are we to feed them? I cant talk religion to a man with bodily hunger in his eyes. [*Almost breaking down.*] It's frightful.

JENNY   [*running to her*]   Major, dear—

BARBARA   [*rebounding*]   No: dont comfort me. It will be all right. We shall get the money.

---

1. A "Cheap Jack" is a street vendor who first puts a high price on his wares and then pretends to be offering a bargain by lowering it.
2. Mephistopheles is the name of a devil, best known as the familiar spirit of Dr. Faustus. Niccolo Machiavelli (1469–1527) was an Italian statesman and political theorist. Both are examples of cunning employed to wicked ends.

UNDERSHAFT How?

JENNY By praying for it, of course. Mrs Baines says she prayed for it last night; and she has never prayed for it in vain: never once. [*She goes to the gate and looks out into the street.*]

BARBARA [*who has dried her eyes and regained her composure*] By the way, dad, Mrs Baines has come to march with us to our big meeting this afternoon; and she is very anxious to meet you, for some reason or other. Perhaps she'll convert you.

UNDERSHAFT I shall be delighted, my dear.

JENNY [*at the gate: excitedly*] Major! Major! heres that man back again.

BARBARA What man?

JENNY The man that hit me. Oh, I hope he's coming back to join us.

> BILL WALKER, *with frost on his jacket, comes through the gate, his hands deep in his pockets and his chin sunk between his shoulders, like a cleaned-out gambler. He halts between* BAR-BARA *and the drum.*

BARBARA Hullo, Bill! Back already!

BILL [*nagging at her*] Bin talkin ever sence, ev you?

BARBARA Pretty nearly. Well, has Todger paid you out for poor Jenny's jaw?

BILL Nao e aint.

BARBARA I thought your jacket looked a bit snowy.

BILL Sao it is snaowy. You want to knaow where the snaow cam from, downt you?

BARBARA Yes.

BILL Well, it cam from orf the grahnd in Pawkinses Corner in Kenintahn. It got rabbed orf be maw shaoulders: see?

BARBARA Pity you didnt rub some off with your knees. Bill! That would have done you a lot of good.

BILL [*with sour mirthless humor*] Aw was sivin anather menn's knees at the tawm. E was kneelin on moy ed, e was.

JENNY Who was kneeling on your head?

BILL Todger was. E was pryin for me: pryin camfortable wiv me as a cawpet. Sow was Mog. Sao was the aol bloomin meetin. Mog she says "Ow Lawd brike his stabborn sperrit; bat downt urt is dear art." Thet was wot she said. "Downt urt is dear art"! An er blowk—thirteen stun four!—kneelin wiv all is wight on me. Fanny, aint it?

JENNY Oh no. We're so sorry, Mr Walker.

BARBARA [*enjoying it frankly*] Nonsense! of course it's funny. Served you right, Bill! You must have done something to him first.

BILL [*doggedly*] Aw did wot Aw said Aw'd do. Aw spit in is eye. E looks ap at the skoy and sez, "Ow that Aw should be fahnd worthy to be spit upon for the gospel's sike!" e sez; an Mog sez "Glaory Allelloolier!"; an then e called me Braddher, an dahned me as if Aw was a kid and e was me mather worshin me a Setterda nawt. Aw ednt jast nao shaow wiv im at all. Arf the street pryed; an the tather arf larfed fit to split theirselves. [*To* BARBARA.] There! are you settisfawd nah?

BARBARA [*her eyes dancing*] Wish I'd been there, Bill.

BILL Yus: youd a got in a hextra bit o talk on me, wouldnt you?

JENNY I'm so sorry, Mr Walker.

BILL [*fiercely*]   Downt you gow bein sorry for me: youve no call. Listen eah. Aw browk your jawr.

JENNY   No, it didnt hurt me: indeed it didnt, except for a moment. It was only that I was frightened.

BILL   Aw downt want to be forgive be you, or be ennybody. Wot Aw did Aw'll py for. Aw trawd to gat me aown jawr browk to settisfaw you—

JENNY [*distressed*]   Oh no—

BILL [*impatiently*]   Tell y' Aw did: cawnt you listen to wots bein taold you? All Aw got be it was bein mide a sawt of in the pablic street for me pines. Well, if Aw cawnt settisfaw you one wy, Aw ken anather. Listen eah! Aw ed two quid sived agen the frost; an Awve a pahnd of it left. A mite o mawn last week ed words with the judy e's gowin to merry. E give er wot-for; an e's bin fawnd fifteen bob. E ed a rawt to itt er cause they was gowin to be merrid; but Aw ednt nao rawt to itt you; sao put anather fawv bob on an call it a pahnd's worth. [*He produces a sovereign.*][3] Eahs the manney. Tike it; and lets ev no more o your forgivin an pryin and your Mijor jawrin me. Let wot Aw dan be dan an pide for; and let there be a end of it.

JENNY   Oh, I couldnt take it, Mr Walker. But if you would give a shilling or two to poor Rummy Mitchens! you really did hurt her; and she's old.

BILL [*contemptuously*]   Not lawkly. Aw'd give her anather as soon as look at er. Let her ev the lawr o me as she threatened! S h e aint forgiven me: not mach. Wot Aw dan to er is not on me mawnd— wot she [*indicating* BARBARA] mawt call on me conscience—no more than stickin a pig. It's this Christian gime o yours that Aw wownt ev plyed agen me: this bloomin forgivin an neggin an jawrin that mikes a menn thet sore that iz lawf's a burdn to im. Aw wownt ev it, Aw tell you; sao tike your manney and stop thraowin your silly beshed fice hap agen me.

JENNY   Major: may I take a little of it for the Army?

BARBARA   No: the Army is not to be bought. We want your soul, Bill; and we'll take nothing less.

BILL [*bitterly*]   Aw knaow. Me an maw few shillins is not good enaff for you. Youre a earl's grendorter, you are. Nathink less than a anderd pahnd for you.

UNDERSHAFT   Come, Barbara! you could do a great deal of good with a hundred pounds. If you will set this gentleman's mind at ease by taking his pound, I will give the other ninety-nine.

BILL, *dazed by such opulence, instinctively touches his cap.*

BARBARA   Oh, youre too extravagant, papa. Bill offers twenty pieces of silver. All you need offer is the other ten.[4] That will make the standard price to buy anybody who's for sale. I'm not; and the Army's not. [*To* BILL.] Youll never have another quiet moment, Bill, until you come round to us. You cant stand out against your salvation.

---

3. "Quid" and "bob" are colloquial terms for pound and shilling, respectively. A sovereign is a gold coin worth one pound.

4. Barbara alludes to the betrayal of Jesus by Judas for thirty pieces of silver. Bill's sovereign is the same as twenty shillings.

BILL [*sullenly*]   Aw cawnt stend aht agen music awl wrastlers and awtful tangued women. Awve offered to py. Aw can do no more. Tike it or leave it. There it is. [*He throws the sovereign on the drum, and sits down on the horse-trough. The coin fascinates* SNOBBY PRICE, *who takes an early opportunity of dropping his cap on it.*]

> MRS BAINES *comes from the shelter. She is dressed as a Salvation Army Commissioner. She is an earnest looking woman of about 40, with a caressing, urgent voice, and an appealing manner.*

BARBARA   This is my father, Mrs Baines. [UNDERSHAFT *comes from the table, taking his hat off with marked civility.*] Try what you can do with him. He wont listen to me, because he remembers what a fool I was when I was a baby. [*She leaves them together and chats with* JENNY.]

MRS BAINES   Have you been shewn over the shelter, Mr Undershaft? You know the work we're doing, of course.

UNDERSHAFT [*very civilly*]   The whole nation knows it, Mrs Baines.

MRS BAINES   No, sir: the whole nation does not know it, or we should not be crippled as we are for want of money to carry our work through the length and breadth of the land. Let me tell you that there would have been rioting this winter in London but for us.

UNDERSHAFT   You really think so?

MRS BAINES   I know it. I remember 1886, when you rich gentlemen hardened your hearts against the cry of the poor. They broke the windows of your clubs in Pall Mall.[5]

UNDERSHAFT [*gleaming with approval of their method*]   And the Mansion House Fund went up next day from thirty thousand pounds to seventy-nine thousand! I remember quite well.

MRS BAINES   Well, wont you help me to get at the people? They wont break windows then. Come here, Price. Let me shew you to this gentleman. [PRICE *comes to be inspected.*] Do you remember the window breaking?

PRICE   My ole father thought it was the revolution, maam.

MRS BAINES   Would you break windows now?

PRICE   Oh no, maam. The windows of eaven av bin opened to me. I know now that the rich man is a sinner like myself.

RUMMY [*appearing above at the loft door*]   Snobby Price!

PRICE   Wot is it?

RUMMY   Your mother's askin for you at the other gate in Cripps's Lane. She's heard about your confession. [PRICE *turns pale.*]

MRS BAINES   Go, Mr Price; and pray with her.

JENNY   You can go through the shelter, Snobby.

PRICE [*to* MRS BAINES]   I couldnt face her now, maam, with all the weight of my sins fresh on me. Tell her she'll find her son at ome, waitin for her in prayer. [*He skulks off through the gate, incidentally*

---

5. Pall Mall is a spacious street extending from St. James Street to the foot of the Haymarket, notable for the many fashionable clubs there. (Pepys went "clubbing" there.) Trafalgar Square is nearby, and on February 8, 1886, a meeting in the Square about unemployment was apparently taken over by a group from the Social Democratic Federation, who turned the crowd into a mob and led them through Pall Mall, St. James Street, Piccadilly, and other nearby areas, breaking the windows of clubs, overturning carriages, and committing other acts of vandalism. It was several hours before the police, who had expected no trouble, were able to bring the crowd under control, with aid from the army.

stealing the sovereign on his way out by picking up his cap from the drum.]

MRS BAINES [*with swimming eyes*] You see how we take the anger and the bitterness against you out of their hearts, Mr Undershaft.

UNDERSHAFT It is certainly most convenient and gratifying to all large employers of labor, Mrs Baines.

MRS BAINES Barbara: Jenny: I have good news: most wonderful news. [JENNY *runs to her.*] My prayers have been answered. I told you they would, Jenny, didnt I?

JENNY Yes, yes.

BARBARA [*moving nearer to the drum*] Have we got money enough to keep the shelter open?

MRS BAINES I hope we shall have enough to keep all the shelters open. Lord Saxmundham has promised us five thousand pounds—

BARBARA Hooray!

JENNY Glory!

MRS BAINES —if—

BARBARA "If!" If what?

MRS BAINES —if five other gentlemen will give a thousand each to make it up to ten thousand.

BARBARA Who is Lord Saxmundham? I never heard of him.

UNDERSHAFT [*who has pricked up his ears at the peer's name, and is now watching* BARBARA *curiously*] A new creation, my dear. You have heard of Sir Horace Bodger?

BARBARA Bodger! Do you mean the distiller? Bodger's whisky!

UNDERSHAFT That is the man. He is one of the greatest of our public benefactors. He restored the cathedral at Hakington. They made him a baronet for that. He gave half a million to the funds of his party: they made him a baron for that.

SHIRLEY What will they give him for the five thousand?

UNDERSHAFT There is nothing left to give him. So the five thousand, I should think, is to save his soul.

MRS BAINES Heaven grant it may! Oh Mr Undershaft, you have some very rich friends. Cant you help us towards the other five thousand? We are going to hold a great meeting this afternoon at the Assembly Hall in the Mile End Road. If I could only announce that one gentleman had come forward to support Lord Saxmundham, others would follow. Dont you know somebody? couldnt you? wouldnt you? [*Her eyes fill with tears.*] Oh, think of those poor people, Mr Undershaft: think of how much it means to them, and how little to a great man like you.

UNDERSHAFT [*sardonically gallant*] Mrs Baines: you are irresistible. I cant disappoint you; and I cant deny myself the satisfaction of making Bodger pay up. You shall have your five thousand pounds.

MRS BAINES Thank God!

UNDERSHAFT You dont thank m e?

MRS BAINES Oh sir, dont try to be cynical: dont be ashamed of being a good man. The Lord will bless you abundantly; and our prayers will be like a strong fortification round you all the days of your life. [*With a touch of caution.*] You will let me have the cheque to shew at the meeting, wont you? Jenny: go in and fetch a pen and ink. [JENNY *runs to the shelter door.*]

UNDERSHAFT Do not disturb Miss Hill: I have a fountain pen. [JENNY

halts. He sits at the table and writes the cheque. CUSINS *rises to make room for him. They all watch him silently.*]

BILL [*cynically, aside to* BARBARA, *his voice and accent horribly debased*] Wot prawce selvytion nah?

BARBARA Stop. [UNDERSHAFT *stops writing: they all turn to her in surprise.*] Mrs Baines: are you really going to take this money?

MRS BAINES [*astonished*] Why not, dear?

BARBARA Why not! Do you know what my father is? Have you forgotten that Lord Saxmundham is Bodger the whisky man? Do you remember how we implored the County Council to stop him from writing Bodger's Whisky in letters of fire against the sky; so that the poor drink-ruined creatures on the Embankment could not wake up from their snatches of sleep without being reminded of their deadly thirst by that wicked sky sign? Do you know that the worst thing I have had to fight here is not the devil, but Bodger, Bodger, Bodger, with his whisky, his distilleries, and his tied houses?[6] Are you going to make our shelter another tied house for him, and ask me to keep it?

BILL Rotten dranken whisky it is too.

MRS BAINES Dear Barbara: Lord Saxmundham has a soul to be saved like any of us. If heaven has found the way to make a good use of his money, are we to set ourselves up against the answer to our prayers?

BARBARA I know he has a soul to be saved. Let him come down here; and I'll do my best to help him to his salvation. But he wants to send his cheque down to buy us, and go on being as wicked as ever.

UNDERSHAFT [*with a reasonableness which* CUSINS *alone perceives to be ironical*] My dear Barbara: alcohol is a very necessary article. It heals the sick—

BARBARA It does nothing of the sort.

UNDERSHAFT Well, it assists the doctor: that is perhaps a less questionable way of putting it. It makes life bearable to millions of people who could not endure their existence if they were quite sober. It enables Parliament to do things at eleven at night that no sane person would do at eleven in the morning. Is it Bodger's fault that this inestimable gift is deplorably abused by less than one per cent of the poor? [*He turns again to the table; signs the cheque; and crosses it.*]

MRS BAINES Barbara: will there be less drinking or more if all those poor souls we are saving come tomorrow and find the doors of our shelters shut in their faces? Lord Saxmundham gives us the money to stop drinking—to take his own business from him.

CUSINS [*impishly*] Pure self-sacrifice on Bodger's part, clearly! Bless dear Bodger! [BARBARA *almost breaks down as* ADOLPHUS, *too, fails her.*]

UNDERSHAFT [*tearing out the cheque and pocketing the book as he rises and goes past* CUSINS *to* MRS BAINES] I also, Mrs Baines, may claim a little disinterestedness. Think of my business! think of the widows and orphans! the men and lads torn to pieces with shrapnel and poisoned with lyddite![7] [MRS BAINES *shrinks; but he goes on remorselessly*] the oceans of blood, not one drop of which is shed in a

6. Inns or public houses whose operators are required to buy their potables from a particular brewery, which often owns the "tied house."

7. A high explosive, made up mainly of picric acid.

really just cause! the ravaged crops! the peaceful peasant forced, women and men, to till their fields, under the fire of opposing armies on pain of starvation! the bad blood of the fierce little cowards at home who egg on others to fight for the gratification of their national vanity! All this makes money for me: I am never richer, never busier than when the papers are full of it. Well, it is your work to preach peace on earth and goodwill to men. [MRS BAINES's *face lights up again*.] Every convert you make is a vote against war. [*Her lips move in prayer*.] Yet I give you this money to help you to hasten my own commercial ruin. [*He gives her the cheque*.]

CUSINS [*mounting the form in an ecstasy of mischief*]   The millennium will be inaugurated by the unselfishness of Undershaft and Bodger.[8] Oh be joyful! [*He takes the drum-sticks from his pocket and flourishes them*.]

MRS BAINES [*taking the cheque*]   The longer I live the more proof I see that there is an Infinite Goodness that turns everything to the work of salvation sooner or later. Who would have thought that any good could have come out of war and drink? And yet their profits are brought today to the feet of salvation to do its blessed work. [*She is affected to tears*.]

JENNY [*running to* MRS BAINES *and throwing her arms around her*]   Oh dear! how blessed, how glorious it all is!

CUSINS [*in a convulsion of irony*]   Let us seize this unspeakable moment. Let us march to the great meeting at once. Excuse me just an instant. [*He rushes into the shelter.* JENNY *takes her tambourine from the drum head*.]

MRS BAINES   Mr Undershaft: have you ever seen a thousand people fall on their knees with one impulse and pray? Come with us to the meeting. Barbara shall tell them that the Army is saved, and saved through you.

CUSINS [*returning impetuously from the shelter with a flag and a trombone, and coming between* MRS BAINES *and* UNDERSHAFT]   You shall carry the flag down the first street, Mrs Baines. [*He gives her the flag*.] Mr Undershaft is a gifted trombonist: he shall intone an Olympian diapason to the West Ham Salvation March.[9] [*Aside to* UNDERSHAFT, *as he forces the trombone on him*.] Blow, Machiavelli, blow.

UNDERSHAFT [*aside to him, as he takes the trombone*]   The trumpet in Zion! [CUSINS *rushes to the drum which he takes up and puts on.* UNDERSHAFT *continues, aloud*.] I will do my best. I could vamp a bass if I knew the tune.

CUSINS   It is a wedding chorus from one of Donizetti's operas; but we have converted it. We convert everything to good here, including Bodger. You remember the chorus. "For thee immense rejoicing— immenso giubilo—immenso giubilo."[1] [*With drum obbligato*.] Rum tum ti tum, tum tum ti ta—

BARBARA   Dolly: you are breaking my heart.

CUSINS   What is a broken heart more or less here? Dionysos Undershaft has descended. I am possessed.

8. A "millennium" is a period of universal harmony and prosperity like that described in *Revelation* 20.
9. "Diapason" is a musical term, used here to imply that Undershaft's trombone will provide a sublime accompaniment to the music of the band.
1. A reference to the wedding chorus in *Lucia di Lammermoor*, Act 2, which begins "Per te d'immenso giubilo."

MRS BAINES   Come, Barbara: I must have my dear Major to carry the flag with me.

JENNY   Yes, yes, Major darling.

CUSINS *snatches the tambourine out of* JENNY's *hand and mutely offers it to* BARBARA.

BARBARA [*coming forward a little as she puts the offer behind her with a shudder, whilst* CUSINS *recklessly tosses the tambourine back to* JENNY *and goes to the gate*]   I cant come.

JENNY   Not come!

MRS BAINES [*with tears in her eyes*]   Barbara: do you think I am wrong to take the money?

BARBARA [*impulsively going to her and kissing her*]   No, no: God help you, dear, you must: you are saving the Army. Go; and may you have a great meeting!

JENNY   But arnt you coming?

BARBARA   No. [*She begins taking off the silver S brooch from her collar.*]

MRS BAINES   Barbara: what are you doing?

JENNY   Why are you taking your badge off? You cant be going to leave us, Major.

BARBARA [*quietly*]   Father: come here.

UNDERSHAFT [*coming to her*]   My dear! [*Seeing that she is going to pin the badge on his collar, he retreats to the penthouse in some alarm.*]

BARBARA [*following him*]   Dont be frightened. [*She pins the badge on and steps back towards the table, shewing him to the others.*]   There! It's not much for £5000, is it?

MRS BAINES   Barbara: if you wont come and pray w i t h us, promise me you will pray f o r us.

BARBARA   I cant pray now. Perhaps I shall never pray again.

MRS BAINES   Barbara!

JENNY   Major!

BARBARA [*almost delirious*]   I cant bear any more. Quick march!

CUSINS [*calling to the procession in the street outside*]   Off we go. Play up, there! I m m e n s o   g i u b i l o. [*He gives the time with his drum; and the band strikes up the march, which rapidly becomes more distant as the procession moves briskly away.*]

MRS BAINES   I must go, dear. Youre overworked: you will be all right tomorrow. We'll never lose you. Now Jenny: step out with the old flag. Blood and Fire! [*She marches out through the gate with her flag.*]

JENNY   Glory Hallelujah! [*Flourishing her tambourine and marching.*]

UNDERSHAFT [*to* CUSINS, *as he marches out past him easing the slide of his trombone*]   "My ducats and my daughter"![2]

CUSINS [*following him out*]   Money and gunpowder!

BARBARA   Drunkenness and Murder! My God: why hast thou forsaken me?

She sinks on the form with her face buried in her hands. The march passes away into silence. BILL WALKER *steals across to her.*

---

2. In Act 2, scene 8 of Shakespeare's *The Merchant of Venice*, Salanio tells Salarino of Shylock's discovery of Jessica's elopement and of the loss of the money she carried with her. Shylock is there reported to have cried, among other things, "My ducats and my daughter!"

BILL [*taunting*]   Wot prawce selvytion nah?

SHIRLEY   Dont you hit her when she's down.

BILL   She itt me wen aw wiz dahn. Waw shouldnt Aw git a bit o me aown beck?

BARBARA [*raising her head*]   I didnt take y o u r money, Bill. [*She crosses the yard to the gate and turns her back on the two men to hide her face from them.*]

BILL [*sneering after her*]   Naow, it warnt enaff for you. [*Turning to the drum, he misses the money.*] Ellow! If you aint took it sammun else ez. Weres it gorn? Bly me if Jenny Ill didnt tike it arter all!

RUMMY [*screaming at him from the loft*]   You lie, you dirty blackguard! Snobby Price pinched it off the drum when he took up his cap. I was up here all the time an see im do it.

BILL   Wot! Stowl maw manney! Waw didnt you call thief on him, you silly aold macker you?

RUMMY   To serve you aht for ittin me acrost the fice. It's cost y'pahnd, that az. [*Raising a paean of squalid triumph.*] I done you. I'm even with you. Ive ad it aht o y— [BILL *snatches up* SHIRLEY's *mug and hurls it at her. She slams the loft door and vanishes. The mug smashes against the door and falls in fragments.*]

BILL [*beginning to chuckle*]   Tell us, aol menn, wot o'clock this mawnin was it wen im as they call Snobby Prawce was sived?

BARBARA [*turning to him more composedly, and with unspoiled sweetness*]   About half past twelve, Bill. And he pinched your pound at a quarter to two. *I* know. Well, you cant afford to lose it. I'll send it to you.

BILL [*his voice and accent suddenly improving*]   Not if Aw wiz to stawve for it. Aw aint to be bought.

SHIRLEY   Aint you? Youd sell yourself to the devil for a pint o beer; ony there aint no devil to make the offer.

BILL [*unshamed*]   Sao Aw would, mite, and often ev, cheerful. But she cawnt baw me. [*Approaching* BARBARA.] You wanted maw saoul, did you? Well, you aint got it.

BARBARA   I nearly got it, Bill. But weve sold it back to you for ten thousand pounds.

SHIRLEY   And dear at the money!

BARBARA   No, Peter: it was worth more than money.

BILL [*salvationproof*]   It's nao good: you cawnt get rahnd me nah. Aw downt blieve in it; and Awve seen tody that Aw was rawt. [*Going.*] Sao long, aol soupkitchener! Ta, ta, Mijor Earl's Grendorter! [*Turning at the gate.*] Wot prawce selvytion nah? Snobby Prawce! Ha! ha!

BARBARA [*offering her hand*]   Goodbye, Bill.

BILL [*taken aback, half plucks his cap off; then shoves it on again defiantly*]   Git aht. [BARBARA *drops her hand, discouraged. He has a twinge of remorse.*] But thets aw rawt, you knaow. Nathink pasnl. Naow mellice. Sao long, Judy. [*He goes.*]

BARBARA   No malice. So long, Bill.

SHIRLEY [*shaking his head*]   You make too much of him, miss, in your innocence.

BARBARA [*going to him*]   Peter: I'm like you now. Cleaned out, and lost my job.

SHIRLEY   Youve youth an hope. Thats two better than me.

BARBARA   I'll get you a job, Peter. Thats hope for you: the youth will

have to be enough for me. [*She counts her money.*] I have just enough left for two teas at Lockharts, a Rowton doss[3] for you, and my tram and bus home. [*He frowns and rises with offended pride. She takes his arm.*] Dont be proud, Peter: it's sharing between friends. And promise me youll talk to me and not let me cry. [*She draws him towards the gate.*]

SHIRLEY   Well, I'm not accustomed to talk to the like of you—

BARBARA [*urgently*]   Yes, yes: you must talk to me. Tell me about Tom Paine's books and Bradlaugh's lectures.[4] Come along.

SHIRLEY   Ah, if you would only read Tom Paine in the proper spirit, miss! [*They go out through the gate together.*]

Act 3

Next day after lunch LADY BRITOMART *is writing in the library in Wilton Crescent.* SARAH *is reading in the armchair near the window.* BARBARA, *in ordinary fashionable dress, pale and brooding, is on the settee.* CHARLES LOMAX *enters. He starts on seeing* BARBARA *fashionably attired and in low spirits.*

LOMAX   Youve left off your uniform!

BARBARA *says nothing; but an expression of pain passes over her face.*

LADY BRITOMART [*warning him in low tones to be careful*]   Charles!

LOMAX [*much concerned, coming behind the settee and bending sympathetically over* BARBARA]   I'm awfully sorry, Barbara. You know I helped you all I could with the concertina and so forth. [*Momentously.*] Still, I have never shut my eyes to the fact that there is a certain amout of tosh about the Salvation Army. Now the claims of the Church of England—

LADY BRITOMART   Thats enough, Charles. Speak of something suited to your mental capacity.

LOMAX   But surely the Church of England is suited to all our capacities.

BARBARA [*pressing his hand*]   Thank you for your sympathy, Cholly. Now go and spoon with Sarah.

LOMAX [*dragging a chair from the writing table and seating himself affectionately by* SARAH's *side*]   How is my ownest today?

SARAH   I wish you wouldnt tell Cholly to do things, Barbara. He always comes straight and does them. Cholly: we're going to the works this afternoon.

LOMAX   What works?

SARAH   The cannon works.

LOMAX   What? your governor's shop!

SARAH   Yes.

3. A Rowton House was a subsidized institution providing inexpensive lodging for indigents. A "doss house" or "doss" is a slang term for a cheap or low-class rooming house.
4. Tom Paine (1737–1809) was the free-thinking author of *Common Sense* and *The Rights of Man*, who figured in both the French and American Revolutions. Charles Bradlaugh (1833–1891) was a notable English Freethinker and leader in the Secularist movement.

LOMAX   Oh I say!

> CUSINS *enters in poor condition. He also starts visibly when he*
> *sees* BARBARA *without her uniform.*

BARBARA   I expected you this morning, Dolly. Didnt you guess that?

CUSINS [*sitting down beside her*]   I'm sorry. I have only just break-
fasted.

SARAH   But weve just finished lunch.

BARBARA   Have you had one of your bad nights?

CUSINS   No: I had rather a good night: in fact, one of the most remarkable nights I have ever passed.

BARBARA   The meeting?

CUSINS   No: after the meeting.

LADY BRITOMART   You should have gone to bed after the meeting.
What were you doing?

CUSINS   Drinking.

LADY BRITOMART	Adolphus!
SARAH	Dolly!
BARBARA	Dolly!
LOMAX	Oh I say!

LADY BRITOMART   What were you drinking, may I ask?

CUSINS   A most devilish kind of Spanish burgundy, warranted free
from added alcohol: a Temperance burgundy in fact. Its richness in
natural alcohol made any addition superfluous.

BARBARA   Are you joking, Dolly?

CUSINS [*patiently*]   No. I have been making a night of it with the
nominal head of this household: that is all.

LADY BRITOMART   Andrew made you drunk!

CUSINS   No: he only provided the wine. I think it was Dionysos who
made me drunk. [*To* BARBARA.] I told you I was possessed.

LADY BRITOMART   Youre not sober yet. Go home to bed at once.

CUSINS   I have never before ventured to reproach you, Lady Brit; but
how could you marry the Prince of Darkness?

LADY BRITOMART   It was much more excusable to marry him than to
get drunk with him. That is a new accomplishment of Andrew's, by
the way. He usent to drink.

CUSINS   He doesnt now. He only sat there and completed the wreck
of my moral basis, the rout of my convictions, the purchase of my
soul. He cares for you, Barbara. That is what makes him so dangerous to me.

BARBARA   That has nothing to do with it, Dolly. There are larger loves
and diviner dreams than the fireside ones. You know that, dont you?

CUSINS   Yes: that is our understanding. I know it. I hold to it. Unless
he can win me on that holier ground he may amuse me for a while;
but he can get no deeper hold, strong as he is.

BARBARA   Keep to that; and the end will be right. Now tell me what
happened at the meeting?

CUSINS   It was an amazing meeting. Mrs Baines almost died of emotion. Jenny Hill simply gibbered with hysteria. The Prince of Darkness played his trombone like a madman: its brazen roarings were
like the laughter of the damned. 117 conversions took place then
and there. They prayed with the most touching sincerity and gratitude for Bodger, and for the anonymous donor of the £5000. Your
father would not let his name be given.

LOMAX   That was rather fine of the old man, you know. Most chaps would have wanted the advertisement.

CUSINS   He said all the charitable institutions would be down on him like kites on a battle-field if he gave his name.

LADY BRITOMART   Thats Andrew all over. He never does a proper thing without giving an improper reason for it.

CUSINS   He convinced me that I have all my life been doing improper things for proper reasons.

LADY BRITOMART   Adolphus: now that Barbara has left the Salvation Army, you had better leave it too. I will not have you playing that drum in the streets.

CUSINS   Your orders are already obeyed, Lady Brit.

BARBARA   Dolly: were you ever really in earnest about it? Would you have joined if you had never seen me?

CUSINS [*disingenuously*]   Well—er—well, possibly, as a collector of religions—

LOMAX [*cunningly*]   Not as a drummer, though, you know. You are a very clearheaded brainy chap, Dolly; and it must have been apparent to you that there is a certain amount of tosh about—

LADY BRITOMART   Charles: if you must drivel, drivel like a grown-up man and not like a schoolboy.

LOMAX [*out of countenance*]   Well, drivel is drivel, dont you know, whatever a man's age.

LADY BRITOMART   In good society in England, Charles, men drivel at all ages by repeating silly formulas with an air of wisdom. Schoolboys make their own formulas out of slang, like you. When they reach your age, and get political private secretaryships and things of that sort, they drop slang and get their formulas out of The Spectator or The Times. Y o u had better confine yourself to The Times. You will find that there is a certain amount of tosh about The Times; but at least its language is reputable.

LOMAX [*overwhelmed*]   You are so awfully strong-minded, Lady Brit—

LADY BRITOMART   Rubbish! [MORRISON *comes in.*] What is it?

MORRISON   If you please, my lady, Mr Undershaft has just drove up to the door.

LADY BRITOMART   Well, let him in. [MORRISON *hesitates.*] Whats the matter with you?

MORRISON   Shall I announce him, my lady; or is he at home here, so to speak, my lady?

LADY BRITOMART   Announce him.

MORRISON   Thank you, my lady. You wont mind my asking, I hope. The occasion is in a manner of speaking new to me.

LADY BRITOMART   Quite right. Go and let him in.

MORRISON   Thank you, my lady. [*He withdraws.*]

LADY BRITOMART   Children: go and get ready. [SARAH *and* BARBARA *go upstairs for their out-of-door wraps.*] Charles: go and tell Stephen to come down here in five minutes: you will find him in the drawing room. [CHARLES *goes.*] Adolphus: tell them to send round the carriage in about fifteen minutes. [ADOLPHUS *goes.*]

MORRISON [*at the door*]   Mr Undershaft.

> UNDERSHAFT *comes in.* MORRISON *goes out.*

UNDERSHAFT   Alone! How fortunate!

LADY BRITOMART [*rising*] Dont be sentimental, Andrew. Sit down. [*She sits on the settee: he sits beside her, on her left. She comes to the point before he has time to breathe.*] Sarah must have £ 800 a year until Charles Lomax comes into his property. Barbara will need more, and need it permanently, because Adolphus hasnt any property.

UNDERSHAFT [*resignedly*] Yes, my dear: I will see to it. Anything else? for yourself, for instance?

LADY BRITOMART I want to talk to you about Stephen.

UNDERSHAFT [*rather wearily*] Dont, my dear. Stephen doesnt interest me.

LADY BRITOMART He does interest me. He is our son.

UNDERSHAFT Do you really think so? He has induced us to bring him into the world; but he chose his parents very incongruously, I think. I see nothing of myself in him, and less of you.

LADY BRITOMART Andrew: Stephen is an excellent son, and a most steady, capable, highminded young man. You are simply trying to find an excuse for disinheriting him.

UNDERSHAFT My dear Biddy: the Undershaft tradition disinherits him. It would be dishonest of me to leave the cannon foundry to my son.

LADY BRITOMART It would be most unnatural and improper of you to leave it to anyone else, Andrew. Do you suppose this wicked and immoral tradition can be kept up for ever? Do you pretend that Stephen could not carry on the foundry just as well as all the other sons of the big business houses?

UNDERSHAFT Yes: he could learn the office routine without understanding the business, like all the other sons; and the firm would go on by its own momentum until the real Undershaft—probably an Italian or a German—would invent a new method and cut him out.

LADY BRITOMART There is nothing that any Italian or German could do that Stephen could not do. And Stephen at least has breeding.

UNDERSHAFT The son of a foundling! Nonsense!

LADY BRITOMART My son, Andrew! And even you may have good blood in your veins for all you know.

UNDERSHAFT True. Probably I have. That is another argument in favor of a foundling.

LADY BRITOMART Andrew: dont be aggravating. And dont be wicked. At present you are both.

UNDERSHAFT This conversation is part of the Undershaft tradition, Biddy. Every Undershaft's wife has treated him to it ever since the house was founded. It is mere waste of breath. If the tradition be ever broken it will be for an abler man than Stephen.

LADY BRITOMART [*pouting*] Then go away.

UNDERSHAFT [*deprecatory*] Go away!

LADY BRITOMART Yes: go away. If you will do nothing for Stephen, you are not wanted here. Go to your foundling, whoever he is; and look after h i m.

UNDERSHAFT The fact is, Biddy—

LADY BRITOMART Dont call me Biddy. I dont call you Andy.

UNDERSHAFT I will not call my wife Britomart: it is not good sense. Seriously, my love, the Undershaft tradition has landed me in a difficulty. I am getting on in years; and my partner Lazarus has at last made a stand and insisted that the succession must be settled one

way or the other; and of course he is quite right. You see, I havnt found a fit successor yet.

LADY BRITOMART [*obstinately*]   There is Stephen.

UNDERSHAFT   Thats just it: all the foundlings I can find are exactly like Stephen.

LADY BRITOMART   Andrew!!

UNDERSHAFT   I want a man with no relations and no schooling: that is, a man who would be out of the running altogether if he were not a strong man. And I cant find him. Every blessed foundling nowadays is snapped up in his infancy by Barnardo homes, or School Board officers, or Boards of Guardians;[5] and if he shews the least ability he is fastened on by schoolmasters; trained to win scholarships like a race-horse; crammed with secondhand ideas; drilled and disciplined in docility and what they call good taste; and lamed for life so that he is fit for nothing but teaching. If you want to keep the foundry in the family, you had better find an eligible foundling and marry him to Barbara.

LADY BRITOMART   Ah! Barbara! Your pet! You would sacrifice Stephen to Barbara.

UNDERSHAFT   Cheerfully. And you, my dear, would boil Barbara to make soup for Stephen.

LADY BRITOMART   Andrew: this is not a question of our likings and dislikings: it is a question of duty. It is your duty to make Stephen your successor.

UNDERSHAFT   Just as much as it is your duty to submit to your husband. Come, Biddy! these tricks of the governing class are of no use with me. I am one of the governing class myself; and it is a waste of time giving tracts to a missionary. I have the power in this matter; and I am not to be humbugged into using it for your purposes.

LADY BRITOMART   Andrew: you can talk my head off; but you cant change wrong into right. And your tie is all on one side. Put it straight.

UNDERSHAFT [*disconcerted*]   It wont stay unless it's pinned— [*He fumbles at it with childish grimaces.*]

STEPHEN *comes in.*

STEPHEN [*at the door*]   I beg your pardon. [*About to retire.*]

LADY BRITOMART   No: come in, Stephen. [STEPHEN *comes forward to his mother's writing table.*]

UNDERSHAFT [*not very cordially*]   Good afternoon.

STEPHEN [*coldly*]   Good afternoon.

UNDERSHAFT [*to* LADY BRITOMART]   He knows all about the tradition, I suppose?

LADY BRITOMART   Yes. [*To* STEPHEN.] It is what I told you last night, Stephen.

UNDERSHAFT [*sulkily*]   I understand you want to come into the cannon business.

STEPHEN   *I* go into trade! Certainly not.

5. The Barnardo Homes (founded 1866–67) are private institutions for the care of orphans. Public responsibility for orphans in Great Britain centered on the Boards of Guardians for the various parish workhouses or poorhouses. In larger parishes or groups of parishes orphans were separated from other paupers. In some cases separate schools were maintained; in others they attended the local schools.

UNDERSHAFT [*opening his eyes, greatly eased in mind and manner*] Oh! in that case—

LADY BRITOMART　Cannons are not trade, Stephen. They are enterprise.

STEPHEN　I have no intention of becoming a man of business in any sense. I have no capacity for business and no taste for it. I intend to devote myself to politics.

UNDERSHAFT [*rising*]　My dear boy: this is an immense relief to me. And I trust it may prove an equally good thing for the country. I was afraid you would consider yourself disparaged and slighted. [*He moves towards* STEPHEN *as if to shake hands with him.*]

LADY BRITOMART [*rising and interposing*]　Stephen: I cannot allow you to throw away an enormous property like this.

STEPHEN [*stiffly*]　Mother: there must be an end of treating me as a child, if you please. [LADY BRITOMART *recoils, deeply wounded by his tone.*] Until last night I did not take your attitude seriously, because I did not think you meant it seriously. But I find now that you left me in the dark as to matters which you should have explained to me years ago. I am extremely hurt and offended. Any further discussion of my intentions had better take place with my father, as between one man and another.

LADY BRITOMART　Stephen! [*She sits down again, her eyes filling with tears.*]

UNDERSHAFT [*with grave compassion*]　You see, my dear, it is only the big men who can be treated as children.

STEPHEN　I am sorry, mother, that you have forced me—

UNDERSHAFT [*stopping him*]　Yes, yes, yes, yes: thats all right, Stephen. She wont interfere with you any more: your independence is achieved: you have won your latchkey. Dont rub it in; and above all, dont apologize. [*He resumes his seat.*] Now what about your future, as between one man and another—I beg your pardon, Biddy: as between two men and a woman.

LADY BRITOMART [*who has pulled herself together strongly*]　I quite understand, Stephen. By all means go your own way if you feel strong enough. [STEPHEN *sits down magisterially in the chair at the writing table with an air of affirming his majority.*]

UNDERSHAFT　It is settled that you do not ask for the succession to the cannon business.

STEPHEN　I hope it is settled that I repudiate the cannon business.

UNDERSHAFT　Come, come! dont be so devilishly sulky: it's boyish. Freedom should be generous. Besides, I owe you a fair start in life in exchange for disinheriting you. You cant become prime minister all at once. Havnt you a turn for something? What about literature, art, and so forth?

STEPHEN　I have nothing of the artist about me, either in faculty or character, thank Heaven!

UNDERSHAFT　A philosopher, perhaps? Eh?

STEPHEN　I make no such ridiculous pretension.

UNDERSHAFT　Just so. Well, there is the army, the navy, the Church, the Bar. The Bar requires some ability. What about the Bar?

STEPHEN　I have not studied law. And I am afraid I have not the necessary push—I believe that is the name barristers give to their vulgarity—for success in pleading.

UNDERSHAFT　Rather a difficult case, Stephen. Hardly anything left but

the stage, is there? [STEPHEN *makes an impatient movement.*] Well, come! is there a n y t h i n g you know or care for?

STEPHEN [*rising and looking at him steadily*]   I know the difference between right and wrong.

UNDERSHAFT [*hugely tickled*]   You dont say so! What! no capacity for business, no knowledge of law, no sympathy with art, no pretension to philosophy; only a simple knowledge of the secret that has puzzled all the philosophers, baffled all the lawyers, muddled all the men of business, and ruined most of the artists: the secret of right and wrong. Why, man, youre a genius, a master of masters, a god! At twentyfour, too!

STEPHEN [*keeping his temper with difficulty*]   You are pleased to be facetious. I pretend to nothing more than any honorable English gentleman claims as his birthright. [*He sits down angrily.*]

UNDERSHAFT   Oh, thats everybody's birthright. Look at poor little Jenny Hill, the Salvation lassie! she would think you were laughing at her if you asked her to stand up in the street and teach grammar or geography or mathematics or even drawing room dancing; but it never occurs to her to doubt that she can teach morals and religion. You are all alike, you respectable people. You cant tell me the bursting strain of a ten-inch gun, which is a very simple matter; but you all think you can tell me the bursting strain of a man under temptation. You darent handle high explosives; but youre all ready to handle honesty and truth and justice and the whole duty of man, and kill one another at that game. What a country! What a world!

LADY BRITOMART [*uneasily*]   What do you think he had better do, Andrew?

UNDERSHAFT   Oh, just what he wants to do. He knows nothing and he thinks he knows everything. That points clearly to a political career. Get him a private secretaryship to someone who can get him an Under Secretaryship; and then leave him alone. He will find his natural and proper place in the end on the Treasury Bench.

STEPHEN [*springing up again*]   I am sorry, sir, that you force me to forget the respect due to you as my father. I am an Englishman and I will not hear the Government of my country insulted. [*He thrusts his hands in his pockets, and walks angrily across to the window.*]

UNDERSHAFT [*with a touch of brutality*]   The government of your country! I am the government of your country: I, and Lazarus. Do you suppose that you and half a dozen amateurs like you, sitting in a row in that foolish gabble shop, can govern Undershaft and Lazarus? No, my friend: you will do what pays u s. You will make war when it suits us, and keep peace when it doesnt. You will find out that trade requires certain measures when we have decided on those measures. When I want anything to keep my dividends up, you will discover that my want is a national need. When other people want something to keep my dividends down, you will call out the police and military. And in return you shall have the support and applause of my newspapers, and the delight of imagining that you are a great statesman. Government of your country! Be off with you, my boy, and play with your caucuses and leading articles and historic parties and great leaders and burning questions and the rest of your toys. *I* am going back to my counting-house to pay the piper and call the tune.

STEPHEN [*actually smiling, and putting his hand on his father's shoulder*

with indulgent patronage] Really, my dear father, it is impossible to be angry with you. You dont know how absurd all this sounds to m e. You are very properly proud of having been industrious enough to make money; and it is greatly to your credit that you have made so much of it. But it has kept you in circles where you are valued for your money and deferred to for it, instead of in the doubtless very old-fashioned and behind-the-times public school and university where I formed my habits of mind. It is natural for you to think that money governs England; but you must allow me to think I know better.

UNDERSHAFT   And what d o e s govern England, pray?

STEPHEN   Character, father, character.

UNDERSHAFT   Whose character? Yours or mine?

STEPHEN   Neither yours nor mine, father, but the best elements in the English national character.

UNDERSHAFT   Stephen: Ive found your profession for you. Youre a born journalist. I'll start you with a high-toned weekly review. There!

> *Before* STEPHEN *can reply* SARAH, BARBARA, LOMAX, *and* CUSINS *come in ready for walking.* BARBARA *crosses the room to the window and looks out.* CUSINS *drifts amiably to the armchair.* LOMAX *remains near the door, whilst* SARAH *comes to her mother.* STEPHEN *goes to the smaller writing table and busies himself with his letters.*

SARAH   Go and get ready, mama: the carriage is waiting. [LADY BRITOMART *leaves the room.*]

UNDERSHAFT [*to* SARAH]   Good day, my dear. Good afternoon, Mr Lomax.

LOMAX [*vaguely*]   Ahdedoo.

UNDERSHAFT [*to* CUSINS]   Quite well after last night, Euripides, eh?

CUSINS   As well as can be expected.

UNDERSHAFT   Thats right. [*To* BARBARA.] So you are coming to see my death and devastation factory, Barbara?

BARBARA [*at the window*]   You came yesterday to see my salvation factory. I promised you a return visit.

LOMAX [*coming forward between* SARAH *and* UNDERSHAFT]   Youll find it awfully interesting. Ive been through the Woolwich Arsenal; and it gives you a ripping feeling of security, you know, to think of the lot of beggars we could kill if it came to fighting. [*To* UNDERSHAFT, *with sudden solemnity.*] Still, it must be rather an awful reflection for you, from the religious point of view as it were. Youre getting on, you know, and all that.

SARAH   You dont mind Cholly's imbecility, papa, do you?

LOMAX [*much taken aback*]   Oh I say!

UNDERSHAFT   Mr Lomax looks at the matter in a very proper spirit, my dear.

LOMAX   Just so. Thats all I meant, I assure you.

SARAH   Are you coming, Stephen?

STEPHEN   Well, I am rather busy—er— [*Magnanimously.*] Oh well, yes: I'll come. That is, if there is room for me.

UNDERSHAFT   I can take two with me in a little motor I am experimenting with for field use. You wont mind its being rather unfashionable. It's not painted yet; but it's bullet proof.

LOMAX [*appalled at the prospect of confronting Wilton Crescent in an unpainted motor*]   Oh I s a y!

SARAH   The carriage for me, thank you. Barbara doesnt mind what she's seen in.

LOMAX   I say, Dolly, old chap: do you really mind the car being a guy?[6] Because of course if you do I'll go in it. Still—

CUSINS   I prefer it.

LOMAX   Thanks awfully, old man. Come, my ownest. [*He hurries out to secure his seat in the carriage.* SARAH *follows him.*]

CUSINS [*moodily walking across to* LADY BRITOMART's *writing table*]   Why are we two coming to this Works Department of Hell? that is what I ask myself.

BARBARA   I have always thought of it as a sort of pit where lost creatures with blackened faces stirred up smoky fires and were driven and tormented by my father? Is it like that, dad?

UNDERSHAFT [*scandalized*]   My dear! It is a spotlessly clean and beautiful hillside town.

CUSINS   With a Methodist chapel? Oh d o say theres a Methodist chapel.

UNDERSHAFT   There are two: a Primitive one and a sophisticated one. There is even an Ethical Society; but it is not much patronized, as my men are all strongly religious.[7] In the High Explosives Sheds they object to the presence of Agnostics as unsafe.

CUSINS   And yet they dont object to you!

BARBARA   Do they obey all your orders?

UNDERSHAFT   I never give them any orders. When I speak to one of them it is "Well, Jones, is the baby doing well? and has Mrs Jones made a good recovery?" "Nicely, thank you, sir." And thats all.

CUSINS   But Jones has to be kept in order. How do you maintain discipline among your men?

UNDERSHAFT   I dont. They do. You see, the one thing Jones wont stand is any rebellion from the man under him, or any assertion of social equality between the wife of the man with 4 shillings a week less than himself, and Mrs Jones! Of course they all rebel against me, theoretically. Practically, every man of them keeps the man just below him in his place. I never meddle with them. I never bully them. I dont even bully Lazarus. I say that certain things are to be done; but I dont order anybody to do them. I dont say, mind you, that there is no ordering about and snubbing and even bullying. The men snub the boys and order them about; the carmen snub the sweepers; the artisans snub the unskilled laborers; the foremen drive and bully both the laborers and artisans; the assistant engineers find fault with the foremen; the chief engineers drop on the assistants; the departmental managers worry the chiefs; and the clerks have tall hats and hymnbooks and keep up the social tone by refusing to associate on equal terms with anybody. The result is a colossal profit, which comes to me.

CUSINS [*revolted*]   You really are a—well, what I was saying yesterday.

BARBARA   What was he saying yesterday?

6. An object of ridicule.

7. The Primitive Methodists (founded 1811) were an offshoot of Methodism which broke away originally because of their practice, under the leadership of Hugh Bourne, of "camp-meetings," services which lasted all day. They were not reunited with the parent group until the 1930s. A Society for Ethical Culture was founded in the United States in 1876. It taught that morality is the fundamental element in religion. It reached Great Britain in 1887.

UNDERSHAFT   Never mind, my dear. He thinks I have made you unhappy. Have I?

BARBARA   Do you think I can be happy in this vulgar silly dress? I! who have worn the uniform. Do you understand what you have done to me? Yesterday I had a man's soul in my hand. I set him in the way of life with his face to salvation. But when we took your money he turned back to drunkenness and derision. [*With intense conviction.*]   I will never forgive you that. If I had a child, and you destroyed its body with your explosives—if you murdered Dolly with your horrible guns—I could forgive you if my forgiveness would open the gates of heaven to you. But to take a human soul from me, and turn it into the soul of a wolf! that is worse than any murder.

UNDERSHAFT   Does my daughter despair so easily? Can you strike a man to the heart and leave no mark on him?

BARBARA   [*her face lighting up*]   Oh, you are right: he can never be lost now: where was my faith?

CUSINS   Oh, clever clever devil!

BARBARA   You may be a devil; but God speaks through you sometimes. [*She takes her father's hands and kisses them.*] You have given me back my happiness: I feel it deep down now, though my spirit is troubled.

UNDERSHAFT   You have learnt something. That always feels at first as if you had lost something.

BARBARA   Well, take me to the factory of death; and let me learn something more. There must be some truth or other behind all this frightful irony. Come, Dolly. [*She goes out.*]

CUSINS   My guardian angel! [*To* UNDERSHAFT.] Avaunt! [*He follows* BARBARA.]

STEPHEN   [*quietly, at the writing table*]   You must not mind Cusins, father. He is a very amiable good fellow; but he is a Greek scholar and naturally a little eccentric.

UNDERSHAFT   Ah, quite so. Thank you, Stephen. Thank you. [*He goes out.*]

> STEPHEN *smiles patronizingly; buttons his coat responsibly; and crosses the room to the door.* LADY BRITOMART, *dressed for out-of-doors, opens it before he reaches it. She looks round for the others; looks at* STEPHEN; *and turns to go without a word.*

STEPHEN   [*embarrassed*]   Mother—

LADY BRITOMART   Dont be apologetic, Stephen. And dont forget that you have outgrown your mother. [*She goes out.*]

> *Perivale St Andrews lies between two Middlesex hills, half climbing the northern one. It is an almost smokeless town of white walls, roofs of narrow green slates or red tiles, tall trees, domes, campaniles, and slender chimney shafts, beautifully situated and beautiful in itself. The best view of it is obtained from the crest of a slope about half a mile to the east, where the high explosives are dealt with. The foundry lies hidden in the depths between, the tops of its chimneys sprouting like huge skittles into the middle distance. Across the crest runs an emplacement of concrete, with a firestep, and a parapet which suggests a fortification, because there is a huge cannon of the obsolete Woolwich Infant pattern peering across it at the town.*

The cannon is mounted on an experimental gun carriage: possibly the original model of the Undershaft disappearing rampart gun alluded to by STEPHEN. *The firestep, being a convenient place to sit, is furnished here and there with straw disc cushions; and at one place there is the additional luxury of a fur rug.*

BARBARA *is standing on the firestep, looking over the parapet towards the town. On her right is the cannon; on her left the end of a shed raised on piles, with a ladder of three or four steps up to the door, which opens outwards and has a little wooden landing at the threshold, with a fire bucket in the corner of the landing. Several dummy soldiers more or less mutilated, with straw protruding from their gashes, have been shoved out of the way under the landing. A few others are nearly upright against the shed; and one has fallen forward and lies, like a grotesque corpse, on the emplacement. The parapet stops short of the shed, leaving a gap which is the beginning of the path down the hill through the foundry to the town. The rug is on the firestep near this gap. Down on the emplacement behind the cannon is a trolley carrying a huge conical bombshell with a red band painted on it. Further to the right is the door of an office, which, like the sheds, is of the lightest possible construction.*

CUSINS *arrives by the path from the town.*

BARBARA   Well?

CUSINS   Not a ray of hope. Everything perfect! wonderful! real! It only needs a cathedral to be a heavenly city instead of a hellish one.

BARBARA   Have you found out whether they have done anything for old Peter Shirley?

CUSINS   They have found him a job as gatekeeper and timekeeper. He's frightfully miserable. He calls the time-keeping brainwork, and says he isnt used to it; and his gate lodge is so splendid that he's ashamed to use the rooms, and skulks in the scullery.

BARBARA   Poor Peter!

STEPHEN *arrives from the town. He carries a fieldglass.*

STEPHEN [*enthusiastically*]   Have you two seen the place? Why did you leave us?

CUSINS   I wanted to see everything I was not intended to see; and Barbara wanted to make the men talk.

STEPHEN   Have you found anything discreditable?

CUSINS   No. They call him Dandy Andy and are proud of his being a cunning old rascal; but it's all horribly, frightfully, immorally, unanswerably perfect.

SARAH *arrives.*

SARAH   Heavens! what a place! [*She crosses to the trolley.*]   Did you see the nursing home!? [*She sits down on the shell.*]

STEPHEN   Did you see the libraries and schools!?

SARAH   Did you see the ball room and the banqueting chamber in the Town Hall!?

STEPHEN   Have you gone into the insurance fund, the pension fund, the building society, the various applications of cooperation!?

UNDERSHAFT *comes from the office, with a sheaf of telegrams in his hand.*

UNDERSHAFT   Well, have you seen everything? I'm sorry I was called away. [*Indicating the telegrams.*] Good news from Manchuria.

STEPHEN   Another Japanese victory?

UNDERSHAFT   Oh, I dont know. Which side wins does not concern us here. No: the good news is that the aerial battleship is a tremendous success. At the first trial it has wiped out a fort with three hundred soldiers in it.

CUSINS [*from the platform*]   Dummy soldiers?

UNDERSHAFT [*striding across to* STEPHEN *and kicking the prostrate dummy brutally out of his way*] No: the real thing.

> CUSINS *and* BARBARA *exchange glances. Then* CUSINS *sits on the step and buries his face in his hands.* BARBARA *gravely lays her hand on his shoulder. He looks up at her in whimsical desperation.*

UNDERSHAFT   Well, Stephen, what do you think of the place?

STEPHEN   Oh, magnificent. A perfect triumph of modern industry. Frankly, my dear father, I have been a fool: I had no idea of what it all meant: of the wonderful forethought, the power of organization, the administrative capacity, the financial genius, the colossal capital it represents. I have been repeating to myself as I came through your streets "Peace hath her victories no less renowned than War."[8] I have only one misgiving about it all.

UNDERSHAFT   Out with it.

STEPHEN   Well, I cannot help thinking that all this provision for every want of your workmen may sap their independence and weaken their sense of responsibility. And greatly as we enjoyed our tea at that splendid restaurant—how they gave us all that luxury and cake and jam and cream for threepence I really cannot imagine!—still you must remember that restaurants break up home life. Look at the continent, for instance! Are you sure so much pampering is really good for the men's characters?

UNDERSHAFT   Well you see, my dear boy, when you are organizing civilization you have to make up your mind whether trouble and anxiety are good things or not. If you decide that they are, then, I take it, you simply dont organize civilization; and there you are, with trouble and anxiety enough to make us all angels! But if you decide the other way, you may as well go through with it. However, Stephen, our characters are safe here. A sufficient dose of anxiety is always provided by the fact that we may be blown to smithereens at any moment.

SARAH   By the way, papa, where do you make the explosives?

UNDERSHAFT   In separate little sheds, like that one. When one of them blows up, it costs very little; and only the people quite close to it are killed.

> STEPHEN, *who is quite close to it, looks at it rather scaredly, and moves away quickly to the cannon. At the same moment the door of the shed is thrown abruptly open; and a foreman in*

---

8. Stephen is quoting John Milton's sonnet, "To the Lord General Cromwell, May 1652."

overalls and list slippers[9] *comes out on the little landing and holds the door for* LOMAX, *who appears in the doorway.*

LOMAX [*with studied coolness*]   My good fellow: you neednt get into a state of nerves. Nothing's going to happen to you; and I suppose it wouldnt be the end of the world if anything did. A little bit of British pluck is what y o u want, old chap. [*He descends and strolls across to* SARAH.]

UNDERSHAFT [*to the foreman*]   Anything wrong, Bilton?

BILTON [*with ironic calm*]   Gentleman walked into the high explosives shed and lit a cigaret, sir: thats all.

UNDERSHAFT   Ah, quite so. [*Going over to* LOMAX.] Do you happen to remember what you did with the match?

LOMAX   Oh come! I'm not a fool. I took jolly good care to blow it out before I chucked it away.

BILTON   The top of it was red hot inside, sir.

LOMAX   Well, suppose it was! I didn't chuck it into any of y o u r messes.

UNDERSHAFT   Think no more of it, Mr Lomax. By the way, would you mind lending me your matches.

LOMAX [*offering his box*]   Certainly.

UNDERSHAFT   Thanks. [*He pockets the matches.*]

LOMAX [*lecturing to the company generally*]   You know, these high explosives dont go off like gunpowder, except when theyre in a gun. When theyre spread loose, you can put a match to them without the least risk: they just burn quietly like a bit of paper. [*Warming to the scientific interest of the subject.*] Did you know that, Undershaft? Have you ever tried?

UNDERSHAFT   Not on a large scale, Mr Lomax. Bilton will give you a sample of gun cotton when you are leaving if you ask him. You can experiment with it at home. [BILTON *looks puzzled.*]

SARAH   Bilton will do nothing of the sort, papa. I suppose it's your business to blow up the Russians and Japs; but you might really stop short of blowing up poor Cholly. [BILTON *gives it up and retires into the shed.*]

LOMAX   My ownest, there is no danger. [*He sits beside her on the shell.*]

LADY BRITOMART *arrives from the town with a bouquet.*

LADY BRITOMART [*impetuously*]   Andrew: you shouldnt have let me see this place.

UNDERSHAFT   Why, my dear?

LADY BRITOMART   Never mind why: you shouldnt have: thats all. To think of all that [*indicating the town*] being yours! and that you have kept it to yourself all these years!

UNDERSHAFT   It does not belong to me. I belong to it. It is the Undershaft inheritance.

LADY BRITOMART   It is not. Your ridiculous cannons and that noisy banging foundry may be the Undershaft inheritance; but all that plate and linen, all that furniture and those houses and orchards and gardens belong to us. They belong to m e: they are not a man's business. I wont give them up. You must be out of your senses to throw them all away; and if you persist in such folly, I will call in a doctor.

9. Cloth coverings for the feet worn for safety in the munitions works.

UNDERSHAFT [*stooping to smell the bouquet*]   Where did you get the flowers, my dear?

LADY BRITOMART   Your men presented them to me in your William Morris Labor Church.[1]

CUSINS   Oh! It needed only that. A Labor Church! [*He mounts the firestep distractedly, and leans with his elbows on the parapet, turning his back to them.*]

LADY BRITOMART   Yes, with Morris's words in mosaic letters ten feet high round the dome. No MAN IS GOOD ENOUGH TO BE ANOTHER MAN'S MASTER. The cynicism of it!

UNDERSHAFT   It shocked the men at first, I am afraid. But now they take no more notice of it than of the ten commandments in church.

LADY BRITOMART   Andrew: you are trying to put me off the subject of the inheritance by profane jokes. Well, you shant. I dont ask it any longer for Stephen: he has inherited far too much of your perversity to be fit for it. But Barbara has rights as well as Stephen. Why should not Adolphus succeed to the inheritance? I could manage the town for him; and he can look after the cannons, if they are really necessary.

UNDERSHAFT   I should ask nothing better if Adolphus were a foundling. He is exactly the sort of new blood that is wanted in English business. But he's not a foundling; and theres an end of it. [*He makes for the office door.*]

CUSINS [*turning to them*]   Not quite. [*They all turn and stare at him.*] I think—Mind! I am not committing myself in any way as to my future course—but I t h i n k the foundling difficulty can be got over. [*He jumps down to the emplacement.*]

UNDERSHAFT [*coming back to him*]   What do you mean?

CUSINS   Well, I have something to say which is in the nature of a confession.

SARAH

LADY BRITOMART

BARBARA   } Confession!

STEPHEN

LOMAX   Oh I s a y!

CUSINS   Yes, a confession. Listen, all. Until I met Barbara I thought myself in the main an honorable, truthful man, because I wanted the approval of my conscience more than I wanted anything else. But the moment I saw Barbara, I wanted her far more than the approval of my conscience.

LADY BRITOMART   Adolphus!

CUSINS   It is true. You accused me yourself, Lady Brit, of joining the Army to worship Barbara; and so I did. She bought my soul like a flower at a street corner; but she bought it for herself.

UNDERSHAFT   What! Not for Dionysos or another?

CUSINS   Dionysos and all the others are in herself. I adored what was divine in her, and was therefore a true worshipper. But I was romantic about her too. I thought she was a woman of the people, and that a marriage with a professor of Greek would be far beyond the wildest social ambitions of her rank.

---

1. The first Labor Church was founded by John Trevor, a Unitarian minister and a socialist, to provide a religious movement for the working classes without the social practices and teachings of other churches. The movement was never large and was nearly dead at the time of the play. William Morris (1834–1896), the English author and artist, was a leader in the Socialist League.

LADY BRITOMART   Adolphus!!

LOMAX   Oh I say!!!

CUSINS   When I learnt the horrible truth—

LADY BRITOMART   What do you mean by the horrible truth, pray?

CUSINS   That she was enormously rich; that her grandfather was an earl; that her father was the Prince of Darkness—

UNDERSHAFT   Chut!

CUSINS   —and that I was only an adventurer trying to catch a rich wife, then I stooped to deceive her about my birth.

BARBARA [*rising*]   Dolly!

LADY BRITOMART   Your birth! Now Adolphus, dont dare to make up a wicked story for the sake of these wretched cannons. Remember: I have seen photographs of your parents; and the Agent General for South Western Australia knows them personally and has assured me that they are most respectable married people.

CUSINS   So they are in Australia; but here they are outcasts. Their marriage is legal in Australia, but not in England. My mother is my father's deceased wife's sister; and in this island I am consequently a foundling. [*Sensation.*][2]

BARBARA   Silly! [*She climbs to the cannon, and leans, listening, in the angle it makes with the parapet.*]

CUSINS   Is the subterfuge good enough, Machiavelli?

UNDERSHAFT [*thoughtfully*]   Biddy: this may be a way out of the difficulty.

LADY BRITOMART   Stuff! A man cant make cannons any the better for being his own cousin instead of his proper self. [*She sits down on the rug with a bounce that expresses her downright contempt for their casuistry.*]

UNDERSHAFT [*to* CUSINS]   You are an educated man. That is against the tradition.

CUSINS   Once in ten thousand times it happens that the schoolboy is a born master of what they try to teach him. Greek has not destroyed my mind: it has nourished it. Besides, I did not learn it at an English public school.

UNDERSHAFT   Hm! Well, I cannot afford to be too particular: you have cornered the foundling market. Let it pass. You are eligible, Euripides: you are eligible.

BARBARA   Dolly: yesterday morning, when Stephen told us all about the tradition, you became very silent; and you have been strange and excited ever since. Were you thinking of your birth then?

CUSINS   When the finger of Destiny suddenly points at a man in the middle of his breakfast, it makes him thoughtful.

UNDERSHAFT   Aha! You have had your eye on the business, my young friend, have you?

CUSINS   Take care! There is an abyss of moral horror between me and your accursed aerial battleships.

UNDERSHAFT   Never mind the abyss for the present. Let us settle the practical details and leave your final decision open. You know that you will have to change your name. Do you object to that?

2. Marriage between a man and the sister of his deceased wife was illegal in Great Britain until 1907. The issue is mentioned in Matthew Arnold's *Culture and Anarchy* (1869) and in W. S. Gilbert's *Iolanthe* (1882). In the latter the Queen of the Fairies distresses some members of the House of Lords by her threat to send her protégé Strephon into Parliament, where with her aid he will do various dreadful things. Along with making dukedoms open to competitive examination, "He shall prick that annual blister / Marriage with deceased wife's sister."

CUSINS Would any man named Adolphus—any man called Dolly!—object to be called something else?

UNDERSHAFT Good. Now, as to money! I propose to treat you handsomely from the beginning. You shall start at a thousand a year.

CUSINS [*with sudden heat, his spectacles twinkling with mischief*] A thousand! You dare offer a miserable thousand to the son-in-law of a millionaire! No, by Heavens, Machiavelli! you shall not cheat m e. You cannot do without m e; and I can do without you. I must have two thousand five hundred a year for two years. At the end of that time, if I am a failure, I go. But if I am a success, and stay on, you must give me the other five thousand.

UNDERSHAFT What other five thousand?

CUSINS To make the two years up to five thousand a year. The two thousand five hundred is only half pay in case I should turn out a failure. The third year I must have ten per cent on the profits.

UNDERSHAFT [*taken aback*] Ten per cent! Why, man, do you know what my profits are?

CUSINS Enormous, I hope: otherwise I shall require twentyfive per cent.

UNDERSHAFT But, Mr Cusins, this is a serious matter of business. You are not bringing any capital into the concern.

CUSINS What! no capital! Is my mastery of Greek no capital? Is my access to the subtlest thought, the loftiest poetry yet attained by humanity, no capital? My character! my intellect! my life! my career! what Barbara calls my soul! are these no capital? Say another word; and I double my salary.

UNDERSHAFT Be reasonable—

CUSINS [*peremptorily*] Mr Undershaft: you have my terms. Take them or leave them.

UNDERSHAFT [*recovering himself*] Very well. I note your terms; and I offer you half.

CUSINS [*disgusted*] Half!

UNDERSHAFT [*firmly*] Half.

CUSINS You call yourself a gentleman; and you offer me half!!

UNDERSHAFT I do not call myself a gentleman; but I offer you half.

CUSINS This to your future partner! your successor! your son-in-law!

BARBARA You are selling your own soul, Dolly, not mine. Leave me out of the bargain, please.

UNDERSHAFT Come! I will go a step further for Barbara's sake. I will give you three fifths; but that is my last word.

CUSINS Done!

LOMAX Done in the eye! Why, *I* get only eight hundred, you know.

CUSINS By the way, Mac, I am a classical scholar, not an arithmetical one. Is three fifths more than half or less?

UNDERSHAFT More, of course.

CUSINS I would have taken two hundred and fifty. How you can succeed in business when you are willing to pay all that money to a University don who is obviously not worth a junior clerk's wages!—well! What will Lazarus say?

UNDERSHAFT Lazarus is a gentle romantic Jew who cares for nothing but string quartets and stalls at fashionable theatres. He will be blamed for your rapacity in money matters, poor fellow! as he has hitherto been blamed for mine. You are a shark of the first order, Euripides. So much the better for the firm!

BARBARA   Is the bargain closed, Dolly? Does your soul belong to him now?

CUSINS   No: the price is settled: that is all. The real tug of war is still to come. What about the moral question?

LADY BRITOMART   There is no moral question in the matter at all, Adolphus. You must simply sell cannons and weapons to people whose cause is right and just, and refuse them to foreigners and criminals.

UNDERSHAFT [*determinedly*]   No: none of that. You must keep the true faith of an Armorer, or you dont come in here.

CUSINS   What on earth is the true faith of an Armorer?

UNDERSHAFT   To give arms to all men who offer an honest price for them, without respect of persons or principles: to aristocrat and republican, to Nihilist and Tsar, to Capitalist and Socialist, to Protestant and Catholic, to burglar and policeman, to black man, white man and yellow man, to all sorts and conditions, all nationalities, all faiths, all follies, all causes and all crimes. The first Undershaft wrote up in his shop IF GOD GAVE THE HAND, LET NOT MAN WITHHOLD THE SWORD. The second wrote up ALL HAVE THE RIGHT TO FIGHT: NONE HAVE THE RIGHT TO JUDGE. The third wrote up TO MAN THE WEAPON: TO HEAVEN THE VICTORY. The fourth had no literary turn; so he did not write up anything; but he sold cannons to Napoleon under the nose of George the Third. The fifth wrote up PEACE SHALL NOT PREVAIL SAVE WITH A SWORD IN HER HAND. The sixth, my master, was the best of all. He wrote up NOTHING IS EVER DONE IN THIS WORLD UNTIL MEN ARE PREPARED TO KILL ONE ANOTHER IF IT IS NOT DONE. After that, there was nothing left for the seventh to say. So he wrote up, simply, UNASHAMED.

CUSINS   My good Machiavelli, I shall certainly write something up on the wall; only, as I shall write it in Greek, you wont be able to read it. But as to your Armorer's faith, if I take my neck out of the noose of my own morality I am not going to put it into the noose of yours. I shall sell cannons to whom I please and refuse them to whom I please. So there!

UNDERSHAFT   From the moment when you become Andrew Undershaft, you will never do as you please again. Dont come here lusting for power, young man.

CUSINS   If power were my aim I should not come here for it. Y o u have no power.

UNDERSHAFT   None of my own, certainly.

CUSINS   I have more power than you, more will. You do not drive this place: it drives you. And what drives the place?

UNDERSHAFT [*enigmatically*]   A will of which I am a part.

BARBARA [*startled*]   Father! Do you know what you are saying; or are you laying a snare for my soul?

CUSINS   Dont listen to his metaphysics, Barbara. The place is driven by the most rascally part of society, the money hunters, the pleasure hunters, the military promotion hunters; and he is their slave.

UNDERSHAFT   Not necessarily. Remember the Armorer's Faith. I will take an order from a good man as cheerfully as from a bad one. If you good people prefer preaching and shirking to buying my weapons and fighting the rascals, dont blame me. I can make cannons: I cannot make courage and conviction. Bah! you tire me, Euripides, with your morality mongering. Ask Barbara: s h e understands.

[*He suddenly reaches up and takes* BARBARA's *hands, looking power-fully into her eyes.*] Tell him, my love, what power really means.

BARBARA [*hypnotized*]   Before I joined the Salvation Army, I was in my own power; and the consequence was that I never knew what to do with myself. When I joined it, I had not time enough for all the things I had to do.

UNDERSHAFT [*approvingly*]   Just so. And why was that, do you suppose?

BARBARA   Yesterday I should have said, because I was in the power of God. [*She resumes her self-possession, withdrawing her hands from his with a power equal to his own.*] But you came and shewed me that I was in the power of Bodger and Undershaft. Today I feel —oh! how can I put it into words? Sarah: do you remember the earthquake at Cannes, when we were little children?[3]—how little the surprise of the first shock mattered compared to the dread and horror of waiting for the second? That is how I feel in this place today. I stood on the rock I thought eternal; and without a word of warning it reeled and crumbled under me. I was safe with an infinite wisdom watching me, an army marching to Salvation with me; and in a moment, at a stroke of your pen in a cheque book, I stood alone; and the heavens were empty. That was the first shock of the earthquake: I am waiting for the second.

UNDERSHAFT   Come, come, my daughter! dont make too much of your little tinpot tragedy. What do we do here when we spend years of work and thought and thousands of pounds of solid cash on a new gun or an aerial battleship that turns out just a hairsbreadth wrong after all? Scrap it. Scrap it without wasting another hour or another pound on it. Well, you have made for yourself something that you call a morality or a religion or what not. It doesnt fit the facts. Well, scrap it. Scrap it and get one that does fit. That is what is wrong with the world at present. It scraps its obsolete steam engines and dynamos; but it wont scrap its old prejudices and its old moralities and its old religions and its old political constitutions. Whats the result? In machinery it does very well; but in morals and religion and politics it is working at a loss that brings it nearer bankruptcy every year. Dont persist in that folly. If your old religion broke down yesterday, get a newer and a better one for tomorrow.

BARBARA   Oh how gladly I would take a better one to my soul! But you offer me a worse one. [*Turning on him with sudden vehemence.*] Justify yourself: shew me some light through the darkness of this dreadful place, with its beautifully clean workshops, and respectable workmen, and model homes.

UNDERSHAFT   Cleanliness and respectability do not need justification, Barbara: they justify themselves. I see no darkness here, no dreadfulness. In your Salvation shelter I saw poverty, misery, cold and hunger. You gave them bread and treacle and dreams of heaven. I give from thirty shillings a week to twelve thousand a year. They find their own dreams; but I look after the drainage.

BARBARA   And their souls?

UNDERSHAFT   I save their souls just as I saved yours.

BARBARA [*revolted*]   Y o u saved my soul! What do you mean?

3. Cannes is a resort town on the Riviera, an area where earthquakes are common. If Barbara is referring to a specific one, there was a major one on Ash Wednesday, February, 23, 1887.

UNDERSHAFT   I fed you and clothed you and housed you. I took care that you should have money enough to live handsomely—more than enough; so that you could be wasteful, careless, generous. That saved your soul from the seven deadly sins.

BARBARA [*bewildered*]   The seven deadly sins!

UNDERSHAFT   Yes, the deadly seven. [*Counting on his fingers.*] Food, clothing, firing, rent, taxes, respectability and children.[4] Nothing can lift those seven millstones from Man's neck but money; and the spirit cannot soar until the millstones are lifted. I lifted them from your spirit. I enabled Barbara to become Major Barbara; and I saved her from the crime of poverty.

CUSINS   Do you call poverty a crime?

UNDERSHAFT   The worst of crimes. All the other crimes are virtues beside it: all the other dishonors are chivalry itself by comparison. Poverty blights whole cities; spreads horible pestilences; strikes dead the very souls of all who come within sight, sound, or smell of it. What you call crime is nothing: a murder here and a theft there, a blow now and a curse then: what do they matter? they are only the accidents and illnesses of life: there are not fifty genuine professional criminals in London. But there are millions of poor people, abject people, dirty people, ill fed, ill clothed people. They poison us morally and physically: they kill the happiness of society: they force us to do away with our own liberties and to organize unnatural cruelties for fear they should rise against us and drag us down into their abyss. Only fools fear crime: we all fear poverty. Pah! [*turning on* BARBARA] you talk of your half-saved ruffian in West Ham: you accuse me of dragging his soul back to perdition. Well, bring him to me here; and I will drag his soul back again to salvation for you. Not by words and dreams; but by thirtyeight shillings a week, a sound house in a handsome street, and a permanent job. In three weeks he will have a fancy waistcoat; in three months a tall hat and a chapel sitting; before the end of the year he will shake hands with a duchess at a Primrose League meeting, and join the Conservative Party.[5]

BARBARA   And will he be the better for that?

UNDERSHAFT   You know he will. Dont be a hypocrite, Barbara. He will be better fed, better housed, better clothed, better behaved; and his children will be pounds heavier and bigger. That will be better than an American cloth mattress in a shelter, chopping firewood, eating bread and treacle, and being forced to kneel down from time to time to thank heaven for it: knee drill, I think you call it. It is cheap work converting starving men with a Bible in one hand and a slice of bread in the other. I will undertake to convert West Ham to Mahometanism[6] on the same terms. Try your hand on m y men: their souls are hungry because their bodies are full.

BARBARA   And leave the east end to starve?

UNDERSHAFT [*his energetic tone dropping into one of bitter and brooding remembrance*]   I was an east ender. I moralized and starved until one day I swore that I would be a full-fed free man at all costs; that nothing should stop me except a bullet, neither reason nor morals

---

4. "Firing" means heat. More traditional lists of the seven deadly sins include pride, envy, anger, covetousness, sloth, lechery, and gluttony.

5. The Primrose League, founded in 1883, was an organization composed of members of the Conservative Party. The name came from the custom at the time of wearing a primrose on the anniversary of Disraeli's death as a commemorative gesture.

6. Another name for Islam.

nor the lives of other men. I said "Thou shalt starve ere I starve"; and with that word I became free and great. I was a dangerous man until I had my will: now I am a useful, beneficent, kindly person. That is the history of most self-made millionaires, I fancy. When it is the history of every Englishman we shall have an England worth living in.

LADY BRITOMART   Stop making speeches, Andrew. This is not the place for them.

UNDERSHAFT [*punctured*]   My dear: I have no other means of conveying my ideas.

LADY BRITOMART   Your ideas are nonsense. You got on because you were selfish and unscrupulous.

UNDERSHAFT   Not at all. I had the strongest scruples about poverty and starvation. Your moralists are quite unscrupulous about both: they make virtues of them. I had rather be a thief than a pauper. I had rather be a murderer than a slave. I dont want to be either; but if you force the alternative on me, then, by Heaven, I'll choose the braver and more moral one. I hate poverty and slavery worse than any other crimes whatsoever. And let me tell you this. Poverty and slavery have stood up for centuries to your sermons and leading articles: they will not stand up to my machine guns. Dont preach at them: dont reason with them. Kill them.

BARBARA   Killing. Is that your remedy for everything?

UNDERSHAFT   It is the final test of conviction, the only lever strong enough to overturn a social system, the only way of saying Must. Let six hundred and seventy fools loose in the streets; and three policemen can scatter them. But huddle them together in a certain house in Westminister; and let them go through certain ceremonies and call themselves certain names until at last they get the courage to kill; and your six hundred and seventy fools become a government. Your pious mob fills up ballot papers and imagines it is governing its masters; but the ballot paper that really governs is the paper that has a bullet wrapped up in it.

CUSINS   That is perhaps why, like most intelligent people, I never vote.

UNDERSHAFT   Vote! Bah! When you vote, you only change the names of the cabinet. When you shoot, you pull down governments, inaugurate new epochs, abolish old orders and set up new. Is that historically true, Mr Learned Man, or is it not?

CUSINS   It is historically true. I loathe having to admit it. I repudiate your sentiments. I abhor your nature. I defy you in every possible way. Still, it is true. But it ought not to be true.

UNDERSHAFT   Ought! ought! ought! ought! ought! Are you going to spend your life saying ought, like the rest of our moralists? Turn your oughts into shalls, man. Come and make explosives with me. Whatever can blow men up can blow society up. The history of the world is the history of those who had courage enough to embrace this truth. Have you the courage to embrace it, Barbara?

LADY BRITOMART   Barbara: I positively forbid you to listen to your father's abominable wickedness. And you, Adolphus, ought to know better than to go about saying that wrong things are true. What does it matter whether they are true if they are wrong?

UNDERSHAFT   What does it matter whether they are wrong if they are true?

LADY BRITOMART [*rising*]   Children: come home instantly. Andrew:

I am exceedingly sorry I allowed you to call on us. You are wickeder than ever. Come at once.

BARBARA [*shaking her head*] It's no use running away from wicked people, mamma.

LADY BRITOMART It is every use. It shews your disapprobation of them.

BARBARA It does not save them.

LADY BRITOMART I can see that you are going to disobey me. Sarah: are you coming home or are you not?

SARAH I daresay it's very wicked of papa to make cannons; but I dont think I shall cut him on that account.

LOMAX [*pouring oil on the troubled waters*] The fact is, you know, there is a certain amount of tosh about this notion of wickedness. It doesnt work. You must look at facts. Not that I would say a word in favor of anything wrong; but then, you see, all sorts of chaps are always doing all sorts of things; and we have to fit them in somehow, dont you know. What I mean is that you cant go cutting everybody; and thats about what it comes to. [*Their rapt attention to his eloquence makes him nervous.*] Perhaps I dont make myself clear.

LADY BRITOMART You are lucidity itself, Charles. Because Andrew is successful and has plenty of money to give to Sarah, you will flatter him and encourage him in his wickedness.

LOMAX [*unruffled*] Well, where the carcase is, there will the eagles be gathered, dont you know. [*To* UNDERSHAFT.] Eh? What?

UNDERSHAFT Precisely. By the way, m a y I call you Charles?

LOMAX Delighted. Cholly is the usual ticket.

UNDERSHAFT [*to* LADY BRITOMART] Biddy—

LADY BRITOMART [*violently*] Dont dare call me Biddy. Charles Lomax: you are a fool. Adolphus Cusins: you are a Jesuit. Stephen: you are a prig. Barbara: you are a lunatic. Andrew: you are a vulgar tradesman. Now you all know my opinion; and m y conscience is clear, at all events. [*She sits down with a vehemence that the rug fortunately softens.*]

UNDERSHAFT My dear: you are the incarnation of morality. [*She snorts.*] Your conscience is clear and your duty done when you have called everybody names. Come, Euripides! it is getting late; and we all want to go home. Make up your mind.

CUSINS Understand this, you old demon—

LADY BRITOMART Adolphus!

UNDERSHAFT Let him alone, Biddy. Proceed, Euripides.

CUSINS You have me in a horrible dilemma. I want Barbara.

UNDERSHAFT Like all young men, you greatly exaggerate the difference between one young woman and another.

BARBARA Quite true, Dolly.

CUSINS I also want to avoid being a rascal.

UNDERSHAFT [*with biting contempt*] You lust for personal righteousness, for self-approval, for what you call a good conscience, for what Barbara calls salvation, for what I call patronizing people who are not so lucky as yourself.

CUSINS I do not: all the poet in me recoils from being a good man. But there are things in me that I must reckon with. Pity—

UNDERSHAFT Pity! The scavenger of misery.

CUSINS Well, love.

UNDERSHAFT   I know. You love the needy and the outcast: you love the oppressed races, the negro, the Indian ryot,[7] the underdog everywhere. Do you love the Japanese? Do you love the French? Do you love the English?

CUSINS   No. Every true Englishman detests the English. We are the wickedest nation on earth; and our success is a moral horror.

UNDERSHAFT   That is what comes of your gospel of love, is it?

CUSINS   May I not love even my father-in-law?

UNDERSHAFT   Who wants your love, man? By what right do you take the liberty of offering it to me? I will have your due heed and respect, or I will kill you. But your love! Damn your impertinence!

CUSINS [grinning]   I may not be able to control my affections, Mac.

UNDERSHAFT   You are fencing, Euripides. You are weakening: your grip is slipping. Come! try your last weapon. Pity and love have broken in your hand: forgiveness is still left.

CUSINS   No: forgiveness is a beggar's refuge. I am with you there: we must pay our debts.

UNDERSHAFT   Well said. Come! you will suit me. Remember the words of Plato.

CUSINS [starting]   Plato! Y o u dare quote Plato to m e!

UNDERSHAFT   Plato says, my friend, that society cannot be saved until either the Professors of Greek take to making gunpowder, or else the makers of gunpowder become Professors of Greek.[8]

CUSINS   Oh, tempter, cunning tempter!

UNDERSHAFT   Come! choose, man, choose.

CUSINS   But perhaps Barbara will not marry me if I make the wrong choice.

BARBARA   Perhaps not.

CUSINS [desperately perplexed]   You hear!

BARBARA   Father: do you love nobody?

UNDERSHAFT   I love my best friend.

LADY BRITOMART   And who is that, pray?

UNDERSHAFT   My bravest enemy. That is the man who keeps me up to the mark.

CUSINS   You know, the creature is really a sort of poet in his way. Suppose he is a great man, after all!

UNDERSHAFT   Suppose you stop talking and make up your mind, my young friend.

CUSINS   But you are driving me against my nature. I hate war.

UNDERSHAFT   Hatred is the coward's revenge for being intimidated. Dare you make war on war? Here are the means: my friend Mr Lomax is sitting on them.

LOMAX [springing up]   Oh I say! You dont mean that this thing is loaded, do you? My ownest: come off it.

SARAH [sitting placidly on the shell]   If I am to be blown up, the more thoroughly it is done the better. Dont fuss, Cholly.

LOMAX [to UNDERSHAFT, strongly remonstrant]   Your own daughter, you know!

UNDERSHAFT   So I see. [To CUSINS.] Well, my friend, may we expect you here at six tomorrow morning?

CUSINS [firmly]   Not on any account. I will see the whole establish-

---

7. An Indian word for peasant.   8. Plato actually spoke of philosophers
                                             and kings.

ment blown up with its own dynamite before I will get up at five. My hours are healthy, rational hours: eleven to five.

UNDERSHAFT Come when you please: before a week you will come at six and stay until I turn you out for the sake of your health. [*Calling.*] Bilton! [*He turns to* LADY BRITOMART, *who rises.*] My dear: let us leave these two young people to themselves for a moment. [BILTON *comes from the shed.*] I am going to take you through the gun cotton shed.

BILTON [*barring the way*] You cant take anything explosive in here, sir.

LADY BRITOMART What do you mean? Are you alluding to me?

BILTON [*unmoved*] No, maam. Mr Undershaft has the other gentleman's matches in his pocket.

LADY BRITOMART [*abruptly*] Oh! I beg your pardon. [*She goes into the shed.*]

UNDERSHAFT Quite right, Bilton, quite right: here you are. [*He gives* BILTON *the box of matches.*] Come, Stephen. Come, Charles. Bring Sarah. [*He passes into the shed.*]

> BILTON *opens the box and deliberately drops the matches into the fire-bucket.*

LOMAX Oh! I say. [BILTON *stolidly hands him the empty box.*] Infernal nonsense! Pure scientific ignorance! [*He goes in.*]

SARAH Am I all right, Bilton?

BILTON Youll have to put on list slippers, miss: thats all. Weve got em inside [*She goes in.*]

STEPHEN [*very seriously to* CUSINS] Dolly, old fellow, think. Think before you decide. Do you feel that you are a sufficiently practical man? It is a huge undertaking, an enormous responsibility. All this mass of business will be Greek to you.

CUSINS Oh, I think it will be much less difficult than Greek.

STEPHEN Well, I just want to say this before I leave you to yourselves. Dont let anything I have said about right and wrong prejudice you against this great chance in life. I have satisfied myself that the business is one of the highest character and a credit to our country. [*Emotionally.*] I am very proud of my father. I—[*Unable to proceed, he presses* CUSINS' *hand and goes hastily into the shed, followed by* BILTON.]

> BARBARA *and* CUSINS, *left alone together, look at one another silently.*

CUSINS Barbara: I am going to accept this offer.

BARBARA I thought you would.

CUSINS You understand, dont you, that I had to decide without consulting you. If I had thrown the burden of the choice on you, you would sooner or later have despised me for it.

BARBARA Yes: I did not want you to sell your soul for me any more than for this inheritance.

CUSINS It is not the sale of my soul that troubles me: I have sold it too often to care about that. I have sold it for a professorship. I have sold it for an income. I have sold it to escape being imprisoned for refusing to pay taxes for hangmen's ropes and unjust wars and things that I abhor. What is all human conduct but the daily and hourly

sale of our souls for trifles? What I am now selling it for is neither money nor position nor comfort, but for reality and for power.

BARBARA You know that you will have no power, and that he has none.

CUSINS I know. It is not for myself alone. I want to make power for the world.

BARBARA I want to make power for the world too; but it must be spiritual power.

CUSINS I think all power is spiritual: these cannons will not go off by themselves. I have tried to make spiritual power by teaching Greek. But the world can never be really touched by a dead language and a dead civilization. The people must have power; and the people cannot have Greek. Now the power that is made here can be wielded by all men.

BARBARA Power to burn women's houses down and kill their sons and tear their husbands to pieces.

CUSINS You cannot have power for good without having power for evil too. Even mother's milk nourishes murderers as well as heroes. This power which only tears men's bodies to pieces has never been so horribly abused as the intellectual power, the imaginative power, the poetic, religious power that can enslave men's souls. As a teacher of Greek I gave the intellectual man weapons against the common man. I now want to give the common man weapons against the intellectual man. I love the common people. I want to arm them against the lawyers, the doctors, the priests, the literary men, the professors, the artists, and the politicians, who, once in authority, are more disastrous and tyrannical than all the fools, rascals, and impostors. I want a power simple enough for common men to use, yet strong enough to force the intellectual oligarchy to use its genius for the general good.

BARBARA Is there no higher power than that? [*Pointing to the shell.*]

CUSINS Yes; but that power can destroy the higher powers just as a tiger can destroy a man: therefore Man must master that power first. I admitted this when the Turks and Greeks were last at war. My best pupil went out to fight for Hellas. My parting gift to him was not a copy of Plato's Republic, but a revolver and a hundred Undershaft cartridges. The blood of every Turk he shot—if he shot any—is on my head as well as on Undershaft's. That act committed me to this place for ever. Your father's challenge has beaten me. Dare I make war on war? I dare. I must. I will. And now, is it all over between us?

BARBARA [*touched by his evident dread of her answer*] Silly baby Dolly! How could it be!

CUSINS [*overjoyed*] Then you—you—you— Oh for my drum! [*He flourishes imaginary drumsticks.*]

BARBARA [*angered by his levity*] Take care, Dolly, take care. Oh, if only I could get away from you and from father and from it all! if I could have the wings of a dove and fly away to heaven!

CUSINS And leave m e!

BARBARA Yes, you, and all the other naughty mischievous children of men. But I cant. I was happy in the Salvation Army for a moment. I escaped from the world into a paradise of enthusiasm and prayer and soul saving; but the moment our money ran short, it all came back to Bodger: it was he who saved our people: he, and the Prince

of Darkness, my papa. Undershaft and Bodger: their hands stretch everywhere: when we feed a starving fellow creature, it is with their bread, because there is no other bread; when we tend the sick, it is in the hospitals they endow; if we turn from the churches they build, we must kneel on the stones of the streets they pave. As long as that lasts, there is no getting away from them. Turning our backs on Bodger and Undershaft is turning our backs on life.

CUSINS   I thought you were determined to turn your back on the wicked side of life.

BARBARA   There is no wicked side: life is all one. And I never wanted to shirk my share in whatever evil must be endured, whether it be sin or suffering. I wish I could cure you of middle-class ideas, Dolly.

CUSINS *[gasping]*   Middle cl—! A snub! A social snub to m e! from the daughter of a foundling!

BARBARA   That is why I have no class, Dolly: I come straight out of the heart of the whole people. If I were middle-class I should turn my back on my father's business; and we should both live in an artistic drawing room, with you reading the reviews in one corner, and I in the other at the piano, playing Schumann:[9] both very superior persons, and neither of us a bit of use. Sooner than that, I would sweep out the guncotton shed, or be one of Bodger's barmaids. Do you know what would have happened if you had refused papa's offer?

CUSINS   I wonder!

BARBARA   I should have given you up and married the man who accepted it. After all, my dear old mother has more sense than any of you. I felt like her when I saw this place—felt that I must have it—that never, never, never could I let it go; only she thought it was the houses and the kitchen ranges and the linen and china, when it was really all the human souls to be saved: not weak souls in starved bodies, sobbing with gratitude for a scrap of bread and treacle, but fullfed, quarrelsome, snobbish, uppish creatures, all standing on their little rights and dignities, and thinking that my father ought to be greatly obliged to them for making so much money for him—and so he ought. That is where salvation is really wanted. My father shall never throw it in my teeth again that my converts were bribed with bread. *[She is transfigured.]* I have got rid of the bribe of bread. I have got rid of the bribe of heaven. Let God's work be done for its own sake: the work he had to create us to do because it cannot be done except by living men and women. When I die, let him be in my debt, not I in his; and let me forgive him as becomes a woman of my rank.

CUSINS   Then the way of life lies through the factory of death?

BARBARA   Yes, through the raising of hell to heaven and of man to God, through the unveiling of an eternal light in the Valley of The Shadow. *[Seizing him with both hands.]* Oh, did you think my courage would never come back? did you believe that I was a deserter? that I, who have stood in the streets, and taken my people to my heart, and talked of the holiest and greatest things with them, could ever turn back and chatter foolishly to fashionable people about nothing in a drawing room? Never, never, never, never: Major

9. Robert Schumann (1810–1856) was a German composer; many of his early works were written for the piano.

Barbara will die with the colors. Oh! and I have my dear little Dolly boy still; and he has found me my place and my work. Glory Hallelujah! [*She kisses him.*]

CUSINS   My dearest: consider my delicate health. I cannot stand as much happiness as you can.

BARBARA   Yes: it is not easy work being in love with me, is it? But it's good for you. [*She runs to the shed, and calls, childlike.*] Mamma! Mamma! [BILTON *comes out of the shed, followed by* UNDERSHAFT.] I want Mamma.

UNDERSHAFT   She is taking off her list slippers, dear. [*He passes on to* CUSINS.] Well? What does she say?

CUSINS   She has gone right up into the skies.

LADY BRITOMART [*coming from the shed and stopping on the steps, obstructing* SARAH, *who follows with* LOMAX. BARBARA *clutches like a baby at her mother's skirt.*] Barbara: when will you learn to be independent and to act and think for yourself? I know as well as possible what that cry of "Mamma, Mamma," means. Always running to me!

SARAH [*touching* LADY BRITOMART'*s ribs with her finger tips and imitating a bicycle horn*] Pip! pip!

LADY BRITOMART [*highly indignant*] How dare you say Pip! pip! to me, Sarah? You are both very naughty children. What do you want, Barbara?

BARBARA   I want a house in the village to live in with Dolly. [*Dragging at the skirt.*] Come and tell me which one to take.

UNDERSHAFT [*to* CUSINS] Six o'clock tomorrow morning, Euripides.

THE END

1905

SHAW'S SPELLING

Shaw has definite notions about the representation of language on the page, including an interest in spelling reform, a cause to which he left a substantial portion of his fortune. Three characteristic features of his own style are represented in *Major Barbara*, and to a lesser extent in *Caesar and Cleopatra:*

1. Certain contractions are printed without an apostrophe, as "cant," "didnt" and "isnt."
2. Certain abbreviations are printed without a period, as in "Who saved you, Mr Price?" and "Have you ever been in love with Poverty, like St Francis?"
3. A word or phrase may be printed with unusual spacing between the letters as a clue to way of speaking the line, as in: "Wot ev I dan to y o u? Aw aint smashed y o u r fice, ev Aw?"

In the last example Shaw uses unusual spelling to indicate, as closely as possible, the actual sounds made by speakers of lower class dialects. This kind of spelling is so common in Act 2 of *Major Barbara* that some help in reading it may be welcome. The four lower class speakers use the dialect in several ways. Peter Shirley, who prides himself on his education, uses relatively few forms. Rummy Mitchens and Snobby Price make some pretension to respectability but do not have Shirley's education. Therefore they use more such forms than he does. Bill Walker, who despises education and respectability, speaks a much more heavily dialectal language. There is more than a hint of defiance in his use of the language.

The following suggestions are offered to help students without training in linguistics follow the dialogue. They are empirical and pragmatic. Using them will not produce flawless speakers of the lower class speech of London's East End.

1. Reading the speech aloud, pronouncing the words with the sounds most commonly associated with the letters, will sometimes help. In some cases Shaw's spelling is more phonetic than the customary spelling of the word, as in *sez* for *says*, *(h)iz* for *his*, *enaff* for *enough*.

2. Initial *h* is frequently dropped from words like *av* for *have*, *appiness*, and *ands*. Less frequently an initial *h* is added to words beginning with a vowel, as in *hintroduced*, *hall hannerstenning* for *all understanding* and *hathers* for *others*. Rummy and Snobby particularly do this because they are trying to mimic people of higher class. They know that lower class speakers drop *h*'s, but they are not sure which words should have them.

3. Initial *wh* may be replaced by *w* as in *wot* for *what* and *wispering*.

4. A final consonant (or final pronounced consonant) may be dropped as in *an* for *and*, *ole* for *old*, *kep* for *kept*, *(h)a* for *(h)ave* and *lea* for *leave*. Less frequently a final consonant may be added, as in *acrost*, or one substituted for another, as in *wiv* for *with*.

5. The substitution of final *n* for final *ng*, common in other dialects, is frequent.

6. In certain words, *r* following a vowel is lost, as in *fust* for *first*, *stawt* for *start*, *aw* for *are*, and *dessay* for *dare say*. In others an *r* is added following a vowel as in *gorn* for *gone*, *lor* for *law*, and *jawr* for *jaw*. Two words add an *r* and drop another consonant, *arter* for *after* and *arf* for *half*.

7. A number of vowel sounds are different from those in Standard English, especially in Bill Walker's speeches. The most common are represented as follows:
   a. the *i* sound in *I* or *lie* as if *aw* or *loy* (two different sounds. He says *maw* and *moy* for *my*).
   b. the *a* sound in *mate* or *waiting* as if *mite* or *witin*.
   c. the *a* sound in *stand* or *am* as if *stend* or *em*.
   d. the *a* sound in *chance*, *cant*, or *ask* as if *chawnce*, *cawnt*, or *awsk*.
   e. the *o* sound in *know* or *go* as if *knaow* or *gow*.
   f. the *u* sound in *up* or *put* as if *ap* or *pat*.
   g. the *ou* sound in *pound* or *now* as if *pahnd* or *nah*.

ANTON CHEKHOV

Three Sisters*

CHARACTERS

ANDREY SERGEYEVITCH PROZOROV[1]
NATALYA IVANOVNA (also called
   NATASHA), his fiancée, after-
   wards his wife
OLGA ⎫
MASHA ⎬ his sisters
IRINA ⎭
FYODOR ILYITCH KULIGIN, a high-
   school teacher, husband of
   Masha
LIEUTENANT COLONEL ALEXANDR
   IGNATYEVITCH VERSHININ, Bat-
   tery Commander
BARON NIKOLAY LVOVITCH TUSEN-
   BACH, Lieutenant

VASSILY VASSILYEVITCH SOLYONY,
   Captain
IVAN ROMANITCH TCHEBUTYKIN,
   army doctor
ALEXEY PETROVITCH FEDOTIK,
   Second Lieutenant
VLADIMIR KARLOVITCH RODDEY,
   Second Lieutenant
FERAPONT, an old porter from the
   Rural Board[2]
ANFISA, the nurse, an old woman
   of eighty

The action takes place in a provincial town.

Act 1

In the house of the PROZOROVS. A drawing room with columns
beyond which a large room is visible. Midday; it is bright and
sunny. The table in the farther room is being laid for lunch.

OLGA, in the dark-blue uniform of a high-school teacher, is correcting exercise books, at times standing still and then walking
up and down; MASHA, in a black dress, with her hat on her knee,
is reading a book; IRINA, in a white dress, is standing plunged in
thought.

OLGA Father died just a year ago, on this very day—the fifth of May,
your name-day, Irina.[3] It was very cold, snow was falling. I felt as
though I should not live through it; you lay fainting as though you
were dead. But now a year has passed and we can think of it calmly;
you are already in a white dress, your face is radiant. [The clock
strikes twelve.] The clock was striking then too. [A pause.] I remember the band playing and the firing at the cemetery as they carried
the coffin. Though he was a general in command of a brigade, yet
there weren't many people there. It was raining, though. Heavy rain
and snow.
IRINA Why recall it!

° Translated by Constance Garnett.
1. See the note on Russian names, p.
1092.
2. The Rural Board was the local arm of
the Imperial government. It was somewhat
more powerful than the locally elected
zemstvo, which is mentioned later in the
play.

3. Like many Europeans, Irina observes
not her birthday but the feast of the saint
whose name she bears. Several Saint Irenes
share May 5 as feast day, including a
Byzantine martyr of the first century, be-
headed during the reign of Domitian or
Trajan and a Greek martyr burned to death
in Thessalonica in 304 A.D.

BARON TUSENBACH, TCHEBUTYKIN, *and* SOLYONY *appear near the table in the dining room, beyond the columns.*

OLGA   It is warm today, we can have the windows open, but the birches are not in leaf yet. Father was given his brigade and came here with us from Moscow eleven years ago and I remember distinctly that in Moscow at this time, at the beginning of May, everything was already in flower; it was warm, and everything was bathed in sunshine. It's eleven years ago, and yet I remember it all as though we had left it yesterday. Oh, dear! I woke up this morning, I saw a blaze of sunshine. I saw the spring, and joy stirred in my heart. I had a passionate longing to be back at home again!

TCHEBUTYKIN   The devil it is!

TUSENBACH   Of course, it's nonsense.

MASHA, *brooding over a book, softly whistles a song.*

OLGA   Don't whistle, Masha. How can you! [*A pause.*] Being all day in school and then at my lessons till the evening gives me a perpetual headache and thoughts as gloomy as though I were old. And really these four years that I have been at the high-school I have felt my strength and my youth oozing away from me every day. And only one yearning grows stronger and stronger. . . .

IRINA   To go back to Moscow. To sell the house, to make an end of everything here, and off to Moscow. . . .

OLGA   Yes! To Moscow, and quickly.

TCHEBUTYKIN *and* TUSENBACH *laugh.*

IRINA   Andrey will probably be a professor, he will not live here anyhow. The only difficulty is poor Masha.

OLGA   Masha will come and spend the whole summer in Moscow every year.

MASHA *softly whistles a tune.*

IRINA   Please God it will all be managed. [*Looking out of window.*] How fine it is today. I don't know why I feel so lighthearted! I remembered this morning that it was my name-day and at once I felt joyful and thought of my childhood when mother was living. And I was thrilled by such wonderful thoughts, such thoughts!

OLGA   You are radiant today and looking lovelier than usual. And Masha is lovely too. Andrey would be nice-looking, but he has grown too fat and that does not suit him. And I have grown older and ever so much thinner. I suppose it's because I get so cross with the girls at school. Today now I am free, I am at home, and my head doesn't ache, and I feel younger than yesterday. I am only twenty-eight. . . . It's all quite right, it's all from God, but it seems to me that if I were married and sitting at home all day, it would be better. [*A pause.*] I should be fond of my husband.

TUSENBACH [*to* SOLYONY]   You talk such nonsense, I am tired of listening to you. [*Coming into the drawing room.*] I forgot to tell you, you will receive a visit today from Vershinin, the new commander of our battery. [*Sits down to the piano.*]

OLGA   Well, I shall be delighted.

IRINA   Is he old?

TUSENBACH   No, nothing to speak of. Forty or forty-five at the most.

[*Softly plays the piano.*] He seems to be a nice fellow. He is not stupid, that's certain. Only he talks a lot.

IRINA   Is he interesting?

TUSENBACH   Yes, he is all right, only he has a wife, a mother-in-law and two little girls. And it's his second wife too. He is paying calls and telling everyone that he has a wife and two little girls. He'll tell you so too. His wife seems a bit crazy, with her hair in a long plait like a girl's, always talks in a high-flown style, makes philosophical reflections and frequently attempts to commit suicide, evidently to annoy her husband. I should have left a woman like that years ago, but he puts up with her and merely complains.

SOLYONY   [*coming into the drawing room with* TCHEBUTYKIN]   With one hand I can only lift up half a hundredweight, but with both hands I can lift up a hundredweight and a half or even a hundredweight and three-quarters.[4] From that I conclude that two men are not only twice but three times as strong as one man, or even more. . . .

TCHEBUTYKIN   [*reading the newspaper as he comes in*]   For hair falling out . . . two ounces of naphthaline in half a bottle of spirit . . . to be dissolved and used daily. . . . [*Puts it down in his notebook.*] Let's make a note of it! No, I don't want it. . . . [*Scratches it out.*] It doesn't matter.

IRINA   Ivan Romanitch, dear Ivan Romanitch!

TCHEBUTYKIN   What is it, my child, my joy?

IRINA   Tell me, why is it I am so happy today? As though I were sailing with the great blue sky above me and big white birds flying over it. Why is it? Why?

TCHEBUTYKIN   [*kissing both her hands, tenderly*]   My white bird. . . .

IRINA   When I woke up this morning, got up and washed, it suddenly seemed to me as though everything in the world was clear to me and that I knew how one ought to live. Dear Ivan Romanitch, I know all about it. A man ought to work, to toil in the sweat of his brow, whoever he may be, and all the purpose and meaning of his life, his happiness, his ecstasies lie in that alone. How delightful to be a workman who gets up before dawn and breaks stones on the road, or a shepherd, or a schoolmaster teaching children, or an engine-driver. . . . Oh, dear! to say nothing of human beings, it would be better to be an ox, better to be a humble horse and work, than a young woman who wakes at twelve o'clock, then has coffee in bed, then spends two hours dressing. . . . Oh, how awful that is! Just as one has a craving for water in hot weather I have a craving for work. And if I don't get up early and work, give me up as a friend, Ivan Romanitch.

TCHEBUTYKIN   [*tenderly*]   I'll give you up, I'll give you up. . . .

OLGA   Father trained us to get up at seven o'clock. Now Irina wakes at seven and lies in bed at least till nine thinking. And she looks so serious! [*Laughs.*]

IRINA   You are used to thinking of me as a child and are surprised when I look serious. I am twenty!

TUSENBACH   The yearning for work, oh dear, how well I understand it! I have never worked in my life. I was born in cold, idle Petersburg, in a family that had known nothing of work or cares of any kind. I

---

4. I.e., 150 to 175 pounds.

remember, when I came home from the school of cadets, a footman used to pull off my boots. I used to be troublesome, but my mother looked at me with reverential awe, and was surprised when other people did not do the same. I was guarded from work. But I doubt if they have succeeded in guarding me completely, I doubt it! The time is at hand, an avalanche is moving down upon us, a mighty clearing storm which is coming, is already near and will soon blow the laziness, the indifference, the distaste for work, the rotten boredom out of our society. I shall work, and in another twenty-five or thirty years everyone will have to work. Everyone!

TCHEBUTYKIN   I am not going to work.

TUSENBACH   You don't count.

SOLYONY   In another twenty-five years you won't be here, thank God. In two or three years you will kick the bucket, or I shall lose my temper and put a bullet through your head, my angel.

> *Pulls a scent-bottle out of his pocket and sprinkles his chest and hands.*

TCHEBUTYKIN [*laughs*]   And I really have never done anything at all. I haven't done a stroke of work since I left the University, I have never read a book, I read nothing but newspapers. . . . [*Takes another newspaper out of his pocket.*] Here . . . I know, for instance, from the newspapers that there was such a person as Dobrolyubov, but what he wrote, I can't say.[5] . . . Goodness only knows. . . .

> *A knock is heard on the floor from the story below.*

There . . . they are calling me downstairs, someone has come for me. I'll be back directly. . . . Wait a minute. . . . [*Goes out hurriedly, combing his beard.*]

IRINA   He's got something up his sleeve.

TUSENBACH   Yes, he went out with a solemn face; evidently he is just going to bring you a present.

IRINA   What a nuisance!

OLGA   Yes, it's awful. He is always doing something silly.

MASHA   By the sea-strand an oak tree green . . . upon that oak a chain of gold . . . upon that oak a chain of gold.[6] [*Gets up, humming softly.*]

OLGA   You are not very cheerful today, Masha.

> MASHA, *humming, puts on her hat.*

OLGA   Where are you going?

MASHA   Home.

IRINA   How queer! . . .

TUSENBACH   To go away from a name-day party!

MASHA   Never mind. . . . I'll come in the evening. Good-bye, my darling. . . . [*Kisses* IRINA.] Once again I wish you, be well and happy. In old days, when father was alive, we always had thirty or forty officers here on name-days; it was noisy, but today there is only a man and a half, and it is as still as the desert. . . . I'll go. . . .

5. Nicholas A. Dobrolyubov (1836–1861) was a distinguished literary critic and advanced social thinker, a forerunner of populism.

6. Masha is quoting from the opening of *Ruslan and Ludmila*, a long narrative poem by Alexander S. Pushkin (1799–1837), the most famous Russian poet of the nineteenth century. Several of the literary quotations in the play, including this one, appear more than once.

I am in the blues today, I am feeling glum, so don't you mind what I say. [*Laughing through her tears.*] We'll talk some other time, and so for now good-bye, darling, I am going. . . .

IRINA [*discontentedly*]   Oh, how tiresome you are. . . .

OLGA [*with tears*]   I understand you, Masha.

SOLYONY   If a man philosophizes, there will be philosophy or sophistry, anyway, but if a woman philosophizes, or two do it, then you may just snap your fingers!

MASHA   What do you mean to say by that, you terrible person?

SOLYONY   Nothing. He had not time to say "alack," before the bear was on his back.[7] [*A pause.*]

MASHA [*to* OLGA, *angrily*]   Don't blubber!

Enter ANFISA *and* FERAPONT *carrying a cake.*

ANFISA   This way, my good man. Come in, your boots are clean. [*To* IRINA.] From the Rural Board, from Mihail Ivanitch Protopopov. . . . A cake.

IRINA   Thanks. Thank him. [*Takes the cake.*]

FERAPONT   What?

IRINA [*more loudly*]   Thank him from me!

OLGA   Nurse dear, give him some pie. Ferapont, go along, they will give you some pie.

FERAPONT   Eh?

ANFISA   Come along, Ferapont Spiridonitch, my good soul, come along . . .

Goes out with FERAPONT.

MASHA   I don't like that Protopopov, that Mihail Potapitch or Ivanitch. He ought not to be invited.

IRINA   I did not invite him.

MASHA   That's a good thing.

Enter TCHEBUTYKIN, *followed by an orderly with a silver samovar; a hum of surprise and displeasure.*

OLGA [*putting her hands over her face*]   A samovar! How awful! [*Goes out to the table in the dining room.*]

IRINA   My dear Ivan Romanitch, what are you thinking about!

TUSENBACH [*laughs*]   I warned you!

MASHA   Ivan Romanitch, you really have no conscience!

TCHEBUTYKIN   My dear girls, my darlings, you are all that I have, you are the most precious treasures I have on earth. I shall soon be sixty, I am an old man, alone in the world, a useless old man. . . . There is nothing good in me, except my love for you, and if it were not for you, I should have been dead long ago. . . . [*To* IRINA.] My dear, my little girl, I've known you from a baby. . . . I've carried you in my arms. . . . I loved your dear mother. . . .

IRINA   But why such expensive presents?

TCHEBUTYKIN [*angry and tearful*]   Expensive presents. . . . Get along with you! [*To the orderly.*] Take the samovar in there. . . . [*Mimicking.*] Expensive presents. . . .

The orderly carries the samovar into the dinng room.

7. A quotation from the fable "The Peasant and the Laborer" by Ivan A. Krylov (1769–1844).

ANFISA [*crossing the room*] My dears, a colonel is here, a stranger. . . . He has taken off his greatcoat, children, he is coming in here. Irinushka, you must be nice and polite, dear. . . . [*As she goes out.*] And it's time for lunch already . . . mercy on us. . . .

TUSENBACH   Vershinin, I suppose.

Enter VERSHININ.

TUSENBACH   Colonel Vershinin.

VERSHININ [*to* MASHA *and* IRINA] I have the honor to introduce myself, my name is Vershinin. I am very, very glad to be in your house at last. How you have grown up! Aie-aie!

IRINA   Please sit down. We are delighted to see you.

VERSHININ [*with animation*] How glad I am, how glad I am! But there are three of you sisters. I remember—three little girls. I don't remember your faces, but that your father, Colonel Prozorov, had three little girls I remember perfectly, and saw them with my own eyes. How time passes! Hey-ho, how it passes!

TUSENBACH   Alexandr Ignatyevitch has come from Moscow.

IRINA   From Moscow? You have come from Moscow?

VERSHININ   Yes. Your father was in command of a battery there, and I was an officer in the same brigade. [*To* MASHA.] Your face, now, I seem to remember.

MASHA   I don't remember you.

IRINA   Olya! Olya! [*Calls into the dining room.*] Olya, come!

OLGA *comes out of the dining room into the drawing room.*

IRINA   Colonel Vershinin is from Moscow, it appears.

VERSHININ   So you are Olga Sergeyevna, the eldest. . . . And you are Marya. . . . And you are Irina, the youngest. . . .

OLGA   You come from Moscow?

VERSHININ   Yes. I studied in Moscow. I began my service there, I served there for years, and at last I have been given a battery here— I have come here as you see. I don't remember you exactly, I only remember you were three sisters. I remember your father. If I shut my eyes, I can see him as though he were living. I used to visit you in Moscow. . . .

OLGA   I thought I remembered everyone, and now all at once . . .

VERSHININ   My name is Alexandr Ignatyevitch.

IRINA   Alexandr Ignatyevitch, you have come from Moscow. . . . What a surprise!

OLGA   We are going to move there, you know.

IRINA   We are hoping to be there by the autumn. It's our native town, we were born there. . . . In Old Basmanny Street.[8] . . . [*Both laugh with delight.*]

MASHA   To see someone from our own town unexpectedly! [*Eagerly.*] Now I remember! Do you remember, Olya, they used to talk of the "love-sick major"? You were a lieutenant at that time and were in love, and for some reason everyone called you "major" to tease you. . . .

VERSHININ [*laughs*] Yes, yes. . . . The love-sick major, that was it.

---

8. Old Basmanny Street (now Karl Marx/Bakunin Street) and Nyemetsky Street (now Bauman Street) were in the part of Moscow called Lefortov (now Baumanski), where many foreigners lived along with army officers and technical and professional people.

MASHA   You only had a moustache then. . . . Oh, how much older you look! [*Through tears.*] How much older!

VERSHININ   Yes, when I was called the love-sick major I was young, I was in love. Now it's very different.

OLGA   But you haven't a single grey hair. You have grown older but you are not old.

VERSHININ   I am in my forty-third year, though. Is it long since you left Moscow?

IRINA   Eleven years. But why are you crying, Masha, you queer girl? . . . [*Through her tears.*] I shall cry too. . . .

MASHA   I am all right. And in which street did you live?

VERSHININ   In Old Basmanny.

OLGA   And that's where we lived too. . . .

VERSHININ   At one time I lived in Nyemetsky Street. I used to go from there to the Red Barracks. There is a gloomy-looking bridge on the way, where the water makes a noise. It makes a lonely man feel melancholy. [*A pause.*] And here what a broad, splendid river! A marvelous river!

OLGA   Yes, but it is cold. It's cold here and there are gnats. . . .

VERSHININ   How can you! You've such a splendid healthy Russian climate here. Forest, river . . . and birches here too. Charming, modest birches, I love them better than any other trees. It's nice to live here. The only strange thing is that the railway station is fifteen miles away. . . . And no one knows why it is so.

SOLYONY   I know why it is. [*They all look at him.*] Because if the station had been near it would not have been so far, and if it is far, it's because it is not near.

An awkward silence.

TUSENBACH   He is fond of his joke, Vassily Vassilyevitch.

OLGA   Now I recall you, too. I remember.

VERSHININ   I knew your mother.

TCHEBUTYKIN   She was a fine woman, the Kingdom of Heaven be hers.

IRINA   Mother is buried in Moscow.

OLGA   In the Novo-Dyevitchy.[9] . . .

MASHA   Would you believe it, I am already beginning to forget her face. So people will not remember us either . . . they will forget us.

VERSHININ   Yes. They will forget us. Such is our fate, there is no help for it. What seems to us serious, significant, very important, will one day be forgotten or will seem unimportant. [*A pause.*] And it's curious that we can't possibly tell what exactly will be considered great and important, and what will seem paltry and ridiculous. Did not the discoveries of Copernicus or Columbus, let us say, seem useless and ridiculous at first,[1] while the nonsensical writings of some wiseacre seemed true? And it may be that our present life, which we accept so readily, will in time seem queer, uncomfortable, not sensible, not clean enough, perhaps even sinful. . . .

TUSENBACH   Who knows? Perhaps our age will be called a great one

9. The most famous nunnery in Moscow, construction of which was begun in 1524 by Grand Duke Vassily III, father of Ivan the Terrible. Many distinguished people are buried there, including Chekhov himself.
1. The Polish astronomer Nicolaus Co-pernicus (1473–1543) and the Italian navigator Christopher Columbus (1451–1506) are popularly believed to have discovered, respectively, that the earth revolves around the sun rather than *vice versa* and that the earth is spherical rather than flat.

and remembered with respect. Now we have no torture-chamber, no executions, no invasions, but at the same time how much unhappiness there is!

SOLYONY [*in a high-pitched voice*] Chook, chook, chook. . . . It's bread and meat to the baron to talk about ideas.

TUSENBACH Vassily Vassilyevitch, I ask you to let me alone. . . . [*Moves to another seat.*] It gets boring, at last.

SOLYONY [*in a high-pitched voice*] Chook, chook, chook. . . .

TUSENBACH [*to* VERSHININ] The unhappiness which one observes now—there is so much of it—does indicate, however, that society has reached a certain moral level.

VERSHININ Yes, yes, of course.

TCHEBUTYKIN You said just now, baron, that our age will be called great; but people are small all the same . . . [*Gets up.*] Look how small I am.

A violin is played behind the scenes.

MASHA That's Andrey playing, our brother.

IRINA He is the learned one of the family. We expect him to become a professor. Father was a military man, but his son has gone in for a learned career.

MASHA It was father's wish.

OLGA We have been teasing him today. We think he is a little in love.

IRINA With a young lady living here. She will come in today most likely.

MASHA Oh, how she dresses! It's not that her clothes are merely ugly or out of fashion, they are simply pitiful. A queer gaudy yellowish skirt with some sort of vulgar fringe and a red blouse. And her cheeks scrubbed till they shine! Andrey is not in love with her— I won't admit that, he has some taste anyway—it's simply for fun, he is teasing us, playing the fool. I heard yesterday that she is going to be married to Protopopov, the chairman of our Rural Board. And a very good thing too. . . . [*At the side door.*] Andrey, come here, dear, for a minute!

Enter ANDREY.

OLGA This is my brother, Andrey Sergeyevitch.

VERSHININ My name is Vershinin.

ANDREY And mine is Prozorov. [*Mops his perspiring face.*] You are our new battery commander?

OLGA Only fancy, Alexandr Ignatyevitch comes from Moscow.

ANDREY Really? Well, then, I congratulate you. My sisters will let you have no peace.

VERSHININ I have had time to bore your sisters already.

IRINA See what a pretty picture-frame Andrey has given me today! [*Shows the frame.*] He made it himself.

VERSHININ [*looking at the frame and not knowing what to say*] Yes . . . it is a thing. . . .

IRINA And that frame above the piano, he made that too!

ANDREY *waves his hand in despair and moves away.*

OLGA He is learned, and he plays the violin, and he makes all sorts of things with the fretsaw. In fact he is good all round. Andrey, don't go! That's a way he has—he always tries to make off! Come here!

MASHA *and* IRINA *take him by the arms and, laughing, lead him back.*

MASHA   Come, come!

ANDREY   Leave me alone, please!

MASHA   How absurd he is! Alexandr Ignatyevitch used to be called the love-sick major at one time, and he was not a bit offended.

VERSHININ   Not in the least!

MASHA   And I should like to call you the love-sick violinist!

IRINA   Or the love-sick professor!

OLGA   He is in love! Andryusha is in love!

IRINA [*claps her hands*]   Bravo, bravo! Encore! Andryusha is in love!

TCHEBUTYKIN [*comes up behind* ANDREY *and puts both arms round his waist*]   Nature our hearts for love created![2] [*Laughs, then sits down and reads the newspaper which he takes out of his pocket.*]

ANDREY   Come, that's enough, that's enough. . . . [*Mops his face.*] I haven't slept all night and this morning I don't feel quite myself, as they say. I read till four o'clock and then went to bed, but it was no use. I thought of one thing and another, and then it gets light so early; the sun simply pours into my bedroom. I want while I am here during the summer to translate a book from the English. . . .

VERSHININ   You read English then?

ANDREY   Yes. Our father, the Kingdom of Heaven be his, oppressed us with education. It's absurd and silly, but it must be confessed I began to get fatter after his death, and I have grown too fat in one year, as though a weight had been taken off my body. Thanks to our father we all know English, French, and German, and Irina knows Italian too. But what it cost us!

MASHA   In this town to know three languages is an unnecessary luxury! Not even a luxury, but an unnecessary encumbrance, like a sixth finger. We know a great deal that is unnecessary.

VERSHININ   What next! [*Laughs.*] You know a great deal that is unnecessary! I don't think there can be a town so dull and dismal that intelligent and educated people are unnecessary in it. Let us suppose that of the hundred thousand people living in this town, which is, of course, uncultured and behind the times, there are only three of your sort. It goes without saying that you cannot conquer the mass of darkness round you; little by little, as you go on living, you will be lost in the crowd. You will have to give in to it. Life will get the better of you, but still you will not disappear without a trace. After you there may appear perhaps six like you, then twelve and so on until such as you form a majority. In two or three hundred years life on earth will be unimaginably beautiful, marvelous. Man needs such a life and, though he hasn't it yet, he must have a presentiment of it, expect it, dream of it, prepare for it; for that he must see and know more than his father and grandfather. [*Laughs.*] And you complain of knowing a great deal that's unnecessary.

MASHA [*takes off her hat*]   I'll stay to lunch.

IRINA [*with a sigh*]   All that really ought to be written down. . . .

ANDREY *has slipped away unobserved.*

TUSENBACH   You say that after many years life on earth will be beauti-

2. A line from a Russian popular song of the 1890s.

ful and marvelous. That's true. But in order to have any share, however far off, in it now one must be preparing for it, one must be working. . . .

VERSHININ [*gets up*] Yes. What a lot of flowers you have! [*Looking round.*] And delightful rooms. I envy you! I've been knocking about all my life from one wretched lodging to another, always with two chairs and a sofa and stoves which smoke. What I have been lacking all my life is just such flowers.·. . . [*Rubs his hands.*] But there, it's no use thinking about it!

TUSENBACH Yes, we must work. I'll be bound you think the German is getting sentimental.[3] But on my honor I am Russian and I can't even speak German. My father belonged to the Orthodox Church. . . . [*A pause.*]

VERSHININ [*walks about the stage*] I often think, what if one were to begin life over again, knowing what one is about! If one life, which has been already lived, were only a rough sketch so to say, and the second were the fair copy! Then, I fancy, every one of us would try before everything not to repeat himself, anyway he would create a different setting for his life; would have a house like this with plenty of light and masses of flowers. . . . I have a wife and two little girls, my wife is in delicate health and so on and so on, but if I were to begin life over again I would not marry. . . . No, no!

Enter KULIGIN *in the uniform of a schoolmaster.*

KULIGIN [*goes up to* IRINA] Dear sister, allow me to congratulate you on your name-day and with all my heart to wish you good health and everything else that one can desire for a girl of your age. And to offer you as a gift this little book. [*Gives her a book.*] The history of our high-school for fifty years, written by myself. An insignificant little book, written because I had nothing better to do, but still you can read it. Good morning, friends. [*To* VERSHININ.] My name is Kuligin, teacher in the high-school here. [*To* IRINA.] In that book you will find a list of all who have finished their studies in our high-school during the last fifty years. *Feci quod potui, faciant meliora potentes.*[4] [*Kisses* MASHA.]

IRINA Why, but you gave me a copy of this book at Easter.

KULIGIN [*laughs*] Impossible! If that's so, give it back, or better still, give it to the Colonel. Please accept it, Colonel. Some day when you are bored you can read it.

VERSHININ Thank you. [*Is about to take leave.*] I am extremely glad to have made your acquaintance. . . .

OLGA You are going? No, no!

IRINA You must stay to lunch with us. Please do.

OLGA Pray do!

VERSHININ [*bows*] I believe I have chanced on a name-day. Forgive me, I did not know and have not congratulated you. . . . [*Walks away with* OLGA *into the dining room.*]

KULIGIN Today, gentlemen, is Sunday, a day of rest. Let us all rest and enjoy ourselves each in accordance with our age and our posi-

---

3. Great numbers of foreigners (known generically as "Germans") immigrated to Russia, beginning early in the 17th century. At various times they were the subject of distrust and prejudice from conservative elements in Russia, particularly the Orthodox Church.

4. Latin for "I have done what I can; let those who are more capable do better things."

tion. The carpets should be taken up for the summer and put away till the winter . . . Persian powder or naphthaline.[5] . . . The Romans were healthy because they knew how to work and they knew how to rest, they had *mens sana in corpore sano*.[6] Their life was molded into a certain framework. Our headmaster says that the most important thing in every life is its framework. . . . What loses its framework, comes to an end—and it's the same in our everyday life. [*Puts his arm round* MASHA's *waist, laughing.*] Masha loves me. My wife loves me. And the window curtains, too, ought to be put away together with the carpets. . . . Today I feel cheerful and in the best of spirits. Masha, at four o'clock this afternoon we have to be at the headmaster's. An excursion has been arranged for the teachers and their families.

MASHA   I am not going.

KULIGIN [*grieved*]   Dear Masha, why not?

MASHA   We'll talk about it afterward. . . . [*Angrily.*] Very well, I will go, only let me alone, please. . . . [*Walks away.*]

KULIGIN   And then we shall spend the evening at the headmaster's. In spite of the delicate state of his health, that man tries before all things to be sociable. He is an excellent, noble personality. A splendid man. Yesterday, after the meeting, he said to me, "I am tired, Fyodor Ilyitch, I am tired." [*Looks at the clock, then at his watch.*] Your clock is seven minutes fast. "Yes," he said, "I am tired."

Sounds of a violin behind the scenes.

OLGA   Come to lunch, please. There's a pie!

KULIGIN   Ah, Olga, my dear Olga! Yesterday I was working from early morning till eleven o'clock at night and was tired out, and today I feel happy. [*Goes up to the table in the dining room.*] My dear. . . .

TCHEBUTYKIN [*puts the newspaper in his pocket and combs his beard*] Pie? Splendid!

MASHA [*to* TCHEBUTYKIN, *sternly*]   Only mind you don't drink today! Do you hear? It's bad for you to drink.

TCHEBUTYKIN   Oh, come, that's a thing of the past. It's two years since I got drunk. [*Impatiently.*] But there, my good girl, what does it matter!

MASHA   Anyway, don't you dare to drink. Don't dare. [*Angrily, but so as not to be heard by her husband.*] Again, damnation take it, I am to be bored a whole evening at the headmaster's!

TUSENBACH   I wouldn't go if I were you. . . . It's very simple.

TCHEBUTYKIN   Don't go, my love.

MASHA   Oh, yes, don't go! . . . It's a damnable life, insufferable. . . . [*Goes to the dining room.*]

TCHEBUTYKIN [*following her*]   Come, come. . . .

SOLYONY [*going to the dining room*]   Chook, chook, chook. . . .

TUSENBACH   Enough, Vassily Vassilyevitch! Leave off!

SOLYONY   Chook, chook, chook. . . .

KULIGIN [*gaily*]   Your health, Colonel! I am a schoolmaster and one of the family here, Masha's husband. . . . She is very kind, really, very kind. . . .

VERSHININ   I'll have some of this dark-colored vodka. . . . [*Drinks.*] To your health! [*To* OLGA.] I feel so happy with all of you!

5. Persian (insect) powder is a form of pyrethrum.　　6. Latin for "a sound mind in a sound body."

No one is left in the drawing room but IRINA *and* TUSENBACH.

IRINA   Masha is in low spirits today. She was married at eighteen, when she thought him the cleverest of men. But now it's not the same. He is the kindest of men, but he is not the cleverest.

OLGA [*impatiently*]   Andrey, do come!

ANDREY [*behind the scenes*]   I am coming. [*Comes in and goes to the table.*]

TUSENBACH   What are you thinking about?

IRINA   Nothing. I don't like that Solyony of yours, I am afraid of him. He keeps on saying such stupid things. . . .

TUSENBACH   He is a queer man. I am sorry for him and annoyed by him, but more sorry. I think he is shy. . . . When one is alone with him he is very intelligent and friendly, but in company he is rude, a bully. Don't go yet, let them sit down to the table. Let me be by you. What are you thinking of? [*A pause.*] You are twenty, I am not yet thirty. How many years have we got before us, a long, long chain of days full of my love for you. . . .

IRINA   Nikolay Lvovitch, don't talk to me about love.

TUSENBACH [*not listening*]   I have a passionate craving for life, for struggle, for work, and that craving is mingled in my soul with my love for you, Irina, and just because you are beautiful it seems to me that life too is beautiful! What are you thinking of?

IRINA   You say life is beautiful. . . . Yes, but what if it only seems so! Life for us three sisters has not been beautiful yet, we have been stifled by it as plants are choked by weeds. . . . I am shedding tears. . . . I mustn't do that. [*Hurriedly wipes her eyes and smiles.*] I must work, I must work. The reason we are depressed and take such a gloomy view of life is that we know nothing of work. We come of people who despised work. . . .

Enter NATALYA IVANOVNA; *she is wearing a pink dress with a green sash.*

NATASHA   They are sitting down to lunch already. . . . I am late. . . . [*Steals a glance at herself in the glass and sets herself to rights.*] I think my hair is all right. [*Seeing* IRINA.] Dear Irina Sergeyevna, I congratulate you! [*Gives her a vigorous and prolonged kiss.*] You have a lot of visitors, I really feel shy. . . . Good day, Baron!

OLGA [*coming into the drawing room*]   Well, here is Natalya Ivanovna! How are you, my dear? [*Kisses her.*]

NATASHA   Congratulations on the name-day. You have such a big party and I feel awfully shy. . . .

OLGA   Nonsense, we have only our own people. [*In an undertone, in alarm.*] You've got on a green sash! My dear, that's not nice!

NATASHA   Why, is that a bad omen?

OLGA   No, it's only that it doesn't go with your dress . . . and it looks queer. . . .

NATASHA [*in a tearful voice*]   Really? But you know it's not green exactly, it's more a neutral color. [*Follows* OLGA *into the dining room.*]

In the dining room they are all sitting down to lunch; there is no one in the drawing room.

KULIGIN   I wish you a good husband, Irina. It's time for you to think of getting married.

TCHEBUTYKIN   Natalya Ivanovna, I hope we may hear of your engagement, too.

KULIGIN   Natalya Ivanovna has got a suitor already.

MASHA [*strikes her plate with her fork*]   Ladies and gentlemen, I want to make a speech!

KULIGIN   You deserve three bad marks for conduct.

VERSHININ   How nice this cordial is! What is it made of?

SOLYONY   Beetles.

IRINA [*in a tearful voice*]   Ugh, ugh! How disgusting.

OLGA   We are going to have roast turkey and apple pie for supper. Thank God I am at home all day and shall be at home in the evening. . . . Friends, won't you come this evening?

VERSHININ   Allow me to come too.

IRINA   Please do.

NATASHA   They don't stand on ceremony.

TCHEBUTYKIN   Nature our hearts for love created! [*Laughs.*]

ANDREY [*angrily*]   Do leave off, I wonder you are not tired of it!

FEDOTIK *and* RODDEY *come in with a big basket of flowers.*

FEDOTIK   I say, they are at lunch already.

RODDEY [*speaking loudly, with a lisp*]   At lunch? Yes, they are at lunch already. . . .

FEDOTIK   Wait a minute. [*Takes a snapshot.*] One! Wait another minute. . . . [*Takes another snapshot.*] Two! Now it's ready.

They take the basket and walk into the dining room, where they are greeted noisily.

RODDEY [*loudly*]   My congratulations! I wish you everything, everything! The weather is delightful, perfectly magnificent. I've been out all the morning for a walk with the high-school boys. I teach them gymnastics.

FEDOTIK   You may move, Irina Sergeyevna, you may move. [*Taking a photograph.*] You look charming today. [*Taking a top out of his pocket.*] Here is a top, by the way. . . . It has a wonderful note. . . .

IRINA   How lovely!

MASHA   By the seashore an oak tree green. . . . Upon that oak a chain of gold. . . . [*Complainingly.*] Why do I keep saying that? That phrase has been haunting me all day. . . .

KULIGIN   Thirteen at table!

RODDEY [*loudly*]   Surely you do not attach importance to such superstitions? [*Laughter.*]

KULIGIN   If there are thirteen at table, it means that someone present is in love. It's not you, Ivan Romanovitch, by any chance? [*Laughter.*]

TCHEBUTYKIN   I am an old sinner, but why Natalya Ivanovna is overcome, I can't imagine . . .

Loud laughter; NATASHA *runs out from the dining room into the drawing room followed by* ANDREY.

ANDREY   Come, don't take any notice! Wait a minute . . . stop, I entreat you. . . .

NATASHA   I am ashamed. . . . I don't know what's the matter with me and they make fun of me. I know it's improper for me to leave the

table like this, but I can't help it. . . . I can't . . . [*Covers her face with her hands.*]

ANDREY My dear girl, I entreat you, I implore you, don't be upset. I assure you they are only joking, they do it in all kindness. My dear, my sweet, they are all kind, warmhearted people and they are fond of me and of you. Come here to the window, here they can't see us . . . [*Looks round.*]

NATASHA I am so unaccustomed to society! . . .

ANDREY Oh youth, lovely, marvelous youth! My dear, my sweet, don't be so distressed! Believe me, believe me. . . . I feel so happy, my soul is full of love and rapture. . . . Oh, they can't see us, they can't see us! Why, why, I love you, when I first loved you—oh, I don't know. My dear, my sweet, pure one, be my wife! I love you, I love you . . . as I have never loved anyone . . . [*A kiss.*]

Two officers come in and, seeing the pair kissing, stop in amazement.

Act 2

The same scene as in Act 1. Eight o'clock in the evening. Behind the scenes in the street there is the faintly audible sound of a concertina. There is no light. NATALYA IVANOVNA *enters in a dressing gown, carrying a candle; she comes in and stops at the door leading to* ANDREY'S *room.*

NATASHA What are you doing, Andryusha? Reading? Never mind, I only just asked. . . .

Goes and opens another door and, peeping into it, shuts it again.

Is there a light?

ANDREY [*enters with a book in his hand*] What is it, Natasha?

NATASHA I was looking to see whether there was a light. . . . It's Carnival, the servants are not themselves; one has always to be on the lookout for fear something goes wrong. Last night at twelve o'clock I passed through the dining room, and there was a candle left burning. I couldn't find out who had lighted it. [*Puts down the candle.*] What's the time?

ANDREY [*looking at his watch*] A quarter past eight.

NATASHA And Olga and Irina aren't in yet. They haven't come in. Still at work, poor dears! Olga is at the teachers' council and Irina at the telegraph office. . . . [*Sighs.*] I was saying to your sister this morning, "Take care of yourself, Irina darling," said I. But she won't listen. A quarter past eight, you say? I am afraid our Bobik is not at all well. Why is he so cold? Yesterday he was feverish and today he is cold all over. . . . I am so anxious!

ANDREY It's all right, Natasha. The boy is quite well.

NATASHA We had better be careful about his food, anyway. I am anxious. And I am told that the mummers are going to be here for the Carnival at nine o'clock this evening. It would be better for them not to come, Andryusha.

ANDREY I really don't know. They've been invited, you know.

NATASHA Baby woke up this morning, looked at me, and all at once

he gave a smile; so he knew me. "Good morning, Bobik!" said I. "Good morning, darling!" And he laughed. Children understand; they understand very well. So I shall tell them, Andryusha, not to let the carnival party come in.

ANDREY [*irresolutely*]   That's for my sisters to say. It's for them to give orders.

NATASHA   Yes, for them too; I will speak to them. They are so kind. . . . [*Is going.*] I've ordered junket for supper. The doctor says you must eat nothing but junket, or you will never get thinner. [*Stops.*] Bobik is cold. I am afraid his room is chilly, perhaps. We ought to put him in a different room till the warm weather comes, anyway. Irina's room, for instance, is just right for a nursery: it's dry and the sun shines there all day. I must tell her; she might share Olga's room for the time. . . . She is never at home, anyway, except for the night. . . . [*A pause.*] Andryushantchik, why don't you speak?

ANDREY   Nothing. I was thinking. . . . Besides, I have nothing to say.

NATASHA   Yes . . . what was it I meant to tell you? . . . Oh, yes; Ferapont has come from the Rural Board, and is asking for you.

ANDREY [*yawns*]   Send him in.

NATASHA *goes out;* ANDREY, *bending down to the candle which she has left behind, reads. Enter* FERAPONT; *he wears an old shabby overcoat, with the collar turned up, and has a scarf over his ears.*

ANDREY   Good evening, my good man. What is it?

FERAPONT   The chairman has sent a book and a paper of some sort here. . . . [*Gives the book and an envelope.*]

ANDREY   Thanks. Very good. But why have you come so late? It is past eight.

FERAPONT   Eh?

ANDREY [*louder*]   I say, you have come late. It is eight o'clock.

FERAPONT   Just so. I came before it was dark, but they wouldn't let me see you. The master is busy, they told me. Well, of course, if you are busy, I am in no hurry. [*Thinking that* ANDREY *has asked him a question.*] Eh?

ANDREY   Nothing. [*Examines the book.*] Tomorrow is Friday. We haven't a sitting, but I'll come all the same . . . and do my work. It's dull at home. . . . [*A pause.*] Dear old man, how strangely life changes and deceives one! Today I was so bored and had nothing to do, so I picked up this book—old university lectures—and I laughed. . . . Good heavens! I am the secretary of the Rural Board of which Protopopov is the chairman. I am the secretary, and the most I can hope for is to become a member of the Board! Me, a member of the local Rural Board, while I dream every night I am professor of the University of Moscow—a distinguished man, of whom all Russia is proud!

FERAPONT   I can't say, sir. . . . I don't hear well. . . .

ANDREY   If you did hear well, perhaps I should not talk to you. I must talk to somebody, and my wife does not understand me. My sisters I am somehow afraid of—I'm afraid they will laugh at me and make me ashamed. . . . I don't drink, I am not fond of restaurants, but how I should enjoy sitting at Tyestov's in Moscow at this moment, dear old chap!

FERAPONT A contractor was saying at the Board the other day that there were some merchants in Moscow eating pancakes; one who ate forty, it seems, died. It was either forty or fifty, I don't remember.

ANDREY In Moscow you sit in a huge room at a restaurant; you know no one and no one knows you, and at the same time you don't feel a stranger. . . . But here you know everyone and everyone knows you, and yet you are a stranger—a stranger. . . . A stranger, and lonely. . . .

FERAPONT Eh? [*A pause.*] And the same contractor says—maybe it's not true—that there's a rope stretched right across Moscow.

ANDREY What for?

FERAPONT I can't say, sir. The contractor said so.

ANDREY Nonsense. [*Reads.*] Have you ever been in Moscow?

FERAPONT [*after a pause*] No, never. It was not God's will I should. [*A pause.*] Am I to go?

ANDREY You can go. Good-bye. [FERAPONT *goes out.*] Good-bye. [*Reading.*] Come tomorrow morning and take some papers here. . . . Go. . . . [*A pause.*] He has gone. [*A ring.*] Yes, it is a business. . . . [*Stretches and goes slowly into his own room.*]

> *Behind the scenes a* NURSE *is singing, rocking a baby to sleep. Enter* MASHA *and* VERSHININ. *While they are talking a maidservant is lighting a lamp and candles in the dining room.*

MASHA I don't know. [*A pause.*] I don't know. Of course habit does a great deal. After father's death, for instance, it was a long time before we could get used to having no orderlies in the house. But apart from habit, I think it's a feeling of justice makes me say so. Perhaps it is not so in other places, but in our town the most decent, honorable, and well-bred people are all in the army.

VERSHININ I am thirsty. I should like some tea.

MASHA [*glancing at the clock*] They will soon be bringing it. I was married when I was eighteen, and I was afraid of my husband because he was a teacher, and I had only just left school. In those days I thought him an awfully learned, clever, and important person. And now it is not the same, unfortunately. . . .

VERSHININ Yes. . . . I see. . . .

MASHA I am not speaking of my husband—I am used to him; but among civilians generally there are so many rude, ill-mannered, badly brought-up people. Rudeness upsets and distresses me: I am unhappy when I see that a man is not refined, not gentle, not polite enough. When I have to be among the teachers, my husband's colleagues, it makes me quite miserable.

VERSHININ Yes. . . . But, to my mind, it makes no difference whether they are civilians or military men—they are equally uninteresting, in this town anyway. It's all the same! If one listens to a man of the educated class here, civilian or military, he is worried to death by his wife, worried to death by his house, worried to death by his estate, worried to death by his horses. . . . A Russian is peculiarly given to exalted ideas, but why is it he always falls so short in life? Why?

MASHA Why?

VERSHININ Why is he worried to death by his children and by his wife? And why are his wife and children worried to death by him?

MASHA You are rather depressed this evening.

VERSHININ   Perhaps. . . . I've had no dinner today, and had nothing to eat since the morning. My daughter is not quite well, and when my little girls are ill I am consumed by anxiety; my conscience reproaches me for having given them such a mother. Oh, if you had seen her today! She is a wretched creature! We began quarreling at seven o'clock in the morning, and at nine I slammed the door and went away. [*A pause.*] I never talk about it. Strange, it's only to you I complain. [*Kisses her hand.*] Don't be angry with me. . . . Except for you I have no one—no one. . . .

A pause.

MASHA   What a noise in the stove! Before father died there was howling in the chimney. There, just like that.

VERSHININ   Are you superstitious?

MASHA   Yes.

VERSHININ   That's strange. [*Kisses her hand.*] You are a splendid, wonderful woman. Splendid! Wonderful! It's dark, but I see the light in your eyes.

MASHA   [*moves to another chair*]   It's lighter here.

VERSHININ   I love you—love, love. . . . I love your eyes, your movements, I see them in my dreams. . . . Splendid, wonderful woman!

MASHA   [*laughing softly*]   When you talk to me like that, for some reason I laugh, though I am frightened. . . . Please don't do it again. . . . [*In an undertone.*] You may say it, though; I don't mind. . . . [*Covers her face with her hands.*] I don't mind. . . . Someone is coming. Talk of something else.

IRINA *and* TUSENBACH *come in through the dining room.*

TUSENBACH   I've got a three-barreled name. My name is Baron Tusenbach-Krone-Altschauer, but I belong to the Orthodox Church and am just as Russian as you. There is very little of the German left in me—nothing, perhaps, but the patience and perseverance with which I bore you. I see you home every evening.

IRINA   How tired I am!

TUSENBACH   And every day I will come to the telegraph office and see you home. I'll do it for ten years, for twenty years, till you drive me away. . . . [*Seeing* MASHA *and* VERSHININ, *delightedly.*] Oh, it's you! How are you?

IRINA   Well, I am home at last. [*To* MASHA.] A lady came just now to telegraph to her brother in Saratov that her son died today, and she could not think of the address. So she sent it without an address—simply to Saratov.[7] She was crying. And I was rude to her for no sort of reason. Told her I had no time to waste. It was so stupid. Are the Carnival people coming tonight?

MASHA   Yes.

IRINA   [*sits down in an armchair*]   I must rest. I am tired.

TUSENBACH   [*with a smile*]   When you come from the office you seem so young, so forlorn. . . . [*A pause.*]

IRINA   I am tired. No, I don't like telegraph work, I don't like it.

MASHA   You've grown thinner. . . . [*Whistles.*] And you look younger, rather like a boy in the face.

---

7. A town of some size, located on the Volga about 450 miles southeast of Moscow.

TUSENBACH That's the way she does her hair.

IRINA I must find some other job, this does not suit me. What I so longed for, what I dreamed of, is the very thing that it's lacking in. . . . It is work without poetry, without meaning. . . . [*A knock on the floor.*] There's the doctor knocking. . . . [*To* TUSENBACH.] Do knock, dear. . . . I can't. . . . I am tired.

TUSENBACH *knocks on the floor.*

IRINA He will come directly. We ought to do something about it. The doctor and our Andrey were at the Club yesterday and they lost again. I am told Andrey lost two hundred roubles.[8]

MASHA [*indifferently*] Well, it can't be helped now.

IRINA A fortnight ago he lost money, in December he lost money. I wish he'd make haste and lose everything, then perhaps we should go away from this town. By God, every night I dream of Moscow, it's perfect madness. [*Laughs.*] We'll move there in June and there is still left February, March, April, May . . . almost half a year.

MASHA The only thing is Natasha must not hear of his losses.

IRINA I don't suppose she cares.

TCHEBUTYKIN, *who has only just got off his bed—he has been resting after dinner—comes into the dining room combing his beard, then sits down to the table and takes a newspaper out of his pocket.*

MASHA Here he is . . . has he paid his rent?

IRINA [*laughs*] No. Not a kopek[9] for eight months. Evidently he has forgotten.

MASHA [*laughs*] How gravely he sits. [*They all laugh; a pause.*]

IRINA Why are you so quiet, Alexandr Ignatyevitch?

VERSHININ I don't know. I am longing for tea. I'd give half my life for a glass of tea. I have had nothing to eat since the morning.

TCHEBUTYKIN Irina Sergeyevna!

IRINA What is it?

TCHEBUTYKIN Come here. *Venez ici.*[1] [IRINA *goes and sits down at the table.*] I can't do without you. [IRINA *lays out the cards for patience.*]

VERSHININ Well, if they won't bring tea, let us discuss something.

TUSENBACH By all means. What?

VERSHININ What? Let us dream . . . for instance of the life that will come after us, in two or three hundred years.

TUSENBACH Well? When we are dead, men will fly in balloons, change the fashion of their coats, will discover a sixth sense, perhaps, and develop it, but life will remain just the same, difficult, full of mysteries and happiness. In a thousand years man will sigh just the same, "Ah, how hard life is," and yet just as now he will be afraid of death and not want it.

VERSHININ [*after a moment's thought*] Well, I don't know. . . . It seems to me that everything on earth is bound to change by degrees

---

8. At the time of the play, one rouble was worth approximately 50 cents in American money. In the States the New York *Times* sold for one cent daily (two cents outside the metropolitan area) and three cents on Sundays. Bedsheets cost from 28 to 45 cents apiece. Old Crow was $1.10 a fifth, and a used grand piano could be purchased for from $175 to $300.

9. There are 100 kopeks in one rouble.

1. French for "Come here." At this period all cultivated, upper-class Russians spoke French.

and is already changing before our eyes. In two or three hundred, perhaps in a thousand years—the time does not matter—a new, happy life will come. We shall have no share in that life, of course, but we are living for it, we are working, well, yes, and suffering for it, we are creating it—and that alone is the purpose of our existence, and is our happiness, if you like.

> MASHA *laughs softly.*

TUSENBACH   What is it?

MASHA   I don't know. I've been laughing all day.

VERSHININ   I was at the same school as you were, I did not go to the Military Academy; I read a great deal, but I do not know how to choose my books, and very likely I read quite the wrong things, and yet the longer I live the more I want to know. My hair is turning gray, I am almost an old man, but I know so little, oh so little! But all the same I fancy that I do know and thoroughly grasp what is essential and matters most. And how I should like to make you see that there is no happiness for us, that there ought not to be and will not be. . . . We must work and work, and happiness is the portion of our remote descendants. [*A pause.*] If it is not for me, at least it is for the descendants of my descendants. . . . [FEDOTIK *and* RODDEY *appear in the dining room; they sit down and sing softly, playing the guitar.*]

TUSENBACH   You think it's no use even dreaming of happiness! But what if I am happy?

VERSHININ   No.

TUSENBACH   [*flinging up his hands and laughing*]   It is clear we don't understand each other. Well, how am I to convince you? [MASHA *laughs softly.* TUSENBACH *holds up a finger to her.*] Laugh! [*To* VERSHININ.] Not only in two or three hundred years but in a million years life will be just the same; it does not change, it remains stationary, following its own laws which we have nothing to do with or which, anyway, we shall never find out. Migratory birds, cranes for instance, fly backward and forward, and whatever ideas, great or small, stray through their minds, they will still go on flying just the same without knowing where or why. They fly and will continue to fly, however philosophic they may become; and it doesn't matter how philosophical they are so long as they go on flying. . . .

MASHA   But still there is a meaning?

TUSENBACH   Meaning. . . . Here it is snowing. What meaning is there in that? [*A pause.*]

MASHA   I think man ought to have faith or ought to seek a faith, or else his life is empty, empty. . . . To live and not to understand why cranes fly; why children are born; why there are stars in the sky. . . . One must know what one is living for or else it is all nonsense and waste. [*A pause.*]

VERSHININ   And yet one is sorry that youth is over. . . .

MASHA   Gogol says: it's dull living in this world, friends![2]

TUSENBACH   And I say: it is difficult to argue with you, my friends, God bless you. . . .

TCHEBUTYKIN   [*reading the newspaper*]   Balzac was married at Berdit-

---

2. The concluding line of the short story "How the Two Ivans Quarreled" by Nikolai V Gogol (1809–1852), best known outside Russia for his novel *Dead Souls* and his play *The Inspector General.*

chev.[3] [IRINA *hums softly.*] I really must put that down in my book. [*Writes.*] Balzac was married at Berditchev. [*Reads the paper.*]

IRINA [*lays out the cards for patience, dreamily*]   Balzac was married at Berditchev.

TUSENBACH   The die is cast. You know, Marya Sergeyevna, I've resigned my commission.

MASHA   So I hear. And I see nothing good in that. I don't like civilians.

TUSENBACH   Never mind . . . [*Gets up.*] I am not good-looking enough for a soldier. But that does not matter, though. . . . I am going to work. If only for one day in my life, to work so that I come home at night tired out and fall asleep as soon as I get into bed. . . . [*Going into the dining room.*] Workmen must sleep soundly!

FEDOTIK [*to* IRINA]   I bought these chalks for you just now as I passed the shop. . . . And this penknife. . . .

IRINA   You've got into the way of treating me as though I were little, but I am grown up, you know. . . . [*Takes the chalks and the penknife, joyfully.*] How lovely!

FEDOTIK   And I bought a knife for myself . . . look . . . one blade, and another blade, a third, and this is for the ears, and here are scissors, and that's for cleaning the nails. . . .

RODDEY [*loudly*]   Doctor, how old are you?

TCHEBUTYKIN   I? Thirty-two. [*Laughter.*]

FEDOTIK   I'll show you another patience. . . . [*Lays out the cards.*]

The samovar is brought in; ANFISA *is at the samovar; a little later* NATASHA *comes in and is also busy at the table;* SOLYONY *comes in and, after greeting the others, sits down at the table.*

VERSHININ   What a wind there is!

MASHA   Yes. I am sick of the winter. I've forgotten what summer is like.

IRINA   It's coming out right, I see. We shall go to Moscow.

FEDOTIK   No, it's not coming out. You see, the eight is over the two of spades. [*Laughs.*] So that means you won't go to Moscow.

TCHEBUTYKIN [*reads from the newspaper*]   Tsi-tsi-kar.[4] Smallpox is raging there.

ANFISA [*going up to* MASHA]   Masha, come to tea, my dear. [*To* VERSHININ.] Come, your honor . . . excuse me, sir, I have forgotten your name. . . .

MASHA   Bring it here, nurse, I am not going there.

IRINA   Nurse!

ANFISA   I am coming!

NATASHA [*to* SOLYONY]   Little babies understand very well. "Good morning, Bobik, good morning, darling," I said. He looked at me in quite a special way. You think I say that because I am a mother, but no, I assure you! He is an extraordinary child.

SOLYONY   If that child were mine, I'd fry him in a frying-pan and eat him.

Takes his glass, comes into the drawing room and sits down in a corner.

3. Honoré de Balzac (1799–1850), the famous French novelist, married Countess Eveline Hanska in the Ukrainian town of Berditchev on March 14, 1850. They had begun to correspond as early as 1832, although she was married to an older man.

Her husband died in 1841, but financial and other considerations delayed their marriage.
4. A city in Manchuria, also called Tsitsihar.

NATASHA [*covers her face with her hands*]   Rude, ill-bred man!

MASHA   Happy people don't notice whether it is winter or summer. I fancy if I lived in Moscow I should not mind what the weather was like. . . .

VERSHININ   The other day I was reading the diary of a French minister written in prison. The minister was condemned for the Panama affair.[5] With what enthusiasm and delight he describes the birds he sees from the prison window, which he never noticed before when he was a minister. Now that he is released, of course, he notices birds no more than he did before. In the same way, you won't notice Moscow when you live in it. We have no happiness and never do have, we only long for it.

TUSENBACH [*takes a box from the table*]   What has become of the sweets?

IRINA   Solyony has eaten them.

TUSENBACH   All?

ANFISA [*handing tea*]   There's a letter for you, sir.

VERSHININ   For me? [*Takes the letter.*] From my daughter. [*Reads.*] Yes, of course. . . . Excuse me, Marya Sergeyevna, I'll slip away. I won't have tea. [*Gets up in agitation.*] Always these upsets. . . .

MASHA   What is it? Not a secret?

VERSHININ [*in a low voice*]   My wife has taken poison again. I must go. I'll slip off unnoticed. Horribly unpleasant it all is. [*Kisses* MASHA's *hand.*] My fine, dear, splendid woman. . . . I'll go this way without being seen. . . . [*Goes out.*]

ANFISA   Where is he off to? I've just given him his tea. . . . What a man.

MASHA [*getting angry*]   Leave off! Don't pester, you give one no peace. . . . [*Goes with her cup to the table.*] You bother me, old lady.

ANFISA   Why are you so huffy? Darling!

ANDREY's *voice:* "Anfisa!"

ANFISA [*mimicking*]   Anfisa! he sits there. . . . [*Goes out.*]

MASHA [*by the table in the dining room, angrily*]   Let me sit down! [*Mixes the cards on the table.*] You take up all the table with your cards. Drink your tea!

IRINA   How cross you are, Masha!

MASHA   If I'm cross, don't talk to me. Don't interfere with me.

TCHEBUTYKIN [*laughing*]   Don't touch her, don't touch her!

MASHA   You are sixty, but you talk rot like a schoolboy.

NATASHA [*sighs*]   Dear Masha, why make use of such expressions in conversation? With your attractive appearance, I tell you straight out, you would be simply fascinating in a well-bred social circle if it were not for the things you say. *Je vous prie, pardonnez-moi, Marie, mais vous avez des manières un peu grossières.*[6]

---

5. From 1880 to 1889 a French group headed by Ferdinand de Lesseps, the builder of the Suez Canal, attempted to dig a canal across the Isthmus of Panama. It was a disaster, both from an engineering standpoint and from a financial one. In 1892 charges of fraud and bribery were made against the principals of the company and a number of politicians; a spectacular scandal resulted. Several officers of the company and Charles Baïhaut (1843–1905), a former Minister of Public Works, were convicted in 1893. After his release from several years in prison, Baïhaut published a book about his experiences called *Impressions Cellulaires* (1898).

6. French for "I beg your pardon, Marie (i.e., Masha), but you have manners which are a bit gross."

TUSENBACH [*suppressing a laugh*]   Give me . . . give me . . . I think there is some brandy there.

NATASHA   *Il paraît que mon Bobik déjà ne dort pas,*[7] he is awake. He is not well today. I must go to him, excuse me. . . . [*Goes out.*]

IRINA   Where has Alexandr Ignatyevitch gone?

MASHA   Home. Something queer with his wife again.

TUSENBACH [*goes up to* SOLYONY *with a decanter of brandy in his hand*]   You always sit alone, thinking, and there's no making out what you think about. Come, let us make it up. Let us have a drink of brandy. [*They drink.*] I shall have to play the piano all night, I suppose, play all sorts of trash. . . . Here goes!

SOLYONY   Why make it up? I haven't quarreled with you.

TUSENBACH   You always make me feel as though something had gone wrong between us. You are a queer character, there's no denying that.

SOLYONY [*declaims*]   I am strange, who is not strange! Be not wroth, Aleko![8]

TUSENBACH   I don't see what Aleko has got to do with it. . . .

SOLYONY   When I am *tête-à-tête*[9] with somebody, I am all right, just like anyone else, but in company I am depressed, ill at ease and . . . say all sorts of idiotic things, but at the same time I am more conscientious and straightforward than many. And I can prove it. . . .

TUSENBACH   I often feel angry with you, you are always attacking me when we are in company, and yet I somehow like you. Here goes, I am going to drink a lot today. Let's drink!

SOLYONY   Let us. [*Drinks.*] I have never had anything against you, Baron. But I have the temperament of Lermontov.[1] [*In a low voice.*] In fact I am rather like Lermontov to look at . . . so I am told. [*Takes out scent-bottle and sprinkles scent on his hands.*]

TUSENBACH   I have sent in my papers. I've had enough of it! I have been thinking of it for five years and at last I have come up to the scratch. I am going to work.

SOLYONY [*declaims*]   Be not wroth, Aleko. . . . Forget, forget thy dreams. . . .

> *While they are talking* ANDREY *comes in quietly with a book and sits down by a candle.*

TUSENBACH   I am going to work.

TCHEBUTYKIN [*coming into the drawing room with* IRINA]   And the food too was real Caucasian stuff: onion soup and for the meat course *tchehartma.* . . .

SOLYONY   *Tcheremsha* is not meat at all, it's a plant rather like our onion.

TCHEBUTYKIN   No, my dear soul, it's not onion, but mutton roasted in a special way.

SOLYONY   But I tell you that *tcheremsha* is an onion.

7. French for "It seems that my Bobik is already no longer asleep." Natasha's unidiomatic French identifies her as coming from a lower social class than the Prozorovs and their friends.

8. The first part of the speech is a quotation from the play *Woe from Wit* or *The Trouble with Reason* by Alexander S. Griboyedov (1795–1829). The second part refers to Aleko, the hero of "The Gypsies," a narrative poem by Pushkin. In the poem, Aleko, a young Russian, joins a Gypsy tribe and lives happily for a while with a Gypsy girl. When she deserts him for another, he stabs both the girl and her new lover and is ostracized by the tribe.

9. French for face-to-face (literally, head to head).

1. Mikhail Yurievitch Lermontov (1814–1841) was the great Romantic poet of 19th-century Russia, known for his melancholy and his fondness for morbid self-examination.

TCHEBUTYKIN   And I tell you that *tchehartma* is mutton.

SOLYONY   And I tell you that *tcheremsha* is an onion.

TCHEBUTYKIN   What's the use of my arguing with you? You have never been to the Caucasus or eaten *tchehartma*.

SOLYONY   I haven't eaten it because I can't bear it. *Tcheremsha* smells like garlic.

ANDREY [*imploringly*]   That's enough! Please!

TUSENBACH   When are the Carnival party coming?

IRINA   They promised to come at nine, so they will be here directly.

TUSENBACH [*embraces* ANDREY *and sings*]   "Oh my porch, oh my new porch . . ."

ANDREY [*dances and sings*]   "With posts of maple wood. . . ."

TCHEBUTYKIN [*dances*] "And lattice work complete. . . ."[2] [*Laughter.*]

TUSENBACH [*kisses* ANDREY]   Hang it all, let us have a drink. Andryusha, let us drink to our everlasting friendship. I'll go to the University when you do, Andryusha.

SOLYONY   Which? There are two universities in Moscow.

ANDREY   There is only one university in Moscow.

SOLYONY   I tell you there are two.

ANDREY   There may be three for aught I care. So much the better.

SOLYONY   There are two universities in Moscow! [*A murmur and hisses.*] There are two universities in Moscow: the old one and the new one. And if you don't care to hear, if what I say irritates you, I can keep quiet. I can even go into another room. [*Goes out at one of the doors.*]

TUSENBACH   Bravo, bravo! [*Laughs.*] Friends, begin, I'll sit down and play! Funny fellow that Solyony. . . . [*Sits down to the piano and plays a waltz.*]

MASHA [*dances a waltz alone*]   The baron is drunk, the baron is drunk, the baron is drunk.

Enter NATASHA.

NATASHA [*to* TCHEBUTYKIN]   Ivan Romanitch!

Says something to TCHEBUTYKIN, *then goes out softly.* TCHEBUTY-KIN *touches* TUSENBACH *on the shoulder and whispers something to him.*

IRINA   What is it?

TCHEBUTYKIN   It's time we were going. Good night.

TUSENBACH   Good night. It's time to be going.

IRINA   But I say . . . what about the Carnival party?

ANDREY [*with embarrassment*]   They won't be coming. You see, dear, Natasha says Bobik is not well, and so. . . . In fact I know nothing about it, and don't care either.

IRINA [*shrugs her shoulders*]   Bobik is not well!

MASHA   Well, it's not the first time we've had to lump it! If we are turned out, we must go. [*To* IRINA.] It's not Bobik that is ill, but she is a bit . . . [*Taps her forehead with her finger.*] Petty, vulgar creature!

ANDREY goes by door on right to his own room, TCHEBUTYKIN following him; they are saying good-bye in the dining room.

2. A traditional Russian dance-song.

FEDOTIK   What a pity! I was meaning to spend the evening, but of course if the child is ill . . . I'll bring him a toy tomorrow.

RODDEY [*loudly*]   I had a nap today after dinner on purpose, I thought I would be dancing all night. . . . Why, it's only nine o'clock.

MASHA   Let us go into the street; there we can talk. We'll decide what to do.

Sounds of "Good-bye! Good night!" The good-humored laugh of TUSENBACH *is heard. All go out.* ANFISA *and the maidservant clear the table and put out the light. There is the sound of the nurse singing.* ANDREY, *in his hat and coat, and* TCHEBUTYKIN *come in quietly.*

TCHEBUTYKIN   I never had time to get married, because life has flashed by like lightning and because I was passionately in love with your mother, who was married.

ANDREY   One shouldn't get married. One shouldn't, because it's boring.

TCHEBUTYKIN   That's all very well, but what about loneliness? Say what you like, it's a dreadful thing to be lonely, my dear boy. . . . But no matter, though!

ANDREY   Let's make haste and go.

TCHEBUTYKIN   What's the hurry? We have plenty of time.

ANDREY   I am afraid my wife may stop me.

TCHEBUTYKIN   Oh!

ANDREY   I am not going to play today, I shall just sit and look on. I don't feel well. . . . What am I to do, Ivan Romanitch, I am so short of breath?

TCHEBUTYKIN   It's no use asking me! I don't remember, dear boy. . . . I don't know. . . .

ANDREY   Let us go through the kitchen. [*They go out.*]

A ring, then another ring; there is a sound of voices and laughter.

IRINA [*enters*]   What is it?

ANFISA [*in a whisper*]   The mummers, all dressed up. [*A ring.*]

IRINA   Nurse, dear, say there is no one at home. They must excuse us.

ANFISA *goes out.* IRINA *walks about the room in hesitation; she is excited. Enter* SOLYONY.

SOLYONY [*in perplexity*]   No one here. . . . Where are they all?

IRINA   They have gone home.

SOLYONY   How queer. Are you alone here?

IRINA   Yes. [*A pause.*] Good night.

SOLYONY   I behaved tactlessly, without sufficient restraint just now. But you are not like other people, you are pure and lofty, you see the truth. You alone can understand me. I love you, I love you deeply, infinitely.

IRINA   Good night! You must go.

SOLYONY   I can't live without you. [*Following her.*] Oh, my bliss! [*Through his tears.*] Oh, happiness! Those glorious, exquisite, marvelous eyes such as I have never seen in any other woman.

IRINA [*coldly*]   Don't, Vassily Vassilyitch!

SOLYONY   For the first time I am speaking of love to you, and I feel as though I were not on earth but on another planet. [*Rubs his fore-*

head.] But there, it does not matter. There is no forcing kindness, of course. . . . But there must be no happy rivals. . . . There must not. . . . I swear by all that is sacred I will kill any rival. . . . O exquisite being!

NATASHA *passes with a candle.*

NATASHA   *peeps in at one door, then at another and passes by the door that leads to her husband's room*] Andrey is there. Let him read. Excuse me, Vassily Vassilyitch, I did not know you were here, and I am in my dressing gown. . . .

SOLYONY   I don't care. Good-bye! [*Goes out.*]

NATASHA   You are tired, my poor, dear little girl! [*Kisses* IRINA.] You ought to go to bed earlier. . . .

IRINA   Is Bobik asleep?

NATASHA   He is asleep, but not sleeping quietly. By the way, dear, I keep meaning to speak to you, but either you are out or else I haven't the time. . . . I think Bobik's nursery is cold and damp. And your room is so nice for a baby. My sweet, my dear, you might move for a time into Olya's room!

IRINA [*not understanding*]   Where?

The sound of a three-horse sledge with bells driving up to the door.

NATASHA   You would be in the same room with Olya, and Bobik in your room. He is such a poppet. I said to him today, "Bobik, you are mine, you are mine!" and he looked at me with his funny little eyes. [*A ring.*] That must be Olya. How late she is!

The maid comes up to NATASHA *and whispers in her ear.*

NATASHA   Protopopov? What a queer fellow he is! Protopopov has come, and asks me to go out with him in his sledge. [*Laughs.*] How strange men are! . . . [*A ring.*] Somebody has come. I might go for a quarter of an hour. . . . [*To the maid.*] Tell him I'll come directly. [*A ring.*] You hear . . . it must be Olya. [*Goes out.*]

The maid runs out; IRINA *sits lost in thought;* KULIGIN, OLGA *and* VERSHININ *come in.*

KULIGIN   Well, this is a surprise! They said they were going to have an evening party.

VERSHININ   Strange! And when I went away half an hour ago they were expecting the Carnival people. . . .

IRINA   They have all gone.

KULIGIN   Has Masha gone too? Where has she gone? And why is Protopopov waiting below with his sledge? Whom is he waiting for?

IRINA   Don't ask questions. . . . I am tired.

KULIGIN   Oh, you little cross-patch. . . .

OLGA   The meeting is only just over. I am tired out. Our headmistress is ill and I have to take her place. Oh, my head, my head does ache; oh, my head! [*Sits down.*] Andrey lost two hundred roubles yesterday at cards. . . . The whole town is talking about it. . . .

KULIGIN   Yes, I am tired out by the meeting too. [*Sits down.*]

VERSHININ   My wife took it into her head to give me a fright, she nearly poisoned herself. It's all right now, and I'm glad, it's a relief.

. . . So we are to go away? Very well, then, I will say good night. Fyodor Ilyitch, let us go somewhere together! I can't stay at home, I absolutely can't. . . . Come along!

KULIGIN   I am tired. I am not coming. [*Gets up.*] I am tired. Has my wife gone home?

IRINA   I expect so.

KULIGIN   [*kisses* IRINA'*s hand*]   Good-bye! I have all day tomorrow and next day to rest. Good night! [*Going.*] I do want some tea. I was reckoning on spending the evening in pleasant company. . . . *O fallacem hominum spem!*³ . . . Accusative of exclamation.

VERSHININ   Well, then, I must go alone. [*Goes out with* KULIGIN, *whistling.*]

OLGA   My head aches, oh, how my head aches. . . . Andrey has lost at cards. . . . The whole town is talking about it. . . . I'll go and lie down. [*Is going.*] Tomorrow I shall be free. . . . Oh, goodness, how nice that is! Tomorrow I am free, and the day after I am free. . . . My head does ache, oh, my head. . . . [*Goes out.*]

IRINA   [*alone*]   They have all gone away. There is no one left.

A concertina plays in the street, the nurse sings.

NATASHA   [*in a fur cap and coat crosses the dining room, followed by the maid*].   I shall be back in half an hour. I shall only go a little way. [*Goes out.*]

IRINA   [*left alone, in dejection*]   Oh, to go to Moscow, to Moscow!

Act 3

The bedroom of OLGA *and* IRINA. *On left and right beds with screens round them. Past two o'clock in the night. Behind the scenes a bell is ringing on account of a fire in the town, which has been going on for some time. It can be seen that no one in the house has gone to bed yet. On the sofa* MASHA *is lying, dressed as usual in black. Enter* OLGA *and* ANFISA.

ANFISA   They are sitting below, under the stairs. . . . I said to them, "Come upstairs; why, you mustn't stay there"—they only cried. "We don't know where father is," they said. "What if he is burned!" What an idea! And the poor souls in the yard . . . They are all undressed too.

OLGA   [*taking clothes out of the cupboard*]   Take this gray dress . . . and this one . . . and the blouse too . . . and that skirt, nurse. . . . Oh, dear, what a dreadful thing! Kirsanov Street is burned to the ground, it seems. . . . Take this . . . take this. . . . [*Throws clothes into her arms.*] The Vershinins have had a fright, poor things. . . . Their house was very nearly burned. Let them stay the night here . . . we can't let them go home. . . . Poor Fedotik has had everything burned, he has not a thing left. . . .

ANFISA   You had better call Ferapont, Olya darling, I can't carry it all.

OLGA   [*rings*]   No one will answer the bell. [*At the door.*] Come here, whoever is there!

3. Latin for "Oh, deceitful hope of mankind!"

Through the open door can be seen a window red with fire; the fire brigade is heard passing the house.

How awful it is! And how sickening!

Enter FERAPONT.

OLGA   Here take these, carry them downstairs. . . . The Kolotilin young ladies are downstairs . . . give it to them . . . and give this too.

FERAPONT   Yes, miss. In 1812 Moscow was burned too. . . . Mercy on us! The French marveled.[4]

OLGA   You can go now.

FERAPONT   Yes, miss. [*Goes out.*]

OLGA   Nurse darling, give them everything. We don't want anything, give it all to them. . . . I am tired, I can hardly stand on my feet. . . . We mustn't let the Vershinins go home. . . . The little girls can sleep in the drawing room, and Alexandr Ignatyevitch down below at the baron's. . . . Fedotik can go to the baron's, too, or sleep in our dining room. . . . As ill-luck will have it, the doctor is drunk, frightfully drunk, and no one can be put in his room. And Vershinin's wife can be in the drawing room too.

ANFISA [*wearily*]   Olya darling, don't send me away; don't send me away!

OLGA   That's nonsense, nurse. No one is sending you away.

ANFISA [*lays her head on* OLGA's *shoulder*]   My own, my treasure, I work, I do my best. . . . I'm getting weak, everyone will say "Be off!" And where am I to go? Where? I am eighty. Eighty-one.

OLGA   Sit down, nurse darling. . . . You are tired, poor thing. . . . [*Makes her sit down.*] Rest, dear good nurse. . . . How pale you are!

Enter NATASHA.

NATASHA   They are saying we must form a committee at once for the assistance of those whose houses have been burned. Well, that's a good idea. Indeed, one ought always to be ready to help the poor, it's the duty of the rich. Bobik and baby Sophie are both asleep, sleeping as though nothing were happening. There are such a lot of people everywhere, wherever one goes, the house is full. There is influenza in the town now; I am so afraid the children may get it.

OLGA [*not listening*]   In this room one does not see the fire, it's quiet here.

NATASHA   Yes . . . my hair must be untidy. [*In front of the looking glass.*] They say I have grown fatter . . . but it's not true! Not a bit! Masha is asleep, she is tired out, poor dear. . . . [*To* ANFISA *coldly.*] Don't dare to sit down in my presence! Get up! Go out of the room! [ANFISA *goes out; a pause.*] Why you keep that old woman, I can't understand!

OLGA [*taken aback*]   Excuse me, I don't understand either. . . .

NATASHA   She is no use here. She is a peasant; she ought to be in the country. . . . You spoil people! I like order in the house! There ought to be no useless servants in the house. [*Strokes her cheek.*] You are tired, poor darling. Our headmistress is tired! When baby Sophie is a big girl and goes to the high-school, I shall be afraid of you.

4. In the summer of 1812 Napoleon invaded Russia. The Russians retreated before him, burning and destroying everything in his path. He reached Moscow to find it abandoned and in flames. His disastrous retreat followed.

OLGA   I shan't be headmistress.

NATASHA   You will be elected, Olya. That's a settled thing.

OLGA   I shall refuse. I can't. . . . It's too much for me. . . . [*Drinks water.*] You were so rude to nurse just now. . . . Excuse me, I can't endure it. . . . It makes me feel faint.

NATASHA [*perturbed*].   Forgive me, Olya; forgive me. . . . I did not mean to hurt your feelings.

MASHA *gets up, takes her pillow, and goes out in a rage.*

OLGA   You must understand, my dear, it may be that we have been strangely brought up, but I can't endure it. . . . Such an attitude oppresses me, it makes me ill. . . . I feel simply unnerved by it. . . .

NATASHA   Forgive me; forgive me. . . . [*Kisses her.*]

OLGA   The very slightest rudeness, a tactless word, upsets me. . . .

NATASHA   I often say too much, that's true, but you must admit, dear, that she might just as well be in the country.

OLGA   She has been thirty years with us.

NATASHA   But now she can't work! Either I don't understand, or you won't understand me. She is not fit for work. She does nothing but sleep or sit still.

OLGA   Well, let her sit still.

NATASHA [*surprised*]   How, sit still? Why, she is a servant. [*Through tears.*] I don't understand you, Olya. I have a nurse to look after the children as well as a wet nurse for baby, and we have a housemaid and a cook, what do we want that old woman for? What's the use of her?

The alarm bell rings behind the scenes.

OLGA   This night has made me ten years older.

NATASHA   We must come to an understanding, Olya. You are at the high-school, I am at home; you are teaching while I look after the house, and if I say anything about the servants, I know what I'm talking about; I do know what I'm talking about. . . . And that old thief, that old hag . . . [*stamps*] that old witch shall clear out of the house tomorrow! . . . I won't have people annoy me! I won't have it! [*Feeling that she has gone too far.*] Really, if you don't move downstairs, we shall always be quarreling. It's awful.

Enter KULIGIN.

KULIGIN   Where is Masha? It's time to be going home. The fire is dying down, so they say. [*Stretches.*] Only one part of the town has been burned, and yet there was a wind; it seemed at first as though the whole town would be destroyed. [*Sits down.*] I am exhausted. Olya, my dear . . . I often think if it had not been for Masha I should have married you. You are so good. . . . I am tired out. [*Listens.*]

OLGA   What is it?

KULIGIN   It is unfortunate the doctor should have a drinking bout just now; he is helplessly drunk. Most unfortunate. [*Gets up.*] Here he comes, I do believe. . . . Do you hear? Yes, he is coming this way. . . . [*Laughs.*] What a man he is, really. . . . I shall hide. [*Goes to the cupboard and stands in the corner.*] Isn't he a ruffian!

OLGA   He has not drunk for two years and now he has gone and done it. . . . [*Walks away with* NATASHA *to the back of the room.*]

TCHEBUTYKIN *comes in; walking as though sober without staggering, he walks across the room, stops, looks round; then goes up to the washing-stand and begins to wash his hands.*

TCHEBUTYKIN [*morosely*]   The devil take them all . . . damn them all. They think I am a doctor, that I can treat all sorts of complaints, and I really know nothing about it, I have forgotten all I did know, I remember nothing, absolutely nothing.

OLGA *and* NATASHA *go out unnoticed by him.*

The devil take them. Last Wednesday I treated a woman at Zasyp— she died, and it's my fault that she died. Yes . . . I did know something twenty-five years ago, but now I remember nothing, nothing. Perhaps I am not a man at all but only pretend to have arms and legs and head; perhaps I don't exist at all and only fancy that I walk about, eat and sleep. [*Weeps.*] Oh, if only I did not exist! [*Leaves off weeping, morosely.*] I don't care! I don't care a scrap! [*A pause.*] Goodness knows. . . . The day before yesterday there was a conversation at the club: they talked about Shakespeare, Voltaire.[5] . . . I have read nothing, nothing at all, but I looked as though I had read them. And the others did the same as I did. The vulgarity! The meanness! And that woman I killed on Wednesday came back to my mind . . . and it all came back to my mind and everything seemed nasty, disgusting and all awry in my soul. . . . I went and got drunk. . . .

Enter IRINA, VERSHININ, *and* TUSENBACH; TUSENBACH *is wearing a fashionable new civilian suit.*

IRINA   Let us sit here. No one will come here.

VERSHININ   If it had not been for the soldiers, the whole town would have been burned down. Splendid fellows! [*Rubs his hands with pleasure.*] They are first-rate men! Splendid fellows!

KULIGIN [*going up to them*]   What time is it?

TUSENBACH   It's past three. It's getting light already.

IRINA   They are all sitting in the dining-room. No one seems to think of going. And that Solyony of yours is sitting there too. . . . [*To* TCHEBUTYKIN.] You had better go to bed, doctor.

TCHEBUTYKIN   It's all right. . . . Thank you! [*Combs his beard.*]

KULIGIN [*laughs*]   You are a bit fuddled, Ivan Romanitch! [*Slaps him on the shoulder.*] Bravo! *In vino veritas,*[6] the ancients used to say.

TUSENBACH   Everyone is asking me to get up a concert for the benefit of the families whose houses have been burned down.

IRINA   Why, who is there? . . .

TUSENBACH   We could get it up, if we wanted to. Marya Sergeyevna plays the piano splendidly, to my thinking.

KULIGIN   Yes, she plays splendidly.

IRINA   She has forgotten. She has not played for three . . . or four years.

TUSENBACH   There is absolutely no one who understands music in this town, not one soul, but I do understand and on my honor I assure you that Marya Sergeyevna plays magnificently, almost with genius.

5. Shakespeare and François Marie Arouet, called Voltaire (1694–1778), the French philosopher and playwright, are cited as examples of the culture of Western Europe as opposed to that of Russia.
6. Latin for "In wine (there is) truth," i.e., that people who have been drinking are likely to speak the truth.

KULIGIN   You are right, Baron. I am very fond of her; Masha, I mean.
She is a good sort.

TUSENBACH   To be able to play so gloriously and to know that no one
understands you!

KULIGIN [*sighs*]   Yes. . . . But would it be suitable for her to take part
in a concert? [*A pause.*] I know nothing about it, my friends. Perhaps
it would be all right. There is no denying that our director is a fine
man, indeed a very fine man, very intelligent, but he has such views.
. . . Of course it is not his business, still if you like I'll speak to him
about it.

TCHEBUTYKIN *takes up a china clock and examines it.*

VERSHININ   I got dirty all over at the fire. I am a sight. [*A pause.*]
I heard a word dropped yesterday about our brigade being transferred ever so far away. Some say to Poland, and others to Tchita.[7]

TUSENBACH   I've heard something about it too. Well! The town will
be a wilderness then.

IRINA   We shall go away too.

TCHEBUTYKIN [*drops the clock, which smashes*]   To smithereens!

KULIGIN [*picking up the pieces*]   To smash such a valuable thing—oh,
Ivan Romanitch, Ivan Romanitch! I should give you minus zero for
conduct!

IRINA   That was mother's clock.

TCHEBUTYKIN   Perhaps. . . . Well, if it was hers, it was. Perhaps I did
not smash it, but it only seems as though I had. Perhaps it only seems
to us that we exist, but really we are not here at all. I don't know
anything—nobody knows anything. [*By the door.*] What are you
staring at? Natasha has got a little affair with Protopopov, and you
don't see it. . . . You sit here and see nothing, while Natasha has a
little affair with Protopopov. . . . [*Sings.*] May I offer you this date?[8]
. . . [*Goes out.*]

VERSHININ   Yes. . . . [*Laughs.*] How very queer it all is, really! [*A
pause.*] When the fire began I ran home as fast as I could. I went up
and saw our house was safe and sound and out of danger, but my
little girls were standing in the doorway in their nightgowns; their
mother was nowhere to be seen, people were bustling about, horses
and dogs were running about, and my children's faces were full of
alarm, horror, entreaty, and I don't know what; it wrung my heart
to see their faces. My God, I thought, what more have these children
to go through in the long years to come! I took their hands and ran
along with them, and could think of nothing else but what more
they would have to go through in this world! [*A pause.*] When I
came to your house I found their mother here, screaming, angry.
[*MASHA comes in with the pillow and sits down on the sofa.*] And
while my little girls were standing in the doorway in their night-
gowns and the street was red with the fire, and there was a fearful
noise, I thought that something like it used to happen years ago
when the enemy would suddenly make a raid and begin plundering
and burning. . . . And yet, in reality, what a difference there is between what is now and has been in the past! And when a little more
time has passed—another two or three hundred years—people will

7. A town in Siberia some 3000 miles
from Moscow; also Chita.
8. Chekhov identified this passage as a
line from an operetta which he had heard
and of which he had forgotten the name.

look at our present manner of life with horror and derision, and everything of today will seem awkward and heavy, and very strange and uncomfortable. Oh, what a wonderful life that will be—what a wonderful life! [*Laughs.*] Forgive me, here I am airing my theories again! Allow me to go on. I have such a desire to talk about the future. I am in the mood. [*A pause.*] It's as though everyone were asleep. And so, I say, what a wonderful life it will be! Can you only imagine? . . . There are only three of your sort in the town now, but in generations to come there will be more and more and more; and the time will come when everything will be changed and be as you would have it; they will live in your way, and later on you too will be out of date—people will be born who will be better than you. . . . [*Laughs.*] I am in such a strange state of mind today. I have a fiendish longing for life. . . . [*Sings.*] Young and old are bound by love, and precious are its pangs[9]. . . . [*Laughs.*]

MASHA   Tram-tam-tam!
VERSHININ   Tam-tam!
MASHA   Tra-ra-ra?
VERSHININ   Tra-ta-ta! [*Laughs.*]

Enter FEDOTIK.

FEDOTIK [*dances*]   Burned to ashes! Burned to ashes! Everything I had in the world. [*Laughter.*]
IRINA   A queer thing to joke about. Is everything burned?
FEDOTIK [*laughs*]   Everything I had in the world. Nothing is left. My guitar is burned, and the camera and all my letters. . . . And the notebook I meant to give you—that's burned too.

Enter SOLYONY.

IRINA   No; please go, Vassily Vassilyitch. You can't stay here.
SOLYONY   How is it the baron can be here and I can't?
VERSHININ   We must be going, really. How is the fire?
SOLYONY   They say it is dying down. No, I really can't understand why the baron may be here and not I. [*Takes out a bottle of scent and sprinkles himself.*]
VERSHININ   Tram-tam-tam!
MASHA   Tram-tam!
VERSHININ [*laughs, to* SOLYONY]   Let us go into the dining room.
SOLYONY   Very well; we'll make a note of it. I might explain my meaning further, but fear I may provoke the geese.[1] . . . [*Looking at* TUSENBACH.] Chook, chook, chook! . . . [*Goes out with* VERSHININ *and* FEDOTIK.]
IRINA   How that horrid Solyony has made the room smell of tobacco! . . . [*In surprise.*] The baron is asleep! Baron, Baron!
TUSENBACH [*waking up*]   I am tired, though. . . . The brickyard. I am not talking in my sleep. I really am going to the brickyard directly, to begin work. . . . It's nearly settled. [*To* IRINA, *tenderly.*] You are so pale and lovely and fascinating. . . . It seems to me as though your paleness sheds a light through the dark air. . . . You are mel-

9. The song is from the opera *Eugene Onegin* by Peter I. Tchaikovsky, based on a novel in verse of the same name by Pushkin. It is sung in the opera by Prince Gremin, the husband of the heroine.
1. A quotation from the fable "The Geese" by Krylov.

ancholy; you are dissatisfied with life. . . . Ah, come with me; let
us go and work together!

MASHA   Nikolay Lvovitch, do go!

TUSENBACH   [*laughing*]   Are you here? I didn't see you. . . . [*Kisses
IRINA's hand.*] Good-bye, I am going. . . . I look at you now, and I
remember as though it were long ago how on your name-day you
talked of the joy of work, and were so gay and confident. . . . And
what a happy life I was dreaming of then! What has become of it?
[*Kisses her hand.*] There are tears in your eyes. Go to bed, it's getting light . . . it is nearly morning. . . . If it were granted to me to
give my life for you!

MASHA   Nikolay Lvovitch, do go! Come, really. . . .

TUSENBACH   I am going. [*Goes out.*]

MASHA   [*lying down*]   Are you asleep, Fyodor?

KULIGIN   Eh?

MASHA   You had better go home.

KULIGIN   My darling Masha, my precious girl! . . .

IRINA   She is tired out. Let her rest, Fedya.

KULIGIN   I'll go at once. . . . My dear, charming wife! . . . I love you,
my only one! . . .

MASHA   [*angrily*]   Amo, amas, amat; amamus, amatis, amant.[2]

KULIGIN   [*laughs*]   Yes, really she is wonderful. You have been my wife
for seven years, and it seems to me as though we were only married
yesterday. Honor bright! Yes, really you are a wonderful woman! I
am content, I am content, I am content!

MASHA   I am bored, I am bored, I am bored! . . . [*Gets up and speaks,
sitting down.*] And there's something I can't get out of my head.
. . . It's simply revolting. It sticks in my head like a nail; I must
speak of it. I mean about Andrey. . . . He has mortgaged this house
in the bank and his wife has grabbed all the money, and you know
the house does not belong to him alone, but to us four! He ought to
know that, if he is a decent man.

KULIGIN   Why do you want to bother about it, Masha? What is it to
you? Andryusha is in debt all round, so there it is.

MASHA   It's revolting, anyway. [*Lies down.*]

KULIGIN   We are not poor. I work—I go to the high-school, and then I
give private lessons. . . . I do my duty. . . . There's no nonsense
about me. *Omnia mea mecum porto,*[3] as the saying is.

MASHA   I want nothing, but it's the injustice that revolts me. [*A
pause.*] Go, Fyodor.

KULIGIN   [*kisses her*]   You are tired, rest for half an hour, and I'll sit
and wait for you. . . . Sleep. . . . [*Goes.*] I am content, I am content,
I am content. [*Goes out.*]

IRINA   Yes, how petty our Andrey has grown, how dull and old he has
become beside that woman! At one time he was working to get a
professorship and yesterday he was boasting of having succeeded at
last in becoming a member of the Rural Board. He is a member, and
Protopopov is chairman. . . . The whole town is laughing and talking
of it and he is the only one who sees and knows nothing. . . . And

2. Latin for "I love, you love, he loves,
we love, you love, they love," the present
tense of the verb *amo*, frequently used as a
sample verb in grammar texts.

3. Latin for "I carry all my (belongings
about) with me."

here everyone has been running to the fire while he sits still in his room and takes no notice. He does nothing but play his violin. . . . [*Nervously.*] Oh, it's awful, awful, awful! [*Weeps.*] I can't bear it anymore, I can't! I can't, I can't! [OLGA *comes in and begins tidying up her table.* IRINA *sobs loudly.*]   Turn me out, turn me out, I can't bear it any more!

OLGA [*alarmed*]   What is it? What is it, darling?

IRINA [*sobbing*]   Where? Where has it all gone? Where is it? Oh, my God, my God! I have forgotten everything, everything . . . everything is in a tangle in my mind. . . . I don't remember the Italian for window or ceiling . . . I am forgetting everything; every day I forget something more and life is slipping away and will never come back, we shall never, never go to Moscow. . . . I see that we shan't go. . . .

OLGA   Darling, darling. . . .

IRINA [*restraining herself*]   Oh, I am wretched. . . . I can't work, I am not going to work. I have had enough of it, enough of it! I have been a telegraph clerk and now I have a job in the town council and I hate and despise every bit of the work they give me. . . . I am nearly twenty-four, I have been working for years, my brains are drying up, I am getting thin and old and ugly and there is nothing, nothing, not the slightest satisfaction, and time is passing and one feels that one is moving away from a real, fine life, moving farther and farther away and being drawn into the depths. I am in despair and I don't know how it is I am alive and have not killed myself yet. . . .

OLGA   Don't cry, my child, don't cry. It makes me miserable.

IRINA   I am not crying, I am not crying. . . . It's over. . . . There, I am not crying now. I won't . . . I won't.

OLGA   Darling, I am speaking to you as a sister, as a friend, if you care for my advice, marry the baron! [IRINA *weeps.* OLGA *speaks softly.*]   You know you respect him, you think highly of him. . . . It's true he is ugly, but he is such a thoroughly nice man, so good. . . . One doesn't marry for love, but to do one's duty. . . . That's what I think, anyway, and I would marry without love. Whoever proposed to me I would marry him, if only he were a good man. . . . I would even marry an old man. . . .

IRINA   I kept expecting we should move to Moscow and there I should meet my real one. I've been dreaming of him, loving him. . . . But it seems that was all nonsense, nonsense. . . .

OLGA [*puts her arms round her sister*]   My darling, lovely sister, I understand it all; when the baron left the army and came to us in a plain coat, I thought he looked so ugly that it positively made me cry. . . . He asked me, "Why are you crying?" How could I tell him! But if God brought you together I should be happy. That's a different thing, you know, quite different.

> NATASHA *with a candle in her hand walks across the stage from door on right to door on left without speaking.*

MASHA [*sits up*]   She walks about as though it were she had set fire to the town.

OLGA   Masha, you are silly. The very silliest of the family, that's you. Please forgive me. [*A pause.*]

MASHA   I want to confess my sins, dear sisters. My soul is yearning. I am going to confess to you and never again to anyone. . . . I'll tell

you this minute. [*Softly.*] It's my secret, but you must know everything. . . . I can't be silent. . . . [*A pause.*] I am in love, I am in love. . . . I love that man. . . . You have just seen him. . . . Well, I may as well say it straight out. I love Vershinin.

OLGA [*going behind her screen*]   Leave off. I don't hear anyway.

MASHA   But what am I to do? [*Clutches her head.*] At first I thought him queer . . . then I was sorry for him . . . then I came to love him . . . to love him with his ·voice, his words, his misfortunes, his two little girls. . . .

OLGA [*behind the screen*]   I don't hear you anyway. Whatever silly things you say I shan't hear them.

MASHA   Oh, Olya, you are silly. I love him—so that's my fate. It means that that's my lot. . . . And he loves me. . . . It's all dreadful. Yes? Is it wrong? [*Takes* IRINA *by the hand and draws her to herself.*] Oh, my darling. . . . How are we going to live our lives, what will become of us? . . . When one reads a novel it all seems stale and easy to understand, but when you are in love yourself you see that no one knows anything and we all have to settle things for ourselves. . . . My darling, my sister. . . . I have confessed it to you, now I'll hold my tongue. . . . I'll be like Gogol's madman[4] . . . silence . . . silence. . . .

Enter ANDREY *and after him* FERAPONT.

ANDREY [*angrily*].   What do you want? I can't make it out.

FERAPONT [*in the doorway, impatiently*]   I've told you ten times already, Andrey Sergeyevitch.

ANDREY   In the first place I am not Andrey Sergeyevitch, but Your Honor, to you!

FERAPONT   The firemen ask leave, Your Honor, to go through the garden on their way to the river. Or else they have to go round and round, an awful nuisance for them.

ANDREY   Very good. Tell them, very good. [FERAPONT *goes out.*] I am sick of them. Where is Olga? [OLGA *comes from behind the screen.*] I've come to ask you for the key of the cupboard, I have lost mine. You've got one, it's a little key.

OLGA *gives him the key in silence;* IRINA *goes behind her screen; a pause.*

ANDREY   What a tremendous fire! Now it's begun to die down. Hang it all, that Ferapont made me so cross I said something silly to him. Your Honor. . . . [*A pause.*] Why don't you speak, Olya? [*A pause.*] It's time to drop this foolishness and sulking all about nothing. . . . You are here, Masha, and you too, Irina—very well, then, let us have things out thoroughly, once for all. What have you against me? What is it?

OLGA   Leave off, Andryusha. Let us talk tomorrow. [*Nervously.*] What an agonizing night!

ANDREY [*greatly confused*]   Don't excite yourself. I ask you quite coolly, what have you against me? Tell me straight out.

[VERSHININ's *voice:* "Tram-tam-tam!"]

MASHA [*standing up, loudly*]   Tra-ta-ta! [*To* OLGA.] Good night, Olya, God bless you. . . .

---

4. The hero of Gogol's story "Memoirs of a Madman."

Goes behind the screen and kisses IRINA.

Sleep well. . . . Good night, Andrey. You'd better leave them now, they are tired out . . . you can go into things tomorrow. [*Goes out.*]

OLGA   Yes, really, Andryusha, let us put it off until tomorrow. . . . [*Goes behind her screen.*] It's time we were in bed.

ANDREY   I'll say what I have to say and then go. Directly. . . . First, you have something against Natasha, my wife, and I've noticed that from the very day of my marriage. Natasha is a splendid woman, conscientious, straightforward, and honorable—that's my opinion! I love and respect my wife, do you understand? I respect her, and I insist on other people respecting her too. I repeat, she is a conscientious, honorable woman, and all your disagreements are simply caprice, or rather the whims of old maids. Old maids never like and never have liked their sisters-in-law—that's the rule. [*A pause.*] Secondly, you seem to be cross with me for not being a professor, not working at something learned. But I am in the service of the Zemstvo,[5] I am a member of the Rural Board, and I consider this service just as sacred and elevated as the service of learning. I am a member of the Rural Board and I am proud of it, if you care to know. . . . [*A pause.*] Thirdly . . . there's something else I have to say. . . . I have mortgaged the house without asking your permission. . . . For that I am to blame, yes, and I ask your pardon for it. I was driven to it by my debts . . . thirty-five thousand. . . . I am not gambling now—I gave up cards long ago; but the chief thing I can say in self-defense is that you are, so to say, of the privileged sex—you get a pension . . . while I had not . . . my wages, so to speak. . . . [*A pause.*]

KULIGIN   [*at the door*]   Isn't Masha here? [*Perturbed.*] Where is she? It's strange. . . . [*Goes out.*]

ANDREY   They won't listen. Natasha is an excellent, conscientious woman. [*Paces up and down the stage in silence, then stops.*] When I married her, I thought we should be happy . . . happy, all of us. . . . But, my God! [*Weeps.*] Dear sisters, darling sisters, you must not believe what I say, you mustn't believe it. . . . [*Goes out.*]

KULIGIN   [*at the door, uneasily*]   Where is Masha? Isn't Masha here? How strange! [*Goes out.*]

The firebell rings in the street. The stage is empty.

IRINA   [*behind the screen*]   Olya! Who is that knocking on the floor?

OLGA   It's the doctor, Ivan Romanitch. He is drunk.

IRINA   What a troubled night! [*A pause.*] Olya! [*Peeps out from behind the screen.*] Have you heard? The brigade is going to be taken away; they are being transferred to some place very far off.

OLGA   That's only a rumor.

IRINA   Then we shall be alone. . . .Olya!

OLGA   Well?

IRINA   My dear, my darling, I respect the baron, I think highly of him, he is a fine man—I will marry him, I consent, only let us go to Moscow! I entreat you, do let us go! There's nothing in the world better than Moscow! Let us go, Olya! Let us go!

5. An elected assembly at the county or provincial level which dealt with local economic and social problems.

Act 4

Old garden of the PROZOROVS' *house. A long avenue of fir trees,
at the end of which is a view of the river. On the farther side of
the river there is a wood. On the right the veranda of the house;
on the table in it are bottles and glasses; evidently they have just
been drinking champagne. It is twelve o'clock noon. People pass
occasionally from the street across the garden to the river; five
soldiers pass rapidly.* TCHEBUTYKIN, *in an affable mood, which
persists throughout the act, is sitting in an easy chair in the garden,
waiting to be summoned; he is wearing a military cap and has a
stick.* IRINA, KULIGIN *with a decoration on his breast and with no
moustache, and* TUSENBACH, *standing on the veranda, are saying
good-bye to* FEDOTIK *and* RODDEY, *who are going down the steps;
both officers are in marching uniform.*

TUSENBACH [*kissing* FEDOTIK] You are a good fellow; we've got on so
happily together. [*Kisses* RODDEY.] Once more. . . . Good-bye, my
dear boy. . . .
IRINA Till we meet again!
FEDOTIK No, it's good-bye for good; we shall never meet again.
KULIGIN Who knows! [*Wipes his eyes, smiles.*] Here I am crying too.
IRINA We shall meet some day.
FEDOTIK In ten years, or fifteen perhaps? But then we shall scarcely
recognize each other—we shall greet each other coldly. . . . [*Takes a
snapshot.*] Stand still. . . . Once more, for the last time.
RODDEY [*embraces* TUSENBACH] We shall not see each other again. . . .
[*Kisses* IRINA's *hand.*] Thank you for everything, everything. . . .
FEDOTIK [*with vexation*] Oh, do wait!
TUSENBACH Please God we shall meet again. Write to us. Be sure to
write to us.
RODDEY [*taking a long look at the garden*] Good-bye, trees! [*Shouts.*]
Halloo! [*A pause.*] Good-bye, echo!
KULIGIN I shouldn't wonder if you get married in Poland. . . . Your
Polish wife will clasp you in her arms and call you *kochany!*[6]
[*Laughs.*]
FEDOTIK [*looking at his watch*] We have less than an hour. Of our
battery only Solyony is going on the barge; we are going with the
rank and file. Three divisions of the battery are going today and
three more tomorrow—and peace and quiet will descend upon the
town.
TUSENBACH And dreadful boredom too.
RODDEY And where is Marya Sergeyevna?
KULIGIN Masha is in the garden.
FEDOTIK We must say good-bye to her.
RODDEY Good-bye. We must go, or I shall begin to cry. . . .

Hurriedly embraces TUSENBACH *and* KULIGIN *and kisses* IRINA's
hand.

We've had a splendid time here.

6. A Polish term of endearment.

FEDOTIK [*to* KULIGIN] This is a little souvenir for you . . . a notebook with a pencil. . . . We'll go down here to the river. . . . [*As they go away both look back.*]

RODDEY [*shouts*] Halloo-oo!

KULIGIN [*shouts*] Good-bye!

RODDEY *and* FEDOTIK *meet* MASHA *in the background and say good-bye to her; she walks away with them.*

IRINA They've gone. . . . [*Sits down on the bottom step of the veranda.*]

TCHEBUTYKIN They have forgotten to say good-bye to me.

IRINA And what were you thinking about?

TCHEBUTYKIN Why, I somehow forget, too. But I shall see them again soon, I am setting off tomorrow. Yes . . . I have one day more. In a year I shall be on the retired list. Then I shall come here again and shall spend the rest of my life near you. . . . There is only one year now before I get my pension. [*Puts a newspaper into his pocket and takes out another.*] I shall come here to you and arrange my life quite differently. . . . I shall become such a quiet . . . God-fearing . . . well-behaved person.

IRINA Well, you do need to arrange your life differently, dear Ivan Romanitch. You certainly ought to somehow.

TCHEBUTYKIN Yes, I feel it. [*Softly hums.*] "Tarara-boom-dee-ay— Tarara-boom-dee-ay."⁷

KULIGIN Ivan Romanitch is incorrigible! Incorrigible!

TCHEBUTYKIN You ought to take me in hand. Then I should reform.

IRINA Fyodor has shaved off his moustache. I can't bear to look at him!

KULIGIN Why, what's wrong?

TCHEBUTYKIN I might tell you what your countenance looks like now, but I really can't.

KULIGIN Well! It's the thing now, *modus vivendi*.⁸ Our headmaster is clean-shaven and now I am second to him I have taken to shaving too. Nobody likes it, but I don't care. I am content. With moustache or without moustache I am equally content. [*Sits down.*]

In the background ANDREY *is wheeling a baby asleep in a perambulator.*

IRINA Ivan Romanitch, darling, I am dreadfully uneasy. You were on the boulevard yesterday, tell me what was it that happened?

TCHEBUTYKIN What happened? Nothing. Nothing much. [*Reads the newspaper.*] It doesn't matter!

KULIGIN The story is that Solyony and the baron met yesterday on the boulevard near the theater. . . .

TUSENBACH Oh, stop it! Really. . . . [*With a wave of his hand walks away into the house.*]

KULIGIN Near the theater. . . . Solyony began pestering the baron and he couldn't keep his temper and said something offensive. . . .

TCHEBUTYKIN I don't know. It's all nonsense.

KULIGIN A teacher at a divinity school wrote "nonsense" at the bottom

---

7. A passage from a popular nonsense song of the 1890s, attributed to Henry J. Sayers, an American, which had its first notable success in England.
8. Latin for "manner of living."

of an essay and the pupil puzzled over it thinking it was a Latin word. . . . [*Laughs.*] It was fearfully funny. . . . They say Solyony is in love with Irina and hates the baron. . . . That's natural. Irina is a very nice girl.

From the background behind the scenes, "Aa-oo! Halloo!"

IRINA [*starts*] Everything frightens me somehow today. [*A pause.*] All my things are ready, after dinner I shall send off my luggage. The baron and I are to be married tomorrow, tomorrow we go to the brickyard and the day after that I shall be in the school. A new life is beginning. God will help me! How will it fare with me? When I passed my exam as a teacher I felt so happy, so blissful, that I cried. . . . [*A pause.*] The cart will soon be coming for my things. . . .

KULIGIN That's all very well, but it does not seem serious. It's all nothing but ideas and very little that is serious. However, I wish you success with all my heart.

TCHEBUTYKIN [*moved to tenderness*] My good, delightful darling. . . . My heart of gold. . . .

KULIGIN Well, today the officers will be gone and everything will go on in the old way. Whatever people may say, Masha is a true, good woman. I love her dearly and am thankful for my lot! . . . People have different lots in life. . . . There is a man called Kozyrev serving in the Excise here.[9] He was at school with me, but he was expelled from the fifth form because he could never understand *ut consecutivum*.[1] Now he is frightfully poor and ill, and when I meet him I say, "How are you, *ut consecutivum?*" "Yes," he says, "just so—*consecutivum*" . . . and then he coughs. . . . Now I have always been successful, I am fortunate, I have even got the order of the Stanislav of the second degree[2] and I am teaching others that *ut consecutivum*. Of course I am clever, cleverer than very many people, but happiness does not lie in that. . . . [*A pause.*]

In the house the "Maiden's Prayer" is played on the piano.[3]

IRINA Tomorrow evening I shall not be hearing that "Maiden's Prayer," I shan't be meeting Protopopov. . . . [*A pause.*] Protopopov is sitting there in the drawing room; he has come again today. . . .

KULIGIN The headmistress has not come yet?

IRINA No. They have sent for her. If only you knew how hard it is for me to live here alone, without Olya. . . . Now that she is headmistress and lives at the high-school and is busy all day long. I am alone, I am bored, I have nothing to do, and I hate the room I live in. . . . I have made up my mind, since I am not fated to be in Moscow, that so it must be. It must be destiny. There is no help for it. . . . It's all in God's hands, that's the truth. When Nikolay Lvovitch made me an offer again . . . I thought it over and made up my mind. . . . He is a

9. The Excise is the local tax office.

1. A reference to the practice in Latin grammar of introducing clauses of result with the conjunction *ut* and of using the subjunctive mood for the verb in the result clauses.

2. The Order of St. Stanislav was originally created in 1765 by Stanislav II, the last king of Poland. It was reestablished in 1815 by Czar Alexander I and included four classes. In 1831 it was made an Imperial and Royal Order (three classes, plus a special class for foreigners). It was an order of merit rather than a military decoration.

3. "The Maiden's Prayer" was a popular piano piece of the period, the best known work of the Polish pianist and composer Teckla Badarzewska (1838–1864).

good man, it's wonderful really how good he is. . . . And I suddenly felt as though my soul had grown wings, my heart felt so light and again I longed for work, work. . . . Only something happened yesterday, there is some mystery hanging over me.

TCHEBUTYKIN   Nonsense.

NATASHA [*at the window*]   Our headmistress!

KULIGIN   The headmistress has come. Let us go in. [*Goes into the house with* IRINA.]

TCHEBUTYKIN [*reads the newspaper, humming softly*]   "Tarara-boom-dee-ay."

> MASHA *approaches; in the background* ANDREY *is pushing the perambulator.*

MASHA   Here he sits, snug and settled.

TCHEBUTYKIN   Well, what then?

MASHA [*sits down*]   Nothing. . . . [*A pause.*] Did you love my mother?

TCHEBUTYKIN   Very much.

MASHA   And did she love you?

TCHEBUTYKIN [*after a pause*]   That I don't remember.

MASHA   Is my man here? It's just like our cook Marfa used to say about her policeman: is my man here?

TCHEBUTYKIN   Not yet.

MASHA   When you get happiness by snatches, by little bits, and then lose it, as I am losing it, by degrees one grows coarse and spiteful. . . . [*Points to her bosom.*] I'm boiling here inside. . . . [*Looking at* ANDREY, *who is pushing the perambulator.*] Here is our Andrey. . . . All our hopes are shattered. Thousands of people raised the bell, a lot of money and of labor was spent on it, and it suddenly fell and smashed.[4] All at once, for no reason whatever. That's just how it is with Andrey. . . .

ANDREY   When will they be quiet in the house? There is such a noise.

TCHEBUTYKIN   Soon. [*Looks at his watch.*] My watch is an old-fashioned one with a repeater. . . . [*Winds his watch, it strikes.*] The first, the second, and the fifth batteries are going at one o'clock. [*A pause.*] And I am going tomorrow.

ANDREY   For good?

TCHEBUTYKIN   I don't know. Perhaps I shall come back in a year. Though goodness knows. . . . It doesn't matter one way or another.

> There is the sound of a harp and violin being played far away in the street.

ANDREY   The town will be empty. It's as though one put an extinguisher over it. [*A pause.*] Something happened yesterday near the theater; everyone is talking of it, and I know nothing about it.

TCHEBUTYKIN   It was nothing. Foolishness. Solyony began annoying the baron and he lost his temper and insulted him, and it came in the end to Solyony's having to challenge him. [*Looks at his watch.*] It's time, I fancy. . . . It was to be at half-past twelve in the Crown forest that we can see from here beyond the river. . . . Piff-paff!

---

4. Masha is perhaps referring to the gigantic bell called the Tsar Kolokol (or "King of Bells") in the Kremlin. It was originally cast at the behest of Boris Godunov to hang in the Ivan Bell Tower of the Kremlin, but it proved too heavy. The platform on which it rested fell on several occasions as a result of fire weakening its supports. It weighs about 200 tons and is over 20 feet high and more than 20 feet in diameter.

[*Laughs.*] Solyony imagines he is a Lermontov and even writes verses. Joking apart, this is his third duel.

MASHA Whose?

TCHEBUTYKIN Solyony's.

MASHA And the baron's?

TCHEBUTYKIN What about the baron? [*A pause.*]

MASHA My thoughts are in a muddle. . . . Anyway, I tell you, you ought not to let them do it. He may wound the baron or even kill him.

TCHEBUTYKIN The baron is a very good fellow, but one baron more or less in the world, what does it matter? Let them! It doesn't matter. [*Beyond the garden a shout of* "Aa-oo! Halloo!"] You can wait. That is Skvortsov, the second, shouting. He is in a boat. [*A pause.*]

ANDREY In my opinion to take part in a duel, or to be present at it even in the capacity of a doctor, is simply immoral.

TCHEBUTYKIN That only seems so. . . . We are not real, nothing in the world is real, we don't exist, but only seem to exist. . . . Nothing matters!

MASHA How they keep on talking, talking all day long. [*Goes.*] To live in such a climate, it may snow any minute, and then all this talk on the top of it. [*Stops.*] I am not going indoors, I can't go in there. . . . When Vershinin comes, tell me. . . . [*Goes down the avenue.*] And the birds are already flying south. . . . [*Looks up.*] Swans or geese. . . . Darlings, happy things. . . . [*Goes out.*]

ANDREY Our house will be empty. The officers are going, you are going, Irina is getting married, and I shall be left in the house alone.

TCHEBUTYKIN What about your wife?

Enter FERAPONT *with papers.*

ANDREY A wife is a wife. She is a straightforward, upright woman, good-natured, perhaps, but for all that there is something in her which makes her no better than some petty, blind, hairy animal. Anyway she is not a human being. I speak to you as to a friend, the one man to whom I can open my soul. I love Natasha, that is so, but sometimes she seems to me wonderfully vulgar, and then I don't know what to think, I can't account for my loving her or, anyway, having loved her.

TCHEBUTYKIN [*gets up*] I am going away tomorrow, my boy, perhaps we shall never meet again, so this is my advice to you. Put on your cap, you know, take your stick and walk off . . . walk off and just go, go without looking back. And the farther you go, the better. [*A pause.*] But do as you like! It doesn't matter. . . .

SOLYONY *crosses the stage in the background with two officers; seeing* TCHEBUTYKIN *he turns toward him; the officers walk on.*

SOLYONY Doctor, it's time! It's half-past twelve. [*Greets* ANDREY.]

TCHEBUTYKIN Directly. I am sick of you all. [*To* ANDREY.] If anyone asks for me, Andryusha, say I'll be back directly. . . . [*Sighs.*] Oho-ho-ho!

SOLYONY He had not time to say alack before the bear was on his back. [*Walks away with the doctor.*] Why are you croaking, old chap?

TCHEBUTYKIN Come!

SOLYONY How do you feel?

TCHEBUTYKIN [*angrily*]   Like a pig in clover.[5]

SOLYONY   The old chap need not excite himself. I won't do anything much, I'll only shoot him like a snipe. [*Takes out scent and sprinkles his hands.*] I've used a whole bottle today, and still they smell. My hands smell like a corpse. [*A pause.*] Yes. . . . Do you remember the poem? "And, restless, seeks the stormy ocean, as though in tempest there were peace."[6] . . .

TCHEBUTYKIN   Yes. He had not time to say alack before the bear was on his back.

> *Goes out with* SOLYONY. *Shouts are heard:* "Halloo! Oo-oo!" AN-DREY *and* FERAPONT *come in.*

FERAPONT   Papers for you to sign. . . .

ANDREY [*nervously*]   Let me alone! Let me alone! I entreat you! [*Walks away with the perambulator.*]

FERAPONT   That's what the papers are for—to be signed. [*Retires into the background.*]

> *Enter* IRINA *and* TUSENBACH *wearing a straw hat;* KULIGIN *crosses the stage shouting* "Aa-oo, Masha, aa-oo!"

TUSENBACH   I believe that's the only man in the town who is glad that the officers are going away.

IRINA   That's very natural. [*A pause.*] Our town will be empty now.

TUSENBACH   Dear, I'll be back directly.

IRINA   Where are you going?

TUSENBACH   I must go into the town, and then . . . to see my comrades off.

IRINA   That's not true. . . . Nikolay, why are you so absentminded to-day? [*A pause.*] What happened yesterday near the theater?

TUSENBACH [*with a gesture of impatience*]   I'll be here in an hour and with you again. [*Kisses her hands.*] My beautiful one . . . [*Looks into her face.*] For five years now I have loved you and still I can't get used to it, and you seem to me more and more lovely. What wonderful, exquisite hair! What eyes! I shall carry you off tomorrow, we will work, we will be rich, my dreams will come true. You shall be happy. There is only one thing, one thing: you don't love me!

IRINA   That's not in my power! I'll be your wife and be faithful and obedient, but there is no love, I can't help it. [*Weeps.*] I've never been in love in my life! Oh, I have so dreamed of love, I've been dreaming of it for years, day and night, but my soul is like a wonderful piano of which the key has been lost. [*A pause.*] You look uneasy.

TUSENBACH   I have not slept all night. There has never been anything in my life so dreadful that it could frighten me, and only that lost key frets at my heart and won't let me sleep. . . . Say something to me. . . . [*A pause.*] Say something to me. . . .

IRINA   What? What am I to say to you? What?

TUSENBACH   Anything.

IRINA   There, there! [*A pause.*]

TUSENBACH   What trifles, what little things suddenly *à propos*[7] of noth-ing acquire importance in life! One laughs at them as before, thinks

---

5. "To turn the pigs into the grass" is a proverbial expression meaning to create a diversion. Tchebutykin means that he is distracted.

6. A quotation from "The Sail," a poem by Lermontov.
7. A French phrase meaning "relating to" or "having to do with."

them nonsense, but still one goes on and feels that one has not the power to stop. Don't let us talk about it! I am happy. I feel as though I were seeing these pines, these maples, these birch trees for the first time in my life, and they all seem to be looking at me with curiosity and waiting. What beautiful trees, and, really, how beautiful life ought to be under them! [*A shout of* "Halloo! Aa-oo!"] I must be off; it's time. . . . See, that tree is dead, but it waves in the wind with the others. And so it seems to me that if I die I shall still have part in life, one way or another. Good-bye, my darling. . . . [*Kisses her hands.*] Those papers of yours you gave me are lying under the calendar on my table.

IRINA   I am coming with you.

TUSENBACH [*in alarm*]   No, no! [*Goes off quickly, stops in the avenue.*] Irina!

IRINA   What is it?

TUSENBACH [*not knowing what to say*]   I didn't have any coffee this morning. Ask them to make me some. [*Goes out quickly.*]

> IRINA *stands lost in thought, then walks away into the background of the scene and sits down on the swing. Enter* ANDREY *with the perambulator, and* FERAPONT *comes into sight.*

FERAPONT   Andrey Sergeyevitch, the papers aren't mine; they are Government papers. I didn't invent them.

ANDREY   Oh, where is it all gone? What has become of my past, when I was young, gay, and clever, when my dreams and thoughts were exquisite, when my present and my past were lighted up by hope? Why on the very threshold of life do we become dull, grey, uninteresting, lazy, indifferent, useless, unhappy? . . . Our town has been going on for two hundred years—there are a hundred thousand people living in it; and there is not one who is not like the rest, not one saint in the past, or the present, not one man of learning, not one artist, not one man in the least remarkable who could inspire envy or a passionate desire to imitate him. . . . They only eat, drink, sleep, and then die . . . others are born, and they also eat and drink and sleep, and not to be bored to stupefaction they vary their lives by nasty gossip, vodka, cards, litigation; and the wives deceive their husbands, and the husbands tell lies and pretend that they see and hear nothing, and an overwhelmingly vulgar influence weighs upon the children, and the divine spark is quenched in them and they become the same sort of pitiful, dead creatures, all exactly alike, as their fathers and mothers. . . . [*To* FERAPONT, *angrily.*] What do you want?

FERAPONT   Eh? There are papers to sign.

ANDREY   You bother me!

FERAPONT [*handing him the papers*]   The porter from the local treasury was saying just now that there was as much as two hundred degrees of frost in Petersburg this winter.[8]

ANDREY   The present is hateful, but when I think of the future, it is so nice! I feel so lighthearted, so free. A light dawns in the distance,

---

8. Two hundred degrees of frost normally means 200 degrees below the freezing point of water, which is very cold even for the Russian winter. Joseph Nicholas Delisle, a French astronomer, was in St. Petersburg from 1725 to 1747 at the invitation of Peter the Great. With the assistance of Josias Weitbrecht, he devised a thermometer which read 0 at the boiling point of water, 150 at the freezing point of water, and was graduated farther down to 200 or 205. Ferapont's temperature reading may have been on his scale.

I see freedom. I see how I and my children will become free from sloth, from kvass,[9] from goose and cabbage, from sleeping after dinner, from mean, parasitic living. . . .

FERAPONT   He says that two thousand people were frozen to death. The people were terrified. It was either in Petersburg or Moscow, I don't remember.

ANDREY [*in a rush of tender feeling*]   My dear sisters, my wonderful sisters! [*Through tears.*] Masha, my sister!

NATASHA [*in the window*]   Who is talking so loud out there? Is that you, Andryusha? You will wake baby Sophie. *Il ne faut pas faire de bruit, la Sophie est dormée déja. Vous êtes un ours.*[1] [*Getting angry.*] If you want to talk, give the perambulator with the baby to somebody else. Ferapont, take the perambulator from the master!

FERAPONT   Yes, ma'am. [*Takes the pram.*]

ANDREY [*in confusion*]   I am talking quietly.

NATASHA [*petting her child, inside the room*]   Bobik! Naughty Bobik! Little rascal!

ANDREY [*looking through the papers*]   Very well, I'll look through them and sign what wants signing, and then you can take them back to the Board. . . .

> *Goes into the house reading the papers;* FERAPONT *pushes the pram farther into the garden.*

NATASHA [*speaking indoors*]   Bobik, what is mamma's name? Darling, darling! And who is this? This is Auntie Olya. Say to Auntie, "Good morning, Olya!"

> *Two wandering musicians, a man and a girl, enter and play a violin and a harp; from the house enter* VERSHININ *with* OLGA *and* ANFISA, *and stand for a minute listening in silence;* IRINA *comes up.*

OLGA   Our garden is like a public passage; they walk and ride through. Nurse, give those people something.

ANFISA [*gives money to the musicians*]   Go away, and God bless you, my dear souls! [*The musicians bow and go away.*] Poor things. People don't play if they have plenty to eat. [*To* IRINA.] Good morning, Irisha! [*Kisses her.*] Aye, aye, my little girl, I am having a time of it! Living in the high-school, in a government flat, with dear Olya— that's what the Lord has vouchsafed me in my old age! I have never lived so well in my life, sinful woman that I am. . . . It's a big flat, and I have a room to myself and a bedstead. All at the government expense. I wake up in the night and, O Lord, Mother of God, there is no one in the world happier than I!

VERSHININ [*looks at his watch*]   We are just going, Olga Sergeyevna. It's time to be off. [*A pause.*] I wish you everything, everything. . . . Where is Marya Sergeyevna?

IRINA   She is somewhere in the garden. . . . I'll go and look for her.

VERSHININ   Please be so good. I am in a hurry.

ANFISA   I'll go and look for her too. [*Shouts.*] Mashenka, aa-oo! [*Goes with* IRINA *into the farther part of the garden.*] Aa-oo! Aa-oo!

---

9. A form of beer.
1. Unidiomatic French for "You mustn't   make so much noise. Sophie is already asleep. You are a bear."

VERSHININ Everything comes to an end. Here we are parting. [*Looks at his watch.*] The town has given us something like a lunch; we have been drinking champagne, the mayor made a speech. I ate and listened, but my heart was here, with you all . . . [*Looks round the garden.*] I've grown used to you. . . .

OLGA Shall we ever see each other again?

VERSHININ Most likely not. [*A pause.*] My wife and two little girls will stay here for another two months; please, if anything happens, if they need anything . . .

OLGA Yes, yes, of course. Set your mind at rest. [*A pause.*] By tomorrow there won't be a soldier in the town—it will all turn into a memory, and of course for us it will be like beginning a new life. . . . [*A pause.*] Nothing turns out as we would have it. I did not want to be a headmistress, and yet I am. It seems we are not to live in Moscow. . . .

VERSHININ Well. . . . Thank you for everything. . . . Forgive me if anything was amiss. . . . I have talked a great deal: forgive me for that too— don't remember evil against me.

OLGA [*wipes her eyes*] Why doesn't Masha come?

VERSHININ What else am I to say to you at parting? What am I to theorize about? . . . [*Laughs.*] Life is hard. It seems to many of us blank and hopeless; but yet we must admit that it goes on getting clearer and easier, and it looks as though the time were not far off when it will be full of happiness. [*Looks at his watch.*] It's time for me to go! In old days men were absorbed in wars, filling all their existence with marches, raids, victories, but now all that is a thing of the past, leaving behind it a great void which there is so far nothing to fill: humanity is searching for it passionately, and of course will find it. Ah, if only it could be quickly! [*A pause.*] If, don't you know, industry were united with culture and culture with industry. . . . [*Looks at his watch.*] But, I say, it's time for me to go. . . .

OLGA Here she comes.

MASHA *comes in.*

VERSHININ I have come to say good-bye. . . .

OLGA *moves a little away to leave them free to say good-bye.*

MASHA [*looking into his face*] Good-bye. . . . [*A prolonged kiss.*]

OLGA Come, come. . . .

MASHA *sobs violently.*

VERSHININ Write to me. . . . Don't forget me! Let me go! . . . Time is up! . . . Olga Sergeyevna, take her, I must . . . go . . . I am late. . . . [*Much moved, kisses* OLGA's *hands; then again embraces* MASHA *and quickly goes off.*]

OLGA Come, Masha! Leave off, darling.

Enter KULIGIN.

KULIGIN [*embarrassed*] Never mind, let her cry—let her. . . . My good Masha, my dear Masha! . . . You are my wife, and I am happy, anyway. . . . I don't complain; I don't say a word of blame. . . . Here Olya is my witness. . . . We'll begin the old life again, and I won't say one word, not a hint. . . .

MASHA [*restraining her sobs*] By the sea-strand an oak tree green. . . .
Upon that oak a chain of gold. . . . Upon that oak a chain of gold.
. . . I am going mad. . . . By the sea-strand . . . an oak tree green. . . .

OLGA Calm yourself, Masha. . . . Calm yourself. . . . Give her some
water.

MASHA I am not crying now. . . .

KULIGIN She is not crying now . . . she is good. . . .

The dim sound of a faraway shot.

MASHA By the sea-strand an oak tree green, upon that oak a chain of
gold. . . . The cat is green . . . the oak is green. . . . I am mixing it
up. . . . [*Drinks water.*] My life is a failure. . . . I want nothing now.
. . . I shall be calm directly. . . . It doesn't matter. . . . What does
"strand" mean? Why do these words haunt me? My thoughts are in
a tangle.

Enter IRINA

OLGA Calm yourself, Masha. Come, that's a good girl. Let us go indoors.

MASHA [*angrily*] I am not going in. Let me alone! [*Sobs, but at once
checks herself.*] I don't go into that house now and I won't.

IRINA Let us sit together, even if we don't say anything. I am going
away tomorrow, you know. . . . [*A pause.*]

KULIGIN I took a false beard and moustache from a boy in the third
grade yesterday, just look. . . . [*Puts on the beard and moustache.*]
I look like the German teacher. . . . [*Laughs.*] Don't I? Funny creatures, those boys.

MASHA You really do look like the German teacher.

OLGA [*laughs*] Yes.

MASHA *weeps.*

IRINA There, Masha!

KULIGIN Awfully like. . . .

Enter NATASHA.

NATASHA [*to the maid*] What? Mr. Protopopov will sit with Sophie,
and let Andrey Sergeyitch wheel Bobik up and down. What a lot
there is to do with children . . . [*To* IRINA.] Irina, you are going
away tomorrow, what a pity. Do stay just another week.

Seeing KULIGIN *utters a shriek; the latter laughs and takes off
the beard and moustache.*

Well, what next, you gave me such a fright! [*To* IRINA.] I am used
to you and do you suppose that I don't feel parting with you? I shall
put Andrey with his violin into your room—let him saw away there!
—and we will put baby Sophie in his room. Adorable, delightful
baby! Isn't she a child! Today she looked at me with such eyes and
said "Mamma"!

KULIGIN A fine child, that's true.

NATASHA So tomorrow I shall be all alone here. [*Sighs.*] First of all I
shall have this avenue of fir trees cut down, and then that maple. . . .
It looks so ugly in the evening. . . . [*To* IRINA.] My dear, that sash
does not suit you at all. . . . It's in bad taste. You want something

light. And then I shall have flowers, flowers planted everywhere, and
there will be such a scent. . . . [*Severely.*] Why is there a fork lying
about on that seat? [*Going into the house, to the maid.*] Why is there
a fork lying about on this seat, I ask you? [*Shouts.*] Hold your
tongue!

KULIGIN   She is at it!

> *Behind the scenes the band plays a march; they all listen.*

OLGA   They are going.

> *Enter* TCHEBUTYKIN.

MASHA   Our people are going. Well . . . a happy journey to them! [*To
her husband.*] We must go home. . . . Where are my hat and cape?

KULIGIN   I took them into the house. . . . I'll get them directly. . . .

OLGA   Yes, now we can go home, it's time.

TCHEBUTYKIN   Olga Sergeyevna!

OLGA   What is it? [*A pause.*] What?

TCHEBUTYKIN   Nothing. . . . I don't know how to tell you. [*Whispers
in her ear.*]

OLGA [*in alarm*]   It can't be!

TCHEBUTYKIN   Yes . . . such a business. . . . I am so worried and worn
out, I don't want to say another word. . . . [*With vexation.*] But
there, it doesn't matter!

MASHA   What has happened?

OLGA [*puts her arms round* IRINA]   This is a terrible day. . . . I don't
know how to tell you, my precious. . . .

IRINA   What is it? Tell me quickly, what is it? For God's sake! [*Cries.*]

TCHEBUTYKIN   The baron has just been killed in a duel.

IRINA [*weeping quietly*]   I knew, I knew. . . .

TCHEBUTYKIN [*in the background of the scene sits down on a garden
seat*]   I am worn out. . . . [*Takes a newspaper out of his pocket.*] Let
them cry. . . . [*Sings softly.*] "Tarara-boom-dee-ay." . . . It doesn't
matter.

> *The three sisters stand with their arms round one another.*

MASHA   Oh, listen to that band! They are going away from us; one has
gone altogether, gone forever. We are left alone to begin our life
over again. . . . We've got to live . . . we've got to live. . . .

IRINA [*lays her head on* OLGA's *bosom*]   A time will come when everyone will know what all this is for, why there is this misery; there will
be no mysteries and, meanwhile, we have got to live . . . we have got
to work, only to work! Tomorrow I shall go alone; I shall teach in the
school, and I will give all my life to those to whom it may be of use.
Now it's autumn; soon winter will come and cover us with snow,
and I will work, I will work.

OLGA [*embraces both her sisters*]   The music is so gay, so confident,
and one longs for life! O my God! Time will pass, and we shall go
away for ever, and we shall be forgotten, our faces will be forgotten,
our voices, and how many there were of us; but our sufferings will
pass into joy for those who will live after us, happiness and peace will
be established upon earth, and they will remember kindly and bless
those who have lived before. Oh, dear sisters, our life is not ended
yet. We shall live! The music is so gay, so joyful, and it seems as

though a little more and we shall know what we are living for, why we are suffering. . . . If we only knew—if we only knew!

The music grows more and more subdued; KULIGIN, *cheerful and smiling, brings the hat and cape;* ANDREY *pushes the perambulator in which* BOBIK *is sitting.*

TCHEBUTYKIN [*humming softly*] "Tarara-boom-dee-ay!" [*Reads his paper.*] It doesn't matter, it doesn't matter.

OLGA   If we only knew, if we only knew!

1901

RUSSIAN NAMES

The use of names in Russian literature will confuse American students unless they bear certain facts in mind. Russian names, generally, consist of three parts: the given name; the patronymic (ending in *itch* for men and *vna* for women) based on the given name of the character's father; and the family name. The name Ivan Romanitch Tchebutykin, for example, tells us that the character's given name is Ivan, that his father's given name was Roman and that the family name is Tchebutykin. In general, strangers, or relative strangers, would use the family name or an appropriate title to refer to or speak to a character.

For example, Tusenbach at first calls Vershinin either "Vershinin" or "Colonel," but later calls him Alexandr Ignatyevitch. Friends of the same rank would use the given name plus patronymic, *e.g.* Ivan Romanitch, as all of the Prozorovs do for Tchebutykin. More intimate relations are indicated by the use of the given name only or by nicknames of varying degrees of intimacy. Andrey, Irina, and Marya, for example, would be called Andryusha, Irisha, and Masha or Andryushantchik, Irinushka, and Mashenka, as dictated by circumstance. Natasha, for example, calls Irina "Irina Sergeyevna" before her marriage to Andrey and "Irina" afterward. In the same way, Irina calls Kuligin either Fyodor, his given name, or Fedya, a nickname, as the particular moment renders appropriate.

The nurse Anfisa shows that in dealing with characters of various ranks, the usual rules may be modified. She calls the three sisters "Olya," "Mashenka," and "Irisha" or "Irinushka" with impunity because she knew them as children. A different view is shown when Andrey takes umbrage at being called Andrey Sergeyevitch, instead of "Your Honor," by Ferapont.

Another point to be noted is that speakers in general use a more formal term in speaking of someone in the second person than they do in the third. Irina, for example, refers to "Solyony" in the third person but calls him "Vassily Vassilyevitch" in person.

ED BULLINS

A Son, Come Home

CHARACTERS

MOTHER, *early 50s*   THE GIRL
SON, *30 years old*   THE BOY

The BOY *and the* GIRL *wear black tights and shirts. They move the
action of the play and express the* MOTHER's *and the* SON's *moods
and tensions. They become various embodiments recalled from
memory and history: they enact a number of personalities and
move from mood to mood. The players are Black.*

*At rise: Scene: Bare stage but for two chairs positioned so as not
to interfere with the actions of the* BOY *and the* GIRL. *The* MOTHER
*enters, sits in chair and begins to use imaginary iron and board.
She hums a spiritual as she works.*

MOTHER   You came three times . . . Michael? It took you three times
to find me at home?

The GIRL *enters, turns and peers through the cracked, imaginary
door.*

SON's VOICE [*offstage*]   Is Mrs. Brown home?
GIRL [*an old woman*]   What?
MOTHER   It shouldn't have taken you three times. I told you that I
would be here by two and you should wait, Michael.

The SON *enters, passes the* GIRL *and takes his seat upon the
other chair. The* BOY *enters, stops on other side of the imaginary
door and looks through at the* GIRL.

BOY   Is Mrs. Brown in?
GIRL   Miss Brown ain't come in yet. Come back later . . . She'll be in
before dark.
MOTHER   It shouldn't have taken you three times . . . You should lis-
ten to me, Michael. Standin' all that time in the cold..
SON   It wasn't cold, Mother.
MOTHER   I told you that I would be here by two and you should wait,
Michael.
BOY   Please tell Mrs. Brown that her son's in town to visit her.
GIRL   You little Miss Brown's son? Well, bless the Lord.

Calls over her shoulder.

Hey, Mandy, do you hear that? Little Miss Brown upstairs got a son
. . . a great big boy . . . He's come to visit her.
BOY   You'll tell her, won't you?
GIRL   Sure, I'll tell her.

Grins and shows gums.

I'll tell her soon as she gets in.
MOTHER   Did you get cold, Michael?
SON   No, Mother. I walked around some . . . sightseeing.

BOY   I walked up Twenty-third Street toward South. I had phoned that I was coming.

MOTHER   Sightseeing? But this is your home, Michael . . . always has been.

BOY   Just before I left New York I phoned that I was taking the bus. Two hours by bus, that's all. That's all it takes. Two hours.

SON   This town seems so strange. Different than how I remember it.

MOTHER   Yes, you have been away for a good while . . . How long has it been, Michael?

BOY   Two hours down the Jersey Turnpike, the trip beginning at the New York Port Authority Terminal . . .

SON   . . . and then straight down through New Jersey to Philadelphia . . .

GIRL   . . . and home . . . Just imagine . . . little Miss Brown's got a son who's come home.

SON   Yes, home . . . an anachronism.

MOTHER   What did you say, Michael?

BOY   He said . . .

GIRL   [*late teens*]   What's an anachronism, Mike?

SON   Anachronism: 1: an error in chronology; *esp:* a chronological misplacing of persons, events, objects, or customs in regard to each other; 2: a person or a thing that is chronologically out of place—anachronistic/ *also* anachronic/ *or* anachronous—anachronistically/ *also* anachronously.

MOTHER   I was so glad to hear you were going to school in California.

BOY   College.

GIRL   Yes, I understand.

MOTHER   How long have you been gone, Michael?

SON   Nine years.

BOY   Nine years it's been. I wonder if she'll know me . . .

MOTHER   You've put on so much weight, son. You know that's not healthy.

GIRL   [*20 years old*]   And that silly beard . . . how . . .

SON   Oh . . . I'll take it off. I'm going on a diet tomorrow.

BOY   I wonder if I'll know her.

SON   You've put on some yourself, Mother.

MOTHER   Yes, the years pass. Thank the Lord.

BOY   I wonder if we've changed much.

GIRL   Yes, thank the Lord.

SON   The streets here seem so small.

MOTHER   Yes, it seems like that when you spend a little time in Los Angeles.

GIRL   I spent eighteen months there with your aunt when she was sick. She had nobody else to help her . . . she was so lonely. And you were in the service . . . away. You've always been away.

BOY   In Los Angeles the boulevards, the avenues, the streets . . .

SON   . . . are wide. Yes, they have some wide ones out West. Here, they're so small and narrow. I wonder how cars get through on both sides.

MOTHER   Why, you know how . . . we lived on Derby Street for over ten years, didn't we?

SON   Yeah, that was almost an alley.

MOTHER   Did you see much of your aunt before you left Los Angeles?

SON   What?

GIRL [*middle-aged woman to* BOY] Have you found a job yet, Michael?

MOTHER Your aunt. My sister.

BOY Nawh, not yet . . . Today I just walked downtown . . . quite a ways . . . this place is plenty big, ain't it?

SON I don't see too much of Aunt Sophie.

MOTHER But you're so much alike.

GIRL Well, your bags are packed and are sitting outside the door.

BOY My bags?

MOTHER You shouldn't be that way, Michael. You shouldn't get too far away from your family.

SON Yes, Mother.

BOY But I don't have any money. I had to walk downtown today. That's how much money I have. I've only been here a week.

GIRL I packed your bags, Michael.

MOTHER You never can tell when you'll need or want your family, Michael.

SON That's right, Mother.

MOTHER You and she are so much alike.

BOY Well, goodbye, Aunt Sophie.

GIRL [*silence*]

MOTHER All that time in California and you hardly saw your aunt. My baby sister.

BOY Tsk tsk tsk.

SON I'm sorry, Mother.

MOTHER In the letters I'd get from both of you there'd be no mention of the other. All these years. Did you see her again?

SON Yes.

GIRL [*on telephone*] Michael? Michael who? . . . Ohhh . . . Bernice's boy.

MOTHER You didn't tell me about this, did you?

SON No, I didn't.

BOY Hello, Aunt Sophie. How are you?

GIRL I'm fine, Michael. How are you? You're looking well.

BOY I'm getting on okay.

MOTHER I prayed for you.

SON Thank you.

MOTHER Thank the Lord, Michael.

BOY Got me a job working for the city.

GIRL You did now.

BOY Yes, I've brought you something.

GIRL What's this, Michael . . . ohhh . . . it's money.

BOY It's for the week I stayed with you.

GIRL Fifty dollars. But, Michael, you didn't have to.

MOTHER Are you still writing that radical stuff, Michael?

SON Radical?

MOTHER Yes . . . that stuff you write and send me all the time in those little books.

SON My poetry, Mother?

MOTHER Yes, that's what I'm talking about.

SON No.

MOTHER Praise the Lord, son. Praise the Lord. Didn't seem like anything I had read in school.

BOY [*on telephone*] Aunt Sophie? . . . Aunt Sophie? . . . It's me, Michael . . .

GIRL   Michael?

BOY   Yes . . . Michael . . .

GIRL   Oh . . . Michael . . . yes . . .

BOY   I'm in jail, Aunt Sophie . . . I got picked up for drunk driving.

GIRL   You did . . . how awful . . .

MOTHER   When you going to get your hair cut, Michael?

BOY   Aunt Sophie . . . will you please come down and sign my bail. I've got the money . . . I just got paid yesterday . . . They're holding more than enough for me . . . but the law says that someone has to sign for it.

MOTHER   You look almost like a hoodlum, Michael.

BOY   All you need to do is come down and sign . . . and I can get out.

MOTHER   What you tryin' to be . . . a savage or something? Are you keeping out of trouble, Michael?

GIRL   Ohhh . . . Michael . . . I'm sorry but I can't do nothin' like that . . .

BOY   But all you have to do is sign . . . I've got the money and everything.

GIRL   I'm sorry . . . I can't stick my neck out.

BOY   But, Aunt Sophie . . . if I don't get back to work I'll lose my job and everything . . . please . . .

GIRL   I'm sorry, Michael . . . I can't stick my neck out . . . I have to go now . . . Is there anyone I can call?

BOY   No.

GIRL   I could call your mother. She wouldn't mind if I reversed the charges on her, would she? I don't like to run my bills up.

BOY   No, thanks.

MOTHER   You and your aunt are so much alike.

SON   Yes, Mother. Our birthdays are in the same month.

MOTHER   Yes, that year was so hot . . . so hot and I was carrying you . . .

> As the MOTHER speaks the BOY comes over and takes her by the hand and leads her from the chair, and they stroll around the stage, arm in arm. The GIRL accompanies them and she and the BOY enact scenes from the MOTHER's mind.

. . . carrying you, Michael . . . and you were such a big baby . . . kicked all the time. But I was happy. Happy that I was having a baby of my own . . . I worked as long as I could and bought you everything you might need . . . diapers . . . and bottles . . . and your own spoon . . . and even toys . . . and even books . . . And it was so hot in Philadelphia that year . . . Your Aunt Sophie used to come over and we'd go for walks . . . sometimes up on the avenue . . . I was living in West Philly then . . . in that old terrible section they called "The Bottom." That's where I met your father.

GIRL   You're such a fool, Bernice. No nigger . . . man or boy's . . . ever going to do a thing to me like that.

MOTHER   Everything's going to be all right, Sophia.

GIRL   But what is he going to do? How are you going to take care of a baby by yourself?

MOTHER   Everything's going to be all right, Sophia. I'll manage.

GIRL   You'll manage? How? Have you talked about marriage?

MOTHER   Oh, please, Sophia!

GIRL   What do you mean "please"? Have you?

MOTHER   I just can't. He might think . . .

GIRL   Think! That dirty nigger better think. He better think before he really messes up. And you better too. You got this baby comin' on. What are you going to do?

MOTHER   I don't know . . . I don't know what I can do.

GIRL   Is he still tellin' you those lies about . . .

MOTHER   They're not lies.

GIRL   Haaaa . . .

MOTHER   They're not.

GIRL   Some smooth-talkin' nigger comes up from Georgia and tell you he escaped from the chain gang and had to change his name so he can't get married 'cause they might find out . . . What kinda shit is that, Bernice?

MOTHER   Please, Sophia. Try and understand. He loves me. I can't hurt him.

GIRL   Loves you . . . and puts you through this?

MOTHER   Please . . . I'll talk to him . . . Give me a chance.

GIRL   It's just a good thing you got a family, Bernice. It's just a good thing. You know that, don't cha?

MOTHER   Yes . . . yes, I do . . . but please don't say anything to him.

SON   I've only seen my father about a half dozen times that I remember, Mother. What was he like?

MOTHER   Down in The Bottom . . . that's where I met your father. I was young and hinkty[1] then. Had big pretty brown legs and a small waist. Everybody used to call me Bernie . . . and me and my sister would go to Atlantic City on the weekends and work as waitresses in the evenings and sit all afternoon on the black part of the beach at Boardwalk and Atlantic . . . getting blacker . . . and having the times of our lives. Your father probably still lives down in The Bottom . . . perched over some bar down there . . . drunk to the world . . . I can see him now . . . He had good white teeth then . . . not how they turned later when he started in drinkin' that wine and wouldn't stop . . . he was so nice then.

BOY   Awwww, listen, kid. I got my problems too.

GIRL   But Andy . . . I'm six months gone . . . and you ain't done nothin'.

BOY   Well, what can I do?

GIRL   Don't talk like that . . . What can you do? . . . You know what you can do.

BOY   You mean marry you? Now lissen, sweetheart . . .

GIRL   But what about our baby?

BOY   Your baby.

GIRL   Don't talk like that! It took more than me to get him.

BOY   Well . . . look . . . I'll talk to you later, kid. I got to go to work now.

GIRL   That's what I got to talk to you about too, Andy. I need some money.

BOY   Money! Is somethin' wrong with your head, woman? I ain't got no money.

GIRL   But I can't work much longer, Andy. You got to give me some money. Andy . . . you just gotta.

BOY   Woman . . . all I got to *ever* do is die and go to hell.

1. A Black slang word which means that she was snobbish or aloof because of her certainly of her own good looks and general worth.

GIRL   Well, you gonna do that, Andy. You sho are . . . you know that, don't you? . . . You know that.

MOTHER   . . . Yes, you are, man. Praise the Lord. We all are . . . All of us . . . even though he ain't come for you yet to make you pay. Maybe he's waitin' for us to go together so I can be a witness to the retribution that's handed down. A witness to all that He'll bestow upon your sinner's head . . . A witness! . . . That's what I am, Andy! Do you hear me? . . . A witness!

SON   Mother . . . what's wrong? What's the matter?

MOTHER   Thank the Lord that I am not blinded and will see the fulfillment of divine . . .

SON   Mother!

MOTHER   Oh . . . is something wrong, Michael?

SON   You're shouting and walking around . . .

MOTHER   Oh . . . it's nothing, son. I'm just feeling the power of the Lord.

SON   Oh . . . is there anything I can get you, Mother?

MOTHER   No, nothing at all.

She sits again and irons.

SON   Where's your kitchen? . . . I'll get you some coffee . . . the way you like it. I bet I still remember how to fix it.

MOTHER   Michael . . . I don't drink anything like that no more.

SON   No?

MOTHER   Not since I joined the service of the Lord.

SON   Yeah? . . . Well, do you mind if I get myself a cup?

MOTHER   Why, I don't have a kitchen. All my meals are prepared for me.

SON   Oh . . . I thought I was having dinner with you.

MOTHER   No. There's nothing like that here.

SON   Well, could I take you out to a restaurant? . . . Remember how we used to go out all the time and eat? I've never lost my habit of liking to eat out. Remember . . . we used to come down to this part of town and go to restaurants. They used to call it home cooking then . . . now, at least where I been out West and up in Harlem . . . we call it soul food. I bet we could find a nice little restaurant not four blocks from here, Mother. Remember that old man's place we used to go to on Nineteenth and South? I bet he's dead now . . . but . . .

MOTHER   I don't even eat out no more, Michael.

SON   No?

MOTHER   Sometimes I take a piece of holy bread to work . . . or some fruit . . . if it's been blessed by my Spiritual Mother.

SON   I see.

MOTHER   Besides . . . we have a prayer meeting tonight.

SON   On Friday?

MOTHER   Every night. You'll have to be going soon.

SON   Oh.

MOTHER   You're looking well.

SON   Thank you.

MOTHER   But you look tired.

SON   Do I?

MOTHER   Yes, those rings around your eyes might never leave. Your father had them.

SON Did he?

MOTHER Yes . . . and cowlicks . . . deep cowlicks on each side of his head.

SON Yes . . . I remember.

MOTHER Do you?

The BOY *and the* GIRL *take crouching positions behind and in front of them. They are in a streetcar. The* BOY *behind the* MOTHER *and* SON, *the* GIRL *across the aisle, a passenger.*

MOTHER [*young woman to the* BOY] Keep your damn hands off him, Andy!

BOY [*chuckles*] Awww, c'mon . . . Bernie. I ain't seen him since he was in the crib.

MOTHER And you wouldn't have seen neither of us . . . if I had anything to do with it . . . Ohhh . . . why did I get on this trolley?

BOY C'mon . . . Bernie . . . don't be so stuckup.

MOTHER Don't even talk to us . . . and stop reaching after him.

BOY Awww . . . c'mon . . . Bernie. Let me look at him.

MOTHER Leave us alone. Look . . . people are looking at us.

The GIRL *across the aisle has been peeking at the trio but looks toward front at the mention of herself.*

BOY Hey, big boy . . . do you know who I am?

MOTHER Stop it, Andy! Stop it, I say . . . Mikie . . . don't pay any attention to him . . . you hear?

BOY Hey, big boy . . . know who I am? . . . I'm your daddy. Hey, there . . .

MOTHER Shut up . . . shut up, Andy . . . you nothin' to us.

BOY Where you livin' at . . . Bernie? Let me come on by and see the little guy, huh?

MOTHER No! You're not comin' near us . . . ever . . . you hear?

BOY But I'm his father . . . look . . . Bernie . . . I've been an ass the way I've acted but . . .

MOTHER He ain't got no father.

BOY Oh, come off that nonsense, woman.

MOTHER Mikie ain't got no father . . . his father's dead . . . you hear?

BOY Dead?

MOTHER Yes, dead. My son's father's dead.

BOY What you talkin' about? . . . He's the spittin' image of me.

MOTHER Go away . . . leave us alone, Andrew.

BOY See there . . . he's got the same name as me. His first name is Michael after your father . . . and Andrew after me.

MOTHER No, stop that, you hear?

BOY Michael Andrew . . .

MOTHER You never gave him no name . . . his name is Brown . . . Brown. The same as mine . . . and my sister's . . . and my daddy . . . You never gave him nothin' . . . and you're dead . . . go away and get buried.

BOY You know that trouble I'm in . . . I got a wife down there, Bernie. I don't care about her . . . what could I do?

MOTHER [*rises, pulling up the* SON] We're leavin' . . . don't you try and follow us . . . you hear, Andy? C'mon . . . Mikie . . . watch your step now.

BOY   Well . . . bring him around my job . . . you know where I work. That's all . . . bring him around on payday.

MOTHER   [*leaving*]   We don't need anything from you . . . I'm working . . . just leave us alone.

The BOY *turns to the* GIRL.

BOY   [*shrugs*]   That's the way it goes . . . I guess. Ships passing on the trolley car . . . Hey . . . don't.I know you from up around 40th and Market?

The GIRL *turns away.*

SON   Yeah . . . I remember him. He always had liquor on his breath.

MOTHER   Yes . . . he did. I'm glad that stuff ain't got me no more . . . Thank the Lord.

GIRL   [*35 years old*]   You want to pour me another drink, Michael?

BOY   [*15 years old*]   You drink too much, Mother.

GIRL   Not as much as some other people I know.

BOY   Well, me and the guys just get short snorts, Mother. But you really hide some port.

GIRL   Don't forget you talkin' to your mother. You gettin' more like your father every day.

BOY   Is that why you like me so much?

GIRL   [*grins drunkenly*]   Oh, hush up now, boy . . . and pour me a drink.

BOY   There's enough here for me too.

GIRL   That's okay . . . when Will comes in he'll bring something.

SON   How is Will, Mother?

MOTHER   I don't know . . . haven't seen Will in years.

SON   Mother.

MOTHER   Yes, Michael.

SON   Why you and Will never got married? . . . You stayed together for over ten years.

MOTHER   Oh, don't ask me questions like that, Michael.

SON   But why not?

MOTHER   It's just none of your business.

SON   But you could be married now . . . not alone in this room . . .

MOTHER   Will had a wife and child in Chester[2] . . . you know that.

SON   He could have gotten a divorce, Mother . . . Why . . .

MOTHER   Because he just didn't . . . that's why.

SON   You never hear from him?

MOTHER   Last I heard . . . Will had cancer.

SON   Oh, he did.

MOTHER   Yes.

SON   Why didn't you tell me? . . . You could have written.

MOTHER   Why?

SON   So I could have known.

MOTHER   So you could have known? Why?

SON   Because Will was like a father to me . . . the only one I've really known.

MOTHER   A father? And you chased him away as soon as you got big enough.

SON   Don't say that, Mother.

MOTHER   You made me choose between you and Will.

---

2. A town in Delaware to the southwest of Philadelphia.

SON   Mother.

MOTHER   The quarrels you had with him . . . the mean tricks you used to play . . . the lies you told to your friends about Will . . . He wasn't much . . . when I thought I had a sense of humor I us'ta call him just plain Will.[3] But we was his family.

SON   Mother, listen.

MOTHER   And you drove him away . . . and he didn't lift a hand to stop you.

SON   Listen, Mother.

MOTHER   As soon as you were big enough you did all that you could to get me and Will separated.

SON   Listen.

MOTHER   All right, Michael . . . I'm listening.

> *Pause.*

SON   Nothing.

> *Pause. Lifts an imaginary object.*

Is this your tambourine?

MOTHER   Yes.

SON   Do you play it?

MOTHER   Yes.

SON   Well?

MOTHER   Everything I do in the service of the Lord I do as well as He allows.

SON   You play it at your meetings.

MOTHER   Yes, I do. We celebrate the life He has bestowed upon us.

SON   I guess that's where I get it from.

MOTHER   Did you say something, Michael?

SON   Yes. My musical ability.

MOTHER   Oh . . . you've begun taking your piano lessons again?

SON   No . . . I was never any good at that.

MOTHER   Yes, three different teachers and you never got past the tenth lesson.

SON   You have a good memory, Mother.

MOTHER   Sometimes, son. Sometimes.

SON   I play an electric guitar in a combo.

MOTHER   You do? That's nice.

SON   That's why I'm in New York. We got a good break and came East.

MOTHER   That's nice, Michael.

SON   I was thinking that Sunday I could rent a car and come down to get you and drive you up to see our show. You'll get back in plenty of time to rest for work Monday.

MOTHER   No, I'm sorry. I can't do that.

SON   But you would like it, Mother. We could have dinner up in Harlem, then go down and . . .

MOTHER   I don't do anything like that any more, Michael.

SON   You mean you wouldn't come to see me play even if I were appearing here in Philly?

MOTHER   That's right, Michael. I wouldn't come. I'm past all that.

SON   Oh, I see.

---

3. The central character of a popular and long-running radio serial *Just Plain Bill* was presented as a man of good heart but without other characteristics to raise him above the average.

MOTHER Yes, thank the Lord.
SON But it's my life, Mother.
MOTHER Good . . . then you have something to live for.
SON Yes.
MOTHER Well, you're a man now, Michael . . . I can no longer live it for you. Do the best with what you have.
SON Yes . . . Yes, I will, Mother.
GIRL'S VOICE [*offstage*] Sister Brown . . . Sister Brown . . . hello.
MOTHER [*uneasy; peers at watch*] Oh . . . it's Mother Ellen . . . I didn't know it was so late.
GIRL [*enters*] Sister Brown . . . how are you this evening?
MOTHER Oh, just fine, Mother.
GIRL Good. It's nearly time for dinner.
MOTHER Oh, yes, I know.
GIRL We don't want to keep the others waiting at meeting . . . do we?
MOTHER No, we don't.
GIRL [*self-assured*] Hello, son.
SON Hello.
MOTHER Oh, Mother . . . Mother . . .
GIRL Yes, Sister Brown, what is it?
MOTHER Mother . . . Mother . . . this is . . . this is . . .

    Pause.

. . . this is . . .
SON Hello, I'm Michael. How are you?
MOTHER [*relieved*] Yes, Mother . . . This is Michael . . . my son.
GIRL Why, hello, Michael. I've heard so much about you from your mother. She prays for you daily.
SON [*embarrassed*] Oh . . . good.
GIRL [*briskly*] Well . . . I have to be off to see about the others.
MOTHER Yes, Mother Ellen.
GIRL [*as she exits; chuckles*] Have to tell everyone that you won't be keeping us waiting, Bernice.

    Silence.

SON Well, I guess I better be going, Mother.
MOTHER Yes.
SON I'll write.
MOTHER Please do.
SON I will.
MOTHER You're looking well . . . Thank the Lord.
SON Thank you, so are you, Mother.

    He moves toward her and hesitates.

MOTHER You're so much like your aunt. Give her my best . . . won't you?
SON Yes, I will, Mother.
MOTHER Take care of yourself, son.
SON Yes, Mother. I will.

    The SON *exits. The* MOTHER *stands looking after him as the lights go slowly down to* . . .

              BLACKNESS

                                             1968

The Gloaming, Oh My Darling

CHARACTERS

MRS. TWEED	⎫ *Patients in a*	SON *of* MRS. WATERMELLON
MRS. WATERMELLON	⎬ *nursing home*	*His* SON *and* DAUGHTER
MR. BIRDSONG	⎭	DAUGHTER *of* MRS. TWEED
A NURSE		*Her* SON *and* DAUGHTER

Two women sit on two chairs in a nursing home. There are two beds in the small sunny room. One of the beds is occupied, but the sheet and blanket are drawn up over the head of the occupant. The two old women speak in Irish accents.

MRS. TWEED   Ah yes, Mrs. Watermellon, and the days go by and the days go by and the days go by and the days go by, and by and by the days go by. My God, how the days go by!

MRS. WATERMELLON   From where I sit . . . I have to agree with you. But they don't go fast enough by, Mrs. Tweed, not by a half sight, not by a full sight. The world is waiting for the sunrise, and I'm the only one who knows where it begins.

MRS. TWEED   Why do you keep it a secret?

MRS. WATERMELLON   No secret. I've told everyone. I've told and told and told everyone.

MRS. TWEED   Where does it begin then?

MRS. WATERMELLON . . [*slapping her breast*]   Here. Right here. Right here it starts! From the old ticker it starts and pumps around and thumps around, coagulates in my belly and once a month bursts out onto the ground . . . but all the color's gone . . . all but one . . . all but . . . one. . .

MRS. TWEED   So that's where the sunrise went.

MRS. WATERMELLON   You three-minute egg. You runny, puny twelve-week's old, three-minute egg. You're underdone and overripe. What do you know? You only learned to speak when you got mad enough . . . I'm going to sleep. I'd as soon live in the mud with the turtles as to have to converse with the likes of you.

MRS. TWEED   Don't talk like that. That hurts me.

MRS. WATERMELLON   Nothing can hurt you if your mind is on a high plain.

MRS. TWEED   If you go to sleep on me, then I'll let him go.

MRS. WATERMELLON   If you let him go, Mrs. Tweed, then I'll tell you where your daughter is.

MRS. TWEED   I won't listen.

MRS. WATERMELLON   Oh yes, you'll listen. You'll listen to me tell you where she is. It makes you cry and you hate to cry. But once you get started crying you wake up everyone, and then they'll give you an enema.

MRS. TWEED   I don't care if they do. There's nothing more to come out. They've tubed, and they've squirted, and they've radiated and they've intravened . . . There's nothing more to come out of me. I haven't had reason to pick my nose in two years.

MRS. WATERMELLON   Do you think he's awake yet?

MRS. TWEED   Mrs. Watermellon, what if someone comes to visit him?

MRS. WATERMELLON   I won't let them see him.

MRS. TWEED   You have to let them see him if they're his folks.

MRS. WATERMELLON   Nope, you dope, I don't.

MRS. TWEED   You do have to let folks see him. What else would folks be coming up here for, if not to see him.

MRS. WATERMELLON   Perhaps he's passed on—passed over. I'll say he's gone West. Anyway, Mrs. Tweed, he's mine now.

MRS. TWEED   Why, he's ours, Mrs. Watermellon. You can't have him all to yourself!

MRS. WATERMELLON   That's what I did in the night. I didn't want you to find out, but since I see what a busybody you finally are, after all these bygone days, I'll tell you once and for all. He's mine!

MRS. TWEED   But we got him together. I carried the bottom end. You weak old tub, you couldn't even have lifted him from his bed by yourself. You'd have dropped and broken him. They'd have put us in jail for stealing and murder. They'd have electrocuted and hung us . . . they'd have . . .

MRS. WATERMELLON   Hush your mouth! Hush up. I won't have him disturbed by your temper.

MRS. TWEED   I'm going to give him back. Tonight I'll carry him back to the men's ward and tuck him in his crib.

MRS. WATERMELLON   No, you won't. He's mine.

MRS. TWEED   Ours.

MRS. WATERMELLON   Mine.

MRS. TWEED   Ours . . .

MRS. WATERMELLON   All right. All right, you pukey squashed robins egg, all right! All right, all right, you leftover maggot mangy mop rag. All right! All right, you dried-up, old snot rag, I'm going to tell you, I'm going to tell you right here and now. Do you hear me? I'm going to tell you right here and now.

MRS. TWEED   I don't want to hear. Not here. Not now.

A recorded voice of a young woman sings. WATERMELLON and TWEED freeze in their places during the song:

VOICE   "In the gloaming, oh my darling,
When the lights are soft and low,
Will you think of me and love me
As you did once long ago?"[1]

MRS. WATERMELLON   [coming back to life]   I'm hungry for canned rhubarb! Never did get enough. My greedy little sister used to get up in the night when we's all asleep and sneak down to the fruit cellar and eat two quarts of rhubarb, every single night.

MRS. TWEED   She must a had the cleanest bowels in the whole country.

MRS. WATERMELLON   My mother had the best dinner. For her last birthday two days before she died my brother asked her what she wanted. She knew it was her last supper.

MRS. TWEED   Chicken baked in cream in the oven?

MRS. WATERMELLON   Nope, you dope. Pheasant she wanted. Cherry-stone clams, six of them, roast pheasant and wild-blackberry pie. She

---

1. "In the Gloaming" is a famous song, written about 1875 with words by Meta Orred and music by Annie Fortescue Harrison.

ate every bit of it. We watched her. She ate it all up, every speck of it. Cherrystone clams, six of them, roast pheasant, and wild-blackberry pie. Licked her lips.

MRS. TWEED   That rings a bell. I had pheasant once. Pheasant under glass. Looked so pretty, I didn't eat it. Where was that?

MRS. WATERMELLON   You had it at the old Biltmore.[2] She licked her lips and closed her eyes. She never opened them again.

MRS. TWEED   That rings a bell. Who'd I have it with? Did I taste it? Under a lovely glass bell. Who was I with?

MRS. WATERMELLON   You were with your husband, Mrs. Tweed. Your second husband. You did that on your anniversary. On your wedding anniversary, you dope. You've told me every one of your anniversary stories five hundred times a year.

MRS. TWEED   [*laughs*]   It's gone from me. All gone from me. Fancy that, but it does ring a bell.

MRS. WATERMELLON   You can eat mushrooms under glass too. Don't you know?

MRS. TWEED   Myrtle Classen used to serve them at her bridge luncheons. Mushrooms, under glass. I didn't eat any of those either.

MRS. WATERMELLON   What have you done with him, Mrs. Tweed?

MRS. TWEED   I made him even.

MRS. WATERMELLON   *What* have you done with him?

MRS. TWEED   What'll you give me if I tell, Mrs. Watermellon?

MRS. WATERMELLON   Tell.

MRS. TWEED   Give.

MRS. WATERMELLON   Tell.

MRS. TWEED   Give.

MRS. WATERMELLON   Tell, tell.

MRS. TWEED   Give, give.

MRS. WATERMELLON   Tell, tell, tell!

MRS. TWEED   Give, give, give!

MRS. WATERMELLON   [*melting*]   I give.

MRS. TWEED   All up?

MRS. WATERMELLON   All.

MRS. TWEED   Say it. Say it all, Mrs. Watermellon.

MRS. WATERMELLON   I give it all up. I give it all up to my uncle. My uncle. Uncle.

MRS. TWEED   Who is he? Who is he, your uncle, uncle?

MRS. WATERMELLON   [*exhausted*]   You are. You . . . are . . . Mrs. Tweed.

MRS. TWEED   Then you've got to tell me what you did to Mr. Birdsong in the night.

MRS. WATERMELLON   Now?

MRS. TWEED   Not a moment too late.

MRS. WATERMELLON   I . . . I married him. I married Mr. Birdsong.

MRS. TWEED   No.

MRS. WATERMELLON   In the night, I lifted the covers from his body and I married him. Mrs. Birdsong. Mrs.

MRS. TWEED   But he was ours. We brought him here together.

MRS. WATERMELLON   In the night . . .

MRS. TWEED   It isn't fair. You didn't do it fair. He was . . .

MRS. WATERMELLON   I didn't want to do it, because we've been such good, such only friends. But I didn't want to tell you 'cause I don't

2. A famous hotel in New York City.

want you to stop rubbing my back on rainy days. I didn't want to tell you because I didn't want you to stop cleaning my nails on Sunday mornings. I didn't want to tell you because you eat those hard-cooked carrots for me on Wednesday nights. I didn't want to tell you 'cause you rub a nipple and make me feel sweet sixteen when we play boy friends. I didn't want to tell you because you're all I've got . . . you're all I've been given in this last twenty years. You're all I've seen in this never-never. I didn't want to tell you because you're the only one who can see *me*. I didn't want to tell you because you were all I had. But now I've got Mr. Birdsong. Mr. and Mrs. Birdsong.

MRS. TWEED Don't tell me that. You shouldn't have told me that.

MRS. WATERMELLON And you don't even know any good lifetime stories. I've been shut up with a life that never moved at all. The only thing you can remember is how . . .

MRS. TWEED . . . Is how I rode out in the Maine snow night with my *Doctor* Father and he held his fur-coat arms around me on his horse and I sat in front of him with his fur-coat arms around me and I held his scratched and leather smelly doctor's bag. Held it tight so's not to drop it in the Maine snow night.

MRS. WATERMELLON That's what I mean, just one sentimental perversion after another.

MRS. TWEED There's nothing perverted about father love.

MRS. WATERMELLON There is if there's something perverted about Father.

MRS. TWEED Who?

MRS. WATERMELLON You. You. You. Mrs. Tweed.

MRS. TWEED [*trying to rise*] That did it. That did it. That just about did it in, all right.

MRS. WATERMELLON Sit down, you old windbag.

MRS. TWEED That did it. That did it, Mrs. Watermellon. That just about did it in, all right.

MRS. WATERMELLON Sit down, you old battle-ax.

MRS. TWEED [*on a rising scale*] That did it. That did it. That just about did it. That did it all right.

MRS. WATERMELLON Sit down, you old blister.

MRS. TWEED [*bursts*] *That did it!* [*She explodes into a convulsive dance. She sings. As she sings her accent disappears.*]
That's done it, that's better.
That's done it,
What ease.
That's done it,
That's better.
What took you so long,
You tease?

MRS. WATERMELLON Don't leave me. I forbid you to go. Don't leave me, Tweed. Come back. Don't leave me here alone with a man.

MRS. TWEED [*dances herself down to the age of sixteen*] I'm so tired. I'm so tired and so done in. We drank and drank so much grape punch and then that gentle Keith Lewiston took me behind the schoolhouse and you know what he did?

MRS. WATERMELLON He hitched you to his buggy and drove you round the yard.

MRS. TWEED [*embracing her*] He soul kissed me. He kissed my soul. Like this.

.MRS. WATERMELLON [*dodges*]   Don't start that mush again.

MRS. TWEED [*still sixteen*]   He kissed my soul. Like this. [*She plants a kiss finally on* MRS. WATERMELLON's *neck.*]

MRS. WATERMELLON [*starts to howl in pain, but the howl changes to a kind of gargle and then to a girlish laugh. Her accent leaves also*] Did it make a strawberry? Did you make me a strawberry on my neck? [*Now* MRS. WATERMELLON *is also sixteen.*] Do it again and make a big red strawberry mark. Then we'll have to wear long scarves around our necks, to school, but everyone will know why. They'll think the boys kissed us behind the schoolhouse. Is it red yet? Is it strawberry red yet?

MRS. TWEED [*coming back to old age, knots an imaginary scarf around* MRS. WATERMELLON's *neck and her Irish accent returns*]   No—not —yet.

MRS. WATERMELLON [*chokes and laughs as if strangling*]   Don't. We're friends. We're best friends. We're girl friends. [*Her Irish accent returns.*] Don't kill me. I'm your mother.

MRS. TWEED   Save all that for Doctor. I'm on to you. Your smart-assed psycho—hology won't work on me any more. Save it for Mr. Birdsong. *If* you can find him.

MRS. WATERMELLON   What have you done with him?

MRS. TWEED   Wouldn't you like to know.

MRS. WATERMELLON   What have you done with him? What have you done with my . . .

MRS. TWEED   *Your* what?

MR. BIRDSONG [*still in a coma, but speaks out in a voice like W. C. Fields[3]*]   Stuck with the cattle through the storm. Dust blowed so hard couldn't see yer hand in front of yer face. Twister blowed us five hundred miles. Caught us in Illinois and set us down in Nebraska. Dust blowed bad, but I never lost a head nor did I even stop to make water.

MRS. WATERMELLON   I'm tired of trying to keep alive.

MRS. TWEED   We'll get off the shelf.

MRS. WATERMELLON   Canned beside the hybrid corn.

MRS. TWEED   And the pickles.

MRS. WATERMELLON   And the piccalilli.

MRS. TWEED   And the bread and butters.

MRS. WATERMELLON   Apple butter.

MRS. TWEED   Watermelon relish.

MR. BIRDSONG   We kept right on putting our lives on the line because some fool gave the order.

MRS. WATERMELLON   Found a family. All I wanted was to found a great family.

MRS. TWEED   I worked hard. The wire factory gave me a good pension. I could still run up and down ladders as good as the men.

MR. BIRDSONG   The heathens want ours. They've infiltrated us in plain clothes. The heathen emissaries of Satan want to sabotage us. Scorch that earth, boys. That's the ticket. I want to get back to my bride.

MRS. TWEED   No one cares what we do now, Mrs. Watermellon, we can share him. We can both be Mrs. Birdsongs. The Mormons done it and God didn't get mad at them.

MRS. WATERMELLON   In the night I climbed into his bed and married him.

3. A comedian (1880–1946), known for his raspy voice and mordant wit. Many of his classic film performances are still widely shown.

MRS. TWEED [*begins to cry very quietly*]   No. No. No. I can't believe it. You promised we'd share him. And to think I trusted you. And to think I loved you like a dear sister. And to think I gave you all my tender feelings for all these whitehouse years. *And to think . . . and to . . .*

MRS. WATERMELLON   Stop that yipping. It's your own fault. You left me all alone in the night. You went to sleep. You didn't keep watch. You turned out the light and went to sleep. They'd have shot you for that in World War I. You stopped guarding. I had to marry someone! I can't die childless. I refuse!

MRS. TWEED   Impossible! You have eleven children living, forty-nine grandchildren living, twenty great grandchildren living and three on the way. There's a lot of biscuit in your oven, and your ovens' ovens.

MRS. WATERMELLON   I just wanted to make it even with you. You had two husbands, you, you white and wizened shrimp. Two husbands! You knew two cocks of the walk in your time. Why should I take a back seat? Why should you know more than me?

MRS. TWEED   Is that your fountain of knowledge? I'll never get over this. Never, never. After all the friends we've been through. I'm going to divorce you.

MRS. WATERMELLON   I don't care. I'm a newlywed. I have security.

MRS. TWEED   I'll say! There's nothing more secure than a coma. *He's been in that coma for eighty days.*

MRS. WATERMELLON   It'll make our adjustment easier.

MRS. TWEED.   Adjustment?

MRS. WATERMELLON   [*inordinately satisfied*]   To married life. Since only one of us has to change his ways, we should become compatible twice as fast.

MRS. TWEED   [*very formal*]   Mrs. Watermellon, I'm going to ring for the nurse to change my room.

MRS. WATERMELLON   [*equally formal*]   Mrs. Tweed, you better ring for the nurse to change your pants. See there, you've messed again.

MRS. TWEED   You're fooling me.

MRS. WATERMELLON   Maybe I am fooling you, but Mother Nature isn't. Ring for the nurse. Ring, ring, ring, ring, ring, ring. Tick a lock, this is a magic spot.

MRS. TWEED   Don't be mad to me any more.

MRS. WATERMELLON   Tick a lock, this is a magic spot.

MRS. TWEED   Don't be mad to me any more.

MR. BIRDSONG   Everywhere you look there's busloads of foreigners. Rats are infiltrating our ranks.

MRS. TWEED   I hear a man's voice. Listen. Did you hear it?

MRS. WATERMELLON   It's your longing. Your longing rising up and talking to you.

MRS. TWEED   Sounds like my granddad. Just like him when he come back from the war.

MRS. WATERMELLON   I don't hear anything but your heart ticks getting fainter and fainter.

MRS. TWEED   Don't be so nice to me. You know I'm going to die, that's why you're so nice to me.

MRS. WATERMELLON   Nonsense. You're not leaving before me. You're not leaving me alone in this hotel.

MR. BIRDSONG   [MRS. TWEED *and* MRS. WATERMELLON *don't react to* MR. BIRDSONG *when he rises from bed.* BIRDSONG *rises from his bed*

and stalks around the room, mounts a box to harangue the crowd—
his voice now sounds like Teddy Roosevelt[4]] As U.S. veteran of
the Indian Wars, I've come here before you to alarm you. Sons of
Liberty unite. Smash the rats of the world. We must cut off their
bloody hands. They're bringing this land that I love to wreck and
ruin. Wreck and ruin to our God-given America. Murderers of
women and children, red rats making balcony speeches. Balcony
speeches by the feeble-minded mockers of God. That's the stink of
Satan, boys. The stink of the murderers of Americans. The stink
smelled is the stink from Satan. Satan who uses the body as a house
to live in. The stink of Satan once smelled coming from these bodies
is never forgotten. They want to make the United States and
Mexico and Canada and Alaska into a death trap. Declare war on
these stinking infiltrators. They've made it easy to burn up American
bodies in the fiery furnaces of every hospital and prison. American
Veterans of foreign wars, boys. Unite to fight. Unite to fight before
they drug every one of us with their poisoned needles. Every man
has been sexually destroyed by the needle while asleep. Fight the
needle, boys. Don't let them burn up our unborn children. Why was
Roosevelt murdered? Why was Kennedy murdered? Why was
Stevenson murdered?[5] The rat bonecrushers of the world are out to
get us, all us American Veterans captive in these hospital jails. Unite
to fight the rats, boys. Unite to fight the rats. [*He returns to his bed
and his coma.*]

    The woman's voice is heard again.

VOICE   "In the gloaming, oh my darling,
    When the lights are soft and low,
    Will you think of me and love me
    As you did once long ago?"

MRS. WATERMELLON   I love President Kennedy.

MRS. TWEED   Makes you feel good just to look at him.

    NURSE *enters with a fixed smile.* MRS. TWEED *and* MRS. WATER-
    MELLON *rush to hide the man. They both get on the bed and
    spread their nightgowns over him. They lapse into their oldest
    age.*

NURSE   All right, you two—smarten up and look alive. [*She man-
    handles them—pushing and pulling them into some sort of erect
    state. They fall back to position like rag dolls—half cackling and
    half gurgling.*] I said look alive! You're going to have a visit. Your
    families have come to pay their monthly respects. Look alive, I said,
    or they'll think we're not taking good care of you.

MRS. WATERMELLON [*frightened of the* NURSE] This woman's molesting me.

NURSE   Hold your head up so I can get some rouge on that pasty cheek.

MRS. WATERMELLON   This woman is molesting me.

NURSE   Hold still, you old hag. I got to get some life in your face.

MRS. WATERMELLON   I'll tell Dr. Sam on you and Dr. Ben and Dr.
Jim, too, and God and everybody.

---

4. Theodore Roosevelt (1858–1919) first
attained fame as a big-game hunter and
cavalry leader of the Rough Riders at the
Battle of San Juan Hill in 1898. He was
elected Vice President of the United States
in 1900 and succeeded to the presidency
on the death of William McKinley in 1901.
    5. John F. Kennedy (1917–1963), 35th
President of the United States, was assas-

sinated in 1963. The other two persons
mentioned are in the same liberal Democratic tradition as Kennedy: Franklin D.
Roosevelt (1882–1945), 32nd President of
the United States, and Adlai E. Stevenson
(1900–1965), Democratic candidate for
President in 1952 and 1956. Both Roosevelt and Stevenson died natural deaths.

NURSE [*to* MRS. TWEED]   Your turn now, you little old crab.

MRS. TWEED [*playfully*]   What'll you give me if I let ya?

NURSE   Dirty-minded old ladies. If your family could only hear you.

MR. BIRDSONG [*under the ladies, belches*]   I rode five hundred miles with my cattle in the dust storm and never stopped once to make water. [WATERMELLON *mouths the lines.*]

NURSE   Who said that?

MRS. TWEED   She did—she always brags about how strong she used to be.

NURSE   Show me a little strength now. Sit up and look out of your eyes.

MRS. TWEED *bites the nurse; the* NURSE *slaps* TWEED.

NURSE   Now there's some real color in your cheeks.

MRS. WATERMELLON [*howls*]   This woman is molesting us! [*The family enters.*]

NURSE [*like an overly cheerful, demented Katherine Hepburn*]   We're feeling very well today. We're glad to see our family today. [*She exits.*] Our family is glad to see us today.

SON WATERMELLON [*accompanied by his* SON *and* DAUGHTER]   Mother! [*He goes to her, ultrabeaming.*] You look wonderful! Doesn't she look wonderful, kids?

SON *and* DAUGHTER [*flatly*]   You look wonderful. You look wonderful. Grandma, you look wonderful.

MRS. WATERMELLON   Who's there? Is there anyone there? Knock once for yes.

DAUGHTER TWEED [*accompanied by her* SON *and* DAUGHTER, *crosses to* MRS. TWEED]   Oh, Mother, you look wonderful. Doesn't she look just wonderful, kids? Tell Mother how wonderful she looks.

SON *and* DAUGHTER [*Run at* TWEED]   You look wonderful, Grandma— you look just wonderful.

They climb all over her.

MRS. TWEED [*Nearly suffocating*]   My dear children—my pretty grand-children. Grandma loves you so much.

DAUGHTER TWEED [*as children swarm all over* TWEED, *kissing and pum-meling her*]   They love you so much, Mother. Isn't it wonderful for them that you're still alive?

GRANDSON *and* GRANDDAUGHTER TWEED   You feel just wonderful, Grandmother—just wonderful. [*They kiss and hug* TWEED *while she chokes and gasps.*]

SON WATERMELLON   Just sign right here, Mother. Here. I'll hold your hand around the pen.

MRS. WATERMELLON   What is it? Who are you?

SON WATERMELLON   I'm so grateful you haven't lost your sense of humor. Mother, you look downright beautiful. Color in your cheeks and everything. This isn't such a bad place after all, is it?

MRS. WATERMELLON [*knocks once for yes*]   You look a bit familiar around the eyes. I kept company with a young man once had shifty eyes kinda like yours.

SON WATERMELLON [*laughs heartily*]   Did you hear that, kids?

KIDS [*flat and bored*]   Hear what, Father?

SON WATERMELLON   Same old doll. What a doll my dear old mother was and still is. Just like the gal that married dear old Dad.[6]

---

6. A phrase from a song, "I Want a Girl Just like the Girl that Married Dear Old Dad," written in 1911 with words by William Dillon and music by Harry von Tilzer.

KIDS [*flat*]   Dear old shifty-eyed Dad.

SON WATERMELLON   Thanks for signing, honey-love. Makes it a lot easier for me now. Now look, sweetheart—you won't be seeing us for three months or so. Marge and the kids and I are going to Europe, but we'll send you a present from every port. How's about that? Give us a big smile and a kiss goodbye.

MRS. WATERMELLON   Then will you go?

SON WATERMELLON [*hurt*]   Mother! I had to take a day off from work and the kids out of school to drive up here! Marge is stuck with booking the passage.

MRS WATERMELLON [*turns off—sighs—lies back down*]   I'll be all right. Don't worry about me.

SON WATERMELLON   Mother, don't be like this.

MRS. WATERMELLON   Don't worry, son, I won't *be* for much longer.

SON WATERMELLON [*kisses her on cheek*]   Goodbye, old girl.

KIDS   Goodbye, old girl. [*They exit.*]

MRS. WATERMELLON   Is there anyone there?

MRS. TWEED [*to* DAUGHTER]   Dorothy, where's your sister, Laura?

DAUGHTER TWEED   She isn't well, Mother. She has a bad cold. She was afraid she'd give it to you—and with your condition you know it could develop into pneumonia and you know . . . [*She makes an explosive gesture.*]

MRS. TWEED   Well, tell her I thank her for her consideration but I'd like to see her face once in a while.

DAUGHTER TWEED   Well, Mother, we got to be getting back, I guess —got the dogs and cats to feed.

KIDS   They sure do get mad at us if they don't get their dinner on time.

DAUGHTER TWEED   It sure was just wonderful to see you and see how good you look and how happy you look. That old lady who shares the room with you looks quiet and nice, too.

MRS. TWEED   Dorothy—take me home.

DAUGHTER TWEED   You know I'd love to, but you know what I'm up against with Harry.

MRS. TWEED   Dorothy, your children tire me.

DAUGHTER TWEED [*freezing up*]   Goodbye, Mother. I'll see you next month. I thought you'd want to see your own grandchildren.

MRS. TWEED   I've seen enough.

DAUGHTER TWEED [*gathering her children and leaving in a hurt rage*] The sun always rose and set on Laura's head and it still does. And she hasn't been to see you in fifty years.

MRS. WATERMELLON   Is there anyone here?

MRS. TWEED   No, thank God. They've gone.

MRS. WATERMELLON   They didn't take him?

MRS. TWEED   I stopped them from it. I told them he'd eloped with a local tramp.

MRS. WATERMELLON   Where is he now?

MRS. TWEED   Under you, you old tub. I hope you haven't smothered him to death.

MRS. WATERMELLON [*feeling* MR. BIRDSONG]   Here's his head. [*She puts her ear to his chest.*] I hear a beat. Far away—a sweet little beat. [*She lifts the sheet and counts his arms.*] One, two. [*Counts his legs*] One, two. [*Counts his sex.*] One, two, three. I'm glad it has a handle on it. My husband said he wouldn't accept the baby otherwise.

MRS. TWEED   Let me see his tiny hands. Oh, oh, the fingernails! [*She kisses the fingernails of* MR. BIRDSONG.]

MRS. WATERMELLON   Why are you crying? A new baby should fill you with joy. Joy!

MRS. TWEED   These fingernails. Look how tiny, the size of a pin head! And sharp! Oh, oh, the fingernails.

MRS. WATERMELLON   God love him. A new life. God love it, God love it, God love it! [*She cuddles* MR. BIRDSONG.]

MRS. TWEED   God spelled backwards is dog.

MRS. WATERMELLON   A son, a son, we have a son. A son from God. [MR. BIRDSONG *gurgles like an infant.*]

MRS. TWEED   Watch out for the teeth. They grow fast. My left nipple still carries a scar.

MR. BIRDSONG   It was scorch the earth . . . scorch the earth of every village we took. After Lieutenant Pike[7] found his brother scalped and his guts strewn across the plain for the wolves to munch, we were ordered to cut down every peach tree, fill every irrigation ditch —burn every lodge and kill every horse, woman, and child of the Navaho.

MRS. WATERMELLON   He'll make his mother proud.

MRS. TWEED   My turn. [*She takes hold of* MR. BIRDSONG. MRS. WATERMELLON *holds on and glares.*] You act as if you did it all yourself.

MRS. WATERMELLON   I did. It was my idea.

MRS. TWEED   Not even you and forty million prayers could have raised him.

MRS. WATERMELLON   It was my idea. All you were was a pair of arms.

MRS. TWEED   And a good strong back—which you lack.

MR. BIRDSONG [*a young officer returning to Illinois on leave*]   Mother! [*To* MRS. WATERMELLON.] It's fine to be home.

MRS. WATERMELLON   You're thin.

MR. BIRDSONG   Not for long. [*To* TWEED.] And what have we here— grown up and pretty as a prairie flower.

MRS. TWEED [*shyly*]   I can still whip you on a fair day, Elijah.

MR. BIRDSONG [*advancing confidently and taking her wrists*]   'Tis fair today, Susan.

MRS. TWEED [*wilts and nearly swoons*]   Mrs. Watermellon, your son's forgot his manners!

MRS. WATERMELLON   Lige! Leave go this gal or marry her.

MR. BIRDSONG [*to* TWEED]   I stayed with our cattle from here to Nebraska. It was the mightiest dust storm with twisters any man could remember. I rode five hundred miles without stopping to make water. I didn't lose a head. Marry me.

MRS. TWEED   Marry me. Marry me. [*She goes into a slow-motion waltz with* BIRDSONG—MRS. WATERMELLON *joins them—while the voice of a woman sings a verse of "In the Gloaming."*]

MR. BIRDSONG [*they are at a picnic on the grass*]   I have my orders, gals—ship out tomorrow. I'll miss your pretty faces—let's have one last roll.

MRS. TWEED *and* MRS. WATERMELLON   You can't go, Donny—you've only been with us a week.

MR. BIRDSONG   Case you didn't hear it, babes, there's a war on. I

---

7. Zebulon M. Pike (1779–1813) was an American army officer who led expeditions to discover the source of the Mississippi River and to the Southwest, which was then a part of Mexico. He is best remembered as the discover of the mountain in Colorado which bears his name, Pike's Peak.

killed off more than my quota of Huns and now good Old Uncle's sending me against the slants. What a secret weapons to throw at the Japs.

MRS. TWEED *and* MRS. WATERMELLON [*leap on him and roll him around in the grass, kissing and stroking him*] The lucky Japs. The lucky Japs. You come back to us, you big, big stud. You hear, you come back to us.

MR. BIRDSONG I rode all night, couldn't see a thing but I heard 'em. The dust so thick I couldn't make out the body of a single cow—but I felt 'em—five hundred miles into the twister and I never lost a head nor did I even stop to make water.

MRS. TWEED I go out of my mind over a man in uniform.

MRS. WATERMELLON I go into my mind with a man in my bed. [*She gets* MR. BIRDSONG *back to bed.*]

MRS. TWEED They'll catch you.

MRS. WATERMELLON If they catch me—they'll have you too.

MR. BIRDSONG [*as he's being put to bed*] The Navaho all got up in their peaked plumed leather caps, blankets draped and heads held high—looked like a battalion of Roman Legionnaires. I felt time had slipped and slided and folded over—there I am in New Mexico fighting Roman warriors.

MRS. WATERMELLON I can see the sunset, can you?

MRS. TWEED Filters through.

MRS. WATERMELLON The older I get the hotter I like it.

MRS. TWEED You'll love it down below.

MRS. WATERMELLON I'll turn you in. I'll tell the doctor.

MRS. TWEED What could you tell the doctor?

MRS. WATERMELLON How you follow him through the hall. How you don't have any pain in your chest and neck. You just crybaby about it so that he'll lift your nightgown and listen to your heartbeat through your dried-up titties.

MRS. TWEED Yes, it's true. I like that.

MRS. WATERMELLON No decency.

MRS. TWEED Nonsense.

MRS. WATERMELLON Of all the billions of Chinese in the world I have to be incarcerated with you. I served my time in the family way, I earned my arms and legs, I could drive from one town to another and visit New York. You'd think I'd have the right to choose my own cellmate, but no, no, I was placed in a place, it was planned and weighed, and examined, and organized for me. It was arranged. You were arranged for my best interests. I'd kill myself if they'd give me a sharp instrument.

MRS. TWEED Your tongue will do.

MRS. WATERMELLON Living with me has done you some improvement.

MRS. TWEED You could do worse. You could be with balmy Mary McLemon. She spends every day picking nits off her clothes and her roommates. How'd you like her monkey hands and eyes all over you twenty-four hours a day. Or whining Mary McOrange who complains if it's hot and complains if it's cold and complains if the sun comes up and complains if it don't and complains if she's dry and complains if she's wet and complains if she lives and complains if she dies.

MRS. WATERMELLON Maybe I am fooling you, but old Mother isn't. Tick a lock, this is a magic spot.

MRS. TWEED   Don't be bad to me anymore.

MRS. WATERMELLON   Maybe I am fooling you.

MRS. TWEED   Don't be mean to me any more.

MRS. WATERMELLON   Maybe I am fooling you, but I'm not responsible. No, I'm not—not any—any more. I'm not.

MRS. TWEED   I'm going to call your mother. I'll fly her here on a plane and have you committed. I'm going to phone your son. I'm going to fly him here and have you committed. I am. I will. You'll be committed.

MRS. WATERMELLON   Dry up, you old fart. I already am.

NURSE [*entering with tray*]   Time for cream of wheat. [*She smiles as she says this, but her voice is flat and mechanical.* TWEED *and* WATERMELLON *dive for their beds to hide* BIRDSONG *again.*] Time for your creamy wheat. Time for your wheat. Your cream's all gone. Time for the heap, the wheat's all dry. Sit up like good wrinkled girls and dribble it down your chins. Time for your cream of wheat, the sugar's all gone.

MRS. WATERMELLON   I'm tired of being a middleman for that pap. Flush it down the nearest john!

NURSE   I'll eat it myself. I'll eat it all up.

MRS. TWEED   It's worms. Look at her eat the pail full of worms.

MRS. WATERMELLON   You got it all wrong, Tweed. That's the worm and she's eating herself.

MRS. TWEED   Herself. And so she is. And to think of that.

MRS. WATERMELLON   [*laughing and slapping* MRS. TWEED *on a knee*] It's rich and richer and so so rich. I'd not thought it possible, but she's beaten us to it.

MRS. TWEED   Beaten us to it.

MRS. WATERMELLON   Yes, she's beaten us to it. Who'd ever have thought that she'd be the first worm. And she's done it before us.

MRS. TWEED   And we're so much older.

MRS. WATERMELLON   Of course we are. Nobody here could dare to be as old as we are. And look at that. Will you just look at that white worm. She's had the audacity to be a worm before us.

MRS. TWEED   And we're so much older.

NURSE   Time for your heat, the salve's all spread. Time for your bed, the sheet's all red. Time for the heap, the wheat's all cooked. Time for the deep, the syringe is plunged.

MRS. WATERMELLON *and* MRS. TWEED   And we're so much older. Nobody would dare to be as old or older. And we're so much older. [*They hold on to one another.*]

MRS. WATERMELLON   And older.

MRS. TWEED   And older.

MRS. WATERMELLON   In order.

MRS. TWEED   And older.

MRS. WATERMELLON   Tonight we'll be older still.

MRS. TWEED   In order.

MRS. WATERMELLON   If you'll stay up with me all night, then I'll let you.

NURSE   Time for the . . .

MRS. WATERMELLON   Keep right on eating and don't interrupt me.

NURSE   Time for the deep, the syringe is plunged. [*She gives them each a shot.*]

MRS. TWEED [*taking* MRS. WATERMELLON's *hand*]   I won't close an eye.

MRS. WATERMELLON   Swear?

MRS. TWEED   I swear by Almighty God and little Lord Jesus asleep in the hay.

MRS. WATERMELLON   Then I'll take you back.

MRS. TWEED   Do you promise?

MRS. WATERMELLON   I promise.

MRS. TWEED   Is he ours?

MRS. WATERMELLON   Since we're older together in order, then I do believe that we can now share him.

MRS. TWEED   Then I'll take *you* back. The two Mrs. Birdsongs!

NURSE   Time for your milk, the white's at night. Time for the drink to put you in the pink. Time for the chalk, you're in the drink.

MRS. WATERMELLON   [*to the* NURSE]   Will you get out of here? Can't you see you're interfering with a honeymoon?

NURSE   [*smiling, leaves*]   Only a few more to pin, then back to my bin. Time for a sleep, the light's turned out. Time for the deep, the syringe is shoved. [*She's gone.*]

MRS. WATERMELLON *and* MRS. TWEED   [*they turn to one another*]   How do you do, Mrs. Birdsong? How do *you* do, Mrs. Birdsong? [*They begin to laugh and burst out of their age. The Irish accents disappear also.*]
THAT DID IT. THAT DID IT. THANK GOD, THAT DID IT.

They jump like young women, leap, float, bump into each other with gaiety, sing and end in a tumble on the floor.

THAT did it, that's better.
That's done it,
What ease.
That did it, that's done it,
That's better.
What took you so long,
What took you so long,
Whatever on earth took you so long?

Two women sing very slowly in harmony while MRS. TWEED *and* MRS. WATERMELLON *freeze.*

VOICES   "In the gloaming, oh my darling,
When the lights are soft and low,
Will you think of me and love me
As you did once long ago?"

MRS. TWEED *and* MRS. WATERMELLON
YOU TEASE
YOU TEASE
YOU TEASE
WHAT TOOK YOU SO LONG?

They jump up fiercely on the last line, still laughing. But now they change to a blank stare and say the final line in a singsong —death has grabbed them by the back of the neck.

WHAT TOOK YOU SO LONG? SO LONG! SO LONG! SO LONG?

Then happily, saying goodbye—their arms around each other— they look out at the audience and smile.

SO LONG . . .

CURTAIN

1967

The Elements of Drama

1. ACTION

The Greek philosopher Aristotle was the first writer on drama whose work has survived. When he began the definition of tragedy, in *The Poetics*, with the phrase "an imitation of an action," he was using terms so basic that they are difficult to define. The term **imitation** (or **mimesis**) can be applied to all art, for art has some relation to reality, no matter how autonomous it may appear as a creation or as an object of experience. The character of this relation, the nature of the imitation, will vary from art to art, for music imitates reality in a different way from painting or literature. Even within a given art form the mode of imitation varies with the individual artist; Ibsen does not imitate reality in the same way that Shakespeare does. Some ways in which the mode of imitation varies, such as treatment of space and use of speech, are discussed elsewhere in this volume.

The playwright imitates by using a series of simulated events which are arranged to make a meaningful whole. The term **action** can be used for one of the events or for the whole series. This action characteristically involves a **conflict** or struggle between two persons, groups of persons, or forces which seems to be moving toward resolution, gaining intensity and complication, until the turning point (**climax** or **peripety**; see STRUCTURE) when the direction of the action changes.

The term **plot** generally refers to the arrangement of the action, the selection and ordering of events which make up the play. When the arrangement involves two or more series of events, which may be more or less discrete, the principal series is referred to as the plot and the other (or others) as the **subplot**.

2. AUDIENCE

When writing, the playwright assumes that some audience will see his play; the character of that audience will be determined, of course, by the social conditions of its age and by the kind of play. In Shakespeare's time early theaters like the Globe, where his works were performed, were open-air structures on the south bank of the Thames, across from London proper. The afternoon performances there drew a more general audience, including poor and uneducated elements of the populace, than the later indoor theaters like the Blackfriars, where some of his later plays were performed and where a sophisticated and affluent audience attended. Some individuals were part of both groups, just as in our time. In the New York theater the audiences for Broadway, Off-Broadway, and Off-Off-Broadway theaters may be as diverse as the plays presented. In cities outside New York there are different, and overlapping, audiences for touring companies with "name" stars,

for local repertory or little theater groups, and for avant-garde or university theater groups.

An equally important distinction in this century has to do with the theoretical notions about the relations between the play and the audience. Four of these are of some importance.

The oldest, and probably still the most widespread, is the attitude of the commercial or "Broadway" theater, where the emphasis is on entertaining the audience, without much consideration of the audience's engagement in the play. The audience sits in the dark and responds. If it is amused, it applauds; if not, there are other ways of indicating its feeling. Entertainment value is not necessarily diminished —it may even be increased—if the audience becomes emotionally involved with the action or the characters, but entertainment comes first.

In the "serious" theater, by contrast, major playwrights, directors, and actors have worked generally toward empathy between the audience and the play, the audience responding to what it sees and hears by experiencing sympathetic emotions toward what is represented on stage. A major influence here is the rise of "The Method," a technique of acting based on or derived from the work of the Russian director Constantin Stanislavsky. In his productions with the Moscow Art Theater around the turn of the century, and particularly in the plays of Chekhov, Stanislavsky taught his actors to feel the emotions of the character rather than to play them and to feel them so intensely that the audience must also feel them. Physical methods such as the theater-in-the round or the thrust stage (see STAGE) help increase the empathy.

A later development in the serious theater toward audience detachment is associated with Bertolt Brecht, who first came into prominence in the 1920s. Brecht was reacting against Stanislavsky, and recently many others have joined the reaction. In his analytical or **epic theater,** Brecht worked to achieve as much detachment of the audience from the stage action as was possible. Then the audience could apply its intellect to the analysis and criticism of what is presented, without the distorting effects of emotional response. Methods of staging and acting should be conducive to the desired **A-effect** or **alienation effect,** a distancing of the audience from the action which permits rational and objective response.

The most recent development in this area aims at mutual participation between the audience and the stage. Still largely limited to the "avant-garde," this style is associated with Antonin Artaud and Jerzy Grotowski. For their followers the stage and the auditorium are regarded as a single theatrical environment in which the actors are the priests and acolytes of a theatrical ritual in which the members of the audience are communicants. The actors may invade the seating areas, and in some cases the audience is invited to take part in the action. Ideally the separation between the stage and auditorium and between actor and audience should disappear.

3. CHARACTER

Most simply a **character** is one of the persons who appears in the play, one of the **dramatis personae** (literally, the persons of the play). In another sense of the term, the treatment of character is a basic part of the playwright's work. Conventions of the period and the author's personal vision will affect the treatment of character. Both Gregers Werle in *The Wild Duck* and Pentheus in *The Bacchae* are partially defined by their relation to their mothers. In Ibsen the relation is described in psychological terms, which though pre-Freudian, express a view of character common in Ibsen's time and in our own. Euripides represents the relation through visual means, having Pentheus put on one of his mother's dresses and ask Dionysus if the resemblance is not striking.

Most plays contain major characters and minor characters. The delineation and development of major characters is essential to the play; the conflict between Hamlet and Claudius depends upon the character of each. A minor character like Marcellus serves a specific function, to inform Hamlet of the appearance of his father's ghost. Once that is done, he can depart in peace, for we need not know what sort of person he is or what happens to him. The distinction between major and minor characters is one of degree, as the character of Horatio might illustrate.

The distinction between heroes (or heroines) and villains, between good guys and bad guys, between virtue and vice is useful in dealing with certain types of plays, but in many modern plays (and some not so modern) it is difficult to make. Is Gregers Werle in *The Wild Duck,* for example, a hero or a villain?

Another common term in drama is **protagonist**. Etymologically it means the first contestant. In the Greek drama, where the term arose, all the parts were played by one, two, or three actors (the more actors, the later the play), and the best actor, who got the principal part(s), was the protagonist. The second best actor was called the **deuteragonist**. Ideally, the term "protagonist" should be used only for the principal character. Several other characters can be defined by their relation to the protagonist. The **antagonist** is his principal rival in the conflict set forth in the play. A **foil** is a character who defines certain characteristics in the protagonist by exhibiting opposite traits or the same traits in a greater or lesser degree. A **confidant(e)** provides a ready ear to which the protagonist can address certain remarks which should be heard by the audience but not by the other characters. In *Hamlet,* for example, Hamlet is the protagonist, Claudius the antagonist, Laertes and Fortinbras foils (observe the way in which each goes about avenging the death or loss of property of his father), and Horatio the confidant.

Certain writers—for example, Molière and Pirandello—use a character type called the **raisonneur,** whose comments express the voice of reason and also, presumably, of the author.

Another type of character is the **stereotype** or stock character, a character who reappears in various forms in many plays. Comedy is

a particularly fruitful source of such figures, including the *miles gloriosus* or boastful soldier (a man who claims great valor but proves to be a coward when tested), the irascible old man (the source of elements in the character of Polonius), the witty servant, the coquette, the prude, the fop, and others. A stock character from another genre is the **revenger** of Renaissance tragedy. The role of Hamlet demonstrates how such a stereotype is modified by an author to create a great role, combining the stock elements with individual ones.

Sometimes groups of actors work together over a long period in relatively stable companies. In such a situation individual members of the group develop expertise in roles of a certain type, such as **leading man** and **leading lady** (those who play the principal parts), **juveniles** or **ingénues** of both sexes (those who specialize as young people), **character actors** (those who perform mature or eccentric types), and **heavies** or villains.

The **commedia dell'arte,** a popular form of the late Middle Ages and early Renaissance, employed actors who had standard lines of business and improvised the particular action in terms of their established characters and a sketchy outline of a plot. Frequently, Pantalone, an older man, generally a physician, was married to a young woman named Columbine. Her lover, Harlequin, was not only younger and more handsome than her husband but also more vigorous sexually. Pantalone's servants, Brighella, Truffaldino, and others, were employed in frustrating or assisting either the lovers in their meetings or the husband in discovering them.

A group of actors who function as a unit, called a **chorus,** was a characteristic feature of the Greek tragedy. The members of the chorus shared a common identity, such as Asian Bacchantes or old men of Thebes. The **choragos** (leader of the chorus) sometimes spoke and acted separately. In some of the plays the chorus participated directly in the action; in others they were restricted to observing the action and commenting on it. The chorus also separated the individual scenes by singing and dancing choral odes, though just what the singing and dancing were like is uncertain. The odes were in strict metrical patterns; sometimes they were direct comments on the action and characters, and at other times they were more general statements and judgments. A chorus in the Greek fashion is not common in later plays, although there are instances such as T. S. Eliot's *Murder in the Cathedral,* in which the Women of Canterbury serve as a chorus.

On occasion a single actor may perform the function of a chorus, as do the aptly named Chorus in Shakespeare's *Henry V* and the Stage Manager in Thornton Wilder's *Our Town.*

4. DIALOGUE

The formal principle of drama is **dialogue,** the imitation of speech, customarily involving two or more persons. Dialogue will have some relation to real speech, but the character of that relation will vary greatly. In his translation of *The Misanthrope* Richard Wilbur uses

heroic couplets to reproduce the effect of Molière's language. Obviously, few real people even in 17th-century France spoke in such a way. The form allows for various rhetorical figures, including one particular to the drama, **stichomythia**, in which two characters exchange short lines of similar structure, as in this exchange:

> ORONTE   If, weighing us, she leans in your direction . . .
> ALCESTE   If she regards you with the least affection . . .
> ORONTE   I swear I'll yield her to you there and then.
> ALCESTE   I swear I'll never see her face again.

Similar kinds of poetic dialogue—that is, speech which has metrical patterns and which is therefore obviously not like real speech—can be seen in Shakespeare and Euripides. Dialogue which aims at reproducing with high accuracy the cadences and patterns of actual speech can be seen in many modern plays; writers like Pirandello and Ibsen imitate actual speech more closely than the writers of poetic dialogue. Within the framework of his characteristic mode of writing dialogue, an author will also write dialogue for an individual character which will set him apart from the others. Examples can be seen in the speeches of Gina in *The Wild Duck* and the gravediggers in *Hamlet*.

Aside from dialogue in general, there are several special uses of stage speech. Occasionally, only one character will speak. A **monologue** is a stage piece written for one character, a relatively rare type of play. More important are the **soliloquy**, which was common in Shakespeare and his contemporaries, in which a single character is left on stage and speaks, and the **aside**, generally associated with 19th-century melodrama, in which a character speaks but cannot be heard by the other characters.

Another special form of dialogue, which is sometimes met in the modern drama, is that in which speech is addressed directly to the audience. In older plays this occurs most frequently in prologues or epilogues (see DIVISION), where the actor may speak in his own person, as was frequent in Restoration drama, or in his dramatic role as Dionysus does in *The Bacchae*. Sometimes a character may turn during the action and speak directly to the audience, or he may drop his role and speak directly to the audience. Both of these tactics occur in Thornton Wilder's *The Skin of Our Teeth*, which also includes scenes in which several actors drop their roles and speak to each other as actors.

5. DIVISION

Most plays can be divided into parts. The basic division is the **act**, either a series of actions occurring in a single place within a consecutive time span or a series of actions separated from the remainder of the play by purely formal considerations. Because Horace in his *Ars Poetica* recommended five acts, most European plays from the 16th to 19th centuries were divided into five acts. For writers like

Shakespeare, whose plays were performed without intervals and with changes of place and time within the presentation, the act divisions seem generally to have been inserted to bring the plays in line with Horace's mandate. Some of the plays, notably *Henry V*, however, do seem to have acts with an organic character.

Greek tragedies and medieval mysteries are examples of plays written in one part, but in each case the play was conceived as a part of a larger structure. The tragedies were performed in groups of three followed by a farcical piece or **satyr play**. The mysteries were presented in cycles, some of which included twenty or more plays, presented consecutively in one day. The Greek tragedies had a formal division into a series of episodes, separated by the choral odes. A mystery play might have more informal divisions, as the three parts of *The Second Shepherds' Play* with scenes on the heath, at Mak's house, and at the stable in Bethlehem.

Playwrights in recent centuries have written **one-act plays**, short plays intended to serve as part of an evening's entertainment. These plays may have formal divisions such as the three scenes of Shaw's *A Village Wooing*, or informal ones such as the two parts of Strindberg's *Miss Julie*, which are separated by a ballet.

A formal division within an act is usually called a **scene**. The term may indicate real differences in time and place, as in *Hamlet,* or may be used for merely formal divisions like those in Molière's comedies, where. as in other French plays, a new scene begins with any entrance or exit of a major character.

The term **part** is used instead of act in some contemporary plays. *The Glass Menagerie* of Tennessee Williams consists of a series of scenes which are more or less closely related episodes of varying length. The scenes are grouped into two parts to allow for an **intermission** or pause in the action. Eugene O'Neill divided *Desire Under the Elms* into three parts, rather than acts, apparently to indicate that each is more self-contained and less closely related to the others than is customary.

Just as some plays are shorter than the length of an average performance, others exceed that length. Such superplays may involve an unusual number of acts, like O'Neill's *Strange Interlude* or a series of smaller "plays," like the five which make up Shaw's *Back to Methuselah*. Such longer plays may be presented in a single day, usually with an extra-long intermission to allow the audience time for a meal, as O'Neill did with *Strange Interlude,* or over a period of several days, as is customary with Richard Wagner's *The Ring of the Nibelung.*

The terms **prologue** and **epilogue** were used by the Greeks to indicate respectively portions of the play before the entrance of the chorus and after their final speech. Later the terms were used for speeches before and after the action, usually addressed to the audience and frequently making some comment about the play itself. The terms may also be used for action widely separated in time from the rest of the play, as in the prologue to Williams' *Summer and Smoke* and the epilogue to Shaw's *Saint Joan.*

6. EFFECT

Certain events in the drama produce the kind of immediate effect in moving the audience strongly which is called **theatrical** or **histrionic.** Aristotle cited the **scene of suffering** and the **scene of recognition** (anagnorisis). The recognition scene is particularly dramatic because the recognition or discovery of the person or fact will automatically change the situation; a recognition scene without its peripety (see STRUCTURE) is hard to imagine. The discovery or recognition may be of a person, as in the brothel scene in *Six Characters,* or of a piece of information. The scene of suffering, often communicated in heightened language, provides an opportunity for the audience to share the feelings of the characters. The appearance of Hjalmar and Gina with the dead body of their child at the end of *The Wild Duck* can hardly fail to move the audience. Many such scenes are related to violence, either offstage, as in *The Wild Duck,* or onstage, as in *Hamlet.* If tastefully and skillfully used, the scene of violence is also powerful theatrically. If there is too much strawberry jam posing as blood, or if it is too obviously strawberry jam, the effect will be dissipated.

Another kind of theatrical effect depends on surprise. The entrance of Madame Pace is an example of a skillfully constructed **coup de théâtre.** An example of a humorous use of the device is the first appearance of Cleopatra in Shaw's *Caesar and Cleopatra.* The interruption of Caesar's windy rhetoric by her "Psst! Old Gentleman!" deflates the conqueror of the world and surprises and delights the audience. A different kind of stage effect is the **deus ex machina.** The name comes from the appearance in the Greek drama of a "god," lowered in a piece of stage machinery, who by his unexpected and often improbable actions straightens out the complications of the plot to provide a suitable conclusion. Examples which do not involve such spectacular devices can be seen in Cusins' announcement that he is a "foundling" in *Major Barbara* or the appearance of the king's messenger in Molière's *Tartuffe.*

Another kind of theatrical effect is based on actualizing some potentiality in the play. When they learn that both the elder Werle and Hedvig in *The Wild Duck* are losing their eyesight, for example, most playgoers will expect more or less consciously that Hjalmar will somehow get the news about Werle. When Mrs. Sørby tells him, the expectation is realized. The term **foreshadowing** is sometimes used for such an effect. **Dramatic irony** is a similar effect in which a character says something with one meaning or with reference to other persons which comes true in another sense or in his own case.

7. GENRE

The notion of **genre** recognizes that certain significant groupings of plays can be made. Aristotle in the *Poetics* attempted to define the kind of play which can be called **tragedy.** Much later dramatic criticism has returned to restate or redefine what Aristotle said. I can-

not here even summarize the various positions, but I will excerpt what seem to me the elements of tragedy.

Basic to tragedy is an order of values which transcends man and which man should obey. Among the Greeks this order rested on the notion of fate, among the Elizabethans on the notion of a highly structured universe in which the individual's place is determined, and among the French classical writers on a concept of honor and duty. A great individual, usually one of high rank, transgresses this order out of **hubris** (or **hybris**), the tendency of the will or the passion of man to step outside the prescribed limits. From this transgression come the tragic events of the work, the result of the order reasserting itself to punish the individual. The proper end of tragedy is the hero's realization that he has transgressed and that his troubles are the result of his guilt. Oedipus achieves a tragic realization which gives dignity and serenity to his exit at the end of *Oedipus Tyrannus*. Two other important terms used by Aristotle are **catharsis** (or **katharsis**), the effect of tragedy on the audience of purging it of such emotions as pity and fear, and **hamartia**, a flaw in an otherwise noble nature—for example, Othello's jealousy.

The history of the drama has included three great tragic periods, the England of Shakespeare, the Athens of Sophocles, and the France of Corneille and Racine. In other periods literary persons have written imitations of these great tragedies or have tried to fit the works of their own time into the definition. Several major contemporary writers seem to have sought to achieve tragic form. The degree of their success is a matter of opinion, but several factors may contribute to the many apparent failures, including the lack of heroic individual figures and the absence of a widely held system of values which transcend man and which can punish transgressors on this earth.

Although it is usually regarded as the polar opposite of tragedy, **comedy** has proved more difficult to define. As a kind of play, comedy is concerned with a system of social, rather than metaphysical, values. A fairly typical plot concerns a young man who is prevented at first from making a suitable marriage but who after difficulty does marry the right girl and is thereby reconciled to his society and restored to his appropriate place in it.

As a mode of apprehending reality, the **comic** is different from, but not inimical to, tragedy. The comic is easy to recognize but difficult to define. Why is it funny for a pompous, middle-aged gentleman, preferably with a top hat, to slip on a banana peel but not funny for an 84-year-old woman walking with a cane to do the same thing? Perhaps the answer is that in first case we see the event in two perspectives. The man seems prosperous and immune to silly accident, but the banana peel exists to remind us that he is only human beneath the signs of prosperity and the air of invulnerability. Only his dignity is likely to be harmed. In the case of the elderly woman, however, her age and condition remind us of her fragility and the real dangers of the accident. We see the event in only one perspective.

The great ages of tragedy have generally been also great eras of

comedy, perhaps because the assumption of established values which is necessary for tragedy is so important for comedy. The lack of such values in our century may explain our lack of true comedy as well as tragedy. Both tragedy and comedy contain more particular kinds. *Hamlet,* for example, belongs to the specific group of **revenge tragedies,** in which the duty to avenge close relatives is a part of the universal order. In the **comedy of manners,** the society represented is composed of persons of wealth, rank, and lack of real occupation, along with occasional servants. These plays are posited on the values of the highly artificial group called high society, with emphasis on wit, the importance of reputation, and the need for secrecy in love affairs. Other common types of comedy are the **comedy of humors,** which is based on a character whose personality is dominated by a single trait, and the **comedy of intrigue,** in which complications of plot and situation are dominant. Another way of discussing comedies divides them into **low comedies,** which depend on vulgar or obscene language and on vigorous physical actions such as pie-throwings, and **high comedies,** which use more elegant language and refined gestures.

The terms **melodrama** and **farce** are used for two large groups of plays which are rather like, respectively, tragedy and comedy, but which are generally regarded as inferior to the other kinds. In both of these "lower" forms, the emphasis is on situation rather than character, events being brought about usually by outside forces rather than the necessities of the individual's personality, and the plot is more episodic.

Two other kinds which bear certain resemblances to comedy are **satire** and **romance.** In both cases, the term is more widely used outside the drama but is sometimes used in dramatic criticism. What the two groups share is their dependence on values other than those of the society which they represent. In satire, the values of the society are the object of attack, in contrast to comedy, where those values are endorsed. One feature of romance is a suggestion that at least one of the characters, like Prospero in *The Tempest,* is aware of and lives by another and higher system of values than that of the society.

A more important group of plays for students of recent drama has affinities with tragedy without being tragedy. They deal in general with life on earth, with metaphysical values either not considered or denied and without endorsing social values. The French term **drame** has been offered as a name for such serious but nontragic plays which do not fit other categories. Others refer to them as **tragicomedies,** though they are not a mixture of tragedy and comedy, but a third something which is neither. Within this area we can distinguish the **problem play,** which treats some social issue, as Ibsen's *A Doll's House* treats the legal position of women, and the **domestic tragedy** (or **bourgeois drama**), in which the central character lacks the insight or heroic stature expected of a tragic hero, as in Arthur Miller's *Death of a Salesman.*

Other generic terms used in the drama are **masque** and **chronicle**

play or **history play.** The masque was generally allegorical in plot and character and relied heavily on elaborate pageantry, including rich costumes, music, dancing, and spectacular sets and stage effects. Many masques were written to commemorate historical events. The chronicle play attempts to imitate historical events and to examine their relation to one another in dramatic terms.

8. GESTURE

The play even on the page contains material for generating the nonverbal elements of the drama. Some of these are prepared and set up before the performance begins, such as make-up, costumes, and sets. Others are prepared beforehand but occur during the performance and are controlled from outside the acting area, such as background music, sound effects, and lighting. All of these might be classed under Aristotle's term **spectacle.**

The other kind of gestural elements occur only during the performance even though they are also set up beforehand. The way in which the actor speaks a given line is a kind of gesture which borders on the verbal. Inflection, loudness, and tempo of speech are on the page only implicitly, and the realization in sound of the speeches greatly influences the character of the performance and its effect on the audience. Generally, for example, in performances of *Hamlet,* Claudius screams for light and runs from the stage, but in at least one version he spoke quietly with a tone of command and moved off stage in a stately manner. Here both the sound of the speech and the accompanying movement contribute to a different understanding of the scene.

The example just noted shows how closely related stage movement is to the words and the way they are spoken. The positions of the actors on stage and their movement from place to place are as important an interpretive element as the spectacle and the interpretation of the speeches. Some of the positions and movements are implicit in the text, as Hamlet's physical isolation from the other members of the court when he first appears. At other times the positions and movements are chosen by the director and his colleagues at rehearsal. The pattern of positions and movements is called the **blocking.** In any single performance of a production there will be small departures from the pre-arranged pattern. However, the overall pattern is generally adhered to because of its significance to the understanding of the play. The term **business** is used for a movement or gesture which occurs at an appropriate point. For example, when Ophelia is set to entrap Hamlet, her business is to walk, to carry a book, and to pretend to be reading.

Action without words is called **pantomime.** The term is also used for an entire play which is presented without words. Such a play may also be called a **mime show.** The term **mime** is used for an actor who specializes in acting without using words and for his art. A special kind of silent performance is the **dumb show,** as in *Hamlet* and other plays of the period. Usually this section of the play introduces the play or a part of it and previews the action to come.

9. LITERARY MOVEMENTS

The history of the drama is partly concerned with the rise and fall of literary movements, some based on dominant styles such as the highly artificial linguistic structures of Euphuism, others on dominant forms such as the comedy of manners of the Restoration period, and others on sets of esthetic principles such as Symbolism. Movements can be traced in every period, but because of the content of this collection, those of the modern period can be traced more easily.

Studies of the modern drama frequently begin with the middle period plays (1870–80) of Henrik Ibsen. The increasing importance of science in explaining man and his environment and the development of such art forms as photography contributed to the rise of **realism,** a literary mode which strives to render persons and things in a manner as lifelike as possible. The expression of this striving in such plays as *The Wild Duck* and *Three Sisters* is typical of this dominant mode of the last hundred years.

Among the reactions to realism, **expressionism** has had the greatest and most lasting influence. The expressionist takes men, events, and things and arranges them not as they exist in the real world but in new ways, distortions of reality which express the artist's individual vision. The movement began with Strindberg and continues to our own time in various forms. The German playwright Bertolt Brecht has been a particularly influential figure in the survival of this dramatic mode.

The major ideological forces in the theater have been the rise of Existentialism and the works of the Italian playwright Luigi Pirandello. Although he was not a systematic philosopher, Pirandello gave dramatic form to a number of important ideas, many of which are the same as or very close to Existentialism: (1) It is impossible to know absolute truth, even if it exists; (2) the personality is the sum of one's experience and therefore constantly changing because every new experience modifies it; (3) language is dangerous because when I use a word, the meaning I ascribe to it is determined by my experience, and when another person hears it, he interprets it in terms of his own different set of experiences; (4) in dealing with each other, men build up **masks** to hide their real selves and thus render real communication impossible. Such ideas have been important in movements like **surrealism** and **dadaism** during the 1920s and the **theater of the absurd** of the 1950s.

An important development in recent years stems from Artaud's **theater of cruelty** and Grotowski's **poor theater.** Plays like the last two in this book are written and performed in ways which stress the ritual and communal aspects of the drama.

10. MYTH

Myth originally meant a story of communal origin which provided an explanation or religious interpretation of man, nature, the universe, and the relation between them. Most frequently the term was applied to the stories of other peoples and therefore implied that

the story was false. However, research in anthropology and comparative religion have revealed underlying identities in myths of diverse places and cultures. The term itself came to be applied to the shared pattern of these stories, whether the individual stories come from the communal experience of a primitive tribe or from the pen of a sophisticated writer. Myth-making is a basic human activity. Myths are not "true" or "false"; they are an expression of that activity. At some level the construction of a dramatic plot will involve elements of myth.

The term **archetype** is widely used to refer to common "mythical" elements in literature, in character, and in plot construction. The term is frequently associated with the Swiss psychologist Carl G. Jung, who used it for the expressions in conscious form of the contents of the "collective unconscious," a part of the unconscious which he posited as being inherited and being held in common by all men. Those who reject the idea of collective unconsciousness suggest that the appearance of archetypal material in diverse cultures may be due to its transmission from one culture to another or to the similarity of human experience in different parts of the world.

The terms **symbol** and **allegory** are related to myth in that they refer to ways of talking about some higher (nonrational, nonconcrete, abstract or religious) reality in concrete ways. Unlike myth, however, they are the products of an individual maker rather than a communal expression. The easiest distinction between symbol and allegory is that in the latter a simple equation can be set up between the object and that which it represents—for example, Spenser's Una = Truth, whereas that for which a symbol stands eludes precise definition. This distinction is unfair to Spenser, since many of his allegorical figures have more than one meaning. The allegorist would tend to regard the surface of the work as a pleasant veil which makes the hidden meaning more palatable, whereas the symbolist would tend to regard the surface as the best, perhaps the only, expression of the unique vision of the artist. Some recent critics seem to regard "symbol" as a term of praise and "allegory" as a term of opprobrium.

The terms **natural symbol** or **conventional symbol** are used for certain common symbolic patterns. The rose is frequently a symbol for beauty on the probable but unprovable assumption that everyone finds roses beautiful. In Western writing the horse is frequently a symbol of sexuality, an identification which Swift used ironically in *Gulliver's Travels*. A **personal symbol** is one set up by an individual author for his own use, as Blake or Yeats did.

The term **ritual**, like myth, refers to communal experience. The drama rose from the rituals of Dionysus and the medieval Christian church. A ritual is a ceremony in which an act or a series of acts are performed on repeated and significant occasions and which is performed with certain elements of exact repetition. Ceremonies in general involve such repetition.

11. RULES

Critics of certain periods have talked about the "correct" way to write a play—that is, a series of rules to which an author should

adhere. Experience has never justified the need of rules. Great writers have written "correctly" as Racine did or "incorrectly" as Shakespeare did.

Among the most famous rules are the three unities of action, place, and time. **Unity of action** requires that the events of the play constitute a single whole, but the term has been understood to refer to a single chain of causes and effects as in *The Bacchae*, several series of events involving the same character as in *Hamlet*, or a series of apparently diverse events which contribute to a central focus as in *Three Sisters*. **Unity of place** requires a single scene as in *The Bacchae* or several scenes closely related in place as in *Three Sisters*. In modern staging conditions, a single setting is often an economic necessity rather than an artistic one. **Unity of time** requires that the elapsed time on stage should not exceed one day, or a little more. *The Bacchae* and *The Wild Duck* have unity of time, whereas *Hamlet* and *Three Sisters* do not.

Three other terms used in talking about the drama may be considered under this heading. Aristotle recommended that tragedy have **probability**, that events follow one another in rational, cause-and-effect order, that unexpected or unprepared-for events be excluded. Characters should observe **decorum**, dressing, speaking, and behaving in a manner appropriate to their rank, age, sex, and previously established traits of character. A play itself should observe **verisimilitude**, for no matter how fantastic the events on stage, they should seem true to the audience.

12. STAGE

In performance a play takes place on a **stage** or acting area, whose design and significance varies in different times and places. In the Greek theater, the audience was seated on a raised semicircle of seats (**amphitheater**) halfway around a circular area (**orchestra**) used primarily for dancing by the chorus. At the back of orchestra was the **skene** or stage house which represented the palace or temple before which the action took place. Shakespeare's stage, in contrast, basically involved a rectangular area built up within a generally round enclosure, so that the audience was on three sides of the principal acting area. However, there were subsidiary acting areas on either side as well a recessed area at the back of the stage which could represent Gertrude's chamber in *Hamlet* or the cave in *The Tempest* and an upper acting area which could serve as Juliet's balcony.

Modern stages are of three types. The **proscenium** stage evolved during the nineteenth century and is still the most common. For such a stage, the proscenium or proscenium arch is an architectural element which separates the auditorium from the stage and which makes the action seem more real because the audience is viewing it through an invisible fourth wall. The proscenium stage lends itself to the use of a curtain which can be lowered and raised or closed and parted between acts or scenes. Sometimes a part of the acting area is on the auditorium side of the proscenium. Such an area is an **apron** or forestage. In an **arena stage**, however, the audience is seated around the acting

area. Entrances and exits are made through the auditorium, and restrictions on the sets are required to insure visibility. The third type of modern stage is the **thrust stage,** in which the audience is seated around three-fourths of the major acting area. All of the action may take place on this projecting area, or some may occur in the extended area on the fourth side.

The proscenium stage has been so dominant in the last hundred years that most stage directions assume it. **Right** and **left** (or **stage right** and **stage left**) assume that the actor is facing the audience directly and mean those directions as perceived by the actor looking through an invisible fourth wall. **Downstage** means nearer the audience, and **upstage** means farther from the audience.

Mise-en-scène refers to the nonpersonal elements of the dramatic presentation, including lighting, costumes, setting, make-up, and properties. **Properties** (or **props**) differ from parts of the setting because they are required by the action. In Ibsen's *Hedda Gabler,* for example, the stage directions call for a picture of Hedda's father above the mantel and a set of pistols which had belonged to him. The picture is a part of the setting because no speech or action refers to it, and the play can be given without it. The pistols, however, are props because Hedda gives one of them to Eilert Lovborg in Act 3 and shoots herself with the other in the final act.

13. STRUCTURE

The action of a play generally falls into five parts, which may or may not coincide with the division into acts and scenes.

The first of these, the **exposition,** presents the situation as it exists at the opening of the play, introducing the characters and defining the relationships among them.

The second part of a play, the **rising action,** consists of a series of events which complicate the original situation and create conflicts among the characters. In *The Bacchae,* for example, the complications include the decision of Cadmus and Teiresias to join the Bacchic worship, the arrest of Dionysus, and the miracle which brings about his release.

During the rising action, the flow of the action is in a single direction, but at some crucial moment an event occurs which changes the direction of the action. This is the third part of the play, the **climax** or **turning point.**

The fourth part of a play is the **falling action,** the changes which characterize the unwinding or unknotting of the complications. Generally the falling action requires less time than the rising action.

The final part of the play is its **conclusion** or **catastrophe.** The conclusion reestablishes a stable situation to end the drama.

The term **denouement** is frequently used by writers about dramatic structure, but some of them use it for the falling action and others for the conclusion or catastrophe.

List of Terms Defined

The Limits
of
Literature

Preface

The division of sections earlier in this volume has assumed generic distinctions between fiction, poetry, and drama, and the prefaces to the genres have attempted to define attributively the nature of each genre. Literature is most often taught by genres, and most of us compare a story to other stories, a poem to other poems, and a play to other plays. But literature does not have to be discussed within generic compartments. The most common way of crossing generic lines is through subject matter or theme, and the works in this section—a story, several poems, and a play—all are concerned with the nature of language and its viability as a means of communication between artist and audience. They may be considered together as treatments of this subject, outside formal and generic considerations, or as examples of how genre refines a subject by its own characteristics or limitations.

Several of the works included here also push at the limits of their own genre. *Pierre Menard, Author of the Quixote*, though it does not resemble a poem or play in any way, appears on the surface to be not a story but an essay, and it "borrows" the conventions of the essay to create specific fictional effects. And similarly a work like *Interview* is, to many people, so unlike their preconceptions of what a play is that it raises the whole issue of the limits of drama. Are the methods of characterization "dramatic" in any sense that is common to those of Euripides, Shakespeare, and Chekhov? Can it be said to have a "plot," and if so, at what points does it resemble the plot of an "ordinary" play? Further, what are the limitations of what one can do on stage? Poems such as *I Dwell in Possibility*, "*It Out-Herods Herod . . . ,*" and *Against the False Magicians* address directly the question of what poetry is and how it relates to other genres. Many of the genre questions raised here are relevant to works included in earlier sections of this book. *Six Characters*, for example, raises many of the same issues as *Interview*.

So this section may be used to show how literature can be considered across generic lines or how an individual work may push at or defy the limits or conventions of its genre. But the subject matter questions not only the limits of genre but of language, of literature itself. Does the word possess the magical quality which we associate with the term "logos," the creative "word" which turns chaos to order and, ultimately, embodies cosmic order? Such magical power would give a value to literature far beyond what we usually attribute to it. On the other hand, is a word merely a sign which possesses no value of its own, which can be the legal tender of communication in only the most trivial sense? In the psychoanalysis scene of *Interview*, for

example, is "hostile" or "penis" more meaningful than the "blah's" which precede it? Do the speeches of the Politician have any meaning? Can the Girl at the Party really hope to make anyone else conscious of her plight? The story *Pierre Menard, Author of the Quixote* additionally tests the limits of language: that an identical passage by Cervantes and "Pierre Menard" must be read differently and have a different "meaning"—while it is a spoof on critics and criticism—also raises the question of whether history and psychological context do not in fact change the meanings of identical language—whether, then, language in and of itself has meaning. Similar questions of verbal possibility are raised by such poems as *anyone lived in a pretty how town, Jabberwocky, A Lesson for Baby,* and *Permanently,* while other poems (*The Cool Web,* for example, and *In the Beginning*) suggest that language is psychologically necessary, whatever its limitations. And poems like *Black Art* and *First Fight. Then Fiddle* prominently raise the question of how poetry (or any literature) relates to other aspects of life that may be more immediately pressing.

Literature attempts an ordered imitation of perceived reality in words, and it is fitting, perhaps inevitable, that so many artists analyze not only the "reality" they hope to "imitate" and "order" but also their medium of expression. Our consciousness of the limitations they face—generic and linguistic—will, we think, enhance the understanding of works whose subject is limitation, and it may also deepen our appreciation of other works where the limits, if not conquered or transcended, are at least dealt with successfully. That literature, like mathematics or physics or philosophy, is but one imperfect way toward knowledge or perception of reality testifies both to its limitations and to its significance.

JORGE LUIS BORGES

Pierre Menard, Author of the *Quixote**

For Silvina Ocampo

The *visible* work left by this novelist is easily and briefly enumerated. Impardonable, therefore, are the omissions and additions perpetrated by Madame Henri Bachelier· in a fallacious catalogue which a certain daily, whose *Protestant* tendency is no secret, has had the inconsideration to inflict upon its deplorable readers—though these be few and Calvinist, if not Masonic and circumcised. The true friends of Menard have viewed this catalogue with alarm and even with a certain melancholy. One might say that only yesterday we gathered before his final monument, amidst the lugubrious cypresses, and already Error tries to tarnish his Memory. . . . Decidedly, a brief rectification is unavoidable.

I am aware that it is quite easy to challenge my slight authority. I hope, however, that I shall not be prohibited from mentioning two eminent testimonies. The Baroness de Bacourt (at whose unforgettable *vendredis*[1] I had the honor of meeting the lamented poet) has seen fit to approve the pages which follow. The Countess de Bagnoregio, one of the most delicate spirits of the Principality of Monaco (and now of Pittsburgh, Pennsylvania, following her recent marriage to the international philanthropist Simon Kautzsch, who has been so inconsiderately slandered, alas! by the victims of his disinterested maneuvers) has sacrificed "to veracity and to death" (such were her words) the stately reserve which is her distinction, and, in an open letter published in the magazine *Luxe*, concedes me her approval as well. These authorizations, I think, are not entirely insufficient.

I have said that Menard's visible work can be easily enumerated. Having examined with care his personal files, I find that they contain the following items:

a) A Symbolist sonnet which appeared twice (with variants) in the review *La conque*[2] (issues of March and October 1899).

b) A monograph on the possibility of constructing a poetic vocabulary of concepts which would not be synonyms or periphrases of those which make up our everyday language, "but rather ideal objects created according to convention and essentially designed to satisfy poetic needs" (Nîmes, 1901).

c) A monograph on "certain connections or affinities" between the thought of Descartes, Leibniz and John Wilkins (Nîmes, 1903).

d) A monograph on Leibniz's *Characteristica universalis*[3] (Nîmes, 1904).

e) A technical article on the possibility of improving the game of chess, eliminating one of the rook's pawns. Menard proposes, recommends, discusses, and finally rejects this innovation.

f) A monograph on Raymond Lully's *Ars magna generalis*[4] (Nîmes, 1906).

* Translated by James E. Irby. Because part of the effect of the story depends upon blurring the line between fact and fiction, annotation will be limited primarily to translation of foreign words and phrases.
1. Literally, "Fridays," indicating a weekly salon or gathering of literary and other notables.
2. *The Conch.*
3. *Universal Characteristics.*
4. *The Great Art of the General* (or *Universal*).

g) A translation, with prologue and notes, of Ruy López de Segura's *Libro de la invención liberal y arte del juego del axedrez*[5] (Paris, 1907).

h) The work sheets of a monograph on George Boole's symbolic logic.

i) An examination of the essential metric laws of French prose, illustrated with examples taken from Saint-Simon (*Revue des langues romanes*,[6] Montpellier, October 1909).

j) A reply to Luc Durtain (who had denied the existence of such laws), illustrated with examples from Luc Durtain (*Revue des langues romanes*, Montpellier, December 1909).

k) A manuscript translation of the *Aguja de navegar cultos* of Quevedo, entitled *La boussole des précieux*.[7]

l) A preface to the Catalogue of an exposition of lithographs by Carolus Hourcade (Nîmes, 1914).

m) The work *Les problèmes d'un problème*[8] (Paris, 1917), which discusses, in chronological order, the different solutions given to the illustrous problem of Achilles and the tortoise.[9] Two editions of this book have appeared so far; the second bears as an epigraph Leibniz's recommendation "*Ne craignez point, monsieur, la tortue*"[1] and revises the chapters dedicated to Russell and Descartes.

n) A determined analysis of the "syntactical customs" of Toulet (*N. R. F.*,[2] March 1921). Menard—I recall—declared that censure and praise are sentimental operations which have nothing to do with literary criticism.

o) A transposition into alexandrines of Paul Valéry's *Le cimetière marin*[3] (*N. R. F.*, January 1928).

p) An invective against Paul Valéry, in the *Papers for the Suppression of Reality* of Jacques Reboul. (This invective, we might say parenthetically, is the exact opposite of his true opinion of Valéry. The latter understood it as such and their old friendship was not endangered.)

q) A "definition" of the Countess de Bagnoregio, in the "victorious volume"—the locution is Gabriele d'Annunzio's, another of its collaborators—published annually by this lady to rectify the inevitable falsifications of journalists and to present "to the world and to Italy" an authentic image of her person, so often exposed (by very reason of her beauty and her activities) to erroneous or hasty interpretations.

r) A cycle of admirable sonnets for the Baroness de Bacourt (1934).

s) A manuscript list of verses which owe their efficacy to their punctuation.[4]

This, then, is the *visible* work of Menard, in chronological order (with no omission other than a few vague sonnets of circumstance written for the hospitable, or avid, album of Madame Henri Bachelier).

---

5. *The Book of Liberal Invention and the Game of Chess.*
6. *Romance Languages Review.*
7. Both titles mean *Guide to* (or *Compass for*) *the Euphuists* (or *Aesthetes*).
8. *The Problems of a Problem.*
9. An Eleatic paradox arguing that there is no such thing as motion; Achilles cannot overtake a tortoise, because as often as he reaches the place occupied by the tortoise at some previous moment the tortoise has already left it.
1. "Don't fear, sir, the tortoise."

2. *Nouvelle Revue Française* (*New French Review*).
3. *The Cemetery by the Sea.*
4. Madame Henri Bachelier also lists a literal translation of Quevedo's literal translation of the *Introduction à la vie dévote* [*Introduction to the Devotional Life*] of St. Francis of Sales. There are no traces of such a work in Menard's library. It must have been a jest of our friend, misunderstood by the lady. (JLB—Borges' own notes will be so indicated.)

I turn now to his other work: the subterranean, the interminably heroic, the peerless. And—such are the capacities of man!—the unfinished. This work, perhaps the most significant of our time, consists of the ninth and thirty-eighth chapters of the first part of *Don Quixote* and a fragment of chapter twenty-two. I know such an affirmation seems an absurdity; to justify this "absurdity" is the primordial object of this note.[5]

Two texts of unequal value inspired this undertaking. One is that philological fragment by Novalis—the one numbered 2005 in the Dresden edition—which outlines the theme of a *total* identification with a given author. The other is one of those parasitic books which situate Christ on a boulevard, Hamlet on Le Cannebière or Don Quixote on Wall Street. Like all men of good taste, Menard abhorred these useless carnivals, fit only—as he would say—to produce the plebeian pleasure of anachronism or (what is worse) to enthrall us with the elementary idea that all epochs are the same or are different. More interesting, though contradictory and superficial of execution, seemed to him the famous plan of Daudet: to conjoin the Ingenious Gentleman and his squire in *one* figure, which was Tartarin. . . . Those who have insinuated that Menard dedicated his life to writing a contemporary *Quixote* calumniate his illustrious memory.

He did not want to compose another *Quixote*—which is easy—but *the Quixote itself*. Needless to say, he never contemplated a mechanical transcription of the original; he did not propose to copy it. His admirable intention was to produce a few pages which would coincide— word for word and line for line—with those of Miguel de Cervantes.

"My intent is no more than astonishing," he wrote me the 30th of September, 1934, from Bayonne. "The final term in a theological or metaphysical demonstration—the objective world, God, causality, the forms of the universe—is no less previous and common than my famed novel. The only difference is that the philosophers publish the intermediary stages of their labor in pleasant volumes and I have resolved to do away with those stages." In truth, not one worksheet remains to bear witness to his years of effort.

The first method he conceived was relatively simple. Know Spanish well, recover the Catholic faith, fight against the Moors or the Turk, forget the history of Europe between the years 1602 and 1918, *be* Miguel de Cervantes. Pierre Menard studied this procedure (I know he attained a fairly accurate command of seventeenth-century Spanish) but discarded it as too easy. Rather as impossible! my reader will say. Granted, but the undertaking was impossible from the very beginning and of all the impossible ways of carrying it out, this was the least interesting. To be, in the twentieth century, a popular novelist of the seventeenth seemed to him a diminution. To be, in some way, Cervantes and reach the *Quixote* seemed less arduous to him—and, consequently, less interesting—than to go on being Pierre Menard and reach the *Quixote* through the experiences of Pierre Menard. (This conviction, we might say in passing, made him omit the autobiographical prologue to the second part of *Don Quixote*. To include that prologue

---

5. I also had the secondary intention of sketching a personal portrait of Pierre Menard. But how could I dare to compete with the golden pages which, I am told, the Baroness de Bacourt is preparing or with the delicate and punctual pencil of Carolus Hourcade? (JLB)

would have been to create another character—Cervantes—but it would also have meant presenting the *Quixote* in terms of that character and not of Menard. The latter, naturally, declined that facility.) "My undertaking is not difficult, essentially," I read in another part of his letter. "I should only have to be immortal to carry it out." Shall I confess that I often imagine he did finish it and that I read the *Quixote*—all of it— as if Menard had conceived it? Some nights past, while leafing through chapter XXVI—never essayed by him—I recognized our friend's style and something of his voice in this exceptional phrase: "the river nymphs and the dolorous and humid Echo." This happy conjunction of a spiritual and a physical adjective brought to my mind a verse by Shakespeare which we discussed one afternoon:

> Where a malignant and a turbaned Turk . . .[6]

But why precisely the *Quixote?* our reader will ask. Such a preference, in a Spaniard, would not have been inexplicable; but it is, no doubt, in a Symbolist from Nîmes, essentially a devoté of Poe, who engendered Baudelaire, who engendered Mallarmé, who engendered Valéry, who engendered Edmond Teste. The aforementioned letter illuminates this point. "The *Quixote*," clarifies Menard, "interests me deeply, but it does not seem—how shall I say it?—inevitable. I cannot imagine the universe without Edgar Allan Poe's exclamation:

> Ah, bear in mind this garden was enchanted!

or without the *Bateau ivre*[7] or the *Ancient Mariner,* but I am quite capable of imagining it without the *Quixote.* (I speak, naturally, of my personal capacity and not of those works' historical resonance.) The *Quixote* is a contingent book; the *Quixote* is unnecessary. I can premeditate writing it, I can write it, without falling into a tautology. When I was ten or twelve years old, I read it, perhaps in its entirety. Later, I have reread closely certain chapters, those which I shall not attempt for the time being. I have also gone through the interludes, the plays, the *Galatea,* the exemplary novels, the undoubtedly laborious tribulations of Persiles and Segismunda and the *Viaje del Parnaso.*[8] . . . My general recollection of the *Quixote,* simplified by forgetfulness and indifference, can well equal the imprecise and prior image of a book not yet written. Once that image (which no one can legitimately deny me) is postulated, it is certain that my problem is a good bit more difficult than Cervantes' was. My obliging predecessor did not refuse the collaboration of chance: he composed his immortal work somewhat *à la diable,*[9] carried along by the inertias of language and invention. I have taken on the mysterious duty of reconstructing literally his spontaneous work. My solitary game is governed by two polar laws. The first permits me to essay variations of a formal or psychological type; the second obliges me to sacrifice these variations to the "original" text and reason out this annihilation in an irrefutable manner. . . . To these artificial hindrances, another—of a congenital kind—must be added. To compose the *Quixote* at the beginning of the seventeenth century was a reasonable undertaking, necessary and perhaps even unavoidable; at the beginning of the twentieth, it is almost impossible. It is not

6. *Othello,* Act V, sc. ii, 353.
7. *The Drunken Boat.* The Poe exclamation not identified.
8. *Voyage to Parnassus.*
9. Like the devil; "off the top of his head."

in vain that three hundred years have gone by, filled with exceedingly complex events. Amongst them, to mention only one, is the *Quixote* itself."

In spite of these three obstacles, Menard's fragmentary *Quixote* is more subtle than Cervantes'. The latter, in a clumsy fashion, opposes to the fictions of chivalry the tawdry provincial reality of his country; Menard selects as his "reality" the land of Carmen during the century of Lepanto and Lope de Vega. What a series of *espagnolades*[1] that selection would have suggested to Maurice Barrès or Dr. Rodríguez Larreta! Menard eludes them with complete naturalness. In his work there are no gypsy flourishes or conquistadors or mystics or Philip the Seconds or *autos da fé*. He neglects or eliminates local color. This disdain points to a new conception of the historical novel. This disdain condemns *Salammbô*, with no possibility of appeal.

It is no less astounding to consider isolated chapters. For example, let us examine Chapter XXXVIII of the first part, "which treats of the curious discourse of Don Quixote on arms and letters." It is well known that Don Quixote (like Quevedo in an analogous and later passage in *La hora de todos*)[2] decided the debate against letters and in favor of arms. Cervantes was a former soldier: his verdict is understandable. But that Pierre Menard's Don Quixote—a contemporary of *La trahison des clercs*[3] and Bertrand Russell—should fall prey to such nebulous sophistries! Madame Bachelier has seen here an admirable and typical subordination on the part of the author to the hero's psychology; others (not at all perspicaciously), a *transcription* of the *Quixote;* the Baroness de Bacourt, the influence of Nietzsche. To this third interpretation (which I judge to be irrefutable) I am not sure I dare to add a fourth, which concords very well with the almost divine modesty of Pierre Menard: his resigned or ironical habit of propagating ideas which were the strict reverse of those he preferred. (Let us recall once more his diatribe against Paul Valéry in Jacques Reboul's ephemeral Surrealist sheet.) Cervantes' text and Menard's are verbally identical, but the second is almost infinitely richer. (More ambiguous, his detractors will say, but ambiguity is richness.)

It is a revelation to compare Menard's *Don Quixote* with Cervantes'. The latter, for example, wrote (**part one**, chapter nine):

. . . truth, whose mother is history, rival of time, depository of deeds, witness of the past, exemplar and adviser to the present, and the future's counselor.

Written in the seventeenth century, written by the "lay genius" Cervantes, this enumeration is a mere rhetorical praise of history. Menard, on the other hand, writes:

. . . truth, whose mother is history, rival of time, depository of deeds, witness of the past, exemplar and adviser to the present, and the future's counselor.

History, the *mother* of truth: the idea is astounding. Menard, a contemporary of William James, does not define history as an inquiry into reality but as its origin. Historical truth, for him, is not what has hap-

---

1. Swashbuckling tales.
2. *La hora de todos y la fortuna con seso*, literally *Everyone's Hour* (or *Time*) *and the Wit of Fortune*, roughly equivalent to *Every Dog Has His Day and the Irony of Fortune.*

3. *The Treason of the Intellectuals*, book by French essayist Julien Benda, attacking European intellectuals for allowing their talents to be used for nationalistic ends.

pened; it is what we judge to have happened. The final phrases—
exemplar and adviser to the present, and the future's counselor—are
brazenly pragmatic.

The contrast in style is also vivid. The archaic style of Menard—
quite foreign, after all—suffers from a certain affectation. Not so that
of his forerunner, who handles with ease the current Spanish of his
time.

There is no exercise of the intellect which is not, in the final analysis,
useless. A philosophical doctrine begins as a plausible description of the
universe; with the passage of the years it becomes a mere chapter—if
not a paragraph or a name—in the history of philosophy. In literature,
this eventual caducity is even more notorious. The *Quixote*—Menard
told me—was, above all, an entertaining book; now it is the occasion
for patriotic toasts, grammatical insolence and obscene de luxe editions.
Fame is a form of incomprehension, perhaps the worst.

There is nothing new in these nihilistic verifications; what is singular
is the determination Menard derived from them. He decided to anticipate the vanity awaiting all man's efforts; he set himself to an undertaking which was exceedingly complex and, from the very beginning,
futile. He dedicated his scruples and his sleepless nights to repeating
an already extant book in an alien tongue. He multiplied draft upon
draft, revised tenaciously and tore up thousands of manuscript pages.[4]
He did not let anyone examine these drafts and took care they should
not survive him. In vain have I tried to reconstruct them.

I have reflected that it is permissible to see in this "final" *Quixote* a
kind of palimpsest, through which the traces—tenuous but not in-
decipherable—of our friend's "previous" writing should be trans-
lucently visible. Unfortunately, only a second Pierre Menard, inverting
the other's work, would be able to exhume and revive those lost
Troys. . . .

"Thinking, analyzing, inventing [he also wrote me] are not anomalous acts; they are the normal respiration of the intelligence. To glorify
the occasional performance of that function, to hoard ancient and alien
thoughts, to recall with incredulous stupor what the *doctor universalis*[5]
thought, is to confess our laziness or our barbarity. Every man should
be capable of all ideas and I understand that in the future this will be
the case."

Menard (perhaps without wanting to) has enriched, by means of a
new technique, the halting and rudimentary art of reading: this new
technique is that of the deliberate anachronism and the erroneous
attribution. This technique, whose applications are infinite, prompts us
to go through the *Odyssey* as if it were posterior to the *Aeneid* and the
book *Le jardin du Centaure*[6] of Madame Henri Bachelier as if it were
by Madame Henri Bachelier. This technique fills the most placid works
with adventure. To attribute the *Imitatio Christi*[7] to Louis Ferdinand
Céline or to James Joyce, is this not a sufficient renovation of its tenuous
spiritual indications?

1942

4. I remember his quadricular notebooks,
his black crossed-out passages, his peculiar typographical symbols and his insect-
like handwriting. In the afternoons he
liked to go out for a walk around the
outskirts of Nîmes; he would take a notebook with him and make a merry bonfire.

(JLB)
5. The universal doctor or savant: sometimes applied to Aristotle or Thomas
Aquinas.
6. *The Garden of the Centaur.*
7. *Imitation of Christ,* generally attributed to Thomas à Kempis (1380?–1471).

ROBERT GRAVES

The Cool Web

Children are dumb to say how hot the day is,
How hot the scent is of the summer rose,
How dreadful the black wastes of evening sky,
How dreadful the tall soldiers drumming by.

But we have speech, to chill the angry day,   5
And speech, to dull the rose's cruel scent.
We spell away the overhanging night,
We spell away the soldiers and the fright.

There's a cool web of language winds us in,
Retreat from too much joy or too much fear: 10
We grow sea-green at last and coldly die
In brininess and volubility.

But if we let our tongues lose self-possession,
Throwing off language and its watery clasp
Before our death, instead of when death comes,   15
Facing the wide glare of the children's day,
Facing the rose, the dark sky and the drums,
We shall go mad no doubt and die that way.

1927

EMILY DICKINSON

I Dwell in Possibility

I dwell in Possibility—
A fairer House than Prose—
More numerous of Windows—
Superior—for Doors—

Of Chambers as the Cedars—   5
Impregnable of Eye—
And for an Everlasting Roof
The Gambrels of the Sky—

Of Visitors—the fairest—
For Occupation—This—   10
The spreading wide my narrow Hands
To gather Paradise—

ca. 1862

ANTHONY HECHT

"It Out-Herods Herod.
Pray You, Avoid It."[1]

Tonight my children hunch
Toward their Western, and are glad
As, with a Sunday punch,
The Good casts out the Bad.

And in their fairy tales   5
The warty giant and witch
Get sealed in doorless jails
And the match-girl strikes it rich.

I've made myself a drink.
The giant and witch are set   10
To bust out of the clink
When my children have gone to bed.

All frequencies are loud
With signals of despair;
In flash and morse they crowd   15
The rondure of the air.

For the wicked have grown strong,
Their numbers mock at death,
Their cow brings forth its young,
Their bull engendereth.   20

Their very fund of strength,
Satan, bestrides the globe;
He stalks its breadth and length
And finds out even Job.[2]

Yet by quite other laws   25
My children make their case;
Half God, half Santa Claus,
But with my voice and face,

A hero comes to save
The poorman, beggarman, thief,   30
And make the world behave
And put an end to grief.

1. *Hamlet*, Act III, sc. ii. Hamlet's advice to the actors about to perform "The Mousetrap" includes a caution against overacting and excessive displays of passion. In medieval mystery plays, the character of Herod was portrayed as wild and bombastic, and the actor who played the part was sometimes allowed to im-provise extravagant and spectacular be-havior.
2. According to the *Book of Job* 1:7–12, Satan has been "going to and fro in the earth, and . . . walking up and down in it" before finding Job, a man of singular righteousness, to torment and tempt.

And that their sleep be sound
I say this childermas[3]
Who could not, at one time,   35
Have saved them from the gas.

1968

JOYCE CAROL OATES

The Dark

A wood breaks to immense flower in blossoms.
The blossoms break to small, fragrant faces.
Above their careful eyes lift a flock of birds
to whom the air is water, layered air,
the texture of clouds lowered.   5

The dancer will not move but uses cries for
leaps and lunges. What is calculated once
breaks with the agony of surprise as the
orchard's blossoms accuse, the faces accuse,
the birds assume faces that are known.   10

Two special animals embrace in the wood's
silence. No trees now but filmy hints
of trees, trees' shapes, only sketches.
They cannot climb the textured air but
rub, wear one another, begging with their teeth.   15

It is a picnic table painted bright green
and surely sticky—*Don't touch.*
On its attached benches sit a crowd, people
known and half-known, the admitted, the loved
and blood-close, the hated. . . . Are these only ideas?   20

Waking, your teeth are dry with a strange lust,
and the tongue is curled upon a forgotten word—
The blossoms were faces, how? Curdled faces wrapped
in a nursery's frail colors? Frozen blossoms,
frozen faces? Single staring eyes of human recognition?   25

The birds were a cloud like buckshot, a spray
of pangs, demands? Don't look. Don't rerun
any spectacle. A dancer deep in sleep performs
miracles of paralysis, muscles ready but
unused, weaponless hand ready and unused.   30

In sleep the hand creates its weapon; swift as thought
the bullet finds its magic mark. Concentrate.
Civilizations' declines are discoveries of books, and
never real as the warm dark of dreams, Egypt's dark
warmth, the cry of horses' deaths in battle, the dark.   35

1969

3. The festival of the Holy Innocents (Childermas) commemmorates Herod's slaughter
of the children; see *Matthew* 2:16.

DANIEL G. HOFFMAN

In the Beginning[1]

On the jetty, our fingers shading
incandescent sky and sea,

my daughter stands with me.
"Boat! Boat!" she cries, her voice

in the current of speech cascading   5
with recognition's joys.

"Boat!" she cries; in spindrift
bobbling sails diminish,

but Kate's a joyous spendthrift
of her language's resources.   10

Her ecstasy's contagion
touches the whirling gulls

and turns their gibbering calls
to "Boat! Boat!" Her passion

to name the nameless pulls her   15
from the syllabic sea.

She points beyond the jetty
where the uncontested sun

wimples the wakeless water
and cries, "Boat!" though there is none.   20

But that makes no difference to Katy,
atingle with vision and word;

and why do I doubt that the harbor,
in the inner design of truth,

is speckled with tops'ls and spinnakers,   25
creased with the hulls of sloops?

Kate's word names the vision
that's hers; I try to share.

That verbal imagination
I've envied, and long wished for: 30

the world without description
is vast and wild as death;

---

1. See *John* 1:1: "In the beginning was the Word. . . ."

the word the tongue has spoken
creates the world and truth.

Child, magician, poet   35
by incantation rule;

their frenzy's spell unbroken
defines the topgallant soul.

          1960

GERTRUDE STEIN

A Lesson for Baby

What is milk. Milk is a mouth. What is a mouth.
Sweet. What is sweet. Baby.
A lesson for baby.
What is a mixture. Good all the time
Who is good all the time. I wonder.   5
A lesson for baby.
What is a melon. A little round.
Who is a little round. Baby.
Sweetly Sweetly sweetly sweetly.
In me baby baby baby   10
Smiling for me tenderly tenderly.
Tenderly sweetly baby baby.
Tenderly tenderly tenderly tenderly.

1918

e. e. cummings

anyone lived in a pretty how town

anyone lived in a pretty how town
(with up so floating many bells down)
spring summer autumn winter
he sang his didn't he danced his did.

Women and men (both little and small)   5
cared for anyone not at all
they sowed their isn't they reaped their same
sun moon stars rain

children guessed (but only a few
and down they forgot as up they grew   10
autumn winter spring summer)
that noone loved him more by more

when by now and tree by leaf
she laughed his joy she cried his grief
bird by snow and stir by still   15
anyone's any was all to her

someones married their everyones
laughed their cryings and did their dance
(sleep wake hope and then) they
said their nevers they slept their dream   20

stairs rain sun moon
(and only the snow can begin to explain
how children are apt to forget to remember
with up so floating many bells down)

one day anyone died i guess   25
(and noone stooped to kiss his face)
busy folk buried them side by side
little by little and was by was

all by all and deep by deep
and more by more they dream their sleep   30
noone and anyone earth by april
wish by spirit and if by yes.

Women and men (both dong and ding)
summer autumn winter spring
reaped their sowing and went their came   35
sun moon stars rain

                                                          1940

LEWIS CARROLL

Jabberwocky[1]

'Twas brillig, and the slithy toves
　　Did gyre and gimble in the wabe;
All mimsy were the borogoves,
　　And the mome raths outgrabe.

"Beware the Jabberwock, my son!   5
　　The jaws that bite, the claws that catch!
Beware the Jubjub bird, and shun
　　The frumious Bandersnatch!"

He took his vorpal sword in hand:
　　Long time the manxome foe he sought—   10
So rested he by the Tumtum tree,
　　And stood awhile in thought.

And as in uffish thought he stood,
　　The Jabberwock, with eyes of flame,
Came whiffling through the tulgey wood,   15
　　And burbled as it came!

---

1. Of the "hard words" in this poem, Carroll wrote: "Humpty-Dumpty's theory, of two meanings packed into one word like a portmanteau, seems to me the right explanation for all. For instance, take the two words 'fuming' and 'furious.' Make up your mind that you will say both words, but leave it unsettled which you will say first. . . . If you have that rarest of gifts, a perfectly balanced mind, you will say 'frumious.'"

One, two! One, two! And through and through
   The vorpal blade went snicker-snack!
He left it dead, and with its head
   He went galumphing back.   20

"And hast thou slain the Jabberwock?
   Come to my arms, my beamish boy!
O frabjous day! Callooh! Callay!"
   He chortled in his joy.

'Twas brillig, and the slithy toves   25
   Did gyre and gimble in the wabe;
All mimsy were the borogoves,
   And the mome raths outgrabe.

                                  1871

KENNETH KOCH

Permanently

One day the Nouns were clustered in the street.
An Adjective walked by, with her dark beauty.
The Nouns were struck, moved, changed.
The next day a Verb drove up, and created the Sentence.

Each Sentence says one thing—for example, "Although it was a dark 5
   rainy day when the Adjective walked by, I shall remember the
   pure and sweet expression on her face until the day I perish from
   the green, effective earth."
Or, "Will you please close the window, Andrew?"
Or, for example, "Thank you, the pink pot of flowers on the window
   sill has changed color recently to a light yellow, due to the heat
   from the boiler factory which exists nearby."

In the springtime the Sentences and the Nouns lay silently on the
   grass.
A lonely Conjunction here and there would call, "And! But!"
But the Adjective did not emerge.   10

As the adjective is lost in the sentence,
So I am lost in your eyes, ears, nose, and throat—
You have enchanted me with a single kiss
Which can never be undone
Until the destruction of language.   15

                                  1962

MICHAEL HAMBURGER

Envoi

Goodbye, words.
I never liked you,
Liking things and places, and
Liking people best when their mouths are shut.

Go out and lose yourselves in a jabbering world,   5
Be less than nothing, a vacuum
Of which words will beware
Lest by suction, your only assertion, you pull them in.

For that I like you, words.
Self-destroyed, self-dissolved   10
You grow true.
To what? You tell me, words.

Run, and I'll follow,
Never to catch you up.
Turn back, and I'll run.   15
So goodbye.

                                                                    1969

DYLAN THOMAS

In My Craft or Sullen Art

In my craft or sullen art
Exercised in the still night
When only the moon rages
And the lovers lie abed
With all their griefs in their arms,   5
I labor by singing light
Not for ambition or bread
Or the strut and trade of charms
On the ivory stages
But for the common wages   10
Of their most secret heart.

Not for the proud man apart
From the raging moon I write
On these spindrift[1] pages
Nor for the towering dead   15
With their nightingales and psalms
But for the lovers, their arms
Round the griefs of the ages,
Who pay no praise or wages
Nor heed my craft or art.   20

                                                                    1946

AMIRI BARAKA (LE ROI JONES)

Black Art

Poems are bullshit unless they are
teeth or trees or lemons piled
on a step. Or black ladies dying
of men leaving nickel hearts
beating them down. Fuck poems   5
and they are useful, they shoot

1. Literally, wind-driven sea spray.

come at you, love what you are,
breathe like wrestlers, or shudder
strangely after pissing. We want live
words of the hip world live flesh &   10
coursing blood. Hearts Brains
Souls splintering fire. We want poems
like fists beating niggers out of Jocks
or dagger poems in the slimy bellies
of the owner-jews. Black poems to   15
smear on girdlemamma mulatto bitches
whose brains are red jelly stuck
between 'lizabeth taylor's toes. Stinking
Whores! We want "poems that kill."
Assassin poems, Poems that shoot   20
guns. Poems that wrestle cops into alleys
and take their weapons leaving them dead
with tongues pulled out and sent to Ireland. Knockoff
poems for dope selling wops or slick halfwhite
politicians. Airplane poems. rrrrrrrrrrrrrrrrrrr   25
rrrrrrrrrr.... tuhtuhtuhtuhtuhtuhtuhtuhtuhtuh
.... rrrrrrrrrrrrrrr... Setting fire and death to
whities ass. Look at the Liberal
Spokesman for the jews clutch his throat
& puke himself into eternity... rrrrrrrrrr   30
There's a negroleader pinned to
a bar stool in Sardi's[1] eyeballs melting
in hot flame. Another negroleader
on the steps of the white house one
kneeling between the sheriff's thighs   35
negotiating cooly for his people.
Aggh ... stumbles across the room ...
Put it on him, poem. Strip him naked
to the world! Another bad poem cracking
steel knuckles in a jewlady's mouth   40
Poem scream poison gas on beasts in green berets
Clean out the world for virtue and love,
Let there be no love poems written
until love can exist freely and
cleanly. Let Black People understand   45
that they are the lovers and the sons
of lovers and warriors and sons
of warriors Are poems & poets &
all the loveliness here in the world.

We want a black poem. And a   50
Black World.
Let the world be a Black Poem
And Let All Black People Speak This Poem
Silently

or LOUD   55
                                                        1966

---

1. A fashionable New York bar and restaurant.

GWENDOLYN BROOKS

First Fight. Then Fiddle.

First fight. Then fiddle. Ply the slipping string
With feathery sorcery; muzzle the note
With hurting love; the music that they wrote
Bewitch, bewilder. Qualify to sing
Threadwise. Devise no salt, no hempen thing   5
For the dear instrument to bear. Devote
The bow to silks and honey. Be remote
A while from malice and from murdering.
But first to arms, to armor. Carry hate
In front of you and harmony behind.   10
Be deaf to music and to beauty blind.
Win war. Rise bloody, maybe not too late
For having first to civilize a space
Wherein to play your violin with grace.

                                                                  1949

THOMAS MC GRATH

Against the False Magicians

The poem must not charm us like a film:
See, in the war-torn city, that reckless, gallant
Handsome lieutenant turn to the wet-lipped blonde
(Our childhood fixation) for one sweet desperate kiss
In the broken room, in blue cinematic moonlight—   5
Bombers across that moon, and the bombs falling,
The last train leaving, the regiment departing—
And their lips lock, saluting themselves and death:
And then the screen goes dead and all go home . . .
Ritual of the false imagination.   10

The poem must not charm us like the fact:
A warship can sink a circus at forty miles,
And art, love's lonely counterfeit, has small dominion
Over those nightmares that move in the actual sunlight.
The blonde will not be faithful, nor her lover ever return,   15
Nor the note be found in the hollow tree of childhood—
This dazzle of the facts would have us weeping
The orphaned fantasies of easier days.

It is the charm which the potential has
That is the proper aura for the poem.   20
Though ceremony fail, though each of your grey hairs
Help string a harp in the landlord's heaven,
And every battle, every augury,
Argue defeat, and if defeat itself
Bring all the darkness level with our eyes—   25
It is the poem provides the proper charm,
Spelling resistance and the living will,
To bring to dance a stony field of fact
And set against terror exile or despair
The rituals of our humanity.   30

                                                                  1955

JEAN-CLAUDE VAN ITALLIE

Interview

A *Fugue for Eight Actors*[1]

FIRST INTERVIEWER

FIRST APPLICANT

SECOND APPLICANT

THIRD APPLICANT

FOURTH APPLICANT

SECOND INTERVIEWER

THIRD INTERVIEWER

FOURTH INTERVIEWER

The set is white and impersonal. Two subway stairs are at the back of the stage. On the sides there is one entrance for APPLICANTS *and another entrance for* INTERVIEWERS. *The only furniture or props needed are eight grey blocks.*

The actors, four men and four women, are dressed in black-and-white street clothes. During the employment agency section only, INTERVIEWERS *wear translucent plastic masks.*

There is an intermittent harpsichord accompaniment: dance variations (minuet, Virginia reel, twist) on a familiar American tune. But much of the music (singing, whistling, humming) is provided by the actors on stage. It is suggested, moreover, that as a company of actors and a director approach the play they find their own variations in rhythmic expression. The successful transition from one setting to the next depends on the actors' ability to play together as a company and to drop character instantaneously and completely in order to assume another character, or for a group effect.

The FIRST INTERVIEWER *for an employment agency, a young woman, sits on stage as the* FIRST APPLICANT, *a Housepainter, enters.*

FIRST INTERVIEWER [*standing*]   How do you do?

FIRST APPLICANT [*sitting*]   Thank you, I said, not knowing where to sit.

The characters will often include the audience in what they say, as if they were being interviewed by the audience.

FIRST INTERVIEWER [*pointedly*]   Won't you sit down?

FIRST APPLICANT [*standing again quickly, afraid to displease*]   I'm sorry.

FIRST INTERVIEWER [*busy with imaginary papers, pointing to a particular seat*]   There. Name, please?

FIRST APPLICANT   Jack Smith.

FIRST INTERVIEWER   Jack what Smith?

FIRST APPLICANT   Beg pardon?

FIRST INTERVIEWER   Fill in the blank space, please. Jack blank space Smith.

1. *Interview* is a revision of an earlier play by the author as modified by his work with Joseph Chaikin and the members of the Open Theatre, of which Chaikin is the head. It was presented and published with two other short plays under the general title *America Hurrah.* The author had written that "*Interview* would not exist in its present form, however, without the collaboration, in rehearsal, of Joseph Chaikin and the actors of *America Hurrah.*"

FIRST APPLICANT   I don't have any.
FIRST INTERVIEWER   I asked you to sit down. [*Pointing.*] There.
FIRST APPLICANT [*sitting*]   I'm sorry.
FIRST INTERVIEWER   Name, please?
FIRST APPLICANT   Jack Smith.
FIRST INTERVIEWER   You haven't told me your *middle* name.
FIRST APPLICANT   I haven't got one.
FIRST INTERVIEWER [*suspicious but writing it down*]   No middle name.

SECOND APPLICANT, *a woman, a Floorwasher, enters.*

FIRST INTERVIEWER   How do you do?
SECOND APPLICANT [*sitting*]   Thank you, I said, not knowing what.
FIRST INTERVIEWER   Won't you sit down?
SECOND APPLICANT [*standing*]   I'm sorry.
FIRST APPLICANT   I am sitting.
FIRST INTERVIEWER [*pointing*]   There. Name, please?
SECOND APPLICANT [*sitting*]   Jane Smith.
FIRST APPLICANT   Jack Smith.
FIRST INTERVIEWER   What blank space Smith?
SECOND APPLICANT   Ellen.
FIRST APPLICANT   Haven't got one.
FIRST INTERVIEWER   What job are you applying for?
FIRST APPLICANT   Housepainter.
SECOND APPLICANT   Floorwasher.
FIRST INTERVIEWER   We haven't many vacancies in that. What experience have you had?
FIRST APPLICANT   A lot.
SECOND APPLICANT   Who needs experience for floorwashing?
FIRST INTERVIEWER   You will help me by making your answers clear.
FIRST APPLICANT   Eight years.
SECOND APPLICANT   Twenty years.

THIRD APPLICANT, *a Banker, enters.*

FIRST INTERVIEWER   How do you do?
SECOND APPLICANT   I'm good at it.
FIRST APPLICANT   Very well.
THIRD APPLICANT [*sitting*]   Thank you, I said, as casually as I could.
FIRST INTERVIEWER   Won't you sit down?
THIRD APPLICANT [*standing again*]   I'm sorry.
SECOND APPLICANT   I am sitting.
FIRST APPLICANT [*standing again*]   I'm sorry.
FIRST INTERVIEWER [*pointing to a particular seat*]   There. Name, please?
FIRST APPLICANT   Jack Smith.
SECOND APPLICANT   Jane Smith.
THIRD APPLICANT   Richard Smith.
FIRST INTERVIEWER   What *exactly* Smith, please?
THIRD APPLICANT   Richard F.
SECOND APPLICANT   Jane Ellen.
FIRST APPLICANT   Jack None.
FIRST INTERVIEWER   What are you applying for?
FIRST APPLICANT   Housepainter.
SECOND APPLICANT   I need money.

THIRD APPLICANT   Bank president.
FIRST INTERVIEWER   How many years have you been in your present job?
THIRD APPLICANT   Three.
SECOND APPLICANT   Twenty.
FIRST APPLICANT   Eight.

FOURTH APPLICANT, *a Lady's Maid, enters.*

FIRST INTERVIEWER   How do you do?
FOURTH APPLICANT   I said thank you, not knowing where to sit.
THIRD APPLICANT   I'm fine.
SECOND APPLICANT   Do I have to tell you?
FIRST APPLICANT   Very well.
FIRST INTERVIEWER   Won't you sit down?
FOURTH APPLICANT   I'm sorry.
THIRD APPLICANT [*sitting again*]   Thank you.
SECOND APPLICANT [*standing again*]   I'm sorry.
FIRST APPLICANT [*sitting*]   Thanks.
FIRST INTERVIEWER [*pointing to a particular seat*]   There. Name, please?

FOURTH APPLICANT *sits.*

ALL APPLICANTS   Smith.
FIRST INTERVIEWER   What Smith?
FOURTH APPLICANT   Mary Victoria.
THIRD APPLICANT   Richard F.
SECOND APPLICANT   Jane Ellen.
FIRST APPLICANT   Jack None.
FIRST INTERVIEWER   How many years' experience have you had?
FOURTH APPLICANT   Eight years.
SECOND APPLICANT   Twenty years.
FIRST APPLICANT   Eight years.
THIRD APPLICANT   Three years four months and nine days not counting vacations and sick leave and the time both my daughters and my wife had the whooping cough.
FIRST INTERVIEWER   Just answer the questions, please.
FOURTH APPLICANT   Yes, sir.
THIRD APPLICANT   Sure.
SECOND APPLICANT   I'm sorry.
FIRST APPLICANT   That's what I'm doing.

SECOND INTERVIEWER, *a young man, enters and goes to inspect* APPLICANTS. *With the entrance of each* INTERVIEWER, *the speed of the action accelerates.*

SECOND INTERVIEWER   How do you do?
FIRST APPLICANT [*standing*]   I'm sorry.
SECOND APPLICANT [*sitting*]   Thank you.
THIRD APPLICANT [*standing*]   I'm sorry.
FOURTH APPLICANT [*sitting*]   Thank you.
SECOND INTERVIEWER   What's your name?
FIRST INTERVIEWER   Your middle name, please.
FIRST APPLICANT   Smith.
SECOND APPLICANT   Ellen.

THIRD APPLICANT   Smith, Richard F.
FOURTH APPLICANT   Mary Victoria Smith.
FIRST INTERVIEWER   What is your exact age?
SECOND INTERVIEWER   Have you any children?
FIRST APPLICANT   I'm thirty-two years old.
SECOND APPLICANT   One son.
THIRD APPLICANT   I have two daughters.
FOURTH APPLICANT   Do I have to tell you that?
FIRST INTERVIEWER   Are you married, single, or other?
SECOND INTERVIEWER   Have you ever earned more than that?
FIRST APPLICANT   No.
SECOND APPLICANT   Never.
THIRD APPLICANT   Married.
FOURTH APPLICANT   Single, NOW.

> THIRD INTERVIEWER, *a woman, enters.*

THIRD INTERVIEWER   How do you do?
FIRST APPLICANT [*sitting*]   Thank you.
SECOND APPLICANT [*standing*]   I'm sorry.
THIRD APPLICANT [*sitting*]   Thank you.
FOURTH APPLICANT [*standing*]   I'm sorry.

> FOURTH INTERVIEWER, *a man, appears on the heels of* THIRD
> INTERVIEWER.

FOURTH INTERVIEWER   How do you do?
FIRST APPLICANT [*standing*]   I'm sorry.
SECOND APPLICANT [*sitting*]   Thank you.
THIRD APPLICANT [*standing*]   I'm sorry.
FOURTH APPLICANT [*sitting*]   Thank you.
ALL INTERVIEWERS   What is your Social Security Number, please?

> APPLICANTS *do the next four speeches simultaneously.*

FIRST APPLICANT   333 dash 6598 dash 5590765439 dash 003.
SECOND APPLICANT   999 dash 5733 dash 699075432 dash 11.
THIRD APPLICANT [*sitting*]   I'm sorry. I left it home. I can call if you
let me use the phone.
FOURTH APPLICANT   I always get it confused with my Checking
Account Number.

> INTERVIEWERS *do the next four speeches in a round.*

FIRST INTERVIEWER   Will you be so kind as to tell me a little about
yourself?
SECOND INTERVIEWER   Can you fill me in on something about your
background please?
THIRD INTERVIEWER   It'd be a help to our employers if you'd give me
a little for our files.
FOURTH INTERVIEWER   Now what would you say, say, to a prospective
employer about yourself?

> APPLICANTS *address parts of the following four speeches, in par-*
> *ticular, directly to the audience.*

FIRST APPLICANT   I've been a Union member twenty years, I said to
them, if that's the kind of thing you want to know. Good health, I
said. Veteran of two wars. Three kids. Wife's dead. Wife's sister, she

takes care of them. I don't know why I'm telling you this, I said smiling.

Sits.

SECOND APPLICANT [*standing*] So what do you want to know, I told the guy. I've been washin' floors for twenty years. Nobody's ever complained. I don't loiter after hours, I said to him. Just because my boy's been in trouble is no reason, I said, no reason—I go right home, I said to him. Right home. Right home.

Sits.

THIRD APPLICANT [*standing*] I said that I was a Republican and we could start right there. And then I said that I spend most of my free time watching television or playing in the garden of my four-bedroom house with our two lovely daughters, aged nine and eleven. I mentioned that my wife plays with us too, and that her name is Katherine, although, I said casually, her good friends call her Kitty. I wasn't at all nervous.

Sits.

FOURTH APPLICANT [*standing*] Just because I'm here, sir, I told him, is no reason for you to patronize me. I've been a lady's maid, I said, in houses you would not be allowed into. My father was a gentleman of leisure, *and* what's more, I said, my references are unimpeachable.

FIRST INTERVIEWER I see.

SECOND INTERVIEWER All right.

THIRD INTERVIEWER That's fine.

FOURTH INTERVIEWER Of course.

APPLICANTS *do the following four speeches simultaneously.*

FIRST APPLICANT Just you call anybody at the Union and ask them. They'll hand me a clean bill of health.

SECOND APPLICANT I haven't been to jail if that's what you mean. Not me. I'm clean.

THIRD APPLICANT My record is impeccable. There's not a stain on it.

FOURTH APPLICANT My references would permit me to be a governess, that's what.

FIRST INTERVIEWER [*going to* FIRST APPLICANT *and inspecting under his arms*] When did you last have a job housepainting?

SECOND INTERVIEWER [*going to* SECOND APPLICANT *and inspecting her teeth*] Where was the last place you worked?

THIRD INTERVIEWER [*going to* THIRD APPLICANT *and inspecting him*] What was your last position in a bank?

FOURTH INTERVIEWER [*going to* FOURTH APPLICANT *and inspecting her*] Have you got your references with you?

APPLICANTS *do the following four speeches simultaneously, with music under.*

FIRST APPLICANT I've already told you I worked right along till I quit.

SECOND APPLICANT Howard Johnson's on Fifty-first Street all last month.

THIRD APPLICANT First Greenfield International and Franklin Banking Corporation Banking and Stone Incorporated.

FOURTH APPLICANT I've got a letter right here in my bag. Mrs. Muggintwat only let me go because she died.

INTERVIEWERS *do the next four speeches in a round.*

FIRST INTERVIEWER [*stepping around and speaking to* SECOND APPLICANT] Nothing terminated your job at Howard Johnson's? No franks, say, missing at the end of the day, I suppose?

SECOND INTERVIEWER [*stepping around and speaking to* THIRD APPLICANT] It goes without saying, I suppose, that you could stand an FBI Security Test?

THIRD INTERVIEWER [*stepping around and speaking to* FOURTH APPLICANT] I suppose there are no records of minor thefts or, shall we say, borrowings from your late employer?

FOURTH INTERVIEWER [*stepping around and speaking to* FIRST APPLICANT] Nothing political in your Union dealings? Nothing Leftist, I suppose? Nothing Rightist either, I hope.

APPLICANTS and INTERVIEWERS *line up for a square dance. Music under the following.*

FIRST APPLICANT [*bowing to* FIRST INTERVIEWER] What's it to you, buddy?

SECOND APPLICANT [*bowing to* SECOND INTERVIEWER] Eleanor Roosevelt wasn't more honest.[2]

THIRD APPLICANT [*bowing to* THIRD INTERVIEWER] My record is lily-white, sir!

FOURTH APPLICANT [*bowing to* FOURTH INTERVIEWER] Mrs. Thumbletwat used to take me to the bank and I'd watch her open her box!

Each INTERVIEWER, *during his next speech, goes upstage to form another line.*

FIRST INTERVIEWER Good!
SECOND INTERVIEWER Fine!
THIRD INTERVIEWER Swell!
FOURTH INTERVIEWER Fine!

APPLICANTS *come downstage together; they do the next four speeches simultaneously and directly to the audience.*

FIRST APPLICANT I know my rights. As a veteran. *And* a citizen. I know my rights. *And* my cousin is very well-known in certain circles, if you get what I mean. In the back room of a certain candy store in the Italian district of this city my cousin is *very* well known, if you get what I mean. I know my rights. And I know my cousin.

SECOND APPLICANT [*putting on a pious act, looking up to heaven*] Holy Mary Mother of God, must I endure all the sinners of this earth? Must I go on a poor washerwoman in this City of Sin? Help me, oh my God, to leave this earthly crust, and damn your silly impudence, young man, if you think you can treat an old woman like this. You've got another thought coming, you have.

THIRD APPLICANT I have an excellent notion to report you to the Junior Chamber of Commerce of this city of which I am the Secre-

2. Eleanor Roosevelt (1884–1962), the wife of President Franklin D. Roosevelt, was a public figure in her own right. An indefatigable supporter of good causes, she wrote, lectured, and traveled. For many years she wrote a widely syndicated newspaper column, "My Day." After her husband's death, she represented the United States at the United Nations for several years.

tary and was in line to be elected Vice President and still will be if you are able to find me gainful and respectable employ!

FOURTH APPLICANT Miss Thumblebottom married into the Twiths and if you start insulting me, young man, you'll have to start in insulting the Twiths as well. A Twith isn't a nobody, you know, as good as a Thumbletwat, *and* they all call me their loving Mary, you know.

ALL INTERVIEWERS [*in a loud raucous voice*] Do you smoke?

Each APPLICANT, *during his next speech, turns upstage.*

FIRST APPLICANT No thanks.
SECOND APPLICANT Not now.
THIRD APPLICANT No thanks.
FOURTH APPLICANT Not now.
ALL INTERVIEWERS [*again in a harsh voice and bowing or curtsying*] Do you mind if I do?
FIRST APPLICANT I don't care.
SECOND APPLICANT Who cares?
THIRD APPLICANT Course not.
FOURTH APPLICANT Go ahead.

INTERVIEWERS *form a little group off to themselves.*

FIRST INTERVIEWER I tried to quit but couldn't manage.
SECOND INTERVIEWER I'm a three-pack-a-day man, I guess.
THIRD INTERVIEWER If I'm gonna go I'd rather go smoking.
FOURTH INTERVIEWER I'm down to five a day.

APPLICANTS *all start to sneeze.*

FIRST APPLICANT Excuse me, I'm gonna sneeze.
SECOND APPLICANT Have you got a hanky?
THIRD APPLICANT I have a cold coming on.
FOURTH APPLICANT I thought I had some tissues in my bag.

APPLICANTS *all sneeze.*

FIRST INTERVIEWER Gezundheit.
SECOND INTERVIEWER God bless you.
THIRD INTERVIEWER Gezundheit.
FOURTH INTERVIEWER God bless you.

APPLICANTS *all sneeze simultaneously.*

FIRST INTERVIEWER God bless you.
SECOND INTERVIEWER Gezundheit.
THIRD INTERVIEWER God bless you.
FOURTH INTERVIEWER Gezundheit.

APPLICANTS *return to their seats.*

FIRST APPLICANT Thanks, I said.
SECOND APPLICANT I said thanks.
THIRD APPLICANT Thank you, I said.
FOURTH APPLICANT I said thank you.

INTERVIEWERS *stand on their seats and say the following as if one person were speaking.*

FIRST INTERVIEWER Do you
SECOND INTERVIEWER speak any

THIRD INTERVIEWER foreign
FOURTH INTERVIEWER languages?
FIRST INTERVIEWER Have you
SECOND INTERVIEWER got a
THIRD INTERVIEWER college
FOURTH INTERVIEWER education?
FIRST INTERVIEWER Do you
SECOND INTERVIEWER take
THIRD INTERVIEWER shorthand?
FOURTH INTERVIEWER Have you
FIRST INTERVIEWER any
SECOND INTERVIEWER special
THIRD INTERVIEWER qualifications?
FIRST INTERVIEWER Yes?
FIRST APPLICANT [*stepping up to* INTERVIEWERS] Sure, I can speak
Italian, I said. My whole family is Italian so I oughta be able to,
and I can match colors, like green to green, so that even your own
mother couldn't tell the difference, begging your pardon, I said,
I went through the eighth grade.

> *Steps back.*

SECOND INTERVIEWER Next.
SECOND APPLICANT [*stepping up to* INTERVIEWERS] My grandmother
taught me some Gaelic, I told the guy. And my old man could rattle
off in Yiddish when he had a load on.[3] I never went to school at all
excepting church school, but I can write my name good and clear.
Also, I said, I can smell an Irishman or a Yid a hundred miles off.

> *Steps back.*

THIRD INTERVIEWER Next.
THIRD APPLICANT [*stepping up to* INTERVIEWERS] I've never had any
need to take shorthand in my position, I said to him. I've a Z.A. in
business administration from Philadelphia, and a Z.Z.A. from M.Y.U.
night school.[4] I mentioned that I speak a little Spanish, of course,
and that I'm a whiz at model frigates and warships.

> *Steps back.*

FOURTH INTERVIEWER Next.
FOURTH APPLICANT [*stepping up to* INTERVIEWERS] I can sew a
straight seam, I said, hand or machine, and I have been exclusively a
lady's maid although I *can* cook and will too if I have someone to
assist me, I said. Unfortunately, aside from self-education, grammar
school is as far as I have progressed.

> *Steps back.*
> *Each* INTERVIEWER, *during his next speech, bows or curtsies to
> the* APPLICANT *nearest him.*

FIRST INTERVIEWER Good.
SECOND INTERVIEWER Fine.
THIRD INTERVIEWER Very helpful.

---

3. Gaelic is the native language of
Ireland. Yiddish is a form of German used
by Jews in Germany and elsewhere. "Yid"
is a derogatory term for a Jew.
4. The abbreviations are made-up ones
which suggest such abbreviations as B.A.
for Bachelor of Arts, B.B.A. for Bachelor
of Business Administration, and N.Y.U. for
New York University.

FOURTH INTERVIEWER Thank you.

Each APPLICANT, *during his next speech, jumps on the back of the* INTERVIEWER *nearest him.*

FOURTH APPLICANT You're welcome, I'm sure.

THIRD APPLICANT Anything you want to know.

SECOND APPLICANT Just ask me.

FIRST APPLICANT Fire away, fire away.

The next eight speeches are spoken simultaneously, with APPLICANTS *on* INTERVIEWERS' *backs.*

FIRST INTERVIEWER Well unless there's anything special you want to tell me, I think—

SECOND INTERVIEWER Is there anything more you think I should know about before you—

THIRD INTERVIEWER I wonder if we've left anything out of this questionnaire or if you—

FOURTH INTERVIEWER I suppose I've got all the information down here unless you can—

FIRST APPLICANT I've got kids to support, you know, and I need a job real quick—

SECOND APPLICANT Do you think you could try and get me something today because I—

THIRD APPLICANT How soon do you suppose I can expect to hear from your agency? Do you—

FOURTH APPLICANT I don't like to sound pressureful, but you know I'm currently on unemploy—

Each APPLICANT, *during his next speech, jumps off* INTERVIEWER'S *back.*

FIRST APPLICANT Beggin' your pardon.

SECOND APPLICANT So sorry.

THIRD APPLICANT Excuse me.

FOURTH APPLICANT Go ahead.

Each INTERVIEWER, *during his next speech, bows or curtsies and remains in that position.*

FIRST INTERVIEWER That's quite all right.

SECOND INTERVIEWER I'm sorry.

THIRD INTERVIEWER I'm sorry.

FOURTH INTERVIEWER My fault.

Each APPLICANT, *during his next speech, begins leap-frogging over* INTERVIEWERS' *backs.*

FIRST APPLICANT My fault.

SECOND APPLICANT My fault.

THIRD APPLICANT I'm sorry.

FOURTH APPLICANT My fault.

Each INTERVIEWER, *during his next speech, begins leap-frogging too.*

FIRST INTERVIEWER That's all right.

SECOD INTERVIEWER My fault.

THIRD INTERVIEWER I'm sorry.

FOURTH INTERVIEWER   Excuse me.

The leap-frogging continues as the preceding eight lines are repeated simultaneously. Then the INTERVIEWERS *confer in a huddle and come out of it.*

FIRST INTERVIEWER   Do you enjoy your work?

FIRST APPLICANT   Sure, I said, I'm proud. Why not? Sure I know I'm no Rembrandt, I said, but I'm proud of my work, I said to him.

SECOND APPLICANT   I told him it stinks. But what am I supposed to do, sit home and rot?

THIRD APPLICANT   Do I like my work, he asked me. Well, I said, to gain time, do I like my work? Well, I said, I don't know.

FOURTH APPLICANT   I told him straight out: for a sensible person, a lady's maid is the *only possible* way of life.

SECOND INTERVIEWER   Do you think you're irreplaceable?

ALL APPLICANTS   Oh, yes indeed.

ALL INTERVIEWERS   Irreplaceable?

ALL APPLICANTS   Yes, yes indeed.

THIRD INTERVIEWER   Do you like me?

FIRST APPLICANT   You're a nice man.

SECOND APPLICANT   Huh?

THIRD APPLICANT   Why do you ask?

FOURTH APPLICANT   It's not a question of *like*.

FIRST INTERVIEWER   Well, we'll be in touch with you.

This is the beginning of leaving the agency. Soft music under. APPLICANTS *and* INTERVIEWERS *push their seats into two masses of four boxes, one on each side of the stage.* APPLICANTS *leave first, joining hands to form a revolving door. All are now leaving the agency, not in any orderly fashion.* INTERVIEWERS *start down one of the subway stairs at the back of the stage and* APPLICANTS *start down the other. The following speeches overlap and are heard indistinctly as crowd noise.*

FOURTH INTERVIEWER   What sort of day will it be?

FIRST APPLICANT   I bet we'll have rain.

SECOND APPLICANT   Cloudy, clearing in the afternoon.

THIRD APPLICANT   Mild, I think, with some snow.

FOURTH APPLICANT   Precisely the same as yesterday.

SECOND APPLICANT   Can you get me one?

FIRST INTERVIEWER   See you tomorrow.

THIRD APPLICANT   When will I hear from you?

SECOND INTERVIEWER   We'll let you know.

FOURTH APPLICANT   Where's my umbrella?

THIRD INTERVIEWER   I'm going to a movie.

FIRST APPLICANT   So how about it?

FOURTH INTERVIEWER   Good night.

THIRD APPLICANT   Can you help me, Doctor, I asked.

When all of the actors are offstage, the FOURTH INTERVIEWER *makes a siren sound and the following speeches continue from downstairs as a loud crowd noise for a few moments; they overlap so that the stage is empty only briefly.*

FIRST INTERVIEWER   It'll take a lot of work on your part.

SECOND INTERVIEWER   I'll do what I can for you.

THIRD INTERVIEWER Of course I'll do my best.
FIRST INTERVIEWER God helps those who help themselves.
FIRST APPLICANT I have sinned deeply, Father, I said.
FIRST INTERVIEWER You certainly have. I hope you truly repent.
SECOND INTERVIEWER In the name of the Father, etcetera, and the Holy Ghost.
THIRD INTERVIEWER Jesus saves.
FOURTH APPLICANT I said can you direct me to Fourteenth Street, please?
FIRST INTERVIEWER Just walk down that way a bit and then turn left.
SECOND INTERVIEWER Just walk down that way a bit and then turn right.
THIRD INTERVIEWER Take a cab!
FOURTH APPLICANT Do you hear a siren?
ALL INTERVIEWERS What time is it?
FIRST APPLICANT Half-past three.
SECOND APPLICANT It must be about four.
THIRD APPLICANT Half-past five.
FOURTH APPLICANT My watch has stopped.
FIRST INTERVIEWER Do you enjoy your work?
SECOND INTERVIEWER Do you think you're irreplaceable?
THIRD INTERVIEWER Do you like me?

> *The actor who played the* FOURTH INTERVIEWER *comes on stage while continuing to make the loud siren noise. The actress who played the* FOURTH APPLICANT *comes on stage and speaks directly to the audience.*

FOURTH APPLICANT Can you direct me to Fourteenth Street, please, I said. I seem to have lost my—I started to say, and then I was nearly run down.

> *The remaining actors return to the stage to play various people on Fourteenth Street: ladies shopping, a panhandler, a man in a sandwich board, a peddler of "franks and orange," a snooty German couple, a lecher, a pair of sighing lovers, and so on. The actors walk straight forward toward the audience and then walk backwards to the rear of the stage. Each time they approach the audience, they do so as a different character. The actor will need to find the essential vocal and physical mannerisms of each character, play them, and drop them immediately to assume another character. The* FOURTH APPLICANT *continues to address the audience directly, to involve them in her hysteria, going up the aisle and back.*

FOURTH APPLICANT I haven't got my Social Security—I started to say, I saw someone right in front of me and I said, could you direct me to Fourteenth Street, I have to get to Fourteenth Street, please, to get a bargain, I explained, although I could hardly remember what it was I wanted to buy. I read about it in the paper today, I said, only they weren't listening and I said to myself, my purpose for today is to get to—and I couldn't remember, I've set myself the task of—I've got to have—it's that I can save, I remembered, I can save if I can get that bargain at—and I couldn't remember where it was so I started to look for my wallet which I seem to have mislaid in my purse, and a man—please watch where you're going, I shouted with

my purse half-open, and I seemed to forget—Fourteenth Street, I remembered, and you'd think with all these numbered streets and avenues a person wouldn't get lost—you'd think a person would *help* a person, you'd think so. So I asked the most respectable looking man I could find, I asked him, please can you direct me to Fourteenth Street. He wouldn't answer. Just wouldn't. I'm lost, I said to myself. The paper said—the television said—they said, I couldn't remember what they said. I turned for help: "Jesus Saves" the sign said, and a man was carrying it, both sides of his body, staring straight ahead. "Jesus Saves" the sign said.

The passers-by jostle her more and more.

FOURTH APPLICANT   I couldn't remember where I was going. "Come and be saved" it said, so I asked the man with the sign, please, sir, won't you tell me how to, dear Lord, I thought, anywhere, please, sir, won't you tell me how to—can you direct me to Fourteenth Street, *please!*

The passers-by have covered the FOURTH APPLICANT. *All actors mill about until they reach designated positions on the stage where they face the audience, a line of women and a line of men, students in a gym class. The* SECOND INTERVIEWER *has stayed coolly out of the crowd during this last; now he is the* GYM INSTRUCTOR.

GYM INSTRUCTOR   I took my last puff and strode resolutely into the room. Ready men, I asked brightly. And one and two and three and four and one and two and keep it up.

The GYM INSTRUCTOR *is trying to help his students mold themselves into the kind of people seen in advertisements and the movies. As he counts to four the students puff out their chests, smile, and look perfectly charming. As he counts to four again, the students relax and look ordinary.*

GYM INSTRUCTOR   You wanna look like the guys in the movies, don't you, I said to the fellahs. Keep it up then. You wanna radiate that kinda charm and confidence they have in the movies, don't you, I said to the girls. Keep it up then, stick 'em out, that's what you got 'em for. Don't be ashamed. All of you, tuck in your butts, I said loudly. That's the ticket, I said, wishing to hell I had a cigarette. You're selling, selling all the time, that right, miss? Keep on selling, I said. And one and two and three and four and ever see that guy on TV, I said. What's his name, I asked them. What's his name? Aw, you know his name, I said, forgetting his name. Never mind, it'll come to you, I said. He comes in here too. See that, I said, grabbing a guy out of line and showing 'em his muscle. See that line, I said, making the guy feel good, know what that is? It's boyishness, I said. You come here, I said, throwing him back into the line, and it'll renew your youthfulness, I said, taking a deep breath. And one and two and three and four and smile, I said, smiling. Not so big, I said, smiling less. You look like creeps, I said, when you smile that big. When you smile, hold something back. Make like you're holding back something big, I said, a secret, I said. That's the ticket. And one and two and three and four and . . .

Accelerating the rhythm to a double count.

Anybody got a cigarette, I said suddenly, without thinking. I was just kidding, I said then, sheepishly. One and two and three and four, I said, wishing I had a cigarette. And one and two and three and four . . .

The rapid movements of the gym class become the vibrations of passengers on a moving subway train. The actors rush to the boxes stage left, continuing to vibrate. Two of the actors stand on the boxes and smile like subway advertisements while the others, directly in front of them, are pushed against each other on the crowded train. They make an appropriate soft subway noise, a kind of rhythmic hiss and, as the subway passengers, form their faces into frozen masks of indifference.

SECOND APPLICANT [*squeezing her way to an uncomfortable front seat and speaking half to herself*] God forgive me . . . you no-good chump, I said to him, I used to love you . . . not now. Not now . . . God forgive me . . . God forgive me for being old. Not now, I said. I wouldn't wipe the smell off your uncle's bottom now, not for turnips, no. God forgive me . . . Remember how we used to ride the roller coaster out at Coney Island, you and me?[5] Remember? Holding hands in the cold and I'd get so scared and you'd get so scared and we'd hug each other and buy another ticket . . . Remember? . . . Look now, I said. Look at me now! God forgive you for leaving me with nothing . . . God forgive you for being dead . . . God forgive me for being alive . . .

The actress who played the THIRD INTERVIEWER *slips out of the subway as though it were her stop and sits on a box, stage right, as a* TELEPHONE OPERATOR. *The other actors form a telephone circuit by holding hands in two concentric circles around the boxes, stage left; they change the hissing sound of the subway into the whistling of telephone circuits.*

TELEPHONE OPERATOR   Just one moment and I will connect you with Information.

The TELEPHONE OPERATOR *alternates her official voice with her ordinary voice; she uses the latter when she talks to her friend Roberta, another operator whom she reaches by flipping a switch. When she is talking to Roberta, the whistling of the telephone circuit changes into a different rhythm and the arms of the actors, which are forming the circuit, move into a different position.*

TELEPHONE OPERATOR   Just one moment and I will connect you with Information. Ow! Listen, Roberta, I said, I've got this terrible cramp. Hang up and dial again, please; we find nothing wrong with that number at all. You know what I ate, I said to her, you were there. Baked macaroni, Wednesday special, maple-nut fudge, I said. I'm sorry but the number you have reached is not—I can feel it

5. Coney Island is a beach and amusement park in New York City. Among its claims to fame is the report that the hotdog was invented there in 1867 by German immigrant Charles Feltman.

gnawing at me at the bottom of my belly, I told her. Do you think it's serious, Roberta? Appendicitis? I asked. Thank you for giving us the area code but the number you have reached is not in this area. Roberta, I asked her, do you think I have cancer? One moment, please, I'm sorry the number you have reached—ow! Well, if it's lunch, Roberta, I said to her, you know what they can do with it tomorrow. Ow! One moment, please, I said. Ow, I said, Roberta, I said, it really hurts.

The TELEPHONE OPERATOR *falls off her seat in pain. The whistling of the telephone circuit becomes a siren. Three actors carry the* TELEPHONE OPERATOR *over to the boxes, stage left, which now serve as an operating table. Three actors imitate the* TELEPHONE OPERATOR'S *breathing pattern while four actors behind her make stylized sounds and movements as surgeons and nurses in the midst of an operation. The* TELEPHONE OPERATOR'S *breathing accelerates, then stops. After a moment the actors begin spreading over the stage and making the muted sounds of a cocktail party: music, laughter, talk. The actors find a position and remain there, playing various aspects of a party in slow motion and muted tones. They completely ignore the* FIRST INTERVIEWER *who, as a* GIRL AT THE PARTY, *goes from person to person as if she were in a garden of living statues.*

GIRL AT THE PARTY [*rapidly and excitedly*] And then after the ambulance took off I went up in the elevator and into the party. Did you see the accident, I asked, and they said they did, and what did he look like, and I said he wore a brown coat and had straight brown hair. He stepped off the curb right in front of me. We had been walking up the same block, he a few feet ahead of me, this block right here, I said, but she wasn't listening. Hi, my name is Jill, I said to somebody sitting down and they looked at me and smiled so I said his arm was torn out of its socket and his face was on the pavement gasping but I didn't touch him and she smiled and walked away and I said after her, you aren't supposed to touch someone before—I *wanted* to help, I said, but she wasn't listening. When a man came up and said was it someone you knew and I said yes, it was someone I knew slightly, someone I knew, yes, and he offered me a drink and I said no thanks, I didn't want one, and he said well how well did I know him, and I said I knew him well, yes, I knew him very well. You were coming together to the party, he said. Yes, I said, excuse me. Hi, my name is Jill, did you hear a siren, and they said oh you're the one who saw it, was he killed?

Becoming resigned to the fact that no one is listening.

And I said yes I was, excuse me, and went back across the room but couldn't find another face to talk to until I deliberately bumped into somebody because I had to tell them one of us couldn't come because of the accident. It was Jill. Jill couldn't come. I'm awfully sorry, I said, because of the accident. She had straight brown hair, I said, and was wearing a brown coat, and two or three people looked at me strangely and moved off. I'm sorry, I said to a man, and I laughed, and moved off. I'm dead, I said to several people and started to push them over, I'm dead, thank you, I said, thank you,

please, I said, I'm dead, until two or three of them got hold of my arms and hustled me out. I'm sorry, I said, I couldn't come because of the accident. I'm sorry. Excuse me.

The GIRL AT THE PARTY *is lowered to the floor by two of the men and then all fall down except the actor who played the* FOURTH INTERVIEWER. *He remains seated as a* PSYCHIATRIST. *The* THIRD APPLICANT, *on the floor, props his head up on his elbow and speaks to the audience.*

THIRD APPLICANT   Can you help me, Doctor, I asked him.

The PSYCHIATRIST *crosses his legs and assumes a professional expression.*

THIRD APPLICANT   Well, it started, well it started, I said, when I was sitting in front of the television set with my feet on the coffee table. Now I've sat there hundreds of times, thousands maybe, with a can of beer in my hand. I like to have a can of beer in my hand when I watch the beer ads. But now for no reason I can think of, the ad was making me sick. So I used the remote control to get to another channel, but each channel made me just as sick. The television was one thing and I was a person, and I was going to be sick. So I turned it off and had a panicky moment. I smelled the beer in my hand and as I vomited I looked around the living room for something to grab on to, something to look at, but there was just our new furniture. I tried to get a hold of myself. I tried to stare straight ahead above the television set, at a little spot on the wall I know. I've had little moments like that before, Doctor, I said, panicky little moments like that when the earth seems to slip out from under, and everything whirls around and you try to hold onto something, some object, some thought, but I couldn't think of anything. Later the panic went away, I told him, it went away, and I'm much better now. But I don't feel like doing anything anymore, except sit and stare at the wall. I've lost my job. Katherine thought I should come and see you. Can you help me, Doctor, I asked him.

PSYCHIATRIST
Blah, blah, blah, blah, blah, blah, HOSTILE.
Blah, blah, blah, blah, blah, blah, PENIS.
Blah, blah, blah, blah, blah, blah, MOTHER.

Holding out his hand.

Blah, blah, blah, blah, blah, blah, MONEY.

The THIRD APPLICANT *takes the* PSYCHIATRIST's *hand and gets up, extending his left hand to the next actor. This begins a grand right and left with all the actors all over the stage.*[6]

ALL [*chanting as they do the grand right and left*]
Blah, blah, blah, blah, blah, blah, HOSTILE.
Blah, blah, blah, blah, blah, blah, PENIS.
Blah, blah, blah, blah, blah, blah, MOTHER.

6. A "grand right and left" is a square dance movement for four couples in which the men move in a circle counterclockwise and the women clockwise. Each dancer passes the first person he meets right shoulder to right shoulder, touching right hands as they pass. He passes the second person left shoulder to left shoulder, touching left hands. This alternation of left and right continues until he meets the fifth person, who is the same as the first one, completing the movement.

Blah, blah, blah, blah, blah, blah, MONEY.
Blah, blah, blah, blah, blah, blah, HOSTILE.
Blah, blah, blah, blah, blah, blah, PENIS.
Blah, blah, blah, blah, blah, blah, MOTHER.
Blah, blah, blah, blah, blah, blah, MONEY.

Forming couples and locking hands with arms crossed, continuing to move, but in a smaller circle.

Blah, blah, blah, blah, blah, blah, blah.
Blah, blah, blah, blah, blah, blah, blah.

Now they slow down to the speed of a church procession. The women bow their heads, letting their hair fall forward over their faces. The "blah, blah, blah" continues, but much more slowly while some of the women accompany it with a descant of "Kyrie Eleison."[7] After they have gone around in a circle once this way, the actor who played the FOURTH INTERVIEWER *sits with his back to the audience as a* PRIEST. *The* FIRST APPLICANT *kneels next to him, facing the audience as if in a confessional booth. The other six actors are at the back of the stage in two lines, swaying slightly, heads down. The women are in front with their hair still down over their faces.*

FIRST APPLICANT [*crossing himself perfunctorily and starting to speak; his manner is not impassioned; it is clear that he comes regularly to repeat this always fruitless ritual*]   Can you help me, Father, I said, as I usually do, and he said, as usual, nothing. I'm your friend, the housepainter, I said, the good housepainter. Remember me, Father? He continued, as usual, to say nothing. Almost the only color you get to paint these days, Father, I said, is white. Only white, Father, I said, not expecting any more from him than usual, but going on anyway. The color I really like to paint, Father, is red, I said. Pure brick red. Now there's a confession, Father. He said nothing. I'd like to take a trip to the country, Father, I said, and paint a barn door red, thinking that would get a rise out of him, but it didn't. God, I said then, deliberately taking the Lord's name in vain, the result of taking a three-inch brush and lightly kissing a coat of red paint on a barn door is something stunning and beautiful to behold. He still said nothing. Father, I said, springing it on him, Father, I'd like to join a monastery. My wife's sister, she could take care of the kids. Still nothing. Father, I said again, I'd like to join a monastery. Can you help me, Father? Nothing. Father, I said, I've tried lots of things in my life, I've gone in a lot of different directions, Father, and none of them seems any better than any other, Father, I said. Can you help me, Father, I said. But he said nothing as usual, and then, as usual, I went away.

The FIRST APPLICANT *and the* FOURTH INTERVIEWER, *who haven't moved at all during the confession, move upstage to join the others as the music starts up violently in a rock beat. The actors do a rock version of the Virginia reel.*

---

7. The Greek words *kyrie eleison* (Lord, have mercy upon us) are used to designate a part of the Mass which begins with those words.

SECOND INTERVIEWER [*loudly*]   My

   All bow to partners.

FOURTH APPLICANT [*loudly*]   fault.

   All dos-à-dos.[8]

SECOND APPLICANT [*loudly*]   Excuse

   All circle around.

FOURTH INTERVIEWER [*loudly*]   me.

   All peel off.[9]

FIRST INTERVIEWER [*loudly*]   Can you
SECOND APPLICANT [*loudly*]   help
FIRST APPLICANT [*loudly*]   me?
FOURTH INTERVIEWER [*loudly*]   Next.

   All continue dancing, joining hands at the center to form a revolving door again. They repeat the preceding eight speeches. Then the SECOND INTERVIEWER *speaks rapidly, as a* SQUARE DANCE CALLER.

SQUARE DANCE CALLER   Step right up, ladies and gents, and shake the hand of the next governor of this state. Shake his hand and say hello. Tell your friends you shook the hand of the next governor of the state. Step right up and shake his hand. Ask him questions. Tell him problems. Say hello. Step right up, shake his hand, shake the hand, ladies and gents, of the next governor of the state. Tell your folks: I shook his hand. When he's famous you'll be proud. Step right up, ladies and gents, and shake his hand. Ask him questions. Tell him problems. Say hello. Step right up, ladies and gents. Don't be shy. Shake the hand of the next governor of this state.

   The actors have formed a crowd, downstage right, facing the audience. They give the impression of being but a few of a great number of people, all trying to squeeze to the front to see and speak to the political candidate. The FOURTH INTERVIEWER, *now playing a* POLITICIAN *stands on a box, stage left, facing the audience. The* SECOND INTERVIEWER *stands by the crowd and keeps it in order.*

POLITICIAN   Thank you very much, I said cheerfully, and good luck to you, I said, turning my smile to the next one.

   The FIRST INTERVIEWER, *panting as the* GIRL AT THE PARTY, *squeezes out of the crowd and rushes up to the* POLITICIAN, *who smiles at her benignly.*

POLITICIAN   Our children *are* our most important asset, I agreed earnestly. Yes they are, I said solemnly. Children, I said, with a long

---

8. *Dos-à-dos* (French for back-to-back) is a square dance movement in which a man and woman approach each other, right shoulder to right shoulder, and circle each other back-to-back.
9. "Peel off" is a square dance movement which begins with the eight dancers arranged in two parallel lines of four. The lines are side by side, and each dancer is facing away from the center of his line. After the movement is completed, the dancers are arranged in two parallel lines again, but now the dancers in each line are side by side and the two lines face each other.

pause, are our most important asset. I only wish I could, madame, I said earnestly, standing tall, but rats, I said regretfully, are a city matter.

The FIRST INTERVIEWER *returns to the crowd while the* THIRD INTERVIEWER, *as the* TELEPHONE OPERATOR, *rushes up to the* POLITICIAN. *She appeals to him, making the same noise she made when her stomach hurt her.*

POLITICIAN   Nobody knows more about red tape than I do, I said knowingly, and I wish you luck, I said, turning my smile to the next one.

The THIRD INTERVIEWER *returns to the crowd and the* FOURTH APPLICANT *goes up to the* POLITICIAN.

POLITICIAN   I certainly will, I said, with my eyes sparkling, taking a pencil out of my pocket. And what's your name, I said, looking at her sweetly and signing my name at the same time. That's a lovely name, I said.

The FOURTH APPLICANT *returns to the crowd while the* THIRD APPLICANT, *as an* OLDER MAN *shakes the* POLITICIAN'S *hand.*

POLITICIAN   Yes sir, I said, those were the days. And good luck to you, sir, I said respectfully but heartily, and look out for the curb, I said, turning my smile to the next one.

The THIRD APPLICANT *returns to the crowd and the* SECOND APPLICANT *approaches the* POLITICIAN.

POLITICIAN   Indeed yes, the air we breathe *is* foul, I said indignantly. I agree with you entirely, I said wholeheartedly. And if my opponent wins it's going to get worse, I said with conviction. We'd all die within ten years, I said. And good luck to you, madame, I said politely, and turned my smile to the next one.

The FIRST APPLICANT *approaches him, his cap in his hand.*

POLITICIAN   Well, I said confidingly, getting a bill through the legislature is easier said than done, and answering violence, I said warningly, with violence, I said earnestly, is not the answer, and how do you do, I said, turning my smile to the next one.

Next, two SIGHING LOVERS—*we saw them on Fourteenth Street —played by the* FIRST *and* SECOND INTERVIEWERS, *approach the* POLITICIAN.

POLITICIAN   No, I said, I never said my opponent would kill us all. No, I said, I never said that. May the best man win, I said manfully.

Half-hearted cheers. The FIRST *and* SECOND INTERVIEWERS *return to the crowd.*

POLITICIAN   I do feel, I said without false modesty, that I'm better qualified in the field of foreign affairs than my opponents are, yes, I said, *but,* I said, with a pause for emphasis, foreign policy is the business of the President, not the Governor, therefore I will say nothing about the war, I said with finality.

The crowd makes a restive sound, then freezes.

POLITICIAN Do you want us shaking hands, I asked the photographer, turning my profile to the left. Goodbye, I said cheerfully, and good luck to you too.

The crowd makes a louder protest, then freezes.

POLITICIAN I'm sorry, I said seriously, but I'll have to study that question a good deal more before I can answer it.

The crowd makes an angry noise, then freezes.

POLITICIAN Of course, I said frowning, we must all support the President, I said as I turned concernedly to the next one.

The crowd makes a very angry sound, then freezes.

POLITICIAN I'm sorry about the war, I said. Nobody could be sorrier than I am, I said sorrowfully. But I'm afraid, I said gravely, that there are no easy answers.

Smiles, pleased with himself.

Good luck to you too, I said cheerfully, and turned my smile to the next one.

The POLITICIAN topples from his box, beginning his speech all over again. Simultaneously, all the other actors lurch about the stage, speaking again in character: the SHOPPER ON FOURTEENTH STREET, the GYM INSTRUCTOR, the SUBWAY RIDER, the TELEPHONE OPERATOR, the GIRL AT THE PARTY, the ANALYSAND, and the HOUSEPAINTER. Simultaneously, they all stop and freeze, continue again, freeze again, then continue with music under. The SECOND INTERVIEWER, acting as policeman, begins to line them up in a diagonal line, like marching dolls, one behind the other. As they are put into line they begin to move their mouths without sound, like fish in a tank. The music stops. When all are in line the SECOND INTERVIEWER joins them.

SECOND INTERVIEWER My
FOURTH APPLICANT fault.
SECOND APPLICANT Excuse
FOURTH INTERVIEWER me.
FIRST INTERVIEWER Can you
SECOND APPLICANT help
FIRST APPLICANT me?
FOURTH INTERVIEWER Next.

All continue marching in place, moving their mouths, and shouting their lines as the lights come slowly down.

SECOND INTERVIEWER My
FOURTH APPLICANT fault.
SECOND APPLICANT Excuse
FOURTH INTERVIEWER me.
FIRST INTERVIEWER Can you
SECOND APPLICANT help
FIRST APPLICANT me?
FOURTH INTERVIEWER Next.

1966

Indices

Index of Authors

Index of Titles and First Lines

Y